THE WORLD ALMANAC®

2010 WORLD ATLAS

The World Almanac® World Atlas

© COPYRIGHT 2010 BY HAMMOND WORLD ATLAS CORPORATION

Published by HAMMOND WORLD ATLAS CORPORATION,
part of the Langenscheidt Publishing Group, 36-36 33rd St., Long Island City, NY, 11106

Printed in Canada.

Library of Congress
Cataloging-in-publication Data
        Hammond World Atlas Corporation.
        The World Almanac world atlas.
            p.   cm.
                Includes index.
                ISBN 978-0843-713640 (softcover : alk. paper)
                1.   Atlases.
                I.   Title: World atlas.
                II. Title.
                G1021. H597 2 0 0 3
                912--dc22   2003056695

HAMMOND

THE WORLD ALMANAC®

2010 WORLD ATLAS

Contents

INTERPRETING MAPS

Designed to enhance your knowledge and enjoyment of maps, these pages explain such cartographic principles as scale, projection and symbology. This section also includes a brief explanation of the boundary and name policies followed in this atlas.

Endsheets Map Locator / World Time Zones
6-7   Using This Atlas
8   Map Projections

FINDING THE FACTS

10-20   **World: Facts and Figures**

For individual subjects in this section, and for Nation Facts and Figues, please see the complete World Almanac Section contents on the opposite page.

Nations: Facts and Figures

22-77   Nations A-Z within each Continent or Region

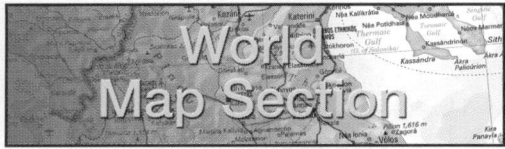

WORLD/CONTINENTS/REGIONS

This collection of regional maps is completely generated from a computer database structured by latitude and longitude. The realistic topography is achieved by combining the political map data with digital bathymetric and hypsometric relief data, and shaded relief. The maps are arranged by continent, and a stunning satellite image and political map of that continent introduce each section. Continent thematic maps are also included in each section, providing for special geographical comparisons. Over 70 inset maps highlight metropolitan and other areas of special interest.

80-81   World - Political Map 1:80.5M
82-83   World - Physical Map 1:80.5M

Europe and Northern Asia

85   Europe 1:20.7M
86   Geographical Comparisons: Temperature, Climate, Vegetation
87   Geographical Comparisons: Rainfall, Population, Land Use, Minerals
88   Metropolitan London, Metropolitan Paris 1:570K
89   United Kingdom, Ireland 1:3.45M
90-91   Southern England and Wales 1:1.15M
92-93   Northeastern Ireland, Northern England and Wales 1:1.15M
94   Central Scotland 1:1.15M
95   Scandinavia and Finland 1:6.9M Iceland 1:6.9M
96-97   Baltic Region 1:3.45M
98-99   North Central Europe 1:3.45M Berlin 1:1.15M
100-101   West Central Europe 1:3.45M
102-103   Spain, Portugal 1:3.45M Barcelona, Madrid, Lisbon 1:1.15M Azores, Canary Islands, Madeira 1:6.9M
104-105   Southern Italy, Albania, Greece 1:3.45M Athens, Malta 1:1.15M
106-107   Hungary, Northern Balkan States 1:3.45M Vienna, Budapest 1:1.15M
108-109   Netherlands, Northwestern Germany 1:1.15M
110-111   Belgium, Northern France, Western Germany 1:1.15M
112-113   Southern Germany, Czech Republic, Upper Austria 1:1.15M
114-115   Central Alps Region 1:1.15M
116-117   Northern Italy 1:1.15M Monaco 1:115K
118-119   Northeastern Europe 1:6.9M St. Petersburg, Moscow 1:1.15M
120-121   Southeastern Europe 1:6.9M
122-123   Russia and Neighboring Countries 1:20.7M

Asia

125   Asia 1:48.3M
126   Geographical Comparisons: Temperature, Climate, Vegetation
127   Geographical Comparisons: Rainfall, Population, Land Use, Minerals
128-129   Eastern Asia 1:13.8M Hong Kong 1:1.15M
130   Northeastern China 1:6.9M Beijing-Tianjin, Shanghai 1:3.45M
131   Korea 1:3.45M Seoul 1:1.15M
132-133   Central and Southern Japan 1:3.45M Ryukyu Islands 1:6.9M
134   Northern Japan 1:3.45M
135   Tokyo-Yokohama, Osaka-Nagoya 1:1.15M
136   Indochina 1:6.9M
137   Southeastern China, Taiwan, Philippines 1:10.3M
138-139   Indonesia, Malaysia 1:10.3M
140-141   Southern Asia 1:10.3M
142-143   Ganges Plain 1:3.45M
144   Punjab Plain 1:10.3M
145   Central Asia 1:3.45M
146-147   Southwestern Asia 1:10.3M
148   Northern Middle East 1:6.9M
159   Eastern Mediterranean Region 1:3.45M Central Israel 1:1.15M

Africa

151   Africa 1:34.5M Cape Verde 1:6.9M
152   Geographical Comparisons: Temperature, Climate, Vegetation
153   Geographical Comparisons: Rainfall, Population, Land Use, Minerals
154-155   Northern Africa 1:17.2M
156-157   Northern West Africa 1:6.9M
158   Northern Morocco, Algeria, Tunisia 1:3.45M
159   Northeastern Africa 1:6.9M
160-161   Southern West Africa 1:6.9M
162   East Africa 1:6.9M
163   Southern Africa 1:17.2M
164-165   South Africa 1:6.9M Cape Town, Johannesburg, Mauritius and Réunion 1:3.45M Madagascar 1:6.9M

Australia, New Zealand and Pacific

167   Australia, New Zealand 1:19.1M

168   Geographical Comparisons: Temperature, Climate, Vegetation

169   Geographical Comparisons: Rainfall, Population, Land Use, Minerals

170-171   Western and Central Australia 1:6.9M
Perth, Adelaide 1:1.15M

172   Northeastern Australia 1:6.9M
Brisbane, Sydney 1:1.15M

173   Southeastern Australia 1:6.9M
Melbourne 1:1.15M

174-175   Central Pacific Ocean 1:31M
New Zealand 1:10.3M

North America

177   North America 1:34.5M

178   Geographical Comparisons: Temperature, Climate, Vegetation

179   Geographical Comparisons: Rainfall, Population, Land Use, Minerals

180-181   Canada 1:13.8M

182-183   United States 1:13.8M
Hawaii 1:3.45M
Oahu 1:1.15M

184-185   Southwestern Canada Northwestern United States 1:6.9M

186-187   Southwestern United States 1:6.9M

188-189   Southeastern Canada, Northeastern United States 1:6.9M
Montreal, Toronto-Buffalo 1:1.15M

190-191   Southeastern United States 1:6.9M

192   Alaska 1:10.3M

193   Seattle-Tacoma, Sacramento-San Francisco-San Jose, Detroit, Chicago-Milwaukee 1:1.15M

194   Los Angeles-San Diego 1:1.15M
Metropolitan Los Angeles 1:570K

195   Denver, Kansas City, New Orleans, Oklahoma City, Phoenix, San Antonio, Salt Lake City, St. Louis 1:1.15M

196-197   New York-Philadelphia-Washington 1:1.15M
Metropolitan New York 1:570K

198-199   Middle America 1:10.3M
Puerto Rico, Lesser Antilles 1:6.9M

200-201   Northern and Central Mexico 1:6.9M
Distrito Federal-Veracruz 1:3.45M
Distrito Federal 1:1.15M

202-203   Southern Mexico, Central America, Western Caribbean 1:6.9M

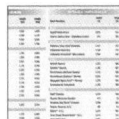

South America and Polar Regions

205   South America 1:27.6M

206   Geographical Comparisons: Temperature, Climate, Vegetation

207   Geographical Comparisons: Rainfall, Population, Land Use, Minerals

208-209   Northern South America 1:14.9M

210-211   Colombia, Venezuela, Ecuador 1:6.9M

212   Northeastern Brazil 1:6.9M

213   Southeastern Brazil 1:6.9M
Rio de Janeiro-São Paulo 1:3.45M

214   Peru 1:6.9M
Galápagos Islands 1:6.9M

215   Southern South America 1:14.9M

216-217   Southern Chile and Argentina 1:6.9M
Santiago-Valparaíso, Buenos Aires 1:3.45M

218   Arctic Regions 1:34.5M
Antarctica 1:57.5M

Looking it Up

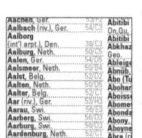 The Master Index at the end of the map section lists 60,000 places and other features appearing in this atlas, complete with page numbers and easy-to-use alpha-numeric references. Preceding the index is a list of abbreviations used in the index.

220   Using the Index and Index Abbreviations

221-292   Index

292   Acknowledgements - Photo Credits

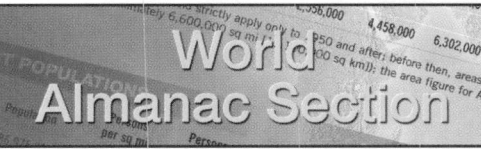

Finding the Facts

These 69 pages – a 12-page section of World Facts and Figures, and a 57-page section of Nation Facts and Figures – provide a wide variety of compelling information selected from The World Almanac® and Book of Facts. The world section (pages 10-20) provides information on the world as a whole; the nations section (pages 22-77) on each individual nation. Nations are arranged by continent and in alphabetical order, and are referenced to the map section for quick access to complementary information.

World: Facts and Figures

10-11   About the World Almanac Sections; Nation Locator Guide

12   Rankings by Population and Area

13   Ocean Areas, Ocean Depths and Islands

14   Rivers and Waterfalls

15   Continental Altitudes and Lakes

16   Reservoirs and Dams

17   Global Temperatures

18   Precipitation and Deserts

19   Languages, Population, and Oil and Gas Reserves

20   Energy Charts

Nations: Facts and Figures

22-77   Nations A-Z within each Continent or Region

22   Africa

36   Asia

51   Australia, New Zealand and the Pacific

55   Europe

67   North America Including Central America and the Islands of the Caribbean

74   South America

Note: Numbers following each entry indicate map scale (M=million, K=thousand).

Using This Atlas

Offering a broad range of features and functions, The World Almanac® World Atlas is more than a geographical reference work of superior quality and a guide for virtual global exploration. It also includes a compendium of compelling facts and figures from The World Almanac® and Book of Facts that will enhance your understanding of the connections in the world around you. The information provided below will help you to get the most enjoyment and benefit from its use.

World Map Section

The detailed maps of all regions of the Earth are arranged by continent. The chapters for each of the continents are introduced with a stunning satellite image and a political continent map, followed by two pages of thematic maps. Eight thematic subjects range from Climate and Land Use to Population Distribution. The detailed regional maps employ a variety of different symbols: Line patterns, surface colors, and textures highlight distinctive features such as mountains, national parks, urban areas, forests, and deserts. These maps also provide a wealth of information on roadways and canals, geographic features, and political divisions. All of the geographic maps and the complex information they contain are the product of modern computer-assisted map development and compilation techniques.

Map Frames

The map frames contain a number of graphic features that make the atlas easy to use. A locator map at the top of the map page shows the position of the individual map section within a larger geographic area. The blue triangles along the four edges of each map refer by page number to the adjacent map sections, and thus make it easy to find neighboring areas quickly in the atlas. The letters and numerals positioned along the outside of the map, in the green map frame, are search coordinates used to locate places and objects listed in the map index. In addition, integrated legends provide basic information about the region covered by each map.

Map Scales

A map's scale describes the relationship of any length on the map to a corresponding length on the Earth's surface. A scale of 1:3,000,000 means that one cm on the map represents 3,000,000 cm (30 km) in nature. Thus a scale of 1:1,000,000 is larger than 1:3,000,000, just as 1/1 is larger than 1/3. The most densely populated areas are shown at a scale of 1:1 M, while selected metropolitan areas are covered at either 1:500,000 or 1:1 M. Other populous areas are presented at 1:3 M and 1:6 M, allowing you to accurately compare areas and distances of similar regions. Remaining regions, including the continent maps, are presented at 1:9 M and smaller scales.

Boundary and Name Policies

The atlas shows the internationally recognized national boundaries. Boundary disputes, armistice lines, and de facto boundaries are indicated by special symbols where appropriate. Generally, the names of places and geographic objects appear in the language of the respective country. Accepted conventional names are used for certain major foreign places names. Name usage also tends to vary depending upon cultural factors, however, and is subject to change over time, not least of all for political reasons. In several cases where, for example, a new name has not gained universal acceptance or the use of a traditional name persists, a second name has been entered in parentheses. Thus, the selection of names is not entirely systematic and reflects important aspects of common usage.

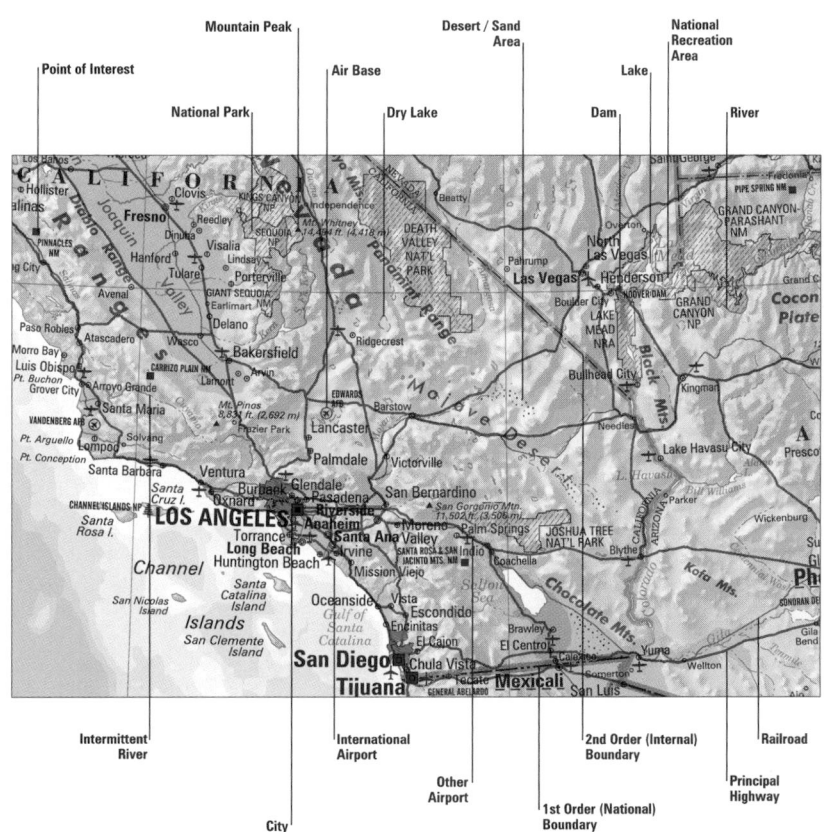

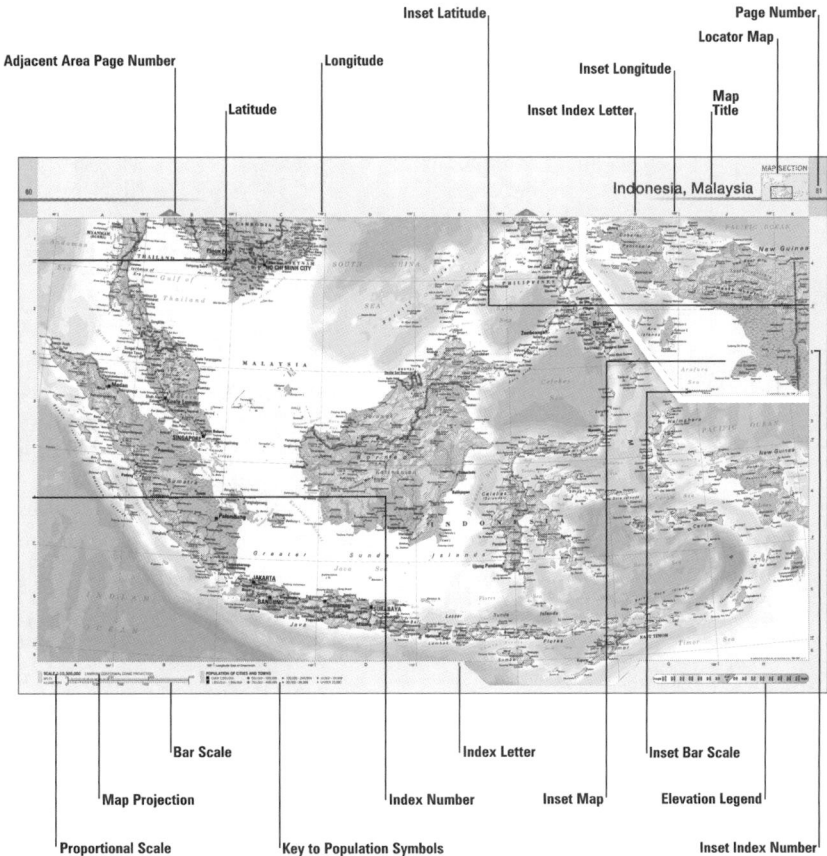

World Locator Map

A simplified world map overlaid with the outlines of all maps in the Map Section is located on the front end sheet. The World Locator Map shows at a glance which maps cover a given area. The page numbers for each map make it easy to locate specific regions quickly.

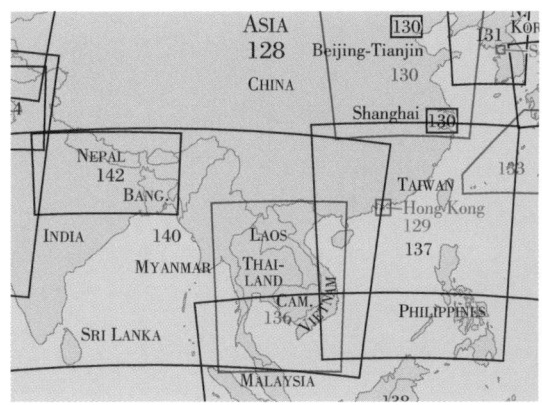

Symbols used on World Maps

FIRST ORDER (NATIONAL) BOUNDARY

- Land Boundary
- Armistice Boundary
- Water Boundary
- De Facto Boundary
- Disputed Boundary
- Undefined

SECOND ORDER (INTERNAL) BOUNDARY

- Land Boundary
- Water Boundary

THIRD ORDER (INTERNAL) BOUNDARY

- Land Boundary
- Water Boundary

CITIES AND TOWNS

- **Stockholm** First Order (National) Capital
- **Salt Lake City** Second Order (Internal) Capital
- **Manchester** Third Order (Internal) Capital
- Towns
- Neighborhood
- City and Urban Area Limits

TRANSPORTATION

- ✈ International Airport
- ✈ Other Airport
- Highways/Roads
- Railroads
- Ferries
- Tunnels (Road, Railroad)

DRAINAGE FEATURES

- Shoreline, River
- Intermittent River
- Canal
- Lake, Reservoir
- Intermittent Lake
- Dry Lake
- Salt Pan
- Swamp/Marsh

OTHER PHYSICAL FEATURES

- ▲ Elevation
- ≍ Pass
- • Falls
- ✳ Rapids
- Desert/Sand Area
- Lava Flow
- Glacier/Ice Shelf

CULTURAL FEATURES

- ∴ Ruins
- • Dam
- ♠ Park
- ✗ Wildlife Area
- ■ Point of Interest
- ⌣ Well
- ⊗ Air Base
- ⊘ Naval Base
- International Date Line
- Ancient Walls
- Native Reservation/Reserve
- Military/Government Reservation
- State Park/Recreation Area
- National Park/Forest/ Recreation/Wildlife Area

ELEVATION LEGEND

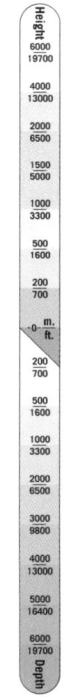

Height
6000 / 19700
4000 / 13000
2000 / 6500
1500 / 5000
1000 / 3300
500 / 1600
200 / 700
0 — m. / ft.
200 / 700
500 / 1600
1000 / 3300
2000 / 6500
3000 / 9800
4000 / 13000
5000 / 16400
6000 / 19700
Depth

The color tints in this bar represent both elevation of land areas and depth of the oceans. The changes between colors are labeled in feet and meters.

Abbreviations used on the maps

Abor. Rsv.	Aboriginal Reserve	Fk.	Fork	NB	National Battlefield	PN	Park National
Admin.	Administration	For.	Forest	NBP	National Battlefield Park	Prom.	Promontory
AFB	Air Force Base	Ft.	Fort	NCA	National Conservation	Prsv.	Preserve
Amm. Dep.	Ammunition Depot	G.	Gulf		Area	Pt.	Point
Arch.	Archipelago	Govt.	Government	NHP	National Historical Park	R.	River
Aut.	Autonomous	Gd.	Grand	NHS	National Historic Site	Rec.	Recreation(al)
B.	Bay	Gt.	Great	NL	National Lakeshore	Ref.	Refuge
Bfld.	Battlefield	Har.	Harbor	NM	National Monument	Reg.	Region
Bk.	Brook	Hist.	Historic(al)	NMEM	National Memorial	Rep.	Republic
Br.	Branch	Hts.	Heights	NMILP	National Military Park	Res.	Reservoir, Reservation
C.	Cape	I., Is.	Island(s)	No.	Northern	Sa.	Sierra
Can.	Canal	Ind. Res.	Indian Reservation	NP	National Park	Sd.	Sound
Cap.	Capital	Int'l	International	NPP	National Park and	So.	Southern
C.G.	Coast Guard	IR	Indian Reservation		Preserve	SP	State Park
Chan.	Channel	Isth.	Isthmus	NPRSV	National Preserve	Spr., Sprgs.	Spring, Springs
Co.	County	Jct.	Junction	NRA	National Recreation Area	St.	State
Consv.	Conservation	L.	Lake	NRIV	National River	Sta.	Station
Cord.	Cordillera	Lag.	Lagoon	NRSV	National Reserve	Stm.	Stream
Cr.	Creek	Mem.	Memorial	NS	National Seashore	Str.	Strait
b	Center	Mil.	Military	NWR	National Wildlife Refuge	Terr.	Territory
Dep.	Depot	Mon.	Monument	Obl.	Oblast	Tun.	Tunnel
Depr.	Depression	Mt.	Mount	Occ.	Occupied	Twp.	Township
Des.	Desert	Mtn.	Mountain	Okr.	Okrug	UNDOF	United Nations
Dist.	District	Mts.	Mountains	Passg.	Passage		Disengagement
DMZ	Demilitarized Zone	Nat.	Natural	Pen.	Peninsula		Observer Force
Est.	Estuary	Nat'l	National	Pk.	Peak	Val.	Valley
Fed.	Federal	Nav.	Naval	Plat.	Plateau	Vill.	Village

Index to the World Map Section

Aa (riv.), Ger.	50/D5
Aach (riv.), Ger.	57/F2
Aach, Ger.	57/E2
Aachen, Ger.	53/F2
Aalbach (riv.), Ger.	54/C3
Aalborg (int'l arpt.), Den.	38/C3
Aalburg, Neth.	50/C5
Aalen, Ger.	54/D5
Aalsmeer, Neth.	50/B4
Aalst, Belg.	52/D2
Aalten, Neth.	50/D5
Aalter, Belg.	52/C1
Aar (riv.), Ger.	53/H3
Aarau, Swi.	56/E3
Aarberg, Swi.	56/D3

The index facilitates the search for a specific place in the atlas. It contains an alphabetical list of place names and geographic objects shown in the maps. Each index entry gives the page and coodinate grid location of the desired place or object. A list of the abbreviations used in the index is found on the first index page.

Map type faces

The use of different type faces helps the reader distinguish between categories of map content.

Major Political Arenas

LUXEMBOURG

Internal Political Divisions

SAXONY-ANHALT

Historical Regions

Polabská Nížina

Cities and Towns

Norfolk Sumter Smyrna

Neighborhoods

BIGGIN HILL

Points of Interest

MISSION SAN BUENAVENTURA

Water Features

L. Elsinore

Capes, Points, Peaks, Passes

Cape Horn...Pt. La Jolla

Mt. Rainier

Islands, Peninsulas

Cape Breton I.

Mountain Ranges, Plateaus, Hills

Serra do Norte

Deserts, Plains, Valleys

San Fernando Valley

Spelling of names

The spelling of geographic names conforms to the rules of the respective official language of each country. Where the official language is written in Latin characters, local spellings, including diacritical marks and modified letters, have been used. For countries with languages written in non-Latin characters, such as China, Russia or the Arabic-speaking countries, an international standard form is used, which may deviate in some cases from conventional American usage.

Rankings by Populat

POPULATION AND LAND AREA OF T

Population Rank as of 2003	Continent or Region	Population (estimated, in thousands)				
		1650	1750	1850	1900	1950
1.	Asia	335,000	476,000	754,000	932,000	1,411,000
2.	Africa	100,000	95,000	95,000	118,000	229,000
3.	Europe	100,000	140,000	265,000	400,000	392,000
4.	North America	5,000	5,000	39,000	106,000	221,000
5.	South America	8,000	7,000	20,000	38,000	111,000
6.	Australia, New Zealand, and the Pacific	2,000	2,000	2,000	6,000	12,000
7.	Antarctic		No indigenous inhabitants			
	WORLD	550,000	725,000	1,175,000	1,600,000	2,556,000

Note: Areas are as defined by the U.S. Bureau of the Census and strictly apply only to 1950 a[...]ureau area for Europe includes all of Russia (approximately 6,600,000 sq mi [17,100,000 s[...]o totals because of rounding.

LARGEST POPULATIONS					
Rank	Country	Population	Persons per sq mi	Persons per sq km	Rank
1.	China[1]	1,286,975,000	357	138	1.
2.	India	1,065,462,000	928	358	2.
3.	United States	288,369,000	81	31	3.
4.	Indonesia	219,883,000	312	120	4.
5.	Brazil	178,470,000	55	21	5.
6.	Pakistan	153,578,000	511	197	6.
7.	Bangladesh	146,736,000	2,838	1,096	7.
8.	Russia	143,246,000	22	8	8.
9.	Japan	127,654,000	838	324	9.

The World Almanac Sections – World and Nations

Two sections – one devoted to World Facts and Figures, and one to Nation Facts and Figures – provide a wide variety of information selected from The World Almanac® and Book of Facts. The 12-page world section (pages 9-20) offers data on the world as a whole. The 57-page nations section (pages 22-77) provides data on each individual nation. Nations are arranged in alphabetical order, and are referenced to the map section for quick access to complementary information. A concurrent reading of maps and related almanac data helps shed light on the impact of geography on the economy, culture, and other spheres of human activity.

Map Projections

Simply stated, the mapmaker's challenge is to project the earth's curved surface onto a flat plane. To achieve this elusive goal, cartographers have developed map projections — formulas that govern this conversion of geographic data. Every point on earth can be identified with the aid of a geographic coordinate grid, and this grid can be projected onto a flat surface. This section explores some of the most widely used projections. It also introduces a new projection, the Hammond Optimal Conformal.

General Principles and Terms

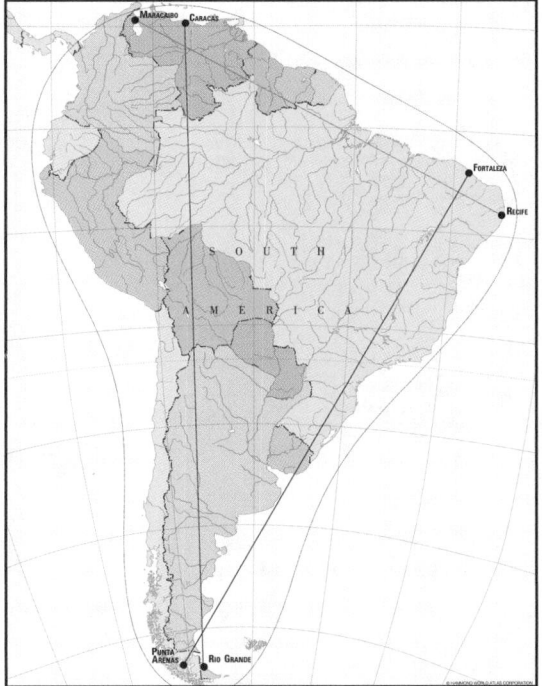

The earth rotates around its axis once a day. Its end points are the north and south poles; the imaginary line circling the earth midway between the poles is the equator. The arc from the equator to either pole is divided into 90 degrees of latitude. The equator represents 0° latitude. Circles of equal latitude, called parallels, are traditionally shown at every fifth or tenth degree. Circles of latitude become progressively smaller toward the poles.

The equator is divided into 360 degrees. Lines circling the globe from pole to pole through the degree points on the equator are called meridians, or great circles. All meridians are equal in length. By international agreement the meridian passing through the Greenwich Observatory near London has been chosen as the prime meridian, or 0° longitude. The distance in degrees from the prime meridian to any point east or west is its longitude.

While meridians are all equal in length, parallels become shorter as they approach the poles. Whereas one degree of latitude represents approximately 69 miles (112 km) anywhere on the globe, a degree of longitude varies from 69 miles (112 km) at the equator to zero at the poles. Each degree of latitude and longitude is divided into 60 minutes. One minute of latitude equals one nautical mile (1.15 land miles or 1.85 km).

How to Flatten a Sphere: The Art of Controlling Distortion

There is only one way to represent the earth's sphere with absolute precision: on a globe. All attempts to project our planet's surface onto a plane result in distortion. Depending upon the map projection selected, distortions appear in shapes and area sizes, angles, or distances between points on the earth.

Only the parallels or the meridians (or some other set of lines) can maintain the same length as on a globe of corresponding scale. All other lines must be either too long or too short. Accordingly, the scale on a flat map cannot be true everywhere; there will always be different scales in different parts of a map. On world maps or maps of very large areas, variations in scale may be extreme. On maps of small areas, variations in scale may be relatively insignificant. Most maps seek to preserve either true area relationships (equal area projections) or true angles and shapes (conformal projections); some attempt to achieve overall balance.

Projections: Selected Examples

Mercator Projection

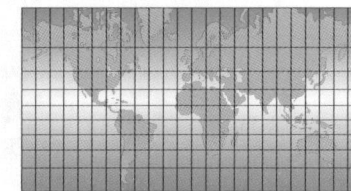

This projection is especially useful because all compass directions appear as straight lines, making it a valuable navigational tool. Moreover, it is a comformal projection – every small region conforms to its shape on a globe. But because its meridians are evenly-spaced vertical lines which never converge (unlike the meridians on a globe), the horizontal parallels must be drawn farther and farther apart at higher latitudes to maintain a correct relationship. Only the equator is true to scale, and the sizes of areas in the higher latitudes are dramatically distorted.

Robinson Projection

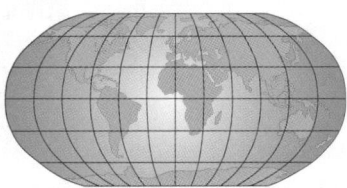

The Robinson is a compromise projection that combines elements of both conformal and equal area projections to show the whole earth with relatively true shapes and reasonably equal areas. The Robinson is used mostly for world maps. To create the World Political and World Physical maps on pages 80-83, this projection has been used.

Conic Projection

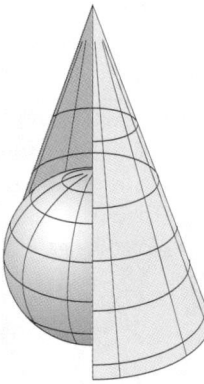

The original idea of this projection is to project lines of latitude and longitude from the planet's center onto a cone. The axis length of the cone is variable. To produce working maps, the cone is simply "cut open" and "laid flat." In the conic projection illustrated here, the cone can be made tangent to any desired parallel. One popular conic projection, the Lambert Conformal Conic, uses two standard parallels of conforming lengths near the top and the bottom of the map to further reduce errors of scale. This projection has been used to create most of the national and regional maps in this atlas.

Hammond Optimal Conformal

As its name implies, this new conformal projection presents the optimal view of an area by reducing shifts in scale over an entire region to the minimum degree possible. While conformal maps generally preserve all small shapes, large shapes can become very distorted because of varying scales, causing considerable inaccuracy in distance measurements. The concept underlying the Optimal Conformal is that for any region on the globe, there is an ideal projection for which scale variation can be made as small as possible. Consequently, unlike other projections, the Optimal Conformal does not use one standard formula to construct a map. Each map is a unique projection — the optimal projection for that particular area.

After a cartographer defines the subject area (in the illustration, left, indicated by the red outline around South America), a sophisticated computer program evaluates the size and shape of the region, and projects the most distortion-free conformal map possible. This projection has been used to create the continent maps in this atlas.

◄ *Hammond Optimal Conformal Projection*

World
Almanac Section

World Facts and Figures
from The World Almanac®

WORLD FACTS AND FIGURES

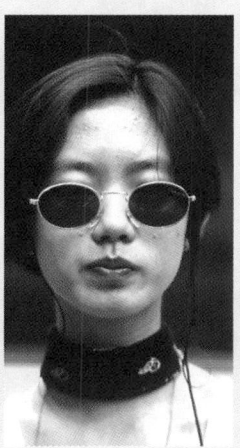

About the World Almanac Sections

The information from *The World Almanac*® is presented in two parts. This first part, preceding the Map Section, contains facts and figures characterizing key aspects of the world and its population. The second part, on pages 22-77, presents detailed information on every nation of the world.

The nations in the second part are arranged in alphabetical order under the heading for the part of the world in which they are located. To find information on a particular nation, turn to the region in which it lies, as indicated by the abbreviation in parentheses below. Note that Russia is covered under Europe, as its capital and the bulk of the population are located in Europe; similarly, Turkey is covered under Asia, since that is where its capital and the majority of its population are found.

Nation Locator Guide—for pages 22-77

(AF) Africa

(AS) Asia

(AU) Australia, New Zealand, and the Pacific

(E) Europe

(NA) North America, including Central America and the islands of the Caribbean

(SA) South America

Afghanistan **(AS)**	Bolivia **(SA)**	Congo, Democratic	Ethiopia **(AF)**
Albania **(E)**	Bosnia and Herzegovina **(E)**	Republic of the **(AF)**	Fiji **(AU)**
Algeria **(AF)**	Botswana **(AF)**	Congo Republic **(AF)**	Finland **(E)**
Andorra **(E)**	Brazil **(SA)**	Costa Rica **(NA)**	France **(E)**
Angola **(AF)**	Brunei **(AS)**	Côte d'Ivoire **(AF)**	Gabon **(AF)**
Antigua and Barbuda **(NA)**	Bulgaria **(E)**	Croatia **(E)**	Gambia **(AF)**
Argentina **(SA)**	Burkina Faso **(AF)**	Cuba **(NA)**	Georgia **(AS)**
Armenia **(AS)**	Burma	Cyprus **(AS)**	Germany **(E)**
Australia **(AU)**	(see Myanmar)	Czech Republic **(E)**	Ghana **(AF)**
Austria **(E)**	Burundi **(AF)**	Denmark **(E)**	Greece **(E)**
Azerbaijan **(AS)**	Cambodia **(AS)**	Djibouti **(AF)**	Grenada **(NA)**
Bahamas **(NA)**	Cameroon **(AF)**	Dominica **(NA)**	Guatemala **(NA)**
Bahrain **(AS)**	Canada **(NA)**	Dominican Republic **(NA)**	Guinea **(AF)**
Bangladesh **(AS)**	Cape Verde **(AF)**	East Timor **(AS)**	Guinea-Bissau **(AF)**
Barbados **(NA)**	Central African Republic **(AF)**	Ecuador **(SA)**	Guyana **(SA)**
Belarus **(E)**	Chad **(AF)**	Egypt **(AF)**	Haiti **(NA)**
Belgium **(E)**	Chile **(SA)**	El Salvador **(NA)**	Honduras **(NA)**
Belize **(NA)**	China **(AS)**	Equatorial Guinea **(AF)**	Hungary **(E)**
Benin **(AF)**	Colombia **(SA)**	Eritrea **(AF)**	Iceland **(E)**
Bhutan **(AS)**	Comoros **(AF)**	Estonia **(E)**	India **(AS)**

Indonesia **(AS)**
Iran **(AS)**
Iraq **(AS)**
Ireland **(E)**
Israel **(AS)**
Italy **(E)**
Jamaica **(NA)**
Japan **(AS)**
Jordan **(AS)**
Kazakhstan **(AS)**
Kenya **(AF)**
Kiribati **(AU)**
Korea, North **(AS)**
Korea, South **(AS)**
Kosovo **(E)**
Kuwait **(AS)**
Kyrgyzstan **(AS)**
Laos **(AS)**
Latvia **(E)**
Lebanon **(AS)**
Lesotho **(AF)**
Liberia **(AF)**
Libya **(AF)**
Liechtenstein **(E)**
Lithuania **(E)**
Luxembourg **(E)**
Macedonia **(E)**
Madagascar **(AF)**
Malawi **(AF)**
Malaysia **(AS)**
Maldives **(AS)**

Mali **(AF)**
Malta **(E)**
Marshall Islands **(AU)**
Mauritania **(AF)**
Mauritius **(AF)**
Mexico **(NA)**
Micronesia **(AU)**
Moldova **(E)**
Monaco **(E)**
Mongolia **(AS)**
Montenegro **(E)**
Morocco **(AF)**
Mozambique **(AF)**
Myanmar **(AS)**
Namibia **(AF)**
Nauru **(AU)**
Nepal **(AS)**
Netherlands **(E)**
New Zealand **(AU)**
Nicaragua **(NA)**
Niger **(AF)**
Nigeria **(AF)**
North Korea
   (see Korea, North)
Norway **(E)**
Oman **(AS)**
Pakistan **(AS)**
Palau **(AU)**
Panama **(NA)**
Papua New Guinea **(AS)**
Paraguay **(SA)**

Peru **(SA)**
Philippines **(AS)**
Poland **(E)**
Portugal **(E)**
Qatar **(AS)**
Romania **(E)**
Russia **(E)**
Rwanda **(AF)**
Saint Kitts and Nevis **(NA)**
Saint Lucia **(NA)**
Saint Vincent and the
   Grenadines **(NA)**
Samoa **(AU)**
San Marino **(E)**
São Tomé and Príncipe **(AF)**
Saudi Arabia **(AS)**
Senegal **(AF)**
Serbia **(E)**
Seychelles **(AF)**
Sierra Leone **(AF)**
Singapore **(AS)**
Slovakia **(E)**
Slovenia **(E)**
Solomon Islands **(AU)**
Somalia **(AF)**
South Africa **(AF)**
South Korea
   (see Korea, South)
Spain **(E)**
Sri Lanka **(AS)**
Sudan **(AF)**

Suriname **(SA)**
Swaziland **(AF)**
Sweden **(E)**
Switzerland **(E)**
Syria **(AS)**
Taiwan **(AS)**
Tajikistan **(AS)**
Tanzania **(AF)**
Thailand **(AS)**
Togo **(AF)**
Tonga **(AU)**
Trinidad and Tobago **(NA)**
Tunisia **(AF)**
Turkey **(AS)**
Turkmenistan **(AS)**
Tuvalu **(AU)**
Uganda **(AF)**
Ukraine **(E)**
United Arab Emirates **(AS)**
United Kingdom **(E)**
United States **(NA)**
Uruguay **(SA)**
Uzbekistan **(AS)**
Vanuatu **(AU)**
Vatican City **(E)**
Venezuela **(SA)**
Vietnam **(AS)**
Yemen **(AS)**
Zambia **(AF)**
Zimbabwe **(AF)**

A WORD ABOUT THE DATA

The facts and figures given here are based on data collected for *The World Almanac®* and represent the latest information available at the time of compilation.

Data on pages 10 through 20 and pages 22 through 77 used under license from *The World Almanac® and Book of Facts*. Copyright by World Almanac Education Group, Inc. All rights reserved.

The World Almanac® and Book of Facts is a registered trademark of World Almanac Education Group, Inc

LOCATIONS PICTURED IN PHOTOS INTRODUCING THE REGIONS OF THE WORLD
AFRICA
page 22 right bottom, *Camel resting by the pyramids at Giza (Al Jizah), Egypt*
ASIA
page 36 left, *Tea harvesting, China;* page 36 mid bottom, *Festival celebration, Hong Kong;* page 36 mid right: *Market stall lantern, Tokyo, Japan*
AUSTRALIA, NEW ZEALAND, AND THE PACIFIC
page 51 left, *Reef formations, South Pacific;* page 51 right bottom, *Opera House, Sydney, Australia*
EUROPE
page 55 left, *Marienplatz, Munich, Germany*
NORTH AMERICA, INCLUDING CENTRAL AMERICA AND THE ISLANDS OF THE CARIBBEAN
page 67 left, *Buffalo near Grand Teton Mountains, Wyoming, United States;* page 67 right top, *Los Angeles, California, United States*
SOUTH AMERICA
page 74 left, *Machu Picchu, Peru;* page 74 mid bottom, *Rio de Janeiro, Brazil*

Chief abbreviations used in the World Almanac Section

cu	cubic	est.	estimate(d)	ft	foot, feet	in	inch(es)	km	kilometer(s)
m	meter(s)	mi	mile(s)	mm	millimeters(s)	NA	not available	Pres.	President
sq	square	yd	yard(s)						

World Facts and Figures

RANKINGS BY POPULATION AND AREA

POPULATION AND LAND AREA OF THE WORLD, 1650–2010

Population Rank	Continent or Region	Population (estimated, in thousands)							Land Area		
		1650	1750	1850	1900	1950	1980	2010*	(1,000 sq mi)	(1,000 sq km)	% of Earth Land Area
1.	Asia	335,000	476,000	754,000	932,000	1,411,000	2,601,000	4,102,170	12,000	31,000	21.4
2.	Africa	100,000	95,000	95,000	118,000	229,000	470,000	996,457	11,500	29,800	20.5
3.	Europe	100,000	140,000	265,000	400,000	392,000	484,000	728,227	8,800	22,800	15.7
4.	North America	5,000	5,000	39,000	106,000	221,000	372,000	534,017	8,300	21,400	14.8
5.	South America	8,000	7,000	20,000	38,000	111,000	242,000	394,352	6,800	17,500	12.1
6.	Australia, New Zealand, and the Pacific	2,000	2,000	2,000	6,000	12,000	23,000	34,839	3,200	8,400	5.8
7.	Antarctic	No indigenous inhabitants							14,000	9.7	
	WORLD	550,000	725,000	1,175,000	1,600,000	2,556,000	4,458,000	6,769,000	56,000	145,000	100.0

Note: Areas are as defined by the U.S. Bureau of the Census and strictly apply only to 1950 and after; before then, areas may be defined differently. The Census Bureau area for Europe includes all of Russia (approximately 6,600,000 sq mi [17,100,000 sq km]); the area figure for Asia excludes Russia. Figures may not add to totals because of rounding.

*Estimate

LARGEST POPULATIONS

Rank	Country	Population	Persons per sq mi[2]	Persons per sq km[2]
1.	China[1]	1,338,612,968	361	139
2.	India	1,166,079,217	919	355
3.	United States	307,212,123	83	32
4.	Indonesia	245,452,739	324	125
5.	Brazil	198,739,269	60	23
6.	Pakistan	176,242,949	568	219
7.	Bangladesh	156,050,883	2,807	1,084
8.	Nigeria	149,229,090	418	162
9.	Russia	140,041,247	21	8
10.	Japan	127,078,679	871	336

[1]Excluding Hong Kong and Macau. [2]Land area only

SMALLEST POPULATIONS

Rank	Country	Population	Persons per sq mi[1]	Persons per sq km[1]
1.	Vatican City	826	*	*
2.	Tuvalu	12,373	1,237	476
3.	Nauru	14,019	1,752	668
4.	Palau	20,796	117	45
5.	San Marino	30,324	1,263	497
6.	Monaco	32,965	43,953	16,905
7.	Liechtenstein	34,761	561	217
8.	Saint Kitts and Nevis	40,131	397	154
9.	Marshall Islands	64,522	922	356
10.	Dominica	72,660	250	96

*Area only 0.17 sq mi (0.4 sq km). [1]Land area only

LARGEST LAND AREAS

Rank	Country	Land Area sq mi	Land Area) (sq km)
1.	Russia	6,562,112	16,995,800
2.	China	3,600,946	9,326,410
3.	United States	3,537,437	9,161,923
4.	Canada	3,511,021	9,093,507
5.	Brazil	3,265,075	8,456,510
6.	Australia	2,941,298	7,617,930
7.	India	1,147,955	2,973,190
8.	Argentina	1,056,641	2,736,690
9.	Kazakhstan	1,030,815	2,669,800
10.	Algeria	919,595	2,381,740

SMALLEST LAND AREAS

Rank	Country	Land Area sq mi	Land Area (sq km)
1.	Vatican City	0.17	0.44
2.	Monaco	0.75	1.95
3.	Nauru	8	21
4.	Tuvalu	10	26
5.	San Marino	24	61
6.	Liechtenstein	62	160
7.	Marshall Islands	70	181
8.	Saint Kitts and Nevis	101	261
9.	Maldives	116	300
10.	Malta	122	316

OCEANS, OCEAN DEPTHS, AND ISLANDS

AREAS AND AVERAGE DEPTHS OF OCEANS, SEAS, AND GULFS

Geographers and mapmakers recognize four major bodies of water: the Pacific, the Atlantic, the Indian, and the Arctic oceans. The Atlantic and Pacific oceans are considered divided at the equator into the North and South Atlantic and the North and South Pacific. The Arctic Ocean is the name for waters north of the continental landmasses in the region of the Arctic Circle.

	Area (sq mi)	Area (sq km)	Average Depth (ft)	Average Depth (m)
Pacific Ocean	64,186,300	166,241,800	12,925	3,940
Atlantic Ocean	33,420,000	86,557,400	11,730	3,575
Indian Ocean	28,350,500	73,427,500	12,598	3,840
Arctic Ocean	5,105,700	13,223,700	3,407	1,038
South China Sea	1,148,500	2,974,600	4,802	1,464
Caribbean Sea	971,400	2,515,900	8,448	2,575
Mediterranean Sea	969,100	2,510,000	4,926	1,501
Bering Sea	873,000	2,261,000	4,893	1,491
Gulf of Mexico	582,100	1,508,000	5,297	1,615
Sea of Okhotsk	537,500	1,392,000	3,192	973
Sea of Japan	391,100	1,013,000	5,468	1,667
Hudson Bay	281,900	730,100	305	93
East China Sea	256,600	664,600	620	189
Andaman Sea	218,100	564,900	3,667	1,118
Black Sea	196,100	507,900	3,906	1,191
Red Sea	174,900	453,000	1,764	538
North Sea	164,900	427,100	308	94

BIGGEST ISLANDS

Island	Area (sq mi)	Area (sq km)
Greenland (Denmark)	840,000	2,175,600
New Guinea (Indonesia, Papua New Guinea)	305,000	789,950
Borneo (Indonesia, Malaysia, Brunei)	286,000	740,740
Madagascar	226,656	587,040
Baffin (Canada)	195,928	507,454
Sumatra (Indonesia)	164,000	424,760
Honshu (Japan)	88,000	227,920
Great Britain (United Kingdom)	84,400	218,896
Victoria (Canada)	83,896	217,290
Ellesmere (Canada)	75,767	196,236
Celebes (Indonesia)	72,986	189,034
South (New Zealand)	58,393	151,238
Java (Indonesia)	48,842	126,501
North (New Zealand)	44,187	114,444
Cuba	42,803	110,860
Newfoundland (Canada)	42,031	108,860
Luzon (Philippines)	40,420	104,688

PRINCIPAL OCEAN DEPTHS

Name of Area	Location (latitude)	Location (longitude)	Depth (m)	Depth (fathoms)	Depth (ft)
PACIFIC OCEAN					
Marianas Trench	11° 22′ N	142° 36′ E	10,924	5,973	35,840
Tonga Trench	23° 16′ S	174° 44′ W	10,800	5,906	35,433
Philippine Trench	10° 38′ N	126° 36′ E	10,057	5,499	32,995
Kermadec Trench	31° 53′ S	177° 21′ W	10,047	5,494	32,963
Bonin Trench	24° 30′ N	143° 24′ E	9,994	5,464	32,788
Kuril Trench	44° 15′ N	150° 34′ E	9,750	5,331	31,988
Izu Trench	31°05′ N	142°10′ E	9,695	5,301	31,808
New Britain Trench	06°19′ S	153°45′ E	8,940	4,888	29,331
Yap Trench	08°33′ N	138°02′ E	8,527	4,663	27,976
Japan Trench	36°08′ N	142°43′ E	8,412	4,600	27,599
Peru-Chile Trench	23°18′ S	71°14′ W	8,064	4,409	26,457
Palau Trench	07°52′ N	134°56′ E	8,054	4,404	26,424
Aleutian Trench	50°51′ N	177°11′ E	7,679	4,199	25,194
ATLANTIC OCEAN					
Puerto Rico Trench	19° 55′ N	65°27′ W	8,605	4,705	28,232
South Sandwich Trench	55°42′ S	25°56′ W	8,325	4,552	27,313
Romanche Gap	0°13′ S	18°26′ W	7,728	4,226	25,354

World Facts and Figures

RIVERS AND WATERFALLS

LONGEST RIVERS

River	Outflow	Length (mi)	Length (km)
AFRICA			
Congo	Atlantic Ocean	2,900	4,670
Niger	Gulf of Guinea	2,590	4,170
Nile	Mediterranean	4,160	6,690
Zambezi	Indian Ocean	1,700	2,740
ASIA			
Amur	Tatar Strait	1,780	2,860
Brahmaputra	Bay of Bengal	1,800	2,900
Chang	East China Sea	3,964	6,380
Euphrates	Shatt al-Arab	1,700	2,740
Huang	Yellow Sea	3,395	5,460
Indus	Arabian Sea	1,800	2,900
Lena	Laptev Sea	2,734	4,400
Mekong	South China Sea	2,700	4,350
Ob	Gulf of Ob	2,268	3,650
Ob-Irtysh	Gulf of Ob	3,362	5,410
Yenisey	Kara Seav	2,543	4,090
AUSTRALIA			
Murray-Darling	Indian Ocean	2,310	3,720
EUROPE			
Danube	Black Sea	1,776	2,860
Volga	Caspian Sea	2,290	3,690
NORTH AMERICA			
Mississippi	Gulf of Mexico	2,340	3,770
Mississippi-Missouri-Red Rock	Gulf of Mexico	3,710	5,970
Missouri	Mississippi River	2,315	3,730
Missouri-Red Rock	Mississippi River	2,540	4,090
Rio Grande	Gulf of Mexico	1,900	3,060
Yukon	Bering Sea	1,979	3,180
SOUTH AMERICA			
Amazon	Atlantic Ocean	4,000	6,440
Japura	Amazon River	1,750	2,820
Madeira	Amazon River	2,013	3,240
Parana	Rio de la Plata	2,485	4,000
Purus	Amazon River	2,100	3,380
Sao Francisco	Atlantic Ocean	1,988	3,200

NOTABLE WATERFALLS

Name (Location)	Height (ft)	Height (m)
AFRICA		
Tugela# (South Africa)	2,014	614
Victoria, Zambezi River* (Zimbabwe-Zambia)	343	105
AUSTRALIA, NEW ZEALAND		
Wallaman, Stony Creek# (Australia)	1,137	347
Wollomombi (Australia)	1,100	335
Sutherland, Arthur River# (New Zealand)	1,904	580
EUROPE		
Krimml# (Austria)	1,312	400
Gavarnie* (France)	1,385	422
Mardalsfossen (Northern) (Norway)	1,535	468
Mardalsfossen (Southern)# (Norway)	2,149	655
Skjeggedal, Nybuai River#** (Norway)	1,378	420
Trummelbach# (Switzerland)	1,312	400
NORTH AMERICA		
Della# (Canada)	1,443	440
Niagara: Horseshoe (Canada)	173	53
Takakkaw, Daly Glacier# (Canada)	1,200	366
Niagara: American (U.S.)	182	55
Ribbon** (U.S.)	1,612	491
Silver Strand, Meadow Brook** (U.S.)	1,170	357
Yosemite#** (U.S.)	2,425	739
SOUTH AMERICA		
Iguazu (Argentina-Brazil)	230	70
Glass (Brazil)	1,325	404
Patos-Maribondo, Grande River (Brazil)	115	35
Paulo Afonso, Sao Francisco River (Brazil)	275	84
Urubupunga, Parana River (Brazil)	39	12
Great, Kamarang River (Guyana)	1,600	488
Kaieteur, Potaro River (Guyana)	741	226
Angel#*(Venezuela)	3,212	979
Cuquenan (Venezuela)	2,000	610

Note: If the river name is not shown, it is the same as that of the falls. "Height" is the total drop in one or more leaps.

#Falls of more than one leap; *falls that diminish greatly seasonally; **falls that reduce to a trickle or are dry for part of each year.

The estimated mean annual flow, in cubic feet per second (cubic meters in parentheses), of major waterfalls is as follows: Niagara, 212,200 (6,000); Paulo Afonso, 100,000 (2,800); Urubupunga, 97,000 (2,700); Iguazu, 61,000 (1,700); Patos-Maribondo, 53,000 (1,500); Victoria, 35,400 (1,000); and Kaieteur, 23,400 (660).

CONTINENTAL ALTITUDES AND LAKES

HIGHEST CONTINENTAL ALTITUDES

Continent	Highest Point	Elevation (ft)	Elevation (m)
Asia	Mount Everest, Nepal-Tibet	29,028	8,848
South America	Mount Aconcagua, Argentina	22,831	6,959
North America	Mount McKinley, Alaska, U.S.	20,320	6,194
Africa	Kilimanjaro, Tanzania	19,340	5,895
Europe	Mount Elbrus, Russia	18,510	5,642
Antarctica	Vinson Massif	16,864	5,140
Australia	Mount Kosciusko, New South Wales	7,310	2,228

LOWEST CONTINENTAL ALTITUDES

Continent	Lowest Point	Feet Below Sea Level	Meters Below Sea Level
Asia	Dead Sea, Israel-Jordan	1,339	408
South America	Valdes Peninsula, Argentina	131	40
North America	Death Valley, California, U.S.	282	86
Africa	Lake Assal, Djibouti	512	156
Europe	Caspian Sea, Russia, Azerbaijan	92	28
Antarctica	Bentley Subglacial Trench	8,327[1]	2,538[1]
Australia	Lake Eyre, South Australia	52	16

[1]Estimated level of the continental floor. Lower points that have yet to be discovered may exist further beneath the ice.

MAJOR NATURAL LAKES OF THE WORLD

Name	Continent	Area (sq mi)	Area (sq km)	Maximum Depth (ft)	Maximum Depth (m)
Caspian Sea[1]	Asia-Europe	143,244	371,000	3,363	1,025
Superior	North America	31,700	82,100	1,330	405
Victoria	Africa	26,828	69,484	270	82
Huron	North America	23,000	59,600	750	229
Michigan	North America	22,300	57,800	923	281
Aral Sea[1]	Asia	13,000[2]	33,700[2]	220	67
Tanganyika	Africa	12,700	32,900	4,823	1,470
Baykal	Asia	12,162	31,500	5,315	1,620
Great Bear	North America	12,096	31,330	1,463	446
Nyasa (Malawi)	Africa	11,150	28,880	2,280	695
Great Slave	North America	11,031	28,570	2,015	614
Erie	North America	9,910	25,670	210	64
Winnipeg	North America	9,417	24,390	60	18
Ontario	North America	7,340	19,010	802	244
Balkhash[1]	Asia	7,115	18,430	85	26
Ladoga	Europe	6,835	17,700	738	225

Note: A lake is generally defined as a body of water surrounded by land.

[1]Salt lake.

[2]Approximate figure, could be less. The diversion of feeder rivers since the 1960s has devastated the Aral—once the world's fourth-largest lake (26,000 sq mi [67,000 sq km]). By 2000, the Aral had effectively become three lakes, with the total area shown.

World Facts and Figures

RESERVOIRS AND DAMS

WORLD'S LARGEST-CAPACITY RESERVOIRS

Rank	Name	Country	Capacity (1,000 acre-ft)	Capacity (1,000,000 cu m)
1.	Kariba	Zimbabwe/ Zambia	146,400	180,600
2.	Bratsk	Russia	137,000	169,000
3.	High Aswan	Egypt	131,300	162,000
4.	Akosombo	Ghana	119,950	147,960
5.	Daniel Johnson	Canada	115,000	141,851
6.	Xinfeng	China	112,660	138,960
7.	Guri	Venezuela	109,400	135,000
8.	W. A. C. Bennett	Canada	60,235	74,300
9.	Krasnoyarsk	Russia	59,425	73,300
10.	Zeya	Russia	55,450	68,400

WORLD'S HIGHEST DAMS

Rank	Name	Country	Height Above Lowest Formation (ft)	Height Above Lowest Formation (m)
1.	Nurek	Tajikistan	984	300
2.	Grand Dixence	Switzerland	935	285
3.	Inguri	Georgia	892	272
4.	Vajont	Italy	860	262
5.	Manuel M. Torres	Mexico	856	261
6.	Alvaro Obregon	Mexico	853	260
7.	Mauvoisin	Switzerland	820	250
8.	Mica	Canada	797	243
9.	Alberto Lleras C	Colombia	797	243
10.	Sayano-Shushensk	Russia	794	242

WORLD'S LARGEST-VOLUME EMBANKMENT DAMS

Rank	Name	Country	Volume (1,000 cu yd)	Volume (1,000 cu m)
1.	Tarbela	Pakistan	194,230	148,500
2.	Fort Peck	U.S.	125,630	96,050
3.	Tucurui	Brazil	111,400	85,200
4.	Ataturk	Turkey	111,200	85,000
5.	Yacireta*	Argentina	105,900	81,000
6.	Rogun*	Tajikistan	98,750	75,500
7.	Oahe	U.S.	92,000	70,339
8.	Guri	Venezuela	91,560	70,000
9.	Parambikulam	India	90,460	69,165
10.	High Island West	China	87,600	67,000

*Under construction.

Photos (from left to right): *Tarbela Dam, Indus River, Pakistan; Grande Dixence Dam, Lac des Dix, Switzerland; Fort Peck Dam, Missouri River, Montana, U.S.; Lake Kariba Dam, Zambezi River, Zambia/Zimbabwe; Vajont Dam, Vajont Valley, Italy*

GLOBAL TEMPERATURES

HIGHEST MOUNTAINS

Rank	Peak	Place	Height (ft)	Height (m)
1.	Everest	Nepal-Tibet	29,028	8,848
2.	K2 (Godwin Austen)	Kashmir	28,250	8,611
3.	Kanchenjunga	India-Nepal	28,208	8,598
4.	Lhotse I (Everest)	Nepal-Tibet	27,923	8,511
5.	Makalu I	Nepal-Tibet	27,789	8,470
6.	Lhotse II (Everest)	Nepal-Tibet	27,560	8,400
7.	Dhaulagiri	Nepal	26,810	8,172
8.	Manaslu I	Nepal	26,760	8,156
9.	Cho Oyu	Nepal-Tibet	26,750	8,153
10.	Nanga Parbat	Kashmir	26,660	8,126

AVERAGE GLOBAL TEMPERATURES, 1900–2000

Decade	Degrees Fahrenheit	Degrees Celsius
1900-09	56.52	13.62
1910-19	56.57	13.65
1920-29	56.74	13.74
1930-39	57.00	13.89
1940-49	57.13	13.96
1950-59	57.06	13.92
1960-69	57.05	13.92
1970-79	57.04	13.91
1980-89	57.36	14.09
1990-99	57.64	14.24
2000	57.60	14.22

HIGHEST MEASURED TEMPERATURE

Continent or Region	Temperature (degrees Fahrenheit)	Temperature (degrees Celsius)	Place	Elevation (ft)	Elevation (m)	Date
Africa	136	58	El Azizia, Libya	367	112	Sept. 13, 1922
North America	134	57	Death Valley, California (Greenland Ranch)	−178	−54	July 10, 1913
Asia	129	54	Tirat Tsvi, Israel	−722	−220	June 21, 1942
Australia	128	53	Cloncurry, Queensland	622	190	Jan. 16, 1889
Europe	122	50	Seville, Spain	26	8	Aug. 4, 1881
South America	120	49	Rivadavia, Argentina	676	206	Dec. 11, 1905
Antarctica	59	15	Vanda Station, Scott Coast	49	15	Jan. 5, 1974

LOWEST MEASURED TEMPERATURE

Continent or Region	Temperature (degrees Fahrenheit)	Temperature (degrees Celsius)	Place	Elevation (ft)	Elevation (m)	Date
Antarctica	−129.0	−89	Vostok	11,220	3,420	July 21, 1983
Asia	−90.0	−68	Oimekon, Russia	2,625	800	Feb. 6, 1933
Asia	−90.0	−68	Verkhoyansk, Russia	350	107	Feb. 7, 1892
Greenland	−87.0	−66	Northice	7,687	2,343	Jan. 9, 1954
North America	−81.4	−63	Snag, Yukon, Canada	2,120	646	Feb. 3, 1947
Europe	−67.0	−55	Ust'-Shchugor, Russia	279	85	Jan.*
South America	−27.0	−33	Sarmiento, Argentina	879	268	June 1, 1907
Africa	−11.0	−24	Ifrane, Morocco	5,364	1,635	Feb. 11, 1935
Australia	−9.4	−23	Charlotte Pass, New South Wales	5,758	1,755	June 29, 1994
Oceania	14.0	−10	Haleakala Summit, Maui, Hawaii	9,750	2,972	Jan. 2, 1961

* Exact day and year unknown.

World Facts and Figures

PRECIPITATION AND DESERTS

HIGHEST AVERAGE ANNUAL PRECIPITATION

Continent or Region	Precipitation (in)	Precipitation (mm)	Place	Elevation (ft)	Elevation (m)	Years of Data
South America	523.6[1,2]	13,300[1,2]	Lloro, Colombia	520[3]	158[3]	29
Asia	467.4[1]	11,870[1]	Mawsynram, India	4,597	1,401	38
Oceania	460.0[1]	11,680[1]	Mt. Waialeale, Kauai, Hawaii	5,148	1,569	30
Africa	405.0	10,290	Debundscha, Cameroon	30	9	32
South America	354.0[2]	8,992[2]	Quibdo, Colombia	120	37	16
Australia	340.0	8,636	Bellenden Ker, Queensland	5,102	1,555	9
North America	256.0	6,502	Henderson Lake, British Columbia	12	4	14
Europe	183.0	4,648	Crkvica, Bosnia-Herzegovina	3,337	1,017	22

[1]The value given is continent's highest and possibly the world's depending on measurement practices, procedures, and period of record variations.

[2]The official greatest average annual precipitation for South America is 354 in (8,992 mm) at Quibdo, Colombia. The 523.6 in (13,300 mm) average at Lloro, Colombia (14 mi [23 km] SE and at a higher elevation than Quibdo) is an estimated amount.

[3]Approximate elevation.

LOWEST AVERAGE ANNUAL PRECIPITATION

Continent or Region	Precipitation (in)	Precipitation (mm)	Place	Elevation (ft)	Elevation (m)	Years of Data
South America	0.03	0.8	Arica, Chile	95	29	59
Africa	< 0.1	< 3	Wadi Halfa, Sudan	410	125	39
Antarctica	0.8[1]	20[1]	Amundsen-Scott South Pole Station	9,186	2,800	10
North America	1.2	30	Batagues, Mexico	16	5	14
Asia	1.8	46	Aden, Yemen	22	7	50
Australia	4.05	103	Mulka (Troudaninna), South Australia	160[2]	49[2]	42
Europe	6.4	163	Astrakhan, Russia	45	14	25
Oceania	8.93	227	Puako, Hawaii	5	2	13

[1]The value given is the average amount of solid snow accumulating in one year as indicated by snow markers. The liquid content of the snow is undetermined.

[2]Approximate elevation.

NOTABLE DESERTS OF THE WORLD

Arabian (Eastern), 70,000 sq mi (181,000 sq km) in Egypt between the Nile River and Red Sea, extending southward into Sudan

Chihuahuan, 140,000 sq mi (363,000 sq km) in Texas, New Mexico, Arizona, and Mexico

Gibson, 120,000 sq mi (311,000 sq km) in the interior of Western Australia

Gobi, 500,000 sq mi (1,295,000 sq km) in Mongolia and China

Great Sandy, 150,000 sq mi (388,000 sq km) in Western Australia

Great Victoria, 150,000 sq mi (388,000 sq km) in South and Western Australia

Kalahari, 225,000 sq mi (583,000 sq km) in southern Africa

Kara Kum, 120,000 sq mi (311,000 sq km) in Turkmenistan

Kyzyl Kum, 100,000 sq mi (259,000 sq km) in Kazakhstan and Uzbekistan

Libyan, 450,000 sq mi (1,165,000 sq km) in the Sahara, extending from Libya through southwestern Egypt into Sudan

Nubian, 100,000 sq mi (259,000 sq km) in the Sahara in northeastern Sudan

Patagonia, 300,000 sq mi (777,000 sq km) in southern Argentina

Rub al-Khali (Empty Quarter), 250,000 sq mi (648,000 sq km) in the southern Arabian Peninsula

Sahara, 3,500,000 sq mi (9,065,000 sq km) in northern Africa, extending westward to the Atlantic; largest desert in the world

Sonoran, 70,000 sq mi (181,000 sq km) in southwestern Arizona and southeastern California extending into northwestern Mexico

Syrian, 100,000 sq mi (259,000 sq km) arid wasteland extending over much of northern Saudi Arabia, eastern Jordan, southern Syria, and western Iraq

Taklimakan, 140,000 sq mi (363,000 sq km) in Xinjiang Province, China

Thar (Great Indian), 100,000 sq mi (259,000 sq km) arid area extending 400 mi (640 km) along the India-Pakistan border

LANGUAGES, POPULATION GROWTH, AND OIL AND GAS RESERVES

TOP TEN LANGUAGES

Language	Major Countries Where Spoken	Native Speakers
Mandarin	China, Taiwan	874,000,000
Hindi	India	366,000,000
English	U.S., Canada, Britain	341,000,000
Spanish	Spain, Latin America	322,000,000
Arabic	Arabian Peninsula	207,000,000
Bengali	India, Bangladesh	207,000,000
Portuguese	Portugal, Brazil	176,000,000
Russian	Russia	167,000,000
Japanese	Japan	125,000,000
German	Germany, Austria	100,000,000

WORLD POPULATION THROUGH HISTORY

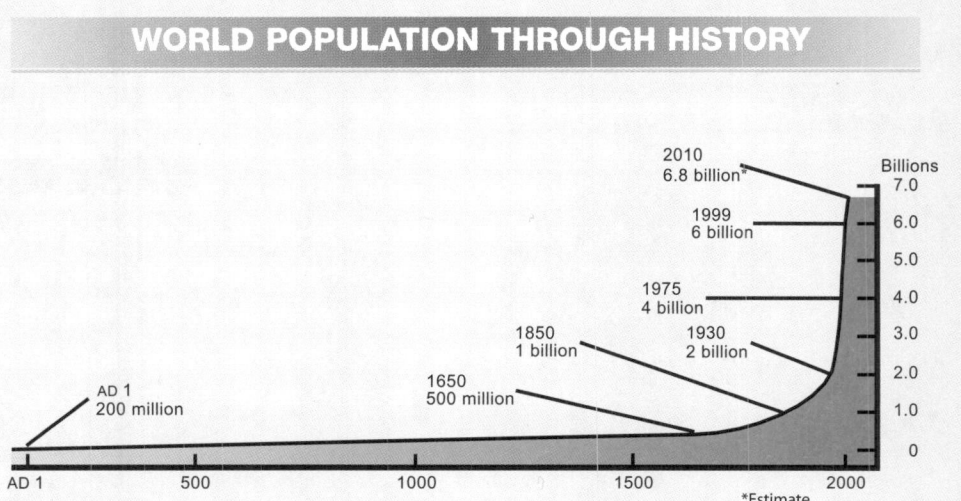

PRINCIPAL KNOWN CRUDE OIL AND NATURAL GAS RESERVES, JANUARY, 2009

	Crude Oil (billion barrels)		Natural Gas (trillion cubic feet)			Crude Oil (billion barrels)		Natural Gas (trillion cubic feet)	
	OGJ	WO	OGJ	WO		OGJ	WO	OGJ	WO
NORTH AMERICA					Iraq	115.0	126.0	111.9	91.0
Canada	178.1	25.2	57.9	58.3	Kuwait	104.0	99.4	63.4	66.3
Mexico	10.5	11.1	13.2	18.1	Oman	5.5	5.7	30.0	32.0
United States	21.3	21.3	237.7	237.7	Qatar	15.2	20.0	891.9	903.2
SOUTH AMERICA					Saudi Arabia	266.7	264.8	258.5	254.0
Argentina	2.6	2.7	15.6	16.5	United Arab Emirates	97.8	68.1	214.4	196.3
Brazil	12.6	12.5	12.9	12.9	**AFRICA**				
Venezuela	99.4	81.0	170.9	152.0	Algeria	12.2	11.9	159.0	160.0
WESTERN EUROPE					Egypt	3.7	3.7	58.5	68.4
Netherlands	0.1	0.2	50.0	48.8	Libya	43.7	36.5	54.4	52.8
Norway	6.7	6.7	81.7	81.7	Nigeria	36.2	37.2	184.2	184.5
United Kingdom	3.4	3.6	12.1	14.0	**ASIA AND OCEANIA**				
EASTERN EUROPE AND FORMER USSR					Australia	1.5	4.2	30.0	151.9
Kazakhstan	30.0	NA	85.0	NA	China	16.0	18.1	80.0	61.8
Russia	60.0	76.0	1,680.0	1,654.0	India	5.6	4.0	38.0	31.8
Turkmenistan	0.6	NA	94.0	NA	Indonesia	4.0	4.5	106.0	92.0
Ukraine	0.4	NA	39.0	NA	Malaysia	4.0	5.5	83.0	88.0
Uzbekistan	0.6	NA	65.0	NA	Pakistan	0.3	0.3	31.3	29.8
MIDDLE EAST					**WORLD**				
Iran	136.2	137.0	991.6	985.0	TOTAL	1,342.2	1,184.2	6,254.4	6,436.0

OGJ = *Oil and Gas Journal*, January 2009

WO = *World Oil*, Year-End 2007

NOTE: Data for Kuwait and Saudi Arabia include one-half of the reserves in the Neutral Zone between Kuwait and Saudi Arabia. All reserve figures except those for the former USSR and natural gas reserves in Canada are *proved reserves* recoverable with present technology and prices at the time of estimation. Former USSR and Canadian natural gas figures include *proved* and some *probable reserves*.

World Facts and Figures

CARBON DIOXIDE EMISSION, AND MAJOR ENERGY USERS AND PRODUCERS

WORLD CARBON DIOXIDE EMISSIONS FROM THE USE OF FOSSIL FUELS, 2006

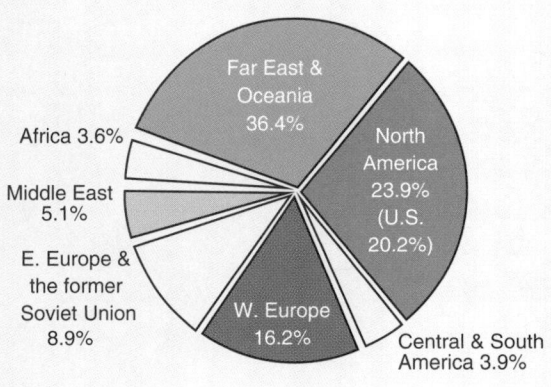

- Far East & Oceania 36.4%
- North America 23.9% (U.S. 20.2%)
- Africa 3.6%
- Middle East 5.1%
- E. Europe & the former Soviet Union 8.9%
- W. Europe 16.2%
- Central & South America 3.9%

NATIONS MOST RELIANT ON NUCLEAR ENERGY, 2008
(nuclear energy generation as % of total electricity generated)

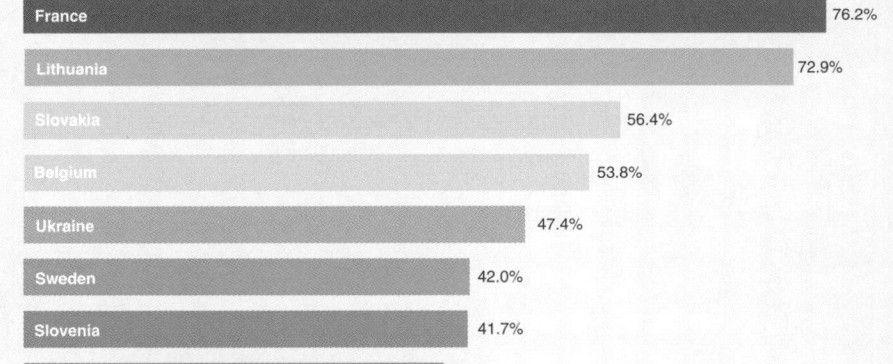

Country	%
France	76.2%
Lithuania	72.9%
Slovakia	56.4%
Belgium	53.8%
Ukraine	47.4%
Sweden	42.0%
Slovenia	41.7%
Armenia	39.4%
Switzerland	39.2%
Hungary	37.2%

0% 10% 20% 30% 40% 50% 60% 70% 80%

WORLD'S MAJOR PRODUCERS OF PRIMARY ENERGY, 2006
(quadrillion Btu)

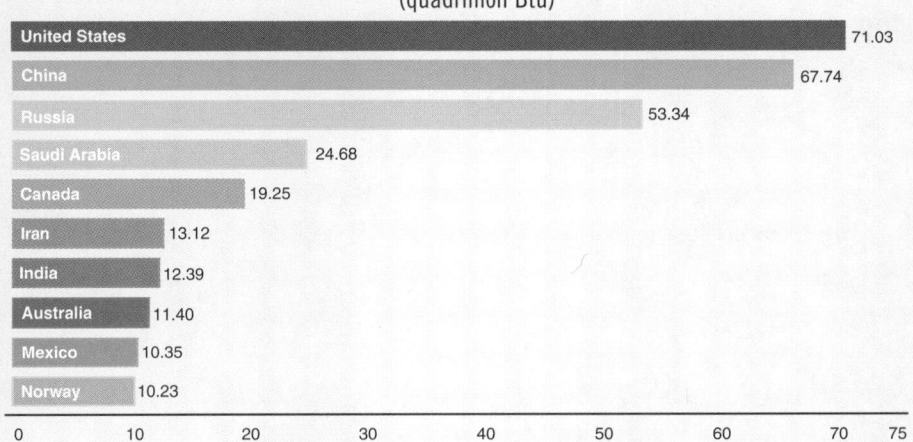

Country	quadrillion Btu
United States	71.03
China	67.74
Russia	53.34
Saudi Arabia	24.68
Canada	19.25
Iran	13.12
India	12.39
Australia	11.40
Mexico	10.35
Norway	10.23

0 10 20 30 40 50 60 70 75

WORLD'S MAJOR CONSUMERS OF PRIMARY ENERGY, 2006
(quadrillion Btu)

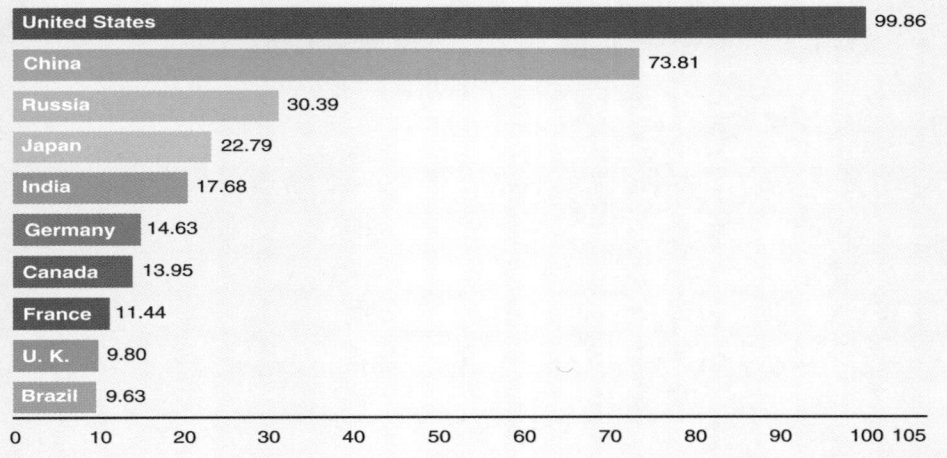

Country	quadrillion Btu
United States	99.86
China	73.81
Russia	30.39
Japan	22.79
India	17.68
Germany	14.63
Canada	13.95
France	11.44
U. K.	9.80
Brazil	9.63

0 10 20 30 40 50 60 70 80 90 100 105

World Almanac Section

Nation Facts and Figures
from The World Almanac®

Nigeria	246,000	2,838	197	5.	Palau	11,000		
ing Hong Kong and Macau.	127,654,000	22	1,096	6.	San Marino	13,000	1,100	
	124,009,000	838	8	7.	Monaco	20,000	1,525	
		353	324	8.	Liechtenstein	28,000	113	
			136	9.	Saint Kitts and Nevis	32,000	1,217	
				10.	Marshall Islands	33,000	41,608	470
					Antigua and Barbuda	39,000	550	16,065
		*Area only 0.17 sq mi (0.4 sq km).		56,000	386	212		
						68,000	800	143
							400	309
								154

LARGEST LAND AREAS

Country	Land Area sq mi	Land Area)
Russia		
China		
Canad	6,59	

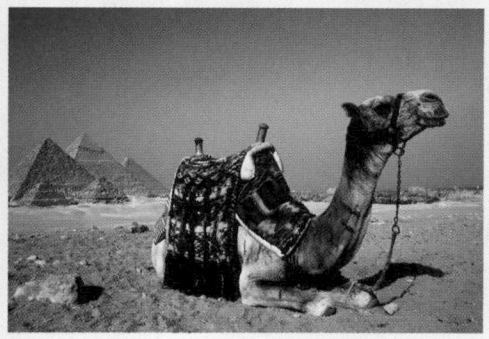

AFRICA

Among African nations, Sudan occupies the largest total area, but Nigeria has the largest population, ranking eighth in the world.

ALGERIA

FOR MAP, SEE PAGE 154

Population: 34,178,188

Ethnic groups: Arab-Berber 99%

Principal languages: Arabic (official), French, Berber dialects

Chief religion: Sunni Muslim (official) 99%

Area: 919,600 sq mi (2,381,741 sq km)

Topography: The Tell, located on the coast, comprises fertile plains 50-100 mi (80-160 km) wide. Two major chains of the Atlas Mountains, running roughly east to west and reaching 7,000 ft (2,100 m), enclose a dry plateau region. Below lies the Sahara, mostly desert with major mineral resources.

Capital: Algiers (pop., 3,060,000)

Independence date: July 5, 1962   **Government type:** republic

Head of state: Pres. Abdelaziz Bouteflika

Head of government: Prime Min. Abdelaziz Belkhadem

Monetary unit: dinar

GDP: $235.5 billion (2008 est.)   **Per capita GDP:** $7,000

Industries: petroleum, natural gas, light industries, mining, electrical, petrochemical, food processing

Chief crops: wheat, barley, oats, grapes, olives, citrus, fruits

Minerals: petroleum, natural gas, iron ore, phosphates, uranium, lead, zinc

Life expectancy at birth (years): male, 69.1; female, 72.0

Literacy rate: 61.6%

Website: www.algeria-us.org

ANGOLA

FOR MAP, SEE PAGE 163

Population: 12,799,293

Ethnic groups: Ovimbundu 37%, Kimbundu 25%, Bakongo 13%

Principal languages: Portuguese (official), Bantu and other African languages

Chief religions: indigenous beliefs 47%, Roman Catholic 38%, Protestant 15%

Area: 481,400 sq mi (1,246,700 sq km)`

Topography: Most of Angola consists of a plateau elevated 3,000 to 5,000 ft (900 to 1,500 m) above sea level, rising from a narrow coastal strip. There is also a temperate highland area in the west-central region, a desert in the south, and a tropical rain forest covering Cabinda.

Capital: Luanda (pop., 2,623,000)

Independence date: November 11, 1975   **Government type:** republic

Head of state: Pres. José Eduardo dos Santos

Head of government: Prime Min. Fernando da Piedade Dias dos Santos

Monetary unit: kwanza

GDP: $110.3 billion (2008 est.)   **Per capita GDP:** $8,800

Industries: petroleum, mining, cement, basic metal products, fish processing, food processing

Chief crops: bananas, sugarcane, coffee, sisal, corn, cotton, manioc, tobacco, vegetables, plantains

Minerals: petroleum, diamonds, iron ore, phosphates, copper, feldspar, gold, bauxite, uranium

Life expectancy at birth (years): male, 36.1; female, 37.6

Literacy rate: 42%   **Website:** www.angola.org

ABOUT THE WORLD ALMANAC DATA: Population figures for cities generally pertain to the entire metropolitan area. Area figures for countries are total area (land and water). GDP (gross domestic product) estimates are based on so-called purchasing power parity calculations, which make use of weighted prices in order to take into account differences in price levels between countries. Please note that the addresses and content of websites are subject to change.

CHIEF ABBREVIATIONS USED IN THE WORLD ALMANAC SECTION

est.	estimate(d)	ft	foot, feet	GovGen. Governor-General	in	inch(es)	km kilometer(s)	m	meter(s)
mi	mile(s)	NA	not available	pop. population	Pres. President	Prime Min. Prime Minister	sq	square

BENIN

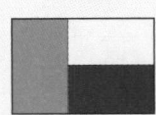

FOR MAP, SEE PAGE 161

Population: 8,791,832

Ethnic groups: 42 groups, including Fon, Adja, Yoruba, and Bariba

Principal languages: French (official), Fon, Yoruba, various tribal languages

Chief religions: indigenous beliefs 50%, Christian 30%, Muslim 20%

Area: 43,480 sq mi (112,620 sq km)

Capital: Porto-Novo (pop., 238,000)

Topography: Most of Benin is flat and covered with dense vegetation. The coast is hot, humid, and rainy.

Independence date: August 1, 1960

Government type: republic

Head of state and government: Pres. Thomas Yayi Boni

Monetary unit: CFA franc

GDP: $12.84 billion (2008 est.)

Per capita GDP: $1,500

Industries: textiles, food processing, chemical production, construction materials

Chief crops: cotton, corn, cassava, yams, beans, palm oil, peanuts

Minerals: offshore oil, limestone, marble

Life expectancy at birth (years): male, 50.3; female, 51.4

Literacy rate: 37.5%

Website: www.beninembassyus.org

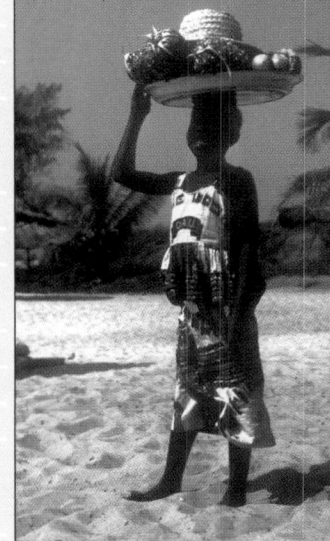

West African fruit seller

BOTSWANA

FOR MAP, SEE PAGE 163

Population: 1,990,876

Ethnic groups: Tswana 79%, Kalanga 11%, Basarwa 3%

Principal languages: English (official), Setswana

Chief religions: indigenous beliefs 85%, Christian 15%

Area: 231,800 sq mi (600,370 sq km)

Topography: The Kalahari Desert, supporting nomadic Bushmen and wildlife, spreads over the southwest; there are swamplands and farming areas in the north, and rolling plains in the east where livestock are grazed.

Capital: Gaborone (pop., 199,000)

Independence date: September 30, 1966

Government type: parliamentary republic

Head of state and government: Pres. Festus Mogae

Monetary unit: pula

GDP: $26.04 billion (2008 est.)   **Per capita GDP:** $13,300

Industries: mining, livestock processing, textiles

Chief crops: sorghum, maize, millet, beans, sunflowers, groundnuts

Minerals: diamonds, copper, nickel, salt, soda ash, potash, coal, iron ore, silver

Life expectancy at birth (years): male, 31.0; female, 30.5

Literacy rate: 69.8%   **Website:** www.gov.bw

BURKINA FASO

FOR MAP, SEE PAGE 161

Population: 15,746,232

Ethnic groups: Mossi (approximately 40%), Gurunsi, Senufo, Lobi, Bobo, Mande, Fulani

Principal languages: French (official), Sudanic languages

Chief religions: Muslim 50%, indigenous beliefs 40%, Christian (mainly Roman Catholic) 10%

Area: 105,900 sq mi (274,200 sq km)

Topography: Landlocked Burkina Faso is in the savanna region of West Africa. The north is arid, hot, and thinly populated.

Capital: Ouagadougou (pop., 821,000)

Independence date: August 5, 1960   **Government type:** republic

Head of state: Pres. Blaise Compaoré

Head of government: Prime Min. Paramanga Ernest Yonli

Monetary unit: CFA franc

GDP: $17.82 billion (2008 est.)   **Per capita GDP:** $1,200

Industries: cotton lint, beverages, agricultural processing, soap, cigarettes, textiles, gold

Chief crops: peanuts, shea nuts, sesame, cotton, sorghum, millet, corn, rice

Minerals: manganese, limestone, marble, gold, antimony, copper, nickel, bauxite, lead, phosphates, zinc, silver

Life expectancy at birth (years): male, 42.6; female, 45.8

Literacy rate: 36%

Website: www.burkinaembassy–usa.org

BURUNDI

FOR MAP, SEE PAGE 162

Population: 8,988,091

Ethnic groups: Hutu 85%, Tutsi 14%, Twa (Pygmy) 1%

Principal languages: Kirundi, French (both official); Swahili

Chief religions: Roman Catholic 62%, indigenous beliefs 23%, Muslim 10%, Protestant 5%

Area: 10,750 sq mi (27,830 sq km)

Topography: Much of the country is grassy highland, with mountains reaching 8,900 ft (2,700 m). The southernmost source of the White Nile is located in Burundi. Lake Tanganyika is the second deepest lake in the world.

Capital: Bujumbura (pop., 346,000)

Independence date: July 1, 1962

Government type: republic

Head of state and government: Pres. Pierre Nkurunziza

Monetary unit: franc

GDP: $3.1 billion (2008 est.)

Per capita GDP: $400

Industries: light consumer goods, assembly of imported components, public works construction, food processing

Chief crops: coffee, cotton, tea, corn, sorghum, sweet potatoes, bananas, manioc

Minerals: nickel, uranium, rare earth oxides, peat, cobalt, copper, platinum (not yet exploited), vanadium

Life expectancy at birth (years): male, 42.7; female, 44.0

Literacy rate: 35.3%

Website: www.burundiembassy-usa.org

CAMEROON

FOR MAP, SEE PAGE 154

Population: 18,879,301

Ethnic groups: Highlanders 31%, Equatorial Bantu 19%, Kirdi 11%, Fulani 10%, northwest Bantu 8%, east Nigritic 7%

Principal languages: English, French (both official); 24 African language groups

Chief religions: indigenous beliefs 40%, Christian 40%, Muslim 20%

Cameroon (continued)

Area: 183,570 sq mi (475,440 sq km)

Topography: A low coastal plain with rain forests is in the south; plateaus in the center lead to forested mountains in the west, including Mt. Cameroon, 13,350 ft (4,070 m); grasslands in the north lead to marshes around Lake Chad.

Capital: Yaoundé (pop., 1,616,000)

Independence date: January 1, 1960   **Government type:** republic

Head of state: Pres. Paul Biya

Head of government: Prime Min. Ephraim Inoni

Monetary unit: CFA franc

GDP: $42.76 billion (2008 est.)   **Per capita GDP:** $2,300

Industries: petroleum production and refining, food processing, light consumer goods, textiles, lumber

Chief crops: coffee, cocoa, cotton, rubber, bananas, oilseed, grains, root starches

Minerals: petroleum, bauxite, iron ore

Life expectancy at birth (years): male, 47.1; female, 48.8

Literacy rate: 63.4%

Website: www.spm.gov.cm

CAPE VERDE

FOR MAP, SEE PAGE 151

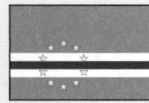

Population: 429,474

Ethnic groups: Creole 71%, African 28%, European 1%

Principal languages: Portuguese (official), Crioulo

Chief religions: Roman Catholic (infused with indigenous beliefs), Protestant (mostly Church of the Nazarene)

Area: 1,560 sq mi (4,030 sq km)

Topography: Cape Verde Islands are 15 in number, volcanic in origin (active crater on Fogo). The landscape is eroded and stark, with vegetation mostly in interior valleys.

Capital: Praia (pop., 82,000)

Independence date: July 5, 1975
Government type: republic

Head of state: Pres. Pedro Pires

Head of government:
Prime Min. José Maria Neves

Monetary unit: escudo

GDP: $1.64 billion (2008 est.)   **Per capita GDP:** $3,800

Industries: food and beverages, fish processing, shoes and garments, salt mining, ship repair

Chief crops: bananas, corn, beans, sweet potatoes, sugarcane, coffee, peanuts

Minerals: salt, basalt rock, limestone, kaolin

Life expectancy at birth (years): male, 66.8; female, 73.5

Literacy rate: 71.6%

Website: www.virtualcapeverde.net

Ripe papayas

CENTRAL AFRICAN REPUBLIC

FOR MAP, SEE PAGE 155

Population: 4,511,488

Ethnic groups: Baya 33%, Banda 27%, Mandjia 13%, Sara 10%, Mboum 7%, M'Baka 4%, Yakoma 4%

Principal languages: French (official), Sangho (national), tribal languages

Chief religions: indigenous beliefs 35%, Protestant 25%, Roman Catholic 25%, Muslim 15%

Area: 240,530 sq mi (622,984 sq km)

Topography: Mostly rolling plateau, average altitude 2,000 ft (600 m), with rivers draining south to the Congo and north to Lake Chad. Open, well-watered savanna covers most of the area, with an arid area in the northeast and tropical rain forest in the southwest.

Capital: Bangui (pop., 689,000)

Independence date: August 13, 1960

Government type: republic

Head of state: Pres. François Bozizé

Head of government: Prime Élie Doté

Monetary unit: CFA franc

GDP: $3.24 billion (2008 est.)   **Per capita GDP:** $700

Industries: diamond mining, sawmills, breweries, textiles, footwear, assembly of bicycles and motorcycles

Chief crops: cotton, coffee, tobacco, manioc, yams, millet, corn, bananas

Minerals: diamonds, uranium, gold, oil

Life expectancy at birth (years): male, 39.7; female, 43.1

Literacy rate: 60%   **Website:** www.state.gov/r/pa/ei/bgn/4007.htm

CHAD

FOR MAP, SEE PAGE 155

Population: 10,329,208

Ethnic groups: about 200 groups; largest are Arabs in north and Sara in south

Principal languages: French, Arabic (both official); Sara; more than 120 different languages and dialects

Chief religions: Muslim 51%, Christian 35%, animist 7%, other 7%

Area: 496,000 sq mi (1,284,000 sq km)

Topography: Wooded savanna, steppe, and desert in the south; part of the Sahara in the north. Southern rivers flow north to Lake Chad, surrounded by marshland.

Capital: N'Djamena (pop., 797,000)

Independence date: August 11, 1960

Government type: republic

Head of state: Pres. Idriss Déby

Head of government: Prime Min. Youssof Saleh Abbas

Monetary unit: CFA franc

GDP: $16.26 billion (2008 est.)   **Per capita GDP:** $1,600

Industries: cotton textiles, meatpacking, beer brewing, natron, soap, cigarettes, construction materials

Chief crops: cotton, sorghum, millet, peanuts, rice, potatoes, manioc

Minerals: petroleum (unexploited but exploration under way), uranium, natron, kaolin

Life expectancy at birth (years): male, 47.0; female, 50.1

Literacy rate: 40%

Website: www.chadembassy.org

COMOROS

FOR MAP, SEE PAGE 165

Population: 752,438

Ethnic groups: Antalote, Cafre, Makoa, Oimatsaha, Sakalava (all are mostly an African-Arab mix)

Principal languages: Arabic, French (both official); Shikomoro (a blend of Swahili and Arabic)

Chief religion: Muslim (official) 98%

Area: 840 sq mi (2,170 sq km)

Topography: The islands are of volcanic origin, with an active volcano on Grande Comore.

Capital: Moroni (pop., 53,000)

Independence date: July 6, 1975

Government type: republic

Head of state and government: Pres. Ahmed Abdallah Mohamed Sambi

Monetary unit: franc

GDP: $741.4 million (2008 est.)   **Per capita GDP:** $1,000

Industries: tourism, perfume distillation

Chief crops: vanilla, cloves, perfume essences, copra, coconuts, bananas, cassava

Life expectancy at birth (years): male, 59.3; female, 63.9

Literacy rate: 57.3%

Website: www.state.gov/r/pa/ei/bgn/5236.htm

CONGO, DEMOCRATIC REPUBLIC OF THE

Population: 68,692,542

FOR MAP, SEE PAGE 151

Ethnic groups: Over 200 groups; the four largest, the Mongo, Luba, Kongo (all Bantu), and Mangbetu-Azande (Hamitic), make up 45% of the population

Principal languages: French (official), Lingala, Kingwana (a Swahili dialect), Kikongo, Tshiluba

Chief religions: Roman Catholic 50%, Protestant 20%, Kimbanguist 10%, Muslim 10%

Area: 905,570 sq mi (2,345,410 sq km)

Topography: Congo includes the bulk of the Congo River basin. The vast central region is a low-lying plateau covered by rain forest. Mountainous terraces in the west, savannas in the south and southeast, grasslands toward the north, and the high Ruwenzori Mountains in the east surround the central region. A short strip of territory borders the Atlantic Ocean. The Congo River is 2,718 mi (4,374 km) long.

Capital: Kinshasa (pop., 5,277,000)

Independence date: June 30, 1960

Government type: republic with strong presidential authority

Head of state and government: Pres. Joseph Kabila

Monetary unit: Congolese franc

GDP: $21.05 billion (2008 est.)

Per capita GDP: $300

Industries: mining, mineral processing, consumer products, cement

Chief crops: coffee, sugar, palm oil, rubber, tea, quinine, cassava, palm oil, bananas, root crops, corn, fruits

Minerals: cobalt, copper, cadmium, petroleum, industrial and gem diamonds, gold, silver, zinc, manganese, tin, germanium, uranium, radium, bauxite, iron ore, coal

Life expectancy at birth (years): male, 47.1; female, 51.3

Literacy rate: 77.3%

Website: www.state.gov/r/pa/ei/bgn/2823.htm

CONGO REPUBLIC

FOR MAP, SEE PAGE 151

Population: 4,012,809

Ethnic groups: Kongo 48%, Sangha 20%, M'Bochi 12%, Teke 17%

Principal languages: French (official), Lingala, Monokutuba, Kikongo, many local languages and dialects

Chief religions: Christian 50%, animist 48%, Muslim 2%

Area: 132,000 sq mi (342,000 sq km)

Topography: Much of the Congo is covered by thick forests. A coastal plain leads to the fertile Niari Valley. The center is a plateau; the Congo River basin consists of flood plains in the lower portion and savanna in the upper.

Capital: Brazzaville (pop., 1,080,000)

Independence date: August 15, 1960   **Government type:** republic

Head of state and government: Pres. Denis Sassou-Nguesso

Monetary unit: CFA franc

GDP: $15.6 billion (2008 est.)   **Per capita GDP:** $4,000

Industries: petroleum extraction, cement, lumber, brewing, sugar, palm oil, soap, flour, cigarettes

Chief crops: cassava, sugar, rice, corn, peanuts, vegetables, coffee, cocoa

Minerals: petroleum, potash, lead, zinc, uranium, copper, phosphates, natural gas

Life expectancy at birth (years): male, 48.5; female, 56.6

Literacy rate: 74.9%   **Website:** www.state.gov/r/pa/ei/bgn/2825.htm

CÔTE D'IVOIRE (IVORY COAST)

FOR MAP, SEE PAGE 160

Population: 20,617,068

Ethnic groups: Akan 42%, Voltaiques (Gur) 18%, north Mandes 17%, Krous 11%, south Mandes 10%

Principal languages: French (official), Dioula, many native dialects

Chief religions: Muslim 35-40%, Christian 20-30%, indigenous beliefs 25-40%

Area: 124,500 sq mi (322,460 sq km)

Familiar wildlife of sub-Saharan Africa: zebras (right) rank among the favorite prey of lions (left)

Nation Facts and Figures

Côte d'Ivoire (Ivory Coast) *(continued)*

Topography: Forests cover the western half of the country, and range from a coastal strip to halfway to the north in the east. A sparse inland plain leads to low mountains in the northwest.

Official capital: Yamoussoukro (pop., 416,000); de facto capital, Abidjan (pop., 3,337,000)

Independence date: August 7, 1960   **Government type:** in transition

Head of state: Pres. Laurent Gbagbo

Head of government: Prime Min. Charles Konan Banny

Monetary unit: CFA franc

GDP: $34.0 billion (2008 est.)   **Per capita GDP:** $1,700

Industries: foodstuffs, beverages, wood products, oil refining, truck and bus assembly, textiles, fertilizer, building materials, electricity

Chief crops: coffee, cocoa beans, bananas, palm kernels, corn, rice, manioc, sweet potatoes, sugar, cotton, rubber

Minerals: petroleum, natural gas, diamonds, manganese, iron ore, cobalt, bauxite, copper

Life expectancy at birth (years): male, 40.3; female, 44.8

Literacy rate: 48.5%

Website: www.state.gov/r/pa/ei/bgn/2846.htm

DJIBOUTI

For map, see page 155

Population: 516,055

Ethnic groups: Somali 60%, Afar 35%

Principal languages: French, Arabic (both official); Afar, Somali

Chief religions: Muslim 94%, Christian 6%

Area: 8,500 sq mi (22,000 sq km)

Topography: The territory—divided into a low coastal plain, mountains behind, and an interior plateau—is arid, sandy, and desolate.

Capital: Djibouti (pop., 502,000)

Independence date: June 27, 1977   **Government type:** republic

Head of state: Pres. Ismail Omar Guelleh

Head of government: Prime Min. Dileita Mohamed Dileita

Monetary unit: Djibouti franc

GDP: $1.9 billion (2008 est.)   **Per capita GDP:** $3,700

Industries: construction, agricultural processing

Chief crops: fruits, vegetables

Life expectancy at birth (years): male, 41.8; female, 44.4

Literacy rate: 46.2%

Website: www.state.gov/r/pa/ei/bgn/5482.htm

EGYPT

For map, see page 155

Population: 83,082,869

Ethnic groups: Egyptian Arab 99%

Principal languages: Arabic (official), English, French

Chief religions: Muslim (official; mostly Sunni) 94%, Coptic Christian and other 6%

Area: 386,660 sq mi (1,001,450 sq km)

Topography: Almost entirely desolate and barren, with hills and mountains in the east and along the Nile. The Nile Valley, where most of the people live, stretches 550 mi (885 km).

Capital: Cairo (pop., 10,834,000)

Independence date: February 28, 1922   **Government type:** republic

Head of state: Pres. Hosni Mubarak

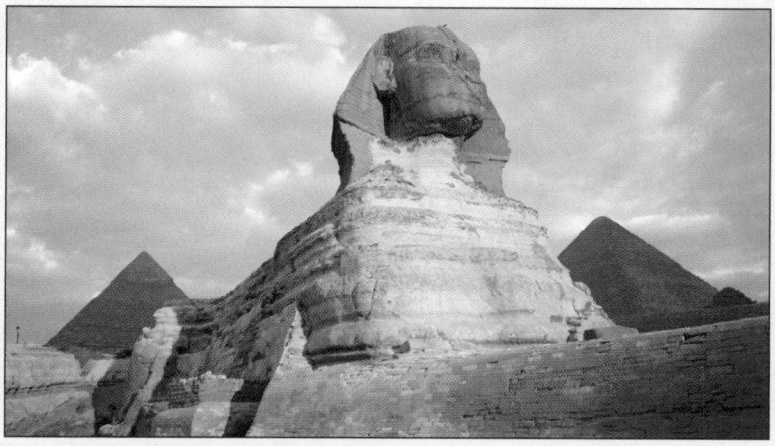

The Great Sphinx and pyramids at Giza (Al Jizah), Egypt

Head of government: Prime Min. Ahmed Nazif

Monetary unit: pound

GDP: $442.6 billion (2008 est.)   **Per capita GDP:** $5,400

Industries: textiles, food processing, tourism, chemicals, hydrocarbons, construction, cement, metals

Chief crops: cotton, rice, corn, wheat, beans, fruits, vegetables

Minerals: petroleum, natural gas, iron ore, phosphates, manganese, limestone, gypsum, talc, asbestos, lead, zinc

Life expectancy at birth (years): male, 68.2; female, 73.3

Literacy rate: 51.4%

Website: www.sis.gov.eg

EQUATORIAL GUINEA

For map, see page 154

Population: 633,441

Ethnic groups: Fang 83%, Bubi 10%

Principal languages: Spanish, French (both official); Fang, Bubi, pidgin English, Portuguese Creole, Ibo

Chief religions: nominally Christian and predominantly Roman Catholic, traditional practices

Area: 10,831 sq mi (95,000 sq km)

Topography: Bioko Island consists of two volcanic mountains and a connecting valley. Rio Muni, with over 90% of the area, has a coastal plain and low hills beyond.

Capital: Malabo (pop., 33,000)

Independence date: October 12, 1968   **Government type:** republic

Head of state: Pres. Teodoro Obiang Nguema Mbasogo

Head of government: Prime Min. Miguel Abia Bieto Borico

Monetary unit: CFA franc

GDP: $19.37 billion (2008 est.)   **Per capita GDP:** $31,400

Industries: petroleum, fishing, sawmilling, natural gas

Chief crops: coffee, cocoa, rice, yams, cassava, bananas, palm oil, nuts

Minerals: oil, petroleum, gold, manganese, uranium

Life expectancy at birth (years): male, 53; female, 57.4

Literacy rate: 78.5%

Website: www.state.gov/r/pa/ei/bgn/7221.htm

ERITREA

For map, see page 155

Population: 5,647,168

Ethnic groups: Tigrinya 50%, Tigre and Kunama 40%, Afar 4%, Saho 3%

Principal languages: Arabic, Tigrinya (both official); Afar, Amharic, Tigre, Kunama, other Cushitic languages

Chief religions: Muslim, Coptic Christian, Roman Catholic, Protestant

Area: 46,840 sq mi (121,320 sq km)

Topography: Eritrea includes many islands of the Dahlak Archipelago. It has low coastal plains in the south and a mountain range with peaks to 9,000 ft (2,700 m) in the north.

Capital: Asmara (pop., 556,000)   Independence date: May 24, 1993

Government type: in transition

Head of state and government: Pres. Isaias Afwerki

Monetary unit: nakfa

GDP: $3.95 billion (2008 est.)   Per capita GDP: $700

Industries: food processing, beverages, clothing and textiles

Chief crops: sorghum, lentils, vegetables, corn, cotton, tobacco, coffee, sisal

Minerals: gold, potash, zinc, copper, salt, possibly oil and natural gas

Life expectancy at birth (years): male, 51.3; female, 54.1

Literacy rate: 25%

Website: www.state.gov/r/pa/ei/bgn/2854.htm

ETHIOPIA

FOR MAP, SEE PAGE 155

Population: 85,237,338

Ethnic groups: Oromo 40%, Amhara and Tigre 32%, Sidamo 9%, Shankella 6%, Somali 6%, Afar 4%, Gurage 2%

Principal languages: Amharic, Tigrinya, Oromigna, Guaragigna, Somali, Arabic, over 200 other languages

Chief religions: Muslim 45-50%, Ethiopian Orthodox 35-40%, animist 12%

Area: 435,190 sq mi (1,127,130 sq km)

Topography: A high central plateau, between 6,000 and 10,000 ft (1,800 and 3,000 m) high, rises to higher mountains near the Great Rift Valley, cutting in from the southwest. The Blue Nile and other rivers cross the plateau, which descends to plains on both the west and southeast.

Capital: Addis Ababa (pop., 2,723,000)

Independence date: more than 2,000 years ago (ancient kingdom of Aksum)

Government type: federal republic

Head of state: Pres. Girma Wolde Giorgis

Head of government: Prime Min. Meles Zenawi

Monetary unit: birr

GDP: $66.29 billion (2008 est.)   Per capita GDP: $800

Industries: food processing, beverages, textiles, chemicals, metals processing, cement

Chief crops: cereals, pulses, coffee, oilseed, sugarcane, potatoes, qat

Minerals: small reserves of gold, platinum, copper, potash, natural gas

Life expectancy at birth (years): male, 40.0; female, 41.8

Literacy rate: 35.5%

Website: www.ethiopianembassy.org

GABON

FOR MAP, SEE PAGE 154

Population: 1,514,993

Ethnic groups: Fang, Bapounou, Nzebi, Obamba, European

Principal languages: French (official), Fang, Myene, Nzebi, Bapounou/Eschira, Bandjabi

Chief religion: Christian 55-75%

Area: 103,350 sq mi (267,670 sq km)

Topography: Heavily forested, the country consists of coastal lowlands; plateaus in the north, east, and south; and mountains in the north, southeast, and center. The Ogooue River system covers most of Gabon.

Capital: Libreville (pop., 611,000)

Independence date: August 17, 1960   Government type: republic

Head of state: Pres. Omar Bongo Ondimba

Head of government: Prime Min. Jean Eyeghe Ndong

Monetary unit: CFA franc

GDP: $21.44 billion (2008 est.)   Per capita GDP: $14,400

Industries: food and beverages, textile, lumber, cement, petroleum extraction and refining, mining, chemicals, ship repair

Chief crops: cocoa, coffee, sugar, palm oil, rubber

Minerals: petroleum, manganese, uranium, gold, iron ore

Life expectancy at birth (years): male, 54.9; female, 58.1

Literacy rate: 63.2%

Website: www.state.gov/r/pa/ei/bgn/2826.htm

THE GAMBIA

FOR MAP, SEE PAGE 160

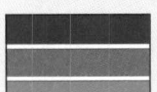

Population: 1,782,893

Ethnic groups: Mandinka 42%, Fula 18%, Wolof 16%, Jola 10%, Serahuli 9%

Principal languages: English (official), Mandinka, Wolof, Fula, other native dialects

Chief religions: Muslim 90%, Christian 9%

Area: 4,400 sq mi (11,300 sq km)

Topography: The country consists of a narrow strip of land on each side of the lower Gambia River.

Capital: Banjul (pop., 372,000)

Independence date: February 18, 1965

Government type: republic

Head of state and government: Pres. Yahya Jammeh

Monetary unit: dalasi

GDP: $2.264 billion (2008 est.)   Per capita GDP: $1,300

Industries: processing of peanuts, fish, and hides; tourism; beverages; agricultural machinery assembly; woodworking; metalworking; clothing

Chief crops: peanuts, millet, sorghum, rice, corn, sesame, cassava, palm kernels

Life expectancy at birth (years): male, 52.8; female, 56.9

Literacy rate: 47.5%

Website: www.visitthegambia.gm

West African craftswoman

Nation Facts and Figures

GHANA

FOR MAP, SEE PAGE 161

Population: 23,832,495

Ethnic groups: Akan 44%, Moshi-Dagomba 16%, Ewe 13%, Ga 8%, Gurma 3%, Yoruba 1%

Principal languages: English (official); about 75 African languages, including Akan, Moshi-Dagomba, Ewe, and Ga

Chief religions: Christian 63%, indigenous beliefs 21%, Muslim 16%

Area: 92,100 sq mi (238,540 sq km)

Topography: Most of Ghana consists of low fertile plains and scrubland, cut by rivers and by the artificial Lake Volta.

Capital: Accra (pop., 1,847,000)

Independence date: March 6, 1957   **Government type:** republic

Head of state and government: Pres. John Atta-Mills

Monetary unit: cedi

GDP: $34.04 billion (2008 est.)   **Per capita GDP:** $1,500

Industries: mining, lumbering, light manufacturing, aluminum smelting, food processing

Chief crops: cocoa, rice, coffee, cassava, peanuts, corn, shea nuts, bananas

Minerals: gold, diamonds, bauxite, manganese

Life expectancy at birth (years): male, 55.4; female, 57.2

Literacy rate: 64.5%

Website: www.ghana.gov.gh

GUINEA

FOR MAP, SEE PAGE 160

Population: 10,057,975

Ethnic groups: Peuhl 40%, Malinke 30%, Soussou 20%

Principal languages: French (official), many African languages

Chief religions: Muslim 85%, Christian 8%, indigenous beliefs 7%

Area: 94,930 sq mi (245,860 sq km)

Topography: A narrow coastal belt leads to the mountainous middle region, the source of the Gambia, Senegal, and Niger rivers. Upper Guinea, farther inland, is a cooler upland. The southeast is forested.

Capital: Conakry (pop., 1,366,000)

Independence date: October 2, 1958   **Government type:** republic

Head of state: Pres. Gen. Lansana Conté

Head of government: Prime Min. Cellou Dalein Diallo

Monetary unit: franc

GDP: $10.44 billion (2008 est.)   **Per capita GDP:** $1,100

Industries: mining, alumina refining, light manufacturing, agricultural processing

Chief crops: rice, coffee, pineapples, palm kernels, cassava, bananas, sweet potatoes

Minerals: bauxite, iron ore, diamonds, gold, uranium

Life expectancy at birth (years): male, 48.5; female, 51.0

Literacy rate: 35.9%

Website: www.state.gov/r/pa/ei/bgn/2824.htm

GUINEA-BISSAU

FOR MAP, SEE PAGE 160

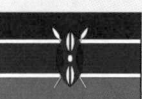

Population: 1,533,964

Ethnic groups: Balanta 30%, Fula 20%, Manjaca 14%, Mandinga 13%, Papel 7%

Principal languages: Portuguese (official), Crioulo, tribal languages

Chief religions: indigenous beliefs 50%, Muslim 45%, Christian 5%

Area: 13,950 sq mi (36,120 sq km)

Topography: A swampy coastal plain covers most of the country; to the east is a low savanna region.

Capital: Bissau (pop., 336,000)   **Independence date:** September 24, 1973

Head of state: Pres. Joao Bernardo Vieira

Head of government: Prime Min. Aristide Gomes

Monetary unit: CFA franc

GDP: $857 million (2008 est.)   **Per capita GDP:** $600

Industries: agricultural processing, beer, soft drinks

Chief crops: rice, corn, beans, cassava, cashew nuts, peanuts, palm kernels, cotton

Minerals: phosphates, bauxite, petroleum

Life expectancy at birth (years): male, 45.1; female, 48.9

Literacy rate: 34%

Website: www.state.gov/r/p/ei/bgn/2824.htm

KENYA

FOR MAP, SEE PAGE 162

Population: 39,002,772

Ethnic groups: Kikuyu 22%, Luhya 14%, Luo 13%, Kalenjin 12%, Kamba 11%, Kisii 6%, Meru 6%

Principal languages: English, Swahili (both official); numerous indigenous languages

Chief religions: Protestant 45%, Roman Catholic 33%, indigenous beliefs 10%, Muslim 10%

Area: 224,960 sq mi (582,650 sq km)

Topography: The northern three-fifths of Kenya is arid. To the south, there are a low coastal area and a plateau varying from 3,000 to 10,000 ft (900 to 3,000 m). The Great Rift Valley enters the country north to south, flanked by high mountains.

Typical door of a residence on the island of Lamu, Kenya

Capital: Nairobi (pop., 2,575,000)

Independence date: December 12, 1963   **Government type:** republic

Head of state: Pres. Mwai Kibaki

Head of government: Prime Min. Raila Amolo Odinga

Monetary unit: shilling

GDP: $61.83 billion (2008 est.)   **Per capita GDP:** $1,600

Industries: small-scale consumer goods, agricultural processing, oil refining, cement, tourism

Chief crops: coffee, tea, corn, wheat, sugarcane, fruit, vegetables

Minerals: gold, limestone, soda ash, salt barites, rubies, fluorspar, garnets

Life expectancy at birth (years): male, 44.8; female, 45.1

Literacy rate: 78.1%

Website: www.kenyaembassy.com

LESOTHO

FOR MAP, SEE PAGE 164

Population: 2,130,819

Ethnic groups: Sotho 99%

Principal languages: Sesotho, English (both official); Zulu, Xhosa

Chief religions: Christian 80%, indigenous beliefs 20%

Area: 11,720 sq mi (30,350 sq km)

Topography: Lesotho is landlocked and mountainous, with altitudes from 5,000 to 11,000 ft (1,500 to 3,300 m).

Capital: Maseru (pop., 170,000)   Independence date: October 4, 1966

Government type: modified constitutional monarchy

Head of state: King Letsie III

Head of government: Prime Min. Pakalitha Mosisili

Monetary unit: loti

GDP: $3.37 billion (2008 est.)   Per capita GDP: $1,600

Industries: food, beverages, textiles, apparel assembly, handicrafts, construction, tourism

Chief crops: corn, wheat, pulses, sorghum, barley

Minerals: diamonds

Life expectancy at birth (years): male, 36.8; female, 36.8

Literacy rate: 83%

Website: www.lesotho.gov.ls

LIBERIA

FOR MAP, SEE PAGE 160

Population: 3,441,790

Ethnic groups: Kpelle, Bassa, Dey, and other tribes 95%; Americo-Liberians 2.5%, Caribbean 2.5%

Principal languages: English (official), Mande, West Atlantic, and Kwa languages

Chief religions: indigenous beliefs 40%, Christian 40%, Muslim 20%

Area: 43,000 sq mi (111,370 sq km)

Topography: Marshy Atlantic coastline rises to low mountains and plateaus in the forested interior; six major rivers flow in parallel courses to the ocean.

Capital: Monrovia (pop., 572,000)

Independence date: July 26, 1847   Government type: republic

Head of state and government: Pres. Ellen Johnson-Sirleaf

Monetary unit: Liberian dollar (LDR)

GDP: $1.53 billion (2008 est.)   Per capita GDP: $500

Industries: rubber processing, palm oil processing, timber, diamonds

Chief crops: rubber, coffee, cocoa, rice, cassava, palm oil, sugarcane, bananas

Minerals: iron ore, diamonds, gold

Life expectancy at birth (years): male, 46.9; female, 49.0

Literacy rate: 38.3%

Website: www.state.gov/r/pa/ei/bgn/6628.htm

LIBYA

FOR MAP, SEE PAGE 155

Population: 6,310,434

Ethnic groups: Arab-Berber 97%

Principal languages: Arabic (official), Italian, English

Chief religion: Muslim (official; mostly Sunni) 97%

Area: 679,360 sq mi (1,759,540 sq km)

Topography: Desert and semidesert regions cover 92% of the land, with low mountains in the north, higher mountains in the south, and a narrow coastal zone.

Capital: Tripoli (pop., 2,006,000)

Independence date: December 24, 1951

Government type: Islamic Arabic Socialist "Mass-State"

Head of state and government: Col. Muammar al-Qaddafi

Monetary unit: dinar

GDP: $88.86 billion (2008 est.)   Per capita GDP: $14,400

Industries: petroleum, food processing, textiles, handicrafts, cement

Chief crops: wheat, barley, olives, dates, citrus, vegetables, peanuts, soybeans

Minerals: petroleum, natural gas, gypsum

Life expectancy at birth (years): male, 74.1; female, 78.6

Literacy rate: 76.2%

Website: www.libya–un.org

MADAGASCAR

FOR MAP, SEE PAGE 165

Population: 20,653,556

Ethnic groups: Mainly Malagasy (Indonesian-African); also Cotiers, French, Indian, Chinese

Principal languages: Malagasy, French (both official)

Chief religions: indigenous beliefs 52%, Christian 41%, Muslim 7%

Area: 226,660 sq mi (587,040 sq km)

Topography: Madagascar has a humid coastal strip in the east, fertile valleys in the mountainous center plateau region, and a wider coastal strip in the west.

Capital: Antananarivo (pop., 1,678,000)

Independence date: June 26, 1960   Government type: republic

Head of state: Pres. Marc Ravalomanana

Head of government: Prime Min. Jacques Sylla

Monetary unit: Malagasy franc

GDP: $20.76 billion (2008 est.)   Per capita GDP: $1,000

Industries: meat processing, soap, breweries, tanneries, sugar, textiles, glassware, cement, automobile assembly, paper, petroleum, tourism

Chief crops: coffee, vanilla, sugarcane, cloves, cocoa, rice, cassava, beans, bananas, peanuts

Minerals: graphite, chromite, coal, bauxite, salt, quartz, tar sands, semiprecious stones, mica

Life expectancy at birth (years): male, 54.2; female, 59.0

Literacy rate: 80%

Website: www.state.gov/r/pa/ei/bgn/5460.htm

MALAWI

FOR MAP, SEE PAGE 163

Population: 14,268,711

Ethnic groups: Chewa, Nyanja, Tumbuka, Yao, Lomwe, Sena, Tonga, Ngoni, Ngonde

Principal languages: Chichewa, English (both official); several African languages

Chief religions: Protestant 55%, Roman Catholic 20%, Muslim 20%

Area: 45,750 sq mi (118,480 sq km)

Topography: Malawi stretches 560 mi (900 m) north to south along Lake Malawi (Lake Nyasa), most of which belongs to Malawi. High plateaus and mountains line the Rift Valley the length of the nation.

Capital: Lilongwe (pop., 587,000)   Independence date: July 6, 1964

Government type: republic

Head of state and government: Pres. Bingu wa Mutharikai

Monetary unit: kwacha

GDP: $11.56 billion (2008 est.)   Per capita GDP: $800

Industries: tobacco, tea, sugar, sawmill products, cement, consumer goods

Chief crops: tobacco, sugarcane, cotton, tea, corn, potatoes, cassava, sorghum, pulses

Minerals: limestone, uranium, coal, and bauxite

Life expectancy at birth (years): male, 37.1; female, 37.9

Literacy rate: 58%

Website: www.malawi.gov.mw

MALI

FOR MAP, SEE PAGE 154

Population: 12,666,987

Ethnic groups: Mande 50% (Bambara, Malinke, Soninke), Peul 17%, Voltaic 12%, Tuareg and Moor 10%, Songhai 6%

Principal languages: French (official), Bambara and other African languages

Chief religions: Muslim 90%, indigenous beliefs 9%

Area: 480,000 sq mi (1,240,000 sq km)

Topography: A landlocked grassy plain in the upper basins of the Senegal and Niger rivers, extending north into the Sahara.

Capital: Bamako (pop., 1,240,000)

Independence date: September 22, 1960 **Government type:** republic

Head of state: Pres. Amadou Toumani Touré

Head of government: Prime Min. Oumane Issoufi Maiga

Monetary unit: CFA franc

GDP: $14.48 billion (2008 est.) **Per capita GDP:** $1,200

Industries: food processing, construction, gold mining

Chief crops: cotton, millet, rice, corn, vegetables, peanuts

Minerals: gold, phosphates, kaolin, salt, limestone, uranium

Life expectancy at birth (years): male, 44.7; female, 45.9

Literacy rate: 38%

Website: www.maliembassy.us

MAURITANIA

FOR MAP, SEE PAGE 154

Population: 3,129,486

Ethnic groups: mixed Maur/black 40%, Maur 30%, black 30%

Principal languages: Hassaniya Arabic, Wolof (both official); Fulani, Pulaar, Soninke (all national); French

Chief religion: predominantly Muslim (official)

Area: 398,000 sq mi (1,030,700 sq km)

Topography: The fertile Senegal River valley in the south gives way to a wide central region of sandy plains and scrub trees. The north is arid and extends into the Sahara.

Capital: Nouakchott (pop., 600,000)

Independence date: November 28, 1960 **Government type:** Islamic republic

Head of state: Pres. Sidi Ould Cheikh Abdallahi

Head of government: Prime Min. Zeine Ould Zeidane

Monetary unit: ouguiya

GDP: $6.31 billion (2008 est.) **Per capita GDP:** $2,100

Industries: fish processing, mining

Chief crops: dates, millet, sorghum, rice, corn, dates

Minerals: iron ore, gypsum, copper, phosphate, diamonds, gold, oil

Life expectancy at birth (years): male, 50.2; female, 54.6

Literacy rate: 41.2%

Website: www.ambarim-dc.org

MAURITIUS

FOR MAP, SEE PAGE 165

Population: 1,284,264

Ethnic groups: Indo-Mauritian 68%, Creole 27%, Sino-Mauritian 3%, Franco-Mauritian 2%

Principal languages: English (official), Creole, French, Hindi, Urdu, Hakka, Bhojpuri

Chief religions: Hindu 52%, Christian 28%, Muslim 17%

Area: 720 sq mi (1,860 sq km)

Topography: Mauritius is a volcanic island nearly surrounded by coral reefs. A central plateau is encircled by mountain peaks.

Capital: Port Louis (pop., 143,000)

Independence date: March 12, 1968 **Government type:** republic

Head of state: Pres. Anerood Jugnauth

Head of government: Prime Min. Navin Ramgoolan

Monetary unit: Mauritian rupee

GDP: $15.36 billion (2008 est.) **Per capita GDP:** $12,100

Industries: food processing, textiles, clothing, chemicals, metal products, transport equipment, nonelectrical machinery, tourism

Chief crops: sugarcane, tea, corn, potatoes, bananas, pulses

Life expectancy at birth (years): male, 68.1; female, 76.1

Literacy rate: 82.9%

Website: www.gov.mut

MOROCCO

FOR MAP, SEE PAGE 156

Population: 34,859,364

Ethnic groups: Arab-Berber 99%

Principal languages: Arabic (official), Berber dialects, French, Spanish, English

Chief religion: Muslim (official) 99%

Area: 172,410 sq mi (446,550 sq km)

Topography: Morocco consists of five natural regions: mountain ranges (Riff in the north, Middle Atlas, Upper Atlas, and Anti-Atlas); rich plains in the west; alluvial plains in the southwest; well-cultivated plateaus in the center; and a pre-Sahara arid zone extending from the southeast.

Capital: Rabat (pop., 1,759,000) **Independence date:** March 2, 1956

Government type: constitutional monarchy

Head of state: King Mohammed VI

Head of government: Prime Min. Driss Jettou

Monetary unit: dirham

GDP: $137.3 billion (2008 est.) **Per capita GDP:** $4,000

Industries: mining, food processing, leather goods, textiles, construction, tourism

Chief crops: barley, wheat, citrus, wine, vegetables, olives

Minerals: phosphates, iron ore, manganese, lead, zinc

Life expectancy at birth (years): male, 68.1; female, 72.7

Literacy rate: 43.7%

Website: www.mincom.gov.ma

Casbah, Ait Ben Haddou, Morocco

MOZAMBIQUE

For map, see page 163

Population: 21,669,278

Ethnic groups: Shangaan, Chokwe, Manyika, Sena, Makua

Principal languages: Portuguese (official) and dialects, English

Chief religions: indigenous beliefs 50%, Christian 30%, Muslim 20%

Area: 309,500 sq mi (801,590 sq km)

Topography: Coastal lowlands make up nearly half the country, with plateaus rising in steps to the mountains along the western border.

Capital: Maputo (pop., 1,221,000)

Independence date: June 25, 1975 **Government type:** republic

Head of state: Pres. Armando Guebuza

Head of government: Prime Min. Luisa Diogo

Monetary unit: metical

GDP: $18.95 billion (2008 est.) **Per capita GDP:** $900

Industries: food, beverages, chemicals, petroleum products, textiles, cement, glass, asbestos, tobacco

Chief crops: cotton, cashew nuts, sugarcane, tea, cassava, corn, coconuts, sisal, citrus and tropical fruits

Minerals: coal, titanium, natural gas, tantalum, graphite

Life expectancy at birth (years): male, 37.8; female, 36.3

Literacy rate: 42.3%

Website: www.embamoc-usa.org

NAMIBIA

For map, see page 163

Population: 2,108,665

Ethnic groups: Ovambo 50%, Kavangos 9%, Herero 7%, Damara 7%, white 6%, mixed 7%

Principal languages: English (official), Afrikaans, German, Oshivambo, Herero, Nama

Chief religions: Lutheran 50%, other Christian 30%, indigenous beliefs 10-20%

Area: 318,700 sq mi (825,420 sq km)

Topography: Three distinct regions include the Namib Desert along the Atlantic coast, a mountainous central plateau with woodland savanna, and the Kalahari Desert in the east. True forests are found in the northeast. There are four rivers, but little other surface water.

Capital: Windhoek (pop., 237,000)

Independence date: March 21, 1990

Government type: republic

Head of state: Pres. Hifikepunye Pohamba

Head of government: Prime Min. Nahas Angula

Monetary unit: Namibia dollar

GDP: $11.23 billion (2008 est.)

Per capita GDP: $5,400

Elephants on the savanna at dawn

Industries: meatpacking, fish processing, dairy products, mining

Chief crops: millet, sorghum, peanuts

Minerals: diamonds, copper, uranium, gold, lead, tin, lithium, cadmium, zinc, salt, vanadium, natural gas

Life expectancy at birth (years): male, 42.4; female, 38.6

Literacy rate: 38%

Website: www.namibianembassyusa.org

NIGER

For map, see page 154

Population: 15,306,252

Ethnic groups: Hausa 56%, Djerma 22%, Fula 9%, Tuareg 8%, Beri Beri (Kanouri) 4%

Principal languages: French (official); Hausa, Djerma, Fulani (all national)

Chief religion: Muslim 80%

Area: 489,000 sq mi (1,267,000 sq km)

Topography: Mostly arid desert and mountains. A narrow savanna in the south and the Niger River basin in the southwest contain most of the population.

Capital: Niamey (pop., 890,000)

Independence date: August 3, 1960 **Government type:** republic

Head of state: Pres. Tandja Mamadou

Head of government: Prime Min. Hama Amadou

Monetary unit: CFA franc

GDP: $9.784 billion (2008 est.) **Per capita GDP:** $700

Industries: mining, cement, brick, textiles, food processing, chemicals

Chief crops: cowpeas, cotton, peanuts, millet, sorghum, cassava, rice

Minerals: uranium, coal, iron ore, tin, phosphates, gold, petroleum

Life expectancy at birth (years): male, 42.4; female, 42.0

Literacy rate: 15.3%

Website: www.nigerembassyusa.org

NIGERIA

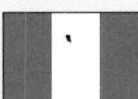

For map, see page 154

Population: 149,229,090

Ethnic groups: more than 250; Hausa and Fulani 29%, Yoruba 21%, Igbo (Ibo) 18%, Ijaw 10%

Principal languages: English (official), Hausa, Yoruba, Igbo (Ibo), Fulani

Chief religions: Muslim 50%, Christian 40%, indigenous beliefs 10%

Area: 356,670 sq mi (923,770 sq km)

Topography: Four east-to-west regions divide Nigeria: a coastal mangrove swamp 10 to 60 mi (16 to 100 km) wide, a tropical rain forest 50 to 100 mi (80 to 160 km) wide, a plateau of savanna and open woodland, and semidesert in the north.

Capital: Abuja (pop., 452,000)

Independence date: October 1, 1960 **Government type:** republic

Head of state and government: Pres. Umaru Musa Yar'Adua

Monetary unit: naira

GDP: $338.1 billion (2008 est.) **Per capita GDP:** $2,300

Industries: petroleum extraction, mining, agricultural processing, cotton, rubber, wood, hides and skins, textiles, cement and other construction materials, footwear, chemicals, fertilizer, printing, ceramics, steel

Chief crops: cocoa, peanuts, palm oil, corn, rice, sorghum, millet, cassava, yams

Minerals: natural gas, petroleum, tin, columbite, iron ore, coal, limestone, lead, zinc

Life expectancy at birth (years): male, 50.9; female, 51.1

Literacy rate: 57.1%

Website: www.nigeriaembassyusa.org

RWANDA

FOR MAP, SEE PAGE 162

Population: 10,473,282

Ethnic groups: Hutu 84%, Tutsi 15%, Twa (Pygmy) 1%

Principal languages: Kinyarwanda, French, English (all official); Swahili

Chief religions: Roman Catholic 57%, Protestant 26%, Adventist 11%, Muslim 5%

Area: 10,170 sq mi (26,340 sq km)

Topography: Grassy uplands and hills cover most of the country, with a chain of volcanoes in the northwest. The source of the Nile River has been located in the headwaters of the Kagera (Akagera) River, southwest of Kigali.

Capital: Kigali (pop., 656,000)

Independence date: July 1, 1962   **Government type:** republic

Head of state: Pres. Paul Kagame

Head of government: Prime Min. Bernard Makuza

Monetary unit: franc

GDP: $9.061 billion (2008 est.)   **Per capita GDP:** $900

Industries: cement, agricultural products, small-scale beverages, soap, furniture, shoes, plastic goods, textiles, cigarettes

Chief crops: coffee, tea, pyrethrum, bananas, beans, sorghum, potatoes

Minerals: gold, tin ore, tungsten ore, methane

Life expectancy at birth (years): male, 38.4; female, 40.0

Literacy rate: 48%

Website: www.gov.rw

Water-loving hippopotamuses

Topography: Low rolling plains cover most of Senegal, rising somewhat in the southeast. Swamp and jungles are in the southwest.

Capital: Dakar (pop., 2,167,000)

Independence date: April 4, 1960   **Government type:** republic

Head of state: Pres. Abdoulaye Wade

Head of government: Prime Min. Macky Sall

Monetary unit: CFA franc

GDP: $21.9 billion (2008 est.)   **Per capita GDP:** $1,600

Industries: agricultural and fish processing, mining, fertilizer production, petroleum refining, construction materials

Chief crops: peanuts, millet, corn, sorghum, rice, cotton, tomatoes, green vegetables

Minerals: phosphates, iron ore

Life expectancy at birth (years): male, 54.9; female, 58.2

Literacy rate: 39.1%

Website: www.senegalembassy.uk

SÃO TOMÉ AND PRÍNCIPE

FOR MAP, SEE PAGE 154

Population: 212,679

Ethnic groups: mestizo, black, Portuguese

Principal languages: Portuguese (official), Creole, Fang

Chief religions: predominantly Roman Catholic

Area: 390 sq mi (1,000 sq km)

Topography: São Tomé and Príncipe islands, part of an extinct volcano chain, are both covered by lush forests and croplands.

Capital: São Tomé (pop., 54,000)   **Independence date:** July 12, 1975

Government type: republic

Head of state: Pres. Fradique Melo de Menezes

Head of government: Prime Min. Tomé Vera Cruz

Monetary unit: dobra

GDP: $276.6 million (2008 est.)   **Per capita GDP:** $1,300

Industries: light construction, textiles, soap, beer, fish processing, timber

Chief crops: cocoa, coconuts, palm kernels, copra, cinnamon, pepper, coffee, bananas, papayas, beans

Life expectancy at birth (years): male, 65.1; female, 68.2

Literacy rate: 79.3%

Website: www.saotome.st

SEYCHELLES

FOR MAP, SEE PAGE 81

Population: 87,476

Ethnic groups: mainly Seychellois (mix of French, African, and Asian)

Principal languages: English, French, Creole (all official)

Chief religions: Roman Catholic 87%, Anglican 7%

Area: 180 sq mi (460 sq km)

Topography: A group of 86 islands, about half of them composed of coral, the other half granite, the latter predominantly mountainous.

Capital: Victoria (pop., 25,000)

Independence date: June 29, 1976

Government type: republic

Head of state and government: Pres. James Michel

Monetary unit: rupee

GDP: $1.47 billion (2008 est.)

A Seychelles beach

Per capita GDP: $17,000

Industries: fishing, tourism, coconut and vanilla processing, rope, boat building, printing, furniture, beverages

Chief crops: coconuts, cinnamon, vanilla, sweet potatoes, cassava, bananas

Life expectancy at birth (years): male, 66.1; female, 77.1

Literacy rate: 58%

Website: www.seychelles.com

SENEGAL

FOR MAP, SEE PAGE 160

Population: 13,711,597

Ethnic groups: Wolof 43%, Pular 24%, Serer 15%, Jola 4%, Mandinka 3%, Soninke 1%

Principal languages: French (official), Wolof, Pulaar, Jola, Mandinka

Chief religions: Muslim 94%, Christian 5%

Area: 75,750 sq mi (196,190 sq km)

SIERRA LEONE

FOR MAP, SEE PAGE 160

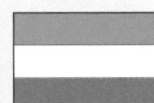

Population: 6,440,053

Ethnic groups: Temne 30%, Mende 30%, other tribes 30%; Creole 10%

Principal languages: English (official), Mende in the south, Temne in the north, Krio (English Creole)

Chief religions: Muslim 60%, indigenous beliefs 30%, Christian 10%

Area: 27,700 sq mi (71,740 sq km)

Topography: The heavily indented, 210-mi (340-km) coastline has mangrove swamps. Behind are wooded hills, rising to a plateau and mountains in the east.

Capital: Freetown (pop., 921,000)

Independence date: April 27, 1961   **Government type:** republic

Head of state and government: Pres. Ernest Bai Koroma

Monetary unit: leone

GDP: $4.307 billion (2008 est.)   **Per capita GDP:** $700

Industries: mining, small-scale manufacturing, petroleum refining

Chief crops: rice, coffee, cocoa, palm kernels, palm oil, peanuts

Minerals: diamonds, titanium ore, bauxite, iron ore, gold, chromite

Life expectancy at birth (years): male, 40.2; female, 45.2

Literacy rate: 31.4%

Website: www.embassyofsierraleone.org

Rural life in Sierra Leone

SOMALIA

FOR MAP, SEE PAGE 155

Population: 9,832,017

Ethnic groups: Somali 85%, Bantu and other 15%

Principal languages: Somali, Arabic (both official); Italian, English

Chief religion: Sunni Muslim (official)

Area: 246,200 sq mi (637,660 sq km)

Topography: The coastline extends for 1,700 mi (2,700 km). Hills cover the north; the center and south are flat.

Capital: Mogadishu (pop., 1,175,000)

Independence date: July 1, 1960   **Government type:** in transition

Head of state: Pres. Abdullahi Yusuf Ahmed

Head of government: Prime Min. Nur Hassan Hussein

Monetary unit: shilling

GDP: $5.524 billion (2008 est.)   **Per capita GDP:** $600

Industries: sugar refining, textiles, wireless communication

Chief crops: bananas, sorghum, corn, coconuts, rice, sugarcane, mangoes, sesame seeds, beans

Minerals: uranium and largely unexploited reserves of iron ore, tin, gypsum, bauxite, copper, salt, natural gas, likely oil reserves

Life expectancy at birth (years): male, 46.0; female, 49.5

Literacy rate: 37.8%   **Website:** www.state.gov/r/pa/ei/bgn/2863.htm

SOUTH AFRICA

FOR MAP, SEE PAGE 163

Population: 49,052,489

Ethnic groups: black 75%, white 14%, mixed 8%, Indian 3%

Principal languages: Afrikaans, English, Ndebele, Pedi, Sotho, Swazi, Tsonga, Tswana, Venda, Xhosa, Zulu (all official)

Chief religions: Christian 68%, indigenous beliefs and animist 29%

Area: 471,010 sq mi (1,219,910 sq km)

Topography: The large interior plateau reaches close to the country's 2,700-mi (4,300-km) coastline. There are few major rivers or lakes; rainfall is sparse in the west, more plentiful in the east.

Capitals: Pretoria (administrative) (pop., 1,590,000), Cape Town (legislative) (pop., 2,993,000), Bloemfontein (judicial) (pop., 1,590,000)

Independence date: May 31, 1910

Government type: republic

Head of state and government: Pres. Thabo Mvuyelwa Mbeki

Monetary unit: rand

GDP: $489.7 billion (2008 est.)   **Per capita GDP:** $10,000

Industries: mining, automobile assembly, metalworking, machinery, textile, iron and steel, chemicals, fertilizer, foodstuffs

Chief crops: corn, wheat, sugarcane, fruits, vegetables

Diamond mining— a key source of South Africa's wealth

Minerals: gold, chromium, antimony, coal, iron ore, manganese, nickel, phosphates, tin, uranium, gem diamonds, platinum, copper, vanadium, salt, natural gas

Life expectancy at birth (years): male, 44.0; female, 44.0

Literacy rate: 85%

Website: www.gov.za

Cape Town, South Africa

Nation Facts and Figures

34

SUDAN

FOR MAP, SEE PAGE 155

Population: 41,087,825

Ethnic groups: black 52%, Arab 39%, Beja 6%

Principal languages: Arabic (official), Nubian, Ta Bedawie; Nilotic, Sudanic dialects; English

Chief religions: Sunni Muslim 70%, indigenous beliefs 25%, Christian 5%

Area: 967,500 sq mi (2,505,810 sq km)

Topography: The north consists of the Libyan Desert in the west and the mountainous Nubia Desert in the east, with the narrow Nile valley between. The center contains large, fertile, rainy areas with fields, pasture, and forest. The south has rich soil and heavy rain.

Capital: Khartoum (pop., 4,286,000)

Independence date: January 1, 1956

Government type: republic with strong military influence

Head of state and government: Pres. Gen. Omar Hassan Ahmad Al-Bashir

Monetary unit: dinar (SDD)

GDP: $87.27 billion (2008 est.)

Per capita GDP: $2,200

Industries: oil, cotton ginning, textiles, cement, edible oils, sugar, soap distilling, shoes, petroleum refining, pharmaceuticals, armaments, automobile/light truck assembly

Chief crops: cotton, groundnuts, sorghum, millet, wheat, gum arabic, sugarcane, cassava, mangos, papaya, bananas, sweet potatoes, sesame

Minerals: petroleum, iron ore, copper, chromium ore, zinc, tungsten, mica, silver, gold

Life expectancy at birth (years): male, 57.0; female, 59.4

Literacy rate: 46.1%

Website: www.sudanembassy.org

SWAZILAND

FOR MAP, SEE PAGE 165

Population: 1,123,913

Ethnic groups: African 97%, European 3%

Principal languages: English, siSwati (both official)

Chief religions: Christian 60%, Muslim 10%, indigenous and other 30%

Area: 6,700 sq mi (17,360 sq km)

Topography: The country descends from W to E in broad belts, becoming more arid in the low veld region, then rising to a plateau in the E.

Capitals: Mbabane (administrative) (pop., 70,000)

Independence date: September 6, 1968

Government type: constitutional monarchy

Head of state: King Mswati III

Head of government: Prime Min. Absalom Themba Dlamini

Monetary unit: lilangeni

GDP: $5.703 billion (2008 est.)

Per capita GDP: $5,100

Industries: mining, wood pulp, sugar, soft drink concentrates, textile and apparel

Chief crops: sugarcane, cotton, corn, tobacco, rice, citrus, pineapples, sorghum, peanuts

Minerals: asbestos, coal, clay, cassiterite, gold, diamonds, quarry stone, talc

Life expectancy at birth (years): male, 39.1; female, 35.9

Literacy rate: 78.3%

Website: www.gov.sz

TANZANIA

FOR MAP, SEE PAGE 162

Population: 41,048,532

Ethnic groups: mainland: Bantu 95%; Zanzibar: Arab, African, mixed

Principal languages: Swahili, English (both official); Arabic, many local languages

Chief religions: Christian 30%, Muslim 35%, indigenous beliefs 35%; Zanzibar is 99% Muslim

Area: 364,900 sq mi (945,090 sq km)

Topography: Hot, arid central plateau, surrounded by the lake region in the west, temperate highlands in the north and south, and the coastal plains. Mt. Kilimanjaro, 19,340 ft (5,895 m), is the highest peak in Africa.

Capital: Dodoma (pop., 155,000)

Independence date: April 26, 1964   **Government type:** republic

Head of state: Pres. Jakaya Mrisho Kikwete

Head of government: Prime Min. Edward Lowassa

Monetary unit: shilling

GDP: $54.26 billion (2008 est.)   **Per capita GDP:** $1,300

Industries: agricultural processing, mining, oil refining, shoes, cement, textiles, wood products, fertilizer, salt

Chief crops: coffee, sisal, tea, cotton, pyrethrum, cashew nuts, tobacco, cloves, corn, wheat, cassava, bananas, fruits, vegetables

Minerals: tin, phosphates, iron ore, coal, diamonds, gemstones, gold, natural gas, nickel

Life expectancy at birth (years): male, 43.2; female, 45.6

Literacy rate: 67.8%

Website: www.tanzania.go.tz/index2E.html

Masai giraffe calf, Serengeti National Park, Tanzania

TOGO

FOR MAP, SEE PAGE 161

Population: 6,019,877

Ethnic groups: 37 African tribes; largest are Ewe, Mina, and Kabre

Principal languages: French (official), Ewe, Mina in the south; Kabye, Dagomba in the north

Chief religions: indigenous beliefs 51%, Christian 29%, Muslim 20%

Area: 21,930 sq mi (56,790 sq km)

Topography: A range of hills running southwest to northeast splits Togo into two savanna plains regions.

Capital: Lomé (pop., 799,000)   **Independence date:** April 27, 1960

Government type: republic

Head of state: Pres. Faure Gnassingbé

Head of government: Prime Min. Edem Kodjo

Monetary unit: CFA franc

GDP: $5.105 billion (2008 est.)   Per capita GDP: $900

Industries: mining, agricultural processing, cement, handicrafts, textiles, beverages

Chief crops: coffee, cocoa, cotton, yams, cassava, corn, beans, rice, millet, sorghum

Minerals: phosphates, limestone, marble

Life expectancy at birth (years): male, 51.1; female, 55.1

Literacy rate: 51.7%

Website: www.state.gov/r/pa/ei/bgn/5430.htm

TUNISIA

For map, see page 157

Population: 10,486,339

Ethnic groups: Arab 98%, European 1%, Jewish and other 1%

Principal languages: Arabic (official), French prevalent

Chief religion: Muslim (official; mostly Sunni) 98%

Area: 63,170 sq mi (163,610 sq km)

Topography: The north is wooded and fertile. The central coastal plains are given to grazing and orchards. The south is arid, merging into the Sahara Desert.

Capital: Tunis (pop., 1,996,000)

Independence date: March 20, 1956   Government type: republic

Head of state: Pres. Gen. Zine al-Abidine Ben Ali

Head of government: Prime Min. Mohamed Ghannouchi

Monetary unit: dinar

GDP: $81.88 billion (2008 est.)   Per capita GDP: $7,900

Industries: petroleum, mining, tourism, textiles, footwear, agribusiness, beverages

Chief crops: olives, olive oil, grain, tomatoes, citrus fruit, sugar beets, dates, almonds

Minerals: petroleum, phosphates, iron ore, lead, zinc, salt

Life expectancy at birth (years): male, 73.0; female, 76.4

Literacy rate: 67.8%

Website: www.state.gov/r/pa/ei/bgn/5439.html

UGANDA

For map, see page 162

Population: 32,369,558

Ethnic groups: Baganda 17%, Ankole 8%, Basoga 8%, Iteso 8%, Bakiga 7%; many other groups

Principal languages: English (official), Swahili, Ganda, many Bantu and Nilotic languages, Arabic

Chief religions: Protestant 33%, Roman Catholic 33%, indigenous beliefs 18%, Muslim 16%

Area: 91,140 sq mi (236,040 sq km)

Topography: Most of Uganda is a high plateau 3,000 to 6,000 ft (900 to 1,800 m) high, with the high Ruwenzori range in the west (Mt. Margherita 16,760 ft [5,109 m]) and volcanoes in the southwest; the northeast is arid, and the west and southwest rainy. Lakes Victoria, Edward, and Albert form much of the borders.

Capital: Kampala (pop., 1,246,000)   Independence date: October 9, 1962

Government type: republic   Head of state: Pres. Yoweri Kaguta Museveni

Head of government: Prime Min. Apollo Nsibambi

Monetary unit: shilling

GDP: $35.88 billion (2008 est.)   Per capita GDP: $1,100

Industries: sugar, brewing, tobacco, cotton textiles, cement

Chief crops: coffee, tea, cotton, tobacco, cassava, potatoes, corn, millet, pulses

Minerals: copper, cobalt, limestone, salt

Life expectancy at birth (years): male, 43.8; female, 46.8

Literacy rate: 62.7%   Website: www.ugandaembassy.com

ZAMBIA

For map, see page 163

Population: 11,862,740

Ethnic groups: more than 70 groups; largest are Bemba, Tonga, Ngoni, and Lozi

Principal languages: English (official), Bemba, Kaonda, Lozi, Lunda, Luvale, Nyanja, Tonga, 70 others

Chief religions: Christian 50-75%, Hindu and Muslim 24-49%

Area: 290,580 sq mi (752,610 sq km)

Topography: Zambia is mostly high plateau country covered with thick forests and drained by several important rivers, including the Zambezi.

Capital: Lusaka (pop., 1,394,000)

Independence date: October 24, 1964   Government type: republic

Head of state and government: Pres. Rupiah Banda

Monetary unit: kwacha

GDP: $17.39 billion (2008 est.)   Per capita GDP: $1,500

Industries: mining, construction, foodstuffs, beverages, chemicals, textiles, fertilizer

Chief crops: corn, sorghum, rice, peanuts, sunflower seed, vegetables, flowers, tobacco, cotton, sugarcane, cassava

Minerals: copper, cobalt, zinc, lead, coal, emeralds, gold, silver, uranium

Life expectancy at birth (years): male, 35.2; female, 35.2

Literacy rate: 78.9%   Website: www.zana.gov.zm

ZIMBABWE

For map, see page 163

Population: 11,392,629

Ethnic groups: Shona 82%, Ndebele 14%

Principal languages: English (official), Shona, Sindebele, numerous dialects

Chief religions: syncretic (Christian-indigenous mix) 50%, Christian 25%, indigenous beliefs 24%

Area: 150,800 sq mi (390,580 sq km)

Topography: Zimbabwe is high plateau country, rising to mountains on the eastern border, sloping down on the other borders.

Capital: Harare (pop., 1,469,000)

Independence date: April 18, 1980

Government type: republic

Head of state and government: Pres. Robert Mugabe (in dispute)

Monetary unit: Zimbabwe dollar

GDP: $1.959 billion (2008 est.)

Per capita GDP: $200

Industries: mining, steel, wood products, cement, chemicals, fertilizer, clothing and footwear, foodstuffs, beverages

Chief crops: corn, cotton, tobacco, wheat, coffee, sugarcane, peanuts

Minerals: coal, chromium ore, asbestos, gold, nickel, copper, iron ore, vanadium, lithium, tin, platinum group metals

Life expectancy at birth (years): male, 40.1; female, 37.9

Literacy rate: 85%

Website: www.state.gov/r/pa/ei/bgn/5479.htm

Devil's Cataract, Victoria Falls, on the Zambesi River between Zambia and Zimbabwe

ASIA

Asia has three of the five most populous countries in the world. China and India, each with more than 1 billion people, rank number 1 and number 2, respectively. Indonesia, with well over 200 million, is number 4.

AFGHANISTAN

FOR MAP, SEE PAGE 147

Population: 33,609,937

Ethnic groups: Pashtun 44%, Tajik 25%, Hazara 10%, Uzbek 8%

Principal languages: Dari (Afghan Persian), Pashtu (both official); Turkic (including Uzbek, Turkmen); Balochi, Pashai, many others

Chief religions: Muslim (official; Sunni 85%, Shi'a 15%)

Area: 250,000 sq mi (647,500 sq km)

Topography: The country is landlocked and mountainous, much of it over 4,000 ft (1,200 m) above sea level. The Hindu Kush Mountains tower 16,000 ft (4,800 m) above Kabul and reach a height of 25,000 ft (7,600 m) to the east. Trade with Pakistan flows through the 35-mi (56-km) Khyber Pass. There are large desert regions, though mountain rivers produce intermittent fertile valleys.

Capital: Kabul (pop., 2,956,000)

Independence date: August 19, 1919

Government type: transitional administration

Head of state and government: Pres. Hamid Karzai

Monetary unit: afghani

GDP: $23.03 billion (2008 est.)   **Per capita GDP:** $800

Industries: textiles, soap, furniture, shoes, fertilizer, cement, handwoven carpets

Chief crops: wheat, fruits, nuts

Minerals: natural gas, petroleum, coal, copper, chromite, talc, barites, sulfur, lead, zinc, iron ore, salt, precious and semiprecious stones

Life expectancy at birth (years): male, 42.3; female, 42.7

Literacy rate: 36%

Website: www.afghanistanembassy.org

ARMENIA

FOR MAP, SEE PAGE 121

Population: 2,967,004

Ethnic groups: Armenian 93%, Russian 2%

Principal languages: Armenian (official), Russian

Chief religions: Armenian Apostolic 94%, other Christian 4%, Yezidi 2%

Area: 11,500 sq mi (29,800 sq km)

Topography: Mountainous, with many peaks above 10,000 ft (3,000 m).

Capital: Yerevan (pop., 1,079,000)

Independence date: September 21, 1991

Government type: republic

Head of state: Pres. Serzh Sargsyan

Head of government: Prime Min. Tigran Sargsyan

Monetary unit: dram

GDP: $18.92 billion (2008 est.)

Per capita GDP: $6,400

Industries: machine tools, forging-pressing machines, electric motors, tires, knitted wear, footwear, silk fabric, chemicals, trucks, instruments, microelectronics, jewelry, software development, food processing

Chief crops: grapes, vegetables

Minerals: gold, copper, molybdenum, zinc, alumina

Life expectancy at birth (years): male, 67.7; female, 75.4

Literacy rate: 99%

Website: www.gov.am/en

AZERBAIJAN

FOR MAP, SEE PAGE 121

Population: 8,238,672

Ethnic groups: Azeri 90%, Dagestani 3%, Russian 3%, Armenian 2%

Principal languages: Azeri (official), Russian, Armenian

Chief religions: Muslim 93%, Russian Orthodox 3%, Armenian Orthodox 2%

Area: 33,440 sq mi (86,600 sq km)

Topography: The Great Caucasus Mountains in the north and the Karabakh Upland in the west border the Kur-Abas Lowland; climate is arid except in the subtropical southeast.

Capital: Baku (pop., 1,816,000)

Independence date: August 30, 1991   **Government type:** republic

Head of state: Pres. Ilham Aliyev

Head of government: Prime Min. Artur Rasizade

Monetary unit: manat

GDP: $73.65 billion (2008 est.)   **Per capita GDP:** $9,000

Industries: petroleum products, oilfield equipment, steel, iron ore, cement, chemicals, textiles

Chief crops: cotton, grain, rice, grapes, fruit, vegetables, tea, tobacco

Minerals: petroleum, natural gas, iron ore, nonferrous metals, alumina

Life expectancy at birth (years): male, 59.1; female, 67.6

Literacy rate: 97%

Website: www.president.az

BAHRAIN

FOR MAP, SEE PAGE 146

Population: 727,785

Ethnic groups: Arab 73%, Asian 19%, Iranian 8%

Principal languages: Arabic (official), English, Farsi, Urdu

Chief religions: Muslim (official; Shi'a 70%, Sunni 30%)

Area: 240 sq mi (620 sq km)

Topography: Bahrain Island, and several adjacent, smaller islands, are flat, hot, and humid, with little rain.

Capital: Manama (pop., 139,000)   **Independence date:** August 15, 1971

Government type: constitutional monarchy

Head of state: King Hamad bin Isa al-Khalifa

Head of government: Prime Min. Khalifa bin Sulman al-Khalifa

Monetary unit: dinar

GDP: $26.7 billion (2008 est.)   **Per capita GDP:** $37,200

Industries: petroleum processing and refining, aluminum smelting, offshore banking, ship repairing, tourism

Chief crops: fruit, vegetables

Minerals: oil, natural gas

Life expectancy at birth (years): male, 71.5; female, 76.5

Literacy rate: 88.5%

Website: www.bahrain.gov.bh/english/index.asp

BANGLADESH

FOR MAP, SEE PAGE 140

Population: 156,050,883

Ethnic groups: Bengali 98%

Principal languages: Bangla (official, also known as Bengali), English

Chief religions: Muslim (official) 83%, Hindu 16%

Area: 56,000 sq mi (144,000 sq km)

Topography: The country is mostly a low plain cut by the Ganges and Brahmaputra rivers and their delta. The land is alluvial and marshy along the coast, with hills only in the extreme southeast and northeast.

Capital: Dhaka (pop., 11,560,000)

Independence date: December 16, 1971

Government type: parliamentary democracy

Head of state: Pres. Iajuddin Ahmed

Head of government: Prime Min. Khaleda Zia

Monetary unit: taka

GDP: $224 billion (2008 est.)   **Per capita GDP:** $1,500

Industries: cotton textiles, jute, garments, tea processing, paper newsprint, cement, chemical fertilizer, light engineering

Chief crops: rice, jute, tea, wheat, sugarcane, potatoes, tobacco, pulses, oilseeds, spices, fruit

Minerals: natural gas, coal

Life expectancy at birth (years): male, 61.8; female, 61.6

Literacy rate: 56%

Website: www.bangladeshgov.com

BHUTAN

FOR MAP, SEE PAGE 143

Population: 691,141

Ethnic groups: Bhote 50%, Nepalese 35%, indigenous tribes 15%

Principal languages: Dzongkha (official), Tibetan, Nepalese dialects

Chief religions: Lamaistic Buddhist (official) 75%, Hindu 25%

Area: 18,000 sq mi (47,000 sq km)

Topography: Bhutan is comprised of very high mountains in the north, fertile valleys in the center, and thick forests in the Duar Plain in the south.

Capital: Thimphu (pop., 35,000)

Independence date: August 8, 1949

Government type: monarchy

Head of state and government: King Jigme Singye Wangchuk

Head of government: Prime Min. Lyonpo Sangay Ngedup

Monetary unit: ngultrum

GDP: $3.789 billion (2008 est.)   **Per capita GDP:** $5,600

Industries: cement, wood products, processed fruits, alcoholic beverages

Chief crops: rice, corn, root crops, citrus, foodgrains

Minerals: gypsum, calcium carbide

Life expectancy at birth (years): male, 54.3; female, 53.7

Literacy rate: 42.2%

Website: www.kingdomofbhutan.com

BRUNEI

FOR MAP, SEE PAGE 138

Population: 388,190

Ethnic groups: Malay 67%, Chinese 15%, indigenous 6%

Principal languages: Malay (official), English, Chinese

Chief religions: Muslim (official) 67%; Buddhist 13%; Christian 10%; indigenous beliefs, other 10%

Area: 2,230 sq mi (5,770 sq km)

Topography: Brunei has a narrow coastal plain, with mountains in the east, hilly lowlands in the west. There are swamps in the west and northeast.

Brunei *(continued)*

Capital: Bandar Seri Begawan (pop., 61,000)

Independence date: January 1, 1984

Government type: independent sultanate

Head of state and government: Sultan Sir Muda Hassanal Bolkiah Mu'izzadin Waddaulah

Monetary unit: Brunei dollar

GDP: $20.25 billion (2008 est.)   **Per capita GDP:** $53,100

Industries: petroleum, petroleum refining, liquefied natural gas, construction

Chief crops: rice, vegetables, fruits

Minerals: petroleum, natural gas

Life expectancy at birth (years): male, 71.9; female, 76.8

Literacy rate: 88.2%   **Website:** www.gov.bn

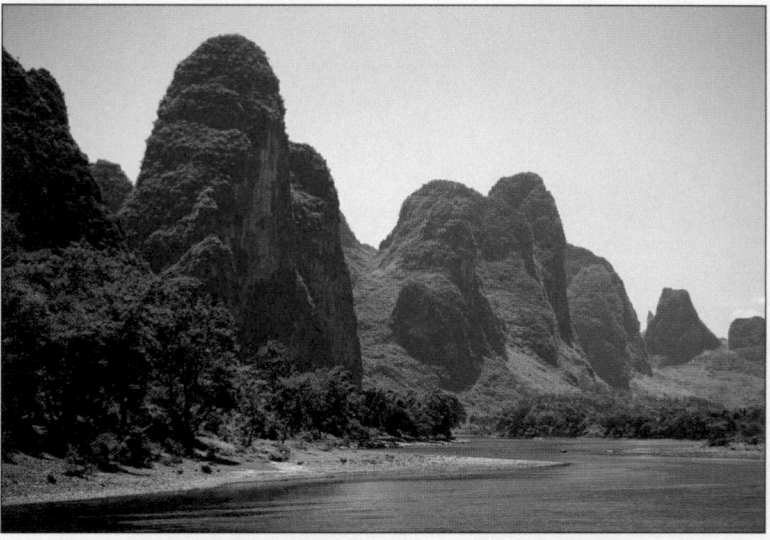

Li River and "pinnacles," China

CAMBODIA

FOR MAP, SEE PAGE 136

Population: 14,494,293

Ethnic groups: Khmer 90%, Vietnamese 5%, Chinese 1%

Principal languages: Khmer (official), French, English

Chief religion: Theravada Buddhist (official) 95%

Area: 69,900 sq mi (181,040 sq km)

Topography: The central area, formed by the Mekong River basin and Tonle Sap lake, is level. Hills and mountains are in the southeast, a long escarpment separates the country from Thailand in the northwest. 76% of the area is forested.

Capital: Phnom Penh (pop., 1,157,000)

Independence date: November 9, 1953

Government type: constitutional monarchy

Head of state: King Norodom Sihanouk

Head of government: Prime Min. Hun Sen

Monetary unit: riel

GDP: $27.95 billion (2008 est.)   **Per capita GDP:** $2,000

Industries: tourism, garments, rice milling, fishing, wood and wood products, rubber, cement, gem mining, textiles

Chief crops: rice, rubber, corn, vegetables

Minerals: gemstones, iron ore, manganese, phosphates

Life expectancy at birth (years): male, 55.7; female, 61.2

Literacy rate: 35%

Website: www.cambodia.gov.kh

Angkor Wat ruins, Cambodia

CHINA

FOR MAP, SEE PAGE 128

(Statistical data do not include Hong Kong or Macau.)

Population: 1,338,612,968

Ethnic groups: 56 groups; Han 92%; also Zhuang, Manchu, Hui, Miao, Uygur, Yi, Tujia, Tong, Tibetan, Mongol, et al.

Principal languages: Mandarin (official), Yue (Cantonese), Wu (Shanghaiese), Minbei (Fuzhou), Minnan (Hokkien-Taiwanese), Xiang, Gan, Hakka, minority languages

Chief religions: officially atheist; Buddhism, Taoism; some Muslims, Christians

Area: 3,705,410 sq mi (9,596,960 sq km)

Topography: Two-thirds of China's vast territory is mountainous or desert; only one-tenth is cultivated. Rolling topography rises to high elevations in the Daxinganlingshanmai separating Manchuria and Mongolia in the north; the Tien Shan in Xinjiang; and the Himalayan range and Kunlunshanmai in the southwest and in Tibet. Length is 1,860 mi (3,000 km) from north to south, width east to west is more than 2,000 mi (3,200 km). The eastern half of China is one of the world's best-watered lands. Three great river systems, the Chang (Yangtze), Huang (Yellow), and Xi, provide water for vast farmlands.

The Forbidden City (former imperial residence), Beijing, China

Capital: Beijing (pop., 10,848,000)

Independence date: 221 BC

Government type: Communist Party-led state

Head of state: Pres. Hu Jintao

Head of government: Premier Wen Jiabao   **Monetary unit:** yuan (renminbi)

GDP: $7,800 billion (2008 est.)   **Per capita GDP:** $6,000

Industries: iron and steel, coal, machine building, armaments, textiles and apparel, petroleum, cement, chemical fertilizers, footwear, toys, food processing, automobiles, consumer electronics, telecommunications

Chief crops: rice, wheat, potatoes, sorghum, peanuts, tea, millet, barley, cotton, oilseed

Minerals: coal, iron ore, petroleum, natural gas, mercury, tin, tungsten, antimony, manganese, molybdenum, vanadium, magnetite, aluminum, lead, zinc, uranium

Life expectancy at birth (years): male, 70.4; female, 73.7

Literacy rate: 81.5%

Website: www.china-embassy.org

HONG KONG, formerly a British dependency, in 1997 became a special administrative region of China, which agreed to allow the territory to keep its capitalist system for 50 years. Hong Kong is a major center for trade and banking and has a per capita GDP of $43,800 (2008 est.), among the highest in the world. Population, 7,055,071 including fewer than 20,000 British; area, 422 sq mi (1,090 sq km); chief executive, Donald Tsang.

MACAU, formerly under Portuguese control, reverted to China in 1999, again with a guarantee of noninterference in its way of life and capitalist system for 50 years. The per capita GDP is $30,000 (2007). Population, 559,846; area, 6 sq mi; chief executive, Fernando Chui.

CYPRUS

FOR MAP, SEE PAGE 149

Population: 796,740

Ethnic groups: Greek 85%, Turkish 12%

Principal languages: Greek, Turkish (both official); English

Chief religions: Greek Orthodox 78%, Muslim 18%

Area: 3,570 sq mi (9,250 sq km)

Topography: Two mountain ranges run east to west, separated by a wide, fertile plain.

Capital: Nicosia (pop., 205,000)

Independence date: August 16, 1960

Government type: republic

Head of state and government: Pres. Demetris Christofias

Monetary unit: euro

GDP: Greek Cypriot area, $22.69 billion (2008 est.); Turkish Cypriot area, $1.829 billion (2007 est.)

Per capita GDP: Greek Cypriot area, $28,600; Turkish Cypriot area, $11,700

Industries: food, beverages, textiles, chemicals, metal products, tourism, wood products

Chief crops: potatoes, citrus, vegetables, barley, grapes, olives, vegetables

Minerals: copper, pyrites, asbestos, gypsum, salt, marble, clay earth pigment

Life expectancy at birth (years): male, 75.1; female, 79.9

Literacy rate: 97%

Website: www.cyprusembassy.net

The TURKISH REPUBLIC OF NORTHERN CYPRUS declared independence in 1983 but failed to gain international recognition. Area, 1,295 sq mi (3,354 sq km); population, 265,000; capital, Lefkosa (Nicosia); president, Mehmet Ali Talat.

EAST TIMOR

FOR MAP, SEE PAGE 139

Population: 1,131,612

Ethnic groups: Austronesian; Papuan

Principal languages: Tetum, Portuguese (both official); Indonesian, English, other native languages

Chief religions: Roman Catholic 90%, Muslim 4%, Protestant 3%

Area: 5,740 sq mi (14,880 sq km)

Topography: Terrain is rugged, rising to 9,721 ft (2,963 m) at Mt. Ramelau.

Capital: Dili (pop., 49,000)

Independence date: May 20, 2002

Government type: republic

Head of state: Pres. José Ramos-Horta

Head of government: Prime Min. Kay Rala Xanana Gusmao

Monetary unit: U.S. dollar and Indonesian rupiah

GDP: $2.713 billion (2008 est.)   Per capita GDP: $2,400

Industries: printing, soap manufacturing, handicrafts, woven cloth

Chief crops: coffee, rice, maize, cassava, sweet potatoes, soybeans, cabbage, mangoes, bananas, vanilla

Minerals: gold, petroleum, natural gas, manganese, marble

Life expectancy at birth (years): male, 63.3; female, 67.9

Literacy rate: 48%

Website: www.timor-leste.gov.tl

GEORGIA

FOR MAP, SEE PAGE 121

Population: 4,615,807

Ethnic groups: Georgian 70%, Armenian 8%, Russian 6%, Azeri 6%

Principal languages: Georgian (official), Russian, Armenian, Azeri, Abkhaz (official in Abkhazia)

Chief religions: Georgian Orthodox 65%, Muslim 11%, Russian Orthodox 10%, Armenian Apostolic 8%

Area: 26,900 sq mi (69,700 sq km)

Topography: Georgia is separated from Russia in the northeast by the main range of the Caucasus Mountains.

Capital: Tbilisi (pop., 1,064,000)

Independence date: April 9, 1991   Government type: republic

Head of state: Pres. Mikhail Saakashvili

Head of government: Prime Min. Lado Gurgenidze

Monetary unit: lari

GDP: $21.6 billion (2008 est.)   Per capita GDP: $4,700

Industries: steel, aircraft, machine tools, electrical appliances, mining, chemicals, wood products, wine

Chief crops: citrus, grapes, tea, vegetables

Minerals: manganese, iron ore, copper, coal, oil

Life expectancy at birth (years): male, 72.4; female, 79.4

Literacy rate: 99%

Website: www.parliament.ge

INDIA

FOR MAP, SEE PAGE 125

Population: 1,166,079,217

Ethnic groups: Indo-Aryan 72%, Dravidian 25%

Principal languages: Hindi, English, Bengali, Telugu, Marathi, Tamil, Urdu, Gujarati, Malayalam, Kannada, Oriya, Punjabi, Assamese, Kashmiri, Sindhi, and Sanskrit (all official); Hindustani, a mix of Hindi and Urdu spoken in the north, is popular but not official

Columned architectural treasures of India: Agra Fort (left); the Qutb Minar complex, near Delhi (right)

India *(continued)*

Taj Mahal, Agra, India

Chief religions: Hindu 82%, Muslim 12%, Christian 2%, Sikh 2%

Area: 1,269,350 sq mi (3,287,590 sq km)

Topography: The Himalaya Mountains, highest in world, stretch across India's northern borders. Below, the Ganges Plain is wide, fertile, and among the most densely populated regions of the world. The area below includes the Deccan Peninsula. Close to one-quarter of the area is forested.

Capital: New Delhi (pop. of city proper, 300,000)

Independence date: August 15, 1947

Government type: federal republic

Head of state: Pres. Pratibha Patil

Head of government: Prime Min. Manmohan Singh

Monetary unit: rupee

GDP: $3,267 billion (2008 est.)   **Per capita GDP:** $2,800

Industries: textiles, chemicals, food processing, steel, transport equipment, cement, mining, petroleum, machinery, software

Chief crops: rice, wheat, oilseed, cotton, jute, tea, sugarcane, potatoes

Minerals: coal, iron ore, manganese, mica, bauxite, titanium ore, chromite, natural gas, diamonds, petroleum, limestone

Life expectancy at birth (years): male, 63.3; female, 64.8

Literacy rate: 52%   **Website:** www.indianembassy.org

INDONESIA

For map, see page 138

Population: 240,271,522

Ethnic groups: Javanese 45%, Sundanese 14%, · Madurese 8%, Malay 8%

Principal languages: Bahasa Indonesia (official, modified form of Malay), English, Dutch, Javanese, other dialects

Chief religions: Muslim 88%, Protestant 5%, Roman Catholic 3%, Hindu 2%, Buddhist 1%

Area: 705,190 sq mi (1,826,440 sq km)

Topography: Indonesia comprises over 13,500 islands (6,000 inhabited), including Java (one of the most densely populated areas in the world with over 2,000 persons per sq mi [770 per sq km]), Sumatra, Kalimantan (most of Borneo), Sulawesi (Celebes), and West Irian (Irian Jaya, the western half of New Guinea). Also: Bangka, Billiton, Madura, Bali, Timor. The mountains and plateaus on the major islands have a cooler climate than the tropical lowlands.

Capital: Jakarta (pop., 12,296,000)   **Independence date:** August 17, 1945

Government type: republic

Head of state and government: Pres. Susilo Bambang Yudhoyono

Monetary unit: rupiah

GDP: $915.9 billion (2008 est.)   **Per capita GDP:** $3,900

Industries: petroleum and natural gas, textiles, apparel, footwear, mining, cement, chemical fertilizers, plywood, rubber, food, tourism

Chief crops: rice, cassava, peanuts, rubber, cocoa, coffee, palm oil, copra

Minerals: petroleum, tin, natural gas, nickel, bauxite, copper, coal, gold, silver

Life expectancy at birth (years): male, 66.8; female, 71.8

Literacy rate: 83.8%

Website: www.embassyofindonesia.org

IRAN

For map, see page 125

Population: 66,429,284

Ethnic groups: Persian 51%, Azeri 24%, Gilaki/Mazandarani 8%, Kurd 7%, Arab 3%, Lur 2%, Balochi 2%, Turkmen 2%

Principal languages: Farsi (Persian; official), Kurdish, Pashto, Luri, Balochi, Gilaki, Mazandarami, Turkic languages (including Azeri and Turkish), Arabic

Chief religions: Muslim (official; Shi'a 89%, Sunni 10%)

Area: 636,000 sq mi (1,648,000 sq km)

Topography: Interior highlands and plains surrounded by high mountains, up to 18,000 ft (5,500 m). Large salt deserts cover much of area, but there are many oases and forest areas. Most of the population inhabits the north and northwest.

Capital: Tehran (pop., 7,190,000)   **Independence date:** April 1, 1979

Rice terraces, Bali, Indonesia

Government type: Islamic republic

Religious head: Ayatollah Sayyed Ali Khamenei

Head of state and government: Pres. Mahmoud Ahmadinejad

Monetary unit: rial

GDP: $842.0 billion (2008 est.)   Per capita GDP: $12,800

Industries: petroleum, petrochemicals, textiles, construction materials, food processing, metal fabricating, armaments

Chief crops: wheat, rice, other grains, sugar beets, fruits, nuts, cotton

Minerals: petroleum, natural gas, coal, chromium, copper, iron ore, lead, manganese, zinc, sulfur

Life expectancy at birth (years): male, 68.3; female, 71.1

Literacy rate: 72.1%

Websites: www.daftar.org   www.iran-un.org

Temple Mount, with the Dome of the Rock shrine, Jerusalem, Israel

---

IRAQ

FOR MAP, SEE PAGE 146

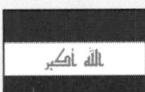

Population: 28,945,657

Ethnic groups: Arab 75%-80%, Kurdish 15%-20%

Principal languages: Arabic (official), Kurdish (official in Kurdish regions), Assyrian, Armenian

Chief religions: Muslim (official; Shi'a 60-65%, Sunni 32-37%)

Area: 168,750 sq mi (437,070 sq km)

Topography: Mostly an alluvial plain, including the Tigris and Euphrates rivers, descending from mountains in the north to desert in the southwest. The Persian Gulf region is marshland.

Capital: Baghdad (pop., 5,620,000)

Independence date: October 3, 1932

Government type: parliamentary democracy

Head of state: Pres. Jalal Talabani

Head of government: Prime Min. Nouri Kamel al-Maliki

Monetary unit: dinar

GDP: $112.8 billion (2008 est.)   Per capita GDP: $4,000

Industries: petroleum, chemicals, textiles, construction materials, food processing

Chief crops: wheat, barley, rice, vegetables, dates, cotton

Minerals: petroleum, natural gas, phosphates, sulfur

Life expectancy at birth (years): male, 67.1; female, 69.5

Literacy rate: 58%

Website: www.state.gov/r/pa/ei/bgn/6804.htm

ISRAEL

FOR MAP, SEE PAGE 149

Population: 7,233,701

Ethnic groups: Jewish 80%, Arab and other 20%

Principal languages: Hebrew, Arabic (both official); English

Chief religions: Jewish 80%, Muslim (mostly Sunni) 15%, Christian 2%

Area: 8,020 sq mi (20,770 sq km)

Topography: The Mediterranean coastal plain is fertile and well-watered. In the center is the Judean Plateau. A triangular-shaped semidesert region, the Negev, extends from south of Beersheba to an apex at the head of the Gulf of Aqaba. The eastern border drops sharply into the Jordan Rift Valley, including Lake Tiberias (Sea of Galilee) and the Dead Sea, which is 1,339 ft (408 m) below sea level, the lowest point on the earth's surface.

Capital: Jerusalem (pop., 686,000)

Independence date: May 14, 1948   Government type: republic

Head of state: Pres. Shimon Peres

Head of government: Prime Min. Ehud Olmert

Monetary unit: new shekel

GDP: $200.7 billion (2008 est.)   Per capita GDP: $28,200

Industries: high-tech design and manufactures, wood and paper products, food, beverages, tobacco, caustic soda, cement, diamond cutting

Chief crops: citrus, vegetables, cotton

Minerals: potash, copper ore, natural gas, phosphate rock, magnesium bromide, clays, sand

Life expectancy at birth (years): male, 77.1; female, 81.4

Literacy rate: 95%

Website: www.israelemb.org

The PALESTINIAN AUTHORITY is responsible for civil government in the Gaza Strip and portions of the West Bank. Gaza: population, 1,551,859; area, 139 sq mi (360 sq km). West Bank: total population, 2,461,267; area, 2,263 sq mi (5,860 sq km).

JAPAN

FOR MAP, SEE PAGE 129

Population: 127,078,679

Ethnic groups: Japanese 99%; Korean, Chinese, and other 1%

Principal languages: Japanese (official), Ainu, Korean

Chief religions: Shinto and Buddhist observed together by 84%

Area: 145,883 sq mi (377,835 sq km)

Topography: Japan consists of four main islands: Honshu ("mainland"), 87,805 sq mi (227,415 sq km); Hokkaido, 30,144 sq mi (78,073 sq km); Kyushu, 14,114 sq mi (36,555 sq km); and Shikoku, 7,049 sq mi (18,257 sq km). The coast, deeply indented, measures 16,654 mi (26,802 km). The northern islands are a continuation of the Sakhalin Mountains. The Kunlun range of China continues into the southern islands, the ranges meeting in the Japanese Alps. In a vast transverse fissure crossing Honshu east to west rises a group of volcanoes, mostly extinct or inactive, including 12,389-ft (3,776-m) Mt. Fuji (Fujiyama) near Tokyo.

Capital: Tokyo (pop., 34,997,000)   Independence date: 660 BC

Government type: parliamentary democracy

Head of state: Emperor Akihito

Head of government: Prime Min. Yasuo Fukuda

Monetary unit: yen

GDP: $4,348 billion (2008 est.)   Per capita GDP: $34,200

Industries: motor vehicles, electronic equipment, machine tools, steel and nonferrous metals, ships, chemicals, textiles, processed foods

Chief crops: rice, sugar beets, vegetables, fruit

Nation Facts and Figures

Three aspects of Japan: Mt. Fuji (top), a lake temple (above left), and Tokyo (above right)

Japan *(continued)*

Life expectancy at birth (years): male, 77.7; female, 84.5

Literacy rate: 99%

Websites: www.us.emb-japan.go.jp
www.jnto.go.jp

JORDAN

FOR MAP, SEE PAGE 146

Population: 6,342,948

Ethnic groups: Arab 98%, Armenian 1%, Circassian 1%

Principal languages: Arabic (official), English

Chief religions: Muslim (official; mostly Sunni) 92%, Christian 6%

Area: 35,300 sq mi (91,540 sq km)

Topography: About 88% of Jordan is arid. Fertile areas are in the west. The only port is on the short Aqaba Gulf coast. The country shares the Dead Sea (1,312 ft [400 m] below sea level) with Israel.

Capital: Amman (pop., 1,237,000)

Independence date: May 25, 1946

Government type: constitutional monarchy

Head of state: King Abdullah II

Head of government: Prime Min. Marouf al-Bakhit

Monetary unit: dinar

GDP: $30.76 billion (2008 est.)

Per capita GDP: $5,000

Industries: mining, petroleum refining, cement, light manufacturing, tourism

Chief crops: wheat, barley, citrus, tomatoes, melons, olives

Minerals: phosphates, potash, shale oil

Life expectancy at birth (years): male, 75.6; female, 80.7

Literacy rate: 86.6%

Websites: www.nic.gov.jo
www.jordanembassyus.org

KAZAKHSTAN

FOR MAP, SEE PAGE 122

Population: 15,399,437

Ethnic groups: Kazakh 53%, Russian 30%, Ukrainian 4%, Uzbek 3%, German 2%, Uighur 1%

Principal languages: Kazakh, Russian (both official); Ukranian, German, Uzbek

Chief religions: Muslim 47%, Russian Orthodox 44%

Area: 1,049,200 sq mi (2,717,300 sq km)

Topography: Kazakhstan extends from the lower reaches of the Volga River in Europe to the Altay Mountains on the Chinese border.

Capital: Astana (pop., 332,000)

Independence date: December 16, 1991

Government type: republic

Head of state: Pres. Nursultan A. Nazarbayev

Head of government: Prime Min. Daniyal Akhmetov

Monetary unit: tenge

GDP: $176.9 billion (2008) **Per capita GDP:** $11,500

Industries: oil, mining, iron and steel, tractors and other agricultural machinery, electric motors, construction materials

Chief crops: spring wheat, cotton

Minerals: petroleum, natural gas, coal, iron ore, manganese, chrome ore, nickel, cobalt, copper, molybdenum, lead, zinc, bauxite, gold, uranium

Life expectancy at birth (years): male, 60.7; female, 71.7

Literacy rate: 98.4%

Website: www.kazakhembus.com

KOREA, NORTH

FOR MAP, SEE PAGE 131

Population: 22,665,345

Ethnic group: Korean

Principal language: Korean (official)

Chief religions: activities almost nonexistent; traditionally Buddhist, Confucianist, Chondogyo

Area: 46,540 sq mi (120,540 sq km)

Topography: Mountains and hills cover nearly all the country, with narrow valleys and small plains in between. The northern and the eastern coasts are the most rugged areas.

Capital: Pyongyang (pop., 3,228,000)

Independence date: September 9, 1948

Government type: Communist state

Leader: Kim Jong Il

Monetary unit: won

GDP: $40.0 billion (2008 est.) **Per capita GDP:** $1,700

Industries: military products, machine building, electric power, chemicals, mining, metallurgy, textiles, food processing

Chief crops: rice, corn, potatoes, soybeans, pulses

Minerals: coal, lead, tungsten, zinc, graphite, magnesite, iron ore, copper, gold, pyrites, salt, fluorspar

Life expectancy at birth (years): male, 68.4; female, 73.9

Literacy rate: 99%

Website: www.korea-dpr.com

KOREA, SOUTH

For map, see page 131

Population: 48,508,972

Ethnic group: Korean

Principal language: Korean (official)

Chief religions: Christian 49%, Buddhist 47%, Confucianist 3%

Area: 38,020 sq mi (98,480 sq km)

Topography: The country is mountainous, with a rugged eastern coast. The western and southern coasts are deeply indented, with many islands and harbors.

Capital: Seoul (pop., 9,895,000)

Independence date: August 15, 1948

Government type: republic

Head of state: Pres. Lee Myung-bak

Head of government: Prime Min. Han Seung-soo

Monetary unit: won

GDP: $1,278 billion (2008 est.)

Per capita GDP: $26,000

Industries: electronics, automobile production, chemicals, shipbuilding, steel, textiles, clothing, footwear, food processing

A painting from a Seoul museum

Chief crops: rice, root crops, barley, vegetables, fruit

Minerals: coal, tungsten, graphite, molybdenum, lead

Life expectancy at birth (years): male, 72.0; female, 79.5

Literacy rate: 98%

Website: www.korea.net

Seoul, South Korea

KUWAIT

For map, see page 146

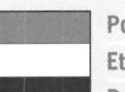

Population: 2,691,158

Ethnic groups: Arab 80%, South Asian 9%, Iranian 4%

Principal languages: Arabic (official), English

Chief religion: Muslim 85% (official; Sunni 70%, Shi'a 30%)

Area: 6,880 sq mi (17,820 sq km)

Topography: The country is flat, very dry, and extremely hot.

Capital: Kuwait City (pop., 1,222,000)

Independence date: June 19, 1961

Government type: constitutional monarchy

Head of state: Emir Sheikh Sabah al-Ahmad al-Jabir al-Sabah

Head of government: Prime Min. Sheikh Nasir Muhammad al-Ahmad al-Sabah

Monetary unit: dinar

GDP: $149.1 billion (2008 est.)   Per capita GDP: $57,400

Industries: petroleum, petrochemicals, desalination, food processing, construction materials

Minerals: petroleum, natural gas

Life expectancy at birth (years): male, 75.9; female, 77.9

Literacy rate: 78.6%   Website: www.kuwait-info.org.uk

KYRGYZSTAN

For map, see page 145

Population: 5,431,747

Ethnic groups: Kyrgyz 52%, Russian 18%, Uzbek 13%, Ukrainian 3%, German 2%

Principal languages: Kyrgyz, Russian (both official); Uzbek

Chief religions: Muslim 75%, Russian Orthodox 20%

Area: 76,600 sq mi (198,500 sq km)

Topography: Kyrgystan is a landlocked country nearly covered by the Tien Shan and Pamir Mountains; the average elevation is 9,020 ft (2,750 m). A large lake, Issyk-Kul, in the northeast is 1 mi (1.6 km) above sea level.

Capital: Bishkek (pop., 806,000)   Independence date: August 31, 1991

Government type: republic

Head of state: Pres. Kurmanbek Bakiyev

Head of government: Prime Min. Feliks Kulov

Monetary unit: som

GDP: $11.41 billion (2008 est.)   Per capita GDP: $2,100

Industries: small machinery, textiles, food processing, cement, shoes, sawn logs, refrigerators, furniture, electric motors

Chief crops: tobacco, cotton, potatoes, vegetables, grapes, fruits and berries

Minerals: gold and rare earth metals, coal, oil, natural gas, nepheline, mercury, bismuth, lead, zinc

Life expectancy at birth (years): male, 63.8; female, 72.1

Literacy rate: 97%

Website: www.kyrgyzstan.org

LAOS

For map, see page 136

Population: 6,834,942

Ethnic groups: Lao Loum 68%, Lao Theung 22%, Lao Soung (includes Hmong and Yao) 9%

Principal languages: Lao (official), French, English, and various ethnic languages

Laos *(continued)*

Chief religions: Buddhism 60%, animist and other 40%

Area: 91,400 sq mi (236,800 sq km)

Topography: Laos is landlocked, dominated by jungle. High mountains along the eastern border are the source of the east to west rivers slicing across the country to the Mekong River, which defines most of the western border.

Capital: Vientiane (pop., 716,000)   **Independence date:** July 19, 1949

Government type: Communist

Head of state: Pres. Khamtai Siphandon

Head of government: Prime Min. Boungnang Vorachith

Monetary unit: kip

GDP: $13.99 billion (2008 est.)   **Per capita GDP:** $2,100

Industries: mining, timber, electric power, agricultural processing, construction, garments, tourism

Chief crops: sweet potatoes, vegetables, corn, coffee, sugarcane, tobacco, cotton, tea, peanuts, rice

Minerals: gypsum, tin, gold, gemstones

Life expectancy at birth (years): male, 52.7; female, 56.8

Literacy rate: 57%

Website: www.laoembassy.com/discover/index.htm

LEBANON

FOR MAP, SEE PAGE 149

Population: 4,017,095

Ethnic groups: Arab 95%, Armenian 4%

Principal languages: Arabic (official), French, English, Armenian

Chief religions: Muslim 70%, Christian 30%

Topography: There is a narrow coastal strip, and two mountain ranges running north to south enclosing the fertile Beqaa Valley. The Litani River runs south through the valley, turning west to empty into the Mediterranean.

Area: 4,000 sq mi (10,400 sq km)

Capital: Beirut (pop., 1,792,000)

Independence date: November 22, 1943   **Government type:** republic

Head of state: Pres. Emile Lahoud

Head of government: Prime Min. Fouad Siniora

Monetary unit: pound

GDP: $44.07 billion (2008 est.)   **Per capita GDP:** $11,100

Industries: banking, food processing, jewelry, cement, textiles, mineral and chemical products, wood and furniture products, oil refining, metal fabricating

Chief crops: citrus, grapes, tomatoes, apples, vegetables, potatoes, olives, tobacco

Minerals: limestone, iron ore, salt

Life expectancy at birth (years): male, 69.6; female, 74.9

Literacy rate: 86.4%

Website: www.lebanonembassyus.org

MALAYSIA

FOR MAP, SEE PAGE 138

Population: 25,715,819

Ethnic groups: Malay and other indigenous 58%, Chinese 24%, Indian 8%

Principal languages: Malay (official), English, Chinese dialects, Tamil, Telugu, Malayalam, Panjabi, Thai; Iban and Kadazan in the east

Thean Hou Temple, Kuala Lumpur, Malaysia

Chief religions: Muslim (official) 60%, Buddhist 19%, Christian 9%, Hindu 6%, Confucianist/Taoist 3%

Area: 127,320 sq mi (329,750 sq km)

Topography: Most of western Malaysia is covered by tropical jungle, including the central mountain range that runs north to soth through the peninsula. The western coast is marshy, the eastern coast, sandy. Eastern Malaysia has a wide, swampy coastal plain, with interior jungles and mountains.

Capital: Kuala Lumpur (pop., 1,352,000)

Independence date: August 31, 1957

Government type: federal parliamentary democracy with a constitutional monarch

Head of state: Paramount Ruler Syed Sirajuddin Syed Putra Jamalullail

Head of government: Prime Min. Datuk Seri Abdullah Ahmad Badawi

Monetary unit: ringgit

GDP: $386.6 billion (2008 est.)   **Per capita GDP:** $15,300

Industries: rubber/oil-palm goods, light manufacturing, electronics, mining, logging

Chief crops: rubber, palm oil, cocoa, rice, coconuts, pepper

Minerals: tin, petroleum, copper, iron ore, natural gas, bauxite

Life expectancy at birth (years): male, 69.3; female, 74.8

Literacy rate: 83.5%

Websites: www.tourism.gov.my
   www.gov.my

MALDIVES

FOR MAP, SEE PAGE 125

Population: 396,334

Ethnic groups: Dravidian, Sinhalese, Arab

Principal languages: Divehi (Sinhala dialect, Arabic script; official), English

Chief religion: Muslim (official; mostly Sunni)

Area: 116 sq mi (300 sq km)

Topography: The Maldives consists of 19 atolls with 1,190 islands, 198 inhabited. None of the islands are over 5 sq mi (13 sq km) in area, and all are nearly flat.

Capital: Male (pop., 83,000)   **Independence date:** July 26, 1965

Government type: republic

Head of state and government: Pres. Mohamed Nasheed

Monetary unit: rufiyaa

GDP: $1.74 billion (2008 est.)   Per capita GDP: $5,000

Industries: fish processing, tourism, shipping, boatbuilding, coconut processing, garments, woven mats, rope, handicrafts, coral and sand mining

Chief crops: coconuts, corn, sweet potatoes

Life expectancy at birth (years): male, 62.4; female, 65.0

Literacy rate: 93.2%   Website: www.themaldives.com

MONGOLIA

FOR MAP, SEE PAGE 128

Population: 3,041,142

Ethnic groups: Mongol 85%, Turkic 7%, Tungusic 5%

Principal languages: Khalkha Mongol, Turkic, Russian

Chief religion: Tibetan Buddhist Lamaism 96%

Area: 604,000 sq mi (1,565,000 sq km)

Topography: Mongolia is mostly a high plateau with mountains, salt lakes, and vast grasslands. Arid lands in the southern are part of the Gobi Desert.

Capital: Ulaanbaatar (pop., 812,000)

Independence date: July 11, 1921

Government type: republic

Head of state: Pres. Tsakhiagiin Elbegdorj

Head of government: Prime Min. Sanjaagiin Bayar

Monetary unit: tugrik

GDP: $9.56 billion (2008 est.)   Per capita GDP: $3,200

Industries: construction materials, mining, food and beverages, processing of animal products

Chief crops: wheat, barley, potatoes, forage crops

Minerals: oil, coal, copper, molybdenum, tungsten, phosphates, tin, nickel, zinc, wolfram, fluorspar, gold, silver, iron, phosphate

Life expectancy at birth (years): male, 62.0; female, 66.5

Literacy rate: 97.8%

Website: www.mongolianembassy.us

MYANMAR (FORMERLY BURMA)

FOR MAP, SEE PAGE 141

Population: 48,137,741

Ethnic groups: Burman 68%, Shan 9%, Karen 7%, Rakhine 4%, Chinese 3%, Indian 2%, Mon 2%

Principal languages: Burmese (official); many ethnic minority languages

Chief religions: Buddhist 89%, Christian 4%, Muslim 4%, animist 1%

Area: 262,000 sq mi (678,500 sq km)

Topography: Mountains surround Myanmar on the west, north, and east, and dense forests cover much of the nation. North to south rivers provide habitable valleys and communications, especially the Irrawaddy, navigable for 900 mi (1,400 km).

Capital: Yangon (Rangoon) (pop., 3,874,000); Nay Pyi Taw (admin. capital)

Independence date: January 4, 1948

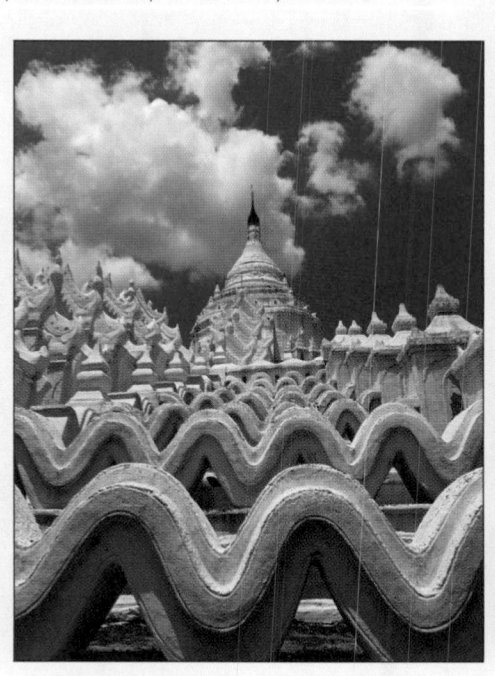

Hsinbyume Pagoda, Mingun, Myanmar

Government type: military

Head of state: Gen. Than Shwe

Head of government: Lt. Gen. Soe Win

Monetary unit: kyat

GDP: $55.04 billion (2008 est.)   Per capita GDP: $1,200

Industries: agricultural processing, knit and woven apparel, wood and wood products, mining, construction materials, pharmaceuticals, fertilizer

Chief crops: rice, pulses, beans, sesame, groundnuts, sugarcane

Minerals: petroleum, tin, antimony, zinc, copper, tungsten, lead, coal, marble, limestone, precious stones, natural gas

Life expectancy at birth (years): male, 54.2; female, 57.9

Literacy rate: 83.1%   Website: www.state.gov/r/pa/ei/bgn/35910.htm

NEPAL

FOR MAP, SEE PAGE 142

Population: 28,563,377

Ethnic groups: Newar, Indian, Gurung, Magar, Tamang, Rai, Limbu, Sherpa, Tharu

Principal languages: Nepali (official); about 30 dialects and 12 other languages

Chief religions: Hindu (official) 86%, Buddhist 8%, Muslim 4%

Area: 54,400 sq mi (140,800 sq km)

Topography: The Himalayas stretch across the north, the hill country with its fertile valleys extends across the center, while the southern border region is part of the flat, subtropical Ganges Plain.

Capital: Kathmandu (pop., 741,000)   Independence date: 1768

Government type: constitutional monarchy

Head of state: King Gyanendra Bir Bikram Shah Dev

Head of government: Prime Min. Girija Prasad Koirala

Monetary unit: rupee

GDP: $31.1 billion (2008 est.)   Per capita GDP: $1,100

Industries: tourism, carpet, textile, rice, jute, sugar, oilseed mills, cigarette, cement and brick production

Chief crops: rice, corn, wheat, sugarcane, root crops

Minerals: quartz, lignite, copper, cobalt, iron ore

Life expectancy at birth (years): male, 59.7; female, 59.1

Literacy rate: 27.5%   Website: www.nepalembassy/usa.org

Machapuchare peak, Nepal

OMAN

For map, see page 147

Population: 3,418,085

Ethnic groups: Arab, Baluchi, South Asian, African

Principal languages: Arabic (official), English, Baluchi, Urdu, Indian dialects

Chief religion: Muslim 75% (official; mostly Ibadhi)

Area: 82,030 sq mi (212,460 sq km)

Topography: Oman has a narrow coastal plain up to 10 mi (16 km) wide, a range of barren mountains reaching 9,900 ft (3,000 m), and a wide, stony, mostly waterless plateau, with an average altitude of 1,000 ft (300 m). Also, an exclave at the tip of the Musandam peninsula controls access to the Persian Gulf.

Capital: Muscat (pop., 638,000)

Independence date: 1650   **Government type:** absolute monarchy

Head of state and government: Sultan Qabus bin Said

Monetary unit: rial Omani

GDP: $67.0 billion (2008 est.)   **Per capita GDP:** $20,200

Industries: oil and gas, construction, cement, copper

Chief crops: dates, limes, bananas, alfalfa, vegetables

Minerals: petroleum, copper, asbestos, marble, limestone, chromium, gypsum, natural gas

Life expectancy at birth (years): male, 70.7; female, 75.2

Literacy rate: approaching 80%

Website: www.state.gov/r/pa/ei/bgn/35834.htm

PAKISTAN

For map, see page 147

Population: 176,242,949

Ethnic groups: Punjabi, Sindhi, Pashtun, Balochi

Principal languages: English, Urdu (both official); Punjabi, Sindhi, Siraiki, Pashtu, Balochi, Hindko, Brahui, Burushaski

Chief religions: Muslim 97% (official; Sunni 77%, Shi'a 20%)

Area: 310,400 sq mi (803,940 sq km)

Topography: The Indus River rises in the Hindu Kush and Himalaya mountains in the north (highest is K2, or Godwin Austen, 28,250 ft [8,611 m], second highest in the world), then flows over 1,000 mi (1,600 km) through fertile valley and empties into Arabian Sea. The Thar Desert and Eastern Plains flank the Indus Valley.

Capital: Islamabad (pop., 698,000)

Independence date: August 14, 1947

Government type: republic with strong military influence

Head of state: Pres. Pervez Musharraf

Head of government: Prime Min. Syed Yousaf Raza Gillani

Monetary unit: rupee

GDP: $452.7 billion (2008 est.)   **Per capita GDP:** $2,600

Industries: textiles, food processing, beverages, construction materials, clothing, paper products

Chief crops: cotton, wheat, rice, sugarcane, fruits, vegetables

Minerals: natural gas, limited petroleum, poor quality coal, iron ore, copper, salt, limestone

Life expectancy at birth (years): male, 61.7; female, 63.6

Literacy rate: 42.7%   **Website:** www.pakistan.gov.pk

PAPUA NEW GUINEA

For map, see page 174

Population: 6,057,263

Ethnic groups: Melanesian, Papuan, Negrito, Micronesian, Polynesian

Principal languages: English (official), pidgin English, Motu; 715 indigenous languages

Chief religions: indigenous beliefs 34%, Roman Catholic 22%, Protestant 44%

Area: 178,700 sq mi (462,840 sq km)

Topography: Thickly forested mountains cover much of the center of the country, with lowlands along the coasts. Included are some islands of the Bismarck and Solomon groups, such as the Admiralty Islands, New Ireland, New Britain, and Bougainville.

Capital: Port Moresby (pop., 275,000)

Independence date: September 16, 1975

Government type: parliamentary democracy

Head of state: Queen Elizabeth II, represented by Gov-Gen. Sir Paulias Matane

Head of government: Prime Min. Sir Michael Somare

Monetary unit: kina

GDP: $13.29 billion (2008 est.)   **Per capita GDP:** $2,200

Industries: copra and palm oil processing, wood products, mining, construction, tourism

Chief crops: coffee, cocoa, coconuts, palm kernels, tea, rubber, sweet potatoes, fruit, vegetables

Minerals: gold, copper, silver, natural gas, oil

Life expectancy at birth (years): male, 62.4; female, 66.8

Literacy rate: 64.5%

Website: www.pngtourism.org.pg

PHILIPPINES

For map, see page 137

Population: 97,976,603

Ethnic groups: Christian Malay 91.5%, Muslim Malay 4%, Chinese 1.5%

Principal languages: Filipino, English (both official); many dialects

Chief religions: Roman Catholic 83%, Protestant 9%, Muslim 5%

Area: 115,830 sq mi (300,000 sq km)

Topography: The country consists of some 7,100 islands stretching 1,100 mi (1,770 km) north to south. About 95% of the area and population are on the 11 largest islands, which are mountainous, except for the heavily indented coastlines and the central plain on Luzon.

Capital: Manila (pop., 10,352,000)

Independence date: July 4, 1946   **Government type:** republic

Head of state and government: Pres. Gloria Macapagal Arroyo

Monetary unit: peso

GDP: $320.6 billion (2008 est.)   **Per capita GDP:** $3,300

Fishing boat, Boracay, Philippines

Industries: textiles, pharmaceuticals, chemicals, wood products, food processing, electronics assembly

Chief crops: rice, coconuts, corn, sugarcane, bananas, pineapples, mangoes

Minerals: petroleum, nickel, cobalt, silver, gold, salt, copper

Life expectancy at birth (years): male, 66.7; female, 72.6

Literacy rate: 94.6%

Websites: www.philippineembassy-usa.org
www.gov.ph

QATAR

FOR MAP, SEE PAGE 146

Population: 833,285

Ethnic groups: Arab 40%, Pakistani 18%, Indian 18%, Iranian 10%

Principal languages: Arabic (official), English

Chief religion: Muslim (official) 95%

Area: 4,420 sq mi (11,440 sq km)

Topography: Qatar is mostly a flat desert, with some limestone ridges; vegetation of any kind is scarce.

Capital: Doha (pop., 286,000)

Independence date: September 3, 1971

Government type: traditional monarchy

Head of state: Emir Hamad bin Khalifa ath-Thani

Head of government: Prime Min. Abdullah bin Khalifa ath-Thani

Monetary unit: riyal

GDP: $85.35 billion (2008 est.)   **Per capita GDP:** $103,500

Industries: oil production and refining, fertilizers, petrochemicals, steel reinforcing bars, cement

Chief crops: fruits, vegetables

Minerals: petroleum, natural gas

Life expectancy at birth (years): male, 70.9; female, 76.0

Literacy rate: 79%

Website: english.mofa.gov.qa

SAUDI ARABIA

FOR MAP, SEE PAGE 146

Population: 28,686,633

Ethnic groups: Arab 90%, Afro-Asian 10%

Principal language: Arabic (official)

Chief religion: Muslim (official)

Area: 756,990 sq mi (1,960,580 sq km)

Topography: Saudi Arabia is bordered by the Red Sea on the west. The highlands on the west, up to 9,000 ft (2,700 m), slope as an arid, barren desert to the Persian Gulf on the east.

Capital: Riyadh (pop., 5,126,000)

Independence date: September 23, 1932

Government type: constitutional monarchy with strong Islamic influence

Head of state and government: King Abdallah bin Abd al-Aziz Al Saud

Monetary unit: riyal

GDP: $582.8 billion (2008 est.)   **Per capita GDP:** $20,700

Industries: oil production and refining, basic petrochemicals, cement, construction, fertilizer, plastics

Chief crops: wheat, barley, tomatoes, melons, dates, citrus

Minerals: petroleum, natural gas, iron ore, gold, copper

Life expectancy at birth (years): male, 73.3; female, 77.3

Literacy rate: 78%

Website: www.saudiembassy.net

SINGAPORE

FOR MAP, SEE PAGE 138

Population: 4,657,542

Ethnic groups: Chinese 77%, Malay 14%, Indian 8%

Principal languages: Chinese, Malay, Tamil, English (all official)

Chief religions: Buddhist, Muslim, Christian, Taoist, Hindu

Area: 250 sq mi (650 sq km)

Topography: Singapore is a flat, formerly swampy island. The nation includes 40 nearby islets.

Capital: Singapore (pop., 4,253,000)

Independence date: August 9, 1965

Government type: republic   **Head of state:** Pres. S. R. Nathan

Head of government: Prime Min. Lee Hsien Loong

Monetary unit: Singapore dollar

GDP: $240.0 billion (2008 est.)   **Per capita GDP:** $52,000

Industries: electronics, chemicals, financial services, oil-drilling equipment, petroleum refining, rubber products, processed food and beverages, ship repair, entrepot trade, biotechnology

Chief crops: rubber, copra, fruit, orchids, vegetables

Life expectancy at birth (years): male, 79.0; female, 84.3

Literacy rate: 93.5%

Website: www.gov.sg

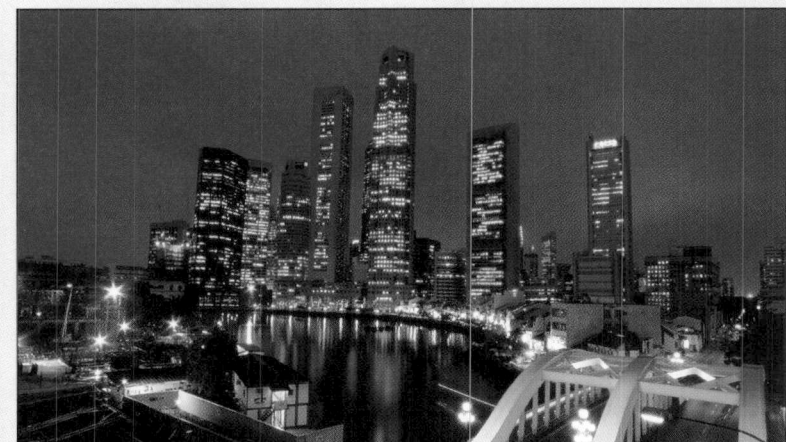

Singapore

SRI LANKA

FOR MAP, SEE PAGE 140

Population: 21,324,791

Ethnic groups: Sinhalese 74%, Tamil 18%, Moor 7%

Principal languages: Sinhala, Tamil (both official); English

Chief religions: Buddhist 70%, Hindu 15%, Christian 8%, Muslim 7%

Area: 25,330 sq mi (65,610 sq km)

Topography: The coastal area and the northern half are flat; the south-central area is hilly and mountainous.

Capitals: Colombo (administrative) (pop., 648,000), Sri Jayawardenepura Kotte (legislative) (pop., 117,000)

Independence date: February 4, 1948

Government type: republic

Head of state: Pres. Mahinda Rajapaksa

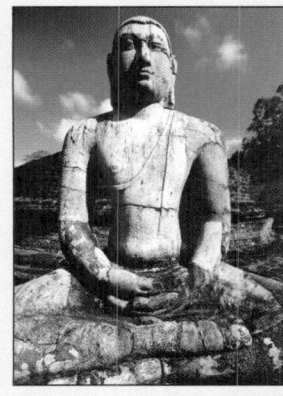

Buddha statue, Polonnaruwa, Sri Lanka

Nation Facts and Figures

Sri Lanka *(continued)*

Tea plantation, Sri Lanka

Head of government: Prime Min. Ratnasiri Wickremanayake

Monetary unit: rupee

GDP: $91.9 billion (2008 est.)   Per capita GDP: $4,300

Industries: rubber processing, agricultural commodities, clothing, cement, petroleum refining, textiles, tobacco

Chief crops: rice, sugarcane, grains, pulses, oilseed, spices, tea, rubber, coconuts

Minerals: limestone, graphite, mineral sands, gems, phosphates, clay

Life expectancy at birth (years): male, 70.3; female, 75.6

Literacy rate: 90.2%   Website: www.slembassyusa.org

Government type: republic (under military regime)

Head of state: Pres. Bashar al-Assad

Head of government: Prime Min. Muhammad Naji al-Otari

Monetary unit: pound

GDP: $95.36 billion (2008 est.)

Per capita GDP: $4,800

Industries: petroleum, textiles, food processing, beverages, tobacco

Chief crops: wheat, barley, cotton, lentils, chickpeas, olives, sugar beets

Minerals: petroleum, phosphates, chrome and manganese ores, asphalt, iron ore, rock salt, marble, gypsum

Life expectancy at birth (years): male, 68.5; female, 71.0

Literacy rate: 70.8%   Website: www.syrianembassy.us

TAIWAN

FOR MAP, SEE PAGE 137

Population: 22,974,347

Ethnic groups: Taiwanese 84%, mainland Chinese 14%, aborigine 2%

Principal languages: Mandarin Chinese (official), Taiwanese (Min), Hakka dialects

Chief religions: Buddhist, Confucian, and Taoist 93%; Christian 5%

Area: 13,890 sq mi (35,980 sq km)

Topography: A mountain range forms the backbone of the island; the eastern half is very steep and craggy, and the western slope is flat, fertile, and well cultivated.

Capital: Taipei (pop., 2,624,00)

Independence date: 1949

Government type: democracy

Head of state: Pres. Ma Ying-jeou

Head of government: Premier Liu Chao-shiuan

Monetary unit: Taiwan dollar (TWD)

GDP: $738.8 billion (2008 est.)

Per capita GDP: $31,900

Industries: electronics, petroleum refining, chemicals, textiles, iron and steel, machinery, cement, food processing

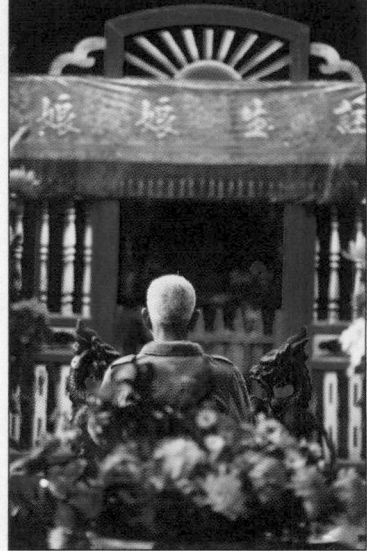

Lungshan Temple, Taipei, Taiwan

Chief crops: rice, corn, vegetables, fruit, tea

Minerals: coal, natural gas, limestone, marble, asbestos

Life expectancy at birth (years): male, 74.3; female, 80.1

Literacy rate: 86%

Website: www.gio.gov.tw

SYRIA

FOR MAP, SEE PAGE 148

Population: 20,178,485

Ethnic groups: Arab 90%, Kurds, Armenians, and other 10%

Principal languages: Arabic (official), Kurdish, Armenian

Chief religions: Sunni Muslim 74%, other Muslims 16%, Christian 10%

Area: 71,500 sq mi (185,180 sq km)

Topography: Syria has a short Mediterranean coastline, then stretches east and south with fertile lowlands and plains, alternating with mountains and large desert areas.

Capital: Damascus (pop., 2,228,000)

Independence date: April 17, 1946

TAJIKISTAN

FOR MAP, SEE PAGE 145

Population: 7,349,145

Ethnic groups: Tajik 65%, Uzbek 25%, Russian 4%

Principal languages: Tajik (official), Russian

Chief religion: Muslim (Sunni 85%, Shi'a 5%)

Area: 55,300 sq mi (143,100 sq km)

Topography: Mountainous region that contains the Pamirs and the Trans-Alai mountain system.

Capital: Dushanbe (pop., 554,000)

Independence date: September 9, 1991

Government type: republic   Head of state: Pres. Imomali Rakhmonov

Head of government: Prime Min. Akil Akilov

Monetary unit: somoni

GDP: $15.4 billion (2008 est.)   Per capita GDP: $2,100

Industries: aluminum, zinc, lead, chemicals and fertilizers, cement, vegetable oil, metal-cutting machine tools, refrigerators and freezers

Chief crops: cotton, grain, fruits, grapes, vegetables

Minerals: petroleum, uranium, mercury, brown coal, lead, zinc, antimony, tungsten, silver, gold

Life expectancy at birth (years): male, 61.5; female, 67.6

Literacy rate: 98%   Website: www.state.gov/r/pa/ei/bgn/5775.htm

THAILAND

FOR MAP, SEE PAGE 136

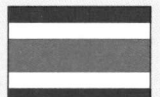

Population: 65,905,410

Ethnic groups: Thai 75%, Chinese 14%

Principal languages: Thai, Chinese, Malay, Khmer

Chief religions: Buddhism (official) 95%, Muslim 4%

Area: 198,000 sq mi (514,000 sq km)

Topography: A plateau dominates the northeast third of Thailand, dropping to the fertile alluvial valley of the Chao Phraya River in the center. Forested mountains are in the north, with narrow fertile valleys. The southern peninsula region is covered by rain forests.

Capital: Bangkok (pop., 6,486,000)   Independence date: 1238

Government type: constitutional monarchy

Head of state: King Bhumibol Adulyadej

Head of government: Prime Min. Thaksin Shinawatra

Monetary unit: baht

GDP: $553.4 billion (2008 est.)   Per capita GDP: $8,500

Industries: tourism, textiles and garments, agricultural processing, beverages, tobacco, cement, light manufacturing, electric appliances and components, computers and parts, integrated circuits, furniture, plastics

Chief crops: rice, cassava, rubber, corn, sugarcane, coconuts, soybeans

Minerals: tin, rubber, natural gas, tungsten, tantalum, lead, gypsum, lignite, fluorite

Life expectancy at birth (years): male, 69.2; female, 73.7

Literacy rate: 93.8%

Website: www.thaiembdc.org

River market, Thailand

Hagia Sophia, Istanbul, Turkey

TURKEY

FOR MAP, SEE PAGE 148

Population: 76,805,524

Ethnic groups: Turk 80%, Kurd 20%

Principal languages: Turkish (official), Kurdish, Arabic, Armenian, Greek

Chief religion: Muslim 99.8% (mostly Sunni)

Area: 301,380 sq mi (780,580 sq km)

Topography: Central Turkey has wide plateaus, with hot, dry summers and cold winters. High mountains ring the interior on all but the west, with more than 20 peaks over 10,000 ft (3,000 m). Rolling plains are in the west; mild, fertile coastal plains are in the south and west.

Capital: Ankara (pop., 3,428,000)

Independence date: October 29, 1923

Government type: republic

Head of state: Pres. Abdullah Gül

Head of government: Prime Min. Recep Tayyip Erdogan

Monetary unit: Turkish lira

GDP: $906.5 billion (2008 est.)   Per capita GDP: $12,000

Industries: textiles, food processing, autos, mining, steel, petroleum, construction, lumber, paper

Chief crops: tobacco, cotton, grain, olives, sugar beets, pulse, citrus

Minerals: antimony, coal, chromium, mercury, copper, borate, sulfur, iron ore

Life expectancy at birth (years): male, 69.7; female, 74.6

Literacy rate: 85%   Website: www.turkey.org

TURKMENISTAN

FOR MAP, SEE PAGE 145

Population: 4,884,887

Ethnic groups: Turkmen 77%, Uzbek 9%, Russian 7%, Kazakh 2%

Principal languages: Turkmen, Russian, Uzbek

Chief religions: Muslim 89%, Eastern Orthodox 9%

Area: 188,500 sq mi (488,100 sq km)

Topography: The Kara Kum Desert occupies 80% of the area. The country is bordered on the west by the Caspian Sea.

Capital: Ashgabat (pop., 574,000)

Turkmenistan (continued)

Independence date: October 27, 1991

Government type: republic with authoritarian rule

Head of state and government: Pres. Gurbanguly Berdimuhamedov

Monetary unit: manat

GDP: $29.65 billion (2008 est.)   Per capita GDP: $6,100

Industries: petroleum products, textiles, food processing

Chief crops: cotton, grain

Minerals: petroleum, natural gas, coal, sulfur, salt

Life expectancy at birth (years): male, 57.9; female, 64.9

Literacy rate: 98%

Website: www.turkmenistanembassy.org

UNITED ARAB EMIRATES

FOR MAP, SEE PAGE 146

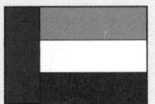

Population: 4,798,491

Ethnic groups: Arab and Iranian 42%, Indian 50%

Principal languages: Arabic (official), Persian, English, Hindi, Urdu

Chief religion: Muslim 96% (official; Shi'a 16%)

Area: 32,000 sq mi (82,880 sq km)

Topography: A barren, flat coastal plain gives way to uninhabited sand dunes on the south. The Hajar Mountains are on the east.

Capital: Abu Dhabi (pop., 475,000)

Independence date: December 2, 1971

Government type: federation of emirates

Head of state: Pres. Khalifa bin Zayid al-Nuhayyan

Head of government: Prime Min. Sheik Muhammad bin Rashid al-Maktum

Monetary unit: dirham

GDP: $184.6 billion (2008 est.)   Per capita GDP: $40,000

Industries: petroleum, fishing, petrochemicals, construction materials, boatbuilding, handicrafts, pearling

Chief crops: dates, vegetables, watermelons

Minerals: petroleum, natural gas

Life expectancy at birth (years): male, 72.5; female, 77.6

Literacy rate: 79.2%

Websites: www.government.ae/gov/en/index.jsp
www.uaeinteract.com

UZBEKISTAN

FOR MAP, SEE PAGE 145

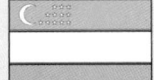

Population: 27,606,007

Ethnic groups: Uzbek 80%, Russian 6%, Tajik 5%, Kazakh 3%, Karakalpak 3%, Tatar 2%

Principal languages: Uzbek (official), Russian, Tajik

Chief religions: Muslim 88% (mostly Sunni), Eastern Orthodox 9%

Area: 172,740 sq mi (447,400 sq km)

Topography: Uzbekistan consists mostly of plains and desert.

Capital: Tashkent (pop., 2,155,000)

Independence date: August 31, 1991

Government type: republic with authoritarian rule

Head of state: Pres. Islam A. Karimov

Head of government: Prime Min. Shavkat Mirziyaev

Monetary unit: som

GDP: $71.63 billion (2008 est.)   Per capita GDP: $2,600

Industries: textiles, food processing, machine building, metallurgy, natural gas, chemicals

Chief crops: cotton, vegetables, fruits, grain

Minerals: natural gas, petroleum, coal, gold, uranium, silver, copper, lead and zinc, tungsten, molybdenum

Life expectancy at birth (years): male, 60.7; female, 67.7

Literacy rate: 97.3%   Website: www.gov.uz

VIETNAM

FOR MAP, SEE PAGE 136

Population: 86,967,524

Ethnic groups: Vietnamese 85%-90%, Chinese, Hmong, Thai, Khmer, Cham

Principal languages: Vietnamese (official), English, French, Chinese, Khmer

Chief religions: Buddhist, Roman Catholic

Area: 127,240 sq mi (329,560 sq km)

Topography: Vietnam is long and narrow, with a 1,400-mi (2,300-km) coast. About 22% of the country is readily arable, including the densely settled Red River valley in the north, narrow coastal plains in the center, and the wide, often marshy Mekong River Delta in the south. The rest consists of semiarid plateaus and barren mountains, with some stretches of tropical rain forest.

Capital: Hanoi (pop., 3,977,000)   Independence date: September 2, 1945

Government type: Communist

Head of state: Pres. Tran Duc Luong

Head of government: Prime Min. Phan Van Khai

Monetary unit: dong

GDP: $241.8 billion (2008 est.)   Per capita GDP: $2,800

Industries: food processing, garments, shoes, machine building, mining, cement, chemical fertilizer, glass, tires, oil, coal, steel, paper

Chief crops: paddy rice, corn, potatoes, rubber, soybeans, coffee, tea, bananas

Minerals: phosphates, coal, manganese, bauxite, chromate, offshore oil and gas

Life expectancy at birth (years): male, 67.9; female, 73.0

Literacy rate: 93.7%

Website: www.vietnamembassy-usa.org

YEMEN

FOR MAP, SEE PAGE 146

Population: 23,822,783

Ethnic groups: Mainly Arab; Afro-Arab, South Asian, European

Principal language: Arabic (official)

Chief religions: Muslim (official; Sunni 60%, Shi'a 40%)

Area: 203,850 sq mi (527,970 sq km)

Topography: A sandy coastal strip leads to well-watered fertile mountains in the interior.

Capital: Sanaa (pop., 1,469,000)   Independence date: May 22, 1990

Government type: republic

Head of state: Pres. Ali Abdullah Saleh

Head of government: Prime Min. Abd-al-Qadir Bajamal

Monetary unit: rial

GDP: $55.29 billion (2008 est.)   Per capita GDP: $2,400

Industries: oil, cotton textiles, leather goods, food processing, handicrafts, aluminum products, cement

Chief crops: grain, fruits, vegetables, pulses, qat, coffee, cotton

Minerals: petroleum, rock salt, marble, coal, gold, lead, nickel, copper

Life expectancy at birth (years): male, 59.5; female, 63.3

Literacy rate: 38%   Website: www.nic.gov.ye

AUSTRALIA, NEW ZEALAND, AND THE PACIFIC

The nation of Australia, which spans the entire continent of Australia, has the sixth biggest land area among the countries of the world. The Pacific island nations of Nauru and Tuvalu fall among the world's five smallest countries in terms of land area. Tuvalu and Nauru, along with Palau, rank among the five smallest countries in terms of population.

AUSTRALIA

FOR MAP, SEE PAGE 167

Population: 21,262,641

Ethnic groups: white 92%, Asian 7%, Aborigine and other 1%

Principal languages: English (official), aboriginal languages

Chief religions: Anglican 26%, Roman Catholic 26%, other Christian 24%

Area: 2,967,910 sq mi (7,686,850 sq km)

Topography: An island continent. The Great Dividing Range along the eastern coast has Mt. Kosciusko, 7,310 ft (2,228 m). The western plateau rises to 2,000 ft (600 m), with arid areas in the Great Sandy and Great Victoria deserts. The northwestern part of Western Australia and the Northern Territory are arid and hot. The northeast has heavy rainfall, and Cape York Peninsula has jungles.

Capital: Canberra (pop., 373,000)

Independence date: January 1, 1901

Government type: democratic, federal state system

Head of state: Queen Elizabeth II, represented by Gov.-Gen. Michael Jeffery

Head of government: Prime Min. John Howard

Monetary unit: Australian dollar

GDP: $800.5 billion (2008 est.)   **Per capita GDP:** $38,100

Industries: mining, industrial and transport equipment, food processing, chemicals, steel

Chief crops: wheat, barley, sugarcane, fruits

Minerals: bauxite, coal, iron ore, copper, tin, silver, uranium, nickel, tungsten, mineral sands, lead, zinc, diamonds, natural gas, petroleum

Life expectancy at birth (years): male, 77.4; female, 83.3

Literacy rate: 100%   **Website:** www.australia.com

Ayers Rock (Uluru), Northern Territory, Australia

Perth, Australia

FIJI

FOR MAP, SEE PAGE 174

Population: 944,720

Ethnic groups: Fijian 51%, Indian 44%

Principal languages: English (official), Fijian, Hindustani

Chief religions: Christian 52%, Hindu 38%, Muslim 8%

Area: 7,050 sq mi (18,270 sq km)

Topography: Fiji consists of 322 islands (106 inhabited), many mountainous, with tropical forests and large fertile areas. Viti Levu, the largest island, has over half the total land area.

Capital: Suva (pop., 210,000)

Independence date: October 19, 1970

Government type: republic

Head of state: Pres. Ratu Josefa Iloilo

Head of government: Prime Min. Laisenia Qarase

Monetary unit: Fiji dollar

GDP $3.62 billion (2008 est.)   **Per capita GDP:** $3,900

Industries: tourism, sugar, clothing, copra, small cottage industries

Chief crops: sugarcane, coconuts, cassava, rice, sweet potatoes, bananas

Minerals: gold, copper, offshore oil potential

Life expectancy at birth (years): male, male, 66.7; female, 71.8

Literacy rate: 92.5%

Websites: www.embassy.org/embassies/fj.html
www.fiji.org.fj

Traditional hut, Lifou Island, New Caledonia (French overseas territory)

Head of state and government: Pres. Kessai Note

Monetary unit: U.S. dollar

GDP: $133.5 million (2008 est.)   **Per capita GDP:** $2,500

Industries: copra, fish, tourism, craft items from shell, wood, and pearls

Chief crops: coconuts, tomatoes, melons, taro, breadfruit, fruits

Minerals: deep seabed minerals

Life expectancy at birth (years): male, 67.8; female, 71.7

Literacy rate: 93.7%   **Website:** www.miembassyus.org

KIRIBATI

FOR MAP, SEE PAGE 174

Population: 112,850

Ethnic groups: Micronesian

Principal languages: English (official), I-Kiribati

Chief religions: Roman Catholic 52%, Protestant 40%

Area: 280 sq mi (720 sq km)

Topography: Kiribati comprises 33 coral islands, all of which, except Banaba (Ocean) Island, are low-lying, with soil of coral sand and rock fragments, subject to erratic rainfall.

Capital: South Tarawa (pop., 42,000)

Independence date: July 12, 1979

Government type: republic

Head of state and government: Pres. Anote Tong

Monetary unit: Australian dollar

GDP: $357.4 million (2008 est.)   **Per capita GDP:** $3,200

Industries: fishing, handicrafts

Chief crops: copra, taro, breadfruit, sweet potatoes, vegetables

Life expectancy at birth (years): male, 58.3; female, 64.4

Literacy rate: NA   **Website:** www.state.gov/r/pa/ei/bgn/1836.htm

MARSHALL ISLANDS

FOR MAP, SEE PAGE 174

Population: 64,522

Ethnic groups: Micronesian

Principal languages: English, Marshallese (both official); Malay-Polynesian dialects, Japanese

Chief religion: mostly Protestant

Area: 70 sq mi (181 sq km)

Topography: The Marshalls are low coral limestone and sand islands.

Capital: Majuro (pop., 25,000)

Independence date: October 21, 1986   **Government type:** republic

MICRONESIA

FOR MAP, SEE PAGE 174

Population: 107,434

Ethnic groups: 9 distinct Micronesian and Polynesian groups

Principal languages: English (official), Trukese, Pohnpeian, Yapese, Kosrean, Ulithian, Woleaian, Nukuoro, Kapingamarangi

Chief religions: Roman Catholic 50%, Protestant 47%

Area: 270 sq mi (700 sq km)

Topography: The country includes both high mountainous islands and low coral atolls; volcanic outcroppings on Pohnpei, Kosrae, and Truk.

Capital: Palikir, on Pohnpei (pop., 7,000)

Independence date: November 3, 1986

Government type: republic

Head of state and government: Pres. Joseph J. Urusemal

Monetary unit: U.S. dollar

GDP: $238.1 million (2008 est.)   **Per capita GDP:** $2,200

Industries: tourism, construction, fish processing, craft items from shell, wood, and pearls

Chief crops: black pepper, tropical fruits and vegetables, coconuts, cassava, sweet potatoes

Minerals: deep-seabed minerals

Life expectancy at birth (years): male, 66.7; female, 71.3

Literacy rate: 89%   **Website:** www.fsmgov.org

NAURU

FOR MAP, SEE PAGE 174

Population: 14,019

Ethnic groups: Nauruan 58%, other Pacific Islander 26%, Chinese 8%, European 8%

Principal languages: Nauruan (official), English

Chief religions: Protestant 66%, Roman Catholic 33%

Area: 8 sq mi (21 sq km)

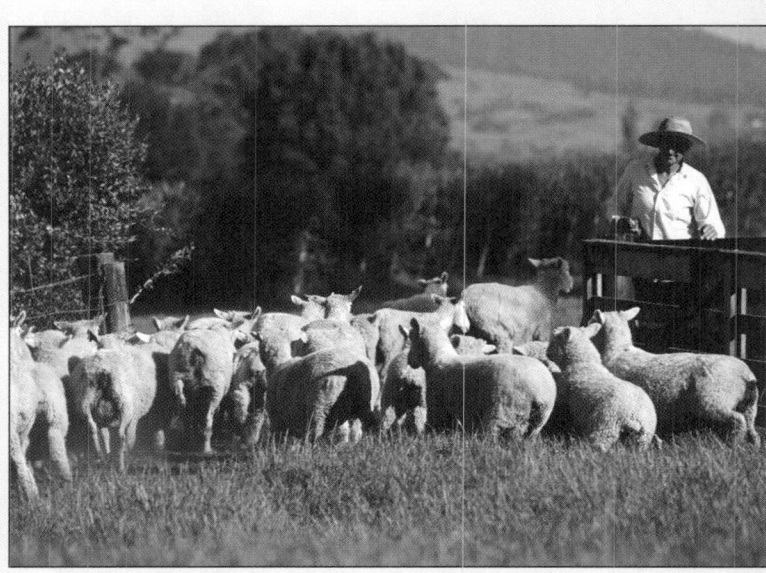
Topography: Mostly a plateau bearing high-grade phosphate deposits, surrounded by a sandy shore and coral reef in concentric rings.

Capital: offices in Yaren District

Independence date: January 31, 1968

Government type: republic

Head of state and government: Pres. Marcus Stephens

Monetary unit: Australian dollar

GDP: $60 million (2005 est.)   **Per capita GDP:** $5,000

Industries: mining, offshore banking, coconut products

Chief crops: rice, corn, wheat, sugarcane, root crops

Minerals: phosphates

Life expectancy at birth (years): male, 58.4; female, 65.7

Literacy rate: NA   **Website:** www.un.int/nauru

NEW ZEALAND

For map, see page 175

Population: 4,213,418

Ethnic groups: New Zealand European 75%, Maori 10%, other European 5%, Pacific Islander 4%

Principal languages: English, Maori (both official)

Chief religions: Protestant 52%, Roman Catholic 15%

Area: 103,740 sq mi (268,680 sq km)

Topography: Each of the two main islands (North and South Islands) is mainly hilly and mountainous. The eastern coasts consist of fertile plains, especially the broad Canterbury Plains on South Island. A volcanic plateau is in the center of North Island. South Island has glaciers and 15 peaks over 10,000 ft (3,000 m).

Capital: Wellington (pop., 343,000)

Independence date: September 26, 1907

Government type: parliamentary democracy

Head of state: Queen Elizabeth II, represented by Gov.-Gen. Dame Anand Satyanand

Head of government: Prime Min. Helen Clark

Monetary unit: New Zealand dollar

GDP: $116.6 billion (2008 est.)

Per capita GDP: $27,900

Industries: food processing, wood and paper products, textiles, machinery, transport equipment, banking and insurance, tourism, mining

Chief crops: wheat, barley, potatoes, pulses, fruits, vegetables

Minerals: natural gas, iron ore, sand, coal, gold, limestone

Life expectancy at birth (years): male, 75.5; female, 81.6

Literacy rate: 99%

Websites: www.govt.nz
www.nzembassy.com

Shotover River, New Zealand

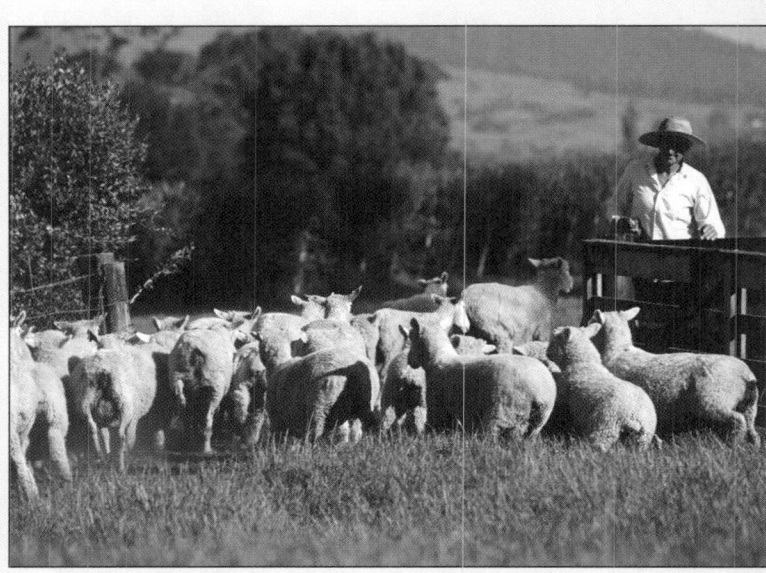

A New Zealand shepherd with his sheep

PALAU

For map, see page 174

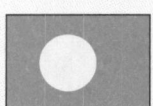

Population: 20,796

Ethnic groups: Palauan (Micronesian/Malayan/Melanesian mix) 70%, Asian 28%, white 2%

Principal languages: English (official); Palauan, Sonsorolese, Tobi, Angaur, Japanese (all official in certain states)

Chief religions: Roman Catholic 49%, Modekngei 30%

Area: 180 sq mi (460 sq km)

Topography: Palau is made up of a mountainous main island and low coral atolls, usually fringed with large barrier reefs.

Capital: Melekeok (pop. 300)

Independence date: October 1, 1994

Government type: republic

Head of state and government: Pres. Johnson Toribiong

Monetary unit: U.S. dollar

GDP: $164.0 million (2008 est.)   **Per capita GDP:** $8,100

Industries: tourism, craft items, construction, garment making

Chief crops: coconuts, copra, cassava, sweet potatoes

Minerals: gold, deep-seabed minerals

Life expectancy at birth (years): male, 66.7; female, 73.2

Literacy rate: 92%   **Website:** www.visit-palau.com

SAMOA

For map, see page 175

Population: 219,998

Ethnic groups: Samoan 92.5%, Euronesians 7%

Principal languages: Samoan, English (both official)

Chief religion: Christian 99.7%

Area: 1,100 sq mi (2,860 sq km)

Topography: Samoa consists of two main islands, Savaii (659 sq mi [1,710 sq km]) and Upolu (432 sq mi [1,120 sq km]), both ruggedly mountainous, and several small islands, of which Manono and Apolima are inhabited.

Capital: Apia (pop., 40,000)   **Independence date:** January 1, 1962

Government type: constitutional monarchy

Head of state: Malietoa Tanumafili II

Head of government: Prime Min. Tuilaepa Sailele Malielegaoi

Samoa (continued)

Monetary unit: tala

GDP: $1.06 billion (2008 est.)   Per capita GDP: $4,900

Industries: food processing, building materials, auto parts

Chief crops: coconuts, bananas, taro, yams

Life expectancy at birth (years): male, 67.6; female, 73.3

Literacy rate: 80%

Website: www.govt.ws

SOLOMON ISLANDS

FOR MAP, SEE PAGE 174

Population: 595,613

Ethnic groups: Melanesian 93%, Polynesian 4%, Micronesian, European, and others 3%

Principal languages: English (official), Melanesian pidgin, and 120 indigenous languages

Chief religions: Anglican 45%, Roman Catholic 18%, other Christian 35%

Area: 10,980 sq mi (28,450 sq km)

Topography: 10 large volcanic and rugged islands and 4 groups of smaller ones.

Capital: Honiara (pop., 56,000)

Independence date: July 7, 1978

Government type: parliamentary democracy

Head of state: Queen Elizabeth II, represented by Gov.-Gen. Sir Nathaniel Waena

Head of government: Prime Min. Derek Sikua

Monetary unit: Solomon Islands dollar (SBD)

GDP: $1.08 billion (2008 est.)   Per capita GDP: $1,900

Industries: fish, mining, timber

Chief crops: cocoa, beans, coconuts, palm kernels, rice, potatoes, vegetables, fruit

Minerals: gold, bauxite, phosphates, lead, zinc, nickel

Life expectancy at birth (years): male, 69.9; female, 75.0

Literacy rate: NA   Website: www.commerce.gov.sb

TONGA

FOR MAP, SEE PAGE 175

Population: 120,898

Ethnic groups: Polynesian

Principal languages: Tongan, English (both official)

Chief religions: Wesleyan 41%, Roman Catholic 16%, Mormon 14%

Area: 290 sq mi (750 sq km)

Topography: Tonga comprises 170 volcanic and coral islands, 36 inhabited.

Capital: Nuku'alofa (pop., 35,000)

Independence date: June 4, 1970

Government type: constitutional monarchy

Head of state: King Taufa'ahau Tupou IV

Head of government: Prime Min. Feleti Seveli

Monetary unit: pa'anga

GDP: $549.1 million (2008 est.)

Per capita GDP: $4,600

Industries: tourism, fishing

Chief crops: squash, coconuts, copra, bananas, vanilla beans, cocoa, coffee, ginger, black pepper

Life expectancy at birth (years): male, 66.7; female, 71.8

Literacy rate: 98.5%

Website: www.pmo.gov.to

TUVALU

FOR MAP, SEE PAGE 174

Population: 12,373

Ethnic group: Polynesian 96%, Micronesian 4%

Principal languages: Tuvaluan, English, Samoan, Kiribati (on the island of Nui)

Chief religion: Church of Tuvalu (Congregationalist) 97%

Area: 10 sq mi (26 sq km)

Topography: Tuvalu's nine islands are all low-lying coral atolls, nowhere rising more than 15 ft (4.6 m) above sea level.

Capital: Funafuti (pop., 6,000)   Independence date: October 1, 1978

Government type: parliamentary democracy

Head of state: Queen Elizabeth II, represented by Gov.-Gen. Filoimea Telito

Head of government: Prime Min. Maatia Toafa

Monetary unit: Australian dollar

GDP: $14.9 million (2002 est.)   Per capita GDP: $1,600

Industries: fishing, tourism, copra

Chief crops: coconuts

Life expectancy at birth (years): male, 65.5; female, 70.0

Literacy rate: 55%   Website: www.timelesstuvalu.com

VANUATU

FOR MAP, SEE PAGE 174

Population: 218,519

Ethnic groups: Melanesian 98%, French, Vietnamese, Chinese, other Pacific Islanders

Principal languages: Bislama, English, French (all official); more than 100 local languages

Chief religions: Presbyterian 37%, Anglican 15%, Roman Catholic 15%, other Christian 10%, indigenous beliefs 8%

Area: 5,700 sq mi (14,760 sq km)

Topography: Dense forest with narrow coastal strips of cultivated land.

Capital: Port-Vila (pop., 34,000)   Independence date: July 30, 1980

Government type: republic

Head of state: Pres. Kalkot Mataskelekele

Head of government: Prime Min. Ham Lini

Monetary unit: vatu

GDP: $983.2 million (2008 est.)   Per capita GDP: $4,600

Industries: food and fish freezing, wood processing, meat canning

Chief crops: copra, coconuts, cocoa, coffee, taro, yams, coconuts, fruits, vegetables

Minerals: manganese

Life expectancy at birth (years): male, 60.6; female, 63.6

Literacy rate: 53%

Website: www.vanuatugovernment.gov.vu

EUROPE

Twenty-seven nations are members of the European Union: Austria, Belgium, Bulgaria, Cyprus, Czech Republic, Denmark, Estonia, Finland, France, Germany, Greece, Hungary, Ireland, Italy, Latvia, Lithuania, Luxembourg, Malta, the Netherlands, Poland, Portugal, Romania, Slovakia, Slovenia, Spain, Sweden, and the United Kingdom.

ALBANIA

FOR MAP, SEE PAGE 105

Population: 3,639,453
Ethnic groups: Albanian 95%, Greek 3%
Principal languages: Albanian (Tosk is the official dialect), Greek
Chief religions: Muslim 70%, Albanian Orthodox 20%, Roman Catholic 10%
Area: 11,100 sq mi (28,750 sq km)
Topography: Apart from a narrow coastal plain, Albania consists of hills and mountains covered with scrub forest, cut by small east to west rivers.
Capital: Tiranë (pop., 367,000)
Independence date: November 28, 1912   **Government type:** republic
Head of state: Pres. Alfred Moisiu
Head of government: Prime Min. Sali Berisha   **Monetary unit:** lek
GDP: $21.82 billion (2008 est.)   **Per capita GDP:** $6,000
Industries: food processing, textiles and clothing, lumber, oil, cement, chemicals, mining, basic metals, hydropower
Chief crops: wheat, corn, potatoes, vegetables, fruits, sugar beets, grapes
Minerals: petroleum, natural gas, coal, chromium, copper, timber, nickel
Life expectancy at birth (years): male, 74.4; female, 80.0
Literacy rate: 93%
Website: www.albaniantourism.com

ANDORRA

FOR MAP, SEE PAGE 103

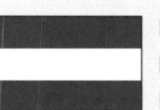

Population: 83,888
Ethnic groups: Spanish 43%, Andorran 33%, Portuguese 11%, French 7%
Principal languages: Catalan (official), Castilian Spanish, French
Chief religion: predominantly Roman Catholic
Area: 174 sq mi (450 sq km)
Topography: High mountains and narrow valleys cover the country.
Capital: Andorra la Vella (pop., 21,000)
Independence date: 1278
Government type: parliamentary co-principality
Heads of state: president of France & bishop of Urgel (Spain), as co-princes
Head of government: Pres. Albert Pintat Santolèria
Monetary unit: euro
GDP: $3.66 billion (2007)   **Per capita GDP:** $42,500
Industries: tourism, cattle raising, timber, tobacco, banking
Chief crops: tobacco, rye, wheat, barley, oats, vegetables
Minerals: iron ore, lead
Life expectancy at birth (years): male, 80.6; female, 86.6
Literacy rate: 100%
Website: www.andorra.ad/ang/home/index.tm

AUSTRIA*

FOR MAP, SEE PAGE 101

Population: 8,210,281
Ethnic groups: German 88%
Principal languages: German (official), Serbo-Croatian, Slovenian
Chief religions: Roman Catholic 78%, Protestant 5%

---

*Member of the European Union

Nation Facts and Figures

Austria (continued)

Area: 32,380 sq mi (83,860 sq km)

Topography: Austria is primarily mountainous, with the Alps and foothills covering the western and southern provinces. The eastern provinces and Vienna are located in the Danube River Basin.

Capital: Vienna (pop., 2,179,000)

Independence date: 1156

Government type: federal republic

Head of state: Pres. Heinz Fischer

Head of government: Chancellor Wolfgang Schüssel

Monetary unit: euro

GDP: $325 billion (2008 est.)   **Per capita GDP:** $39,200

Industries: construction, machinery, vehicles and parts, food, chemicals, lumber and wood processing, paper and paperboard, commercial equipment, tourism

Chief crops: grains, potatoes, sugar beets, fruit

Minerals: iron ore, oil, timber, magnesite, lead, coal, copper

Life expectancy at birth (years): male, 75.0; female, 81.5

Literacy rate: 98%   **Website:** www.austria.org

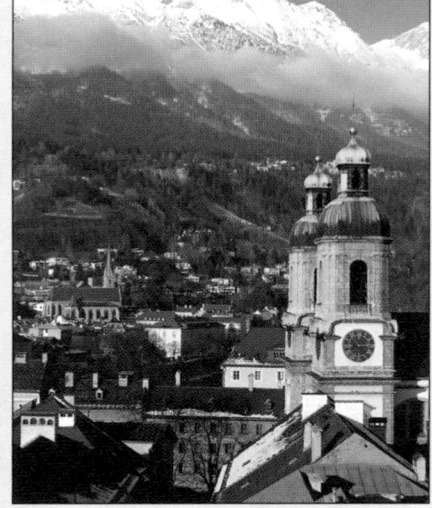

Innsbruck, Austria

BELARUS

For map, see page 85

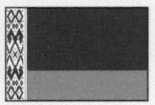

Population: 9,648,533

Ethnic groups: Belarusian 81%, Russian 11%

Principal languages: Belarusian, Russian

Chief religions: Eastern Orthodox 80%, other 20%

Area: 80,200 sq mi (207,600 sq km)

Topography: Belarus is a landlocked country consisting mostly of hilly lowland with significant marsh areas in the south.

Capital: Minsk (pop., 1,705,000)   **Independence date:** August 25, 1991

Government type: republic

Head of state: Pres. Aleksandr Lukashenko

Head of government: Prime Min. Sergey Sidorsky

Monetary unit: ruble

GDP: $114.1 billion (2008 est.)   **Per capita GDP:** $11,800

Industries: machine tools, tractors, trucks, earthmovers, motorcycles, domestic appliances, chemical fibers, fertilizer, textiles

Chief crops: grain, potatoes, vegetables, sugar beets, flax

Minerals: oil and natural gas, granite, dolomitic limestone, marl, chalk, sand, gravel, clay

Life expectancy at birth (years): male, 62.8; female, 74.7

Literacy rate: 98%

Website: www.belarusembassy.org

BELGIUM*

For map, see page 98

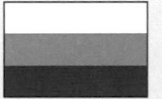

Population: 10,414,336

Ethnic groups: Fleming 58%, Walloon 31%

Principal languages: Dutch, French, German (all official); Flemish, Luxembourgish

*Member of the European Union

Chief religions: Roman Catholic 75%; Protestant, other 25%

Area: 11,780 sq mi (30,510 sq km)

Topography: Mostly flat, the country is trisected by the Scheldt and Meuse, major commercial rivers. The land becomes hilly and forested in the southeast (Ardennes) region.

Capital: Brussels (pop., 998,000)

Independence date: October 4, 1830

Government type: parliamentary democracy under a constitutional monarch

Head of state: King Albert II

Head of government: Premier Guy Verhofstadt

Monetary unit: euro

GDP: $390.5 billion (2008 est.)   **Per capita GDP:** $37,500

Industries: engineering and metal products, motor vehicle assembly, processed food and beverages, chemicals, basic metals, textiles, glass, petroleum, coal

Chief crops: sugar beets, fresh vegetables, fruits, grain, tobacco

Minerals: coal, natural gas

Life expectancy at birth (years): male, 75.3; female, 81.8

Literacy rate: 98%

Website: www.diplobel.us

BOSNIA AND HERZEGOVINA

For map, see page 106

Population: 4,613,414

Ethnic groups: Bosniak 48%, Serbian 37%, Croatian 14%

Principal languages: Bosnian (official), Croatian, Serbian

Chief religions: Muslim 40%, Orthodox 31%, Roman Catholic 15%, Protestant 4%

Area: 19,740 sq mi (51,130 sq km)

Topography: Hilly with some mountains. About 36% of the land is forested.

Capital: Sarajevo (pop., 579,000)

Independence date: March 1, 1992

Government type: federal republic

Heads of state: collective presidency with rotating leadership

Head of government: Prime Min. Nikola Špirič

Monetary unit: converted marka (BAM)

GDP: $29.9 billion (2008 est.)   **Per capita GDP:** $6,500

Industries: steel, mining, vehicle assembly, textiles, tobacco products, wooden furniture, tank and aircraft assembly, domestic appliances, oil refining

Chief crops: wheat, corn, fruits, vegetables

Minerals: coal, iron, bauxite, manganese, copper, chromium, lead, zinc

Life expectancy at birth (years): male, 69.8; female, 75.5

Literacy rate: NA

Website: www.bhembassy.org

BULGARIA*

For map, see page 107

Population: 7,204,687

Ethnic groups: Bulgarian 84%, Turk 10%, Roma 5%

Principal languages: Bulgarian (official), Turkish

Chief religions: Bulgarian Orthodox 84%, Muslim 12%

Area: 42,820 sq mi (110,910 sq km)

Topography: The Stara Planina (Balkan) Mountains stretch east to west across the center of the country, with the Danubian plain on the north, the Rhodope Mountains on the southwest, and the Thracian Plain on the southeast.

Capital: Sofia (pop., 1,076,000)

Independence date: March 3, 1878

Government type: republic

Head of state: Pres. Georgi Parvanov

Head of government: Prime Min. Sergei Stanishev

Monetary unit: lev

GDP: $93.78 billion (2008 est.)

Per capita GDP: $12,900

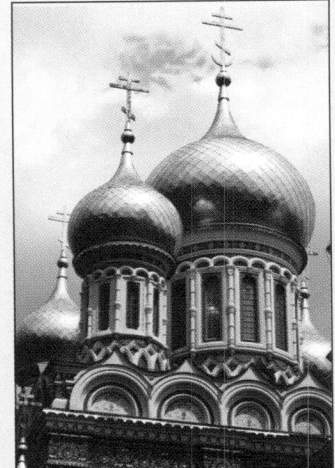

A Bulgarian cathedral

Industries: electricity, gas and water, food, beverages and tobacco, machinery and equipment, base metals, chemical products, coke, refined petroleum, nuclear fuel

Chief crops: vegetables, fruits, tobacco, wheat, barley, sunflowers, sugar beets

Minerals: bauxite, copper, lead, zinc, coal

Life expectancy at birth (years): male, 68.1; female, 75.6

Literacy rate: 98%

Website: www.government.bg/English

CROATIA

FOR MAP, SEE PAGE 106

Population: 4,489,409

Ethnic groups: Croat 78%, Serb 12%, Bosniak 1%

Principal languages Croatian (official), Serbian

Chief religions: Roman Catholic 88%, Orthodox 5%

Area: 21,830 sq mi (56,540 sq km)

Topography: Flat plains in the northeast; highlands, low mountains along the Adriatic coast.

Capital: Zagreb (pop., 688,000)   Independence date: June 25, 1991

Government type: parliamentary democracy

Head of state: Pres. Stipe Mesic

Head of government: Prime Min. Jadranka Kosor

Monetary unit: kuna

GDP: $73.36 billion (2008 est.)   Per capita GDP: $16,100

Industries: chemicals and plastics, machine tools, fabricated metal, electronics, pig iron and rolled steel products, aluminum, paper, wood products, construction materials, textiles, shipbuilding, tourism

Chief crops: wheat, corn, sugar beets, sunflower seed, barley, alfalfa, clover, olives, citrus, grapes, soybeans, potatoes

Minerals: oil, coal, bauxite, iron ore, calcium, natural asphalt, silica, mica, clays, salt

Life expectancy at birth (years): male, 70.2; female, 78.3

Literacy rate: 97%

Website: www.vlada.hr/default.asp?ru=2

CZECH REPUBLIC*

FOR MAP, SEE PAGE 99

Population: 10,211,904

Ethnic groups: Czech 81%, Moravian 13%, Slovak 3%

Principal languages: Czech (official), German, Polish, Romani

Chief religions: atheist 40%, Roman Catholic 39%, Protestant 5%, Orthodox 3%

Area: 30,350 sq mi (78,870 sq km)

Topography: Bohemia, in the west, is a plateau surrounded by mountains; Moravia is hilly.

Capital: Prague (pop., 1,170,000)

Independence date: January 1, 1993   Government type: republic

Head of state: Pres. Václav Klaus

Head of government: Prime Min. Jiri Paroubek

Monetary unit: koruna

GDP: $266.3 billion (2008 est.)   Per capita GDP: $26,100

Industries: metallurgy, machinery and equipment, motor vehicles, glass, armaments

Chief crops: wheat, potatoes, sugar beets, hops, fruit

Minerals: coal, kaolin, clay, graphite

Life expectancy at birth (years): male, 72.5; female, 79.2

Literacy rate: 99.9%   Website: www.czech.cz

Prague, Czech Republic

DENMARK*

FOR MAP, SEE PAGE 96

Population: 5,500,510

Ethnic groups: Mainly Danish; German minority in south

Principal languages: Danish (official), Faroese, Greenlandic (an Inuit dialect), German

Chief religions: Evangelical Lutheran (official) 95%, other Christian 3%, Muslim 2%

Area: 16,640 sq mi (43,090 sq km)

Topography: Denmark consists of the Jutland Peninsula and about 500 islands, 100 inhabited. The land is flat or gently rolling and is almost all in productive use.

Capital: Copenhagen (pop., 1,066,000)

Independence date: 10th century

Government type: constitutional monarchy

Head of state: Queen Margrethe II

Head of government: Prime Min. Anders Fogh Rasmussen

Monetary unit: krone

GDP: $204.9 billion (2008 est.)   Per capita GDP: $37,400

Industries: food processing, machinery and equipment, textiles and clothing, chemical products, electronics, construction, furniture, shipbuilding

Chief crops: barley, wheat, potatoes, sugar beets

Minerals: petroleum, natural gas, salt, limestone, stone, gravel and sand

Life expectancy at birth (years): male, 75.2; female, 79.8

Literacy rate: 100%

Website: www.ambwashington.um.dk/en

GREENLAND (Kalaallit Nunaat), a huge island situated between the North Atlantic and the Polar Sea and separated from the North American continent by the Davis Strait and Baffin Bay, is part of the Danish realm but possesses home rule. Population, 57,600; area, 836,330 sq mi (2,166,086 sq km), 81% of which is ice-capped; capital, Nuuk (Godthab).

―――――

*Member of the European Union

ESTONIA*

FOR MAP, SEE PAGE 97

Population: 1,299,371

Ethnic groups: Estonian 65%, Russian 28%

Principal languages: Estonian (official), Russian, Ukrainian, Finnish

Chief religions: Evangelical Lutheran, Russian Orthodox, Estonian Orthodox

Area: 17,460 sq mi (45,230 sq km)

Topography: Estonia is a marshy lowland with numerous lakes and swamps; about 40% forested. Elongated hills show evidence of former glaciation. There are more than 800 islands on the Baltic coast.

Capital: Tallinn (pop., 391,000)

Independence date: August 20, 1991   **Government type:** republic

Head of state: Pres. Arnold Rüütel

Head of government: Prime Min. Andrus Ansip

Monetary unit: kroon

GDP: $27.72 billion (2008 est.)   **Per capita GDP:** $21,200

Industries: engineering, electronics, wood and wood products, textile, information technology, telecommunications

Chief crops: potatoes, vegetables

Minerals: oil shale, peat, phosphorite, clay, limestone, sand, dolomite, sea mud

Life expectancy at birth (years): male, 65.8; female, 77.3

Literacy rate: 100%   **Website:** www.riik.ee/en/

FINLAND*

FOR MAP, SEE PAGE 95

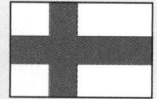

Population: 5,250,275

Ethnic groups: Finnish 93%, Swedish 6%

Principal languages: Finnish, Swedish (both official); Russian, Sami

Chief religion: Evangelical Lutheran 89%

Area: 130,130 sq mi (337,030 sq km)

Topography: South and central Finland are generally flat areas with low hills and many lakes. The north has mountainous areas, 3,000 to 4,000 ft (900 to 1,200 m) above sea level.

Capital: Helsinki (pop., 1,075,000)

Independence date: December 6, 1917

Government type: republic   **Head of state:** Pres. Tarja Halonen

Head of government: Prime Min. Matti Vanhanen

Monetary unit: euro

GDP: $195.2 billion (2008 est.)   **Per capita GDP:** $37,200

Industries: metal products, electronics, shipbuilding, pulp and paper, copper refining, foodstuffs, chemicals, textiles, clothing

Chief crops: barley, wheat, sugar beets, potatoes

Minerals: copper, zinc, iron ore, silver

Life expectancy at birth (years): male, 74.7; female, 81.9

Literacy rate: 100%

Website: www.finland.org/en/

The ÅLAND ISLANDS (Ahvenanmaa), constituting an autonomous province, are a group of small islands in the Gulf of Bothnia. Population 26,923; area, 590 sq mi (1,500 sq km); capital, Mariehamn.

FRANCE*

FOR MAP, SEE PAGE 100

Population: 64,420,073

Ethnic groups: French, with Slavic, North African, Indochinese, Basque minorities

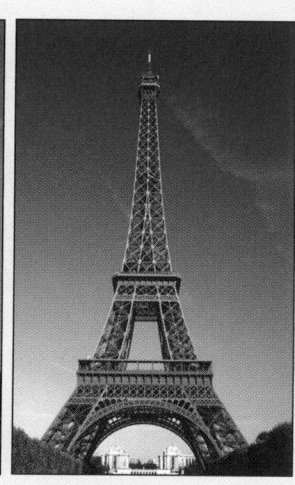

Parisian landmarks: Arc de Triomphe (left), Eiffel Tower (right)

Principal languages: French (official), Italian, Breton, Alsatian (German), Corsican, Gascon, Portuguese, Provençal, Dutch, Flemish, Catalan, Basque, Romani

Chief religions: Roman Catholic 83-88%, Muslim 5-10%

Area: 211,210 sq mi (547,030 sq km)

Topography: A wide plain covers more than half of the country, in the north and west, drained to the west by the Seine, Loire, and Garonne rivers. The Massif Central is a mountainous plateau in the center. In the east are the Alps (Mt. Blanc is the tallest peak in Western Europe, 15,771 ft [4,807 m]), the lower Jura range, and the forested Vosges. The Rhone flows from Lake Geneva to the Mediterranean. The Pyrenees are in the southwest, on the border with Spain.

Capital: Paris (pop., 9,794,000)   **Independence date:** 486

Government type: republic

Head of state: Pres. Nicholas Sarkosy

Head of government: Prime Min. François Fillon

Monetary unit: euro

GDP: $2,097 billion (2008 est.)   **Per capita GDP:** $32,700

Industries: machinery, chemicals, automobiles, metallurgy, aircraft, electronics, textiles, food processing, tourism

Chief crops: wheat, cereals, sugar beets, potatoes, wine grapes

Minerals: coal, iron ore, bauxite, zinc, potash

Life expectancy at birth (years): male, 75.8; female, 83.3

Literacy rate: 99%   **Website:** www.info-france-usa.org

GERMANY*

FOR MAP, SEE PAGE 98

Population: 82,329,758

Ethnic groups: German 92%, Turkish 2%

Principal languages: German (official), Turkish, Italian, Greek, English, Danish, Dutch, Slavic languages

Chief religions: Protestant 34%, Roman Catholic 34%, Muslim 4%

Area: 137,890 sq mi (357,070 sq km)

Topography: Germany is flat in the north, hilly in the center and west, and mountainous in Bavaria in the south. The chief rivers are the Elbe, Weser, Ems, Rhine, and Main, all flowing toward the North Sea, and the Danube, flowing toward the Black Sea.

Capital: Berlin (pop., 3,327,000)

Independence date: January 18, 1871

Government type: federal republic

Head of state: Pres. Horst Köhler

Head of government: Chancellor Angela Merkel

Monetary unit: euro

*Member of the European Union

Looking down a German street

GDP: $2,863 billion (2008 est.)
Per capita GDP: $34,800

Industries: mining, steel, cement, chemicals, machinery, vehicles, machine tools, electronics, food and beverages, shipbuilding, textiles

Chief crops: potatoes, wheat, barley, sugar beets, fruit, cabbages

Minerals: iron ore, coal, potash, lignite, uranium, copper, natural gas, salt, nickel

Life expectancy at birth (years): male, 75.6; female, 81.7

Literacy rate: 99%

Website: www.germany–info.org

Bavarian village church, Germany

GREECE*

FOR MAP, SEE PAGE 105

Population: 10,737,428

Ethnic groups: Greek 98%

Principal languages: Greek (official), English, French

Chief religions: Greek Orthodox (official) 98%, Muslim 1%

Area: 50,940 sq mi (131,940 sq km)

Topography: About three-quarters of Greece is nonarable, with mountains in all areas. Pindus Mountains run through the country north to south. The heavily indented coastline is 9,385 mi (15,100 km) long. Of over 2,000 islands, only 169 are inhabited, among them Crete, Rhodes, Milos, Kerkira (Corfu), Chios, Lesbos, Samos, Euboea, Delos, and Mykonos.

Capital: Athens (pop., 3,215,000)   Independence date: 1829

Government type: parliamentary republic

Head of state: Pres. Karolos Papoulias

Head of government: Prime Min. Konstantinos (Kostas) Karamanlis

Monetary unit: euro

GDP: $343.6 billion (2008 est.)   Per capita GDP: $32,000

Industries: tourism, food and tobacco processing, textiles, chemicals, metal products, mining, petroleum

Chief crops: wheat, corn, barley, sugar beets, olives, tomatoes, tobacco, potatoes

Minerals: bauxite, lignite, magnesite, petroleum, marble

Life expectancy at birth (years): male, 76.4; female, 81.6

Literacy rate: 97%   Website: www.greekembassy.org

HUNGARY*

FOR MAP, SEE PAGE 106

Population: 9,905,596

Ethnic groups: Hungarian 90%, Roma 4%, German 3%, Serb 2%

Principal languages: Hungarian (official), Romani, German, Slavic languages, Romanian

Chief religions: Roman Catholic 68%, Protestant 25%

Area: 35,920 sq mi (93,030 sq km)

Topography: The Danube River forms the Slovak border in the northwest, then swings south to bisect the country. The eastern half of Hungary is mainly a great fertile plain, the Alfold; the west and north are hilly.

Capital: Budapest (pop., 1,708,000)

Independence date: 1001   Government type: parliamentary democracy

Head of state: Pres. László Sólyom

Head of government: Prime Min. Ferenc Gyurcsány

Monetary unit: forint

GDP: $205.7 billion (2008 est.)   Per capita GDP: $19,800

Industries: mining, metallurgy, construction materials, processed foods, textiles, pharmaceuticals, motor vehicles

Chief crops: wheat, corn, sunflower seed, potatoes, sugar beets

Minerals: bauxite, coal, natural gas

Life expectancy at birth (years): male, 68.1; female, 76.7

Literacy rate: 99%   Website: www.hungary.hu

ICELAND

FOR MAP, SEE PAGE 95

Population: 306,694

Ethnic groups: Icelandic 94%

Principal language: Icelandic (official)

Chief religion: Evangelical Lutheran 93%

Area: 40,000 sq mi (103,000 sq km)

Topography: Iceland is of recent volcanic origin. Three-quarters of the surface is wasteland: glaciers, lakes, a lava desert. There are geysers and hot springs.

Capital: Reykjavík (pop., 184,000)

Independence date: June 17, 1944

Government type: constitutional republic

Head of state: Pres. Olafur Ragnar Grímsson

Head of government: Prime Min. Halldór Ásgrímsson

Monetary unit: krona

GDP: $12.15 billion (2008 est.)   Per capita GDP: $39,900

Industries: fish processing, aluminum smelting, ferrosilicon production, geothermal power, tourism

Chief crops: potatoes, turnips   Minerals: diatomite

Life expectancy at birth (years): male, 78.2; female, 82.3

Literacy rate: 99.9%

Website: www.iceland.is

Parthenon, Athens, Greece

*Member of the European Union

IRELAND*

FOR MAP, SEE PAGE 89

Population: 4,203,200

Ethnic groups: Celtic; English minority

Principal languages: English, Irish Gaelic (both official); Irish Gaelic spoken by small number in western areas

Chief religions: Roman Catholic 92%, Anglican 3%

Area: 27,140 sq mi (70,280 sq km)

Topography: Ireland consists of a central plateau surrounded by isolated groups of hills and mountains. The coastline is heavily indented by the Atlantic Ocean.

Capital: Dublin (pop., 1,015,000)   **Independence date:** December 6, 1921

Government type: parliamentary republic

Head of state: Pres. Mary McAleese

Head of government: Prime Min. Bertie Ahern

Monetary unit: euro

GDP: $191.9 billion (2008 est.)   **Per capita GDP:** $46,200

Industries: food products, brewing, textiles, clothing, chemicals, pharmaceuticals, machinery, transport equipment, glass and crystal, software

Chief crops: turnips, barley, potatoes, sugar beets, wheat

Minerals: zinc, lead, natural gas, barite, copper, gypsum, limestone, dolomite, peat, silver

Life expectancy at birth (years): male, 74.7; female, 80.2

Literacy rate: 98%

Websites: www.irlgov.ie   www.irelandemb.org

ITALY*

FOR MAP, SEE PAGE 85

Population: 58,126,212

Ethnic groups: mostly Italian; small minorities of German, Slovene, Albanian

Principal languages: Italian (official), German, French, Slovenian, Albanian

Chief religion: predominantly Roman Catholic

Area: 116,310 sq mi (301,230 sq km)

Topography: Italy occupies a long boot-shaped peninsula, extending southeast from the Alps into the Mediterranean, with the islands of Sicily and Sardinia offshore. The alluvial Po Valley drains most of the north. The rest of the country is rugged and mountainous, except for intermittent coastal plains, like the Campania, south of Rome. The Apennine Mountains run down through the center of the peninsula.

Capital: Rome (pop., 2,665,000)

Independence date: March 17, 1861

Government type: republic

Head of state: Pres. Giorgio Napolitano

Head of government: Prime Min. Silvio Berlusconi

Monetary unit: euro

GDP: $1,821 billion (2008 est.)

Per capita GDP: $31,000

Industries: tourism, machinery, iron and steel, chemicals, food processing, textiles, motor vehicles, clothing, footwear, ceramics

Chief crops: fruits, vegetables, grapes, potatoes, sugar beets, soybeans, grain, olives

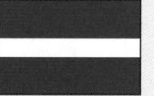

Leaning Tower of Pisa, Italy

---

*Member of the European Union

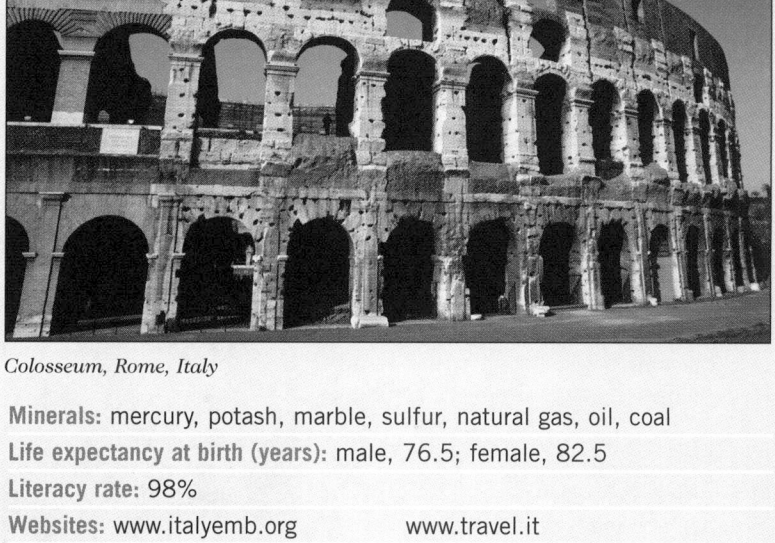

Colosseum, Rome, Italy

Minerals: mercury, potash, marble, sulfur, natural gas, oil, coal

Life expectancy at birth (years): male, 76.5; female, 82.5

Literacy rate: 98%

Websites: www.italyemb.org   www.travel.it

KOSOVO

FOR MAP, SEE PAGE 106

Population: 1,804,838

Ethnic groups: Albanian 88%, Serbian 7%, Bosniak 2%

Principal languages: Albanian, Serbian

Chief religions: Muslim 90%, Serbian Orthodox 10%

Area: 4,203 sq mi (10,887 sq km)

Topography: Kosovo is mostly highland with canyons and wide valleys. The principal river, the Beli Drim, bisects the southwest region. Arable land is found in the west and northwest.

Capital: Priština (pop., 250,000)

Independence date: February 17, 2008

Government type: UN protectorate   **Head of state:** Pres. Fatmir Sejdiu

Head of government: Prime Min. Hashim Thaçi

Monetary unit: euro

GDP: $5 billion (2007 est.)   **Per capita GDP:** $2,300

Industries: Mining and smelting, leather products, machinery, appliances

Chief crops: grains, fruit, nuts, tobacco, potatoes

Minerals: lead, zinc, lignite, chromite, magnesite, halloysite, nickel

Life expectancy at birth (years): male, 71.0; female, 77.2

Literacy rate: 94.1%

Websites: www.state.gov/r/pa/ei/bgn/100931.htm

LATVIA*

FOR MAP, SEE PAGE 97

Population: 2,231,503

Ethnic groups: Latvian 58%, Russian 30%, Belarusian 4%, Ukrainian 3%, Polish 2%, Lithuanian 1%

Principal languages: Latvian (official), Russian, Belarusian, Ukrainian, Polish

Chief religions: Lutheran, Roman Catholic, Russian Orthodox

Area: 24,900 sq mi (64,590 sq km)

Topography: Latvia is a lowland with numerous lakes, marshes and peat bogs. The principal river, the Western Dvina (Daugava), rises in Russia. There are glacial hills in the east.

Capital: Riga (pop., 733,000)

Independence date: August 21, 1991

Government type: republic   **Head of state:** Pres. Vaira Vike-Freiberga

Head of government: Prime Min. Aigars Kalvitis

Monetary unit: lat

GDP: $38.98 billion (2008 est.)   Per capita GDP: $17,800

Industries: motor vehicles, railroad cars, synthetic fibers, agricultural machinery, fertilizers, household appliances, pharmaceuticals, processed foods, textiles

Chief crops: grain, sugar beets, potatoes, vegetables

Minerals: peat, limestone, dolomite, amber

Life expectancy at birth (years): male, 65.9; female, 76.1

Literacy rate: 99.8%

Websites: www.latvia-usa.org

LIECHTENSTEIN

FOR MAP, SEE PAGE 115

Population: 34,761

Ethnic groups: Alemannic 86%; Italian, Turkish, and other 14%

Principal languages: German (official), Alemannic dialect

Chief religions: Roman Catholic 80%, Protestant 7%

Area: 62 sq mi (161 sq km)

Topography: The Rhine Valley occupies one-third of the country; the Alps cover the rest.

Capital: Vaduz (pop., 5,000)   Independence date: January 23, 1719

Government type: hereditary constitutional monarchy

Head of state: Prince Hans-Adam II   Head of government: Otmar Hasler

Monetary unit: Swiss franc

GDP: $4.16 billion (2007) Per capita GDP: $118,000

Industries: electronics, metal manufacturing, textiles, ceramics, pharmaceuticals, food products, precision instruments, tourism

Chief crops: wheat, barley, corn, potatoes

Life expectancy at birth (years): male, 75.8; female, 83

Literacy rate: 100%

Website: www.liechtenstein.li/en

LITHUANIA*

FOR MAP, SEE PAGE 97

Population: 3,555,179

Ethnic groups: Lithuanian 81%, Russian 9%, Polish 7%, Belarusian 2%

Principal languages: Lithuanian (official), Belarusian, Russian, Polish

Chief religion: predominantly Roman Catholic

Area: 25,200 sq mi (65,200 sq km)

Topography: Lithuania is a lowland with hills in the west and south; fertile soil; many small lakes and rivers, with marshes especially in the north and west.

Capital: Vilnius (pop., 549,000)   Independence date: March 11, 1990

Government type: republic   Head of state: Pres. Dalia Grybauskaite

Head of government: Prime Min. Andrius Kubilius

Monetary unit: litas

GDP: $63.25 billion (2008 est.)   Per capita GDP: $17,700

Industries: machine tools, electric motors, household appliances, petroleum refining, shipbuilding, furniture making, textiles, food processing, fertilizers, agricultural machinery, optical equipment, electronic components, computers, amber

Chief crops: grain, potatoes, sugar beets, flax, vegetables

Minerals: peat

Life expectancy at birth (years): male, 68.2; female, 79.0

Literacy rate: 98%

Websites: www.president.lt/en   www.ltembassyus.org

LUXEMBOURG*

FOR MAP, SEE PAGE 111

Population: 491,775

Ethnic groups: Mixture of French and German

Principal languages: Luxembourgish (national), German, French (official)

Chief religion: majority is Roman Catholic; 1979 law forbids collection of such statistics

Area: 1,000 sq mi (2,590 sq km)

Topography: Heavy forests (Ardennes) cover the north; the south is a low, open plateau.

Capital: Luxembourg (pop., 77,000)   Independence date: 1839

Government type: constitutional monarchy

Head of state: Grand Duke Henri

Head of government: Prime Min. Jean-Claude Juncker

Monetary unit: euro

GDP: $39.42 billion (2008 est.)   Per capita GDP: $81,100

Industries: banking, iron and steel, food processing, chemicals, metal products, tires, glass, aluminum

Chief crops: barley, oats, potatoes, wheat, fruits, wine grapes

Life expectancy at birth (years): male, 75.3; female, 82.1

Literacy rate: 100%   Website: www.luxembourg-usa.org

MACEDONIA (FORMER YUGOSLAV REPUBLIC OF MACEDONIA)

FOR MAP, SEE PAGE 105

Population: 2,066,718

Ethnic groups: Macedonian 67%, Albanian 23%, Turkish 4%, Roma 2%, Serb 2%

Principal languages: Macedonian (official), Albanian, Turkish, Romani, Serbo-Croatian

Chief religions: Macedonian Orthodox 67%, Muslim 30%

Area: 9,780 sq mi (25,330 sq km)

Topography: Macedonia is a landlocked, mostly mountainous country, with deep river valleys and three large lakes; the country is bisected by the Vardar River.

Capital: Skopje (pop., 447,000)   Independence date: September 17, 1991

Government type: republic   Head of state: Pres. Gjorge Ivanov

Head of government: Prime Min. Nikola Gruevski

Monetary unit: euro

GDP: $18.52 billion (2008 est.)   Per capita GDP: $9,000

Industries: mining, textiles, wood products, tobacco, food processing, buses

Chief crops: rice, tobacco, wheat, corn, millet, cotton, sesame, mulberry leaves, citrus, vegetables

Minerals: chromium, lead, zinc, manganese, tungsten, nickel, iron ore, asbestos, sulfur

Life expectancy at birth (years): male, 72.5; female, 77.2

Literacy rate: NA   Website: www.macedonia.co/uk/mcic

MALTA*

FOR MAP, SEE PAGE 104

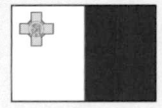

Population: 405,165

Ethnic group: Maltese, other Mediterranean

Principal languages: Maltese (a Semitic dialect), English (both official)

---

*Member of the European Union

Malta *(continued)*

Chief religion: Roman Catholic (official) 91%

Area: 124 sq mi (321 sq km)

Topography: The island of Malta is 95 sq mi (246 sq km); other islands in the group: Gozo, 26 sq mi (67 sq km); Comino, 1 sq mi (2.6 sq km). The coastline is heavily indented. Low hills cover the interior.

Capital: Valletta (pop., 83,000)

Independence date: September 21, 1964

Government type: parliamentary democracy

Head of state: Pres. Edward (Eddie) Fenech-Adami

Head of government: Prime Min. Lawrence Gonzi

Monetary unit: euro

GDP: $9.8 billion (2008 est.)   **Per capita GDP:** $24,200

Industries: tourism, electronics, shipbuilding, construction, food and beverages, textiles, footwear, clothing, tobacco

Chief crops: potatoes, cauliflower, grapes, wheat, barley, tomatoes, citrus, cut flowers, green peppers

Minerals: limestone, salt

Life expectancy at birth (years): male, 76.5; female, 81.0

Literacy rate: 88.76%   **Website:** www.gov.mt/index.asp?l=2

MOLDOVA

FOR MAP, SEE PAGE 107

Population: 4,320,748

Ethnic groups: Moldovan/Romanian 65%, Ukrainian 14%, Russian 13%

Principal languages: Moldovan (official), Russian, Gagauz (a Turkish dialect)

Chief religion: Eastern Orthodox 99%

Area: 13,000 sq mi (33,700 sq km)

Topography: The country is landlocked; mainly hilly plains, with steppelands in the south near the Black Sea.

Capital: Chisinau (pop., 662,000)   **Independence date:** August 27, 1991

Government type: republic

Head of state: Pres. Vladimir Voronin

Head of government: Prime Min. Vasile Tarlev

Monetary unit: leu

GDP: $10.63 billion (2008 est.)   **Per capita GDP:** $2,500

Industries: food processing, agricultural machinery, foundry equipment, household appliances, hosiery, sugar, vegetable oil, shoes, textiles

Chief crops: vegetables, fruits, wine, grain, sugar beets, sunflower seed, tobacco

Minerals: lignite, phosphorites, gypsum, limestone

Life expectancy at birth (years): male, 60.9; female, 69.4

Literacy rate: 96%   **Website:** www.tourism.md/eng

MONACO

FOR MAP, SEE PAGE 116

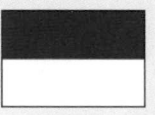

Population: 32,965

Ethnic groups: French 47%, Monegasque 16%, Italian 16%

Principal languages: French (official), English, Italian, Monegasque

Chief religion: Roman Catholic (official) 90%

Area: 0.75 sq mi (1.9 sq km)

Topography: Monaco-Ville sits atop a high promontory; the rest of the principality rises from the port up the hillside.

Capital: Monaco (pop., 32,000)   **Independence date:** 1419

Government type: constitutional monarchy

Head of state: Prince Rainier III

Head of government: Min. of State Patrick Leclercq

Monetary unit: euro

GDP: $976.3 million (2006 est.)   **Per capita GDP:** $30,000

Industries: tourism, construction, small-scale industrial and consumer products

Life expectancy at birth (years): male, 75.5; female, 83.5

Literacy rate: 99%   **Website:** www.monaco-consulate.com

MONTENEGRO

FOR MAP, SEE PAGE 106

Population: 672,180

Ethnic groups: Montenegrins 43%, Serbs 32%, Bosniaks 8%, Albanians 5%

Principal languages: Serbian of the Ijekavian dialect (official), Albanian

Chief religions: Orthodox 74%, Muslim 18%, Roman Catholic 2%

Area: 5,333 sq mi (13,812 sq km)

Topography: From high peaks along the borders with Kosovo and Albania, to a narrow coastal plain only one to four miles wide, Montenegro contains some of Europe's most diverse and rugged terrain.

Capital: Prodgorica (pop., 179,500)

Independence date: June 3, 2006   **Government type:** republic

Head of state: Pres. Filip Vujanovic

Head of government: Prime Min. Milo Dukanovic

Monetary unit: euro

GDP: $6.6 billion (2008 est.)   **Per capita GDP:** $9,700

Industries: Mining, manufacturing, chemicals, clothing, textiles, forestry

Chief crops: olives, wine, potatoes, corn, citrus fruit, vegetables

Minerals: coal, bauxite, aluminum

Life expectancy at birth (years): male, 71.0; female, 76.0

Literacy rate: 93%   **Website:** www.gom.cg.yu/eng.com

NETHERLANDS*

FOR MAP, SEE PAGE 108

Population: 16,715,999

Ethnic groups: Dutch 83%

Principal languages: Dutch (official), Frisian, Flemish

Chief religions: Roman Catholic 31%, Protestant 21%, Muslim 4%

Area: 16,030 sq mi (41,530 sq km)

Topography: The land is flat, with an average altitude of 37 ft (11 m) above sea level. Much land is below sea level, reclaimed and protected by some 1,500 mi (2,400 km) of dikes. Since 1920 the government has been draining the IJsselmeer, formerly the Zuider Zee.

Capital: Amsterdam (pop., 1,145,00); seat of government, The Hague (pop., 705,00)

Independence date: 1579

Government type: parliamentary democracy under a constitutional monarch

Head of state: Queen Beatrix

Head of government: Prime Min. Jan Peter Balkenende

Monetary unit: euro

GDP: $670.2 billion (2008 est.)

Per capita GDP: $40,300

Traditional attributes of the Netherlands: tulips (top, with windmill in background) and wooden shoes (bottom)

*Member of the European Union

Industries: agroindustries, metal and engineering products, electrical machinery and equipment, chemicals, petroleum, construction, micro-electronics, fishing

Chief crops: grains, potatoes, sugar beets, fruits, vegetables

Minerals: natural gas, petroleum

Life expectancy at birth (years): male, 76.2; female, 81.3

Literacy rate: 99%   **Website:** www.netherlands-embassy.org

NETHERLANDS DEPENDENCIES, constitutionally on a level of equality with the Netherlands homeland within the kingdom, are Aruba and the Netherlands Antilles. ARUBA: population, 103,065; area, 75 sq mi (193 sq km); capital, Oranjestad. NETHERLANDS ANTILLES (CURAÇAO, BONAIRE, SAINT EUSTATIUS, SABA, southern part of SAINT MAARTEN): population, 227,049; area, 371 sq mi (960 sq km), capital, Willemstad, on Curaçao.

NORWAY

FOR MAP, SEE PAGE 95

Population: 4,660,539

Ethnic groups: Norwegian, Sami

Principal languages: Norwegian (official), Sami, Finnish

Chief religion: Evangelical Lutheran (official) 86%

Area: 125,180 sq mi (324,220 sq km)

Topography: A highly indented coast is lined with tens of thousands of islands. Mountains and plateaus cover most of the country, which is only 25% forested.

Capital: Oslo (pop., 795,000)

Independence date: June 7, 1905

Government type: hereditary constitutional monarchy

Norwegian coast

Head of state: King Harald V

Head of government: Prime Min. Jens Stoltenberg

Monetary unit: krone

GDP: $256.5 billion (2008 est.)   **Per capita GDP:** $55,200

Industries: petroleum and gas, food processing, shipbuilding, pulp and paper products, metals, chemicals, timber, mining, textiles, fishing

Chief crops: barley, wheat, potatoes

Minerals: petroleum, copper, natural gas, pyrites, nickel, iron ore, zinc, lead

Life expectancy at birth (years): male, 76.6; female, 82.2

Literacy rate: 100%   **Website:** www.norway.no

POLAND*

FOR MAP, SEE PAGE 99

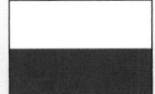

Population: 38,482,919

Ethnic groups: Polish 98%, German 1%

Principal languages: Polish (official), Ukrainian, German

Chief religion: Roman Catholic 95%

Area: 120,730 sq mi (312,680 sq km)

Topography: Poland consists mostly of lowlands forming part of the Northern European Plain. The Carpathian Mountains along the southern border rise to 8,200 ft (2,500 m).

Capital: Warsaw (pop., 2,200,000)

Independence date: November 11, 1918   **Government type:** republic

Head of state: Pres. Lech Kaczynski

Head of government: Prime Min. Donald Tusk

Monetary unit: zloty

GDP: $667.4 billion (2008 est.)   **Per capita GDP:** $17,300

Industries: machine building, iron and steel, mining, chemicals, ship-building, food processing, glass, beverages, textiles

Chief crops: potatoes, fruits, vegetables, wheat

Minerals: coal, sulfur, copper, natural gas, silver, lead, salt

Life expectancy at birth (years): male, 70.0; female, 78.5

Literacy rate: 99%

Websites: www.polandembassy.org;   www.poland.pl

PORTUGAL*

FOR MAP, SEE PAGE 102

Population: 10,707,924

Ethnic groups: mainly Portuguese

Principal language: Portuguese (official)

Chief religion: Roman Catholic 94%

Area: 35,670 sq mi (92,390 sq km)

Topography: Portugal north of the Tajus River, which bisects the country northeast to southwest, is mountainous, cool, and rainy. To the south there are drier, rolling plains and a warm climate.

Capital: Lisbon (pop., 1,962,000)

Independence date: 1143   **Government type:** republic

Head of state: Pres. Aníbal Cavaco Silva

Head of government: Prime Min. José Sócrates Carvalho Pinto de Sousa

Monetary unit: euro

GDP: $237.3 billion (2008 est.)   **Per capita GDP:** $22,000

Industries: textiles, footwear, pulp and paper, cork, metalworking, oil refining, chemicals, fish canning, wine, tourism

Chief crops: grain, potatoes, olives, grapes

Minerals: tungsten, iron ore, uranium ore, marble

Life expectancy at birth (years): male, 74.9; female, 80.9

Literacy rate: 87.4%

Website: www.presidenciarepublica.pt/en/main.html

ROMANIA*

FOR MAP, SEE PAGE 107

Population: 22,215,421

Ethnic groups: Romanian 90%, Hungarian, Roma, and others 10%

Principal languages: Romanian (official), Hungarian, German, Romani

Chief religions: Romanian Orthodox 70%, Roman Catholic 6%, Protestant 6%

Area: 91,700 sq mi (237,500 sq km)

Topography: The Carpathian Mountains encase the north-central Transylvanian plateau. There are wide plains south and east of the mountains, through which flow the lower reaches of the rivers of the Danube system.

Capital: Bucharest (pop., 1,853,000)

Independence date: May 9, 1877   **Government type:** republic

Head of state: Pres. Traian Basescu

Head of government: Prime Min. Calin Constantin Anton Popescu-Tariceanu

Monetary unit: lei

GDP: $271.2 billion (2008 est.)   **Per capita GDP:** $12,200

Industries: textiles, footwear, light machinery, auto assembly, mining, timber, construction materials, metallurgy, chemicals, food processing, petroleum refining

Chief crops: wheat, corn, sugar beets, sunflower seed, potatoes, grapes

Minerals: petroleum, natural gas, coal, iron ore, salt

Life expectancy at birth (years): male, 67.6; female, 74.8

---

*Member of the European Union

Romania *(continued)*

Literacy rate: 97%

Websites: www.gov.ro/engleza/index.html;   www.roembus.org

RUSSIA

FOR MAP, SEE PAGE 122

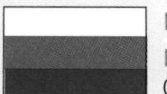

Population: 140,041,247

Ethnic groups: Russian 82%, Tatar 4%, Ukrainian 3%, Chuvash 1%, Bashkir 1%, Belarusian 1%, Moldavian 1%

Principal languages: Russian (official), many others

Chief religions: Russian Orthodox, Muslim

Area: 6,592,800 sq mi (17,075,400 sq km)

Topography: Russia contains every type of climate except the distinctly tropical and has a varied topography. The European portion is a low plain, grassy in the south, wooded in the north, with the Ural Mountains on the east and the Caucasus Mountains on the south. The Urals stretch north to south for 2,500 mi (4,000 km). The Asiatic portion is also a vast plain, with mountains on the south and in the east; tundra covers the extreme north, with forest belt below; plains, marshes are in the west, desert in the southwest.

Capital: Moscow (pop., 10,469,000)

Independence date: August 24, 1991

Government type: federal republic

Head of state: Pres. Dmitry Medvedev

Head of government: Prime Min. Vladimir Putin

Monetary unit: ruble

GDP: $2,225 billion (2008 est.)

Per capita GDP: $15,800

Industries: mining, extractive industries, machine building, shipbuilding, vehicles, commercial equipment, agricultural machinery, construction equipment, instruments, consumer durables, textiles, foodstuffs, handicrafts

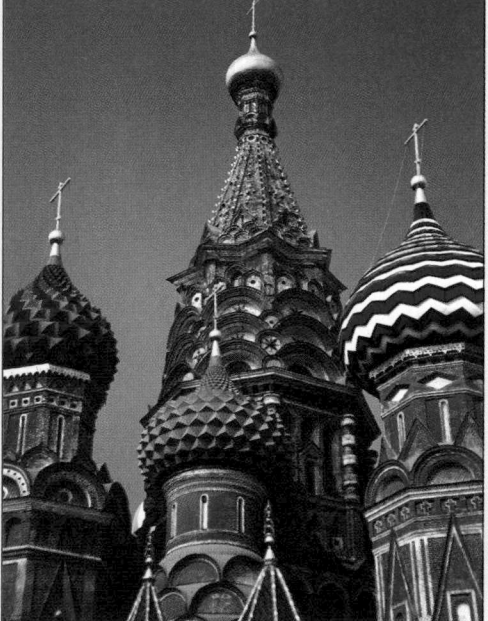

St. Basil's Cathedral, Moscow, Russia

Chief crops: grain, sugar beets, sunflower seed, vegetables, fruits

Minerals: large variety, including oil, natural gas, coal, strategic minerals

Life expectancy at birth (years): male, 59.9; female, 73.3

Literacy rate: 98%   Website: www.russiaembassy.org

SAN MARINO

FOR MAP, SEE PAGE 117

Population: 30,324

Ethnic groups: Sammarinese, Italian

Principal language: Italian (official)

Chief religion: predominantly Roman Catholic

Area: 23 sq mi (60 sq km)

Topography: The country lies on the slopes of Mt. Titano.

Capital: San Marino (pop., 5,000)

Independence date: September 3, 301   **Government type:** republic

Heads of state and government: two co-regents appointed every 6 months

Monetary unit: euro

GDP: 1.662 billion (2007 est.)   **Per capita GDP:** $41,900

Industries: tourism, banking, textiles, electronics, ceramics, wine

Chief crops: wheat, grapes, corn, olives

Minerals: building stone

Life expectancy at birth (years): male, 78.0; female, 85.3

Literacy rate: 96%   Website: www.visitsanmarino.com

SERBIA

FOR MAP, SEE PAGE 106

Population: 7,379,339

Ethnic groups: Serb 63%, Albanian 14%

Principal languages: Serbian (official), Albanian, Hungarian

Chief religions: Orthodox 65%, Muslim 19%, Roman Catholic 4%

Area: 34,185 sq mi (88,538 sq km)

Topography: The terrain of this landlocked country varies widely, with fertile plains drained by the Danube and other rivers in the north, limestone basins in the east ancient mountains and hills in the southeast.

Capital: Belgrade (pop., 1,118,000)

Independence date: February 4, 2003   **Government type:** federal republic

Head of state and government: Pres. Svetozar Marović

Monetary unit: new dinar

GDP: $80.74 billion (2008 est.)   **Per capita GDP:** $10,900

Industries: machine building, metallurgy, mining, consumer goods, electronics, petroleum products, chemicals, pharmaceuticals

Chief crops: cereals, fruits, vegetables, tobacco, olives

Minerals: oil, gas, coal, antimony, copper, lead, zinc, nickel, gold, pyrite, chrome

Life expectancy at birth (years): male, 71.0; female, 77.2

Literacy rate: 93%   Website: www.gov.yu

SLOVAKIA*

FOR MAP, SEE PAGE 99

Population: 5,463,046

Ethnic groups: Slovak 86%, Hungarian 11%, Roma 2%

Principal languages: Slovak (official), Hungarian

Chief religions: Roman Catholic 60%, Protestant 8%, Orthodox 4%

Area: 18,860 sq mi (48,850 sq km)

Topography: Mountains (Carpathians) in the north, and the fertile Danube plane in the south.

Capital: Bratislava (pop., 425,000)

Independence date: January 1, 1993   **Government type:** republic

Head of state: Pres. Ivan Gašparovič

Head of government: Prime Min. Mikulás Dzurinda

Monetary unit: koruna

GDP: $119.5 billion (2008 est.)   **Per capita GDP:** $21,900

Industries: metal and metal products, food and beverages, electricity, chemicals and manmade fibers, machinery, paper and printing, earthenware and ceramics, transport vehicles, textiles, electrical and optical apparatus, rubber products

Chief crops: grains, potatoes, sugar beets, hops, fruit

Minerals: coal, iron ore, copper, manganese, salt

Life expectancy at birth (years): male, 70.2; female, 78.4

Literacy rate: NA

Websites: www.government.gov.sk/english/
www.slovakembassy-us.org

SLOVENIA*

FOR MAP, SEE PAGE 106

Population: 2,005,692

Ethnic groups: Slovene 88%, Croat 3%, Serb 2%, Bosniak 1%

Principal languages: Slovenian (official), Serbo-Croatian

Chief religion: Roman Catholic 71%

Area: 7,820 sq mi (20,250 sq km)

Topography: Mostly hilly; 42% of the land is forested.

Capital: Ljubljana (pop., 256,000)

Independence date: June 25, 1991   Government type: republic

Head of state: Pres. Danilo Türk

Head of government: Prime Min. Janez Jansa

Monetary unit: euro

GDP: $59.14 billion (2008 est.)   Per capita GDP: $29,500

Industries: metallurgy and metal products, electronics, trucks, electric power equipment, wood products, textiles, chemicals, machine tools

Chief crops: potatoes, hops, wheat, sugar beets, corn, grapes

Minerals: coal, lead, zinc, mercury, uranium, silver

Life expectancy at birth (years): male, 72.2; female, 79.9

Literacy rate: 99%   Website: www.sigov.si

SPAIN*

FOR MAP, SEE PAGE 102

Population: 40,525,002

Ethnic groups: Castilian, Catalan, Basque, Galician

Principal languages: Castilian Spanish (official), Catalan, Galician, Basque

Chief religion: Roman Catholic 94%

Area: 194,890 sq mi (504,780 sq km)

Topography: The interior is a high, arid plateau broken by mountain ranges and river valleys. The northwest is heavily watered; the south has lowlands and a Mediterranean climate.

Capital: Madrid (pop., 5,103,000)   Independence date: 1492

Government type: constitutional monarchy

Head of state: King Juan Carlos I de Borbon y Borbon

Head of government: Prime Min. José Luis Rodriguez Zapatero

Monetary unit: euro

GDP: $1,378 billion (2008 est.)   Per capita GDP: $34,600

Industries: textiles and apparel, food and beverages, metals and metal manufacture, chemicals, shipbuilding, automobiles, machine tools, tourism

Chief crops: grain, vegetables, olives, wine grapes, sugar beets, citrus

Spanish olive groves

*Member of the European Union

Minerals: coal, iron ore, uranium, mercury, pyrites, fluorspar, gypsum, zinc, lead, tungsten, copper, kaolin, potash

Life expectancy at birth (years): male, 76.0; female, 82.9

Literacy rate: 97%   Website: www.embaspain.ca

SWEDEN*

FOR MAP, SEE PAGE 95

Population: 9,059,651

Ethnic groups: Swedish 89%, Finnish 2%; Sami and others 9%

Principal languages: Swedish (official), Sami, Finnish

Chief religion: Lutheran 87%

Area: 173,730 sq mi (449,960 sq km)

Topography: Mountains along the northwestern border cover 25% of Sweden; flat or rolling terrain covers the central and southern areas, which include several large lakes.

Capital: Stockholm (pop., 1,697,000)

Independence date: June 6, 1523

Government type: constitutional monarchy

Head of state: King Carl XVI Gustaf

Head of government: Prime Min. Goran Persson

Monetary unit: krona

GDP: $348.6 billion (2008 est.)   Per capita GDP: $38,500

Industries: iron and steel, precision equipment, pulp and paper products, processed foods, motor vehicles

Chief crops: barley, wheat, sugar beets

Minerals: zinc, iron ore, lead, copper, silver, uranium

Life expectancy at birth (years): male, 78.1; female, 82.6

Literacy rate: 99%   Website: www.sweden.se

SWITZERLAND

FOR MAP, SEE PAGE 114

Population: 7,604,467

Ethnic groups: German 65%, French 18%, Italian 10%, Romansch 1%

Principal languages: German, French, Italian (all official); Romansch (semi-official)

Chief religions: Roman Catholic 46%, Protestant 40%

Area: 15,940 sq mi (41,290 sq km)

Topography: The Alps cover 60% of the land area; the Jura, near France, 10%. Running between, from northeast to southwest, are midlands, 30%.

Capitals: Bern (administrative) (pop., 320,000), Lausanne (judicial) (pop., 285,000)

Matterhorn, Switzerland

Switzerland *(continued)*

Independence date: August 1, 1291

Government type: federal republic

Head of state and government: the president is elected by the Federal Assembly to a nonrenewable one-year term

Monetary unit: franc

GDP: $309.9 billion (2008 est.)   **Per capita GDP:** $40,900

Industries: machinery, chemicals, watches, textiles, precision instruments

Chief crops: grains, fruits, vegetables   **Minerals:** salt

Life expectancy at birth (years): male, 77.5; female, 83.3

Literacy rate: 99%   **Website:** www.swissemb.org

Stonehenge, England

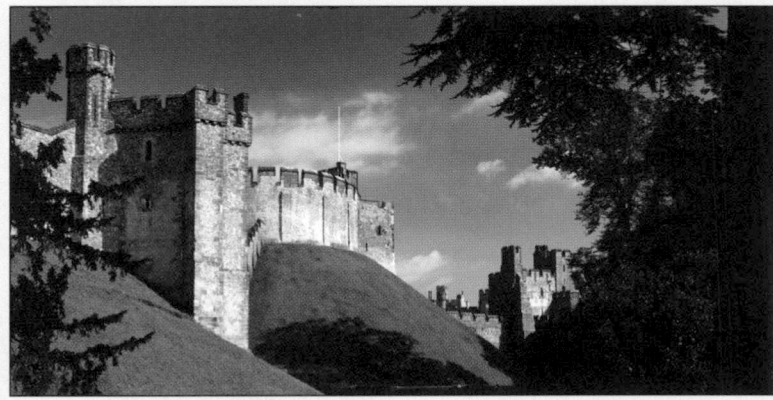

Arundel Castle, England

UKRAINE

FOR MAP, SEE PAGE 120

Population: 45,700,395

Ethnic groups: Ukrainian 78%, Russian 17%

Principal languages: Ukrainian (official), Russian, Romanian, Polish, Hungarian

Chief religions: Ukrainian Orthodox (Kiev patriarchate and Russian patriarchate), Autocephalous Orthodox, Ukrainian Greek Catholic

Area: 233,100 sq mi (603,700 sq km)

Topography: Ukraine is part of the East European plain. Mountainous areas include the Carpathians in the southwest and the Crimean chain in the south. Arable black soil constitutes a large part of the country.

Capital: Kiev (pop., 2,618,000)   **Independence date:** August 24, 1991

Government type: constitutional republic

Head of state: Pres. Viktor Yushchenko

Head of government: Prime Min. Yuriy Yekhanurov

Monetary unit: hryvnia

GDP: $337 billion (2008 est.)   **Per capita GDP:** $6,900

Industries: mining, electric power, ferrous and nonferrous metals, machinery and transport equipment, chemicals, food processing

Chief crops: grain, sugar beets, sunflower seeds, vegetables

Minerals: iron ore, coal, manganese, natural gas, oil, salt, sulfur, graphite, titanium, magnesium, kaolin, nickel, mercury

Life expectancy at birth (years): male, 61.4; female, 72.3

Literacy rate: 98%

Websites: www.ukraineinfo.us;   www.kmu.gov.ua/control/en

UNITED KINGDOM*

FOR MAP, SEE PAGE 89

Population: 61,113,205

Ethnic groups: English 81.5%, Scottish 9.6%, Irish 2.4%, Welsh 1.9%, Ulster 1.9%; West Indian, Indo-Pakistani, and other 2.8%

Principal languages: English (official), Welsh and Scottish Gaelic

Chief religions: Christian 72%, Muslim 3%, many others

Area: 94,530 sq mi (244,820 sq km)

Topography: England is mostly rolling land, rising to the Uplands of southern Scotland; the Lowlands are in the center of Scotland, and the granite Highlands are in the north. The coast is

Houses of Parliament with Big Ben, London, United Kingdom

heavily indented, especially on the west. The Severn, 220 mi (354 km), and the Thames, 215 mi (346 km), are the longest rivers.

Capital: London (pop., 7,619,000)

Independence date: 1801   **Government type:** constitutional monarchy

Head of state: Queen Elizabeth II

Head of government: Prime Min. Gordon Brown

Monetary unit: pound

GDP: $2,231 billion (2008 est.)   **Per capita GDP:** $36,600

Industries: machine tools, electric power and automation equipment, rail, shipbuilding, aircraft, motor vehicles and parts, electronics and communication equipment, mining, chemicals, paper and paper products, food processing, textiles, clothing and other consumer goods

Chief crops: cereals, oilseed, potatoes, vegetables

Minerals: coal, petroleum, natural gas, tin, limestone, iron ore, salt, clay, chalk, gypsum, lead, silica

Life expectancy at birth (years): male, 75.8; female, 80.8

Literacy rate: 99%   **Website:** www.britainusa.com

The CHANNEL ISLANDS—Jersey, Guernsey, and the dependencies of Guernsey (Alderney, Brechou, Great Sark, Little Sark, Herm, Jethou, and Lihou)—are situated off the northwest coast of France. Jersey and Guernsey have separate legal existences and lieutenant governors named by the Crown. Population, 157,496; area, 75 sq mi (194 sq km).

The ISLE OF MAN, in the Irish Sea, has its own laws and a lieutenant governor appointed by the Crown. Population, 76,512; area 221 sq mi (572 sq km).

VATICAN CITY (THE HOLY SEE)

FOR MAP, SEE PAGE 104

Population: 826

Ethnic groups: Italian, Swiss, other

Principal languages: Latin (official), Italian, French, Monastic Sign Language, various others

Chief religion: Roman Catholic

Area: 0.17 sq mi (0.4 sq km)

Independence date: February 11, 1929

Government type: ecclesiastical state   **Sovereign:** Pope Benedict XVI

Monetary unit: euro   **Website:** www.vatican.va/phome_en.htm

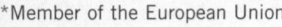
*Member of the European Union

NORTH AMERICA
Including Central America and the Islands of the Caribbean

Two of the world's five biggest countries, in terms of land area, are in North America: the United States, which ranks Number 3, and Canada, Number 4. The United States, has the third largest population in the world, while Canada is the world's ninth most sparsely populated country.

ANTIGUA AND BARBUDA

FOR MAP, SEE PAGE 199

Population: 85,632

Ethnic groups: black, British, Portuguese, Lebanese, Syrian

Principal languages: English (official), local dialects

Chief religions: predominantly Protestant, some Roman Catholic

Area: 174 sq mi (440 sq km)

Topography: These are mostly low-lying and limestone coral islands. Antigua is mostly hilly with an indented coast; Barbuda is a flat island with a large lagoon on the west.

Capital: Saint John's (pop., 28,000)

Independence date: November 1, 1981

Government type: constitutional monarchy with British-style parliament

Head of state: Queen Elizabeth II, represented by Gov.-Gen. James Carlisle

Head of government: Prime Min. Baldwin Spencer

Monetary unit: East Caribbean dollar

GDP: $1.61 billion (2008 est.)   **Per capita GDP:** $19,000

Industries: tourism, construction, light manufacturing

Chief crops: cotton, fruits, vegetables, bananas, coconuts, cucumbers, mangoes, sugarcane

Life expectancy at birth (years): male, 69.3; female, 74.1

Literacy rate: 89%   **Website:** www.antigua-barbuda.com

Chief religions: Baptist 32%, Anglican 20%, Roman Catholic 19%, other Christian 24%

Area: 5,380 sq mi (13,940 sq km)

Topography: Nearly 700 islands (29 inhabited) and over 2,000 islets in the western Atlantic Ocean extend 760 mi (1,220 km) northwest to southeast.

Capital: Nassau (pop.,222,000)

Independence date: July 10, 1973

Government type: independent commonwealth

Head of state: Queen Elizabeth II, represented by Gov.-Gen. Arthur D. Hanna

Head of government: Prime Min. Perry Christie

Monetary unit: Bahamas dollar

GDP: $8.78 billion (2008 est.)

Per capita GDP: $28,600

Industries: tourism, banking, cement, oil refining and transshipment, pharmaceuticals, steel pipe

Chief crops: citrus, vegetables

Minerals: salt, aragonite

Life expectancy at birth (years): male, 62.3; female, 69.1

Literacy rate: 98.2%

Website: www.bahamas.gov.bs

Nassau, the Bahamas

THE BAHAMAS

FOR MAP, SEE PAGE 199

Population: 309,156

Ethnic groups: black 85%, white 12%

Principal languages: English, Creole (among Haitian immigrants)

BARBADOS

FOR MAP, SEE PAGE 199

Population: 284,589

Ethnic groups: black 90%, white 4%

Principal language: English

Nation Facts and Figures

BELIZE – COSTA RICA

Barbados *(continued)*

Chief religions: Protestant 67%, Roman Catholic 4%

Area: 165 sq mi (430 sq km)

Topography: The island lies alone in the Atlantic almost completely surrounded by coral reefs. The highest point is Mt. Hillaby, 1,115 ft (340 m).

Capital: Bridgetown (pop., 140,000)

Independence date: November 30, 1966

Government type: parliamentary democracy

Head of state: Queen Elizabeth II, represented by Gov.-Gen. Sir Clifford Husbands

Head of government: Prime Min. Owen Arthur

Monetary unit: Barbados dollar

GDP: $5.47 billion (2008 est.)   **Per capita GDP:** $19,300

Industries: tourism, sugar, light manufacturing, component assembly for export

Chief crops: sugarcane, vegetables, cotton

Minerals: petroleum, natural gas

Life expectancy at birth (years): 69.5; female, 73.8

Literacy rate: 97.4%

Website: www.barbados.gov.bb

BELIZE

FOR MAP, SEE PAGE 202

Population: 307,899

Ethnic groups: mestizo 49%, Creole 25%, Maya 11%, Garifuna 6%

Principal languages: English (official), Spanish, Mayan, Creole, Garifuna (Carib)

Chief religions: Roman Catholic 50%, Protestant 27%

Area: 8,860 sq mi (22,960 sq km)

Topography: Belize has swampy lowlands in the north, Maya Mountains in the south, coral reefs and cays near the coast.

Capital: Belmopan (pop., 9,000)

Independence date: September 21, 1981

Government type: parliamentary democracy

Head of state: Queen Elizabeth II, represented by Gov.-Gen. Sir Colville Young

Head of government: Prime Min. Said Musa

Monetary unit: Belize dollar

GDP: $2.82 billion (2008 est.)   **Per capita GDP:** $8,600

Industries: garment production, food processing, tourism, construction

Chief crops: bananas, coca, citrus, sugarcane

Life expectancy at birth (years): male, 65.1; female, 69.9

Literacy rate: 70.3%   **Website:** www.belize.gov.bz

CANADA

FOR MAP, SEE PAGE 180

Population: 33,489,208

Ethnic groups: British 28%, French 23%, other European 15%, Amerindian 2%

Principal languages: English, French (both official)

Chief religions: Roman Catholic 46%, Protestant 36%, other 18%

Area: 3,851,810 sq mi (9,976,140 sq km)

Topography: Canada stretches 3,426 mi (5,514 km) from east to west and extends south from the North Pole to the U.S. border. Its seacoast includes 36,356 mi (58,509 km) of mainland and 115,133 mi (185,289 km) of islands, including the Arctic islands almost from Greenland to near the Alaskan border.

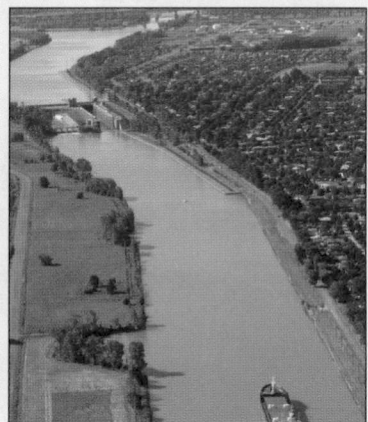

Images of Canada: Vancouver, British Columbia (top); Manitoba farmland (middle); lobster traps in Nova Scotia (above left); Welland Canal, Ontario (above right)

Capital: Ottawa (pop., 1,093,000)

Independence date: July 1, 1867

Government type: confederation with parliamentary democracy

Head of state: Queen Elizabeth II, represented by Gov.-Gen. Michaelle Jean

Head of government: Prime Min. Stephen Harper

Monetary unit: Canadian dollar

GDP: $1,307 billion (2008 est.)   **Per capita GDP:** $39,300

Industries: transport equipment, chemicals, mining, food products, wood and paper products, fish products, petroleum and natural gas

Chief crops: wheat, barley, oilseed, tobacco, fruits, vegetables

Minerals: iron ore, nickel, zinc, copper, gold, lead, molybdenum, potash, silver, coal, petroleum, natural gas

Life expectancy at birth (years): male, 76.6; female, 83.5

Literacy rate: 97%

Websites: www.statcan.ca   www.canada.gc.ca

COSTA RICA

FOR MAP, SEE PAGE 203

Population: 4,253,877

Ethnic groups: European and mestizo 94%, black 3%, Amerindian 1%, Chinese 1%

Principal languages Spanish (official), English spoken around Puerto Limon

Chief religions: Roman Catholic (official) 76%, Protestant 14%

Area: 19,700 sq mi (51,100 sq km)

Topography: Lowlands by the Caribbean are tropical. The interior plateau, with an altitude of about 4,000 ft (1,200 m), is temperate.

Capital: San José (pop., 1,085,000)

Independence date: September 15, 1821   Government type: republic

Head of state and government: Pres. Óscar Arias Sánchez

Monetary unit: colon

GDP: $48.48 billion (2008 est.)

Per capita GDP: $11,600

Industries: microprocessors, food processing, textiles and clothing, construction materials, fertilizer, plastic products

Chief crops: coffee, pineapples, bananas, sugar, corn, rice, beans, potatoes

Life expectancy at birth (years): male, 74.1; female, 79.3

Literacy rate: 95.5%

Website: www.costarica-embassy.com

CUBA

FOR MAP, SEE PAGE 203

Population: 11,451,652

Ethnic groups: Creole 51%, white 37%, black 11%, Chinese 1%

Principal language: Spanish (official)

Chief religions: Roman Catholic, Santeria

Area: 42,800 sq mi (110,860 sq km)

Topography: The coastline is about 2,500 mi (4,000 km). The northern coast is steep and rocky, and the southern coast low and marshy. Low hills and fertile valleys cover more than half the country. The Sierra Maestra, in the east, is the highest of three mountain ranges.

Capital: Havana (pop., 2,189,000)

Independence date: May 20, 1902   Government type: Communist state

Head of state and government: Pres. Raúl Castro Ruz

Monetary unit: peso

GDP: $108.2 billion (2008 est.)

Per capita GDP: $9,500

Industries: sugar, petroleum, tobacco, chemicals, construction, mining, cement, agricultural machinery, biotechnology

Chief crops: sugar, tobacco, citrus, coffee, rice, potatoes, beans

Minerals: cobalt, nickel, iron ore, copper, manganese, salt, silica, petroleum

Life expectancy at birth (years): male, 74.8; female, 79.4

Literacy rate: 95.7%

Website: www.cubagob.cu/ingles/default.htm

Scuba diving in the Caribbean

DOMINICA

FOR MAP, SEE PAGE 199

Population: 72,660

Ethnic groups: black, Carib Amerindian

Principal languages: English (official), French patois

Chief religions: Roman Catholic 77%, Protestant 15%

Area: 290 sq mi (750 sq km)

Topography: Mountainous, with a central ridge running from north to south, terminating in cliffs. Dominica is volcanic in origin, with numerous thermal springs; there is rich deep topsoil on the leeward side, red tropical clay on the windward coast.

Capital: Roseau (pop., 27,000)

Independence date: November 3, 1978

Government type: parliamentary democracy

Head of state: Pres. Nicholas Liverpool

Head of government: Prime Min. Roosevelt Skerrit

Monetary unit: East Caribbean dollar

GDP: $719.8 million (2008 est.)   Per capita GDP: $9,900

Industries: soap, coconut oil, tourism, copra, furniture, cement blocks, shoes

Chief crops: bananas, citrus, mangoes, root crops, coconuts, cocoa

Life expectancy at birth (years): male, 71.5; female, 77.4

Literacy rate: 94%

Website: www.ndcdominica.dm

DOMINICAN REPUBLIC

FOR MAP, SEE PAGE 199

Population: 9,650,054

Ethnic groups: Creole 73%, white 16%, black 11%

Principal language: Spanish (official)

Chief religion: Roman Catholic 95%

Area: 18,810 sq mi (48,730 sq km)

Topography: The Cordillera Central range crosses the center of the country, rising to over 10,000 ft (3,000 m), the highest mountains in the Caribbean. The Cibao Valley to the north is a major agricultural area.

Capital: Santo Domingo (pop., 1,865,000)

Independence date: February 27, 1844

Government type: republic

Head of state and government: Pres. Leonel Fernández Reyna

Monetary unit: peso

GDP: $77.43 billion (2008 est.)

Per capita GDP: $8,100

Industries: tourism, sugar processing, mining, textiles, cement, tobacco

Chief crops: sugarcane, coffee, cotton, cocoa, tobacco, rice, beans, potatoes, corn, bananas

Minerals: nickel, bauxite, gold, silver

Life expectancy at birth (years): male, 66.0; female, 69.4

Literacy rate: 82.1%

Website: www.domrep.org

EL SALVADOR

FOR MAP, SEE PAGE 202

Population: 7,185,218

Ethnic groups: mestizo 90%, white 9%, Amerindian 1%

Principal languages: Spanish (official), Nahua

Chief religions: Roman Catholic 83%, many Protestant groups

Area: 8,120 sq mi (21,040 sq km)

El Salvador *(continued)*

Topography: A hot Pacific coastal plain in the south rises to a cooler plateau and valley region, densely populated. The north is mountainous, including many volcanoes.

Capital: San Salvador (pop., 1,424,000)

Independence date: September 15, 1821   **Government type:** republic

Head of state and government: Pres. Mauricio Funes

Monetary unit: colon

GDP: $43.94 billion (2008 est.)   **Per capita GDP:** $6,200

Industries: food processing, beverages, petroleum, chemicals, fertilizer, textiles, furniture, light metals

Chief crops: coffee, sugar, corn, rice, beans, oilseed, cotton, sorghum

Minerals: petroleum

Life expectancy at birth (years): male, 67.3; female, 74.7

Literacy rate: 71.5%

Website: www.elsalvador.org

GRENADA

FOR MAP, SEE PAGE 199

Population: 90,739

Ethnic groups: black 82%, Creole 13%

Principal languages: English (official), French patois

Chief religions: Roman Catholic 53%, Anglican 14%, other Protestant 33%

Area: 131 sq mi (339 sq km)

Topography: The main island is mountainous; the country includes Carriacou and Petit Martinique islands.

Capital: Saint George's (pop., 33,000)

Independence date: February 7, 1974

Government type: parliamentary democracy

Head of state: Queen Elizabeth II, represented by Gov.-Gen. Daniel Williams

Head of government: Prime Min. Keith Mitchell

Monetary unit: East Caribbean dollar

GDP: $1.21 billion (2008 est.)

Per capita GDP: $13,400

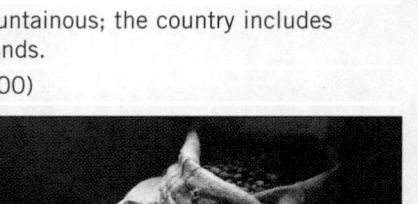

Nutmeg factory, Grenada

Industries: food and beverages, textiles, light assembly operations, tourism, construction

Chief crops: bananas, cocoa, nutmeg, mace, citrus, avocados, root crops, sugarcane, corn, vegetables

Life expectancy at birth (years): male, 62.7; female, 66.3

Literacy rate: 98%

Website: www.grenadagrenadines.com

GUATEMALA

FOR MAP, SEE PAGE 202

Population: 13,276,517

Ethnic groups: mestizo 55%, Amerindian 43%

Principal languages: Spanish (official); more than 20 Amerindian languages, including Quiche, Cakchiquel, Kekchi, Mam, Garifuna, and Xinca

Chief religions: mostly Roman Catholic; some Protestant, indigenous Mayan beliefs

Area: 42,040 sq mi (108,890 sq km)

Topography: The central highland and mountain areas are bordered by the narrow Pacific coast and the lowlands and fertile river valleys on the Caribbean. There are numerous volcanoes in the south, more than half a dozen over 11,000 ft (3,350 m).

Capital: Guatemala City (pop., 951,000)

Independence date: September 15, 1821

Government type: republic

Head of state and government: Pres. Álvaro Colom

Monetary unit: quetzal

GDP: $68.02 billion (2008 est.)

Per capita GDP: $5,200

Industries: sugar, textiles and clothing, furniture, chemicals, petroleum, metals, rubber, tourism

Chief crops: sugarcane, corn, bananas, coffee, beans, cardamom

Minerals: petroleum, nickel

Life expectancy at birth (years): male, 64.3; female, 66.1

Literacy rate: 63.6%

Website: www.guatemala-embassy.org

HAITI

FOR MAP, SEE PAGE 203

Population: 9,035,536

Ethnic groups: black 95%, Creole and other 5%

Principal languages: French, Creole (both official)

Chief religions: Roman Catholic 80%, Protestant 16%; voodoo widely practiced

Area: 10,710 sq mi (27,750 sq km)

Topography: About two-thirds of Haiti is mountainous. Much of the rest is semiarid. Coastal areas are warm and moist.

Capital: Port-au-Prince (pop., 1,961,000)

Independence date: January 1, 1804   **Government type:** republic

Head of state: Pres. René Préval

Head of government: Prime Min. Jacques Édouard Alexis

Monetary unit: gourde

GDP: $11.59 billion (2008 est.)   **Per capita GDP:** $1,300

Industries: sugar refining, flour milling, textiles, cement, light assembly industries

Chief crops: coffee, mangoes, sugarcane, rice, corn, sorghum

Minerals: bauxite, copper, calcium carbonate, gold, marble

Life expectancy at birth (years): male, 50.5; female, 53.1

Literacy rate: 45%

Website: www.haiti.org

HONDURAS

FOR MAP, SEE PAGE 202

Population: 7,792,854

Ethnic groups: mestizo 90%, Amerindian 7%, black 2%, white 1%

Principal languages: Spanish (official), Garífuna, Amerindian dialects

Chief religion: Roman Catholic 97%

Area: 43,280 sq mi (112,090 sq km)

Topography: The Caribbean coast is 500 mi (800 km) long. The Pacific coast, on the Gulf of Fonseca, is 40 mi (65 km) long. Honduras is mountainous, with wide fertile valleys and rich forests.

Capital: Tegucigalpa (pop., 1,007,000)

Independence date: September 15, 1821

Government type: republic

Head of state and government: Pres. José Manuel Zelaya Rosales (ousted) Roberto Micheletti (acting)

Monetary unit: lempira

GDP: $33.63 billion (2008 est.)   Per capita GDP: $4,400

Industries: sugar, coffee, textiles, clothing, wood products

Chief crops: bananas, coffee, citrus

Minerals: gold, silver, copper, lead, zinc, iron ore, antimony, coal

Life expectancy at birth (years): male, 65.0; female, 67.4

Literacy rate: 74%

Website: www.hondurasemb.org

JAMAICA

FOR MAP, SEE PAGE 203

Population: 2,825,928

Ethnic groups: black 91%, mixed 7%, East Indian and other 2%

Principal languages: English, patois English

Chief religions: Protestant 61%, Roman Catholic 4%, spiritual cults and other 35%

Area: 4,240 sq mi (10,990 sq km)

Topography: Four-fifths of Jamaica is covered by mountains.

Capital: Kingston (pop., 575,000)   Independence date: August 6, 1962

Government type: parliamentary democracy

Head of state: Queen Elizabeth II, represented by Gov.-Gen. Sir Kenneth Hall

Head of government: Prime Min. Portia Simpson Miller

Monetary unit: Jamaican dollar

GDP: $20.88 billion (2008 est.)   Per capita GDP: $7,400

Industries: tourism, bauxite, textiles, food processing, light manufactures, rum, cement, metal, paper, chemical products

Chief crops: sugarcane, bananas, coffee, citrus, potatoes, vegetables

Minerals: bauxite, gypsum, limestone

Life expectancy at birth (years): male, 74.0; female, 78.2

Literacy rate: 85%

Websites: www.cabinet.gov.jm
www.jis.gov.jm

MEXICO

FOR MAP, SEE PAGE 177

Population: 111,211,789

Ethnic groups: mestizo 60%, Amerindian 30%, white 9%

Principal languages: Spanish (official), Náhuatl, Maya, Zaptec, Otomi, Miztec, other indigenous

Mayan ruins, Chichen Itza, Mexico

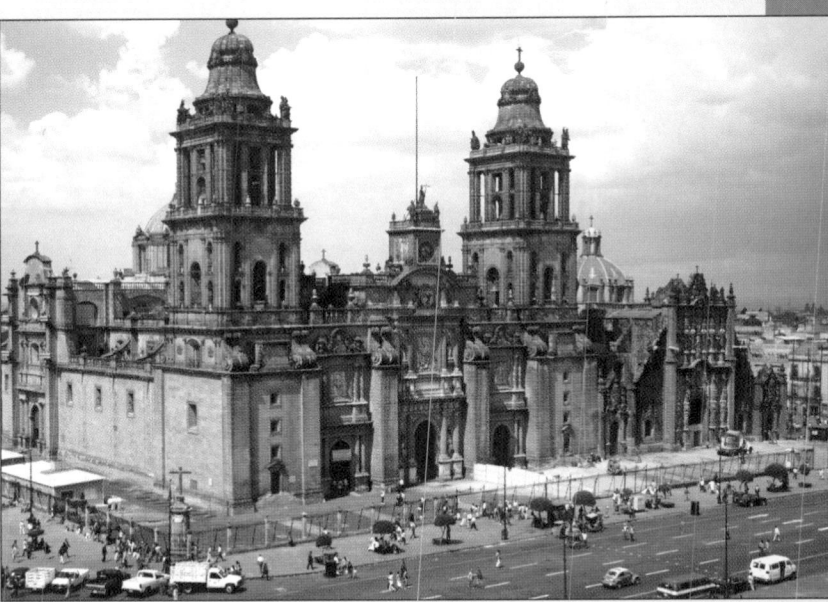

Cathedral on the Zocalo (main square), Mexico City, Mexico

Chief religions: Roman Catholic 89%, Protestant 6%

Area: 761,610 sq mi (1,972,550 sq km)

Topography: The Sierra Madre Occidental Mountains run northwest to southeast near the west coast; the Sierra Madre Oriental Mountains run near the Gulf of Mexico. They join south of Mexico City. Between the two ranges lies the dry central plateau, 5,000 to 8,000 ft (1,500 to 2,400 m) in altitude, rising toward the south, with temperate vegetation. Coastal lowlands are tropical. About 45% of the land is arid.

Capital: Mexico City (pop., 19,493,000)

Independence date: September 16, 1810

Government type: federal republic

Head of state and government: Pres. Felipe de Jesús Calderón Hinojosa

Monetary unit: new peso

GDP: $1,559 billion (2009 est.)   Per capita GDP: $14,200

Industries: food and beverages, tobacco, chemicals, iron and steel, petroleum, mining, textiles, clothing, motor vehicles, consumer durables, tourism

Chief crops: corn, wheat, soybeans, rice, beans, cotton, coffee, fruit, tomatoes

Minerals: petroleum, silver, copper, gold, lead, zinc, natural gas

Life expectancy at birth (years): male, 72.2; female, 77.8

Literacy rate: 89.6%

Website: www.presidencia.gob.mx/?NLang=en

NICARAGUA

FOR MAP, SEE PAGE 203

Population: 5,891,199

Ethnic groups: mestizo 69%, white 17%, black 9%, Amerindian 5%

Principal languages: Spanish (official), indigenous languages, English on Atlantic coast

Chief religion: Roman Catholic 85%

Area: 50,000 sq mi (129,490 sq km)

Topography: Both the Caribbean and the Pacific coasts are over 200 mi (320 m) long. The Cordillera Mountains, with many volcanic peaks, run northwest to southeast through the middle of the country. Between this and a volcanic range to the east lie Lakes Managua and Nicaragua.

Capital: Managua (pop., 1,098,000)

Independence date: September 15, 1821

Nicaragua *(continued)*

Government type: republic

Head of state and government: Pres. José Daniel Ortega Saavedra

Monetary unit: gold cordoba

GDP: $16.83 billion (2008 est.)   **Per capita GDP:** $2,900

Industries: food processing, chemicals, machinery and metal products, textiles, clothing, petroleum refining and distribution, beverages, footwear, wood

Chief crops: coffee, bananas, sugarcane, cotton, rice, corn, tobacco, sesame, soya, beans

Minerals: gold, silver, copper, tungsten, lead, zinc

Life expectancy at birth (years): male, 68.0; female, 72.2

Literacy rate: 68.2%   **Website:** www.consuladodenicaragua.com

PANAMA

FOR MAP, SEE PAGE 203

Population: 3,360,474

Ethnic groups: mestizo 70%, Amerindian-West Indian 14%, white 10%, Amerindian 6%

Principal languages: Spanish (official), English

Chief religions: Roman Catholic 85%, Protestant 15%

Area: 30,200 sq mi (78,200 sq km)

Topography: 2 mountain ranges run the length of the isthmus. Tropical rain forests cover the Caribbean coast and eastern Panama.

Capital: Panamá (pop., 930,000)

Independence date: November 3, 1903   **Government type:** republic

Head of state and government: Pres. Ricardo Martinelli Berrocal

Monetary unit: balboa

GDP: $38.49 billion (2008 est.)   **Per capita GDP:** $11,600

Industries: construction, petroleum refining, brewing, cement, sugar milling

Chief crops: bananas, rice, corn, coffee, sugarcane, vegetables

Minerals: copper

Life expectancy at birth (years): male, 69.8; female, 74.6

Literacy rate: 90.8%   **Website:** www.embassyofpanama.org

Panama Canal

SAINT KITTS AND NEVIS

FOR MAP, SEE PAGE 199

Population: 40,131

Ethnic group: black, British, Portuguese, Lebanese

Principal language: English (official)

Chief religions: Anglican, other Protestant, Roman Catholic

Area: 101 sq mi (261 sq km)

Topography: Saint Kitts has forested volcanic slopes; Nevis rises from beaches to a central peak.

Capital: Basseterre (pop., 13,000)

Independence date: September 19, 1983

Government type: constitutional monarchy

Head of state: Queen Elizabeth II, represented by Gov.-Gen. Sir Cuthbert Montraville Sebastian

Head of government: Prime Min. Denzil Llewellyn Douglas

Monetary unit: East Caribbean dollar

GDP: $784.9 million (2008 est.)   **Per capita GDP:** $19,700

Industries: sugar processing, tourism, cotton, salt, copra, clothing, footwear, beverages

Chief crops: sugarcane, rice, yams, vegetables, bananas

Life expectancy at birth (years): male, 69.0; female, 74.9

Literacy rate: 97%

Website: www.stkittsnevis.net

SAINT LUCIA

FOR MAP, SEE PAGE 199

Population: 160,267

Ethnic groups: black 90%, mixed 6%, East Indian 3%, white 1%

Principal languages: English (official), French patois

Chief religions: Roman Catholic 90%, Protestant 10%

Area: 240 sq mi (620 sq km)

Topography: Saint Lucia is mountainous, volcanic in origin; Soufriere, a volcanic crater, is in the south. Wooded mountains run north to south to Mt. Gimie, 3,143 ft (958 m), with streams through fertile valleys.

Capital: Castries (pop., 14,000)

Independence date: February 22, 1979

Government type: parliamentary democracy

Head of state: Queen Elizabeth II, represented by Gov.-Gen. Calliopa Pearlette Louisy

Head of government: Prime Min. Kenny Anthony

Monetary unit: East Caribbean dollar

GDP: $1.8 billion (2008 est.)   **Per capita GDP:** $11,300

Industries: clothing, assembly of electronic components, beverages, corrugated cardboard boxes, tourism

Chief crops: bananas, coconuts, vegetables, citrus, root crops, cocoa

Minerals: pumice

Life expectancy at birth (years): male, 69.5; female, 76.9

Literacy rate: 67%

Website: www.stlucia.gov.lc

SAINT VINCENT AND THE GRENADINES

FOR MAP, SEE PAGE 199

Population: 104,574

Ethnic groups: black 66%, mixed 19%, East Indian 6%, Carib Amerindian 2%

Principal languages: English (official), French patois

Chief religions: Anglican 47%, Methodist 28%, Roman Catholic 13%

Area: 131 sq mi (339 sq km)

Topography: St. Vincent is volcanic, with a ridge of thickly wooded mountains running its length.

Capital: Kingstown (pop., 29,000)

Independence date: October 27, 1979

Government type: constitutional monarchy

Head of state: Queen Elizabeth II, represented by Gov.-Gen. Sir Frederick Nathaniel Ballantyne

Head of government: Prime Min. Ralph Gonsalves

Monetary unit: East Caribbean dollar

GDP: $1.1 billion (2008 est.)   **Per capita GDP:** $10,500

Industries: food processing, cement, furniture, clothing

Chief crops: bananas, coconuts, sweet potatoes, spices

Life expectancy at birth (years): male, 71.3; female, 74.9

Literacy rate: 96%   **Website:** www.svgtourism.com

TRINIDAD AND TOBAGO

For map, see page 199

Population: 1,229,953

Ethnic groups: black 40%, East Indian 40%, mixed 18%

Principal languages: English (official), Hindi, French, Spanish, Chinese

Chief religions: Roman Catholic 29%, Hindu 24%, Protestant 14%, Muslim 6%

Area: 1,980 sq mi (5,130 sq km)

Topography: Three low mountain ranges cross Trinidad east to west, with a well-watered plain between the north and central ranges. Parts of the east and west coasts are swamps. Tobago, 116 sq mi (300 sq km), lies 20 mi (30 km) northeast.

Capital: Port-of-Spain (pop., 55,000)

Independence date: August 31, 1962

Government type: parliamentary democracy

Head of state: Pres. George Maxwell Richards

Head of government: Prime Min. Patrick Augustus Mervyn Manning

Monetary unit: Trinidad and Tobago dollar

GDP: $24.19 billion (2008 est.)   **Per capita GDP:** $18,600

Industries: petroleum products, chemicals, tourism, food processing, cement, beverage, cotton textiles

Chief crops: cocoa, sugarcane, rice, citrus, coffee, vegetables

Minerals: petroleum, natural gas, asphalt

Life expectancy at birth (years): male, 65.9; female, 71.8

Literacy rate: 94%   **Website:** www.gov.tt

UNITED STATES

For map, see page 182

Population: 307,212,123 (50 states and District of Columbia)

Ethnic groups: white 75.1%, black 12.3%, Asian 3.6%, Amerindian and Alaska native 0.9% (Hispanics of any race or group 12.5%)

Principal languages: English, Spanish

Chief religions: Protestant 56%, Roman Catholic 28%, Jewish 2%

Area: 3,794,085 sq mi (9,826,635 sq km)

Topography: The area comprising the contiguous 48 states has a vast central plain, mountains in the west, and hills and low mountains in the east. Rugged mountains and broad river valleys are found in Alaska, and rugged, volcanic topography in Hawaii.

Capital: Washington, D.C. (pop., 4,098,000)

Independence date: July 4, 1776

Government type: federal republic

Head of state and government: Pres. Barack H. Obama

Monetary unit: U.S. dollar

GDP: $14,290 billion (2008 est.)   **Per capita GDP:** $47,000

Industries: petroleum, steel, motor vehicles, aerospace, telecommunications, chemicals, electronics, food processing, consumer goods, lumber, mining

Chief crops: wheat, other grains, corn, fruits, vegetables, cotton

Minerals: coal, copper, lead, molybdenum, phosphates, uranium, bauxite, gold, iron, mercury, nickel, potash, silver, tungsten, zinc, petroleum, natural gas

Life expectancy at birth (years): male, 74.6; female, 80.4

Literacy rate: 97%

Websites: www.census.gov
www.whitehouse.gov
www.firstgov.gov

MAJOR OUTLYING U.S. AREAS include two commonwealths—the Northern Mariana Islands in the Pacific Ocean and Puerto Rico in the West Indies—as well as the unincorporated territories American Samoa and Guam in the Pacific and the Virgin Islands in the West Indies.

AMERICAN SAMOA: population, 65,628; area, 77 sq mi; capital, Pago Pago on island of Tutuila

GUAM: population, 178,430; area, 212 sq mi; capital, Hagåtña

NORTHERN MARIANA ISLANDS: population, 88,662; area, 184 sq mi; seat of government, Saipan

PUERTO RICO: population, 3,971,020; area, 3,515 sq mi; capital: San Juan

VIRGIN ISLANDS (ST. JOHN, ST. CROIX, ST. THOMAS): population, 109,825; area, 136 sq mi; capital: Charlotte Amalie on St. Thomas

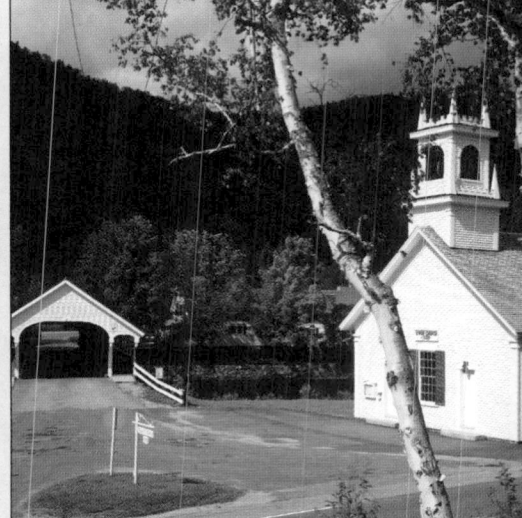

Three U.S. hallmarks: Statue of Liberty, New York Harbor (left); cable car, San Francisco (middle); New England church, New Hampshire (right)

SOUTH AMERICA

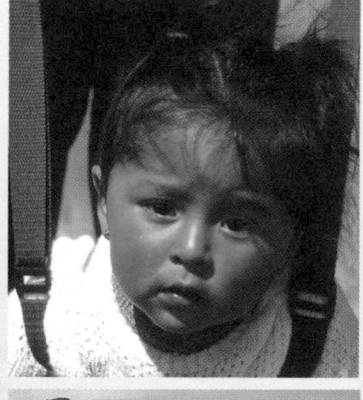

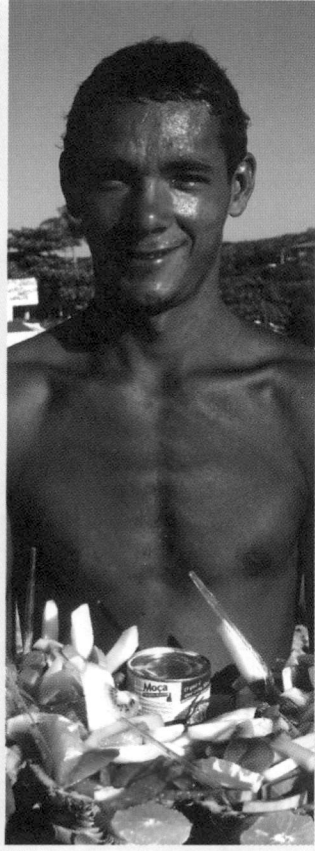

Brazil is the biggest nation in South America, and the fifth biggest in the world, in terms of both land area and population. It also has the continent's largest economy.

ARGENTINA

FOR MAP, SEE PAGE 215

Population: 40,913,584

Ethnic groups: European 97%, Amerindian 3%

Principal languages: Spanish (official), English, Italian, German, French

Chief religion: Roman Catholic 92% (official)

Area: 1,068,300 sq mi (2,766,890 sq km)

Topography: Mountains in the west are the Andean, Central, Misiones, and Southern ranges. Aconcagua is the highest peak in the western hemisphere, altitude 22,834 ft (6,959 m). East of the Andes are heavily wooded plains, called the Gran Chaco in the north, and the fertile, treeless Pampas in the central region. Patagonia, in the south, is bleak and arid. Rio de la Plata, an estuary in the northeast, 170 by 140 mi (270 by 225 km), is mostly fresh water, from the 2,485-mi (4,000-km) Parana and 1,000-mi (1,600-km) Uruguay rivers.

Capital: Buenos Aires (pop., 13,047,000)

Iguaçú Falls, Argentine-Brazilian border

Independence date: July 9, 1816   **Government type:** republic

Head of state and government: Pres. Cristina Fernández de Kirchner

Monetary unit: peso

GDP: $575.6 billion (2008 est.)   **Per capita GDP:** $14,200

Industries: food processing, motor vehicles, consumer durables, textiles, chemicals and petrochemicals, printing, metallurgy, steel

Chief crops: sunflower seeds, lemons, soybeans, grapes, corn, tobacco, peanuts, tea, wheat

Minerals: lead, zinc, tin, copper, iron ore, manganese, petroleum, uranium

Life expectancy at birth (years): male, 72.0; female, 79.7

Literacy rate: 96.2%

Websites: www.turismo.gov.ar/eng/menu.htm

BOLIVIA

FOR MAP, SEE PAGE 208

Population: 9,775,246

Ethnic groups: Quechua 30%, mestizo 30%, Aymara 25%, white 15%

Principal languages: Spanish, Quechua, Aymara (all official)

Chief religion: Roman Catholic (official) 95%

Area: 424,160 sq mi (1,098,580 sq km)

Topography: The great central plateau, at an altitude of 12,000 ft (3,600 m), over 500 mi (800 km) long, lies between two great cordilleras having three of the highest peaks in South America. Lake Titicaca, on the Peruvian border, is the highest lake in the world on which steamboats ply (12,506 ft [3,812 m]). The east-central region has semitropical forests; the llanos, or Amazon-Chaco lowlands, are in the east.

Capitals: La Paz (adminstrative) (pop., 1,477,000), Sucre (judicial) (pop., 212,000)

Independence date: August 6, 1825

Government type: republic

Head of state and government: Pres. Juan Evo Morales Aima

Monetary unit: boliviano

GDP: $43.08 billion (2008 est.)   Per capita GDP: $4,500

Industries: mining, smelting, petroleum, food and beverages, tobacco, handicrafts, clothing

Chief crops: soybeans, coffee, coca, cotton, corn, sugarcane, rice, potatoes

Minerals: tin, natural gas, petroleum, zinc, tungsten, antimony, silver, iron, lead, gold

Life expectancy at birth (years): male, 62.5; female, 67.9

Literacy rate: 83.1%

Website: www.state.gov/r/pa/ei/bgn/35751.htm

BRAZIL

FOR MAP, SEE PAGE 205

Population: 198,739,269

Ethnic groups: European 55%, Creole 38%, African 6%

Principal languages: Portuguese (official), Spanish, English, French

Chief religion: Roman Catholic (nominal) 80%

Area: 3,286,490 sq mi (8,511,970 sq km)

Topography: Brazil's Atlantic coastline stretches 4,603 mi (7,408 km). In the north is the heavily wooded Amazon basin covering half the country. Its network of rivers is navigable for 15,814 mi (25,450 km). The Amazon itself flows 2,093 mi (3,368 km) in Brazil, all navigable. The northeast region is semiarid scrubland, heavily settled and poor. The south-central region, favored by climate and resources, has almost half of the population and produces 75% of farm goods and 80% of industrial output. The narrow coastal belt includes most of the major cities.

Capital: Brasília (pop., 3,099,000)

Independence date: September 7, 1822

Government type: federal republic

Head of state and government: Pres. Luis Inacio Lula da Silva

Monetary unit: real

GDP: $1,990 billion (2008 est.)

Per capita GDP: $10,100

Ipanema Beach and Rio de Janeiro, Brazil

Industries: textiles, shoes, chemicals, cement, lumber, aircraft, motor vehicles and parts, other machinery and equipment

Chief crops: coffee, soybeans, wheat, rice, corn, sugarcane, cocoa, citrus

Minerals: bauxite, gold, iron ore, manganese, nickel, phosphates, platinum, tin, uranium, petroleum

Life expectancy at birth (years): male, 67.5; female, 75.6

Literacy rate: 83.3%

Website: www.brasilemb.org

CHILE

FOR MAP, SEE PAGE 215

Population: 16,601,707

Ethnic groups: European and mestizo 95%, Amerindian 3%

Principal languages: Spanish (official), Araucanian

Chief religions: Roman Catholic 89%, Protestant 11%

Area: 292,260 sq mi (756,950 sq km)

Topography: The Andes Mountains on the eastern border include some of the world's highest peaks; on the west is the 2,650 mi (4,265 km) Pacific coast. The country's width varies between 100 and 250 mi (160 and 400 km). In the north is the Atacama Desert, in the center are agricultural regions, in the south, forests and grazing lands.

Capital: Santiago (pop., 5,478,000)

Independence date: September 18, 1810

Government type: republic

Head of state and government: Pres. Verónica Michelle Bachelet Jeria

Monetary unit: peso

GDP: $245.3 billion (2008 est.)

Per capita GDP: $14,900

Industries: mining, food-stuffs, fish processing, iron and steel, wood and wood products, transport equipment, cement, textiles

Chief crops: wheat, corn, grapes, beans, sugar beets, potatoes, fruit

Minerals: copper, timber, iron ore, nitrates, precious metals, molybdenum

Life expectancy at birth (years): male, 73.1; female, 79.8

Literacy rate: 95.2%

Website: www.chileangovernment.cl

Torres del Paine National Park, Chile

TIERRA DEL FUEGO is the largest (18,800 sq mi [48,700 sq km]) island in the archipelago of the same name at the southern tip of South America, an area of majestic mountains, tortuous channels, and high winds. Part of the island is in Chile, part in Argentina. Punta Arenas, on a mainland peninsula, is the world's southernmost city (population about 70,000); Puerto Williams is the southern-most settlement.

COLOMBIA

FOR MAP, SEE PAGE 210

Population: 45,644,023

Ethnic groups: mestizo 58%, European 20%, Creole 14%, black 4%, black-Amerindian 1%, Amerindian 3%

Principal language: Spanish (official)

Chief religion: Roman Catholic 90%

Colombia *(continued)*

Area: 439,740 sq mi (1,138,910 sq km)

Topography: Three ranges of Andes—Western, Central, and Eastern Cordilleras—run through the country from north to south. The eastern range consists mostly of high tablelands, densely populated. The Magdalena River rises in the Andes and flows north to the Caribbean through a rich alluvial plain. Sparsely settled plains in the east are drained by the Orinoco and Amazon systems.

Capital: Bogotá (pop., 7,290,000)

Independence date: July 20, 1810

Government type: republic

Head of state and government: Pres. Álvaro Uribe Vélez

Monetary unit: peso

GDP: $399.4 billion (2008 est.)   **Per capita GDP:** $8,900

Industries: textiles, food processing, oil, clothing and footwear, beverages, chemicals, cement, gold, coal, emeralds

Chief crops: coffee, cut flowers, bananas, rice, tobacco, corn, sugarcane, cocoa beans, oilseed, vegetables

Minerals: petroleum, natural gas, coal, iron ore, nickel, gold, copper, emeralds

Life expectancy at birth (years): male, 67.6; female, 75.4

Literacy rate: 91.3%

Website: www.colombiaembassy.org

ECUADOR

FOR MAP, SEE PAGE 208

Population: 14,451,101

Ethnic groups: mestizo 65%, Amerindian 25%, black 3%

Principal languages: Spanish (official), Amerindian languages (especially Quechua)

Chief religion: Roman Catholic 95%

Area: 109,480 sq mi (283,560 sq km)

Topography: Two ranges of Andes run north and south, splitting the country into three zones: hot, humid lowlands on the coast; temperate highlands between the ranges; and rainy, tropical lowlands to the east.

Capital: Quito (pop., 1,451,000)

Independence date: May 24, 1822

Government type: republic

Head of state and government: Pres. Rafael Correa

Monetary unit: U.S. dollar

GDP: $107.1 billion (2008 est.)

Per capita GDP: $7,500

Industries: petroleum, food processing, textiles, metal work, paper and wood products, chemicals, plastics, fishing, lumber

Chief crops: bananas, coffee, cocoa, rice, potatoes, manioc (tapioca), plantains, sugarcane

Minerals: petroleum

Life expectancy at birth (years): male, 73.2; female, 79.0

Literacy rate: 90.1%

Website: www.ecuador.org

An Ecuadoran market

GUYANA

FOR MAP, SEE PAGE 211

Population: 772,298

Ethnic groups: East Indian 50%, black 36%, Amerindian 7%

Principal languages: English (official), Amerindian dialects, Creole, Hindi, Urdu

Chief religions: Christian 50%, Hindu 35%, Muslim 10%

Area: 83,000 sq mi (214,970 sq km)

Topography: Dense tropical forests cover much of the land, although a flat coastal area up to 40 mi (65 km) wide, where 90% of the population lives, provides rich alluvial soil for agriculture. A grassy savanna divides the two zones.

Capital: Georgetown (pop., 231,000)

Independence date: May 26, 1966   **Government type:** republic

Head of state: Pres. Bharrat Jagdeo

Head of government: Prime Min. Samuel Hinds

Monetary unit: Guyana dollar

GDP: $3.01 billion (2008 est.)   **Per capita GDP:** $3,900

Industries: sugar, rice milling, timber, textiles, mining

Chief crops: sugar, rice, wheat, vegetable oils

Minerals: bauxite, gold, diamonds

Life expectancy at birth (years): male, 60.1; female, 64.8

Literacy rate: 98.1%

Website: www.guyana.org

Guyanese rain forest

PARAGUAY

FOR MAP, SEE PAGE 205

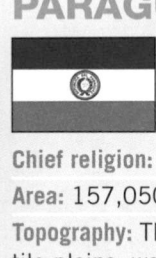

Population: 6,995,655

Ethnic groups: mestizo 95%

Principal languages: Spanish, Guaraní (both official)

Chief religion: Roman Catholic 90%

Area: 157,050 sq mi (406,750 sq km)

Topography: The Paraguay River bisects the country. To the east are fertile plains, wooded slopes, and grasslands. To the west is the Gran Chaco plain, with marshes and scrub trees. The extreme west is arid.

Capital: Asunción (pop., 1,639,000)

Independence date: May 14, 1811

Government type: republic

Head of state and government: Pres. Fernando Lugo

Monetary unit: guarani

GDP: $28.71 billion (2008 est.)   **Per capita GDP:** $4,200

Industries: sugar, cement, textiles, beverages, wood products

Chief crops: cotton, sugarcane, soybeans, corn, wheat, tobacco, cassava, fruits, vegetables

Minerals: iron ore, manganese, limestone

Life expectancy at birth (years): male, 72.1; female, 77.3

Literacy rate: 92.1%

Website: www.paraguay.com

PERU

For map, see page 214

Population: 29,546,963

Ethnic groups: Amerindian 45%, mestizo 37%, white 15%

Principal languages: Spanish, Quechua (both official); Aymara

Chief religion: Roman Catholic (official) 90%

Area: 496,230 sq mi (1,285,220 sq km)

Topography: An arid coastal strip, 10 to 100 mi (16 to 160 km) wide, supports much of the population thanks to widespread irrigation. The Andes cover 27% of the land area. The uplands are well-watered, as are the eastern slopes reaching to the Amazon basin, which covers half the country with its forests and jungles.

Capital: Lima (pop., 7,899,000)

Independence date: July 28, 1821   **Government type:** republic

Head of state: Pres. Alan García Pérez

Head of government: Prime Min. Jorge Alfonso Alejandro Del Castillo Gálvez

Monetary unit: new sol

GDP: $238.9 billion (2008 est.)   **Per capita GDP:** $8,400

Industries: mining, petroleum, fishing, textiles, clothing, food processing, cement, auto assembly, steel, shipbuilding, metal fabrication

Chief crops: coffee, cotton, sugarcane, rice, wheat, potatoes, corn, plantains, coca

Minerals: copper, silver, gold, petroleum, iron ore, coal, phosphate, potash

Life expectancy at birth (years): male, 67.5; female, 71.0

Literacy rate: 88.3%

Website: www.peru.info/perueng.asp

SURINAME

For map, see page 211

Population: 481,267

Ethnic groups: East Indians 37%, Creole 31%, Javanese 15%, Maroons 10%, Amerindian 2%, Chinese 2%, white 1%

Principal languages: Dutch (official), English, Sranang Tongo (an English Creole), Hindustani, Javanese

Chief religions: Hindu 27%, Protestant 25%, Roman Catholic 23%, Muslim 20%

Area: 63,040 sq mi (163,270 sq km)

Topography: A flat Atlantic coast, where dikes permit agriculture. Inland is a forest belt; to the south, largely unexplored hills cover 75% of the country.

Capital: Paramaribo (pop., 253,000)

Independence date: November 25, 1975   **Government type:** republic

Head of state and government: Pres. Runaldo Ronald Venetiaan

Monetary unit: guilder

GDP: $4.256 billion (2008 est.)   **Per capita GDP:** $8,900

Industries: mining, alumina production, oil, lumbering, food processing, fishing

Chief crops: paddy rice, bananas, palm kernels, coconuts, plantains, peanuts

Minerals: kaolin, bauxite, gold, nickel, copper, platinum, iron ore

Life expectancy at birth (years): male, 66.8; female, 71.6

Literacy rate: 93%   **Website:** www.surinameembassy.org

URUGUAY

For map, see page 215

Population: 3,494,382

Ethnic groups: white 88%, mestizo 8%, black 4%

Principal languages: Spanish (official), Portunol/Brazilero (Portuguese-Spanish)

Chief religion: Roman Catholic 66%

Area: 68,040 sq mi (176,220 sq km)

Topography: Uruguay is composed of rolling, grassy plains and hills, well watered by rivers flowing west to the Uruguay River.

Capital: Montevideo (pop., 1,341,000)

Independence date: August 25, 1825   **Government type:** republic

Head of state and government: Pres. Tabaré Ramón Vázquez Rosas

Monetary unit: peso

GDP: $42.46 billion (2008 est.)   **Per capita GDP:** $12,200

Industries: food processing, electrical machinery, transport equipment, petroleum products, textiles, chemicals, beverages

Chief crops: rice, wheat, corn, barley

Life expectancy at birth (years): male, 72.7; female, 79.2

Literacy rate: 97.3%

Website: www.uruwashi.org

VENEZUELA

For map, see page 210

Population: 26,814,843

Ethnic groups: Spanish, Italian, Portuguese, Arab, German, black, indigenous

Principal languages: Spanish (official), numerous indigenous dialects

Chief religion: Roman Catholic 96%

Area: 352,140 sq mi (912,050 sq km)

Topography: The flat coastal plain and Orinoco Delta are bordered by the Andes Mountains and hills. Plains, called llanos, extend between the mountains and the Orinoco. The Guiana Highlands and plains are south of the Orinoco, which stretches 1,600 mi (2,600 km) and drains 80% of Venezuela.

Capital: Caracas (pop., 3,226,000)

Independence date: July 5, 1811

Caracas, Venezuela

Government type: federal republic

Head of state and government: Pres. Hugo Rafael Chávez Frías

Monetary unit: bolivar

GDP: $357.9 billion (2008 est.)

Per capita GDP: $13,500

Industries: petroleum, mining, construction materials, food processing, textiles, steel, aluminum, motor vehicle assembly

Chief crops: corn, sorghum, sugarcane, rice, bananas, vegetables, coffee

Minerals: petroleum, natural gas, iron ore, gold, bauxite

Life expectancy at birth (years): male, 71.0; female, 77.3

Literacy rate: 91.1%

Website: www.embavenez-us.org

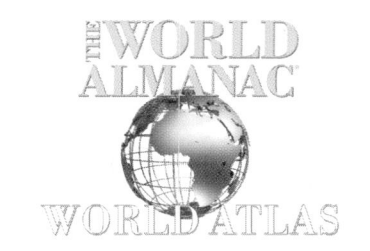

World
Map Section

World

Continents

Regions / Nations

POPULATION OF CITIES AND TOWNS
- ◉ OVER 5,000,000
- ⊙ 500,000 - 1,999,999
- ⊕ 2,000,000 - 4,999,999
- ○ UNDER 500,000

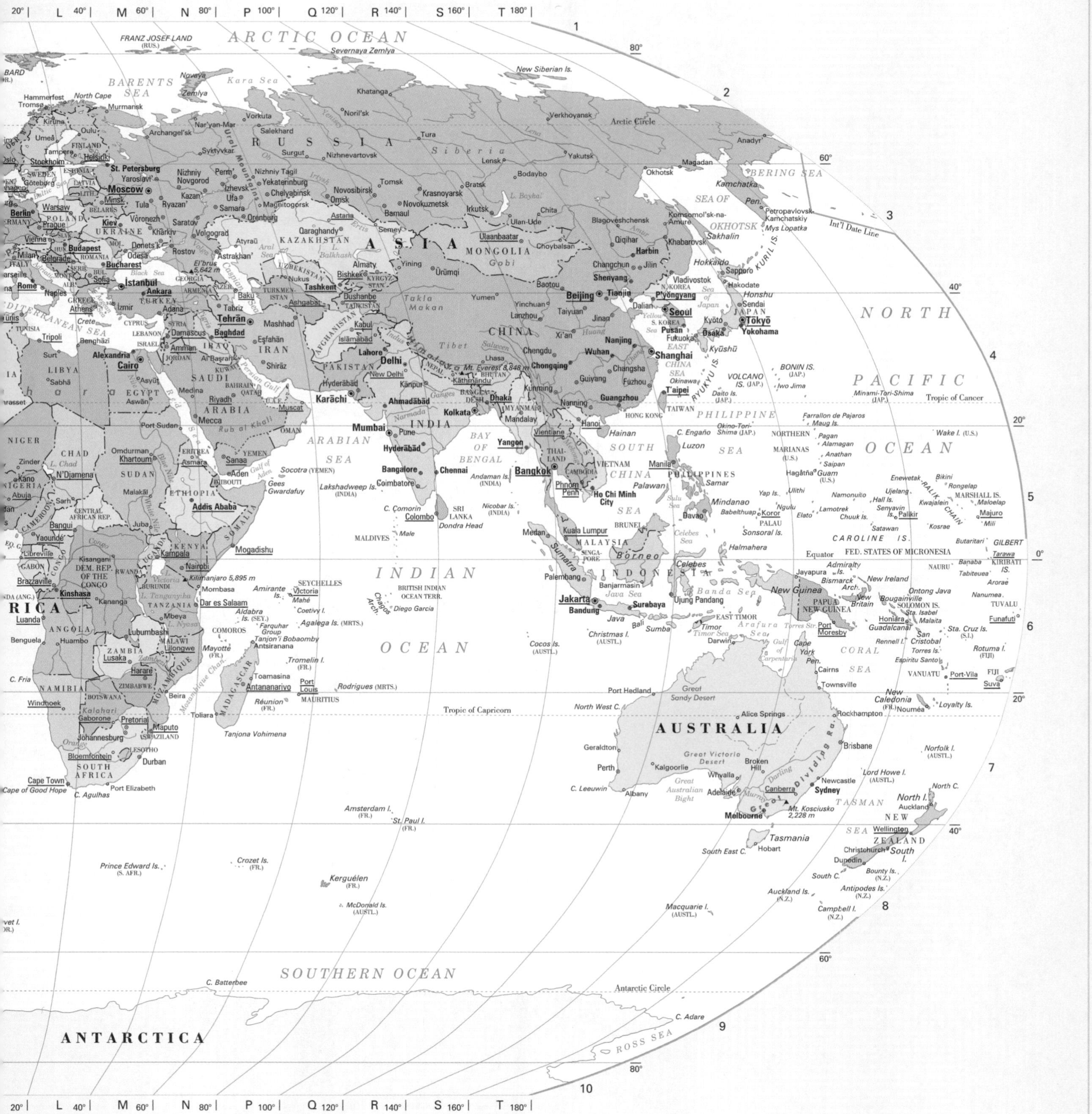

SCALE 1:80,500,000 ROBINSON PROJECTION STANDARD PARALLELS 38° N and 38° S

MILES 0 1000 2000 3000 4000
KILOMETERS 0 1000 2000 3000 4000

© HAMMOND WORLD ATLAS CORPORATION   CM-1 · A·A·A

ARCTIC OCEAN

Queen Elizabeth Is.

Greenland

Beaufort
Sea

Baffin
Bay

Wrangel I.
CHUKCHI
SEA

Pt. Barrow

Victoria I.

Arctic Circle

Denmark

Str.

Iceland

Mt. McKinley
6194 m

Great Bear L.

Hudson
Bay

Ungava
Pen.

LABRADOR

Kap Farvel

ICELAND BASIN

BERING SEA

Gulf of
Alaska

Great Slave L.

NORTH

SEA

Ireland

Aleutian Is.

ALEUTIAN TRENCH

L. Winnipeg

Churchill

Newfoundland

NORTH

Vancouver

Seattle

Great
Lakes

Montreal

C. Race

ATLANTIC

MENDOCINO FRACTURE ZONE

NORTH

Denver

Chicago

Ohio

New York

RIDGE

Azores

OCEAN

San Francisco

Dallas

C. Hatteras

Mississippi

Madeira

Rabat

MURRAY FRACTURE ZONE

PACIFIC

Baja
California

Gulf of Mexico

Miami
Bahamas

MID-ATLANTIC

Tropic of Cancer

Canary Is.

Cap Blanc

HAWAIIAN RIDGE

Hawaiian Is.

MOLOKAI FRACTURE ZONE

Mexico

Yucatan
Pen.

Cuba

Greater Antilles

Hispaniola

West
Milwaukee Deep
-8,605 m

Indies

Cape Verde Is.

Cape
Verde

Honolulu

CLARION FRACTURE ZONE

OCEAN

CARIBBEAN
SEA

Lesser
Antilles

CENTRAL

Clipperton I.

GUATEMALA
BASIN

MIDDLE-AMERICAN TRENCH

Trinidad

PACIFIC

CLIPPERTON FRACTURE ZONE

Bogotá

Llanos

Guiana Highlands

ROMANCHE FRACTURE ZONE

BASIN

Equator

Galápagos Is.

Cordillera

Selvas

Marajó

Belém

BRASIL

Ascension

Phoenix
Is.

C. de São Roque

BASIN

MID-

Line Islands

Northern
Cook Is.

Marquesas
Is.

PERU

Amazon

SOUTH

Brazilian
Highlands

SOUTH

PERU-CHILE

AMERICA

ATLANTIC

Samoan
Is.

BASIN

ATLANTIC

Southern
Cook Is.

Tahiti
Society
Is.

Tuamotu Arch.

Tropic of Capricorn

NAZCA RIDGE

Gran
Choco

Rio de Janeiro

RIDGE

TONGA TRENCH

Pitcairn I.

Sala y Gomez

Easter I.

RIO GRANDE

ATLANT

Tubuai Is.

CHILE

Cerro Aconcagua
6,959 m

PLATEAU

KERMADEC TRENCH

LOUISVILLE RIDGE

SOUTH PACIFIC OCEAN

Is. Juan Fernández

Santiago

BASIN

R. de la Plata

Pampas

ARGENTINE
BASIN

OCEAN

Tristan

Chatham Is.

SOUTHWEST
PACIFIC
BASIN

Pen.
Valdés

C. Tres Puntas

PACIFIC-ANTARCTIC RIDGE

Str. of Magellan

Tierra
del Fuego

Falkland Is.

S. Georgia

Meteor Deep
-8,325 m

Cape Horn

Drake Passage

SCOTIA SEA

S. Sandwich Is.

AMUNDSEN ABYSSAL PLAIN

S. Shetland
Is.

Antarctic
Pen.

WEDDELL
ABYSSAL
PLAIN

C. Norvegia

ROSS SEA

WEDDELL SEA

ARCTIC OCEAN

Svalbard · Franz Josef Land · Severnaya Zemlya · New Siberian Is.

BARENTS SEA · Nordkapp · Novaya Zemlya · Kara Sea · Yamal Pen. · Kola Pen. · White Sea · Yenisey · Ob'

Stockholm · L. Ladoga · Moscow · Ural Mountains · West Siberian Plain · Central Siberian Plateau · Lena · BERING SEA · Kamchatka Pen. · Kolyma Ra.

EUROPE · Carpathians · Alps · Dnipro · Kirgiz Steppe · Aral Sea · A S I A · Altai Mts. · Gobi Desert · SEA OF OKHOTSK · Kuril Is. · EMPEROR SEAMOUNTAIN CHAIN

Rome · Istanbul · Black Sea · Caucasus · El'brus 5,642 m · Caspian Sea · L. Balkhash · Tian Shan · Hokkaidō · NORTHWEST PACIFIC BASIN

MEDITERRANEAN SEA · Sicily · Cyprus · Taurus Mts. · Zagros Mts. · Tehrān · Hindu Kush · Takla Makan · Kunlun Mts. · Beijing · Sea of Japan · Tōkyō · Honshū · NORTH

Cairo · Nile · Red Sea Hills · Arabian Pen. · Persian Gulf · Himalaya · Mt. Everest 8,848 m · Ganges · Yellow Sea · East China Sea · PACIFIC

A F R I C A · L. Chad · Blue Nile · Sudan · Rub' al Khali · ARABIAN SEA · Mumbai (Bombay) · BAY OF BENGAL · Andaman Is. · Hainan · Taiwan · Tropic of Cancer · RYUKYU TRENCH · OCEAN

Ethiopian Plateau · Gulf of Aden · SOMALI BASIN · CARLSBERG RIDGE · Maldive Is. · Sri Lanka · C. Comorin · Isthmus of Kra · SOUTH CHINA SEA · PHILIPPINE SEA · Luzon · Manila · PHILIPPINE BASIN · Mariana Is. · Challenger Deep 11,033 m · MARIANA TRENCH · CENTRAL PACIFIC BASIN · Marshall Is.

Congo · Congo Basin · Kinshasa · Kilimanjaro 5,895 m · L. Victoria · L. Tanganyika · Seychelles · Chagos Arch. · Equator · INDIAN · Malay Pen. · Sumatra · Borneo · Palawan · Sulu Sea · Mindanao · Celebes Sea · Halmahera · Caroline Is. · MELANESIAN BASIN

Lusaka · Zambezi · Comoros Is. · Madagascar · Mozambique Chan. · Réunion · Mauritius · Cocos Is. · OCEAN · JAVA TRENCH · 7,450 m · Jakarta · Java Sea · Celebes · Banda Sea · New Guinea · Bismarck Arch. · New Britain · Solomon Is.

Johannesburg · Drakensberg · Cape of Good Hope · SOUTHWEST INDIAN RIDGE · CENTRAL INDIAN RIDGE · NINETYEAST RIDGE · BROKEN PLATEAU · C. Leeuwin · Great Victoria Desert · AUSTRALIA · Darling · Great Dividing Ra. · Sydney · Arafura Sea · Timor Sea · Gulf of Carpentaria · Cape York Pen. · Torres Str. · Great Barrier Reef · CORAL SEA · New Hebrides · New Caledonia · Fiji Is.

Kerguélen · McDonald Is. · KERGUÉLEN PLATEAU · SOUTHEAST INDIAN RIDGE · Great Australian Bight · Murray · Melbourne · Mt. Kosciusko 2,228 m · Tasmania · TASMAN SEA · North C. · North I. · South I.

ENDERBY ABYSSAL PLAIN · AUSTRALIAN-ANTARCTIC BASIN · Antarctic Circle · C. Batterbee · C. Adare · ROSS SEA

A N T A R C T I C A

20° L 40° M 60° N 80° P 100° Q 120° R 140° S 160° T 180°

POPULATION OF CITIES AND TOWNS
- ◉ OVER 5,000,000
- ◉ 2,000,000 - 4,999,999
- ◉ 500,000 - 1,999,999
- ○ UNDER 500,000

SCALE 1:80,500,000 ROBINSON PROJECTION STANDARD PARALLELS 38° N and 38° S

MILES 0 1000 2000 3000 4000
KILOMETERS 0 1000 2000 3000 4000

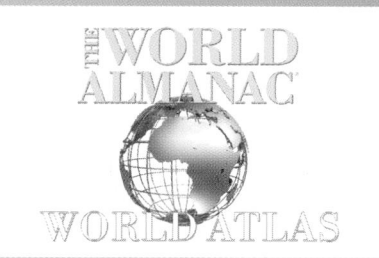

Europe

The terrain in this high-oblique, northwest-looking image, is indicative of the rugged, mountainous landscape characterizing most of Greece. Two major landform regions are captured in this image: the northwest to southeast-trending Mountains of Pindus in central Greece (north of the Gulf of Corinth), and the Peloponnisos Peninsula (south of the Gulf of Corinth). The Pindus, a massive continuation of the Dinaric Alps of Albania and the former Yugoslavia, make the land inhospitable and travel difficult. This rugged terrain caused the Greeks to become a seafaring people.

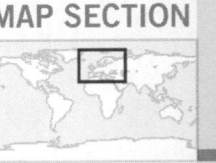

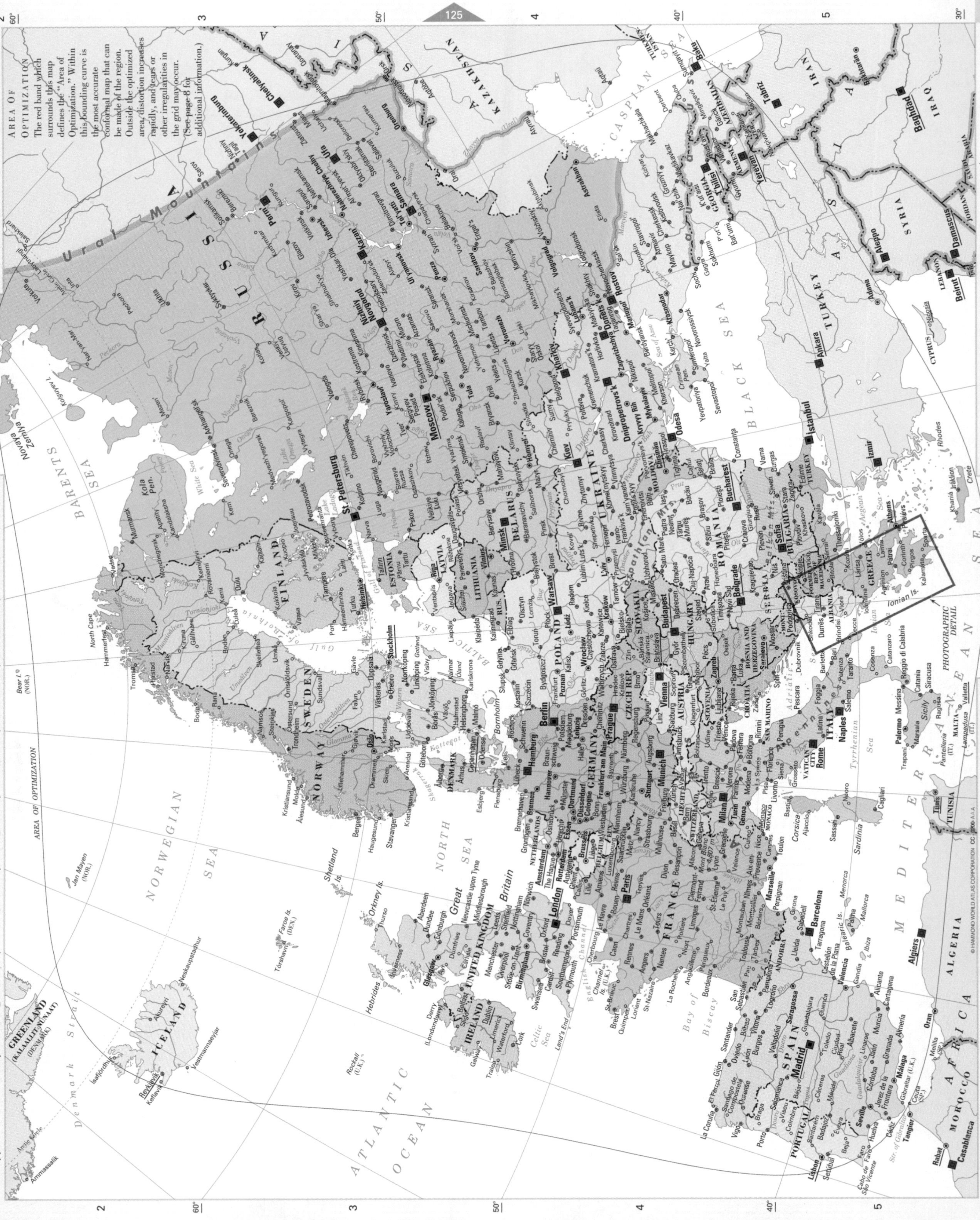

POPULATION OF CITIES AND TOWNS

■ OVER 3,000,000	● 500,000 - 999,999
■ 1,000,000 - 2,999,999	● 100,000 - 499,999
	○ UNDER 100,000

SCALE 1:20,700,000 OPTIMAL CONFORMAL PROJECTION

MILES

KILOMETERS

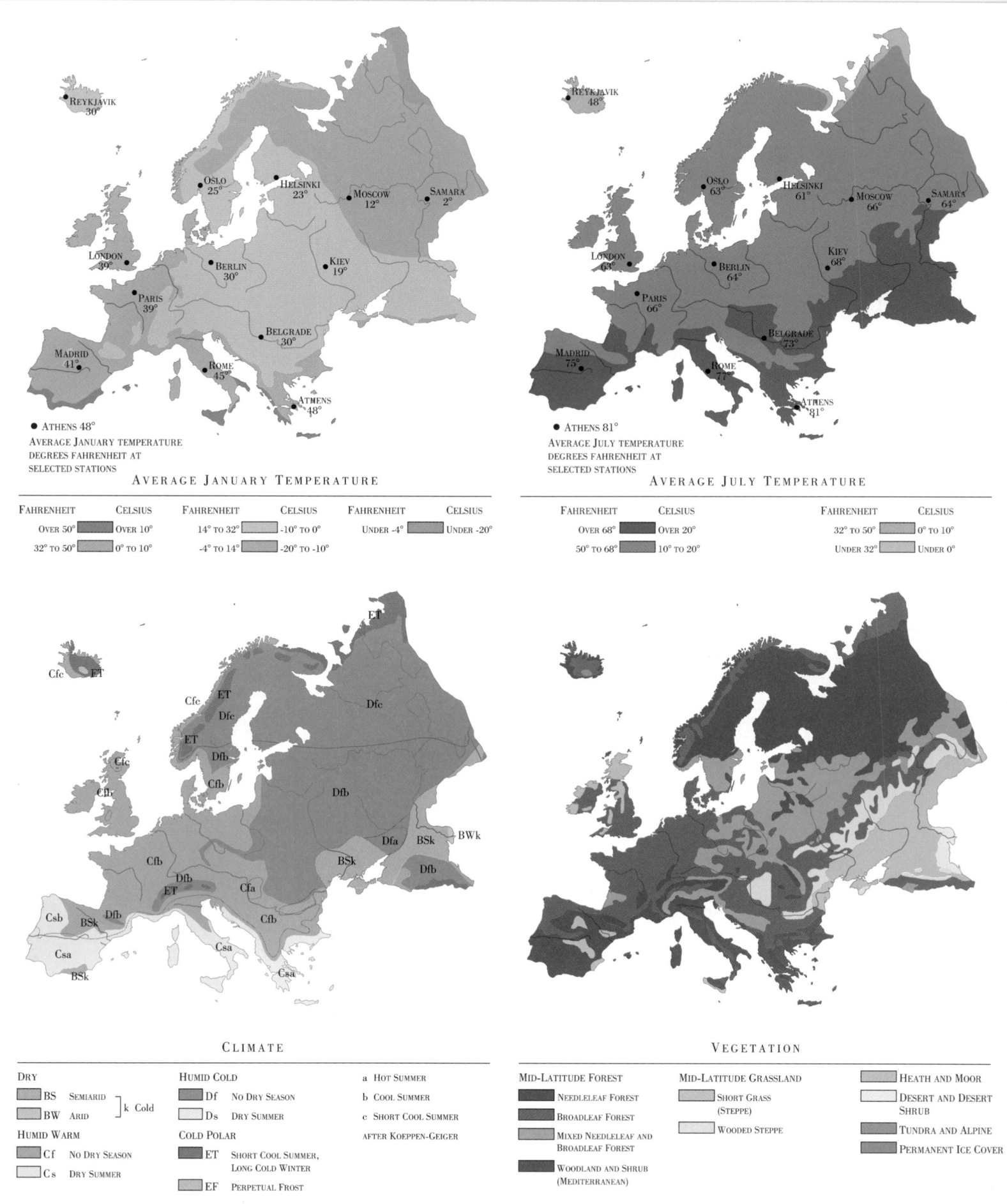

AVERAGE JANUARY TEMPERATURE

REYKJAVIK 30°
OSLO 25°
HELSINKI 23°
MOSCOW 12°
SAMARA 2°
LONDON 39°
BERLIN 30°
KIEV 19°
PARIS 39°
BELGRADE 30°
MADRID 41°
ROME 45°
ATHENS 48°

● ATHENS 48°
AVERAGE JANUARY TEMPERATURE
DEGREES FAHRENHEIT AT
SELECTED STATIONS

FAHRENHEIT	CELSIUS	FAHRENHEIT	CELSIUS	FAHRENHEIT	CELSIUS
OVER 50°	OVER 10°	14° TO 32°	-10° TO 0°	UNDER -4°	UNDER -20°
32° TO 50°	0° TO 10°	-4° TO 14°	-20° TO -10°		

AVERAGE JULY TEMPERATURE

REYKJAVIK 48°
OSLO 63°
HELSINKI 61°
MOSCOW 66°
SAMARA 64°
LONDON 63°
BERLIN 64°
KIEV 68°
PARIS 66°
BELGRADE 73°
MADRID 75°
ROME 77°
ATHENS 81°

● ATHENS 81°
AVERAGE JULY TEMPERATURE
DEGREES FAHRENHEIT AT
SELECTED STATIONS

FAHRENHEIT	CELSIUS	FAHRENHEIT	CELSIUS
OVER 68°	OVER 20°	32° TO 50°	0° TO 10°
50° TO 68°	10° TO 20°	UNDER 32°	UNDER 0°

CLIMATE

ET
Cfc   ET
Cfc   ET   Dfc
Dfc
Cfc   ET
Dfb
Cfc   Dfb
Dfb
Cfb
Dfa   BSk   BWk
Cfb   BSk
Dfb   Dfb
Csb   Dfb   ET   Cfa
BSk   Cfb
Csa
Csa
Csa
BSk

DRY

BS   SEMIARID
BW   ARID   } k Cold

HUMID WARM

Cf   NO DRY SEASON
Cs   DRY SUMMER

HUMID COLD

Df   NO DRY SEASON
Ds   DRY SUMMER

COLD POLAR

ET   SHORT COOL SUMMER,
     LONG COLD WINTER
EF   PERPETUAL FROST

a   HOT SUMMER
b   COOL SUMMER
c   SHORT COOL SUMMER

AFTER KOEPPEN-GEIGER

VEGETATION

MID-LATITUDE FOREST

NEEDLELEAF FOREST
BROADLEAF FOREST
MIXED NEEDLELEAF AND
BROADLEAF FOREST
WOODLAND AND SHRUB
(MEDITERRANEAN)

MID-LATITUDE GRASSLAND

SHORT GRASS
(STEPPE)
WOODED STEPPE

HEATH AND MOOR
DESERT AND DESERT
SHRUB
TUNDRA AND ALPINE
PERMANENT ICE COVER

REYKJAVIK
31

MURMANSK
15

BERGEN
77

HELSINKI
27

MOSCOW
22

KILLARNEY
67

LONDON
23

KIEV
24

BERLIN
23

ASTRAKHAN
6

PARIS
25

ODESSA
15

LUGANO
69

BELGRADE
27

MADRID
17

ROME
26

TIRANE
46

● BERLIN 23

AVERAGE ANNUAL RAINFALL
IN INCHES AT SELECTED STATIONS

AVERAGE ANNUAL RAINFALL

INCHES	CM	INCHES	CM	INCHES	CM
OVER 80	OVER 200	40 TO 60	100 TO 150	10 TO 20	25 TO 50
60 TO 80	150 TO 200	20 TO 40	50 TO 100	UNDER 10	UNDER 25

● CITIES WITH OVER 2,000,000
INHABITANTS

POPULATION DISTRIBUTION

DENSITY PER		SQ. MI.	SQ. KM.	SQ. MI.	SQ. KM.
SQ. MI.	SQ. KM.	130 TO 260	50 TO 100	3 TO 25	1 TO 10
OVER 260	OVER 100	25 TO 130	10 TO 50	UNDER 3	UNDER 1

FURS

FURS

FURS

OATS

FLAX

RYE

RYE

HEMP

WHEAT

DAIRY

RYE

POTATOES

WHEAT

SHEEP

RYE

POTATOES

RYE

SUGAR BEETS

CATTLE

WHEAT

OATS

HOGS

OATS

WHEAT

CORN

HOGS

CORN

SHEEP

DAIRY

WINE

CORN

BARLEY

TOBACCO
TEA

WHEAT

WINE

DAIRY

DAIRY

WHEAT

CORN

WHEAT

WINE

WINE

WINE

SHEEP
TOBACCO

WINE

FRUIT

OLIVES
WINE

OLIVES

LAND USE

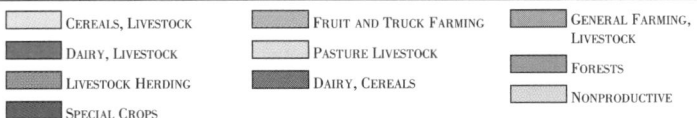

CEREALS, LIVESTOCK	FRUIT AND TRUCK FARMING	GENERAL FARMING, LIVESTOCK
DAIRY, LIVESTOCK	PASTURE LIVESTOCK	FORESTS
LIVESTOCK HERDING	DAIRY, CEREALS	NONPRODUCTIVE
SPECIAL CROPS		

MINERAL RESOURCES

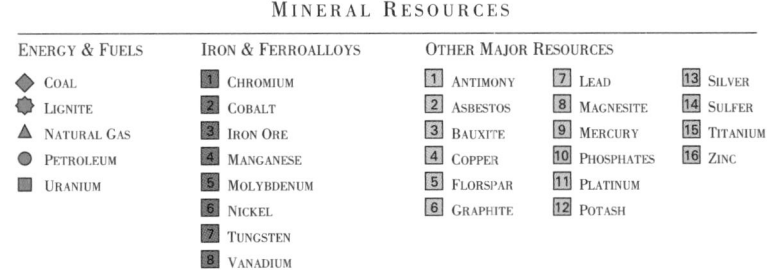

ENERGY & FUELS

◆ COAL
⬟ LIGNITE
▲ NATURAL GAS
● PETROLEUM
■ URANIUM

IRON & FERROALLOYS

1 CHROMIUM
2 COBALT
3 IRON ORE
4 MANGANESE
5 MOLYBDENUM
6 NICKEL
7 TUNGSTEN
8 VANADIUM

OTHER MAJOR RESOURCES

1 ANTIMONY
2 ASBESTOS
3 BAUXITE
4 COPPER
5 FLORSPAR
6 GRAPHITE
7 LEAD
8 MAGNESITE
9 MERCURY
10 PHOSPHATES
11 PLATINUM
12 POTASH
13 SILVER
14 SULFER
15 TITANIUM
16 ZINC

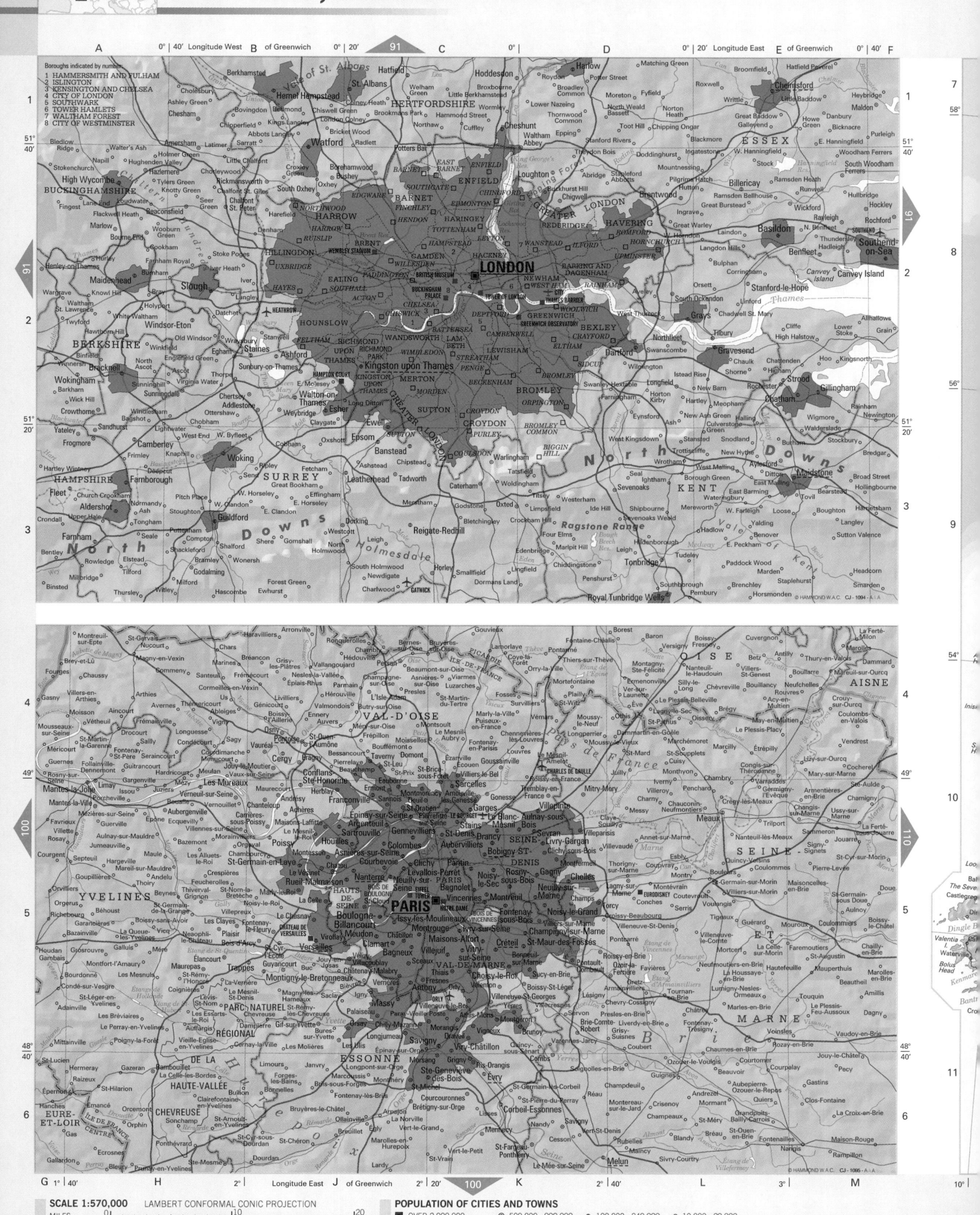

Boroughs indicated by number:
1 HAMMERSMITH AND FULHAM
2 ISLINGTON
3 KENSINGTON AND CHELSEA
4 CITY OF LONDON
5 SOUTHWARK
6 TOWER HAMLETS
7 WALTHAM FOREST
8 CITY OF WESTMINSTER

SCALE 1:570,000   LAMBERT CONFORMAL CONIC PROJECTION

MILES
KILOMETERS

POPULATION OF CITIES AND TOWNS

OVER 2,000,000   500,000 - 999,999   100,000 - 249,999   10,000 - 29,999
1,000,000 - 1,999,999   250,000 - 499,999   30,000 - 99,999   UNDER 10,000

United Kingdom, Ireland

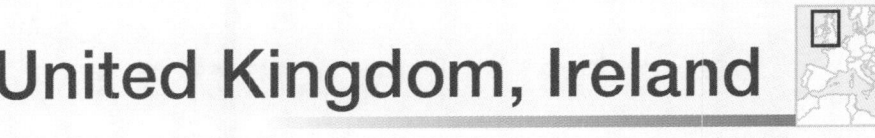

Same scale as main map

SCALE 1:3,450,000   LAMBERT CONFORMAL CONIC PROJECTION

MILES

KILOMETERS

© HAMMOND WORLD ATLAS CORPORATION   CM-1004-A-A

Longitude West of Greenwich   Longitude East of Greenwich

Southern England and Wales

POPULATION OF CITIES AND TOWNS

■ OVER 2,000,000
■ 1,000,000 - 1,999,999
● 500,000 - 999,999
● 250,000 - 499,999
● 100,000 - 249,999
● 30,000 - 99,999
○ 10,000 - 29,999
○ UNDER 10,000

SCALE 1:1,150,000 LAMBERT CONFORMAL CONIC PROJECTION

© HAMMOND WORLD ATLAS CORPORATION

NORTH SEA

POPULATION OF CITIES AND TOWNS

| ■ | OVER 2,000,000 | ⊚ | 500,000 - 999,999 | ⊙ | 100,000 - 249,999 | ○ | 10,000 - 29,999 |
| ■ | 1,000,000 - 1,999,999 | ⊙ | 250,000 - 499,999 | • | 30,000 - 99,999 | ∘ | UNDER 10,000 |

SCALE 1:1,150,000   LAMBERT CONFORMAL CONIC PROJECTION

MILES

KILOMETERS

Longitude West of Greenwich

© HAMMOND WORLD ATLAS CORPORATION   CM - A / A

Central Scotland

SCALE 1:1,150,000   LAMBERT CONFORMAL CONIC PROJECTION

MILES 0 10 20 30 40 50

KILOMETERS 0 10 20 30 40 50

POPULATION OF CITIES AND TOWNS

■ OVER 2,000,000	◉ 500,000 - 999,999
▪ 1,000,000 - 1,999,999	● 250,000 - 499,999
● 100,000 - 249,999	○ 10,000 - 29,999
• 30,000 - 99,999	○ UNDER 10,000

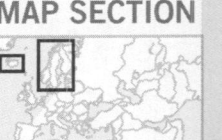

Baltic Region

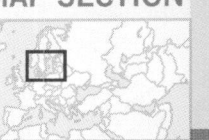

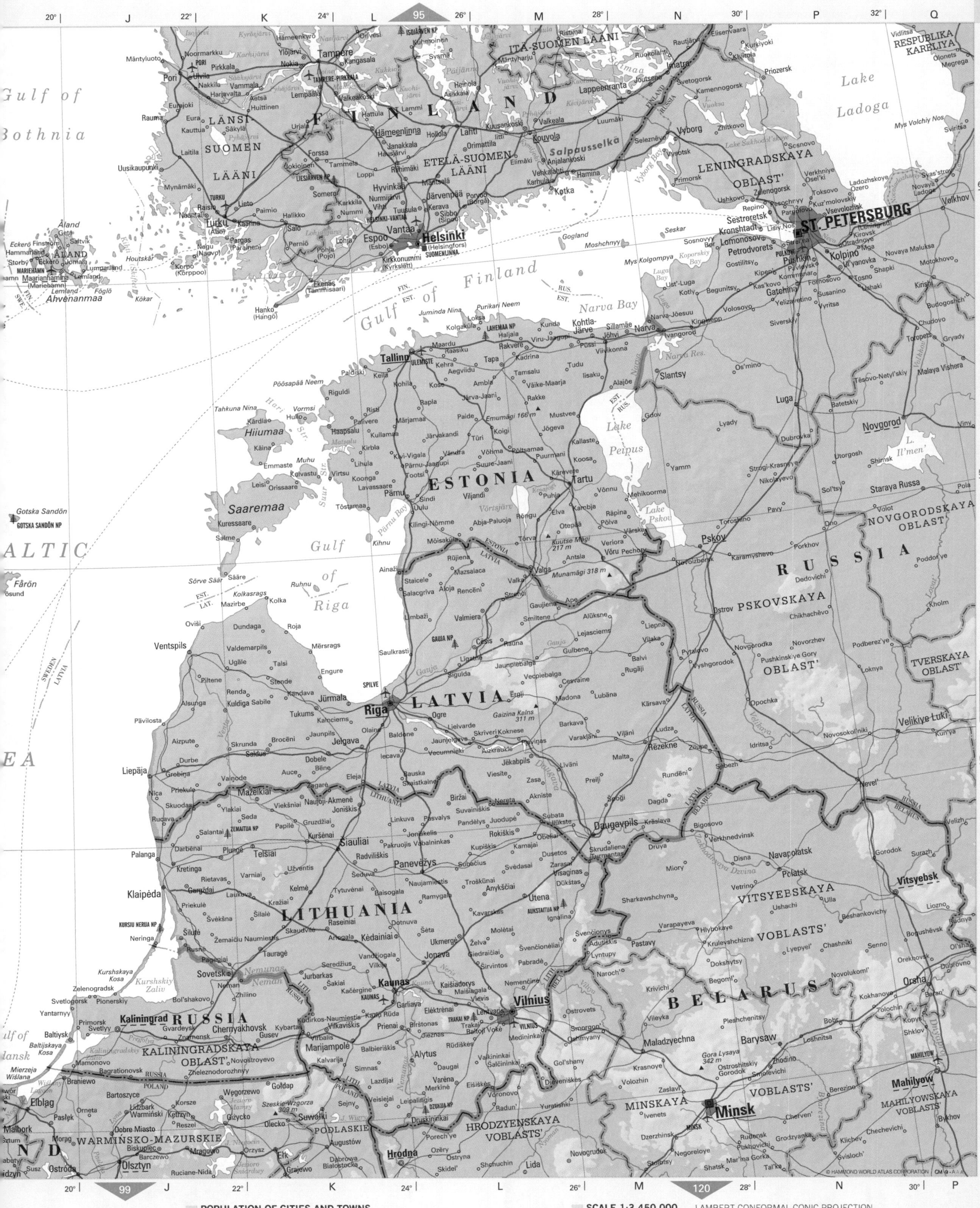

POPULATION OF CITIES AND TOWNS

OVER 2,000,000	500,000 - 999,999	100,000 - 249,999	10,000 - 29,999
1,000,000 - 1,999,999	250,000 - 499,999	30,000 - 99,999	UNDER 10,000

SCALE 1:3,450,000 LAMBERT CONFORMAL CONIC PROJECTION

MILES 0 50 100 150

KILOMETERS 0 50 100 150

POPULATION OF CITIES AND TOWNS

| ■ OVER 2,000,000 | ● 500,000 - 999,999 | ● 100,000 - 249,999 | ○ 10,000 - 29,999 |
| ■ 1,000,000 - 1,999,999 | ● 250,000 - 499,999 | ● 30,000 - 99,999 | ○ UNDER 10,000 |

SCALE 1:3,450,000   LAMBERT CONFORMAL CONIC PROJECTION

MILES

KILOMETERS

0   50   100   150

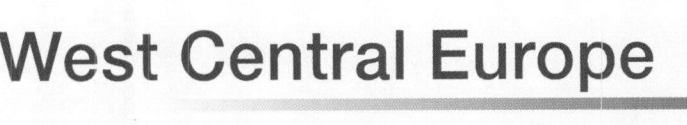
(Map of West Central Europe — showing parts of Germany, Switzerland, Austria, Czech Republic, Slovakia, Slovenia, Croatia, and Italy. Major cities include Frankfurt, Stuttgart, Munich, Nürnberg, Prague, Vienna, Bratislava, Zürich, Milan, Turin, Genoa, Venice, Bologna, Florence, Zagreb, Ljubljana. Bodies of water include the Adriatic Sea, Ligurian Sea, Golfo di Venezia, and Golfo di Genova.)

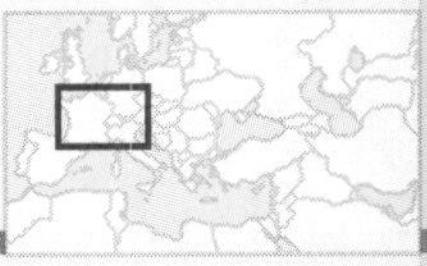

POPULATION OF CITIES AND TOWNS

■ OVER 2,000,000	◉ 500,000 - 999,999
■ 1,000,000 - 1,999,999	◉ 250,000 - 499,999
● 100,000 - 249,999	
● 30,000 - 99,999	◦ 10,000 - 29,999
	○ UNDER 10,000

SCALE 1:3,450,000   LAMBERT CONFORMAL CONIC PROJECTION

MILES 0 50 100 150

KILOMETERS 0 50 100 150

© HAMMOND WORLD ATLAS CORPORATION   CM -1015 - A-A-A

FRANCE

MIDI-PYRÉNÉES · LANGUEDOC-ROUSSILLON · PROVENCE-ALPES-CÔTE D'AZUR · Côte d'Azur

Toulouse · Montpellier · Marseille · Toulon · Nice · Cannes · Monaco

Gulf of Lion

Perpignan · ANDORRA · Andorra la Vella · PN DES PYRÉNÉES · PN D'ORDESA Y MONTE PERDIDO

Huesca · Saragossa (Zaragoza) · ARAGÓN · Lleida (Lérida) · CATALUÑA · Girona (Gerona) · Figueres

COSTA BRAVA · Costa Brava · Sabadell · Terrassa · **Barcelona** · L'Hospitalet de Llobregat · El Prat de Llobregat · Tarragona · Costa Dorada

Reus · Tortosa · Sierra de Gúdar · Peñarroya 2,019 m

MEDITERRANEAN SEA

Castellón de la Plana · Costa del Azahar · Golfo de Valencia · **Valencia** · Costa del Azahar

Alicante · Elche · Costa Blanca · Benidorm · Torrevieja · Cabo de Palos · Cartagena

Minorca (Menorca) · Mahón · MENORCA · Pollença · Alcúdia · Sóller · Inca · Manacor · **Palma de Mallorca** · Mallorca · Cabrera

ISLAS BALEARES · Ibiza · Ibiza (Eivissa) · San Antonio de Portmany · Formentera

Balearic Islands (Islas Baleares)

Barcelona inset (K–L / 6–7)

CATALUÑA · Montserrat 1,236 m · Terrassa · Sabadell · Granollers · Mataró · Badalona · Santa Coloma de Gramenet · **Barcelona** · L'Hospitalet de Llobregat · Sant Boi de Llobregat · El Prat de Llobregat · Gavà · Castelldefels · Sitges · Vilanueva i la Geltrú

MEDITERRANEAN SEA · Mahón · Palma · Ibiza

© HAMMOND W.A.C. CJ-1103-A-A-A

Madrid inset (M–Q / 8–9)

Sierra de Guadarrama · El Escorial · Las Rozas de Madrid · Alcobendas · Alcalá de Henares · **MADRID** · Móstoles · Alcorcón · Leganés · Getafe · Fuenlabrada · Parla · Pinto · CASTILLA-LA MANCHA

© HAMMOND W.A.C. CJ-1106-A-A-A

Lisbon inset (P–Q / 10–11)

LISBOA · Mafra · Loures · Odivelas · Amadora · **Lisbon** (Lisboa) · Belém · Almada · Cascais · Estoril · Costa da Caparica · Setúbal · SANTARÉM · Baía de Setúbal

ATLANTIC OCEAN · Cabo da Roca · Cabo Espichel

© HAMMOND W.A.C. CJ-1101-A-A-A

Madeira inset (U–V / 14–15)

ATLANTIC OCEAN · MADEIRA (PORT.) · Madeira · Porto Moniz · Santana · Funchal · Porto Santo · Ilhas Desertas

© HAMMOND W.A.C. CJ-1105-A-A-A

Azores inset (R–T / 12–13)

ATLANTIC OCEAN · Corvo · Flores · Graciosa · Terceira · São Jorge · Faial · Pico 2,351 m · Horta · Angra do Heroísmo · São Miguel · Ponta Delgada · Santa Maria

AZORES (PORTUGAL)

© HAMMOND W.A.C. CJ-1102-A-A-A

Canary Islands inset (W–Y / 16–17)

ATLANTIC OCEAN · CANARY ISLANDS (SPAIN) · La Palma · Santa Cruz de la Palma · PARQUE NACIONAL DE TIMANFAYA · Lanzarote · Arrecife · Tenerife · La Laguna · Santa Cruz de Tenerife · PN DEL TEIDE · Pico de Teide 3,718 m · Gran Canaria · **Las Palmas de Gran Canaria** · Fuerteventura · Hierro · Gomera · MOROCCO · WESTERN SAHARA

© HAMMOND W.A.C. CJ-1104-A-A-A

POPULATION OF CITIES AND TOWNS

- ■ OVER 2,000,000
- ■ 1,000,000 - 1,999,999
- ● 500,000 - 999,999
- ● 250,000 - 499,999
- ● 100,000 - 249,999
- ● 30,000 - 99,999
- ◉ 10,000 - 29,999
- ○ UNDER 10,000

SCALE 1:3,450,000 · LAMBERT CONFORMAL CONIC PROJECTION

MILES · KILOMETERS

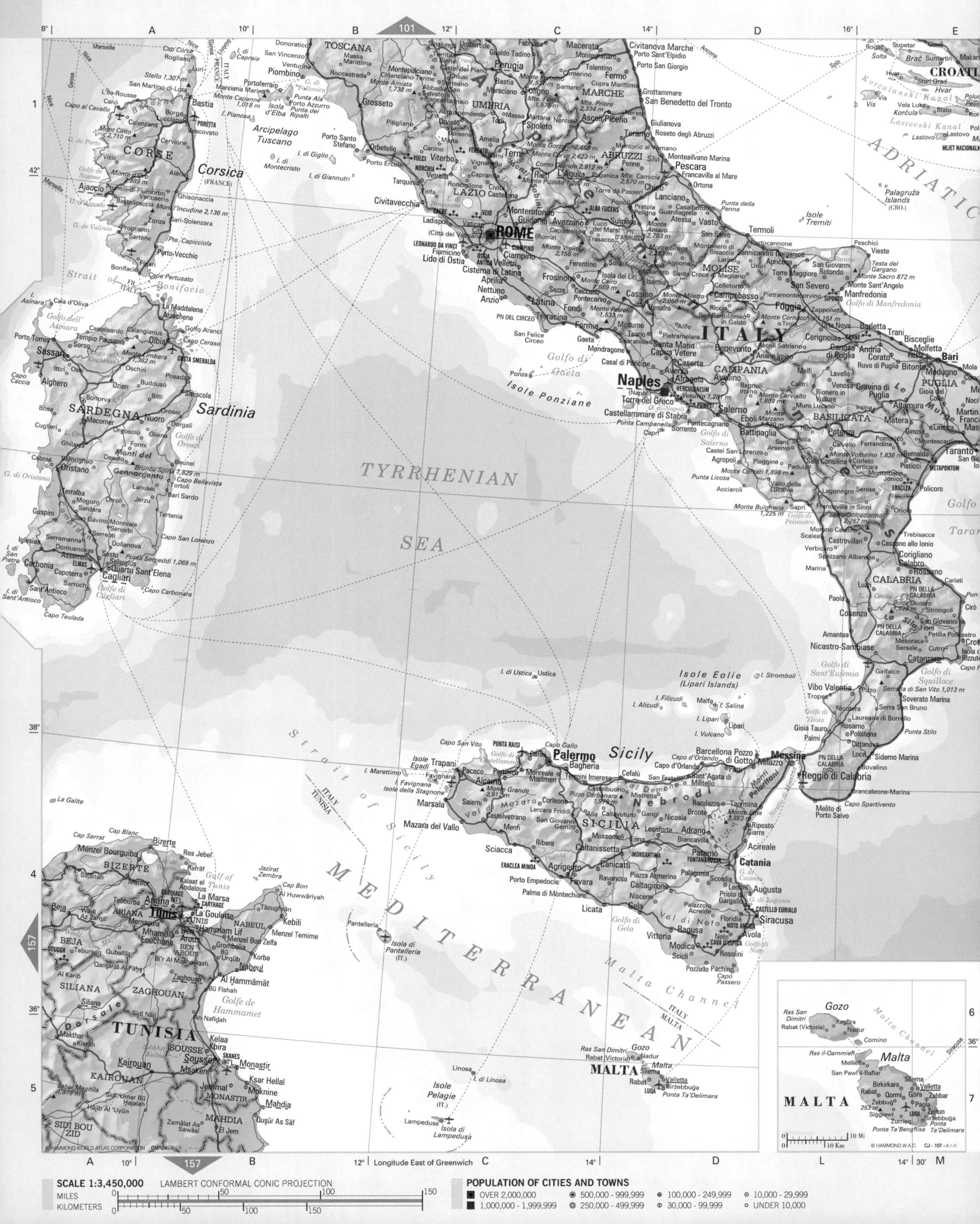

POPULATION OF CITIES AND TOWNS

■ OVER 2,000,000	● 500,000 - 999,999
■ 1,000,000 - 1,999,999	◉ 250,000 - 499,999
	● 100,000 - 249,999
	● 30,000 - 99,999
	○ 10,000 - 29,999
	○ UNDER 10,000

Southern Italy, Albania, Greece

SCALE 1:3,450,000   LAMBERT CONFORMAL CONIC PROJECTION

MILES

KILOMETERS

0   50   100   150

POPULATION OF CITIES AND TOWNS

■ OVER 2,000,000	◉ 500,000 - 999,999 ● 100,000 - 249,999 ○ 10,000 - 29,999
■ 1,000,000 - 1,999,999	◉ 250,000 - 499,999 ● 30,000 - 99,999 ○ UNDER 10,000

Longitude East of Greenwich

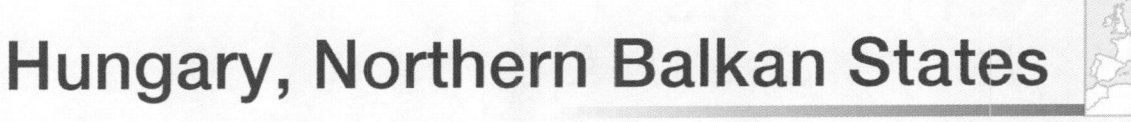

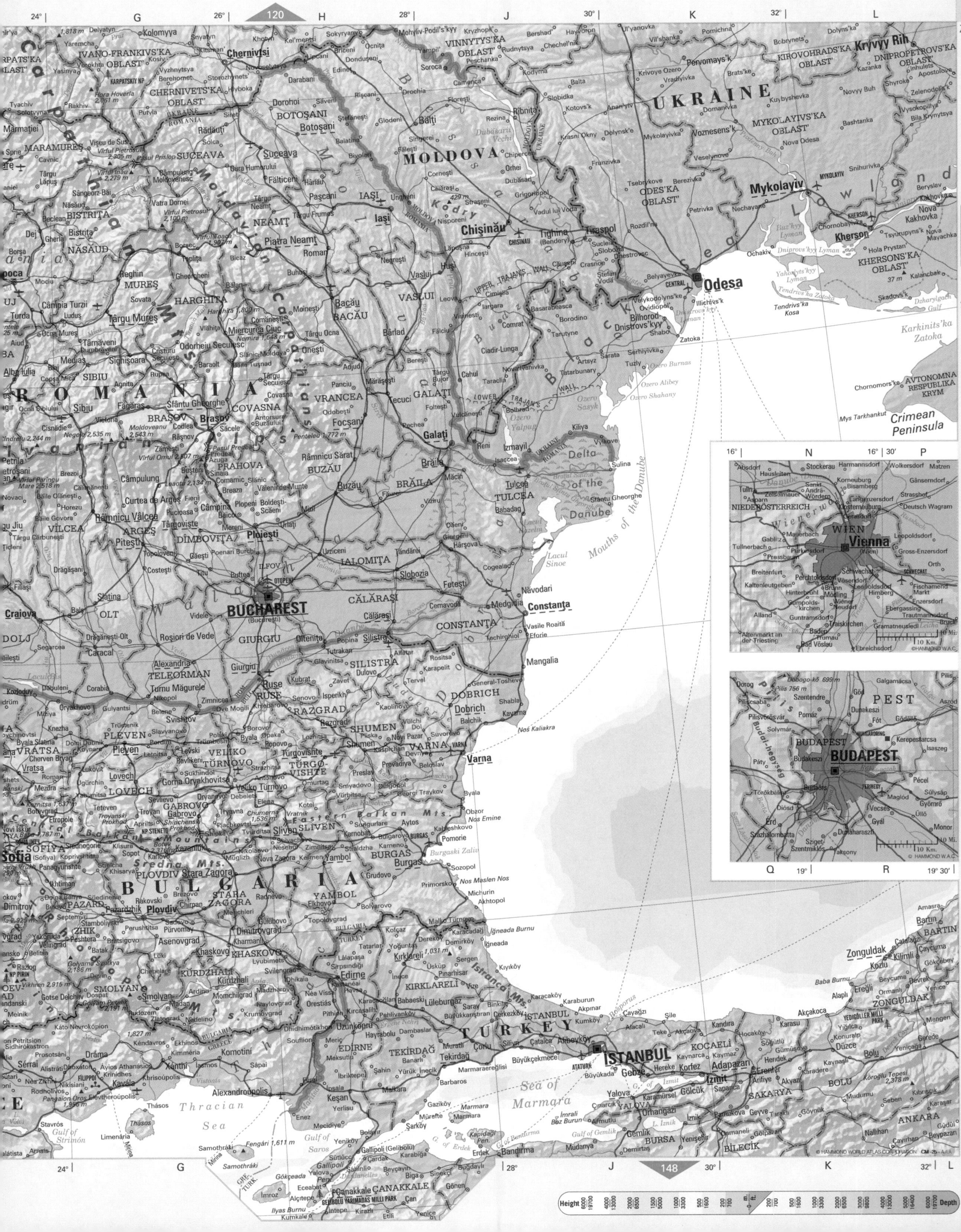

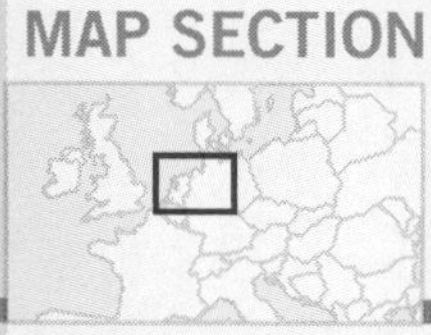

Netherlands, Northwestern Germany

NORTH SEA

West Frisian Islands

Waddenzee

GRONINGEN
FRIESLAND
DRENTHE
OVERIJSSEL
FLEVOLAND
NOORD-HOLLAND
GELDERLAND
UTRECHT
ZUID-HOLLAND
N E T H E R L A N D S
ZEELAND
NOORD-BRABANT
LIMBURG

IJsselmeer
Markerwaard
Hoornse Hop
Waddenzee

Amsterdam
The Hague
Rotterdam
Utrecht
Leiden
Haarlem
Alkmaar
Den Helder
Leeuwarden
Groningen
Assen
Zwolle
Apeldoorn
Arnhem
Nijmegen
's Hertogenbosch
Eindhoven
Tilburg
Breda
Middelburg
Vlissingen

ANTWERPEN
Antwerpen
OOST-VLAANDEREN
Ghent
B E L G I U M
VLAAMS-BRABANT
LIMBURG

Duisburg
Düsseldorf
Mönchengladbach
Essen

Westerschelde
Oosterschelde

Height   Depth

NETHERLANDS

UNITED KINGDOM

Strait of Dover

BELGIË

WEST-VLAANDEREN

OOST-VLAANDEREN

Brussels

Antwerp

Ghent (Gent)

Brugge

HAINAUT

NORD

PAS-DE-CALAIS

CALAIS

PICARDIE

SOMME

AISNE

Picardy

OISE

SEINE-MARITIME

EURE

HAUTE-NORMANDIE

ÎLE-DE-FRANCE

VAL-D'OISE

YVELINES

PARIS

SEINE-ET-MARNE

MARNE

Champagne

Brie

AUBE

EURE-ET-LOIR

CENTRE

Reims (Champagne)

Amiens

Beauvais

Boulogne-sur-Mer

Calais

Dunkirk (Dunkerque)

Dover

Folkestone

Dieppe

Abbeville

Arras

Cambrai

Saint-Quentin

Soissons

Compiègne

Creil

Versailles

Thiérache

Vimeu

Ponthieu

Collines de l'Artois

Flandre

Longitude East of Greenwich

Height   Depth

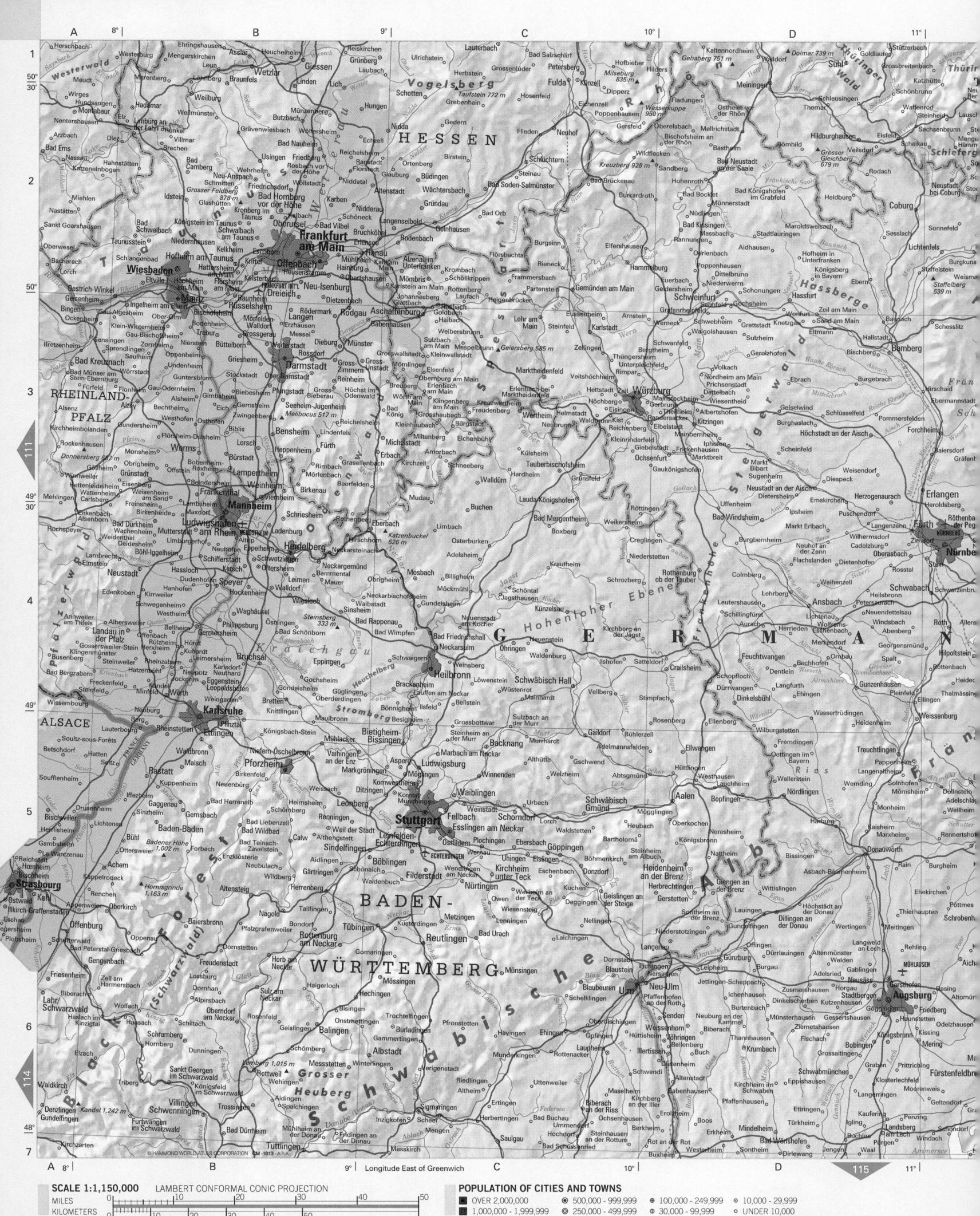

SCALE 1:1,150,000   LAMBERT CONFORMAL CONIC PROJECTION
MILES
KILOMETERS

POPULATION OF CITIES AND TOWNS
■ OVER 2,000,000   ● 500,000 - 999,999   ○ 100,000 - 249,999   ○ 10,000 - 29,999
■ 1,000,000 - 1,999,999   ● 250,000 - 499,999   ○ 30,000 - 99,999   ○ UNDER 10,000

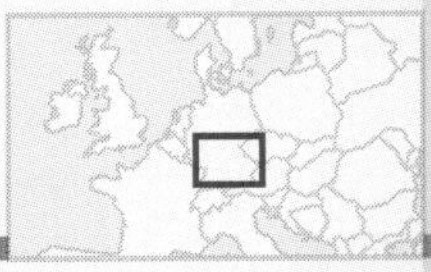

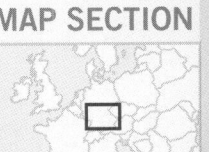

SCALE 1:1,150,000   LAMBERT CONFORMAL CONIC PROJECTION

MILES 0   10   20   30   40   50

KILOMETERS 0   10   20   30   40   50

POPULATION OF CITIES AND TOWNS

■ OVER 2,000,000	◉ 500,000 - 999,999
■ 1,000,000 - 1,999,999	◎ 250,000 - 499,999
◉ 100,000 - 249,999	○ 10,000 - 29,999
◎ 30,000 - 99,999	∘ UNDER 10,000

Longitude East of Greenwich

© HAMMOND W.A.C.   CJ - 1004 - A - A - A   © HAMMOND WORLD ATLAS CORPORATION   CM - A - A - A

101
106
104

ADRIATIC SEA

Golfo di Venezia

Golfo di Trieste

Mouths of the Po

SLOVENIA

CROATIA

Istria

UDINE
GORIZIA
PORDENONE
TREVISO
VENEZIA
VICENZA
PADOVA
VERONA
BELLUNO
ROVIGO
FERRARA
BOLOGNA
RAVENNA
FORLÌ-CESENA
RIMINI
SAN MARINO
PESARO E URBINO
ANCONA
MACERATA
PERUGIA
AREZZO
FIRENZE
PRATO
PISTOIA
SIENA

VENETO
FRIULI VENEZIA GIULIA
LOMBARDIA
EMILIA-ROMAGNA
TOSCANA
MARCHE
UMBRIA

Po
Polesine
Romagna
Montefeltro

Verona
Vicenza
Padova
Venice (Venezia)
Treviso
Belluno
Pordenone
Udine
Gorizia
Trieste
Koper
Pula
Rovinj
Poreč
Umag
Piran
Izola
Chioggia
Ferrara
Modena
Carpi
Bologna
Ravenna
Cervia
Cesenatico
Rimini
Riccione
Pesaro
Fano
Senigallia
Ancona
Jesi
Florence (Firenze)
Prato
Pistoia
Arezzo
Siena

Monti Appennino Tosco-Emiliano
Appennino Umbro-Marchigiano
Alpe di San Benedetto
Monti Palomago
Monti del Chianti

Height / Depth scale

Height | Depth

Longitude East of Greenwich

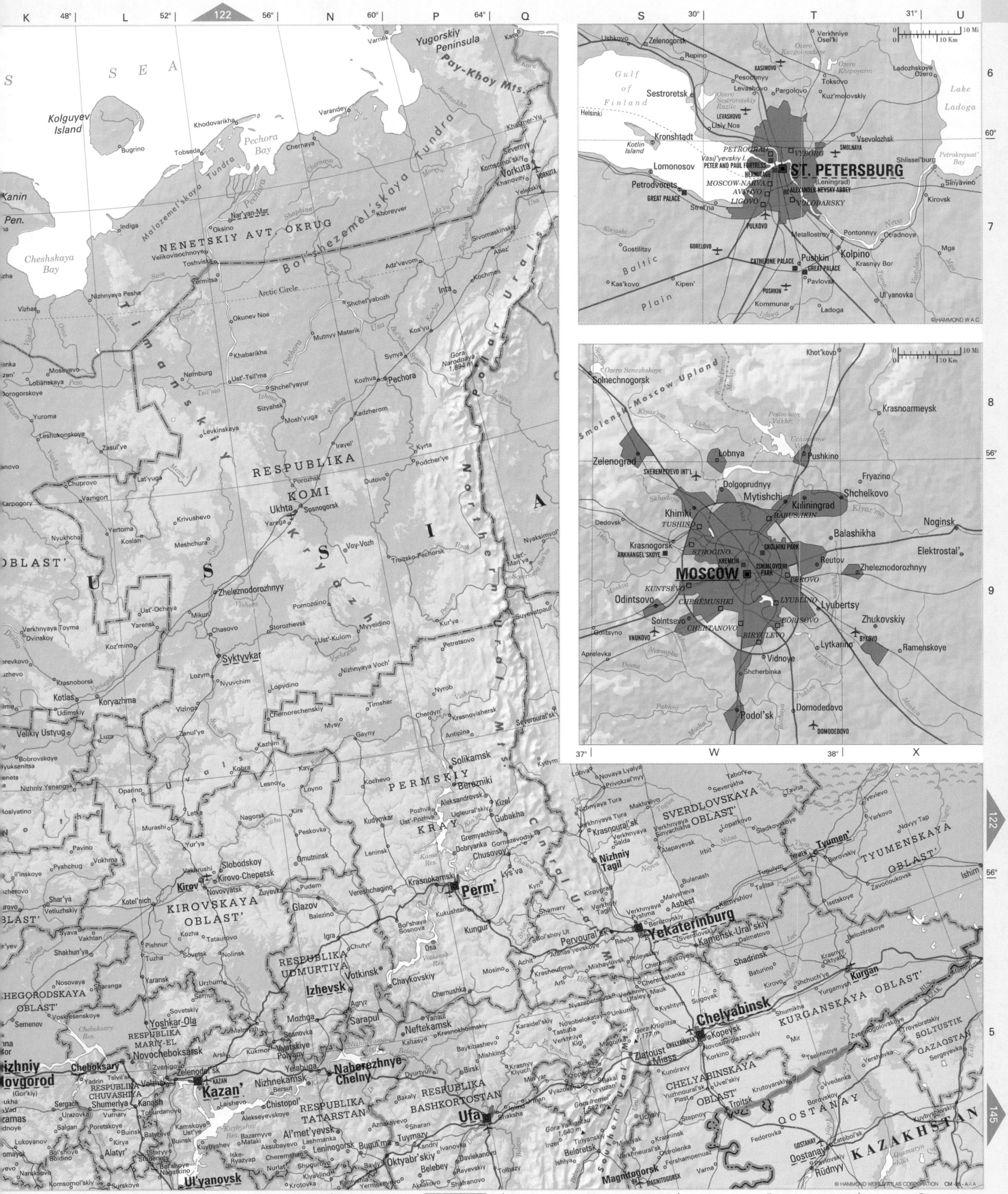

POPULATION OF CITIES AND TOWNS

- OVER 2,000,000
- 1,000,000 - 1,999,999
- 500,000 - 999,999
- 250,000 - 499,999
- 100,000 - 249,999
- 30,000 - 99,999
- 10,000 - 29,999
- UNDER 10,000

SCALE 1:6,900,000   LAMBERT CONFORMAL CONIC PROJECTION

MILES   0   100   200   300

KILOMETERS   0   100   200   300

SCALE 1:6,900,000 LAMBERT CONFORMAL CONIC PROJECTION

MILES

KILOMETERS

0   100   200   300

0   100   200   300

POPULATION OF CITIES AND TOWNS

■ OVER 2,000,000	◉ 500,000 - 999,999	● 100,000 - 249,999	○ 10,000 - 29,999
■ 1,000,000 - 1,999,999	◎ 250,000 - 499,999	● 30,000 - 99,999	○ UNDER 10,000

Height
9000 6500 5000 4000 3000 2000 1000 700 500 200
m ft.
200 700 1000 2000 3000 4000 5000 6000 7000 8000 9000 10000
Depth

Russia and Neighboring Countries

RUSSIA
(Administrative divisions are named only when they differ from their respective capitals.)

1. RESPUBLIKA ADYGEYA
2. RESPUBLIKA KARACHAYEVO-CHERKESIYA
3. RESPUBLIKA KABARDINO-BALKARIYA
4. RESPUBLIKA SEVERNAYA OSETIYA-ALANIYA
5. RESPUBLIKA INGUSHETIYA
6. RESPUBLIKA CHECHNYA
7. RESPUBLIKA DAGESTAN
8. RESPUBLIKA MORDOVIYA
9. RESPUBLIKA CHUVASHIYA
10. RESPUBLIKA MARIY-EL
11. RESPUBLIKA TATARSTAN
12. RESPUBLIKA BASHKORTOSTAN
13. RESPUBLIKA UDMURTIYA
14. RESPUBLIKA KHAKASIYA
15. YEVREYSKAYA AVTONOMNAYA OBLAST'

© HAMMOND WORLD ATLAS CORPORATION   CM-29-A-A

POPULATION OF CITIES AND TOWNS

■ OVER 2,000,000	● 500,000 - 999,999	◉ 50,000 - 99,999
■ 1,000,000 - 1,999,999	● 100,000 - 499,999	○ UNDER 50,000

SCALE 1:20,700,000   LAMBERT CONFORMAL CONIC PROJECTION

MILES   0   300   600   900

KILOMETERS   0   300   600   900

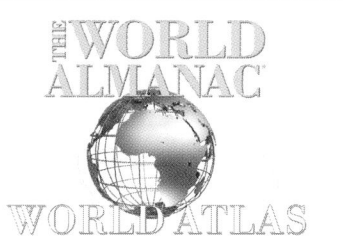

The delta of the Indus River, the longest river in southwest Asia, is the highlight of this southeast-looking, low-oblique image. Fed by snowmelt and glacial meltwater from the mountains of the Tibet Plateau, the Indus River flows nearly 1800 miles (2897 km.) before emptying into the Arabian Sea. After leaving the Tibet Plateau, the river flows onto the Punjab Plains of western Pakistan and through a vast alluvial lowland where it receives its major tributary, the Panjnad (five streams). In this severely arid landscape the rivers form precarious strips of fertile land.

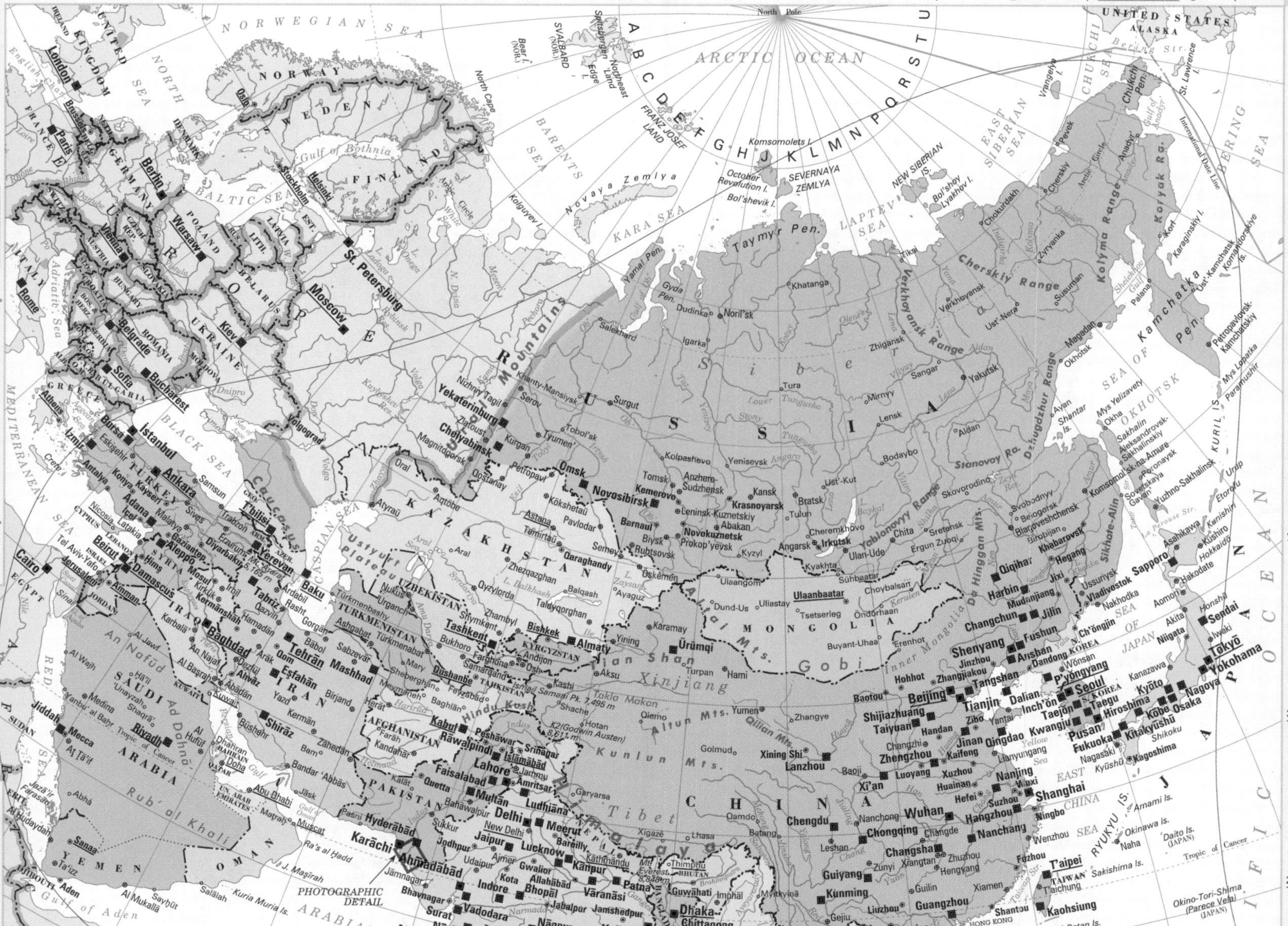

AREA OF OPTIMIZATION

The red band which surrounds this map defines the "Area of Optimization." Within this bounding curve is the most accurate conformal map that can be made of the region. Outside the optimized area, distortion increases rapidly, and tears or other irregularities in the grid may occur. (See page 8 for additional information.)

Longitude East F of Greenwich

POPULATION OF CITIES AND TOWNS

■ OVER 3,000,000	⊕ 500,000 - 999,999
■ 1,000,000 - 2,999,999	⊕ 100,000 - 499,999
	○ UNDER 100,000

SCALE 1:48,300,000 OPTIMAL CONFORMAL PROJECTION

MILES

KILOMETERS

© HAMMOND WORLD ATLAS CORPORATION   CC - 1030 - A A

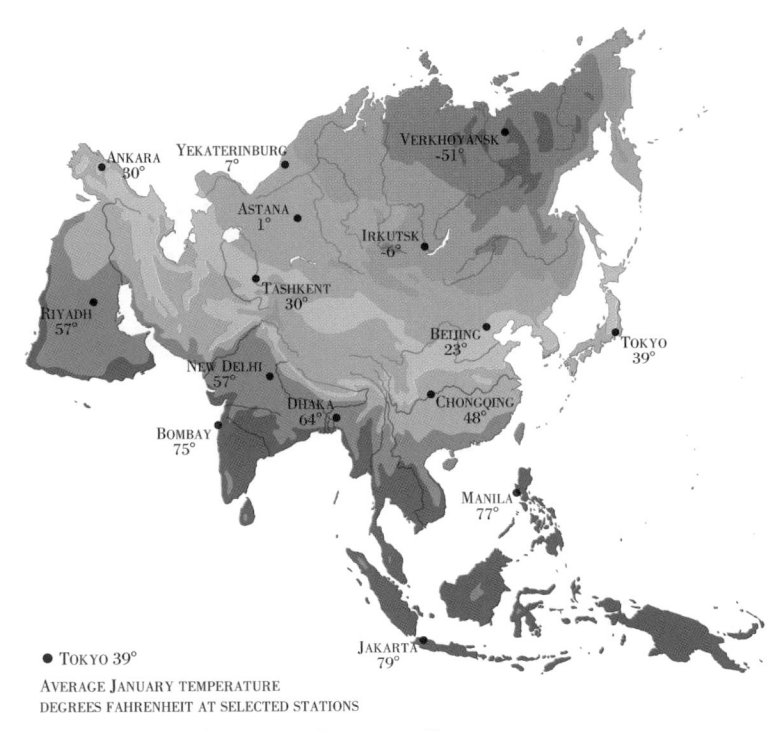

● Tokyo 39°
Average January temperature
degrees Fahrenheit at selected stations

AVERAGE JANUARY TEMPERATURE

FAHRENHEIT	CELSIUS	FAHRENHEIT	CELSIUS	FAHRENHEIT	CELSIUS
OVER 68°	OVER 20°	14° TO 32°	-10° TO 0°	-40° TO -22°	-40° TO -30°
50° TO 68°	10° TO 20°	-4° TO 14°	-20° TO -10°	UNDER -40°	UNDER -40°
32° TO 50°	0° TO 10°	-22° TO -4°	-30° TO -20°		

● Tokyo 77°
Average July temperature
degrees Fahrenheit at selected stations

AVERAGE JULY TEMPERATURE

FAHRENHEIT	CELSIUS	FAHRENHEIT	CELSIUS	FAHRENHEIT	CELSIUS
OVER 86°	OVER 30°	50° TO 68°	10° TO 20°	UNDER 32°	UNDER 0°
68° TO 86°	20° TO 30°	32° TO 50°	0° TO 10°		

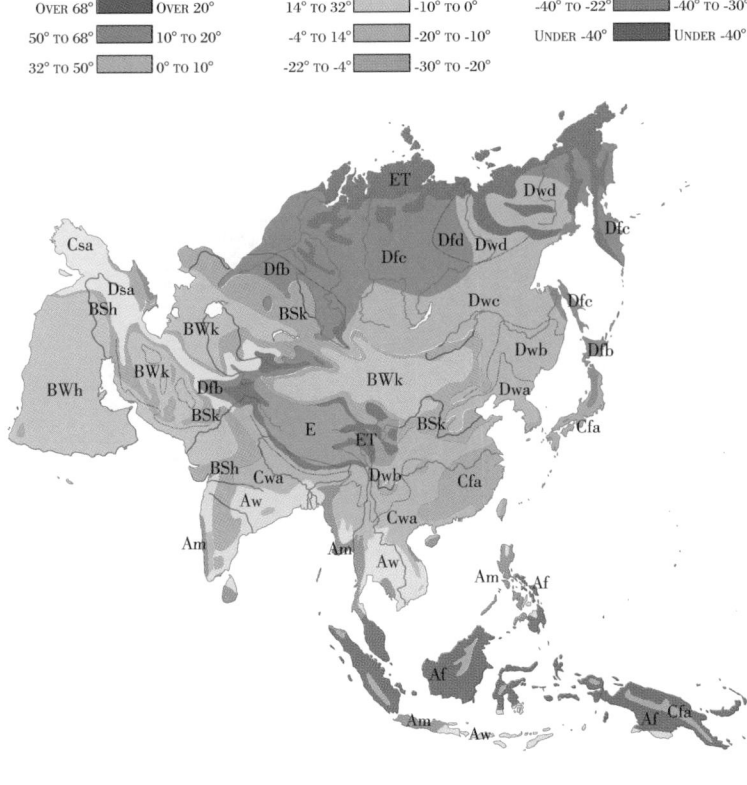

CLIMATE

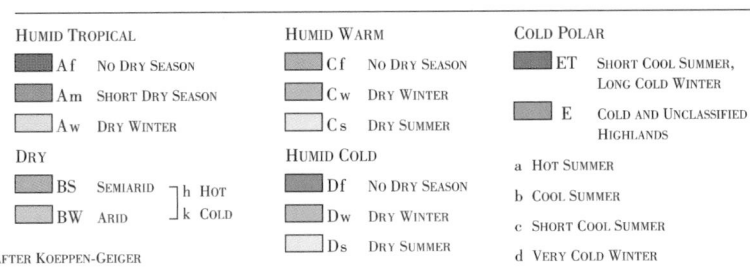

HUMID TROPICAL
- Af NO DRY SEASON
- Am SHORT DRY SEASON
- Aw DRY WINTER

DRY
- BS SEMIARID ⎤ h HOT
- BW ARID   ⎦ k COLD

AFTER KOEPPEN-GEIGER

HUMID WARM
- Cf NO DRY SEASON
- Cw DRY WINTER
- Cs DRY SUMMER

HUMID COLD
- Df NO DRY SEASON
- Dw DRY WINTER
- Ds DRY SUMMER

COLD POLAR
- ET SHORT COOL SUMMER, LONG COLD WINTER
- E   COLD AND UNCLASSIFIED HIGHLANDS

- a HOT SUMMER
- b COOL SUMMER
- c SHORT COOL SUMMER
- d VERY COLD WINTER

VEGETATION

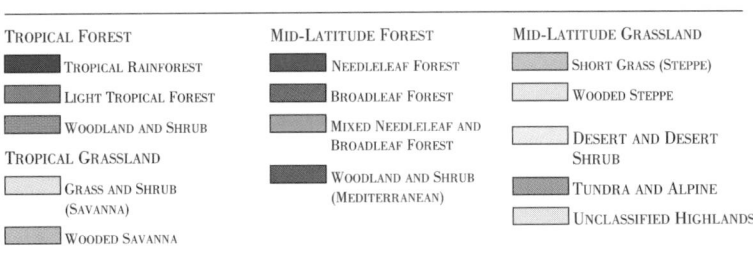

TROPICAL FOREST
- TROPICAL RAINFOREST
- LIGHT TROPICAL FOREST
- WOODLAND AND SHRUB

TROPICAL GRASSLAND
- GRASS AND SHRUB (SAVANNA)
- WOODED SAVANNA

MID-LATITUDE FOREST
- NEEDLELEAF FOREST
- BROADLEAF FOREST
- MIXED NEEDLELEAF AND BROADLEAF FOREST
- WOODLAND AND SHRUB (MEDITERRANEAN)

MID-LATITUDE GRASSLAND
- SHORT GRASS (STEPPE)
- WOODED STEPPE
- DESERT AND DESERT SHRUB
- TUNDRA AND ALPINE
- UNCLASSIFIED HIGHLANDS

Asia – Geographical Comparisons

● Tokyo 61

AVERAGE ANNUAL RAINFALL
IN INCHES AT SELECTED STATIONS

AVERAGE ANNUAL RAINFALL

INCHES	CM	INCHES	CM	INCHES	CM
OVER 80	OVER 200	40 TO 60	100 TO 150	10 TO 20	25 TO 50
60 TO 80	150 TO 200	20 TO 40	50 TO 100	UNDER 10	UNDER 25

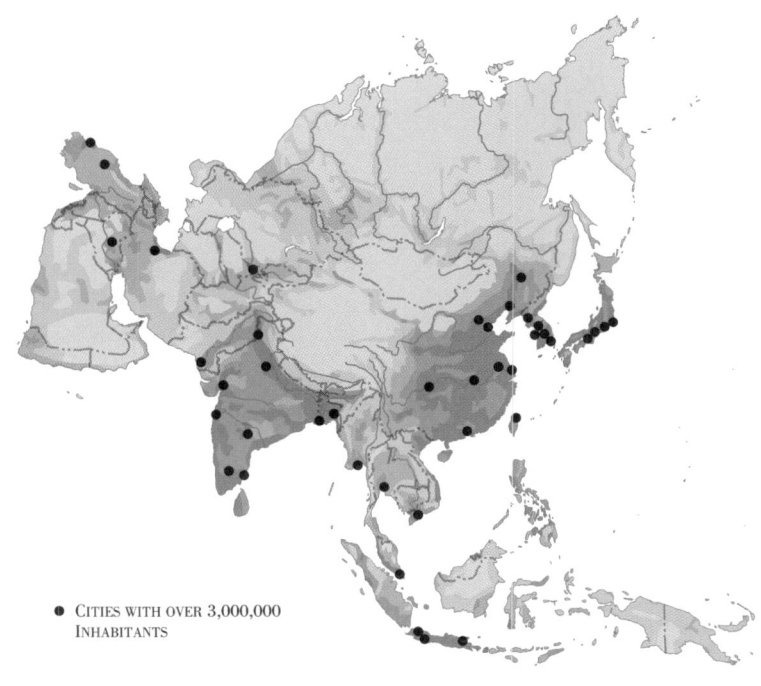

● CITIES WITH OVER 3,000,000
INHABITANTS

POPULATION DISTRIBUTION

DENSITY PER		SQ. MI.	SQ. KM.	SQ. MI.	SQ. KM.
SQ. MI.	SQ. KM.	130 TO 260	50 TO 100	3 TO 25	1 TO 10
OVER 260	OVER 100	25 TO 130	10 TO 50	UNDER 3	UNDER 1

LAND USE

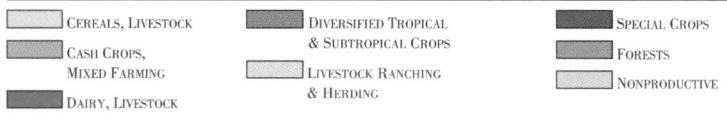

	CEREALS, LIVESTOCK		DIVERSIFIED TROPICAL & SUBTROPICAL CROPS		SPECIAL CROPS
	CASH CROPS, MIXED FARMING		LIVESTOCK RANCHING & HERDING		FORESTS
	DAIRY, LIVESTOCK				NONPRODUCTIVE

MINERAL RESOURCES

ENERGY & FUELS	IRON & FERROALLOYS	OTHER MAJOR RESOURCES		
◆ COAL	1 CHROMIUM	1 ANTIMONY	8 GRAPHITE	15 POTASH
⬠ LIGNITE	2 COBALT	2 ASBESTOS	9 LEAD	16 SILVER
▲ NATURAL GAS	3 IRON ORE	3 BAUXITE	10 MAGNESITE	17 SULFER
● PETROLEUM	4 MANGANESE	4 BORAX	11 MERCURY	18 TIN
■ URANIUM	5 MOLYBDENUM	5 COPPER	12 MICA	19 TITANIUM
	6 NICKEL	6 DIAMONDS	13 PHOSPHATES	20 ZINC
	7 TUNGSTEN	7 GOLD	14 PLATINUM	

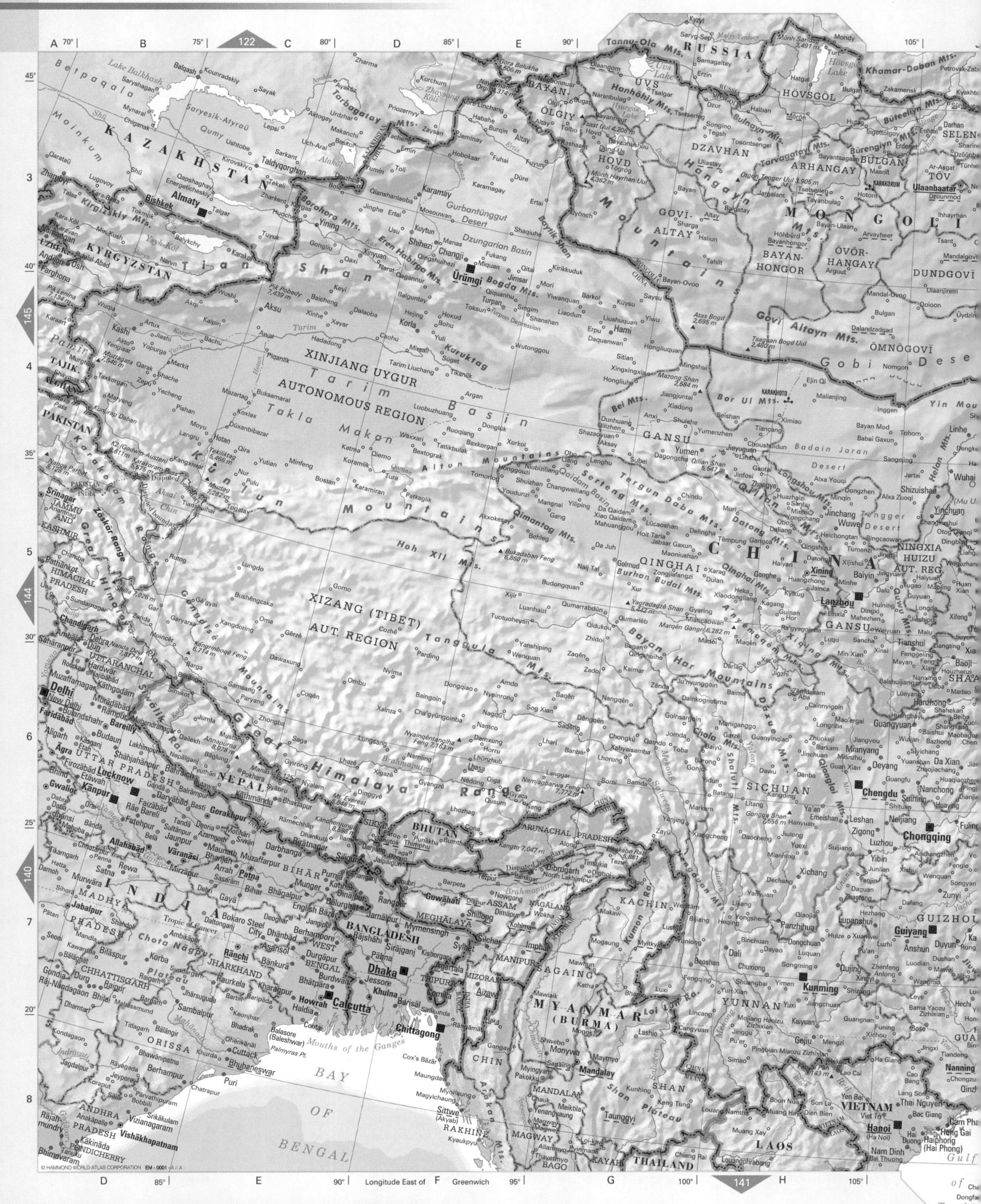

RUSSIA

DORNOD · SÜHBAATAR · Nei Monggol Plateau · NEI MONGGOL AUT. REG. · Mongolia

HEILONGJIANG · Qiqihar · Daqing · Harbin · Mudanjiang · Jixi · Hegang · Yichun

JILIN · Changchun · Jilin · LIAONING · Shenyang · Fushun · Benxi · Anshan · Dandong

Vladivostok · Khabarovsk · Sikhote-Alin · Sakhalin

NORTH KOREA · P'yŏngyang · Namp'o · Wŏnsan · Ch'ŏngjin · Hamhŭng

SOUTH KOREA · Seoul (Sŏul) · Inch'ŏn · Taejŏn · Taegu · Kwangju · Pusan · Ulsan · Chŏnju

HEBEI · Beijing · Tianjin · Tangshan · Baoding · Zhangjiakou

SHANXI · Taiyuan · SHANDONG · Jinan · Qingdao · Zibo · Dalian

Shijiazhuang · Handan · HENAN · Zhengzhou · Luoyang · Kaifeng

JIANGSU · Nanjing · Xuzhou · ANHUI · Hefei · Shanghai · Wuxi · Suzhou · Changzhou

Hangzhou · ZHEJIANG · Ningbo · HUBEI · Wuhan · HUNAN · Changsha · JIANGXI · Nanchang

FUJIAN · Fuzhou · GUANGDONG · Guangzhou · Shantou · Macau · Victoria · HONG KONG

TAIWAN · T'aipei · T'aichung · T'ainan · Kaohsiung · Keelung

JAPAN · Hokkaidō · Sapporo · Hakodate · Honshū · Tōkyō · Yokohama · Nagoya · Kyōto · Ōsaka · Kōbe · Sendai · Niigata · Hiroshima · Kitakyūshū · Fukuoka · Shikoku · Kyūshū · Kagoshima · Nagasaki · Kumamoto

SEA OF OKHOTSK · SEA OF JAPAN · PACIFIC OCEAN · YELLOW SEA · EAST CHINA SEA · SOUTH CHINA SEA · Bo Hai (Gulf of Chihli) · Korea Bay · Korea Strait · Ryukyu Islands · Okinawa · Hainan Dao · Tropic of Cancer

Hong Kong inset:
GUANGDONG · Shenzhen · Sheung Shui · Fanling · Yuen Long · Tai Po · Tin Shui Wai · Tuen Mun · Tsuen Wan · Sha Tin · New Kowloon · Kowloon · Victoria · HONG KONG · Lantau Island · Lantau Peak 934 m · Tai Mo Shan 957 m

POPULATION OF CITIES AND TOWNS

■ OVER 2,000,000 · ● 500,000 - 999,999 · ● 50,000 - 99,999
■ 1,000,000 - 1,999,999 · ● 100,000 - 499,999 · ○ UNDER 50,000

SCALE 1:13,800,000 — LAMBERT CONFORMAL CONIC PROJECTION

MILES 0 — 200 — 400 — 600
KILOMETERS 0 — 200 — 400

SCALE 1:6,900,000   LAMBERT CONFORMAL CONIC PROJECTION

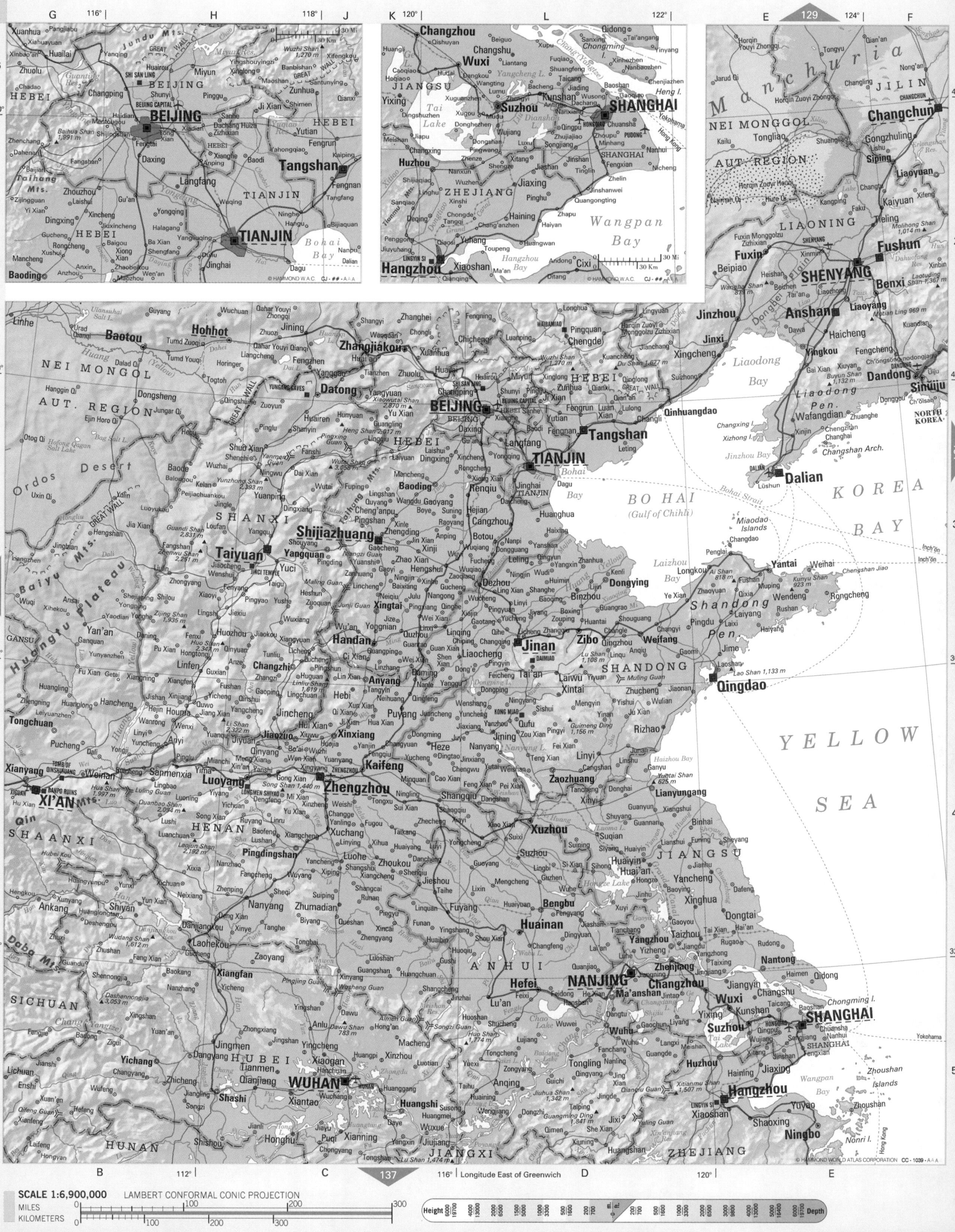

Central and Southern Japan

© HAMMOND WORLD ATLAS CORPORATION CM -1035 - A·A

© HAMMOND W.A.C. CJ -1116 - A·A

POPULATION OF CITIES AND TOWNS

■ OVER 2,000,000	● 500,000 - 999,999	● 100,000 - 249,999	● 10,000 - 29,999
■ 1,000,000 - 1,999,999	● 250,000 - 499,999	● 30,000 - 99,999	○ UNDER 10,000

SCALE 1:3,450,000 LAMBERT CONFORMAL CONIC PROJECTION

MILES

KILOMETERS

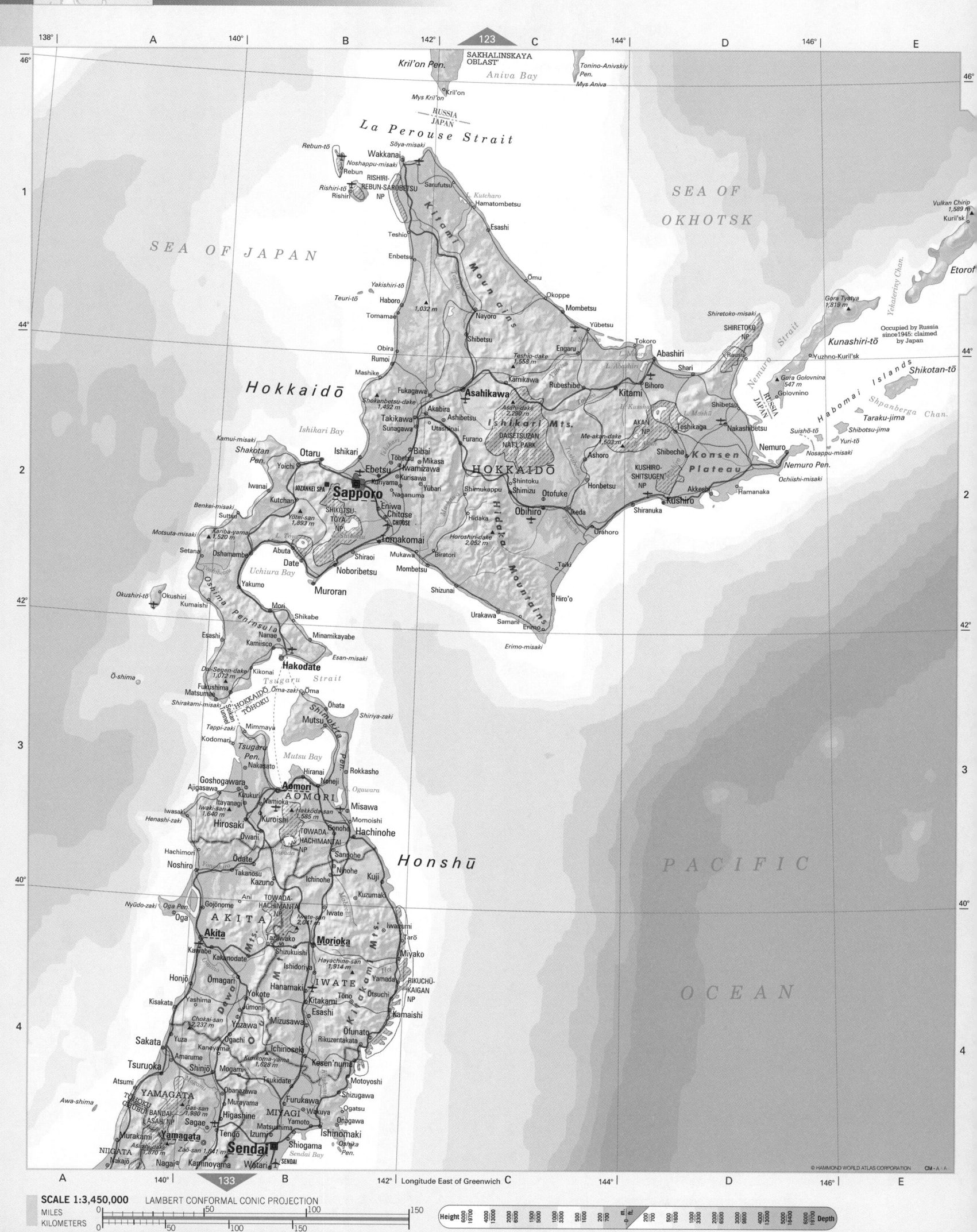

SCALE 1:3,450,000
LAMBERT CONFORMAL CONIC PROJECTION

MILES

KILOMETERS

© HAMMOND WORLD ATLAS CORPORATION

Tokyo – Yokohama, Osaka – Nagoya

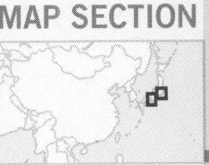

POPULATION OF CITIES AND TOWNS

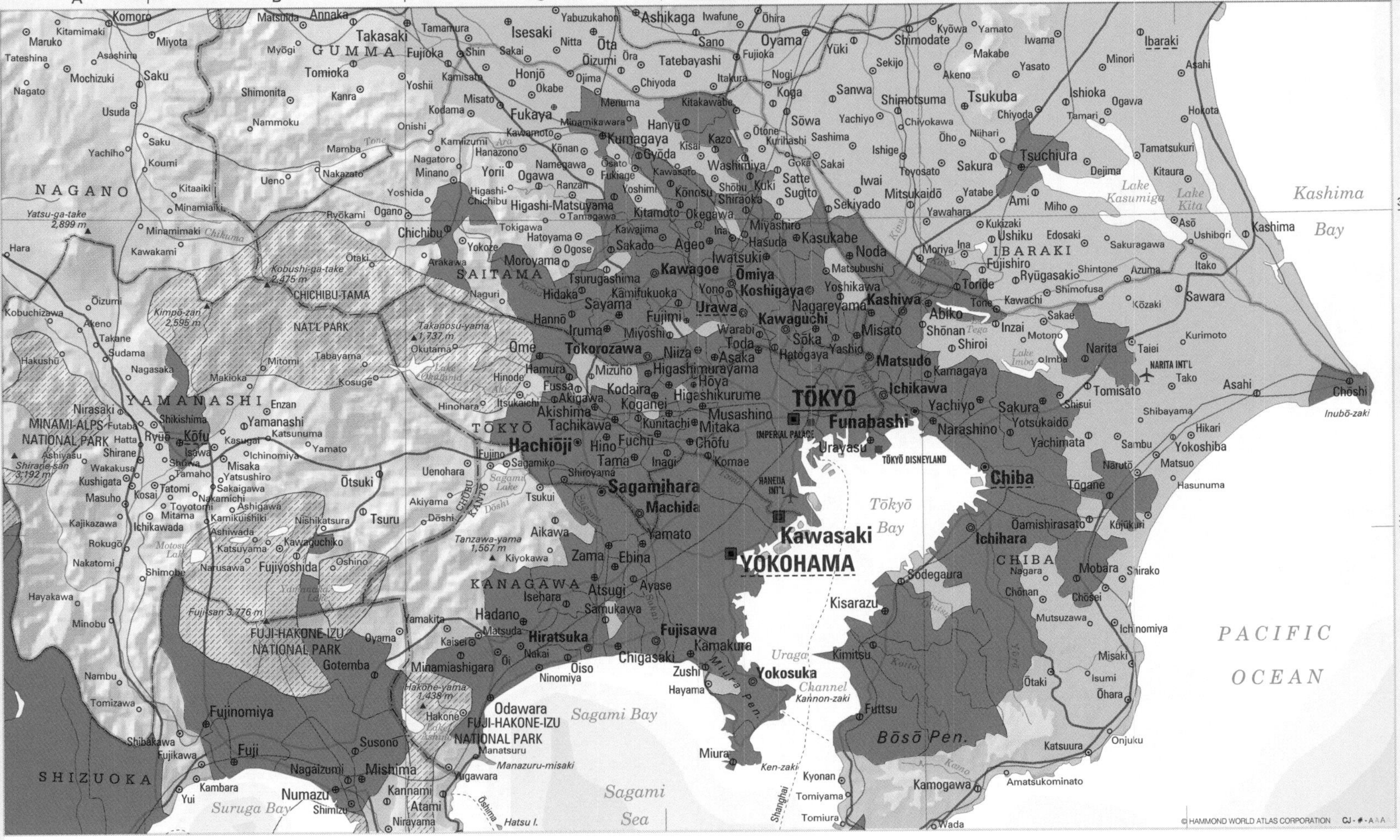

| ■ OVER 2,000,000 | ● 500,000 - 999,999 | ◉ 100,000 - 249,999 | ○ 10,000 - 29,999 |
| ■ 1,000,000 - 1,999,999 | ● 250,000 - 499,999 | ◎ 30,000 - 99,999 | ○ UNDER 10,000 |

SCALE 1:1,150,000   LAMBERT CONFORMAL CONIC PROJECTION

MILES 0 10 20 30 40 50

KILOMETERS 0 10 20 30 40 50

© HAMMOND WORLD ATLAS CORPORATION

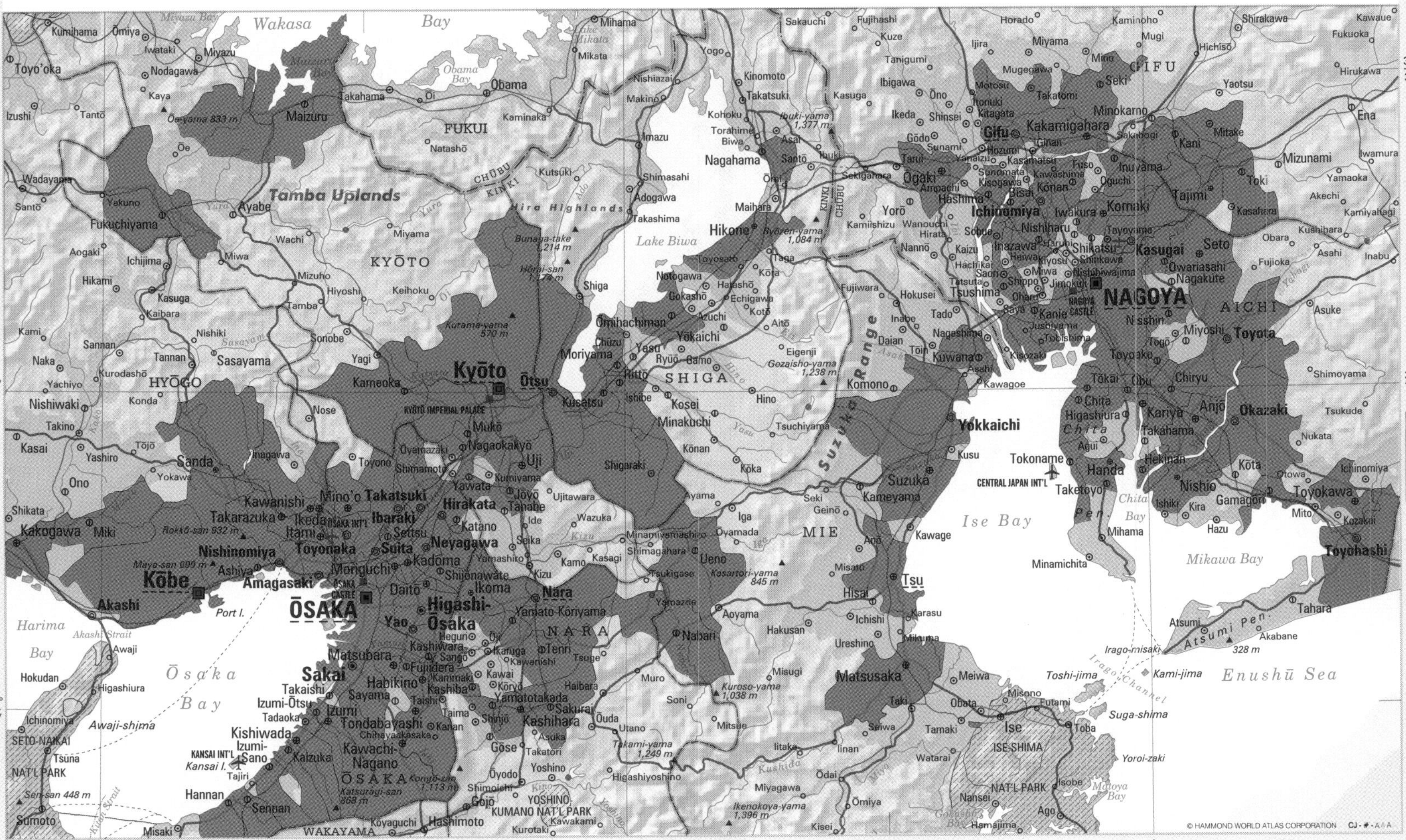

Indochina

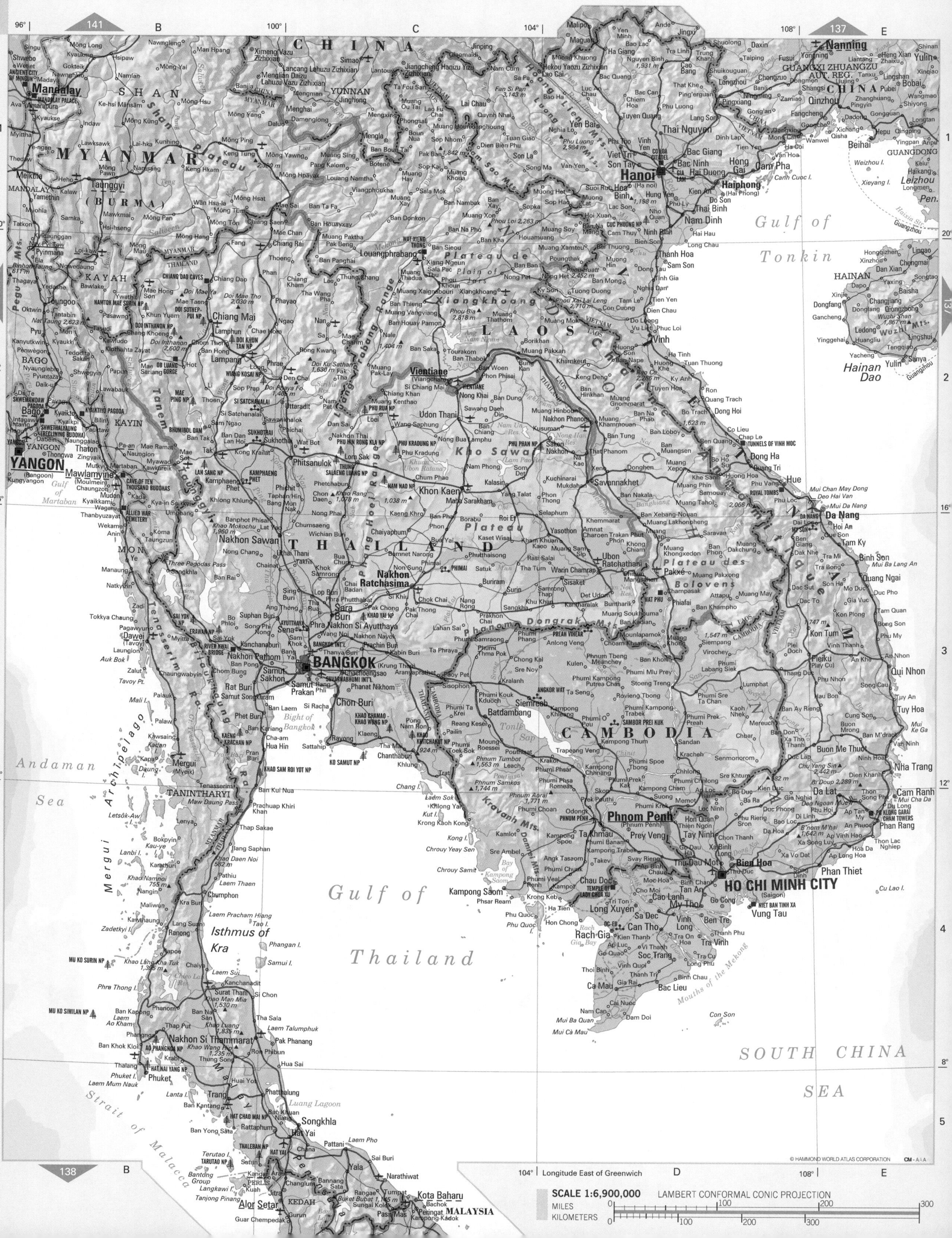

SCALE 1:6,900,000 LAMBERT CONFORMAL CONIC PROJECTION

© HAMMOND WORLD ATLAS CORPORATION

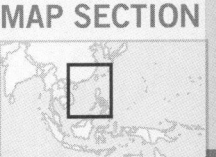
SCALE 1:10,300,000 LAMBERT CONFORMAL CONIC PROJECTION

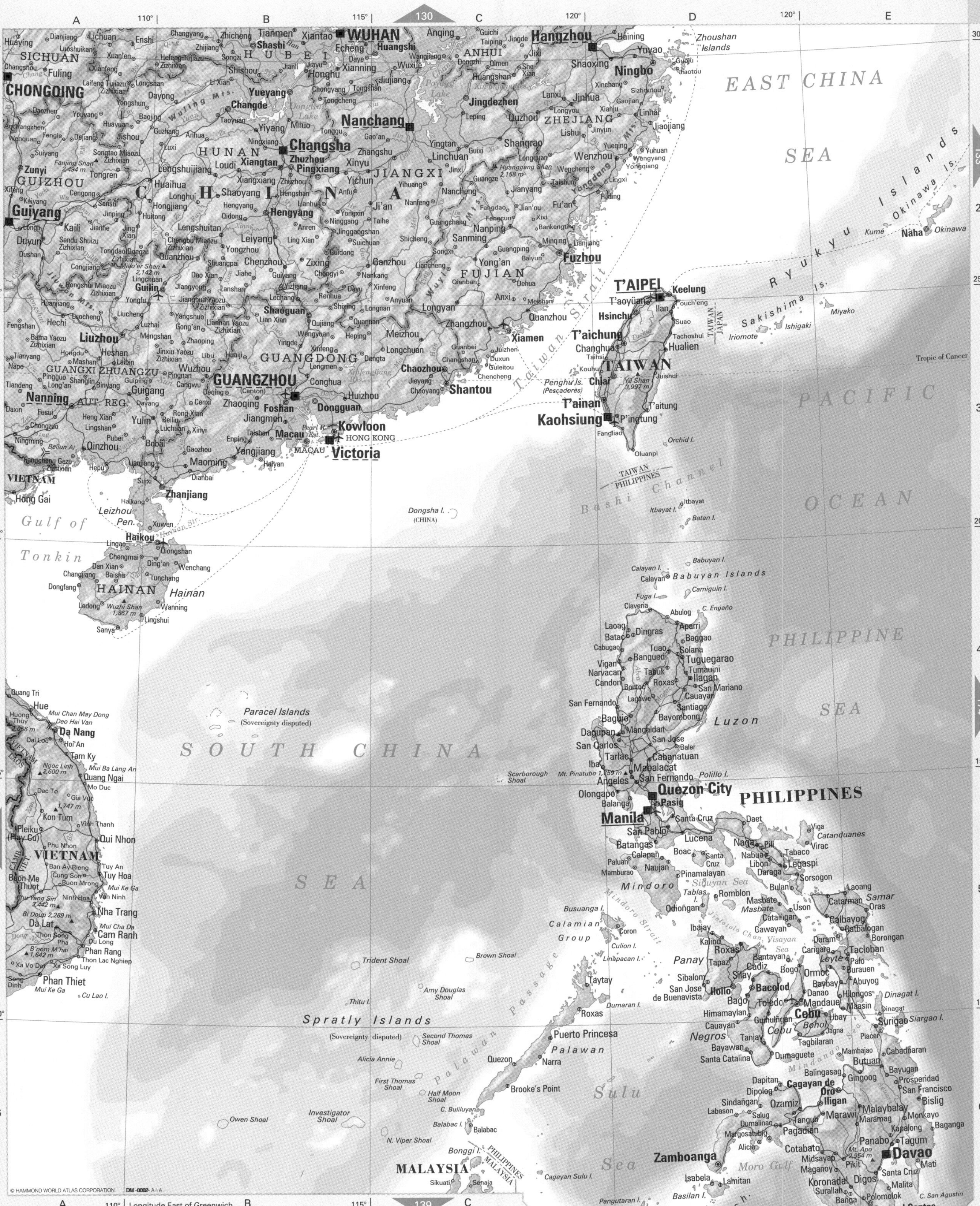

MILES

KILOMETERS

0 150 300 450

© Hammond World Atlas Corporation

SCALE 1:10,300,000   LAMBERT CONFORMAL CONIC PROJECTION

MILES

KILOMETERS

POPULATION OF CITIES AND TOWNS

■ OVER 2,000,000
■ 1,000,000 - 1,999,999
⬤ 500,000 - 999,999
⬤ 250,000 - 499,999
● 100,000 - 249,999
● 30,000 - 99,999
○ 10,000 - 29,999
○ UNDER 10,000

Indonesia, Malaysia

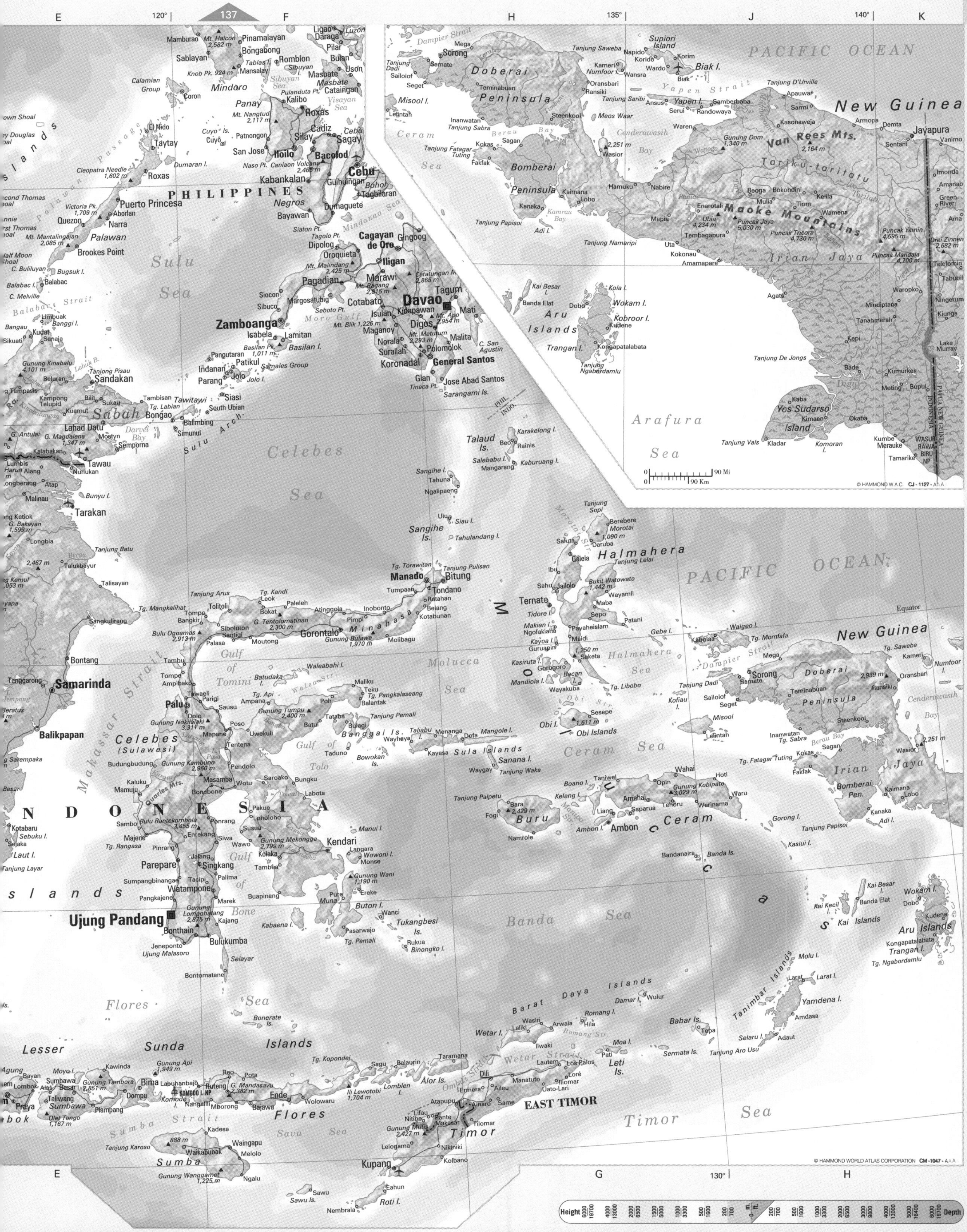

Southern Asia

POPULATION OF CITIES AND TOWNS
- ■ OVER 2,000,000
- ■ 1,000,000 - 1,999,999
- ● 500,000 - 999,999
- ◉ 250,000 - 499,999
- ● 100,000 - 249,999
- ◦ 30,000 - 99,999
- • 10,000 - 29,999
- ◦ UNDER 10,000

SCALE 1:10,300,000 LAMBERT CONFORMAL CONIC PROJECTION

MILES 0 — 150 — 300 — 450
KILOMETERS 0 — 150 — 300 — 450

© HAMMOND WORLD ATLAS CORPORATION   CM · A · A

A 78° B 80° C 82° D 84°

Pūndri · Karnāl
Gharaunda
Safidon · Thāna Bhawan
Pānipat · Kairāna
Samālkha
Gohāna · Sardhana
Rohtak
Bahādurgarh
Jhajjar
DELHI
New Delhi
INDIRA GANDHI
RUINS OF TUGHLAKABAD
Pataudi
Farrukhnagar
Faridābad
Rewāri
Tijāra
Kishangarh
Alwar
Mālākhera
Rājgarh

Gangoh · Nanauta
Jalālābad · Deoband
Thāna Bhawan · Thithāwal
Budhāna · Jānsath
Khatāuli · Jhālu
Phalauda · Mīrānpur
Bāghpat
Khekra
Mawāna Khurd
Pilkhua
Hāpur
Gulaothi

MEERUT
Ghaziābād
Murādnagar

Manglaur
Kotdwāra
Nagina · Najibābād
Afzalgarh
Bijnor
Amroha
Moradābad

LANSDOWNE

CORBETT NP

UTTARANCHAL

MAHAKALI

RARA NAT'L PARK

KARNALI

DHAWALĀGIRI

Annapurna 8,078 m

NEPAL

SCALE 1:3,450,000   LAMBERT CONFORMAL CONIC PROJECTION

MILES 0 50 100 150
KILOMETERS 0 50 100 150

Longitude East of Greenwich

POPULATION OF CITIES AND TOWNS

- ■ OVER 2,000,000
- ■ 1,000,000 - 1,999,999
- ◉ 500,000 - 999,999
- ◉ 250,000 - 499,999
- ⊙ 100,000 - 249,999
- ⊙ 30,000 - 99,999
- ○ 10,000 - 29,999
- ○ UNDER 10,000

Punjab Plain

AFGHANISTAN
NORTH-WEST FRONTIER
FEDERALLY ADMINISTERED TRIBAL AREAS
PAKISTAN
PUNJAB
Thal Desert
Punjab Plains
Thar Desert
Great Indian Desert
RĀJASTHĀN
HARYANA
PUNJAB
UTTAR PRADESH
HIMĀCHAL PRADESH
JAMMU AND KASHMĪR
AZAD KASHMIR*
NORTHERN AREAS*
CHINA
INDIA
Karakoram Ra.
Great Himalaya Ra.
Zāskār Ra.
Siwālik Range
Salt Range
Safed Koh Range
Pir Panjal Range

Peshāwar, Islāmābād, Rāwalpindi, Srinagar, Jammu, Sargodha, Faisalābād, Gujrānwāla, Lahore, Amritsar, Jalandhar, Ludhiāna, Chandigarh, Multān, Bahāwalpur, Delhi, New Delhi, Meerut, Faridābād, Ghaziābād

SCALE 1:3,450,000
LAMBERT CONFORMAL CONIC PROJECTION
MILES
KILOMETERS
0 50 100 150

Height   Depth

* AZAD KASHMIR AND THE NORTHERN AREAS ARE ADMINISTERED BY PAKISTAN BUT DO NOT HAVE PROVINCIAL STATUS.

© HAMMOND WORLD ATLAS CORPORATION

SCALE 1:10,300,000   LAMBERT CONFORMAL CONIC PROJECTION

POPULATION OF CITIES AND TOWNS

Southwestern Asia

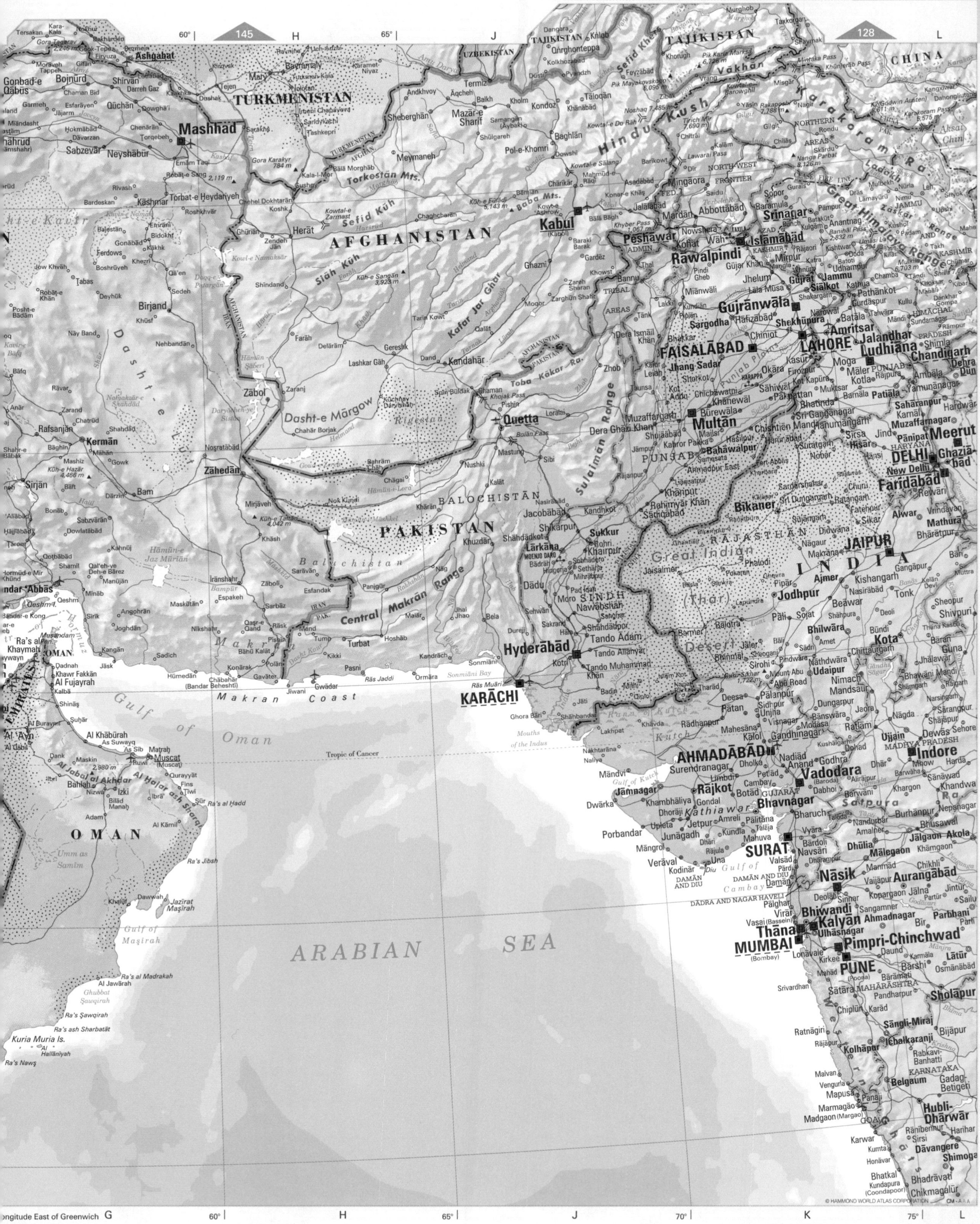

POPULATION OF CITIES AND TOWNS

| ■ OVER 2,000,000 | ◉ 500,000 - 999,999 | ● 100,000 - 249,999 | ○ 10,000 - 29,999 |
| ■ 1,000,000 - 1,999,999 | ◉ 250,000 - 499,999 | ● 30,000 - 99,999 | ○ UNDER 10,000 |

SCALE 1:10,300,000 LAMBERT CONFORMAL CONIC PROJECTION

MILES
KILOMETERS

© Hammond World Atlas Corporation   CM–A·A·A

SCALE 1:6,900,000   LAMBERT CONFORMAL CONIC PROJECTION

MILES   0   100   200   300

KILOMETERS   0   100   200   300

© HAMMOND WORLD ATLAS CORPORATION

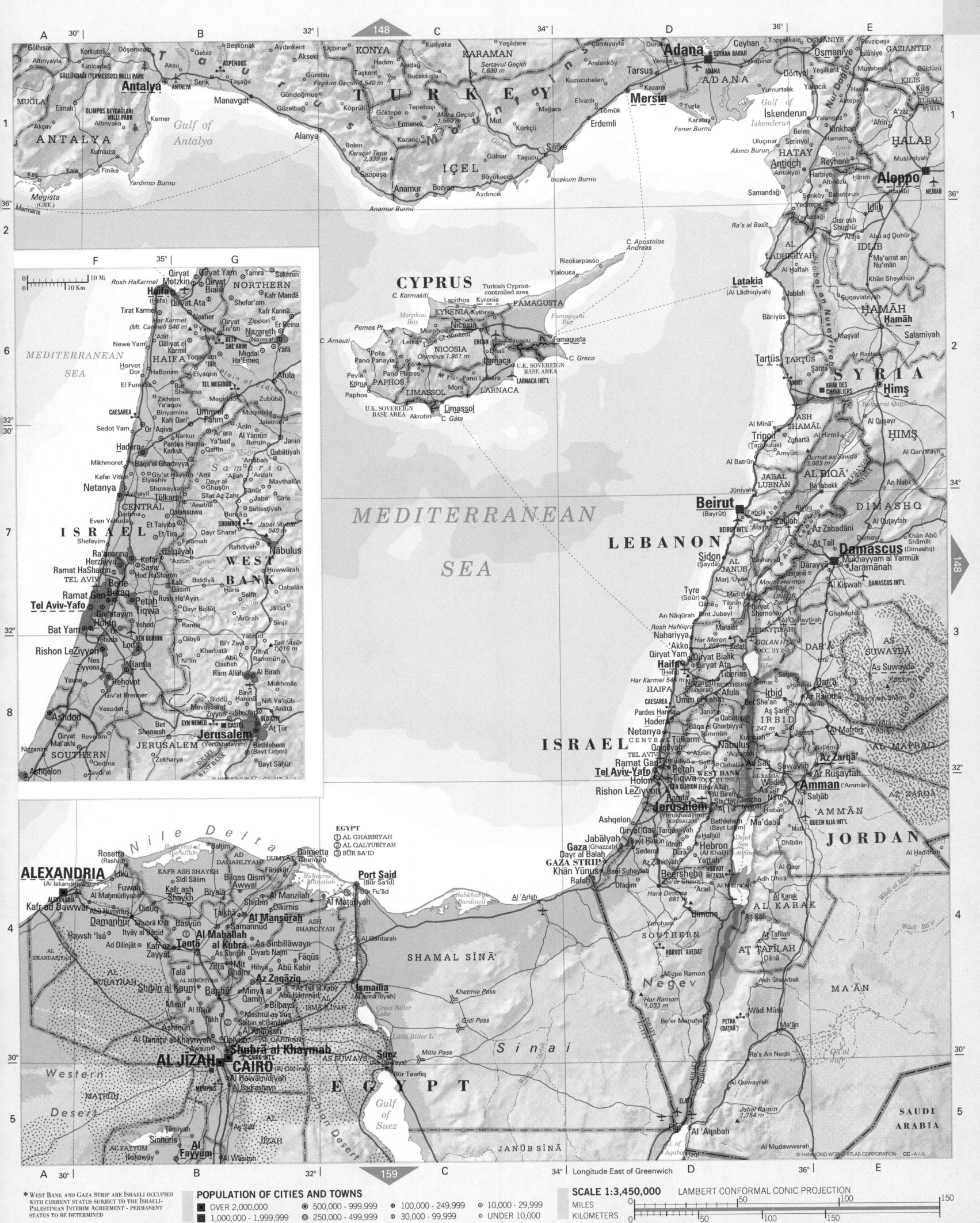

Africa

Several physiographic features are captured in this southeast-looking, high-oblique image. The Nile River Delta, the large, dark area at the bottom of the image, extends from the capital city of Cairo at the apex of the delta to the Suez Canal. The entire region is classified as desert (less than 10 inches [25 cm.] of rainfall per year). Desert-like areas are visible southwest of the delta and in the northwestern Sinai. Major rock outcrops (darker areas) are seen encircling the Red Sea. The two bodies of water flanking the southern end of the Sinai Peninsula are the Gulf of Suez and the Gulf of Aqaba.

AREA OF OPTIMIZATION

The red band which surrounds this map defines the "Area of Optimization." Within this bounding curve is the most accurate conformal map that can be made of the region. Outside the optimized area, distortion increases rapidly, and tears or other irregularities in the grid may occur. (See page 8 for additional information.)

POPULATION OF CITIES AND TOWNS

- ■ OVER 3,000,000
- ■ 1,000,000 - 2,999,999
- ● 500,000 - 999,999
- ● 100,000 - 499,999
- ○ UNDER 100,000

SCALE 1:34,500,000 OPTIMAL CONFORMAL PROJECTION

MILES

KILOMETERS

LAMBERT CONFORMAL CONIC PROJECTION

© HAMMOND W.A.C.   CJ - 1136 - A·A·A

© HAMMOND WORLD ATLAS CORPORATION   CC - A·A·A

152

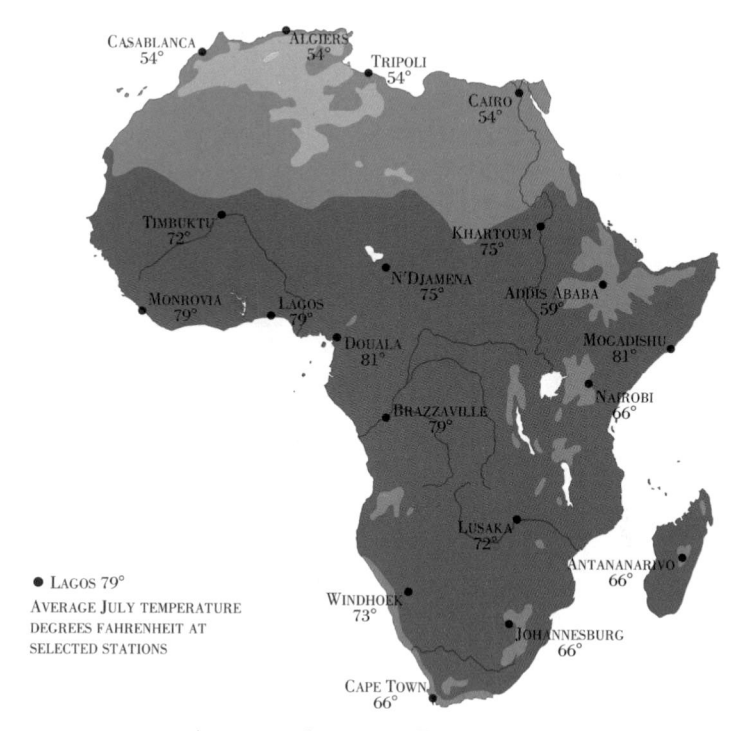

● LAGOS 79°
AVERAGE JULY TEMPERATURE
DEGREES FAHRENHEIT AT
SELECTED STATIONS

AVERAGE JANUARY TEMPERATURE

FAHRENHEIT	CELSIUS		FAHRENHEIT	CELSIUS
OVER 68°	OVER 20°		32° TO 50°	0° TO 10°
50° TO 68°	10° TO 20°		UNDER 32°	UNDER 0°

● LAGOS 75°
AVERAGE JULY TEMPERATURE
DEGREES FAHRENHEIT AT
SELECTED STATIONS

AVERAGE JULY TEMPERATURE

FAHRENHEIT	CELSIUS		FAHRENHEIT	CELSIUS
OVER 86°	OVER 30°		50° TO 68°	10° TO 20°
68° TO 86°	20° TO 30°		UNDER 50°	UNDER 10°

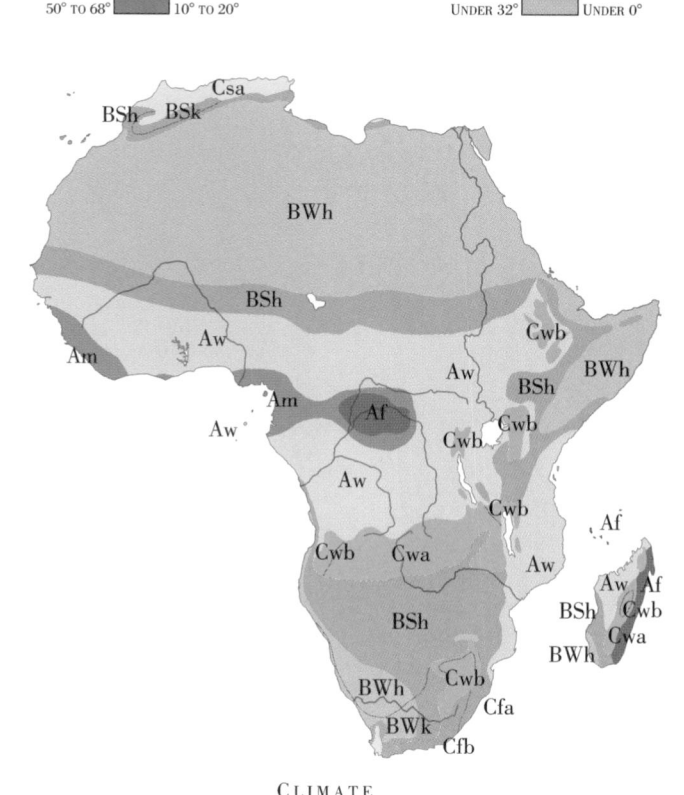

CLIMATE

HUMID TROPICAL

Af   NO DRY SEASON

Am   SHORT DRY SEASON

Aw   DRY WINTER

DRY

BS   SEMIARID

BW   ARID

} h HOT
  k COLD

HUMID WARM

Cf   NO DRY SEASON

Cw   DRY WINTER

Cs   DRY SUMMER

a   HOT SUMMER

b   COOL SUMMER

AFTER KOEPPEN-GEIGER

VEGETATION

TROPICAL FOREST

TROPICAL RAINFOREST

LIGHT TROPICAL FOREST

WOODLAND AND SHRUB

TROPICAL GRASSLAND

GRASS AND SHRUB
(SAVANNA)

WOODED SAVANNA

MID-LATITUDE FOREST

MIXED NEEDLELEAF AND
BROADLEAF FOREST

WOODLAND AND SHRUB
(MEDITERRANEAN)

MID-LATITUDE GRASSLAND

SHORT GRASS (STEPPE)

DESERT AND DESERT
SHRUB

RIVER VALLEY AND OASIS

UNCLASSIFIED
HIGHLANDS

Africa – Geographical Comparisons

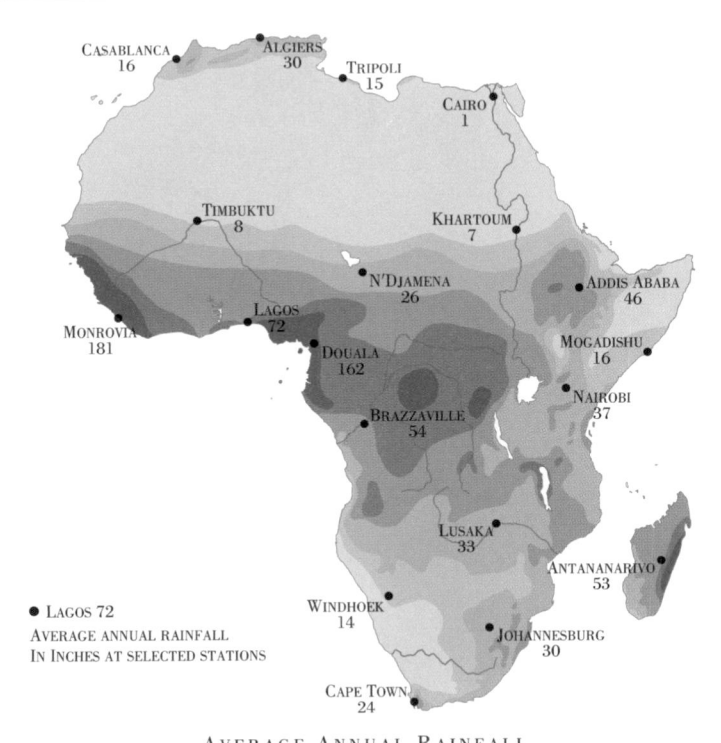

CASABLANCA 16
ALGIERS 30
TRIPOLI 15
CAIRO 1
TIMBUKTU 8
KHARTOUM 7
N'DJAMENA 26
ADDIS ABABA 46
LAGOS 72
MONROVIA 181
DOUALA 162
MOGADISHU 16
BRAZZAVILLE 54
NAIROBI 37
LUSAKA 33
ANTANANARIVO 53
WINDHOEK 14
JOHANNESBURG 30
CAPE TOWN 24

● LAGOS 72
AVERAGE ANNUAL RAINFALL
IN INCHES AT SELECTED STATIONS

AVERAGE ANNUAL RAINFALL

INCHES	CM	INCHES	CM	INCHES	CM
OVER 80	OVER 200	40 TO 60	100 TO 150	10 TO 20	25 TO 50
60 TO 80	150 TO 200	20 TO 40	50 TO 100	UNDER 10	UNDER 25

● CITIES WITH OVER 1,000,000
INHABITANTS

POPULATION DISTRIBUTION

DENSITY PER		SQ. MI.	SQ. KM.	SQ. MI.	SQ. KM.
SQ. MI.	SQ. KM.	130 TO 260	50 TO 100	3 TO 25	1 TO 10
OVER 260	OVER 100	25 TO 130	10 TO 50	UNDER 3	UNDER 1

SHEEP
FRUIT WINE
CORN COTTON DATES
SHEEP
PEANUTS
CATTLE
CATTLE
COTTON
CATTLE
PEANUTS
HOGS
COFFEE
COFFEE COCOA COCOA
PALM OIL
COCOA
BANANAS
SHEEP
SHEEP
COFFEE
CATTLE
PALM OIL
SISAL
COFFEE
CORN TOBACCO COPRA
SHEEP
CORN CATTLE
SHEEP SHEEP

LAND USE

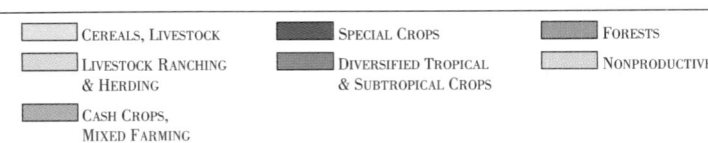

- CEREALS, LIVESTOCK
- LIVESTOCK RANCHING & HERDING
- CASH CROPS, MIXED FARMING
- SPECIAL CROPS
- DIVERSIFIED TROPICAL & SUBTROPICAL CROPS
- FORESTS
- NONPRODUCTIVE

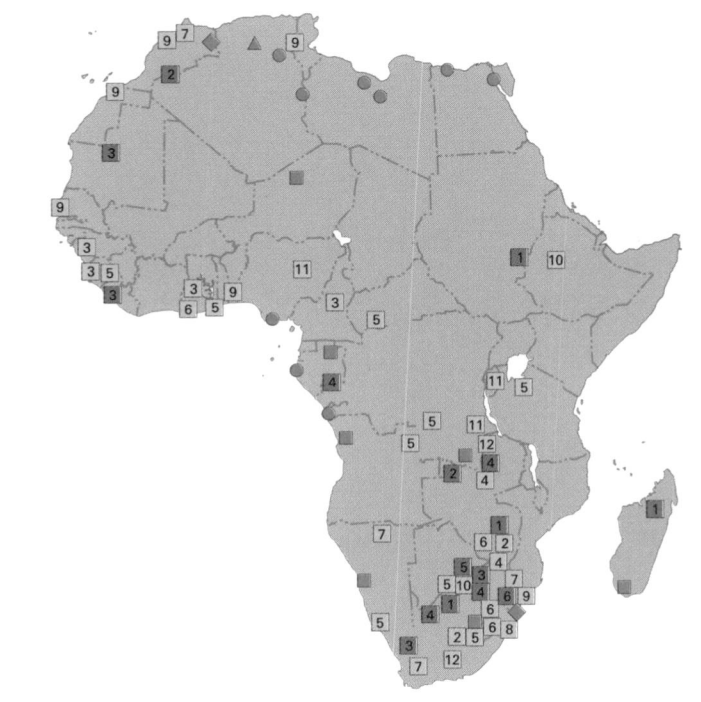

MINERAL RESOURCES

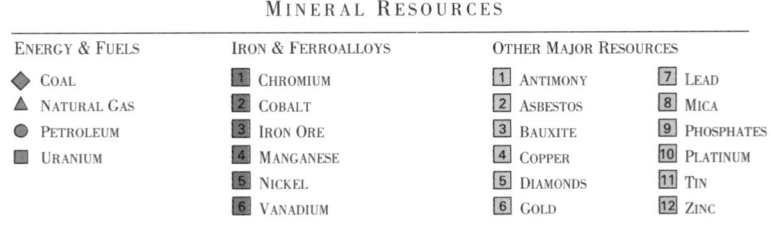

ENERGY & FUELS
- ◆ COAL
- ▲ NATURAL GAS
- ● PETROLEUM
- ■ URANIUM

IRON & FERROALLOYS
- 1 CHROMIUM
- 2 COBALT
- 3 IRON ORE
- 4 MANGANESE
- 5 NICKEL
- 6 VANADIUM

OTHER MAJOR RESOURCES
- 1 ANTIMONY
- 2 ASBESTOS
- 3 BAUXITE
- 4 COPPER
- 5 DIAMONDS
- 6 GOLD
- 7 LEAD
- 8 MICA
- 9 PHOSPHATES
- 10 PLATINUM
- 11 TIN
- 12 ZINC

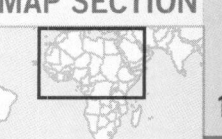
POPULATION OF CITIES AND TOWNS

- ■ OVER 2,000,000
- ■ 1,000,000 - 1,999,999
- ● 500,000 - 999,999
- ◉ 100,000 - 499,999
- ◎ 50,000 - 99,999
- ○ UNDER 50,000

SCALE 1:17,200,000   POLYCONIC PROJECTION

MILES   0   250   500   750

KILOMETERS   0   250   500   750

© HAMMOND WORLD ATLAS CORPORATION   CM-2103-A-A

ATLANTIC

OCEAN

SPAIN

MOROCCO

CASABLANCA
(Dar-el-Beida)

Rabat
Salé
RABAT (SALE)

Marrakech

Agadir (AL MASSIRA)

Tangier

Fès
Meknès

Madeira Is.
(PORT.)

Funchal

Canary Islands
(SPAIN)

Las Palmas
de Gran Canaria

Santa Cruz
de Tenerife

Tenerife

WESTERN
SAHARA
(Occupied by Morocco)

EL AAIÚN (HASSANI)
El Aaiún

Ad Dakhla

Nouâdhibou

MAURITANIA

MALI

TIRIS ZEMMOUR

ADRAR

TOMBOUC

Tropic of Cancer

MOROCCO is divided into 7 non-administrative
regions shown here. Scale does not permit
showing the boundaries and names of Morocco's
provinces and prefectures.

Longitude West of Greenwich 4°

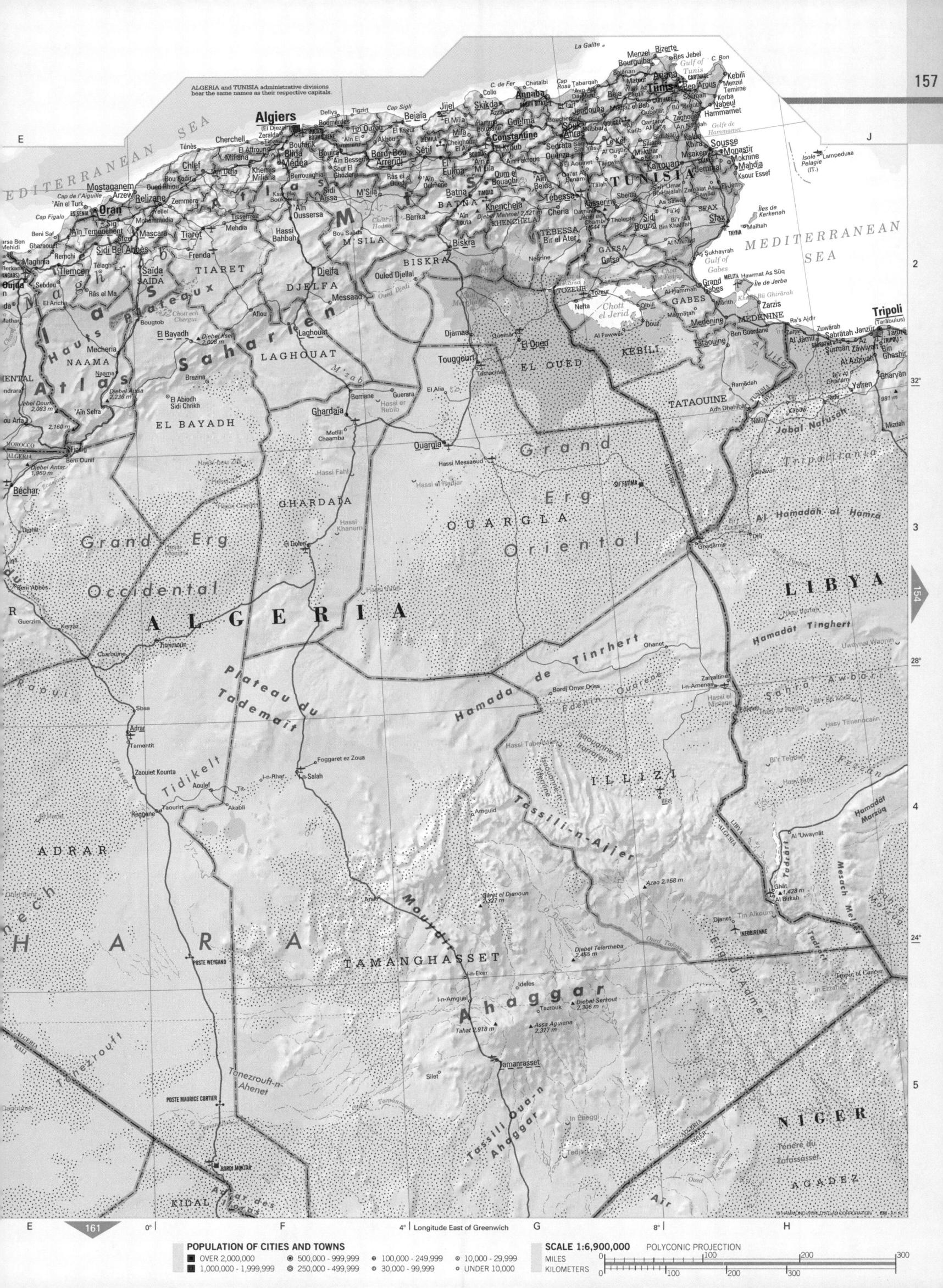

ALGERIA and TUNISIA administrative divisions
bear the same names as their respective capitals.

MEDITERRANEAN SEA

E J

La Galite
C. de Fer   Chetaibi   Cap   Tabarqah   Bizerte   Menzel   Res Jebel
Collo   Annaba   Ava   Bourguiba   C. Bon
Cap Sigli   Jijel   Skikda   Souk   Carthage   **Tunis**   Ben Arous   Kebili
Dellys   Tigzirt   El Milia   Guelma   Jendouba   Nabeul
Algiers   Tizi Ouzou   Bejaïa   Ramma   Kef   Hammamet
Boumerdes   El Kseur   Constantine   Kairouan   Sousse
Cherchell   Bordj Bou   Sétif   Sidi   Monastir
Ténès   Bouira   Arrendj   Bouzid   Mahdia
Chlef   Medea   Ksar el Oued   Sfax
Khemis   M'Sila   Batna   Khenchela   **TUNISIA**   Îles de Kerkenah
Miliana   Barika   Biskra   Gafsa
Mostaganem   Djelfa   Gabes   **MEDITERRANEAN SEA**
Oran   Mascara   Tiaret   Négrine
Sidi Bel Abbès   SAIDA   DJELFA   BISKRA   TOZEUR   GABES   2
Tlemcen   TIARET   Touggourt   Nefta   MEDENINE
Oujda   Saïda   EL OUED   KEBILI   Medenine   **Tripoli**
NAAMA   Laghouat   Djamaa   Tataouine
El Bayadh   LAGHOUAT   El Oued   32°
ADRAR   Ghardaïa   Ouargla   TATAOUINE
EL BAYADH   Hassi Messaoud
MOROCCO   GHARDAÏA   Grand Erg Oriental   **LIBYA**
Béchar   3
ADRAR   Grand Erg Occidental   154
ALGERIA   Plateau du Tademaït   Hamada de Tinrhert
ILLIZI   28°
Adrar   Tidikelt   I-n-Salah   Bordj Omar Driss   I-n-Amenas
ADRAR   24°
TAMANGHASSET   Ahaggar   Tahat 2,918 m
Tamanrasset   Silet   5
SAHARA
NIGER
KIDAL   AGADEZ

E 161   0°   4° Longitude East of Greenwich   G   8°   H

POPULATION OF CITIES AND TOWNS

| ■ OVER 2,000,000 | ◉ 500,000 - 999,999 | ● 100,000 - 249,999 | ○ 10,000 - 29,999 |
| ■ 1,000,000 - 1,999,999 | ◉ 250,000 - 499,999 | ● 30,000 - 99,999 | ○ UNDER 10,000 |

SCALE 1:6,900,000   POLYCONIC PROJECTION

MILES   0   100   200   300
KILOMETERS   0   100   200   300

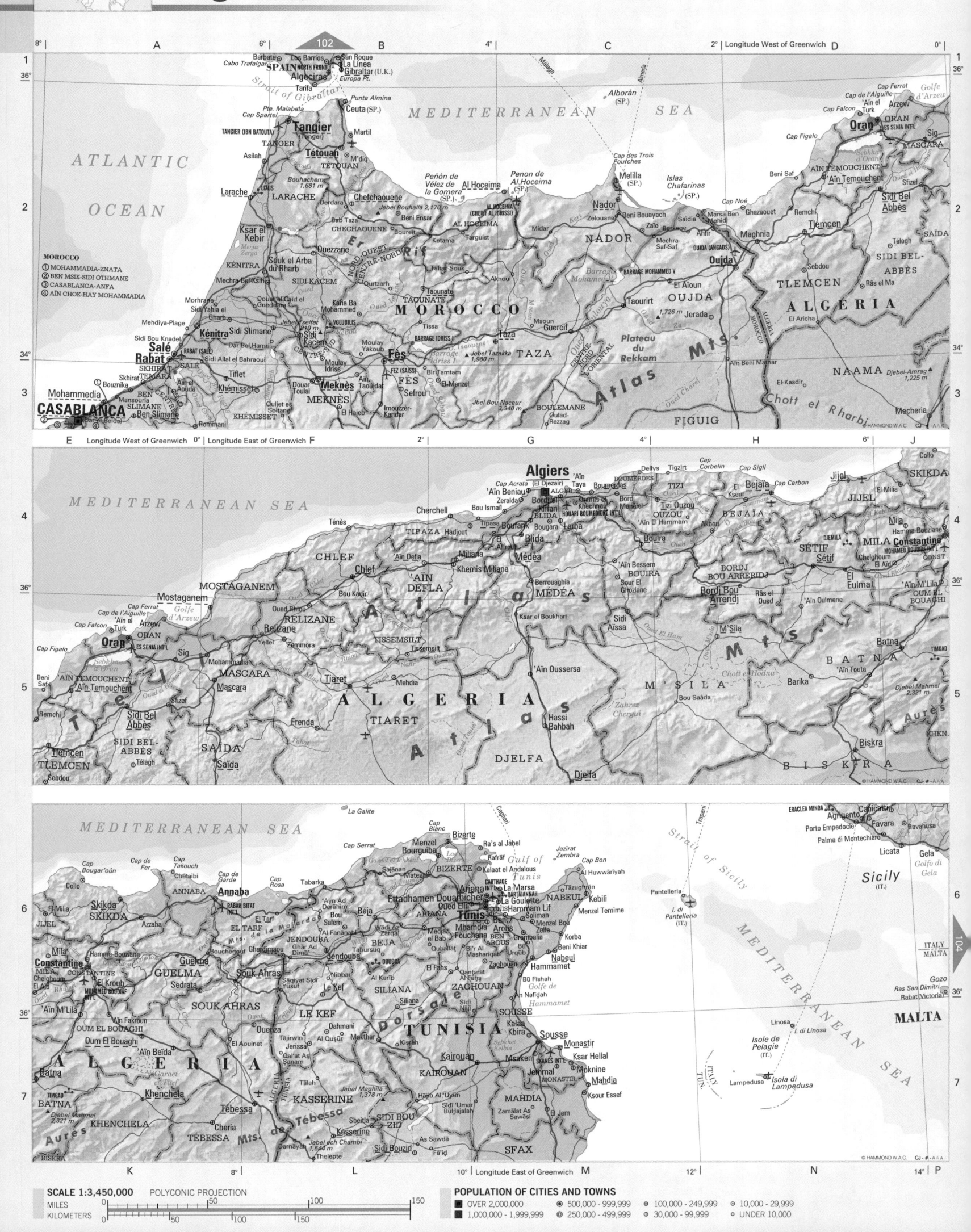

POPULATION OF CITIES AND TOWNS

| ■ OVER 2,000,000 | ● 500,000 - 999,999 | ⊙ 100,000 - 249,999 | ⊙ 10,000 - 29,999 |
| ■ 1,000,000 - 1,999,999 | ● 250,000 - 499,999 | ⊙ 30,000 - 99,999 | ○ UNDER 10,000 |

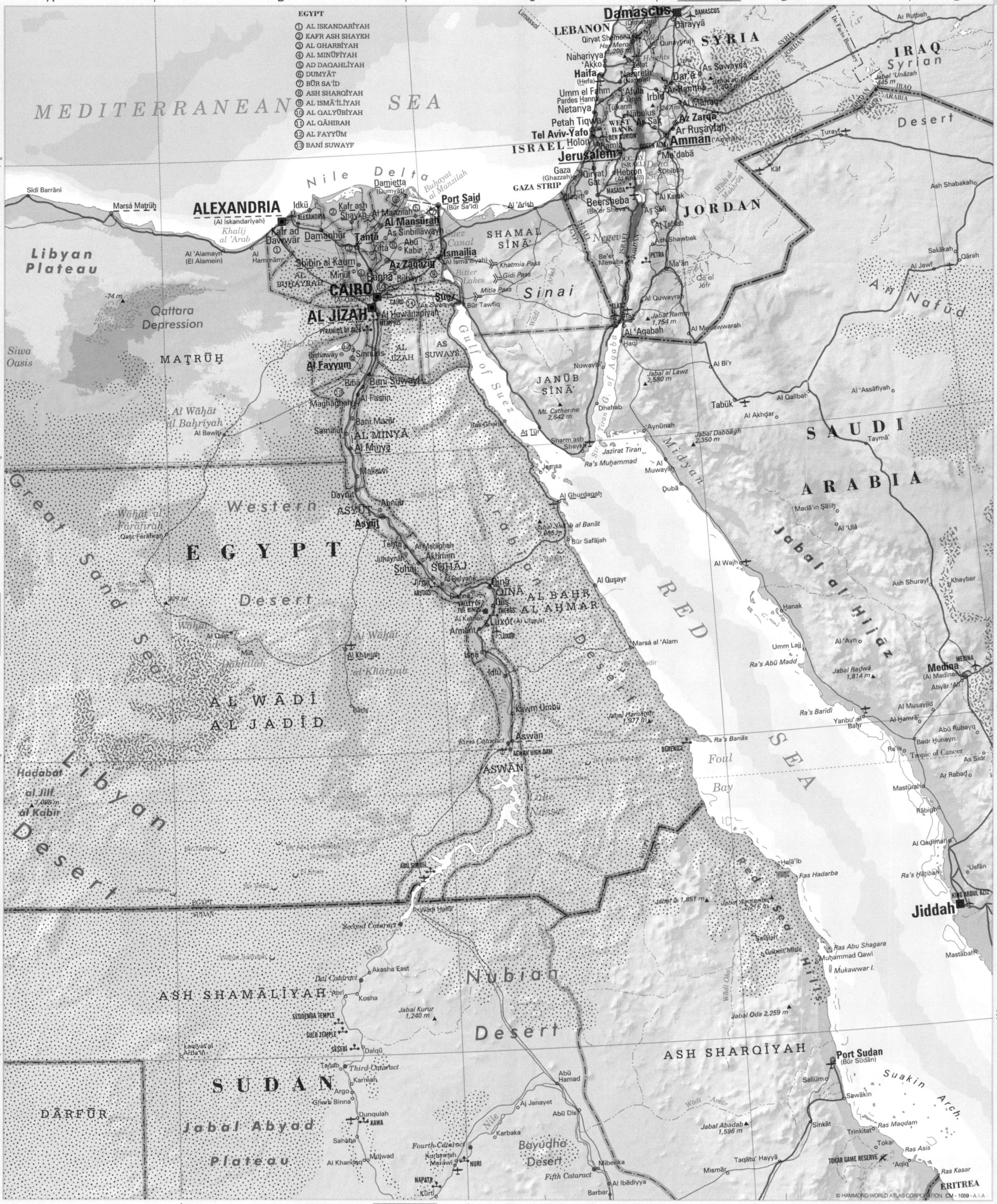

EGYPT
① AL ISKANDARĪYAH
② KAFR ASH SHAYKH
③ AL GHARBĪYAH
④ AL MINŪFĪYAH
⑤ AD DAQAHLĪYAH
⑥ DUMYĀT
⑦ BŪR SA'ĪD
⑧ ASH SHARQĪYAH
⑨ AL ISMĀ'ĪLĪYAH
⑩ AL QALYŪBĪYAH
⑪ AL QĀHIRAH
⑫ AL FAYYŪM
⑬ BANĪ SUWAYF

MEDITERRANEAN SEA

Libyan Plateau

Qattara Depression

Siwa Oasis

MAṬRŪḤ

ALEXANDRIA (Al Iskandarīyah)

Nile Delta

Port Said (Būr Sa'īd)

Al Manṣūrah

Tanta

CAIRO (Al Qāhirah)

AL JĪZAH

Al Fayyūm

Banī Suwayf

AL MINYĀ

Al Minyā

ASYŪṬ

Asyūṭ

Western Desert

E G Y P T

AL WĀDĪ AL JADĪD

SUHĀJ

QINĀ

AL BAHR AL AHMAR

Luxor (Al Uqṣur)

Aswan

ASWĀN

ASWAN HIGH DAM

Lake Nasser

ABŪ SIMBEL

Great Sand Sea

Libyan Desert

Ḥaḍabat al Jilf al Kabīr

ASH SHAMĀLĪYAH

Nubian Desert

SUDAN

DĀRFŪR

Jabal Abyaḍ Plateau

ASH SHARQĪYAH

Port Sudan (Būr Sūdān)

ERITREA

RED SEA

Gulf of Suez

Gulf of Aqaba

Sinai

SHAMAL SĪNĀ'

JANŪB SĪNĀ'

Mt. Catherine 2,642 m

Sharm ash Shaykh

Ra's Muḥammad

Al Ghurdaqah

ISRAEL

Tel Aviv-Yafo

Jerusalem

GAZA STRIP

Gaza (Ghazzah)

Beersheba (Be'er Sheva)

Negev

WEST BANK

Haifa (Hefa)

Netanya

LEBANON

Damascus (Dimashq)

SYRIA

Syrian Desert

IRAQ

JORDAN

Amman

Az Zarqā'

Al Karak

Ma'ān

Al 'Aqabah

SAUDI ARABIA

An Nafūd

Jabal al Hijaz

Medina (Al Madīnah)

Jiddah

Tropic of Cancer

Suakin Arch.

POPULATION OF CITIES AND TOWNS
- ■ OVER 2,000,000
- ■ 1,000,000 - 1,999,999
- ◉ 500,000 - 999,999
- ◉ 250,000 - 499,999
- ⊕ 100,000 - 249,999
- ⊕ 30,000 - 99,999
- • 10,000 - 29,999
- ○ UNDER 10,000

SCALE 1:6,900,000   POLYCONIC PROJECTION
MILES
KILOMETERS
100   200   300

© HAMMOND WORLD ATLAS CORPORATION

ATLANTIC

OCEAN

© HAMMOND WORLD ATLAS CORPORATION   CM-A-A-A

Longitude West of Greenwich

SCALE 1:6,900,000

POLYCONIC PROJECTION

MILES

KILOMETERS

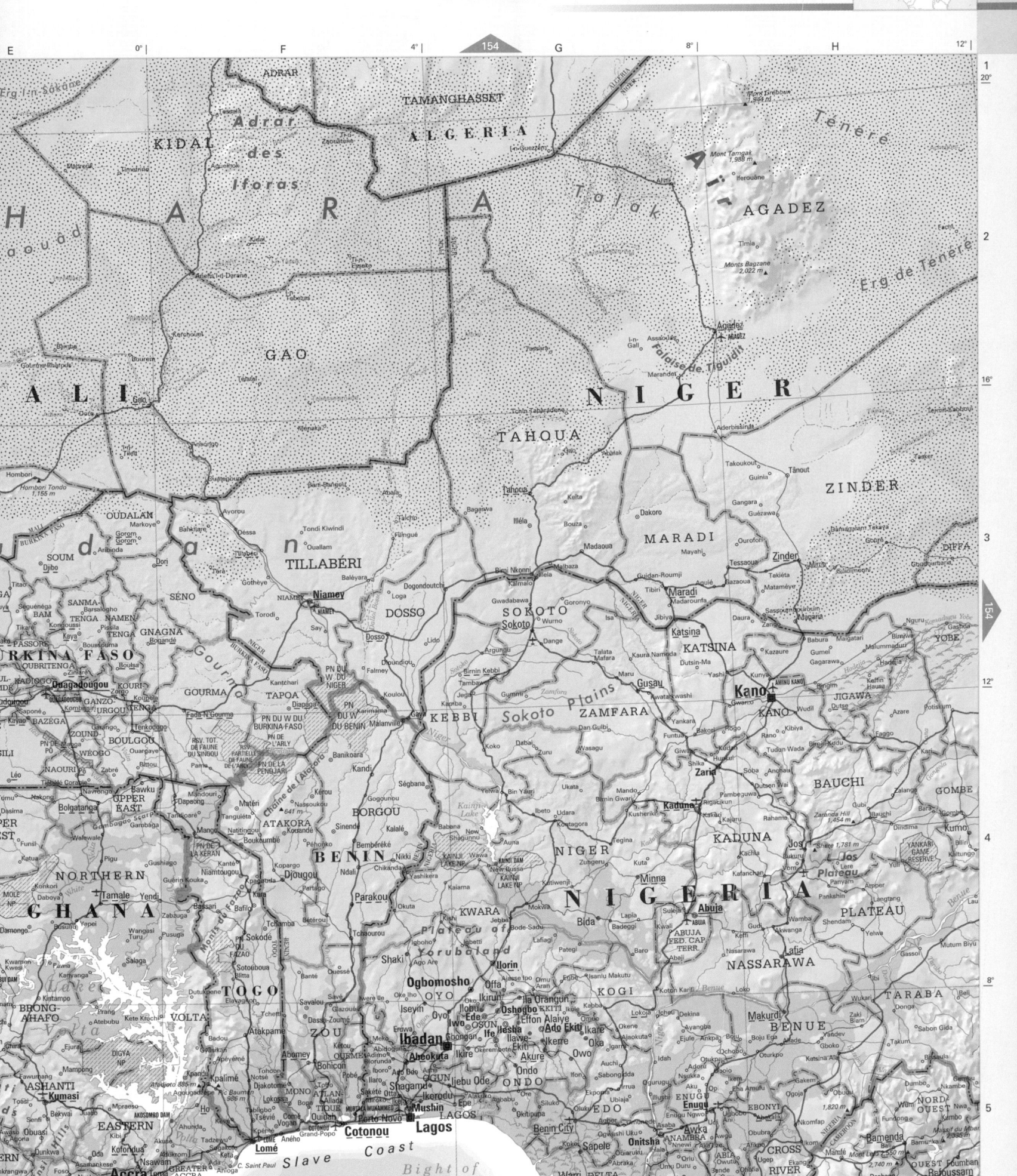

POPULATION OF CITIES AND TOWNS

■ OVER 2,000,000	● 500,000 - 999,999	● 100,000 - 249,999	○ 10,000 - 29,999
■ 1,000,000 - 1,999,999	● 250,000 - 499,999	● 30,000 - 99,999	○ UNDER 10,000

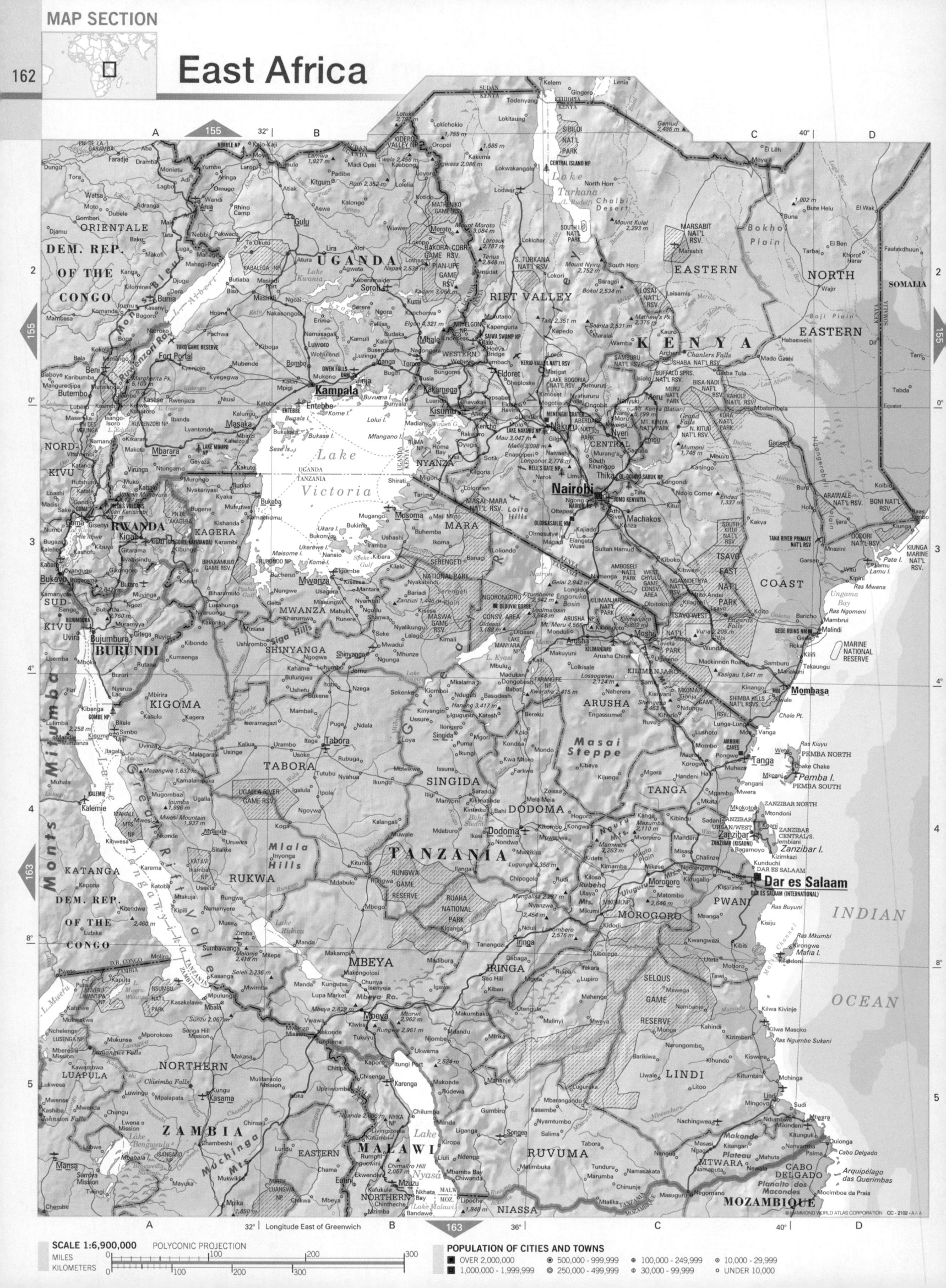

POPULATION OF CITIES AND TOWNS

■ OVER 2,000,000	⊚ 500,000 - 999,999
■ 1,000,000 - 1,999,999	⊚ 250,000 - 499,999

⊙ 100,000 - 249,999	⊙ 10,000 - 29,999
⊙ 30,000 - 99,999	○ UNDER 10,000

Southern Africa

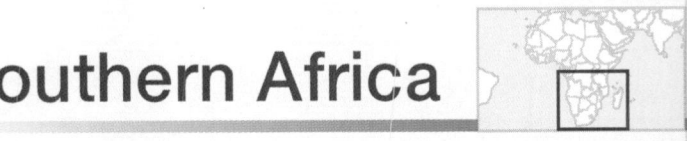

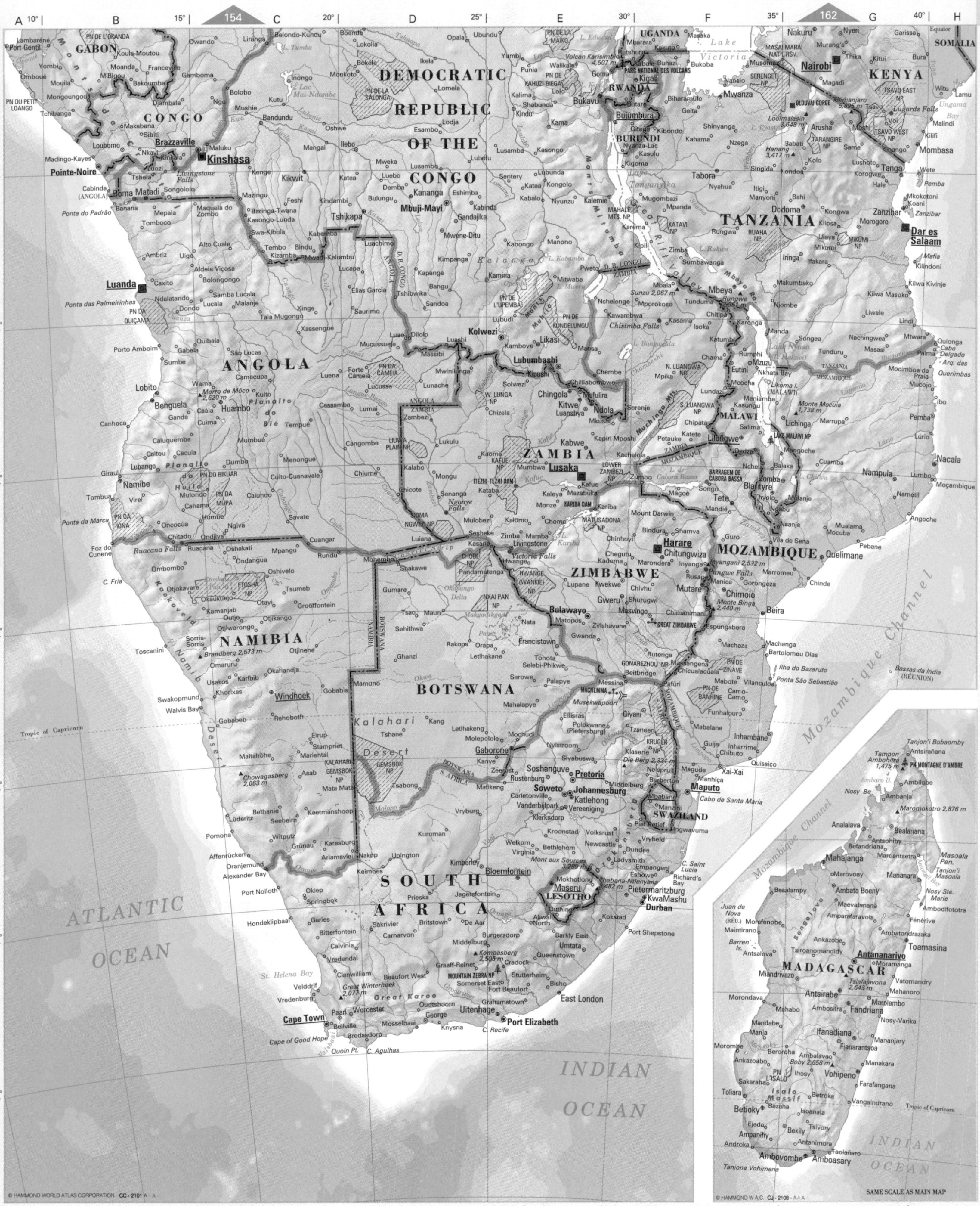

POPULATION OF CITIES AND TOWNS

■ OVER 2,000,000	◉ 500,000 - 999,999
■ 1,000,000 - 1,999,999	⊕ 100,000 - 499,999
⊙ 50,000 - 99,999	○ UNDER 50,000

SCALE 1:17,200,000 POLYCONIC PROJECTION

MILES 0 250 500 750

KILOMETERS 0 250 500 750

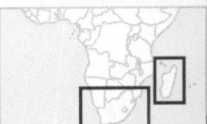
POPULATION OF CITIES AND TOWNS

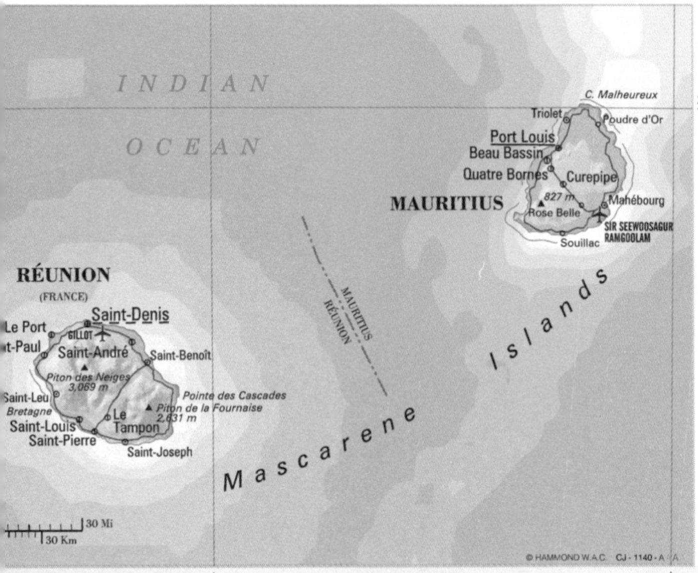

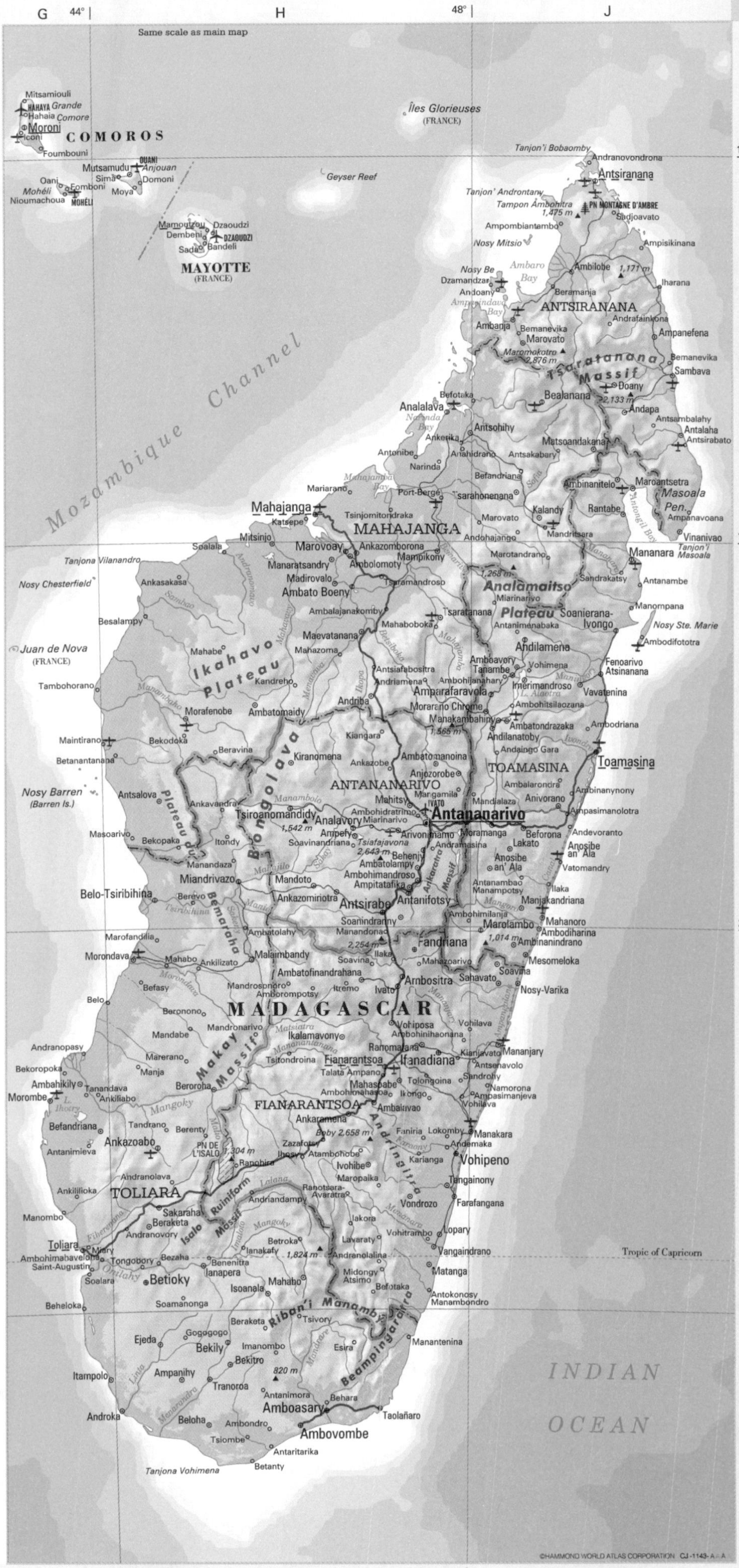

■ OVER 2,000,000   ● 500,000 - 999,999   ● 100,000 - 249,999   ● 10,000 - 29,999
■ 1,000,000 - 1,999,999   ● 250,000 - 499,999   ○ 30,000 - 99,999   ○ UNDER 10,000

SCALE 1:6,900,000   POLYCONIC PROJECTION

MILES
KILOMETERS

© HAMMOND WORLD ATLAS CORPORATION

Longitude East of Greenwich

Australia, New Zealand and the Pacific

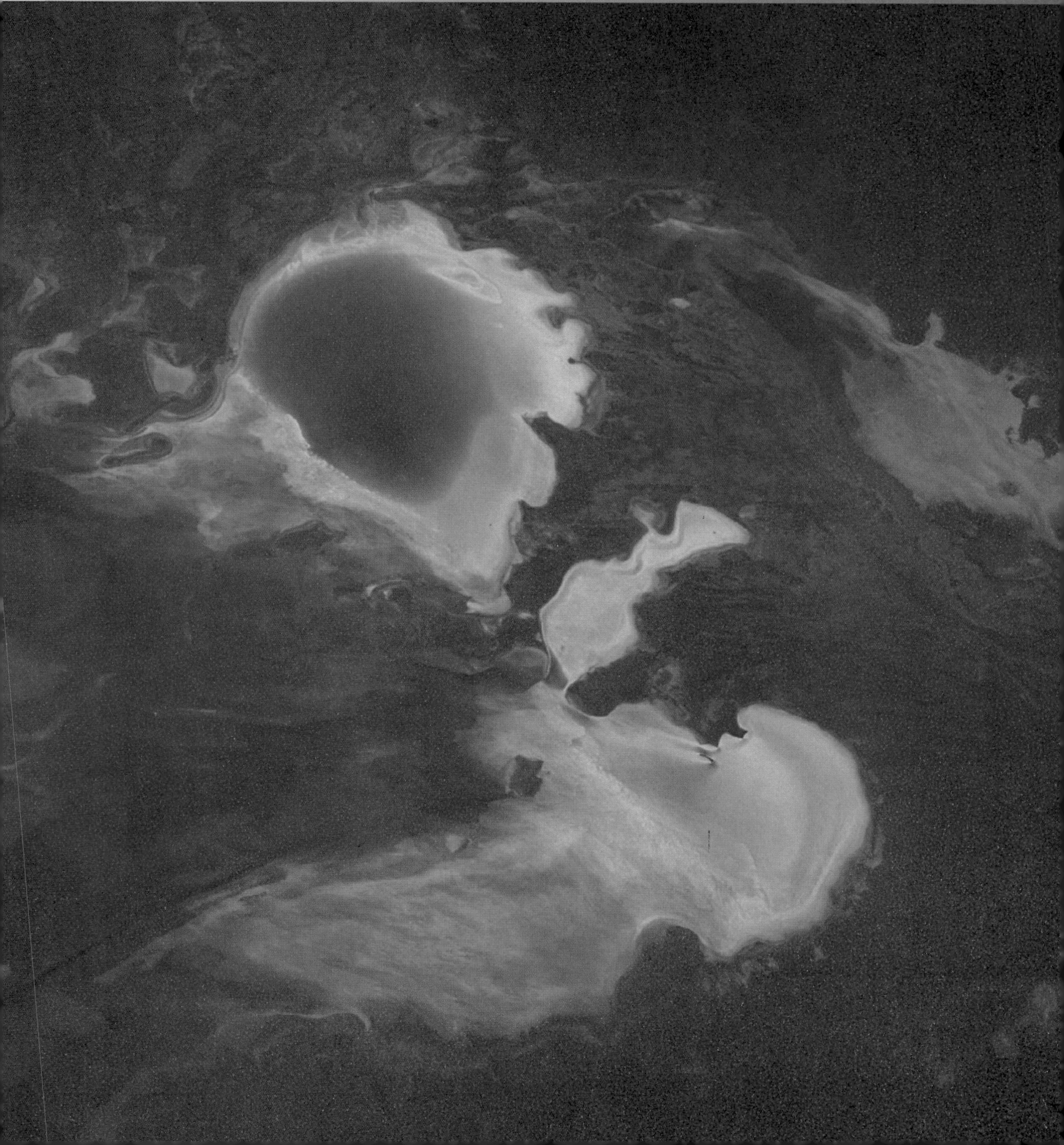

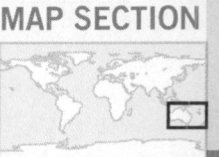
The Lake Eyre Basin is located in the arid interior of south central Australia. This basin is one of the largest areas of internal drainage in the world. It consists of two distinct, but interrelated basins: the north basin and the south basin. The much larger north basin shown here (the highly reflective areas) consists of two very large, normally dry lakebeds. The western lobe (bottom of the image) is Belt Bay, and the eastern lobe is Madigan Bay. The color change, especially in the Madigan Bay lobe, indicates that there was some water in this lobe at the time the image was taken.

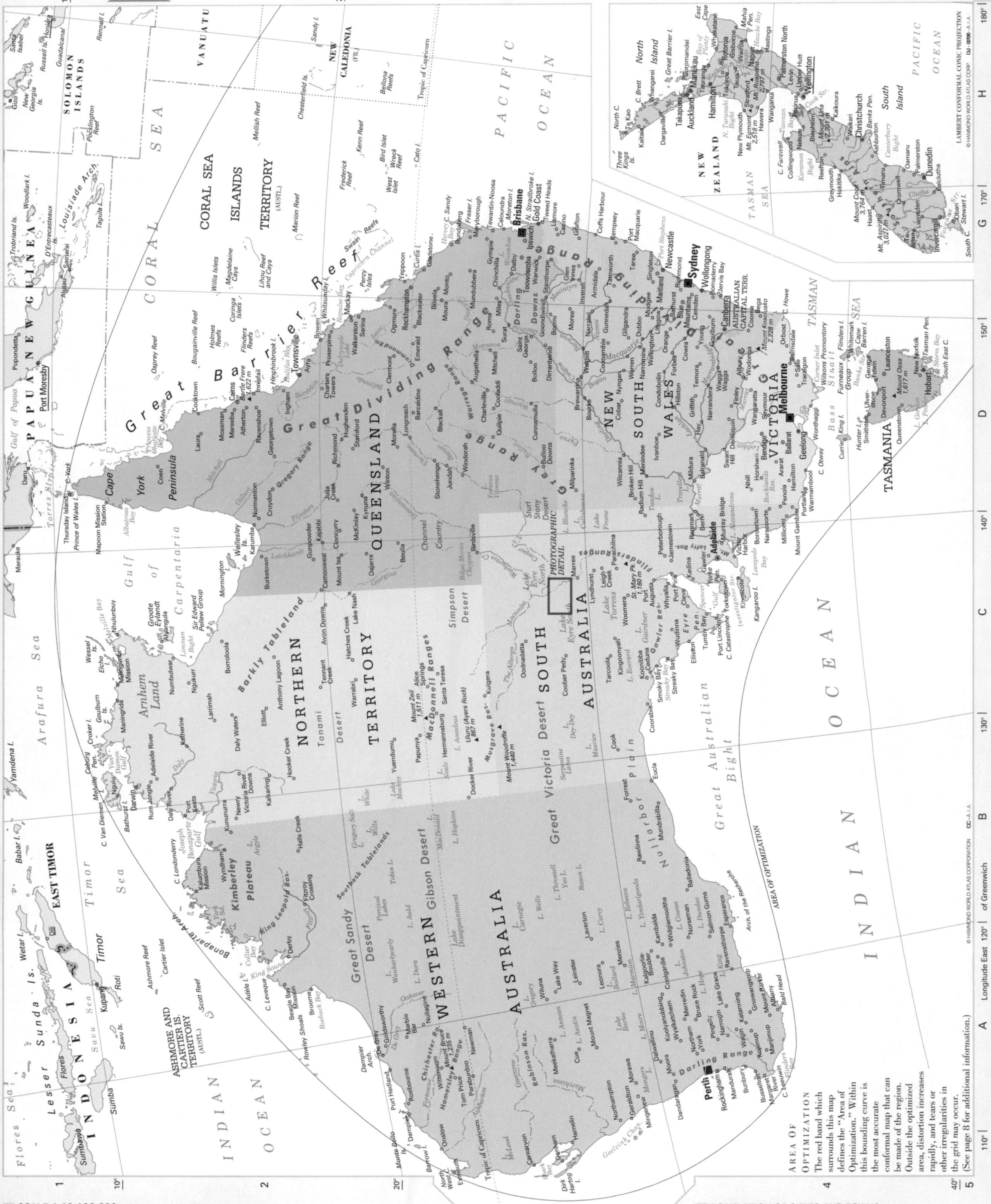

SCALE 1:19,100,000   OPTIMAL CONFORMAL PROJECTION

MILES

KILOMETERS

POPULATION OF CITIES AND TOWNS

■ OVER 2,000,000   ⬤ 500,000 - 999,999   ⊙ 50,000 - 99,999
■ 1,000,000 - 1,999,999   ● 100,000 - 499,999   ○ UNDER 50,000

AREA OF OPTIMIZATION

The red band which surrounds this map defines the "Area of Optimization." Within this bounding curve is the most accurate conformal map that can be made of the region. Outside the optimized area, distortion increases rapidly, and tears or other irregularities in the grid may occur. (See page 8 for additional information.)

© HAMMOND WORLD ATLAS CORPORATION

LAMBERT CONFORMAL CONIC PROJECTION   © HAMMOND WORLD ATLAS CORP.

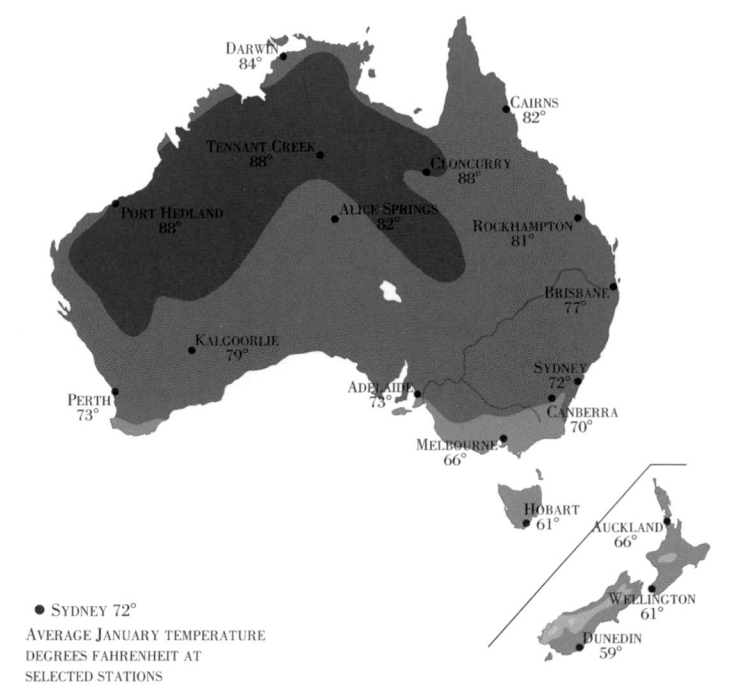

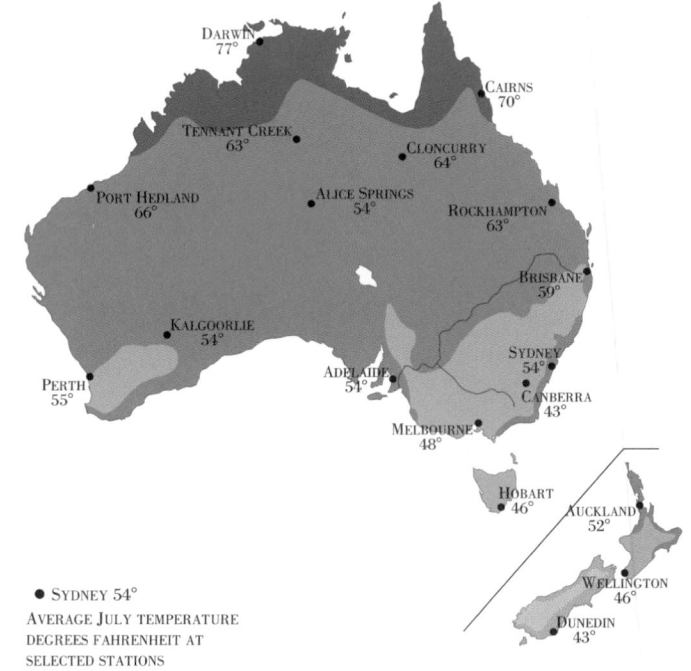

AVERAGE JANUARY TEMPERATURE

- SYDNEY 72°
AVERAGE JANUARY TEMPERATURE
DEGREES FAHRENHEIT AT
SELECTED STATIONS

AVERAGE JULY TEMPERATURE

- SYDNEY 54°
AVERAGE JULY TEMPERATURE
DEGREES FAHRENHEIT AT
SELECTED STATIONS

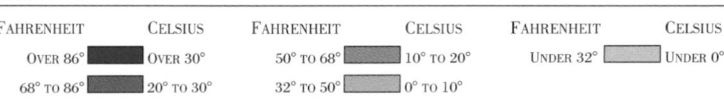

FAHRENHEIT	CELSIUS	FAHRENHEIT	CELSIUS	FAHRENHEIT	CELSIUS
OVER 86°	OVER 30°	50° TO 68°	10° TO 20°	UNDER 32°	UNDER 0°
68° TO 86°	20° TO 30°	32° TO 50°	0° TO 10°		

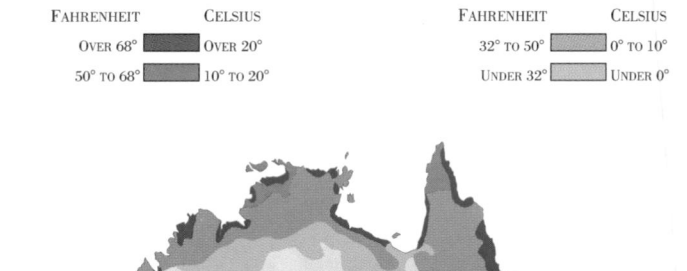

FAHRENHEIT	CELSIUS	FAHRENHEIT	CELSIUS
OVER 68°	OVER 20°	32° TO 50°	0° TO 10°
50° TO 68°	10° TO 20°	UNDER 32°	UNDER 0°

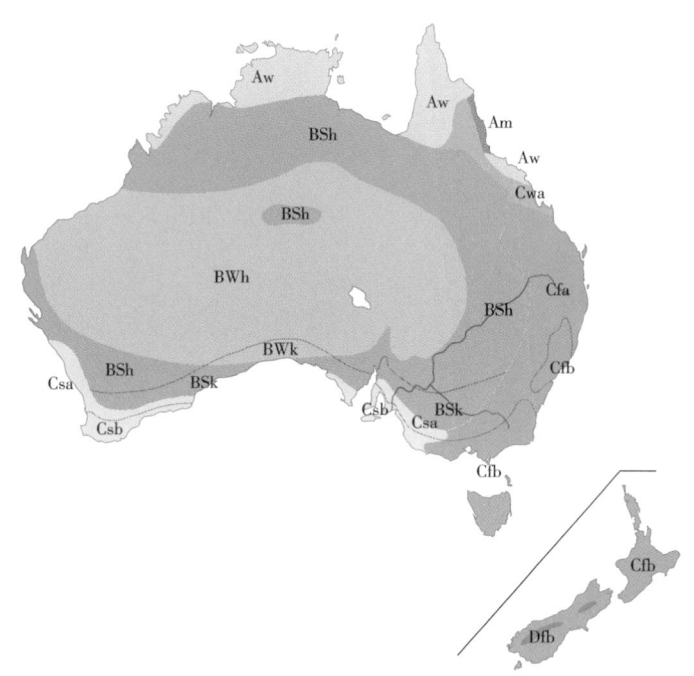

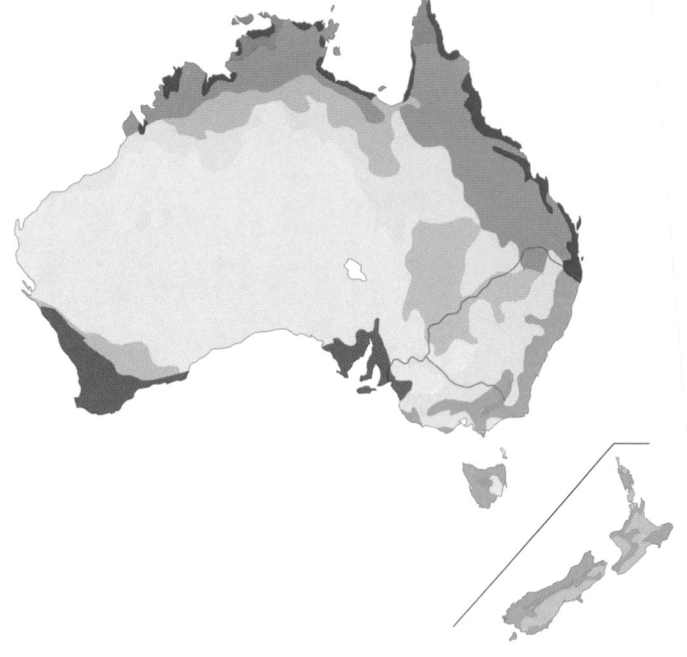

CLIMATE

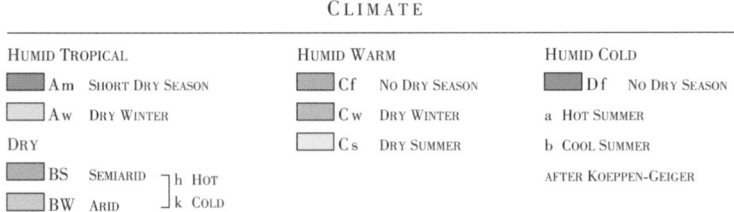

VEGETATION

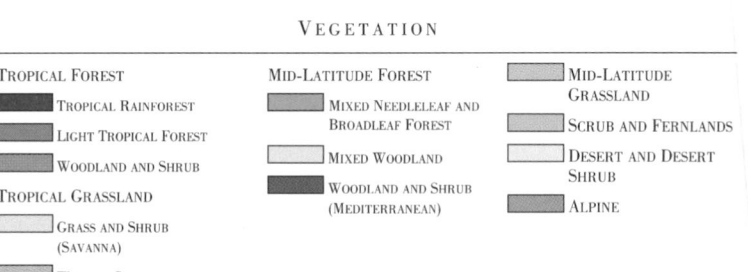

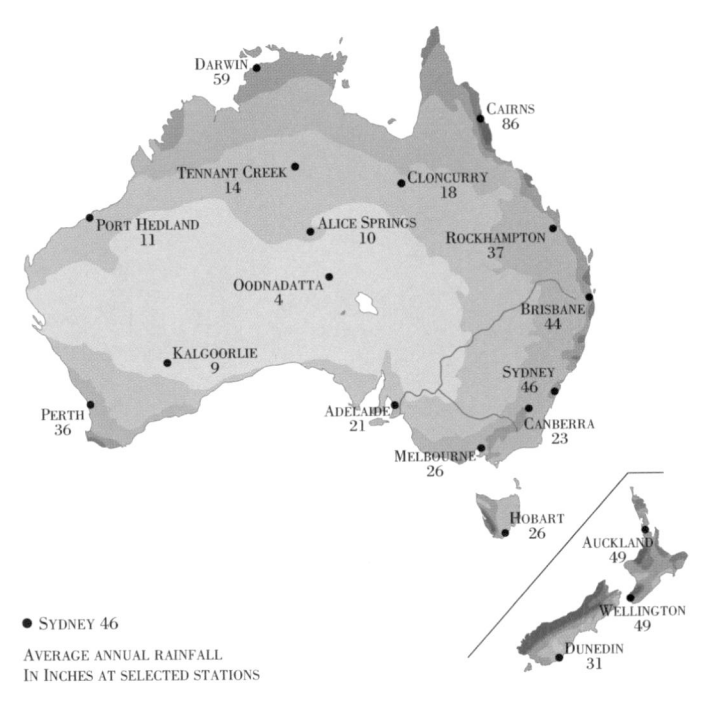

● SYDNEY 46

AVERAGE ANNUAL RAINFALL
IN INCHES AT SELECTED STATIONS

● CITIES WITH OVER 500,000
  INHABITANTS

AVERAGE ANNUAL RAINFALL

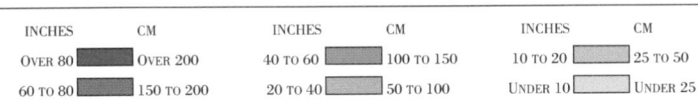

INCHES	CM	INCHES	CM	INCHES	CM
OVER 80	OVER 200	40 TO 60	100 TO 150	10 TO 20	25 TO 50
60 TO 80	150 TO 200	20 TO 40	50 TO 100	UNDER 10	UNDER 25

POPULATION DISTRIBUTION

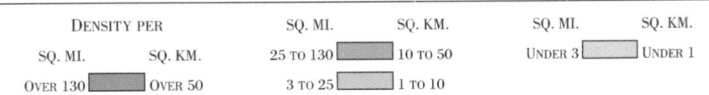

DENSITY PER		SQ. MI.	SQ. KM.	SQ. MI.	SQ. KM.
SQ. MI.	SQ. KM.	25 TO 130	10 TO 50	UNDER 3	UNDER 1
OVER 130	OVER 50	3 TO 25	1 TO 10		

LAND USE

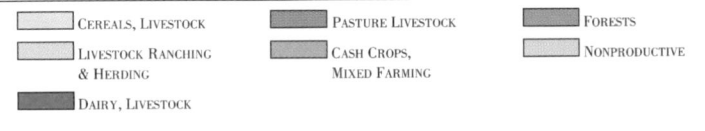

	CEREALS, LIVESTOCK		PASTURE LIVESTOCK		FORESTS
	LIVESTOCK RANCHING & HERDING		CASH CROPS, MIXED FARMING		NONPRODUCTIVE
	DAIRY, LIVESTOCK				

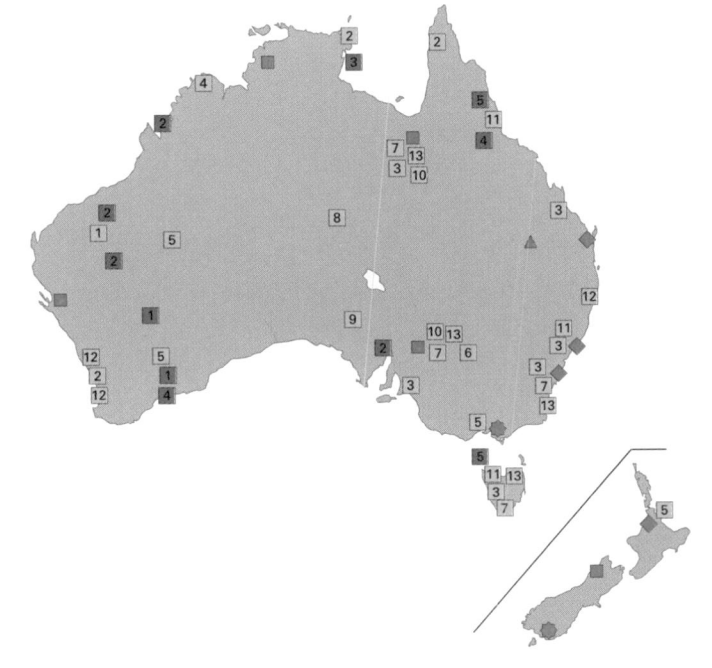

MINERAL RESOURCES

ENERGY & FUELS	IRON & FERROALLOYS	OTHER MAJOR RESOURCES		
◆ COAL	1 COBALT	1 ASBESTOS	6 GYPSUM	11 TIN
⬣ LIGNITE	2 IRON ORE	2 BAUXITE	7 LEAD	12 TITANIUM
▲ NATURAL GAS	3 MANGANESE	3 COPPER	8 MICA	13 ZINC
▪ URANIUM	4 NICKEL	4 DIAMONDS	9 OPALS	
	5 TUNGSTEN	5 GOLD	10 SILVER	

Height [scale bar] Depth

© HAMMOND WORLD ATLAS CORPORATION   CM·A

120° | Longitude East of Greenwich

POPULATION OF CITIES AND TOWNS

| ■ OVER 2,000,000 | ◉ 500,000 - 999,999 | ● 100,000 - 249,999 | ○ 10,000 - 29,999 |
| ■ 1,000,000 - 1,999,999 | ◉ 250,000 - 499,999 | ◉ 30,000 - 99,999 | ○ UNDER 10,000 |

SCALE 1:6,900,000   LAMBERT CONFORMAL CONIC PROJECTION

MILES

KILOMETERS

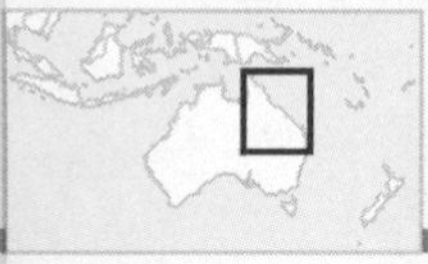

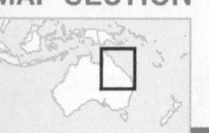

Northeastern Australia

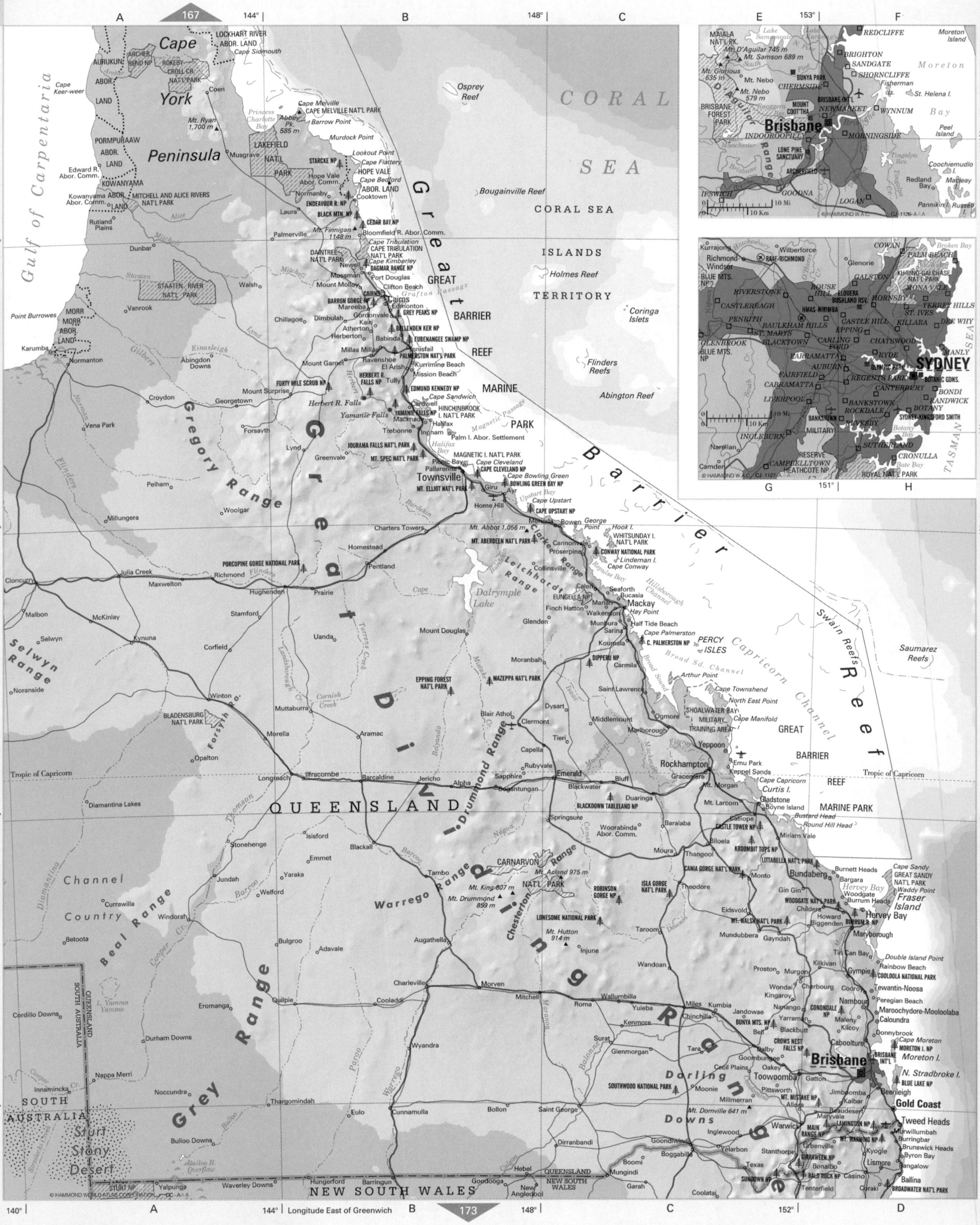

SCALE 1:6,900,000 LAMBERT CONFORMAL CONIC PROJECTION

MILES 0 100 200 300

KILOMETERS 0 100 200 300

Southeastern Australia

POPULATION OF CITIES AND TOWNS

■ OVER 2,000,000	◉ 500,000 - 999,999	● 100,000 - 249,999	◉ 10,000 - 29,999
■ 1,000,000 - 1,999,999	◉ 250,000 - 499,999	◉ 30,000 - 99,999	○ UNDER 10,000

SCALE 1:6,900,000 LAMBERT CONFORMAL CONIC PROJECTION

MILES 100 200 300
KILOMETERS 100 200 300

© HAMMOND WORLD ATLAS CORPORATION CC - A/LA

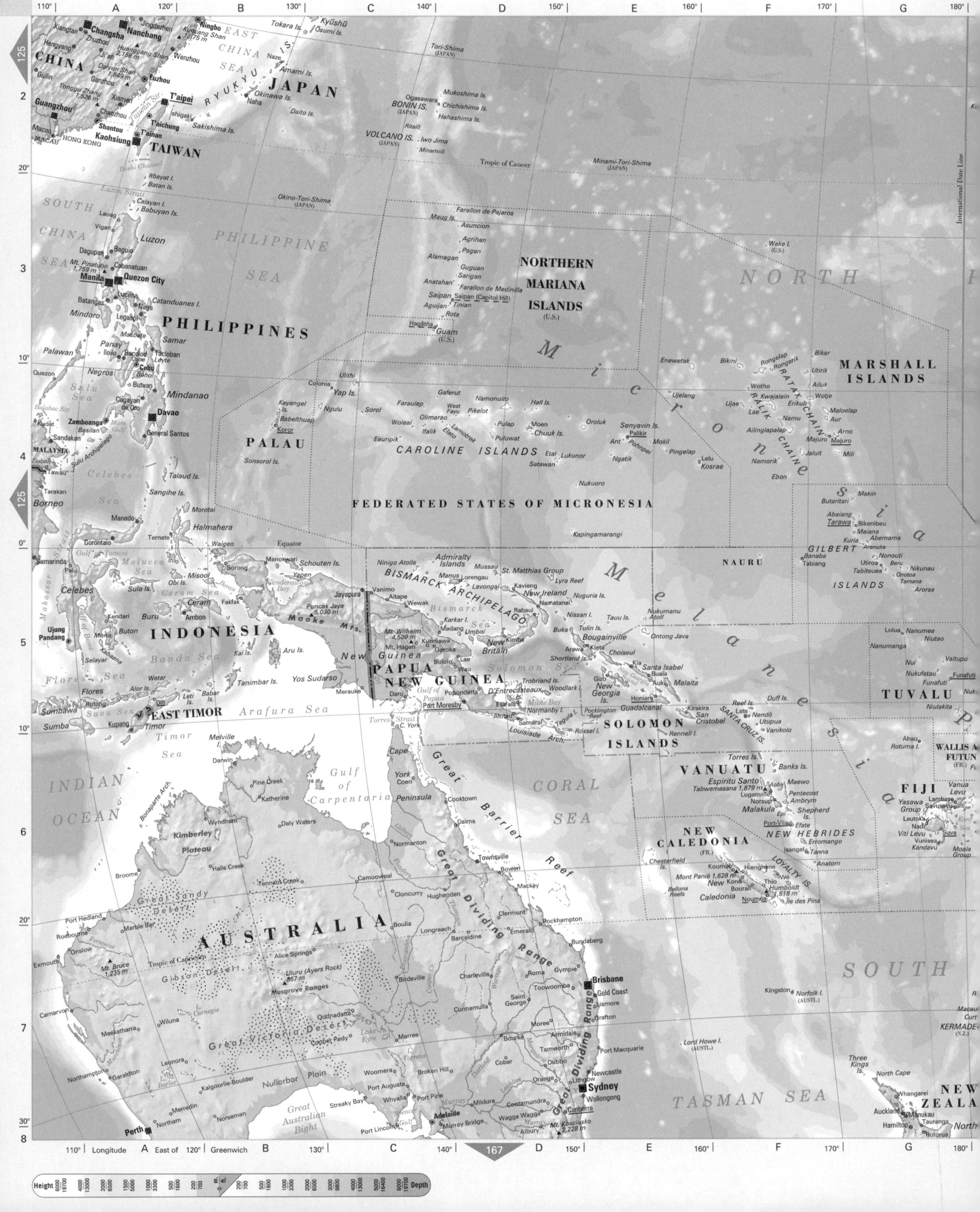

CHINA
Changsha
Nanchang
Ningbo
Wenzhou
Fuzhou
Guangzhou
Xiamen
Shantou
Kaohsiung
Macau
HONG KONG
T'aipei
T'aichung
T'ainan
TAIWAN
EAST CHINA SEA
RYUKYU IS.
JAPAN
Kyūshū
Ōsumi Is.
Tokara Is.
Amami Is.
Okinawa Is.
Naha
Sakishima Is.
Daito Is.
Tori-Shima (JAPAN)
Mukoshima Is.
Chichishima Is.
Hahashima Is.
BONIN IS. (JAPAN)
VOLCANO IS. (JAPAN)
Iwo Jima
Minamiiō
Tropic of Cancer
Minami-Tori-Shima (JAPAN)
International Date Line
Okino-Tori-Shima (JAPAN)
Bashi Channel
Luzon Strait
Itbayat I.
Batan Is.
Calayan I.
Babuyan Is.
SOUTH CHINA SEA
Luzon
Laoag
Vigan
Baguio
Dagupan
Cabanatuan
Mt. Pinatubo 1,759 m
Manila
Quezon City
Lucena
Batangas
Naga
Catanduanes I.
Mindoro
Legaspi
PHILIPPINE SEA
PHILIPPINES
Masbate
Samar
Panay
Iloilo
Bacolod
Cebu
Tacloban
Leyte
Palawan
Negros
Bohol
Butuan
Mindanao
Cagayan de Oro
Davao
Zamboanga
General Santos
Sulu Sea
Sulu Archipelago
Basilan
Sandakan
Kudat
MALAYSIA
Sabah
Tawau
Tarakan
Borneo
Celebes Sea
Talaud Is.
Sangihe Is.
Manado
Morotai
Halmahera
Ternate
Gorontalo
Samarinda
Palu
Molucca Sea
Waigeo
Sorong
Manokwari
Schouten Is.
Yapen
Misool
Obi Is.
Sula Is.
Celebes
Ceram Sea
Ceram
Fakfak
Ambon
Buru
Kendari
Buton
Ujung Pandang
Makassar Strait
Gulf of Bone
Muna
Kabaena
Selayar
INDONESIA
Banda Sea
Kai Is.
Aru Is.
Tanimbar Is.
Yos Sudarso
Merauke
Wetar
Alor Is.
Flores Sea
Flores
Ruteng
Sumbawa
Savu Sea
Sumba
Kupang
Timor
Dili
EAST TIMOR
Leti Is.
Babar Is.
Arafura Sea
Timor Sea
INDIAN OCEAN
Equator
Tropic of Capricorn
Farallon de Pajaros
Maug Is.
Asuncion
Agrihan
Pagan
Alamagan
Guguan
Sarigan
Anatahan
Farallon de Medinilla
Saipan
Saipan (Capitol Hill)
Tinian
Aguijan
Rota
Hagåtña
Guam (U.S.)
NORTHERN MARIANA ISLANDS (U.S.)
Wake I. (U.S.)
NORTH
Micronesia
Ulithi
Colonia
Yap Is.
Ngulu
Sorol
Faraulep
Gaferut
West Fayu
Pikelot
Namonuito
Hall Is.
Woleai
Olimarao
Ifalik
Elato
Lamotrek
Pulap
Puluwat
Moen
Chuuk Is.
Oroluk
Senyavin Is.
Palikir
Pohnpei
Mokil
Pingelap
Ant
Ngatik
Lelu
Kosrae
Eauripik
CAROLINE ISLANDS
Etal
Satawan
Lukunor
Nukuoro
Kayangel Is.
Babelthuap
Koror
PALAU
Sonsorol Is.
FEDERATED STATES OF MICRONESIA
Kapingamarangi
Enewetak
Bikini
Rongelap
Rongerik
Bikar
Utirik
Ailuk
Wotho
Ujelang
Ujae
Lae
Kwajalein
Erikub
Wotje
RALIK CHAIN
RATAK CHAIN
Maloelap
Aur
Namu
Ailinglapalap
Arno
Majuro
Jaluit
Mili
Namorik
Ebon
MARSHALL ISLANDS
Makin
Butaritari
Abaiang
Tarawa
Bikenibeu
Maiana
Abemama
Kuria
Aranuka
Nonouti
Banaba
Tabiang
Utiroa
Tabiteuea
Beru
Nikunau
Onotoa
Tamana
Arorae
GILBERT ISLANDS
NAURU
Ninigo Atolls
Admiralty Islands
Mussau
St. Matthias Group
Manus
Lorengau
Lavongai
Kavieng
New Ireland
Lyra Reef
Namatanai
Nuguria Is.
Vanimo
Aitape
Wewak
Jayapura
Puncak Jaya 5,030 m
Maoke Mts.
Mt. Wilhelm 4,509 m
Mt. Hagen
Madang
Karkar I.
Bismarck Sea
BISMARCK ARCHIPELAGO
Rabaul
Umboi
Kundiawa
Goroka
Lae
Bulolo
Wau
New Britain
Kimbe
New Guinea
PAPUA NEW GUINEA
Solomon Sea
Nissan I.
Buka
Tulin Is.
Tauu Is.
Nukumanu Atoll
Bougainville
Kieta
Ontong Java
Arawa
Shortland Is.
Choiseul
Kia
Santa Isabel
Buala
Gizo
New Georgia Is.
Auki
Malaita
Honiara
Guadalcanal
Daru
Gulf of Papua
Popondetta
D'Entrecasteaux Is.
Trobriand Is.
Woodlark I.
Port Moresby
Esa'ala
Normanby I.
Alotau
Samarai
Tagula I.
Rossel I.
Louisiade Arch.
Pocklington Reef
SOLOMON ISLANDS
Rennell I.
Kirakira
San Cristobal
Reef Is.
Lata
Nendö
Utupua
Vanikolo
Duff Is.
SANTA CRUZ IS.
Torres Strait
C. York
Cape York Peninsula
Melville I.
Darwin
Gulf of Carpentaria
Pine Creek
Katherine
Cooktown
Great Barrier Reef
CORAL SEA
Bonaparte Arch.
Wyndham
Daly Waters
Kimberley Plateau
Cairns
Normanton
Halls Creek
Broome
Tennant Creek
Camooweal
Townsville
Bowen
Cloncurry
Hughenden
Mackay
Great Sandy Desert
Great Dividing Range
Port Hedland
Marble Bar
Roebourne
AUSTRALIA
Boulia
Longreach
Clermont
Emerald
Rockhampton
Barcaldine
Onslow
Exmouth
Mt. Bruce 1,235 m
Gibson Desert
Alice Springs
Uluru (Ayers Rock) 867 m
Musgrave Ranges
Birdsville
Charleville
Roma
Gympie
Bundaberg
Brisbane
Gold Coast
Toowoomba
Saint George
Cunnamulla
Lismore
Grafton
Carnarvon
Wiluna
Meekatharra
Oodnadatta
Coober Pedy
Lake Eyre
Great Victoria Desert
Marree
Bourke
Moree
Armidale
Tamworth
Port Macquarie
Dubbo
Cobar
Broken Hill
Leonora
Geraldton
Northampton
Kalgoorlie-Boulder
Nullarbor Plain
Woomera
Port Augusta
Whyalla
Port Pirie
Orange
Lithgow
Newcastle
Sydney
Wollongong
Cootamundra
Wagga Wagga
Mildura
Adelaide
Murray Bridge
Canberra
Mt. Kosciusko 2,228 m
Albury
Streaky Bay
Port Lincoln
Great Australian Bight
Merredin
Northam
Norseman
Perth
Nanumea
Niutao
Lolua
Nanumanga
Nui
Vaitupu
Nukufetau
Funafuti
TUVALU
Niulakita
VANUATU
Torres Is.
Banks Is.
Espiritu Santo
Tabwemasana 1,879 m
Aoba
Maewo
Luganville
Pentecost
Ambrym
Malakula
Norsup
Shepherd Is.
Epi
Port-Vila
Efate
NEW HEBRIDES
Erromango
Tanna
Anatom
Isangel
NEW CALEDONIA (FR.)
Chesterfield Is.
LOYALTY IS.
Hienghène
Koumac
Mont Panié 1,628 m
Koné
Bourail
Thio
Humboldt 1,618 m
Nouméa
Île des Pins
New Caledonia
Bellona Reefs
Ahau
Rotuma I.
WALLIS AND FUTUNA (FR.)
FIJI
Vanua Levu
Yasawa Group
Lambasa
Savusavu
Lautoka
Nadi
Viti Levu
Vunisea
Suva
Kandavu
Moala Group
Kingston
Norfolk I. (AUSTL.)
SOUTH
Lord Howe I. (AUSTL.)
TASMAN SEA
Three Kings Is.
North Cape
Whangarei
Auckland
Manukau
Hamilton
Tauranga
Rotorua
NEW ZEALAND
KERMADEC

125
125
167

Left Map (Central Pacific Ocean)

170° J 160° K 150° L

and Hermes Reef
Lisianski I.
Laysan I. Maro Reef
French Frigate Shoals
Necker I.
Nihoa
Kauai
Niihau Oahu Molokai
Honolulu Lanai Maui
Hilo
Hawaii

HAWAII (U.S.)

HAWAIIAN ISLANDS

Tropic of Cancer

P A C I F I C   O C E A N

Johnston Atoll (U.S.)

Kingman Reef (U.S.)
Palmyra Atoll (U.S.)

Teraina (Washington I.)
Tabuaeran (Fanning I.)

Kiritimati (Christmas I.)

Equator

Jarvis I. (U.S.)

P O L Y N E S I A

L I N E   I S L A N D S

International Date Line

I. (U.S.)

B A T I

PHOENIX IS.
Abariringa (Canton I.)
Enderbury
Birnie
Rawaki (Phoenix I.)
Orona (Hull I.)
Manra (Sydney I.)

Malden I.

Starbuck I.

Vostok I.

Caroline I.

Flint I.

Atafu
TOKELAU (N.Z.)
Nukunonu
Fakaofo
Swains I.

Rakahanga
Pukapuka
Manihiki
Nassau
Tongareva (Penrhyn)

NORTHERN COOK IS.

Suwarrow

SAMOA
Mt. Silisili 1,858 m
AMERICAN SAMOA
Savai'i
Apia
Upolu
Manua Is.
Tutuila
Pago Pago

Rose I.

COOK ISLANDS (N.Z.)

Bellingshausen

Îles Sous le Vent
Tupai
Maupiti Bora Bora Makatea
Huahine
Raiatea Uturoa
Tahaa Moorea
Faaa Papeete
SOCIETY IS.
Îles du Vent
Tahiti
Anaa

Tikehau Rangiroa Manihi
Tiputa Arutua Takaroa
Apataki Takapoto
Kaukura Toau
Tetiaroa
Fakarava
Tahanea Makemo
Hikueru
Marokau

TUAMOTU
Disappointment Is.
Tepoto Napuka
Pukapuka
Fangatau
Fakahina
Raroia
Tatakoto

M E L A N E S I A

ou
Neiafu
Vava'u Group
Atofi
Niue
atoputapu Group
Pangai
Ha'apai Group
aku'alofa
Eua

NIUE (N.Z.)

Amuri
Aitutaki Atoll
Manuae Atoll
Palmerston Atoll
SOUTHERN COOK IS.
Atiu
Mitiaro
Mauke
Avarua
Rarotonga
Mangaia

Maria
Moerai
Rurutu
Mataura
Rimatara
Tubuai
TUBUAÏ ISLANDS (Austral Islands)
Raivavae

Hereheretue

Vanavaro
Tureia
Fangataufa

Rapa
Marotiri Is. (Bass I.)

Amanu
Otepa
Hao
Vahitahi
Nukutavake
Pukarua Reao

Aktueon Group
Marutea

Actaeon Group
Rikitea Tarava
Morane
Mangareva
GAMBIER IS.
Maria
Temoe

MARQUESAS IS.

TUAMOTU ARCHIPELAGO

FRENCH POLYNESIA

PITCAIRN ISLANDS (U.K.)
Oeno Atoll
Adamstown Pitcairn I.
Henderson I.
Ducie I.

Tropic of Capricorn

P A C I F I C   O C E A N

International Date Line

Easter Island (Isla de Pascua) (CHILE)

170° J 160° K 150° L 140° M 130° N 120° Longitude P West of 110° Greenwich Q 100°

10°
6
20°
7
30°
8

Right Map (New Zealand)

R 170° S 175° T

Three Kings Is.
North C.
C. Maria van Diemen
Te Kao
C. Kerikeri
Kaitaia
Kaikohe
C. Brett
Whangarei
Dargaville
Great Barrier I.
Warkworth
Hauraki Gulf
Kaipara Har.
Takapuna
Auckland
Manukau
Coromandel Pen.
Thames
Te Aroha
Bay of Plenty
Huntly
Te Araroa
Hamilton
Tauranga
Whakatane
Te Awamutu
Cambridge
Whakatane
East C.
Ngaruawahia
Rotorua
UREWERA NP
Hikurangi 1,754 m
Te Kuiti
Murupara
TASMAN SEA

North Island

Taupo

New Plymouth
Mt. Egmont 2,518 m
C. Egmont
Stratford
Hawera
North Taranaki Bight
Mt. Ruapehu 2,797 m
TONGARIRO NP
Turangi
Gisborne
Wairoa
Napier
Mahia Pen.
Hawke Bay
Hastings

NEW ZEALAND

South Taranaki Bight
Wanganui
Waipukurau
Dannevirke
Ashhurst
Palmerston North
Levin
Masterton

C. Farewell
Collingwood
Tasman Bay
Karamea Bight
Karamea
Motueka
Porirua
Upper Hutt
Wellington
Lower Hutt

Westport
Mt. Owen 1,875 m
NELSON LAKES NP
Nelson
Blenheim
Ward
Cook Strait
C. Palliser

Moreland
Reefton
Mt. Una 2,301 m
Clarence
Greymouth
Lewis Pass
Kaikoura
Hokitika
ARTHUR'S PASS NP
Otira
Waikari
Arthur's Pass
Rangiora
Pegasus Bay
Fox Glacier
WESTLAND NP
Mt. Cook 3,764 m
Haast
MT. COOK NP
Darfield
Kaiapoi
Christchurch
Banks Pen.
MT. ASPIRING NP
Mt. Aspiring 3,027 m
Ashburton
Geraldine
Temuke
Canterbury Bight
Twizel
Timaru
FIORDLAND
Queenstown
Wanaka
Cromwell
Alexandra
Waimate
NAT'L PARK
Te Anau
Lumsden
Oamaru
Palmerston
West C.
Gore
Mosgiel
Dunedin
Riverton
Milton
Invercargill
Balclutha
Mt. Anglem 980 m
Bluff
Foveaux Strait
Oban
Stewart I.
South C.
Snares Is.

S O U T H E R N   A L P S

South Island

P A C I F I C   O C E A N

LAMBERT CONFORMAL CONIC PROJECTION

0 ___ 90 Mi
0 ___ 90 Km

© HAMMOND W.A.C. CJ-1200-A-A-A

9
35°
10
40°
11
45°
12

Legend

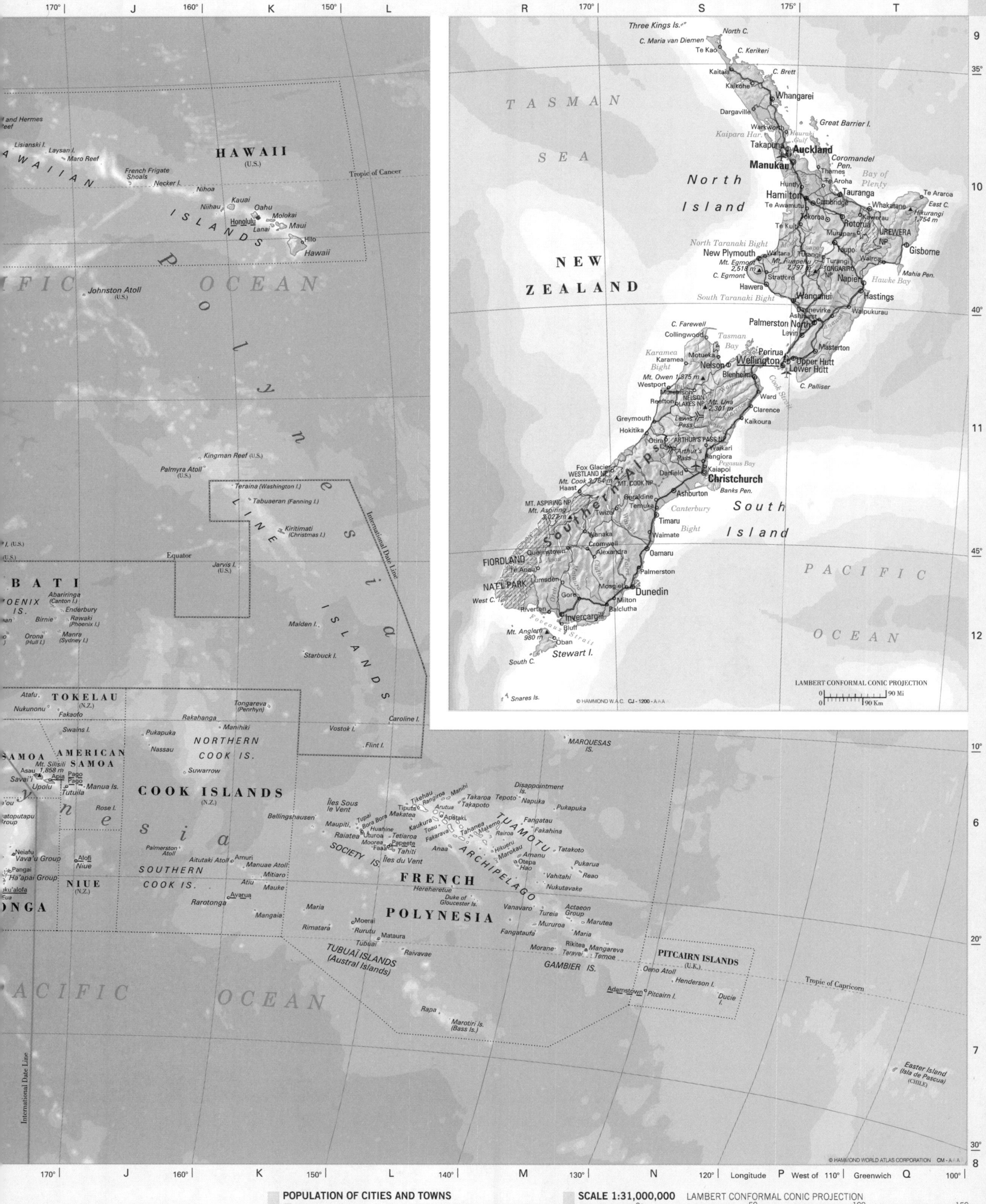

POPULATION OF CITIES AND TOWNS

■ OVER 3,000,000
■ 1,000,000 - 2,999,999
● 500,000 - 999,999
● 100,000 - 499,999
∘ UNDER 100,000

SCALE 1:31,000,000 LAMBERT CONFORMAL CONIC PROJECTION

MILES
0   50   100   150
KILOMETERS
0   50   100   150

© HAMMOND WORLD ATLAS CORPORATION CM-A-A-A

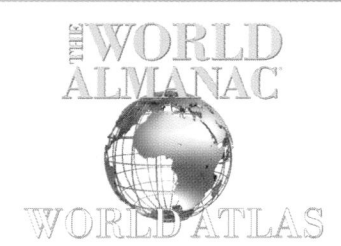

North America

The Grand Canyon, one of the deepest canyons in the world, with a depth of 1 mile (1.6 km.), can be seen in this spectacular, west-looking, low-oblique image. The Colorado River cut through rocks billions of years old to create this canyon. The Grand Canyon is 277 miles (466 km.) long and averages nearly 10 miles (16 km.) in width. The snow-covered, forested Kaibab Plateau (north of the canyon) and the Coconino Plateau (south of the canyon) are visible. Western portions of the Painted Desert can be seen east of the canyon where the Little Colorado joins the Colorado River.

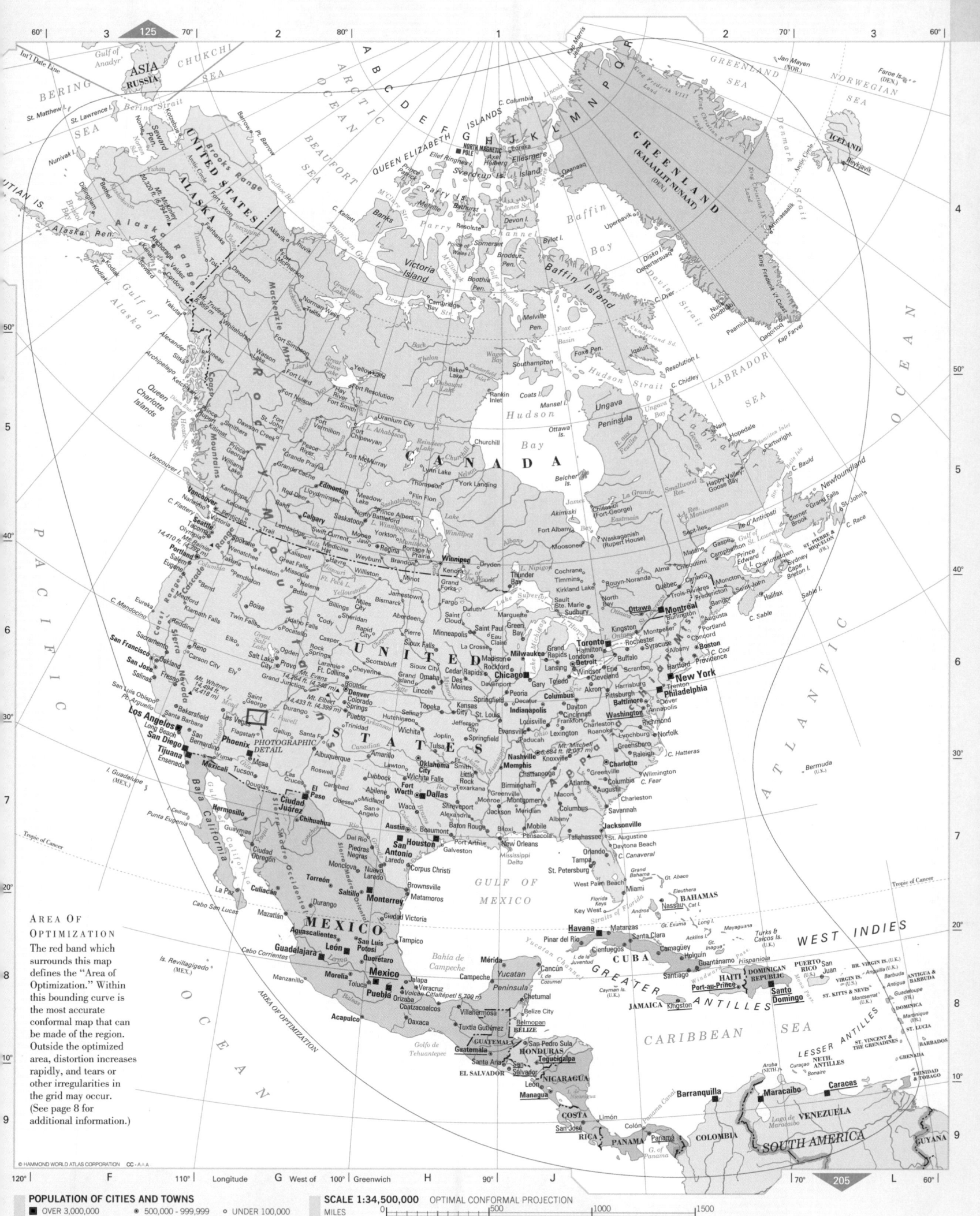

AREA OF OPTIMIZATION
The red band which surrounds this map defines the "Area of Optimization." Within this bounding curve is the most accurate conformal map that can be made of the region. Outside the optimized area, distortion increases rapidly, and tears or other irregularities in the grid may occur. (See page 8 for additional information.)

© HAMMOND WORLD ATLAS CORPORATION   CC - A·A·A

POPULATION OF CITIES AND TOWNS
■ OVER 3,000,000   ● 500,000 - 999,999   ○ UNDER 100,000
■ 1,000,000 - 2,999,999   ◉ 100,000 - 499,999

SCALE 1:34,500,000   OPTIMAL CONFORMAL PROJECTION
MILES   0   500   1000   1500
KILOMETERS   0   500   1000   1500

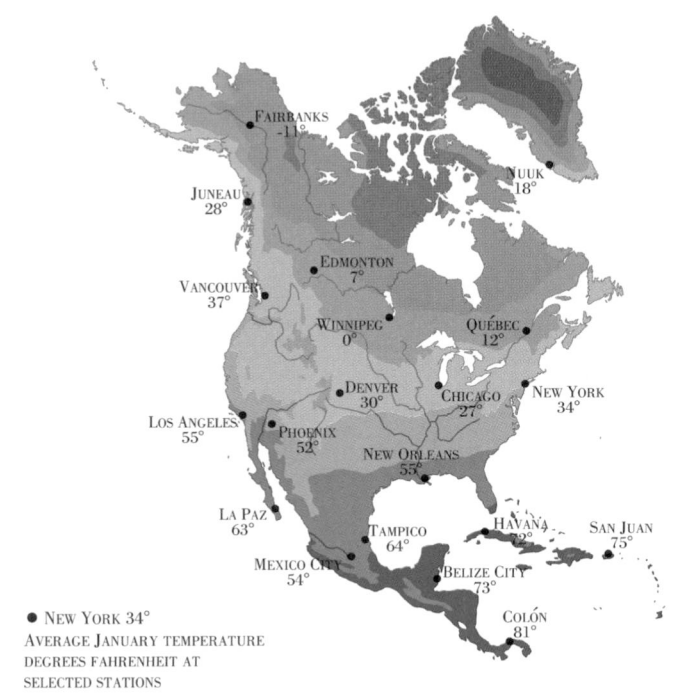

● NEW YORK 34°
AVERAGE JANUARY TEMPERATURE
DEGREES FAHRENHEIT AT
SELECTED STATIONS

AVERAGE JANUARY TEMPERATURE

FAHRENHEIT	CELSIUS	FAHRENHEIT	CELSIUS	FAHRENHEIT	CELSIUS
OVER 68°	OVER 20°	14° TO 32°	-10° TO 0°	-40° TO -22°	-40° TO -30°
50° TO 68°	10° TO 20°	-4° TO 14°	-20° TO -10°	UNDER -40°	UNDER -40°
32° TO 50°	0° TO 10°	-22° TO -4°	-30° TO -20°		

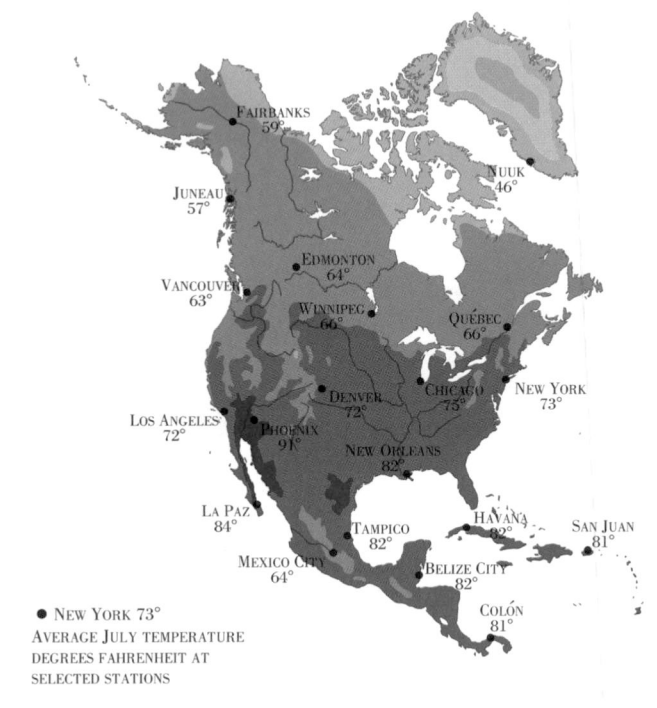

● NEW YORK 73°
AVERAGE JULY TEMPERATURE
DEGREES FAHRENHEIT AT
SELECTED STATIONS

AVERAGE JULY TEMPERATURE

FAHRENHEIT	CELSIUS	FAHRENHEIT	CELSIUS	FAHRENHEIT	CELSIUS
OVER 86°	OVER 30°	50° TO 68°	10° TO 20°	14° TO 32°	-10° TO 0°
68° TO 86°	20° TO 30°	32° TO 50°	0° TO 10°	UNDER 14°	UNDER -10°

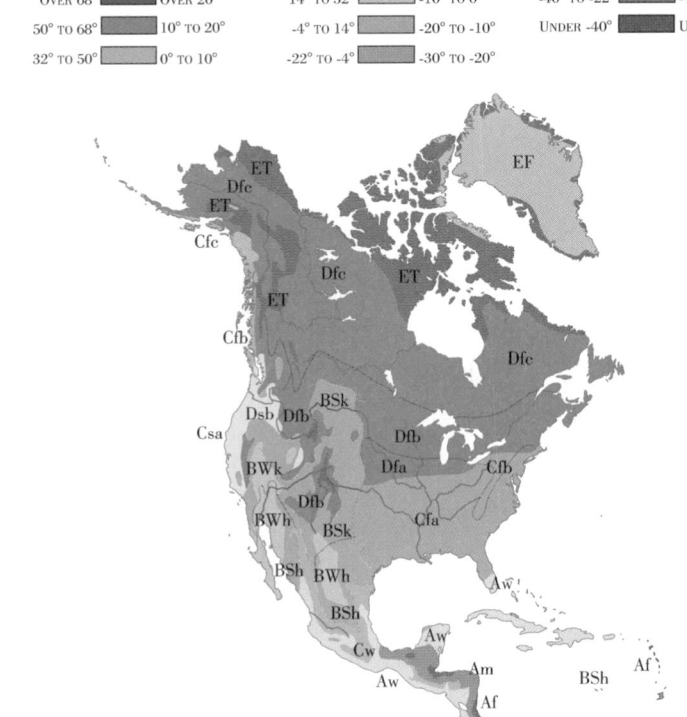

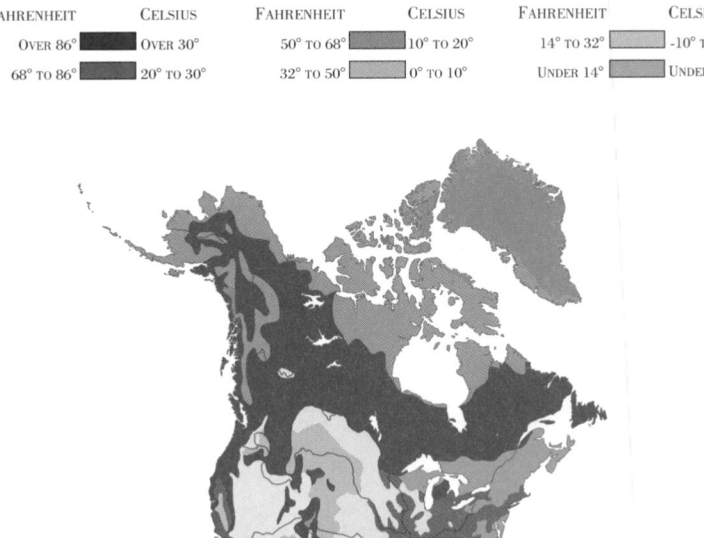

CLIMATE

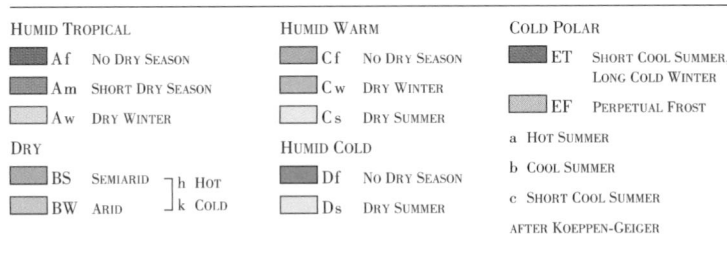

HUMID TROPICAL
- Af NO DRY SEASON
- Am SHORT DRY SEASON
- Aw DRY WINTER

DRY
- BS SEMIARID   ⎤ h HOT
- BW ARID   ⎦ k COLD

HUMID WARM
- Cf NO DRY SEASON
- Cw DRY WINTER
- Cs DRY SUMMER

HUMID COLD
- Df NO DRY SEASON
- Ds DRY SUMMER

COLD POLAR
- ET SHORT COOL SUMMER, LONG COLD WINTER
- EF PERPETUAL FROST

a HOT SUMMER
b COOL SUMMER
c SHORT COOL SUMMER

AFTER KOEPPEN-GEIGER

VEGETATION

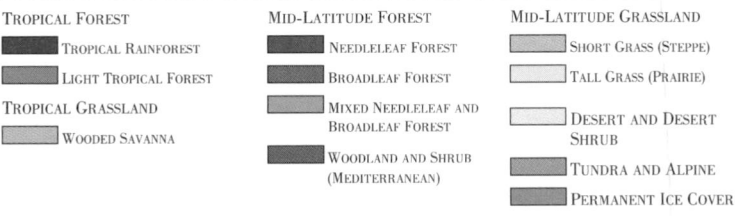

TROPICAL FOREST
- TROPICAL RAINFOREST
- LIGHT TROPICAL FOREST

TROPICAL GRASSLAND
- WOODED SAVANNA

MID-LATITUDE FOREST
- NEEDLELEAF FOREST
- BROADLEAF FOREST
- MIXED NEEDLELEAF AND BROADLEAF FOREST
- WOODLAND AND SHRUB (MEDITERRANEAN)

MID-LATITUDE GRASSLAND
- SHORT GRASS (STEPPE)
- TALL GRASS (PRAIRIE)
- DESERT AND DESERT SHRUB
- TUNDRA AND ALPINE
- PERMANENT ICE COVER

North America – Geographical Comparisons

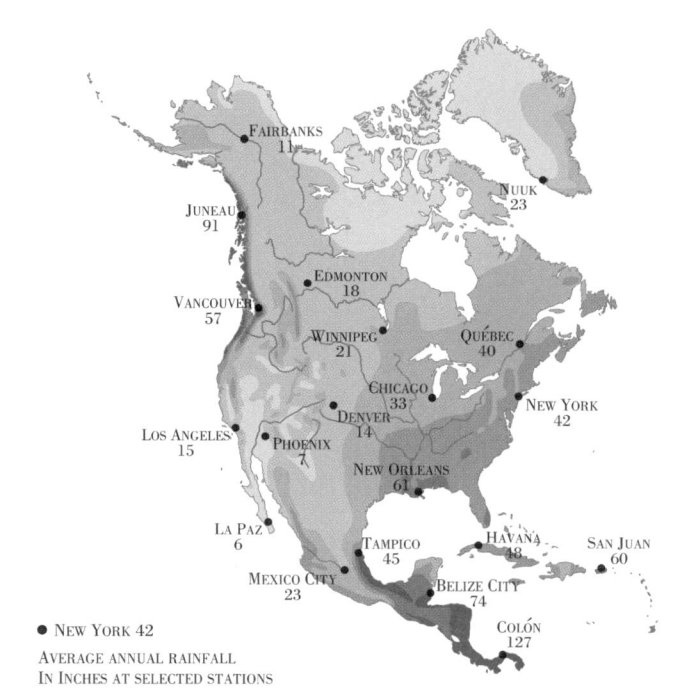

● NEW YORK 42
AVERAGE ANNUAL RAINFALL
IN INCHES AT SELECTED STATIONS

AVERAGE ANNUAL RAINFALL

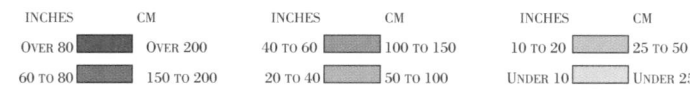

INCHES	CM	INCHES	CM	INCHES	CM
OVER 80	OVER 200	40 TO 60	100 TO 150	10 TO 20	25 TO 50
60 TO 80	150 TO 200	20 TO 40	50 TO 100	UNDER 10	UNDER 25

● CITIES WITH OVER 2,000,000
INHABITANTS

POPULATION DISTRIBUTION

DENSITY PER		SQ. MI.	SQ. KM.	SQ. MI.	SQ. KM.
SQ. MI.	SQ. KM.	130 TO 260	50 TO 100	3 TO 25	1 TO 10
OVER 260	OVER 100	25 TO 130	10 TO 50	UNDER 3	UNDER 1

LAND USE

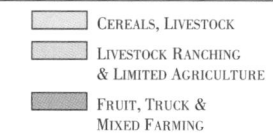

CEREALS, LIVESTOCK	
LIVESTOCK RANCHING & LIMITED AGRICULTURE	
FRUIT, TRUCK & MIXED FARMING	

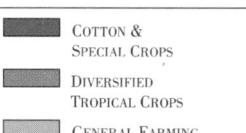

COTTON & SPECIAL CROPS	
DIVERSIFIED TROPICAL CROPS	
GENERAL FARMING	

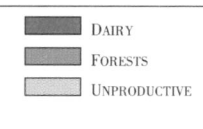

DAIRY	
FORESTS	
UNPRODUCTIVE	

MINERAL RESOURCES

ENERGY & FUELS
◆ COAL
▲ NATURAL GAS
● PETROLEUM
■ URANIUM

IRON & FERROALLOYS
1 COBALT
2 IRON ORE
3 MANGANESE
4 MOLYBDENUM
5 NICKEL
6 TUNGSTEN
7 VANADIUM

OTHER MAJOR RESOURCES
1 ANTIMONY
2 ASBESTOS
3 BAUXITE
4 BORAX
5 COPPER
6 FLUORSPAR
7 GOLD
8 GRAPHITE
9 LEAD
10 MERCURY
11 MICA
12 PHOSPHATES
13 PLATINUM
14 POTASH
15 SILVER
16 SULFUR
17 TITANIUM
18 ZINC

POPULATION OF CITIES AND TOWNS

■ OVER 2,000,000	◉ 500,000 - 999,999	◦ 50,000 - 99,999
■ 1,000,000 - 1,999,999	◉ 100,000 - 499,999	∘ UNDER 50,000

SCALE 1:13,800,000 LAMBERT CONFORMAL CONIC PROJECTION

MILES 0 — 200 — 400 — 600
KILOMETERS 0 — 200 — 400 — 600

Height 6000 4000 2000 1500 1000 500 200 0 200 700 1000 2000 3000 4000 6000 Depth

POPULATION OF CITIES AND TOWNS

■ OVER 2,000,000
■ 1,000,000 - 1,999,999
● 500,000 - 999,999
● 100,000 - 499,999
○ 50,000 - 99,999
○ UNDER 50,000

SCALE 1:13,800,000   LAMBERT CONFORMAL CONIC PROJECTION

MILES 0   200   400   600
KILOMETERS 0   200   400   600

© HAMMOND WORLD ATLAS CORPORATION   CM – A·A

Longitude West of Greenwich

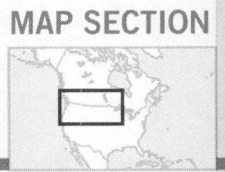
POPULATION OF CITIES AND TOWNS

■ OVER 2,000,000	● 500,000 - 999,999	⊕ 100,000 - 249,999	○ 10,000 - 29,999
■ 1,000,000 - 1,999,999	● 250,000 - 499,999	⊕ 30,000 - 99,999	○ UNDER 10,000

SCALE 1:6,900,000   LAMBERT CONFORMAL CONIC PROJECTION

MILES   0   100   200   300

KILOMETERS   0   100   200   300

© HAMMOND WORLD ATLAS CORPORATION

PACIFIC OCEAN

POPULATION OF CITIES AND TOWNS

■ OVER 2,000,000 ⊛ 500,000 - 999,999 ⦿ 100,000 - 249,999 ⊙ 10,000 - 29,999

■ 1,000,000 - 1,999,999 ⊛ 250,000 - 499,999 ⦿ 30,000 - 99,999 ∘ UNDER 10,000

SCALE 1:6,900,000   LAMBERT CONFORMAL CONIC PROJECTION

MILES   100   200   300

KILOMETERS   100   200   300

© HAMMOND WORLD ATLAS CORPORATION   CM–A•A

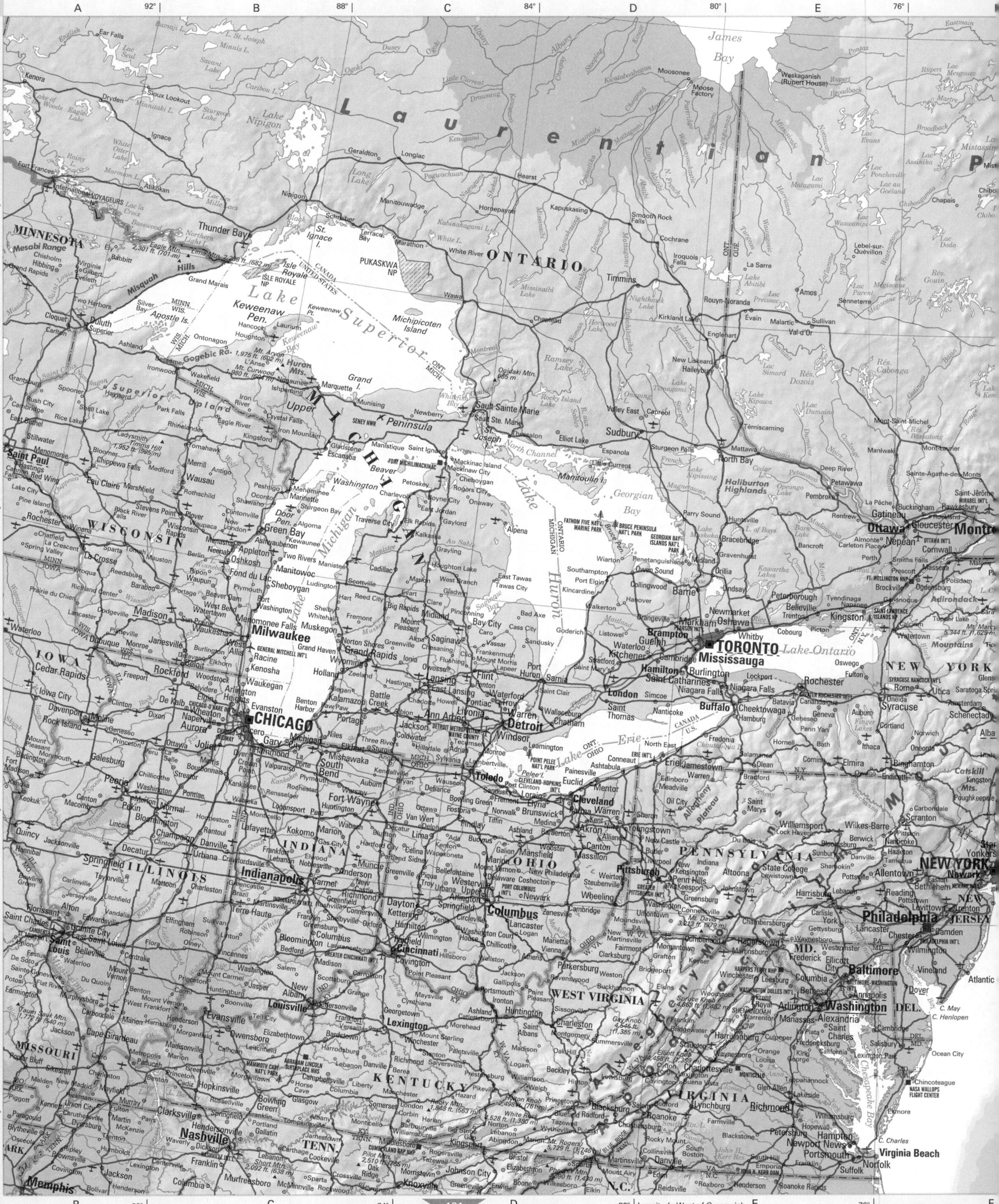

POPULATION OF CITIES AND TOWNS

- ■ OVER 2,000,000
- ■ 1,000,000 - 1,999,999
- ◉ 500,000 - 999,999
- ◉ 250,000 - 499,999
- ⊕ 100,000 - 249,999
- ⊙ 30,000 - 99,999
- ○ 10,000 - 29,999
- ○ UNDER 10,000

SCALE 1:6,900,000   LAMBERT CONFORMAL CONIC PROJECTION

MILES 0 100 200 300
KILOMETERS 0 100 200 300

Southeastern United States

POPULATION OF CITIES AND TOWNS

■ OVER 2,000,000
■ 1,000,000 - 1,999,999
● 500,000 - 999,999
● 250,000 - 499,999
⊕ 100,000 - 249,999
⊕ 30,000 - 99,999
○ 10,000 - 29,999
○ UNDER 10,000

SCALE 1:6,900,000 LAMBERT CONFORMAL CONIC PROJECTION

MILES 0 100 200 300
KILOMETERS 0 100 200 300

© Hammond World Atlas Corporation — CM·A·A·A

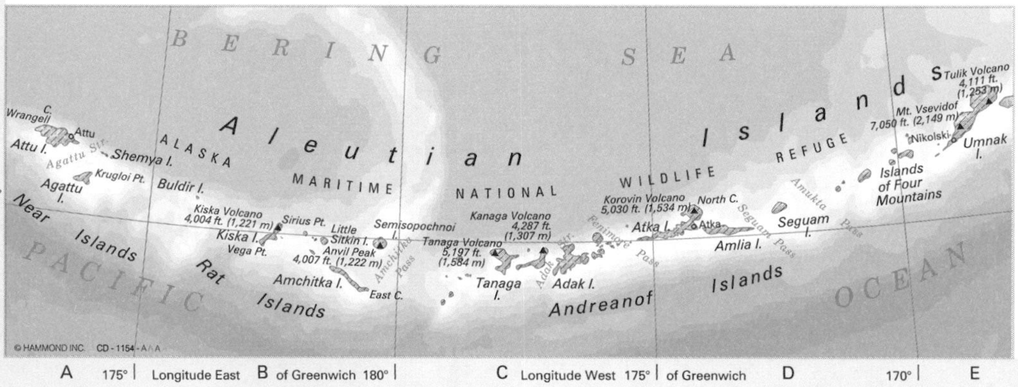

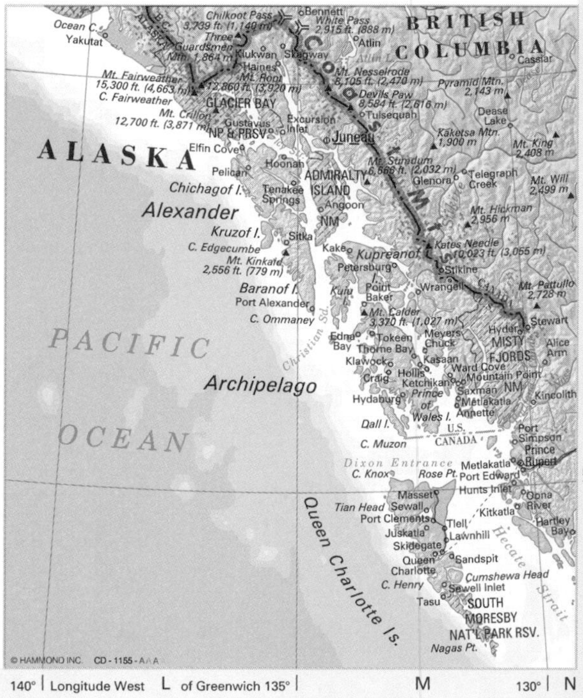

SCALE 1:10,300,000 LAMBERT CONFORMAL CONIC PROJECTION

MILES 0 | 150 | 300 | 450

KILOMETERS 0 | 150 | 300 | 450

POPULATION OF CITIES AND TOWNS

| ■ OVER 2,000,000 | ● 500,000 - 999,999 | ● 100,000 - 249,999 | ○ 10,000 - 29,999 |
| ■ 1,000,000 - 1,999,999 | ● 250,000 - 499,999 | ● 30,000 - 99,999 | ○ UNDER 10,000 |

Longitude West of Greenwich

© HAMMOND WORLD ATLAS CORPORATION   CC - 1077 A A A

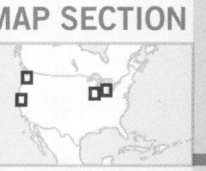
SCALE 1:1,150,000 LAMBERT CONFORMAL CONIC PROJECTION

MILES
KILOMETERS

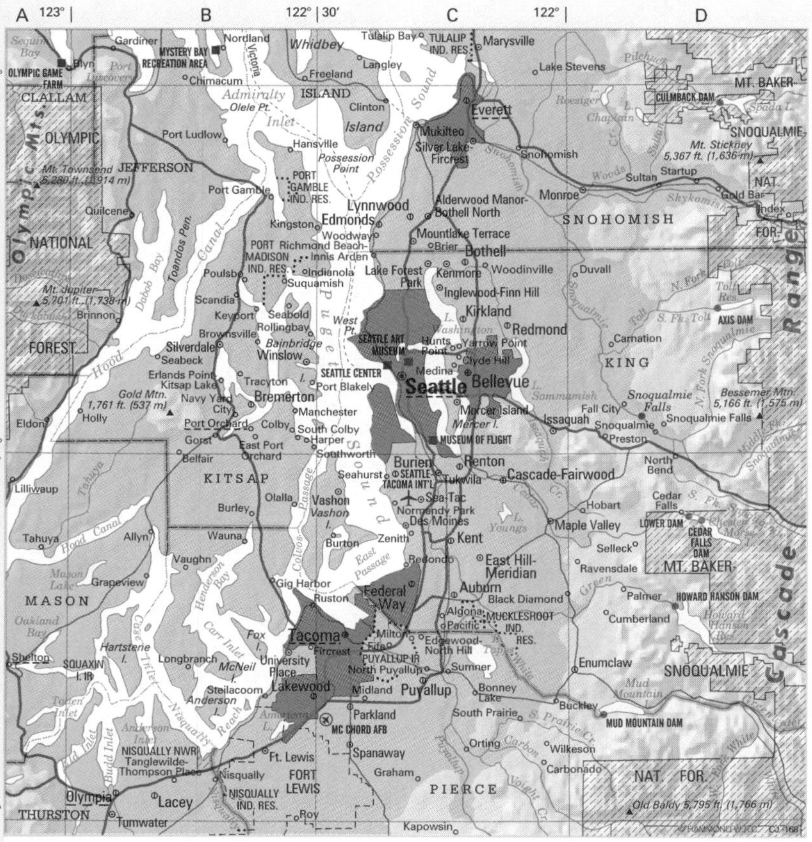

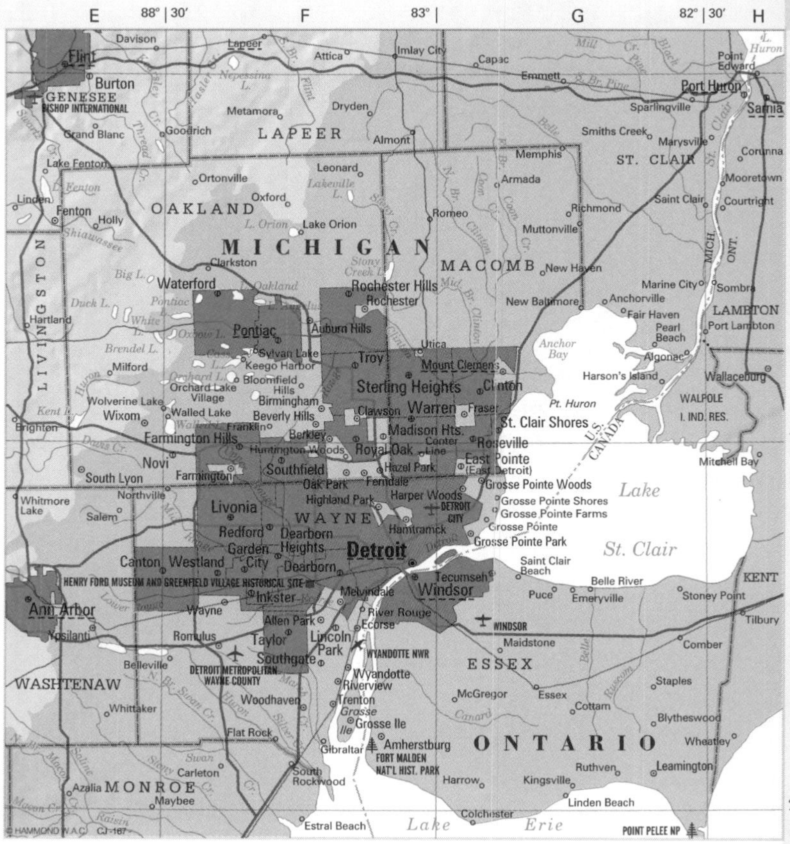

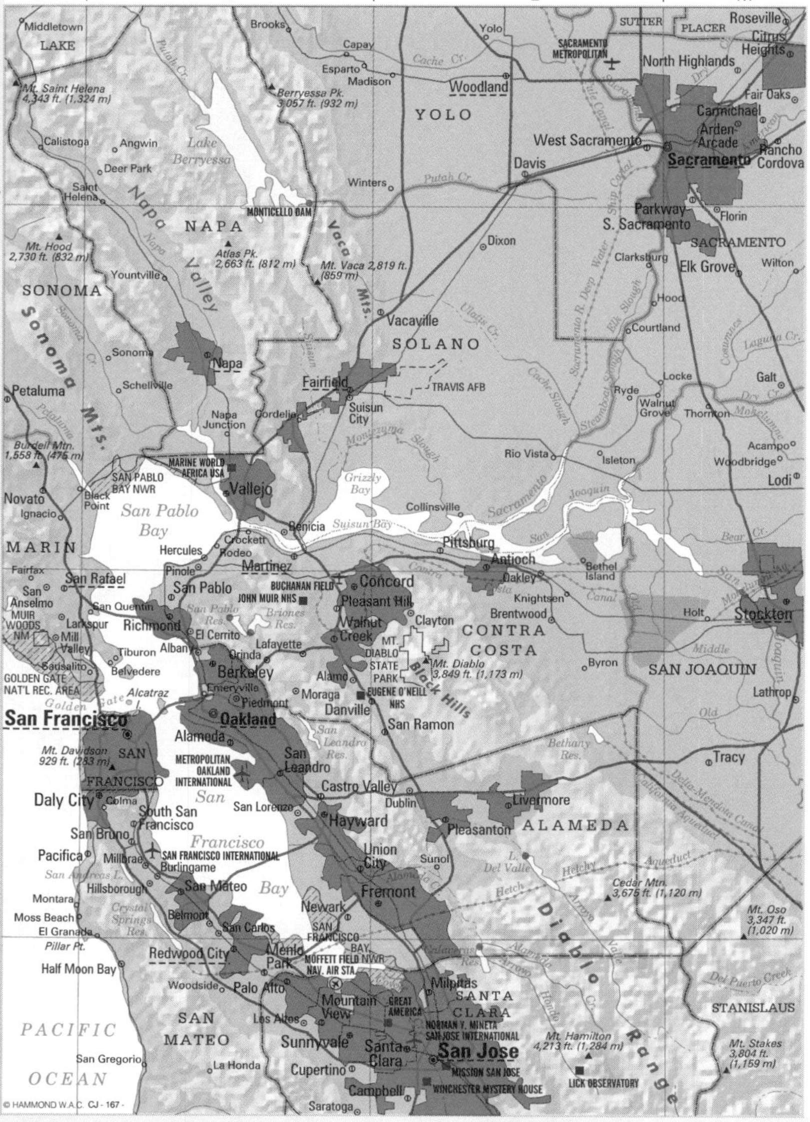

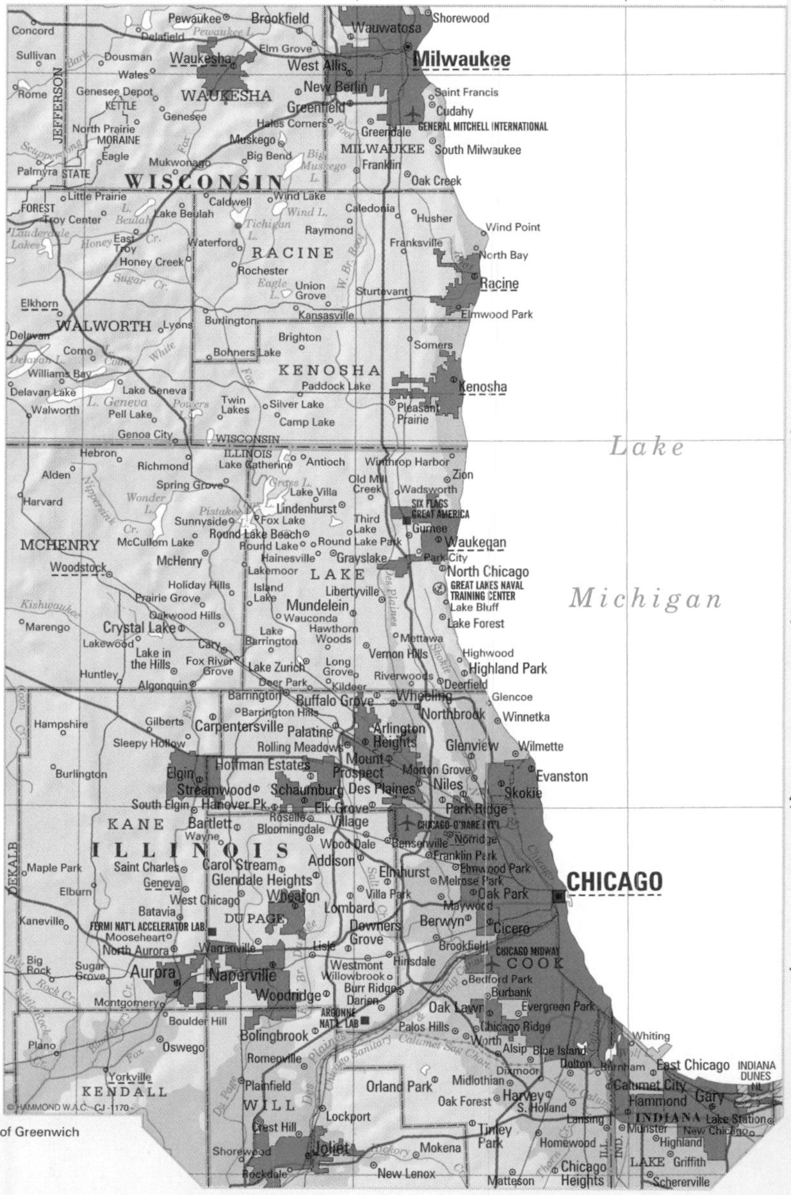

Longitude West of Greenwich

© HAMMOND W.A.C. CJ-167

Los Angeles – San Diego

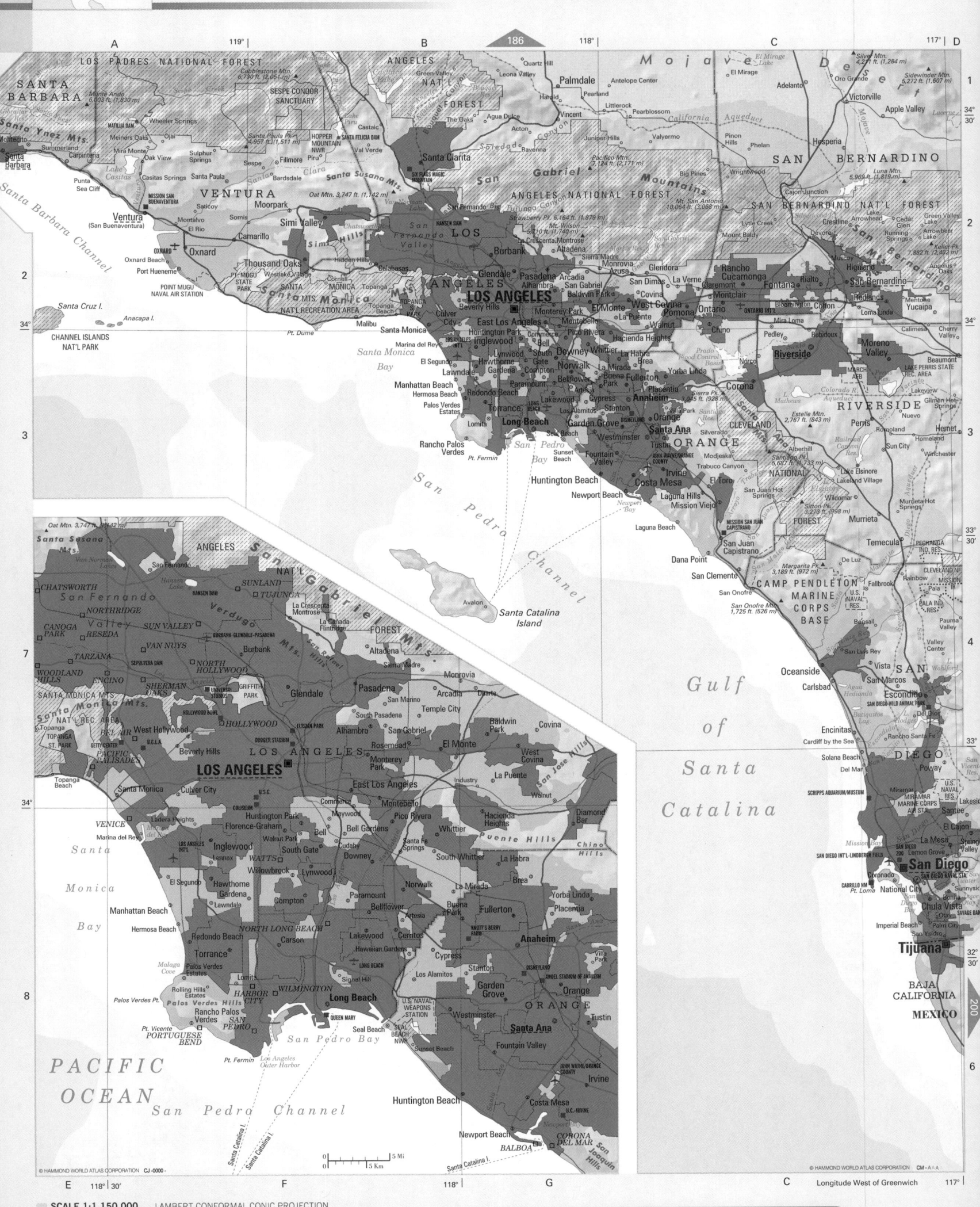

Longitude West of Greenwich   117°

SCALE 1:1,150,000   LAMBERT CONFORMAL CONIC PROJECTION

MILES
KILOMETERS

Height   Depth

Denver, Kansas City, New Orleans, Oklahoma City, Phoenix, San Antonio, Salt Lake City, St. Louis

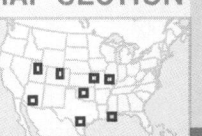

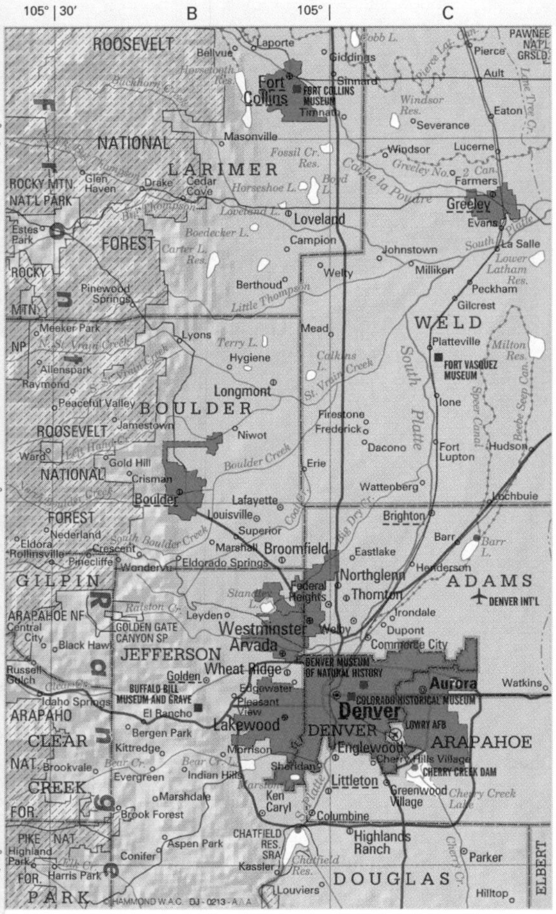

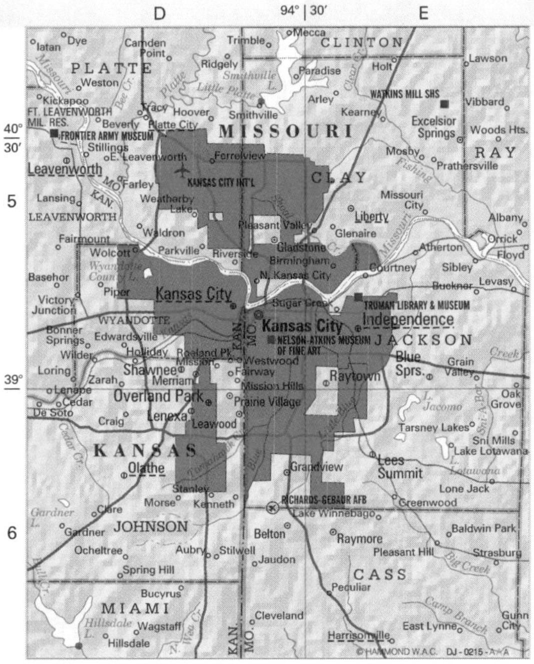

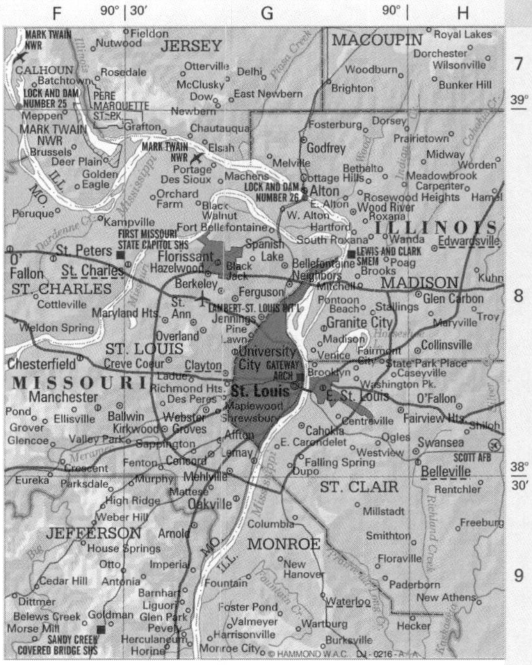

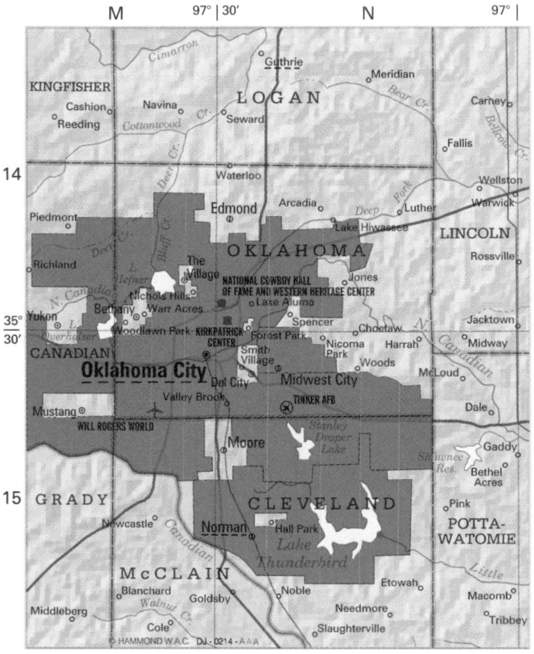

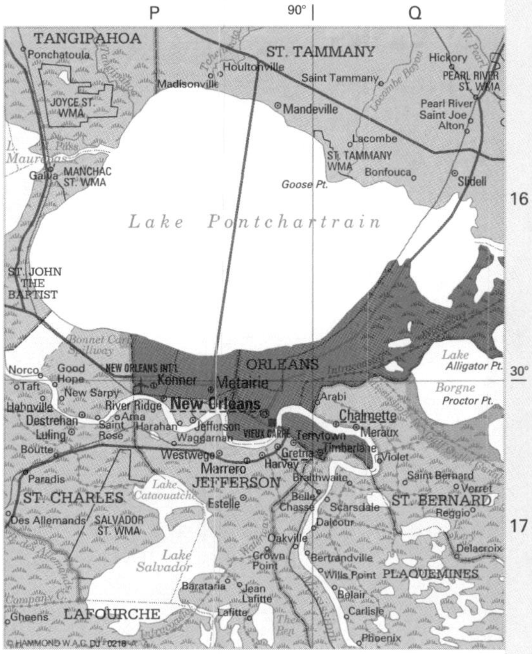

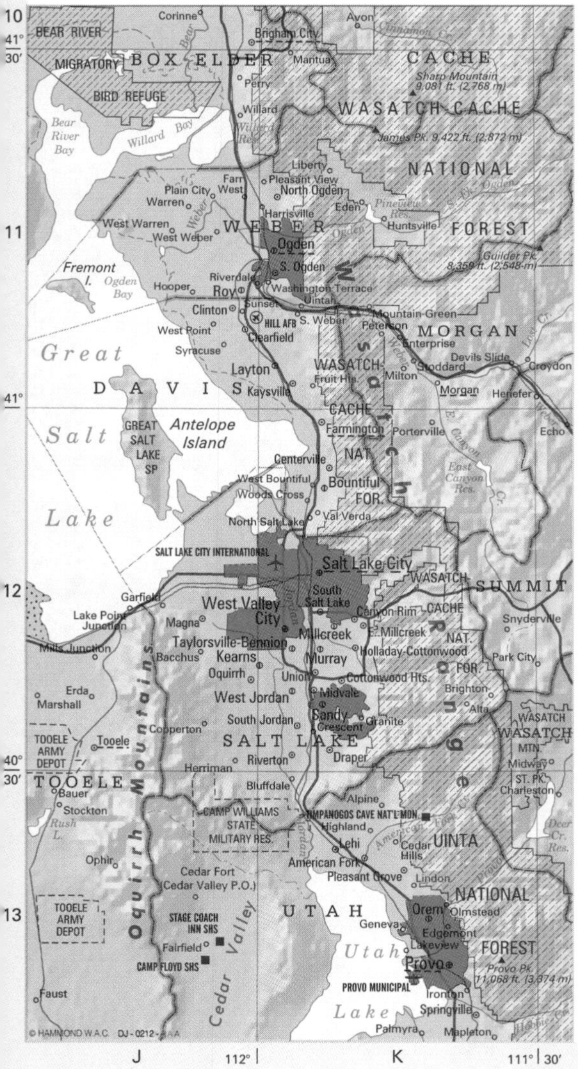

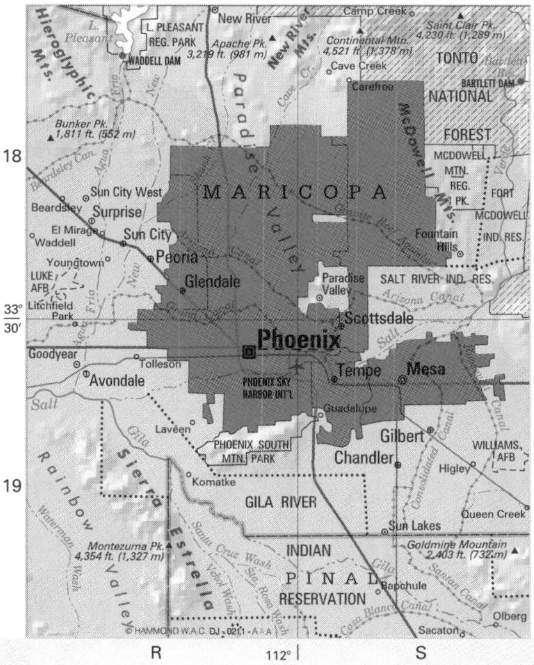

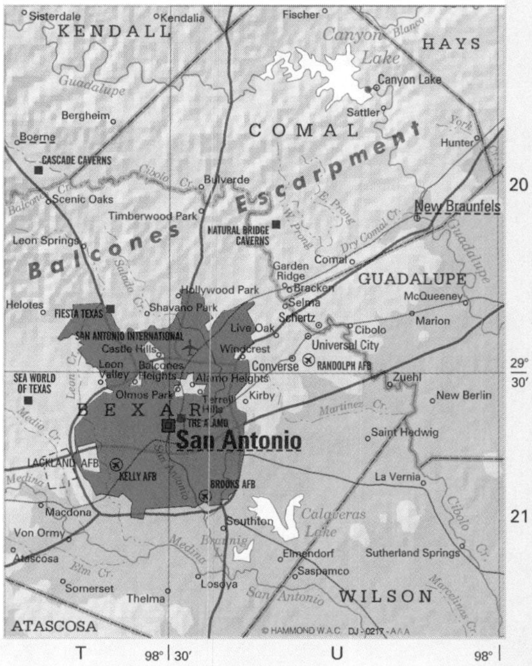

Longitude West of Greenwich

POPULATION OF CITIES AND TOWNS

- OVER 2,000,000
- 1,000,000 - 1,999,999
- 500,000 - 999,999
- 250,000 - 499,999
- 100,000 - 249,999
- 30,000 - 99,999
- 10,000 - 29,999
- UNDER 10,000

SCALE 1:1,150,000 LAMBERT CONFORMAL CONIC PROJECTION

MILES 0 10 20 30 40 50

KILOMETERS 0 10 20 30 40 50

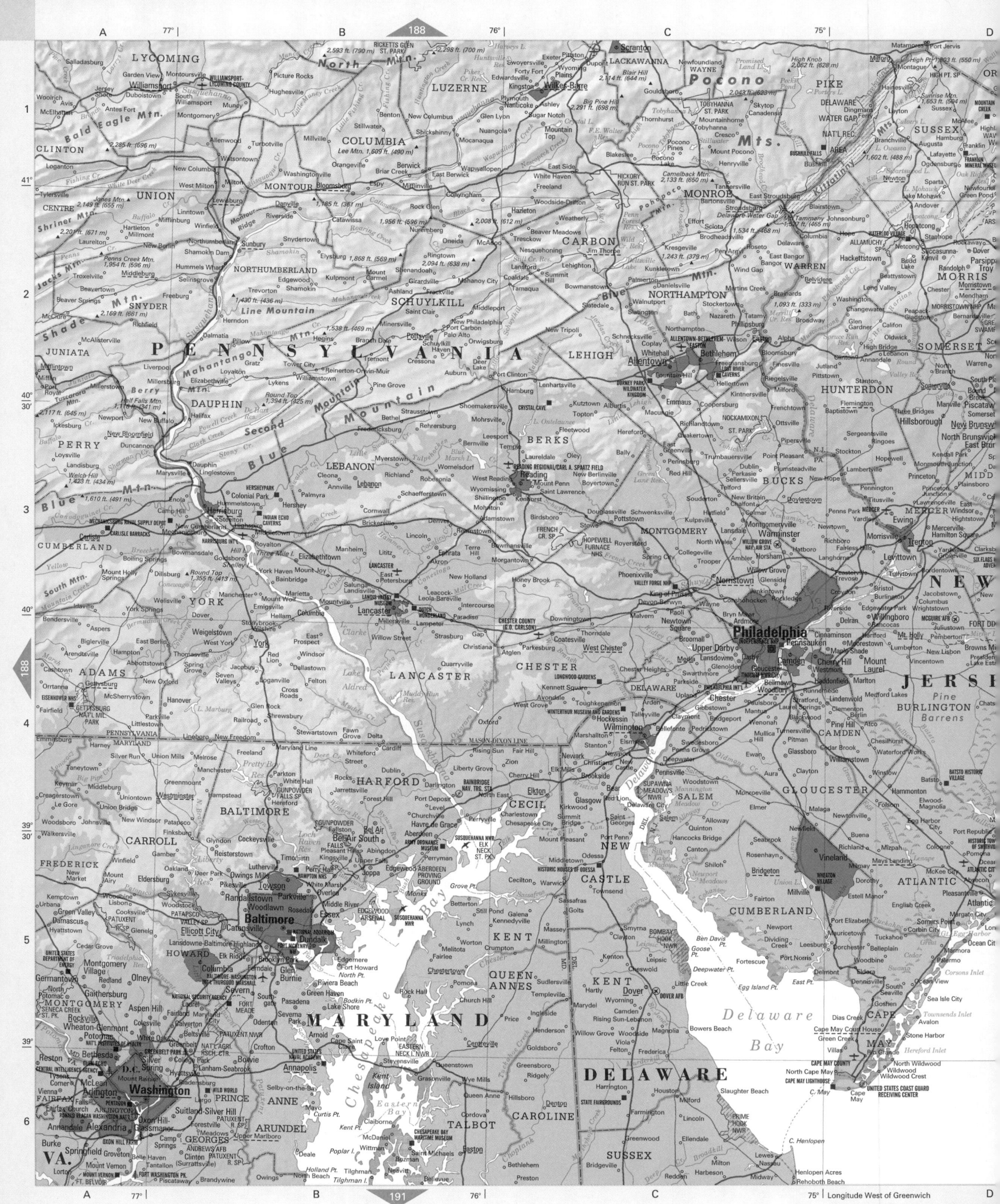

New York – Philadelphia – Washington

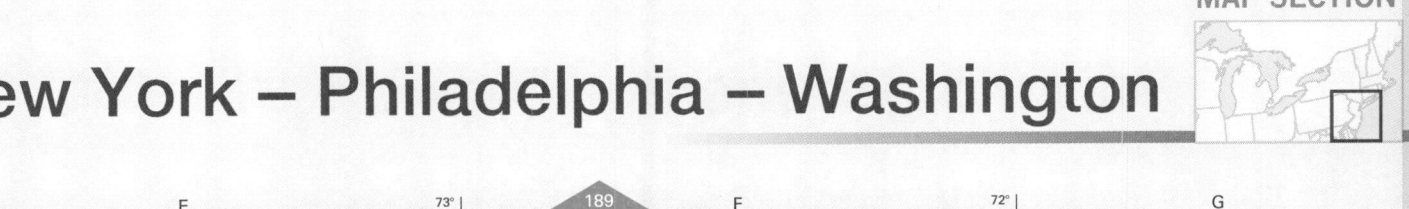

POPULATION OF CITIES AND TOWNS

Symbol	Population
■	OVER 2,000,000
■	1,000,000 - 1,999,999
●	500,000 - 999,999
●	250,000 - 499,999
●	100,000 - 249,999
●	30,000 - 99,999
○	10,000 - 29,999
○	UNDER 10,000

SCALE 1:1,150,000 LAMBERT CONFORMAL CONIC PROJECTION

MILES   0 10 20 30 40 50
KILOMETERS 0 10 20 30 40 50

© HAMMOND W.A.C.   CJ - 1171 -

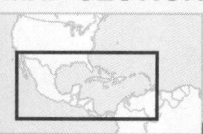

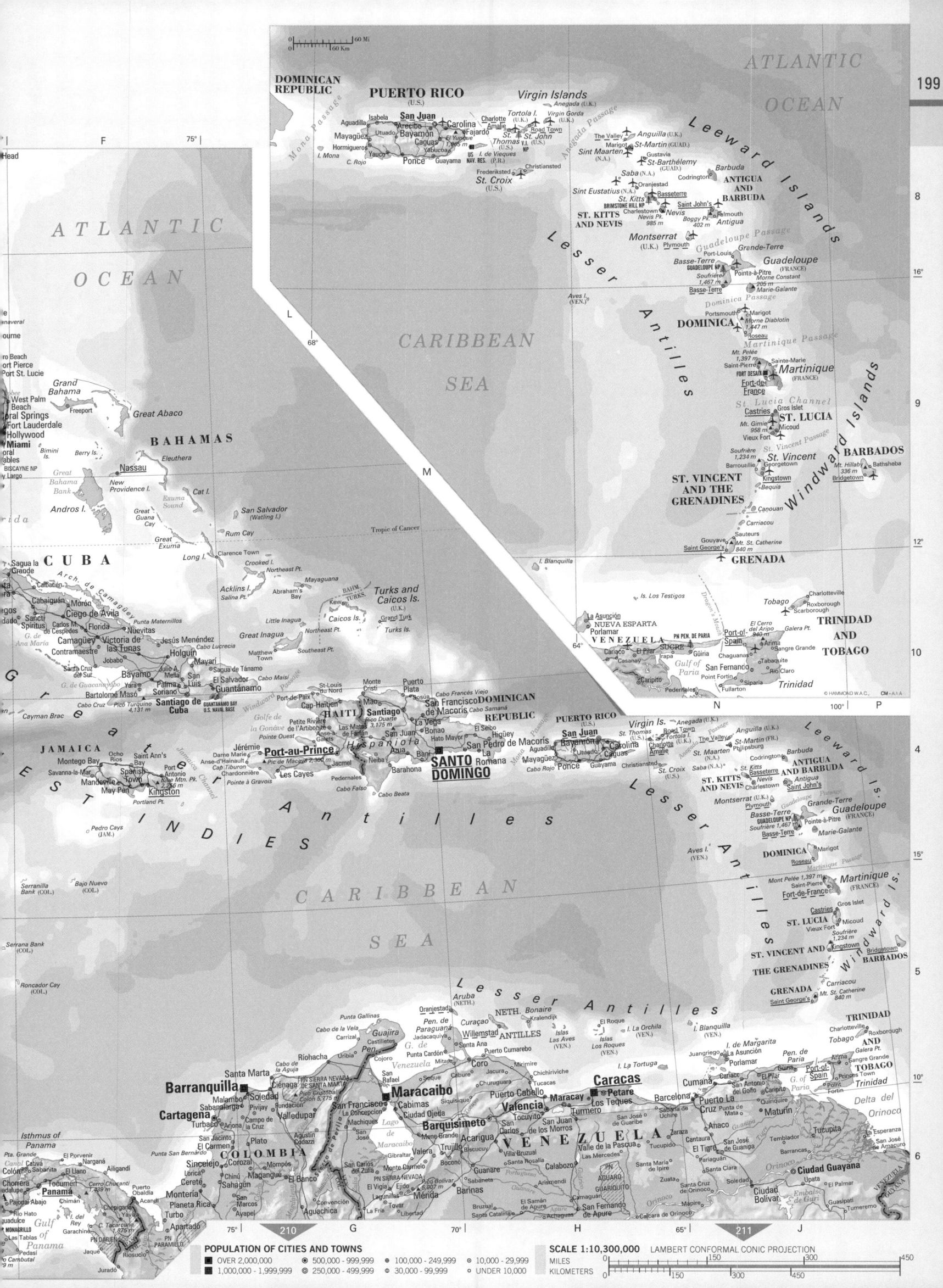

PACIFIC

OCEAN

Islas Revillagigedo
(MEXICO)

Tropic of Cancer

Longitude West of Greenwich

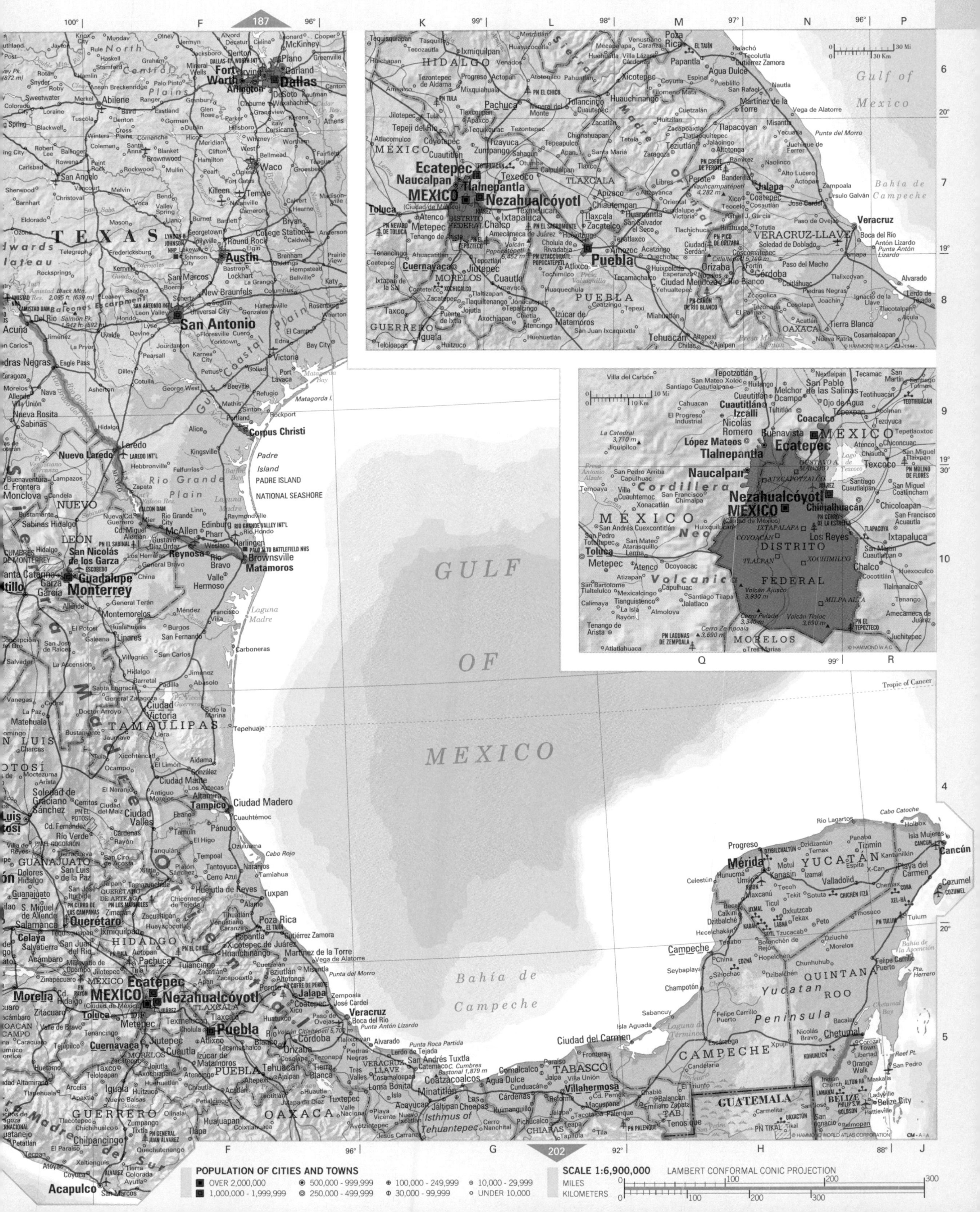

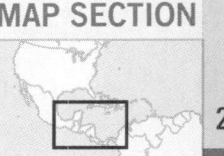

South America

The highest mountain peak in the Americas, Mount Aconcagua, at 22,831 feet (6959 m.) above sea level, is visible in this northeast-looking, low-oblique image. Several major snow-covered peaks with summits exceeding 20,000 feet (6100 m.) rise along the north-south axis of the cohesive and massive structure of the Andes Mountains through this area of Argentina and Chile. The narrow east-west valley immediately south of Mount Aconcagua contains a section of the American Highway that connects Mendoza, Argentina, with Santiago, Chile.

MAP SECTION

205

CARIBBEAN SEA

NETHERLANDS ANTILLES
Punta Gallinas
Aruba (NETH.)
Pen. de la
Guajira
Santa Marta
Pico Cristóbal Colón
5,775 m
Willemstad

Barranquilla
Cartagena
Valledupar
Maracaibo
Cabimas
Coro
Los Teques
Caracas
Cumaná
Port of Spain
TRINIDAD AND TOBAGO

COSTA
San José
RICA
Panama
Panama Canal
Gulf of Panama
PANAMA

Montería
Cabo Corrientes
Bello
Medellín
Manizales
Pereira
Armenia
Ibagué

Cúcuta
San Cristóbal
Mérida
Valera
Barinas
Bucaramanga
Arauca
Barquisimeto
Valencia
Maracay
Barcelona
Maturín
Delta del Orinoco

VENEZUELA

Pico Bolívar 5,007 m
Ciudad Bolívar
San Fernando de Apure
PRESA GURI
El Tigre
Ciudad Guayana
Morawhanna

Isla de Malpelo
(COL.)

Buenaventura
Cali
Palmira
Neiva
Villavicencio
Puerto Ayacucho

Georgetown
New Amsterdam
Nieuw Nickerie
Paramaribo
Cayenne
Bartica
Saint-Laurent du Maroni

Popayán
Nevado del Huila 5,750 m
Alto Ritacuba 5,493 m

GUYANA
Salto del Ángel
Mt. Roraima 2,772 m
SURINAME
FRENCH GUIANA

COLOMBIA
Tumaco
Pasto
Florencia
Mitú
Boa Vista
Caracaraí

Amapá

Esmeraldas
Puenta Galera
Ibarra
Quito
Pico de la Neblina 3,014 m

Equator

ECUADOR
Manta
Portoviejo
Ambato
Riobamba
Chimborazo 6,310 m

Macapá
Ilha de Marajó
B. de Marajó
Belém
Castanhal
Abaetetuba
Bragança

Guayaquil
G. de Guayaquil
Machala
Cuenca
Milagro
Iquitos

Tumbes
Tulcán
Loja

Manaus
Manacapuru
Tefé
Itacoatiara
Óbidos
Alenquer
Santarém
Parintins
Maués
Novo Aripuanã

Parnaíba
São Luís
Tucurui
Represa de Tucuruí
Bacabal
Imperatriz

Sobral
Codó
Teresina
Crateús
Quixadá
Messoró
Açu
Macau
Cabo de São Roque
Ceará-Mirim
I. Fernando de Noronha (BRAZIL)

Talara
Sullana
Piura
Chiclayo
Cajamarca
PERU

Punta Aguja
Chiclayo
Moyobamba
Tarapoto

Manicoré
Humaitá
Maloca
Caxias
Floriano
Picos
Sousa
Crato
Patos
Natal
João Pessoa

BRAZIL

Porto Velho
Aripuanã
Marabá
Tocantinópolis
Concepção do Araguaia

Balsas
Gradaús

Petrolina
Juazeiro
Jaboatão
Recife
Olinda

Trujillo
Chimbote
Nevado Huascarán 6,768 m
Huaraz
Huánuco
Cerro de Pasco
La Oroya
Huancayo

Cruzeiro do Sul
Tarauacá
Eirunepé
Benjamin Constant

Rio Branco
Cobija
Riberalta
Guajará-Mirim

Porto Nacional
Xique-Xique
Jacobina
Senhor do Bonfim
Barreiras

Aracajú
Estância
Maceió

Callao
Lima
Ayacucho
Cusco

Puerto Maldonado
Madre de Dios

Gurupi
Serra das Parecis

Serrinha
Alcobinhas
Feira de Santana

Salvador
Candeias

Chincha Alta
Pisco
Ica
Nazca
Juliaca
Lago Titicaca
Puno
Nevado Ancohuma 6,550 m

Trinidad
Vila Bela da Santíssima Trindade
Cuiabá
Cáceres

Planalto do
Porangatu
Bom Jesus da Lapa
Guanambi
Itabuna
Ilhéus
Itapetinga

Brazilian

Volcán Misti 5,822 m
Arequipa
Tacna
Arica
La Paz
Cochabamba
Oruro
Llallagua

BOLIVIA
Santa Cruz
Sucre
Vallegrande
Roboré

Rondonópolis
Mato Grosso
Iporá
Goiás
Anápolis
Brasília
Taguatinga
Januária
Montes Claros
Highlands
Teófilo Otoni
Nanuque

Iquique
Potosí
Pulacayo
Camiri
Corumbá
Aquidauana

Rio Verde
Jataí
Mineiros
Itumbiara
Goiânia
Uberlândia
Patos de Minas
Pirapora
Governador Valadares
Coletina

Tocopilla
Tupiza
Tarija
Villamontes
Villazón
Yacuba
Mariscal Estigarribia
Tartagal
Pedro Juan Caballero

Uberaba
Sete Lagoas
Divinópolis
Belo Horizonte
Itabira
Pico da Bandeira 2,890 m
Cachoeiro de Itapemirim

Antofagasta
Chuquicamata
Villarrica
Puerto Olimpo
Bela Vista
Concepción
Dourados
PARAGUAY
Poços de Caldas
Barbacena
Juiz de Fora
Valença
Vitória

Tropic of Capricorn

San Salvador de Jujuy
Salta
Fuerte Olimpo
Presidente Prudente
Marília
Londrina
Piracicaba
Campinas
Volta Redonda
Nova Iguaçu
Cabo de São Tomé
Cabo Frio

Volcán Llullaillaco 6,723 m
Chañaral
Copiapó
Cerro Ojos del Salado 6,880 m

Asunción
Formosa
Presidencia Roque Sáenz Peña
Resistencia
Pilar
Corrientes
Posadas
Encarnación
Foz do Iguaçu
Cataratas del Iguazú
Ciudad del Este

Maringá
Ponta Grossa
Sorocaba
São Paulo
Santos
Rio de Janeiro
Niterói

Tafí Viejo
San Miguel de Tucumán
Santiago del Estero
Catamarca
La Rioja

Goya
Curuzú Cuatiá
Santa Fe
Paraná

Lages
Blumenau
Itajaí
Curitiba
Joinville
Paranaguá
Florianópolis

La Serena
Coquimbo
Ovalle

Cruz del Eje
Rafaela
San Francisco
Villa María
Córdoba
Río Cuarto

Cruz Alta
Passo Fundo
Tubarão
Santa Maria
Canoas

PACIFIC

Is. Juan Fernández (CHILE)
I. Robinson Crusoe
I. Alejandro Selkirk

Cerro Aconcagua 6,959 m
Viña del Mar
Valparaíso
Santiago
Rancagua

San Juan
Mendoza
San Luis
Mercedes
Pergamino
Rosario
San Nicolás de los Arroyos
Santa Fe
Paraná

Uruguaiana
Alegrete
Santana do Livramento
Rivera
Bagé
Pelotas
Río Grande
Porto Alegre

AREA OF OPTIMIZATION

CHILE
PHOTOGRAPHIC DETAIL
San Rafael
Curicó
Talca
Linares
Chillán
Malargüe
San Luis
Junín
Buenos Aires
Lanús
La Plata
Olavarría
Azul
Tandil

Concepción del Uruguay
Mercedes
San José de Mayo
Melo
URUGUAY
Montevideo
Rocha
Punta del Este

I. de San Félix (CHILE)
I. de San Ambrosio (CHILE)

OCEAN
Tropic of Capricorn

Talcahuano
Concepción
Los Ángeles
Temuco

ARGENTINA

Tres Arroyos
Bahía Blanca
Punta Alta
Mar del Plata
Necochea
Dolores
Cabo San Antonio

Valdivia
Osorno
Neuquén
Zapala
General Roca
Río Colorado

Viedma

ATLANTIC

Puerto Montt
San Carlos de Bariloche
Ancud
Chiloé
G. de Corcovado

San Antonio Oeste
Península Valdés
Puerto Madryn

Golfo San Matías

Rawson

Arch. de los Chonos
Pen. de Taitao
Cabo Tres Montes

Sarmiento
Comodoro Rivadavia
Golfo San Jorge
Cabo Tres Puntas
Puerto Deseado

OCEAN

Isla Wellington
Arch. Reina Adelaida

San Julián
Santa Cruz

Falkland Islands (U.K.) (Claimed by Arg.)
Stanley
West Falkland
East Falkland

Río Gallegos
Str. of Magellan
Tierra del Fuego
Río Grande
Punta Arenas
Ushuaia
C. San Diego
Cape Horn

AREA OF OPTIMIZATION The red band which surrounds this map defines the "Area of Optimization." Within this bounding curve is the most accurate conformal map that can be made of the region. Outside the optimized area, distortion increases rapidly, and tears or other irregularities in the grid may occur. (See page 8 for additional information.)

© HAMMOND WORLD ATLAS CORPORATION   CM - A A A

POPULATION OF CITIES AND TOWNS

■ OVER 3,000,000   ● 500,000 - 999,999
■ 1,000,000 - 2,999,999   ● 100,000 - 499,999   ○ UNDER 100,000

SCALE 1:27,600,000   OPTIMAL CONFORMAL PROJECTION
MILES   0   400   800   1200
KILOMETERS   0   400   800   1200

Longitude West G of Greenwich

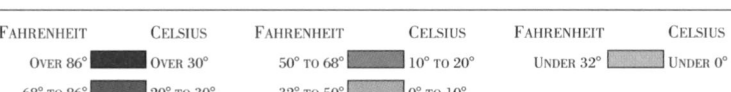

AVERAGE JANUARY TEMPERATURE

FAHRENHEIT	CELSIUS	FAHRENHEIT	CELSIUS	FAHRENHEIT	CELSIUS
OVER 86°	OVER 30°	50° TO 68°	10° TO 20°	UNDER 32°	UNDER 0°
68° TO 86°	20° TO 30°	32° TO 50°	0° TO 10°		

AVERAGE JULY TEMPERATURE

FAHRENHEIT	CELSIUS	FAHRENHEIT	CELSIUS	FAHRENHEIT	CELSIUS
OVER 86°	OVER 30°	50° TO 68°	10° TO 20°	UNDER 32°	UNDER 0°
68° TO 86°	20° TO 30°	32° TO 50°	0° TO 10°		

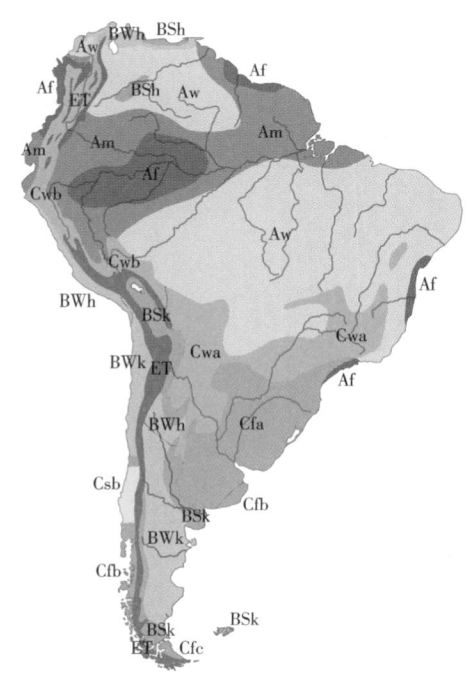

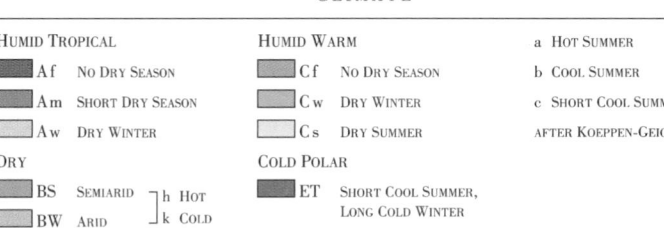

CLIMATE

HUMID TROPICAL
- Af NO DRY SEASON
- Am SHORT DRY SEASON
- Aw DRY WINTER

DRY
- BS SEMIARID ⎤ h HOT
- BW ARID ⎦ k COLD

HUMID WARM
- Cf NO DRY SEASON
- Cw DRY WINTER
- Cs DRY SUMMER

COLD POLAR
- ET SHORT COOL SUMMER, LONG COLD WINTER

- a HOT SUMMER
- b COOL SUMMER
- c SHORT COOL SUMMER

AFTER KOEPPEN-GEIGER

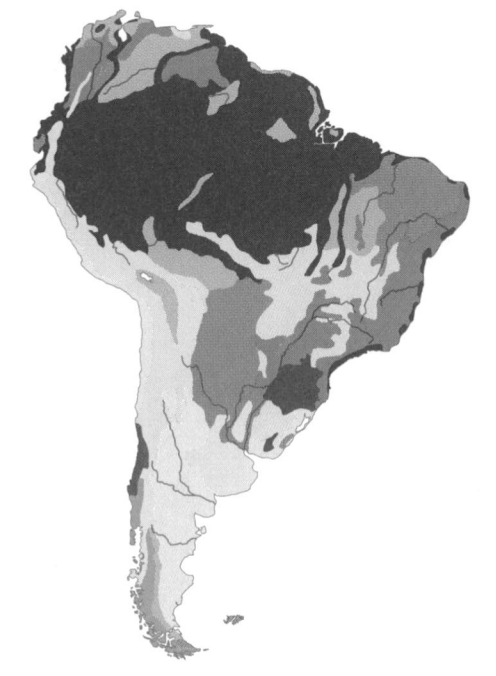

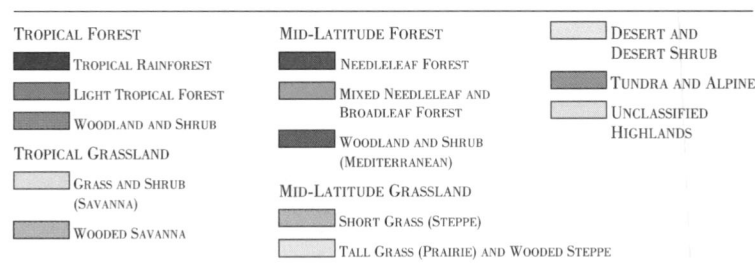

VEGETATION

TROPICAL FOREST
- TROPICAL RAINFOREST
- LIGHT TROPICAL FOREST
- WOODLAND AND SHRUB

TROPICAL GRASSLAND
- GRASS AND SHRUB (SAVANNA)
- WOODED SAVANNA

MID-LATITUDE FOREST
- NEEDLELEAF FOREST
- MIXED NEEDLELEAF AND BROADLEAF FOREST
- WOODLAND AND SHRUB (MEDITERRANEAN)

MID-LATITUDE GRASSLAND
- SHORT GRASS (STEPPE)
- TALL GRASS (PRAIRIE) AND WOODED STEPPE

- DESERT AND DESERT SHRUB
- TUNDRA AND ALPINE
- UNCLASSIFIED HIGHLANDS

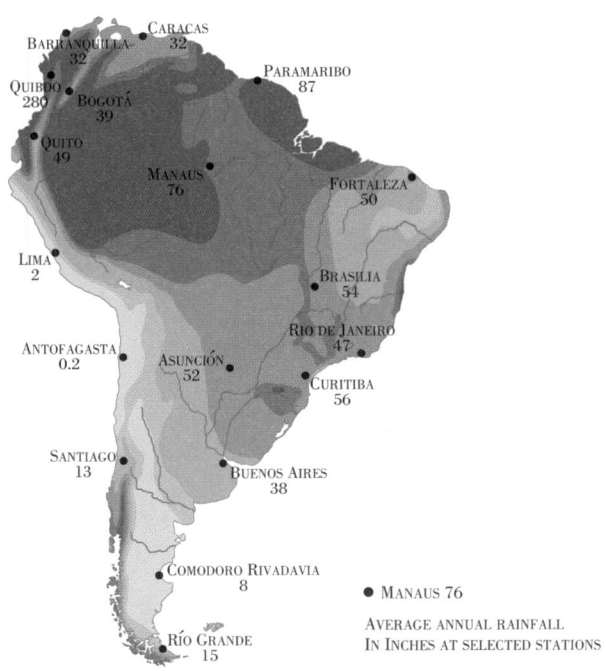

● MANAUS 76
AVERAGE ANNUAL RAINFALL
IN INCHES AT SELECTED STATIONS

● CITIES WITH OVER 1,000,000
INHABITANTS

AVERAGE ANNUAL RAINFALL

INCHES	CM	INCHES	CM	INCHES	CM
OVER 80	OVER 200	40 TO 60	100 TO 150	10 TO 20	25 TO 50
60 TO 80	150 TO 200	20 TO 40	50 TO 100	UNDER 10	UNDER 25

POPULATION DISTRIBUTION

DENSITY PER		SQ. MI.	SQ. KM.	SQ. MI.	SQ. KM.
SQ. MI.	SQ. KM.	130 TO 260	50 TO 100	3 TO 25	1 TO 10
OVER 260	OVER 100	25 TO 130	10 TO 50	UNDER 3	UNDER 1

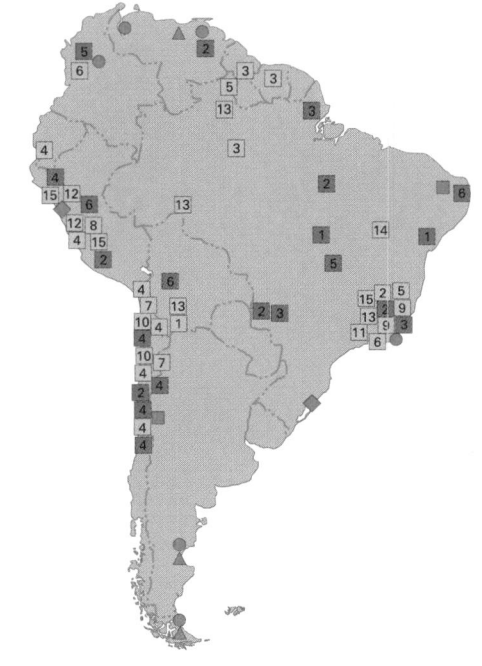

LAND USE

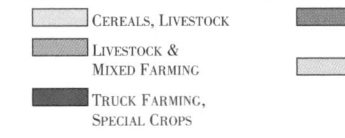 CEREALS, LIVESTOCK

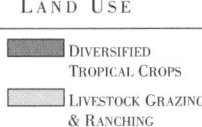 LIVESTOCK & MIXED FARMING

TRUCK FARMING, SPECIAL CROPS

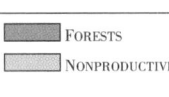 DIVERSIFIED TROPICAL CROPS

LIVESTOCK GRAZING & RANCHING

FORESTS

NONPRODUCTIVE

MINERAL RESOURCES

ENERGY & FUELS
◆ COAL
▲ NATURAL GAS
● PETROLEUM
■ URANIUM

IRON & FERROALLOYS
1 CHROMIUM
2 IRON ORE
3 MANGANESE
4 MOLYBDENUM
5 NICKEL
6 TUNGSTEN

OTHER MAJOR RESOURCES
1 ANTIMONY 7 IODINE 13 TIN
2 ASBESTOS 8 LEAD 14 TITANIUM
3 BAUXITE 9 MICA 15 ZINC
4 COPPER 10 NITRATES
5 DIAMONDS 11 PHOSPHATES
6 GOLD 12 SILVER

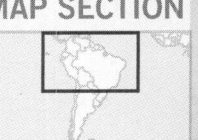
ATLANTIC OCEAN

ATLANTIC OCEAN

POPULATION OF CITIES AND TOWNS

■ OVER 2,000,000	● 500,000 - 999,999
■ 1,000,000 - 1,999,999	● 100,000 - 499,999
◉ 50,000 - 99,999	○ UNDER 50,000

SCALE 1:14,900,000   LAMBERT CONFORMAL CONIC PROJECTION

MILES   0   200   400   600

KILOMETERS   0   200   400   600

© Hammond World Atlas Corporation   CM-2107-A

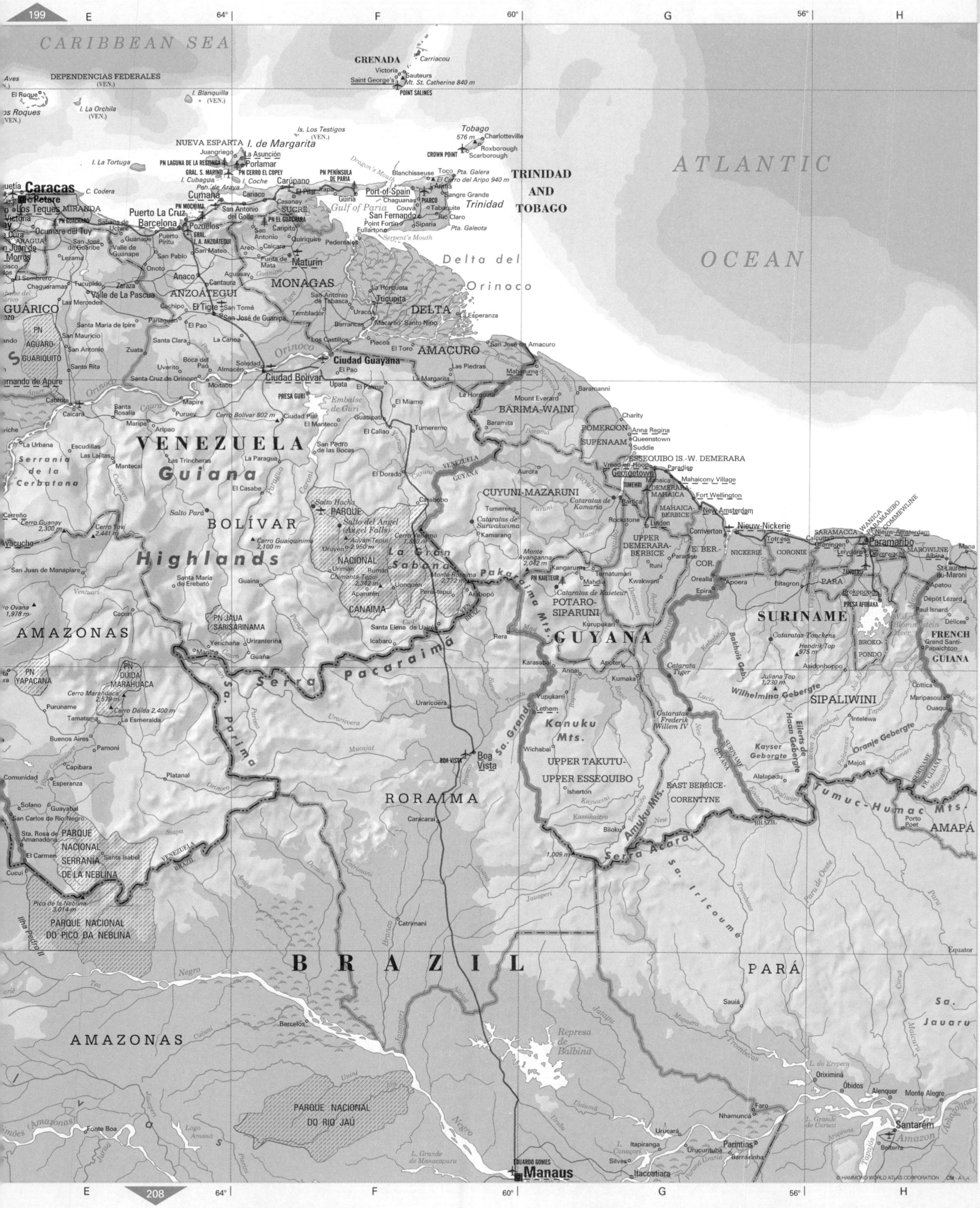

Northeastern Brazil

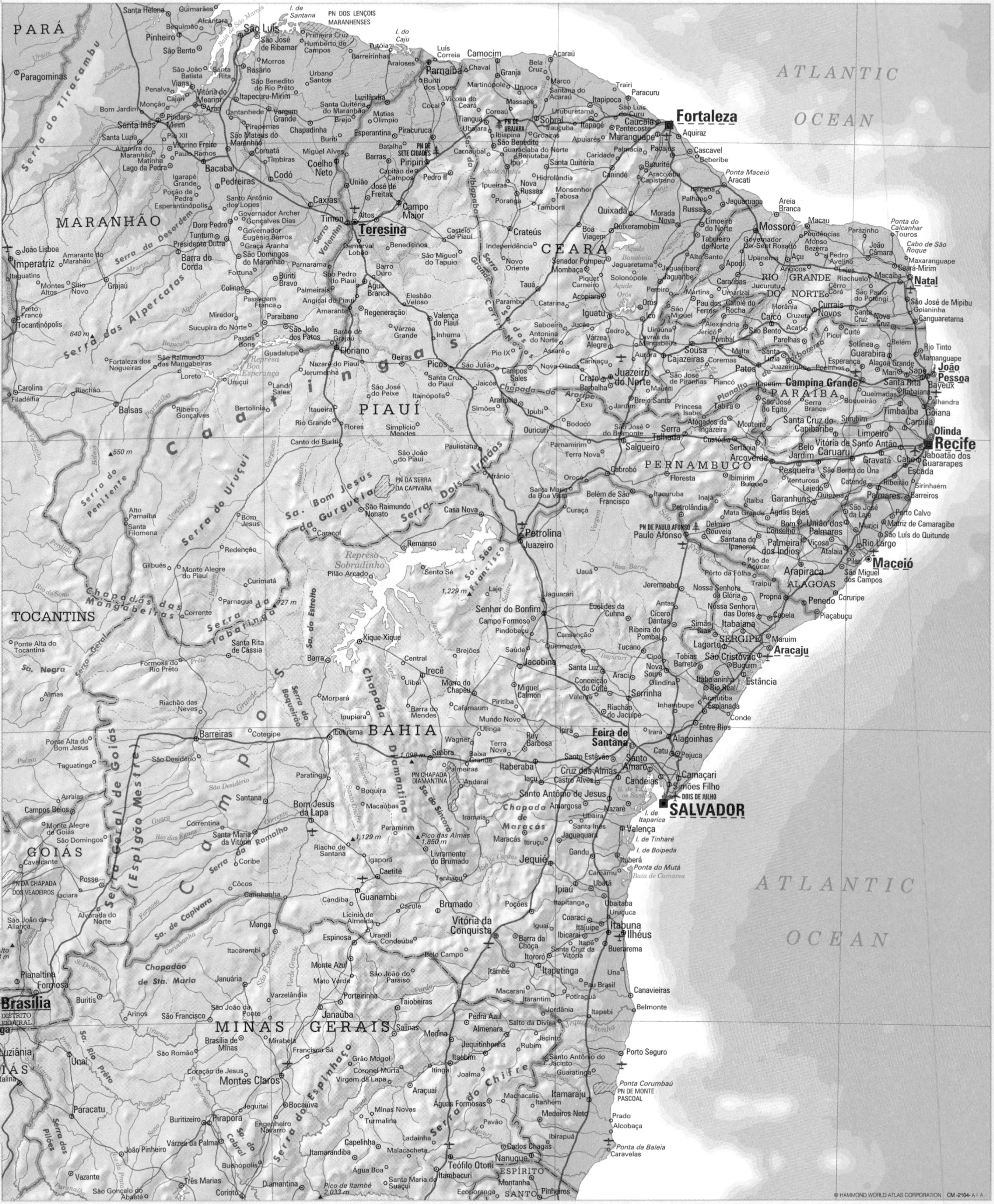

SCALE 1:6,900,000 LAMBERT CONFORMAL CONIC PROJECTION

© HAMMOND WORLD ATLAS CORPORATION

Southeastern Brazil

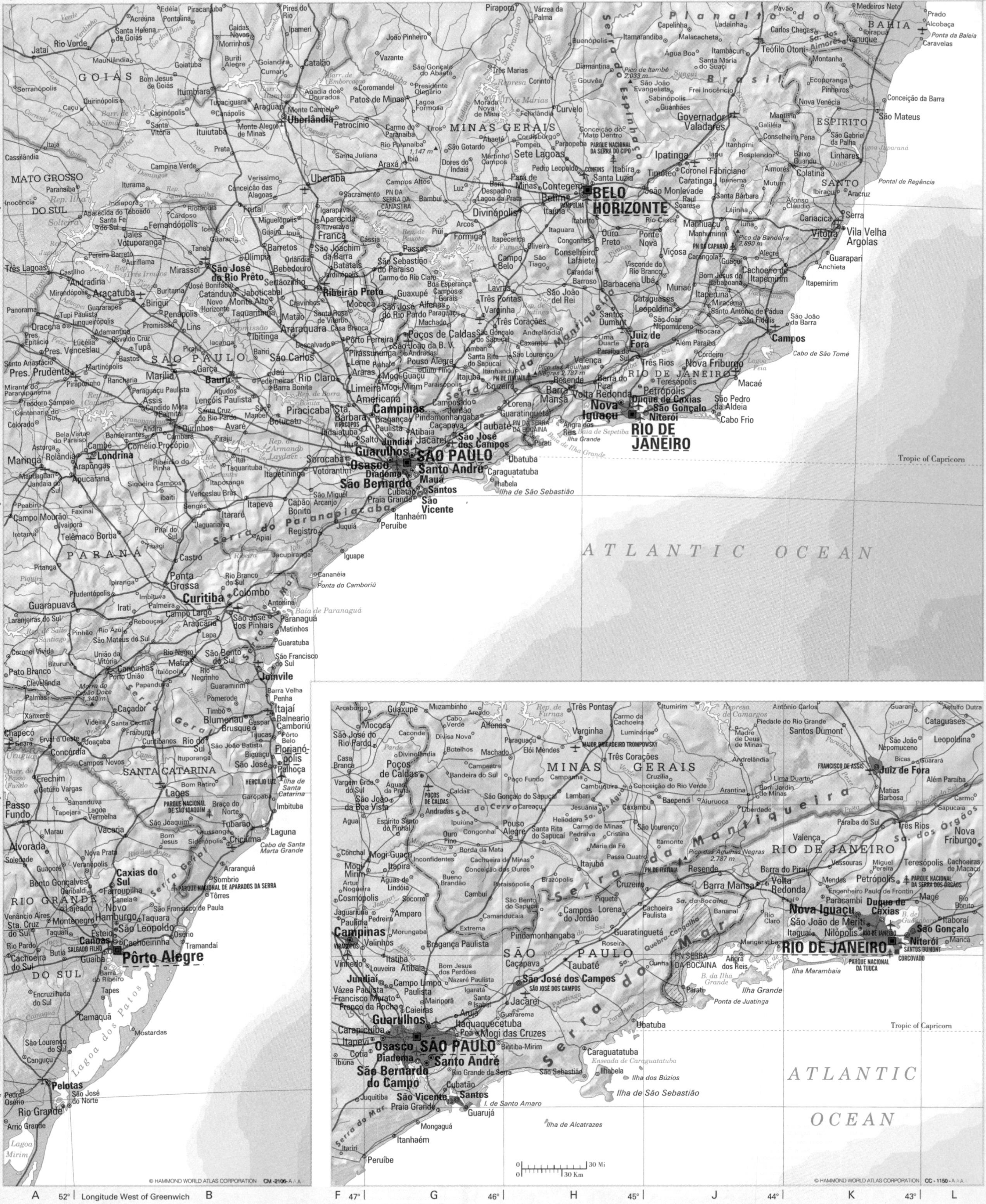

POPULATION OF CITIES AND TOWNS

- ■ OVER 2,000,000
- ■ 1,000,000 - 1,999,999
- ● 500,000 - 999,999
- ● 250,000 - 499,999
- ● 100,000 - 249,999
- ● 30,000 - 99,999
- ● 10,000 - 29,999
- ○ UNDER 10,000

SCALE 1:6,900,000 LAMBERT CONFORMAL CONIC PROJECTION

MILES

KILOMETERS

© HAMMOND WORLD ATLAS CORPORATION

Longitude West of Greenwich

Peru

210

208

PACIFIC OCEAN

COLOMBIA

ECUADOR

BRAZIL

AMAZONAS

ACRE

PERU

LORETO

AMAZONAS

SAN MARTÍN

CAJAMARCA

LAMBAYEQUE

PIURA

LA LIBERTAD

ANCASH

HUÁNUCO

UCAYALI

PASCO

JUNÍN

LIMA

MADRE DE DIOS

CUSCO

HUANCAVELICA

AYACUCHO

APURÍMAC

ICA

PUNO

AREQUIPA

MOQUEGUA

TACNA

CHILE

BOLIVIA

Golfo de Guayaquil

Desierto de Sechura

Cordillera central

Cordillera azul

Cordillera oriental

Andes

Cordillera Real

Lago Titicaca

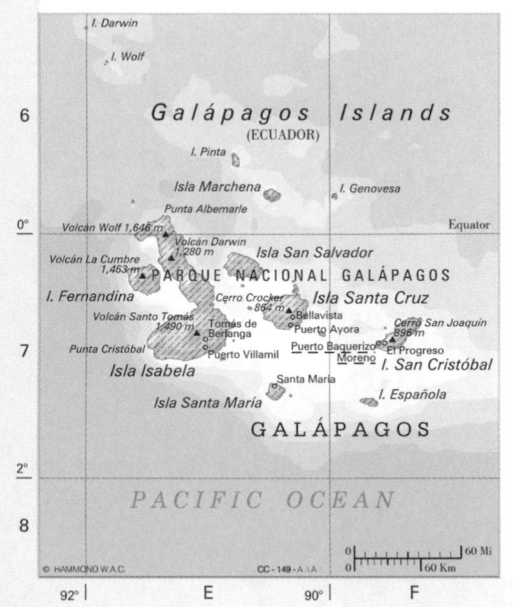

I. Darwin
I. Wolf

Galápagos Islands
(ECUADOR)

I. Pinta
Isla Marchena
Punta Albemarle
I. Genovesa

Volcán Wolf 1,646 m
Volcán Darwin 1,280 m
Isla San Salvador

Equator

I. Fernandina
Volcán La Cumbre 1,463 m
Volcán Santo Tomás 1,490 m
Cerro Crocker 864 m
Isla Santa Cruz
Cerro San Joaquín 896 m
I. San Cristóbal

Tomás de Berlanga
Puerto Ayora
Bellavista
El Progreso
Puerto Baquerizo Moreno

Punta Cristóbal
Puerto Villamil
Santa María

Isla Isabela
Isla Santa María
I. Española

GALÁPAGOS

PACIFIC OCEAN

© HAMMOND W.A.C.

CC-149-A-A

© HAMMOND WORLD ATLAS CORPORATION   CM -1072-A-A

SCALE 1:6,900,000   LAMBERT CONFORMAL CONIC PROJECTION

MILES
KILOMETERS
0   100   200   300

POPULATION OF CITIES AND TOWNS

| ■ OVER 2,000,000 | ● 500,000 - 999,999 | ● 100,000 - 249,999 | ○ 10,000 - 29,999 |
| ■ 1,000,000 - 1,999,999 | ● 250,000 - 499,999 | ● 30,000 - 99,999 | ○ UNDER 10,000 |

Longitude West of Greenwich

Southern South America

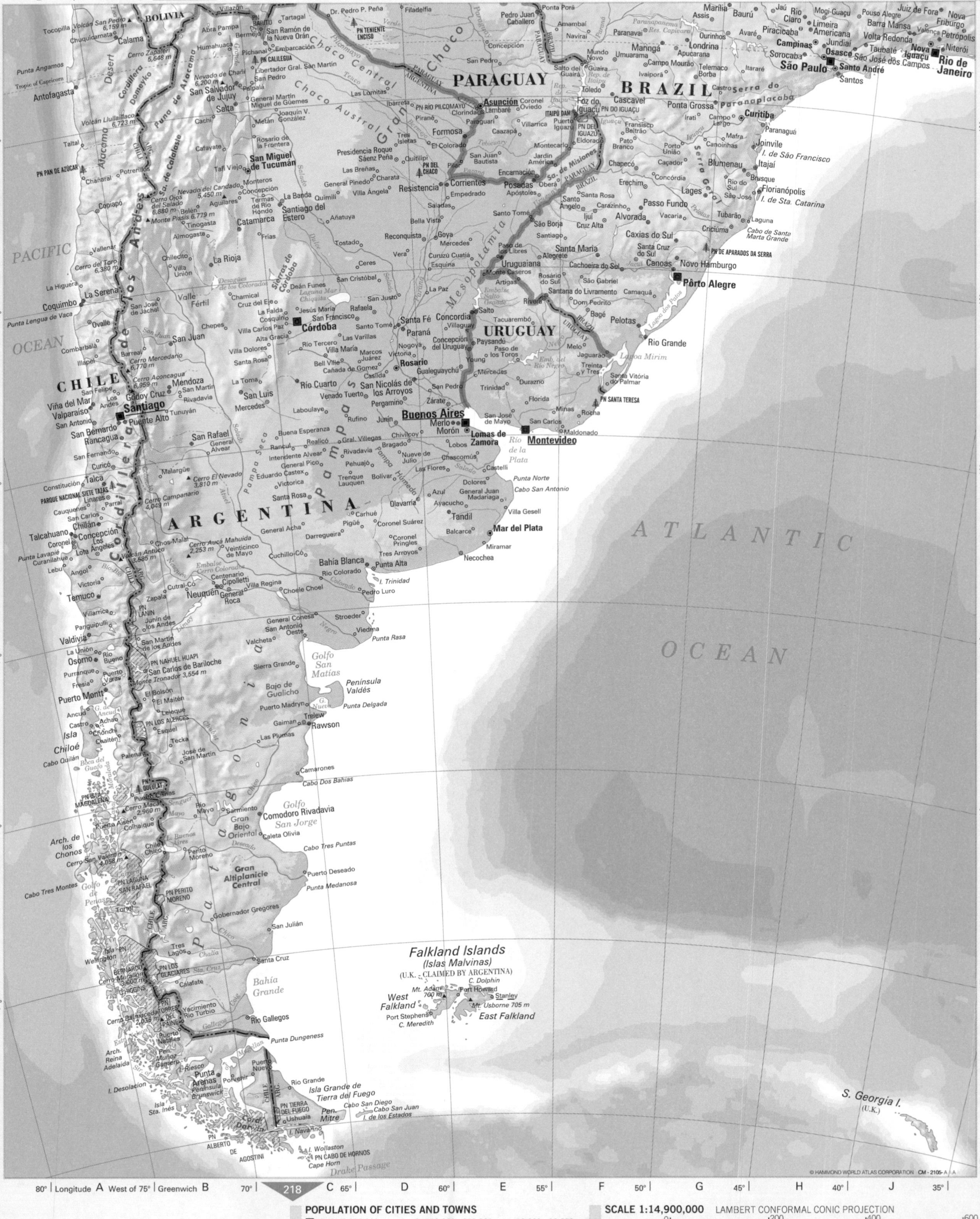

POPULATION OF CITIES AND TOWNS
- OVER 2,000,000
- 1,000,000 - 1,999,999
- 500,000 - 999,999
- 100,000 - 499,999
- 50,000 - 99,999
- UNDER 50,000

SCALE 1:14,900,000 LAMBERT CONFORMAL CONIC PROJECTION

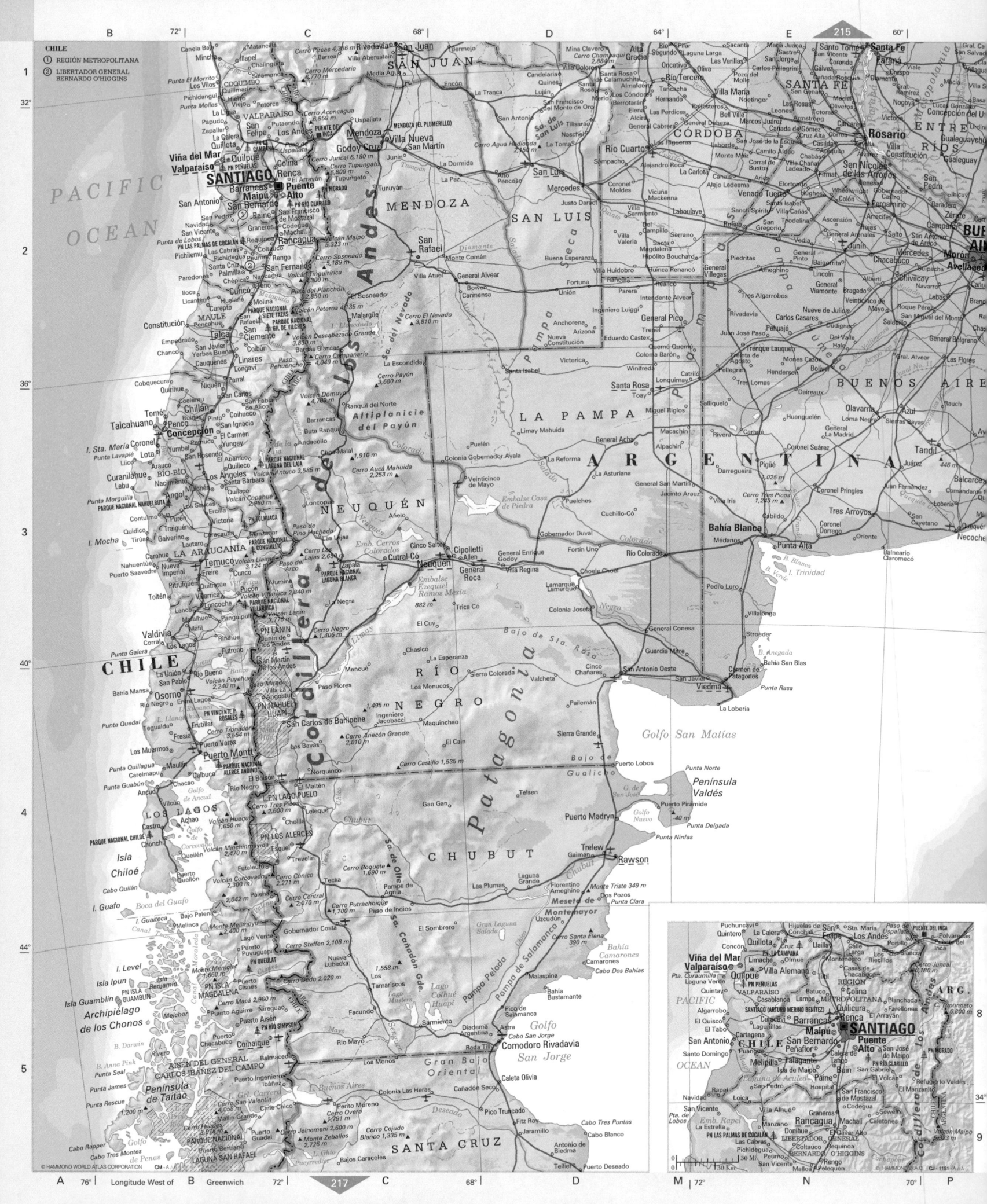

POPULATION OF CITIES AND TOWNS

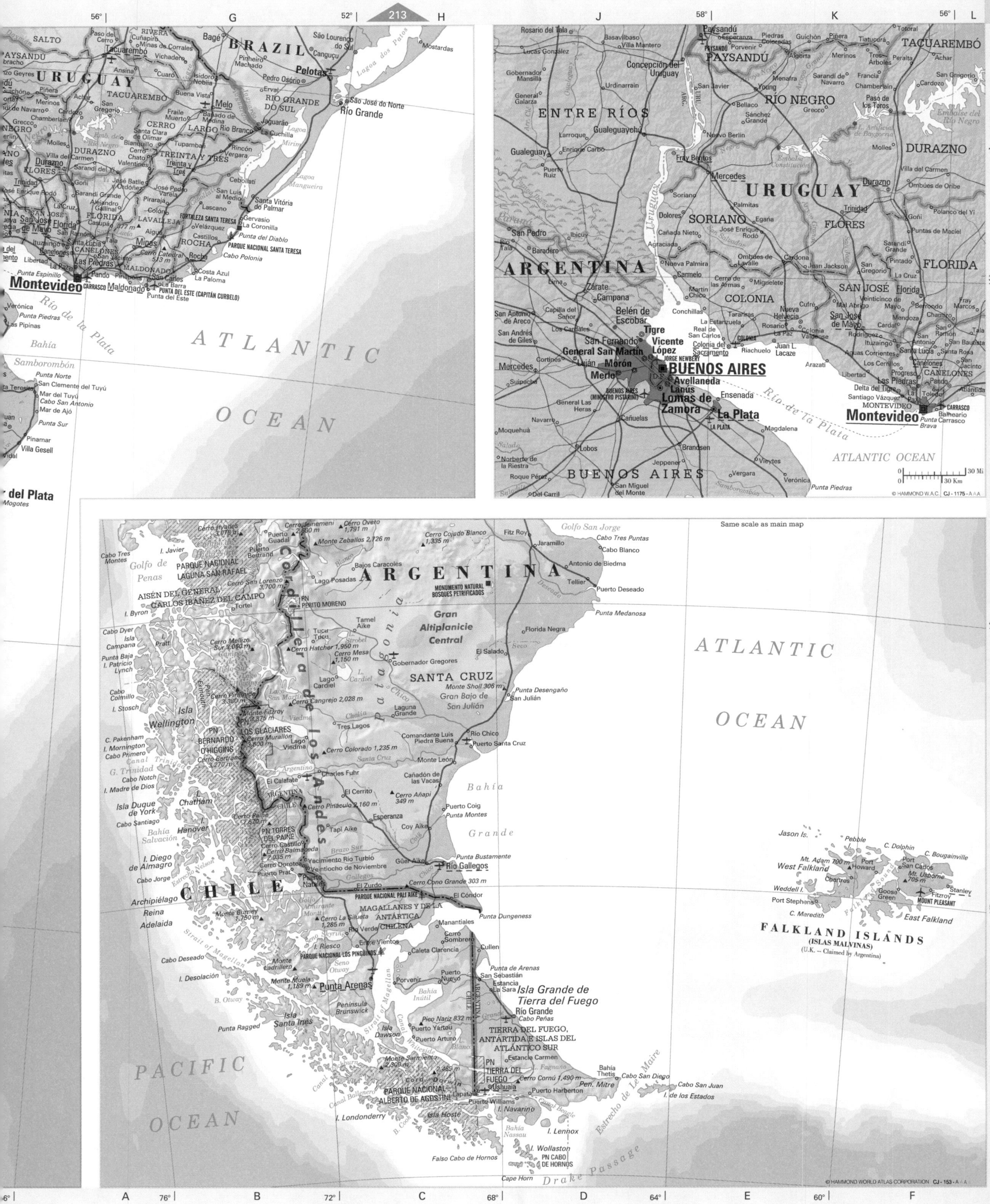

- ■ OVER 2,000,000
- ■ 1,000,000 - 1,999,999
- ● 500,000 - 999,999
- ● 250,000 - 499,999
- ⊕ 100,000 - 249,999
- Φ 30,000 - 99,999
- ◉ 10,000 - 29,999
- ○ UNDER 10,000

SCALE 1:6,900,000   LAMBERT CONFORMAL CONIC PROJECTION

MILES
KILOMETERS

© HAMMOND WORLD ATLAS CORPORATION   CJ - 153 - A - A

Arctic Regions, Antarctica

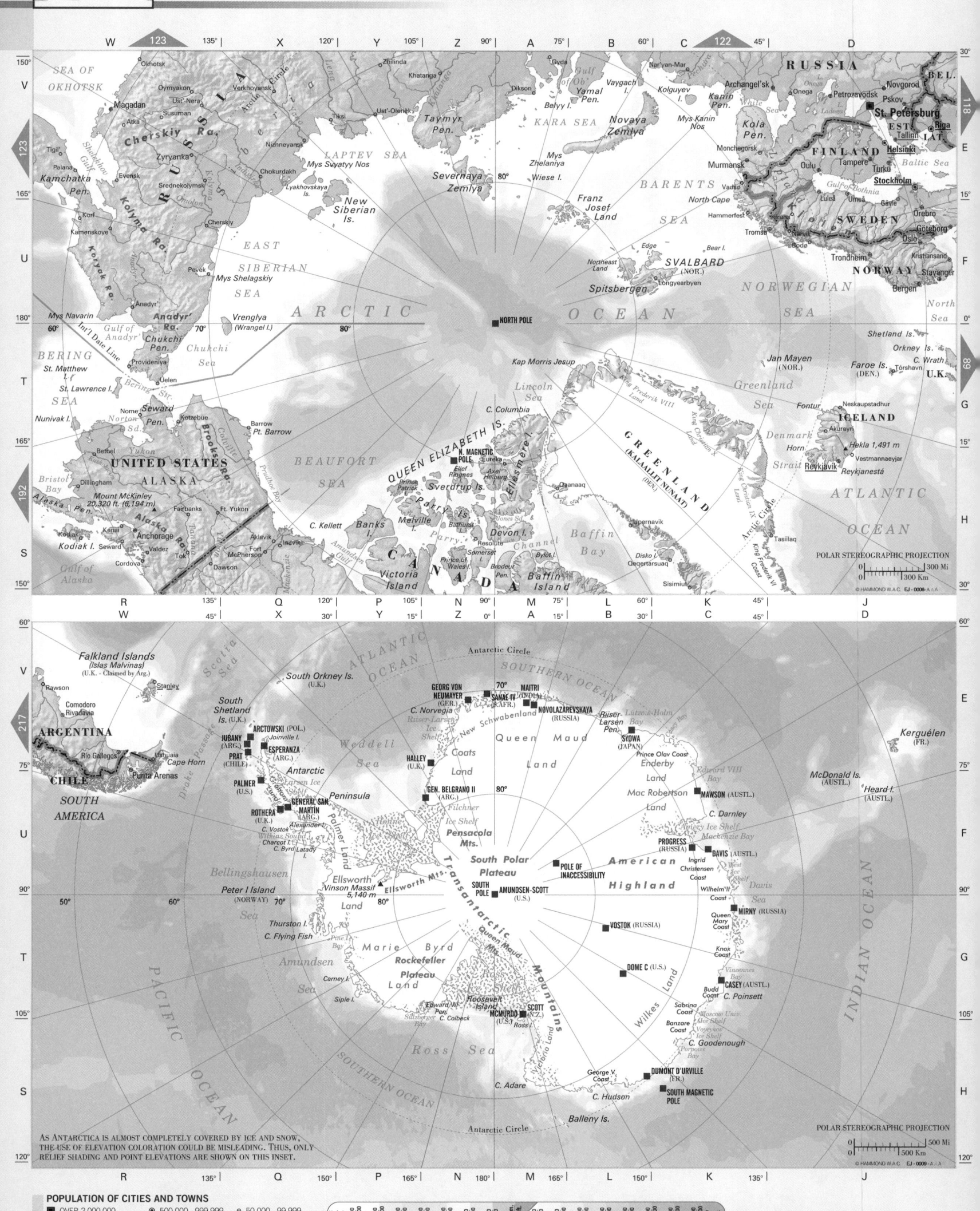

POLAR STEREOGRAPHIC PROJECTION

AS ANTARCTICA IS ALMOST COMPLETELY COVERED BY ICE AND SNOW, THE USE OF ELEVATION COLORATION COULD BE MISLEADING. THUS, ONLY RELIEF SHADING AND POINT ELEVATIONS ARE SHOWN ON THIS INSET.

POLAR STEREOGRAPHIC PROJECTION

POPULATION OF CITIES AND TOWNS

■ OVER 2,000,000	◉ 500,000 - 999,999	○ 50,000 - 99,999
■ 1,000,000 - 1,999,999	◉ 100,000 - 499,999	○ UNDER 50,000

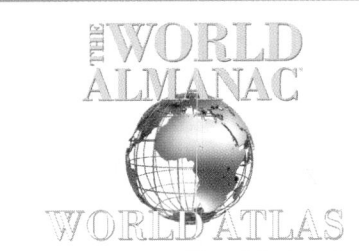

Index to the
World Map Section

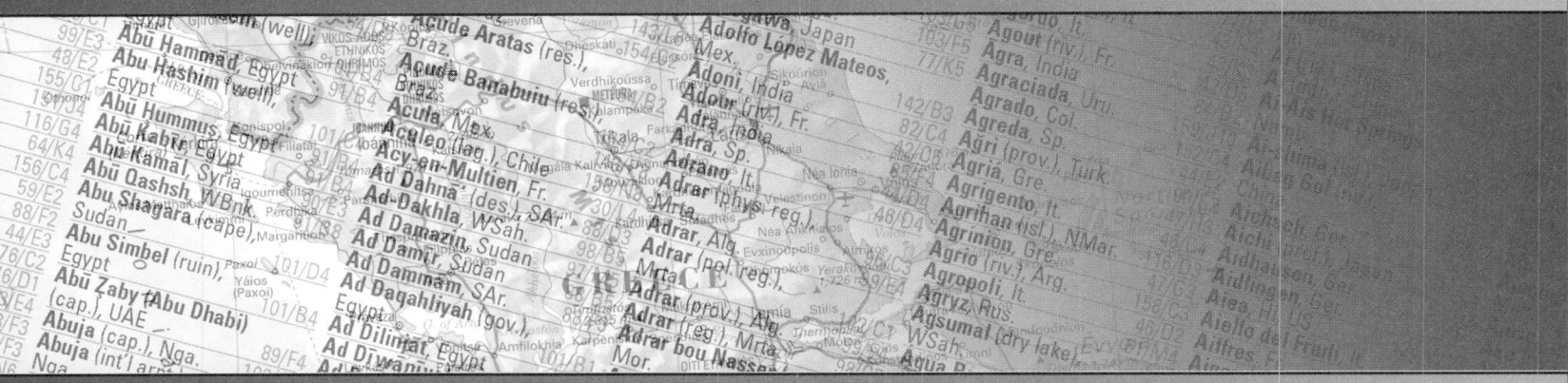

Using the Index

This index is a comprehensive listing of the places and geographic features found in the atlas. Names are arranged in strict alphabetical order, without regard to hyphens or spaces. Every name is followed by the country or area to which it belongs. Except for cities, towns, countries and cultural areas, all entries include a reference to feature type, such as province, river, island, peak, and so on. The page number and alpha-numeric code appear in blue to the right of each listing. The page number directs you to the largest scale map on which the name can be found, or in the case of a nation, on which the nation is depicted in its entirety. The code refers to the grid squares formed by the horizontal and vertical lines of latitude and longitude on each map. Following the letters from left to right and the numbers from top to bottom helps you to locate quickly the square containing the place or feature. Inset maps have their own alpha-numeric codes. Names that are accompanied by a point symbol are indexed to the symbol's location on the map. Other names are indexed to the initial letter of the name. When a map name contains a subordinate or alternate name, both names are listed in the index. To conserve space and provide room for more entries, many abbreviations are used in this index. The primary abbreviations are listed below.

Abbreviations

A

Ab,Can	Alberta
Abor.	Aboriginal
Acad.	Academy
ACT	Australian Capital Territory
A.F.B.	Air Force Base
Afld.	Airfield
Afg.	Afghanistan
Afr.	Africa
Ak,US	Alaska
Al,US	Alabama
Alb.	Albania
Alg.	Algeria
Amm. Dep.	Ammunition Depot
And.	Andorra
Ang.	Angola
Angu.	Anguilla
Ant.	Antarctica
Anti.	Antigua and Barbuda
Ar,US	Arkansas
Arch.	Archipelago
Arg.	Argentina
Arm.	Armenia
Arpt.	Airport
Aru.	Aruba
ASam.	American Samoa
Ash.	Ashmore and Cartier Islands
Aus.	Austria
Austl.	Australia
Aut.	Autonomous
Az,US	Arizona
Azer.	Azerbaijan
Azor.	Azores

B

Bahm.	Bahamas, The
Bahr.	Bahrain
Bang.	Bangladesh
Bar.	Barbados
BC,Can	British Columbia
Bela.	Belarus
Belg.	Belgium
Belz.	Belize
Ben.	Benin
Berm.	Bermuda
Bfld.	Battlefield
Bhu.	Bhutan
Bol.	Bolivia
Bor.	Borough
Bosn.	Bosnia and Herzegovina
Bots.	Botswana
Braz.	Brazil
BrIn.	British Indian Ocean Territory
Bru.	Brunei
Bul.	Bulgaria
Burk.	Burkina Faso
Buru.	Burundi
BVI	British Virgin Islands

C

Ca,US	California
CAfr.	Central African Republic
Camb.	Cambodia
Camr.	Cameroon
Can.	Canada
Can.	Canal
Canl.	Canary Islands
Cap.	Capital
Cap. Dist.	Capital District
Cap. Terr.	Capital Territory
Cay.	Cayman Islands
C.d'Iv.	Côte d'Ivoire
C.G.	Coast Guard
Chan.	Channel
Chl.	Channel Islands
Co.	County
Co,US	Colorado
Col.	Colombia
Com.	Comoros
Cont.	Continent
CpV.	Cape Verde Islands
CR	Costa Rica
Cr.	Creek
Cro.	Croatia
CSea.	Coral Sea Islands Territory
Ct,US	Connecticut
Ctr.	Center
Ctry.	Country
Cyp.	Cyprus
Czh.	Czech Republic

D

DC,US	District of Columbia
De,US	Delaware
Den.	Denmark
Depr.	Depression
Dept.	Department
Des.	Desert
DF	Distrito Federal
Dist.	District
Djib.	Djibouti
Dom.	Dominica
Dpcy.	Dependency
D.R.Congo	Democratic Republic of the Congo
DRep.	Dominican Republic

E

Ecu.	Ecuador
Emb.	Embankment
Eng.	Engineering
Eng,UK	England
EqG.	Equatorial Guinea
Erit.	Eritrea
ESal.	El Salvador
Est.	Estonia
Eth.	Ethiopia
ETim.	East Timor
Eur.	Europe

F

Falk.	Falkland Islands
Far.	Faroe Islands
Fed. Dist.	Federal District
Fin.	Finland
Fl,US	Florida
For.	Forest
Fr.	France
FrAnt.	French Southern and Antarctic Lands
FrG.	French Guiana
FrPol.	French Polynesia
FYROM	Former Yugoslav Rep. of Macedonia

G

Ga,US	Georgia
Galp.	Galapagos Islands
Gam.	Gambia, The
Gaza	Gaza Strip
GBis.	Guinea-Bissau
Geo.	Georgia
Ger.	Germany
Gha.	Ghana
Gib.	Gibraltar
Glac.	Glacier
Gov.	Governorate
Govt.	Government
Gre.	Greece
Grld.	Greenland
Gren.	Grenada
Grsld.	Grassland
Guad.	Guadeloupe
Guat.	Guatemala
Gui.	Guinea
Guy.	Guyana

H

Har.	Harbor
Hi,US	Hawaii
Hist.	Historic(al)
Hon.	Honduras
Hts.	Heights
Hun.	Hungary

I

Ia,US	Iowa
Ice.	Iceland
Id,US	Idaho
Il,US	Illinois
IM	Isle of Man
In,US	Indiana
Ind. Res.	Indian Reservation
Indo.	Indonesia
Int'l	International
Ire.	Ireland
Isl., Isls.	Island, Islands
Isr.	Israel
Isth.	Isthmus
It.	Italy

J

Jam.	Jamaica
Jor.	Jordan

K

Kaz.	Kazakhstan
Kiri.	Kiribati
Kos.	Kosovo
Ks,US	Kansas
Kuw.	Kuwait
Ky,US	Kentucky
Kyr.	Kyrgyzstan

L

La,US	Louisiana
Lab.	Laboratory
Lag.	Lagoon
Lakesh.	Lakeshore
Lat.	Latvia
Lcht.	Liechtenstein
Ldg.	Landing
Leb.	Lebanon
Les.	Lesotho
Libr.	Liberia
Lith.	Lithuania
Lux.	Luxembourg

M

Ma,US	Massachusetts
Madg.	Madagascar
Madr.	Madeira
Malay.	Malaysia
Mald.	Maldives
Malw.	Malawi
Mart.	Martinique
May.	Mayotte
Mb,Can	Manitoba
Md,US	Maryland
Me,US	Maine
Mem.	Memorial
Mex.	Mexico
Mi,US	Michigan
Micr.	Micronesia, Federated States of
Mil.	Military
Mn,US	Minnesota
Mo,US	Missouri
Mol.	Moldova
Mon.	Monument
Mona.	Monaco
Mong.	Mongolia
Mont.	Montenegro
Monts.	Montserrat
Mor.	Morocco
Moz.	Mozambique
Mrsh.	Marshall Islands
Mrta.	Mauritania
Mrts.	Mauritius
Ms,US	Mississippi
Mt.	Mount
Mt,US	Montana
Mtn., Mts.	Mountain, Mountains
Mun. Arpt.	Municipal Airport
Myan.	Myanmar

N

NAm.	North America
Namb.	Namibia
NAnt.	Netherlands Antilles
Nat'l	National
Nav.	Naval
NB,Can	New Brunswick
Nbrhd.	Neighborhood
NC,US	North Carolina
NCal.	New Caledonia
ND,US	North Dakota
Ne,US	Nebraska
Neth.	Netherlands
Nf,Can	Newfoundland
Nga.	Nigeria
NH,US	New Hampshire
NI,UK	Northern Ireland
Nic.	Nicaragua
NJ,US	New Jersey
NKor.	North Korea
NM,US	New Mexico
NMar.	Northern Mariana Islands
Nor.	Norway
NS,Can	Nova Scotia
Nv,US	Nevada
Nun.,Can	Nunavut
NW,Can	Northwest Territories
NY,US	New York
NZ	New Zealand

O

Obl.	Oblast
Oh,US	Ohio
Ok,US	Oklahoma
On,Can	Ontario
Or,US	Oregon

P

Pa,US	Pennsylvania
PacUS	Pacific Islands, U.S.
Pak.	Pakistan
Pan.	Panama
Par.	Paraguay
Par.	Parish
PE,Can	Prince Edward Island
Pen.	Peninsula
Phil.	Philippines
Phys. Reg.	Physical Region
Pitc.	Pitcairn Islands
Plat.	Plateau
PNG	Papua New Guinea
Pol.	Poland
Port.	Portugal
Poss.	Possession
Pkwy.	Parkway
PR	Puerto Rico
Pref.	Prefecture
Prov.	Province
Prsv.	Preserve
Pt.	Point

Q

Qu,Can	Quebec

R

Rec.	Recreation(al)
Ref.	Refuge
Reg.	Region
Rep.	Republic
Res.	Reservoir, Reservation
Reun.	Réunion
RI,US	Rhode Island
Riv.	River
Rom.	Romania
Rsv.	Reserve
Rus.	Russia
Rvwy.	Riverway
Rwa.	Rwanda

S

SAfr.	South Africa
Sam.	Samoa
SAm.	South America
SaoT.	São Tomé and Príncipe
SAr.	Saudi Arabia
Sc,UK	Scotland
SC,US	South Carolina
SD,US	South Dakota
Seash.	Seashore
Sen.	Senegal
Serb.	Serbia
Sey.	Seychelles
SGeo.	South Georgia and Sandwich Islands
Sing.	Singapore
Sk,Can	Saskatchewan
SKor.	South Korea
SLeo.	Sierra Leone
Slov.	Slovenia
Slvk.	Slovakia
SMar.	San Marino
Sol.	Solomon Islands
Som.	Somalia
Sp.	Spain
Spr., Sprs.	Spring, Springs
SrL.	Sri Lanka
Sta.	Station
StH.	Saint Helena
Str.	Strait
StK.	Saint Kitts and Nevis
StL.	Saint Lucia
StP.	Saint Pierre and Miquelon
StV.	Saint Vincent and the Grenadines

T

Tah.	Tahiti
Tai.	Taiwan
Taj.	Tajikistan
Tanz.	Tanzania
Ter.	Terrace
Terr.	Territory
Thai.	Thailand
Tn,US	Tennessee
Tok.	Tokelau
Trg.	Training
Trin.	Trinidad and Tobago
Trkm.	Turkmenistan
Trks.	Turks and Caicos Islands
Tun.	Tunisia
Tun.	Tunnel
Turk.	Turkey
Tuv.	Tuvalu
Twp.	Township
Tx,US	Texas

U

UAE	United Arab Emirates
Ugan.	Uganda
UK	United Kingdom
Ukr.	Ukraine
Uru.	Uruguay
US	United States
USVI	U.S. Virgin Islands
Ut,US	Utah
Uzb.	Uzbekistan

V

Va,US	Virginia
Val.	Valley
Van.	Vanuatu
VatC.	Vatican City
Ven.	Venezuela
Viet.	Vietnam
Vill.	Village
Vol.	Volcano
Vt,US	Vermont

W

Wa,US	Washington
Wal,UK	Wales
Wall.	Wallis and Futuna
WBnk.	West Bank
Wi,US	Wisconsin
Wild.	Wildlife, Wilderness
WSah.	Western Sahara
WV,US	West Virginia
Wy,US	Wyoming

Y

Yem.	Yemen
Yk,Can	Yukon Territory

Z

Zam.	Zambia
Zim.	Zimbabwe

A

100 Mile House, BC, Can. 184/C3
Aa (riv.), Ger. 108/D5
Aach (riv.), Ger. 115/F2
Aach, Ger. 115/E2
Aachen, Ger. 111/F2
Aalbach (riv.), Ger. 112/C3
Aalborg (int'l arpt.), Den. 96/C3
Aalburg, Neth. 108/C5
Aalen, Ger. 112/D5
Aalsmeer, Neth. 108/B4
Aalst, Belg. 110/D2
Aalten, Neth. 108/D5
Aalter, Belg. 110/C1
Aar (riv.), Ger. 111/H3
Aarau, Swi. 114/E3
Aarberg, Swi. 114/D3
Aarburg, Swi. 114/D3
Aardenburg, Neth. 110/C1
Aare (riv.), Swi. 101/H3
Aargau (canton), Swi. 115/E3
Aarred (lake), WSah. 156/B4
Aarschot, Belg. 111/D2
Aartselaar, Belg. 111/D1
Aarwangen, Swi. 114/D3
Aba, China 128/H5
Aba, D.R. Congo 162/A2
Aba, Nga. 161/G5
Abā as Su'ūd, SAr. 146/D5
Abacaxis (riv.), Braz. 208/G5
Abadab (peak), Sudan 159/C5
Ābādān, Iran 146/E2
Ābādeh, Iran 146/F2
Abadia dos Dourados, Braz. 213/C1
Abadla, Alg. 157/E3
Abádszalók, Hun. 106/E2
Abaeté, Braz. 213/C1
Abaetetuba, Braz. 209/J4
Abaiang (isl.), Kiri. 174/G4
Abakan, Rus. 122/K4
Abancay, Peru 214/C4
Abano Terme, It. 117/E2
Abar Kūh, Iran 146/F2
Abarán, Sp. 102/E3
Abashiri (lake), Japan 134/C2
Abashiri, Japan 134/D1
Abasolo, Mex. 201/E4
Abasolo, Mex. 201/F3
Abay, Kaz. 145/F3
Ābaya Hayk (lake), Eth. 155/N6
Abbadia Lariana, It. 115/F6
Abbadia San Salvatore, It. 101/J5
Abbeville, La, US 187/J5
Abbeville, SC, US 191/H3
Abbeville, Fr. 110/A3
Abbey (peak), Austl. 171/B1
Abbeyfeale, Ire. 89/P10
Abbeyleix, Ire. 89/Q10
Abbiategrasso, It. 116/B2
Abbot (mt.), Austl. 171/B3
Abbotsinch (int'l arpt.), Sc, UK 94/B5
Abbottābād, Pak. 144/B2
Abbottstown, Pa, US 196/B4
Abcoude, Neth. 108/B4
Abdul Hakīm, Pak. 144/B4
Abdulino, Rus. 121/K1
Abéché, Chad 155/K5
Abemama (isl.), Kiri. 174/G4
Abenberg, Ger. 112/D4
Abengourou, C.d'Iv. 160/E5
Åbenrå, Den. 96/C4
Abens (riv.), Ger. 98/F4
Abensberg, Ger. 113/E5
Abeokuta, Nga. 161/F5
Abercarn, Wal, UK 90/C3
Aberchirder, Sc, UK 94/D1
Aberdare, Wal, UK 90/C3
Aberdare NP, Kenya 162/C3
Aberdeen, Austl. 173/D2
Aberdeen (lake), Nun., Can. 180/F2
Aberdeen, SAfr. 164/D4
Aberdeen, Sc, UK 94/D2
Aberdeen (pol. reg.), Sc, UK 94/D2
Aberdeen, SD, US 185/J4
Aberdeen, Ms, US 191/F3
Aberdeen, Md, US 196/B5
Aberdeen, Wa, US 184/C4
Aberdeen Proving Ground, Md, US 196/B5
Aberdeenshire, Sc, UK 94/D2
Aberdeenshire (pol. reg.), Sc, UK 94/D2
Aberdour, Sc, UK 94/C4
Aberdour (bay), Sc, UK 94/D1
Aberfeldy, Sc, UK 94/C3
Aberfoyle, Sc, UK 94/B4
Abergavenny, Wal, UK 90/C3
Abergele, Wal, UK 92/E5
Aberlour, Sc, UK 94/C2
Abernethy, Sc, UK 94/C4
Abert (lake), Or, US 184/C5
Abertillery, Wal, UK 90/C3
Aberystwyth, Wal, UK 90/B2
Abhá, SAr. 146/D5
Abhar, Iran 146/E1
Abhayāpuri, India 143/H2
Abhe Bad (lake), Djib.,Eth. 155/P5
Abia (prov.), Nga. 161/G5
Abidjan, C.d'Iv. 160/D5
Abiko, Japan 135/E2
Abilene, Tx, US 187/H4
Abilene, Ks, US 187/H3
Abingdon, Eng, UK 91/E3
Abingdon, Md, US 196/B5
Abington (reef), Austl. 171/C2
Abington, Sc, UK 94/C6
Abino (pt.), On, Can. 189/R10
Abiquiu, NM, US 190/B2
Abitibi (lake), On,Qu, Can. 181/H4
Abitibi (riv.), On, Can. 181/H4
Abkhazia Aut. Rep., Geo. 121/G4
Ableiges, Fr. 88/H4
Abnūb, Egypt 159/B3
Åbo (Turku), Fin. 97/K1
Abohar, India 144/C4
Aboisso, C.d'Iv. 160/E5
Abomey, Ben. 161/F5
Abondance, Fr. 114/C5
Abony, Hun. 106/D2
Aboyne, Sc, UK 94/D2
Abra (riv.), Phil. 137/D4
Abra Pampa, Arg. 215/C1
Abraham Gonzalez (int'l arpt.), Mex. 184/D2
Abrantes, Port. 102/A3
Abreojos (pt.), Mex. 184/B3
Abrud, Rom. 107/F2
Abruzzi (prov.), It. 101/K5
Abruzzo, PN de, It. 104/C2
Absam, Aus. 115/H3
Absaroka (range), Mt,Wy, US 184/F4
Absecon, NJ, US 196/D5
Abtsgmünd, Ger. 112/D5
Abu Dhabi (Abū Ẓaby) (cap.), UAE 147/F4
Abu el-Husein (well), Egypt 159/B4
Abū Ḩammād, Egypt 149/B4
Abu Hashim (well), Egypt 159/C4
Abū Ḩummuş, Egypt 149/B4
Abū Kabīr, Egypt 149/B4
Abū Kamāl, Syria 148/E3
Abū Qashsh, WBnk. 149/G8
Abu Shagara (cape), Sudan 159/D4
Abu Simbel (ruin), Egypt 159/B4
Abuja (cap.), Nga. 161/G4
Abuja (int'l arpt.), Nga. 161/G4
Abuja Capital Territory, Nga. 161/G4
Abukuma (riv.), Japan 133/G2
Abukuma (plat.), Japan 133/G2
Abulog, Phil. 137/D4
Abunã (riv.), Braz. 208/E6
Abuta, Japan 134/B2
Ābuyē Mēda (peak), Eth. 155/N5
Abuyog, Phil. 137/E5
Åby, Swe. 96/G2
Abybro, Den. 96/C3
Abydos (ruin), Egypt 159/B3
Acacías, Col. 210/C4
Acacoyagua, Mex. 202/C3
Acadia NP, Me, US 189/G2
Acadian Village, La, US 187/J5
Acajutiba, Braz. 212/C3
Acámbaro, Mex. 201/E4
Acampo, Ca, US 193/M10
Acandí, Col. 210/B2
Acaponeta (riv.), Mex. 184/D4
Acaponeta, Mex. 184/D4
Acapulco de Juárez, Mex. 198/B4
Acaraí (mts.), Braz.,Guy. 211/G4
Acaraí, Serra (mts.), Braz. 208/G3
Acaraú (riv.), Braz. 212/B1
Acaraú, Braz. 212/B1
Acari, Braz. 212/C2
Acari (riv.), Braz. 208/G5
Acari, Peru 214/C4
Acarigua, Ven. 210/D2
Acatlán de Osorio, Mex. 202/B2
Acatlán de Pérez Figueroa, Mex. 201/N8
Acatzingo, Mex. 201/M7
Acayucan, Mex. 202/C2
Accha, Peru 214/D4
Acciaroli, It. 104/D2
Accra (cap.), Gha. 161/E5
Accrington, Eng, UK 93/F4
Aceuchal, Sp. 102/B3
Ach (riv.), Aus. 113/G6
Achacachi, Bol. 208/E7
Achaguas, Ven. 210/D3
Achao, Chile 216/B4
Achar, Uru. 217/K10
Achegour (well), Niger 154/H4
Achen (pass), Ger. 115/H2
Acheng, China 129/N2
Achères, Fr. 88/J5
Achhnera, India 142/A2
Achicourt, Fr. 110/B3
Achill (isl.), Ire. 88/N10
Achill Head (pt.), Ire. 88/N9
Achiltibuie, Sc, UK 89/R7
Achinsk, Rus. 122/K4
Achmîm (well), Mrta. 160/D2
Achnasheen, Sc, UK 94/A1
Achoma, Peru 214/D4
A'chràlaig (peak), Sc, UK 94/A2
Achuapa, Nic. 202/E3
Achupallas, Ecu. 214/B1
Acireale, It. 104/D4
Acklins (isl.), Bahm. 199/G3
Acland (mt.), Austl. 171/C4
Acobamba, Peru 214/C4
Acolla, Peru 214/C3
Acolman, Mex. 201/R9
Acomayo, Peru 214/D4
Acomayo, Peru 214/B3
Aconcagua (peak), Arg. 216/C2
Aconchi, Mex. 184/C2
Acopiara, Braz. 212/C2
Acora, Peru 214/D4
Acqualagna, It. 117/F5
Acquanegra sul Chiese, It. 116/D2
Acquapendente, It. 104/B1
Acqui Terme, It. 116/B3
Acraman (lake), Austl. 171/G5
Acrata (pt.), Alg. 158/G4
Acre (riv.), Braz. 208/E6
Acre (state), Braz. 214/D3
Acreúna, Braz. 213/B1
Acropolis, Gre. 105/N9
Actaeon Group (isls.), FrPol. 175/M7
Acton, Ca, US 194/B2
Actopan, Mex. 201/N7
Actopan, Mex. 201/L6
Açu, Braz. 212/C2
Açude Aratas (res.), Braz. 212/B2
Açude Banabuiu (res.), Braz. 212/C2
Acula, Mex. 201/P8
Aculeo (lag.), Chile 216/N8
Acy-en-Multien, Fr. 88/L4
Ad Dahnā' (des.), SAr. 146/D3
Ad-Dakhla, WSah. 156/B5
Ad Damazin, Sudan 155/M5
Ad Dāmir, Sudan 146/B5
Ad Dammām, SAr. 146/F3
Ad Daqahliyah (gov.), Egypt 159/B1
Ad Dilinjāt, Egypt 149/B4
Ad Dīwānīyah, Iraq 148/F4
Ad Dujayl, Iraq 148/F3
Ad Duwaym, Sudan 155/M5
Ada, Gha. 161/F5
Ada, Serb. 106/E3
Ada, Oh, US 188/D3
Ada, Ok, US 187/H4
Adainville, Fr. 88/G5
Adair (cape), Nun., Can. 181/J1
Adair, Bahia del (bay), Mex. 144/D5
Adaja (riv.), Sp. 102/C2
Adak (isl.), Ak, US 192/C6
Adak (str.), Ak, US 192/C6
Adam (mt.), Falk., UK 217/E6
Adamantina, Braz. 213/B2
Adamaoua (plat.), Camr.,Nga. 151/D4
Adamello (peak), It. 115/G5
Adaminaby, Austl. 173/D3
Adams (lake), BC, Can. 184/D3
Adams (co.), Co, US 195/C3
Adams (co.), Pa, US 196/A4
Adams (mt.), Wa, US 184/C4
Adamstown (cap.), Pitc. 175/M7
Adamstown, Pa, US 196/B3
Adamwa (plat.), Nga. 161/H5
'Adan, Yem. 146/D6
Adana, Turk. 149/D1
Adana (prov.), Turk. 148/C2
Adana (int'l arpt.), Turk. 149/D1
Adapazarı, Turk. 107/K5
Adare, Ire. 89/P10
Adare (cape), Ant. 218/M
Adarza (peak), Fr. 102/E1
Add (riv.), Sc, UK 94/A4
Adda (riv.), It. 101/H4
Addison, Il, US 193/P16
Addlestone, Eng, UK 88/B2
Addo Elephant NP, SAfr. 164/D4
Adekeieh (Ādī K'eyih), Erit. 146/C6
Adelaide, SAfr. 164/D4
Adelaide (pen.), Nun., Can. 180/G2
Adelaide (int'l arpt.), Austl. 171/M8
Adelaide, Austl. 171/M8
Adelaide Zoo, Austl. 171/M8
Adelanto, Ca, US 194/C1
Adelebsen, Ger. 109/G5
Adelheidsdorf, Ger. 109/H3
Adelmannsfelden, Ger. 112/D5
Adelong, Austl. 173/D2
Adelschlag, Ger. 112/E5
Adelsheim, Ger. 112/C4
Adelsried, Ger. 112/D6
Aden (gulf), Afr.,Asia 125/D8
Adenau, Ger. 111/F3
Adendorf, Ger. 109/H2
Adh Dhirā', Jor. 149/D4
Adi (isl.), Indo. 139/H4
Ādī Ugrī, Erit. 146/C6
Adieu (cape), Austl. 171/G5
Adige (riv.), It. 101/J4
Adige (Etsch) (riv.), It. 115/G4
Ādīgrat, Eth. 146/C6
Adilābād, India 140/C4
Adilcevaz, Turk. 148/E2
Adiora (well), Mali 161/E2
Adirondack (mts.), NY, US 183/L3
Ādīs Ābeba (Addis Ababa) (cap.), Eth. 155/N6
Adıyaman, Turk. 148/D2
Adıyaman (prov.), Turk. 148/D2
Adjud, Rom. 107/H2
Adjuntas, Presa de la (res.), Mex. 201/F4
Adler/Sochi (int'l arpt.), Rus. 120/F4
Adliswil, Swi. 115/E3
Admiralty (inlet), Nun., Can. 181/H1
Admiralty (isl.), Ak, US 180/C3
Admiralty Island Nat'l Mon., Ak, US 192/M4
Admiralty (isls.), PNG 174/D5
Admiralty (inlet), Wa, US 193/B2
Adnan Menderes (int'l arpt.), Turk. 148/A2
Ado (riv.), Japan 135/J5
Ado Ekiti, Nga. 161/G5
Ado Odo, Nga. 161/F5
Adogawa, Japan 135/K5
Adolfo López Mateos, Mex. 184/B3
Ādoni, India 140/C4
Adour (riv.), Fr. 100/C5
Adra, India 143/F4
Adra, Sp. 102/D4
Adrano, It. 104/D4
Adrar (phys. reg.), Mrta. 154/C3
Adrar, Alg. 157/E4
Adrar (pol. reg.), Mrta. 160/C1
Adrar (prov.), Alg. 157/E4
Adrar (reg.), Mrta. 156/C5
Adrar bou Nasser (peak), Mor. 156/E2
Adrar Sotuf (mts.), WSah. 156/B5
Adria, It. 117/F2
Adrian, Mi, US 188/C3
Adriatic (sea), Eur. 85/F4
Adro, It. 116/C1
Adulis (ruin), Erit. 146/C5
Adur (riv.), Eng, UK 91/F5
Ādwa, Eth. 146/C6
Adwick le Street, Eng, UK 93/G4
Adycha (riv.), Rus. 123/P3
Adygeya, Resp., Rus. 120/F3
Adz'va (riv.), Rus. 119/P2
Aegean (sea), Gre.,Turk. 105/J3
Aerø (isl.), Den. 96/D4
Aeron (riv.), Wal, UK 90/B2
Aesch, Swi. 114/D3
Aeschi bei Spiez, Swi. 114/D4
Äetsä, Fin. 97/K1
Afadjoto (peak), Gha. 161/F5
'Afak, Iraq 146/E2
Afándou, Gre. 148/B2
Aff (riv.), Fr. 100/B3
Affoltern im Emmental, Swi. 114/D3
Affric (lake), Sc, UK 94/A2
Affton, Mo, US 195/G8
Afghanistan (ctry.) 147/H2
Afmadow, Som. 155/P7
Afogados da Ingàzeira, Braz. 212/C2
Afognak (mtn.), Ak, US 192/H4
Afognak (isl.), Ak, US 192/H4
Afollé, Massif de (phys. reg.), Mrta. 160/C2
Afonso Bezerra, Braz. 212/C2
Afonso Cláudio, Braz. 213/D2
Afragola, It. 104/D2
Afrânio, Braz. 212/B3
Africa (cont.) 109
Afrin (riv.), Turk. 149/E1
'Afrīn, Syria 149/E1
Afrique (peak), Fr. 114/A3
Afsluitdijk (dam), Neth. 108/C2
Afte (riv.), Ger. 109/F5
Afton, Wy, US 184/F5
Afuidich (lake), WSah. 156/B5
'Afula, Isr. 149/G6
Afyon, Turk. 148/B2
Afyon (prov.), Turk. 148/B2
Afzalgarh, India 142/B1
Agades (int'l arpt.), Niger 161/G2
Agadez, Niger 161/G2
Agadez (dept.), Niger 157/H5
Agadir, Mor. 156/C3
Agago (riv.), Ugan. 162/B2
Agamor (well), Mali 161/F2
Agano (riv.), Japan 133/F2
Agassiz Ice Cap (ice field), Nun., Can. 181/T6
Agattu (isl.), Ak, US 192/A5
Agattu (str.), Ak, US 192/A5
Agbabu, Nga. 161/G5
Agboville, C.d'Iv. 160/D5
Ağdam, Azer. 121/H5
Agde, Fr. 100/E5
Agen, Fr. 100/D4
Ageo, Japan 135/D2
Ager (riv.), Aus. 113/G7
Ageræk, Den. 96/C4
Agerisee (lake), Swi. 115/E3
Agger (riv.), Ger. 111/G1
Aggteleki NP, Slvk. 106/E1
Āghā Jārī, Iran 146/E2
Aghagallon, NI, UK 92/B3
Aghagower, Ire. 89/P10
Agiabampo, Mex. 184/C3
Ağınskiy Buryatskiy Aut. Okrug, Rus. 123/Q7
Aginskoye, Rus. 129/K1
Agliana, It. 117/D5
Ağlıköy, Turk. 148/C1
Agly (riv.), Fr. 100/E5
Agna, It. 117/E2
Agnanderón, Gre. 105/G3
Agnita, Rom. 107/G3
Agno (riv.), It. 117/E1
Agno (int'l arpt.), Swi. 115/E6
Agnone, It. 104/D2
Ago, Japan 135/L7
Agogna (riv.), It. 101/H4
Agordo, It. 101/K3
Agout (riv.), Fr. 100/D5
Agra, India 142/B2
Agraciada, Uru. 217/J10
Agrado, Col. 210/C4
Agreda, Sp. 102/E2
Ağri (prov.), Turk. 148/E2
Agriá, Gre. 105/H3
Agrigento, It. 104/C4
Agrihan (isl.), NMar. 174/D3
Agrínion, Gre. 105/G3
Agrio (riv.), Arg. 216/C3
Agropoli, It. 104/D2
Agryz, Rus. 119/M4
Agsumal (dry lake), WSah. 156/B4
Água Boa, Braz. 212/B5
Água Branca, Braz. 212/B2
Agua Dulce, Ca, US 194/B2
Agua Dulce, Mex. 202/C2
Agua Fria (riv.), Az, US 195/R19
Agua Fria NM, Az, US 186/E4
Agua Hedionda (lake), Ca, US 194/C4
Agua Larga, Ven. 210/D2
Agua Prieta, Mex. 184/C2
Aguachica, Col. 210/C2
Aguadilla, PR 199/M8
Aguadulce, Pan. 210/A2
Aguaí, Braz. 213/G7
Agualva-Cacém, Port. 103/P10
Aguan (riv.), Hon. 198/D4
Aguanus (riv.), Qu, Can. 189/J1
Aguapeí (riv.), Braz. 213/B2
Aguarico (riv.), Peru 210/B5
Águas Belas, Braz. 212/C3
Aguas Corrientes, Uru. 217/K11
Águas da Prata, Braz. 213/G6
Águas de Lindóia, Braz. 213/G7
Águas Formosas, Braz. 212/B5
Aguas, Serra das (hills), Braz. 213/H7
Aguasay, Ven. 211/F2
Aguascalientes, Mex. 184/E4
Aguascalientes (state), Mex. 198/A3
Aguavermelha, Represa (res.), Braz. 213/B1
Aguaytía (riv.), Peru 214/C3
Agudos, Braz. 213/B2
Agueda (riv.), Sp. 102/B2
Águeda, Port. 102/A2
Aguêraktem (well), Mali 156/D5
Agugliano, It. 117/G5
Agui, Japan 135/L6
Aguijan (isl.), NMar. 174/D3
Aguilar, Sp. 102/C4
Aguilar de Campóo, Sp. 102/C1
Aguilares, Arg. 215/C2
Aguilas, Sp. 102/E4
Aguililla, Mex. 184/E5
Aguja (pt.), Peru 214/A2
Agulhas (cape), SAfr. 164/M11
Agulhas Negras, Pico das (peak), Braz. 213/J7
Agung (vol.), Indo. 139/E5
Agusan (riv.), Phil. 137/E6
Agustín Codazzi, Col. 210/C2
Ahaggar (plat.), Arg. 154/F3
Ahaggar (mts.), Alg. 157/G5
Ahal (pol. reg.), Trkm. 145/C5
Aham, Ger. 113/F5
Ahar, Iran 121/H5
Ahaus, Ger. 108/E4
Ahfir, Mor. 158/C2
Ahırlı, Turk. 148/C2
Ahlat, Turk. 148/E2
Ahlen, Ger. 109/E5
Ahlerstedt, Ger. 109/G2
Ahmadābād, India 147/K4
Ahmadpur East, Pak. 144/A5
Ahmadpur Siāl, Pak. 144/A4
Ahmar (mts.), Eth. 155/P6
Ahmar, 'Erg el (des.), Mali 156/D4
Ahmed (well), WSah. 156/B5
Ahmeyine (well), Mrta. 156/B5
Ahoghill, NI, UK 92/B2
Ahome, Mex. 184/C3
Ahr (riv.), Ger. 101/G1
Ahraurā, India 142/D3
Ahrensburg, Ger. 109/H1
Ahse (riv.), Ger. 109/F5
Ahuacatitlán, Mex. 201/K8
Ahuacatlán, Mex. 184/D4
Ahuachapán, ESal. 202/D3
Ahualulco, Mex. 201/E4
Ahuimanu, Hi, US 182/W13
Ahumada, Mex. 184/D2
Ahun, Fr. 100/E3
Åhus, Swe. 96/F4
Ahvāz, Iran 146/E2
Ahvenanmaa (prov.), Fin. 95/F4
Ai (riv.), China 131/C2
Ai (mtn.), China 130/E3
Ai-Ais Hot Springs, Namb. 164/B2
Ai-shima (isl.), Japan 132/B3
Aibag Gol (riv.), China 130/B2
Aichach, Ger. 112/E6
Aichi (pref.), Japan 133/E3
Aidhausen, Ger. 112/D2
Aidlingen, Ger. 112/B5
Aiea, Hi, US 182/W13
Aiello del Friuli, It. 117/G1
Aiffres, Fr. 100/C3
Aigen im Mühlkreis, Aus. 113/G5
Aigle, Pic de l' (peak), Fr. 114/B4
Aiglemont, Fr. 111/D4
Aigoual (peak), Fr. 100/E4
Aiguá, Uru. 217/G2
Aigues (riv.), Fr. 100/F4
Aigües Tortes y Lago de San Mauricio, PN de, Sp. 103/F1
Aiguille, Cap de l' (cape), Alg. 158/E5
Aiguillon, Fr. 100/D4
Aikawa, Japan 133/F1
Aikawa, Japan 135/C2
Aiken, SC, US 191/H3
Ailigandí, Pan. 210/B2
Ailinglapalap (isl.), Mrsh. 174/F4
Aillevillers-et-Lyaumont, Fr. 114/C2
Ailly-sur-Noye, Fr. 110/B4
Ailsa Craig (isl.), Sc, UK 94/A6
Ailuk (isl.), Mrsh. 174/G3
Aimen (pass), China 130/D5
Aimogasta, Arg. 215/C2
Aimorés, Braz. 213/D1
Aimorés, Serra dos (mts.), Braz. 213/D1
Ain (riv.), Fr. 100/F4
'Aïn Beïda, Alg. 158/K7
'Aïn Beniau, Alg. 158/G4
'Aïn Bessem, Alg. 158/G4
Aïn Chok-Hay Mohammadia (prov.), Mor. 158/A2
'Aïn Defla, Alg. 158/F4
'Aïn Defla (prov.), Alg. 158/F4
Aïn el Aouda, Mor. 158/A3
'Aïn el Bey (int'l arpt.), Alg. 158/K6
'Aïn el Hammam, Alg. 158/H4
'Aïn el Turk, Alg. 158/D4
'Aïn Fakroun, Alg. 158/K6
'Aïn M'lila, Alg. 158/K6
'Aïn Oulmene, Alg. 158/H5
'Aïn Oussersa, Alg. 158/G5
'Aïn Sefra, Alg. 157/E2
'Aïn Taoujdat, Mor. 158/B3
'Aïn Taya, Alg. 158/G4
'Aïn Temouchent, Alg. 158/D2
'Aïn Touta, Alg. 158/H5
Aina Haina, Hi, US 182/W13
Aincourt, Fr. 88/H4
Aínos (peak), Gre. 105/G3
Aínos NP, Gre. 105/G3
Aipe, Col. 210/C4
Aïr (plat.), Niger 154/G4
Air Force (isl.), Nun., Can. 181/J2
Airaines, Fr. 110/A4
Airdrie, Ab, Can. 184/E3
Airdrie, Sc, UK 94/C5
Aire (riv.), Fr. 100/F2
Aire, Canal d' (canal), Fr. 110/B2
Aire-sur-la-Lys, Fr. 110/B2
Aire-sur-l'Adour, Fr. 100/C5
Airolo, Swi. 115/E4
Airuno, It. 116/C1
Airvault, Fr. 100/C3
Aisch (riv.), Ger. 101/J2
Aiseau-Presles, Belg. 111/D3
Aisén del General Carlos Ibáñez del Campo (pol. reg.), Chile 216/B5
Aisne (riv.), Fr. 98/B4
Aïssa (peak), Alg. 157/E2
Aist (riv.), Aus. 113/H6
Aït Ourir, Mor. 156/D3
Aitape, PNG 174/D5
Aitō, Japan 135/K5
Aitolikón, Gre. 105/G3
Aitrach, Ger. 115/G2
Aitrang, Ger. 115/G2
Aitutaki Atoll (isl.), Cookls. 175/J6
Aiud, Rom. 107/F2
Aiuruoca, Braz. 213/J6
Aiuruoca (riv.), Braz. 213/J7
Aix-en-Provence, Fr. 100/F5
Aiyina, Gre. 105/H4
Aiyínion, Gre. 105/H2
Aiyion, Gre. 105/H3
Aīzawl, India 141/F3
Aizu-Wakamatsu, Japan 133/F2
Ajaccio, Fr. 104/A2
Ajaccio, Golfe d' (gulf), Fr. 104/A2
Ajaigarh, India 142/C3
Ajalpan, Mex. 201/M8
Ajaria Aut. Rep., Geo. 121/G4
Ajax, On, Can. 189/R8
Ajay (riv.), India 143/F3
Ajdābiyā, Libya 155/K1
Ajdovščina, Slov. 101/K4
Ajigasawa, Japan 134/B3
'Ajjah, WBnk. 149/G7
Ajka, Hun. 106/C2
Ajo, Az, US 186/D4
Ajo (cape), Sp. 102/D1
Ajuchitlán del Progreso, Mex. 198/A4
Ajusco (vol.), Mex. 201/Q10
Aka (riv.), Japan 133/F1
Akabane, Japan 135/M6
Akabira, Japan 134/C2
Akaishi-dake (peak), Japan 133/F3
Akaltara, India 142/D4
Akan (lake), Japan 134/D2
Akan NP, Japan 134/D2
Åkarp, Swe. 96/E4
Akarsu, Turk. 148/D2
Akashi, Japan 135/G6
Akashi (str.), Japan 135/G6
Akbarpur, India 142/D2
Akbarpur, India 142/B2
Akbaytal (pass), Taj. 145/F5
Akbou, Alg. 158/H4
Akçaabat, Turk. 148/D1
Akçakale, Turk. 148/D2
Akçakoca, Turk. 107/K5
Akçaova, Turk. 107/K5
Akçapınar, Turk. 148/D2
Akçay, Turk. 149/A1
Akchâr (riv.), Mrta. 154/B4
Akchâr (phys. reg.), Mrta. 156/B5
Akdağmadeni, Turk. 120/E5
Akechi, Japan 135/M5
Akeno, Japan 135/E1
Akeno, Japan 135/A2
Åkersberga, Swe. 96/H2
Akershus (co.), Nor. 95/D3
Aketi, D.R. Congo 155/K7
Akhalts'ikhe, Geo. 121/G4
Akharnaí, Gre. 105/N8
Akhelóos (riv.), Gre. 105/G3
Akhiok, Ak, US 192/H4
Akhisar, Turk. 148/A2
Akhnūr, India 144/C3
Akhtopol, Bul. 107/H4
Akhtuba (riv.), Rus. 121/H3
Akhtubinsk, Rus. 121/H2
Aki, Japan 132/C4
Aki (riv.), Japan 135/C2
Akiachak, Ak, US 192/F3
Akigawa, Japan 135/C2
Akimiski (isl.), On, Can. 181/H3
Akıncı (pt.), Turk. 149/D1
Akıncılar, Turk. 148/D2
Äkirkeby, Den. 96/F4
Akishima, Japan 135/C2
Akita, Japan 134/B4
Akita (pref.), Japan 134/B4
Akiyama, Japan 135/C2
Akjoujt, Mrta. 160/B2
Akka, Mor. 156/C3
Akkaraipattu, SrL. 140/D6
Akkerhaugen, Nor. 96/C2
Akkeshi, Japan 134/D2
'Akko, Isr. 149/D3
Akkrum, Neth. 108/C2
Aklavik, NW, Can. 192/L2
Akō, Japan 132/D3
Akora, Pak. 144/B2
Ak'ordat, Erit. 146/C5
Akören, Turk. 148/C2
Akosombo (dam), Gha. 161/F5
Akpatok (isl.), Qu, Can. 181/K2
Akpınar, Turk. 107/J5
Akqi, China 145/G4
Akranes, Ice. 95/M7
Akrathos (cape), Gre. 105/J2
Åkrehamn, Nor. 96/A2
Akrítas (cape), Gre. 105/G4
Akron, Co, US 187/G2
Akron, Oh, US 188/D3
Akron, Pa, US 196/B3
Aksai Chin (reg.), China,India 128/C4
Aksaray, Turk. 148/C2
Aksaray (prov.), Turk. 148/C2
Aksay Kazakzu Zizhixian, China 128/F4
Akşehir, Turk. 148/B2
Akşehir Lake (lake), Turk. 148/B2
Akseki, Turk. 149/B1
Aksoran (peak), Kaz. 145/G3
Aksu, China 128/D3
Aksu, Turk. 149/B1
Aksu (riv.), Turk. 149/B1
Āksum, Eth. 146/C6
Aktepe, Turk. 149/E1
Aktí (pen.), Gre. 105/J2
Akto, China 145/G5
Akune, Japan 132/B4
Akure, Nga. 161/G5
Akureyri, Ice. 95/N6
Akuse, Gha. 161/F5
Akutan (isl.), Ak, US 192/E5
Akutan, Ak, US 192/E5
Akutan Pass (chan.), Ak, US 192/E5
Akwa Ibom (state), Nga. 161/G5
Akyab (Sittwe), Myan. 141/F3
Akyazı, Turk. 107/K5
Āl, Nor. 96/C1
Al 'āl, Jor. 149/D4
Al 'Amārah, Iraq 146/E2
Al Anbār (gov.), Iraq 148/E3
Al 'Aqabah, Jor. 149/D5
Al 'Arīsh, Egypt 149/C4
Al 'Ayn, UAE 147/G4
Al 'Azīzīyah, Libya 154/H1
Al 'Azīzīyah, Iraq 148/F3
Al Bāb, Syria 148/D2
Al Badrashayn, Egypt 149/B5
Al Baḩr Al Aḩmar (gov.), Egypt 159/C3
Al Bājūr, Egypt 149/B4
Al Balqā' (gov.), Jor. 149/D4
Al Balyanā, Egypt 159/B3
Al Başrah, Iraq 146/E2
Al Batrūn, Leb. 149/D2
Al Bayḑā, Libya 155/K1
Al Biqā' (gov.), Leb. 149/E2
Al Biqā' (valley), Leb. 149/D3
Al Bīrah, WBnk. 149/G8
Al Birkah, Libya 157/H4
Al Buḩayrah (gov.), Egypt 159/B2
Al Fāsher, Sudan 155/L5
Al Fatḩah, Iraq 148/E3
Al Fāw, Iraq 146/E3
Al Fayyūm, Egypt 149/B5
Al Fayyūm (gov.), Egypt 159/B1
Al Ghurdaqah, Egypt 159/C3
Al Ḩadīthah, Iraq 148/E3
Al Ḩaḑr, Iraq 148/E3
Al Ḩaffah, Syria 149/E2
Al Ḩajar ash Sahrqī (mts.), Oman 147/G4
Al Ḩamādah al Ḩamrā' (upland), Libya 154/H2
Al Ḩammāmāt, Tun. 104/B4
Al Ḩasakah, Syria 148/E2
Al Ḩasakah (prov.), Syria 148/E2
Al Ḩawāmidīyah, Egypt 149/B5
Al Ḩayy, Iraq 146/E2
Al Ḩillah, Iraq 148/F3
Al Hindīyah, Iraq 148/F3
Al Hirmil, Leb. 149/E2
Al Hoceima (prov.), Mor. 158/B2
Al Hoceima, Mor. 158/C2
Al Ḩudaydah, Yem. 146/D6
Al Hufūf, SAr. 146/E3
Al Iskandarīyah, Iraq 148/F3
Al Iskandarīyah (Alexandria), Egypt 149/A4
Al Iskandarīyah (gov.), Egypt 159/B1
Al Ismā'īlīyah, Egypt 149/C4
Al Ismā'īlīyah (gov.), Egypt 149/C4
Al Jabal Akaur (mts.), Oman 147/G4
Al Jaghbūb, Libya 155/K2
Al Janub (gov.), Leb. 149/D3
Al Jifārah (plain), Libya 157/H2
Al Jīzah, Egypt 149/B4
Al Junaynah, Sudan 155/K5
Al Karak (gov.), Jor. 149/D4
Al Karak, Jor. 149/D4
Al Khābūrah, Oman 147/G4
Al Khalīl (Hebron), WBnk. 149/D4
Al Khāliş, Iraq 148/F3
Al Khānkah, Egypt 149/B4
Al Khārijah, Egypt 159/B3
Al Kharṭūm Baḩrī (Khartoum North), Sudan 155/M4
Al Khubar, SAr. 146/F3
Al Khums, Libya 154/H1
Al Kiswah, Syria 149/E3
Al Kūfah, Iraq 148/F3
Al Kufrah, Libya 155/K3
Al Lādhiqīyah (gov.), Syria 148/C3
Al Lādhiqīyah (Latakia), Syria 149/D2
Al Madīnah, SAr. 146/C4
Al Madīnah al Fikrīyah, Egypt 146/B3

INDEX SECTION
222
Al Maf – Amiat

Al Mafraq (gov.), Jor. 149/E3
Al Mafraq, Jor. 149/E3
Al Maghrib (reg.), Mor. 154/E1
Al Maḩallah al Kubrá, Egypt 149/B4
Al Maḩmūdīyah, Egypt 149/B4
Al Mālikīyah, Syria 148/E2
Al Manşūrah, Egypt 149/B4
Al Manzilah, Egypt 149/B4
Al Marāghah, Egypt 159/B3
Al Marj, Libya 155/K1
Al Maţarīyah, Egypt 149/C4
Al Mawşil (Mosul), Iraq 148/E2
Al Mayādīn, Syria 148/E3
Al Mazra'ah, Jor. 149/D4
Al Minyā (gov.), Egypt 159/B2
Al Miqdādīyah, Iraq 148/F3
Al Mubarraz, SAr. 146/E4
Al Mudawwarah, Jor. 149/D5
Al Mukallā, Yem. 146/E6
Al Munastīr (prov.), Alg. 158/M7
Al Musayyib, Iraq 148/F3
Al Muthanná (gov.), Iraq 148/F4
Al Qābil, Oman 147/G4
Al Qaḑārif, Sudan 146/C6
Al Qādisīyah (gov.), Iraq 148/F4
Al Qāhirah (gov.), Egypt 159/B1
Al Qāhirah (Cairo) (cap.), Egypt 159/B2
Al Qā'im, Iraq 148/E3
Al Qāmishlī, Syria 148/E2
Al Qanāţir al Khayrīyah, Egypt 149/B4
Al Qanţarah, Egypt 149/C4
Al Qaşr, Jor. 149/D4
Al Qunayţirah (prov.), Syria 149/D3
Al Qunayţirah, Syria 149/D3
Al Qurnah, Iraq 146/E2
Al Quşayr, Syria 149/E2
Al Quţayfah, Syria 149/E3
Al Quwayrah, Jor. 149/D5
Al Ubayyiḑ, Sudan 155/M5
Al 'Uwaynāt (peak), Sudan 155/L3
Al Wādī Al Jadīd (gov.), Egypt 159/B3
Al Wāḩāt al Baḩrīyah (oasis), Egypt 159/B2
Al Wāḩāt al Khārijah (oasis), Egypt 159/B3
Al Wāsiţah, Egypt 149/B5
Al Yāmūn, WBnk. 149/G7
Ala (pt.), It. 104/B1
Ala, It. 117/E1
Alabama (riv.), Al,Ga, US 191/G4
Alabama (state), US 191/G3
Alabaster, Al, US 191/G3
Alaca, Turk. 148/C1
Alacalı, Turk. 107/J5
Alaçam, Turk. 148/C1
Alaçatı, Turk. 105/K3
Alachua, Fl, US 191/H4
Alacrán (reef), Mex. 202/D1
Alacranes (res.), Cuba 203/F1
Aladağ, Turk. 149/C1
Alaejos, Sp. 102/C2
Alagir, Rus. 121/H4
Alagna Valsesia, It. 116/A1
Alagnon (riv.), Fr. 100/E4
Alagoa Grande, Braz. 212/D2
Alagoas (state), Braz. 212/C3
Alagoinhas, Braz. 212/C4
Alagón (riv.), Sp. 102/C2
Alagón, Sp. 103/E2
Alajärvi, Fin. 118/D3
Alajuela, CR 203/E4
Alakanuk, Ak, US 192/F3
Alakol' (lake), Kaz. 128/D2
Alakol (lake), Kaz. 122/J5
Alalaú (riv.), Braz. 211/F5
Alamagan (isl.), NMar. 174/D3
'Alāmarvdasht (riv.), Iran 146/F3
Alameda, Ca, US 193/K11
Alaminos, Phil. 137/C4
Alamo (lake), Az, US 186/D4
Alamo, Mex. 202/B1
Alamo, Ca, US 193/K11
Alamo Heights, Tx, US 195/U21
Alamogordo, NM, US 187/F4
Alamor, Ecu. 214/A2
Alamos, Mex. 184/C3
Åland (isl.), Fin. 95/G3
Aland (riv.), Ger. 98/F2
Alanya, Turk. 149/C1
Alaotra (lake), Madg. 165/J7
Alapaha (riv.), Fl,Ga, US 191/H4
Alaplı, Turk. 107/K5
Alarcón, Embalse de (res.), Sp. 102/D3
Alaşehir, Turk. 148/B2
Alaska (state), US 192/G2
Alaska (range), Ak, US 192/G4
Alaska (pen.), Ak, US 192/G4
Alaska, Gulf of (gulf), Ak, US 192/J4
Alassio, It. 116/B5
Alatyr', Rus. 119/K5
Alaverdi, Arm. 121/H4
Alavus, Fin. 118/D3
Alaw (riv.), Wal, UK 92/D5
Alaw, Llyn (lake), Wal, UK 92/D5
Alayor, Sp. 102/C3
Alayskiy (mts.), Kyr. 145/F5
Alazeya (riv.), Rus. 123/R3
Alb (riv.), Ger. 112/B5
Alba, It. 101/H4
Alba (prov.), Rom. 107/F2
Alba de Tormes, Sp. 102/C2
Alba Fucens (ruin), It. 104/C1
Alba Iulia, Rom. 107/F2
Albacete, Sp. 102/E3
Albaida, Sp. 103/E3
Albairate, It. 116/B2
Ålbæk, Den. 96/D3
Albalate del Arzobispo, Sp. 103/E2
Alban, Fr. 100/E5
Albanel (lake), Qu, Can. 188/F1
Albania (ctry.) 105/F2
Albany, Austl. 170/C5
Albany (riv.), On, Can. 180/H3
Albany, Ca, US 193/K11
Albany, Ga, US 191/G4
Albany, Ky, US 188/C4
Albany, Mo, US 195/E5
Albany (cap.), NY, US 188/F3
Albany, Or, US 184/C4
Albany County (int'l arpt.), NY, US 188/F3
Albaredo d'Adige, It. 117/E2
Albarine (riv.), Fr. 114/B5
Albarracín, Sp. 102/E2
Albatross (bay), Austl. 167/D2
Albatross Rock (pt.), Namb. 164/A2
Albbruck, Ger. 114/E2
Albemarle (sound), NC, US 191/J2
Albemarle, NC, US 191/H3
Albemarle (pt.), Ecu. 214/E6
Alben (peak), It. 101/H4
Albenga, It. 116/B4
Alberche (riv.), Sp. 102/C2
Alberhill, Ca, US 194/C3
Alberndorf in der Riedmark, Aus. 113/H6
Alberschwende, Aus. 115/F3
Albersdorf, Ger. 96/C4
Albersweiler, Ger. 112/B4
Albert (lake), Austl. 173/A2
Albert (lake), D.R.Congo,Ugan. 155/M7
Albert, Fr. 110/B3
Albert Kanaal (riv.), Belg. 111/E2
Albert Nile (riv.), Ugan. 155/M7
Alberta (prov.), Can. 180/E3
Alberti, Arg. 216/E2
Albertinia, SAfr. 164/C4
Albertirsa, Hun. 106/D2
Alberto de Agostini, PN, Chile 215/B7
Alberton, SAfr. 164/Q13
Albertshofen, Ger. 112/D3
Albertville, Al, US 191/G3
Albertville, Fr. 101/G4
Albestroff, Fr. 111/F6
Albeuve, Swi. 114/D4
Albi, Fr. 100/E5
Albignasego, It. 117/E2
Albina, Sur. 209/H2
Albinea, It. 116/D3
Albino, It. 116/C1
Albion, Mi, US 188/C3
Albisola Marina, It. 116/B4
Albisola Superiore, It. 116/B4
Alblasserdam, Neth. 108/B5
Albocácer, Sp. 103/E2
Alborán (isl.), Mor. 156/E2
Ålborg (bay), Den. 96/D3
Ålborg, Den. 96/C3
Albox, Sp. 102/D4
Albright-Knox Art Gallery, NY, US 189/S10
Albristhorn (peak), Swi. 114/D5
Albufeira, Port. 102/A4
Albula (riv.), Swi. 101/H3
Albuñol, Sp. 102/D4
Albuquerque (int'l arpt.), NM, US 186/F4
Albuquerque, NM, US 186/F4
Albuquerque, Cayos de (isls.), Col. 203/F3
Alburquerque, Sp. 102/B3
Alburtis, Pa, US 196/C3
Albury, Austl. 173/C3
Alby-sur-Chéran, Fr. 114/C6
Alca, Peru 214/C4
Alcabideche, Port. 103/P10
Alcácer do Sal, Port. 102/A3
Alcalá de Chivert, Sp. 103/F2
Alcalá de Guadaira, Sp. 102/C4
Alcalá de Henares, Sp. 103/N9
Alcalá de los Gazules, Sp. 102/C4
Alcalá la Real, Sp. 102/D4
Alcamo, It. 104/C4
Alcanadre (riv.), Sp. 103/E2
Alcanar, Sp. 103/F2
Alcañices, Sp. 102/B2
Alcañiz, Sp. 103/E2
Alcântara, Braz. 212/A1
Alcántara, Sp. 102/B3
Alcántara, Embalse de (res.), Sp. 102/B3
Alcantarilla, Sp. 102/E4
Alcaraz, Sp. 102/D3
Alcaraz, Sierra de (range), Sp. 102/D3
Alcatraz (isl.), Ca, US 193/K11
Alcaudete, Sp. 102/C4
Alcázar de San Juan, Sp. 102/D3
Alcira, Sp. 103/E3
Alcira, Arg. 216/D2
Alçıtepe, Turk. 105/K2
Alcoa, Tn, US 191/H3
Alcobaça, Braz. 212/C5
Alcobaça, Port. 102/A3
Alcobendas, Sp. 103/N8
Alcochete, Port. 103/Q10
Alcora, Sp. 103/E2
Alcorcón, Sp. 103/N9
Alcorisa, Sp. 103/E2
Alcoutim, Port. 102/B4
Alcoy, Sp. 103/E3
Alcúdia, Sp. 103/G3
Aldabra (isls.), Sey. 151/G5
Aldama, Mex. 184/D2
Aldama, Mex. 201/F4
Aldan (plat.), Rus. 123/N4
Aldan, Rus. 123/N4
Aldan (riv.), Rus. 125/N3
Alde (riv.), Eng, UK 91/H2
Aldeburgh, Eng, UK 91/H2
Aldeia Nova de São Bento, Port. 102/B4
Alden, Il, US 193/N15
Aldenhoven, Ger. 111/F2
Aldeno, It. 115/H6
Aldergrove (int'l arpt.), NI, UK 92/B2
Aldergrove, NI, UK 92/B2
Alderley Edge, Eng, UK 93/F5
Alderney (isl.), Chl, UK 100/B2
Aldershot, Eng, UK 91/F4
Alderwood Manor-Bothell North, Wa, US 193/C2
Aldine, Tx, US 187/J5
Aldingen, Ger. 115/E1
Aldred (lake), Pa, US 196/B4
Aldridge, Eng, UK 91/E1
Ale Water (riv.), Sc, UK 94/D6
Aleg, Mrta. 160/B2
Alegre, Braz. 213/D2
Alegrete, Braz. 215/E2
Alejandro Gallinal, Uru. 217/G2
Alejandro Roca, Arg. 216/E2
Alejandro Selkirk (isl.), Chile 205/A6
Alejo Ledesma, Arg. 216/E2
Aleknagik, Ak, US 192/G4
Aleksandrov, Rus. 118/H4
Aleksandrovac, Serb. 106/E4
Aleksandrovsk, Rus. 119/N4
Aleksandrów Kujawski, Pol. 99/K2
Aleksandrów Lódzki, Pol. 99/K3
Alekseyevka, Kaz. 145/F2
Alekseyevka, Kaz. 145/E2
Alekseyevka, Rus. 120/F2
Aleksin, Rus. 118/H5
Aleksinac, Serb. 106/E4
Além Paraíba, Braz. 213/L6
Alençon, Fr. 100/D2
Alenquer, Braz. 209/H4
Alenuihaha (chan.), Hi, US 182/T10
Alerce Andino, PN, Chile 216/B4
Aléria, Fr. 104/A1
Alert (pt.), Nun., Can. 181/S6
Aleşd, Rom. 106/F2
Alessandria (prov.), It. 116/B3
Alessandria, It. 116/B3
Ålestrup, Den. 96/C3
Ålesund, Nor. 95/C3
Aletschhorn (peak), Swi. 114/D5
Aleutian (range), Ak, US 192/G4
Aleutian (isls.), Ak, US 192/B5
Alexander (mt.), Austl. 170/B2
Alexander (arch.), Ak, US 192/L4
Alexander (isl.), Ant. 218/V
Alexander Bay, SAfr. 164/B3
Alexander City, Al, US 191/G3
Alexander Nevsky Abbey, Rus. 119/T7
Alexandria, Braz. 212/C2
Alexandria (Al Iskandarīyah), Egypt 149/A4
Alexandria (int'l arpt.), Egypt 149/A4
Alexándria, Gre. 105/H2
Alexandria, NZ 175/R12
Alexandria, Rom. 107/G4
Alexandria, SAfr. 164/D4
Alexandria, La, US 187/J5
Alexandria, Mn, US 185/K4
Alexandria, Sc, UK 94/B5
Alexandria, Va, US 196/A6
Alexandrina (lake), Austl. 167/C4
Alexandroúpolis, Gre. 105/J2
Alexis Creek, BC, Can. 184/C2
Alfaro, Sp. 102/E1
Alfatar, Bul. 107/H4
Alfbach (riv.), Ger. 111/F3
Alfeld, Ger. 109/G5
Alfenas, Braz. 213/H6
Alfhausen, Ger. 109/E3
Alfiós (riv.), Gre. 105/G4
Alfonsine, It. 117/F3
Alfonso Bonilla Aragón (int'l arpt.), Col. 210/B4
Alfred NP, Austl. 173/D3
Alfreton, Eng, UK 93/G5
Alfter, Ger. 111/G2
Alga, Kaz. 121/L2
Ålgård, Nor. 96/A2
Algarrobo, Chile 216/N8
Algarve (reg.), Port. 102/A4
Algeciras, Sp. 102/C4
Algeciras, Col. 210/C4
Algemesí, Sp. 103/E3
Alger (prov.), Alg. 158/G4
Algeria (ctry.) 154/F2
Algermissen, Ger. 109/G4
Algete, Sp. 103/N8
Alghero, It. 104/A2
Algiers (El Djezair) (cap.), Alg. 158/G4
Algoa (bay), SAfr. 164/D4
Algodón (riv.), Peru 208/D4
Algodonales, Sp. 102/C4
Algoma, Wi, US 185/M4
Algona, Wa, US 193/C3
Algonac, Mi, US 193/G6
Algonquin, Il, US 193/P14
Algorta, Uru. 217/K10
Algueirão, Port. 103/P10
Algund (Lagundo), It. 115/H4
Alhama de Granada, Sp. 102/D4
Alhama de Murcia, Sp. 102/E4
Alhambra, Ca, US 194/F7
Alhandra, Braz. 212/D2
Alhandra, Port. 103/P10
Alhaurín el Grande, Sp. 102/C4
'Alī al Gharbī, Iraq 146/E2
'Alī ash Sharqī, Iraq 146/E2
Ali Bayramlı, Azer. 121/J5
Alia, It. 104/C4
Alía, Sp. 102/C3
Aliağa, Turk. 148/A2
Aliákmon (riv.), Gre. 105/G2
Aliákmonos (lake), Gre. 105/G2
Aliartos, Gre. 105/H3
Alibates Flint Quarries Nat'l Mon., Tx, US 187/G4
Alibey (lake), Ukr. 107/K3
Alibeyköy, Turk. 107/J5
Alicante, Sp. 103/E3
Alicante (int'l arpt.), Sp. 103/E3
Alice, Tx, US 190/D5
Alice (pt.), It. 105/E3
Alice Arm, BC, Can. 192/N4
Alice Springs, Austl. 171/G2
Aliceville, Al, US 191/F3
Alicia, Phil. 137/D6
Alicudi (isl.), It. 104/D3
Alicurá (res.), Arg. 216/C4
Alife, It. 104/D2
Alīganj, India 142/B2
Alijó, Port. 102/B2
Alima (riv.), Congo 154/J8
Alingār (riv.), Afg. 144/A2
Alingsås, Swe. 96/E3
Alīpur, Pak. 144/A5
Alīpur Duār, India 143/G2
Alirājpur, India 147/K4
Alisos (riv.), Mex. 186/E5
Alistráti, Gre. 105/H2
Alivérion, Gre. 105/J3
Aliwal North, SAfr. 164/D3
Aljezur, Port. 102/A4
Aljustrel, Port. 102/A4
Alken, Belg. 111/E2
Alkmaar, Neth. 108/B3
Alkoum (well), Alg. 157/H4
Alkoven, Aus. 113/H6
Allada, Ben. 161/F5
Allahābād, India 142/C3
Allakaket, Ak, US 192/H2
Allaman, Swi. 114/C5
Allan (hills), Sk, Can. 185/G3
Allan, Sk, Can. 185/G3
Alland, Aus. 107/N7
Allanmyo, Myan. 141/G4
Allanridge, SAfr. 164/D2
Allanson, Austl. 170/C5
'Allāq (well), Libya 154/H1
Allariz, Sp. 102/B1
Alle, Swi. 114/D3
Allegan, Mi, US 188/C3
Allegheny (mts.), US 183/K4
Allegheny (plat.), US 188/E3
Allegheny (riv.), US 188/D3
Allen (riv.), Eng, UK 90/B5
Allen, Arg. 216/D3
Allen Park, Mi, US 193/F7
Allendale, SC, US 191/H3
Allendale, NJ, US 197/J7
Allende, Mex. 201/E2
Allende, Mex. 201/E3
Allendorf, Ger. 109/F6
Allensbach, Ger. 115/F2
Allenspark, Co, US 195/A2
Allentown, Pa, US 196/C2
Allentsteig, Aus. 99/H4
Allenwood, Pa, US 196/B1
Alleppey, India 140/C6
Aller (riv.), Ger. 109/H3
Allerkanal (canal), Ger. 109/H4
Allersberg, Ger. 112/E4
Allershausen, Ger. 113/E6
Allgäu Alps (range), Aus.,Ger. 98/F5
Alliance, Ne, US 185/H5
Alliance, Oh, US 188/D3
Allied War Cemetery, Myan. 136/B2
Allier (riv.), Fr. 100/E3
Alligator (pt.), La, US 195/Q16
Allingåbro, Den. 96/D3
Allinges, Fr. 114/C5
Alloa, Sc, UK 94/C4
Allonnes, Fr. 100/D3
Allora, Austl. 171/C5
Allos, Fr. 101/G4
Alloway, NJ, US 196/C4
Allschwil, Swi. 114/D2
Alm (riv.), Aus. 113/G7
Alma, Mi, US 188/C3
Alma, Qu, Can. 189/G1
Alma, Ga, US 191/H4
Almacelles, Sp. 103/F2
Almada, Port. 103/P10
Almadén, Sp. 102/C3
Almafuerte, Arg. 216/D2
Almagro, Sp. 102/D3
Almanor (lake), Ca, US 186/B2
Almansa, Sp. 103/E3
Almanza, Sp. 102/C1
Almanzor, Pico de (peak), Sp. 102/C2
Almanzora (riv.), Sp. 102/D4
Almas (riv.), Braz. 209/J6
Almas, Braz. 212/A3
Almas, Pico das (peak), Braz. 212/B4
Almaty (int'l arpt.), Kaz. 145/G4
Almaty, Kaz. 145/G4
Almazán, Sp. 102/D2
Almazora, Sp. 103/E3
Almeida, Port. 102/B2
Almeirim, Braz. 209/H4
Almeirim, Port. 102/A3
Almelo, Neth. 108/D4
Almenara, Braz. 212/B5
Almenara (peak), Sp. 102/D3
Almenara, Sp. 103/E3
Almendra, Embalse de (res.), Sp. 102/B2
Almendralejo, Sp. 102/B3
Almenno San Salvatore, It. 116/C1
Almere, Neth. 108/C4
Almería, Sp. 102/D4
Almería, Golfo de (gulf), Sp. 102/D4
Al'met'yevsk, Rus. 119/M5
Älmhult, Swe. 96/F3
Almina (pt.), Sp. 158/B2
Almirós, Gre. 105/H3
Almiroú (gulf), Gre. 105/J5
Almodôvar, Port. 102/A4
Almodóvar del Campo, Sp. 102/C3
Almodóvar del Río, Sp. 102/C4
Almoharín, Sp. 102/B3
Almond (riv.), Sc, UK 94/C4
Almont (riv.), Fr. 88/L6
Almonte, On, Can. 188/E2
Almonte, Sp. 102/B4
Almora, India 142/B1
Almoradí, Sp. 103/E3
Almorox, Sp. 102/C2
Almte. Montt (gulf), Chile 217/B7
Almudévar, Sp. 103/E1
Almuñécar, Sp. 102/D4
Almus, Turk. 148/D1
Alness, Sc, UK 94/B1
Alness (riv.), Sc, UK 94/B1
Alnwick, Eng, UK 94/E6
Alofi (isl.), Wall., Fr. 174/H6
Alofi, NZ 175/J6
Along, India 141/G2
Alónnisos (isl.), Gre. 105/H3
Alor (isls.), Indo. 139/F5
Alor Setar, Malay. 141/H6
Álora, Sp. 102/C4
Alotau, PNG 174/E6
Aloysius (mt.), Austl. 171/F3
Alpachiri, Arg. 216/E3
Alpe di Poti (peak), It. 117/E6
Alpedrete, Sp. 103/M8
Alpen, Ger. 108/D5
Alpena, Mi, US 188/D2
Alpercatas (riv.), Braz. 212/A2
Alpercatas, Serra das (mts.), Braz. 209/J5
Alperschällihorn (peak), Swi. 115/F4
Alpes de Provence (range), Fr. 101/G5
Alpha, Austl. 171/B3
Alpha, NJ, US 196/C2
Alphen aan de Rijn, Neth. 108/B4
Alpi Apuane (range), It. 101/J4
Alpi Dolomitiche (range), It. 101/J3
Alpi Orobie (range) It. 101/J3
Alpiarça, Port. 102/A3
Alpine, NJ, US 197/K8
Alpine, Ut, US 195/K13
Alpine, Wy, US 184/F5
Alpirsbach, Ger. 115/E1
Alpnach, Swi. 115/E4
Alps (mts.), Eur. 85/E4
Alqōsh, Iraq 148/E2
Als (isl.), Den. 98/F1
Alsace (pol. reg.), Fr. 98/D4
Alsager, Eng, UK 93/F5
Alsask, Sk, Can. 184/F3
Alsasua, Sp. 102/D1
Alsdorf, Ger. 111/F2
Alsenz (riv.), Ger. 111/G4
Alsenz, Ger. 111/G4
Alsfeld, Ger. 101/H1
Alsheim, Ger. 112/B3
Alsip, Il, US 193/Q16
Alstahaug, Nor. 95/E2
Alster (riv.), Ger. 109/H1
Alsting, Fr. 111/F5
Alstonville, Austl. 173/E1
Alt (riv.), Eng, UK 93/E4
Alta, Ut, US 195/K12
Alta, Nor. 95/G1
Alta Floresta, Braz. 209/G5
Alta Gracia, Arg. 215/D3
Altach, Aus. 115/F3
Altadena, Ca, US 194/F7
Altagracia, Nic. 202/E4
Altai (mts.), Asia 128/E2
Altamaha (riv.), Ga, US 191/H4
Altamira, Braz. 209/H4
Altamira, Mex. 202/B1
Altamira do Maranhão, Braz. 212/A2
Altamonte Springs, Fl, US 191/H4
Altamura, It. 104/E2
Altar, Mex. 184/C2
Altar (vol.), Ecu. 210/B5
Altar de los Sacrificios (ruin), Guat. 202/D2
Altar, Desierto de (des.), Mex. 186/D4
Altare, It. 116/B4
Altavilla Vicentina, It. 117/E1
Altay, China 128/E2
Altay, Mong. 128/E2
Altay, Mong. 128/G2
Altay, Resp., Rus. 122/J4
Altayskiy Kray, Rus. 145/G2
Altdorf, Swi. 115/E4
Altdorf bei Nürnberg, Ger. 113/E4
Altea, Sp. 103/E3
Altedo, It. 117/E3
Altena, Ger. 109/E6
Altenahr, Ger. 111/G2
Altenau, Ger. 109/H5
Altenau (riv.), Ger. 109/F5
Altenbeken, Ger. 109/F5
Altenberg bei Linz, Aus. 113/H6
Altenburg, Ger. 98/G3
Altenfelden, Aus. 113/G6
Altenglan, Ger. 111/G4
Altengottern, Ger. 109/H6
Altenkirchen, Ger. 111/G2
Altenmünster, Ger. 112/D6
Altenstadt, Ger. 115/G1
Altenstadt, Ger. 112/B2
Altensteig, Ger. 112/B5
Altentreptow, Ger. 96/E5
Altepexi, Mex. 201/M8
Alter Rhein (riv.), Ger. 108/D5
Altes Land (phys. reg.), Ger. 109/G1
Althengstett, Ger. 112/B5
Althofen, Aus. 101/L3
Althütte, Ger. 112/C5
Altındere NP, Turk. 148/D1
Altınözü, Turk. 149/E1
Altıntaş, Turk. 148/B2
Altınyaka, Turk. 149/B1
Altınyayla, Turk. 149/A1
Altiplano (plat.), Bol.,Peru 205/C4
Altkirch, Fr. 114/D2
Altlandsberg, Ger. 98/Q6
Altmark (phys. reg.), Ger. 98/F2
Altmühl (riv.), Ger. 101/J2
Altmünster, Aus. 113/G7
Altnaharra, Sc, UK 89/R7
Alto (peak), Braz. 212/A4
Alto (peak), It. 115/G4
Alto Araguaia, Braz. 209/H7
Alto de Tamar (peak), Col. 210/C3
Alto Garças, Braz. 209/H7
Alto Lucero, Mex. 201/N7
Alto Parnaíba, Braz. 212/A3
Alto Purús (riv.), Peru 208/D6
Alto Santo, Braz. 212/C2
Alto Yuruá (riv.), Peru 214/C3
Altomünster, Ger. 112/E6
Alton, La, US 195/Q16
Alton, Il, US 195/G8
Alton, Eng, UK 91/F4
Altona, Mb, Can. 185/J3
Altoona, Pa, US 188/E3
Altopascio, It. 117/D5
Altos, Braz. 212/B2
Altos de Campana NP, Pan. 210/B2
Altotonga, Mex. 201/M7
Altötting, Ger. 113/F6
Altrincham, Eng, UK 93/F5
Altrip, Ger. 112/B4
Altun (mts.), China 125/H6
Altun Ha (ruin), Belz. 202/D2
Alturas, Ca, US 184/C5
Altus (res.), Ok, US 187/H4
Altus, Ok, US 187/H4
Altzayanca, Mex. 201/M7
Alucra, Turk. 148/D1
Aluminé, Arg. 216/C3
Alunda, Swe. 96/H1
Ālūs, Iraq 148/E3
Alushta, Ukr. 120/E3
Alva, Ok, US 187/H3
Alva, Sc, UK 94/C4
Alvalade, Port. 102/A4
Älvängen, Swe. 96/E3
Alvarado, Mex. 201/P8
Álvarez, Arg. 216/E2
Alvaro Obregón, Presa (dam), Mex. 184/C2
Alvdal, Nor. 95/D3
Älvdalen, Swe. 96/F1
Alverca, Port. 103/P10
Alveringem, Belg. 110/B1
Alvesta, Swe. 96/F3
Ålvik, Nor. 96/B1
Alvin, Tx, US 187/J5
Alvito, Port. 102/B3
Älvkarleby, Swe. 96/G1
Alvorada, Braz. 213/A4
Alvorada do Norte, Braz. 212/A4
Älvsborg (co.), Swe. 95/E4
Älvsbyn, Swe. 95/G2
Alwen (riv.), Wal, UK 92/E5
Alxa Youqi, China 128/H4
Alxa Zuoqi, China 128/J4
Alyawarra Abor. Land, Austl. 171/G2
Alyth, Sc, UK 94/C3
Alytus, Lith. 97/L4
Alz (riv.), Ger. 101/K2
Alzano Lombardo, It. 116/C1
Alzenau in Unterfranken, Ger. 112/C2
Alzette (riv.), Lux. 111/F4
Alzey, Ger. 112/B3
Am Timan, Chad 155/K5
Ama, La, US 195/P17
Amacayacú, PN, Col. 208/D4
Amacuro (riv.), Ven. 211/F2
Amacuro (delta), Ven. 211/F2
Amacuzac (riv.), Mex. 201/K8
Amadeus (lake), Austl. 167/C3
Amadjuak (lake), Nun., Can. 181/J2
Amadora, Port. 103/P10
Amagansett, NY, US 197/F2
Amagansett NWR, NY, US 197/F2
Amagasaki, Japan 135/H6
Amagi, Japan 132/B4
Amagi-san (peak), Japan 133/F3
Amaguaña, Ecu. 210/B5
Amajac (riv.), Mex. 201/M7
Åmål, Swe. 96/E2
Amala (riv.), Kenya 162/B3
Amalfi, Col. 210/C3
Amalia, SAfr. 164/D2
Amaliás, Gre. 105/G4
Amaluza, Ecu. 214/B2
Amambaí, Braz. 215/E1
Amambaí (riv.), Braz. 209/H8
Amami (isls.), Japan 125/M7
Amami-O-Shima (isl.), Japan 133/K6
Amanā (lake), Braz. 208/F4
Amance, Fr. 114/C2
Amānganj, India 142/C3
Amāngarh, Pak. 144/A2
Amantea, It. 104/E3
Amanu (isl.), FrPol. 175/L6
Amanzimtoti, SAfr. 165/E3
Amapá, Braz. 209/H3
Amapá (state), Braz. 211/H4
Amarante, Braz. 212/B2
Amarante, Port. 102/A2
Amarante do Maranhão, Braz. 212/A2
Amarapura, Myan. 141/G3
Amareleja, Port. 102/B3
Amargosa, Braz. 212/C4
Amargosa (riv.), Ca, US 186/C3
Amarillo, Tx, US 187/G4
Amaro (peak), It. 104/D1
Amarpātan, India 142/C3
Amarume, Japan 134/A4
Amarwāra, India 142/B4
Amasra, Turk. 107/L5
Amasya, Turk. 148/C1
Amasya (prov.), Turk. 148/C1
Amata, Austl. 171/F3
Amatlán de Cañas, Mex. 184/D4
Amatsukominato, Japan 135/E3
Amawalk (res.), NY, US 197/E1
Amay, Belg. 111/E2
Amayuca, Mex. 201/L8
Amazon (Amazonas) (riv.), Braz.,Peru 214/C1
Amazonas, Cuba 203/G1
Amazonas (state), Braz. 210/C5
Amazonas (Amazon) (riv.), Braz.,Peru 214/C1
Amazônia, PN da (Tapajós), Braz. 209/G4
Ambāh, India 142/B2
Ambahikily, Madg. 165/G8
Ambajogai, India 147/L5
Ambāla Sadar, India 144/D4
Ambalangoda, SrL. 140/D6
Ambalavao, Madg. 165/H8
Ambam, Camr. 154/H7
Ambanja, Madg. 165/J6
Ambaro (bay), Madg. 165/J6
Ambato, Ecu. 210/B5
Ambato Boeny, Madg. 165/H7
Ambatofinandrahana, Madg. 165/H8
Ambatolampy, Madg. 165/H7
Ambatomaidy, Madg. 165/H7
Ambatomanoina, Madg. 165/H7
Ambatondrazaka, Madg. 165/J7
Ambazac, Fr. 100/D4
Ámbelos (cape), Gre. 105/H3
Amberg, Ger. 113/E4
Ambergris Cay (isl.), Belz. 202/E2
Ambérieu-en-Bugey, Fr. 114/B6
Amberloup, Belg. 111/E3
Ambikāpur, India 142/D4
Ambilobe, Madg. 165/J6
Ambinanindrano, Madg. 165/J8
Ambinanitelo, Madg. 165/J6
Ambler, Ak, US 192/G2
Ambler, Pa, US 196/C3
Amblève (riv.), Belg. 98/C3
Amblève, Belg. 111/F3
Ambo, Peru 214/B3
Amboasary, Madg. 165/H9
Amboavory, Madg. 165/J7
Ambodifototra, Madg. 165/J7
Ambodiharina, Madg. 165/J8
Ambohidratrimo, Madg. 165/H7
Ambohijanahary, Madg. 165/J7
Ambohimahasoa, Madg. 165/H8
Ambohimandroso, Madg. 165/H7
Ambohinihaonana, Madg. 165/H8
Ambohitsilaozana, Madg. 165/J7
Ambolomoty, Madg. 165/H7
Ambon (isl.), Indo. 139/G4
Ambon, Indo. 139/G4
Ambondro, Madg. 165/H9
Amboni Caves, Tanz. 162/C4
Amborompotsy, Madg. 165/H8
Amboseli NP, Kenya 162/C3
Ambositra, Madg. 165/H8
Ambovombe, Madg. 165/H9
Ambrym (isl.), Van. 174/F6
Amchitka (isl.), Ak, US 192/B6
Amchitka Pass (chan.), Ak, US 192/B6
Amealco, Mex. 201/K6
Ameca, Mex. 184/D4
Amecameca de Juárez, Mex. 201/R10
Ameghino, Arg. 216/E2
Ameglia, It. 116/C4
Ameisberg (peak), Aus. 113/G5
Ameland (isl.), Neth. 108/C2
Amelia, It. 104/C1
Amelinghausen, Ger. 109/H2
Amer (chan.), Neth. 108/B5
American (lake), Wa, US 193/B3
American (riv.), Ca, US 193/M9
American Falls (mts.), Id, US 186/D2
American Fork, Ut, US 195/K13
American, North Fork (riv.), Ca, US 186/B3
American Samoa (dpcy.), US 175/H6
American, South Fork (riv.), Ca, US 186/B3
Americana, Braz. 213/C2
Americus, Ga, US 191/G3
Ameringkogel (peak), Aus. 101/L3
Amersfoort, SAfr. 165/E2
Amersfoort, Neth. 108/C4
Amersham, Eng, UK 91/F3
Amery Ice Shelf, Ant. 218/E
Amesbury, Eng, UK 91/E4
Amet, India 147/K3
Amethi, India 142/C2
Amfiklia, Gre. 105/H3
Amfilokhía, Gre. 105/G3
Ámfissa, Gre. 105/H3
Amga (riv.), Rus. 123/N3
Amguema (riv.), Rus. 123/T3
Amgun' (riv.), Rus. 123/P4
Amherst, NS, Can. 189/H2
Amherst, NY, US 189/S10
Amherstburg, On, Can. 193/F7
Ami, Japan 135/E1
Amiata (peak), It. 101/J5

Amiens, Fr. 110/B4
Amik (lake), Turk. 148/D2
Amila (isl.), Ak, US 192/D6
Amilcar Cabral (int'l arpt.), CpV. 151/K10
Amillis, Fr. 88/M5
Amindaion, Gre. 105/G2
Nga. 161/H3
Amisk (lake), Sk, Can. 185/H2
Amistad (res.), Mex.,US 190/D4
Amistad Nat'l Rec. Area, Tx, US 187/G5
Amite, La, US 187/K5
Amityville, NY, US 197/M9
Amla, India 142/B5
Amlâgora, India 143/F4
Âmli, Nor. 96/C2
'Ammān (gov.), Jor. 149/E4
Amman (riv.), Wal, UK 90/C3
Amman ('Ammān) (cap.), Jor. 149/E4
Ammanford, Wal, UK 90/C3
Ammarfjället (peak), Swe. 95/E2
Ammassalik, Grld 218/J
Ammer (riv.), Ger. 112/B5
Ammerman (mtn.), Yk, Can. 192/K2
Ammersee (lake), Ger. 101/J3
Amnéville, Fr. 111/F5
Âmol, Iran 146/F2
Amora, Port. 103/P10
Amorbach, Ger. 112/C3
Amorgós, Gre. 105/J5
Amorgós (isl.), Gre. 105/J4
Amory, Ms, US 191/F3
Amos, Qu, Can. 188/E1
Âmot, Nor. 96/B2
Amotfors, Swe. 96/E2
Amozoc, Mex. 201/L7
Ampachi, Japan 135/L5
Ampanefena, Madg. 165/J6
Ampangalana (canal), Madg. 165/J8
Ampanihy, Madg. 165/H9
Amparafaravola, Madg. 165/J7
Amparai, SrL. 140/D6
Amparo, Braz. 213/G7
Ampasindava (bay), Madg. 165/H6
Ampato (peak), Peru 214/D4
Ampefy, Madg. 165/J7
Amper (riv.), Ger. 113/E6
Ampfing, Ger. 113/F6
Ampflwang im Hausruckwald, Aus. 113/G6
Ampitatafika, Madg. 165/H7
Amposta, Sp. 103/F2
Amqui, Qu, Can. 189/H1
Amravati, India 140/C3
Amreli, India 147/K4
'Amrît (ruin), Syria 149/D2
Amritsar, India 144/C4
Amroha, India 142/B1
Amrum (isl.), Ger. 98/C1
Amstel (riv.), Neth. 108/B4
Amstelveen, Neth. 108/B4
Amsterdam, NY, US 188/B1
Amsterdam, SAfr. 165/E2
Amsterdam (cap.), Neth. 108/B4
Amsterdam (isl.), Fr. 81/N7
Amsterdam Rijnkanaal (riv.), Neth. 108/C4
Amsterdam (Schipol) (int'l arpt.), Neth. 108/B4
Amstetten, Aus. 101/L2
Amu Darya (riv.), Asia 125/F3
Amudat, Ugan. 162/B2
Amukta Pass (chan.), Ak, US 192/D5
Amuku (mts.), Guy. 211/G4
Amund Ringnes (isl.), Nun., Can. 181/S7
Amundsen (gulf), NW, Can. 180/D1
Amundsen (bay), Ant. 218/D
Amundsen (sea), Ant. 218/S
Amundsen-Scott, US, Ant. 218/A
Amunge (lake), Swe. 96/F1
Amur (riv.), Rus. 129/P2
Amurrío, Sp. 102/D1
Amurskaya Oblast, Rus. 123/N4
Amyûn, Leb. 149/D2
An Nabk, Syria 149/E2
An Nahûd, Sudan 155/L5
An Najaf, Iraq 148/E4
An Najaf (gov.),Iraq 148/E4
An Nâşiriyah,Iraq 146/F2
An Nu'maniyah,Iraq 148/E3
An Teallach (peak), Sc, UK 94/A1
An Uaimh, Ire. 89/Q10
Ana María (gulf), Cuba 199/F3
Anaa (isl.), FrPol. 175/L6
Anabar (riv.), Rus. 123/L3
'Anabtâ, WBnk. 149/G7
Anachucuna (mtn.), Pan. 210/B2
Anaco, Ven. 211/F2
Anaconda-Deer Lodge County, Mt, US 184/E4
Anadarko, Ok, US 187/H4
Anadyr' (gulf), Rus. 125/T3

Anadyr' (range), Rus. 218/U
Anadyr' (riv.), Rus. 125/S3
Anadyr', Rus. 123/T3
Anáfi (isl.), Gre. 105/J4
Anafi, Gre. 105/J3
Anaheim, Ca, US 194/G8
Anahim Lake, BC, Can. 184/B2
Anáhuac, Mex. 190/C5
Anahuac, Tx, US 190/E4
Anáhuac, Mex. 184/D2
Anak, NKor. 131/C3
Anakāpalle, India 140/D4
Anaktuvuk Pass, Ak, US 192/H2
Analalava, Madg. 165/H6
Analamaitso (plat.), Madg. 165/J7
Anambas (isls.), 138/C3
Anambra (state), Nga. 161/G5
Anamur, Turk. 149/C1
Anamur (pt.), Turk. 149/C1
Anan, Japan 132/D4
Anand, India 147/K4
Ananea, Peru 214/D4
Ananea, Bol. 214/D4
Anantapur, India 140/C5
Anantnag, India 144/C3
Anapa, Rus. 120/F3
Anápolis, Braz. 209/J7
Anápu (riv.), Braz. 209/H4
Anār, Iran 147/G2
Anārak, Iran 146/F2
'Anātā, WBnk. 149/G7
Anathan (isl.), NMar. 174/D3
Anatolia (reg.), Turk. 148/B2
Añatuya, Arg. 215/D2
Anaué (riv.), Braz. 208/F3
Ancash (dept.), Peru 214/B3
Anchieta, Braz. 213/D2
Anchor (bay), Mi, US 193/G6
Anchor Point, Ak, US 192/H4
Anchorage, Ak, US 192/J3
Anchorville, Mi, US 193/G6
Anchovy, Jam. 203/G2
Ancient City of Oc-Eo, Viet. 136/D4
Ancoeur (riv.), Fr. 88/L6
Ancohuma (peak), Bol. 214/D4
Ancón, Peru 214/B3
Ancón de Sardinas (bay), Col. 210/B4
Ancona (prov.), It. 117/G5
Ancona, It. 117/G5
Ancoraimes, Bol. 214/D4
Ancre (riv.), Fr. 110/B3
Ancud, Chile 216/B4
Ancud, Golfo de (gulf), Chile 216/B5
Anda, China 129/N2
Andacollo, Arg. 216/C3
Andagua, Peru 214/C4
Andahuaylas, Peru 214/C4
Andāl, India 143/F4
Åndalsnes, Nor. 95/C3
Andalucia (aut. comm.), Sp. 102/C4
Andalusia, Al, US 191/G4
Andalusia (reg.), Sp. 102/C4
Andaman (sea), Asia 141/F5
Andaman and Nicobar (isls.), India 141/F5
Andaman (isl.), India 141/F4
Andamarca, Peru 214/C3
Andamooka, Austl. 171/H4
Andapa, Madg. 165/J6
Andaraí, Braz. 212/B4
Andau, Aus. 101/M3
Andebu, Nor. 96/D2
Andechs, Ger. 115/H2
Andeer, Swi. 115/F4
Andelfingen, Swi. 115/E2
Andelot-Blancheville, Fr. 114/B1
Andelsbach (riv.), Ger. 115/F2
Andelu, Fr. 88/H5
Andemaka, Madg. 165/H8
Andenne, Belg. 111/E3
Anderlues, Belg. 111/D3
Andermatt, Swi. 115/E4
Andernach, Ger. 111/G3
Anderson (res.), Mex. 198/C4
Anderson, Ak, US 192/J3
Anderson, Ca, US 186/B2
Anderson, In, US 188/C3
Anderson, SC, US 191/H3
Anderson, Tx, US 187/J5
Anderson (inlet), Wa, US 193/B3
Anderson (isl.), Wa, US 193/B3
Andes (mts.), SAm. 205/C5
Andes, Cordillera de los (mts.), SAm. 205/C5
Andevoranto, Madg. 165/J7
Andfjorden (chan.), Nor. 95/F1
Andhra Pradesh (state), India 140/C4
Andijk, Neth. 108/C3
Andijon (pol. reg.), Uzb. 145/F4
Andijon, Uzb. 145/G4
Andikíthira (isl.), Gre. 105/H5
Andilamena, Madg. 165/J7

Andilanatoby, Madg. 165/J7
Andīmeshk, Iran 146/E2
Andíparos (isl.), Gre. 105/J4
Andira, Braz. 213/B2
Andissa, Gre. 105/J3
Andkhvoy, Afg. 145/K5
Andohajango, Madg. 165/J6
Andorf, Aus. 113/G6
Andorno Micca, It. 116/B1
Andorra (ctry.) 103/F1
Andorra, It. 103/E2
Andorra la Vella (cap.), And. 100/D5
Andover, Eng, UK 91/E4
Andover, NJ, US 196/D2
Andøya (isl.), Nor. 95/E1
Andradas, Braz. 213/G7
Andradina, Braz. 213/B2
Andraitx, Sp. 103/G3
Andramasina, Madg. 165/H7
Andranolava, Madg. 165/H8
Andranomavo (riv.), Madg. 165/H7
Andranopasy, Madg. 165/G8
Andreanof (isls.), Ak, US 192/C6
Andrelândia, Braz. 213/J6
Andrespol, Pol. 99/K3
Andrésy, Fr. 88/J5
Andrezel, Fr. 88/L6
Andria, It. 104/E2
Andriba, Madg. 165/H7
Andringitra (mts.), Madg. 165/H8
Andrítsaina, Gre. 105/G4
Androka, Madg. 165/H9
Androntany (cape), Madg. 165/J6
Andros (isl.), Bahm. 199/F3
Andros, Gre. 105/J4
Andros (isl.), Gre. 105/J4
Androscoggin (riv.), Me,NH, US 189/G2
Andújar, Sp. 102/C3
Aneby, Swe. 96/F3
Anecón Grande (peak), Arg. 216/C4
Anegada (bay), Arg. 216/E4
Anegada (isl.), UK 199/J4
Anegada Passage (chan.), NAm. 199/J4
Aného, Togo 161/F5
Aneityum (isl.), Van. 174/F7
Añelo, Arg. 216/C3
Aneto, Pico de (peak), Sp. 103/F1
Anfu, China 141/K2
Ang Nam Ngum (res.), Laos 141/H4
Ang Thong, Thai. 136/C3
Angamos (pt.), Chile 215/B1
Angara (riv.), Rus. 125/J4
Angaston, Austl. 171/H5
Angel (riv.), Ger. 109/E5
Angel (falls), Ven. 211/F3
Angeles, Phil. 137/D4
Angeles National Forest, Ca, US 194/C1
Angelholm, Swe. 96/E3
Angelholm (int'l arpt.), Swe. 96/E3
Angelina (riv.), Tx, US 187/J5
Angeln (reg.), Ger. 98/E1
Angelus (lake), Mi, US 193/F6
Angera, It. 116/B1
Angermanalven (riv.), Swe. 95/E2
Angermünde, Ger. 99/H2
Angers, Fr. 100/C3
Anghiari, It. 117/F5
Angical do Piauí, Braz. 212/B2
Angicos, Braz. 212/C2
Angkor (ruin), Camb. 136/C3
Anglem (mt.), NZ 175/R12
Anglès, Sp. 103/G2
Anglesea, Austl. 173/C3
Anglesey (isl.), Wal, UK 92/D5
Angleton, Tx, US 187/J5
Anglin (riv.), Fr. 100/D3
Anóyia, Gre. 105/J5
Angol, Chile 216/B3
Angola (ctry.) 163/C3
Angola, In, US 188/D3
Angoon, Ak, US 192/M4
Angostura (res.), Mex. 198/C4
Angostura, Mex. 184/C3
Angoulême, Fr. 100/D4
Angra do Heroísmo, Azor., Port. 103/S12
Angra dos Reis, Braz. 213/J7
Angren, Uzb. 145/F4
Anguilla (isl.), UK 199/N8
Anguillara Veneta, It. 117/E2
Angus (pol. reg.), Sc,UK 94/C3
Angutikada (peak), Ak, US 192/G2
Anhée, Belg. 111/D3
Anholt (isl.), Den. 96/D3
Anhui (prov.), China 129/L5
Ani, Japan 134/B4
Aniak, Ak, US 192/G3
Aniákchak (crater), Ak, US 192/G4
Andilamena, Madg. 165/J7

Aniakchak Nat'l Mon. and Prsv., Ak, US 192/F4
Aniche, Fr. 110/C2
Animas (riv.), Co,NM, US 186/F3
Animas, Punta De Las (pt.), Mex. 184/B2
'Ānîn, Isr. 149/G6
Anina, Rom. 106/E3
Aniva (cape), Rus. 129/R2
Aniva (bay), Rus. 134/C1
Anivorano, Madg. 165/J7
Anizy-le-Château, Fr. 110/C4
Anjalankoski, Fin. 97/M1
Anjär, India 147/K4
Anjō, Japan 135/M6
Anjou (reg.), Fr. 100/C3
Anjou, Qu, Can. 189/N6
Anjouan (isl.), Com. 165/H6
Anjozorobe, Madg. 165/H7
Anju, NKor. 131/C3
Ankang, China 128/J5
Ankara (cap.), Turk. 148/C2
Ankara (prov.), Turk. 148/C1
Ankaramena, Madg. 165/H8
Ankaratra (mass.), Madg. 165/H7
Ankarsrum, Swe. 96/G3
Ankavandra, Madg. 165/H7
Ankazoabo, Madg. 165/H8
Ankazobe, Madg. 165/H7
Ankazomborona, Madg. 165/H7
Ankazomiriotra, Madg.165/H7
Ankerika, Madg. 165/H6
Ankililioka, Madg. 165/G8
Ankilizato, Madg. 165/H8
Anklam, Ger. 96/E5
Ankum, Ger. 109/E3
Anlong, China 141/J2
Anloo, Neth. 108/D2
Anlu, China 130/C3
Anma (isl.), SKor. 131/D5
Ann (cape), Ma, US 189/G3
Ann Arbor, Mi, US 188/D3
Anna (lake), Va, US 188/E4
Anna Bay, Austl. 173/E2
Anna Pavlowna, Neth. 108/B3
Anna Pink (bay), Chile 216/B5
Anna Regina, Guy. 211/G3
Annaba, Alg. 158/K6
Annaba (prov.), Alg. 158/K6
Annaberg-Buchholz, Ger. 113/G1
Annaclone, NI, UK 92/B3
Annai, Guy. 211/G4
Annaka, Japan 135/B1
Annalong, NI, UK 92/C3
Annan, Mo, US 195/G9
Annan (riv.), Sc, UK 94/C6
Annandale, Va, US 196/A6
Annandale, NJ, US 196/D2
Annapolis (cap.), Md, US 196/B6
Annapurna (peak), Nepal 142/D1
Annbank Station, Sc, UK 94/B6
Anne (mt.), Austl. 173/C4
Anne Arundel (co.), Md, US 196/B6
Annean (lake), Austl. 167/A3
Annecy, Fr. 114/C6
Annecy (lake), Fr. 114/C6
Annecy-le-Vieux, Fr. 114/C5
Annemasse, Fr. 114/C5
Annet-sur-Marne, Fr. 88/L5
Annette, Al, US 192/M4
Annezin, Fr. 110/B2
Anniston, Al, US 191/G3
Annobón (isl.), EqG. 151/C5
Annonay, Fr. 100/F4
Annville, Pa, US 196/B3
Annweiler, Ger. 111/G5
Ano, Japan 135/K6
Ano Viánnos, Gre. 105/J5
Anoia (riv.), Sp. 103/K7
Anoka, Mn, US 185/K4
Anosibe An' Ala, Madg. 165/J7
Anou-Zeggarene (riv.), Niger 161/G2
Anould, Fr. 114/C1
Anping, China 130/D3
Anqiu, China 130/D3
Anren, China 141/K2
Anrhomer (peak), Mor. 156/D3
Anröchte, Ger. 109/F5
Ans, Belg. 111/E2
Ansai, China 130/B3
Ansan, SKor. 131/F7
Ansbach, Ger. 112/D4
Anse-à-Galets, Haiti 203/H2
Anse-d'Hainault, Haiti 203/G2
Anse Rouge, Haiti 203/H2
Ansfelden, Aus. 113/H6
Anshan, China 131/B2
Anshun, China 141/H3
Anson, Tx, US 187/H4
Ansŏng, SKor. 131/D4
Ansongo, Mali 160/E2
Ant (riv.), Eng, UK 91/H1
Ant (isl.), Anti. 199/N8
Anta, Peru 214/C4
Antabamba, Peru 214/C4
Antakya, Turk. 149/E1
Antalaha, Madg. 165/J6
Antalya (prov.), Turk. 148/B2
Antalya (int'l arpt.), Turk. 149/B1
Antalya, Turk. 149/B1

Antalya, Gulf of (gulf), Turk. 149/B1
Antanambao Manampotsy, Madg. 165/J7
Antananarivo (prov.), Madg. 165/H7
Antananarivo (cap.), Madg. 165/H7
Antanifotsy, Madg. 165/H7
Antanimieva, Madg. 165/G8
Antanimora, Madg. 165/H9
Antar (peak), Alg. 157/E3
Antarctic (pen.), Ant. 218/W
Antarctic Circle 218/Z
Antarctica (cont.) 176
Antas, Braz. 212/C3
Antas, Rio das (riv.), Braz. 213/B4
Antella, It. 117/E5
Antelope (isl.), Ut, US 195/J12
Antelope Center, Ca, US 194/C1
Antequera, Sp. 102/C4
Antes Fort, Pa, US 196/A1
Anthering, Aus. 113/G7
Anthony, NM, US 186/F4
Anti-Atlas (mts.), Mor. 154/C2
Anti-Lebanon (mts.), Leb. 149/D3
Antibes, Fr. 101/G5
Anticosti, Île d' (isl.), Qu, Can. 181/K4
Antiesen (riv.), Aus. 113/G6
Antifer, Cap d' (cape), Fr. 100/C2
Antigo, Wi, US 185/L4
Antigonish, NS, Can. 189/J2
Antigua, Canl., Sp. 156/B3
Antigua (isl.), Anti. 199/N8
Antigua and Barbuda (ctry.) 199/N8
Antigua Guatemala, Guat. 202/D3
Antiguo Morelos, Mex. 201/K7
Antilly, Fr. 88/L4
Antioquia, Sp. 103/J5
Antioquia (dept.), Col. 210/C3
Antioniesberg (peak), SAfr. 164/C4
Antonina, Braz. 213/B3
Antonina do Norte, Braz. 212/C2
Antônio Carlos, Braz. 213/K6
Antônio Lizardo, Mex. 201/P7
Antón Lizardo (pt.), Mex. 201/P7
Antongil (bay), Madg. 165/J6
Antonia, Mo, US 195/G9
Antonibe, Madg. 165/H6
Antonito, Co, US 190/B2
Antonovo, Bul. 107/H4
Antony, Fr. 88/J5
Antrim, NI, UK 92/B2
Antrim (mts.), NI, UK 92/B1
Antrim (dist.), NI, UK 92/B2
Antronapiana, It. 114/E5
Antsalova, Madg. 165/H7
Antsambalahy, Madg. 165/J6
Antsenavolo, Madg. 165/J8
Antsirabe, Madg. 165/H7
Antsiranana, Madg. 165/J6
Antsiranana (prov.), Madg. 165/J6
Antsohihy, Madg. 165/H6
Antucco (vol.), Chile 216/C3
Antulai (mtn.), Malay. 139/E3
Antwerp (Deurne) (int'l arpt.), Belg. 108/B6
Antwerpen, Belg. 108/B6
Anūpgarh, India 144/B5
Anūpshahr, India 142/B1
Anuradhapura, SrL. 140/D6
Anvik, Ak, US 192/F3
Anvil Peak (vol.), Ak, US 192/B6
Anxi, China 137/C2
Anxi, China 128/G3
Anyang, China 130/C3
Anyang, SKor. 131/F7
Anyi, China 130/D3
Anyuan, China 130/C4
Anza (riv.), It. 114/E6
'Anzah, WBnk. 149/G7
Anzegem, Belg. 110/C2
Anzin, Fr. 110/C3
Anzing, Ger. 113/E6
Anzio, It. 104/C2
Anzoátegui, Ven. 210/D2
Anzoátegui (state), Ven. 211/E2
Anzoátegui (int'l arpt.), Ven. 211/E2
Anzola dell'Emilia, It. 117/E3
Ao Kham (pt.), Thai. 136/B4
Ao Phangnga NP, Thai. 136/B4
Aoba (isl.), Van. 174/F6
Aoga (isl.), Japan 133/F4
Aogaki, Japan 135/H5
Aoiz, Sp. 102/E1

Aomori (pref.), Japan 134/B3
Aomori, Japan 134/B3
Aonla, India 142/B1
Aoral (peak), Camb. 136/D3
Aos, Gre. 105/J4
Aosta, It. 101/G4
Aosta, Valle d' (valley), It. 116/A1
Aoudaghast (ruin), Mrta. 160/C2
Aouk, Bahr (riv.), Chad 155/K6
Aoukar (pol. reg.), Mrta. 154/C4
Aoulef, Alg. 157/F4
Aoyama, Japan 135/K6
Apache (peak), Az, US 195/R18
Apalachicola, Fl, US 191/G4
Apan, Mex. 201/L7
Apaporis (riv.), Col. 208/D3
Apapa, Braz. 213/C2
Aparados da Serra, PN de, Braz. 213/B4
Aparecida, Braz. 213/C2
Aparecida do Taboado, Braz. 213/B2
Aparición, Ven. 210/D2
Aparri, Phil. 137/D4
Apartadó, Col. 210/B3
Apátfalva, Hun. 106/E2
Apatin, Serb. 106/D3
Apatity, Rus. 118/G2
Apatzingán de la Constitución, Mex. 184/D4
Apaxco, Mex. 201/K7
Apeldoorn, Neth. 108/C4
Apelern, Ger. 109/G4
Apennines (mts.), It. 85/F4
Apensen, Ger. 109/G2
Aphrodisias (ruin), Turk. 148/B2
Api (peak), Indo. 139/E5
Api (cape), Indo. 139/F4
Api (cape), Indo. 138/C3
Apiacás, Serra dos (mts.), Braz. 209/G6
Apiaí, Braz. 213/B3
Apia (cap.), Hi, US 182/U11
Apishapa (riv.), Co, US 187/J4
Aplao, Peru 214/C4
Apo (mt.), Phil. 137/E6
Apodi, Braz. 212/C2
Apodi (riv.), Braz. 212/C2
Apollo Bay, Austl. 173/B3
Apollonía, Gre. 105/J4
Apopa, Bol. 214/D4
Apóstoles, Arg. 215/E2
Apostle (isls.), Wi, US 185/L4
Apostle Islands Nat'l Lakeshore, Wi, US 185/L4
Apostolos Andreas (cape), Cyp. 149/D2
Apoteri, Guy. 211/G3
Appalachian (mts.), US 183/K4
Appen, Ger. 109/G1
Appennino Ligure (mts.), It. 101/H4
Appennino Tosco-Emiliano (mts.), It. 101/J4
Appennino Umbro-Marchigiano (mts.), It. 101/K5
Appenweier, Ger. 114/D1
Appenzell, Swi. 115/F3
Appenzell (canton), Swi. 115/F3
Appignano, It. 117/G6
Appingedam, Neth. 108/D2
Apple Valley, Ca, US 194/C1
Appleton, NY, US 189/S9
Aprica, It. 115/G5
Aprica, Passo dell' (pass), It. 115/G5
Aprilia, It. 104/C2
Apriltsi, Bul. 105/J1
Apsheronsk, Rus. 120/F3
Apsley Gorge NP, Austl. 173/E1
'Apua, US, Hi, US 182/U11
Apucarana, Braz. 213/B2
Apuiarés, Braz. 212/C1
Apure (riv.), Ven. 208/D2
Apure (prov.), Ven. 210/D3
Apurímac (dept.), Peru 214/C4
Apurímac (riv.), Peru 205/D3
Aqaba (gulf), Asia 125/B7
Aqmola (gulf), Kaz. 145/E2
'Aqrabah, WBnk. 149/G7
Aqsay, Kaz. 121/K2
Aqtau, Kaz. 121/J4
Aqtöbe, Kaz. 145/C2
Aqtöbe (obl.), Kaz. 145/C2
Aquanaval (riv.), Mex. 184/D3
Aquaro-Guariquito, PN, Ven. 208/E2
Aquia, Peru 214/B3
Aquidauana, Braz. 209/G8
Aquidauana (riv.), Braz. 209/G8
Aquila, Swi. 115/F4
Aquileia, It. 117/G1
Aquiles Serdán, Mex. 184/D2
Aquin, Haiti 203/H2
Aquiraz, Braz. 212/D1

Aquitaine (pol. reg.), Fr. 100/C4
Ar-Asgat, Mong. 128/K2
Ar Horqin Qi, China 130/E2
Ar Ramādī, Iraq 148/E3
Ar Ramthā, Jor. 149/D3
Ar Raqqah, Syria 148/D2
Ar Raqqah (prov.), Syria 148/D2
Ar Rastan, Syria 149/E2
Ar Rayyān, Qatar 147/F4
Ar Riyād (Riyadh) (cap.), SAr. 146/E4
Ar Rumaythah, Iraq 148/E4
Ar Ruşayfah, Jor. 149/E3
Ar Ruţbah, Iraq 148/D3
Arab, Syria 148/D3
Arab, US 191/G3
'Arab, Bahr al (riv.), Sudan 155/L6
Arabi, La, US 195/Q17
Arabian (sea), Asia 125/F8
Arabian (pen.), SAr. 146/D3
Arabian Egypt 155/M2
Arabian (pen.), SAr. 146/A1
Araç, Turk. 120/C4
Araç (riv.), Turk. 120/C4
Araca, Bol. 208/E7
Araçá (riv.), Braz. 211/F4
Aracaju, Braz. 212/C3
Aracataca, Col. 210/C2
Aracati, Braz. 212/C2
Araçatuba, Braz. 213/B2
Aracena, Sp. 102/B4
Araçoiaba, Braz. 212/C2
Aracruz, Braz. 213/D1
Araçuaí, Braz. 212/B5
Araça (riv.), Braz. 211/F4
Arad, Rom. 106/E2
Arad (prov.), Rom. 106/E2
'Arad, Isr. 149/D4
'Arad, Iran 146/F1
Arafura (sea), Indo. 139/E5
Aragarças, Braz. 209/H7
Aragats (peak), Arm. 121/H4
Aragón (aut. comm.), Sp. 103/E2
Aragón (riv.), Sp. 103/E1
Aragua (state), Ven. 211/E2
Araguaia (riv.), Braz. 205/D3
Araguaia, PN do, Braz. 209/H6
Araguaiana, Braz. 209/H7
Araguari, Braz. 213/B1
Araguari (riv.), Braz. 209/H3
Araguatins, Braz. 209/J5
Arai, Japan 133/F2
Araioses, Braz. 212/B1
Arak, Iran 146/F2
Arakamchechan (isl.), Rus. 192/D3
Arakawa, Japan 135/C2
Arakht (riv.), Gre. 105/G3
Araklı, Turk. 148/D1
Aral, Kaz. 145/D3
Aral (sea), Asia 145/C2
Aral, Kaz. 145/C3
Aral Mangy Qaraqumy (des.), Kaz. 145/C3
Aralık, Turk. 148/F2
Aralsor (lake), Kaz. 121/H2
Arāmbāgh, India 143/F4
Aran (isls.), Ire. 89/P10
Aran Fawddwy (peak), Wal, UK 92/E6
Aranda de Duero, Sp. 102/D2
Arandelovac, Serb. 106/E3
Arani, India 140/C5
Aranjuez, Sp. 102/D2
Aransas Pass, Tx, US 190/D5
Arantina, Braz. 213/K6
Aranuka (isl.), Kiri. 174/G5
Arapaho, Ok, US 187/H4
Arapiraca, Braz. 212/C3
Arapongas, Braz. 213/B2
Arapoti, Braz. 213/B3
Araranguá, Braz. 213/B4
Araraquara, Braz. 213/B2
Araras, Braz. 213/C2
Ararat, Austl. 173/B3
Ararí, Braz. 212/A1
Arária, India 143/F3
Araripe, Chapada do (uplands), Braz. 212/B2
Araripina, Braz. 212/B2
Aras (riv.), Iran 121/H4
Aratane (well), Mrta. 160/C2
Arauá (riv.), Braz. 210/D4
Arauca (riv.), Col., Ven. 211/E3
Arauca, Col. 210/D3
Araucária, Braz. 213/B3
Arauco, Chile 216/B3
Arauquita, Col. 210/D3
Araure, Ven. 210/D2
Aravis, Col des (pass), Fr. 114/C6
Araxá, Braz. 213/B1
Araya (riv.), Japan 134/B4
Arba Minch', Eth. 155/N6
Arbeca, Sp. 103/F2
Arbil (gov.), Iraq 148/E2
Arboga, Swe. 96/F2

Arbois, Fr. 114/B4
Arbois, Mont d' (peak), Fr. 114/C6
Arboletes, Col. 210/B2
Arbon, Swi. 115/F2
Arborfield, Sk, Can. 185/H2
Arborg, Mb, Can. 185/J3
Arbrå, Swe. 96/G1
Arbroath, Sc, UK 94/D3
Arc (riv.), Fr. 100/F5
Arc-en-Barrois, Fr. 114/B2
Arc-et-Senans, Fr. 114/B3
Arc-lès-Gray, Fr. 114/B3
Arc-sur-Tille, Fr. 114/B3
Arcachon, Fr. 100/C4
Arcachon, Bassin d' (lag.), Fr. 100/C4
Arcachon, Pointe d' (pt.), Fr. 100/C4
Arcadia, Ca, US 194/F7
Arcadia, Fl, US 191/H5
Arcadia, Ok, US 195/N14
Arcas, Cayos (isl.), Mex. 202/D1
Arcata, Ca, US 184/B5
Arceburgo, Braz. 213/G6
Arcelia, Mex. 201/K7
Arcene, It. 116/C1
Arceto, It. 117/D3
Arches, Fr. 114/C1
Arches NP, Ut, US 186/E3
Archena, Sp. 102/E3
Archer City, Tx, US 187/H4
Archidona, Sp. 102/C4
Archman, Trkm. 121/J5
Arcipelago Toscano (isl.), It. 101/H5
Arcisate, It. 115/E6
Arco, It. 115/G5
Arco, Paso del (pass), Chile 216/C3
Arcola, It. 116/C4
Arcole, It. 117/E2
Arcos, Braz. 213/C2
Arcos de Jalón, Sp. 102/D2
Arcos de la Frontera, Sp. 102/C4
Arcos de Valdevez, Port. 102/A2
Arcoverde, Braz. 212/C3
Arctic (ocean) 218/U
Arctic (plain), Ak, US 192/F2
Arctic Bay, Nun., Can. 181/H1
Arctic Circle 218/J
Arctic Red (riv.), NW, Can. 192/M2
Arctic Village, Ak, US 192/J2
Arctowski, Pol., Ant. 218/W
Arda (riv.), Bul. 120/C4
Ardabīl, Iran 121/J5
Ardahan, Turk. 148/E1
Ardal, Iran 146/F2
Ardalstangen, Nor. 96/B1
Ardanuç, Turk. 148/E1
Ardèche (riv.), Fr. 100/F4
Ardee, Ire. 92/B4
Arden (mt.), Austl. 171/H5
Arden, De, US 196/C4
Arden, Sc, UK 96/C3
Arden-Arcade, Ca, US 193/M9
Ardennes (for.), Belg. 100/F3
Ardennes (dept.), Fr. 111/D4
Ardennes, Canal des (canal), Fr. 111/D4
Ardentes, Fr. 100/D3
Ardersier, Sc, UK 94/B1
Ardeşen, Turk. 148/E1
Ardesio, It. 115/F5
Ardestān, Iran 146/F2
Ardez, Swi. 115/G4
Ardila (riv.), Sp. 102/B3
Ardino, Bul. 107/G5
Ardivachar (pt.), Sc, UK 89/Q8
Ardle (riv.), Sc, UK 94/C3
Ardlethan, Austl. 173/C2
Ardmore, Ok, US 187/H4
Ardmore, Pa, US 196/C4
Ardnamurchan (pt.), Sc, UK 89/Q8
Ardon, Swi. 114/D5
Ardooie, Belg. 110/C2
Ardres, Fr. 110/A2
Ardrossan, Austl. 171/H5
Ardrossan, Sc, UK 94/B5
Ards (pen.), NI, UK 92/C3
Ards (dist.), NI, UK 92/C3
Ardsley, NY, US 197/K7
Åre, Swe. 95/E3
Areado, Braz. 213/G6
Arecibo, PR 199/M8
Areia Branca, Braz. 212/D1
Arena (pt.), Ca, US 186/B3
Arena de la Ventana Punta (pt.), Mex. 184/C3
Arenal (vol.), CR 203/E4
Arenápolis, Braz. 209/G6
Arenas de San Pedro, Sp. 102/C2
Arenas, Punta de (pt.), Arg. 217/C7
Arendal, Nor. 96/C2
Arendonk, Belg. 108/C6
Arendtsville, Pa, US 196/A4
Arenig Fawr (peak), Wal, UK 92/E6
Arenys de Mar, Sp. 103/L6
Arenzano, It. 116/B4
Areo, Ven. 211/F2
Areópolis, Gre. 105/H4
Arequipa (dept.), Peru 214/C5

Arequipa, Peru 214/D5
Arequito, Arg. 216/E2
Aresing, Ger. 112/E5
Arezzo, It. 117/E6
Arezzo (prov.), It. 117/E5
Arga (riv.), Sp. 102/E1
Argalasti, Gre. 105/H3
Argamasilla de Alba, Sp. 102/D3
Argamasilla de Calatrava, Sp. 102/C3
Arganda, Sp. 103/N9
Argegno, It. 115/F6
Argelès-Gazost, Fr. 100/C5
Argelès-sur-Mer, Fr. 100/E5
Argen (riv.), Ger. 115/F2
Argenbühl, Ger. 115/F2
Argens (riv.), Fr. 101/G5
Argenta, It. 117/E3
Argentan, Fr. 100/C2
Argentat, Fr. 100/D4
Argentera (peak), It. 101/G4
Argentière, Aiguille d' (peak), Swi. 114/D6
Argentina (ctry.) 215/C4
Argentina (riv.), It. 116/K5
Argentino (lake), Arg. 217/B6
Argenton-sur-Creuse, Fr. 100/D3
Argentona, Sp. 103/L6
Arges (riv.), Rom. 107/G3
Arges (prov.), Rom. 107/G3
Arghandab (riv.), Afg. 147/J2
Argithani, Turk. 148/B2
Argolis (gulf), Gre. 105/H4
Argonne (for.), Fr. 98/C4
Argonne National Laboratory, Il, US 193/P16
Árgos, Gre. 105/G4
Argos Orestikón, Gre. 105/G2
Argostólion, Gre. 105/G3
Arguello (pt.), Ca, US 186/B4
Arguin, Cap d' (cape), Mrta. 156/A5
Argun' (riv.), Rus. 123/M4
Arguut, Mong. 128/F2
Argyle (lake), Austl. 167/E2
Argyll and Bute (pol. reg.), Sc, UK 94/A4
Arhangay (prov.), Mong. 128/G2
Arhreijit (well), Mrta. 156/B5
Århus, Den. 96/D3
Århus (co.), Den. 96/D3
Ariana, Tun. 158/M6
Ariano Irpino, It. 104/D2
Ariari (riv.), Col. 210/C4
Arias, Arg. 216/E2
Arica, Chile 214/D5
Arıcak, Turk. 148/E2
Arid (cape), Austl. 170/D5
Arida, Japan 132/D3
Aridhaia, Gre. 105/H2
Arido (peak), Ca, US 194/K1
Aridol (lake), WSah. 156/B3
Ariège (riv.), Fr. 100/D5
Arifiye, Turk. 107/K5
Arîfwâla, Pak. 144/B4
Arîhâ, Syria 149/E2
Arikaree (riv.), Co, US 187/G5
Arilje, Serb. 106/E4
Arima, Trin. 211/F2
Arinos (riv.), Braz. 209/G6
Arinos, Braz. 212/A4
Arinthod, Fr. 114/B5
Ario de Rosales, Mex. 201/E5
Aripao, Ven. 211/E3
Aripuanã, Braz. 208/G6
Aripuanã (riv.), Braz. 205/C3
Ariquemes, Braz. 208/F5
Arish, Austl. 171/B2
Arismendi, Ven. 210/D2
Arivechi, Mex. 184/C2
Arivonimamo, Madg. 165/H7
Ariza, Sp. 102/D2
Arizona, Arg. 216/D2
Arizona (canal), Az, US 195/R18
Arizona (state), US 186/D4
Arizpe, Mex. 184/C2
Arjäng, Swe. 96/E2
Arjeplog, Swe. 95/F2
Arjona, Sp. 102/C4
Arjona, Col. 210/C2
Arkadelphia, Ar, US 187/J4
Arkaig (lake), Sc, UK 94/A3
Arkalokhórion, Gre. 105/J5
Arkansas (riv.), US 190/E3
Arkansas (state), US 187/J4
Arkansas City, Ar, US 187/K4
Arkansas City, Ks, US 187/H3
Arkanü (peak), Libya 155/K3
Arkhángelos, Gre. 148/B2
Arkhangel'sk (int'l arpt.), Rus. 118/J2
Arkhangel'sk (Archangel), Rus. 118/J2
Arkhangel'skaya Oblast, Rus. 118/H3
Arkhangel'skoye, Rus. 119/W9
Arklow, Ire. 92/B6
Arkona (cape), Ger. 96/E4
Arkonam, India 140/C5
Arkticheskiy Institut (isls.), Rus. 122/H2
Arla, Swe. 96/G2
Arlan (peak), Trkm. 145/B5
Arlanda (int'l arpt.), Swe. 96/G2
Arlanza (riv.), Sp. 102/C1

Arlazón (riv.), Sp. 102/D1
Arlbergpass (pass), Aus. 115/G3
Arles, Fr. 100/F5
Arlesheim, Swi. 114/D3
Arley, Mo, US 195/K4
Arlington, Mn, US 185/K4
Arlington, Ga, US 191/G4
Arlington, Va, US 196/A6
Arlington Heights, Il, US 188/C3
Arló, Hun. 99/L4
Arlon, Belg. 111/E4
Arluno, It. 115/B1
Arly (riv.), Fr. 114/C6
Arly, PN de l', Burk. 161/F4
Arly, Réserve Totale de Faune de l', Burk. 161/F4
Armada, Mi, US 193/G6
Armadale, Sc, UK 94/C5
Armagh (dist.), NI, UK 92/B3
Armagh, NI, UK 92/B3
Armando Laydner, Reprêsa de (res.), Braz. 213/B2
Armant, Egypt 159/C3
Armavir, Rus. 121/G3
Arme, Cap d' (cape), Fr. 101/G5
Armenia, Col. 208/C3
Armenia (ctry.) 121/H5
Armentières, Fr. 110/B2
Armentières-en-Brie, Fr. 88/M5
Armería, Mex. 184/E5
Armidale, Austl. 173/D1
Armilla, Sp. 102/D4
Armstrong, Arg. 216/E2
Armstrong, BC, Can. 184/D3
Armthorpe, Eng, UK 93/G4
Armur, India 140/C4
Armutlu, Turk. 107/J5
Army Ordnance Museum, Md, US 196/B5
Arnage, Fr. 100/D3
Arnager (int'l arpt.), Den. 96/H4
Arnaia, Gre. 105/H2
Arnaud (riv.), Qu, Can. 181/J3
Arnauti (cape), Cyp. 149/C2
Arnedo, Sp. 102/D1
Arnett, Ok, US 187/H3
Arnhem, Neth. 108/C5
Arnhem Land (reg.), Austl. 167/C2
Arnø (isl.), Mi, US 185/L4
Arno (riv.), It. 101/J5
Arno (isl.), Mrsh. 174/G4
Arnold, Eng, UK 93/G6
Arnold, Md, US 196/B5
Arnold, Mo, US 195/G9
Arnoldstein, Aus. 101/K3
Arnprior, On, Can. 188/E2
Arnsberg, Ger. 109/F6
Arnstadt, Ger. 101/J1
Arnstein, Ger. 112/C3
Arnstorf, Ger. 113/F5
Aroab, Namb. 164/B2
Aroche, Sp. 102/B4
Arolsen, Ger. 109/G6
Aron (riv.), Fr. 100/E3
Arona, Canl. 103/X16
Arona, It. 116/B1
Aronde (riv.), Fr. 110/B5
Arorae (isl.), Kiri. 174/G5
Aroser Rothern (peak), Swi. 115/F4
Ærøskøbing, Den. 96/D4
Arpaçay, Turk. 148/E1
Arpajon, Fr. 88/J6
Arpajon-sur-Cère, Fr. 100/E4
Arqalyq, Kaz. 145/E2
Arquata Scrivia, It. 116/B3
Arques, Fr. 110/B3
'Arrābah, WBnk. 149/G7
Arrah, India 143/E3
Arraias (riv.), Braz. 209/H6
Arraias, Braz. 212/A4
Arraiján, Pan. 210/B2
Arran (isl.), Sc, UK 89/R8
Arrancabarba (peak), Nic. 203/E4
Arras, Fr. 110/B3
Arreau, Fr. 100/D5
Arrecife, Canl., Sp. 156/B3
Arrecifes, Arg. 216/E2
Arrée, Monts d' (mts.), Fr. 100/B2
Arriaga, Mex. 202/C2
Arriondas, Sp. 102/C1
Arrochar, Sc, UK 94/B4
Arroio Grande, Braz. 213/A5
Arronville, Fr. 88/J4
Arroscia (riv.), It. 116/B4
Arroux (riv.), Fr. 100/D5
Arrow (riv.), Eng, UK 90/C2
Arrowbear Lake, Ca, US 194/C2
Arroyo de la Luz, Sp. 102/B3
Arroyo Grande, Ca, US 186/B4
Arroyo Hondo (riv.), Ca, US 193/L12
Arroyo Trabuco (riv.), Ca, US 194/C3
Ars, Den. 96/C3
Ars-sur-Moselle, Fr. 111/F5
Arsen'yev, Rus. 129/P3
Arsiero, It. 117/E1
Arslanköy, Turk. 149/D1

Arta (gulf), Gre. 105/G3
Árta, Gre. 105/G3
Artá, Sp. 103/G3
Arteaga, Mex. 184/E5
Arteixo, Sp. 102/A1
Artem, Rus. 129/P3
Artemisa, Cuba 203/F1
Arth, Swi. 115/E3
Arthies, Fr. 88/H4
Arthur (pt.), Austl. 173/B3
Arthur (riv.), Austl. 170/C5
Arthur Kill (riv.), NJ,NY, US 197/J9
Arthur's (pass), NZ 175/S11
Arthur's Pass NP, NZ 175/S11
Artigas, Uru. 215/E3
Artois (reg.), Fr. 98/A3
Artogne, It. 116/D1
Artova, Turk. 148/D1
Artur Nogueira, Braz. 213/F7
Arturo Merino Benítez (Santiago) (int'l arpt.), Chile 216/N8
Artux, China 145/G5
Artvin, Turk. 148/E1
Artvin (prov.), Turk. 148/E1
Aru (isls.), Indo. 139/H5
Arua, Ugan. 162/A2
Aruba (isl.), Aru., Neth. 199/H5
Arucas, Canl., Sp. 156/X16
Arudy, Fr. 100/C5
Arujá, Braz. 213/G8
Arun (riv.), China 143/F2
Arunáchal Pradesh (state), India 141/F2
Arundel, Eng, UK 91/F5
Aruppukkottai, India 140/C6
Arus (cape), Indo. 139/F3
Arusha, Tanz. 162/C3
Arusha (pol. reg.), Tanz. 162/C4
Arusha NP, Tanz. 162/C3
Arutua (isl.), FrPol. 175/L6
Aruwimi (riv.), D.R. Congo 155/K7
Arvada, Co, US 195/B3
Arvayheer, Mong. 128/H2
Arve (riv.), Fr. 114/C6
Arviat, Nun., Can. 180/G2
Arvidsjaur, Swe. 95/F2
Arvika, Swe. 96/E2
Arvin, Ca, US 186/C4
Arvon (mt.), Mi, US 185/L4
Arys', Kaz. 145/E4
Arz (riv.), Fr. 100/B3
Arzachena, It. 104/A2
Arzamas, Rus. 119/K5
Arzbach, Ger. 111/G3
Arzberg, Ger. 113/F2
Ärzen, Ger. 109/G4
Arzew, Alg. 158/E5
Arzignano, It. 117/E1
Arzl im Pitztal, Aus. 115/G3
Arzúa, Sp. 102/A1
Aš, Czh. 113/F2
Ås, Nor. 96/D2
As Sabkhah, Syria 148/D3
As Sālimīyah, Kuw. 146/E3
As Sallūm, Egypt 155/L1
As Salmān, Iraq 148/F4
As Salt, Jor. 149/D3
As Santah, Egypt 149/B4
As Sarih, Jor. 149/E3
As Sinbillāwayn, Egypt 149/B4
As Sudd (reg.), Sudan 155/M6
As Sulaymānīyah (gov.), Iraq 148/F3
As Sulaymānīyah, Iraq 148/F3
As Suwaydā' (prov.), Syria 149/D3
As Suwaydā', Syria 149/E3
As Suwayrah, Iraq 148/F3
As Suways, Egypt 159/C2
As Suways (gov.), Egypt 159/C2
Asaba, Nga. 161/G5
Asadābād, Afg. 144/A2
Asadābād, Iran 146/E2
Asagny, PN d', C.d'Iv. 160/D5
Asahan (riv.), Indo. 139/A4
Asahi, Japan 133/G3
Asahi, Japan 135/K5
Asahi, Japan 132/C3
Asahi, Japan 135/F1
Asahi, Japan 135/L5
Asahi, Japan 135/M5
Asahi-dake (peak), Japan 134/C2
Asahikawa, Japan 134/C2
Asai, Japan 135/K5
Asaka, Japan 135/K2
Asake (riv.), Japan 135/K5
Asama-yama (peak), Japan 133/F2
Asan (riv.), SKor. 131/D4
Asansol, India 143/F4
Asashi-dake (peak), Japan 133/F1
Asashina, Japan 135/A1
Asawanwah (well), Libya 155/J3
Asbach, Ger. 111/G2
Asbach-Bäumenheim, Ger. 112/D5
Asbest, Rus. 119/P4
Asbestos (mts.), SAfr. 164/C3
Asbury Park, NJ, US 196/D3
Ascensión, Bol. 208/F7

Ascensión (bay), Mex. 198/D4
Ascensión, Mex. 184/D2
Ascensión, Arg. 216/E2
Aschach an der Donau, Aus. 113/H6
Aschaffenburg, Ger. 112/C3
Aschau am Inn, Ger. 113/F6
Ascheberg, Ger. 109/E2
Aschendorf, Ger. 109/E2
Aschersleben, Ger. 98/F3
Ascoli Piceno, It. 101/K5
Ascoli Satriano, It. 104/D2
Ascona, Swi. 115/E3
Ascope, Peru 214/B2
Aseda, Swe. 96/F3
Asela, Eth. 155/N6
Asele, Swe. 95/F2
Asendorf, Ger. 109/G2
Asendorf, Ger. 109/F3
Aseral, Nor. 96/B2
Asera, Mor. 156/C3
Aserei (peak), It. 116/C3
Asfeld, Fr. 111/D5
Ash, Eng, UK 88/A3
Ash Shabakah, Iraq 148/E4
Ash Shamal (gov.), Leb. 149/E2
Ash Shāmīyah, Iraq 148/F4
Ash Shāriqah, UAE 147/G3
Ash Sharqāt, Iraq 148/E3
Ash Sharqīyah (state), Sudan 159/C5
Ash Shawbak, Jor. 149/D4
Asha, Nga. 161/F5
Asha (uplands), C.d'Iv. 154/E6
Ashanti (pol. reg.), Gha. 161/E5
Asharoken, NY, US 197/M8
Ashbourne, Ire. 92/B4
Ashbourne, Eng, UK 93/G5
Ashburton (riv.), Austl. 167/A3
Ashburton, NZ 175/S11
Ashby (canal), Eng, UK 91/E1
Ashby-de-la-Zouch, Eng, UK 91/E1
Ashcroft, BC, Can. 184/C3
Ashdod, Isr. 149/F8
Asheboro, NC, US 191/J3
Ashern, Mb, Can. 185/J3
Asheville, NC, US 191/H3
Asheweig (riv.), On, Can. 185/M2
Ashford, Austl. 173/D1
Ashford, Eng, UK 91/G4
Ashford, Eng, UK 88/B2
Ashford, Ire. 92/B5
Ashington, Eng, UK 93/G1
Ashino (lake), Japan 135/C3
Ashiwada, Japan 135/B3
Ashiya, Japan 135/H6
Ashizuri-misaki (cape), Japan 132/C4
Ashland, Ks, US 187/H3
Ashland, Ky, US 188/D4
Ashland, Oh, US 188/D3
Ashland, Or, US 184/C5
Ashland, Pa, US 196/B2
Ashley, ND, US 185/J4
Ashley, Pa, US 196/C1
Ashmore (reef), Austl. 167/B2
Ashmore and Cartier Islands Territory (dpcy.), Austl. 167/B2
Ashmūn, Egypt 149/B4
Ashoknagar, India 142/A3
Ashoro, Japan 134/C2
Ashqelon, Isr. 149/F8
Ashta, India 140/C3
Ashtabula, Oh, US 188/D3
Ashton, Id, US 184/C4
Ashton, SAfr. 164/M10
Ashton-in-Makerfield, Eng, UK 93/F5
Ashton-under-Lyne, Eng, UK 93/F5
Asia (cont.) 83
Asia, Peru 214/B4
Asiago, It. 115/H6
Asikkala, Fin. 97/L1
Asilah, Mor. 158/A2
Asillo, Peru 214/C4
Asinara (isl.), It. 104/A2
Asinara, Golfo dell' (gulf), It. 104/A2
Asino, Rus. 122/J4
Asipovichy, Bela. 120/C1
Asir (mts.), SAr. 146/D5
Asis (cape), Sudan 159/D5
Aşkale, Turk. 148/E2
Askeaton, Ire. 89/P10
Asker, Nor. 96/C2
Askersund, Swe. 96/F2
Askim, Swe. 96/D3
Askion (peak), Gre. 105/G2
Askja (crater), Ice. 95/P6
Askold, Den. 96/D3
Askov, Den. 96/C3
Askvoll, Nor. 95/C3
Asmara (cap.), Erit. 146/C5
Asnen (lake), Swe. 96/F3
Asnières-sur-Oise, Fr. 88/K4
Asnières-sur-Seine, Fr. 88/J5
Asó, Japan 135/E2

Aso NP, Japan 132/B4
Aso-san (peak), Japan 132/B4
Asola, It. 116/D2
Asolo, It. 117/E1
Asosa, Eth. 155/M5
Asoteriba (peak), Sudan 159/D4
Aspach, Aus. 113/G6
Aspe, Sp. 103/E3
Aspen Hill, Md, US 196/A5
Aspen Park, Co, US 195/B1
Aspendos (ruin), Turk. 149/B1
Asperg, Ger. 112/C5
Aspermont, Tx, US 187/G4
Aspers, Pa, US 196/A4
Aspiring (mt.), NZ 175/R11
Asprópirgos, Gre. 105/H3
Asquith, Sk, Can. 184/G2
Assa Aguiene (peak), Alg. 157/G5
Assab, Erit. 146/D6
Assaba (pol. reg.), Mrta. 160/C2
Assam (state), India 141/F2
Assaré, Braz. 212/C2
Assemini, It. 104/A3
Asse, Belg. 111/D2
Assen, Neth. 108/D3
Assenede, Belg. 110/C1
Assens, Den. 96/C4
Assens, Den. 96/D3
Assentoft, Den. 96/D3
Assiniboia, Sk, Can. 185/G3
Assiniboine (mt.), BC, Can. 184/D3
Assiniboine (riv.), Mb,Sk, Can. 185/H3
Assinika (lake), Qu, Can. 188/F1
Assis, Braz. 213/B2
Assisi, It. 101/J6
Assling, Ger. 113/F6
Asso, It. 116/C1
Assomada, CpV. 151/K10
Astakós, Gre. 105/G3
Astana (cap.), Kaz. 145/F2
Asten, Neth. 108/C6
Asten, Aus. 113/H6
Asti (prov.), It. 116/B3
Asti, It. 101/H4
Astico (riv.), It. 117/E1
Astipálaia, Gre. 148/A2
Astolfo Dutra, Braz. 213/L6
Astorga, Braz. 213/B2
Astorga, Sp. 102/B1
Astoria, Or, US 184/C4
Astorp, Swe. 96/E3
Astrakhan', Rus. 121/J3
Astrakhanskaya Oblast, Rus. 121/H3
Astros, Gre. 105/H4
Astudillo, Sp. 102/C1
Asturias (aut. comm.), Sp. 102/B1
Asuka, Japan 135/J7
Asuke, Japan 135/M5
Asunción (cap.), Par. 215/E2
Asunción Ixtaltepec, Mex. 202/C2
Asunden (lake), Swe. 96/F3
Aswa (riv.), Ugan. 155/M7
Aswān (gov.), Egypt 159/C3
Aswān, Egypt 159/C3
Aswan High (dam), Egypt 159/C4
Asyūt (gov.), Egypt 159/B3
Asyūt, Egypt 159/B3
Aszód, Hun. 107/R9
At Tafilah, Jor. 149/D4
At Tafilah (gov.), Jor. 149/D4
At Ta'if, SAr. 146/D4
At Tall, WBnk. 149/G8
At Tall al Kabīr, Egypt 149/B4
At Ta'mīn (gov.), Iraq 148/E3
Aṭ Ṭūr, WBnk. 149/G8
Atami, Japan 133/F2
Atar, Mrta. 154/B3
Atarfe, Sp. 102/D4
Atarra, India 142/C2
Atas Bogd (peak), Mong. 128/C3
Atascadero, Ca, US 186/B4
Atascosa (co.), Tx, US 195/T21
Atascosa, Tx, US 195/T21
Aṭbara (riv.), Eth. 155/N5
Atbara, Sudan 155/M4
Atbasar, Kaz. 145/E2
Atchafalaya (riv.), La, US 187/K5
Atchafalaya (bay), La, US 187/K5
Atchison, Ks, US 187/J2
Atco, NJ, US 196/D4
Ateca, Sp. 102/D2
Atebubu, Gha. 161/E5

Ateelva (riv.), Nor. 95/G1
Atén, Bol. 214/D4
Atencingo, Mex. 201/Q10
Atenco, Mex. 201/Q10
Atenco, Mex. 201/R9
Atengo (riv.), Mex. 184/D4
Atessa, It. 104/D1
Atglen, Pa, US 196/C4
Ath, Belg. 111/C2
Ab, Can. 180/E2
Athabasca, Ab, Can. 184/E2
Athabasca (riv.), Ab, Can. 180/D2
Athabasca (lake), Ab,Sk, Can. 180/E3
Athapapuskow (lake), Mb, Can. 185/H2
Athār Tulmaythah (Ptolemaïs) (ruin), Libya 155/K1
Athboy, Ire. 89/Q10
Athenry, Ire. 89/P10
Athens (Athínai) (cap.), Gre. 105/N9
Athens, Al, US 191/G3
Athens, Ga, US 191/H3
Athens, Tn, US 191/G3
Athens, Oh, US 191/H2
Atherstone, Eng, UK 91/E1
Atherton, Austl. 171/B2
Atherton, Eng, UK 93/F4
Atherton, Mo, US 195/E5
Athgarh, India 140/E3
Athi (riv.), Kenya 162/C3
Athína (Athens) (cap.), Gre. 105/N9
Athis-Mons, Fr. 88/K5
Athlone, Ire. 89/Q10
Atholl (for.), Sc, UK 94/B3
Athos (peak), Gre. 105/J2
Athy, Ire. 89/Q10
Ati, Chad 155/J5
Atibaia, Braz. 213/G8
Atibaia (riv.), Braz. 213/G7
Atico, Peru 214/C5
Atienza, Sp. 102/D2
Atikokan, On, Can. 185/L3
Atil, Mex. 184/C2
Aṭîl, Isr. 149/G6
Atitlán (lake), Guat. 202/D3
Atiu (isl.), Cooks. 175/K7
Atizapan, Mex. 201/Q10
Atka, Ak, US 192/D5
Atka (isl.), Ak, US 192/C5
Atkarsk, Rus. 121/H2
Atkinson (pt.), NW, Can. 192/M2
Atlacomulco de Fabela, Mex. 201/K7
Atlanta (cap.), Ga, US 191/G3
Atlántida, Uru. 217/B4
Atlantic (ocean) 80/G3
Atlantic (co.), NJ, US 196/D4
Atlantic Beach, NY, US 197/L9
Atlantic City, NJ, US 196/D5
Atlantic Highlands, NJ, US 197/J10
Atlántico (dept.), Col. 210/C2
Atlantique (prov.), Ben. 161/F5
Atlas (mts.), Mor. 154/E1
Atlas (peak), Ca, US 193/K10
Atlas Saharien (mts.), Alg. 154/E1
Atlatlahuaca, Mex. 201/Q10
Atlin, BC, Can. 192/M3
Atlin (lake), BC, Can. 192/M3
'Atlit, Isr. 149/F6
Atlixco, Mex. 201/L8
Atmore, Al, US 191/G4
Atocha, Bol. 208/E8
Atoka, Ok, US 187/H4
Atomium, The, Belg. 111/D2
Atonilco, Mex. 201/K6
Atouila, 'Erg (des.), Mali 156/D5
Atoyac, Mex. 201/K7
Atoyac (riv.), Mex. 202/B2
Atqasuk, Ak, US 192/G1
Atrai (riv.), Bang. 143/G3
Atrak (riv.), Iran 147/G1
Atran (riv.), Swe. 96/E3
Atrato (riv.), Col. 208/C2
Atrauli, India 142/B1
Atri, It. 104/C1
Atsugi, Japan 135/K2
Atsumi, Japan 135/M6
Atsumi (pen.), Japan 135/M6
Attalens, Swi. 114/C4
Attalla, Al, US 191/G3
Attalándi, Gre. 105/H3
Attawapiskat (lake), On, Can. 185/L2
Attawapiskat (riv.), On, Can. 185/L2
Attendorn, Ger. 111/G1
Atteridgeville, SAfr. 164/Q12
Attersee (lake), Aus. 101/K3
Attica, Mi, US 193/G6
Attigny, Fr. 111/D5
'Attil, WBnk. 149/G7
Attleboro, Ma, US 197/H2
Attock, Pak. 144/B3
Attu, Ak, US 192/A5
Attu (isl.), Ak, US 192/A5
Attur, India 140/C5
Atuel (riv.), Arg. 215/C4
Atuntaqui, Ecu. 210/B4
Atvidaberg, Swe. 96/G2
Au (isl.), Mrsh. 174/G4
Au, Swi. 115/F3
Au, Aus. 115/F3
Au in der Hallertau, Ger. 113/E5

Au Sable (riv.), Mi, US 188/D2
Auari (riv.), Braz. 211/E3
Aubange, Belg. 111/E4
Aube (dept.), Fr. 111/D6
Aube (riv.), Fr. 98/C4
Aubenas, Fr. 100/F4
Aubepierre-Ozouer-le-Repos, Fr. 88/L6
Aubergenville, Fr. 88/H5
Aubert (peak), Swi. 114/C4
Aubervilliers, Fr. 88/K5
Aubetin (riv.), Fr. 110/C6
Aubette (riv.), Fr. 88/H5
Aubette de Magny (riv.), Fr. 88/H4
Aubin, Fr. 100/E4
Aubonne, Swi. 114/C5
Auboué, Fr. 111/E5
Aubrac, Monts du (mts.), Fr. 100/E4
Aubrives, Fr. 111/D3
Aubry, Ks, US 195/D6
Auburn, Austl. 171/H4
Auburn, Al, US 191/G3
Auburn, Ca, US 186/B3
Auburn, In, US 188/C3
Auburn, Me, US 189/G2
Auburn, Ne, US 187/J2
Auburn, NY, US 188/E3
Auburn, Pa, US 196/B2
Auburn, Wa, US 184/C4
Auburn Hills, Mi, US 193/G6
Aucá Mahuida (peak), Arg. 216/C3
Auch, Fr. 100/D5
Auchel, Fr. 110/B2
Auchinleck, Sc, UK 94/C4
Auchterarder, Sc, UK 94/C4
Auchtermuchty, Sc, UK 94/C4
Auchy-lès-Hesdin, Fr. 110/B2
Auckland, NZ 175/S10
Auckland (int'l arpt.), NZ 175/S10
Auckland (isls.), NZ 81/T8
Aude (riv.), Fr. 100/E5
Audenge, Fr. 100/C4
Auderghem, Belg. 111/D2
Audeux (riv.), Fr. 114/C3
Audierne (bay), Fr. 100/A3
Audincourt, Fr. 114/C3
Audo (range), Eth. 155/P6
Audruicq, Fr. 110/B2
Audun-le-Roman, Fr. 111/E5
Audun-le-Tiche, Fr. 111/E5
Aue, Ger. 109/G2
Aue (riv.), Ger. 113/F1
Auer (Ora), It. 115/H5
Auerbach, Ger. 113/F1
Auerbach in der Oberpfalz, Ger. 113/E3
Auersberg (peak), Ger. 113/F2
Auffargis, Fr. 88/H5
Augathella, Austl. 171/B4
Augher, NI, UK 92/A3
Aughnacloy, NI, UK 92/B3
Aughrim, Ire. 92/B6
Augrabies Falls NP, SAfr. 164/C3
Augrabiesvalle (falls), SAfr. 164/C3
Augsburg, Ger. 112/D6
Augub (peak), Namb. 164/A2
Augusta, Ga, US 191/H3
Augusta (cap.), Me, US 189/G2
Augusta, It. 104/D4
Augusta, Austl. 170/B5
Augusta, NJ, US 196/D1
Augustdorf, Ger. 109/F5
Augustenborg, Den. 96/C4
Augusto César Sandino (int'l arpt.), Nic. 202/E3
Augustów, Pol. 97/K5
Augustus (mt.), Austl. 170/C3
Auki, Sol. 174/F5
Aukstaitija NP, Lith. 97/M4
Auld (lake), Austl. 167/B3
Aulendorf, Ger. 115/F2
Aulla, It. 116/C2
Aulnay-sous-Bois, Fr. 88/K5
Aulnay-sur-Mauldre, Fr. 88/H5
Aulne (riv.), Fr. 100/A3
Aulnoy, Fr. 88/M5
Aulnoye-Aymeries, Fr. 110/C3
Aulnut (int'l arpt.), Fr. 100/E2
Ault, Co, US 195/C1
Ault, Fr. 110/A3
Aumale, Fr. 110/A4
Aumetz, Fr. 111/E5
Aumühle, Ger. 109/H1
Aunay-sur-Odon, Fr. 100/C2
Auneau, Fr. 100/D2
Auneuil, Fr. 110/B5
Auning, Den. 96/D3
Aur (isl.), Mrsh. 174/G4
Aura, NJ, US 196/D4
Aurach, Ger. 112/D4
Auraiya, India 142/B2
Aurangābād, India 143/E3
Aurangābād, India 140/B4
Auray, Fr. 100/B3

Aureilhan, Fr. 100/D5
Aurich, Ger. 109/E2
Auriflama, Braz. 213/B2
Aurillac, Fr. 100/E4
Aurisina, It. 117/G1
Aurland, Nor. 96/B1
Aurolzmünster, Aus. 113/G6
Aurora, Braz. 212/C2
Aurora, Guy. 211/G3
Aurora, Co, US 195/C3
Aurora, Il, US 187/K2
Aurora, Mo, US 187/J3
Aurora Lodge, Ak, US 192/J3
Aus, Namb. 164/B2
Ausa (riv.), It. 117/G1
Aussillon, Fr. 100/E5
Aust-Agder (co.), Nor. 95/C4
Austin, Nv, US 186/D3
Austin (lake), Austl. 167/A3
Austral (Tubuaï Islands) (isls.), FrPol. 175/K7
Australia (cont.) 125
Australia (ctry.) 125
Australian Alps (range), Austl. 173/C3
Australian Capital Territory (cap. terr.), Austl. 173/D2
Australind, Austl. 170/B5
Austria (ctry.) 101/L3
Austurhorn (pt.), Ice. 95/P7
Auterive, Fr. 100/D5
Authie (riv.), Fr. 110/D1
Autlán de Navarro, Mex. 184/D5
Automne (riv.), Fr. 88/L5
Autreppe, Belg. 110/C3
Autun, Fr. 100/F3
Auvergne (pol. reg.), Fr. 100/E4
Auvers-sur-Oise, Fr. 88/J4
Auvézère (riv.), Fr. 100/D4
Aux Sables (riv.), On, Can. 188/D2
Auxerre, Fr. 100/E3
Auxi-le-Château, Fr. 110/B3
Auxonne, Fr. 114/B3
Auyán-Tepuí (peak), Ven. 211/F3
Auyuittuq NP, Nun., Can. 181/K2
Auzangate (peak), Peru 214/D4
Avaj, Iran 146/E1
Avallon, Fr. 100/E3
Avalon (pen.), Nf, Can. 181/L4
Avalon, Ca, US 194/B4
Avalon, NJ, US 196/D5
Avanne-Aveney, Fr. 114/B3
Avaré, Braz. 213/B2
Avarua, NZ 175/K7
Avdat (ruin), Isr. 149/D4
Avebury Stone Circle, Eng, UK 91/E4
Aveiro, Port. 102/A2
Aveiro (dist.), Port. 102/A2
Aveley, Eng, UK 88/D2
Avelgem, Belg. 110/C2
Avellaneda, Arg. 217/J11
Avellino, It. 104/D2
Avelon (riv.), Fr. 110/B5
Avenal, Ca, US 186/B3
Avenches, Swi. 114/D4
Avenel, NJ, US 197/H9
Avernes, Fr. 88/H4
Aversa, It. 104/D2
Aves (isl.), Ven. 199/J4
Avesnes-le-Comte, Fr. 110/B3
Avesnes-sur-Helpe, Fr. 110/C3
Avesta, Swe. 96/G1
Aveyron (riv.), Fr. 100/D4
Avezzano, It. 104/C1
Avich (lake), Sc, UK 94/A4
Aviemore, Sc, UK 94/C2
Avignon, Fr. 100/F5
Avihayil, Isr. 149/F7
Avila de los Caballeros, Sp. 102/C2
Avilés, Sp. 102/C1
Avio, It. 117/D1
Avion, Fr. 110/B2
Avis, Pa, US 196/A1
Avisio (riv.), It. 115/H5
Avize, Fr. 110/D6
Avlum, Den. 96/C3
Avoca, Austl. 173/C4
Avoca, Austl. 173/A3
Avola, Austl. 171/H4
Avola, It. 104/D4
Avon, Fr. 88/L6
Avon (riv.), Eng, UK 90/C6
Avon (riv.), Eng, UK 94/C1
Avon, Ct, US 197/G2
Avon, NJ, US 196/D3
Avon Valley NP, Austl. 170/C4
Avon Water (riv.), Sc, UK 94/B5
Avonbeg (riv.), Ire. 92/B6
Avondale, Az, US 195/R19
Avondale, NJ, US 196/C4
Avonlea, Sk, Can. 185/G3
Avonmore (riv.), Ire. 92/B5
Avranches, Fr. 100/C2
Avre (riv.), Fr. 98/B4
Avrillé, Fr. 100/C3
Awa-shima (isl.), Japan 134/A4
A'waj (riv.), Syria 149/E3
Awaji, Japan 135/H6

Awans, Belg. 111/E2
Awasa, Eth. 155/N6
Awash, Eth. 155/P6
Awash Wenz (riv.), Eth. 155/P5
Awaso, Gha. 161/E5
Awat, China 128/D3
Awbārī, Libya 154/H2
Awbārī (des.), Libya 157/H4
Awe (lake), Sc, UK 94/A4
Awjilah, Libya 155/K2
Awka, Nga. 161/G5
Awsīm, Egypt 149/B4
Ax-les-Thermes, Fr. 100/D5
Axamo (int'l arpt.), Swe. 96/F3
Axams, Aus. 115/H3
Axarfjördhur (inlet), Ice. 95/N6
Axel, Neth. 108/A6
Axel Heiberg (isl.), Nun., Can. 181/S7
Axim, Gha. 161/E5
Axios (riv.), Gre. 105/H2
Axis (dam), Wa, US 193/D2
Axminster, Eng, UK 90/D5
Axochiapan, Mex. 201/L8
Ay (riv.), Rus. 119/N5
Ay, Fr. 110/C5
Ayabaca, Peru 214/B2
Ayabe, Japan 135/H5
Ayacucho, Peru 214/C4
Ayacucho (dept.), Peru 214/C4
Ayacucho, Arg. 216/F3
Ayagöz, Kaz. 128/D2
Ayaguz (riv.), Kaz. 128/C2
Ayama, Japan 135/K6
Ayamé I, Barrage d' (dam), C.d'Iv. 160/E5
Ayamé II, Barrage d' (dam), C.d'Iv. 160/E5
Ayamonte, Sp. 102/B4
Ayancık, Turk. 148/C1
Ayanganna (mtn.), Guy. 211/G3
Ayapel, Col. 210/C2
Ayaş, Turk. 148/C1
Ayase, Japan 135/C3
Ayaviri, Peru 214/D4
Āybak, Afg. 145/E5
'Aybāl, Jabal (peak), WBnk. 149/G7
Aybastı, Turk. 148/D1
Aydar Kŭli (lake), Trkm. 145/E4
Aydın, Turk. 148/A2
Aydin (prov.), Turk. 148/B2
Aydıncık, Turk. 148/C1
Aydıncık, Turk. 149/C1
Aydınkent, Turk. 149/B1
Ayer, Swi. 114/D5
Ayers Rock (Uluru) (peak), Austl. 171/F3
Ayeyarwady (div.), Myan. 141/F4
Ayeyarwady (Irrawaddy) (riv.) Myan. 141/G4
Ayiá, Gre. 105/H3
Ayia Paraskeví, Gre. 105/K3
Ayiásos, Gre. 105/K3
Ayios Ioánnis (cape), Gre. 105/J5
Ayios Kírikos, Gre. 105/K4
Ayios Konstandínos, Gre. 105/H3
Ayios Matthaíos, Gre. 105/F3
Ayios Nikólaos, Gre. 105/J5
Aylesbury, Eng, UK 91/F3
Aylesford, Eng, UK 91/G4
Ayllón, Sp. 102/D2
Aylmer (lake), NW, Can. 180/F2
'Ayn al 'Arab, Syria 148/D2
'Ayn Zuwayyah (well), Libya 155/K3
Ayna, Peru 214/C4
Ayon (isl.), Rus. 123/S3
Ayora, Sp. 103/E3
Ayotzintepec, Mex. 202/B2
'Ayoûn 'Abd el Mâlek (well), Mrta. 156/D4
'Ayoûn el 'Atroûs, Mrta. 160/C2
Ayr, Austl. 171/B2
Ayr, Sc, UK 94/B6
Ayr (riv.), Sc, UK 94/B5
Aytré, Fr. 100/C3
Ayubia NP, Pak. 144/B3
Ayutla, Mex. 184/D4
Ayutla de los Libres, Mex. 198/B4
Ayutthaya (ruin), Thai. 136/C3
Ayvacık, Turk. 105/K3
Ayvalık, Turk. 148/A2
Aywaille, Belg. 111/E3
Az Zabadānī, Syria 149/E3
Az Ẓāhirīyah, WBnk. 149/D4
Az Zaqāzīq, Egypt 149/B4
Az Zarqā' (gov.), Jor. 149/E3
Az Zarqā', Jor. 149/E3
Az Zāwiyah, Libya 154/H1
Az Zaydīyah, Yem. 146/D5
Azad Kashmir (terr.), Pak. 144/B3
Azahar (coast), Sp. 103/F3
Azalea, Or, US 184/C5
Azalia, Mi, US 193/E7
Azamgarh, India 142/D2
Azángaro (riv.), Peru 214/D4
Azángaro, Peru 214/D4
Azao (peak), Alg. 157/H4
Azaouâd (phys. reg.), Mali 154/E4
Āzarān, Iran 146/E1
Āzarbāyjān-e Gharbī (prov.), Iran 148/F2
A'zāz, Syria 149/E1
Azemmour, Mor. 156/C2
Azerbaijan (ctry.) 121/H4
Azilal, Mor. 156/D3
Azīmganj, India 143/G3
Azogues, Ecu. 210/B5
Azores (dpcy.), Port. 103/R12
Azourki (peak), Mor. 156/D3
Azov, Rus. 120/F3
Azov (sea), Rus.,Ukr. 120/E3
Azoyú, Mex. 202/B2
Azpeitia, Sp. 102/D1
Azrou, Mor. 156/D2
Aztec, NM, US 186/F3
Aztec Ruins Nat'l Mon., NM, US 186/E3
Azua de Compostela, DRep. 199/G4
Azuaga, Sp. 102/C3
Azuara, Sp. 103/E2
Azuay (dept.), Ecu. 210/B5
Azuchi, Japan 135/K5
Azuero, Peninsula de (pen.), Pan. 208/B2
Azuga, Rom. 107/G3
Azul (mtn.), CR 203/E4
Azul (riv.), Guat. 202/D2
Azul, Arg. 216/F3
Azul, Cordillera (mts.), Peru 214/B2
Azuma, Japan 135/E2
Azuma-san (peak), Japan 133/G2
Azumaya-san (peak), Japan 133/F2
Azur, Côte d' (coast), Fr. 101/G5
Azusa, Ca, US 194/C2
Azzaba, Alg. 158/K6
Azzano Decimo, It. 117/F1
Azzano San Paolo, It. 116/C1
Azzate, It. 116/B1
'Azzūn, WBnk. 149/G7

B

Ba (riv.), Viet. 136/E3
Ba Lang An (cape), Viet. 136/E3
Ba Quan (cape), Viet. 136/D4
Baar, Swi. 115/E3
Baarle-Hertog, Belg. 108/B6
Baarle-Nassau, Neth. 108/B6
Baarn, Neth. 108/C4
Bab el Mandeb (str.), Asia 146/D6
Baba (mts.), Afg. 147/J2
Baba (peak), Bul. 105/H1
Baba (pt.), Turk. 107/K5
Baba Burnu (pt.), Turk. 105/K3
Babadag, Rom. 107/J3
Babaeski, Turk. 107/H5
Babahoyo, Ecu. 210/B5
Babai Khola (riv.), Nepal 142/C1
Babakale, Turk. 105/K3
Babar (isls.), Indo. 139/G5
Babatorun, Turk. 149/E1
Babatpur (int'l arpt.), India 142/D3
Babbacombe (bay), Eng, UK 90/C6
Babbitt, Mn, US 185/L4
B'abdā, Leb. 149/D3
Babelthuap (isl.), Palau 174/C4
Babenhausen, Ger. 115/G1
Babenhausen, Ger. 112/B3
Babensham, Ger. 113/F6
Baberu, India 142/C3
Babia (peak), Pol. 120/A2
Babian (riv.), China 141/H3
Bābil (gov.), Iraq 148/F3
Bābil (Babylon) (ruin), Iraq 148/F3
Babīna, India 142/B3
Babinda, Austl. 171/B2
Babine (riv.), BC, Can. 180/D3
Bābol, Iran 146/F1
Babruysk, Bela. 120/D1
Babuyan (isl.), Phil. 137/D4
Babylon, NY, US 197/E2
Bac Giang, Viet. 136/D1
Bac Lieu, Viet. 136/D4
Bac Ninh, Viet. 141/J3
Bacabal, Braz. 212/A2
Bacadéhuachi, Mex. 184/C2
Bacajá (riv.), Braz. 209/H4
Bacalar, Mex. 202/D2
Bacalar (lag.), Mex. 202/D2
Bacan (isl.), Indo. 139/G4
Bacău, Rom. 107/H2
Bacău (prov.), Rom. 107/H2
Baccarat, Fr. 114/C1
Bacchiglione (riv.), It. 117/E2
Bacchus, Ut, US 195/J12
Bacerac, Mex. 184/C2
Bacharach, Ger. 111/G3
Bachhraon, India 142/B1
Bachíniva, Mex. 184/D2
Back (riv.), Md, US 196/B5
Back (riv.), Nun., Can. 180/F2
Bačka (reg.), Serb. 106/D3
Bačka Palanka, Serb. 106/D3
Bačka Topola, Serb. 106/D3
Bäckefors, Swe. 96/E2
Backnang, Ger. 112/C5
Bacobampa, Mex. 184/C3
Bacolod, Phil. 139/F1
Bács-Kiskun (prov.), Hun. 106/D2
Bácsalmás, Hun. 106/D2
Bacup, Eng, UK 93/F4
Bad (riv.), SD, US 185/H5
Bad Abbach, Ger. 113/F5
Bad Axe, Mi, US 188/D3
Bad Bellingen, Ger. 114/D2
Bad Bergzabern, Ger. 112/A4
Bad Berneck, Ger. 113/E2
Bad Bocklet, Ger. 112/D2
Bad Brambach, Ger. 113/F2
Bad Breisig, Ger. 111/G3
Bad Brückenau, Ger. 112/C2
Bad Buchau, Ger. 115/F1
Bad Camberg, Ger. 112/B2
Bad Doberan, Ger. 96/D4
Bad Driburg, Ger. 109/G5
Bad Dürkheim, Ger. 112/B4
Bad Dürrheim, Ger. 115/E1
Bad Ems, Ger. 111/G3
Bad Endorf, Ger. 113/F7
Bad Essen, Ger. 109/F4
Bad Freienwalde, Ger. 99/H2
Bad Gandersheim, Ger. 109/H5
Bad Goisern, Aus. 101/K3
Bad Grund, Ger. 109/H5
Bad Hall, Aus. 113/H6
Bad Harzburg, Ger. 109/H5
Bad Heilbrunn, Ger. 115/H2
Bad Herrenalb, Ger. 112/B5
Bad Hersfeld, Ger. 101/H1
Bad Hofgastein, Aus. 101/K3
Bad Homburg vor der Höhe, Ger. 112/B2
Bad Honnef, Ger. 111/G2
Bad Hönningen, Ger. 111/G2
Bad Ischl, Aus. 101/K3
Bad Karlshafen, Ger. 109/G5
Bad Kissingen, Ger. 112/D2
Bad Kohlgrub, Ger. 115/H2
Bad König, Ger. 112/C3
Bad Königshofen, Ger. 112/D2
Bad Kreuznach, Ger. 111/G4
Bad Krozingen, Ger. 114/D2
Bad Langensalza, Ger. 109/H6
Bad Lauterberg, Ger. 109/H5
Bad Leonfelden, Aus. 113/H5
Bad Liebenzell, Ger. 112/B5
Bad Lippspringe, Ger. 109/F5
Bad Marienberg, Ger. 111/G2
Bad Mergentheim, Ger. 112/C4
Bad Munder am Deister, Ger. 109/G4
Bad Nauheim, Ger. 112/B2
Bad Nenndorf, Ger. 109/G4
Bad Neuenahr-Ahrweiler, Ger. 111/G2
Bad Neustadt an der Saale, Ger. 112/D2
Bad Oeynhausen, Ger. 109/F4
Bad Orb, Ger. 112/C2
Bad Peterstal-Griesbach, Ger. 114/E1
Bad Plaas, SAfr. 165/E2
Bad Pyrmont, Ger. 109/G5
Bad Ragaz, Swi. 115/F4
Bad Rappenau, Ger. 112/C4
Bad Reichenhall, Ger. 101/K3
Bad Rothenfelde, Ger. 109/F4
Bad Sachsa, Ger. 109/H5
Bad Salzdetfurth, Ger. 109/G4
Bad Salzschlirf, Ger. 112/C1
Bad Salzuflen, Ger. 109/F4
Bad Salzungen, Ger. 98/F3
Bad Sankt-Leonhard im Lavanttal, Aus. 101/L3
Bad Sassendorf, Ger. 109/F5
Bad Schallerbach, Aus. 113/G6
Bad Schwalbach, Ger. 111/H3
Bad Schwartau, Ger. 96/D5
Bad Segeberg, Ger. 96/D5
Bad Soden-Salmünster, Ger. 112/C2
Bad Sooden-Allendorf, Ger. 109/G6
Bad Tölz, Ger. 115/H2
Bad Vilbel, Ger. 112/B2
Bad Vöslau, Aus. 101/M3
Bad Waldsee, Ger. 115/F2
Bad Wildungen, Ger. 109/G6
Bad Wimpfen, Ger. 112/C4
Bad Wimsbach-Neydharting, Aus. 113/G6
Bad Windsheim, Ger. 112/D3
Bad Wörishofen, Ger. 115/G1
Bad Wurzach, Ger. 115/F2
Bad Zell, Aus. 113/H6
Bad Zwischenahn, Ger. 109/F2
Badagara, India 140/C5
Badain Jaran (des.), China 128/H3
Badajoz, Sp. 102/B3
Badalona, Sp. 103/L7
Badalucco, It. 116/A5
Badbergen, Ger. 109/E3
Baddeckenstedt, Ger. 109/H4
Baddomalhi, Pak. 144/C4
Baden, Aus. 101/M2
Baden, Swi. 115/E3
Baden-Baden, Ger. 112/B5
Baden-Württemberg (state), Ger. 101/H2
Badener (peak), Ger. 112/B5
Badenoch (reg.), Sc, UK 94/B3
Badenweiler, Ger. 114/D2
Badgastein, Aus. 101/K3
Badgingarra NP, Austl. 170/B4
Badia Polesine, It. 117/E2
Badiar, PN du, Gui. 160/B3
Badile (peak), It. 115/F5
Badīn, Pak. 147/J4
Badiraguato, Mex. 184/D3
Badlands (plat.), SD, US 185/H5
Badlands NP, SD, US 185/H5
Badonviller, Fr. 114/C1
Badou, Togo 161/F5
Badovinci, Serb. 106/D3
Bādrāh, Pak. 147/J3
Badrah, Iraq 146/E2
Badua (riv.), India 143/F3
Badulla, SrL. 140/D6
Bāduria, India 143/G4
Baena, Sp. 102/C4
Baependi, Braz. 213/J6
Baerenkopf (peak), Fr. 114/C2
Baesweiler, Ger. 111/F2
Baeza, Sp. 102/D4
Baffa, Pak. 144/B2
Baffin (bay), Can.,Grld. 177/K2
Baffin (isl.), Nun., Can. 181/H1
Baffin (bay), Tx, US 190/D5
Bafia, Camr. 154/H7
Bafilo, Togo 161/F4
Bafing (riv.), Gui. 154/C5
Bafoulabé, Mali 160/C3
Bafoussam, Camr. 154/H6
Bāfq, Iran 147/G2
Bafra, Turk. 148/C1
Bafra (cape), Turk. 148/C1
Bāft, Iran 147/G3
Bag Salt (lake), China 130/B3
Bagaces, CR 203/E4
Bagadó, Col. 210/B3
Bagaha, India 143/E2
Bagamoyo, Tanz. 162/C4
Baganga, Phil. 137/E6
Bagda (mts.), China 128/E3
Bagé, Braz. 215/F3
Bagenkop, Den. 96/D4
Baggao, Phil. 137/D4
Baggy (pt.), Eng, UK 90/B4
Bāgh, Pak. 144/B4
Baghain (riv.), India 142/C3
Baghdād (Baghdad) (cap.), Iraq 148/F3
Bagheria, It. 104/C3
Baghlān, Afg. 147/J1
Bāghpat, India 144/D5
Bağırpaşa (peak), Turk. 148/E2
Bagley, Mn, US 185/K4
Bāglung, Nepal 142/D1
Bāgmati (riv.), India 143/E2
Bāgmati (zone), Nepal 143/E2
Bagn, Nor. 96/C1
Bagnacavallo, It. 117/F4
Bagnasco, It. 116/B4
Bagnères-de-Bigorre, Fr. 100/D5
Bagnères-de-Luchon, Fr. 100/D5
Bagneux, Fr. 88/J5
Bagni di Lucca, It. 116/D4
Bagno a Ripoli, It. 117/E5
Bagnolet, Fr. 88/K5
Bagnoli Irpino, It. 104/D2
Bagnolo Cremasco, It. 116/C2
Bagnolo in Piano, It. 117/D3
Bagnolo Mella, It. 116/D2
Bagnolo San Vito, It. 117/D2
Bagnols-sur-Cèze, Fr. 100/F4
Bagnone, It. 116/C4
Bago, Phil. 137/D5
Bago (Pegu), Myan. 141/G4
Bago (div.), Myan. 141/G4
Bagoe (riv.), Mali 154/D5
Bagolino, It. 116/D1
Bagshot, Eng, UK 88/A3
Bagua Grande, Peru 214/B2
Baguio, Phil. 137/D4
Baguirmi (reg.), Chad 154/J5
Bagzane (peak), Niger 161/H2
Bāh, India 142/B2
Bahādurganj, India 143/F2
Bahādurgarh, India 144/D5
Bahamas, The (ctry.) 199/F2
Bahāwalnagar, Pak. 144/B5
Bahāwalpur, Pak. 144/A5
Bahçe, Turk. 148/D2
Bahçesaray, Turk. 148/E2
Baheri, India 142/B1
Bahi (swamp), Tanz. 162/B4
Bahia (state), Braz. 212/B4
Bahía Asunción, Mex. 184/B3
Bahía Blanca, Arg. 216/E3
Bahía de Caráquez, Ecu. 210/A5
Bahía de los Angeles, Mex. 184/B2
Bahía de Tortugas, Mex. 184/B3
Bahía, Islas de la (isls.), Hon. 198/D4
Bahía Solano, Col. 210/B3
Bahir Dar, Eth. 155/N5
Bahjoi, India 142/B1
Bahlah, Oman 147/G4
Baḩr al 'Arab (riv.), Sudan 155/L6
Baḩr al Milḩ (lake), Iraq 148/E3
Bahraich, India 142/C2
Bahrain (ctry.) 146/F3
Bahrain, Gulf of (gulf), Asia 146/F3
Baia de Aramă, Rom. 107/F3
Baia Mare, Rom. 107/F2
Baia Sprie, Rom. 107/F2
Baïbokoum, Chad 154/J6
Baicheng, China 128/D3
Baicheng, China 129/M2
Băicoi, Rom. 107/G3
Baidong (lake), China 130/D5
Baie-Comeau, Qu, Can. 189/G1
Baie-Saint-Paul, Qu, Can. 189/G2
Baienfurt, Ger. 115/F2
Baiersbronn, Ger. 112/B5
Baiersdorf, Ger. 112/E3
Baigorrita, Arg. 216/E2
Baigou (riv.), China 130/G7
Baihar, India 142/C4
Baihua (mtn.), China 130/G7
Ba'ījī, Iraq 148/E3
Baikunthpur, India 142/D4
Bailadores, Ven. 210/D2
Baildon, Eng, UK 93/G4
Băile Govora, Rom. 107/G3
Băile Herculane, Rom. 106/F3
Băile Olănești, Rom. 107/G3
Băile Tușnad, Rom. 107/G2
Bailén, Sp. 102/D3
Băilești, Rom. 107/F3
Bailieborough, Ire. 89/Q10
Bailleul, Fr. 110/B2
Bailong (riv.), China 128/H5
Bailu (riv.), China 130/C4
Baima, China 128/H5
Bain (riv.), Eng, UK 93/H5
Bainang, China 143/G1
Bainbridge, Ga, US 191/G4
Bainbridge, Pa, US 196/B3
Bainbridge (isl.), Wa, US 193/B2
Bainbridge Naval Training Sta., Md, US 196/B4
Baingoin, China 128/E5
Bains-les-Bains, Fr. 114/C2
Bairāgnia, India 143/E2
Baird (inlet), Ak, US 192/F3
Baird, Tx, US 187/H4
Bairin Youqi, China 129/L3
Bairnsdale, Austl. 173/C3
Baïse (riv.), Fr. 100/D5
Baixa da Banheira, Port. 103/P10
Baixa Grande, Braz. 212/B4
Baixiang, China 130/C3
Baixo Guandu, Braz. 213/D1
Baiyin, China 128/H4
Baiyu (mts.), China 130/B3
Baiyun (int'l arpt.), China 137/B3
Baja (pt.), Mex. 184/B2
Baja, Hun. 106/D2
Baja (pt.), Chile 217/B6
Baja California (state), Mex. 184/B2
Baja California (pen.), Mex. 184/B2
Baja California Sur (state), Mex. 184/B3
Bajánsenye, Hun. 101/M3
Bajestān, Iran 147/G2
Bājil, Yem. 146/D5
Bajina Bašta, Serb. 106/D4
Bajmbat (mt.), Austl. 173/E1
Bajmok, Serb. 106/D3
Bajo Boquete, Pan. 203/F4
Bajo de Gualicho (plain), Arg. 215/C5
Bajram Curri, Alb. 105/G1
Bakanas (riv.), Kaz. 145/G3
Bakau, Gam. 160/A3
Bakayan (peak), Indo. 139/E3
Bakel, Sen. 160/B3
Baker (lake), Nun., Can. 180/G2
Baker (riv.), Chile 217/B5
Baker (isl.), Pac., US 175/H4
Baker, La, US 187/K5
Baker, Mt, US 185/G4
Baker (mt.), Wa, US 184/C3
Baker City, Or, US 184/D4
Baker Lake, Nun., Can. 180/G2
Bakersfield, Ca, US 186/C4
Bakhchysaray, Ukr. 120/E3
Bakhmach, Ukr. 120/E2
Bākhtarān, Iran 146/E2
Bakhtiyārpur, India 143/E3
Bakhuis (mts.), Sur. 211/G4
Bakkaflói (bay), Ice. 95/P6
Baklan, Turk. 148/B2
Bakonyszombathely, Hun. 106/C2
Bakora Corridor Game Rsv., Ugan. 162/B2
Bakovský Potok (riv.), Czh. 113/G2
Bakoye (riv.), Gui. 160/C4
Baku (cap.), Azer. 121/J4
Baku (int'l arpt.), Azer. 121/J4
Balâ, Turk. 148/C2
Bala, Wal, UK 92/E6
Balabac, Phil. 139/E2
Balabac (str.), Malay.,Phil. 139/E2
Balabac (isl.), Phil. 139/E2
Ba'labakk, Leb. 149/E2
Bālāghāt, India 142/C5
Balaguer, Sp. 103/F2
Balaïtous (peak), Fr. 100/C5
Balaka, Malw. 163/F3
Balakhna, Rus. 119/J4
Balaklava, Austl. 171/H5
Balakovo, Rus. 121/H1
Bal'amā, Jor. 149/E3
Bălan, Rom. 107/G2
Balancán, Mex. 202/D2
Balanga, Phil. 137/D5
Bālāngīr, India 140/D3
Balao, Ecu. 214/B1
Balarāmpur, India 143/F4
Balashikha, Rus. 119/W9
Balashov, Rus. 121/G2
Balasore (Baleshwar), India 140/E3
Balassagyarmat, Hun. 99/K4
Balaton (lake), Cro. 106/C2
Balatonföldvár, Hun. 106/C2
Balatonfüred, Hun. 106/C2
Balatonszabadi, Hun. 106/D2
Balatonszentgyörgy, Hun. 106/C2
Balbina (res.), Braz. 205/D3
Balbriggan, Ire. 92/B4
Balcarce, Arg. 216/F3
Balcary (pt.), Sc, UK 92/E2
Balchik, Bul. 107/J4
Balclutha, NZ 175/R12
Balcones Escarpment (plat.), Tx, US 195/T20
Balcones Heights, Tx, US 195/T21
Bald (pt.), Austl. 170/C5
Bald Eagle Mtn. (mtn.), Pa, US 196/A1
Bald Rock NP, Austl. 173/E1
Baldock, Eng, UK 91/F3
Baldwin, NY, US 197/L9
Baldwin Harbour, NY, US 197/L9
Baldwin Park, Mo, US 195/E6
Baldwin Park, Ca, US 194/G7
Baldy (mtn.), Mb, Can. 185/H3
Baldy Beacon (peak), Belz. 202/D2
Bale Mountains NP, Eth. 155/N6
Baleares (Balearic) (isls.), Sp. 103/G3
Baleia, Ponta da (pt.), Braz. 212/C5
Baleine, Grand Rivière de la (riv.), Qu, Can. 181/J3
Baleine, Petite Rivière de la (riv.), Qu, Can. 181/J3
Baleine, Rivière à la (riv.), Qu, Can. 181/K3
Balen, Belg. 111/E1
Baler, Phil. 137/D4
Balerna, Swi. 115/F6
Balesa (riv.), Kenya 162/C2
Baleshwar (Balasore), India 140/E3
Balfour, SAfr. 164/E2
Balfron, Sc, UK 94/B4
Balgatay, Mong. 128/G2
Balhannah, Austl. 171/M8
Bali (sea), Indo. 138/D5
Bali (isl.), Indo. 138/D5
Bāli Chak, India 143/F4
Balice (int'l arpt.), Pol. 99/K3
Baliem (riv.), Indo. 139/J4
Balıkesir, Turk. 148/A2
Balıkesir (prov.), Turk. 148/A2
Balikpapan, Indo. 139/E4
Balimbing, Phil. 139/E2
Baling, Malay. 141/H6
Balingasag, Phil. 137/D6
Bälinge, Swe. 96/G2
Balingen, Ger. 115/E1
Balk, Neth. 108/C3
Balkan (pol. reg.), Trkm. 145/B4
Balkan (mts.), Bul.,Serb. 85/F3
Balkhash (lake), Kaz. 125/G5
Ballagan (pt.), Ire. 92/B4
Ballaghaderreen, Ire. 89/P10
Ballangen, Nor. 95/F1
Ballantrae, Sc, UK 92/C1
Ballarat, Austl. 173/B3
Ballard (lake), Austl. 167/B3
Ballarpur, India 140/C4
Ballater, Sc, UK 94/C2
Ballaugh, IM, UK 92/D3
Ballens, Swi. 114/C4
Balleny (isls.), Ant. 218/L
Ballia, India 143/E3
Ballina, Austl. 173/E1
Ballinamallard, NI, UK 89/Q9
Ballinasloe, Ire. 89/P10
Ballinderry (riv.), NI, UK 92/B2
Ballinger, Tx, US 187/H5
Ballingry, Sc, UK 94/C4
Ballinrobe, Ire. 89/P10
Balloch, Sc, UK 94/B2
Ballon, Col du (pass), Fr. 114/C2
Ballon d'Alsace (peak), Fr. 114/C2
Ballon de Sevance (peak), Fr. 114/C2
Ballwin, Mo, US 195/F8
Bally, Pa, US 196/C3
Ballycarry, NI, UK 92/C2
Ballycastle, NI, UK 92/B1
Ballycastle, Ire. 89/P9
Ballyclare, NI, UK 92/B2
Ballyeaston, NI, UK 92/B2
Ballygawley, NI, UK 92/A3
Ballygeary, Ire. 89/Q10
Ballygowan, NI, UK 92/C3
Ballyhaunis, Ire. 89/P10
Ballyheigue, Ire. 88/P10
Ballyliffin, Ire. 92/A1
Ballymena (dist.), NI, UK 92/B2
Ballymena, NI, UK 92/B2
Ballymoney (dist.), NI, UK 92/B1
Ballymoney, NI, UK 92/B1
Ballynahinch, NI, UK 92/C3
Ballynure, NI, UK 92/C2
Ballyquintin (pt.), NI, UK 92/C3
Ballyshannon, Ire. 89/P9
Balmaceda (peak), Chile 217/B6
Balmazújváros, Hun. 99/L5
Balmhorn (peak), Swi. 114/D5
Balmoral, Austl. 173/B3
Balmoral Castle, Sc, UK 94/C2
Balneário Camboriú, Braz. 213/B3
Balneario Claromecó, Arg. 216/E3
Balneario de los Novillos, PN, Mex. 187/G5
Balochistān (reg.), Pak. 147/J3
Balonne (riv.), Austl. 167/D3
Bālotra, India 147/K3
Balqash, Kaz. 145/G3
Balrāmpur, India 142/D2
Balranald, Austl. 173/B2
Balș, Rom. 107/G3
Bálsamo (pt.), Ecu. 210/A5
Balsapuerto, Peru 214/B2
Balsas, Braz. 212/A2
Balsas (riv.), Mex. 201/F5
Balsthal, Swi. 114/D3
Baltanás, Sp. 102/C2
Bălți, Mol. 107/H2
Baltic (sea), Swe. 95/F5
Baltic (plain), Rus. 119/S7
Baltic Spit (bar), Pol.,Rus. 97/H4
Baltīm, Egypt 149/B4
Baltimore, Md, US 196/B5
Baltimore (co.), Md, US 196/B4
Baltimore-Washington (int'l arpt.), Md, US 196/B5
Baltiysk, Rus. 97/H4
Baltray, Ire. 92/B4
Baltrum (isl.), Ger. 109/E1
Bælum, Den. 96/D3
Bālurghāt, India 143/G3
Balve, Ger. 109/E6
Balya, Turk. 120/C5
Balykshi, Kaz. 121/J3
Balzar, Ecu. 210/B5
Balzers, Lcht. 115/F3
Bam (prov.), Burk. 161/E3
Bam, Iran 147/G3
Bama Yaozu Zizhixian, China 141/J3
Bamaji (lake), On, Can. 185/K3
Bamako (cap.), Mali 160/D3
Bamako (Senou) (int'l arpt.), Mali 160/D3
Bambamarca, Peru 214/B2
Bambana (riv.), Nic. 203/E3
Bambari, CAfr. 155/K6
Bamberg, Ger. 112/D3
Bamberg, SC, US 191/H3
Bamble, Nor. 96/C2
Bambuí, Braz. 213/C2
Bamenda, Camr. 161/H5
Bāmīān, Afg. 145/E6
Bamingui-Bangoran, PN du, CAfr. 155/J6
Bammental, Ger. 112/B4
Bampūr (riv.), Iran 147/H3
Ban Boun Tai, Laos 141/H3
Ban Chiang (ruin), Thai. 136/C2
Ban Houayxay, Laos 141/H3
Ban Kantang, Thai. 136/B5
Ban Kengkok, Laos 141/J4
Ban Pak Phanang, Thai. 136/C4
Banaba (isl.), Kiri. 174/F5
Banagher, Ire. 89/Q10
Banamba, Mali 160/D3
Banana (isls.), SLeo. 160/B4
Bananal, Braz. 213/J7
Bananal, Ilha do (isl.), Braz. 209/H6
Banar (riv.), Bang. 143/H3
Banarlı, Turk. 107/H5
Banās (pt.), Egypt 159/C4
Banās (riv.), India 147/L3
Banat (reg.), Serb. 106/E3
Banatsko Novo Selo, Serb. 106/E3
Banaz, Turk. 148/B2
Banbar, China 128/G5
Banbridge, NI, UK 92/B3
Banbridge (dist.), NI, UK 92/B3
Banbury, Eng, UK 91/E2
Banc d'Arguin, Mrta. 156/A5
Banc d'Arguin, PN du, Mrta. 154/B3
Banc d'Arguin, PN du, Mrta. 160/A2
Banchette, It. 116/A2
Banchory, Sc, UK 94/D2
Banco Chinchorro (isls.), Mex. 198/D4
Bancroft, On, Can. 188/E2
Banda (isls.), Indo. 139/H4
Bāndā, India 142/C3
Banda, India 142/B3
Banda (sea), Indo. 139/G5
Banda Aceh, Indo. 138/A2
Bandai-san (peak), Japan 133/G2
Bandama (riv.), C.d'Iv. 154/D6
Bandama Blanc (riv.), C.d'Iv. 160/D4
Bandama Rouge (riv.), C.d'Iv. 160/D4
Bandar Beheshtī, Iran 147/H3
Bandar-e 'Abbās, Iran 147/G3
Bandar-e Anzalī, Iran 146/E1
Bandar-e Deylam, Iran 146/F2
Bandar-e Lengeh, Iran 147/F3
Bandar-e Māhshahr, Iran 146/E2
Bandar-e Torkeman, Iran 146/F1
Bandar Seri Begawan (cap.),Bru. 138/D3
Bande, Sp. 102/B1
Bandeira do Sul, Braz. 213/G6
Bandeira, Pico da (peak), Braz. 213/D2
Bandeirantes, Braz. 213/B2
Bandelier Nat'l Mon., NM, US 187/F4
Bandera, Tx, US 187/H5
Banderilla, Mex. 201/N7
Bandhavgarh NP, India 142/C4
Bandholm, Den. 96/D4
Bandiagara, Mali 160/E3
Bandipura, India 144/C2
Bandırma (gulf), Turk. 107/H5
Bandırma, Turk. 107/H5
Bandon, Ire. 89/P11
Bandon (riv.), Ire. 89/P11
Bandundu, D.R. Congo 163/C1
Bandung, Indo. 138/C5
Bañeres, Sp. 103/E3
Banes, Cuba 203/H1
Banff, Ab, Can. 184/E3
Banff, Sc, UK 94/D1
Banff NP, Ab, Can. 184/E3
Banfora, Burk. 160/D4
Bang Lang (res.), Thai. 136/C5
Banga, Phil. 137/D6
Banga, India 144/C4
Bangalore, India 140/C5
Bangalow, Austl. 171/D5
Bangaon, India 143/G4
Bangarmau, India 142/C2
Bangassou, CAfr. 155/K7
Bangau (cape), Malay. 139/E2
Banggai (isls.), Indo. 139/F4
Banghiang (riv.), Laos 136/D2
Bangka (str.), Indo. 138/B4
Bangka (isl.), Indo. 138/C4
Bangkok (Krung Thep) (cap.),Thai. 136/C3
Bangkok (int'l arpt.), Thai. 136/C3
Bangkok, Bight of (bay), Thai. 141/H5
Bangladesh (ctry.) 140/E3
Bangor, NI, UK 92/C2
Bangor (int'l arpt.), Me, US 189/G2
Bangor, Me, US 189/G2
Bangor, Pa, US 196/C2
Bangor, Wal, UK 92/D5
Bangued, Phil. 137/D4
Bangui (cap.), CAfr. 155/J7
Bangweulu (swamp), Zam. 162/A5
Bangweulu (lake), Zam. 163/E3
Banhā, Egypt 149/B4
Banhine, PN de, Moz. 163/F5
Bani (riv.), Mali 154/D5
Baní, DRep. 199/G4
Banī Mazār, Egypt 159/B2
Banī Suhaylah, Gaza 149/D4
Banī Suwayf (gov.), Egypt 159/B1
Banī Suwayf, Egypt 159/B2
Bánica, DRep. 203/J2
Banifing (riv.), Mali 160/D3
Banihāl (pass), India 144/C3
Banikoara, Ben. 161/F4
Banister (riv.), Va, US 191/J2
Bāniyās, Syria 149/D2
Banja Koviljača, Serb. 106/D3
Banja Luka, Bosn. 106/C3
Banjarmasin, Indo. 138/D4
Banjul (cap.), Gam. 160/A3
Bānka, India 143/F3
Bankas, Mali 160/E3
Bankeryd, Swe. 96/F3
Bankfoot, Sc, UK 94/C3
Bankhead, Sc, UK 94/D2
Bānki, India 143/E4

Banks (cape), Austl. 173/B3
Banks (str.), Austl. 173/C4
Banks (isl.), NW, Can. 180/D2
Banks (pen.), NZ 175/S11
Banks (pt.), Ak, US 192/H4
Banks (lake), Wa, US 184/D4
Banks (isls.), Van. 174/F6
Bānkurā, India 143/F4
Bankya, Bul. 105/H1
Banmankhi, India 143/F3
Bann (riv.), Ire. 89/Q10
Bann (riv.), NI, UK 92/B3
Banna (riv.), It. 116/A3
Bannockburn, Sc, UK 94/C4
Bannockburn Battlesite, Sc, UK 94/C4
Bannu, Pak. 144/A3
Baños, Ecu. 214/B1
Banpo Ruins, China 130/B4
Bansberia, India 143/G4
Bānsdīh, India 143/E3
Bānsi, India 142/D2
Bansin, Ger. 96/F5
Banská Bystrica, Slvk. 99/K4
Banská Štiavnica, Slvk. 106/D1
Bansko, Bul. 105/H2
Banskobystrický (pol. reg.), Slvk. 99/K4
Banstead, Eng, UK 88/C3
Bānswāra, India 147/K4
Bantayan, Phil. 137/D5
Banté, Ben. 161/F4
Bantenan (cape), Indo. 138/D5
Bantong Group (isls.), Thai. 136/B5
Bantry, Ire. 89/P11
Bañuelo (peak), Sp. 102/C3
Banyak (isls.), Indo. 138/A3
Banyoles, Sp. 103/G1
Banyuwangi, Indo. 138/D5
Banzare (coast), Ant. 218/J
Baode, China 130/B3
Baodi, China 130/H7
Baoding, China 130/G7
Baofeng, China 130/C4
Baoji, China 128/J5
Baojing, China 141/J2
Baokang, China 130/B5
Baoruco (mts.), DRep. 203/J2
Baoshan, China 141/G2
Baoshan, China 130/L8
Baotou, China 130/B2
Baoulé (riv.), Mali 154/D5
Baoying, China 130/D4
Bapaume, Fr. 110/B3
Bapchule, Az, US 195/S19
Baptistown, NJ, US 196/C2
Bāqa el Gharbiyya, Isr. 149/G7
Baqên, China 128/F5
Ba'qūbah, Iraq 148/F3
Bar, Mont. 106/D4
Bar (riv.), Fr. 98/C4
Bar Bigha, India 143/E3
Bar el Ksaïb (well), Mali 156/D5
Bar Harbor, Me, US 189/G2
Bar-le-Duc, Fr. 111/E6
Bar-sur-Aube, Fr. 100/F2
Bar-sur-Seine, Fr. 100/F2
Bara, Swe. 96/E4
Bāra Banki, India 142/C2
Bārā Lācha La (pass), India 144/D3
Barabai, Indo. 138/E4
Barabinsk, Rus. 145/G1
Baraboo, Wi, US 185/L5
Baracaldo, Sp. 102/D1
Baracoa, Cuba 203/H1
Barada (riv.), Syria 149/E3
Baradero, Arg. 217/J10
Baradine, Austl. 173/D1
Baragoi, Kenya 162/C2
Baraguá, Cuba 203/G1
Baragua, Ven. 210/D2
Barajas (int'l arpt.), Sp. 103/N9
Barajevo, Serb. 106/E3
Barākar (riv.), India 143/F3
Barakī Barak, Afg. 147/J2
Baralaba, Austl. 171/C4
Baram (cape), Malay. 138/D3
Baram (riv.), Malay. 138/D3
Barama (riv.), Guy. 208/F2
Baramanni, Guy. 211/G3
Baramula, India 144/C2
Bāran, India 147/L3
Baranagar, India 143/G4
Baranavichy, Bela. 120/C1
Barani (well), Alg. 156/E4
Baranoa, Col. 210/C2
Baranof (isl.), Ak, US 192/L4
Baranya (prov.), Hun. 106/C3
Barão de Cocais, Braz. 213/D1
Barão de Grajaú, Braz. 212/B2
Baraolt, Rom. 107/G2
Baraque de Fraiture (hill), Belg. 111/E3
Barat Daya (isls.), Indo. 139/G5
Barataria, La, US 195/P17
Barauli, India 143/E2
Baraut, India 144/D5
Baraya, Col. 210/C4
Barbacena, Braz. 213/D2
Barbacoas, Col. 210/B4
Barbados (ctry.) 199/P9
Barbalha, Braz. 212/C2
Barbaros, Turk. 107/H5
Barbas (cape), Mor. 156/A5
Barbastro, Sp. 103/F1
Barbate de Franco, Sp. 102/C4
Barbeau (peak), Nun., Can. 181/T6
Barberà del Vallès, Sp. 103/L6
Barberino di Mugello, It. 117/E5
Barbers (pt.), Hi, US 182/V13
Barberton, Oh, US 188/D3
Barberton, SAfr. 165/E2
Barbona (peak), It. 116/D5
Barbosa, Col. 210/C3
Barbourville, Ky, US 188/D4
Barbuda (isl.), Anti. 199/N8
Barcaldine, Austl. 171/B3
Barcarrota, Sp. 102/B3
Barcău (riv.), Rom. 106/F2
Barcellona Pozzo di Gotto, It. 104/D3
Barcelona, Ven. 211/E2
Barcelona, Sp. 103/L7
Barcelona (int'l arpt.), Sp. 103/L7
Barcelos, Port. 102/A2
Barcelos, Braz. 211/F5
Barcin, Pol. 99/J2
Barcoo (riv.), Austl. 167/D3
Barcs, Hun. 106/C3
Barczewo, Pol. 97/J5
Bardejov, Slvk. 99/L4
Bardi, It. 116/C3
Bardīyah, Libya 155/L1
Bārdoli, India 147/K4
Bardolino, It. 117/D1
Bardonia, NY, US 197/K7
Bardsdale, Ca, US 194/B2
Bardsey (isl.), Wal, UK 92/D6
Bardstown, Ky, US 188/C4
Bareggio, It. 116/B2
Bareli, India 142/B4
Barellan, Austl. 173/C2
Barendrecht, Neth. 108/B5
Barentin, Fr. 100/D2
Barents (sea), Eur. 122/D2
Barentu, Erit. 146/C5
Bäretswil, Swi. 115/E3
Barfleur, Pointe de (pt.), Fr. 100/C2
Barga, It. 116/D4
Bargara, Austl. 171/D4
Bargarh, India 140/D3
Bargfeld-Stegen, Ger. 109/H1
Bargi, India 142/B4
Bargo, Austl. 173/D2
Bargteheide, Ger. 109/H1
Bārh, India 143/E3
Barhaj, India 142/D2
Barhalganj, India 142/D2
Barham, Austl. 173/C2
Barhiya, India 143/F3
Bāri, India 142/A2
Bari, It. 104/E2
Bari Sardo, It. 104/A3
Bariano, It. 116/C1
Baricella, It. 117/E3
Barichara, Col. 210/C3
Barīdī (pt.), SAr. 146/C4
Barigazzo (peak), It. 116/C3
Barika, Alg. 158/H5
Barillas, Guat. 202/D3
Barima (riv.), Guy. 211/G2
Barima-Waini (pol. reg.), Guy. 211/F3
Barinas (state), Ven. 210/D2
Barinas, Ven. 210/D2
Barinitas, Ven. 210/D2
Bariri, Braz. 213/B2
Barisāl (pol. reg.), Bang. 143/H4
Barisan Mountains (mts.), Indo. 138/B4
Barito (riv.), Indo. 138/D4
Baritu, PN, Arg. 215/D1
Bark (lake), On, Can. 188/E2
Bark (riv.), Wi, US 193/N13
Barka Kāna, India 143/E4
Barker, NY, US 189/S9
Barki Saria, India 143/E3
Barking and Dagenham (bor.), Eng, UK 88/D2
Barkley (sound), BC, Can. 184/B3
Barkley (lake), Ky,Tn, US 191/G2
Barkly East, SAfr. 164/D3
Barkly Tableland (plat.), Austl. 167/C2
Barkly West, SAfr. 164/D3
Barkol Kazak Zizhixian, China 128/F3
Barlee (lake), Austl. 167/A3
Barlee (range), Austl. 170/B2
Barlee Range Nature Rsv., Austl. 170/B2
Barletta, It. 104/E2
Barlin, Fr. 110/B3
Barlinek, Pol. 99/H2
Barmedman, Austl. 173/C2
Barmera, Austl. 171/J5
Barmstedt, Ger. 109/G1
Barnāla, India 144/C4
Bärnbach, Aus. 101/L3
Barnegat (inlet), NJ, US 196/D4
Barnegat (bay), NJ, US 196/D4
Barnegat, NJ, US 196/D4
Barnegat Light, NJ, US 196/D4
Barneveld, Neth. 108/C4
Barnhart, Mo, US 195/G9
Barnoldswick, Eng, UK 93/F4
Barnsley, Eng, UK 93/G4
Barnsley (co.), Eng, UK 93/G5
Barnstaple, Eng, UK 90/B4
Barnstaple (Bideford) (bay), Eng, UK 90/B4
Barnstorf, Ger. 109/F3
Barntrup, Ger. 109/G5
Barnwell, SC, US 191/H3
Baroghil (pass), Pak. 145/F5
Baron, Fr. 88/L4
Barone (peak), It. 116/B1
Barow (riv.), Ire. 92/A5
Barowghīl (pass), Afg. 147/K1
Barquisimeto, Ven. 210/D2
Barquisimeto (int'l arpt.), Ven. 210/D2
Barr (lake), Co, US 195/C3
Barr, Co, US 195/C3
Barr, Fr. 114/D1
Barra, Braz. 212/B3
Barra (isl.), Sc, UK 89/Q8
Barra Bonita, Braz. 213/B2
Barra Bonita, Represa de (res.), Braz. 213/B2
Barra da Choça, Braz. 212/B4
Barra del Colorado, PN, CR 198/E5
Barra do Bugres, Braz. 209/G7
Barra do Corda, Braz. 212/A2
Barra do Garças, Braz. 209/H7
Barra do Mendes, Braz. 212/B3
Barra do Piraí, Braz. 213/K7
Barra do Ribeiro, Braz. 213/B4
Barra Head (pt.), Sc, UK 89/Q8
Barra Mansa, Braz. 213/J7
Barra Velha, Braz. 213/B3
Barraba, Austl. 173/D1
Barrackpur, India 143/G4
Barrage de Lagdo (dam), Camr. 154/H6
Barranca, Peru 214/B3
Barranca, Peru 214/B2
Barranca de Upía, Col. 210/C3
Barranca del Cobre PN, Mex. 184/D3
Barrancabermeja, Col. 210/C3
Barrancas, Ven. 211/F2
Barrancas, Col. 210/C2
Barrancas, Chile 216/N8
Barranco de Loba, Col. 210/C2
Barrancos, Port. 102/B3
Barranquilla, Col. 210/C2
Barras, Braz. 212/B2
Barreal, Arg. 215/C3
Barreiras, Braz. 212/A4
Barreirinhas, Braz. 212/B1
Barreiro, Port. 103/P10
Barreiros, Braz. 212/D3
Barren (isl.), Madg. 165/G7
Barren, Nosy (Barren Islands) (isls.), Madg. 165/G7
Barretal, Mex. 201/F3
Barretos, Braz. 213/B2
Barrhead, Ab, Can. 184/E2
Barrhead, Sc, UK 94/B5
Barrie, On, Can. 188/E2
Barrier (range), Austl. 171/J4
Barrington, Il, US 193/P15
Barrington Hills, Il, US 193/P15
Barrington Tops (peak), Austl. 173/D1
Barrington Tops NP, Austl. 173/D1
Barro Duro, Braz. 212/B2
Barron Gorge NP, Austl. 171/B2
Barroso, Braz. 213/D2
Barrouallie, StV. 199/N9
Barrow, Ak, US 192/G1
Barrow (pt.), Ak, US 192/G1
Barrow (isl.), Austl. 167/A3
Barrow (riv.), Ire. 89/Q10
Barrow (pt.), Austl. 171/B1
Barrow (str.), Nun., Can. 180/G1
Barrow-in-Furness, Eng, UK 93/E3
Barrow Island, Austl. 170/B2
Barrowford, Eng, UK 93/F4
Barruelo de Santullán, Sp. 102/C1
Barry, Wal, UK 90/C4
Barsakel'mes (lake), Uzb. 145/C4
Barsinghausen, Ger. 109/G4
Barssel, Ger. 109/E2
Barstow, Ca, US 186/C4
Bartang (riv.), Taj. 145/F5
Bartenheim, Fr. 114/D2
Barth, Ger. 96/E4
Bartholomä, Ger. 112/C5
Bartholomäberg, Aus. 115/F3
Bartica, Guy. 211/G3
Bartın, Turk. 107/L5
Bartle Frere (peak), Austl. 167/D2
Bartlesville, Ok, US 187/J3
Bartlett, Tx, US 187/H5
Bartlett (dam), Az, US 195/S18
Bartlett (res.), Az, US 195/S18
Bartlett, Il, US 193/P16
Bartolomé Masó, Cuba 203/G1
Bartolomeu Dias, Moz. 163/G5
Bartonsville, Pa, US 196/C2
Bartoszyce, Pol. 97/J4
Bartow, Fl, US 191/H5
Bartow, Ger. 96/E5
Barú (vol.), Pan. 203/F4
Bāruipur, India 143/G4
Barumun (riv.), Indo. 138/B3
Barus, Indo. 138/A3
Baruun-Urt, Mong. 129/K2
Barwa Sāgar, India 142/B3
Barwāha, India 147/L4
Barwāla, India 144/C5
Barwon (riv.), Austl. 167/D3
Barycz (riv.), Pol. 99/J3
Barysaw, Bela. 97/N4
Barysh, Rus. 121/H1
Barzanò, It. 116/C1
Bas-Rhin (dept.), Fr. 114/D1
Basaldella, It. 117/G1
Basauri, Sp. 102/D1
Basavilbaso, Arg. 217/J10
Bascharage, Lux. 111/E4
Basehor, Ks, US 195/D5
Basel, Swi. 114/D2
Basel/Mulhouse (int'l arpt.), Fr. 114/D2
Baselga di Pinè, It. 115/H5
Baselland (canton), Swi. 114/D3
Bashee (riv.), SAfr. 164/E3
Bashi (chan.), Phil.,Tai. 137/C3
Bashkortostan, Resp., Rus. 122/Q6
Bāsht, Iran 146/F2
Basilan (isl.), Phil. 139/F2
Basilan (peak), Phil. 139/F2
Basildon, Eng, UK 91/G3
Basilica di Fieschi, It. 116/C4
Basilicata (reg.), It. 104/D2
Basingstoke, Eng, UK 91/E4
Basingstoke (canal), Eng, UK 88/A3
Basīrhāt, India 143/G4
Basīrpur, Pak. 144/B4
Başkale, Turk. 148/F2
Baskatong (res.), Qu, Can. 188/F2
Baskil, Turk. 148/D2
Başkomutan NP, Turk. 148/B2
Bāsoda, India 142/A4
Basodino (peak), It. 115/E5
Basoko, D.R. Congo 155/K7
Basoli, India 144/C3
Bass (str.), Austl. 167/D4
Bass Rock (isl.), Sc, UK 94/D4
Bassae (Vassés) (ruin), Gre. 105/G4
Bassano, Ab, Can. 184/E3
Bassano del Grappa, It. 117/E1
Bassari, Togo 161/F4
Bassas da India (isl.), Reun., Fr. 163/G5
Basse-Normandie (pol. reg.), Fr. 100/C2
Basse Santa Su, Gam. 160/B3
Basse-Terre, Guad., Fr. 199/N8
Basse-Terre (isl.), Guad., Fr. 199/J4
Bassecourt, Swi. 114/D3
Bassein (riv.), Myan. 141/F4
Bassein (Vasai), India 147/K5
Bassenge, Belg. 111/E2
Bassenheim, Ger. 111/G3
Bassenthwaite (lake), Eng, UK 93/E2
Basseterre (cap.), StK. 199/N8
Bassum, Ger. 109/F3
Basswood (lake), Can.,US 188/B1
Båstad, Swe. 96/E3
Bastak, Iran 147/F3
Bastām, Iran 147/G1
Bastelicaccia, Fr. 104/A2
Bastheim, Ger. 112/D2
Bastī, India 142/D2
Bastia, Fr. 104/A1
Bastia, It. 101/K5
Bastogne, Belg. 111/E4
Bastos, Braz. 213/B2
Bastrop, Tx, US 187/H5
Basyūn, Egypt 149/B4
Bat Shelomo, Isr. 149/F6
Bat Yam, Isr. 149/F7
Bata, EqG. 154/G7
Batabanó (gulf), Cuba 198/E3
Batac, Phil. 137/D4
Batagay, Rus. 123/P3
Batai (pass), Pak. 144/A3
Batalha, Braz. 212/B2
Batalha, Port. 102/A3
Batan (isls.), Phil. 137/D3
Batang, China 128/G6
Batangafo, CAfr. 155/J6
Batangas, Phil. 137/D5
Batarasa, Phil. 137/C6
Batatais, Braz. 213/C2
Batavia, NY, US 188/E3
Batavia, Il, US 193/P16
Bataysk, Rus. 120/F3
Batchtown, Il, US 195/F7
Bătdâmbang, Camb. 136/C3
Bate (bay), Austl. 171/H9
Batéké (plat.), Congo 154/H8
Batemans Bay, Austl. 173/D2
Batesburg-Leesville, SC, US 191/H3
Batesville, Ms, US 187/K4
Bath, Me, US 189/G3
Bath, NY, US 188/E3
Bath, Eng, UK 90/D4
Bath, Pa, US 196/C2
Bath and Northeast Somerset (co.), Eng, UK 90/D4
Bathgate, Sc, UK 94/C5
Bathmen, Neth. 108/D4
Bathurst, Austl. 173/D2
Bathurst (cape), NW, Can. 192/N1
Bathurst, NB, Can. 189/H2
Bathurst (isl.), Nun., Can. 181/R7
Bathurst (inlet), Nun., Can. 180/F2
Bathurst Inlet, Nun., Can. 180/F2
Batian (Mt. Kenya) (peak), Kenya 162/C3
Batiquitos (lag.), Ca, US 194/C4
Batiscan (riv.), Qu, Can. 189/F2
Batley, Eng, UK 93/G4
Batlow, Austl. 173/D2
Batman, Turk. 148/E2
Batman (dam), Turk. 148/E2
Batna (prov.), Alg. 157/G2
Batna, Alg. 158/J5
Baton Rouge (cap.), La, US 187/K5
Batopilas, Mex. 184/D3
Batoti, India 144/C3
Batouri, Camr. 154/H7
Baṭrā' (Petra) (ruin), Jor. 149/D4
Båtsfjord, Nor. 95/J1
Batsto (riv.), NJ, US 196/D4
Batsto, NJ, US 196/D4
Batsto Historic Village, NJ, US 196/D4
Battaglia Terme, It. 117/E2
Battenberg, Ger. 109/F6
Bätterkinden, Swi. 114/D3
Batticaloa, SrL. 140/D6
Battipaglia, It. 104/D2
Battle, Eng, UK 91/G5
Battle (riv.), Ab,Sk, Can. 180/E3
Battle Creek, Mi, US 188/C3
Battle Mountain, Nv, US 184/D5
Battleford, Sk, Can. 184/F2
Battock (mt.), Sc, UK 94/D3
Batu (peak), Eth. 155/N6
Batu (cape), Indo. 139/E3
Batu (isls.), Indo. 138/A4
Batu (bay), Malay. 138/D3
Batu (peak), Malay. 138/D3
Batu Gajah, Malay. 138/B3
Batu Pahat, Malay. 138/B3
Batu Puteh (peak), Malay. 138/B3
Batudaka (isl.), Indo. 139/F4
Batuensambang (peak), Indo. 138/D3
Bat'umi, Geo. 121/G4
Bat'umi (int'l arpt.), Geo. 121/G4
Baturaja, Indo. 138/B4
Baturité, Braz. 212/C2
Batys Qazaqstan, Kaz. 122/E5
Bauchi (state), Nga. 161/H4
Bauchi, Nga. 161/H4
Baudette, Mn, US 185/K3
Baudó (mts.), Col. 210/B3
Baudó (riv.), Col. 210/B3
Bauer, Ut, US 195/J13
Bauld (cape), Nf, Can. 189/L1
Baulmes, Swi. 114/C4
Bauman (peak), Togo 161/F5
Baume-les-Dames, Fr. 114/C3
Baumholder, Ger. 111/G4
Baunach, Ger. 112/D3
Baunach (riv.), Ger. 112/D2
Baunatal, Ger. 109/G6
Baunei, It. 104/A2
Baurú, Braz. 213/B2
Bautzen, Ger. 99/H3
Bavans, Fr. 114/C3
Bavarian Alps (mts.), Aus.,Ger. 115/G3
Bavay, Fr. 110/C3
Båven (lake), Swe. 96/G2
Baveno, It. 115/E6
Baviácora, Mex. 184/C2
Bavilliers, Fr. 114/C2
Bavispe, Río de (riv.), Mex. 184/C2
Baw Baw (mt.), Austl. 173/C3
Baw Baw NP, Austl. 173/C3
Bawāna, India 144/D5
Bawang (cape), Indo. 138/C4
Bawean (isl.), Indo. 138/D5
Bawku, Gha. 161/E4
Baxoi, China 141/G2
Bay City, Mi, US 188/D3
Bay City, Tx, US 187/J5
Bay Minette, Al, US 191/G4
Bay Roberts, Nf, Can. 189/L2
Bay Saint Louis, Ms, US 191/F4
Bayamo, Cuba 203/G1
Bayamón, PR 199/M8
Bayan, Mong. 128/G2
Bayan Har (mts.), China 128/G5
Bayan-Hongor (prov.), Mong. 128/G2
Bayan-Ölgiy (prov.), Mong. 128/E2
Bayan-Ulaan, Mong. 128/H2
Bayanaul'skiy NP, Kaz. 145/G2
Bayanhongor, Mong. 128/H2
Bayanhushuu, Mong. 128/F2
Bayannuur, Mong. 128/F2
Bayano (lake), Pan. 203/G4
Bayanterem, Mong. 129/K2
Bayantsagaan, Mong. 128/H2
Bayard, Ne, US 185/H5
Bayat, Turk. 148/C1
Bayawan, Phil. 139/F2
Baybach (riv.), Ger. 111/G3
Baybay, Phil. 137/D5
Bayburt, Turk. 148/E1
Bayburt (prov.), Turk. 148/E1
Baydaratskaya (bay), Rus. 122/G2
Baydhabo (Baidoa), Som. 155/P7
Bayel, Fr. 114/A1
Bayerischer Wald (hills), Ger. 113/F4
Bayerischer Wald NP, Ger. 113/G5
Bayern (state), Ger. 98/F4
Bayeux, Braz. 212/D2
Bayeux, Fr. 100/C2
Baygorria (res.), Uru. 217/K10
Baykal (mts.), Rus. 123/L4
Baykal (lake), Rus. 125/L4
Baykan, Turk. 148/E2
Bayombong, Phil. 137/D4
Bayon, Fr. 114/C1
Bayona, Sp. 102/A1
Bayonet Point, Fl, US 191/H4
Bayonne, Fr. 100/C5
Bayonne, NJ, US 197/J9
Bayport, NY, US 197/E2
Bayramaly, Trkm. 147/H1
Bayramıç, Turk. 105/K3
Bayreuth, Ger. 113/E3
Bayrūt (Beirut) (cap.), Leb. 149/D3
Bays, Lake of (lake), On, Can. 188/E2
Bayşehir (lake), Turk. 148/B2
Bayt Ḥanīnā, WBnk. 149/G8
Bayt Ḥānūn, Gaza 149/D4
Bayt Laḥm (Bethlehem), WBnk. 149/G8
Bayt Sāḥūr, WBnk. 149/G8
Baytik Shan (mts.), China,Mong. 128/E2
Baytown, Tx, US 187/J5
Bayudha (des.), Sudan 159/C5
Bayugan, Phil. 137/E6
Bayville, NY, US 197/L8
Baza, Sp. 102/D4
Bazainville, Fr. 88/G5
Bazardüzü (peak), Azer. 121/H4
Bazaruto, Ilha do (isl.), Moz. 163/G5
Bazèga (prov.), Burk. 161/E4
Bazemont, Fr. 88/H5
Bazet, Fr. 100/D5
Bazhong, China 128/J5
Bazin (riv.), Qu, Can. 188/F2
Bāzpur, India 142/B1
Bazzano, It. 117/E3
Be, Nosy (isl.), Madg. 165/H6
Beach Haven, NJ, US 196/D4
Beachport, Austl. 173/B3
Beachwood, NJ, US 196/D4
Beachy Head (pt.), Eng, UK 91/G5
Beacon (peak), Wal, UK 90/C2
Beaconsfield, Austl. 173/C4
Beaconsfield, Eng, UK 91/F3
Beaconsfield, Qu, Can. 189/N7
Beal (range), Austl. 171/A4
Bealanana, Madg. 165/J6
Beale (cape), BC, Can. 184/B3
Beampingaratra (ridge), Madg. 165/H9
Bear (isl.), Nor. 218/E
Bear (riv.), US 186/E2
Bear (mt.), Ak, US 192/K3
Bear (mtn.), Ak, US 192/K2
Bear, De, US 196/C4
Bear (lake), Ut, US 186/E2
Bear Creek (lake), Co, US 195/B3
Bear River (bay), Ut, US 195/J11
Bear River Migratory Bird Refuge (nat'l wild. ref.), Ut, US 195/J10
Beardsley, Az, US 195/R18
Beardsley (canal), Az, US 195/R18
Bearfort (mtn.), NJ, US 197/H7
Bearma (riv.), India 142/B4
Bearpaw (mts.), Mt, US 184/F3
Bearsden, Sc, UK 94/B5
Beartooth (mts.), Mt,Wy, US 184/F4
Beās (riv.), India 142/B3
Beas de Segura, Sp. 102/D3
Beasain, Sp. 102/D1
Beata (isl.), DRep. 203/J2
Beata (cape), DRep. 203/J2
Beatenberg, Swi. 114/D4
Beatty, Nv, US 186/C3
Beattystown, NJ, US 196/D2
Beau Bassin-Rose Hill, Mrts. 165/T15
Beaucaire, Fr. 100/F5
Beaucamps-le-Vieux, Fr. 110/A4
Beauchamp, Fr. 88/J4
Beaucourt, Fr. 114/C3
Beaudesert, Austl. 171/D4
Beaufort, Austl. 173/B3
Beaufort (sea), Can.,US 177/C2
Beaufort, Fr. 114/B4
Beaufort, Lux. 111/F4
Beaufort, SC, US 191/H3
Beaufort West, SAfr. 164/C4
Beaugency, Fr. 100/D3
Beaujolais, Monts du (mts.), Fr. 100/F4
Beauly (riv.), Sc, UK 94/B2
Beauly, Sc, UK 94/B2
Beauly Firth (lake), Sc, UK 94/B2
Beaumaris, Wal, UK 92/D5
Beaume, Fr. 100/F3
Beaumont, Tx, US 187/J5
Beaumont, Ca, US 194/D3
Beaumont, Fr. 100/E4
Beaumont, Belg. 111/D3
Beaumont-de-Lomagne, Fr. 100/D5
Beaumont-sur-Oise, Fr. 88/J4
Beaupréau, Fr. 100/C3
Beauquesne, Fr. 110/B3
Beauraing, Belg. 111/D3
Beaurainville, Fr. 110/A3
Beaurevoir, Fr. 110/C4
Beausejour, Mb, Can. 185/J3
Beautheil, Fr. 88/M5
Beautor, Fr. 110/C4
Beauvais, Fr. 110/B5
Beauval, Sk, Can. 184/G2
Beauval, Fr. 110/B3
Beauvoir, Fr. 88/L6
Beaver (lake), Ar, US 190/E2
Beaver (riv.), Yk, Can. 180/D2
Beaver, Ak, US 192/J2
Beaver (isl.), Mi, US 188/C2
Beaver (riv.), Ok, US 186/G3
Beaver (riv.), On, Can. 185/L2
Beaver, Ut, US 186/D3
Beaver Creek, Yk, Can. 192/K3
Beaver Meadows, Pa, US 196/C2
Beaver Springs, Pa, US 196/A2
Beaverhead (riv.), Mt, US 184/E4
Beaverlodge, Ab, Can. 184/D2
Beavertown, Pa, US 196/A2
Bebedouro, Braz. 213/B2
Beberibe, Braz. 212/C2
Bebington, Eng, UK 93/E5
Bebra, Ger. 109/G7
Becal, Mex. 202/D1
Beccles, Eng, UK 91/H2
Bečej, Serb. 106/E3
Becerreá, Sp. 102/B1
Bechar (prov.), Alg. 156/E3
Bechar, Alg. 157/E3
Becharof (lake), Ak, US 192/G4
Bechhofen, Ger. 111/G5
Bechtheim, Ger. 112/B3
Bechyně, Czh. 113/H4
Beckdorf, Ger. 109/G2
Beckenried, Swi. 115/E4
Beckingen, Ger. 111/F5
Beckley, WV, US 188/D4
Beckum, Ger. 109/F5
Beclean, Rom. 107/G2
Becs de Bosson (peak), Swi. 114/D5
Bédarieux, Fr. 100/E5
Bedburg, Ger. 111/F2
Bedburg-Hau, Ger. 108/D5
Beder, Den. 96/D3
Bedford (cape), Austl. 171/B1
Bedford, Qu, Can. 188/F2
Bedford, Eng, UK 91/F2
Bedford, In, US 188/C4
Bedford, SAfr. 164/D4
Bedford, Va, US 188/E4
Bedford Hills, NY, US 197/E1
Bedford Level (phys. reg.), Eng, UK 91/F2
Bedford Park, Il, US 193/Q16
Bedfordshire (co.), Eng, UK 91/F2
Bedlington, Eng, UK 93/G1
Bedonia, It. 116/C3
Bedouaram (well), Niger 154/H4
Bedretto, Swi. 115/E5
Bedsted, Den. 96/C3
Bedum, Neth. 108/D2
Bedworth, Eng, UK 91/E2
Beebe Seep (canal), Co, US 195/C2
Beechworth, Austl. 173/C3
Beek, Neth. 111/E2
Beelen, Ger. 109/F5
Beelitz, Ger. 98/P7
Beenleigh, Austl. 171/D4
Beer (pt.), Eng, UK 90/C5
Be'er Sheva', Isr. 149/D4
Beerfelden, Ger. 112/B3
Beernem, Belg. 110/C1
Beerzel, Belg. 111/D1
Beesel, Neth. 108/D6
Beeville, Tx, US 190/D4
Befandriana, Madg. 165/J6
Befandriana, Madg. 165/G8
Beforona, Madg. 165/J7
Befotaka, Madg. 165/J6
Beg (lake), NI, UK 92/B2
Bega, Austl. 173/D3
Bega (riv.), Ger. 109/F5
Bega Veche (riv.), Cro. 106/E3
Begamganj, Bang. 143/H4
Begamganj, India 142/B4
Bégard, Fr. 100/B2
Begarslan (peak), Trkm. 121/K4
Begejci, Serb. 106/E3
Begichev (isl.), Rus. 123/M2
Begna (riv.), Nor. 95/D3
Begusarai, India 143/F3
Béhague (pt.), FrG. 209/H3
Behala (str.), Indo. 138/B4
Behāla, India 140/E3
Behamberg, Aus. 113/H6
Behat, India 144/D4
Behbahān, Iran 146/F2
Behenjy-Afovany, Madg. 165/H7
Béhoust, Fr. 88/H5
Behren-lès-Forbach, Fr. 111/F5
Behri (riv.), Nepal 142/C1
Behshahr, Iran 146/F1
Bei (riv.), China 137/A2
Bei (mts.), China 128/F3
Bei'an, China 129/N2
Beierfeld, Ger. 113/F1
Beigua (peak), It. 116/B4
Beijing (mun.), China 129/L3
Beijing (cap.), China 130/H7
Beijing Capital (int'l arpt.), China 130/H6
Beilen, Neth. 108/D3
Beiliu, China 141/K3
Beilngries, Ger. 113/E4
Beilstein, Ger. 112/C4
Beilun (pass), China 137/A3
Bein Tharsuinn (peak), Sc, UK 94/B1
Beindersheim, Ger. 112/B3
Beinn a' Chuallaich (peak), Sc, UK 94/B3
Beinn a' Ghlò (peak), Sc, UK 94/C3
Beinn a' Mheadhoin (lake), Sc, UK 94/B2
Beinn Bhàn (peak), Sc, UK 94/A3
Beinn Bheula (peak), Sc, UK 94/B4
Beinn Bhrotain (peak), Sc, UK 94/C2
Beinn Bhuidhe (peak), Sc, UK 94/B4
Beinn Bhuidhe Mhór (peak),Sc, UK 94/B2
Beinn Dearg (peak), Sc, UK 94/B1
Beinn Dearg (peak), Sc, UK 94/C3
Beinn Dòrain (peak), Sc, UK 94/B4
Beinn Eighe (peak), Sc, UK 94/A1
Beinn Heasgarnich (peak), Sc, UK 94/B3
Beinn Mholach (peak), Sc, UK 94/B3
Beinn Mhór (peak), Sc, UK 94/A4
Beinwil am See, Swi. 114/E3
Beipiao, China 130/E2
Beira, Moz. 163/F4
Beiru (riv.), China 130/C4
Beirut (Bayrūt), (cap.), Leb. 149/D3
Beirut (int'l arpt.), Leb. 149/D3
Beitbridge, Zim. 163/E5
Beith, Sc, UK 94/B5
Beiuş, Rom. 106/F2
Beizhen, China 131/A2
Beja, Port. 102/B3
Beja (dist.), Port. 102/A4
Beja, Tun. 158/L6
Beja (gov.), Tun. 158/L6
Bejaïa (prov.), Alg. 158/H4
Bejaïa, Alg. 158/H4
Béjar, Sp. 102/C2
Bejhi (riv.), Pak. 147/J3
Bekabad, Uzb. 145/E4
Bekasi, Indo. 138/C5
Békés, Hun. 106/E2
Békés (prov.), Hun. 106/E2
Békéscsaba, Hun. 106/E2
Bekilli, Turk. 148/B2
Bekily, Madg. 165/H9
Bekitro, Madg. 165/H9
Bekwai, Gha. 161/E5
Bel Air, Md, US 196/B4
Bel Air South, Md, US 196/B5
Belā, India 140/D2
Bela, Pak. 147/J3
Belá, Slvk. 99/K4
Bela Crkva, Serb. 106/E3
Bela Cruz, Braz. 212/B1
Bela Palanka, Serb. 106/F4
Bělá pod Bezdězem, Czh. 113/H1
Belā Pratāpgarh, India 142/C3
Bela Vista, Braz. 209/G8
Bela Vista, Moz. 165/F2
Bela Vista do Paraíso, Braz. 213/B2
Belair, La, US 195/Q17
Belair Rec. Pk., Austl. 171/M9
Belan (riv.), India 142/D3

Belarus (ctry.) 85/G3
Belas, Port. 103/P10
Belaya (riv.), Rus. 122/F4
Belbo (riv.), It. 116/B3
Bełchatów, Pol. 99/K3
Belchen (peak), Ger. 114/C2
Belcher (chan.), Nun., Can. 181/S7
Belcher (isls.), On, Can. 181/H3
Belchite, Sp. 103/E2
Belcourt, ND, US 185/J3
Beldānga, India 143/G4
Belebey, Rus. 119/M5
Beled Weyne, Som. 155/Q7
Belém, Braz. 209/J4
Belém, Braz. 212/D2
Belém de São Francisco, Braz. 212/C3
Belem Tower, Port. 103/P10
Belén, Arg. 215/C2
Belén, NM, US 186/F4
Belén, Chile 214/D5
Belen, Nic. 198/D5
Belen, Turk. 149/E1
Belen, Turk. 149/C1
Belén de Escobar, Arg. 217/J11
Belene, Bul. 107/G4
Beles Wenz (riv.), Eth. 155/N5
Belesar, Embalse de (res.), Sp. 102/B1
Belev, Rus. 120/F1
Belews Creek, Mo, US 195/G9
Belfair, Wa, US 193/B3
Belfast (cap.), NI, UK 92/C2
Belfast (dist.), NI, UK 92/B2
Belfast, SAfr. 165/E2
Belfast, Me, US 189/G2
Belfast Lough (bay), NI, UK 92/C2
Belfaux, Swi. 114/D4
Belfield, ND, US 185/H4
Belfort (dept.), Fr. 114/C2
Belfort, Fr. 114/C2
Belgioioso, It. 116/C2
Belgium (ctry.) 98/C3
Belgorod, Rus. 120/F2
Belgorodskaya Oblast, Rus. 120/F2
Belgrade, Mt, US 184/F4
Belgrade (Beograd) (cap.), Serb. 106/E3
Beli (riv.), Kos. 106/E4
Beli Manastir, Cro. 106/D3
Beli Timok (riv.), Serb. 106/F4
Belitsa, Bul. 105/H2
Belitung (isl.), Indo. 138/C4
Belize (riv.), Belz. 202/D2
Belize (ctry.) 202/D2
Belize City, Belz. 202/D2
Beljanica (peak), Serb. 106/E3
Bel'kovskiy (isl.), Rus. 123/N2
Bell, Austl. 171/C4
Bell (riv.), Austl. 171/G5
Bell (pen.), Nun., Can. 181/H2
Bell (riv.), Qu, Can. 181/J4
Bell, Ca, US 194/F8
Bell, Ger. 111/G3
Bell Gardens, Ca, US 194/F8
Bell Rock (Inchcape) (isl.), Sc, UK 94/D4
Bell Ville, Arg. 215/D3
Bella Coola, BC, Can. 184/B2
Bella Vista, Arg. 215/E2
Bellac, Fr. 100/D3
Bellaghy, NI, UK 92/B2
Bellagio, It. 115/F6
Bellano, It. 115/F5
Bellary, India 140/C4
Bellavista, Peru 214/B2
Bellavista, Peru 214/B2
Bellavista (cape), It. 104/A3
Bellavista, Ecu. 214/E7
Belle (riv.), On, Can. 193/G7
Belle-Anse, Haiti 203/H2
Belle Chasse, La, US 195/Q17
Belle Fourche (riv.), Wy, US 185/G5
Belle Glade, Fl, US 191/H5
Belle Haven, Va, US 196/A6
Belle-Ile (isl.), Fr. 100/B3
Belle Isle (str.), NF, Can. 189/K1
Belle Terre, NY, US 197/E2
Belleek, NI, UK 92/B3
Bellefontaine, Oh, US 188/D3
Bellefonte, De, US 196/C4
Bellegarde-sur-Valserine, Fr. 114/B5
Bellenberg, Ger. 115/G1
Bellenden Ker NP, Austl. 171/B2
Belleplain, NJ, US 196/D5
Bellerive-sur-Allier, Fr. 100/E3
Bellerose, NY, US 197/L9
Belleu, Fr. 110/C5
Belleville, On, Can. 188/E2
Belleville, Fr. 114/A5
Belleville, Il, US 195/H8
Belleville, NJ, US 197/J8
Belleville-sur-Meuse, Fr. 111/E5
Bellevue, Md, US 196/B6
Bellevue, Ca, US 194/F8
Bellflower, Ca, US 194/F8
Bellheim, Ger. 112/B4
Bellignat, Fr. 114/B5
Bellinge, Den. 96/D4
Bellingen, Austl. 173/E1

Bellingham, Wa, US 184/C3
Bellingshausen (isl.), FrPol. 175/K6
Bellingshausen (sea), Ant. 218/U
Bellingwolde, Neth. 109/E2
Bellinzago Novarese, It. 116/B1
Bellinzona, Swi. 115/F5
Bellmawr, NJ, US 196/C4
Bellmead, Tx, US 187/H5
Bellmore, NY, US 197/L9
Bello, Col. 208/C2
Bellona Reefs (reef),
Bellot (str.), Nun., Can. 180/G1
Bellport, NY, US 197/F2
Bellshill, Sc, UK 94/B5
Belluno (prov.), It. 117/E1
Belluno, It. 101/K3
Bellville, Tx, US 187/H5
Bellvue, Co, US 195/B1
Bellwald, Swi. 114/E5
Belm, Ger. 109/F4
Belmar, NJ, US 196/D3
Belmez, Sp. 102/C3
Belmont, Ca, US 193/K11
Belmonte, Braz. 212/C4
Belmonte, Sp. 102/D3
Belmonte, Port. 102/B2
Belmopan (cap.), 202/D2
Belmullet, Ire. 89/P9
Belo Campo, Braz. 212/B4
Belo Horizonte, Braz. 213/D1
Belo-Tsiribihina, Madg. 165/H7
Beloeil, Qu, Can. 189/P6
Beloeil, Belg. 110/C2
Belogorsk, Rus. 129/N1
Beloha, Madg. 165/H9
Beloit, Wi, US 185/L5
Beloit, Ks, US 187/H3
Belomorsk, Rus. 118/G2
Belorado, Sp. 102/D1
Belorechensk, Rus. 120/F3
Belören, Turk. 148/C2
Beloretsk, Rus. 119/N5
Beloslav, Bul. 107/H4
Belovo, Bul. 105/J1
Belovo, Rus. 122/J4
Beloye (lake), Rus. 122/D3
Belper, Eng, UK 93/G5
Belsand, India 143/E2
Belt, Mt, US 184/F4
Belterwijde (lake), Neth. 108/D3
Beltheim, Ger. 111/G3
Belton, Tx, US 187/H5
Belton, Mo, US 195/D6
Beltsville, Md, US 196/B5
Beltzville (lake), Pa, US 196/C2
Belukha (peak), Rus. 128/E2
Belvedere, Ca, US 193/K11
Belvidere, NJ, US 196/C2
Belyando (riv.), Austl. 167/D3
Belyy (isl.), Rus. 218/A
Belzig, Ger. 98/G2
Bełżyce, Pol. 99/M3
Bemaraha (plat.), Madg. 165/H7
Bemarivo (riv.), Madg. 165/H7
Bembéréké, Ben. 161/F4
Bembibre, Sp. 102/B1
Bemboka, Austl. 173/D3
Bemetāra, India 140/D3
Bemidji, Mn, US 185/K4
Bemmel, Neth. 108/C5
Ben Aigan (hill), Sc, UK 94/C1
Ben Alder (peak), Sc, UK 94/B3
Ben Améra (well), Mrta. 156/B5
Ben Avon (peak), Sc, UK 94/C2
Ben Boyd NP, Austl. 173/D3
Ben Chonzie (peak), Sc, UK 94/C4
Ben Cleuch (peak), Sc, UK 94/C4
Ben Cruachan (peak), Sc, UK 94/A4
Ben Davis (pt.), NJ, US 196/C5
Ben Gurion (int'l arpt.), Isr. 149/F7
Ben Hope (peak), Sc, UK 89/R7
Ben Ime (peak), Sc, UK 94/B4
Ben Lawers (peak), Sc, UK 94/B3
Ben Ledi (peak), Sc, UK 94/B4
Ben Lomond (peak), Sc, UK 94/B4
Ben Lomond NP, Austl. 173/C4
Ben Lui (peak), Sc, UK 94/B4
Ben Macdui (peak), Sc, UK 94/C2
Ben More (peak), Sc, UK 89/Q8
Ben More (peak), Sc, UK 94/B4
Ben More Assynt (peak), Sc, UK 89/R7
Ben Msik-Sidi Othmane (prov.), Mor. 158/A2

Ben Nevis (peak), Sc, UK 94/B3
Ben Rinnes (peak), Sc, UK 94/C2
Ben Slimane, Mor. 156/D2
Ben Slimane (prov.), Mor. 158/A3
Ben Starav (peak), Sc, UK 94/A3
Ben Tee (peak), Sc, UK 94/B2
Ben Tirran (peak), Sc, UK 94/C3
Ben Tre, Viet. 136/D4
Ben Vane (peak), Sc, UK 94/B4
Ben Vorlich (peak), Sc, UK 94/B4
Ben Vrackie (peak), Sc, UK 94/C3
Ben Wyvis (peak), Sc, UK 94/B1
Ben Zohra (well), Alg. 156/E3
Benabarre, Sp. 103/F1
Benahmed, Mor. 156/D2
Benalla, Austl. 173/C3
Benalmádena, Sp. 102/C4
Benambra (peak), Indo. 139/E4
Benavente, Sp. 102/C1
Benavides, Tx, US 190/D5
Benbane (pt.), NI, UK 92/B1
Benbecula (isl.), Sc, UK 89/Q8
Benbonyathe (peak), Austl. 171/H4
Benburb, NI, UK 92/B3
Bend, Or, US 184/C4
Bendeleben (mt.), Ak, US 192/F2
Bendemeer, Austl. 173/D1
Bendersville, Pa, US 196/A4
Bendigo, Austl. 173/C3
Bendorf, Ger. 96/C4
Bene Beraq, Isr. 149/F7
Benedict (mt.), Nf, Can. 181/L3
Benediktbeuern, Ger. 115/H2
Benediktenwand (peak), Ger. 115/H2
Beneditinos, Braz. 212/B2
Benenitra, Madg. 165/H8
Benešov, Czh. 113/H3
Benevento, It. 104/D2
Benfeld, Fr. 114/D1
Bengal, Bay of (gulf), Asia 140/E4
Bengbu, China 130/D4
Benghāzī, Libya 154/K1
Bengkalis, Indo. 138/B3
Bengkalis (isl.), Indo. 138/B3
Bengkayang, Indo. 138/C3
Bengkulu, Indo. 138/B4
Bengough, Sk, Can. 185/G3
Bengtsfors, Swe. 96/E2
Benguela, Ang. 163/B3
Benguerir, Mor. 156/D2
Beni, D.R. Congo 162/E1
Beni (riv.), Bol. 205/C4
Beni Abbes, Alg. 157/E3
Beni Bouayach, Mor. 158/C2
Beni Ensar, Mor. 158/C1
Beni Khiar, Tun. 158/M6
Beni Mellal, Mor. 156/D2
Beni Ounif, Alg. 157/F2
Benicarló, Sp. 103/F2
Benicia, Ca, US 193/K10
Benidorm, Sp. 103/E3
Benifayó, Sp. 103/E3
Benin (ctry.) 161/F4
Benin, Bight of (bay), Afr. 151/C4
Benin City, Nga. 161/G5
Benisa, Sp. 103/F3
Benito Juárez, Mex. 184/D2
Benjamin, Tx, US 187/H4
Benjamin Constant, Braz. 214/D2
Benjamin Hill, Mex. 184/C2
Benjamin, Isla (isl.), Chile 216/B5
Benkei-misaki (cape), Japan 134/B2
Benkelman, Ne, US 187/G2
Bennachie (hill), Sc, UK 94/D2
Bennett (pt.), Sc, UK 94/A6
Bennett (isl.), Rus. 123/O2
Bennettsville, SC, US 191/J3
Bennington, Vt, US 188/F3
Bénoué, PN de la, Camr. 154/H6
Bensenville, Il, US 193/Q16
Bensheim, Ger. 112/B3
Benson, Mn, US 185/K5
Benson, Az, US 186/E5
Benta (riv.), Hun. 107/Q10
Bentheim, Ger. 109/E4
Bentley, Eng, UK 93/G4
Bento Gonçalves, Braz. 213/B4
Benton, Ar, US 187/J4
Benton, La, US 187/J4
Benton, Mo, US 195/B1
Benton Harbor, Mi, US 188/C3
Bentong, Malay. 138/B3
Benue (state), Nga. 161/H5
Benue (riv.), Nga. 154/G6
Benxi, China 131/C2
Beočin, Serb. 106/D3
Beograd (int'l arpt.), Serb. 106/E3
Beohāri, India 142/C3
Beppu, Japan 132/B4
Beppu (bay), Japan 132/B4

Beppu, Japan 132/B4
Bequia (isl.), StV. 199/N9
Bequimão, Braz. 212/A1
Beraber (well), Alg. 154/E1
Beragh, NI, UK 92/A2
Beraketa, Madg. 165/H8
Berane, Serb. 106/D4
Berasia, India 142/A4
Beratus (peak), Indo. 139/E4
Beratzhausen, Ger. 113/E4
Berau (riv.), Indo. 139/E3
Berau (bay), Indo. 139/H4
Berbenno di Valtellina, It. 115/F5
Berbera, Som. 155/Q5
Berbérati, CAfr. 154/J7
Berbice (riv.), Guy. 208/G2
Berceto, It. 116/C3
Berchem, Belg. 108/B6
Bercher, Swi. 114/C4
Berching, Ger. 113/E4
Berchtesgaden, Ger. 101/K3
Berchtesgaden, NP, Ger. 101/K3
Berck, Fr. 110/A3
Berdsk, Rus. 145/H2
Berdyans'k, Ukr. 120/F3
Berdychiv, Ukr. 120/D2
Berea, Ky, US 188/C4
Bereguardo, It. 116/C2
Berehove, Ukr. 99/M4
Berekum, Gha. 161/E5
Berenguela, Bol. 214/D5
Berenice (ruin), Egypt 159/C4
Beresford, SD, US 185/J5
Beresford, NB, Can. 189/H2
Berești, Rom. 107/H2
Berettyóújfalu, Hun. 106/F2
Berevo, Madg. 165/H7
Berezina (riv.), Bela. 120/D1
Berezniki, Rus. 119/N4
Berezovo, Rus. 122/G3
Berg (riv.), SAfr. 164/B4
Berg, Swi. 115/F2
Berg, Lux. 111/F4
Berg bei Rohrbach, Ger. 112/B5
Berga, Sp. 103/F1
Bergama, Turk. 148/A2
Bergamo, It. 116/C1
Bergamo (prov.), It. 115/F6
Bergara, Sp. 102/D1
Bergatruete, Ger. 115/F2
Bergen, Ger. 109/G3
Bergen, Ger. 96/E4
Bergen, Neth. 108/B3
Bergen, Nor. 96/A1
Bergen (co.), NJ, US 196/D2
Bergen op Zoom, Neth. 108/B5
Bergen Park, Co, US 195/B3
Bergenfield, NJ, US 197/K8
Bergerac, Fr. 100/D4
Bergeyk, Neth. 108/C6
Bergheim, Tx, US 195/T20
Bergheim, Aus. 113/G7
Bergheim, Ger. 111/F2
Bergisch Gladbach, Ger. 111/G2
Bergkamen, Ger. 109/E5
Bergneset, Swe. 118/D2
Bergneustadt, Ger. 111/G1
Bergrheinfeld, Ger. 98/F4
Bergse Maas (riv.), Neth. 108/B5
Bergshamra, Swe. 96/H2
Bergsviken, Swe. 96/H2
Bergtheim, Ger. 112/D3
Berguent, Mor. 158/C2
Bergues, Fr. 110/B2
Bergum, Neth. 108/D2
Bergumermeer (lake), Neth. 108/D2
Bergün-Bravuonga, Swi. 115/H4
Bergviken (lake), Swe. 96/G1
Berh, Mong. 129/K2
Berikat (cape), Indo. 138/C4
Bering (isl.), Rus. 123/S4
Bering (str.), Rus.,US 125/U3
Bering Land Bridge Nat'l Prsv., Ak, US 192/E2
Beringen, Belg. 111/E1
Beritarikap (cape), Indo. 138/B4
Berja, Sp. 102/D4
Berkel, Neth. 108/B5
Berkel (riv.), Ger. 98/D2
Berkeley, Ca, US 186/B3
Berkeley, Mo, US 195/G8
Berkeley Heights, NJ, US 197/H9
Berkhamsted, Eng, UK 88/B1
Berkheim, Ger. 115/G1
Berkhout, Neth. 108/B3
Berkley, Mi, US 193/F6
Berkovitsa, Bul. 105/H1
Berks (co.), Pa, US 196/C3
Berkshire (co.), Eng, UK 91/E3
Berkshire Downs (hills), Eng, UK 90/D5
Berlaimont, Fr. 110/C3
Berlanga de Duero, Sp. 102/D2
Berlare, Belg. 110/D1
Berleburg, Ger. 109/F6
Berlicum, Neth. 108/C5
Berlin (cap.), Ger. 98/Q6
Berlin (state), Ger. 98/Q6

Berlin, NH, US 189/G2
Berlin, NJ, US 196/D4
Berlin, Wi, US 185/L5
Bermagui, Austl. 173/D3
Bermejo, Bol. 215/D1
Bermejo (riv.), Arg. 205/D5
Bermeo, Sp. 102/D1
Bermillo de Sayago, Sp. 102/B2
Bermuda (isl.), UK 177/L6
Bern (canton), Swi. 114/D4
Bern (cap.), Swi. 114/D4
Bern-Belp (int'l arpt.), Swi. 114/D4
Bernal, Peru 214/A2
Bernalda, It. 104/E2
Bernalillo, NM, US 186/F4
Bernard (riv.), NW, Can. 180/D1
Bernardo O'Higgins, PN, Chile 215/B6
Bernardsville, NJ, US 196/D2
Bernau, Ger. 114/E2
Bernau, Ger. 98/Q6
Bernay, Fr. 100/D2
Bernburg, Ger. 98/F3
Berne, Fr. 110/A3
Berne, Ger. 109/F3
Berneck, Ger. 115/G2
Bernes-sur-Oise, Fr. 88/J4
Bernese Alps (mtn.), Swi. 101/G3
Bernhardswald, Ger. 113/F4
Bernice, La, US 187/J4
Bernier (isl.), Austl. 170/B3
Bernier (bay), Nun., Can. 180/G1
Bernina (peak), Swi. 115/F5
Bernina, Passo del (pass), Swi. 115/G5
Bernissart, Belg. 110/C2
Bernkastel-Kues, Ger. 111/G4
Bernsbach, Ger. 113/F1
Bernville, Pa, US 196/B3
Beromünster, Swi. 114/E3
Beroroha, Madg. 165/H8
Beroun, Czh. 113/H3
Berounka (riv.), Czh. 99/G4
Berovo, FYROM 105/H2
Berra, It. 117/E3
Berre, Étang de (lake), Fr. 100/F5
Berrechid, Mor. 156/D2
Berri, Austl. 171/J5
Berriane, Alg. 157/F2
Berridale, Austl. 173/D3
Berriedale, Sc, UK 89/S7
Berrigan, Austl. 173/C2
Berriozábal, Mex. 202/C2
Berrouaghia, Alg. 158/G4
Berry, Austl. 173/D2
Berry (isls.), Bahm. 199/F2
Berry (reg.), Fr. 100/D3
Berry (pt.), Nu, Can. 90/C6
Berry (mtn.), Pa, US 196/A2
Berryessa (peak), Ca, US 193/K9
Bersenbrück, Ger. 109/E3
Berthoud, Co, US 195/B2
Bertinoro, It. 117/F4
Bertiolo, It. 117/G1
Bertogne, Belg. 111/E3
Bertolinia, Braz. 212/B2
Bertoua, Camr. 154/H7
Bertrand (peak), Arg. 217/B6
Bertrix, Belg. 111/E4
Bertry, Fr. 110/C3
Beru (isl.), Kiri. 174/G5
Berwick, NS, Can. 189/H2
Berwick, Pa, US 196/B1
Berwick-upon-Tweed, Eng, UK 94/D5
Berwyn, Il, US 193/Q16
Berwyn (mts.), Wal, UK 92/E6
Berzence, Hun. 106/C2
Bès (riv.), Fr. 100/F2
Besalampy, Madg. 165/H7
Besançon, Fr. 114/C3
Besar (mount), Indo. 139/E4
Besbre (riv.), Fr. 100/E3
Beşiri, Turk. 148/E2
Beška, Serb. 106/E3
Besna Kobila (peak), Serb. 106/F4
Besozzo, It. 116/B1
Bessacarr, Eng, UK 93/G5
Bessancourt, Fr. 88/H4
Bessarabia (reg.), Mol. 107/J2
Bessbrook, NI, UK 92/B3
Bessemer, Al, US 191/G3
Bessemer (mtn.) 144/B3
Bessines-sur-Gartempe, Fr. 100/D3
Best, Neth. 108/C5
Bestensee, Ger. 98/Q7
Bet She'an, Isr. 149/D3
Bet Shemesh, Isr. 149/D4
Betanzos, Sp. 102/A1
Beth She'arim (ruin), Isr. 149/G6

Bethal, SAfr. 164/E2
Bethalto, Il, US 195/G8
Bethanie, Namb. 164/B2
Bethany (res.), Ca, US 193/L11
Bethany, Mo, US 185/K5
Bethany, Ok, US 195/M14
Bethel, Ak, US 192/F3
Bethel, Pa, US 196/B3
Bethel Acres, Ok, US 195/N15
Bethel Island, Ca, US 193/L10
Bétheniville, Fr. 111/D5
Bétheny, Fr. 110/D5
Bethesda, Md, US 196/A6
Bethesda-Wal, UK 92/D5
Béthisy-Sainte-Pierre, Fr. 110/B5
Bethlehem, SAfr. 164/E3
Bethlehem, Pa, US 196/C2
Bethlehem, Md, US 196/C6
Bethoncourt, Fr. 114/C2
Bethpage, NY, US 197/M9
Bethulie, SAfr. 164/D3
Béthune (riv.), Fr. 100/D2
Béthune, Fr. 110/B2
Bhutan (ctry.) 143/G2
Betim, Braz. 213/C1
Betioky, Madg. 165/H8
Betpaqala (plain), Kaz. 128/A2
Betroka, Madg. 165/H8
Betschdorf, Fr. 112/A5
Betsiamites (riv.), Qu, Can. 189/G1
Betsiboka (riv.), Madg. 165/H7
Bettancourt-la-Ferrée, Fr. 111/D6
Bette (peak), Libya 155/J3
Bettembourg, Lux. 111/F4
Betterton, Md, US 196/B5
Bettiah, India 143/E2
Bettlach, Swi. 114/D3
Bettles, Ak, US 192/H2
Betuwe (phys. reg.), Neth. 108/C5
Betwa (riv.), India 142/B3
Betz, Fr. 88/J4
Betzdorf, Ger. 111/G2
Betzenstein, Ger. 113/E3
Beulah, Austl. 173/B3
Beulah, ND, US 185/H4
Beulah (lake), Wi, US 193/P14
Beulakerwijde (lake), Neth. 108/D3
Beuningen, Neth. 108/C5
Beure, Fr. 114/C3
Beuvray (peak), Fr. 100/F3
Beuvron (riv.), Fr. 100/D3
Beuvron (riv.), Fr. 88/L5
Beuvry, Fr. 110/B2
Bevensen, Ger. 109/H2
Bever (riv.), Ger. 109/E4
Beveren, Belg. 108/B6
Beverin (peak), Swi. 115/F4
Beverley, Austl. 170/C5
Beverley, Eng, UK 93/H4
Beverly, Mo, US 195/D5
Beverly Hills, Ca, US 194/F7
Beverly Hills, Mi, US 193/F6
Beverstedt, Ger. 109/F2
Beverungen, Ger. 109/G5
Beverwijk, Neth. 108/B4
Bewar, India 142/B3
Bewl Bridge (res.), Eng, UK 91/G4
Bexar (co.), Tx, US 195/T21
Bexbach, Ger. 111/G5
Bexhill, Eng, UK 91/G5
Bexley (bor.), Eng, UK 88/D2
Beyçayırı, Turk. 107/H5
Beycuma, Turk. 107/K5
Beyne-Heusay, Belg. 111/E2
Beynes, Fr. 88/H5
Beyoneisu-Retsugan (isl.), Japan 133/F5
Beypazarı, Turk. 148/B2
Beyşehir, Turk. 148/B2
Bezaha, Madg. 165/H8
Bezau, Aus. 115/F3
Bezdan, Serb. 106/D3
Bezdrev (lake), Czh. 113/H4
Bezhetsk, Rus. 118/H4
Béziers, Fr. 100/E5
Bhabua, India 142/D3
Bhadarwāh, India 144/C3
Bhadaur, India 144/C4
Bhadohī, India 142/D3
Bhādra, India 144/C5
Bhadreswar, India 140/A3
Bhāgalpur, India 143/F3
Bhai Pheru, Pak. 144/B4
Bhairab (riv.), Bang. 143/G4
Bhairab Bāzār, Bang. 143/H3
Bhakkar, Pak. 144/B3
Bhaktapur, Nepal 143/F2
Bhalwāl, Pak. 144/B3
Bhamo, Myan. 141/G3
Bhānder, India 142/B3
Bhānder (range), India 142/B3
Bhānwad, India 140/A3
Bharatpur, Nepal 143/E2
Bharthana, India 142/B2
Bharuch, India 147/K4
Bhasāwar, India 142/B2
Bhātāpāra, India 140/D3
Bhatgaon, India 142/D4
Bhatkal, India 147/K6
Bhātpāra, India 143/G4

Bhavāni, India 140/C5
Bhavnagar, India 147/K4
Bhawāna, Pak. 144/B3
Bhawāni Mandi, India 147/L4
Bhera, Pak. 144/B3
Bheri (zone), Nepal 142/C1
Bhilai, India 140/D3
Bhīlwāra, India 147/L5
Bhīma (riv.), India 147/L5
Bhimavaram, India 140/D4
Bhima (riv.), India 147/L5
Bhimunipatnam, India 140/D4
Bhinga, India 142/C2
Bhiwandi, India 147/K5
Bhiwāni, India 144/D5
Bhojpur, Nepal 143/F2
Bhokardan, India 140/C3
Bhola, Bang. 143/H4
Bhongaon, India 142/B2
Bhopāl, India 140/C3
Bhor, India 147/K5
Bhraoin (lake), India 140/D4
Bhuban, India 140/D4
Bhumibol (dam), Thai. 136/B2
Bhusawal, India 147/L4
Bhutan (ctry.) 143/G2
Bi Doup (peak), Viet. 136/D3
Biá (riv.), Braz. 208/E4
Bia (riv.), C.d'Iv. 160/E5
Biafra, Bight of (bay), Camr. 154/G7
Biak (isl.), Indo. 139/J4
Biak (int'l arpt.), Indo. 139/J4
Biała Podlaska, Pol. 99/M2
Biała (riv.), Pol. 99/L3
Białobrzegi, Pol. 99/L3
Białogard, Pol. 96/C3
Białowieski NP, Pol. 99/K4
Białowieski NP, Pol. 99/M2
Białystok, Pol. 99/M2
Bianca (peak), It. 115/G4
Biancavilla, It. 104/D4
Bigge (riv.), Ger. 111/G1
Biandronno, It. 116/B1
Bianze, It. 116/B2
Biarritz, Fr. 100/C5
Biasca, Swi. 115/F5
Bibā, Egypt 159/B2
Bibai, Japan 134/B2
Bibbiano, It. 116/D3
Bibbiena, It. 117/E5
Biberach, Ger. 114/E1
Biberach, Ger. 115/G1
Biberach an der Riss, Ger. 115/F1
Biberist, Swi. 114/D3
Bibione, It. 117/G1
Biblián, Ecu. 210/B5
Biblis, Ger. 112/B3
Bicas, Braz. 213/K6
Bicester, Eng, UK 91/E3
Bicheno, Austl. 173/D4
Bicknacre, Eng, UK 88/E1
Bicske, Hun. 106/D2
Bida, Nga. 161/G4
Bīdar, India 140/C4
Biddeford, Me, US 189/G3
Biddiyā, WBnk. 149/G7
Biddū, WBnk. 149/G8
Biddulph, Eng, UK 93/F5
Bidean nam Bian (peak), Sc, UK 94/A3
Bideford, Eng, UK 90/B4
Bidente (riv.), It. 117/E4
Bidhūna, India 142/B2
Bīdokht, Iran 147/G2
Biebesheim am Rhein, Ger. 112/B3
Biebra (riv.), Pol. 99/M2
Biel, Swi. 114/D3
Bielawa, Pol. 99/J3
Bielefeld, Ger. 109/F4
Biella (prov.), It. 116/B1
Biella, It. 116/B1
Bielsk Podlaski, Pol. 99/M2
Bielsko-Biała, Pol. 99/K4
Bien Hoa, Viet. 136/D4
Bienenbüttel, Ger. 109/H2
Bienne (riv.), Fr. 114/B5
Bienno, It. 115/G6
Bientina, It. 116/D5
Bienville (lake), Qu, Can. 181/J3
Bière, Swi. 114/C4
Bierset (int'l arpt.), Belg. 111/E2
Bierum, Neth. 108/D2
Bierutów, Pol. 99/J3
Biesbosch (reg.), Neth. 108/B5
Biesenthal, Ger. 98/Q6
Biesles, Fr. 114/B1
Biesme, Fr. 111/K2
Bieszczadzki NP, Pol. 99/M4
Bietigheim, Ger. 112/B5
Bietschhorn (peak), Swi. 114/D5
Bièvre (riv.), Fr. 88/J5
Bièvre, Belg. 111/E4
Bièvres, Fr. 88/H5
Big (des.), Austl. 173/B2
Big (isl.), On, Can. 180/G4
Big (isl.), Nu, Can. 181/J2
Big (riv.), Mo, US 195/F6
Big Belt (mts.), Mt, US 184/F4
Big Bend, Swaz. 165/E2
Big Bend, Wi, US 193/P14

Big Bend NP, Tx, US 187/C5
Big Blue (riv.), Ks,Ne, US 187/H2
Big Diomede (isl.), Rus. 192/E2
Big Fork (riv.), Mn, US 185/K4
Big Hole (riv.), Mt, US 184/E4
Big Hole, SAfr. 187/G5
Big Lake, Tx, US 187/G5
Big Lost (riv.), Id, US 186/D2
Big Muskego (lake), Wi, US 193/P14
Big Pine (hill), Pa, US 196/C1
Big Pines, Ca, US 194/C2
Big Rapids, Mi, US 188/C3
Big River, Sk, Can. 184/G2
Big Rock, Il, US 193/N16
Big Sandy (riv.), Wy, US 186/E2
Big Sioux (riv.), Ia,SD, US 185/J5
Big Spring, Tx, US 187/G4
Big Stone (lake), Mn,SD, US 185/J4
Big Thompson (riv.), Co, US 195/B2
Big Thompson, North Fork (riv.), Co, US 195/A2
Big Timber, Mt, US 184/F4
Big Trout (lake), On, US 180/H3
Big Tujunga Canyon (canyon), Ca, US 194/C3
Big Wood (riv.), Id, US 186/D2
Biga, Turk. 107/H5
Bigadiç, Turk. 148/B2
Bigbury (bay), Eng, UK 90/C6
Biggar, Sk, Can. 184/G2
Biggar, Sc, UK 94/C5
Biggenden, Austl. 171/D4
Biggleswade, Eng, UK 91/F2
Bighorn (basin), Wy, US 186/E1
Bighorn (lake), Mt,Wy, US 184/F4
Bighorn (mts.), Wy, US 182/E3
Bighorn (riv.), Wy, US 184/G4
Biglerville, Pa, US 196/A4
Bignona, Sen. 160/A3
Biguaçu, Braz. 213/B3
Bihać, Bosn. 101/L4
Bihar, India 143/E3
Biharamulo, Tanz. 162/A3
Biharamulo Game Rsv., Tanz. 162/A3
Bihāriganj, India 143/F3
Biharkeresztes, Hun. 106/F2
Bihor (co.), Rom. 99/M5
Bihorel, Fr. 110/D2
Bihoro, Japan 134/D2
Bijagós (arch.), GBis. 151/A3
Bijagós, Arquipélago do (isl.) GBis. 154/B5
Bijapur, India 146/D4
Bījār, Iran 146/E2
Bijāwar, India 142/B3
Bijbiara, India 144/C3
Bijeljina, Bosn. 106/D3
Bijelo Polje, Mont. 106/D4
Bijiang, China 141/G2
Bijie, China 141/J2
Bijni, India 143/H2
Bijnor, India 142/B1
Bikaner, India 147/K3
Bikar (isl.), Mrsh. 174/G3
Bikin, Rus. 129/P2
Bikin (riv.), Rus. 129/N2
Bikini (isl.), Mrsh. 174/F3
Bikramganj, India 142/D3
Bikuar, PN do, Ang. 163/C4
Bila Tserkva, Ukr. 120/D2
Bilāra, India 140/B2
Bilāri, India 142/B1
Bilāsīpāra, India 143/H2
Bilāspur, India 142/D4
Bilāspur, India 143/H2
Bilāspur, India 144/D4
Bilaukraung (range), Myan. 141/G5
Bilauktaung (range), Myan.,Thai. 136/B3
Bilba Morea Claypan (lake), Austl. 167/C3
Bilbays, Egypt 149/B4
Bileća, Bosn. 105/F1
Bilecik (prov.), Turk. 148/B1
Bilgoraj, Pol. 99/M3
Bilgrām, India 142/C2
Bilhaur, India 142/C2
Bilhorod-Dnistrovs'kyy, Ukr. 107/K2
Bilibino, Rus. 123/S3
Bilin (riv.), Myan. 136/B2
Bilin, Czh. 113/G1
Biliri (riv.), Myan. 131/B3
Bill of Portland (pt.), Eng, UK 90/D5
Bill Williams (riv.), Az, US 186/D4
Bille (riv.), Ger. 109/H1
Billère, Fr. 100/C5
Billericay, Eng, UK 88/E2
Billiat Conservation Park, Austl. 173/B2

Billiat Consv. Park, Austl. 171/J5
Billigheim, Ger. 112/C4
Billinge, Eng. UK 93/F4
Billingham, Eng. UK 91/G3
Billings, Mt, US 184/F4
Billingsfors, Swe. 96/E2
Billund (int'l arpt.), Den. 96/C4
Billund, Den. 96/C4
Bilma, Niger 154/H4
Biloela, Austl. 171/C4
Biloku, Guy. 211/G4
Biloxi, Ms, US 191/F4
Bilpa Morea Claypan (lake), Austl. 171/H3
Bilqas Qism Awwal, Egypt 149/B4
Bilsi, India 142/B1
Biltine, Chad 155/K5
Bilzen, Belg. 111/E2
Bima, Indo. 139/E5
Bimberi (peak), Austl. 173/D2
Bimbo, CAfr. 155/J7
Bimini (isls.), Bahm. 199/F2
Bina (riv.), Ger. 113/F6
Bina-Etāwa, India 142/B3
Binalong, Austl. 173/D2
Binasco, It. 116/C2
Binbrook, On, Can. 189/Q9
Binche, Belg. 111/D3
Binchuan, China 141/H2
Bindki, India 142/C2
Bindura, Zim. 163/F4
Binéfar, Sp. 103/F2
Binga (mtn.), Moz. 163/F4
Bingara, Austl. 173/D1
Bingen, Ger. 111/G4
Bingerville, C.d'Iv. 160/E5
Binghamton, NY, US 188/F3
Bingley, Eng, UK 93/G4
Bingöl, Turk. 148/E2
Bingöl (prov.), Turk. 148/E2
Binh Son, Viet. 136/E3
Binhai, China 130/D4
Binhon (peak), Myan. 141/G4
Binisalem, Sp. 103/G3
Binjai, Indo. 138/A3
Binkılıç, Turk. 107/J5
Binnaway, Austl. 173/D1
Binningen, Swi. 114/D2
Binongko (isl.), Indo. 139/F5
Bintang (peak), Malay. 138/B2
Binyamina, Isr. 149/F6
Bio-Bío (riv.), Chile 215/B4
Bio-Bío (pol. reg.), Chile 216/B3
Biograd, Cro. 106/C3
Biogradska NP, Mont. 106/D4
Bioko (isl.), EqG. 151/C4
Biougra, Mor. 156/C3
Bipoint (Bissau) (int'l arpt.), GBis. 160/B4
Bippen, Ger. 109/E3
Bīr, India 147/L5
Bīr Abu Minqār (well), Egypt 159/A3
Bir Aïdiat (well), Mrta. 156/C4
Bir Bel Guerdâne (well), Mrta. 156/C4
Bi'r Ghadir (well), Egypt 159/A3
Bîr Ounâne (well), Mali 156/C5
Bi'r Zayt, WBnk. 149/G8
Birāk, Libya 154/H2
Birao, CAfr. 155/K5
Birātnagar, Nepal 143/F2
Biratori, Japan 134/C2
Birch (mts.), Ab, Can. 180/E2
Birch Creek, Ak, US 192/J2
Birch Hills, Sk, Can. 185/H2
Birch River, Mb, Can. 185/H2
Birchip, Austl. 173/B2
Bird Islet (isl.), Austl. 167/E3
Birds Rock (peak), Austl. 173/D2
Birdsboro, Pa, US 196/C3
Birdwood, Austl. 171/M8
Birecik, Turk. 148/D2
Bīrganj, Nepal 143/F2
Biritiba-Mirim, Braz. 213/G8
Birjand, Iran 147/G2
Birkat Qārūm (lake), Egypt 148/B4
Birken-Honigsessen, Ger. 111/G2
Birkenau, Ger. 112/B3
Birkenfeld, Ger. 111/G4
Birkenhead, Eng. UK 93/E5
Birkenheide, Ger. 112/B4
Birkenwerder, Ger. 98/Q6
Birkirkara, Malta 104/L7
Birkkarspitze (peak), Aus. 115/H3
Bîrlad, Rom. 107/H2
Birmingham, Eng. UK 91/E2
Birmingham (co.), Eng. UK 91/E2
Birmingham (int'l arpt.), Eng. UK 91/E2
Birmingham, Al, US 191/G3
Birmingham, Mi, US 193/F6
Birmingham, Mo, US 195/T5
Birmitrapur, India 143/E4
Birnam, Sc, UK 94/C1
Birnhorn (peak), Aus. 101/K3
Birni Nkonni, Niger 161/G3
Birnie (isl.), Kiri. 175/H5

Birnin Kebbi, Nga. 161/G3
Birobijan, Rus. 129/P2
Bīrpur, India 143/F2
Birr, Ire. 89/Q10
Birs (riv.), Swi. 101/G3
Birsk, Rus. 119/M5
Birstein, Ger. 112/C2
Biruaca, Ven. 211/E3
Biržai, Lith. 97/L3
Birżebbuġa, Malta 104/M7
Bis (lake), Rom. 107/F4
Bisai, Japan 135/L5
Bīsalpur, India 142/B1
Bisamberg, Aus. 107/N7
Bisauli, India 142/B1
Biscarrosse, Fr. 100/C4
Biscarrosse,Étang de (lake), Fr. 100/C4
Biscay (bay), Fr.,Sp. 100/B4
Biscayne NP, Fl, US 191/H5
Bisceglie, It. 104/E2
Bischberg, Ger. 112/D3
Bischheim, Fr. 111/G6
Bischofsgrün, Ger. 113/E2
Bischofsheim, Ger. 112/B3
Bischofsheim an der Rhön, Ger. 112/D2
Bischofshofen, Aus. 101/K3
Bischofszell, Swi. 115/F3
Bischwiller, Fr. 114/D2
Biscubio (riv.), It. 117/F5
Biscucuy, Ven. 210/D2
Bīshah (riv.), SAr. 146/D4
Bishkek (cap.), Kyr. 145/F4
Bishnupur, India 143/F4
Bishop, Ca, US 186/C3
Bishop Auckland, Eng. UK 93/G2
Bishopbriggs, Sc, UK 94/B5
Bishop's Falls, Nf, Can. 189/L1
Bishop's Stortford, Eng. UK 91/G3
Bishopton, Sc, UK 94/B5
Bisingen, Ger. 112/B6
Biskra, Alg. 158/H5
Biskupiec, Pol. 97/J5
Bislig, Phil. 137/E6
Bismarck (cap.), ND, US 185/H4
Bismarck, On, Can. 189/Q9
Bismarck (arch.), PNG 174/D5
Bismarck (sea), PNG 174/D5
Bismil, Turk. 148/E2
Bispgarden, Swe. 95/F3
Bispingen, Ger. 109/G2
Bissau (cap.), GBis. 160/B4
Bissau, India 144/C5
Bissendorf, Ger. 109/F4
Bissett, Mb, Can. 185/K3
Bissingen, Ger. 112/D5
Bistagno, It. 116/B3
Bistrița (riv.), Rom. 107/G2
Bistrița, Rom. 107/G2
Bistrița-Năsăud (prov.), Rom. 107/G2
Biswān, India 142/C2
Bita (riv.), Col. 208/E2
Bitam, Gabon 154/H7
Bitburg, Ger. 111/F4
Bitche, Fr. 111/G5
Bitkin, Chad 155/J5
Bitlis (prov.), Turk. 148/E2
Bitlis, Turk. 148/E2
Bitola, FYROM 105/G2
Bitonto, It. 104/E2
Bitter (lakes), Egypt 159/C2
Bitterfontein, SAfr. 164/B3
Bitterroot (range), Id,Mt, US 184/E4
Bitti, It. 104/A2
Bitung, Indo. 139/G3
Biwa, Japan 135/K5
Bixby, Ok, US 190/E3
Biyalā, Egypt 149/B4
Biyang, China 130/C4
Bizard (isl.), Qu, Can. 189/M7
Bizerte, Tun. 158/L6
Bizerte (gov.), Tun. 158/L6
Bizerte (lake), Tun. 158/L6
Bjärred, Swe. 96/E4
Bjelovar, Cro. 106/C3
Bjerkvik, Nor. 95/F1
Bjerringbro, Den. 96/C1
Bjørkelangen, Nor. 96/D2
Bjørnafjorden (estu.), Nor. 96/A1
Bjørne (pen.), Nun., Can. 181/N2
Bjugn, Nor. 95/C3
Bjuv, Swe. 96/E3
Blå Jungfrun NP, Swe. 96/G3
Blace, Serb. 105/K3
Blachownia, Pol. 99/K3
Black (sea), Asia,Eur. 107/J5
Black (bay), On, Can. 185/L3
Black (riv.), On, Can. 189/R7
Black (mt.), Yk, Can. 192/M3
Black (riv.), China,Viet. 136/D2
Black (for.), Ger. 98/D5
Black (pt.), Eng, UK 90/A6
Black (pt.), NI, UK 92/C2
Black (mts.), Wal, UK 90/C3
Black (mesa), Az, US 187/D4
Black (mts.), Az, US 187/D4
Black (pt.), Ct, US 197/F1
Black (range), NM, US 186/F4

Black (riv.), NY, US 188/F3
Black (hills), SD, US 182/F3
Black (riv.), Wi, US 185/L4
Black Canyon of the Gunnison Nat'l Park, Co, US 186/F3
Black Diamond, Ab, Can. 184/E3
Black Diamond, Wa, US 193/C3
Black Eagle, Mt, US 184/F4
Black Forest (Schwarzwald) (for.), Ger. 112/B6
Black Hawk, Co, US 195/B3
Black Jack, Mo, US 195/B3
Black Mountain NP, Austl. 171/B1
Black Mtn. (mtn.), Wal, UK 90/C3
Black Point, Ca, US 193/K10
Black River, Jam. 203/G2
Black River Falls, Wi, US 185/L4
Black Rock (des.), Nv, US 186/C2
Black Rock (pt.), RI, US 197/G1
Black Sea Lowland (reg.), Mol.,Ukr. 107/J3
Black Sugarloaf (peak), Austl. 173/D1
Black Volta (riv.), Burk. 154/E6
Black Walnut, Mo, US 195/G8
Black Warrior (riv.), Al, US 191/G3
Blackadder Water (riv.), Sc, UK 94/D5
Blackall, Austl. 171/B4
Blackburn, Eng, UK 93/F4
Blackburn, Sc, UK 94/C5
Blackburn with Darwen (co.), Eng, UK 93/F4
Blackbutt, Austl. 171/D4
Blackcraig (peak), Sc, UK 94/B6
Blackdown (hills), Eng, UK 90/C5
Blackdown (hill), Eng, UK 91/F4
Blackdown Tableland NP, Austl. 171/C3
Blackfoot (res.), Id, US 184/F5
Blackheath, Austl. 173/D2
Blackmoor (upland), Eng, UK 90/B5
Blackpool, Eng, UK 93/E4
Blackpool (co.), Eng, UK 93/E4
Blackshear (lake), Ga, US 191/H3
Blackstone, Va, US 188/E4
Blackville, NB, Can. 189/H2
Blackwater, Austl. 171/C3
Blackwater (riv.), Ire. 89/P10
Blackwater (riv.), Eng, UK 88/A2
Blackwater (res.), Sc, UK 94/B3
Blackwater (riv.), RI, US 189/G3
Block Island C. G. Sta., RI, US 197/G1
Blackwell, Ok, US 187/H3
Blackwood (riv.), Austl. 170/B5
Blackwood, NJ, US 196/C4
Bladensburg, Md, US 196/B6
Bladensburg NP, Austl. 171/A3
Bladnoch (riv.), Sc, UK 92/D2
Blaenau Gwent (co.), Wal, UK 90/C3
Blagnac, Fr. 100/D5
Blagnac (int'l arpt.), Fr. 100/D5
Blagny, Fr. 111/F4
Blagoevgrad, Bul. 105/H1
Blagoveshchensk, Rus. 129/N1
Blaine Lake, Sk, Can. 184/G2
Blainville, Qu, Can. 189/N6
Blair (hill), Pa, US 196/C1
Blair Atholl, Sc, UK 94/C3
Blairstown, NJ, US 196/D2
Blaise (riv.), Fr. 100/F2
Blaj, Rom. 107/F2
Blakely, Ga, US 191/G4
Blakeslee, Pa, US 196/C1
Blamont, Fr. 114/C3
Blanc (cape), Fr. 101/G5
Blanc (peak), Fr. 114/C6
Blanc (cape), Mrta. 154/B3
Blanc, Cap (cape), Tun. 158/L6
Blanc Nez (cape), Fr. 110/A2
Blanca (peak), NM, US 184/B2
Blanca (bay), Arg. 205/C6
Blanca, Cordillera (mts.), Peru 208/C4
Blanca, Costa (coast), Sp. 103/E4
Blanchard, Ok, US 190/E3
Blanche (lake), Austl. 171/A1
Blanche (peak), Swi. 114/D5
Blanche (cape), Austl. 171/G5

Blanco (cape), CR 203/E4
Blanco (cape), Mor. 156/A5
Blanco (cape), Peru 208/B4
Blanco (lake), Chile 217/C7
Blanco (riv.), Bol. 208/F6
Blanco (riv.), Tx, US 187/H5
Blanding, Ut, US 186/E3
Blandy, Fr. 88/L6
Blanes, Sp. 103/G2
Blangy-sur-Bresle, Fr. 110/A4
Blankenberge, Belg. 110/C1
Blankenfelde, Ger. 98/Q7
Blankenheim, Ger. 111/F3
Blanquilla (isl.), Ven. 208/F1
Blanquillo, Uru. 217/G2
Blansko, Czh. 99/J4
Blantyre, Malw. 163/G4
Blantyre, Sc, UK 94/B5
Blanzy, Fr. 100/F3
Blaricum, Neth. 108/C4
Blas (riv.), Swi. 115/E4
Blatná, Czh. 113/G4
Blato, Cro. 104/E1
Blatten, Swi. 114/D5
Blau (riv.), Ger. 112/C6
Blaubeuren, Ger. 112/C6
Blauen (peak), Ger. 114/D2
Blaustein, Ger. 112/C6
Blauvelt, NY, US 197/K7
Blåvands (pt.), Den. 96/C4
Blavet (riv.), Fr. 100/B3
Blaye, Fr. 100/C4
Blayney, Austl. 173/D2
Bleckede, Ger. 109/G4
Bled, Slov. 101/L3
Blefjell (peak), Nor. 96/C2
Blégny, Belg. 111/E2
Bléharies, Belg. 110/C2
Bleiburg, Aus. 106/B2
Bleicherode, Ger. 109/H6
Bleik (peak), Ger. 115/G2
Bleiswijk, Neth. 108/B4
Blekinge (co.), Swe. 95/E4
Blendecques, Fr. 110/B2
Blender, Ger. 109/G3
Blenheim, NZ 175/S11
Blénod-lès-Pont-à-Mousson, Fr. 111/F6
Bléone (riv.), Fr. 101/G4
Blesberg (peak), SAfr. 164/C4
Blessington (lake), Ire. 92/B5
Bletterans, Fr. 114/B4
Bleury, Fr. 88/H6
Bleus (mts.), D.R. Congo 155/L7
Bleus, Monts (mts.), D.R. Congo 162/A2
Blida (prov.), Alg. 158/G4
Blida, Alg. 158/G4
Blies (riv.), Ger. 111/G5
Blieskastel, Ger. 111/G5
Blik (mt.), Phil. 139/F2
Blinnenhorn (peak), Swi. 115/E5
Blithe (riv.), Eng, UK 93/F6
Blitfield (res.), Eng, UK 93/G6
Block Island, RI, US 189/G3
Block Island (New Shoreham), RI, US 197/G1
Block Island NWR, RI, US 197/G1
Blodelsheim, Fr. 114/D2
Bloemendaal, Neth. 108/B4
Bloemfontein (cap.), SAfr. 164/D3
Bloemhof, SAfr. 164/D2
Bloemhofdam (res.), SAfr. 164/D2
Blois, Fr. 100/D3
Blomberg, Ger. 109/E1
Blomberg, Ger. 109/G5
Blomstermåla, Swe. 96/G3
Blonay, Swi. 114/C5
Blönduós, Ice. 95/N6
Bloodvein (riv.), Mb,On, Can. 180/G3
Bloody Foreland (pt.), Ire. 89/P9
Bloomfield, NJ, US 197/J8
Bloomfield, NM, US 186/F3
Bloomfield Hills, Mi, US 193/F6
Bloomingdale, NJ, US 197/H7
Bloomingdale, Il, US 193/P16
Bloomington, Mn, US 185/K4
Bloomington, Il, US 185/L5
Bloomington, Ca, US 194/C2
Bloomsburg, Pa, US 196/B2
Bloomsbury, NJ, US 196/C2
Blora, Indo. 138/D5
Blossburg, Pa, US 196/B1
Blountstown, Fl, US 191/G4
Blovice, Czh. 113/G3
Blšanka (riv.), Czh. 101/K1
Blue (mtn.), India 141/G4
Blue (riv.), Ok, US 190/D3
Blue (pt.), Or,Wa, US 182/C2
Blue Head (pt.), Sc, UK 94/C1
Blue Island, Il, US 193/Q16
Blue Lake NP, Austl. 171/D4
Blue Marsh Lake (res.), Pa, US 196/B3
Blue Mesa (res.), Co, US 186/F3
Blue Mountain (peak), Jam. 203/G2

Blue Mountain (ridge), Pa, US 196/A3
Blue Mountains, Austl. 173/D2
Blue Mountains NP, Austl. 173/D2
Blue Nile (riv.), Sudan, Eth. 155/M5
Blue Ridge (mts.), US 191/H3
Blue Ridge Parkway, US 188/D4
Blue Springs, Mo, US 195/E5
Bluefield, WV, US 188/D4
Bluefields, Nic. 203/F4
Bluefields (bay), Nic. 203/F4
Bluejoint (lake), Or, US 186/C2
Bluenose (lake), Nun., Can. 180/E2
Bluff, NZ 175/R12
Bluff (pt.), Austl. 170/B3
Bluff, Austl. 171/C3
Bluff (peak), Austl. 170/C5
Bluffdale, Ut, US 195/K13
Bluffton, In, US 188/C3
Blumberg, Ger. 115/E2
Blümlisalp (peak), Swi. 114/D5
Blyn, Wa, US 193/B1
Blyth (pt.), Austl. 171/H5
Blyth, Eng, UK 93/G1
Blythe, Ca, US 186/D4
Blytheville, Ar, US 187/K4
Bnom Mhai (peak), Viet. 136/D4
Bo, SLeo. 160/C5
Bø, Nor. 96/C2
Bo Hai (Chihli) (gulf), China 130/D3
Boa Esperança, Braz. 213/C2
Boa Esperança, Reprêsa (res.), Braz. 209/J5
Boa Viagem, Braz. 212/C2
Boa Vista, Braz. 211/F4
Boa Vista (int'l arpt.), Braz. 211/F4
Boa Vista (isl.), CpV. 151/K10
Boac, Phil. 137/D5
Boaco, Nic. 202/E3
Boadilla del Monte, Sp. 103/N9
Bo'ai, China 130/C4
Boano (isl.), Indo. 139/G4
Boas (riv.), Nun., Can. 181/H2
Boavita, Col. 191/G3
Boaz, Al, US 191/G3
Boba, Hun. 106/C2
Bobai, China 141/J3
Bobaomby (cape), Madg. 165/J5
Bobbili, India 140/D4
Bobbio, It. 116/C3
Bobenheim-Roxheim, Ger. 112/B3
Bobigny, Fr. 88/K5
Bobingen, Ger. 115/G1
Böblingen, Ger. 112/C5
Bobo Dioulasso, Burk. 160/D4
Boboshevo, Bul. 105/H1
Bobotov Kuk (peak), Mont. 106/D4
Bobovdol, Bul. 105/H1
Bóbr (riv.), Pol. 99/H3
Bobrov, Rus. 120/D2
Bobures, Ven. 210/D2
Boby (peak), Madg. 165/H8
Boca de Aroa, Ven. 210/D1
Boca del Guafo (chan.), Chile 216/B4
Boca del Pao, Ven. 211/E2
Boca del Rio, Mex. 201/N7
Bôca do Acre, Braz. 208/E5
Boca Raton, Fl, US 191/H5
Bocaina, Serra da (mts.), Braz. 213/J7
Bocairente, Sp. 103/E3
Bocas del Toro, Pan. 203/F4
Bocay (riv.), Nic. 203/E3
Bochil, Mex. 202/C2
Bochnia, Pol. 99/L4
Bocholt, Ger. 108/D5
Bocholt, Belg. 111/E1
Bochum, Ger. 109/E5
Bockau, Ger. 113/F2
Bockenem, Ger. 109/H4
Bockenheim an der Weinstrasse, Ger. 111/H4
Bockhorn, Ger. 109/F2
Bockhorn, Ger. 113/E6
Boconó, Ven. 210/D2
Bocq (riv.), Belg. 111/D3
Boda, CAfr. 155/J7
Bodafors, Swe. 96/F3
Bodalla, Austl. 173/D3
Bodaybo, Rus. 123/M4
Boddam, Sc, UK 94/E2
Boddington, Austl. 170/C5
Bode (riv.), Ger. 98/F3
Bodegraven, Neth. 108/B4
Bodélé (depr.), Chad 154/J4
Bodenheim, Ger. 112/B3
Bodenkirchen, Ger. 113/F6
Bodensee (Constance) (lake), Swi 101/H3
Bodenteich, Ger. 109/H3
Bodh Gaya, India 143/E3
Bodhan, India 140/C4
Bodināyakkanūr, India 140/C6
Bodio, Swi. 115/E5
Bodkin (pt.), Md, US 196/B5
Bodmin, Eng, UK 90/B6

Bodmin Moor (upland), Eng, UK 90/B6
Bodø, Nor. 95/E2
Bodocó, Braz. 212/C2
Bodrog (riv.), Hun.,Slvk. 99/L4
Bodrum, Turk. 148/A2
Bódvaszilas, Hun. 99/L4
Boedecker (lake), Co, US 195/B2
Boëge, Fr. 114/C5
Boegoeberg (peak), Namb. 164/A2
Boekel, Neth. 108/C5
Boende, D.R. Congo 155/K8
Boerne, Tx, US 195/T20
Boeuf (riv.), Ar, US 187/K4
Bog of Allen (swamp), Ire. 92/A5
Bogalusa, La, US 191/F4
Bogan (riv.), Austl. 167/D4
Bogan Gate, Austl. 173/C2
Bogandé, Burk. 161/E3
Bogatić, Serb. 106/D3
Bogatynia, Pol. 99/H3
Bogazkale-Alacahöyük NP, Turk. 148/C1
Boğazlıyan, Turk. 148/C2
Bogdanci, FYROM 105/H2
Bogdo, India 143/F4
Bogen, Ger. 113/F5
Bogen, Nor. 95/F1
Bogense, Den. 96/D4
Boggabilla, Austl. 171/C5
Boggabri, Austl. 173/D1
Boggy (peak), Anti. 199/N8
Boglárielle, Hun. 106/C2
Bogliasco, It. 116/C3
Bognor Regis, Eng, UK 91/F5
Bogny-sur-Meuse, Fr. 111/D4
Bogo, Phil. 137/D5
Bogong (mt.), Austl. 173/C3
Bogong NP, Austl. 173/C3
Bogor, Indo. 138/C5
Bogotá (cap.), Col. 208/D3
Bogota, NJ, US 197/J8
Bogovino, FYROM 105/G2
Bogra (pol. reg.), Bang. 143/G3
Bogra, Bang. 143/G3
Bogué, Mrta. 160/B2
Bogy (riv.), Nun., Can. 181/H2
Bohain-en-Vermandois, Fr. 111/D4
Bohemia (reg.), Czh. 99/G4
Bohemian (for.), Czh.,Ger. 98/G4
Bohicon, Ben. 161/F5
Böhme (riv.), Ger. 109/G3
Böhmenkirch, Ger. 112/C5
Bohmte, Ger. 109/F4
Bohners Lake, Wi, US 193/P14
Bohol (isl.), Phil. 137/D6
Böhönye, Hun. 106/C2
Bohu, China 128/E3
Boiling Springs, Pa, US 196/A3
Boipeda, Ilha de (isl.), Braz. 212/C4
Boiro, Sp. 102/A1
Bois-d'Amont, Fr. 114/C4
Bois-d'Arcy, Fr. 88/J5
Bois de Boulogne (dept.), Fr. 88/J5
Bois de Vincennes (dept.), Fr. 88/K5
Bois-des-Filion, Qu, Can. 189/N6
Bois, Rios dos (riv.), Braz. 213/B1
Boisbriand, Qu, Can. 189/N6
Boise (riv.), Id, US 184/E5
Boise City, Ok, US 187/G3
Boissevain, Mb, Can. 185/H3
Boissy-Fresnoy, Fr. 88/L4
Boissy-L'Aillerie, Fr. 88/J4
Boissy-le-Châtel, Fr. 88/M5
Boissy-Saint-Léger, Fr. 88/K5
Boissy-Sans-Avoir, Fr. 88/H5
Boizenburg, Ger. 109/G4
Bojador (cape), Mor. 154/C2
Bojano, It. 106/B5
Boji (plain), Kenya 162/C2
Bojnúrd, Iran 147/G1
Bokaro Steel City, India 143/F4
Boké (pol. reg.), Gui. 160/B4
Boké, Gui. 160/B4
Bokhol (plain), Kenya 162/C2
Boknafjorden (estu.), Nor. 95/C4
Bokol (plain), Kenya 162/C2
Bokoro, Chad 154/J5
Bokpyin, Myan. 136/B4
Boksburg, SAfr. 164/Q13
Bokspits, Bots. 164/C2
Bol, Chad 154/H5
Bolama, GBis. 160/B4
Bolān (pass), Pak. 147/J3
Bolaños de Calatrava, Sp. 102/D3
Bolayır, Turk. 105/K2
Boldești-Scăeni, Rom. 107/H3
Boldon, Eng, UK 93/G2
Bole, China 128/D3
Bole, Gha. 161/E4
Bolesławiec, Pol. 99/H3
Bolgatanga, Gha. 161/E4
Boli, China 129/P2
Boliden, Swe. 95/G2
Bolinao, Phil. 137/C4
Bolívar, Arg. 216/E3

Bolívar, Col. 210/B3
Bolívar (dept.), Col. 210/C2
Bolívar, Ecu. 210/A4
Bolívar, Peru 214/B2
Bolívar, Mo, US 187/J3
Bolívar (peak), Ven. 210/D2
Bolívar (peak), Ven. 211/F3
Bolívar (state), Ven. 211/E3
Bolivia (ctry.), Bol. 208/F7
Bolivia (ctry.), Bol. 195/B2
Bollate, It. 116/C1
Bollène, Fr. 100/F4
Bollington, Swi. 116/C1
Bollin (riv.), Eng, UK 93/F5
Bollnäs, Swe. 96/G1
Bollullos Par del Condado, Sp. 102/B4
Bolmen (lake), Swe. 96/E3
Bolobo, D.R. Congo 154/J8
Bologna, It. 117/E4
Bologna (prov.), It. 117/E4
Bologne, Fr. 114/B1
Bolognesi, Peru 214/C2
Bologoye, Rus. 118/E4
Bolomba, D.R. Congo 155/J7
Bolonchén de Rejón, Mex. 202/D2
Bolovens (plat.), Laos 136/D3
Bolsena, It. 104/B1
Bolsena (lake), It. 104/B1
Bol'shaya Kinel' (riv.), Rus. 121/K1
Bol'shaya Rogovaya (riv.), Rus. 119/P2
Bol'shaya Synya (riv.), Rus. 119/N2
Bol'shevik (isl.), Rus. 125/K2
Bol'shezemel'skaya (tundra), Rus. 119/M2
Bol'shoy Bolvanskiy Nos (pt.), Rus. 122/F2
Bol'shoy Irgiz (riv.), Rus. 121/J1
Bol'shoy Lyakhov (isl.), Rus. 125/P2
Bol'shoy Lyakhovskiy (isl.), Rus. 125/P2
Bol'shoy Uzen' (riv.), Rus. 121/J2
Bolsover, Eng, UK 93/G5
Bolsward, Neth. 108/C2
Bolt (pt.), Eng, UK 90/C6
Boltaña, Sp. 103/F1
Bolton (co.), Eng, UK 93/F4
Bolton, Turk. 107/H5
Bolu (prov.), Turk. 107/K5
Bolu, Turk. 107/K5
Bolungavik, Ice. 95/M6
Bolvadin, Turk. 148/B2
Bóly, Hun. 106/D3
Bolzano, It. 115/H5
Bolzano-Bozen (prov.), It. 115/H4
Bom Conselho, Braz. 212/C3
Bom Despacho, Braz. 213/C2
Bom Jardim, Braz. 213/D4
Bom Jardim de Minas, Braz. 213/J6
Bom Jesus, Braz. 212/A3
Bom Jesus da Gurguéia, Serra (mts.), Braz. 209/K5
Bom Jesus de Goiás, Braz. 213/B1
Bom Jesus do Itabapoana, Braz. 213/D4
Bom Jesus dos Perdões, Braz. 213/G6
Bom Retiro, Braz. 213/B3
Boma, D.R. Congo 163/B2
Bomaderry, Austl. 173/D2
Bombala, Austl. 173/D3
Bombay Hook NWR, De, US 196/C5
Bombay (Mumbai), India 147/K5
Bomberai (pen.), Indo. 139/J4
Bombo, Ugan. 162/A2
Bombo, China 141/G2
Bomlitz, Ger. 109/G3
Bømlo (isl.), Nor. 96/A1
Bomu (riv.), D.R. Congo 155/L6
Bon-Encontre, Fr. 100/D4
Bonaduz, Swi. 115/F4
Bonaire (isl.), NAnt. 199/H5
Bonalbo, Austl. 173/E1
Bonampak (ruin), Mex. 202/D2
Bonao, DRep. 199/G4
Bonao, Ben. 161/F5
Bonaparte (arch.), Austl. 167/B2
Bonaparte (isls.), Austl. 167/B2
Bonasila, Ak, US 192/D3
Bonaventure, Qu, Can. 189/H1
Bonaventure (bay), Qu, Can. 189/H1
Bonavista, Braz. 208/G4
Bonavista, Nf, Can. 189/L1
Bonavista (bay), Nf, Can. 189/L1
Bonavista (cape), Nf, Can. 189/L1
Boncourt, Swi. 114/D3
Bondeno, It. 117/D3
Bondo, D.R. Congo 155/K7
Bondoukou, C.d'Iv. 160/E4
Bondowoso, Indo. 138/D5
Bonen, Ger. 109/E5
Bönen, Ger. 109/E5
Bonerate (isls.), Indo. 139/F5

Bonfol, Swi. 114/D3
Bonfouca, La, US 195/Q16
Bong (co.), Libr. 160/C5
Bong (range), Libr. 160/C5
Bongabong, Phil. 139/F1
Bongaigaon, India 143/H2
Bongandanga, D.R. Congo 155/K7
Bongao, Phil. 139/E3
Bonggi (isl.), Malay. 139/E3
Bongka (riv.), Indo. 139/F4
Bongo, Massif des (plat.), CAfr. 155/K6
Bongolava (uplands), Madg. 165/H7
Bongor, Chad 154/J5
Bonham, Tx, US 187/H4
Bonheiden, Belg. 111/D1
Bonhill, Sc, UK 94/B5
Bonhomme, Col du (pass), Fr. 114/C1
Boni Nat'l Rsv., Kenya 162/D3
Bonifacio, Fr. 104/A2
Bonifacio (str.), It. 104/A2
Bonifay, Fl, US 191/G4
Bönigen, Swi. 114/D4
Bonin (isls.), Japan 174/C2
Bonita, Ca, US 194/C5
Bonita Springs, Fl, US 191/H5
Bonito (peak), Hon. 202/E3
Bonn, Ger. 111/G2
Bonndorf im Schwarzwald, Ger. 115/E2
Bonne, Fr. 114/C5
Bonnelles, Fr. 88/J6
Bonner Springs, Ks, US 195/D5
Bonner-West Riverside, Mt, US 184/E4
Bonners Ferry, Id, US 184/D3
Bonnet Carré Spillway, La, US 195/P16
Bonnet, Lac du (lake), Mb, Can. 185/K3
Bonneuil-sur-Marne, Fr. 88/K5
Bonneval, Fr. 100/D2
Bonneville (dam), Wa,Or, US 184/C4
Bonneville, Fr. 114/C5
Bonney Lake, Wa, US 193/C3
Bönnigheim, Ger. 112/C4
Bonnybridge, Sc, UK 94/C5
Bonorva, It. 104/A2
Bons-en-Chablais, Fr. 114/C5
Bontberg (peak), SAfr. 164/C4
Bontebok NP, SAfr. 164/C4
Bonthain, Indo. 139/E5
Bonthe, SLeo. 160/B5
Bontoc, Phil. 137/D4
Bonyhád, Hun. 106/D2
Booker T. Washington Nat'l Mon., Va, US 191/J2
Boom, Belg. 111/D1
Boone, Ia, US 185/K5
Boone, NC, US 188/D4
Booneville, Ms, US 191/F3
Boonton, NJ, US 197/H8
Boorabbin NP, Austl. 170/D4
Boorama, Som. 155/P6
Booroondara (mt.), Austl. 173/C1
Boorowa, Austl. 173/D2
Boos (int'l arpt.), Fr. 100/D2
Boos, Fr. 115/G1
Boosaaso (Bender Cassim), Som. 155/Q5
Boostedt, Ger. 96/D4
Boothbay Harbor, Me, US 189/G3
Boothia (pen.), Nun., Can. 180/G1
Boothia (gulf), Nun., Can. 180/G1
Bootle, Eng, UK 93/E5
Booué, Gabon 154/H8
Bopa, Ben. 161/F5
Bopfingen, Ger. 112/D5
Boppard, Ger. 111/G3
Boppy (mt.), Austl. 173/C1
Boqueirão, Braz. 212/C2
Boqueirão, Serra do (mts.), Braz. 212/B3
Boquete (peak), Arg. 216/C4
Boquillas del Carmen, Mex. 190/C4
Boquira, Braz. 212/B4
Bor, Rus. 119/K4
Bor, Turk. 148/C2
Bor Ul (mts.), China 128/D3
Bora Bora (isl.), FrPol. 175/V4
Borah (peak), Id, US 184/F4
Borås, Swe. 96/E3
Borāzjān, Iran 146/F3
Borba, Braz. 208/G4
Borba, Port. 102/B3
Borba (riv.), It. 116/B3
Borbore (riv.), It. 116/B3
Borborema, Planalto da (plat.), Braz. 209/L5
Borča, Serb. 106/E2
Borcea Branch (riv.), Rom. 107/H3
Borchen, Ger. 109/F5
Borçka, Turk. 121/C4
Borculo, Neth. 108/D4
Borda da Mata, Braz. 213/G7

Bordeaux, Fr. 100/C4
Borden (isl.), NW,Nun., Can. 181/R7
Borden (pen.), Nun., Can. 181/H1
Bordentown, NJ, US 196/D3
Bordertown, Austl. 173/B3
Bordj Bou Arreridj, Alg. 158/H4
Bordj Bou Arreridj (prov.), Alg. 158/H4
Bordj el Kiffan, Alg. 158/G4
Bordj Manaïel, Alg. 158/G4
Bordj Moktar, Alg. 157/F5
Bordj Omar Driss, Alg. 157/G3
Bordj Sainte-Marie, Alg. 156/E4
Borehamwood, Eng, UK 88/C2
Borest, Fr. 88/L4
Boretto, It. 116/D3
Borgå (Porvoo), Fin. 97/L1
Borgaretto, It. 116/A2
Borgaro Torinese, It. 116/A2
Borgarnes, Ice. 95/N7
Borgefjell NP, Nor. 95/E2
Borgentreich, Ger. 109/G5
Borger, Tx, US 187/G4
Börger, Ger. 109/E3
Borger, Neth. 108/D3
Borgerhout, Belg. 108/B6
Borges Blanques, Sp. 103/F2
Borghetto Lodigiano, It. 116/B4
Borghetto Santo Spirito, It. 116/B4
Borgholm, Swe. 96/G3
Borgholzhausen, Ger. 109/F4
Borghorst, Ger. 109/E4
Borgloon, Belg. 111/E2
Borgne (lake), La, US 195/Q17
Borgne (riv.), Swi. 114/D5
Borgo (int'l arpt.), Burk. 160/D4
Borgo, Fr. 104/A1
Borgo, It. 115/H5
Borgo a Mozzano, It. 116/D5
Borgo San Dalmazzo, It. 101/G4
Borgo San Giacomo, It. 116/C2
Borgo San Lorenzo, It. 116/D5
Borgo Tossignano, It. 117/E4
Borgo Val di Taro, It. 116/C4
Borgo Vercelli, It. 116/B2
Borgofranco d'Ivrea, It. 116/A1
Borgomanero, It. 116/B1
Borgonovo Val Tidone, It. 116/C2
Borgosatollo, It. 116/D2
Borgosesia, It. 116/B1
Borgou (prov.), Ben. 161/F4
Borgund, Nor. 96/B1
Borio, India 143/F3
Borisoglebsk, Rus. 121/G2
Borispol (int'l arpt.), Ukr. 120/D2
Borja, Peru 214/B2
Borja, Sp. 102/E2
Borken, Ger. 108/D5
Borken, Ger. 109/G6
Børkop, Den. 96/C4
Borkum, Ger. 100/D1
Borkum (isl.), Ger. 108/D1
Borlänge, Swe. 96/F1
Bormida (riv.), It. 101/H4
Bormida, It. 116/B4
Bormida di Millesimo (riv.), It. 116/B4
Bormio, It. 115/G5
Born, Neth. 111/E1
Borna, Ger. 98/G3
Borndiep (chan.), Neth. 108/C2
Borne, Neth. 108/D4
Borne (riv.), Fr. 114/C6
Bornel, Fr. 110/B5
Bornem, Belg. 111/D1
Bornemouth, Eng, UK 91/E5
Bornemouth (co.), Eng, UK 91/E5
Borneo (isl.), Indo.,Malay. 138/D3
Bornheim, Ger. 109/E1
Bornholm (co.), Den. 96/F4
Bornholm (isl.), Den. 96/F4
Bornholmsgat (chan.), Den.,Swi. 99/H1
Borno, It. 115/G6
Bornos, Sp. 102/C4
Börnsen, Ger. 109/H2
Bornu (plain), Nga. 154/H5
Boro (riv.), Sudan 155/L6
Borohoro (mts.), China 128/D3
Borongan, Phil. 137/E3
Borough Green, Eng, UK 88/B3
Borovany, Czh. 113/H5
Borovichi, Rus. 118/G4
Borovo, Bul. 107/G4
Borovo, Cro. 106/D3
Borre, Nor. 96/C2
Borrisokane, Ire. 89/H10
Borrnida (riv.), It. 116/B3
Borşa, Rom. 107/G2
Borsec, Rom. 107/G2
Borso del Grappa, It. 117/E1
Borsod-Abaúj-Zemplén (co.), Hun. 106/E1
Borssele, Neth. 108/A4
Borstel, Ger. 109/F3
Bort-les-Orgues, Fr. 100/D4
Boruca, CR 203/F4

Borūjerd, Iran 146/E2
Boryslav, Ukr. 99/M4
Borzonasca, It. 116/C4
Borzya, Rus. 129/L1
Bosa, It. 104/A2
Bosanska Dubica, Bosn. 106/C3
Bosanska Gradiška, Bosn. 106/C3
Bosanska Kostajnica, Bosn. 106/C3
Bosanska Krupa, Bosn. 106/C3
Bosanski Brod, Bosn. 106/D3
Bosanski Petrovac, Bosn. 106/C3
Bosanski Šamac, Bosn. 106/D3
Bōsō (pen.), Japan 133/G3
Bosco Mesola, It. 117/F3
Bosconero, It. 116/A2
Bose, China 141/J3
Boshof, SAfr. 164/D3
Boskoop, Neth. 108/B4
Boskovice, Czh. 99/J4
Bosna (riv.), Bosn. 106/D3
Bosnia and Herzegovina (ctry.) 106/C3
Bošnjaci, Cro. 106/D3
Bōsō (pen.) 133/G3
Bosobolo, D.R. Congo 155/J7
Bosporus (str.), Turk. 107/J5
Bosque Farms, NM, US 186/F4
Bosques Petrificados, Mon. Natural, Arg. 217/C5
Bossangoa, CAfr. 155/J6
Bossier City, La, US 187/J4
Bostān, Iran 146/E2
Bostānābād-e Bālā, Iran 146/E1
Boston (mts.), Ar, US 187/J4
Boston (cap.), Ma, US 189/G3
Boston, Eng, UK 93/H6
Bosut (riv.), Cro. 106/D3
Boswil, Swi. 115/E3
Botād, India 147/K4
Boteler (peak), NC, US 191/H3
Botelerpunt (pt.), SAfr. 165/F2
Botelhos, Braz. 213/G6
Botev (peak), Bul. 105/J1
Botevgrad, Bul. 105/H1
Bothaspas (pass), SAfr. 165/E2
Bothaville, SAfr. 164/D2
Bothel, Ger. 109/G2
Bothell, Wa, US 193/C2
Bothnia (gulf), Fin.,Swe. 218/E
Bothwell, Austl. 173/C4
Botoşani (prov.), Rom. 107/H2
Botoşani, Rom. 107/H2
Botou, China 130/D3
Botrange (peak), Belg. 111/F3
Botrivier, SAfr. 164/L11
Botsford, Ct, US 197/E1
Botswana (ctry.) 163/D5
Bottanuco, It. 116/C1
Botte Donato (peak), It. 104/E3
Botticino, It. 116/D1
Bottineau, ND, US 185/H4
Bottrighe, It. 117/F2
Bottrop, Ger. 108/D5
Botucatu, Braz. 213/B2
Botwood, Nf, Can. 189/L1
Bou (riv.), C.d'Iv. 160/D4
Bou Arfa, Mor. 157/E2
Boû Djébéha (well), Mali 160/E2
Bou Hamdane, Oued (riv.), Alg. 158/K6
Bou Ismaïl, Alg. 158/G4
Bou Izakarn, Mor. 156/C5
Bou Kadir, Alg. 158/F4
Bou Laber (well), Alg. 156/D4
Bou Naceur (peak), Mor. 158/C3
Bou Regreg (riv.), Mor. 158/A3
Bou Salem, Tun. 158/L6
Bou Sellam, Oued (riv.), Alg. 158/H4
Bouaflé, C.d'Iv. 160/D5
Bouaflé, Fr. 88/H5
Bouaké, C.d'Iv. 160/D5
Bouar, CAfr. 154/J6
Boubin (peak), Czh. 113/G5
Bouca, CAfr. 155/J6
Bouchain, Fr. 110/C3
Bouchegouf, Alg. 158/K6
Boucherville, Qu, Can. 189/P6
Boucle du Baoulé, PN de la, Mali 154/D5
Boucle Du Baoulé, PN de la, Mali 160/C3
Boudry, Swi. 114/C4
Boufarik, Alg. 158/G4
Bouffémont, Fr. 88/J4
Bougainville (reef), Austl. 167/D2
Bougainville (isl.), PNG 174/E5
Bougainville (cape), Falk., UK 217/F6

Bougara, Alg. 158/G4
Bougar'oûn (cape), Alg. 158/K6
Bough Beech (res.), Eng, UK 88/D3
Bougouni, Mali 160/D4
Bougouriba (prov.), Burk. 160/E4
Bouguenais, Fr. 100/C3
Bouhachem (peak), Mor. 158/B2
Bouhalla (peak), Mor. 158/B2
Bouillancy, Fr. 88/L4
Bouillon, Belg. 111/E4
Bouira (prov.), Alg. 158/G4
Bouira, Alg. 158/G4
Boujad, Mor. 156/D2
Boukhalf (Tangier) (int'l arpt.), Mor. 158/B2
Boukoumbé, Ben. 161/F4
Boulaide, Lux. 111/E4
Boulaouane, Mor. 156/C2
Boulay-Moselle, Fr. 111/F5
Boulazac, Fr. 100/D4
Boulder, Co, US 195/B2
Boulder (co.), Co, US 195/B2
Boulder, Mt, US 184/E4
Boulder City, Nv, US 186/D4
Boulder Hill, Il, US 193/P16
Boulemane, Mor. 156/D2
Boulemane (prov.), Mor. 158/C3
Bouleurs, Fr. 88/L5
Boulgou (prov.), Burk. 161/E4
Boulia, Austl. 171/H2
Bouligny, Fr. 111/E5
Boulkiemde (prov.), Burk. 161/E3
Boullarre, Fr. 88/M4
Boulogne (riv.), Fr. 100/C3
Boulogne-Billancourt, Fr. 88/J5
Boulogne-sur-Mer, Fr. 110/A2
Boulsworth (hill), Eng, UK 93/F4
Boumalne, Mor. 156/D3
Boumerdas (prov.), Alg. 158/G4
Boumerdas, Alg. 158/G4
Boun Nua, Laos 141/H3
Bouna, C.d'Iv. 160/E4
Bound Brook, NJ, US 196/D2
Boundary (peak), Nv, US 186/C3
Boundiali, C.d'Iv. 160/D4
Bountiful, Ut, US 195/K12
Bouquet (res.), Ca, US 194/B1
Bouquet (canyon), Ca, US 194/B2
Bourbon l'Archambault, Fr. 100/E3
Bourbonnais (reg.), Fr. 100/D3
Bourbonne-les-Bains, Fr. 114/B2
Bourbourg, Fr. 110/B2
Bourdonné, Fr. 88/G5
Bourem, Mali 161/E2
Bouressa (riv.), Mali 161/F2
Bourg-en-Bresse, Fr. 114/B5
Bourg-lès-Valence, Fr. 100/F4
Bourg-Saint-Andéol, Fr. 100/F4
Bourg-Saint-Maurice, Fr. 101/G4
Bourg-Saint-Pierre, Swi. 114/D6
Bourganeuf, Fr. 100/D4
Bourges, Fr. 100/E3
Bourget (lake), Fr. 114/B6
Bourget (bay), Fr. 100/B3
Bourgogne (pol. reg.), Fr. 100/F3
Bourgogne (canal), Fr. 114/B3
Bourgoin-Jallieu, Fr. 100/F4
Bourke, Austl. 173/C1
Bourmont, Fr. 114/B1
Bourne, Eng, UK 91/E4
Bourne End, Eng, UK 91/F3
Bourne, The (riv.), Eng, UK 88/B3
Bournemouth, Eng, UK 91/E5
Bournezeau, Fr. 100/C3
Bourscheid, Lux. 111/F4
Bourtanger Moor (reg.), Ger. 109/E3
Bousbecque, Fr. 110/C3
Bousso, Chad 154/J5
Boussois, Fr. 110/D3
Boutilimit, Mrta. 160/B2
Boutte, La, US 195/P17
Bouvard (cape), Austl. 170/B5
Bouvet (isl.), Nor. 81/K8
Bouxières-aux-Dames, Fr. 111/F6
Bouxwiller, Fr. 111/G6
Bouznika, Mor. 158/A3
Bouzonville, Fr. 111/F5
Bovalino, It. 104/E3
Bovegno, It. 116/D1
Boven Tapanahoni (riv.), Sur. 211/H4
Bovenden, Ger. 109/G5
Bovenwijde (lake), Neth. 108/D3
Boves, Fr. 110/B4
Bovezzo, It. 116/D1

Bovingdon, Eng, UK 88/B1
Bovino, It. 106/B5
Bovolone, It. 117/E2
Bow (riv.), Ab, Can. 180/E3
Bow Island, Ab, Can. 180/E3
Bowdle, SD, US 185/J4
Bowdon, Eng, UK 93/F5
Bowen, Austl. 171/C3
Bowen, Arg. 216/D2
Bowers Beach, De, US 196/C5
Bowie, Az, US 186/F4
Bowie, Md, US 196/B6
Bowling Green (cape), Austl. 171/B2
Bowling Green, Ky, US 188/C4
Bowling Green, Mo, US 187/K3
Bowling Green, Oh, US 188/D3
Bowling Green Bay NP, Austl. 171/B2
Bowman, ND, US 185/H4
Bowman (bay), Nun., Can. 181/J2
Bowmansdale, Pa, US 196/B3
Bowmanstown, Pa, US 196/C2
Bowmansville, Pa, US 196/C2
Bowmore, Sc, UK 89/Q9
Bowokan (isls.), Indo. 139/F4
Bowral, Austl. 173/D2
Bowron (riv.), BC, Can. 184/C2
Box Elder (co.), Ut, US 195/J11
Boxberg, Ger. 112/C4
Boxholm, Swe. 96/F2
Boxing, China 130/D3
Boxmeer, Neth. 108/C5
Boxtel, Neth. 108/C5
Boyabat, Turk. 148/C1
Boyaca (dept.), Col. 210/C3
Boyanup, Austl. 170/B5
Boye, China 130/C3
Boyer (riv.), Ia, US 185/K5
Boyertown, Pa, US 196/C2
Boyle, Ab, Can. 184/E2
Boyle, Ire. 89/P10
Boyne (riv.), Ire. 89/Q10
Boyne City, Mi, US 188/C2
Boynton Beach, Fl, US 191/H5
Boysen (res.), Wy, US 184/F5
Boyup Brook, Austl. 170/C5
Boz (pt.), Turk. 121/J3
Bozashchy Tübegi (pen.), Kaz. 121/J3
Bozcaada (isl.), Gre. 105/J3
Bozcaada, Turk. 148/A2
Bozeman, Mt, US 184/F4
Bozkir, Turk. 148/C2
Bozkurt, Turk. 120/E4
Bozman, Md, US 196/B6
Bozoum, CAfr. 154/J6
Bozova, Turk. 148/D2
Bozüyük, Turk. 148/B2
Bozyazı, Turk. 149/C1
Bozzolo, It. 116/D2
Bra, It. 116/A3
Braan (riv.), Sc, UK 94/C3
Brač (isl.), Cro. 104/E1
Bracciano (lake), It. 104/B1
Bracebridge, On, Can. 188/E2
Bracken, Tx, US 115/U20
Brackenheim, Ger. 112/B1
Brackettville, Tx, US 187/G5
Bracknell, Eng, UK 91/F4
Bracknell Forest (co.), Eng, UK 91/F4
Braço do Norte, Braz. 213/B4
Brad, Rom. 107/F2
Bradano (riv.), It. 106/B5
Bradda (pt.), IM, UK 92/D3
Bradenton, Fl, US 191/H5
Bradford, Ma, US 197/G2
Bradford (co.), Eng, UK 93/G4
Bradford, Eng, UK 93/G4
Bradford, Pa, US 188/E3
Bradley (int'l arpt.), Ct, US 189/F3
Bradley Beach, NJ, US 196/D3
Brady, Tx, US 187/H5
Braemar (reg.), Sc, UK 94/C2
Braeriach (peak), Sc, UK 94/C2
Braga (dist.), Port. 102/A2
Braga, Port. 102/A2
Bragado, Arg. 216/E2
Bragança (dist.), Port. 102/B2
Bragança, Port. 102/B2
Brāhmanbāria, Bang. 143/H4

Brahmaputra (riv.), Asia 141/F2
Braich-y-Pwll (pt.), Wal, UK 92/D6
Braid (riv.), NI, UK 92/B2
Brăila (prov.), Rom. 107/H3
Brăila, Rom. 107/H3
Brainards, NJ, US 196/C2
Braine, Fr. 110/C5
Braine-l'Alleud, Belg. 111/D2
Braine-le-Comte, Belg. 111/D2
Brainerd, Mn, US 185/K4
Braintree, Eng, UK 91/G3
Braithwaite, La, US 195/Q17
Brak (riv.), SAfr. 164/C3
Brake, Ger. 109/F2
Brakel, Belg. 110/C2
Brakel, Ger. 109/G5
Brakel, Neth. 108/C5
Brakna (pol. reg.), Mrta. 160/B2
Brålanda, Swe. 96/E2
Bram, Fr. 100/E5
Bramdrupdam, Den. 96/C4
Bramley, Eng, UK 88/B3
Brampton, On, Can. 189/Q8
Bramsche, Ger. 109/F4
Bramstedt, Ger. 109/F2
Bran (riv.), Sc, UK 94/A1
Brancaleone-Marina, It. 104/E3
Branch Dale, Pa, US 196/B2
Branchville, NJ, US 196/D1
Branchville, Ct, US 197/E1
Branco (riv.), Chile 217/C7
Branco (riv.), Braz. 205/C2
Brand, Aus. 115/F3
Brandberg (peak), Namb. 163/B5
Brandbu, Nor. 96/D1
Brande, Den. 96/C4
Brandenburg (state), Ger. 98/P6
Brandenburg, Ger. 98/G2
Brander, Pass of (pass), Sc, UK 94/A4
Brandizzo, It. 116/A2
Brandon, Mb, Can. 185/J3
Brandon, Fl, US 191/H5
Brandon, Ms, US 191/F3
Brandsen, Arg. 217/J11
Brandvlei, SAfr. 164/C3
Brandýs nad Labem, Czh. 113/H2
Brandywine, Md, US 196/B6
Brandywine (riv.), Pa, US 196/C4
Branford, Ct, US 197/F1
Branges, Fr. 114/B4
Braniewo, Pol. 97/H4
Brannenburg, Ger. 101/K3
Brant Beach, NJ, US 196/D4
Branxholm, Austl. 173/C4
Branzoll (Bronzolo), It. 115/H4
Bras d'Or (lake), NS, Can. 189/J2
Brasiléia, Braz. 208/E6
Brasília de Minas, Braz. 212/A5
Brasília, PN de, Braz. 212/B1
Braşov, Rom. 107/G3
Braşov (prov.), Rom. 107/G3
Brasschaat, Belg. 108/B6
Brassey (mt.), Austl. 171/G2
Brasstown Bald (peak), Ga, US 191/H3
Brastad, Swe. 96/D2
Bratislava (cap.), Slvk. 101/M2
Bratislava (Ivanka) (int'l arpt.), Slvk. 106/C1
Bratislavský (pol. reg.), Slvk. 99/J4
Bratsk, Rus. 123/L4
Brattleboro, Vt, US 189/F3
Bratunac, Bosn. 106/D3
Braubach, Ger. 111/G3
Braulio Carrillo, PN, CR 198/E5
Braunau am Inn, Aus. 113/G6
Braunfels, Ger. 112/B1
Braunig (lake), Tx, US 195/U21
Bräunlingen, Ger. 115/E2
Braunschweig, Ger. 109/H4
Brava (pt.), Chile 217/C7
Brava (riv.), Uru. 217/K11
Brava, Costa (coast), Sp. 103/G2
Bråviken (inlet), Swe. 96/G2
Bravo (peak), Bol. 208/F7
Bravo del Norte (riv.), Mex. 198/A2
Brawley, Ca, US 186/D4
Bray (isl.), Nun., Can. 181/J2
Bray, Ire. 92/B5
Bray (pt.), Ire. 92/B5

Bray-Dunes, Fr. 110/B1
Braye (riv.), Fr. 100/D3
Brazey-en-Plaine, Fr. 114/B3
Brazil (ctry.) 205/D3
Brazilian Highlands (uplands), Braz. 205/E4
Brazo Casiquiare (riv.), Ven. 211/E4
Brazo Sur (riv.), Arg. 217/C6
Brazópolis, Braz. 213/H7
Brazos (riv.), Tx, US 190/D3
Brazos, Salt Fork (riv.), Tx, US 190/C3
Brazzaville (cap.), Congo 163/C1
Brčko, Bosn. 106/D3
Brda (riv.), Pol. 96/G5
Brdy (mts.), Czh. 99/G4
Brea, Ca, US 194/G8
Breadalbane (dist.), Sc, UK 94/B3
Breamish (riv.), Eng, UK 94/C6
Bréancon, Fr. 88/J4
Breaza, Rom. 107/G3
Brebbia, It. 116/B1
Brèche (riv.), Fr. 110/B5
Brechen, Ger. 112/B2
Brechin, Sc, UK 94/D3
Brecht, Belg. 108/B6
Breckenridge, Mn, US 185/J4
Breckenridge, Tx, US 187/H4
Breckerfeld, Ger. 109/E6
Breckland (phys. reg.), Eng, UK 91/G2
Brecknock (pen.), Chile 217/C7
Brecon, Wal, UK 90/C3
Brecon Beacons (mts.), Wal, UK 90/C3
Breda, Neth. 108/B5
Bredaryd, Swe. 96/E3
Bredasdorp, SAfr. 164/M11
Bredene, Belg. 110/B1
Bredstedt, Ger. 96/C4
Bree (riv.), SAfr. 164/B4
Breë (riv.), SAfr. 164/B4
Bree, Belg. 111/E1
Breg (riv.), Ger. 98/E5
Bregagno (peak), It. 115/F5
Bregalnica (riv.), FYROM 105/H2
Breganze, It. 117/E1
Bregenz, Aus. 115/F3
Bregenzer Ache (riv.), Aus. 115/F3
Brégy, Fr. 88/L4
Breidhafjördhur (bay), Ice. 95/M6
Breil-Brigels, Swi. 115/F4
Breisach, Ger. 114/D1
Breitbrunn am Chiemsee, Ger. 113/F2
Breitenauriegel (peak), Ger. 113/G5
Breitenbach, Swi. 114/D3
Breitenbrunn, Ger. 113/E4
Breitenfurt bei Wien, Aus. 107/N7
Breitenworbis, Ger. 109/H6
Breithorn (peak), Swi. 114/D6
Breithorn (peak), Swi. 114/D6
Brejo Santo, Braz. 212/B2
Brejões, Braz. 212/B3
Brembate di Sopra, It. 116/C1
Brembilla, It. 116/C1
Brembo (riv.), It. 115/F6
Bremen (int'l arpt.), Ger. 109/F2
Bremen (state), Ger. 96/C5
Bremen, Ger. 109/F2
Bremer (riv.), Austl. 171/F1
Bremerhaven, Ger. 109/F1
Bremerton, Wa, US 184/C4
Bremervörde, Ger. 109/G2
Bremgarten bei Bern, Swi. 114/D4
Bremnes, Nor. 96/A2
Brendel (lake), Mi, US 193/E7
Brendola, It. 117/E2
Brendon (hills), Eng, UK 90/C4
Brenes, Sp. 102/C4
Brenham, Tx, US 190/D4
Brenig, Llyn (lake), Wal, UK 92/C5
Brenne (riv.), Fr. 98/C5
Brenner (pass), Aus. 115/H3
Brenner (riv.), Austl. 171/N9
Brenno (riv.), Swi. 115/F4
Breno, It. 115/G6
Brent (bor.), Eng, UK 88/C2
Brent (res.), Eng, UK 88/C2
Brentwood, Ca, US 193/L11

Brentwood, Eng, UK 88/D2
Brenz (riv.), Ger. 112/D5
Brescello, It. 116/D3
Brescia (prov.), It. 115/G6
Brescia, It. 116/D1
Bresle (riv.), Fr. 100/D1
Bresles, Fr. 110/B5
Bressana, It. 116/C2
Bressanone, It. 101/J3
Bressay (isl.), Sc, UK 89/W13
Bressuire, Fr. 100/C3
Brest, Fr. 100/A2
Brest, Bela. 99/M2
Brest (int'l arpt.), Bela. 99/M2
Bretagne (pol. reg.), Fr. 100/B2
Bretagne, Monts de (mts.), Fr. 100/B2
Bretagne, Pointe de (pt.), Reun., Fr. 165/S15
Bretaña, Peru 214/C2
Brétigny-sur-Orge, Fr. 88/J6
Bréau, Fr. 88/L6
Breton (cape), NS, Can. 184/E2
Breton (chan.), Can. 189/K2
Brett (cape), NZ 175/S10
Brett (riv.), Eng, UK 91/G2
Brettach (riv.), Ger. 112/C4
Bretten, Ger. 112/B4
Bretzenheim, Ger. 111/G4
Breuberg, Ger. 112/C3
Breuillet, Fr. 88/J6
Breukelen, Neth. 108/B4
Breuna, Ger. 109/G6
Breuvannes-en-Bassigny, Fr. 114/B1
Breves, Braz. 209/H4
Brevig Mission, Ak, US 192/E2
Brevik, Nor. 96/C2
Brevoort (isl.), Nun., Can. 181/K2
Brewarrina, Austl. 173/C1
Brewer, Me, US 189/G2
Brewster, Ne, US 185/J5
Brewton, Al, US 191/G4
Brey-et-Lü, Fr. 88/G4
Breyten, SAfr. 165/E2
Brežice, Slov. 101/L4
Brezina, CAfr. 155/K6
Březnice, Czh. 113/H3
Breznik, Bul. 105/H1
Brezno, Slvk. 99/K4
Brezoi, Rom. 107/G3
Brezovo, Bul. 105/J1
Briançon, Fr. 101/G4
Brianne, Llyn (res.), Wal, UK 90/C2
Briar Creek, Pa, US 196/B1
Briare, Fr. 100/E3
Brickerville, Pa, US 196/B3
Bricktown, NJ, US 196/D3
Bride (riv.), Ire. 89/P10
Bride, IM, UK 92/D3
Bridge City, Tx, US 190/E4
Bridge of Allan, Sc, UK 94/C2
Bridge of Don, Sc, UK 94/C2
Bridge of Weir, Sc, UK 94/B5
Bridgehampton, NY, US 197/F2
Bridgend, Wal, UK 90/C3
Bridgend (co.), Wal, UK 90/C3
Bridgeport, Ca, US 186/C3
Bridgeport, Ct, US 197/E1
Bridgeport, Ne, US 185/H5
Bridgeton, NJ, US 196/D4
Bridger, Mt, US 184/F4
Bridgeton, Me, US 189/G2
Bridgetown, Austl. 170/C5
Bridgetown (cap.), Bar. 199/P9
Bridgeville, De, US 196/C5
Bridgewater, Austl. 173/C4
Bridgewater, NS, Can. 189/H2
Bridgnorth, Eng, UK 90/D4
Bridgton, Me, US 189/G2
Bridgwater, Eng, UK 90/D4
Bridgwater (bay), Eng, UK 90/D4
Bridlington, Eng, UK 93/H3
Bridlington (bay), Eng, UK 93/H3
Bridport, Austl. 173/C4
Bridport, Eng, UK 90/D5
Brie, Swi. 115/E3
Brie-Comte-Robert, Fr. 88/K6
Brieg Brzeg, Pol. 99/J3
Brielle, Neth. 108/B5
Brielle, NJ, US 196/D3
Brienz, Swi. 114/E4
Brier, Wa, US 193/C2
Brierfield, Eng, UK 93/F4
Brieselang, Ger. 98/O6
Brig, Swi. 114/D4
Brigantine, NJ, US 196/D4
Brigg, Eng, UK 93/H4
Brighouse, Eng, UK 93/G4
Bright, Austl. 173/C3
Brightlingsea, Eng, UK 91/H3
Brighton, Austl. 173/A2
Brighton and Hove (co.), Eng, UK 91/F5
Brighton, Co, US 195/C3
Brighton, Il, US 195/H13
Brighton, Ut, US 195/K12
Brighton, Wi, US 193/P14
Brignais, Fr. 100/F4
Brignoles, Fr. 100/G5
Brihuega, Sp. 102/D2

Briis-sous-Forges, Fr. 88/J6
Brikama, Gam. 160/A3
Brilhante (riv.), Braz. 209/G8
Brilon, Ger. 109/F6
Brimstone Hill NP, StK. 199/N8
Brindisi, It. 105/E2
Brinkworth, Austl. 171/H5
Brinnon, Wa, US 193/B2
Brión, Sp. 102/A1
Brione, Swi. 115/E4
Briones (res.), Ca, US 193/K11
Brisbane, Austl. 171/F6
Brisbane (int'l arpt.), Austl. 171/F6
Brisbane (riv.), Austl. 171/E7
Brisbane Forest Park, Austl. 171/E6
Brisbane Ranges NP, Austl. 173/C3
Brisbane Water NP, Austl. 173/D2
Brisighella, It. 117/E4
Brissago, Swi. 115/E4
Bristol, Eng, UK 90/D4
Bristol (chan.), Eng,Wal, UK 90/B4
Bristol (co.), Eng, UK 90/D4
Bristol (bay), Ak, US 192/F4
Bristol, Pa, US 196/D3
Bristol, Tn, US 188/D4
Bristow, Ok, US 187/H4
British Columbia (prov.), Can. 180/D3
British Empire (range), Nun., Can. 181/S6
British Indian Ocean Territory (dpcy.), UK 125/G10
British Museum, Eng, UK 88/C2
Britstown, SAfr. 164/C3
Brittany (reg.), Fr. 100/B3
Britton, SD, US 185/J4
Brive-la-Gaillarde, Fr. 100/D4
Brives-Charensac, Fr. 100/E4
Briviesca, Sp. 102/D1
Brivio, It. 116/C1
Brněnský (pol. reg.), Slvk. 99/J4
Brnik (int'l arpt.), Slov. 101/L3
Brno, Czh. 99/J4
Broa (bay), Cuba 203/F1
Broad (pass), Ak, US 192/J3
Broad (riv.), NC,SC, US 191/H3
Broad Law (peak), Sc, UK 94/C5
Broad Sound (isls.), Austl. 171/C2
Broadback (riv.), Qu, Can. 188/E1
Broadford, Austl. 173/C3
Broadkill (riv.), De, US 196/C6
Broads NP, The, Eng, UK 91/H1
Broadstairs, Eng, UK 91/H4
Broadus, Mt, US 185/G4
Broadwater NP, Austl. 173/E1
Broadway (hill), Eng, UK 91/E3
Broadway, NJ, US 196/C2
Broc, Swi. 114/D4
Brochet, Mb, Can. 180/F3
Brock (isl.), NW, Can. 181/R7
Brocken (peak), Ger. 109/H6
Brockman (mt.), Austl. 170/C2
Brockton, Ma, US 189/G3
Brockville, On, Can. 188/F2
Brodeur (pen.), Nun., Can. 181/J2
Brodheadsville, Pa, US 196/C2
Brodnica, Pol. 99/K2
Broek in Waterland, Neth. 108/B4
Broek Op Langedijk, Neth. 108/B3
Bröhn (peak), Ger. 109/G4
Broken (bay), Austl. 173/D2
Broken Arrow, Ok, US 187/J3
Broken Bow, Ne, US 185/J5
Broken Bow (lake), Ok, US 187/J4
Broken Bow, Ok, US 187/J4
Broken Hill, Austl. 173/B1
Brokeoff (mts.), NM, US 190/B3
Brokopondo, Sur. 211/H3
Brokopondo (dist.), Sur. 211/H3
Brome, Ger. 98/F2
Bromölla, Swe. 96/F3
Bromsgrove, Eng, UK 90/D2
Bromskirchen, Ger. 109/F6
Bron, Fr. 114/A6
Brønderslev, Den. 96/C3
Brong-Ahafo (pol. reg.), Gha. 161/E5
Broni, It. 116/C2
Bronkhorstspruit, SAfr. 164/E2

Brønnøy, Nor. 95/E2
Brøns, Den. 96/C4
Bronschhofen, Swi. 115/F3
Bronte, It. 104/D4
Bronx (bor.), NY, US 197/K2
Bronx Zoo, NY, US 197/K8
Bronxville, NY, US 197/K8
Brook Forest, Co, US 195/B3
Brooke's Point, Phil. 139/E2
Brookfield, Il, US 193/Q16
Brookhaven, Ms, US 187/K5
Brooklyn (bor.), NY, US 196/D2
Brooklyn, Il, US 195/G8
Brooklyn Park, Md, US 196/B5
Brookmans Park, Eng, UK 88/C1
Brooks (mtn.), Ak, US 192/E2
Brooks, Ab, Can. 184/F3
Brooks, Il, US 195/G8
Brooks (range), Ak, US 192/F2
Brookside, De, US 196/C4
Brooksville, Fl, US 191/H4
Brookton, Austl. 170/C5
Brookvale, Co, US 195/B3
Brookville, NY, US 197/L8
Broomall, Pa, US 196/C4
Broomfield, Co, US 195/B3
Brørup, Den. 96/C4
Brösarp, Swe. 96/F4
Brossard, Qu, Can. 185/P7
Brough (pt.), Sc, UK 89/V14
Broughshane, NI, UK 92/B2
Brousseval, Fr. 114/A1
Brouwersdam (dam), Neth. 108/A5
Brouwershaven, Neth. 108/A5
Brovst, Den. 96/C3
Brown (mt.), Austl. 171/H5
Brown (pt.), Austl. 171/G5
Brown Clee (hill), Eng, UK 90/D2
Brown Shoal (bar), Asia 137/C5
Brownfield, Tx, US 187/G4
Brownhills, Eng, UK 91/E1
Browning, Mt, US 184/E3
Browns Mills, NJ, US 196/D4
Brownsea (isl.), Eng, UK 91/E5
Brownsville, Tn, US 188/B5
Brownsville, Tx, US 190/D5
Brownsville, Wa, US 193/B2
Broxburn, Sc, UK 94/C5
Broye (riv.), Swi. 114/C4
Brozas, Sp. 102/B3
Bruay-la-Buissière, Fr. 110/C3
Bruay-sur-L'Escaut, Fr. 110/C3
Bruce (pen.), On, Can. 188/D2
Bruce (mt.), Austl. 170/B3
Bruce Rock, Austl. 170/C5
Bruchberg (peak), Ger. 109/H5
Bruche (riv.), Fr. 101/G2
Bruchhausen-Vilsen, Ger. 109/G3
Bruchköbel, Ger. 111/G5
Bruchmühlbach-Miesau, Ger. 111/F5
Bruchsal, Ger. 112/B4
Brucht (riv.), Ger. 109/G5
Bruck, Aus. 107/P7
Bruck an der Grossglocknerstrasse, Aus. 101/K3
Bruck an der Mur, Aus. 101/L3
Bruckberg, Ger. 113/F5
Bruckmühl, Ger. 101/J3
Brue (riv.), Eng, UK 90/D4
Bruflat, Nor. 96/C1
Brügg, Swi. 114/D3
Brugg, Swi. 114/E3
Brugge, Belg. 110/C1
Brüggen, Ger. 108/D6
Brugnera, It. 117/F1
Brühl, Ger. 111/F2
Bruinisse, Neth. 108/B5
Brukkaros (peak), Namb. 164/B2
Brukunga, Austl. 171/M8
Brumado, Braz. 212/B4
Brumath, Fr. 111/G6
Brummen, Neth. 108/D4
Brumunddal, Nor. 96/D1
Brune (riv.), Fr. 110/C4
Bruneau (riv.), Id,Nv, US 184/E5
Brunei (ctry.) 138/D3
Brunete, Sp. 103/M9
Brunflo, Swe. 95/E3
Brunico, It. 101/J3
Brünigpass (pass), Swi. 114/E4
Brunn am Gebirge, Aus. 107/N7
Brunoy, Fr. 88/K5
Brunsbüttel, Ger. 109/G1
Brunssum, Neth. 111/E2
Brunstatt, Fr. 114/D2
Brunswick, Ga, US 191/H4

Brunswick, Me, US 189/G3
Brunswick, Oh, US 188/D3
Brunswick Heads, Austl. 171/D5
Brunswick Junction, Austl. 170/B5
Brunswick, Península de (pen.), Chile 215/B7
Brus (lake), Hon. 203/E3
Brusartsi, Bul. 106/F4
Brushy Creek, Tx, US 187/J5
Brusio, Swi. 115/G5
Brussels, Il, US 195/F8
Brussels (int'l arpt.), Belg. 111/D2
Brussels (Bruxelles) (cap.), Belg. 111/D2
Brusson, It. 116/A1
Bruthen, Austl. 173/C3
Bruyères, Fr. 114/C1
Bruyères-le-Châtel, Fr. 88/J6
Bruyères-sur-Oise, Fr. 88/K4
Bruz, Fr. 100/C2
Bruzual, Ven. 210/D2
Bryan, Tx, US 187/H5
Bryan, Oh, US 188/C3
Bryan (mt.), Austl. 171/H5
Bryansk, Rus. 120/E1
Bryanskaya Oblast, Rus. 120/E1
Bryce Canyon NP, Ut, US 186/D3
Bryn Brawd (peak), Wal, UK 90/C2
Bryn Mawr, Pa, US 196/C3
Bryne, Nor. 96/A2
Brzeg Dolny, Pol. 99/J3
Brzesko, Pol. 99/L4
Brzozów, Pol. 99/M4
Bua, Swe. 96/E3
Buala, Sol. 174/E5
Buba, GBis. 160/B4
Bubaque, GBis. 160/B4
Bubendorf, Swi. 114/D3
Bubikon, Swi. 115/E3
Bubu (riv.), Tanz. 162/B4
Buc, Fr. 88/J5
Bucak, Turk. 148/B2
Bucakkışla, Turk. 149/C1
Bucasia, Austl. 171/C3
Bucelas, Port. 103/P10
Buch, Ger. 115/G1
Buchan (gulf), Nun., Can. 181/J1
Buchan (reg.), Sc, UK 94/D1
Buchan Ness (pt.), Sc, UK 94/E2
Buchanan, Libr. 160/C5
Buchanan (lake), Tx, US 187/H5
Buchans, Nf, Can. 189/K1
Bucharest (București) (cap.), Rom. 107/H4
Buchbach, Ger. 113/F6
Büchen, Ger. 109/H2
Buchen, Ger. 112/C3
Buchenberg, Ger. 115/G2
Buchholz, Ger. 111/G3
Buchholz in der Nordheide, Ger. 109/G2
Buchloe, Ger. 115/G1
Buchon (pt.), Ca, US 186/B4
Buchs, Swi. 115/F3
Buckden Pike (peak), Eng, UK 93/F3
Bückeburg, Ger. 109/G4
Buckie, Sc, UK 94/D1
Buckingham, Qu, Can. 188/F2
Buckingham Palace, Eng, UK 88/C2
Buckland, Ak, US 192/F2
Buckley, Wal, UK 93/E5
Buckley, Wa, US 193/C3
Buckner, Mo, US 195/E5
Bucks (co.), Pa, US 196/C3
Bucksburn, Sc, UK 94/D2
Bucquoy, Fr. 110/B3
Buctouche, NB, Can. 189/H2
București (co.), Rom. 107/G3
Bucy-le-Long, Fr. 110/C5
Bucyrus, Oh, US 188/D3
Bucyrus, Ks, US 195/D6
Budai hegy (hill), Hun. 107/Q9
Budakeszi, Hun. 107/Q9
Budaörs, Hun. 107/R10
Budapest (cap.), Hun. 107/R9
Budapest (co.), Hun. 107/R9
Budaun, India 142/B1
Budd (coast), Ant. 218/H
Budd (inlet), Wa, US 193/B3
Budd Lake, NJ, US 196/D2
Buddon Ness (pt.), Sc, UK 94/D4
Buddusò, It. 104/A2
Bude, Eng, UK 90/B5
Bude (bay), Eng, UK 90/B5
Budějovický (pol. reg.), Slvk. 99/H4

Budel, Neth. 108/C6
Büdelsdorf, Ger. 96/C4
Budge-Budge, India 143/G4
Budhana, India 142/D5
Budhanilantha, Nepal 143/E2
Budhlada, India 144/C5
Budia, Sp. 102/D2
Büdingen, Ger. 112/C2
Budrio, It. 117/E3
Budva, Mont. 106/D4
Budzhak (reg.), Mol. 107/J2
Buea, Camr. 154/G7
Buelna (int'l arpt.), Mex. 184/D4
Buena, NJ, US 196/D4
Buena Esperanza, Arg. 216/D2
Buena Fe, Ecu. 210/B5
Buena Park, Ca, US 194/G8
Buena Vista, Co, US 187/F3
Buenaventura, Mex. 184/D4
Buenaventura, Col. 210/B4
Buenavista, Mex. 201/Q9
Buenavista, Phil. 137/E6
Bueno (riv.), Chile 216/B4
Bueno Brandão, Braz. 213/G7
Buenópolis, Braz. 212/A5
Buenos Aires (cap.), Arg. 217/J11
Buenos Aires (lake), Arg.,Chile 205/B7
Buenos Aires (prov.), Arg. 216/E3
Buenos Aires, Col. 210/B4
Buenos Aires, Peru 214/B2
Buenos Aires (Jorge Newbery) (int'l arpt.), Arg. 217/J11
Buenos Aires (Ministro Pistarini) (int'l arpt.), Arg. 217/J11
Buerarema, Braz. 212/C4
Buesaco, Col. 210/B4
Buet (peak), Fr. 114/C5
Bueu, Sp. 102/A1
Buffalo (mt.), Austl. 173/C3
Buffalo (lake), Ab, Can. 184/E2
Buffalo (riv.), SAfr. 165/E2
Buffalo (riv.), Ar, US 190/E3
Buffalo, Mn, US 185/K4
Buffalo, NY, US 189/S10
Buffalo, Ok, US 187/H3
Buffalo, SD, US 185/H4
Buffalo, Wy, US 184/G4
Buffalo Bill Museum and Grave, Co, US 195/B3
Buffalo Narrows, Sk, Can. 184/F2
Buffalo Springs Nat'l Rsv., Kenya 162/C2
Buffelsrivier (riv.), SAfr. 164/B3
Buford, Ga, US 191/G3
Buftea, Rom. 107/G3
Bug (riv.), Pol. 99/M2
Buga, Col. 210/B4
Bugaba, Pan. 203/F4
Bugac, Hun. 106/D2
Bugala (isl.), Ugan. 162/B3
Bugalagrande, Col. 210/B3
Bugat, Mong. 128/F2
Buğdaylı, Turk. 107/H5
Bugel (pt.), Indo. 138/D5
Buggenhout, Belg. 111/D1
Bugojno, Bosn. 106/C3
Bugosa (prov.), Ugan. 162/B2
Bugsuk (isl.), Phil. 139/E2
Bugul'ma, Rus. 119/M5
Buguruslan, Rus. 121/K1
Buh (riv.), Ukr. 99/M3
Buhayrat al Asad (lake), Syria 148/D2
Buḩayrat ath Tharthār (res.), Iraq 148/E3
Buhi, Phil. 137/D5
Buhl, Fr. 114/D2
Bühl, Ger. 115/E2
Bühler (riv.), Ger. 112/C4
Bühlerzell, Ger. 112/C5
Buhuşi, Rom. 107/H2
Buí (dam), Gha. 161/E4
Bui Gorge (res.), Gha. 161/E4
Bui NP, Gha. 161/E4
Buin (peak), Swi. 115/G4
Buin, Chile 216/N8
Buíque, Braz. 212/B3
Bujalance, Sp. 102/C4
Bujanovac, Serb. 106/E4
Bujumbura (cap.), Buru. 162/A3
Bujumbura (int'l arpt.), Buru. 162/A3
Buk, Pol. 99/J2
Buka (isl.), PNG 174/E5
Bukadaban (peak), China 128/F4
Bükän, Iran 146/E1
Bukasa (isl.), Ugan. 162/B3
Bukavu, D.R. Congo 162/B4
Bukene, Tanz. 162/B4
Buket Bubat (peak), Malay. 141/H6
Bukhoro (pol. reg.), Uzb. 145/D4
Bukhoro (prov.), Uzb. 145/D4
Bukhovo, Bul. 105/H1
Bukidnon (prov.), Phil. 137/D5
Bukit Gantang, Malay. 141/H6
Bukittinggi, Indo. 138/B4
Bükk NP, Hun. 99/L4
Bukoba, Tanz. 162/A3

Buku (cape), Indo. 138/B4
Bülach, Swi. 115/E2
Bulahdelah, Austl. 173/D2
Bulan, Phil. 139/F1
Bulancak, Turk. 148/D1
Bulandshahr, India 142/A1
Bulanık, Turk. 148/E2
Bulawa (peak), Indo. 139/F3
Bulawayo, Zim. 163/E5
Buldan, Turk. 148/B2
Buldibuyo, Peru 214/B3
Bulgan, Mong. 128/H1
Bulgan (prov.), Mong. 128/H2
Bulgan, Mong. 128/H3
Bulgan, Mong. 128/H3
Bulgaria (ctry.) 107/G4
Bŭlgarovo, Bul. 107/H4
Bulgheria (peak), It. 104/D2
Buliluyan (cape), Phil. 139/E2
Bulkley (riv.), BC, Can. 184/B2
Bull (pt.), NI, UK 92/B1
Bull Shoals (lake), Ar,Mo, US 187/J3
Bullange, Belg. 111/F3
Bullas, Sp. 102/E3
Bulle, Swi. 114/D4
Buller (isl.), NZ 175/S11
Bullerup, Den. 96/D4
Bullhead City, Az, US 186/D4
Bullion, Fr. 88/H6
Bulloo (riv.), Austl. 167/D3
Bulloo River Overflow (swamp), Austl. 171/A5
Bully-les-Mines, Fr. 110/B3
Bulnayn (mts.), Mong. 128/G2
Bulnes, Chile 216/B2
Bulolo (riv.), SAfr. 164/D3
Bulukumba, Indo. 139/F5
Bulverde, Tx, US 195/U20
Bumba, D.R. Congo 155/K7
Bumtang (riv.), Bhu. 143/G2
Bumthang, Bhu. 143/H2
Bunaga-take (peak), Japan 135/J5
Bunbury, Austl. 170/B5
Bundaberg, Austl. 171/D4
Bundarra, Austl. 173/D1
Bünde, Ger. 109/F4
Bunde, Ger. 109/F2
Bundoran, Ire. 89/P9
Bündü, India 143/E4
Bungendore, Austl. 173/D2
Bunguran (isl.), Indo. 138/C3
Bunia, D.R. Congo 162/A2
Bunker (peak), Az, US 195/R18
Bunker Hill, Il, US 195/H7
Bunkie, La, US 187/J5
Bunnell, Fl, US 191/H4
Bunnik, Neth. 108/C4
Buñol, Sp. 103/E3
Bunschoten, Neth. 108/C4
Bunya, Austl. 171/E6
Bunya Mountains NP, Austl. 171/C4
Bünyan, Turk. 148/C2
Bunyu (isl.), Indo. 139/E3
Buochs, Swi. 115/E4
Buon Me Thuot, Viet. 136/E4
Buonconvento, It. 101/J5
Bugala (pt.), Pan. 203/F4
Bür Sa'īd (gov.), Egypt 149/C4
Bür Sa'īd (Port Said), Egypt 149/C4
Bür Südān (Port Sudan), Sudan 159/D5
Burang, China 128/D5
Buranga (pass), Ugan. 155/M7
Burano (riv.), It. 117/F2
Burano, It. 117/F2
Buras-Triumph, La, US 191/F4
Burauen, Phil. 137/D5
Buraydah, SAr. 146/D3
Burbach, Ger. 111/H2
Burbank, Ca, US 194/F7
Burbure, Fr. 110/B3
Burco (Burao), Som. 155/O6
Burdekin (riv.), Austl. 167/D2
Burdell (mtn.), Ca, US 193/J10
Burdur (lake), Turk. 148/B2
Burdur (prov.), Turk. 148/B2
Burdur, Turk. 148/B2
Burdwān, India 143/F4
Büren (riv.), Eng, UK 91/H1
Büren, Neth. 108/C5
Büren an der Aare, Swi. 114/D3
Bürengiyn (mts.), Mong. 128/H2
Bürewäla, Pak. 144/B4
Bureya (riv.), Rus. 123/N4
Burg, Ger. 96/C4
Burg, Ger. 96/C4
Burgas (prov.), Bul. 105/K1
Burgas (bay), Bul. 107/H4
Burgas (int'l arpt.), Burgas, Bul. 107/H4
Burgau, Ger. 112/D6
Burgaw, NC, US 191/J3
Burgberg im Allgäu, Ger. 115/G2
Burgbernheim, Ger. 112/D3
Burgbrohl, Ger. 111/G3
Burgdorf, Ger. 112/D3
Burgdorf, Swi. 114/D3
Burgebrach, Ger. 112/D3

Burgenland (prov.), Eng, UK 99/J5
Burgeo, Nf, Can. 189/K2
Burgersdorp, SAfr. 164/D3
Burgess (mt.), Austl. 170/D4
Burgess Hill, Eng, UK 91/F5
Burgess, Yk, Can. 192/L2
Burgfjället (peak), Swe. 95/E2
Burghaslach, Ger. 112/D3
Burghausen, Ger. 113/F6
Burghead, Sc, UK 94/C1
Burghead (bay), Sc, UK 94/C1
Burgheim, Ger. 112/E5
Burgkirchen, Aus. 113/G6
Burgkirchen an der Alz, Ger. 113/F6
Burgkunstadt, Ger. 112/E2
Bürglen, Swi. 115/F2
Burglengenfeld, Ger. 113/F4
Burgos, Mex. 201/F3
Burgos, Sp. 102/D1
Burgsinn, Ger. 112/C2
Burgstall (Postal), It. 115/H4
Burgsteinfurt, Ger. 109/E4
Burgsvik, Swe. 96/H3
Burgundy (reg.), Fr. 100/F3
Burhä Balang (riv.), India 143/F4
Burhan Budai (mts.), China 128/G4
Burhaniye, Turk. 148/A2
Burhänpur, India 147/L4
Burhar-Dhanpuri, India 142/C4
Burhi Gandak (riv.), India 143/E2
Burica (pen.), Pan. 203/F4
Burica (pt.), Pan. 203/F4
Burin, Nf, Can. 189/L2
Burin (pen.), Nf, Can. 181/L4
Buriram, Thai. 136/C3
Buritama, Braz. 213/B2
Buriti, Braz. 212/B1
Buriti Alegre, Braz. 213/B1
Buriti Bravo, Braz. 212/B2
Buriti dos Lopes, Braz. 212/B2
Buritis, Braz. 212/A4
Buritizeiro, Braz. 212/A5
Burjasot, Sp. 103/E3
Burka, Rwa. 162/A3
Burke (chan.), BC, Can. 184/B2
Burketown, Austl. 167/C2
Burkina Faso (ctry.) 161/E3
Burksville, Il, US 195/G9
Burladingen, Ger. 115/F1
Burley, Wa, US 193/B3
Burli, It. 116/B1
Burlingame, Ca, US 193/K11
Burlington, On, Can. 189/D9
Burlington, Co, US 187/G3
Burlington, Ia, US 185/L5
Burlington, Il, US 193/N15
Burlington, Ks, US 187/J3
Burlington, NC, US 191/J2
Burlington, NJ, US 196/D3
Burlington (co.), NJ, US 196/D4
Burlington, Vt, US 188/F2
Burlington, Wi, US 188/B3
Burma (Myanmar) (ctry.) 141/G3
Bürmoos, Aus. 113/F7
Burnas (lake), Ukr. 107/K3
Burnet, Tx, US 187/H5
Burnet Heads, Austl. 171/D4
Burney, Ca, US 186/B2
Burney (peak), Chile 217/B7
Burnham, Il, US 193/Q16
Burnham-on-Sea, Eng, UK 90/D4
Burnie-Somerset, Austl. 173/C4
Burnley, Eng, UK 93/F4
Burns, Or, US 184/D4
Burns Lake, BC, Can. 184/B2
Burnside (riv.), Nun., Can. 180/E2
Burntisland, Sc, UK 94/C4
Burntwood, Eng, UK 91/E1
Burntwood (riv.), Mb, Can. 180/G3
Buronga, Austl. 173/B2
Buronzo, It. 116/B2
Burqä, WBnk. 149/G7
Burqīn, WBnk. 149/G7
Burr Ridge, Il, US 193/Q16
Burra, Austl. 171/H5
Burrel, Alb. 105/G2
Burrendong (res.), Austl. 173/D2
Burrewarra (pt.), Austl. 173/D2
Burriana, Sp. 103/E3
Burringbar, Austl. 171/D4
Burrinjuck (res.), Austl. 173/D2
Burrow (pt.), Sc, UK 92/D2
Burrowes (pt.), Austl. 173/C4
Burrum Heads, Austl. 171/D4
Burrum River NP, Austl. 171/D4
Bursa, Turk. 148/B1
Bursa (prov.), Turk. 148/B1
Burscheid, Ger. 111/G1
Bürstadt, Ger. 112/B4
Burt, NY, US 189/S9
Burtenbach, Ger. 112/D6
Burton, Wa, US 193/C3

Burton Latimer, Eng, UK 91/F2
Burton upon Trent, Eng, UK 91/E1
Buru (isl.), Indo. 139/G4
Buru (isl.), Indo. 139/G4
Burundi (ctry.) 162/B3
Bururi, Buru. 162/A3
Buruticupu (riv.), Braz. 212/A2
Burwash Landing, Yk, Can. 192/L3
Bury, Eng, UK 93/F4
Bury (co.), Eng, UK 93/F4
Bury, Fr. 110/B5
Bury Saint Edmunds, Eng, UK 91/G2
Burynshyk (pt.), Kaz. 121/J3
Busalla, It. 116/B3
Busca, It. 116/A3
Busembatia, Ugan. 162/B2
Busenberg, Ger. 111/G5
Buseno, Swi. 115/F5
Bushy, India 143/J3
Bush (riv.), Md, US 196/B5
Bush Kill (riv.), Pa, US 196/C1
Bushey, Eng, UK 88/B2
Bushkill, Pa, US 196/C1
Bushkill Falls, Pa, US 196/C1
Bushmanland (reg.), SAfr. 164/B3
Bushmills, NI, UK 92/B1
Busigny, Fr. 110/C4
Businga, D.R. Congo 155/K7
Buskerud (co.), Nor. 95/D3
Busko-Zdrój, Pol. 99/L3
Buss Craig (pt.), Sc, UK 94/D5
Busselton, Austl. 170/B5
Busseri (riv.), Sudan 155/L6
Busseto, It. 116/D3
Bussolengo, It. 117/D2
Bussum, Neth. 108/C4
Bustamante, Mex. 201/E3
Bustamante, Mex. 201/F4
Bustamante (pt.), Arg. 217/C6
Bustard (pt.), Austl. 171/C4
Buşteni, Rom. 107/G3
Busto Arsizio, It. 116/B1
Busto Garolfo, It. 116/B1
Busuanga (isl.), Phil. 137/C5
Büsum, Ger. 96/C4
Buta, D.R. Congo 155/K7
Buta Ranquil, Arg. 216/C3
Butaritari (isl.), Kiri. 174/G4
Butawal, Nepal 142/D2
Bute (inlet), BC, Can. 184/B3
Bute, Austl. 171/H5
Bute (isl.), Sc, UK 94/A5
Bute, Sound of (sound), Sc, UK 94/A5
Büteeliyn (mts.), Mong. 128/H2
Butembo, D.R. Congo 162/A2
Bütgenbach, Belg. 111/F3
Buti, It. 116/D5
Butiaba, Ugan. 162/A2
Butler, NJ, US 197/H8
Butler, Pa, US 188/E3
Butmir (int'l arpt.), Bosn. 106/C4
Buton (isl.), Indo. 139/F5
Bütschelegg (peak), Swi. 114/D4
Bütschwil, Swi. 115/F3
Butt of Lewis (pt.), Sc, UK 89/Q7
Butte, Mt, US 184/F4
Butte-Silver Bow County, Mt, US 184/F4
Butterhude, Ger. 109/G2
Butterworth, Malay. 138/B2
Buttes, Swi. 114/C4
Buttevant, Ire. 89/P10
Buttrio, It. 117/F1
Butuan, Phil. 137/E6
Buturlinovka, Rus. 121/G2
Butzbach, Ger. 112/B2
Bützow, Ger. 96/D5
Büüech (riv.), Fr. 100/F4
Buulo Berde, Som. 155/O6
Buuma (isl.), Ugan. 162/B3
Buxar, India 142/D3
Buxheim, Ger. 115/G2
Buxtehude, Ger. 109/G2
Buxton, Eng, UK 93/G5
Buxton, Austl. 173/C3
Buy, Rus. 118/J4
Buyant-Uhaa, Mong. 129/K3
Buynaksk, Rus. 121/H4
Buyo, Barrage de (dam), C.d'Iv. 160/D5
Büyük Anafarta, Turk. 105/K2
Büyükarmutlu, Turk. 148/B2
Büyükçekmece, Turk. 148/B1
Büyükceli, Turk. 149/C1
Büyükkarıştıran, Turk. 107/J5
Büyükyurt, Turk. 148/D2
Buyun Shan (peak), China 131/B2
Buyuni (riv.), Tanz. 162/B4
Büzău, Rom. 107/H3
Büzău (prov.), Rom. 107/H3
Büzău (riv.), Rom. 106/H3
Buzău, Rom. 107/H3
Buzescu, Rom. 107/G4
Buz'ky Lyman (estu.), Ukr. 107/K2
Buzuluk, Rus. 121/K1
Buzuluk, Rus. 121/K1
Byala, Bul. 107/G4

Byala, Bul. 107/H4
Byala Slatina, Bul. 107/F4
Byam Martin (chan.), Nun., Can. 181/R7
Byam Martin (isl.), Nun., Can. 181/R7
Byarezina (riv.), Bela. 118/E5
Bydgoszcz, Pol. 99/J2
Byfleet, Eng, UK 88/B3
Byford, Austl. 170/L7
Bygland, Nor. 96/B2
Bykhov, Bela. 97/P5
Bykle, Nor. 96/B2
Bykovo (int'l arpt.), Rus. 119/X9
Bylot (isl.), Nun., Can. 181/J1
Bynum Run (riv.), Md, US 196/B4
Byram (riv.), Ct, US 197/L7
Byram (pt.), Ct, US 197/L8
Byram (lake), NY, US 197/L7
Byrd, US, Ant. 218/S
Byrd (cape), Ant. 218/U
Byron, Ca, US 193/L11
Byron (isl.), Chile 217/B5
Byron Bay, Austl. 171/D5
Byrranga (mts.), Rus. 122/K2
Byrum, Den. 96/D3
Bystřice (riv.), Czh. 113/F2
Bystrá (peak), Slvk. 99/K4
Bystřice, Czh. 113/H3
Bytantay (riv.), Rus. 123/N3
Bytom, Pol. 99/K3
Bytów, Pol. 96/G4

C

C.F. Secada (int'l arpt.), Peru 214/C1
Ca (riv.), Viet. 141/J4
Ca Mau, Viet. 136/D4
Ca Mau (cape), Viet. 136/D4
Caála, Ang. 163/C3
Caatingas (phys. reg.), Braz. 205/G4
Caazapá, Par. 215/E2
Cabadbaran, Phil. 137/E6
Cabaiguán, Cuba 203/G1
Caballo (res.), NM, US 186/F4
Caban-Coch (res.), Wal, UK 90/C2
Cabanaconde, Peru 214/C4
Cabañaquinta, Sp. 102/C1
Cabanatuan, Phil. 137/D4
Cabanes, Sp. 103/F2
Cabano, Qu, Can. 189/G2
Cabella Ligure, It. 116/C3
Cabestany, Fr. 100/E5
Cabeza del Buey, Sp. 102/C3
Cabeza Lagarto (pt.), Peru 214/B3
Cabezón de la Sal, Sp. 102/C1
Cabildo, Arg. 216/E3
Cabimas, Ven. 210/D2
Cabinda, Ang. 163/B2
Cabo, Braz. 212/D3
Cabo Corrientes, Cabo (cape), Mex. 184/D4
Cabo de Hornos, PN, Chile 215/C8
Cabo Delgado (prov.), Moz. 162/C5
Cabo Frio, Braz. 213/D2
Cabo Gracias a Dios, Nic. 203/F3
Cabo Orange, PN do, Braz. 209/H3
Cabo San Lucas, Mex. 184/C4
Cabo Verde, Braz. 213/G6
Cabonga (res.), Qu, Can. 181/J4
Caboolture, Austl. 172/D4
Cabora Bassa (lake), Moz. 163/F4
Cabora Bassa, Barragem de (dam), Moz. 163/F4
Cabot (str.), NS,Nf, Can. 181/K4
Cabra, Sp. 102/C4
Cabra de Santo Cristo, Sp. 102/D4
Cabral, Serra do (range), Braz. 212/A5
Cabras, It. 104/A3
Cabrera, Isla de (isl.), Sp. 103/G3
Cabri, Sk, Can. 184/F3
Cabriel (riv.), Sp. 102/E3
Cabrillo Nat'l Mon., Ca, US 194/C5
Cabrobó, Braz. 212/B3
Cabruta, Ven. 211/E3
Cabudare, Ven. 210/D2
Caburé, Ven. 210/D2
Caçador, Braz. 213/B3
Cačak, Serb. 106/E3
Cacalotán, Mex. 200/D4
Caccia (cape), It. 104/A2
Cacequi, Braz. 213/A4
Cáceres, Sp. 102/B3
Cáceres (prov.), Sp. 102/B3
Cáceres, Col. 210/C3
Cachapoal (riv.), Chile 216/N9
Cachari, Arg. 217/J12
Cache (peak), Id, US 184/E5
Cache (co.), Ut, US 195/K11
Cache Creek, BC, Can. 184/C3

Cache la Poudre (riv.), Co, US 195/C2
Cache Slough (riv.), Ca, US 193/L10
Cacheu, GBis. 160/A3
Cachí, Arg. 215/C2
Cachicadán, Peru 214/B3
Cachimbo, Serra do (mts.), Braz. 209/G5
Cachipo, Ven. 211/E2
Cachoeira de Minas, Braz. 213/H7
Cachoeira do Sul, Braz. 213/A4
Cachoeira Paulista, Braz. 213/H7
Cachoeiras de Macacu, Braz. 213/L7
Cachoeirinha, Braz. 213/B4
Cachoeirinha, Braz. 213/G6
Caçu, Braz. 213/B1
Caculé, Braz. 212/B4
Caddo (mts.), Ar, US 190/E3
Cadelbosco di Sopra, It. 116/D3
Cadelle (peak), It. 115/F5
Cadenberge, Ger. 109/G1
Cader Idris (peak), Wal, UK 90/C1
Cadibarrawirracanna (lake), Austl. 171/G4
Cadillac, Mi, US 188/C2
Cadiz, Phil. 139/F1
Cadiz, Ky, US 188/C4
Cádiz, Sp. 102/B4
Cádiz, Golfo de (gulf), Port.,Sp. 102/B4
Cadolzburg, Ger. 112/D4
Cadria (peak), It. 115/G4
Caen, Fr. 100/C2
Caerano di San Marco, It. 117/F1
Caernarfon (bay), Wal, UK 92/D5
Caernarfon, Wal, UK 92/D5
Caernarfon Castle, Wal, UK 92/D5
Caerphilly, Wal, UK 90/C3
Caerphilly (co.), Wal, UK 90/C3
Caesarea (ruin), Isr. 149/G6
Caesarea (ruin), Isr. 149/D3
Caetité, Braz. 212/B4
Cafarnaum, Braz. 212/B3
Cafayate, Arg. 215/C2
Cagayan Sulu (isl.), Phil. 137/C6
Cagli, It. 117/F5
Cagliari, It. 104/A3
Cagliari, Golfo di (gulf), It. 104/A3
Cagnes-sur-Mer, Fr. 101/G5
Caguán (riv.), Col. 208/D3
Caguas, PR 199/M8
Caher, Ire. 89/Q10
Cahirsiveen, Ire. 88/N11
Cahokia, Il, US 195/G8
Cahore (pt.), Ire. 89/Q10
Cahors, Fr. 100/D4
Cahuacan, Mex. 200/T10
Cahuapanas, Peru 214/B2
Cahuinari (riv.), Col. 210/D5
Cahuita, PN, CR 203/F4
Cahul, Mol. 107/J3
Cai (riv.), Braz. 213/B4
Caia, Moz. 163/G4
Caiapó (riv.), Braz. 213/B1
Caiapó, Serra (mts.), Braz. 209/H7
Caibarién, Cuba 203/G1
Caicara, Ven. 211/E3
Caicara, Ven. 211/E3
Caicó, Braz. 212/C2
Caicos (isls.), UK 199/G3
Caicos Passage (chan.), Bahm. 203/H1
Caieiras, Braz. 213/G8
Cailloma, Peru 214/C4
Cailly (riv.), Fr. 110/A4
Caio (peak), It. 116/B1
Cairate, It. 116/B1
Cairn (mtn.), Ak, US 192/G3
Cairn Curran (dam), Austl. 173/B3
Cairn Gorm (peak), Sc, UK 94/C2
Cairn Table (peak), Sc, UK 94/B6
Cairn Toul (peak), Sc, UK 94/C2
Cairndow, Sc, UK 94/B4
Cairngorm (mts.), Sc, UK 94/B2
Cairns (int'l arpt.), Austl. 172/B2
Cairns, Austl. 172/B2
Cairns (mt.), Austl. 171/G2
Cairnsmore of Carsphairn (peak), Sc, UK 94/B6
Cairo, Ga, US 191/G4
Cairo (Al Qāhirah) (cap.), Egypt 159/B2
Cairo (cap.), Egypt 159/B2
Cairo Montenotte, It. 116/B3

Cairo (peak), It. 104/C2
Cairo (Al Qāhirah) (cap.), Egypt 159/B2
Cairo (int'l arpt.), Egypt 159/B2
Cairo Montenotte, It. 116/B4
Caistor Centre, On, Can. 189/Q9
Caistorville, On, Can. 189/Q9
Caizi (lake), China 130/D3
Cajabamba, Peru 214/B2
Cajabamba, Ecu. 210/B5
Cajacay, Peru 214/B3
Cajamarca (ruin), Peru 214/B2
Cajamarca, Peru 214/B2
Cajamarca (dept.), Peru 214/B2
Cajari, Braz. 212/A1
Cajatambo, Peru 214/B3
Cajazeiras, Braz. 212/C2
Cajibío, Col. 210/B4
Cajon Junction, Ca, US 194/C2
Cajones, Cayos (isl.), Hon. 198/C4
Caju (isl.), Braz. 212/B1
Çal, Turk. 148/B2
Cala d'Oliva, It. 104/A2
Calabar, Nga. 161/H5
Calabar (int'l arpt.), Nga. 161/H5
Calabasas, Ca, US 194/B2
Calabozo, Ven. 211/E2
Calabria, PN della, It. 104/D3
Calaburras (pt.), Sp. 102/C4
Calaceite, Sp. 103/F2
Calacoto, Bol. 214/D5
Calafat, Rom. 106/F4
Calahorra, Sp. 102/E1
Calais, Me, US 189/H2
Calais, Fr. 110/C3
Calais, Canal de (canal), Fr. 110/C2
Calalaste, Sierra de (mts.), Arg. 215/C2
Calama, Chile 215/C1
Calamar, Col. 210/C2
Calamian Group (isls.), Phil. 139/E1
Calamocha, Sp. 102/E2
Calamonte, Sp. 102/B3
Calañas, Sp. 102/B4
Calanda, Sp. 103/E2
Calangianus, It. 104/A2
Calapan, Phil. 137/D5
Călăraşi (prov.), Rom. 107/H3
Călăraşi, Rom. 107/H3
Calasparra, Sp. 102/E3
Calatorao, Sp. 102/E2
Calauag, Phil. 137/D5
Calaveras (lake), Tx, US 195/U21
Calaveras (res.), Ca, US 193/L12
Calayan, Phil. 137/D4
Calayan (isl.), Phil. 137/D4
Calbayog, Phil. 137/D5
Calberlah, Ger. 109/H4
Calbuco, Chile 216/N8
Calca, Peru 214/D4
Calcanhar, Ponta do (pt.), Braz. 212/D2
Calcasieu (riv.), La, US 187/J5
Calceta, Ecu. 210/A5
Calci, It. 116/D5
Calcinate, It. 116/C1
Calcinato, It. 116/D2
Calcinelli, It. 117/F5
Calcio, It. 116/C2
Calcium, NY, US 188/F2
Calçoene, Braz. 209/H3
Calcutta (Kolkata), India 143/G4
Calcutta (Kolkata) (int'l arpt.), India 143/G4
Calcutta, Sur. 211/H3
Caldaro (Kaltern), It. 101/J3
Caldas, Braz. 213/G6
Caldas (dept.), Col. 210/C3
Caldas da Rainha, Port. 103/P10
Caldas Novas, Braz. 213/B1
Calden, Ger. 109/G6
Calder (mt.), Ak, US 192/M4
Calder (riv.), Eng, UK 93/F3
Caldera de Taburiente, PN de la, Canl., Sp. 156/A3
Calderara di Reno, It. 117/E3
Calderas, Ven. 210/D2
Caldercruix, Sc, UK 94/C5
Calderdale (co.), Eng, UK 93/F4
Caldes de Montbui, Sp. 103/L6
Caldew (riv.), Eng, UK 93/F2
Caldicot, Wal, UK 90/D5
Caldiero, It. 117/E2
Çaldıran, Turk. 148/E2
Caldonazzo, It. 115/H6
Caldono, Col. 210/B4
Caldwell, NJ, US 197/H8
Caldwell, Tx, US 187/H5
Caldwell, Wi, US 193/P14
Caldy (isl.), Wal, UK 90/B3
Caledon, NI, UK 92/B3
Caledon (riv.), SAfr. 164/L11
Caledon, SAfr. 164/L11
Caledonia (hills), NB, Can. 189/H2
Caledonia, Wi, US 193/P14
Caledonian (canal), Sc, UK 94/B2

Calella, Sp. 103/G2
Calen, Austl. 172/C3
Calenzana, Fr. 104/A1
Calenzano, It. 117/E5
Calera de Tango, Chile 216/N8
Calestano, It. 116/D3
Caleta de Campos, Mex. 200/E5
Caleta Olivia, Arg. 216/D5
Calexico, Ca, US 186/D4
Calf of Man (isl.), IM, UK 92/C3
Calf, The (peak), Eng, UK 93/F3
Calgary (int'l arpt.), Ab, Can. 184/E3
Calgary, Ab, Can. 184/E3
Calheta, Azor., Port. 103/S12
Calhoun, Ga, US 191/G3
Calhoun (co.), Il, US 195/F7
Calhoun, Ky, US 188/C4
Cali, Col. 210/B4
Calicut (Kozhikode), India 140/C5
Calida, Costa (coast), Sp. 102/E4
Caliente, Nv, US 186/D3
Califon, NJ, US 196/D2
California (gulf), Mex. 200/C2
California (state), US 186/B3
California, Md, US 188/E4
California, Mo, US 187/J3
Calilegua, PN, Arg. 215/D1
Calima, Ven. 211/E2
Calimaya, Mex. 201/Q10
Calimere (pt.), India 140/C5
Calimesa, Ca, US 194/C2
Calitri, It. 104/D2
Calixa-Lavallée, 189/P6
Calkiní, Mex. 202/D1
Calkins (lake), Co, US 195/B2
Çalköy, Turk. 148/B2
Callabonna (lake), Austl. 173/A1
Callahonna (lake), Austl. 167/D3
Callalli, Peru 214/D4
Callan, Ire. 89/Q10
Callander, Sc, UK 94/B4
Callantsoog, Neth. 108/B3
Callao, Peru 214/B4
Callapa, Bol. 214/D5
Callaway, Fl, US 191/G4
Calle Larga, Chile 216/N8
Calliope, Austl. 172/C4
Callosa de Segura, Sp. 103/E3
Calne, Eng, UK 90/E4
Calolziocorte, It. 116/C1
Calonne-Ricouart, Fr. 110/B3
Calore (riv.), It. 104/D2
Caloundra, Austl. 172/D4
Calpe, Sp. 103/F3
Calpulálpan, Mex. 201/L7
Caltagirone, It. 104/D4
Caltanissetta, It. 104/D4
Caltavuturo, It. 104/C4
Caluire-et-Cuire, Fr. 100/F4
Calumet Sag (chan.), Il, US 193/Q16
Caluso, It. 116/A2
Calvados (dept.), Fr. 110/C2
Calvenzano, It. 116/C2
Calvert (isl.), BC, Can. 184/A3
Calvert, Tx, US 187/H5
Calverton, Md, US 196/B5
Calvi, Fr. 104/A1
Calvià, Sp. 103/G3
Calvillo, Mex. 200/E4
Calvinia, SAfr. 164/B3
Calvisano, It. 116/D2
Calvitero (peak), Sp. 102/C2
Calvörde, Ger. 112/B5
Calzada de Calatrava, Sp. 102/D3
Cam or Rhee (riv.), Eng, UK 91/F2
Cam Pha, Viet. 136/D1
Cam Ranh, Viet. 136/E4
Camaçari, Braz. 212/C4
Camacho, Mex. 200/E3
Camacupa, Ang. 163/C3
Camaguán, Ven. 211/E2
Camagüey (arch.), Cuba 199/F3
Camagüey, Cuba 203/G1
Camaiore, It. 116/D5
Camajuaní, Cuba 203/G1
Camamu, Braz. 212/C4
Camamu, Baía de (bay), Braz. 212/C4
Camanã, Peru 214/C5
Camanducaia, Braz. 213/G3
Camaquã (riv.), Braz. 213/A4
Camaquã, Braz. 213/B4
Camargo, Sp. 102/D1
Camariñas, Sp. 102/A1
Camarones (cape), Hon. 203/E3
Camarones, Arg. 216/D5
Camas, Sp. 102/B4
Cambados, Sp. 102/A1
Cambará, Braz. 213/B2
Cambay, Gulf of (gulf), India 140/D3
Cambé, Braz. 213/B2
Camberley, Eng, UK 88/A3

Cambiano, It. 116/A3
Cambodia (ctry.) 141/H5
Camboriú, Ponta do (pt.), Braz. 213/C3
Cambrai, Fr. 110/C3
Cambrian (mts.), Wal, UK 92/E5
Cambridge, Eng, UK 91/G3
Cambridge (int'l arpt.), Eng, UK 91/G2
Cambridge, NZ 175/T10
Cambridge, Ma, US 189/G3
Cambridge, Md, US 188/E4
Cambridge, Oh, US 188/D3
Cambridge, On, Can. 188/D3
Cambridge Bay, Nun., Can. 180/D2
Cambridgeshire (co.), Eng, UK 91/F2
Cambrils, Sp. 103/F2
Cambuí, Braz. 213/G7
Cambuquira, Braz. 213/H6
Cambuslang, Sc, UK 94/B5
Cambutal (mtn.), Pan. 210/A3
Camden, Austl. 172/G9
Camden (co.), Eng, UK 88/C2
Camden, Al, US 191/G4
Camden, De, US 196/C5
Camden, Me, US 189/G2
Camden, NJ, US 196/C4
Camden (co.), NJ, US 196/C4
Camden, SC, US 191/H3
Camden Haven, Austl. 173/E1
Camden Point, Mo, US 195/D5
Cameia, PN da, Ang. 163/D3
Camel (riv.), Eng, UK 90/B6
Camelback (mtn.), Sc, UK 94/B4
Camerano, It. 117/G5
Cameri, It. 116/B2
Cameron (isl.), Nun., Can. 181/R7
Cameron, Mo, US 187/J3
Cameron, Tx, US 187/H5
Cameron (ctry.) 154/H7
Cametá, Braz. 209/J4
Camicia (peak), It. 104/C1
Camiguin (isl.), Phil. 137/D4
Camilla, Ga, US 191/G4
Camilo Aldao, Arg. 216/E2
Caminha, Port. 102/A2
Camino, Peru 214/B4
Camiri, Bol. 208/F8
Camisano Vicentino, It. 117/E1
Çamlıdere, Turk. 148/C1
Çamlık, Turk. 148/C2
Çamlıyayla, Turk. 149/D1
Camoapa, Nic. 203/E3
Camogli, It. 116/C4
Camon, Fr. 110/B4
Camorta (isl.), India 141/F6
Camp Angelus (Angelus Oaks), Ca, US 194/D2
Camp Creek, Az, US 195/S18
Camp Lake, Wi, US 193/P14
Camp Springs, Md, US 196/B6
Campagna Lupia, It. 117/F2
Campagnola Emilia, It. 117/D3
Campana, Arg. 217/J11
Campana (isl.), Chile 217/B6
Campana, PN de la, Chile 216/N8
Campanario, Sp. 102/C3
Campanario (peak), Arg. 216/C2
Campanella (cape), It. 104/D2
Campanha, Braz. 213/H6
Campania (prov.), It. 104/D2
Campbell, Ca, US 193/L12
Campbell (isl.), NZ 81/T8
Campbell River, BC, Can. 184/B3
Campbell Town, Austl. 173/C4
Campbellsville, Ky, US 188/C4
Campbellton, NB, Can. 189/H1
Campbelltown, Sc, UK 94/R9
Campden, On, Can. 189/R9
Campeche (state), Mex. 198/C4
Campeche, Mex. 202/D2
Campeche (bay), Mex. 201/G5
Camperdown, Austl. 173/B3
Camperville, Mb, Can. 185/H3
Campestre, Braz. 213/G6
Campi Bisenzio, It. 117/E5
Campidano (range), It. 104/A3
Campillo de Altobuey, Sp. 102/E2
Campillos, Sp. 102/C4
Campina Verde, Braz. 213/B1
Campione d'Italia, It. 115/E6
Campo (int'l arpt.), Braz. 214/C2
Campo Belo, Braz. 213/C2
Campo de Criptana, Sp. 102/D3
Campo de la Cruz, Col. 210/C2
Campo dei Fiori (peak), It. 116/B1

Campo Grande, Braz. 209/H8
Campo Ligure, It. 116/B3
Campo Limpo Paulista, Braz. 213/G8
Campo Maior, Port. 102/B3
Campo Mourão, Braz. 213/A3
Campo Tencia (peak), Swi. 115/E5
Campo Tizzoro, It. 117/D4
Campoalegre, Col. 210/C4
Campobasso, It. 104/D2
Campodarsego, It. 117/E2
Campodolcino, It. 115/F5
Campogalliano, It. 117/D3
Campomorone, It. 116/B3
Componogara, It. 117/F2
Camporosso, It. 116/A5
Camporredondo, Peru 214/B2
Camporredondo, Embalse de (res.), Sp. 102/C1
Campos (phys. reg.), Braz. 205/D5
Campos Altos, Braz. 213/C1
Campos Belos, Braz. 212/A4
Campos de Hielo Norte (glacier), Chile 217/B5
Campos de Hielo Sur (glacier), Chile 217/B6
Campos del Puerto, Sp. 103/G3
Campos do Jordão, Braz. 213/H7
Campos Gerais, Braz. 213/C2
Campos Novos, Braz. 213/B3
Campos Sales, Braz. 212/B2
Camposampiero, It. 117/E2
Camposanto, It. 117/E3
Campsie Fells (hills), Sc, UK 94/B4
Campti, La, US 190/E4
Camrose, Ab, Can. 184/E2
Can, Turk. 107/H5
Can Tho, Viet. 136/D4
Canaçari (lake), Braz. 211/G5
Canada (ctry.) 180
Cañada de Gómez, Arg. 216/E2
Cañada Nieto, Uru. 217/J10
Cañada Rosquín, Arg. 216/E2
Canadensis, Pa, US 196/C1
Canadian (riv.), US 187/F3
Canadian (co.), Ok, US 195/M15
Canadian, Tx, US 187/G4
Canadian, North (riv.), Ok, US 187/H3
Cañadón Grande (mts.), Arg. 216/C5
Cañadón Seco, Arg. 216/D5
Canaima, PN, Ven. 208/F2
Canajoharie, NY, US 188/E3
Cananea, Mex. 200/C2
Cananéia, Braz. 213/C3
Canápolis, Braz. 213/B1
Cañar, Ecu. 214/B1
Cañar (dept.), Ecu. 210/B5
Canard (riv.), On, Can. 193/G7
Canary (isls.), Sp. 156/A3
Cañas, CR 203/E4
Cañasgordas, Col. 210/B3
Canatlán de las Manzanas, Mex. 200/D3
Canaveral (cape), Fl, US 191/H4
Canberra, Austl. 173/D2
Canchaque, Peru 214/B2
Canche (riv.), Fr. 100/E1
Cancún (int'l arpt.), Mex. 202/E1
Cancun (int'l arpt.), Mex. 202/E1
Candado, Nevado del (peak), Arg. 215/C2
Candarave, Peru 214/D5
Çandarlı (gulf), Gre.,Turk. 148/A2
Candás, Sp. 102/C1
Candeias, Braz. 212/C4
Candelaria, Mex. 202/D2
Candelaria (riv.), Mex. 202/D2
Candelaria, Arg. 216/D2
Candeleda, Sp. 102/C2
Candelo, Austl. 173/D3
Candelo, It. 116/B1
Candia Lomellina, It. 116/B2
Candía, Qu, Can. 189/N7
Candiba, Braz. 212/B3
Cândido Mota, Braz. 213/B2
Canding (cape), Indo. 138/D5
Candir, Turk. 148/C2
Candlewood, NJ, US 196/D3
Cando, ND, US 185/J3
Candon, Phil. 137/D4
Canegrate, It. 116/B1
Canela, Braz. 213/B4
Canelli, It. 116/B3

Canelones (dept.), Uru. 217/F2
Canelones, Uru. 217/K11
Cañete, Sp. 102/C2
Canete, Rio de (riv.), Peru 214/B4
Cangallo, Peru 214/C4
Cangas, Sp. 102/A1
Cangas de Narcea, Sp. 102/A1
Cangas de Onis, Sp. 102/C1
Cangkuang (cape), Indo. 138/C5
Cango Caves, SAfr. 164/C4
Cangrejo (peak), Arg. 217/B6
Cangshan, China 130/D4
Canguaretama, Braz. 212/D2
Canguçu, China 141/K3
Cangwu, China 141/K3
Cangyuan (Cangyuan Vazu Zizhixian), China 141/G3
Cangzhou, China 130/D3
Canh Cuoc (isl.), Viet. 136/D1
Cania Gorge NP, Austl. 172/C4
Caniapiscau (lake), Qu, Can. 181/K3
Caniapiskau (riv.), Qu, Can. 181/J3
Canicatti, It. 104/C4
Canik (mts.), Turk. 148/C1
Caniles, Sp. 102/D4
Canindé (riv.), Braz. 209/K5
Canindé, Braz. 213/H7
Canino, It. 104/B1
Canistear (res.), NJ, US 196/D1
Canistro, It. 104/C1
Cañitas de Felipe Pescador, Mex. 200/E4
Canjáyar, Sp. 102/D4
Çankırı, Turk. 148/C1
Çankırı (prov.), Turk. 148/C1
Canlaon (vol.), Phil. 139/F1
Canmore, Ab, Can. 184/E3
Cann River, Austl. 173/D3
Canna (isl.), Sc, UK 89/Q8
Cannanore, India 140/C5
Canne (ruin), It. 104/E2
Canner (riv.), Fr. 111/F5
Cannero Riviera, It. 115/E5
Cannes, Fr. 101/G5
Canneto sull'Oglio, It. 116/D2
Canneto (peak), It. 104/B1
Canning, Austl. 170/C4
Canning (dam), Austl. 170/L7
Canning (riv.), Austl. 170/K7
Cannobio, It. 115/E5
Cannock, Eng, UK 90/D1
Cannon Falls, Mn, US 185/K4
Cannonball (riv.), ND, US 185/H4
Cannondale, Ct, US 197/E1
Cannonvale, Austl. 172/C3
Caño Guaritico (riv.), Ven. 210/D3
Caño Negro NWF, CR 203/E4
Canoas, Braz. 213/B4
Canoas (riv.), Braz. 213/B3
Canobolas (mt.), Austl. 173/D2
Canoinhas, Braz. 213/B3
Cañón de Río Blanco, PN, Mex. 201/M8
Cañón del Sumidero, PN, Mex. 202/C2
Canora, Sk, Can. 185/H3
Canosa di Puglia, It. 104/E2
Canouan (isl.), StV. 199/N9
Canowindra, Austl. 173/D2
Cansahcan, Braz. 212/C4
Canso (cape), NS, Can. 189/J2
Canta, Peru 214/B3
Cantabria (aut. comm.), Sp. 102/C1
Cantabria, Cordillera (mts.), Sp. 102/B1
Cantal, Massif du (mass.), Fr. 100/E4
Cantalejo, Sp. 102/D2
Cantanhede, Braz. 212/A1
Cantanhede, Port. 102/A2
Cantaura, Ven. 211/E2
Canterbury, Eng, UK 91/H4
Canterbury Bight (bay), NZ 175/S11
Canterbury Cathedral, Eng, UK 91/H4
Cantillana, Sp. 102/C4
Canto do Buriti, Braz. 212/B3
Canton, Mi, US 193/F7
Canton, Ms, US 187/K4
Canton, NY, US 188/F2
Canton, Oh, US 190/D2
Canton, Tx, US 187/H4
Canton (Abariringa) (isl.), Kiri. 175/H5
Cantoria, Sp. 102/D4
Cantù, It. 116/C1
Cantwell, Ak, US 192/J3
Cañuelas, Arg. 217/J11
Canunda NP, Austl. 173/B3
Canvey (isl.), Eng, UK 88/E2
Canvey Island, Eng, UK 88/E2
Canwood, Sk, Can. 184/G2
Canyon, Tx, US 187/F4
Canyon (lake), Tx, US 195/U20
Canyon de Chelly Nat'l Mon., Az, US 186/E3
Canyon Lake, Tx, US 195/U20
Canyonlands Nat'l Park, Ut, US 186/E3

Canyon of the Ancients Nat'l Mon., Co, US 186/E3
Canzo, It. 116/C1
Cao Bang, Viet. 141/J3
Cao Lanh, Viet. 136/D4
Cao Xian, China 130/C4
Caodu (riv.), China 137/A2
Caorle, It. 117/F1
Caorso, It. 116/C2
Cap-Chat, Qu, Can. 189/H1
Cap d'Agde (cape), Fr. 100/E5
Cap-de-la-Madeleine, Qu, Can. 189/H2
Cap-Haïtien, Haiti 203/H2
Cap Rock Escarpment (cliff), Tx, US 190/C3
Cap-Rouge, Qu, Can. 189/G2
Cap Roux, Pointe du (pt.), Fr. 101/G5
Capac, Mi, US 193/G5
Capanaparo (riv.), Ven. 208/E2
Capanema, Braz. 209/J4
Capanne (peak), It. 104/B1
Capannoli, It. 117/D5
Capannori, It. 116/D5
Capão Bonito, Braz. 213/B3
Capão Doce, Morro do (peak), Braz. 213/B3
Caparaó, PN do, Braz. 213/A4
Caparica, Port. 103/P10
Caparo (riv.), Ven. 210/D3
Capay, Ca, US 193/K9
Capbreton, Fr. 100/C5
Capdenac-Gare, Fr. 100/E4
Capdepera, Sp. 103/G3
Cape Arid NP, Austl. 170/D5
Cape Barren (isl.), Austl. 173/C4
Cape Breton (isl.), NS, Can. 189/J2
Cape Breton Highlands (uplands), NS, Can. 189/J2
Cape Breton Highlands NP, NS, Can. 189/J2
Cape Cleveland NP, Austl. 172/B2
Cape Coast, Gha. 161/E5
Cape Cod Nat'l Seashore, Ma, US 189/H3
Cape Coral, Fl, US 191/H5
Cape Dorset, Nun., Can. 181/J2
Cape Fear (riv.), NC, US 191/J3
Cape Hatteras Nat'l Seashore, NC, US 191/K3
Cape Krusenstern Nat'l Mon., Ak, US 192/E2
Cape Le Grand NP, Austl. 170/D5
Cape Lookout Nat'l Seashore, NC, US 191/J3
Cape May, NJ, US 196/D6
Cape May (co.), NJ, US 196/D5
Cape May Court House, NJ, US 196/D5
Cape May Lighthouse, NJ, US 196/D6
Cape Melville NP, Austl. 172/B1
Cape Palmerston NP, Austl. 172/C3
Cape Range NP, Austl. 170/B2
Cape Saint Claire, Md, US 196/B5
Cape Town, Qu, Can.
Cape Town (D.F. Malan) (int'l arpt.), SAfr. 164/L10
Cape Tribulation NP, Austl. 172/B1
Cape Upstart NP, Austl. 172/B2
Cape Verde (ctry.) 151/J9
Cape Yakataga, Ak, US 192/K3
Cape York (pen.), Austl. 167/D2
Capel, Austl. 170/B5
Capela, Braz. 212/C3
Capelinha, Braz. 212/B5
Capella, Austl. 172/C3
Capellades, Sp. 103/K6
Capestang, Fr. 100/E5
Capicciola (pt.), Fr. 104/A2
Capilla del Señor, Arg. 217/J11
Capim (riv.), Braz. 209/J4
Capinópolis, Braz. 213/B1
Capirara (res.), Braz. 215/F1
Capistrano, Braz. 213/A4
Capistrello, It. 104/C2
Capitan (mts.), NM, US 190/B3
Capitán Poço, Braz. 209/J4
Capitol Reef NP, Ut, US 186/E3
Capivara, Represa (res.), Braz. 209/H8
Capivara, Serra de (range), Braz. 212/A4
Capivari (riv.), Braz. 213/L6
Čapljina, Bosn. 105/E1
Caplone (peak), It. 116/D1
Capodichino (int'l arpt.), It. 104/D2

Capolona, It. 117/E5
Capoterra, It. 104/A3
Cappella Maggiore, It. 117/F1
Cappoquin, Ire. 89/Q10
Capraia (isl.), It. 104/A1
Caprarola, It. 104/C1
Capreol, On, Can. 188/D2
Capri (isl.), It. 167/E3
Capricorn (chan.), Austl. 172/C3
Capricorn (cape), Austl. 172/C3
Caprino Veronese, It. 117/D1
Caprivi Strip (reg.), Namb. 163/D2
Captain Cook, Hi, US 182/U11
Captain (har.), Ct, US 197/L7
Captainganj, India 143/D2
Captains Flat, Austl. 173/D2
Capua, It. 106/B5
Capuá, Braz. 212/A4
Capulhuac, Mex. 201/Q10
Capulhuac, Mex. 201/Q10
Caputh, Ger. 98/Q7
Caquetá (riv.), Col. 210/D5
Caquetá (dept.), Col. 210/C5
Car Nicobar (isl.), India 141/F6
Carabobo (state), Ven. 210/D2
Caracal, Rom. 107/G3
Caracaraí, Braz. 211/F4
Caracas (cap.), Ven. 208/E1
Carache, Ven. 210/D2
Caracol, Braz. 212/B3
Caracolí, Col. 210/C3
Carácuaro de Morelos, Mex. 201/L8
Caradon (hill), Eng, UK 90/B5
Caraguatatuba, Braz. 213/J8
Caraguatatuba, Enseada de (bay), Braz. 213/H8
Carahue, Chile 216/B3
Carajás, Serra dos (mts.), Braz. 209/H5
Caranavi, Bol. 208/E7
Carandaí, Braz. 213/D2
Carangola, Braz. 213/D2
Carapicuíba, Braz. 213/G8
Carapó, Braz. 213/A2
Caras-Severin (prov.), Rom. 106/E3
Carasco, It. 116/C4
Caratasca (lag.), Hon. 198/E4
Caratinga, Braz. 213/D1
Caraúbas, Braz. 212/C2
Caravaca de la Cruz, Sp. 102/E3
Caravaggio, It. 116/C2
Caravela, Ilha (isl.), GBis. 160/A4
Caravelas, Braz. 212/C5
Caravelí, Peru 214/C4
Caraz, Peru 214/B3
Carazinho, Braz. 215/F2
Carballino, Sp. 102/A1
Carballo, Sp. 102/A1
Carberry, Mb, Can. 185/J3
Carbo, Mex. 200/C2
Carbon (cape), Alg. 158/H4
Carbon (co.), Pa, US 196/C2
Carbon (riv.), Wa, US 193/C3
Carbonara (cape), It. 104/A3
Carbonara (peak), It. 104/C4
Carbondale, Pa, US 196/C2
Carbonear, Nf, Can. 189/L2
Carbonera, It. 117/F1
Carboneras, Mex. 201/F3
Carbonia, It. 104/A3
Carbonne, Fr. 100/D5
Carbost, Sc, UK 89/Q8
Carcagente, Sp. 103/E3
Carcaraña, Arg. 216/E2
Carcare, It. 116/B3
Carcassonne, Fr. 100/E5
Carche (peak), Sp. 102/E3
Carcross, Yk, Can. 192/M3
Cardak, Turk. 107/H5
Cardal, Uru. 217/K11
Cardedeu, Sp. 103/L6
Cárdenas, Mex. 201/L6
Cárdenas, Cuba 203/F1
Cárdenas, Mex. 202/C2
Cardener, Sc, UK 94/B2
Cardiel (lake), Arg. 217/C5
Cardiff (cap.), Wal, UK 90/C4
Cardiff, Md, US 196/B4
Cardiff by the Sea, Ca, US 194/C4
Cardigan, Sp. 103/F2
Cardona, Uru. 217/K10
Cardona, Sp. 103/F2
Cardoso, Braz. 213/B2
Cardoso, Uru. 217/K10
Cardston, Ab, Can. 184/E3
Cardwell, Austl. 172/B2

Cariaco, Ven. 211/F2
Cariamanga, Ecu. 214/B2
Cariati, It. 104/E3
Caribbean (sea), NAm.,SAm. 177/L8
Cariboo (mts.), BC, Can. 184/C2
Caribou, Me, US 189/G2
Caribou (range), Id, US 184/F5
Caribou (mts.), Ab, Can. 180/D3
Caridade, Braz. 212/C2
Carigara, Phil. 137/D5
Carignan, Qu, Can. 189/P7
Carignan, Fr. 111/E4
Carignano, It. 116/A3
Cariñena, Sp. 102/E2
Carinhanha, Braz. 212/B4
Carinhanha (riv.), Braz. 212/A4
Carini, It. 104/C3
Caripito, Ven. 211/F2
Caririaçu, Braz. 212/C2
Cariris Novos, Serra dos (mts.), Braz. 212/B2
Carleton (mt.), NB, Can. 189/H2
Carleton (riv.), NS, Can. 189/H2
Carleton, Qu, Can. 189/H1
Carleton, Mi, US 193/F7
Carleton Place, On, Can. 188/E2
Carletonville, SAfr. 164/Q12
Carlin, Nv, US 184/D5
Carlindie Abor. Land, Austl. 170/C2
Carling, Fr. 111/F5
Carlingford, Ire. 92/B3
Carlingford (lake), Ire. 92/B3
Carlingford (mtn.), Ire. 92/B3
Carlinville, Il, US 187/K3
Carlisle, Pa, US 188/E3
Carlisle, La, US 195/Q17
Carlisle, Eng, UK 93/F2
Carlisle Barracks Mil. Res., Pa, US 196/A3
Carlit (peak), Fr. 100/D5
Carlos Casares, Arg. 216/E2
Carlos Chagas, Braz. 212/B5
Carlos M. de Cespedes, Rom. 203/G1
Carlow, Ire. 89/Q10
Carlow (co.), Ire. 92/B4
Carloway, Sc, UK 89/Q7
Carlsbad, Ca, US 194/C4
Carlsbad, Eng, UK 93/F2
Carlsbad Caverns NP, NM, US 187/F4
Carlsberg, Ger. 112/B3
Carlsfeld, Ger. 113/F2
Carlton, Eng, UK 93/G6
Carluke, Sc, UK 94/B5
Carlton, Mn, US 185/K4
Carlyle, Il, US 187/K3
Carlyle, Sk, Can. 185/H3
Carmacks, Yk, Can. 192/L3
Carmagnola, It. 116/A3
Carman, Mb, Can. 185/J3
Carmarthen, Wal, UK 90/B3
Carmarthen (bay), Wal, UK 90/B3
Carmarthenshire (co.), Wal, UK 90/B3
Carmaux, Fr. 100/E4
Carmel (pt.), Wal, UK 92/D5
Carmelo, Uru. 217/J11
Carmen (isl.), Mex. 200/C2
Carmen, It. 190/B4
Carmen de Patagones, Arg. 216/E4
Carmensa, Arg. 216/C2
Carmo, Braz. 213/L6
Carmo da Cachoeira, Braz. 213/H6
Carmo de Minas, Braz. 213/H7
Carmo do Paranaíba, Braz. 213/C1
Carmo do Rio Claro, Braz. 213/C2
Carmona, Sp. 102/C4
Carn Ban (peak), Sc, UK 94/B2
Carn Easgann Bàna (peak), Sc, UK 94/A2
Càrn Eige (peak), Sc, UK 94/A2
Càrn Glas-choire (peak), Sc, UK 94/B2
Carn Kitty (hill), Sc, UK 94/C2
Carn Mairg (peak), Sc, UK 94/B3
Carn Mór (peak), Sc, UK 94/C2
Carn na Cailliche (hill), Sc, UK 94/B1
Carn na Saobhaidhe (peak), Sc, UK 94/B2
Carnago, It. 116/B1
Carnamah, Austl. 170/A3
Carnarvon, Austl. 167/A3
Carnarvon NP, Austl. 172/B4
Carnarvon, SAfr. 164/C3
Carnarvonleep (riv.), SAfr. 164/C3
Carnation, Wa, US 193/D2
Carnaubal, Braz. 212/B2
Carnaxide, Port. 103/P10
Carncastle, NI, UK 92/C2
Carndonagh, Ire. 92/A1

Carnduff, Sk, Can. 185/H3
Carnedd Llewelyn (peak), Wal, UK 92/E5
Carnegie (lake), Austl. 167/B3
Carney, Ok, US 195/N14
Carney (isl.), Ant. 218/S
Carnforth, Eng, UK 93/F3
Carnlough, NI, UK 92/B2
Carnot (cape), Austl. 171/G5
Carnot, CAfr. 154/J7
Carnota, Sp. 102/A1
Carnsore (pt.), Ire. 89/Q10
Carnwath (riv.), NW, Can. 180/D2
Carnwath, Sc, UK 94/C5
Caro, Mi, US 188/D3
Carol Stream, Il, US 193/P16
Carolina, Braz. 212/A2
Carolina, PR 199/M8
Carolina, SAfr. 165/E2
Carolina Beach, NC, US 191/J3
Caroline, Ok, US, Kiri. 175/K5
Caroline (isls) Micr. 174/D4
Caroní (riv.), Ven. 205/C2
Carora, Ven. 210/D2
Carouge, Swi. 114/C5
Carpaneto Piacentino, It. 116/C3
Carpathian (mts.), Eur. 85/G4
Carpegna (peak), It. 117/F5
Carpegna, It. 117/F5
Carpenedolo, It. 116/D2
Carpentaria, Gulf of (gulf), Austl. 167/G2
Carpenter, Il, US 195/H8
Carpentersville, Il, US 193/P15
Carpentras, Fr. 100/F4
Carpi, It. 117/D3
Carpignano Sesia, It. 116/B1
Carpina, Braz. 212/D2
Carpinteria, Ca, US 194/A2
Carpiquet (int'l arpt.), Fr. 100/C2
Carr (inlet), Wa, US 193/B3
Carrabelle, Fl, US 191/G4
Carrantuohill (peak), Ire. 89/P10
Carrara, It. 116/D4
Carrasco (int'l arpt.), Uru. 217/K11
Carrasquero, Ven. 210/D2
Carreg Ddu (pt.), Wal, UK 92/D6
Carriacou (isl.), Gren. 208/F1
Carrick (reg.), Sc, UK 94/B6
Carrick on Shannon, Ire. 89/P10
Carrick on Suir, Ire. 89/Q10
Carrickalinga, Austl. 171/H5
Carrickfergus, NI, UK 92/C2
Carrickfergus (dist.), NI, UK 92/C2
Carrickmacross, Ire. 89/Q10
Carrickmore, NI, UK 92/A2
Carrières-sous-Poissy, Fr. 88/J5
Carrigaholt, Ire. 89/P10
Carrigaline, Ire. 89/P11
Carrington, ND, US 185/J4
Carrión (riv.), Sp. 102/C1
Carrión de los Condes, Sp. 102/C1
Carrizo (mts.), Az, US 182/D4
Carrizo Plain Nat'l Mon. Ca, US 186/C4
Carrizo Springs, Tx, US 190/D4
Carrizo Wash (riv.), Az,NM, US 186/E4
Carrizozo, NM, US 187/F4
Carroll (co.), Md, US 196/A5
Carrollton, Ky, US 188/C4
Carrollton, Ga, US 191/G3
Carron (lake), Sc, UK 94/A2
Carron (riv.), Sc, UK 94/A2
Carrot (riv.), Sk, Can. 185/H2
Carrot River, Sk, Can. 185/H2
Carrowdore, NI, UK 92/C2
Carrowkeel, Ire. 92/A1
Carrù, It. 116/A4
Carrum Downs, Austl. 173/G6
Carryduff, NI, UK 92/C2
Carşamba, Turk. 148/D1
Carse of Forth (plain), Sc, UK 94/B4
Carse of Gowrie (plain), Sc, UK 94/C4
Carson (riv.), Nv, US 186/C3
Carson, Ca, US 194/F8
Carson City (cap.), Nv, US 186/C3
Carson Sink (dry lake), Nv, US 186/C3
Carstairs, Ab, Can. 184/E3
Cartagena, Chile 216/N8
Cartagena, Col. 210/C2
Cartago, Col. 208/C3
Cartago, CR 203/F4
Cártama, Sp. 102/C4
Cartaya, Sp. 102/B4
Carter Bar (hill), Eng, UK 94/D6
Carter Lake (res.), Co, US 195/B2
Carteret, NJ, US 197/J9
Carterton, Eng, UK 91/E3

Carthage (int'l arpt.), Tun. 158/M6
Carthage, Mo, US 187/J3
Carthage, Ms, US 191/F3
Carthage, Tn, US 188/C4
Carthage, Tx, US 187/J4
Carthage (Qarṭājannah) (ruin), Tun. 158/M6
Carti (mtn.), Pan. 210/B2
Cartier Islet (isl.), Austl. 167/B2
Cartwright, Nf, Can. 181/L3
Caruaru, Braz. 212/D3
Carumás, Peru 214/D5
Carúpano, Ven. 211/F2
Caruthersville, Mo, US 187/K3
Carvico, It. 116/C1
Carvin, Fr. 110/B2
Carvoeiro (cape), Port. 102/A3
Cary, NC, US 191/J3
Cary, Il, US 193/P15
Casa Blanca (canal), Az, US 195/S19
Casa Branca, Braz. 213/F6
Casa de Piedra (res.), Arg. 216/D3
Casa Grande, Az, US 186/E4
Casa Grande Nat'l Mon., Az, US 186/E4
Casa Nova, Braz. 212/B3
Casablanca, Chile 216/N8
Casablanca-Anfa (prov.), Mor. 158/A2
Casal di Principe, It. 104/D2
Casalbordino, It. 104/D1
Casalbuttano, It. 116/C2
Casale di Scodosia, It. 117/E2
Casale Monferrato, It. 116/B2
Casale sul Sile, It. 117/F1
Casalecchio di Reno, It. 117/E4
Casaleone, It. 117/E2
Casalmaggiore, It. 116/D3
Casalpusterlengo, It. 116/C2
Casalserugo, It. 117/E2
Casamance (riv.), Sen. 160/A3
Casanare (riv.), Col. 208/D2
Casanare (dept.), Col. 210/D3
Casanay, Ven. 211/F2
Casar de Cáceres, Sp. 102/B3
Casarano, It. 105/F2
Casarsa della Delizia, It. 117/F1
Casarza Ligure, It. 116/C4
Casas Grande (riv.), Mex. 186/E5
Casas Grandes, Mex. 200/C2
Casas Grandes (ruin), Mex. 200/C2
Casas-Ibáñez, Sp. 102/E3
Ca'Savio, It. 117/F2
Casazza, It. 116/C1
Cascada de Bassaseachic, PN, Mex. 200/C2
Cascade (res.), Id, US 184/D4
Cascade (range), Or,Wa, US 184/C5
Cascade Caverns, Tx, US 195/T20
Cascade-Fairwood, Or, US 193/C3
Cascade-Siskiyou Nat'l Mon., Or, US 184/C5
Cascades (pt.), Reun., Fr. 165/S15
Cascais, Port. 103/P10
Cascapédia (riv.), Qu, Can. 189/H1
Cascas, Peru 214/B3
Cascavel, Braz. 215/F1
Cascavel, Braz. 212/C2
Casciago, It. 116/B1
Casciana Terme, It. 116/D5
Cascina, It. 116/D5
Case (inlet), Wa, US 193/B3
Casella, It. 116/B3
Caselle, It. 117/E2
Casentino (valley), It. 117/E5
Caserta, It. 104/D2
Casey (bay), Ant. 218/D
Casey, Austl., Ant. 218/H
Caseyr (cape), Som. 155/R5
Caseyville, Il, US 195/F5
Cashel, Ire. 89/Q10
Cashion, Ok, US 195/M14
Cashmere, Wa, US 184/C4
Cashtown, Pa, US 196/A4
Casigua, Ven. 210/C2
Casilda (pt.), Cuba 203/F1
Casilda, Arg. 216/E2
Casimiro Castillo, Mex. 200/D5
Casina, It. 116/D3
Casinalbo, It. 117/D3
Casino, Austl. 173/E1
Casino and Opera House, Mona. 116/J8
Casitas (lake), Ca, US 194/A2
Casitas Springs, Ca, US 194/A2
Casma, Peru 214/B3
Casnigo, It. 116/C1
Casole d'Elsa, It. 117/E6
Casorate Primo, It. 116/C2
Casorate Sempione, It. 116/B1
Caspe, Sp. 103/E2
Casper, Wy, US 185/G3
Caspian (sea), Asia 125/E5
Cass (co.), Mo, US 195/E6

Cass (lake), Mi, US 193/F6
Cass City, Mi, US 188/D3
Cassano allo Ionio, It. 104/E3
Cassano d'Adda, It. 116/C1
Cassano Magnago, It. 116/B1
Cassano Spinola, It. 116/B3
Cassel, Fr. 110/B2
Cássia, Braz. 213/F6
Cassiar, BC, Can. 192/N3
Cassiar (mts.), BC, Can. 180/C3
Cassilândia, Braz. 213/B1
Cassine, It. 116/B3
Cassino, It. 104/C2
Cassolnovo, It. 116/B1
Castagnaro, It. 117/E2
Castagneto Carducci, It. 101/J5
Castagnole delle Lanze, It. 116/B3
Castaic, Ca, US 194/B2
Castalla, Sp. 103/E3
Castanet-Tolosan, Fr. 100/D5
Castanhal, Braz. 209/J4
Castaños, Mex. 201/E3
Castegnato, It. 116/C2
Casteggio, It. 116/D1
Castel Bolognese, It. 117/E4
Castel d'Ario, It. 117/D2
Castel di Sangro, It. 104/D2
Castel Goffredo, It. 116/D2
Castel Mella, It. 116/D2
Castel San Giovanni, It. 116/C2
Castel San Lorenzo, It. 104/D2
Castel San Pietro Terme, It. 117/E4
Castelbuono, It. 104/D4
Castelcovati, It. 116/C2
Castelfidardo, It. 117/G6
Castelfiorentino, It. 117/D5
Castelfranco di Sopra, It. 117/E5
Castelfranco Emilia, It. 117/E3
Castelfranco Veneto, It. 117/E1
Castelgomberto, It. 117/E1
Casteljaloux, Fr. 100/D4
Castell de Montjuic, Sp. 103/L7
Castellammare di Stabia, It. 104/D2
Castellammare, Golfo di (gulf), It. 104/C3
Castellamonte, It. 116/A2
Castellanza, It. 116/B1
Castellar del Vallès, Sp. 103/G2
Castellarano, It. 117/D3
Castell'Arquato, It. 116/C2
Castellazzo Bormida, It. 116/B3
Castelldefels, Sp. 103/K7
Castelleone, It. 116/C2
Castelli, Arg. 217/K12
Castellina in Chianti, It. 117/E6
Castello di Godego, It. 117/E1
Castello di Miramare, It. 117/G1
Castello Eurialo (ruin), It. 104/D4
Castello, Monte il (peak), It. 117/E5
Castellón de la Plana, Sp. 103/E3
Castellote, Sp. 103/E2
Castellucchio, It. 116/D2
Castelmassa, It. 117/E2
Castelnau-le-Lez, Fr. 100/E5
Castelnaudary, Fr. 100/D5
Castelnovo di Sotto, It. 116/D3
Castelnovo ne'Monti, It. 116/D4
Castelnuovo Berardenga, It. 117/E5
Castelnuovo di Garfagnana, It. 116/D4
Castelnuovo Don Bosco, It. 116/A2
Castelnuovo Scrivia, It. 116/B3
Castelo Branco, Port. 102/B3
Castelo Branco (dist.), Port. 102/B2
Castelo de Vide, Port. 102/B3
Castelo do Piauí, Braz. 212/B2
Castelsardo, It. 104/A2
Castelvetrano, It. 104/C4
Castelvetro di Modena, It. 117/D3
Castelvetro Piacentino, It. 116/D2
Castenaso, It. 117/E3
Castenedolo, It. 116/D2
Casterton, Austl. 173/B3
Castiglion Fiorentino, It. 117/E5
Castiglione, It. 117/F4
Castiglione d'Adda, It. 116/C2
Castiglione dei Pepoli, It. 117/E4
Castiglione delle Stiviere, It. 116/D2
Castiglione Torinese, It. 116/A2
Castilho, Braz. 213/B2
Castilla, Peru 214/A2
Castilla-La Mancha (aut. comm.), Sp. 102/C3

Castilla y León (aut. comm.), Sp. 102/D2
Castilla y Léon Treviño, Sp. 102/D1
Castillo (peak), Arg. 216/C4
Castillo de San Marcos Nat'l Mon., Fl, US 191/H4
Castillos, Uru. 217/G2
Castione della Presolana, It. 115/G6
Castions, It. 117/F1
Castions di Strada, It. 117/G1
Castle Dale, Ut, US 186/E3
Castle Douglas, Sc, UK 92/E1
Castle Hills, Tx, US 195/T20
Castle Rock, Co, US 187/F3
Castle Rock, Wa, US 184/C4
Castle Rock (lake), Wi, US 185/L5
Castle Tower NP, Austl. 172/C4
Castlebar, Ire. 89/P10
Castlebay, Sc, UK 89/Q8
Castlebellingham, Ire. 89/Q10
Castlebridge, Ire. 89/Q10
Castlecaufield, NI, UK 92/B2
Castlecomer, Ire. 89/Q10
Castledawson, NI, UK 92/B2
Castleford, Eng, UK 93/G4
Castlegar, BC, Can. 184/D3
Castlegregory, Ire. 88/N10
Castleisland, Ire. 89/P10
Castlemaine, Austl. 173/C3
Castlereagh, Ire. 89/P10
Castletown, IM, UK 92/D3
Castlewellan, NI, UK 92/C3
Castor, Ab, Can. 184/F2
Castos (riv.), Libr. 154/D6
Castres, Fr. 100/E5
Castricum, Neth. 108/B3
Castries (cap.), StL. 199/N9
Castro, Braz. 213/B3
Castro, Chile 216/B4
Castro Alves, Braz. 212/C4
Castro Daire, Port. 102/B2
Castro de Rey, Sp. 102/B1
Castro del Rio, Sp. 102/C4
Castro-Urdiales, Sp. 102/D1
Castro Verde, Port. 102/A4
Castrojeriz, Sp. 102/C1
Castrop-Rauxel, Ger. 109/E5
Castropol, Sp. 102/B1
Castrovillari, It. 104/E3
Castrovirreyna, Peru 214/C4
Castuera, Sp. 102/C3
Casupá, Uru. 217/G2
Cat (isl.), Bahm. 199/F3
Cat (lake), On, Can. 185/K3
Cat Law (peak), Sc, UK 94/C3
Catacamas, Hon. 202/E3
Catacaos, Peru 214/A2
Catacocha, Ecu. 214/B2
Cataduanes (isl.), Phil. 137/D5
Cataguases, Braz. 213/L6
Catalão, Braz. 213/B1
Catalca, Turk. 107/J5
Catalçam, Turk. 148/D2
Catalina, Az, US 186/E4
Catalonia (reg.), Sp. 103/F2
Cataluña (aut. comm.), Sp. 103/F2
Catamarca, Arg. 215/C2
Catamayo, Ecu. 214/B1
Catanduanes (isl.), Phil. 137/D5
Catanduva, Braz. 213/B2
Catania, It. 104/D4
Catania, Golfo di (gulf), It. 104/D4
Catanzaro, It. 104/E3
Cataouatche (lake), La, US 195/P17
Catarina, Braz. 212/C2
Cataraman, Phil. 137/D5
Catastrophe (cape), Austl. 171/G5
Catatumbo (riv.), Col. 199/G6
Catatungan (mtn.), Phil. 139/F2
Catawba (riv.), NC,SC, US 191/H3
Catawissa, Pa, US 196/B2
Catbalogan, Phil. 137/D5
Catedral (peak), Uru. 217/G2
Catemaco (lake), Mex. 202/C2
Catemaco, Mex. 202/C2
Catende, Braz. 212/D3
Cateran (hill), Eng, UK 94/E5
Caterham, Eng, UK 88/C3
Caterham and Warlingham, Eng, UK 91/F4
Cathcart, SAfr. 164/D4
Cathédrale de Reims, Fr. 110/D2
Catherine (Kātrīna) (mtn.), Egypt 159/C2
Catherine Palace, Rus. 119/T7
Ca'Tiepolo, It. 117/F3
Catió, Pan. 203/G4
Çatköyü, Turk. 148/E2
Catlettsburg, Ky, US 188/D4
Cato (isl.), Austl. 167/E3
Catoche, Cabo (cape), Mex. 202/E1

Catolé do Rocha, Braz. 212/C2
Catonsville, Md, US 196/B5
Catria (peak), It. 117/F6
Catrimani (riv.), Braz. 208/F3
Catriló, Arg. 216/C4
Catrine, Sc, UK 94/B6
Catskill, NY, US 188/F3
Catskill (mts.), NY, US 188/F3
Cattolica, It. 117/F5
Catu, Braz. 212/C4
Cauayan, Phil. 137/D6
Cauayan, Phil. 137/D6
Cauca (dept.), Col. 210/B4
Cauca (riv.), Col. 210/C3
Caucaia, Braz. 212/C1
Caucasia, Col. 210/C3
Caucasus (mts.), Geo. 121/G4
Caudete, Sp. 103/E3
Caudry, Fr. 110/C3
Cauldcleuch Head (peak), Sc, UK 94/D6
Cauquenes, Chile 216/B2
Caura (riv.), Ven. 208/F2
Caussade, Fr. 100/D4
Cauterets, Fr. 100/C5
Cauto (riv.), Cuba 203/G1
Cauvery (riv.), India 140/C5
Cava d'Ispica, It. 104/D4
Cavaillon, Fr. 100/F5
Cavalaire-sur-Mer, Fr. 100/G5
Cavalcante, Braz. 212/A4
Cavalese, It. 115/H5
Cavalier, ND, US 185/J3
Cavalla (riv.), Libr. 154/D6
Cavallermaggiore, It. 116/A3
Cavallino, It. 117/F2
Cavallo, Capo al (cape), Fr. 104/A1
Cavally (riv.), C.d'Iv. 160/D5
Cavan, Ire. 89/Q10
Cavan (co.), Ire. 89/Q10
Cavarzere, It. 117/F2
Cave Creek, Az, US 195/S18
Cave of Ten Thousand Buddhas, Myan. 136/B2
Cavezzo, It. 117/E3
Caviana (isl.), Braz. 209/J3
Cavite, Phil. 137/D5
Cavriana, It. 116/D2
Cawdor, Sc, UK 94/C1
Caxias do Sul, Braz. 213/B4
Caxinas (pt.), Hon. 202/E2
Caxias (pt.), Ang. 163/B2
Caxito, Ang. 163/B2
Çay, Turk. 148/B2
Çayağzı, Turk. 107/K5
Cayambe, Ecu. 210/B4
Cayambe (vol.), Ecu. 210/B4
Cayce, SC, US 191/H3
Cayce, Ky, US 187/K3
Çayeli, Turk. 148/E1
Cayenne (cap.), FrG. 209/H3
Çayırhan, Turk. 110/A4
Cayman (isls.), UK 198/E4
Cayman Brac (isl.), UK 199/F4
Cazalla de la Sierra, Sp. 102/C4
Cazères, Fr. 100/D5
Cazin, Bosn. 101/L4
Cazis, Swi. 115/F4
Cazones (riv.), Mex. 202/B1
Cazorla, Sp. 102/D4
Cazzago San Martino, It. 116/C1
Cea (riv.), Sp. 102/C1
Ceanannus Mór (kells), Ire. 89/Q10
Ceará (state), Braz. 212/B2
Cébaco (isl.), Pan. 203/F5
Ceballos, Mex. 200/D3
Cebollati (riv.), Uru. 217/G2
Cebollati, Uru. 217/G2
Cebreros, Sp. 102/C2
Cebu, Phil. 137/D5
Cebu (int'l arpt.), Phil. 137/D6
Cebu (isl.), Phil. 137/D6
Ceccano, It. 104/C2
Cecil (co.), Md, US 196/C4
Cecil Macks (pass), Swaz. 165/E2
Cecil Plains, Austl. 172/C4
Cecil Rhodes (mt.), Austl. 170/D3
Cecilton, Md, US 196/C5
Cecina (lake), Mex. 202/D2
Cecina, It. 101/J5
Cecita (lake), It. 104/E3
Ceclavín, Sp. 102/B3
Cedar (co.), Ia, US 185/L5
Cedar, Ks, US 195/D6
Cedar (valley), Ut, US 195/J13
Cedar (lake), Mb,Sk, Can. 180/F3
Cedar (mtn.), Ca, US 193/L11
Cedar Bay NP, Austl. 172/B2
Cedar Bluff (res.), Ks, US 187/H3
Cedar Breaks Nat'l Mon., Ut, US 186/D3
Cedar Brook, NJ, US 196/D4
Cedar City, Ut, US 186/D3
Cedar Cove, Co, US 195/B2
Cedar Creek (res.), Tx, US 191/D3

Cedar Falls (dam), Wa, US 193/D3
Cedar Falls, Wa, US 196/B5
Cedar Fort (Cedar Valley), Ut, US 195/J13
Cedar Glen, Ca, US 194/C2
Cedar Grove, Md, US 196/A5
Cedar Grove, NJ, US 197/J8
Cedar Hill, Mo, US 195/F9
Cedar Hills, Ut, US 195/K13
Cedar Key, Fl, US 191/H4
Cedar Island, NY, US 197/L8
Cedarhurst, NY, US 197/L9
Cedartown, Ga, US 191/G3
Cedarville, Ca, US 184/C5
Cedegolo, It. 115/G5
Cedeira, Sp. 102/A1
Cedral, Mex. 201/E4
Cedro, Braz. 212/C2
Cedros (isl.), Mex. 200/B2
Ceduna, Austl. 171/G5
Cee, Sp. 102/A1
Čepin, Cro. 106/D3
Cefalù, It. 104/D3
Cefni (riv.), Wal, UK 92/D5
Cega (riv.), Sp. 102/C2
Cegléd, Hun. 106/D2
Cegrane, FYROM 105/G2
Cehegín, Sp. 102/E3
Cehu Silvaniei, Rom. 107/F2
Ceiriog (riv.), Wal, UK 92/D5
Cekerek (riv.), Turk. 120/F4
Çelákovice, Czh. 113/H2
Celanova, Sp. 102/B1
Celaya, Mex. 201/E4
Celebes (isl.), Indo. 139/E4
Celebes (sea), Asia 139/F3
Celendín, Peru 214/B2
Celestún, Mex. 202/D1
Celica, Ecu. 214/B2
Céligny, Swi. 114/C5
Celina, Tx, US 187/H4
Celina, Oh, US 188/C3
Celje, Slov. 101/L3
Cella, Sp. 102/E2
Celldömölk, Hun. 106/C2
Celle (riv.), It. 98/B4
Celle, Ger. 109/H4
Celle Ligure, It. 116/B4
Celles, Belg. 110/C2
Čelopek, FYROM 106/C5
Celorico da Beira, Port. 102/B2
Celtic (sea), Eur. 89/P11
Cemaes (pt.), Wal, UK 90/B2
Cemaru (peak), Indo. 138/C3
Cembra, It. 115/H5
Cenajo, Embalse del (res.), Sp. 102/E3
Cenderawasih (bay), Indo. 139/H4
Cene, It. 116/C1
Cenepa (riv.), Peru 214/B1
Cengong, China 141/J2
Cenia, Sp. 103/F2
Cenicero, Sp. 102/D1
Cenia, Turk. 107/L5
Cento, It. 117/E3
Cento Croci, Passo di (pass), It. 116/C4
Central (peak), Arg. 216/C4
Central, Braz. 212/B3
Central (pol. reg.), Gha. 161/E5
Central (prov.), Kenya 162/C3
Central (int'l arpt.), Ukr. 107/K2
Central, Ak, US 192/K2
Central, NM, US 186/E4
Central African Republic (ctry.) 155/J6
Central Australia Abor. Land, Austl. 171/F2
Central Australia (Warburton) Abor. Rsv., Austl. 171/E3
Central Butte, Sk, Can. 184/G3
Central City, Ne, US 185/J5
Central City, Co, US 195/A3
Central Cordillera (mts.), SAm. 208/C3
Central Desert Abor. Rsv., Austl. 171/F2
Central Intelligence Agency Fed. Govt. Res., Va, US 196/A6
Central Islip, NY, US 197/F2
Central Makrān (range), Pak. 147/H3
Central, Massif (mass.), Fr. 100/E4
Central Mount Stuart (peak), Austl. 171/G2
Central Mount Wedge (peak), Austl. 171/F2
Central Park, NY, US 197/K8
Central, Planalto (plat.), Braz. 209/J7
Central Point, Or, US 184/C5

Central Siberian (plat.), Rus. 123/L3
Central Ural (mts.), Rus. 119/N4
Central Valley, NY, US 196/D1
Centralia, Wa, US 184/C4
Centralia, Il, US 187/K3
Centre (pol. reg.), Fr. 100/D2
Centre (pol. reg.), Mor. 156/D2
Centre (co.), Pa, US 196/A2
Centre-Nord (pol. reg.), Mor. 158/B2
Centre-Sud (pol. reg.), Mor. 158/B2
Centreville, Al, US 191/G3
Centreville, Il, US 195/G8
Centreville, Md, US 196/B5
Cenxi, China 141/K3
Ceram (isl.), Indo. 139/G4
Ceram (sea), Indo. 139/G4
Cerano, It. 116/B2
Ceraso (cape), It. 104/A2
Cerbère, Fr. 100/E5
Cercal, Port. 102/A4
Cercedilla, Sp. 103/M8
Čerchov (peak), Czh. 113/F4
Cerea, It. 117/E2
Ceredigion (co.), Wal, UK 90/B2
Ceres, Braz. 209/J7
Ceres, SAfr. 164/L10
Ceres, It. 116/A2
Cerese, It. 117/D2
Céret, Fr. 100/E5
Cerfontaine, Belg. 111/D3
Cergy, Fr. 88/J4
Cerignola, It. 104/D2
Cerigo (isl.), It. 105/H5
Čermik, Turk. 148/D2
Cerná (riv.), Czh. 113/H5
Černá (peak), Czh. 113/G5
Cernavodă, Rom. 107/J3
Cernay, Fr. 114/D2
Cernier, Swi. 114/C3
Cerralvo, Mex. 201/E3
Cerralvo (isl.), Mex. 200/C3
Cerreto Guidi, It. 117/D5
Cerreto, Passo del (pass), It. 116/C4
Cérrik, Alb. 105/F2
Cerritos, Mex. 201/E4
Cerritos, Ca, US 194/F8
Cerro Azul, Peru 214/B4
Cerro Azul, Mex. 202/B1
Cerro Castillo, Chile 217/B6
Cerro Chato, Uru. 217/G2
Cerro Corá, Braz. 212/C2
Cerro de la Estrella, PN, Mex. 201/Q10
Cerro de las Campanas, PN, Mex. 201/E4
Cerro de Pasco, Peru 214/B3
Cerro de San Antonio, Col. 210/C2
Cerro El Copey, PN, Ven. 211/F2
Cerro Maggiore, It. 116/B1
Cerro Nanchital, Mex. 202/C2
Cerro del Pinacate (peak), Mex. 200/B1
Cerros Colorados (res.), Arg. 215/C4
Cerros de Amotape, PN, Peru 214/A2
Certaldo, It. 117/E5
Certosa di Pavia, It. 116/C2
Certosa di Pisa, It. 116/D5
Cervantes, Austl. 170/B4
Cervaro, It. 104/D2
Cervati (peak), It. 104/D2
Cervera, Sp. 103/F2
Cervera de Pisuerga, Sp. 102/C1
Cervera del Río Alhama, Sp. 102/E1
Cervia, It. 117/F4
Cervialto (peak), It. 104/D2
Cervignano del Friuli, It. 117/G1
Cervino (peak), It. 115/H4
Cervione, It. 104/A1
Cervo (riv.), It. 116/B1
Cervo, Sp. 102/B1
Cervo, It. 116/B5
Cervo, Serra do (hills), Braz. 213/G7
Cesano (riv.), It. 117/G5
Cesano Boscone, It. 116/C1
Cesano Maderno, It. 116/C1
César (dept.), Col. 210/C2
Cesar (riv.), Col. 210/C2
Cesen (peak), It. 117/F1
Cesena, It. 117/F4
Cesenatico, It. 117/F4
Cēsis, Lat. 97/L3
České Budějovice, Czh. 113/H5
České Středohoří (mts.), Czh. 113/G2
Českomoravská Vysočina (plat.), Czh. 99/H4
Český Brod, Czh. 113/H2

Český Krumlov, Czh. 113/H5
Český Les Sumava (mts.), Czh. 113/F3
Česma (riv.), Cro. 106/C3
Çeşme, Turk. 105/K3
Cesson, Fr. 88/K6
Cesson-Sévigné, Fr. 100/C2
Cestos (riv.), Libr. 160/C5
Cetinje, Mont. 106/D4
Cetraro, It. 104/E3
Çetinkaya, Turk. 148/D2
Ceuta, Sp. 158/B2
Ceva, It. 116/B4
Cevedale (peak), It. 115/G5
Cévennes (mts.), Fr. 100/E4
Cevio, Swi. 115/E5
Ceyhan, Turk. 149/D1
Ceylânpınar, Turk. 148/E2
Ceylon (isl.), SrL. 140/D6
Cèze (riv.), Fr. 114/B5
Cha Da (cape), Viet. 136/C3
Chabás, Arg. 216/E2
Chabjuwardoo (bay), Austl. 170/B2
Chablé, Mex. 202/D2
Chacabuco, Arg. 216/E2
Chachani (peak), Peru 214/D5
Chachapoyas, Peru 214/B2
Chachoengsao, Thai. 136/C3
Chaclacayo, Peru 214/B3
Chaco (riv.), NM, US 186/E3
Chaco (mesa), NM, US 190/B3
Chaco Austral (plain), Arg. 215/D1
Chaco Boreal (plain), Par. 208/F8
Chaco Central (plain), Arg. 215/D1
Chaco, PN, Arg. 215/E2
Chacuapi (ruin), Guat. 202/D3
Chad (lake), Niger 154/H5
Chad (ctry.) 155/J4
Chafarinas (isl.), Sp. 158/C2
Chagang-do (prov.), NKor. 131/D2
Chagda, Rus. 123/P4
Chaghcharān, Afg. 145/K2
Chagny, Fr. 114/A3
Chagos (arch.) 125/G10
Chaguanas, Trin. 211/F2
Chaguarpamba, Ecu. 214/B2
Chahuites, Mex. 202/C2
Chaibāsā, India 143/E4
Chailly-en-Brie, Fr. 88/M5
Chain, SKor. 131/E5
Chainat, Thai. 136/C3
Chaîne Annamitique (mts.), Laos 141/H4
Chaîne de la Selle (peak), Haiti 203/J2
Chaine de l'Atacora (mts.), Ben. 161/F4
Chaitén, Chile 215/B5
Chaiyaphum, Thai. 136/C3
Chākdaha, India 162/C4
Chākia, India 143/E3
Chakradharpur, India 143/E4
Chakrāta, India 144/B3
Chakwāl, Pak. 144/B3
Chala, Peru 214/C4
Chalain (lake), Fr. 114/C3
Chalais, Swi. 114/D5
Chālakudi, India 140/C5
Chalaronne (riv.), Fr. 114/A5
Chalatenango, ESal. 202/D3
Chalbi (des.), Kenya 155/N7
Chalchihuites, Mex. 200/D4
Chalco, Mex. 201/R10
Chale (pt.), Kenya 162/C4
Chaleur (bay), NB,Qu, Can. 189/H2
Chalfont, Pa, US 196/C3
Chalfont Saint Giles, Eng, UK 88/B2
Chalfont Saint Peter, Eng, UK 88/B2
Chalhuanca, Peru 214/C4
Chalifert (canal), Fr. 88/L5
Chalindrey, Fr. 114/B2
Chalk (riv.), Tx, US 190/C4
Chalkyitsik, Ak, US 192/K2
Challans, Fr. 100/C3
Challapata, Bol. 208/E7
Challenger (mts.), Nun., Can. 181/T6
Chalmette, La, US 195/Q17
Chālna Port, Bang. 143/G4
Chalon-sur-Saône, Fr. 114/A3
Châlons-sur-Marne, Fr. 111/D6
Châlus, Iran 146/F1
Cham, Ger. 113/F4
Cham (riv.), Ger. 113/F4
Chama, Zam. 162/B5
Chama (riv.), NM, US 186/E3
Chamah (peak), Malay. 138/B2
Chaman, Pak. 144/D3
Chamba, India 144/D3
Chambal (riv.), India 144/D3
Chambaran, Plateau de (plat.), Fr. 100/F4
Chambas, Cuba 203/G1
Chamberlain (lake), Me, US 189/G2
Chamberlin (mt.), Ak, US 192/K2
Chambersburg, Pa, US 188/E4

Chambéry, Fr. 100/F4
Chambeshi (riv.), Zam. 163/F3
Chambly, Qu, Can. 189/P7
Chambly, Fr. 88/J4
Chambourcy, Fr. 88/J5
Chambry, Fr. 88/L5
Chamchamāl, Iraq 146/D1
Chamechaude (peak), Fr. 100/F4
Chamical, Arg. 215/C3
Chamigny, Fr. 88/M5
Chamizal Nat'l Mem., Tx, US 190/B4
Chamizo, Uru. 217/L11
Chamonix-Mont-Blanc, Fr. 114/C6
Champagne, Yk, Can. 192/L3
Champagne (reg.), Fr. 98/C4
Champagne-Ardenne (pol. reg), Fr. 100/F2
Champagne-sur-Oise, Fr. 88/J4
Champagney, Fr. 114/C2
Champagnole, Fr. 114/B4
Champasak, Laos 136/D3
Champawat, India 142/C1
Champdeuil, Fr. 88/L6
Champeaux, Fr. 88/L6
Champéry, Swi. 114/C5
Champigneulles, Fr. 111/F6
Champigny-sur-Marne, Fr. 88/K5
Champlain (lake), NY,Vt, US 186/F2
Champlitte, Fr. 114/B2
Champotón, Mex. 202/D2
Champotón (riv.), Mex. 202/D2
Champs-sur-Marne, Fr. 88/K5
Champsevraine, Fr. 114/B2
Champvans, Fr. 114/B3
Chamusca, Port. 102/A3
Chan Chan (ruin), Peru 214/B3
Chan May Dong (cape), Viet. 136/E2
Chañaral, Chile 215/B2
Chança (riv.), Port. 102/B4
Chancay, Peru 214/B3
Chanco, Chile 216/B2
Chancy, Swi. 114/B5
Chandalar, Ak, US 192/J2
Chandalar (riv.), Ak, US 192/J2
Chandalar, East Fork (riv.), Ak, US 192/J2
Chandannagar, India 143/G4
Chandausi, India 142/B1
Chanderi, India 142/B3
Chandīgarh, India 144/D4
Chandīgarh (state), India 144/D4
Chandlees (riv.), Braz. 208/D6
Chandler (riv.), Ak, US 192/H2
Chandler, Ok, US 190/D3
Chandler, Qu, Can. 189/H1
Chandler, Az, US 195/S19
Chandolin, Swi. 114/D5
Chāndpur, Bang. 143/H4
Chāndpur, India 142/B1
Chandrapur, India 140/C4
Chanduy, Ecu. 210/A5
Chang (lake), China 130/C5
Chang (riv.), China 130/B5
Changan, SKor. 131/E5
Changbai (peak), China 131/E2
Changbai Chaoxianzu Zizhixian, China 131/E2
Changchun, China 129/N3
Changdang (lake), China 130/D5
Changdao, China 130/E3
Changde, China 137/B2
Changé, Fr. 100/D3
Changewater, NJ, US 196/D2
Changfeng, China 130/D4
Changge, China 130/C4
Changgi-ap (cape), SKor. 132/A2
Changhai, China 131/B3
Changhang, SKor. 131/D4
Changhowŏn, SKor. 131/D4
Changhua, Tai. 137/D3
Changhŭng, SKor. 131/D5
Changis-sur-Marne, Fr. 88/M5
Changji, China 128/E3
Changjiang, China 141/J4
Changjin (res.), NKor. 131/D2
Changjin (lake), NKor. 131/D2
Changle, China 130/D3
Changli, China 130/D3
Changling, China 130/E1
Changning, China 141/H2
Changning, China 141/G3
Ch'angnyŏng, SKor. 131/E5
Changping, China 130/H6
Changqing, China 130/D3
Changsan-got (cape), NKor. 131/C3
Changsha, China 141/K2
Changshou, China 137/A2
Changshu, China 130/L8
Changshun, China 141/J2
Changsŏng, SKor. 131/D5
Changsu, SKor. 131/D5
Changsŭngp'o, SKor. 131/E5
Changtai, China 137/C3
Changtu, China 130/F2
Changuinola, Pan. 203/F4
Ch'angwŏn, SKor. 131/E5
Changxing, China 130/K8
Changyang, China 137/B1
Changyi, China 130/D3
Changyŏn, NKor. 131/C3
Changyuan, China 130/C4
Changzhi, China 130/C3
Changzhou, China 130/K8
Chañi, Nevado de (peak), Arg. 215/C1
Chanlers (falls), Kenya 162/C2
Channel (isls.), UK 100/B2
Channel Country (phys. reg.), Austl. 167/C3
Channel Islands NP, Ca, US 186/C4
Channel-Port aux Basques, Nf, Can. 189/K2
Channel Tunnel, Eng, Fr.,UK 91/H5
Channing, Tx, US 187/G4
Chantada, Sp. 102/B1
Chanteloup-les-Vignes, Fr. 88/J5
Chanthaburi, Thai. 136/C3
Chantilly, Fr. 110/B5
Chantraine, Fr. 114/C1
Chantrey (inlet), Nun., Can. 180/G2
Chao (lake), China 130/D5
Chao Phraya (riv.), Thai. 136/C3
Chaoyang, China 137/C3
Chaoyang, China 130/E2
Chapacura, Bol. 214/D3
Chapada Diamantina, PN, Braz. 209/K6
Chapada dos Veadeiros, PN da, Braz. 209/J6
Chapadinha, Braz. 212/B1
Chapais, Qu, Can. 188/F1
Chapala (lake), Mex. 200/E4
Chapala, Mex. 200/E4
Chaparral, Col. 210/C4
Chaparrosa, Mex. 200/E4
Chapayevsk, Rus. 121/J1
Chapel Hill, NC, US 191/J3
Chapel Ness (pt.), Sc, UK 94/D4
Chapelfell Top (peak), Eng, UK 93/F2
Chapelle-lez-Herlaimont, Belg. 111/D3
Chapeltown, Eng, UK 93/G5
Chaplain (lake), Wa, US 193/D2
Chapleau, On, Can. 188/D2
Chaplin, Sk, Can. 184/G3
Chāpra, India 143/E3
Char (well), Mrta. 156/B5
Chara (riv.), Rus. 123/M4
Charambirá (pt.), Col. 210/B3
Charaña, Bol. 214/D5
Charandra (riv.), Gre. 105/N8
Charata, Arg. 215/D2
Charcas, Mex. 201/E4
Charcot (isl.), Ant. 218/U
Chardonnière, Haiti 203/H2
Charente (riv.), Fr. 100/C4
Chari (riv.), Chad 154/J5
Chārīkār, Afg. 147/J1
Chariton (riv.), Ia,Mo, US 187/J2
Charity, Guy. 211/G3
Charjew, Trkm. 145/D5
Charkhāri, India 142/B3
Charkhi Dādri, India 144/D5
Charlemagne, Qu, Can. 189/P6
Charlemont, NI, UK 92/B3
Charleroi, Belg. 111/D3
Charleroi à Bruxelles, Canal de (canal), Belg. 111/D2
Charles (peak), Austl. 170/D5
Charles (mt.), Austl. 170/C3
Charles (isl.), Qu, Can. 181/J2
Charles City, Ia, US 185/K5
Charles de Gaulle (int'l arpt.), Fr. 88/K4
Charleston, Ms, US 187/K4
Charleston, Nv, US 184/E5
Charleston, SC, US 191/J3
Charleston, Ut, US 195/L13
Charleston (cap.), WV, US 188/D4
Charlestown, StK. 199/N8
Charlestown, Md, US 196/C4
Charleville, Austl. 172/B4
Charleville-Mézières, Fr. 111/D4
Charlevoix, Mi, US 188/C2
Charlotte (lake), BC, Can. 184/B2
Charlotte, Mi, US 188/C3
Charlotte, NC, US 191/H3
Charlotte Amalie, USVI 199/M8
Charlotte/Douglas (int'l arpt.), NC, US 191/H3
Charlottenberg, Swe. 96/E2
Charlottenburg, Ger. 98/Q6
Charlottetown (cap.), PE, Can. 189/J2
Charlton, Austl. 173/B3
Charlton (isl.), On, Can. 181/H3
Charlton Kings, Eng, UK 90/D3
Charly, Fr. 110/C6
Charmes (res.), Fr. 114/B2
Charmes, Fr. 114/C1
Charmey, Swi. 114/D4
Charnay-lès-Mâcon, Fr. 100/F3
Charny, Fr. 88/L5
Charny-sur-Meuse, Fr. 111/E5
Charolais, Monts du (mts.), Fr. 100/F3
Charouine, Alg. 157/E3
Charquemont, Fr. 114/C3
Chars, Fr. 88/H4
Chārsadda, Pak. 144/A2
Charters Towers, Austl. 172/B3
Charthāwal, India 144/D5
Chartres, Fr. 100/D2
Chās, India 143/F4
Chaschauna (peak), Swi. 115/G4
Chascomús, Arg. 216/F2
Chase, BC, Can. 184/D3
Chasŏng, NKor. 131/D2
Chassezac (riv.), Fr. 100/F4
Chastre-Villeroux-Blanmont, Belg. 111/D2
Chatanika, Ak, US 192/J2
Château Bougon (int'l arpt.), Fr. 100/C3
Chateau de Versailles, Fr. 88/J5
Château-d'Olonne, Fr. 100/C3
Château-du-Loir, Fr. 100/D3
Château-Porcien, Fr. 111/D4
Château-Renault, Fr. 100/D3
Château-Salins, Fr. 111/F6
Château-Thierry, Fr. 110/C5
Châteaubriant, Fr. 100/C3
Châteaudun, Fr. 100/D2
Châteauguay, Qu, Can. 189/N7
Châteauneuf-sur-Charente, Fr. 100/C4
Châteaurenard, Fr. 100/F5
Châteauroux, Fr. 100/D3
Châteauvillain, Fr. 114/A1
Châtel-Saint-Denis, Swi. 114/C4
Châtelaillon-Page, Fr. 100/C3
Châtelet, Belg. 111/D3
Châtellerault, Fr. 100/D3
Châtenay-Malabry, Fr. 88/J5
Châtenois, Fr. 114/B1
Châtenois-les-Forges, Fr. 114/C2
Chatfield (res.), Co, US 195/B3
Chatham (isls.), Chile 217/B6
Chatham, On, Can. 188/D3
Chatham, Eng, UK 91/G4
Chatham, NJ, US 197/H9
Châtillon, It. 101/G4
Châtillon, Fr. 88/J5
Châtillon-sur-Chalaronne, Fr. 114/A5
Châtillon-sur-Marne, Fr. 110/C5
Châtillon-sur-Seine, Fr. 100/F3
Chatkal (riv.), Kyr. 145/F4
Chatou, Fr. 88/J5
Chatra, India 143/E3
Chatrapur, India 140/E4
Châtres, Fr. 88/L5
Chatsworth (res.), Ca, US 194/B2
Chatsworth, NJ, US 196/D4
Chattahoochee (riv.),US 191/G4
Chattahoochee, Fl, US 191/G4
Chattanooga, Tn, US 191/G3
Chatteris, Eng, UK 91/G2
Chau Doc, Viet. 136/D4
Chaucey, Îles (isls.), Fr. 100/C2
Chauconin-Neufmontiers, Fr. 88/L5
Chaudfontaine, Belg. 111/E2
Chaudière (riv.), Qu, Can. 189/G2
Chauk, Myan. 141/F3
Chaukan (pass), India 141/G2
Chaumes-en-Brie, Fr. 88/L5
Chaumont, Fr. 114/B1
Chaumont-en-Vexin, Fr. 110/A5
Chaunskaya (bay), Rus. 123/T3
Chauny, Fr. 110/C4
Chaussin, Fr. 114/B4
Chaussy, Fr. 88/H4
Chautauqua (lake), NY, US 188/E3
Chautauqua, Il, US 195/G8
Chauvigny, Fr. 100/D3
Chaval, Braz. 212/B1
Chavanoz, Fr. 114/B6
Chaves, Port. 102/B2
Chavín de Huantar (ruin), Peru 214/B3
Chaviña, Peru 214/C4
Chavinillo, Peru 214/B3
Chavornay, Swi. 114/C4
Chawinda, Pak. 144/C3
Chay (riv.), Viet. 136/D1
Chayanta (riv.), Bol. 208/E7
Chaykovskiy, Rus. 119/M4
Chazuta, Peru 214/B2
Cheadle, Eng, UK 93/G6
Cheaha (mtn.), Al, US 191/G3
Cheb, Czh. 113/F2
Cheboksary, Rus. 119/K4
Cheboksary (res.), Rus. 119/K4
Cheboygan, Mi, US 188/C2
Chechaouene, Mor. 158/B2
Chechaouene (prov.), Mor. 158/B2
Chechen' (isl.), Rus. 121/H3
Chechnya, Resp., Rus. 122/G6
Chech'ŏn, SKor. 131/E4
Checotah, Ok, US 187/J4
Chedabucto (bay), NS, Can. 189/J2
Cheduba (isl.), Myan. 141/F4
Cheektowaga, NY, US 189/S10
Cheepash (riv.), On, Can. 188/D1
Cheepay (riv.), On, Can. 188/D1
Chefornak, Ak, US 192/F3
Chegutu, Zim. 163/F4
Chehalis, Wa, US 184/C4
Cheïkh (well), Alg. 157/F3
Cheju, SKor. 129/N5
Cheju (isl.), SKor. 129/N5
Cheju (str.), SKor. 129/N5
Cheka (peak), Rus. 145/C2
Chelan, Wa, US 184/C4
Chelan (lake), Wa, US 184/C4
Chelghoum El Aïd, Alg. 158/J4
Chelles, Fr. 88/K5
Chełm, Pol. 99/M3
Chełmno, Pol. 99/K2
Chelmsford, Eng, UK 91/G3
Chełmża, Pol. 99/K2
Cheltenham, Eng, UK 90/D3
Chelva, Sp. 103/E3
Chelyabinsk (int'l arpt.), Rus. 119/P5
Chelyabinsk, Rus. 119/P5
Chelyabinskaya Oblast, Rus. 145/D2
Chelyuskina (cape), Rus. 123/L2
Chemaïa, Mor. 156/C2
Chemax, Mex. 202/E1
Chemnitz, Ger. 98/G3
Chen (riv.), China 137/A2
Chena Hot Springs, Ak, US 192/J2
Chenāb (riv.), Pak. 147/K2
Chenachane (well), Alg. 156/D4
Cheney, Wa, US 184/D4
Cheng'anpu, China 130/C3
Chengbu Miaozu Zizhixian, China 141/K2
Chengde, China 130/D2
Chengdu, China 128/H5
Chengkou, China 128/J5
Chengmai, China 141/J4
Chengshan Jiao (cape), China 131/B4
Chengwu, China 130/C4
Cheniménil, Fr. 114/C1
Chennai (Madras), India 140/D5
Chennevières-lès-Louvres, Fr. 88/K4
Chenòve, Fr. 114/A3
Chenxi, China 141/K2
Chenzhou, China 141/K2
Chep Lak Kok (int'l arpt.), China 129/T10
Chepelare, Bul. 105/J2
Chepén, Peru 214/B2
Chepes, Arg. 215/C3
Chépica, Chile 216/C2
Chepigana, Pan. 210/B2
Chepo, Pan. 210/B2
Chepstow, Wal, UK 90/D3
Cheptsa (riv.), Rus. 119/M4
Cher (riv.), Fr. 100/E3
Chéran (riv.), Fr. 114/C6
Cherasco, It. 116/A3
Cherāt, Pak. 144/A3
Cheraw, SC, US 191/J3
Cherbourg, Fr. 100/C2
Cherbourg, Austl. 172/C4
Cherchell, Alg. 158/G4
Cherepovets, Rus. 118/H4
Cherf, Oued (riv.), Alg. 158/K6
Cheria, Alg. 158/K7
Cherkas'ka Oblasti, Ukr. 120/D2
Cherkasy, Ukr. 120/E2
Cherkessk, Rus. 121/G3
Chermignon, Swi. 114/D5
Chernaya (riv.), Rus. 119/N1
Cherni Lom (riv.), Bul. 107/H4
Cherni Vrŭkh (peak), Bul. 105/H1
Chernihiv, Ukr. 120/D2
Chernihivs'ka Oblasti, Ukr. 120/D2
Chernivets'ka Oblasti, Ukr. 120/C2
Chernivtsi, Ukr. 107/G1
Chernushka, Rus. 119/N4
Cherokee, Ok, US 187/H3
Cherry Creek (dam), Co, US 195/C3
Cherry Creek (lake), Co, US 195/C3
Cherry Hill, Md, US 196/C4
Cherry Hill, NJ, US 196/C4
Cherry Valley, Ca, US 194/D3
Cherski (range), Rus. 125/P3
Chertsey, Eng, UK 88/B2
Cherven Bryag, Bul. 107/G4
Chervonohrad, Ukr. 120/C2
Cherwell (riv.), Eng, UK 91/E3
Chesaning, Mi, US 188/C3
Chesapeake (bay), US 188/E4
Chesapeake and Delaware (canal), De,Md, US 196/C4
Chesapeake Bay Maritime Museum, Md, US 196/B6
Chesapeake City, Md, US 196/C4
Chesham, Eng, UK 91/F3
Cheshire (co.), Eng, UK 93/F5
Cheshire (plain), Eng, UK 93/F5
Cheshskaya (bay), Rus. 122/E3
Cheshunt, Eng, UK 88/C1
Chesilhurst, NJ, US 196/D4
Chester, Eng, UK 93/F5
Chester, Ca, US 184/C5
Chester (riv.), Md, US 196/B5
Chester, Mt, US 184/F3
Chester, NJ, US 196/D2
Chester, Pa, US 196/C4
Chester (co.), Pa, US 196/C4
Chester, SC, US 191/H3
Chester Heights, Pa, US 196/C4
Chester-le-Street, Eng, UK 93/G2
Chester Morse (lake), Wa, US 193/D3
Chesterfield (inlet), Nun., Can. 180/G2
Chesterfield, Eng, UK 93/G5
Chesterfield, Mo, US 195/F8
Chesterfield (isls.), NCal., Fr. 174/E6
Chesterfield Inlet, Nun., Can. 180/G2
Chesterfield, Nosy (isl.), Madg. 165/G7
Chesterton (range), Austl. 172/B4
Chestertown, Md, US 196/B5
Chesuncook (lake), Me, US 189/G2
Cheswold, De, US 196/C5
Chetumal (bay), Mex. 198/D4
Chetumal, Mex. 202/D2
Chetwynd, BC, Can. 184/C2
Cheung Chau (isl.), China 129/T11
Chevak, Ak, US 192/E3
Cheval Blanc (pt.), Haiti 203/H2
Chevigny-Saint-Sauveur, Fr. 114/B3
Cheviot (hills), Sc, UK 94/D6
Cheviot, The (peak), Eng, UK 94/D6
Chevreuse, Fr. 88/J5
Chevry-Cossigny, Fr. 88/K5
Chew (riv.), Eng, UK 90/D4
Chew Valley (lake), Eng, UK 90/D4
Chewelah, Wa, US 184/D3
Chexbres, Swi. 114/C5
Cheyenne (riv.), SD,Wy, US 185/H5
Cheyenne (cap.), Wy, US 185/G5
Cheyenne, Ok, US 187/H4
Cheyenne Wells, Co, US 187/G3
Cheyres, Swi. 114/C4
Chhabra, India 142/A3
Chhaprauli, India 144/D5
Chhāta, India 142/A2
Chhatarpur, India 142/B3
Chhattisgarh (state), India 140/D3
Chhibrāmau, India 142/B2
Chhindwāra, India 142/B4
Chi (riv.), Thai. 141/H4
Chi, Tai. 137/D3
Ch'iak-san NP, SKor. 131/E4
Chiampo, It. 117/E1
Chianciano Terme, It. 101/J5
Chiang Kai Shek (int'l arpt.), Tai. 137/D2
Chiang Mai, Thai. 141/G4
Chiang Rai, Thai. 141/G4
Chianti (reg.), It. 117/E5
Chianti, Monti del (mts.), It. 117/E5
Chiapa de Corzo, Mex. 202/C2
Chiapas (state), Mex. 198/C4
Chiappa (pt.), It. 116/C4
Chiaravalle, It. 117/G5
Chiari, It. 116/C1
Chiasso, Swi. 115/F6
Chiat'ura, Geo. 121/G4
Chiautempan, Mex. 201/L7
Chiautla, Mex. 201/R9
Chiautla de Tapia, Mex. 202/B2
Chiavari, It. 116/C4
Chiavenna, It. 115/F5
Chiba, Japan 133/G3
Chibougamau, Qu, Can. 188/F1
Chibougamau (riv.), Qu, Can. 188/F1
Chibougamau (lake), Qu, Can. 188/F1
Chibukak (pt.), Ak, US 192/D3
Chibuto, Moz. 163/F5
Chicago, Il, US 185/M5
Chicago Heights, Il, US 193/Q16
Chicago Midway (int'l arpt.), Il, US 187/L2
Chicago, North Branch (riv.), Il, US 193/Q15
Chicago-O'Hare (int'l arpt.), Il, US 185/M5
Chicago Ridge, Il, US 193/Q16
Chicago Sanitary and Ship Canal, Il, US 193/P16
Chicama, Peru 214/B2
Chichagof (isl.), Ak, US 180/C3
Chichaoua, Mor. 156/C3
Chīchāwatni, Pak. 144/B4
Chichén Itzá (ruin), Mex. 202/D1
Chicheng, China 129/L3
Chichester (range), Austl. 167/A3
Chichester, Eng, UK 91/F5
Chichibu, Japan 133/F3
Chichicastenango, Guat. 202/D3
Chichigalpa, Nic. 202/E3
Chichihualco, Mex. 201/F5
Chichiriviche, Ven. 210/D2
Chichishima (isls.), Japan 174/D2
Chickaloon, Ak, US 192/J3
Chickamauga (lake), Tn, US 191/G3
Chickasaw Nat'l Rec. Area, Ok, US 187/H4
Chickasha, Ok, US 187/H4
Chicla, Peru 214/B3
Chiclana de la Frontera, Sp. 102/B4
Chiclayo, Peru 214/B2
Chico, Ca, US 186/B3
Chico (riv.), Arg. 205/B7
Chicoloapan, Mex. 201/R10
Chicomostoc (ruin), Mex. 200/E4
Chicomuselo, Mex. 202/C3
Chiconcuac, Mex. 201/R9
Chicontepec de Tejeda, Mex. 202/B1
Chicopee, Ma, US 189/F3
Chicoutimi, Qu, Can. 189/G1
Chicualacuala, Moz. 163/F5
Chidley (cape), Nf, Can. 181/K2
Chido, SKor. 131/D5
Chiefland, Fl, US 191/H4
Chiemsee (lake), Ger. 101/K3
Chieo Lan (res.), Thai. 141/G6
Chieri, It. 116/A2
Chierry, Fr. 110/C5
Chiers (riv.), Fr. 111/E5
Chiesa in Valmalenco, It. 115/F5
Chiese (riv.), It. 101/J3
Chieti, It. 104/D1
Chietla, Mex. 201/L8
Chièvres, Belg. 110/C2
Chifeng, China 129/L3
Chifre, Serra do (mts.), Braz. 209/K7
Chigasaki, Japan 133/F3
Chiginagak (mt.), Ak, US 192/G4
Chignahuapan, Mex. 201/L7
Chignecto (bay), NB,NS, Can. 189/H2
Chignik, Ak, US 192/G4
Chignik Lake, Ak, US 192/G4
Chigorodó, Col. 210/B3
Chigu (lake), China 143/H1
Chigwell, Eng, UK 88/D2
Chihayaakasaka, Japan 135/J7
Chihli (Bo Hai) (gulf), China 130/D3
Chihuahua, Mex. 200/D2
Chihuahua (state), Mex. 200/D2
Chikaskia (riv.), Ks,Ok, US 187/H3
Chikballāpur, India 140/C5
Chikhli, India 147/L5
Chikmagalūr, India 147/K5
Chikoy (riv.), Rus. 123/L5
Chikugo (riv.), Japan 132/B4
Chikuma (riv.), Japan 133/F2
Chilac, Mex. 201/M8
Chilaw, SrL. 140/C6
Chilbo-san (peak), NKor. 131/E2
Chilca, Peru 214/B4
Chilcotin (riv.), BC, Can. 180/D3
Childers, Austl. 172/D4
Childersburg, Al, US 191/G3
Childress, Tx, US 187/G4
Chile (ctry.) 215/B3
Chile Chico, Chile 216/C5
Chile, Monte el (peak), Hon. 202/E3
Chilecito, Arg. 215/C2
Chilete, Peru 214/B2
Ch'ilgap-san NP, SKor. 131/D4
Chililabombwe, Zam. 163/E3
Chilka (lake), India 140/E4
Chilko (lake), BC, Can. 180/D3
Chilkoot (pass), Can.,US 192/L4
Chilkoot (pass), Ak, US 192/L3
Chilla Well Abor. Land, Austl. 171/F2
Chillán, Chile 216/B3
Chillanes, Ecu. 214/B1
Chillicothe, Il, US 185/L5
Chilliwack, BC, Can. 184/C3
Chillon, Swi. 114/C5
Chilly-Mazarin, Fr. 88/J5
Chiloé (isl.), Chile 216/B4
Chiloé, PN, Chile 216/B4
Chiloquin, Or, US 184/C5
Chilpancingo de los Bravos, Mex. 201/F5
Chiltern (hills), Eng, UK 91/E3
Chiltern Hundreds (reg.), Eng, UK 88/A2
Chilung La (pass), India 144/D3
Chilwa (lake), Malw. 163/G4
Chimacum, Wa, US 193/B1
Chimalhuacán, Mex. 201/R10
Chimaliro (hill), Malw. 162/B5
Chimaltenango, Guat. 202/D3
Chimán, Pan. 210/B2
Chimanimani, Zim. 163/F4
Chimantá-Tepuí (peak), Ven. 211/F3
Chimay, Belg. 111/D3
Chimbay, Uzb. 145/C4
Chimborazo (dept.), Ecu. 210/B5
Chimborazo (vol.), Ecu. 210/B5
Chimbote, Peru 214/B3
Chimichaqua, Col. 210/C2
Chimoio, Moz. 163/F4
Chimtarga (peak), Taj. 145/E5
Chin (state), Myan. 141/F3
China (ctry.) 128/G4
China, Mex. 201/F3
China, Mex. 202/D2
Chinácota, Col. 210/C3
Chinan, SKor. 131/D5
Chinandega, Nic. 202/E3
Chinati (mts.), Tx, US 190/B4
Chincha Alta, Peru 214/B4
Chinchaga (riv.), Ab,BC, Can. 180/E3
Chinchilla, Sp. 102/E3
Chinchilla, Austl. 172/C4
Chinch'ŏn, SKor. 131/D4
Chinchón, Sp. 102/D2
Chincoteague, Va, US 188/F4
Chinde, Moz. 163/G4
Chindo, SKor. 131/D5
Chindrieux, Fr. 114/B6
Chindu, China 128/G4
Chindwin (riv.), Myan. 141/F3
Chingaza, PN, Col. 210/C3
Chingleput, India 140/C5
Chingola, Zam. 163/E3
Chinguetti, Dhar de (cliff), Mrta. 156/B5
Chinhae, SKor. 131/E5
Chinhoyi, Zim. 163/F4
Chiniak (cape), Ak, US 192/H4
Chiniot, Pak. 144/B4
Chinit (riv.), Camb. 136/D3
Chinju, SKor. 131/D5
Chinko (riv.), CAfr. 155/K6
Chinle, Az, US 186/E3
Chinnor, Eng, UK 91/F3
Chino, Japan 133/F3
Chino, Ca, US 194/C2
Chino (hills), Ca, US 194/G8
Chinook, Mt, US 184/F3
Chinsali, Zam. 162/B5
Chinú, Col. 210/C2
Chiny, Belg. 111/E4
Chinyŏng, SKor. 131/E5
Chioggia, It. 117/F2
Chipata, Zam. 163/F3
Chiping, China 130/D3
Chipiona, Sp. 102/B4
Chipley, Fl, US 191/G4
Chiplūn, India 147/K5
Chippenham, Eng, UK 90/D4
Chippewa (co.), Wi, US 185/L4
Chippewa (riv.), Wi, US 185/L4
Chipping Ongar, Eng, UK 88/D1
Chiprovtsi, Bul. 106/F4
Chiputneticook (lakes), US,Can. 189/H2
Chiquián, Peru 214/B3
Chiquimula, Guat. 202/D3
Chiquimulilla, Guat. 202/D3
Chiquinquirá, Col. 208/D2
Chiquita (sea), Arg. 205/C6
Chirāla, India 140/D4
Chirāwa, India 142/A1
Chirchiq, Uzb. 145/E4
Chirgaon, India 142/B3
Chiri-san (peak), SKor. 131/D5
Chiri-san NP, SKor. 131/D5
Chiricahua Nat'l Mon., Az, US 186/E4
Chiriguaná, Col. 210/C2
Chirikof (isl.), Ak, US 192/G4
Chirinos, Peru 214/B2
Chirip (peak), Rus. 134/E1
Chiripa (peak), Nic. 203/E4
Chiriquí (lag.), Pan. 203/F4
Chiriquí, Golfo de (gulf), Pan. 208/B2
Chirkunda, India 143/F4
Chirnside, Sc, UK 94/D5
Chironico, Swi. 115/E5
Chirpan, Bul. 105/J1
Chirripó (mtn.), CR 203/F4
Chirripó, PN, CR 198/E6
Chiryu, Japan 135/M6
Chisana, Ak, US 192/K3
Chisasibi (Fort-George), Qu, Can. 181/J3
Chisholm, Mn, US 188/A2
Chishtiān Mandi, Pak. 144/B5
Chisimba (falls), Zam. 162/A5
Chişinău (cap.), Mol. 107/J2
Chişinău (int'l arpt.), Mol. 107/J2
Chişineu Criş, Rom. 106/E2
Chistochina, Ak, US 192/K3
Chistopol', Rus. 119/L5
Chita, Col. 210/C3
Chita, Japan 135/L6
Chita (bay), Japan 135/L6
Chita (pen.), Japan 135/L6
Chitina, Ak, US 192/K3
Chitinskaya Oblast, Rus. 123/M4
Chitipa, Malw. 162/B5
Chitose, Japan 134/B2
Chitose (int'l arpt.), Japan 134/B2
Chitradurga, India 140/C5
Chitrakut, India 142/C3
Chitral Gol NP, Pak. 144/A2
Chitré, Pan. 210/A3
Chittagong (pol. div.), Bang. 143/H4
Chittagong, Bang. 141/F3
Chittaranjan, India 143/F4
Chittoor, India 140/C5
Chitungwiza, Zim. 163/F4
Chiuduno, It. 116/C1
Chiuppano, It. 117/E1
Chiusa di Pesio, It. 116/A4
Chiusella (riv.), It. 116/A1
Chiusi, It. 101/J5
Chivacoa, Ven. 210/D2
Chivasso, It. 116/A2
Chivato (pt.), Mex. 200/C3
Chivay, Peru 214/D4
Chivé, Bol. 214/D4
Chivhu, Zim. 163/F4
Chivilcoy, Arg. 216/E2
Chixoy (riv.), Guat. 202/D3
Chiyoda, Japan 135/E1
Chiyoda, Japan 135/E1
Chiyokawa, Japan 135/D1
Chizela, Zam. 163/E3
Chlef (riv.), Alg. 158/F4
Chlef (prov.), Alg. 158/F4
Chlef, Alg. 158/F4
Chlum (peak), Czh. 113/H5
Chno Dearg (peak), Sc, UK 94/B3
Ch'o (isl.), NKor. 131/C3
Cho Oyu (peak), Nepal 143/F1
Chobe NP, Bots. 163/D4
Chobham, Eng, UK 88/B3
Choceň, Czh. 99/J4
Choch'iwŏn, SKor. 131/D4
Chocianów, Pol. 99/H3
Chocó (dept.), Col. 203/G5
Chocolate (mts.), Ca, US 186/D4
Chocontá, Col. 210/C3
Chocope, Peru 214/B2
Choctaw, Ok, US 195/N15
Chodavaram, India 140/D4
Chodov, Czh. 113/F2
Chodzież, Pol. 99/J2
Choele Choel, Arg. 216/D3
Chōfu, Japan 133/F3
Choiseul (isl.), Sol. 174/E5
Choisy-au-Bac, Fr. 110/B5
Choisy-le-Roi, Fr. 88/K5
Choix, Mex. 200/C3
Chojna, Pol. 99/H2
Chojnice, Pol. 96/G5
Chojnów, Pol. 99/H3
Chokai-san (peak), Japan 134/B4
Choke Canyon (res.), Tx, US 190/D4
Chola (mts.), China 128/G5
Cholet, Fr. 100/C3
Cholila, Arg. 216/C4
Chŏlla-bukto (prov.), SKor. 131/D5
Ch'ŏlla-namdo (prov.), SKor. 131/D5
Cholula de Rivadabia, Mex. 201/L7
Choluteca, Hon. 202/E3
Choluteca (riv.), Hon. 202/E3
Choma, Zam. 163/E4
Chŏmch'ŏn, SKor. 131/E4
Chomo Lhāri (peak), Bhu. 143/G2
Chomutov, Czh. 113/G2
Chomutovka (riv.), Czh. 113/G2
Chon Buri, Thai. 136/C3
Ch'ŏnan, SKor. 131/D4
Chōnan, Japan 135/E3
Chonchi, Chile 216/B4
Ch'ŏnch'ŏn, NKor. 131/D2
Chone, Ecu. 210/A5

Ch'ŏng-yang, SKor. 131/D4
Chong'an, China 137/C2
Ch'ŏngch'ŏn (riv.), NKor. 131/D2
Ch'ŏngdo, SKor. 131/E5
Ch'ŏngjin, NKor. 131/E2
Ch'ŏngjin -si (prov.), NKor. 131/E2
Chŏngju, SKor. 131/D5
Ch'ŏngju, NKor. 131/C3
Chongli, China 130/C2
Chongmyo Shrine, SKor. 131/G6
Chongoyape, Peru 214/B2
Chŏngsŏn, SKor. 131/E4
Ch'ŏngsong, SKor. 131/E4
Chongyi, China 141/K2
Chongzuo, China 141/J3
Chŏnju, SKor. 131/D5
Ch'ŏnma-san (peak), SKor. 131/G6
Chonos, Archipiélago de los (arch.), Chile 216/B5
Chopan, India 142/D3
Chorcha (mtn.), Pan. 203/F4
Chorley, Eng. UK 93/F4
Chorleywood, Eng, UK 88/B2
Choroszcz, Pol. 99/M2
Chortkiv, Ukr. 120/C2
Ch'ŏrwŏn, SKor. 131/D3
Chorzele, Pol. 99/L2
Chorzów, Pol. 99/K3
Chos-Malal, Arg. 216/C3
Ch'osan, NKor. 131/C2
Chōsei, Japan 135/E3
Chōshi, Japan 133/G3
Choszczno, Pol. 99/H2
Chota, Peru 214/B2
Chota Nāgpur (plat.), India 140/D3
Choteau, Mt, US 184/E4
Chott el Rharbi (depr.), Alg. 158/D3
Chotyšanka (riv.), Czh. 113/H3
Chowagasberg (peak), Namb. 163/C6
Chowan (riv.), NC, US 191/J2
Choybalsan, Mong. 129/K2
Choyr, Mong. 128/J2
Chreirik (well), Mrta. 156/B5
Christchurch, NZ 175/S11
Christchurch (int'l arpt.), NZ 175/S11
Christchurch, Eng, UK 91/E5
Christchurch (bay), Eng, UK 91/E5
Christian (sound), Ak, US 192/M4
Christiana, Jam. 203/G2
Christiana, SAfr. 164/D2
Christiana, De, US 196/C4
Christiana, Pa, US 196/C4
Christiansfeld, Den. 96/C4
Christiansted, USVI 199/M8
Christina (riv.), De, US 196/C5
Christmas (isl.), Austl. 125/K11
Chrudim, Czh. 99/H4
Chryston, Sc, UK 94/B5
Chrzanów, Pol. 99/K3
Chu Yang Sin (peak), Viet. 136/E3
Chuādanga, Bang. 143/G4
Chuansha, China 130/L8
Chuathbaluk, Ak, US 192/G3
Chubut (riv.), Arg. 216/C4
Chubut (prov.), Arg. 216/C4
Chucanti (peak), Pan. 210/B2
Chūgoku (mts.), Japan 132/C3
Chūgoku (prov.), Japan 132/B4
Chūhar Kāna, Pak. 144/B4
Chukai, Malay. 138/B3
Chukchi (sea), Rus. 125/T3
Chukchi (pen.), Rus. 125/T3
Chukotskiy Aut. Okrug, Rus. 123/S3
Chukotskiy (cape), Rus. 192/D3
Chula Vista, Ca, US 194/C5
Ch'ulp'o, SKor. 131/D5
Chulucanas, Peru 214/A2
Chulym (riv.), Rus. 122/J4
Chuma, Bol. 214/D4
Chumerna (peak), Bul. 105/J1
Chumphon, Thai. 136/B4
Chuna (riv.), Rus. 122/K4
Chunār, India 142/D3
Ch'unch'ŏn, SKor. 131/D4
Ch'ungch'ŏng-bukto (prov.), SKor. 131/D4
Ch'ungch'ŏng-namdo (prov.), SKor. 131/D4
Ch'ungju (lake), SKor. 131/D4
Ch'ungju, SKor. 131/D4
Ch'ungman (riv.), NKor. 131/C2
Ch'ungmu, SKor. 131/E5
Ch'ungsan, NKor. 131/C3
Chunhuhub, Mex. 202/D2
Chūnián, Pak. 144/B4
Chunya, Tanz. 162/B5
Chunya (riv.), Rus. 123/L3
Ch'unyang, SKor. 131/E4
Chupa, Peru 214/D4
Chupaca, Peru 214/C4
Chuquibamba, Peru 214/C4

Chuquibambilla, Peru 214/C4
Chuquicamata, Chile 215/C1
Chur, Swi. 115/F4
Churachandpur, India 141/F3
Churcampa, Peru 214/C4
Church, Eng, UK 93/F4
Church Hill, Md, US 196/C4
Churchill, Austl. 173/C3
Churchill (peak), BC, Can. 180/D3
Churchill, Mb, Can. 180/G3
Churchill (cape), Mb, Can. 180/G3
Churchill, Mb, Can. 180/G3
Churchill (lake), Sk, Can. 180/F3
Churchill Falls, Nf, Can. 181/K3
Churchill NP, Austl. 173/G5
Churchville, Md, US 196/B4
Churia Ghats (mts.), Nepal 143/E2
Churin, Peru 214/B3
Churnet (riv.), Eng, UK 93/G5
Churu, India 144/C5
Churuguara, Ven. 210/D2
Churumuco de Morelos, Mex. 201/E5
Churwalden, Swi. 115/F4
Chuschi, Peru 214/C4
Chuska (mts.), Az,NM, US 186/E3
Chusovaya (riv.), Rus. 119/N4
Chusovoy, Rus. 119/N4
Chutung, Tai. 137/D3
Chuvashiya, Resp., Rus. 122/Q6
Chuwang-san NP, SKor. 131/H2
Chuxiong, China 141/H2
Chüy (obl.), Kyr. 145/F4
Chūzu, Japan 135/K5
Ci Xian, China 130/C3
Ciadir-Lunga, Mol. 107/J2
Ciamis, Indo. 138/C5
Ciampino (int'l arpt.), It. 104/C2
Ciampino, It. 104/C2
Cianjur, Indo. 138/C5
Cibolo, Tx, US 195/U20
Cicagna, It. 116/C4
Cicero, Il, US 188/C3
Cicero Dantas, Braz. 212/C3
Ćićevac, Serb. 106/E4
Cide, Turk. 148/C1
Ciechanów, Pol. 99/L2
Ciechocinek, Pol. 99/K2
Ciego de Ávila, Cuba 203/G1
Ciénaga, Col. 210/C2
Ciénaga de Oro, Col. 210/C2
Cienfuegos, Cuba 203/F1
Cieplice Śląskie Zdrój, Pol. 99/H3
Cieszyn, Pol. 99/K4
Cieza, Sp. 102/E3
Çifteler, Turk. 148/B2
Cifuentes, Sp. 102/D2
Cifuentes, Cuba 203/F1
Cigánd, Hun. 99/L4
Cigliano, It. 116/B1
Cigüela (riv.), Sp. 102/D3
Cihanbeyli, Turk. 148/C2
Cihuatlán, Mex. 200/D5
Cijara, Embalse de (res.), Sp. 102/C3
Cijulang, Indo. 138/C5
Cilacap, Indo. 138/C5
Cilavegna, It. 116/B2
Çıldır (lake), Turk. 148/E1
Cilfaesty (peak), Wal, UK 90/C2
Cili, China 137/B2
Cilleros, Sp. 102/B2
Cima della Laurasca (peak), It. 115/E5
Cima de'Piazzi (peak), It. 115/G5
Cima la Casina (peak), It. 115/G4
Cimarron (range), NM, US 190/B2
Cimarron (riv.), Ks,Ok, US 190/D3
Cime du Cheiron (peak), Fr. 101/G5
Cime du Diable (peak), Fr. 101/G4
Cimone (peak), It. 117/D4
Çimpeni, Rom. 107/F2
Cimpia Turzii, Rom. 107/F2
Cimpina, Rom. 107/G3
Cimpulung, Rom. 107/G3
Cimpulung Moldovenesc, Rom. 107/G2
Çınar, Turk. 148/E2
Çınarcık, Turk. 107/J5
Cinaruco (riv.), Ven. 210/D3
Cinca (riv.), Sp. 103/F1
Cincar (peak), Bosn. 106/C4
Cincinnati, Oh, US 188/D4
Cinco Saltos, Arg. 216/C3
Cindrelu (peak), Rom. 107/F3
Çine, Turk. 148/B2
Ciney, Belg. 111/E3
Cingia de'Botti, It. 116/D2
Cingoli, It. 117/G6

Cinisello Balsamo, It. 116/C1
Cinnaminson, NJ, US 196/D4
Cintalapa de Figueroa, Mex. 202/C2
Cinto (peak), Fr. 104/A1
Cinto Caomaggiore, It. 117/F1
Cintruénigo, Sp. 102/E1
Ciovo (isl.), Cro. 106/C4
Cipó, Braz. 212/C3
Cipolletti, Arg. 216/D3
Circeo, PN del, It. 104/C2
Circle, Ak, US 192/K2
Circle, Mt, US 185/G4
Circle Hot Springs, Ak, US 192/K2
Cirebon, Indo. 138/C5
Cirencester, Eng, UK 90/E3
Cires-lès-Mello, Fr. 110/B5
Ciriè, It. 116/A2
Cirò Marina, It. 105/E3
Ciron (riv.), Fr. 100/C4
Ciserano, It. 116/C1
Cisnădie, Rom. 107/G3
Cisneros, Col. 210/C3
Cisnes (riv.), Chile 216/B5
Cisse (riv.), Fr. 100/D3
Cisterna di Latina, It. 104/C2
Cistierna, Sp. 102/C1
Citlaltépetl (vol.), Mex. 201/M7
Citrus Heights, Ca, US 186/B3
Citrusdal, SAfr. 164/L10
Città del Vaticano (Vatican City) (cap.), VatC. 104/C2
Città di Castello, It. 117/F6
Città di Torino (int'l arpt.), It. 101/G4
Cittadella, It. 117/E1
Cittanova, It. 104/E3
Cittiglio, It. 116/C1
City (isl.), NY, US 197/K8
City (int'l arpt.), NI, UK 92/C2
Ciudad Acuña, Mex. 201/E2
Ciudad Altamirano, Mex. 201/E5
Ciudad Bolívar, Ven. 211/F2
Ciudad Bolivia, Ven. 210/D2
Ciudad Camargo, Mex. 200/D3
Ciudad Constitución, Mex. 200/C3
Ciudad Cortés, CR 203/F4
Ciudad Cuauhtémoc, Mex. 202/B1
Ciudad de Dolores Hidalgo, Mex. 201/E4
Ciudad de México (Mexico) (cap.), Mex. 201/Q10
Ciudad de Nutrias, Ven. 210/D2
Ciudad de Río Grande, Mex. 200/E4
Ciudad del Carmen, Mex. 202/D2
Ciudad del Maíz, Mex. 201/E4
Ciudad Delicias, Mex. 200/D2
Ciudad Fernández, Mex. 201/E4
Ciudad Frontera, Mex. 201/E3
Ciudad Guayana, Ven. 211/F2
Ciudad Guzmán, Mex. 201/E5
Ciudad Hidalgo, Mex. 201/E5
Ciudad Hidalgo, Mex. 202/C3
Ciudad Insurgentes, Mex. 200/C3
Ciudad Ixtepec, Mex. 202/C2
Ciudad Juárez, Mex. 200/D2
Ciudad Lerdo, Mex. 200/E3
Ciudad Madero, Mex. 202/B1
Ciudad Mante, Mex. 202/B1
Ciudad Mendoza, Mex. 201/M8
Ciudad Miguel Alemán, Mex. 201/F3
Ciudad Obregón, Mex. 200/C3
Ciudad Ojeda, Ven. 210/D2
Ciudad Pemex, Mex. 202/C2
Ciudad Piar, Ven. 211/F3
Ciudad, PN de la, Mex. 200/D4
Ciudad Real, Sp. 102/D3
Ciudad Rodrigo, Sp. 102/B2
Ciudad Serdán, Mex. 201/M8
Ciudad Valles, Mex. 202/G4
Ciudad Victoria, Mex. 201/F4
Ciudadela de Menorca, Sp. 103/G3
Civa Burnu (pt.), Turk. 139/E1
Civate, It. 116/C1
Civezzano, It. 115/H5
Cividale del Friuli, It. 117/K3
Cividate Camuno, It. 115/G6
Civita Castellana, It. 104/C1
Civitavecchia, It. 100/D3
Civray, Fr. 100/D3
Çivril, Turk. 148/B2
Cixi, China 130/L9
Cize, Fr. 114/B4
Cizre (dam), Turk. 148/E2
Cizur, Sp. 102/E1
Clackmannan, Sc, UK 94/C4
Clackmannanshire (pol. reg.), Sc, UK 94/C4
Claerwen (res.), Wal, UK 90/C2
Claiborne, Md, US 196/B6
Clain (riv.), Fr. 100/D3

Clair Engle (lake), Ca, US 186/B2
Claire (lake), Ab, Can. 180/E3
Clairefontaine-en-Yvelines, Fr. 88/H6
Clairvaux-les-Lacs, Fr. 114/B4
Claise (riv.), Fr. 100/D3
Clallam (co.), Wa, US 193/A2
Clamart, Fr. 88/J5
Clamecy, Fr. 100/F3
Clane, Ire. 89/Q10
Clanton, Al, US 191/G3
Clanwilliam, SAfr. 164/B4
Clara (pt.), Arg. 216/D4
Clara, Ire. 89/Q10
Clare, Austl. 171/H5
Clare (isl.), Ire. 88/N5
Clare (riv.), Ire. 89/P10
Clare, Ks, US 195/D6
Clare, Mi, US 188/C3
Claremont, NH, US 189/F3
Claremont, Ca, US 194/C2
Claremore, OK, US 187/J3
Claremorris, Ire. 89/P10
Clarence (pt.), Nun., Can. 181/T7
Clarence, NZ 175/S11
Clarence (riv.), NZ 175/S11
Clarence, NY, US 189/S9
Clarence Town, Bahm. 199/G3
Clarendon, Tx, US 187/G4
Clarendon, Mo, US 187/J3
Clarenville, Nf, Can. 189/L1
Claresholm, Ab, Can. 184/C3
Clarion (isl.), Mex. 200/B5
Clark, SD, US 185/J4
Clark, NJ, US 197/H9
Clark Fork (riv.), Id,Mt, US 184/E3
Clarke (isl.), Austl. 173/D4
Clarke (lake), Pa, US 196/B4
Clarks Point, Ak, US 192/G4
Clarksburg, WV, US 188/D4
Clarksburg, Ca, US 193/M9
Clarksburg, Ca, US 193/L10
Clarksdale, Ms, US 187/K4
Clarkston, Wa, US 184/D4
Clarkston, Mi, US 193/F6
Clarksville, Ar, US 187/J4
Clarksville, Tn, US 188/C4
Clarksville, Tx, US 187/J4
Claro (riv.), Braz. 209/H7
Claro, Swi. 115/F6
Clatteringshaws Loch (lake), Sc, UK 92/D1
Claudy, NI, UK 92/A2
Clausen, Ger. 111/G5
Clausthal-Zellerfeld, Ger. 109/H5
Claveria, Phil. 137/D4
Clawson, Mi, US 193/F6
Clay (pt.), IM, UK 92/D3
Clay (co.), Mo, US 195/C5
Clay Center, Ks, US 187/H3
Clay Cross-North Wingfield, Eng, UK 93/G5
Claye-Souilly, Fr. 88/L5
Claymont, De, US 196/C4
Clayton, Ca, US 193/L11
Clayton, De, US 196/C5
Clayton, Ga, US 191/H3
Clayton, Mo, US 195/G8
Clayton, NJ, US 196/C4
Clayton, NM, US 187/G3
Clayton, Ok, US 190/E3
Clayton-le-Moors, Eng, UK 93/F4
Clear (lake), Ca, US 186/B3
Clear (hills), Ab, Can. 180/E3
Clear (cape), Ire. 89/P11
Clear Fork Brazos (riv.), Tx, US 187/H4
Clear Lake, SD, US 185/J4
Cleare (cape), Ak, US 192/J4
Clearfield, Ut, US 195/J11
Clearwater, BC, Can. 184/C3
Clearwater, Fl, US 191/H5
Clearwater (mts.), Id, US 184/D4
Clearwater (riv.), Mn, US 185/K4
Clearwater NP, Austl. 171/G5
Cleburne, Tx, US 187/H4
Cleethorpes, Eng, UK 93/H4
Cleeve (hill), Eng, UK 90/D3
Cleland Rec. Area, Austl. 171/M8
Clementon, NJ, US 196/C4
Clemson, SC, US 191/H3
Cleona, Pa, US 196/B3
Cleopatra Needle (peak), Phil. 139/E1
Clermont, Austl. 172/B3
Clermont, Fr. 110/B5
Clermont-en-Argonne, Fr. 111/E5
Clermont-Ferrand, Fr. 100/E4
Clerval, Fr. 114/C3
Clervaux, Lux. 111/F3
Cles, It. 115/H5
Cleve, Austl. 171/H5
Clevedon, Eng, UK 90/D4
Cleveland (cape), Austl. 172/B2
Cleveland (hills), Eng, UK 93/G3
Cleveland, Mo, US 195/D8
Cleveland, Ms, US 187/K4
Cleveland (mt.), Mt, US 184/E3
Cleveland, Oh, US 188/D4
Cleveland (co.), Ok, US 195/N15

Cleveland, Tn, US 191/G3
Cleveland, Tx, US 187/J5
Cleveland-Hopkins (int'l arpt.), Oh, US 188/D4
Cleveland National Forest, Ca, US 194/C3
Clevelândia, Braz. 213/A3
Cleviscook, Qu, Can. 189/G2
Clew (bay), Ire. 89/P10
Clewiston, Fl, US 191/H5
Clichy, Fr. 88/J5
Clichy-sous-Bois, Fr. 88/K5
Cliffden, Ire. 88/F10
Cliffside Park, NJ, US 197/K8
Cliffwood, NJ, US 197/J10
Clifton, Az, US 186/E4
Clifton, NJ, US 197/J8
Clifton Beach, Austl. 172/B2
Clifton Forge, Va, US 191/J2
Clignon (riv.), Fr. 110/C5
Clingmans (peak), NC,Tn, US 191/H3
Clinton, BC, Can. 184/C3
Clinton, Ct, US 197/F1
Clinton, Ia, US 185/L5
Clinton, La, US 187/K5
Clinton, Mi, US 193/G6
Clinton (riv.), Mi, US 193/F6
Clinton, Mo, US 187/J3
Clinton (co.), Mo, US 195/C5
Clinton, Ms, US 187/K4
Clinton, NC, US 191/J3
Clinton, Ok, US 187/H3
Clinton, Ut, US 195/J11
Clinton, Wa, US 193/C2
Clinton (res.), NJ, US 196/D1
Clinton, Mi, US 193/F6
Clinton, Middle Branch (riv.), Mi, US 193/G6
Clinton, North Branch (riv.), Mi, US 193/G6
Clintonville, Wi, US 188/B2
Clints Dod (hill), Sc, UK 94/D5
Clio, Mi, US 188/D3
Clitheroe, Eng, UK 93/F4
Cloates (pt.), Austl. 170/B2
Clocolan, SAfr. 164/D3
Clogherhead, Ire. 92/B4
Clonakilty, Ire. 89/P11
Cloncurry, Austl. 172/A3
Clondalkin, Ire. 92/B5
Clonmany, Ire. 92/A1
Clonmel, Ire. 89/Q10
Cloppenburg, Ger. 109/F3
Clorinda, Arg. 215/E2
Clos-Fontaine, Fr. 88/M6
Closter, NJ, US 197/K8
Cloudcroft, NM, US 190/B3
Cloudy (riv.), Ak, US 192/G3
Cloughmills, NI, UK 92/B2
Cloverdale, Ca, US 186/B3
Cloverdale, In, US 188/C4
Clovis, Ca, US 186/C3
Clovis, NM, US 187/G4
Cluanie (lake), Sc, UK 94/A2
Cluj (co.), Rom. 107/F2
Cluj-Napoca, Rom. 107/F2
Cluses, Fr. 114/C5
Clusone, It. 115/F6
Clutha (riv.), NZ 175/R12
Clwyd (co.), Wal, UK 93/E5
Clwyd (riv.), Wal, UK 93/E5
Clwyd, Vale of, Wal, UK 93/E5
Clwydian (range), Wal, UK 93/E5
Clyde (riv.), NS, Can. 189/H2
Clyde, Sc, UK 94/B5
Clyde, Firth of (inlet), Sc, UK 89/R8
Clyde Hill, Wa, US 193/C2
Clydesdale (valley), Sc, UK 94/C5
Clywedog (riv.), Wal, UK 90/C2
Clynnog (hill), Eng, UK 90/B5
CN Tower, On, Can. 189/R8
Co Loa Citadel, Viet. 136/D7
Côa (riv.), Port. 102/B2
Coacalco, Mex. 201/Q9
Coachella, Ca, US 186/C4
Coagh, NI, UK 92/B2
Coahuayana de Hidalgo, Mex. 200/D5
Coahuila de Zaragoza (state), Mex. 200/D3
Coahuila, Mex. 200/B1
Coalcomán de Matamoros, Mex. 200/D5
Coaldale, Ab, Can. 184/E3
Coaldale, Pa, US 196/C2
Coalhurst, Ab, Can. 184/E3
Coalisland, NI, UK 92/B2
Coalville, Eng, UK 91/E1
Coalville, Ut, US 186/E2
Coaraci, Braz. 212/D4
Coari, Braz. 208/F4
Coari (riv.), Braz. 208/F5
Coasa, Peru 214/D4
Coast (mts.), Can.,US 180/C2
Coast (prov.), Kenya 162/C2
Coast (ranges), Ca, US 184/C5

Coatbridge, Sc, UK 94/B5
Coatepec, Mex. 201/N7
Coatepec Harinas, Mex. 201/K8
Coatesville, Pa, US 196/C4
Coatetelco, Mex. 201/K8
Coaticook, Qu, Can. 189/G2
Coats Land (pol. reg.), Ant. 218/Y
Coatzacoalcos, Mex. 202/C2
Coatzingo, Mex. 201/L8
Coba (ruin), Mex. 202/E1
Coba de Serpe, Sierra de (peak), Sp. 102/B1
Cobán, Guat. 202/D3
Cobar, Austl. 173/C1
Cobb (lake), Co, US 195/C1
Cobberas (mt.), Austl. 173/D3
Cobblestone (mtn.), Ca, US 194/B1
Cobden, Austl. 173/B3
Cóbh, Ire. 89/P11
Cobham (riv.), Mb,On, Can. 185/K2
Cobija, Bol. 208/E6
Cobourg, On, Can. 188/E3
Cobquecura, Chile 216/B3
Coburg (pen.), Austl. 167/C2
Coburg (isl.), Nun., Can. 181/T7
Coburg, Ger. 112/D2
Coca, Ecu. 210/B5
Coca (riv.), Ecu. 210/B5
Cocachacra, Peru 214/D5
Cocal, Braz. 212/B1
Coccaglio, It. 116/C1
Cocentaina, Sp. 103/E3
Cochabamba, Bol. 208/E7
Coche (isl.), Ven. 211/F2
Cochem, Ger. 111/G3
Cocherel, Fr. 88/M4
Cochin, India 140/C6
Cochrane, On, Can. 188/D1
Cochrane, Ab, Can. 184/D3
Cock Cairn (peak), Sc, UK 94/D3
Cockatoo, Austl. 173/G5
Cockburn (sound), Austl. 170/K7
Cockburn (chan.), Chile 217/B7
Cockeysville, Md, US 196/B5
Cockscomb (peak), SAfr. 164/D4
Coclé del Norte, Pan. 203/F4
Coco (riv.), Hon. 198/C5
Coco, Cayo (isl.), Cuba 203/G1
Coco, Isla del (isl.), CR 208/A2
Cocoa, Fl, US 191/H4
Coconino (plat.), Az, US 186/D4
Cocoparra NP, Austl. 173/C2
Cocorocuma, Cayo (isl.), Hon. 203/F3
Cocos (isls.), Austl. 125/J11
Côcos, Braz. 212/A4
Cocotitlán, Mex. 201/R10
Cocula, Mex. 200/E4
Cod (isl.), Nf, Can. 181/K3
Codajás, Braz. 208/F4
Codegua, Chile 216/N9
Codigoro, It. 117/F3
Codlea, Rom. 107/G3
Codó, It. 116/C2
Codsall, Eng, UK 90/D1
Coelemu, Chile 216/B3
Coelho Neto, Braz. 212/B2
Coesfeld, Ger. 109/E5
Coevorden, Neth. 108/D3
Coffin Bay, Austl. 171/G5
Coffin Bay NP, Austl. 171/G5
Coffs Harbour, Austl. 173/E1
Cofre de Perote, PN, Mex. 201/M7
Coggiola, It. 116/B1
Coghinas (lake), It. 104/A2
Cognac, Fr. 100/C4
Cogolin, Fr. 101/G5
Cogollo del Cengio, It. 117/E1
Cogolludo, Sp. 102/D2
Cohansey (riv.), NJ, US 196/C5
Cohuna, Austl. 173/C2
Cohuna NP, Austl. 170/L7
Coiba, Isla de (isl.), Pan. 208/B2
Coig (riv.), Arg. 215/C7
Coignières, Fr. 88/H5
Coihaique, Chile 216/B5
Coihueco, Chile 216/B3
Coimbatore, India 140/C5
Coimbra (dist.), Port. 102/A2
Coimbra, Port. 102/A2
Coín, Sp. 102/C4
Coina (riv.), Port. 103/P10
Coise (riv.), Fr. 100/F4
Cojedes (riv.), Ven. 210/D2

Cojedes (state), Ven. 210/D2
Colomiers, Fr. 100/D5
Colomoncagua, Hon. 202/D3
Colón, Arg. 216/E2
Colón, Cuba 203/F1
Colón (mts.), Hon. 203/G4
Colón, Pan. 203/G4
Colón, Uru. 217/K11
Colonche, Ecu. 214/A1
Colonelganj, India 142/C2
Colonia, Micr. 174/C4
Colonia (dept.), Uru. 217/K11
Colonia, NJ, US 197/H9
Colonia Barón, Arg. 216/E3
Colonia del Sacramento, Uru. 217/K11
Colonia Juárez, Mex. 200/C2
Colonia Las Heras, Arg. 216/C5
Colonial Park, Pa, US 196/B3
Colonsay (isl.), Sc, UK 89/Q8
Colorado (peak), Arg. 217/C6
Colorado, Braz. 215/C4
Colorado (plat.), US 186/E3
Colorado (riv.), US 186/D4
Colorado, Braz. 213/B3
Colorado (state), US 186/F3
Colorado City, Tx, US 187/G4
Colorado Historical Museum, Co, US 195/C3
Colorado Springs, Co, US 187/F3
Colorno, It. 116/D3
Colotlán, Mex. 200/E4
Colquiri, Bol. 208/E7
Colson (pt.), Belz. 202/D2
Colstrip, Mt, US 184/G4
Colt (hill), Sc, UK 94/B6
Coltauco, Chile 216/N9
Colton, Ca, US 194/C2
Colts Neck, NJ, US 196/D3
Coluene (riv.), Braz. 205/D4
Columbe, Ecu. 214/B1
Columbia (riv.), Can.,US 184/C4
Columbia (plat.), US 184/C4
Columbia, Il, US 195/G9
Columbia, Ky, US 188/C4
Columbia, La, US 187/J4
Columbia, Md, US 196/B5
Columbia, Ms, US 191/F4
Columbia, NJ, US 196/C2
Columbia, Pa, US 196/B3
Columbia (co.), Pa, US 196/B1
Columbia (cap.), SC, US 191/H3
Columbia, Tn, US 188/C5
Columbia Falls, Mt, US 184/E3
Columbine (cape), SAfr. 164/K10
Columbus, Ga, US 191/G3
Columbus, In, US 188/C4
Columbus, Ms, US 191/F3
Columbus, Mt, US 184/F4
Columbus, Ne, US 185/J5
Columbus, NM, US 190/B4
Columbus (cap.), Oh, US 188/D4
Columbus, Tx, US 187/H5
Colunga, Sp. 102/C1
Colusa, Ca, US 186/B3
Colville (riv.), Ak, US 192/G2
Colville, Wa, US 184/D3
Colville (lake), NW, Can. 180/D2
Colvos (passg.), Wa, US 193/B3
Colwyn Bay, Wal, UK 92/E5
Comacchio, It. 117/F3
Comacchio, Valli di (lag.), It. 101/K4
Comai, China 143/H1
Comal, Tx, US 195/U20
Comal (co.), Tx, US 195/U20
Comala, Mex. 200/E5
Comalcalco, Mex. 202/C2
Comanche, Tx, US 187/H5
Comandante Luis Piedra Buena, Arg. 217/C6
Comandante Nicanor Otamendi, Arg. 216/F3
Comănești, Rom. 107/H2
Comarnic, Rom. 107/G3
Comas, Peru 214/C3
Comas, Peru 214/B3
Comayagua, Hon. 202/D3
Comayagua (mts.), Hon. 202/D3
Combapata, Peru 214/D4
Combarbalá, Chile 215/B3
Combeaufontaine, Fr. 114/B3
Comber, On, Can. 193/G7
Comber, NI, UK 92/C2
Comblain-au-Pont, Belg. 111/E3
Combloux, Fr. 114/C5
Combs-la-Ville, Fr. 88/K6
Comé, Ben. 161/F5
Comendador, DRep. 203/J2
Comilla (pol. reg.), Bang. 143/H4
Comines, Fr. 110/C2
Comines, Belg. 110/C2
Comino (isl.), Malta 104/L6
Comitán de Domínguez, Mex. 202/C2

Commack, NY, US 197/E2
Commentry, Fr. 100/E3
Commeny, Fr. 88/H4
Commerce, Ca, US 194/F7
Commerce City, Co, US 195/C3
Commercy, Fr. 111/E6
Commewijne (dist.), Sur. 211/H3
Committee (bay), Nun., Can. 181/H2
Como (lake), It. 101/H3
Como, It. 115/F6
Como, Wi, US 193/P14
Comodoro Rivadavia, Arg. 216/D5
Comoé (prov.), Burk. 160/D4
Comoe, PN de la, C.d'Iv. 154/E6
Comoé, PN de la, C.d'Iv. 160/D4
Comorin (cape), India 140/C6
Comoros (ctry.) 165/G5
Comox, BC, Can. 184/B3
Compiègne, Fr. 110/B5
Compostela, Phil. 137/E6
Compostela, Mex. 200/D4
Compton, Ca, US 194/F8
Comrat, Mol. 107/J2
Comrie, Sc, UK 94/C4
Comstock, Tx, US 190/C4
Con Son (isl.), Viet. 141/J6
Cona, China 141/F2
Conaica, Peru 214/C4
Conakry (pol. reg.), Gui. 160/B4
Conakry (cap.), Gui. 160/B4
Conakry (int'l arpt.), Gui. 160/B4
Conambo (riv.), Ecu. 210/B5
Conca (riv.), It. 117/F5
Concarneau, Fr. 100/B3
Conceição da Barra, Braz. 213/E1
Conceição das Alagoas, Braz. 213/B1
Conceição do Araguaia, Braz. 209/J5
Conceição do Coité, Braz. 212/C3
Conceição do Mato Dentro, Braz. 213/D1
Conceição do Rio Verde, Braz. 213/H6
Conceição dos Ouros, Braz. 213/H7
Concepción (lake), Bol. 208/F7
Concepción, Arg. 215/C2
Concepción, Bol. 208/E6
Concepción, Chile 216/B3
Concepción (pt.), Mex. 200/C3
Concepción, Par. 215/E1
Concepción, Peru 208/C6
Concepción (bay), Mex. 200/B3
Concepción de La Vega, DRep. 199/G4
Concepción del Oro, Mex. 201/E3
Concepción del Uruguay, Arg. 217/J10
Conception (pt.), Ca, US 186/B4
Concesio, It. 116/D1
Conchal, Braz. 213/F7
Conchas (lake), NM, US 187/F4
Conches, Fr. 88/L5
Conchillas, Uru. 217/J11
Concho (riv.), Tx, US 187/G5
Conchos (riv.), Mex. 200/D2
Concord, Ca, US 186/B3
Concord, NC, US 191/H3
Concord (cap.), NH, US 189/G3
Concord, Wi, US 193/N13
Concordia, Arg. 215/E3
Concórdia, Braz. 213/A3
Concordia, Mex. 200/D4
Concordia, Peru 214/C2
Concordia Sagittaria, It. 117/F1
Concordia sulla Secchia, It. 117/D3
Concrete, Wa, US 184/C3
Condado, Cuba 203/G1
Condamine (riv.), Austl. 167/E3
Condamine, Austl. 172/C3
Conde, Braz. 212/D3
Condé-sur-l'Escaut, Fr. 110/C3
Condé-sur-Noireau, Fr. 100/C2
Condé-sur-Vesgre, Fr. 88/G5
Condé-sur-Vire, Fr. 100/C2
Condécourt, Fr. 88/H4
Condeúba, Braz. 212/B4
Condino, It. 115/G6
Condobolin, Austl. 173/C2
Condom, Fr. 100/D5
Condon, Or, US 184/C4
Condroz (plat.), Belg. 98/C3
Conecuh (riv.), Al, US 191/G4
Conegliano, It. 117/F1
Conejos, Co, US 187/F3
Conesa, Arg. 216/E2
Conestoga (riv.), Pa, US 196/B3
Conewago (lake), Pa, US 196/A3
Confins (int'l arpt.), Braz. 213/D1
Conflans-en-Jarnisy, Fr. 111/E5
Conflans-Sainte-Honorine, Fr. 88/J5
Congaree Swamp Nat'l Mon., SC, US 191/H3
Congers, NY, US 197/K7
Congis-sur-Thérouanne, Fr. 88/L4
Congjiang, China 141/J2
Congleton, Eng, UK 93/F5
Congo (basin), D.R. Congo 155/K7
Congo, Rep. of the (ctry.) 151/D4
Congo (riv.), Afr. 151/D4
Congo, Democratic Republic of the (ctry.) 151/E5
Congonhal, Braz. 213/G7
Congonhas, Braz. 213/D2
Congonhas (int'l arpt.), Braz. 213/G8
Conguillío, PN, Chile 216/C3
Conic (hill), Sc, UK 94/B4
Cónico (peak), Arg. 216/C4
Conifer, Co, US 195/B3
Conil de la Frontera, Sp. 102/B4
Conisbrough, Eng, UK 93/G5
Conlig, NI, UK 92/C2
Conn (lake), Nun., Can. 181/J1
Connacht (reg.), Ire. 89/P10
Connah's Quay, Wal, UK 93/E5
Connantre, Fr. 110/C6
Conneaut, Oh, US 188/D3
Connecticut (riv.), US 189/G2
Connecticut (state), US 189/F3
Connellsville, Pa, US 188/E3
Connemara NP, Ire. 89/P10
Connersville, In, US 188/C4
Cono Grande (peak), Arg. 217/C6
Conocoto, Ecu. 210/B5
Conon, Falls of (falls), Sc, UK 94/B1
Cononbridge, Sc, UK 94/B1
Conondale NP, Austl. 172/D4
Čonoplja, Serb. 106/D3
Conrad, Mt, US 184/F3
Conroe, Tx, US 187/J5
Consandolo, It. 117/E3
Conscience Point NWR, NY, US 197/F2
Consdorf, Lux. 111/F4
Conselheiro Pena, Braz. 213/D1
Conselice, It. 117/E3
Conselve, It. 117/E2
Conservation Park, Austl. 171/F4
Consett, Eng, UK 93/G2
Conshohocken, Pa, US 196/C3
Consolación del Sur, Cuba 203/F1
Consolidated (canal), Az, US 195/S19
Constance (lake), Swi. 101/H3
Constance (Bodensee) (lake), Swi. 101/H3
Constant (mtn.), Guad., Fr. 199/N9
Constanța (prov.), Rom. 107/H3
Constanța, Rom. 107/J3
Constantí, Sp. 103/F2
Constantina, Sp. 102/C4
Constantine (cape), Ak, US 192/G4
Constantine, Alg. 158/K6
Constitución, Chile 216/B2
Constitución (res.), Uru. 217/K10
Constitución de 1857, PN, Mex. 200/B2
Consuegra, Sp. 102/D3
Contai, India 143/F5
Contamana, Peru 214/C2
Contarina, It. 117/F2
Contas, Rio de (riv.), Braz. 209/K6
Contegem, Braz. 213/C1
Contes, Fr. 101/G5
Conthey, Swi. 114/D5
Continental (range), Ab,BC, Can. 184/C2
Continental (mtn.), Az, US 195/S18
Contoy (isl.), Mex. 202/E1
Contra Costa (canal), Ca, US 193/L10
Contra Costa (co.), Ca, US 193/L11
Contramaestre, Cuba 203/G1
Contratación, Col. 210/C3
Contrecoeur, Qu, Can. 189/P6
Contreras, Embalse de (res.), Sp. 102/E3
Contrexéville, Fr. 114/B1
Controller (bay), Ak, US 192/J3
Contulmo, Chile 216/B3
Contumazá, Peru 214/B2
Contwig, Ger. 111/G5
Contwoyto (lake), Nun., Can. 180/F2
Conty, Fr. 110/B4
Convención, Col. 210/C2
Conversano, It. 105/E2
Converse, Tx, US 195/U20
Conway, Ar, US 187/J4
Conway, SC, US 191/J3
Conway, NH, US 189/G3
Conway (cape), Austl. 172/C3
Conway NP, Austl. 172/C3
Conwy (bay), Wal, UK 92/D5
Conwy (co.), Wal, UK 92/E5
Conwy (riv.), Wal, UK 92/E5
Conwy, Vale of (valley), Wal, UK 92/E5
Conyngham, Pa, US 196/B2
Coober Pedy, Austl. 171/G4
Cooch Behār, India 143/G2
Coochiemudlo (isl.), Austl. 172/F7
Cook (bay), Chile 217/C7
Cook (mt.), NZ 175/S11
Cook (str.), NZ 175/S11
Cook (inlet), Ak, US 180/A3
Cook (co.), Il, US 193/Q16
Cook Islands (dpcy.), NZ 175/J6
Cooke (mt.), Austl. 170/C5
Cookeville, Tn, US 188/C4
Cookham, Eng, UK 88/A2
Cookhouse, SAfr. 164/D4
Cookstown, NI, UK 92/B2
Cookstown (dist.), NI, UK 92/B2
Cooksville, Md, US 196/A5
Cooktown, Austl. 172/B1
Coola Coola (swamp), Austl. 173/B3
Coolah, Austl. 173/D1
Coolamon, Austl. 173/C2
Coolangatta, Austl. 173/E1
Cooley (pt.), Ire. 92/B4
Coolgardie, Austl. 170/D4
Cooloola NP, Austl. 172/D4
Cooloongup (lake), Austl. 170/K7
Cooma, Austl. 173/D3
Coonabarabran, Austl. 173/D1
Coonalpyn, Austl. 173/A2
Coonamble, Austl. 173/D1
Coonana Abor. Land, Austl. 170/D4
Coondapoor (Kundapura), India 147/K6
Coongan Abor. Land, Austl. 170/C2
Coonoor, India 140/C5
Cooper, Tx, US 187/J4
Coopersburg, Pa, US 196/C2
Cooperstown, ND, US 185/J4
Coordewandy (peak), Austl. 170/C3
Coorong NP, Austl. 173/A3
Coorow, Austl. 170/C4
Cooroy, Austl. 172/D4
Coosa (riv.), Al, US 191/G3
Cootamundra, Austl. 173/D2
Coot'tha (mt.), Austl. 172/E6
Copacabana, Bol. 214/D5
Copahué (vol.), Chile 216/C3
Copainalá, Mex. 202/C2
Copala, Mex. 198/B4
Copán (ruin), Hon. 202/D3
Cope (cape), Sp. 102/E4
Copeland (isl.), NI, UK 92/C2
Copenhagen (København) (cap.), Den. 96/E4
Copertino, It. 105/F2
Copeton (dam), Austl. 173/D1
Copiague, NY, US 197/M9
Copiapó, Chile 215/B2
Coplay, Pa, US 196/C2
Copparo, It. 117/E3
Coppename (riv.), Sur. 211/H3
Coppenbrügge, Ger. 109/G4
Copper (riv.), Ak, US 180/B2
Copper Center, Ak, US 192/J3
Copperas Cove, Tx, US 187/H5
Coppermine (riv.), NW,Nun., Can. 180/E2
Copperton, Ut, US 195/J12
Coppet, Swi. 114/C5
Copșa Mică, Rom. 107/G2
Coqên, China 128/E5
Coquet (riv.), Eng, UK 94/D6
Coquet Dale (valley), Eng, UK 93/G1
Coquimbo, Chile 215/B2
Coquitlam, BC, Can. 184/C3
Corabia, Rom. 107/G4
Coração de Jesus, Braz. 212/A5
Coracora, Peru 214/C4
Corail, Haiti 203/H2
Coraki, Austl. 173/E1
Coral (sea) 174/E6
Coral Gables, Fl, US 191/H5
Coral Harbour, Nun., Can. 181/H2
Coral Sea Islands Territory (dpcy.), Austl. 167/E2
Coral Springs, Fl, US 191/H5
Corales del Rosario, PN, Col. 210/C2
Coram, NY, US 197/E2
Corato, It. 104/E2
Corbeil-Essonnes, Fr. 88/K6
Corbelin (cape), Alg. 158/H4
Corbenay, Fr. 114/C2
Corbet (peak), Swi. 115/F5
Corbett NP, India 142/B1
Corbetta, It. 116/B2
Corbie, Fr. 110/B4
Corbieres (mts.), Fr. 100/E5
Corbin, Ky, US 188/C4
Corbin City, NJ, US 196/D5
Corby, Eng, UK 91/F2
Corcovado, Braz. 213/K7
Corcovado (vol.), Chile 216/B4
Corcovado (gulf), Chile 205/B7
Corcovado, PN, CR 203/E4
Cordeiro, Braz. 213/D2
Cordele, Ga, US 191/H4
Cordelia, Ca, US 193/K10
Cordell, Ok, US 187/H4
Cordenons, It. 101/K4
Cordignano, It. 117/F1
Cordillera de Los Picachos, PN, Col. 208/D3
Cordillera Oriental (mts.), SAm. 210/B5
Cordisburgo, Braz. 213/C1
Córdoba, Arg. 215/D3
Córdoba (dept.), Col. 203/H4
Córdoba, Mex. 201/N8
Córdoba (plain), SAm. 216/E2
Córdoba, Sp. 102/C4
Córdoba, Sierra de (mts.), Arg. 215/D3
Cordova, Ak, US 192/J3
Cordova (peak), Ak, US 192/J3
Cordova, Md, US 196/C6
Coreaú, Braz. 212/B1
Corella, Sp. 102/E1
Coremas, Braz. 212/C2
Corentyne (riv.), Guy. 208/G3
Corfu (Kérika) (isl.), Gre. 105/F3
Corgémont, Swi. 114/D3
Corgo, Sp. 102/B1
Coria, Sp. 102/B3
Coria del Río, Sp. 102/B4
Coriano, It. 117/F5
Coribe, Braz. 212/A4
Coricudgy (mt.), Austl. 173/D2
Corigliano Calabro, It. 104/E3
Corinaldo, It. 117/G5
Coringa Islets (isls.), Austl. 172/C2
Corinne, Ut, US 195/J10
Corinth, Ms, US 191/F3
Corinth (gulf), Gre. 105/H3
Corinth (Kórinthos) (ruin), Gre. 105/H4
Corinto, Nic. 202/E3
Cork, Ire. 89/P11
Corleone, It. 104/C4
Corleto Perticara, It. 104/E2
Çorlu, Turk. 107/H5
Cormeilles-en-Vexin, Fr. 88/J4
Cormons, It. 117/G1
Cormontreuil, Fr. 110/D5
Cormorant, Mb, Can. 185/H2
Cormorant (lake), Mb, Can. 185/H2
Cornacchia (peak), It. 104/D2
Cornaredo, It. 116/C2
Cornberg, Ger. 109/G6
Corndon (peak), Wal, UK 90/C1
Cornedo Vicentino, It. 117/E1
Cornélio Procópio, Braz. 213/B2
Cornelius Grinnell (bay), Nun., Can. 181/K2
Cornell, Ca, US 194/B2
Cornella, Sp. 103/L7
Corner (inlet), Austl. 167/D4
Corner Brook, Nf, Can. 189/K1
Cornetto (peak), It. 115/H6
Cornfield (pt.), Ct, US 197/F1
Corniglio, It. 116/D4
Cornimont, Fr. 114/C2
Corning, NY, US 188/E3
Corno alle Scale (peak), It. 101/J4
Corno di Rosazzo, It. 117/G1
Cornone di Blumone (peak), It. 115/G6
Cornú (peak), Arg. 217/D7
Cornuda, It. 117/F1
Cornwall (isl.), Nun., Can. 181/S7
Cornwall, On, Can. 188/F2
Cornwall, PE, Can. 189/J2
Cornwall (cape), Eng, UK 90/A6
Cornwall (co.), Eng, UK 90/A6
Cornwall, Pa, US 196/B3
Cornwallis (isl.), Nun., Can. 181/S7
Corny (pt.), Austl. 171/H5
Coro, Ven. 210/D2
Coroatá, Braz. 212/A2
Corocoro, Bol. 214/D5
Coromandel, Braz. 213/C1
Coromandel (pen.), NZ 175/T10
Coromandel (coast), India 140/D5
Coron, Phil. 139/F1
Corona, Ca, US 194/C3
Coronado (bay), CR 198/E6
Coronado, Ca, US 194/C5
Coronation, Ab, Can. 184/F2
Coronation (gulf), Nun., Can. 180/E2
Coronel, Chile 216/B3
Coronel Dorrego, Arg. 216/E3
Coronel Fabriciano, Braz. 213/D1
Coronel Moldes, Arg. 216/D2
Coronel Murta, Braz. 212/B5
Coronel Oviedo, Par. 215/E2
Coronel Pringles, Arg. 216/E3
Coronel Suárez, Arg. 216/E3
Coronel Vidal, Arg. 216/F3
Coronel Vivida, Braz. 213/A3
Corongo, Peru 214/B3
Coronie (dist.), Sur. 211/G3
Coropuna (peak), Peru 214/C4
Çorovodë, Alb. 105/G2
Corozal, Col. 210/C2
Corozal, Belz. 202/D2
Corpach, Sc, UK 94/A3
Corpus Christi, Tx, US 190/D5
Corral, Chile 216/B3
Corral de Almaguer, Sp. 102/D3
Corral de Bustos, Arg. 216/E2
Corrales, Col. 210/C3
Corralillo, Cuba 203/F1
Corre, Fr. 114/C2
Correa, Arg. 216/E2
Corredor, CR 203/F4
Correggio, It. 117/D3
Corrente (riv.), Braz. 212/A4
Corrente, Braz. 212/A3
Correntina, Braz. 212/A4
Corrib (lake), Ire. 89/P10
Corrientes (riv.), Peru 208/C4
Corrientes, Arg. 215/E2
Corrientes (cape), Cuba 203/E1
Corrientes (pt.), Col. 210/B3
Corrigan, Tx, US 187/J5
Corrigin, Austl. 170/C5
Corriverton, Guy. 211/G3
Corryhabbie (peak), Sc, UK 94/C2
Corryong, Austl. 173/C3
Corse (hill), Sc, UK 94/B5
Corse (cape), Fr. 101/H5
Corse (dept.), Fr. 101/H5
Corserine (peak), Sc, UK 92/D1
Corsewall (pt.), NI, UK 92/C1
Corsham, Eng, UK 90/D4
Corsica (isl.), Fr. 104/A1
Corsicana, Tx, US 187/H4
Corsico, It. 116/C2
Corsons (inlet), NJ, US 196/D5
Cortaillod, Swi. 114/C4
Cortegana, Sp. 102/B4
Cortemaggiore, It. 116/C3
Cortemilia, It. 116/B3
Cortez, Co, US 186/E3
Cortina d'Ampezzo, It. 101/K3
Cortines, Arg. 217/J11
Cortland, NY, US 188/E3
Corubal (riv.), GBis. 160/B3
Coruche, Port. 102/A3
Çoruh (riv.), Turk. 121/G4
Çorum, Turk. 148/C1
Çorum (prov.), Turk. 148/C1
Corumbá, Braz. 208/G7
Corumbá (riv.), Braz. 209/J7
Corumbaú (pt.), Braz. 212/C5
Coruripe, Braz. 212/C3
Corvallis, Or, US 184/C4
Corve (riv.), Eng, UK 90/D2
Corvo (peak), It. 104/C1
Corvo (isl.), Azor., Port. 103/R12
Corzoneso, Swi. 115/E5
Cosalá, Mex. 200/D3
Cosamaloapan, Mex. 201/P8
Cosautlán, Mex. 201/N7
Coscomatepec, Mex. 201/M7
Cosenza, It. 104/E3
Coshocton, Oh, US 188/D3
Cosigüina (pt.), Nic. 202/E3
Coslada, Sp. 103/N9
Cosmo Newberry Abor. Rsv., Austl. 170/D3
Cosmópolis, Braz. 213/F7
Cosne-Cours-sur-Loire, Fr. 100/E3
Cosne d'Allier, Fr. 100/E3
Cosolapa, Mex. 201/N8
Cospeito, Sp. 102/B1
Cosquín, Arg. 215/D3
Cossato, It. 116/B1
Cosson (riv.), Fr. 100/D3
Cossonay, Swi. 114/C4
Costa Azul, Uru. 217/G2
Costa Brava (int'l arpt.), Sp. 103/G2
Costa da Caparica, Port. 103/P10
Costa de Mosquitos (phys. reg.), Nic. 203/E4
Costa di Rovigo, It. 117/E2
Costa Masnaga, It. 116/C1
Costa Mesa, Ca, US 194/G8
Costa Rica (ctry.) 203/F4
Costa Smeralda (int'l arpt.), It. 104/A2
Costa Volpino, It. 116/D1
Costabissara, It. 117/E1
Costești, Rom. 107/G3
Costigliole d'Asti, It. 116/B3
Cotabambas, Peru 214/C4
Cotabato, Phil. 139/F2
Cotacachi (peak), Ecu. 210/B4
Cotahuasi, Peru 214/C4
Cotatumbo (riv.), Col. 203/H4
Côte d'Azur (int'l arpt.), Fr. 101/G5
Côte de Hautmont (hill), Fr. 114/B1
Côte d'Ivoire (ctry.) 160/D5
Côte d'Or (uplands), Fr. 100/F3
Côte du Rif (Al Hoceima) (int'l arpt.), Mor. 158/C2
Côte-Saint-Luc, Qu, Can. 189/N7
Coteau des Prairies (plat.), SD, US 185/J4
Coteau-du-Lac, Qu, Can. 189/M7
Coteau du Missouri (plat.), ND, US 185/H3
Coteau-Landing, Qu, Can. 189/M7
Cotegipe, Braz. 212/A4
Cotentin (pen.), Fr. 100/C2
Côtes de Meuse (uplands), Fr. 100/F2
Cothi (riv.), Wal, UK 90/B3
Cotia, Braz. 213/G8
Cotignola, It. 117/E4
Cotonou, Ben. 161/F5
Cotonou (int'l arpt.), Ben. 161/F5
Cotopaxi (dept.), Ecu. 210/B5
Cotopaxi (vol.), Ecu. 210/B5
Cotopaxi, PN, Ecu. 210/B5
Cotswolds (hills), Eng, UK 90/D3
Cottage Grove, Or, US 184/C5
Cottage Hills, Il, US 195/G8
Cottam, On, Can. 193/G7
Cottbus, Ger. 99/H3
Cottian Alps (mts.), Fr. 101/G4
Cottleville, Mo, US 195/F8
Cottonport, La, US 187/J5
Cottonwood, Az, US 186/D4
Cottonwood (riv.), Tx, US 187/F5
Cotulla, Tx, US 190/D4
Coubert, Fr. 88/L6
Coubre, Pointe de la (pt.), Fr. 100/C4
Couchey, Fr. 114/A3
Coudekerque-Branche, Fr. 110/B1
Coulee City, Wa, US 184/D4
Coulee Dam Nat'l Rec. Area, Wa, US 184/D3
Coulogne, Fr. 110/A2
Coulombs-en-Valois, Fr. 88/M4
Coulommes, Fr. 88/L5
Coulommiers, Fr. 110/C6
Coulonge (riv.), Qu, Can. 188/E2
Coulounieix-Chamiers, Fr. 100/D4
Council, Ak, US 192/F3
Council, Id, US 184/D4
Council Grove, Ks, US 187/H3
Coupar Angus, Sc, UK 94/C3
Coupvray, Fr. 88/L5
Courantyne (riv.), Guy.,Sur. 211/G3
Courbevoie, Fr. 88/J5
Courcelles, Belg. 111/D3
Courcouronnes, Fr. 88/K6
Courdimanche, Fr. 88/H4
Courgenay, Swi. 114/D3
Courgent, Fr. 88/G5
Courmayeur, It. 114/C6
Cournon-d'Auvergne, Fr. 100/E4
Courpalay, Fr. 88/L6
Courrendlin, Swi. 114/D3
Courroux, Swi. 114/D3
Coursan, Fr. 100/E5
Courtelary, Swi. 114/D3
Courtepin, Swi. 114/D4
Courtice, On, Can. 189/S8
Courtisols, Fr. 111/D6
Courtland, Ca, US 193/L10
Courtmacsherry, Ire. 89/P11
Courtney, Mo, US 195/E5
Courtomer, Fr. 88/L6
Cousance, Fr. 114/B4
Coushatta, La, US 187/J4
Cousolre, Fr. 111/D3
Coutances, Fr. 100/C2
Coutevroult, Fr. 88/L5
Coutras, Fr. 100/C4
Coutts, Ab, Can. 184/F3
Couva, Trin. 211/F2
Couvet, Swi. 114/C4
Couvin, Belg. 111/D3
Couzeix, Fr. 100/D4
Covadonga NP, Sp. 102/C1
Covasna, Rom. 107/H3
Covasna (prov.), Rom. 107/G3
Cove Bay, Sc, UK 94/D2
Cove Neck, NY, US 197/L8
Coventry, Eng, UK 91/E2
Coventry (canal), Eng, UK 91/E1
Coventry (co.), Eng, UK 91/E2
Covilhã, Port. 102/B2
Covina, Ca, US 194/G7
Covington, Ga, US 191/H3
Covington, Tn, US 187/K4
Covo, It. 116/C2
Cow Green (res.), Eng, UK 93/F2
Cowal (reg.), Sc, UK 94/A4
Cowan (lake), Austl. 167/B4
Cowdenbeath, Sc, UK 94/C4
Cowell, Austl. 171/H5
Cowes, Eng, UK 91/E5
Cowie, Sc, UK 94/C4
Cowlitz (riv.), Wa, US 184/C4
Cowra, Austl. 173/D2
Coxim, Braz. 209/H7
Cox's Bāzār, Bang. 141/F3
Coyame, Mex. 200/D2
Coye-la-Forêt, Fr. 88/K4
Coyotepec, Mex. 201/K7
Coyuca de Benítez, Mex. 201/E5
Coyutla, Mex. 201/M6
Cozumel, Mex. 202/E1
Cozumel (int'l arpt.), Mex. 202/E1
Cozumel (isl.), Mex. 202/E1
Cradle (mtn.), Austl. 173/C4
Cradle Mountain-Lake Saint Clair NP, Austl. 173/C4
Cradock, SAfr. 164/D4
Crag (mtn.), Yk, Can. 192/K3
Crag (peak), Eng, UK 93/F3
Craig, Co, US 186/F2
Craig, Ak, US 192/M4
Craig, Ks, US 195/D6
Craigavon (dist.), NI, UK 92/B3
Craigavon, NI, UK 92/B3
Craigieburn, Austl. 173/F5
Craik, Sk, Can. 185/G3
Crail, Sc, UK 94/D4
Crailsheim, Ger. 112/D4
Craiova, Rom. 107/F3
Cramalina (peak), Swi. 115/E5
Cramlington, Eng, UK 93/G1
Cran-Gevrier, Fr. 114/C6
Crana (riv.), Ire. 92/A1
Cranberry Portage, Mb, Can. 185/H2
Cranborne Chase (for.), Eng, UK 90/D5
Cranbourne, Austl. 173/G6
Cranbrook, BC, Can. 184/E3
Cranbrook, Austl. 170/C5
Cranbury, NJ, US 196/D3
Crane, Tx, US 190/C4
Crane Neck (pt.), NY, US 197/E2
Crane River, Mb, Can. 185/J3
Cranford, NJ, US 197/H9
Cranleigh, Eng, UK 91/F4
Craponne, Fr. 100/F4
Crasna (riv.), Rom. 106/F2
Crater (lake), Or, US 186/B2
Crater Lake NP, Or, US 186/B2
Craters of the Moon Nat'l Mon., Id, US 186/D2
Crateús, Braz. 212/B2
Crati (riv.), It. 104/E3
Crato, Port. 102/B3
Cravinhos, Braz. 213/C2
Crawfordsville, In, US 188/C3
Crawfordville, Fl, US 191/G4
Crawley, Eng, UK 91/F4
Cray (riv.), Eng, UK 88/D2
Crazy (mts.), Mt, US 184/F4
Creag Meagaidh (peak), Sc, UK 94/B3
Creagerstown, Md, US 196/A4
Creasy (Mifflinville), Pa, US 196/B1
Creazzo, It. 117/E2
Crêches-sur-Saône, Fr. 114/A5
Crécy-sur-Serre, Fr. 110/C4
Credit (riv.), On, Can. 189/Q8
Cree (lake), Sk, Can. 180/F3
Cree (riv.), Sk, Can. 180/F3
Cree (riv.), Sc, UK 92/D2
Creel, Mex. 200/D3
Creetown, Sc, UK 92/D2
Creglingen, Ger. 112/D4
Crégy-lès-Meaux, Fr. 88/L5
Créhange, Fr. 111/F5
Creighton, Sk, Can. 185/H2
Creil, Fr. 110/B5
Crema, It. 116/C2
Crémieu, Fr. 114/B6
Cremlingen, Ger. 109/H4
Cremona (prov.), It. 116/C2
Cremona, It. 116/D2
Crepaja, Serb. 106/E3
Crépy, Fr. 110/C4
Creran (lake), Sc, UK 94/A3
Cres (isl.), Cro. 106/B3
Crescent, Mo, US 195/F8
Crescent, Co, US 195/B3
Crescent, Ut, US 195/K12
Crescent City, Ca, US 184/B5
Crescentino, It. 116/B2
Cresco, Pa, US 196/C1
Crespano del Grappa, It. 117/E1
Crespellano, It. 117/E3
Crespières, Fr. 88/H5
Crespin, Fr. 110/C3
Cresskill, NJ, US 197/K8
Cressona, Pa, US 196/B2
Cressy, Austl. 173/C4
Crest, Fr. 100/F4
Crest Hill, Il, US 193/P16
Crestline, Ca, US 194/C2
Creston, Ia, US 185/K5
Creston, BC, Can. 184/D3
Crestview, Fl, US 191/G4
Crestwood Village, NJ, US 196/D4
Creswick, Austl. 173/B3
Crete (sea), Gre. 105/J4
Crete (isl.), Gre. 105/J5
Créteil, Fr. 88/K5
Creuch (hill), Sc, UK 94/B5
Creus (cape), Sp. 103/G1
Creuse (riv.), Fr. 100/D3
Creussen, Ger. 113/E3
Creussen (riv.), Ger. 113/E3
Creutzwald-la-Croix, Fr. 111/F5
Creuzburg, Ger. 109/H6
Crevacuore, It. 116/B1
Crevalcore, It. 117/E3
Creve Coeur, Mo, US 195/G8
Crèvecœur-le-Grand, Fr. 110/B4
Crevillente, Sp. 103/E3
Crevoladossola, It. 115/E5
Crewe, Eng, UK 93/F5
Crib Point, Austl. 173/C3
Criciúma, Braz. 213/B4
Crieff, Sc, UK 94/C4
Criffell (hill), Sc, UK 92/E2
Crikvenica, Cro. 106/B3
Crillon (mt.), Ak, US 192/L4
Crimean (pen.), Ukr. 107/L3
Crimeanpen (pen.), Ukr. 120/E3
Crimond, Sc, UK 94/E1
Crisenoy, Fr. 88/L6
Crisman, Co, US 195/B2
Crissier, Swi. 114/C4
Cristal, Monts de (mts.), Gabon 163/B1
Cristalina, Braz. 212/A5
Cristina, Braz. 213/H7
Cristóbal (pt.), Ecu. 214/E7
Cristóbal Colón (peak), Col. 210/C2
Cristoforo Colombo (int'l arpt.), It. 116/B4
Cristuru Secuiesc, Rom. 107/G2
Crișul Alb (riv.), Rom. 106/F2
Crișul Negru (riv.), Rom. 106/E2
Crixás-Açu (riv.), Braz. 209/H6
Crna Reka (riv.), FYROM 105/G2
Črnomelj, Slov. 101/L4
Croajingolong NP, Austl. 173/D3
Croatia (ctry.) 106/B3
Croce (peak), It. 115/H5
Croce, Pico di (peak), It. 115/H4
Croche (peak), Fr. 114/C6
Croche (riv.), Qu, Can. 189/F2
Crocker (range), Malay. 139/E3
Crocker (peak), Ecu. 214/E7
Crockett, Tx, US 187/J5
Crockett, Ca, US 193/K10
Crocodile Head (pt.), Austl. 173/D2
Crodo, It. 115/E5
Crofton, Md, US 196/B6
Croghan (mtn.), Ire. 92/B6
Croisette (cape), Fr. 100/F5
Croisilles, Fr. 110/B3
Croissy-Beaubourg, Fr. 88/K5
Croker (isl.), Austl. 167/C2

Cromarty Firth (bay), Sc, UK 94/B1
Crombie (mt.), Austl. 171/F3
Cromdale (hills), Sc, UK 94/C2
Cromwell, NZ 175/R12
Crong A Na (riv.), Viet. 136/D3
Crooked (riv.), Bahm. 199/G3
Crooked Creek, Ak, US 192/G3
Crooked Island Passage (chan.), Bahm. 203/H1
Crookston, Mn, US 185/J4
Crookwell, Austl. 173/D2
Croom, Ire. 89/P10
Crosby, ND, US 185/H3
Crosby, Eng, UK 93/E5
Crosbyton, Tx, US 187/G4
Cross (lake), Mb, Can. 185/J2
Cross City, Fl, US 191/H4
Cross Fell (peak), Eng, UK 93/F2
Cross Plains, Tx, US 187/H4
Cross River (state), Nga. 161/H5
Cross River (res.), NY, US 197/E1
Cross Roads, Pa, US 196/B4
Crossfield, Ab, Can. 184/E3
Crossford, Sc, UK 94/C4
Crosshouse, Sc, UK 94/B5
Crossroads, Ire. 89/P9
Crossville, Tn, US 191/G3
Crostolo (riv.), It. 116/D3
Croton-on-Hudson (Croton-Harmon), NY, US 197/E1
Crotone, It. 105/E3
Crottendorf, Ger. 113/F1
Croult (riv.), Fr. 88/K5
Crouy, Fr. 110/C5
Crouy-sur-Ourcq, Fr. 88/M4
Crow Agency, Mt, US 184/G4
Crowborough, Eng, UK 91/G4
Crowdy Bay NP, Austl. 173/E1
Crowe (riv.), On, Can. 188/E2
Crowley, La, US 187/J5
Crowley's (ridge), Ar, US 191/F3
Crown Point, In, US 188/C3
Crown Point, La, US 195/P17
Crown Point (int'l arpt.), Trin. 211/F2
Crown Prince Frederik (isl.), Nun., Can. 181/H1
Crownpoint, NM, US 186/E4
Crows Nest Falls NP, Austl. 172/D4
Crowthorne, Eng, UK 91/F4
Croydon, Austl. 172/A2
Croydon (bor.), Eng, UK 88/C2
Croydon, Pa, US 196/C4
Croydon, Ut, US 195/K11
Crozet (isls.), Fr. 81/M8
Crozon, Fr. 100/A2
Cruach Mhór (peak), Sc, UK 94/A4
Cruach nan Capull (peak), Sc, UK 94/A5
Crucero, Peru 214/D4
Cruden Bay, Sc, UK 94/E2
Cruick Water (riv.), Sc, UK 94/D3
Crumlin, NI, UK 92/B2
Crummock Water (lake), Eng, UK 93/E2
Crumpton, Md, US 196/C5
Cruseilles, Fr. 114/C5
Crusnes (riv.), Fr. 111/E5
Cruz (cape), Cuba 203/G2
Cruz Alta, Braz. 215/F2
Cruz Alta, Arg. 216/E2
Cruz Alta (peak), Port. 103/P10
Cruz das Almas, Braz. 212/C4
Cruz del Eje, Arg. 215/D3
Cruz Grande, Mex. 202/B2
Cruzeiro, Braz. 213/J7
Cruzeiro do Sul, Braz. 214/C2
Cruzeta, Braz. 212/C2
Cruzília, Braz. 213/J6
Crvenka, Serb. 106/D3
Cryn-y-Brain (peak), Wal, UK 93/E5
Crystal (lake), Pa, US 196/C1
Crystal Bay, Nv, US 186/C3
Crystal Brook, Austl. 171/H5
Crystal Cave, Ca, US 196/C2
Crystal City, Tx, US 190/D4
Crystal Springs, Ms, US 187/K5
Crystal Springs (res.), Ca, US 193/K11
Csenger, Hun. 99/M5
Csepreg, Hun. 101/M3
Csongrád, Hun. 106/E2
Csorna, Hun. 106/C2
Csorvás, Hun. 106/E2
Csóványos (peak), Hun. 106/D2
Csurgó, Hun. 106/C2
Cu Lao (isl.), Viet. 136/E4
Cuajinicuilapa, Mex. 202/B2
Cualedro, Sp. 102/B2
Cuamba, Moz. 163/G3
Cuando (riv.), Ang. 163/D4

Cuango (riv.), Ang. 163/C2
Cuanza (riv.), Ang. 163/B2
Cuart de Poblet, Sp. 103/E3
Cuarto (riv.), Arg. 216/D2
Cuatrociénagas de Carranza, Mex. 190/C5
Cuauhtémoc, Mex. 200/E5
Cuauhtémoc, Mex. 200/D2
Cuautepec, Mex. 201/L6
Cuautitlán, Mex. 201/Q9
Cuautitlán Izcalli, Mex. 201/Q9
Cuautla, Mex. 201/L8
Cuba, Mo, US 187/K3
Cuba, Port. 103/B3
Cuba (ctry.) 203/F1
Cubagua (isl.), Ven. 211/E2
Cuballing, Austl. 170/C5
Cubango (riv.), Ang. 163/C4
Çubuk, Turk. 148/C1
Cucamonga (Rancho Cucamonga), Ca, US 194/C2
Cuccurano, It. 117/F5
Cuchivero (riv.), Ven. 208/E2
Cuchumatanes (mts.), Guat. 202/D3
Cuckmere (riv.), Eng, UK 91/G5
Cucq, Fr. 100/D1
Cúcuta, Col. 210/C3
Cucuyagua, Hon. 202/D3
Cudahy, Ca, US 194/F8
Cuddalore, India 140/C5
Cudgewa, Austl. 173/C3
Cudillero, Sp. 102/B1
Cudrefin, Swi. 114/D4
Cudworth, Eng, UK 93/G4
Cue, Austl. 170/C3
Cuéllar, Sp. 102/C2
Cuéllar-Baza, Sp. 102/D4
Cuenca, Sp. 102/D2
Cuenca, Ecu. 210/B5
Cuenca, Sierra de (range), Sp. 102/E2
Cuencamé de Ceniceros, Mex. 200/E3
Cuernavaca, Mex. 201/K8
Cuero, Tx, US 187/H5
Cuers, Fr. 100/G5
Cueto, Cuba 203/H1
Cupertino, Ca, US 193/K12
Cuetzalán, Mex. 201/M6
Cueva de los Guácharos, PN, Col. 208/C3
Cuevas de Vinromá, Sp. 103/F2
Cuevas del Almanzora, Sp. 102/E4
Cuffley, Eng, UK 88/C1
Cufré, Uru. 217/K11
Cugir, Rom. 107/F3
Cuglieri, It. 104/A2
Cugnaux, Fr. 100/D5
Cuiabá, Braz. 209/G2
Cuiabá (riv.), Braz. 209/G7
Cuicas, Ven. 210/D2
Cuijk, Neth. 108/C5
Cuilapa, Guat. 202/D3
Cuilco (riv.), Guat. 202/C3
Cuillin (sound), Sc, UK 89/Q8
Cuilo (riv.), Ang. 163/C3
Cuisance (riv.), Fr. 114/A4
Cuise-la-Motte, Fr. 110/C5
Cuiseaux, Fr. 114/B5
Cuisery, Fr. 88/L4
Cuisy, Fr. 88/L4
Cuité, Braz. 212/C2
Cuitláhuac, Mex. 201/N8
Cuito (riv.), Ang. 163/C4
Cuiuni (riv.), Braz. 208/F4
Culcairn, Austl. 173/C2
Culdaff (riv.), Ire. 92/A1
Culemborg, Neth. 108/C5
Culgoa (riv.), Austl. 167/D3
Culiacán Rosales, Mex. 200/D3
Culion (isl.), Phil. 137/D5
Cullen, Sc, UK 94/D2
Cullera, Sp. 103/E3
Culleredo, Sp. 102/A1
Cullman, Al, US 191/G3
Culloden Battlesite, Sc, UK 94/B2
Cully, Swi. 114/C5
Cullybackey, NI, UK 92/B2
Culmback (dam), Wa, US 193/D2
Culmore, NI, UK 92/A1
Culoz, Fr. 114/B6
Culpeper, Va, US 188/E4
Culross, Sc, UK 94/C4
Cults, Sc, UK 94/D2
Culver (pt.), Austl. 170/E5
Culver City, Ca, US 194/F7
Culvers (lake), NJ, US 196/D1
Cumaná, Ven. 211/E1
Cumari, Braz. 213/H5
Cumba, Peru 214/B2
Cumbal, Col. 210/B4
Cumbal, Nevado de (peak), Col. 210/B4
Cumberland (pen.), Nun., Can. 181/J2
Cumberland (plat.), US 191/G3
Cumberland (isl.), Ga, US 191/H4
Cumberland (falls), Ky, US 191/G2

Cumberland (lake), Ky, US 188/C4
Cumberland (riv.), Ky,Tn, US 183/J4
Cumberland, Md, US 188/E4
Cumberland (co.), NJ, US 196/A3
Cumberland, Wa, US 193/D3
Cumberland House, Sk, Can. 185/H2
Cumbernauld, Sc, UK 94/C5
Cumbres Bastonal, Cerro (peak), Mex. 202/C2
Cumbres de Majalca, PN, Mex. 200/D2
Cumbres de Monterrey, PN de, Mex. 201/E3
Cumbria (co.), Eng, UK 93/E2
Cumbrian (mts.), Eng, UK 93/E2
Cumbum, India 140/C4
Cummins, Austl. 171/G5
Cumnock, Austl. 173/D2
Cumpas, Mex. 200/C2
Çumra, Turk. 148/C2
Cumshewa (pt.), BC, Can. 192/M5
Cunaviche, Ven. 211/E3
Cunco, Chile 216/B3
Cundeelee Abor. Rsv., Austl. 170/D4
Cunderdin, Austl. 170/C5
Cundinamarca (dept.), Col. 210/C3
Cunduacán, Mex. 202/C2
Cunene (riv.), Ang. 163/B4
Cuneo (prov.), It. 116/A3
Cuneo, It. 101/G4
Cunha, Braz. 213/J8
Cunnamulla, Austl. 172/B5
Cunninghame (reg.), Sc, UK 94/B5
Čuokkaraš'ša (peak), Nor. 95/H1
Cuorgnè, It. 101/G4
Cupar, Sc, UK 94/C4
Cupra Marittima, It. 101/K5
Cupramontana, It. 117/G6
Cuprija, Serb. 106/E4
Cuprija, Serb. 106/E4
Cuquenán (riv.), Ven. 211/F3
Curaçá, Braz. 212/C3
Curaçao (isl.) 210/D2
Curacautín, Chile 216/C3
Curacaví, Chile 216/N8
Curahuara de Carangas, Bol. 214/D5
Curanilahue, Chile 216/B2
Curaray (riv.), Ecu. 208/C4
Curaray (riv.), Ecu. 208/C4
Curaré, Peru 210/C5
Curarén, Hon. 202/E3
Curaumilla (pt.), Chile 216/N8
Curcubăta (peak), Rom. 107/F2
Cure (riv.), Fr. 88/B5
Curecanti Nat'l Rec. Area, Co, US 190/B2
Curepipe, Mrts. 165/T15
Curepto, Chile 216/B2
Curicó, Chile 216/C2
Curimatá, Braz. 212/B3
Curitibanos, Braz. 213/B3
Curno, It. 116/C1
Curone (riv.), It. 116/C3
Curral Velho, CpV. 151/K10
Current (riv.), Ar,Mo, US 187/K3
Currie, Austl. 173/B3
Currie, Sc, UK 94/C5
Curry, Ak, US 192/H3
Curtea de Argeş, Rom. 107/G3
Curtici, Rom. 106/E2
Curtis, It. 102/A1
Curtis (isls.), Austl. 172/D4
Curtis, Sp. 102/A1
Curtis (pt.), Md, US 196/B6
Curú NWR, CR 203/E4
Curuá (riv.), Braz. 209/H3
Curuá Una (riv.), Braz. 211/H5
Curuçá (riv.), Braz. 208/D5
Curup, Indo. 138/B4
Cururupu, Braz. 209/K4
Curuzú Cuatiá, Arg. 215/E2
Curvelo, Braz. 213/C1
Cusco, Peru 214/D4
Cusher (riv.), NI, UK 92/B3
Cushet Law (peak), Eng, UK 94/D6
Cushing, Ok, US 187/H4
Cusna (mt.), It. 116/D4
Cusset, Fr. 100/E3
Cusseta, Ga, US 191/G3
Custer, Mt, US 184/G4
Custer, SD, US 185/H5
Custines, Fr. 111/F6
Custódia, Braz. 212/C2
Cut (hill), Eng, UK 90/C5
Cut Bank, Mt, US 184/E3
Cut Knife, Sk, Can. 184/F2
Cutchogue, NY, US 197/F2
Cutervo, Peru 214/B2
Cuthbert, Ga, US 191/G4
Cutral-Có, Arg. 216/C3
Cutro, It. 105/E3

Cuttack, India 140/E3
Cuvergnon, Fr. 88/L4
Cuvier (cape), Austl. 170/B3
Cuxhaven, Ger. 109/F1
Cuyabeno, Ecu. 210/C5
Cuyama (riv.), Ca, US 186/C4
Cuyo, Phil. 139/F1
Cuyo (isls.), Phil. 139/F1
Cuyocuyo, Peru 214/D4
Cuyuni (riv.), Ven. 208/F2
Cuyuni (riv.), Guy., Ven. 211/G3
Cuyuni-Mazaruni (pol. reg.), Guy. 211/F3
Cuzco (ruin), Peru 214/D4
Cwmbran, Wal, UK 90/C3
Cyangugu, Rwa. 162/A3
Cyclades (isls.), Gre. 105/J4
Cypress (hills), Ab,Sk, Can. 184/F3
Cypress, Ca, US 194/F8
Cyprus (ctry.) 149/C2
Cyrenaica (reg.), Libya 155/K1
Cywyn (riv.), Wal, UK 90/B3
Czaplinek, Pol. 99/J2
Czarna Białostocka, Pol. 99/M2
Czarnków, Pol. 99/J2
Czech Republic (ctry.) 99/G3
Częstochowa, Pol. 99/K3
Człuchów, Pol. 96/G5

D

Da (riv.), China 137/D2
Da Hinggan (mts.), China 129/M2
Da Lat, Viet. 136/E4
Da Nang (cape), Viet. 136/E2
Da Nang, Viet. 136/E2
Da Xian, China 128/J5
Daaden, Ger. 111/G2
Da'an, China 129/M2
Daanbantayan, Phil. 137/D5
Daba (mts.), China 128/J5
Dabajuro, Ven. 210/D2
Dabakala, C.d'Iv. 195/N15
Dabas, Hun. 106/D2
Dabbāgh, Jabal (peak), SAr. 146/C3
Dabeiba, Col. 210/B3
Dabob (bay), Wa, US 193/B2
Dabou, C.d'Iv. 160/D5
Daboya, Gha. 161/E4
Dabra, India 142/B3
Dąbrowa Białostocka, Pol. 97/K5
Dąbrowa Górnicza, Pol. 99/K3
Dabu, China 137/C3
Dachang Huizu Zizhixian, China 130/H7
Dachau, Ger. 113/E6
Dacono, Co, US 195/C2
Dade City, Fl, US 191/H4
Dades, Oued (riv.), Mor. 156/D3
Dadi (cape), Indo. 139/H4
Dādra and Nagar Haveli (state), India 140/B4
Dādri, India 144/C3
Dādri, India 144/C3
Dādu (riv.), China 128/G4
Dadu, Pak. 147/J3
Daduru (riv.), SrL. 140/C6
Daen Noi (peak), Thai. 136/B4
Daet, Phil. 137/D5
Dafang, China 141/J2
Dafeng, China 130/E4
Dafla (mts.), Niger,Mali 161/F3
Dagana, Sen. 160/B2
Dağardı, Turk. 148/B2
Dağbaşı, Turk. 148/D2
Dagda, Lat. 97/M4
Dagestan, Resp., Rus. 121/H4
Daggaboersnek (pass), SAfr. 164/C4
Dagmar Range NP, Austl. 172/B2
Dagny, Fr. 88/M5
Dagu, China 130/H7
Dagua, Col. 210/B3
Dagupan, Phil. 137/D4
Daguragu, Austl. 167/D3
Dahanu, Bangl. 143/F4
Daharki, Pak. 140/A2
Dahei (riv.), China 130/D3
Dahlak (arch.), Erit. 155/N4
Dahlem, Ger. 111/F3
Dahlenburg, Ger. 109/F2
Dahlonega, Ga, US 191/H3
Dahmani, Tun. 158/L7
Dahme, Ger. 109/G3
Dahme (riv.), Ger. 111/G5
Dāhod, India 142/B4
Dahūk, Iraq 148/E2
Dahūk (gov.), Iraq 148/E2
Dahuofang (res.), China 130/D2
Dai (lake), China 130/D2
Dai-Segen-dake (peak), Japan 134/B3

Dai-sen (peak), Japan 132/C3
Dai Xian, China 130/C3
Daian, Japan 135/L5
Daicheng, China 130/D3
Daigo, Japan 133/G2
Dailekh, Nepal 142/C1
Dailly, Sc, UK 94/B6
Daimao, China 130/D3
Daimiel, Sp. 102/D3
Daingerfield, Tx, US 187/J4
Dāira Dīn Panāh, Pak. 144/A4
Daireaux, Arg. 216/E3
Daisen-Oki NP, Japan 132/C3
Daisetsuzan NP, Japan 134/C2
Daishan, China 137/D1
Damongo, Gha. 161/E4
Damparis, Fr. 114/B3
Daitō (isl.), Japan 125/N7
Daitō, Japan 135/J6
Daiyun (peak), China 129/L6
Dajabón, DRep. 203/J2
Dampier, Austl. 170/C2
Dakar (cap.), Sen. 160/A3
Dakar (pol. reg.), Sen. 160/A3
Dākhilah, Wāḥāt ad (oasis), Egypt 159/B3
Dakhin Shābāzpur (isl.), Bang. 143/H4
Dakhlet Nouadhibou (pol. reg.), Mrta. 156/A5
Dakoro, Niger 161/G3
Dakota City, Ne, US 185/J5
Dakovica, Kos. 106/E4
Dakovo, Cro. 106/D3
Dal (falls), Sudan 159/B4
Dala-Järna, Swe. 96/F1
Dalälven (riv.), Swe. 122/B3
Dalaas, Aus. 115/F3
Dalad Qi, China 130/B2
Dalaman, Turk. 148/B2
Dalaman (int'l arpt.), Turk. 148/B2
Dalandzadgad, Mong. 128/H3
Dalarna (reg.), Swe. 95/E3
Dalatangi (pt.), Ice. 95/Q6
Dalbeattie, Sc, UK 92/E2
Dalby, Austl. 172/C4
Dalby, Swe. 96/E4
Dalcour, La, US 195/Q17
Dalcross (int'l arpt.), Sc, UK 94/B1
Dale, Ok, US 195/N15
Dale, Nor. 96/A1
Dalen, Neth. 108/D3
Dalen, Nor. 96/C2
Dalfsen, Neth. 108/D3
Dalgaranger (mt.), Austl. 170/C3
Dalhart, Tx, US 187/G3
Dalhousie (cape), NW, Can. 192/N1
Dalhousie, NB, Can. 189/H1
Dalhousie, India 144/C3
Dali, China 141/H2
Dali, China 130/B4
Dalian (bay), China 131/A3
Dalian, China 131/A3
Dalian (int'l arpt.), China 130/E3
Dalías, Sp. 102/D4
Dalidag (peak), Azer. 121/H5
Dāliyat el Karmil, Isr. 149/G6
Dalj, Cro. 106/D3
Dalkeith, Sc, UK 94/C5
Dalkola, India 143/F3
Dall (lake), Ak, US 192/F3
Dall (isl.), Ak, US 180/C3
Dallas, Or, US 184/B1
Dallastown, Pa, US 196/B4
Dallgow, Ger. 98/Q6
Dallol Bosso (riv.), Niger,Mali 161/F3
Dalmatia (reg.), Cro. 106/B3
Dalmatia, Pa, US 196/B2
Dalmellington, Sc, UK 94/B6
Dar-el-Beida (Casablanca), Mor. 156/D2
Dalmeny, Austl. 173/D3
Dalmine, It. 116/C1
Dalnegorsk, Rus. 129/Q3
Dal'nerechensk, Rus. 129/P2
Daloa, C.d'Iv. 160/D5
Dalry, Sc, UK 94/B5
Dalrymple (lake), Austl. 167/D3
Dalrymple, Sc, UK 94/B6
Dals Långed, Swe. 96/C2
Dalsingh Sarai, India 143/E3
Dalsjöfors, Swe. 96/E3
Dāltāb, Iran 146/G2
Daltonganj, India 143/E3
Dalvík, Ice. 95/N6
Daly (riv.), Austl. 167/C2
Daly (bay), Nun., Can. 180/F2
Damak, Nepal 143/F2
Daman and Diu (state), India 142/B4
Damān, India 140/A2
Damanhūr, Egypt 149/B4
Damar (isl.), Indo. 139/G5
Damascus (int'l arpt.), Syria 149/E3
Damascus, Md, US 196/A5
Damascus (Dimashq) (cap.), Syria 149/D3
Damaturu, Nga. 154/H5
Damavānd (mtn.), Iran 146/F1

Dambach-la-Ville, Fr. 114/D1
Dambaslar, Turk. 107/H5
Dame Marie (cape), Haiti 203/H2
Dame Marie, Haiti 203/H2
Dämghän, Iran 147/F1
Damietta (riv.), Egypt 149/B4
Damietta (Dumyāṭ), Egypt 149/B4
Daming, China 130/C3
Damion (peak), Fr. 111/D4
Dammard, Fr. 88/M4
Dammartin-en-Goële, Fr. 88/L4
Dammastock (peak), Swi. 115/E4
Damme, Ger. 109/F3
Damme, Belg. 110/C1
Dāmodar (riv.), India 140/E3
Damoh, India 142/B4
Damongo, Gha. 161/E4
Damparis, Fr. 114/B3
Dampier (arch.), Austl. 167/A2
Dampier, Austl. 170/C2
Dampierre, Fr. 88/H5
Dampierre-sur-Salon, Fr. 114/B2
Damprichard, Fr. 114/C3
Damrei (mts.), Camb. 136/C4
Damsterdiep (riv.), Neth. 108/D2
Damvant, Swi. 114/C3
Damxung, China 128/F5
Dan (riv.), NC,Va, US 191/H2
Dan Xian, China 141/J4
Dāna, Jor. 149/D4
Dana Point, Ca, US 194/C4
Danané, C.d'Iv. 160/C5
Danao, Phil. 137/D5
Danba, China 128/H5
Danbury, Eng, UK 91/G3
Dancheng, China 130/C4
Dandaragan, Austl. 170/B4
Dandeldhurā, Nepal 142/C1
Dandenong (mt.), Austl. 173/G5
Danderhall, Sc, UK 94/C5
Dandong, China 131/C2
Dane (riv.), Eng, UK 93/F5
Danger (pt.), SAfr. 164/L11
Dangla, Belz. 202/D2
Dangrek (mts.), Camb. 128/J5
Dangshan, China 130/D4
Dangyang, China 129/K5
Danielskuil, SAfr. 164/C3
Danielsville, Pa, US 196/C2
Danilov, Rus. 118/J4
Daning, China 130/B3
Danjoutin, Fr. 114/C2
Dankaur, India 144/D5
Dankov, Rus. 120/F1
Danlí, Hon. 202/E3
Dannelly (res.), Al, US 191/G3
Dannemora, Swe. 96/G1
Dannenberg, Ger. 98/F2
Dannes, Fr. 110/A2
Dannevirke, NZ 175/T11
Dannhauser, SAfr. 165/E3
Danube (riv.), Eur. 85/F4
Danube, Delta of the (delta), Rom. 107/J3
Danube (Donau) (riv.), Ger. 101/H2
Danube, Mouths of the (delta), Rom.,Ukr. 107/J3
Danville, Il, US 188/C3
Danville, Ky, US 188/C4
Danville, Pa, US 196/B2
Dao Xian, China 141/H3
Daora (riv.), Alg. 156/D3
Dapaong, Togo 161/F4
Dapitan, Phil. 137/D6
Daqing, China 129/N2
Daqing (riv.), China 130/H7
Dar-el-Beida (Casablanca), Mor. 156/D2
Dātāgaṇj, India 142/B1
Datchet, Eng, UK 88/B2
Date, Japan 134/B2
Datia, India 142/B3
Datian, China 137/C3
Datil, NM, US 190/B3
Datong (mts.), China 128/G4
Datong, China 128/H4
Datong, China 130/C2
Datteln, Ger. 109/E5
Datu (cape), Indo. 138/B3
Datuk (cape), Indo. 138/C3
Daugavpils, Lat. 97/M4
Daule, Ecu. 210/B5
Daule (riv.), Ecu. 210/B5
Daun, Ger. 111/F3
Daund, India 140/B4
Daung (isl.), Myan. 136/B4
Dauphin (lake), Mb, Can. 185/J3
Dauphin, Pa, US 196/B3
Dauphin (co.), Pa, US 196/B3
Dauphiné (reg.), Fr. 100/F4
Dauphiné, Alpes du (range), Fr. 100/F4

Dārfūr (state), Sudan 159/A5
Dargaville, NZ 175/S10
Dargle (riv.), Ire. 92/B5
D'Arguin (bay), Austl. 171/F2
Daventry, Eng, UK 91/E2
Daverdisse, Belg. 111/E3
Darie (hills), Som. 155/Q6
Daveyton, SAfr. 164/E2
Davgaard-Jensen Land (phys. reg.), Grld. 181/T6
Darien, Ga, US 191/H4
Darien, Il, US 193/P16
Darien, PN, Pan. 208/C2
Darién, Serranía del (mts.), Pan. 208/C2
Darkan, Austl. 170/C5
Darlag, China 128/G5
Darling (range), Austl. 167/A4
Darling, Austl., Ant. 218/F
Darling (riv.), Austl. 186/B3
Darling, SAfr. 164/L10
Darling Downs (reg.), Austl. 167/D3
Darling Downs (range), Austl. 172/C3
Darlington, Eng, UK 93/G2
Darlington (co.), Eng, UK 93/G2
Darlington, Md, US 196/B4
Darlington, SC, US 191/J3
Darlington Point, Austl. 173/C2
Darłowo, Pol. 96/G4
Darmstadt, Ger. 112/B3
Darnah, Libya 155/K1
Darney, Fr. 114/C1
Darnley (bay), NW, Can. 180/D2
Darnley (cape), Ant. 218/E
Dartmoor NP, Eng, UK 90/B5
Dartmouth (dam), Austl. 173/C3
Dayr al Balaḥ, Gaza 149/D4
Dartmouth (res.), WBnk. 149/G7
Dayr Az Zawr (prov.), Syria 148/E3
Dartmouth, NS, Can. 189/J2
Dayr Ballūṭ, WBnk. 149/G7
Darton, Eng, UK 93/G4
Dartuch (cape), Sp. 103/G2
Dayr Sharaf, WBnk. 149/G7
Darvel (bay), Malay. 139/E3
Dayrūṭ, Egypt 159/B3
Darvel, Sc, UK 94/B5
Daysland, Ab, Can. 184/E2
Darwen, Eng, UK 93/F4
Dayton, Wa, US 184/D4
Darwin (bay), Chile 216/B5
Dayton, Tn, US 191/G3
Darwin (isl.), Ecu. 214/E6
Dayton, NJ, US 196/D3
Darwin (vol.), Ecu. 214/E7
Daytona Beach, Fl, US 191/H4
Darwin, Cordillera (mts.), Chile 215/B7
Dayu, China 141/K2
Dazhizhu Dau (isl.), China 129/T11
Darya Khan, Pak. 144/A4
D.C. (fed. dist.), US 196/A6
Daryābād, India 142/C2
De Aar, SAfr. 164/D3
Dashennongjia (peak), China 130/B5
De Bilt, Neth. 108/C4
De Doorns, SAfr. 164/L10
De Funiak Springs, Fl, US 191/G4
Dasht-e Kavīr (des.), Iran 147/F2
De Grey (riv.), Austl. 167/A3
De Haan, Belg. 110/C1
De Hart (res.), Pa, US 196/B3
Dasht-e Lūt (des.), Iran 147/G2
De Hoge Veluwe, NP, Neth. 108/C4
Dasht-e Mārgow (des.), Afg. 147/H2
De Kalb, Il, US 193/N16
Dasht Kaur (riv.), Pak. 147/H3
De Land, Fl, US 191/H4
De Leijen (lake), Neth. 108/D2
Dasing, Ger. 112/E6
De Lier, Neth. 108/B5
Daska, Pak. 144/C3
De Luz, Ca, US 194/C4
Dassa-Zoumé, Ben. 161/F5
De Panne, Belg. 110/B1
Dassel, Ger. 109/G5
De Peel (phys. reg.), Neth. 108/C6
Dassendorf, Ger. 109/H1
De Pinte, Belg. 110/C2
Dasseneiland (isl.), SAfr. 164/B4
De Ridder, La, US 187/J5
Dasūya, India 144/C4
De Soto, Ks, US 195/D6
De Soto, Mo, US 187/K3
De Wijk, Neth. 108/D3
Dead Sea (sea), Isr.,Jor. 149/D4
Deadhorse, Ak, US 192/J1
Deadman (peak), Austl. 170/C2
Deadwood, SD, US 185/H4
Deal (isl.), Austl. 173/C3
Deal, NJ, US 196/D3
Deale, Md, US 196/B6
Dean (riv.), BC, Can. 184/B2
Dean (chan.), BC, Can. 184/B2
De'an, China 137/C2
Deán Funes, Arg. 215/D3
Deanmill, Austl. 170/C5
Dearborn Heights, Mi, US 193/G7
Dearne, Eng, UK 93/G4
Dease (riv.), Nun., Can. 180/F2
Dease (riv.), BC, Can. 180/D3
Dease Lake, BC, Can. 192/M4
Death Valley NP, Ca, US 186/C3
Debar, FYROM 105/G2
Debauch (mtn.), Ak, US 192/F3
Davel, SAfr. 165/E2
Debe Habe, Nga. 154/H5

Debelets, Bul. 105/J1
Deben (riv.),
Eng, UK 91/H2
Dębica, Pol. 99/L3
Deblin, Pol. 99/L3
Dębno, Pol. 99/H2
Débo (lake), Mali 160/E3
Deborah (mt.), Ak, US 192/J3
Debre Birhan, Eth. 155/N5
Debre Mark'os, Eth. 155/N6
Debre Tabor, Eth. 155/N6
Debre Zeyit, Eth. 155/N6
Debrecen, Hun. 99/L5
Decatur (lake), India 191/G3
Decatur, Il, US 185/L6
Decatur, In, US 188/C3
Decatur, Ga, US 191/G3
Decatur, Tx, US 187/H4
Decazeville, Fr. 100/E4
Deccan (plat.), India 140/C5
Decima, It. 117/E3
Děčín, Czh. 99/H3
Décines-Charpieu, Fr. 114/A6
Decize, Fr. 100/E3
Dedemsvaart, Neth. 108/D3
Dedo (peak), Arg. 216/C2
Dédougou, Burk. 160/E3
Dedza, Malw. 163/F3
Dee (riv.), Sc, UK 94/C3
Deel (riv.), Ire. 92/A4
Deep Fork (riv.),
Ok, US 195/N14
Deep River,
On, Can. 188/E2
Deepcut, Eng, UK 88/F3
Deepwater, Austl. 173/D1
Deepwater, NJ, US 196/C4
Deepwater (pt.),
De, US 196/C5
Deer (isl.), Ak, US 192/F5
Deer Creek (res.),
Ut, US 195/L13
Deer Lake, Nf, Can. 189/K1
Deer Lake, Pa, US 196/B2
Deer Lodge,
Mt, US 184/E4
Deer Park, Il, US 193/P15
Deer Park, Md, US 196/B5
Deer Park, NY, US 197/E2
Deer Park, Wa, US 184/D4
Deer Plain, Il, US 195/F8
Deerfield, Il, US 193/P15
Deering, Ak, US 192/F2
Deerlijk, Belg. 110/C2
Deeside (valley),
Sc, UK 94/D2
Deex Nugaaleed (riv.),
Som. 155/Q6
Defensores del Chaco,
Par. 208/F8
Defiance, Oh, US 188/C3
Dégelis, Qu, Can. 189/G2
Degerfors (res.),
Swe. 96/F2
Degersheim, Swi. 115/F3
Deggendorf, Ger. 113/F5
Deggingen, Ger. 112/C5
Dego, It. 116/B4
DeGrey (riv.),
Austl. 170/C2
Deh Bīd, Iran 146/F2
Dehalak (isl.), Erit. 155/P4
Dehalak Marine NP,
Erit. 155/P4
Deheq, Iran 146/F2
Dehra Dūn, India 147/L2
Dehri, India 143/E3
Dehua, China 137/C2
Deidesheim, Ger. 112/B4
Deinste, Ger. 109/G1
Deinze, Belg. 110/C2
Deister (mts.),
Ger. 109/G4
Deiva Marina, It. 116/C4
Dej, Rom. 107/F2
Deje, Swe. 96/E2
Dejiang, China 141/J2
Dejima, Japan 135/E1
Dekemhare (Dek'emhāre),
Erit. 146/C5
Del Campillo, Arg. 216/D2
Del Carril, Arg. 217/J11
Del City, Ok, US 195/N15
Del Dios, Ca, US 194/C4
Del Gran Paradiso, It. 116/A2
Del Mar, Ca, US 194/C5
Del Norte, Co, US 187/F3
Del Rio, Tx, US 187/G5
Del Valle, Arg. 216/E2
Del Valle (lake),
Ca, US 193/L11
Delacroix, La, US 195/Q17
Delafield, Wi, US 193/P13
Delano, Ca, US 186/C4
Delareyville, SAfr. 164/D3
Delarode (lake),
Sk, Can. 184/G2
Delavan, Wi, US 187/K2
Delavan (lake),
Wi, US 193/P14
Delavan Lake,
Wi, US 193/N14
Delaware (riv.), US 188/F3
Delaware (state), US 188/F4
Delaware, NJ, US 196/C2
Delaware (bay),
NJ, US 188/F4
Delaware, Oh, US 188/D3
Delaware (co.),
Pa, US 196/C4
Delaware (pass),
Pa, US 196/C2
Delaware City,
De, US 196/C4
Delaware Water Gap
Nat'l Rec. Area, Pa, US 188/F3

Delbrück, Ger. 109/F5
Delčevo, FYROM 105/H2
Delden, Neth. 108/D4
Dent de Lys (peak),
Swi. 114/C4
Delebio, It. 115/F5
Delegate, Austl. 173/D3
Delft, Neth. 108/B4
Delfzijl, Neth. 108/D2
Delgada (pt.),
Arg. 216/E4
Delgado (cape),
Moz. 162/D5
Delhi, India 144/D5
Delhi (state), India 140/C2
Delhi, Il, US 195/G7
Delhi, La, US 187/K4
Delice, Turk. 148/C2
Delice (riv.), Turk. 120/E5
Delījān, Iran 146/F2
Delisle, Sk, Can. 184/G3
Dell Rapids, SD, US 185/J4
Delligsen, Ger. 109/G5
Delmas, SAfr. 164/Q13
Delme, Fr. 111/F4
Delmenhorst, Ger. 109/F2
Delmiro Gouveia,
Braz. 212/C3
Delmont, NJ, US 196/D5
Delnice, Cro. 106/B3
Deloraine, Austl. 173/C4
Deloraine,
Mb, Can. 185/H4
Delphi (Dhelfoí)
(ruin), Gre. 105/H3
Delphos, Oh, US 188/C3
Delportshoop, SAfr. 164/D3
Delran, NJ, US 196/D4
Delray Beach,
Fl, US 191/H5
Delson, Qu, Can. 189/N7
Delta, Ut, US 186/D3
Delta (state), Nga. 161/G5
Delta, Pa, US 196/B4
Dolj del Tigre, Uru. 217/K11
Dera Ghāzi Khān,
Pak. 144/A4
Dera Gopipur, India 144/D4
Dera Ismāīl Khān,
Pak. 144/A4
Derbent, Rus. 121/J4
Derby, Eng, UK 93/G4
Derby (co.), Eng, UK 93/G6
Derby, Ct, US 197/E1
Derbyshire (co.),
Eng, UK 93/G6
Derdap NP, Serb. 106/F3
Derecske, Hun. 106/E2
Derdingen, Swi. 114/D3
Derg, Lough (lake),
Ire. 89/P10
Derik, Turk. 148/E2
Derinkuyu, Turk. 148/C2
Dermerara (riv.) Guy. 211/G3
Déroute, Passage de la
(chan.), Fr. 100/B2
Derrevaragh
(lake), Ire. 92/A4
Derry, NH, US 189/G3
Derryboy, NI, UK 92/C3
Derventa, Bosn. 106/C3
Dervio, It. 115/F5
Derwent (riv.),
Austl. 173/C4
Derwent (riv.),
Eng, UK 93/E2
Derwent (res.),
Eng, UK 93/F2
Derwent Water
(lake), Eng, UK 93/E2
Des Allemands,
La, US 195/P17
Des Moines (cap.),
Ia, US 185/K5
Des Moines (riv.),
Ia,Mn, US 185/J2
Des Peres, Mo, US 195/G8
Desaguadero (riv.),
Bol. 208/E7
Desaguadero, Peru 214/D5
Desagües de los Colorados
(dry lake), Arg. 215/C2
Desana, It. 116/B2
Descabezado Grande
(vol.), Chile 216/C2
Descalvado, Braz. 213/C2
Descartes, Fr. 100/D3
Deschambault,
Sk, Can. 185/H2
Deschambault Lake,
Sk, Can. 184/G2
Deschutes (riv.),
Or, US 184/C4
Desdunes, Haiti 203/H2
Dese, Eth. 155/N5
Dese (riv.), It. 117/F2
Deseado (riv.), Arg. 205/C7
Deseado (cape),
Chile 217/B7
Desengaño (pt.), Arg. 217/D6
Desenzano del
Garda, It. 116/D1
Désertines, Fr. 100/D3
Desio, It. 116/C1
Desna (riv.), Ukr. 120/D2
Desolación (isl.),
Chile 215/A7
Desordem, Serra da
(range), Braz. 212/A2
Despatch, SAfr. 164/D4
Dessau, Ger. 98/G3
Dessel, Belg. 108/C6
Dessoubre (riv.), Fr. 114/C3
Destelbergen, Belg. 110/C1

Dennisville, NJ, US 196/D5
Denpasar, Indo. 138/E5
Dent de Lys (peak),
Swi. 114/C4
Dent d'Hérens
(peak), It. 114/C6
Dentergem, Belg. 110/C2
Dentlein am Forst,
Ger. 112/D4
Denton, Eng, UK 93/F5
Denton, Md, US 196/C6
Denton, Tx, US 190/D3
Denton, Tx, US 187/H4
Detroit Metropolitan Wayne
County (int'l arpt.),
Mi, US 188/D3
Dettelbach, Ger. 112/D3
Dettifoss (falls),
Ice. 95/P6
Dettwiller, Fr. 111/G6
Deua NP, Austl. 173/D2
Deuil-la-Barre, Fr. 88/J5
Deûle (riv.), Fr. 110/B2
Deurne, Belg. 190/B4
Deurne, Neth. 108/C6
Deustua, Peru 214/D4
Deutsch Evern,
Ger. 109/H2
Deutsch Wagram,
Aus. 107/P7
Deutschkreutz,
Aus. 101/M3
Deutschlandsberg,
Aus. 101/L3
Deux-Montagnes,
Qu, Can. 189/N6
Deux-Montagnes (co.),
Qu, Can. 189/M6
Deux-Montagnes, Lac des
(lake), Qu, Can. 189/M7
Deva, Rom. 106/F3
Dévaványa, Hun. 106/E2
Develi, Turk. 148/C2
Deventer, Neth. 108/D4
Deveron (riv.),
Sc, UK 94/D2
Deville, Fr. 111/D4
Devil's (isl.), FrG. 209/H2
Devils (riv.), Mex. 201/E2
Devil's Elbow
(pass), Sc, UK 94/C3
Devils Lake,
ND, US 185/J3
Dias Creek, NJ, US 196/D5
Devils Paw (peak),
Ak, US 192/L4
Devils Postpile Nat'l Mon.,
Ca, US 186/C3
Devils Slide,
Ut, US 195/K11
Devine, Tx, US 187/H5
Devizes, Eng, UK 90/E4
Devnya, Bul. 107/H4
Devoll (riv.), Alb.,Gre. 106/E5
Devon, Ab, Can. 184/E2
Devon (isl.),
Nun., Can. 181/S7
Devon (co.), Eng, UK 90/C5
Devon (riv.), Sc, UK 94/C4
Devon-Berwyn,
Pa, US 196/C3
Devonport, Austl. 173/C4
Devore, Ca, US 194/C2
Devrek, Turk. 107/K5
Devrek (riv.), Turk. 107/K5
Devrez (riv.), Turk. 120/E4
Dewa (pt.), Indo. 138/A3
Dewa (mts.), Japan 134/B4
Dewās, India 147/L4
Dewetsdorp, SAfr. 164/D3
Dewsbury, Eng, UK 93/G4
Dexter, Me, US 189/G2
Dey-Dey (lake),
Austl. 167/C3
Deyang, China 128/H5
Dez (riv.), Iran 122/E6
Dezfūl, Iran 146/E2
Dezhneva (cape),
Rus. 192/E2
Dezhou, China 130/D3
Dhabān Singh, Pak. 144/B4
Dhākā (div.),
Bang. 143/H4
Dhāka, India 143/E2
Dhaleswari (riv.),
Bang. 143/H4
Dhali, Cyp. 149/C2
Dhāmpur, India 142/B1
Dhamtari, India 140/D3
Dhanaula, India 144/C4
Dhanbād, India 143/F4
Dhangadhī, Nepal 142/C1
Dhānkutā, Nepal 143/F2
Dhār, India 147/L4
Dhārān, Nepal 143/F2
Dhāriwāl, India 144/C4
Dharmapuri, India 140/C5
Dharmavaram, India 140/C5
Dharmjaygarh, India 143/E4
Dharmsāla, India 144/D3
Dhasan (riv.), India 142/B3
Dhaulāgiri (peak),
Nepal 142/D1
Dhaulāgiri (zone),
Nepal 142/D1
Dhaurahra, India 142/D2
Dhelfoí, Gre. 105/H3
Dhelvinákion, Gre. 105/G3
Dheskáti, Gre. 105/G3
Dheune (riv.), Fr. 114/A4
Dhībān, Jor. 149/D4
Dhidhimótikhon, Gre. 105/K2
Dhikaía, Gre. 105/K2
Dhílos (ruin), Gre. 105/J4

Dhimitsána, Gre. 105/H4
Dhirfis (peak), Gre. 105/H3
Dhistomon, Gre. 105/H3
Dhofar (reg.), Oman 146/F5
Dhokímion, Gre. 105/J3
Dholka, India 147/K4
Dhomokós, Gre. 105/H3
Dhonoúsa (isl.),
Gre. 105/J5
Dhorāji, India 147/K4
Dhronbach (riv.),
Ger. 111/F4
Dhūlia, India 147/K4
Dhuliān, India 143/F3
Dhulikhel, Nepal 143/E2
Dhupgāri, India 143/G2
Dhūri, India 144/C4
Di Linh, Viet. 136/E4
Dia (isl.), Gre. 105/J5
Diablo (mt.), Ak, US 192/H4
Diablo (range),
Ca, US 186/B3
Diablo (plat.), Tx, US 190/B4
Diablo, Punta del
(pt.), Uru. 217/G2
Diablotin (peak),
Dom. 199/N9
Diadema, Braz. 213/G8
Diadema Argentina,
Arg. 216/D5
Diamante (riv.),
Arg. 216/D2
Diamantina, Braz. 212/B5
Diamantina
(riv.), Austl. 167/D3
Diamantina, Chapada
(hills), Braz. 209/K6
Diamantino, Braz. 209/G6
Diamond Bar,
Ca, US 194/G8
Diamond Harbour,
India 143/G4
Diamond Head (pt.),
Hi, US 182/W13
Dianalund, Den. 96/D4
Dianbai, China 141/K3
Dianjiang, China 137/A1
Diano Marina, It. 116/B5
Dianshan (lake),
China 130/L8
Diapaga, Burk. 161/F3
Dinder NP, Sudan 155/N5
Dias Creek, NJ, US 196/D5
Diavolezza (peak),
Swi. 115/F5
Dibai, India 142/B1
Dibeng, SAfr. 164/C2
Dibiāpur, India 142/B2
Dibis (well), Egypt 159/B4
Dibis, Iraq 148/F3
Dickens, Tx, US 187/H6
Dickens (pt.),
RI, US 197/G1
Dickinson, ND, US 185/H4
Dickson, Tn, US 188/C4
Dicle (dam), Turk. 148/E2
Dicomano, It. 117/E5
Didam, Neth. 108/D5
Didcot, Eng, UK 91/E3
Diddington, Austl. 173/D4
Didesbury, Ab, Can. 184/E3
Didwāna, India 147/K3
Didyma (ruin), Turk. 148/A2
Die (dam), Turk. 148/E2
Die Berg (peak),
SAfr. 163/F6
Dieblich, Ger. 111/G3
Diébougou, Burk. 160/E4
Dieburg, Ger. 112/B3
Diedersdorf, Ger. 98/G7
Diefenbaker (lake),
Sk, Can. 184/G3
Diekirch (dist.), Lux. 111/E4
Diekirch, Lux. 111/F4
Diemen, Neth. 108/B4
Diemtigen, Swi. 114/D4
Diepenbeek, Belg. 111/E2
Diepenveen, Neth. 108/D4
Diepholz, Ger. 109/F3
Dieppe, Fr. 100/D2
Dierdorf, Ger. 111/G2
Diespeck, Ger. 112/D3
Diessen am Ammersee,
Ger. 115/H2
Diest, Belg. 111/E1
Dique (canal), Col. 203/H4
Dirē, Mali 160/E2
Dirê Dawa, Eth. 155/P6
Diriamba, Nic. 202/E4
Dirj, Libya 157/H3
Dirk Hartog (isl.),
Austl. 170/A3
Dirksland, Neth. 108/B5
Dirlewang, Ger. 115/G2
Dirranbandi, Austl. 173/C1
Dirrington Great Law
(hill), Sc, UK 94/D5
Dirty Devil (riv.),
Ut, US 186/E3
Disappointment
(lake), Austl. 167/B3
Disappointment
(isls.), FrPol. 175/L6
Discovery
(bay), Austl. 173/B3
Discovery Bay, Jam. 203/G2
Digby, NS, Can. 189/H2
Discovery Bay, China 130/R18
Disentis-Muster, Swi. 115/F4
Disgrazi (peak), It. 115/F5
Disko (isl.), Grld. 177/M3
Disko (Qeqertarsuaq)
(isl.), Grld. 181/L2
Disneyland, Ca, US 194/G8
Dison, Belg. 111/F2
Dispur, India 141/F2

Diklosmta (peak),
Geo. 121/H4
Diksmuide, Belg. 110/B1
Dilbeek, Belg. 110/D2
Dilek Yarımadası NP,
Turk. 154/A2
Dili (cap.), ETim. 139/G5
Dillenburg, Ger. 111/H2
Dillingen, Ger. 111/F5
Dillingen an der Donau,
Ger. 112/D5
Dillingham, Ak, US 192/G4
Dillon, Mt, US 184/E4
Dillon, SC, US 191/J3
Dillsburg, Pa, US 196/A3
Dilolo, D.R. Congo 163/D3
Dilsen, Belg. 111/E1
Dīmāpur, India 141/F2
Dimaro, It. 115/G5
Dimas, Mex. 200/D4
Dimashq (prov.),
Syria 148/D3
Dimbokro, C.d'Iv. 160/D5
Dimboola, Austl. 173/B3
Dimbovița (prov.),
Rom. 107/G3
Dimbulah, Austl. 172/B2
Dimitriya Lapteva (str.),
Rus. 123/P2
Dimitrovgrad, Bul. 105/J1
Dimitrovgrad, Rus. 121/J1
Dimitrovgrad, Serb. 105/J1
Dimlang (peak), Nga. 154/H6
Dimmitt, Tx, US 187/G4
Dimona, Isr. 149/D4
Dimovo, Bul. 107/F4
Dina, Pak. 144/C3
Dinagat (isl.), Phil. 137/E5
Dinagat, Phil. 137/E6
Dinājpur (pol. reg.),
Bang. 143/G3
Dinan, Fr. 100/B2
Dinant, Belg. 111/D3
Dinapur, India 143/F3
Dinar, Turk. 148/B2
Dinard, Fr. 100/B2
Dinaric Alps (mts.),
Cro. 106/C3
Dinas (pt.), Wal, UK 90/B3
Dindigul, India 140/C5
Dindori, India 142/C4
Dinga, Pak. 144/B3
Ding'an, China 141/K4
Dingbian, China 128/J4
Dingelstädt, Ger. 109/H6
Dinggyê, China 143/F1
Dingle, Ire. 88/N10
Dingle (bay), Ire. 88/N10
Dingmans Ferry,
Pa, US 196/D1
Dingnan, China 137/C3
Dingolfing, Ger. 113/F5
Dingras, Phil. 137/D4
Dingtao, China 130/C4
Dingwall, Sc, UK 94/B1
Dingxi, China 128/H4
Dingxiang, China 130/C3
Dingxing, China 130/C3
Dingyuan, China 130/D7
Dinkel (riv.), Ger. 108/E4
Dinkelsbühl, Ger. 112/D4
Dinkelscherben,
Ger. 112/D6
Dinklage, Ger. 109/F3
Dinosaur Nat'l Mon.,
US 186/E2
Dinslaken, Ger. 108/D5
Dinsmore, Sk, Can. 184/G3
Dintel Mark (riv.),
Neth. 108/B5
Dinuba, Ca, US 186/C3
Dinxperlo, Neth. 108/D5
Dioïla, Mali 160/D3
Dion (riv.), Gui. 160/C4
Diósd, Hun. 107/Q10
Diourbel (pol. reg.),
Sen. 160/A3
Diphu, India 141/F2
Diplo, Pak. 147/J4
Dipni (dam), Turk. 148/E2
Dipperu NP, Austl. 172/C3
Dipperz, Ger. 112/C1
Dique (canal), Col. 203/H4
Diré, Mali 160/E2
Dirê Dawa, Eth. 155/P6
Discovery Bay, China 130/R18
Disentis-Muster, Swi. 115/F4

Disraëli, Qu, Can. 189/G2
Dissen am Teutoburger
Wald, Ger. 109/F4
District of Columbia
(fed. dist.), US 196/A6
Distrito Féderal
(fed. dist.), Braz. 212/A4
Distrito Federal
(fed. dist.), Col. 210/C3
Distrito Federal
(fed. dist.), Mex. 201/Q10
Distrito Federal
(fed. dist.), Ven. 211/E2
Ditchling Beacon
(hill), Eng, UK 91/F5
Dittaino (riv.), It. 104/D4
Dittelbrunn, Ger. 112/D2
Dittmer, Mo, US 195/F9
Ditzingen, Ger. 112/C5
Diu, India 140/B3
Dive (riv.), Fr. 100/D3
Dividing Creek,
NJ, US 196/D5
Divinolândia, Braz. 213/G6
Divinopolis, Braz. 213/C2
Divisa Nova, Braz. 213/G6
Divisor, Serra do
(mts.), Braz. 208/D5
Divo, C.d'Iv. 160/D5
Divonne-les-Bains, Fr. 114/C5
Dīwānīya, Turk. 148/D2
Dix (lake), Swi. 114/D5
Dixmoor, Il, US 193/Q16
Dixon, Il, US 185/L5
Dixon Entrance (chan.),
Can., US 192/M4
Diyadin, Turk. 148/E2
Diyāla (gov.), Iraq 148/E3
Diyarb Najm, Egypt 149/B4
Diyarbakir (prov.),
Turk. 148/E2
Diyarbakir, Turk. 148/E2
Djado (plat.), Niger 151/G2
Djakotomé, Ben. 161/F5
Djamaa, Alg. 157/G2
Djambala, Congo 154/H8
Djanet, Alg. 157/G3
Djebel-Amrag
(mtn.), Alg. 158/D3
Djebel Tichka
(peak), Mor. 156/C3
Djedi, Oued (riv.), Alg. 157/G2
Djelfa, Alg. 157/G1
Djema, CAfr. 155/L6
Djemila (ruin), Alg. 158/H4
Djénné, Mali 160/D3
Djibo, Burk. 161/E3
Djibouti (ctry.) 155/P5
Djibouti (cap.), Djib. 155/P5
Djougou, Ben. 161/F4
Djúpivogur, Ice. 95/P7
Dnepr (riv.), Ukr. 85/H3
Dnipro (riv.), Ukr. 120/E2
Dniprodzerzhyns'k,
Ukr. 120/E2
Dnipropetrovs'k, Ukr. 120/E2
Dnipropetrovs'ka
Oblasti, Ukr. 120/E2
Dniprovs'kyy Lyman
(estu.), Ukr. 107/K2
Dnistrovs'kyy Lyman
(str.), Nun., Can. 180/E2
Dno Sol, Viet. 136/D1
Dolton, Il, US 193/Q16
Dnyapro (riv.), Bela. 97/P4
Do (lake), Mali 160/D3
Do Rāh (pass), Afg. 147/K1
Do Son, Viet. 136/D1
Doany, Madg. 165/J6
Doba, Chad 154/J6
Dobbs Ferry,
NY, US 197/K7
Dobel, Lat. 97/J3
Döbeln, Ger. 98/G3
Doberan (pen.),
Ger. 109/G1
Dobiegniew, Pol. 99/H2
Dobogo-kő (peak),
Hun. 107/Q10
Doboj, Bosn. 106/D3
Dobřany, Czh. 113/G3
Dobre Miasto, Pol. 97/L5
Dobre C, US, Ant. 218/J
Döbrich, Bul. 107/H4
Dobříš, Czh. 113/G3
Dobruja (reg.), Bul. 107/H4
Dobrush, Bela. 97/P4
Dobryanka, Rus. 119/N4
Doce (riv.), Braz. 209/K7
Dochart (riv.), Sc, UK 94/B4
Dock Junction,
Ga, US 191/H4
Docker River, Austl. 171/F3
Doctor Arroyo, Mex. 201/E4
Doctor Pedro P. Peña,
Par. 215/D1
Doctor Petru Groza,
Rom. 106/F2
Doda, India 144/C3
Doda (lake), India 144/D3
Dodder (riv.), Ire. 92/B5
Doddinghurst,
Eng, UK 88/D2
Dodecanese (isl.),
Gre. 148/A2
Dodge City,
Ks, US 187/G3
Dodger Stadium,
Ca, US 194/F7
Dodgeville, Wi, US 185/L5
Dodman
(pt.), Eng, UK 90/B6
Dodoma (pol. reg.),
Tanz. 162/B4

Dodori Nat'l Rsv.,
Kenya 162/D3
Dodsland, Sk, Can. 184/F3
Dodworth, Eng, UK 93/G4
Doesburg, Neth. 108/D4
Doetinchem, Neth. 108/D5
Doğankent (riv.), Turk. 148/D1
Doğanhisar, Turk. 148/B2
Doğankent (riv.), Turk. 148/D1
Doğanşar, Turk. 148/D1
Doğanşehir, Turk. 148/D1
Doğanyurt, Turk. 148/C1
Döğer, Turk. 148/B2
Dogliani, It. 116/A3
Dogondoutchi,
Niger 161/G3
Doğubayazit, Turk. 148/F2
Doğukaradeniz
(mts.), Turk. 148/D1
Dohad, India 147/K4
Dohrīghāt, India 142/D2
Doi Khun Tan NP,
Thai. 136/B2
Doilungdêqên, China 140/F2
Doiras, Embalse de
(res.), Sp. 102/B1
Dois de Julho
(int'l arpt.), Braz. 212/B1
Dois Irmãos, Serra
(mts.), Braz. 209/K5
Doische, Belg. 111/D3
Dokka, Nor. 96/D1
Dokkum, Neth. 108/D2
Dokkumer Ee (riv.),
Neth. 108/C2
Doksy, Czh. 113/H1
Dolbeau, Qu, Can. 189/F1
Dolcedorme
(peak), It. 104/E3
Dole, Fr. 114/B3
Dolent (peak), Swi. 114/C6
Dolgellau, Wal, UK 90/C1
Dolgoprudnyy, Rus. 119/W9
Dolinsk, Rus. 129/R2
Dollar, Sc, UK 94/C4
Dollar Law (peak),
Sc, UK 94/C5
Dollard-des-Ormeaux,
Qu, Can. 189/N7
Dollard (Dollart) (bay),
Ger.,Neth. 109/E2
Doller (riv.), Fr. 98/D5
Dollnstein, Ger. 112/E5
Dolmar (peak), Ger. 112/D1
Dolmen (ruin), It. 104/E2
Dolna Banya, Bul. 105/H1
Dolni Dübnik, Bul. 107/G4
Dolnoslaskie
(prov.), Pol. 99/J3
Dolo, Eth. 155/P7
Dolo, It. 117/F2
Dolol (riv.), Rom. 107/F3
Doloon, Mong. 128/J3
Dolores, Arg. 216/F3
Dolores (riv.), Co, US 186/E3
Dolores, Guat. 202/D2
Dolores (riv.), Co, US 190/A2
Dolores, Co, US 190/A2
Dolores, Uru. 217/J10
Dolphin (cape), UK 217/F6
Dolphin and Union
(str.), Nun., Can. 180/E2
Dölsach, Aus. 101/K3
Dolton, Il, US 193/Q16
Dom (peak), Swi. 114/D6
Dom (peak), Indo. 139/J4
Dom Noi
(res.), Thai. 136/D3
Dom Pedrito, Braz. 215/B3
Dom Pedro, Braz. 212/A2
Domat-Ems, Swi. 115/F4
Domažlice, Czh. 113/F3
Dombasle-sur-Meurthe,
Fr. 111/F2
Dombay-Ul'gen
(peak), Geo. 121/G4
Dombes (lake), Fr. 114/B5
Dombóvár, Hun. 106/E2
Dombrád, Hun. 106/F1
Domburg, Neth. 108/A5
Domérat, Fr. 100/E3
Domeyko, Cordillera
(mts.), Chile 215/C1
Dominica (ctry.) 199/N9
Dominica Passage
(chan.), Dom.,Guad. 199/N9
Dominican Republic
(ctry.) 199/J4
Dommartin-lès-Remiremont,
Fr. 114/C2
Dommartin-lès-Toul, Fr. 111/E1
Dommel (riv.), Neth. 111/E1
Domodedovo
(int'l arpt.), Rus. 119/W9
Domodossola, It. 115/E5
Domondina, India 143/G2
Domont, Fr. 88/J4
Dompu, Indo. 139/E5
Domrémy-la-
Pucelle, Fr. 114/B1
Dömsöd, Hun. 106/D2
Domusnovas, It. 104/A3
Domvilk (mt.), Austl. 172/C5
Domvraia, Slov. 101/L3
Don (riv.), Eng, UK 93/G5
Don (ridge), Rus. 85/J4
Don Benito, Sp. 102/C3
Donabate, Ire. 92/B5
Donada, It. 117/F2
Donaghadee,
NI, UK 92/C2

Donaghmore, NI, UK 92/B2
Donald, Austl. 173/B3
Donaldsonville, La, US 187/K5
Doñana NP, Sp. 102/C3
Donath, Swi. 115/F4
Donau (Danube) (riv.), Ger. 101/H2
Donaueschingen, Ger. 115/E2
Donauwörth, Ger. 112/D5
Doncaster, Eng, UK 93/G4
Doncaster (co.), Eng, UK 93/G4
Donchery, Fr. 111/D4
Dondra Head (pt.), SrL. 140/D6
Donegal, Ire. 89/P9
Donegal (dist.), Ire. 92/A1
Donegal (bay), Ire. 89/P9
Donets (riv.), Rus., Ukr. 121/G2
Donets'k, Ukr. 120/F2
Donets'k (int'l arpt.), Ukr. 120/F2
Donets'ka Oblasti, Ukr. 120/F3
Dong (riv.), Viet. 141/J5
Dong Ha, Viet. 136/D2
Dong Hoi, Viet. 136/D2
Dong Noi (riv.), Viet. 136/D4
Donga (riv.), Nga. 161/H4
Dongar Parãsia, India 142/B4
Dongara, Austl. 170/B4
Dongbei (plain), China 130/E2
Dongchuan, China 141/H2
Dong'e, China 130/D3
Dongen, Neth. 108/B5
Dongfang, China 141/J4
Donggou, China 131/C3
Dongguan, China 141/K3
Dongguang, China 130/D3
Donghai, China 130/D4
Dongio, Swi. 115/E5
Dongkya (pass), China 143/G2
Donglan, China 137/A3
Dongliao (riv.), China 130/F2
Dongming, China 130/C4
Dongo, It. 115/F5
Dongping, China 130/D4
Dongsha (isl.), China 137/C3
Dongshan, China 137/C3
Dongtai, China 130/E4
Dongtiao (riv.), China 130/L9
Dongting (lake), China 137/C1
Dongzhi, China 137/C1
Donihue, Chile 216/N9
Donjek (riv.), Yk, Can. 180/C2
Donji Komren, Serb. 106/E4
Donji Vakuf, Bosn. 106/C3
Donnas, It. 116/A1
Donnersberg (peak), Ger. 111/G4
Donnybrook, Austl. 172/D4
Donnybrook, Austl. 170/B5
Donon (peak), Fr. 114/D1
Donoratico, It. 101/J5
Donzdorf, Ger. 112/C5
Donzy, Fr. 100/E3
Dooleena (peak), Austl. 170/C2
Doon (riv.), Sc, UK 94/B6
Doon (lake), Sc, UK 94/B6
Doonbeg, Ire. 89/P10
Doonerak (mt.), Ak, US 192/H2
Door (pen.), Wi, US 185/M4
Doorn (riv.), SAfr. 164/B3
Doorn, Neth. 108/C4
Doppo (peak), It. 116/D1
Doğen (lake), China 143/G1
Dora (lake), Austl. 167/B3
Dora Riparia (riv.), It. 101/G4
Dorada (coast), Sp. 103/F2
Dorchester, NB, Can. 189/H2
Dorchester, Il, US 195/H7
Dorchester, Eng, UK 90/D5
Dorchester (cape), Nun., Can. 181/J2
Dorchester, NJ, US 196/D5
Dordogne (riv.), Fr. 100/D4
Dordrecht, SAfr. 164/D3
Dordrecht, Neth. 108/B5
Dore (lake), Sk, Can. 184/G2
Dore, Monts (mts.), Fr. 100/E4
Dores do Indaiá, Braz. 213/C1
Dorfen, Ger. 113/F6
Dorfen (riv.), Ger. 113/E6
Dorgali, It. 104/A2
Dori, Burk. 161/E3
Dorion, Qu, Can. 189/M7
Dorking, Eng, UK 91/H5
Dorlisheim, Fr. 114/D1
Dormagen, Ger. 111/F1
Dormans, Fr. 110/C5
Dornach, Swi. 114/D3
Dornbirn, Aus. 115/F3
Dorney Park/ Wildwater Kingdom, Pa, US 196/C2
Dornhan, Ger. 115/E1
Dorno, It. 116/B2

Dornoch Firth (inlet), Sc, UK 94/B1
Dornod (prov.), Mong. 129/K2
Dornogoví (prov.), Mong. 129/J3
Dornstadt, Ger. 112/C6
Dornstetten, Ger. 112/B6
Dorog, Hun. 107/Q9
Dorothy, NJ, US 196/D5
Dörpen, Ger. 109/E3
Dorre (isl.), Austl. 170/B3
Dorrigo, Austl. 173/E1
Dorrigo NP, Austl. 173/E1
Dorsale (mts.), Tun. 158/L7
Dorset (co.), Eng, UK 90/D5
Dorsey, Il, US 195/G8
Dorsten, Ger. 108/D5
Dortan, Fr. 114/B5
Dortmund, Ger. 109/E5
Dortmund-Ems (canal), Ger. 109/E4
Dortmund (Wickede) (int'l arpt.), Ger. 109/E5
Dörtyol, Turk. 149/E1
Dorum, Ger. 109/F1
Dorval, Qu, Can. 189/N7
Dörverden, Ger. 109/G3
Dos Bahías (cape), Arg. 216/D5
Dos de Mayo, Peru 214/C2
Dos Hermanas, Sp. 102/C4
Döşemealtı, Turk. 149/B1
Dosewallips (riv.), Wa, US 193/A2
Dōshi, Japan 135/C2
Dōshi (riv.), Japan 135/C2
Dosso, Niger 161/F3
Dosso (dept.), Niger 161/F3
Dosson, It. 117/F1
Dossor, Kaz. 121/K3
Dot Lake, Ak, US 192/K3
Dothan, Al, US 191/G4
Dötlingen, Ger. 109/G3
Döttingen, Swi. 115/E2
Douai, Fr. 110/C3
Douala, Camr. 154/G7
Douar el Cãid el Gueddara, Mor. 158/A2
Douar Toulal, Mor. 158/B3
Douarnenez, Fr. 100/A2
Douarnenez, Baie de (bay), Fr. 100/A2
Double Island (pt.), Austl. 172/D4
Double Mountain Fork Brazos (riv.), Tx, US 187/G4
Doubs (riv.), Fr. 100/F3
Doubs (dept.), Fr. 114/C3
Doubs, Fr. 114/C4
Doubtful Island (bay), Austl. 170/C5
Douchy-les-Mines, Fr. 110/C3
Doue, Fr. 88/M5
Doué-la-Fontaine, Fr. 100/D3
Douentza, Mali 160/E3
Dougga (ruin), Tun. 158/L6
Douglas, SAfr. 164/C3
Douglas (cap.), IM, UK 92/C3
Douglas, Sc, UK 94/C5
Douglas (mt.), Ak, US 192/H4
Douglas (co.), Co, US 195/C4
Douglas, Ga, US 191/H4
Douglas, Wy, US 185/G5
Douglassville, Pa, US 196/C3
Doulaincourt-Saucourt, Fr. 114/B1
Doullens, Fr. 110/B3
Doune, Sc, UK 94/B4
Doune (peak), Sc, UK 94/B4
Doupovské Hory (mts.), Czh. 101/K1
Dour, Belg. 110/C3
Dourados, Braz. 209/H8
Dourdan, Fr. 88/J6
Dourdou (riv.), Fr. 100/E4
Douro (riv.), Port. 102/B2
Dousman, Wi, US 193/P13
Doussard, Fr. 114/C6
Douvaine, Fr. 114/C5
Douvrin, Fr. 110/B2
Doux (riv.), Fr. 100/F4
Douze (riv.), Fr. 100/C4
Dove Creek, Co, US 186/E3
Dover, Austl. 173/C4
Dover (pt.), Austl. 170/C5
Dover, Eng, UK 91/H4
Dover (cap.), De, US 196/C5
Dover, NJ, US 196/D2
Dover, Pa, US 196/B4
Dover-Foxcroft, Me, US 189/G2
Dover, Strait of (str.), Fr., UK 91/H5
Dovrefjell NP, Nor. 95/D3
Dow, Il, US 195/G7
Dowerin, Austl. 170/B4
Dowlatãbãd, Iran 147/G3
Down (dist.), NI, UK 92/C3
Downers Grove, Il, US 193/P16
Downey, Ca, US 194/F8
Downieville, Ca, US 186/B3
Downingtown, Pa, US 196/C4

Downpatrick, NI, UK 92/C3
Doylestown, Pa, US 196/C3
Dözen (isl.), Japan 132/C3
Dozois (res.), Qu, Can. 188/E2
Drāa (cape), Mor. 156/C3
Drāa, Oued (riv.), Mor. 156/C3
Drac (riv.), Fr. 100/F4
Dracena, Braz. 213/B2
Drachten, Neth. 108/D2
Drăgănești-Olt, Rom. 107/G3
Dragoman, Bul. 105/H1
Dragon's Mouth (str.), Trin.,Ven. 211/F2
Draguignan, Fr. 101/G5
Drake (passg.) 215/C8
Drake, Co, US 195/B2
Drake (passg.), SAm. 217/D8
Drakensberg (mts.), SAfr. 164/D3
Dráma, Gre. 105/J2
Drammen, Nor. 96/D2
Drance (riv.), Swi. 114/D5
Drancy, Fr. 88/K5
Drangedal, Nor. 96/C2
Dransfeld, Ger. 109/G5
Draper, Ut, US 195/K12
Drau (riv.), Aus. 101/K3
Drâva (riv.), Slov. 101/L3
Drava (riv.), Slov. 101/L3
Draveil, Fr. 88/K5
Drawa (riv.), Pol. 99/H2
Drawieński NP, Pol. 99/H2
Drawsko Pomorskie, Pol. 99/H2
Drayton, ND, US 185/J3
Drayton Valley, Ab, Can. 184/E2
Dreghorn, Sc, UK 94/B5
Drei Zinnen (peak), PNG 139/K4
Dreieselsberg (peak), Ger. 113/G5
Dreisam (riv.), Ger. 114/D2
Drensteinfurt, Ger. 109/E5
Drenthe (prov.), Neth. 108/D3
Drentse Hoofdvaart (riv.), Neth. 108/D3
Drentwede, Ger. 109/F3
Dresano, It. 116/C2
Dresden, Ger. 99/G3
Drezdenko, Pol. 99/H2
Driebergen, Neth. 108/C4
Driedorf, Ger. 111/H2
Drigh Road, Pak. 147/J4
Drimoleague, Ire. 89/P11
Drina (riv.), Bosn., Serb. 106/D4
Drini (gulf), Alb. 105/F2
Drini (riv.), Alb. 105/F1
Drniš, Cro. 106/C4
Dro, It. 115/G6
Drøbak, Nor. 96/D2
Drobeta-Turnu Severin, Rom. 106/F3
Drochtersen, Ger. 109/G1
Drocourt, Fr. 88/H4
Drogheda, Ire. 92/B4
Drohobych, Ukr. 120/B2
Droitwich, Eng, UK 90/D2
Drolshagen, Ger. 111/G1
Dromiskin, Ire. 92/B4
Dromore (riv.), Ire. 92/A3
Dromore, NI, UK 92/B3
Dronero, It. 101/G4
Dronfield, Eng, UK 93/G5
Drongan, Sc, UK 94/B6
Dronne (riv.), Fr. 100/D4
Dronten, Neth. 108/C3
Dropt (riv.), Fr. 100/D4
Drouetien (riv.), Fr. 110/A6
Drowning (riv.), On, Can. 188/C1
Drumbeg, NI, UK 92/C2
Drumcar, Ire. 92/B4
Drumheller, Ab, Can. 184/E3
Drumleck (pt.), Ire. 92/B5
Drummond (range), Austl. 167/D3
Drummond (pt.), Austl. 171/G5
Drummond (mt.), Austl. 172/B4
Drummondville, Qu, Can. 189/F2
Drumochter, Pass of (pass), Sc, UK 94/B3
Drunen, Neth. 108/C5
Druridge (bay), Eng, UK 93/G1
Drusenheim, Fr. 111/G6
Druskininkai, Lith. 97/K4
Druten, Neth. 108/C5
Drvar, Bosn. 106/C3
Drweca (riv.), Pol. 99/K2
Dry Fork Cheyenne (riv.), Wy, US 187/F2
Dry Tortugas (isl.), Fl, US 191/H5
Dry Tortugas NP, Fl, US 191/H5
Dryanovo, Bul. 105/J1
Dryden, On, Can. 185/K3
Dryden, Tx, US 190/C4
Dryden, Mi, US 193/H6
Drygarn Fawr (peak), Wal, UK 90/C2
Du Bois, Pa, US 188/E3

Du Page (co.), Il, US 193/P16
Du Page (riv.), Il, US 193/P16
Du Page, East Br. (riv.), Il, US 193/P16
Du Quoin, Il, US 187/K3
Duaringa, Austl. 172/C3
Duarte (peak), DRep. 199/G4
Duarte, Ca, US 194/G7
Dubawnt (riv.), NW, Can. 180/F2
Dubawnt (lake), Nun., Can. 180/F2
Dubayy, UAE 147/G3
Dubbo, Austl. 173/D2
Dublin (cap.), Ire. 92/B5
Dublin (co.), Ire. 92/B5
Dublin, Ca, US 193/L11
Dublin, Ga, US 191/H3
Dublin, Md, US 196/B4
Dublin, Tx, US 190/D3
Dubna, Rus. 118/H4
Dubnica nad Váhom, Slvk. 99/K4
Dubno, Ukr. 120/C2
Dubois, Wy, US 184/F5
Duboistown, Pa, US 196/A1
Dubossary (res.), Mol. 107/J2
Dubrãjpur, India 143/F4
Dubrovnik, Cro. 105/F1
Dubrovnik (int'l arpt.), Cro. 105/F1
Dubuque, Ia, US 185/L5
Duchang, China 137/C2
Duchcov, Czh. 113/G1
Duchesne, Ut, US 186/E2
Duchesne (riv.), Ut, US 186/E2
Ducie (isl.), Pitc. 175/N7
Duck (riv.), Tn, US 188/C5
Duck (lake), Mi, US 193/E7
Duckabush (riv.), Wa, US 193/A2
Duda (riv.), Col. 210/C4
Duddon (riv.), Eng, UK 93/E3
Dudelange, Lux. 111/F5
Dudenhofen, Ger. 112/B4
Duderstadt, Ger. 109/H5
Dudh Kosi (riv.), Nepal 143/F2
Dudhi, India 142/D3
Dudhwa NP, India 142/C1
Dudignac, Arg. 216/E2
Dudinka, Rus. 122/J3
Dudley, Eng, UK 90/D1
Dudley (co.), Eng, UK 90/D2
Dueñas, Sp. 102/C2
Duero (riv.), Sp. 102/C2
Dueville, It. 117/E1
Dufaja (riv.), Kenya 162/C3
Duff (isls.), Sol. 174/F5
Duffel, Belg. 111/D1
Dufftown, Sc, UK 94/C2
Dufour (Dufourspitze) (peak), Swi. 116/A1
Dufourspitze (peak), Swi. 101/G4
Dugi Otok (isl.), Cro. 106/B3
Dugny-sur-Meuse, Fr. 111/E5
Dugo Selo, Cro. 106/C3
Dugway, Ut, US 186/D2
Duich (lake), Sc, UK 94/A2
Duida (peak), Ven. 211/E4
Duida Marahuaca, PN, Ven. 208/E3
Duingen, Ger. 109/G4
Duisburg, Ger. 108/D6
Duitama, Col. 210/C3
Duiven, Neth. 108/D5
Duke of Gloucester (isls.), FrPol. 175/L7
Duke's (pass), Sc, UK 94/B4
Dukielska (Dukla Pass) (pass), Pol. 99/L4
Dulan, China 128/G4
Dulce (riv.), Arg. 215/D2
Dulce, NM, US 186/F3
Dulce (gulf), Pan. 203/F4
Dulce Nombre de Culmí, Hon. 203/E3
Dülgopol, Bul. 107/H4
Dülmen, Ger. 109/E5
Duluth, MN, US 185/H3
Dulovo, Bul. 107/H4
Dulqula, Sudan 159/C5
Dumaguete, Phil. 137/D6
Dumai, Indo. 138/B4
Dumaran (isl.), Phil. 139/E1
Dumaresq (riv.), Austl. 173/D1
Dumas, Ar, US 187/K4
Dumas, Tx, US 187/F4
Dumbarton, Sc, UK 94/B5
Dúmbier (peak), Slvk. 99/K4
Dumbleyung, Austl. 170/B5
Dumbrãveni, Rom. 107/G2
Dume (pt.), Ca, US 194/B2
Dūrã, WBnk. 149/D4

Dumfries, Sc, UK 92/E1
Dumfries and Galloway (pol. reg.), Sc, UK 94/C6
Dumka, India 143/F3
Dumlu, Turk. 121/G4
Dumoine (riv.), Qu, Can. 188/E2
Dumoine (lake), Qu, Can. 187/H4
Dumont, NJ, US 197/K8
Dumont d'Urville, Fr., Ant. 218/K
Dumraon, India 143/E3
Dún Laoghaire, Ire. 92/B5
Dumyãt (gov.), Egypt 159/N7
Dun Rig (peak), Sc, UK 94/C5
Dunaföldvár, Hun. 106/D2
Dunaharaszti, Hun. 107/R10
Dunajec (riv.), Pol. 99/L4
Dunakeszi, Hun. 107/R9
Dunany (riv.), Ire. 92/B4
Dunaszekcso, Hun. 106/D2
Dunaújváros, Hun. 106/D2
Dunavecse, Hun. 106/D2
Dunavtsi, Bul. 106/F4
Dunbar, Sc, UK 94/D5
Dunblane, Sc, UK 94/C4
Dunboyne, Ire. 92/B5
Duncan, BC, Can. 184/C3
Duncan, Ok, US 187/H4
Duncannon, Pa, US 196/A3
Duncansby Head (pt.), Sc, UK 89/V14
Duncanville, Tx, US 190/D3
Dunchurch, On, Can. 189/P2
Dundalk (bay), Ire. 89/Q10
Dundalk, Md, US 196/B5
Dundalk, Ire. 92/B4
Dundas (lake, Austl.) 167/B4
Dundas, On, Can. 189/D9
Dundas (pen.), NW, Can. 181/R7
Dundee, SAfr. 165/E3
Dundee (pol. reg.), Sc, UK 94/D4
Dundee, Sc, UK 94/D4
Dundgovi (prov.), Mong. 128/J2
Dundo, Ang. 99/J3
Dundonald, Sc, UK 94/B5
Dundrum, NI, UK 92/C3
Dundrum (bay), NI, UK 92/C3
Dundurn, Sk, Can. 184/G3
Dundwa (range), Nepal 142/D2
Dunedin, Fl, US 191/H4
Dunedin, NZ 175/S12
Dunedoo, Austl. 173/D2
Düzce, Turk. 107/K5
Düzici, Turk. 148/D2
Dunfanaghy, Ire. 89/O9
Dunfermline, Sc, UK 94/C4
Dunga Bunga, Pak. 144/B5
Dungannon, NI, UK 92/B3
Dungannon (co.), NI, US 92/B3
Dungarpur, India 147/K4
Dungarvan, Ire. 89/Q10
Dungau (reg.), Ger. 113/F5
Dungeness (pt.) 91/G5
Dungeness (pt.), Arg. 217/C7
Dungiven, NI, UK 92/B2
Dunglow, Ire. 89/P9
Dungog, Austl. 173/D2
Dungu, D.R. Congo 162/A2
Dungu (riv.), D.R. Congo 162/A2
Dunhua, China 129/N3
Dunhuang, China 128/F3
Dunkeld, Sc, UK 94/C3
Dunkerque (Dunkirk), Fr. 100/E1
Dunkery (hill), Eng, UK 90/C4
Dunkirk (Dunkerque), Fr. 100/E1
Dunkirk, NY, US 188/E3
Dunkwa, Gha. 161/E5
Dunlap, In, US 193/G5
Dunloy, NI, UK 92/B2
Dunmanway, Ire. 89/P11
Dunmurry, NI, UK 92/B3
Dunn, NC, US 191/J3
Dunnamanagh, NI, UK 92/A2
Dunnet Head (pt.), Sc, UK 89/V14
Dunningen, Ger. 115/E1
Dunnville, On, Can. 189/Q10
Dunolly, Austl. 173/B3
Dunoon, Sc, UK 94/B5
Dunnula, Sudan 159/C5
Duns, Sc, UK 94/D5
Dunsborough, Austl. 170/B5
Dunshaughlin, Ire. 92/B4
Dunsmuir, Ca, US 186/B2
Dunstable, Eng, UK 91/F3
Dunster, Eng, UK 90/C4
Dunure, Sc, UK 94/B6
Dunvegan, Sc, UK 89/V14
Duolun, China 129/L3
Dupo, Il, US 195/G8
Dupree, SD, US 185/H4
Dupuy (cape), Austl. 170/B2

Durağan, Turk. 148/C1
Durak, Turk. 149/D1
Durance (riv.), Fr. 100/F5
Durango (state), Mex. 198/A3
Durango, Sp. 102/D1
Durango de Victoria, Mex. 200/D3
Durant, Ok, US 181/J4
Durazno (dept.), Uru. 217/E2
Durazno, Uru. 217/K10
Durban, SAfr. 165/E3
Durbanville, SAfr. 164/L10
Durbion (riv.), Fr. 114/C1
Durbuy, Belg. 111/E3
Dúrcal, Sp. 102/D4
Durdevac, Cro. 106/C2
Durdevo, Serb. 106/E3
Düren, Ger. 111/F2
Durg, India 140/D3
Durgãpur, India 143/F4
Durham, NH, US 189/G3
Durham, NC, US 191/J3
Durham, Eng, UK 93/G2
Durham (co.), Eng, UK 93/F2
Durlston (pt.), Eng, UK 90/E5
Durmitor NP, Mont. 106/D4
Durnford (pt.), Wa, US 184/C4
Dürrenroth, Swi. 114/D3
Durrës, Alb. 105/F2
Dürrlauingen, Ger. 112/D6
Dürrwangen, Ger. 112/D4
Dursunbey, Turk. 148/B2
Durüz (peak), Syria 149/E3
D'Urville (cape), Indo. 139/J4
Dusanovac, Kos. 106/E4
Dusey (riv.), On, Can. 185/M3
Dushan, China 137/B2
Dushanbe (cap.), Taj. 145/E5
Dushanbe (int'l arpt.), Taj. 145/E5
Düsseldorf (int'l arpt.), Ger. 108/D6
Düsseldorf, Ger. 108/D6
Dutch (riv.), Eng, UK 93/H4
Dutch Harbor, Ak, US 192/E5
Dutch Wonderland, Pa, US 196/B3
Dutoitspiek (peak), SAfr. 164/L10
Dutse, Nga. 161/H4
Dutywa, SAfr. 164/C4
Dve Mogili, Bul. 107/G4
Dvina (riv.), Rus. 118/H2
Dvořiště (lake), Czh. 113/H4
Dwãrka, India 147/J4
Dwãrkeswar (riv.), India 143/F4
Dworshak (res.), Id, US 184/D4
Dwyer (riv.), SAfr. 164/C4
Dwyfor (riv.), Wal, UK 92/D2
Dyat'kovo, Rus. 120/E1
Dybvad, Den. 96/D3
Dyce (int'l arpt.), Sc, UK 94/D2
Dyce, Sc, UK 94/D2
Dye, Nu, US 195/D5
Dyer (cape), Nun., Can. 181/K2
Dyer (cape), Chile 217/B6
Dyer, In, US 188/C3
Dyersburg, Tn, US 188/C4
Dyersville, Ia, US 185/L5
Dyje (riv.), Czh. 99/J4
Dykh-tau (peak), Rus. 121/G4
Dyle (riv.), Belg. 98/C3
Dyleń (peak), Czh. 113/F3
Dylewska (peak), Pol. 99/K2
Dysart, Austl. 172/C3
Dysselsdorp, SAfr. 164/C4
Dyul'tydag (peak), Rus. 121/H4
Dzaoudzi (cap.), May. 165/H6
Dzaoudzi (int'l arpt.), May. 165/H6
Dzavhan (prov.), Mong. 128/G2
Dzavhan (riv.), Mong. 128/G2
Dzerzhinsk, Rus. 118/J4
Dzhankoy, Ukr. 120/E3
Dzharylgach (gulf), Ukr. 107/L2
Dzhebel, Bul. 105/H2
Dzhugdzhur (range), Rus. 125/N4
Działdowo, Pol. 99/L2
Dzierżoniów, Pol. 99/J3
Dzitbalché, Mex. 202/D1
Dziuché, Mex. 202/D2
Dzükija NP, Lith. 97/L4
Dzüünbayan, Mong. 129/K3
Dzüünbulag, Mong. 129/K2

Dzüünharaa, Mong. 128/J2
Dzuunmod, Mong. 128/J2

E

Eads, Co, US 187/G3
Eagle (riv.), Nf, Can. 181/L3
Eagle (lake), On, Can. 188/A1
Eagle, Ak, US 192/K3
Eagle (lake), Ca, US 184/C5
Eagle, Co, US 186/F3
Eagle (mtn.), Mn, US 185/L4
Eagle Butte, SD, US 185/H4
Eagle Pass, Tx, US 190/C4
Eagle River, Wi, US 185/L4
Eaglesham, Sc, UK 94/B5
Ealing (bor.), Eng, UK 88/B2
Ear Falls, On, Can. 185/K3
Earl's Seat (peak), Sc, UK 94/B4
Earle Naval Weapons Center, NJ, US 196/D3
Earlimart, Ca, US 186/C4
Earlston, Sc, UK 94/D5
Earn (riv.), Sc, UK 94/C4
Earn (lake), Sc, UK 94/B4
Easley, SC, US 191/H3
East (mt.), Austl. 170/D4
East (cape), NZ 175/T10
East (cape), Ak, US 192/C3
East (cape), Ak, US 192/K3
East (riv.), NY, US 197/K8
East (passg.), Wa, US 193/C3
East Alton, Il, US 195/G8
East Anglia (reg.), Eng, UK 91/H2
East Angus, Qu, Can. 189/G2
East Ayrshire (pol. reg.), Sc, UK 94/B6
East Bangor, Pa, US 196/C2
East Berbice-Corentyne (pol. reg.), Guy. 211/G3
East Berlin, Pa, US 196/B4
East Berwick, Pa, US 196/B1
East Brunswick, NJ, US 197/H10
East Canyon (res.), Ut, US 195/K12
East Carondelet, Il, US 195/G8
East China (sea), Asia 125/M6
East Dart (riv.), Eng, UK 90/C5
East Dereham, Eng, UK 91/G1
East Dunbartonshire (pol. reg.), Sc, UK 94/B5
East Falkland (isl.), UK 217/F7
East Farmingdale, NY, US 197/M9
East Frisian (isls.), Ger. 98/D2
East Glen (riv.), Eng, UK 93/H6
East Greenville, Pa, US 196/C3
East Grinstead, Eng, UK 91/F4
East Hampton, NY, US 197/F2
East Haven, Ct, US 197/F1
East Helena, Mt, US 184/F4
East Hill-Meridian, Wa, US 193/C3
East Hills, NY, US 197/L8
East Jordan, Mi, US 188/C2
East Kilbride, Sc, UK 94/B5
East Lamma (chan.), China 129/U11
East Lansing, Mi, US 188/C3
East Leavenworth, Mo, US 195/D5
East Linton, Sc, UK 94/D5
East Liverpool, Oh, US 188/D3
East London, SAfr. 164/D4
East Los Angeles, Ca, US 194/F7
East Lothian (pol. reg.), Sc, UK 94/D5
East Lynne, Mo, US 195/E6
East Meadow, NY, US 197/L9
East Midlands (int'l arpt.), Eng, UK 93/G6
East Millcreek, Ut, US 195/K12
East Millinocket, Me, US 189/G2
East Newark, NJ, US 197/J9
East Nishnabotna (riv.), Ia, US 185/J5
East Northport, NY, US 197/F2
East Orange, NJ, US 197/J8
East Peckham, Eng, UK 88/C5
East Petersburg, Pa, US 196/B3

East Point, Ga, US 191/G3
East Pointe (East Detroit), Mi, US 193/G4
East Port Orchard, Wa, US 193/B2
East Prospect, Pa, US 196/B4
East Quogue, NY, US 197/F2
East Renfrewshire (pol. reg.), Sc, UK 94/B5
East Retford, Eng, UK 93/H4
East Riding of Yorkshire (co.), Eng, UK 93/H4
East Rockaway, NY, US 197/L9
East Rutherford, NJ, US 197/J8
East Saint Louis, Il, US 195/G8
East Side, Pa, US 196/C1
East Siberian (sea), Rus. 123/S2
East Stroudsburg, Pa, US 196/C2
East Sussex (co.), Eng, UK 91/G5
East Tawas, Mi, US 188/D2
East Timor (ctry.) 139/G5
East Troy, Wi, US 193/P14
East Wemyss, Sc, UK 94/C4
East Wenatchee, Wa, US 184/C4
East Windsor, NJ, US 196/D3
Eastbourne, Eng, UK 91/G5
Eastern (plain), Eng, UK 93/H4
Eastern (pol. reg.), Gha. 161/E5
Eastern (chan.), Japan 132/A4
Eastern (prov.), SLeo. 160/C4
Eastern (bay), Md, US 196/B6
Eastern (prov.), Zam. 162/B3
Eastern Ghats (mts.), India 196/C2
Eastern Neck Island NWR, Md, US 196/B5
Eastern Sayans (mts.), Rus. 122/K4
Easterville, Mb, Can. 185/J2
Eastlake, Co, US 195/C3
Eastleigh (int'l arpt.), Eng, UK 91/E5
Eastleigh, Eng, UK 91/E5
Eastmain (riv.), Qu, Can. 181/J3
Eastman, Ga, US 191/H3
Easton, Ct, US 197/E1
Easton, Pa, US 196/C2
Easton, Md, US 196/B6
Eastport, Me, US 189/H2
Eastport, NY, US 197/F2
Eastriggs, Sc, UK 93/E2
Eastwood, Eng, UK 93/G6
Eaton, Co, US 195/C1
Eatonia, Sk, Can. 184/F3
Eatons Neck (pt.), NY, US 197/M8
Eatontown, NJ, US 196/D3
Eau (riv.), Eng, UK 93/H5
Eau Claire (lake), Qu, Can. 181/J3
Eau d'Heure (riv.), Belg. 111/D3
Eau d'Heure, Barrage de l' (dam), Belg. 111/D3
Eaubonne, Fr. 88/J5
Eaulne (riv.), Fr. 110/A4
Eauripik (isl.), Micr. 174/D4
Eauze, Fr. 100/D5
Ebano, Mex. 202/B1
Ebble (riv.), Eng, UK 91/E4
Ebbw Vale, Wal, UK 90/C3
Ebebiyín, EqG. 154/H7
Ebeggi (well), Alg. 157/H5
Ebeleben, Ger. 109/H6
Ebeltoft, Den. 96/D3
Ebensee, Aus. 101/K3
Eberbach, Ger. 112/B4
Ebergassing, Aus. 107/P7
Ebergötzen, Ger. 109/H5
Ebermannstadt, Ger. 112/E3
Ebern, Ger. 112/D2
Ebersbach an der Fils, Ger. 112/C5
Ebersberg, Ger. 113/E6
Eberschwang, Aus. 113/F6
Ebersheim, Fr. 114/D1
Eberswalde-Finow, Ger. 99/G2
Ebetsu, Japan 134/B2
Ebian, China 141/H2
Ebina, Japan 135/C2
Ebnat-Kappel, Swi. 115/F3
Eboli, It. 104/D2
Ebolowa, Camr. 154/H7
Ebonyi (state), Nga. 161/H5
Ebrach, Ger. 112/D3
Ebro (riv.), Sp. 103/F2
Ebstorf, Ger. 109/H2
Ecatepec, Mex. 201/Q9
Ecclefechan, Sc, UK 93/E1
Eccles, Eng, UK 93/F5
Eceabat, Turk. 107/H5
Echallens, Swi. 114/C4
Echarate, Peru 214/C4
Echaz (riv.), Ger. 112/C6
Eché Fadadinga (riv.), Niger 161/H3

Echigawa, Japan 135/K5
Eching, Ger. 113/E6
Échirolles, Fr. 100/F4
Echo (lake), NJ, US 196/D1
Echo, Ut, US 195/L12
Echoing (riv.), Mb,On, Can. 185/L2
Echt, Neth. 111/E1
Echterdingen (int'l arpt.), Ger. 112/C5
Echternach, Lux. 111/F4
Echuca, Austl. 173/C3
Echunga, Austl. 171/M9
Echzell, Ger. 112/B2
Écija, Sp. 102/C4
Ečka, Serb. 106/E3
Eckernförde, Ger. 96/C4
Eckerö (isl.), Fin. 97/H1
Eckerö, Fin. 97/H1
Eclipse Sound (bay), Nun., Can. 181/H1
Écommoy, Fr. 100/D3
Ecoporanga, Braz. 212/B5
Ecorse (riv.), Mi, US 193/F7
Ecorse, Mi, US 193/F7
Écouen, Fr. 88/K4
Ecquevilly, Fr. 88/H5
Ecrins, PN des, Fr. 101/G4
Écrosnes, Fr. 88/H6
Écrouves, Fr. 111/E6
Ecuador (ctry.) 208/C4
Ecublens, Swi. 114/C4
Ed, Swe. 96/D2
Eday (isl.), Sc, UK 89/V14
Eddystone (pt.), Austl. 173/D4
Eddystone Rocks (isls.), Eng, UK 90/B6
Ede, Nga. 161/G5
Ede, Neth. 108/C4
Edéa, Camr. 154/H7
Edegem, Belg. 111/D1
Edehin Ouarene (des.), Alg. 157/G4
Edéia, Braz. 213/B1
Edelény, Hun. 99/L4
Edemissen, Ger. 109/H4
Eden, Austl. 173/D3
Eden (riv.), Sc, UK 94/D4
Eden, NC, US 188/E4
Eden, Ut, US 195/K11
Edenbridge, Eng, UK 88/D3
Edenburg, SAfr. 164/D3
Edendale, SAfr. 165/E3
Edenhope, Austl. 173/B3
Edenkoben, Ger. 112/B4
Edenside (valley), Eng, UK 93/F2
Edenton, NC, US 191/J2
Eder (riv.), Ger. 98/E3
Eder-Stausee (lake), Ger. 109/F6
Edewecht, Ger. 109/E2
Edgar (mt.), Austl. 170/D2
Edge (isl.), Sval. 218/E
Edgecumbe (cape), Ak, US 192/L4
Edgell (isl.), Nun., Can. 181/K2
Edgemere, Md, US 196/B5
Edgemont, Ut, US 195/K13
Edgerton, Wy, US 185/G5
Edgewater, Co, US 195/B3
Edgewater Park, NJ, US 196/D3
Edgewood, Pa, US 196/B2
Edgewood, Md, US 196/B5
Edgewood Arsenal, Md, US 196/B5
Edgewood-North Hill, Wa, US 193/C3
Édhessa, Gre. 105/H2
Edinboro, Pa, US 188/D3
Edinburg, Tx, US 190/D5
Edinburgh (cap.), Sc, UK 94/C5
Edinburgh (pol. reg.), Sc, UK 94/C5
Edirne (prov.), Turk. 107/H5
Edirne, Turk. 107/H5
Edison, NJ, US 197/H9
Edison International Field, Ca, US 194/G8
Edison Nat'l Hist. Site, NJ, US 197/J8
Edisto Island, SC, US 191/H3
Edisto, South Fork (riv.), SC, US 191/H3
Edithburgh, Austl. 171/H5
Édjérir (riv.), Mali 161/F2
Edmond, Ok, US 195/N14
Edmonds, Wa, US 184/C4
Edmonton (int'l arpt.), Ab, Can. 184/E2
Edmonton (cap.), Ab, Can. 184/E2
Edmund Kennedy NP, Austl. 172/B2
Edmundston, NB, Can. 189/G2
Edna, Tx, US 187/H5
Edna Bay, Ak, US 192/M4
Edo (state), Nga. 161/G5
Edo (riv.), Japan 135/D2
Edolo, It. 115/G5
Edosaki, Japan 135/E2
Edremit, Turk. 148/A2
Edremit (gulf), Gre.,Turk. 148/A2
Edsbyn, Swe. 96/F1
Edson, Ab, Can. 184/D2
Eduardo Castex, Arg. 216/D2
Edward (mt.), Austl. 171/F2
Edward (lake), D.R. Congo 162/A3
Edward River Aboriginal Community, Austl. 172/A1
Edward VII (pen.), Ant. 218/P
Edward VIII (bay), Ant. 218/D
Edwards (riv.), Il, US 187/K2
Edwards (plat.), Tx, US 187/G5
Edwardsville, Il, US 195/H8
Edwardsville, Ks, US 195/D5
Edwardsville, Pa, US 196/C1
Edzell, Sc, UK 94/D3
Edzná (ruin), Mex. 202/D2
Eek, Ak, US 192/F3
Eeklo, Belg. 110/C1
Eel (riv.), Ca, US 186/B3
Eelde-Paterswolde, Neth. 108/D2
Eem (riv.), Neth. 108/C4
Eemenes, Neth. 108/C4
Eems (Ems) (riv.), Ger., Neth 108/D2
Eemshaven (har.), Neth. 108/D2
Eemskanaal (riv.), Neth. 108/D2
Eersel, Neth. 108/C6
Efate (isl.), Van. 174/F6
Eferding, Aus. 113/H6
Effigy Mounds Nat'l Mon., Ia, US 185/L5
Effingham, Il, US 187/K3
Effingham, On, Can. 189/R9
Effon Alaiye, Nga. 161/G5
Effort, Pa, US 196/C2
Eforie, Rom. 107/J3
Efringen-Kirchen, Ger. 114/D2
Efyrnwy, Llyn (lake), Wal, UK 92/E6
Egadi (isls.), It. 104/B3
Egan (range), Nv, US 186/D3
Egan (riv.), Ger. 112/D5
Egaña, Uru. 217/K10
Egegik, Ak, US 192/G4
Eger (riv.), Ger. 98/G3
Eger, Hun. 99/L5
Egeskov, Den. 96/D4
Egestorf, Ger. 109/H2
Egg, Aus. 115/F3
Egg, Swi. 115/E3
Egg Harbor City, NJ, US 196/D4
Egg Island (pt.), NJ, US 196/C5
Eggebek, Ger. 96/C4
Eggegebirge (ridge), Ger. 109/F5
Eggelsberg, Aus. 113/F6
Eggenburg, Aus. 101/L2
Eggenfelden, Ger. 113/F6
Eggenstein-Leopoldshafen, Ger. 112/B4
Eggesin, Ger. 96/F5
Eggiwil, Swi. 114/D4
Egglescliffe, Eng, UK 93/G3
Eggstätt, Ger. 113/F7
Egham, Eng, UK 88/B2
Eghezée, Belg. 111/D2
Egilsstadhir, Ice. 95/P6
Egletons, Fr. 100/E4
Eglinton (isl.), NW, Can. 181/R7
Eglinton, NI, UK 92/A1
Eglisau, Swi. 115/E2
Egly, Fr. 88/J6
Egmond aan Zee, Neth. 108/B3
Egmont (cape), NZ 175/S10
Egmont (mt.), NZ 175/S10
Egna (Neumarkt), It. 115/H5
Egnach, Swi. 115/F2
Eğridir, Turk. 148/B2
Eğridir (lake), Turk. 148/B2
Éguas, Rio das (riv.), Braz. 212/A4
Egypt (ctry.) 155/L2
Ehebach (riv.), Ger. 112/D3
Ehekirchen, Ger. 112/D5
Ehime (pref.), Japan 132/C4
Ehingen, Ger. 115/F1
Ehingen, Ger. 112/D4
Ehringshausen, Ger. 112/B1
Ehrwald, Aus. 115/G3
Eibar, Sp. 102/D1
Eibelstadt, Ger. 112/C3
Eibenstock, Ger. 113/F1
Eibergen, Neth. 108/D4
Eich, Ger. 112/B3
Eichel (riv.), Fr. 111/G6
Eichenau, Ger. 112/E6
Eichenbühl, Ger. 112/C3
Eichendorf, Ger. 113/F5
Eichenzell, Ger. 112/C2
Eichstätt, Ger. 112/E5
Eichwalde, Ger. 98/Q7
Eicklingen, Ger. 109/H3
Eid, Nor. 95/C3
Eidfjord, Nor. 96/B1
Eidsvold, Austl. 172/C4
Eidsvoll, Nor. 96/D1
Eifel (plat.), Ger. 98/D3
Eiffel Tower, Fr. 88/J5
Eigenji, Japan 135/K5
Eiger (peak), Swi. 114/D4
Eigersund, Nor. 96/A2
Eigg (isl.), Sc, UK 89/Q8
Eight Degree (chan.), India,Mald. 140/B6
Eijerlandse Gat (chan.), Neth. 108/B2
Eijsden, Neth. 111/E2
Eikelandsosen, Nor. 96/A1
Eil, Loch (inlet), Sc, UK 94/A3
Eildon (lake), Austl. 173/C3
Eildon, Austl. 173/C3
Eilerts de Haan (mts.), Sur. 211/G4
Einbeck, Ger. 109/G5
Eindhoven (int'l arpt.), Neth. 108/C6
Eindhoven, Neth. 108/C6
Einsiedeln, Swi. 115/E3
Einville-au-Jard, Fr. 111/F6
Eirunepé, Braz. 214/D2
Eisch (riv.), Lux. 111/E4
Eisenach, Ger. 109/H7
Eisenberg, Ger. 112/B3
Eisenhower Nat'l Hist. Site, Pa, US 196/A4
Eisenhüttenstadt, Ger. 99/H2
Eiserfeld, Ger. 111/G2
Eisfeld, Ger. 112/D2
Eisingen, Ger. 112/C3
Eislingen, Ger. 112/C5
Eitelborn, Ger. 111/G3
Eiter (riv.), Ger. 109/F3
Eitorf, Ger. 111/G2
Eitting, Ger. 113/E6
Ejea de los Caballeros, Sp. 103/E1
Ejeda, Madg. 165/H9
Ejido, Ven. 210/D2
Ejin Horo Qi, China 130/B3
Ejin Qi, China 128/H3
Ejutla de Crespo, Mex. 202/B2
Ekeby, Swe. 96/E3
Ekenäs (Tammisaari), Fin. 97/K2
Ekeren, Belg. 108/B6
Ekhínos, Gre. 105/J2
Ekibastuz, Kaz. 145/G2
Eksjö, Swe. 96/F3
Ekuk, Ak, US 192/G4
Ekwan (riv.), On, Can. 181/H3
Ekwok, Ak, US 192/G4
El Aaiún, WSah. 156/B4
El Aatf (reg.), WSah. 156/B5
El Abiodh Sidi Chrikh, Alg. 157/F2
El 'Açâba (mass.), Mrta. 160/C2
El Affroun, Alg. 158/G4
El Águila, Mex. 190/B5
El Aïoun, Mor. 158/C2
El Alto, Peru 214/A2
El Amparo de Apure, Ven. 210/D3
El Anegado, Ecu. 210/A5
El Aouinet, Alg. 158/K7
El Arahal, Sp. 102/C4
El Arhlaf (well), Mrta. 160/D2
El Astillero, Sp. 102/D1
El Bagre, Col. 210/C3
El Banco, Col. 210/C2
El Barco, Sp. 102/B1
El Barco de Ávila, Sp. 102/C2
El Baúl, Ven. 210/D2
El Bayadh (prov.), Alg. 157/F2
El Bayadh, Alg. 157/F2
El Bolsón, Arg. 216/C4
El Bonillo, Sp. 102/D3
El Borouj, Mor. 156/D2
El Burgo de Osma, Sp. 102/D2
El Cajon, Ca, US 194/D5
El Cajón (res.), Hon. 202/E3
El Calafate, Arg. 217/B6
El Callao, Ven. 211/F3
El Capitan (peak), Mt, US 184/E4
El Carmen, Chile 216/B3
El Carmen, Col. 210/B3
El Carmen, Peru 214/B4
El Carmen de Bolívar, Col. 210/C2
El Casar de Talamanca, Sp. 103/N8
El Centro, Ca, US 186/D4
El Cerrito, Col. 210/B4
El Cerrito, Ca, US 193/K11
El Cerro del Aripo (peak), Trin. 211/F2
El Cerrón (peak), Ven. 210/D2
El Chico, PN, Mex. 201/L6
El Cocuy, Col. 210/C3
El Cocuy, PN, Col. 208/D2
El Colorado, Arg. 215/E2
El Difícil, Col. 210/C2
El Djouf (des.), Mrta. 154/D3
El Dorado, Mex. 200/D3
El Dorado, Ar, US 187/J4
El Dorado, Ks, US 187/H3
El Dorado, Ven. 211/F3
El Eglab (plat.), Alg. 154/D2
El Empedrado, Ven. 210/D2
El Escorial, Sp. 103/M8
El Espinar, Sp. 102/C2
El Eulma, Alg. 158/H4
El Fahs, Tun. 158/L6
El Ferrol, Sp. 102/A1
El Fuerte, Mex. 200/C3
El Fureidîs, Isr. 149/F6
El Gogorrón, PN, Mex. 198/A3
El Golea, Alg. 157/F3
El Golfete (lake), Guat. 202/D3
El Granada, Ca, US 193/K11
El Grullo, Mex. 200/D5
El Guachara, PN, Ven. 211/F2
El Hajeb, Mor. 158/B3
El Hank (cliff), Mali 156/D4
El Harino, Pan. 210/A2
El Harta (well), Alg. 157/E4
El Higo, Mex. 202/B1
El Indio, Tx, US 190/C4
El Jadida, Mor. 156/C2
El Jem, Tun. 158/M7
El Kelaâ des Srarhna, Mor. 156/D2
El Khatt (cliff), Mrta. 154/C3
El Khatt (depr.), Mrta. 160/C2
El Khnâchîch (cliff), Mali 156/E5
El Kroub, Alg. 158/K6
El Kseur, Alg. 158/H4
El Libertador General Bernardo O'Higgins (pol. reg.), Chile 216/N8
El Limón, Mex. 201/F4
El Mahia (phys. reg.), Mali 157/E5
El Maitén, Arg. 216/C4
El Malpais Nat'l Mon., NM, US 186/F4
El Manteco, Ven. 211/F3
El-Menzel, Mor. 158/B3
El Miamo, Ven. 211/F3
El Milia, Alg. 158/J4
El Mirage, Az, US 195/R18
El Mirage, Ca, US 194/C1
El Montcau (peak), Sp. 103/K6
El Monte, Ca, US 194/F7
El Morrito (pt.), Chile 216/C1
El Mrâyer (well), Mrta. 156/C5
El Mreyyé (phys. reg.), Mrta. 160/C2
El Mzereb (well), Mali 156/D4
El Naranjo de Carlos Sarabia, Mex. 201/F4
El Nayar, Mex. 200/D4
El Nevado (peak), Arg. 216/C2
El Nido, Phil. 139/E1
El Olivar Alto, Chile 216/N9
El Oro (prov.), Ecu. 214/A1
El Oued (prov.), Alg. 157/G2
El Oued, Alg. 157/G2
El Palmar, Ven. 211/F3
El Pao, Ven. 211/F2
El Pao, Ven. 211/E2
El Paraíso, Mex. 201/E5
El Paraíso, Hon. 202/E3
El Paso, Tx, US 186/F5
El Paso International (int'l arpt.), Tx, US 187/F5
El Pilar, Ven. 211/F2
El Porvenir, Mex. 200/D2
El Porvenir, Pan. 210/B2
El Potosí, Mex. 201/E3
El Potosí, PN, Mex. 198/B3
El Prat de Llobregat, Sp. 103/L7
El Progreso, Ecu. 214/F7
El Progreso, Guat. 202/D3
El Progreso, Hon. 202/E3
El Progreso Industrial, Mex. 201/Q9
El Puerto de Santa María, Sp. 102/B4
El Quelite, Mex. 200/D4
El Quisco, Chile 216/N8
El Rama, Nic. 203/E3
El Rancho, Co, US 195/B3
El Reno, Ok, US 187/H4
El Rio, Ca, US 194/A2
El Roble, Pan. 210/A2
El Rosario de Arriba, Mex. 200/B2
El Sacromonte, PN, Mex. 201/L7
El Salto, Mex. 200/D4
El Salvador (ctry.) 202/D3
El Salvador, Mex. 201/E3
El Salvador, Cuba 203/H1
El Salvador (int'l arpt.), ESal. 202/D3
El Samán de Apure, Ven. 210/D3
El Sauz, Mex. 200/D2
El Sauzal, Mex. 200/A2
El Segundo, Ca, US 194/F8
El Shab (well), Egypt 159/B4
El Tabo, Chile 216/N8
El Tajín (ruin), Mex. 201/M6
El Tama, PN, Ven. 210/C3
El Tambo, Ecu. 210/B5
El Tarf (prov.), Alg. 158/K6
El Tarf, Alg. 158/L6
El Teleno (peak), Sp. 102/B1
El Tepozteco, PN, Mex. 201/R10
El Tiemblo, Sp. 102/C2
El Tigre, Ven. 211/E2
El Tocuyo, Ven. 210/D2
El Toro, Ca, US 194/C3
El Triunfo, Ecu. 210/B5
El Triunfo, Mex. 202/D2
El Tucuche (peak), Trin. 211/F2
El Tuito, Mex. 200/D4
El Tuparro, PN, Col. 208/E3
El Valle, Pan. 210/A2
El Venado (isl.), Nic. 203/F4
El Viejo (peak), Col. 210/C3
El Viejo, Nic. 202/E3
El Vigía, Ven. 210/D2
El Yagual, Ven. 210/D3
El Yunque (peak), PR 199/M8
El Zacatón, Mex. 200/E4
Elan (riv.), Wal, UK 90/C2
Elancourt, Fr. 88/H5
Elandsrivier (riv.), SAfr. 164/Q12
Elassón, Gre. 105/H3
Elat (int'l arpt.), Isr. 149/D5
Elat, Isr. 149/D5
Elátia, Gre. 105/H3
Elato (isl.), Micr. 174/D4
Elazığ, Turk. 148/D2
Elazig (prov.), Turk. 148/D2
Elba, Al, US 191/G4
Elba (isl.), It. 101/H5
Elbasan, Alb. 105/G2
Elbbach (riv.), Ger. 111/G2
Elbe (riv.), Ger. 98/F2
Elbe (Labe) (riv.), Czh.,Ger. 99/H2
Elbe-Seitenkanaal (canal), Ger. 109/H2
Elbert (co.), Co, US 195/C4
Elberton, Ga, US 191/H3
Elbeuf, Fr. 100/D2
Elbigenalp, Aus. 115/G3
Elbląg, Pol. 97/H4
Elbow, Sk, Can. 184/G3
El'brus (peak), Rus. 121/G4
Elburg, Neth. 108/C4
Elburn, Il, US 193/N16
Elburz (mts.), Iran 146/E1
Elche, Sp. 103/E3
Elche de la Sierra, Sp. 102/D3
Elchingen, Ger. 112/D6
Elcho (isl.), Austl. 167/C2
Eld (inlet), Wa, US 193/A3
Elda, Sp. 103/E3
Elde (riv.), Ger. 98/G2
Eldersburg, Md, US 196/B5
Eldivan, Turk. 148/C1
Eldon, Wa, US 193/A2
Eldora, Co, US 195/A3
Eldora, NJ, US 196/D5
Eldorado, Arg. 215/F2
Eldorado, Tx, US 187/G5
Eldorado Springs, Co, US 195/B3
Eldoret, Kenya 162/B2
Eleao (peak), Hi, US 182/W13
Elefsís, Gre. 105/H3
Elek, Hun. 106/E2
Elektrostal', Rus. 119/X9
Elena, Arg. 216/D2
Elesbão Veloso, Braz. 212/B2
Eleşkirt, Turk. 148/E2
Eleuthera (isl.), Bahm. 199/F2
Eleven Point (riv.), Mo, US 187/K3
Elevsís (ruin), Gre. 105/N8
Elevtheroúpolis, Gre. 105/J2
Elfershausen, Ger. 112/C2
Elgg, Swi. 115/E3
Elgin, ND, US 185/H4
Elgin, Il, US 185/L5
Elgin, Tx, US 187/H5
Elgin, Sc, UK 94/C1
Elgóibar, Sp. 102/D1
Elgon (Wagagai) (peak), Ugan. 162/B2
Elida, NM, US 190/C3
Elim, Ak, US 192/F3
Elimäki, Fin. 97/M1
Elista, Rus. 121/H3
Elixhausen, Aus. 113/G7
Elizabeth (bay), Namb. 164/A2
Elizabeth, NJ, US 197/J9
Elizabeth City, NC, US 191/J2
Elizabethan Village Hist. Site, Austl. 170/L7
Elizabethton, Tn, US 188/D4
Elizabethtown, Pa, US 196/B3
Elizabethville, Pa, US 196/B2
Elk (mts.), Co, US 190/B2
Elk (riv.), WV, US 191/H2
Ełk, Pol. 97/K5
Elk City, Ok, US 187/H4
Elk Grove, Ca, US 193/M10
Elk Grove Village, Il, US 193/P16
Elk Island NP, Ab, Can. 184/E2
Elk Mills, Md, US 196/C4
Elk Point, Ab, Can. 184/F2
Elk Rapids, Mi, US 188/C2
Elk Ridge, Md, US 196/B5
Elk River, Mn, US 185/K4
Elk Slough (riv.), Ca, US 193/L10
Elkenroth, Ger. 111/G2
Elkhart, In, US 188/C3
Elkhart, Ks, US 187/G3
Elkhart, Tx, US 187/J5
Elkhorn, Mb, Can. 185/H3
Elkhorn, Wi, US 188/B3
Elkhorn (riv.), Ne, US 185/H2
Elkhovo, Bul. 105/K1
Elkin, NC, US 188/D4
Elko, Nv, US 184/E5
Elkton, Md, US 196/C4
Ellamar, Ak, US 192/J3
Elland, Eng, UK 93/G4
Elle (riv.), Ger. 111/F2
Ellef Ringnes (isl.), Nun., Can. 181/R7
Ellefeld, Ger. 113/F2
Ellen (riv.), Eng, UK 93/E2
Ellenberg, Ger. 112/D4
Ellendale, ND, US 185/J4
Ellendale, De, US 196/C6
Ellensburg, Wa, US 184/C4
Eller (riv.), Ger. 109/H5
Ellerbach (riv.), Ger. 111/G4
Ellero (riv.), It. 116/A4
Ellery (mt.), Austl. 173/D3
Ellesmere (isl.), Nun., Can. 181/S6
Ellesmere Port, Eng, UK 93/F5
Ellezelles, Belg. 110/C2
Ellice (riv.), Nun., Can. 180/F2
Ellicott City, Md, US 196/B5
Ellinikón (int'l arpt.), Gre. 105/N9
Elliot, SAfr. 164/D3
Elliot Lake, On, Can. 188/D2
Elliot Price Consv. Park, Austl. 171/H4
Elliott (peak), Va, US 191/J2
Ellis Island, NJ,NY, US 197/J9
Ellisras, SAfr. 163/E5
Elliston, Austl. 171/G5
Ellisville, Mo, US 195/F8
Ellon, Sc, UK 94/D2
Ellrich, Ger. 109/H5
Ellsworth (mts.), Ant. 218/U
Ellsworth, Ks, US 187/H3
Ellsworth, Me, US 189/G2
Ellsworth, Wi, US 188/A2
Ellsworth Land (phys. reg.), Ant. 218/U
Ellwangen, Ger. 112/D5
Elm, Swi. 115/F4
Elm Grove, Wi, US 193/P13
Elma, NY, US 189/S10
Elmadağ, Turk. 120/E5
Elmalı, Turk. 148/B2
Elmas (int'l arpt.), It. 104/A3
Elmendorf, Tx, US 195/U21
Elmer, NJ, US 196/C4
Elmhurst, Il, US 193/Q16
Elmina, Gha. 161/E5
Elmira, NY, US 188/E3
Elmont, NY, US 197/L9
Elmore, Austl. 173/C3
Elmsford, NY, US 197/K7
Elmshorn, Ger. 109/G1
Elmstein, Ger. 111/G5
Elmwood Park, Wi, US 193/Q14
Elmwood Park, NJ, US 197/J8
Elmwood Park, Il, US 193/Q16
Elne, Fr. 100/E5
Elói Mendes, Braz. 213/H6
Elorn (riv.), Fr. 100/A2
Elortondo, Arg. 216/E2
Elorza, Ven. 210/D3
Elouera Nat'l Rsv., Austl. 172/H8
Eloy, Az, US 186/E4
Eloy Alfaro, Ecu. 210/B5
Eloyes, Fr. 114/C1
Elpitiya, SrL. 140/D6
Elrose, Sk, Can. 184/F3
Elsa, Yk, Can. 192/L3
Elsa (riv.), It. 101/J5
Elsa, Embalse de (res.), Sp. 102/B2
Elsah, Il, US 195/G8
Elsdorf, Ger. 109/G2
Elsdorf, Ger. 111/F2
Else (riv.), Ger. 109/F4
Elsenfeld, Ger. 112/C3
Elsenz (riv.), Ger. 112/B4
Elsfleth, Ger. 109/F2
Elsinore (lake), Ca, US 194/C3
Elsmere, De, US 196/C4
Elst, Neth. 108/C5
Elstal, Ger. 98/Q6
Elstead, Eng, UK 91/F4
Elsterberg, Ger. 113/F1
Eltmann, Ger. 112/D3
El'ton (lake), Rus. 121/H2
Eltville am Rhein, Ger. 112/B2
Elūru, India 140/D4
Elvanlı, Turk. 149/D1
Elvas, Port. 102/B3
Elverum, Nor. 96/D1
Elvire (riv.), Austl. 170/C2
Elvo (riv.), It. 116/B2
Elwell (lake), Mt, US 184/F3
Elwood, In, US 188/C3
Elwood-Magnolia, NJ, US 196/D4
Elwy (riv.), Wal, UK 92/E5
Ely, Nv, US 186/D3
Ely, Eng, UK 91/G2
Elyaqim, Isr. 149/G6
Elyashiv, Isr. 149/F7
Elyria, Oh, US 188/D3
Elysburg, Pa, US 196/B2
Elysian Park, Ca, US 194/F7
Elz (riv.), Ger. 112/B6
Elz, Ger. 112/B2
Elzach, Ger. 114/E1
Elzbach (riv.), Ger. 111/G3
Elze, Ger. 109/G4
Emajõgi (riv.), Est. 97/M2
Emāmshahr (Shāhrūd), Iran 147/F1
Emån (riv.), Swe. 96/F3
Emancé, Fr. 88/H6
Emas, PN das, Braz. 209/H7
Emba (riv.), Kaz. 120/K3
Embarcación, Arg. 215/D1
Embarras (riv.), Il, US 191/F2
Embi, Kaz. 121/L2
Embi (riv.), Kaz. 122/F5
Embira (riv.), Braz. 208/D5
Emborcação, Barragem de (res.), Braz. 213/C1
Embrach, Swi. 115/E3
Embrun, Fr. 101/G4
Embsen, Ger. 109/H2
Embu, Kenya 162/C3
Emden, Ger. 109/E2
Emeishan, China 141/H2
Emerald, Austl. 172/C3
Emerald, Austl. 173/G5
Emerson, Mb, Can. 185/J3
Emerson, NJ, US 197/J8
Emeryville, Ca, US 193/K11
Emet, Turk. 148/B2
Emigsville, Pa, US 196/B3
Emilia-Romagna (pol. reg.), It. 101/J4
Emiliano Zapata, Mex. 202/D2
Emin, China 128/D2
Emīnābād, Pak. 144/C3
Eminence, Mo, US 187/K3
Emir Pasha (gulf), Tanz. 162/A3
Emirdağ, Turk. 148/B2
Emirgazi, Turk. 148/C2
Emlembe (peak), Swaz. 165/E2
Emlichheim, Ger. 108/D3
Emma (riv.), Sur. 211/H4
Emmaboda, Swe. 96/F3
Emmanuel Head (pt.), Eng, UK 94/E5
Emmaus, Pa, US 196/C2
Emme (riv.), Swi. 114/D4
Emmeloord, Neth. 108/C3
Emmen, Neth. 108/D3
Emmendingen, Ger. 114/D1
Emmental (valley), Swi. 114/D3
Emmer (riv.), Ger. 109/G4
Emmerbach (riv.), Ger. 109/E5
Emmerich, Ger. 108/D5
Emmett, Mi, US 193/G6
Emmingen-Liptingen, Ger. 115/E2
Emmitsburg, Md, US 196/A4
Emmonak, Ak, US 192/F3
Emneth, Eng, UK 91/G1
Emőd, Hun. 106/E2
Emory, Tx, US 187/J4
Emosson (lake), Swi. 114/C5
Empalme, Mex. 200/C3
Empangeni, SAfr. 165/E3
Empedrado, Arg. 215/E2
Empedrado, Chile 216/B2
Empoli, It. 117/D5
Emporia, Ks, US 187/H3
'Emrānī, Iran 147/G2
Ems (Eems) (riv.), Ger.,Neth. 108/D2
Ems-Jade (canal), Ger. 109/E2
Emsbüren, Ger. 109/E4
Emsdetten, Ger. 109/E4
Emskirchen, Ger. 112/D3
Emsland (reg.), Ger. 98/D2
Emstek, Ger. 109/F3
Emu Park, Austl. 172/C3
Emumägi (hill), Est. 97/M2
Emyvale, Ire. 92/B3
Ena, Japan 133/E3
Enbetsu, Japan 134/B1
Encantada, Cerro (peak), Mex. 200/B3
Encantada, Cerro de la (peak), Mex. 200/B2
Encarnación, Par. 215/E2
Encarnación de Díaz, Mex. 200/E4
Enchi, Gha. 160/E5
Encinitas, Ca, US 194/C4
Enciso, Col. 210/C3
Encontrados, Ven. 210/C2
Encounter (bay), Austl. 173/A2
Encruzilhada do Sul, Braz. 213/A4
Encs, Hun. 99/L4
Endau (peak), Kenya 162/C3
Ende, Indo. 139/F5
Endeavour River NP, Austl. 172/B1
Enderbury (isl.), Kiri. 175/H5
Enderby, BC, Can. 184/D3
Enderby Land (phys. reg.), Ant. 218/D
Enderlin, ND, US 185/J4
Endicott, NY, US 188/E3
Endingen, Ger. 114/D1
Ene (riv.), Peru 208/D6
Eneabba, Austl. 170/B4
Enebakk, Nor. 96/D2
Enewetak (isl.), Mrsh. 174/F3
Enez, Turk. 105/K2
Enfield (bor.), Eng, UK 88/C2
Engaño (cape), Phil. 137/D4
Engaru, Japan 134/C1
Engaruka (basin), Tanz. 162/B3
Engelberg, Swi. 115/E4
Engelhartszell, Aus. 113/G5
Engel's, Rus. 121/H2
Engelskirchen, Ger. 111/G2
Engelsmanplaat (isl.), Neth. 108/D2
Engen, Ger. 115/E2
Engenheiro Navarro, Braz. 212/B5
Engenheiro Paulo de Frontin, Braz. 213/K7
Enger, Ger. 109/F4
Engerwitzdorf, Aus. 113/H6
Enggano (isl.), Indo. 138/B5
Enghershatu (peak), Erit. 146/C5
Enghien, Belg. 110/D2
Engi, Swi. 115/F4
England, UK 90/D2
Englefontaine, Fr. 110/C3
Englehart, On, Can. 188/E2
Englewood, Co, US 195/C3
Englewood, NJ, US 197/K8
Englewood Cliffs, NJ, US 197/K8
English (riv.), On, Can. 185/K3
English (chan.), Fr.,UK 100/B2
English Bay, Ak, US 192/H4
English Bāzār, India 143/G3
English Creek, NJ, US 196/D5
Englishtown, NJ, US 196/D3
Enguera, Sp. 103/E3
Enguri (riv.), Geo. 121/G4
Enhtal, Mong. 128/J2
Enid, Ok, US 187/H3
Eniwa, Japan 134/B2
Enkenbach-Alsenborn, Ger. 111/G5
Enkhuizen, Neth. 108/C3
Enkirch, Ger. 111/G4
Enköping, Swe. 96/G2
Enna, It. 104/D4
Ennedi (plat.), Chad 155/K4
Ennepe (riv.), Ger. 109/E6
Ennepetal, Ger. 109/E6
Ennery, Fr. 88/J4
Enningerloh, Ger. 109/F5
Ennis, Mt, US 184/F4
Ennis, Tx, US 187/H4
Ennis, Ire. 89/P10
Enniscorthy, Ire. 89/Q10
Enniskerry, Ire. 92/B5
Enniskillen, NI, UK 89/Q9
Ennistimon, Ire. 89/P10
Enns, Aus. 113/H6
Enns (riv.), Aus. 99/H5
Enogger (res.), Austl. 172/E6
Enola, Pa, US 196/B3
Enontekiö, Fin. 95/G1
Enoree (riv.), SC, US 191/H3
Enping, China 141/K3
Enrick (riv.), Sc, UK 94/B2
Enrique Carbó, Arg. 217/J10
Enriquillo, DRep. 203/J2
Enschede, Neth. 108/D4
Ensdorf, Ger. 113/E4
Ense, Ger. 109/E5
Enseleni, SAfr. 165/F3
Ensenada, Mex. 200/A2
Ensenada, Arg. 217/K11
Enshi, China 137/A1
Ensisheim, Fr. 114/D2
Entebbe (int'l arpt.), Ugan. 162/B2
Entebbe, Ugan. 162/B2
Entenbühl (peak), Ger. 113/F3
Enterprise, Al, US 191/G4
Enterprise, Ut, US 195/K11
Entlebuch, Swi. 114/E4
Entre Ríos, Braz. 212/C3
Entre Ríos (mts.), Hon. 203/E3
Entroncamento, Port. 102/A3
Entzheim, Fr. 114/D1
Enugu, Nga. 161/G5
Enugu (state), Nga. 161/G5
Enumclaw, Wa, US 193/D3
Enshū (sea), Japan 135/M6
Envira, Braz. 214/D2
Enz (riv.), Ger. 101/H2
Enza (riv.), It. 116/D4
Enzan, Japan 133/F3
Enzbach (riv.), Ger. 111/F4
Enzersdorf an der Fischa, Aus. 107/P7
Enzklösterle, Ger. 112/B5
Epalinges, Swi. 114/C4
Epáno Arkhánai, Gre. 105/J5
Epanomí, Gre. 105/H2
Epe, Nga. 161/F5
Epe, Neth. 108/C4
Epehy, Fr. 110/C3
Epernay, Fr. 110/C5
Epfig, Fr. 114/D1
Ephrata, Pa, US 196/B3
Epi (isl.), Van. 174/F6
Epiais-Rhus, Fr. 88/J4

Epídhavros (Epidaurus) (ruin), Gre. 105/H4
Épinal, Fr. 114/C1
Épinay-sur-Orge, Fr. 88/J6
Épinay-sur-Seine, Fr. 88/J5
Epira, Guy. 211/G3
Epirus (reg.), Gre. 105/G3
Epône, Fr. 110/A6
Eppelborn, Ger. 111/F5
Eppelheim, Ger. 112/B4
Eppenbrunn, Ger. 111/G5
Eppeville, Fr. 110/C4
Epping (for.), Eng. UK 88/D2
Epping, Eng. UK 88/D1
Epping Forest NP, Austl. 172/B3
Eppingen, Ger. 112/B4
Eppishausen, Ger. 115/G1
Epsom, Eng. UK 88/C3
Epsom and Ewell, Eng, UK 91/F4
Epte (riv.), Fr. 110/A4
Equator (fall), Ecu. 210/A4
Equatorial Guinea (ctry.) 154/G7
Equihen-Plage, Fr. 110/A2
Er Rachidia, Mor. 156/D3
Er Reina, Isr. 149/G6
Er Rif (mts.), Mor. 154/D1
Era (riv.), It. 117/D6
Eraclea, It. 117/F1
Eraclea (ruin) It. 104/E2
Eraclea Minoa (ruin), It. 104/C4
Eragny, Fr. 88/J4
Erandique, Hon. 202/D3
Eravur, SrL. 140/D6
Erawan NP, Thai. 136/B3
Erba, It. 116/C1
Erbaa, Turk. 148/D1
Erbach, Ger. 112/B3
Erbendorf, Ger. 113/F3
Erbeskopf (peak), Ger. 111/G4
Ercan (int'l arpt.), Cyp. 149/C2
Erçek, Turk. 148/E2
Erçek (lake), Turk. 148/E2
Ercilla, Chile 216/B3
Erciş, Turk. 148/E2
Erciyes (peak), Turk. 148/C2
Erclin (riv.), Fr. 110/C3
Erd, Hun. 107/Q10
Erda, Ut, US 195/J12
Erdek (gulf), Turk. 107/H5
Erdek, Turk. 107/H5
Erdemli, Turk. 149/D1
Erdenet, Mong. 128/H2
Erdi-Ma (plat.), Chad 155/K4
Erding, Ger. 113/E6
Erdre (riv.), Fr. 100/C3
Erdweg, Ger. 112/E6
Erechim, Braz. 213/A3
Ereen Davaanï (mts.), Mong. 129/K2
Ereğli, Turk. 148/C2
Ereğli, Turk. 107/K5
Eremo di Camaldoli, It. 117/E5
Erenhaberga (mts.), China 128/D3
Erenhot, China 129/K3
Erenler, Turk. 107/K5
Erentepe, Turk. 148/E2
Erepecu, Lago do (lake), Braz. 209/G4
Eresma (riv.), Sp. 102/C2
Erétria, Gre. 105/H3
Ereymentaü, Kaz. 145/F2
Érezée, Belg. 111/E3
Erfa (riv.), Ger. 112/C3
Erfoud, Mor. 156/D3
Erft (riv.), Ger. 98/D3
Erftstadt, Ger. 111/F2
Erfurt, Ger. 98/F3
'Erg Chech (des.), Mali,Alg. 154/E3
'Erg Iguidi (des.), Alg.,Mrta. 156/D4
Ergene Nehri (riv.), Turk. 107/H5
Erguig (riv.), Chad 154/J5
Ergun Youqi, China 129/M1
Ergun Zuoqi, China 129/M1
Ericeira, Port. 103/P10
Ericht (lake), Sc, UK 94/B3
Ericht (riv.), Sc, UK 94/B3
Erickson, Mb, Can. 185/J3
Erickson, BC, Can. 184/D3
Erie (lake), Can.,US 188/D3
Erie, Co, US 195/B2
Erie (canal), NY, US 189/S9
Erie (,) NY, US 189/S10
Erie (int'l arpt.), Pa, US 188/D3
Eriksdale, Mb, Can. 185/J3
Eriksmalä, Swe. 96/F3
Erikub (isl.), Mrsh. 174/F4
Erimanthos (peak), Gre. 105/G4
Erimo, Japan 134/C2
Erimo-misaki (cape), Japan 134/C3
Erithraí, Gre. 105/H3
Eritrea (ctry.) 155/N5
Erkelenz, Ger. 111/F1
Erken (isl.), Swe. 97/H1
Erkheim, Ger. 115/G1
Erkner, Ger. 98/Q7
Erkrath, Ger. 108/D6
Erlach, Swi. 114/D3

Erlands Point-Kitsap Lake, Wa, US 193/B2
Erlangen, Ger. 112/E3
Erlau (riv.), Ger. 113/G5
Erlenbach (riv.), Ger. 112/B4
Erlenbach am Main, Ger. 112/C3
Erlenbach bei Marktheidenfeld, Ger. 112/C3
Erlenbach im Simmental, Swi. 114/D4
Erlinsbach, Swi. 114/E3
Erlongshan (res.), China 130/F2
Erme (riv.), Eng, UK 90/C6
Ermelo, SAfr. 165/E2
Ermelo, Neth. 108/C4
Ermenek (riv.), Turk. 149/C1
Ermenek, Turk. 149/C1
Ermenonville, Fr. 88/L4
Ermióni, Gre. 105/H4
Ermont, Fr. 88/J5
Ermoúpolis, Gre. 105/J4
Erms (riv.), Ger. 112/C6
Erndtebrück, Ger. 111/H2
Ernée (riv.), Fr. 100/C2
Ernée, Fr. 100/C2
Ernesto Cortissoz (int'l arpt.), Col. 210/C2
Ernsthofen, Aus. 113/H6
Erode, India 140/C5
Erolzheim, Ger. 115/G1
Erowal Bay, Austl. 173/D2
Erpel, Ger. 111/G2
Erquelinnes, Belg. 111/D3
Errigal (mtn.), Ire. 89/P9
Erris Head (pt.), Ire. 89/P9
Erro (riv.), It. 116/B4
Errochty (lake), Sc, UK 94/B3
Erromango (isl.), Van. 174/F6
Erse (riv.), Ger. 109/H4
Ersekë, Alb. 105/G2
Erstein, Fr. 114/D1
Erstfeld, Swi. 115/E4
Ertingen, Ger. 115/F1
Ertis (riv.), Kaz. 122/H4
Ertix (riv.), China 128/E2
Eruh, Turk. 148/E2
Eruwa, Nga. 161/F5
Erwin, Tn, US 188/B2
Erwitte, Ger. 109/F5
Eryuan, China 141/G2
Erzgebirge (Krušné Hory) (mts.), Czh.,Ger. 101/K1
Erzen (riv.), Alb. 105/F2
Erzhausen, Ger. 112/B3
Erzincan, Turk. 148/D2
Erzurum (prov.), Turk. 148/E1
Es Senia (int'l arpt.), Alg. 158/E5
Esan-misaki (cape), Japan 134/B3
Esashi, Japan 134/C1
Esashi, Japan 134/B2
Esashi, Japan 134/B4
Esbjerg, Den. 96/C4
Esbjerg (int'l arpt.), Den. 96/C4
Esbly, Fr. 88/L5
Esbo (Espoo), Fin. 97/L1
Escada, Braz. 212/D3
Escalante (riv.), Ut, US 186/E3
Escalón, Mex. 200/D3
Escalona, Sp. 102/C2
Escambia (riv.), Fl, US 191/G4
Escaudain, Fr. 110/C3
Escaut (riv.), Fr. 98/B3
Esch (riv.), Ger. 111/E6
Esch-sur-Alzette, Lux. 111/E4
Esch-sur-Sure, Lux. 111/E4
Eschach (riv.), Ger. 115/E1
Eschau, Fr. 114/D1
Eschborn, Ger. 112/B2
Eschede, Ger. 109/H3
Eschen, Lcht. 115/F3
Eschenbach, Ger. 112/C5
Eschenbach in der Oberpfalz, Ger. 113/E3
Eschershausen, Ger. 109/G5
Esches (riv.), Fr. 110/B5
Escholzmatt, Swi. 114/D4
Eschwege, Ger. 109/H6
Eschweiler, Ger. 111/F2
Escobedo (int'l arpt.), Mex. 201/K3
Escoma, Bol. 214/D4
Escondido, Ca, US 194/C4
Escuinapa de Hidalgo, Mex. 200/D4
Escuintla, Guat. 202/D3
Esdraelon, Plain of (plain), Isr. 149/G6
Eséka, Camr. 154/H7
Esenboga (int'l arpt.), Turk. 148/C1
Esence (peak), Turk. 148/D2
Esens, Ger. 109/F1
Esera (riv.), Sp. 103/F1
Eşfahān, Iran 146/F2
Esfandak, Iran 147/H3
Esgair Ddu (peak), Wal, UK 90/C1
Esha Ness (cape), Sc, UK 89/W13
Esher, Eng, UK 88/B2

Eshowe, SAfr. 165/E3
Esil, Kaz. 145/E2
Esil (riv.), Kaz. 145/E2
Esine, It. 115/G6
Esino (riv.), It. 117/G6
Esk (riv.), Eng, UK 93/E2
Eskdale (valley), Sc, UK 94/C6
Eskifjördhur, Ice. 95/Q6
Eskil, Turk. 148/C2
Eskilstuna, Swe. 96/G2
Eskimalatya, Turk. 148/D2
Eskimo (lakes), NW, Can. 180/C2
Eskipazar, Turk. 148/C1
Eskişehir, Turk. 148/B2
Eskişehir (prov.), Turk. 148/B2
Esla (riv.), Sp. 102/C1
Eslāmābād, Iran 146/E2
Eslohe, Ger. 109/F6
Eslöv, Swe. 96/E4
Esme, Turk. 148/B2
Esmeralda, Cuba 203/G1
Esmeraldas, Ecu. 210/B4
Esmeraldas (dept.), Ecu. 210/B4
Esneux, Belg. 111/E2
Espada (pt.), Col. 210/D1
Espalion, Fr. 100/E4
Española, NM, US 187/F4
Española, On, Can. 188/D2
Española (isl.), Ecu. 214/F7
Esparraguera, Sp. 103/K6
Esparta, Hon. 202/E3
Esparto, Ca, US 193/K9
Espejo, Sp. 102/C4
Espelkamp, Ger. 109/F4
Esperança, Braz. 212/D2
Esperance (bay), Austl. 170/D5
Esperance, Austl. 170/D5
Esperantina, Braz. 212/B1
Esperantinópolis, Braz. 212/A2
Esperanza, Arg., Ant. 218/W
Esperanza (inlet), BC, Can. 184/B3
Esperanza (mts.), Hon. 202/E3
Esperanza, Mex. 200/C3
Esperanza, Mex. 201/M8
Esperanza, Peru 214/D3
Espichel (cape), Port. 103/P11
Espinal, Mex. 201/M6
Espinal, Col. 210/C3
Espinar, Peru 214/D4
Espinhaço, Serra do (mts.), Braz. 209/K7
Espinho, Port. 102/A2
Espinosa, Braz. 212/B4
Espírito Santo (state), Braz. 213/D2
Espiritu Santo (isl.), Van. 174/F6
Espíritu Santo (bay), Mex. 202/E2
Espita, Mex. 202/D1
Esplanada, Braz. 212/C3
Espluga de Francolí, Sp. 103/E2
Espluges, Sp. 103/L7
Esposende, Port. 102/A2
Espungabera, Moz. 163/F5
Espy, Pa, US 196/B1
Esquel, Arg. 216/C4
Esquimalt, Mex. 200/C2
Esquipulas, Sp. 102/C2
Essaouira, Mor. 156/C3
Esse (riv.), Ger. 109/G5
Essen, Belg. 108/B6
Essen, Ger. 108/E6
Essen, Ger. 109/E3
Essenbach, Ger. 113/F5
Essendon (mt.), Austl. 170/D3
Essenheim, Ger. 111/H4
Essequibo (riv.), Guy. 205/D2
Essequibo Island-West Demerara (pol. reg.), Guy. 211/G3
Essex, On, Can. 193/G7
Essex (co.), Eng, UK 88/E1
Essex, Md, US 196/B5
Essex (co.), NJ, US 196/D2
Essex Fells, NJ, US 197/H8
Esslingen, Ger. 112/C5
Essômes-sur-Marne, Fr. 110/C5
Essonne (riv.), Fr. 100/C2
Est, Canal de l' (canal), Fr. 114/C2
Estaca de Bares, Punta de la (cape), Sp. 102/B1
Estación Santa Engracia, Mex. 201/F3
Estados, Isla de los (isl.), Arg. 215/D7
Eşṭahbān, Iran 146/F3
Estaires, Fr. 110/B2
Estats, Pico de (peak), Sp. 103/F1
Estavayer-le-Lac, Swi. 114/C4
Estcourt, SAfr. 165/E3
Este, It. 117/E2

Este, Punta del (pt.), Cuba 198/E3
Este Sudeste, Cayos del (isls.), Col. 203/F3
Esteio, Braz. 213/B4
Estelí, Nic. 202/E3
Estell Manor (Risley), NJ, US 196/D5
Estella, Sp. 102/D1
Estelle (mtn.), Ca, US 194/C3
Estelle, La, US 195/P17
Estepa, Sp. 102/C4
Estepona, Sp. 102/C4
Ester, Ak, US 192/J3
Esterhazy, Sk, Can. 185/H3
Esterias (cape), Gabon 154/G7
Esternay, Fr. 110/C6
Estero de Agiabampo (lag.), Mex. 200/C3
Estéron (riv.), Fr. 101/G5
Esterwegen, Ger. 109/E3
Estes Park, Co, US 195/A2
Estevan, Sk, Can. 185/H3
Estinnes-au-Mont, Belg. 111/D3
Eston, Sk, Can. 184/F3
Estonia (ctry.) 97/L2
Estoril, Port. 103/P10
Estral Beach, Mi, US 193/F8
Estrées-Saint-Denis, Fr. 110/B5
Estrela, Serra da (mts.), Port. 102/A3
Estrela, Serra da (peak), Port. 102/B2
Estrella (pt.), Mex. 200/B2
Estrelto, Serra do (range), Braz. 212/B3
Estremoz, Port. 102/B3
Estrondo, Serra do (mts.), Braz. 209/J5
Esztergom, Hun. 106/D2
Et Taiyiba, Isr. 149/G7
Et Tira, Isr. 149/F7
Etah, India 142/B2
Etain, Fr. 111/E5
Etal (isl.), Micr. 174/E4
Étalle, Belg. 111/E4
Étampes, Fr. 110/A2
Etāwah, India 142/B2
Etāwah Branch (riv.), India 142/B2
Etchojoa, Mex. 200/C3
Ethelbert, Mb, Can. 185/H3
Ethiopia (ctry.) 155/N5
Ethiopian (plat.), Eth. 155/N6
Eti (riv.), Japan 135/K5
Etili, Turk. 107/H6
Etival-Clairefontaine, Fr. 114/C1
Étive, Loch (inlet), Sc, UK 94/A4
Etna (peak), It. 104/D4
Etna, Monte (Mount Etna) (vol.), It. 104/D4
Etne, Nor. 96/A2
Etobicoke, Can. 189/Q8
Etolin (str.), Ak, US 192/E3
Etorofu (isl.), Rus. 129/S2
Etosha (salt pan), Namb. 163/C4
Etosha NP, Namb. 163/C4
Etowah, Ok, US 195/N15
Étrépilly, Fr. 88/L4
Etropole, Bul. 105/J1
Etroubles, It. 114/D6
Ettadhamen Douarhicher, Tun. 158/M6
Ettelbruck, Lux. 111/F4
Etten-Leur, Neth. 108/B5
Ettenheim, Ger. 114/D1
Etterbeek, Belg. 111/D2
Etters (Goldsboro), Pa, US 196/B3
Ettington, Ger. 112/B5
Ettrick Pen (peak), Sc, UK 94/C6
Ettrick Water (riv.), Sc, UK 94/C6
Ettringen, Ger. 115/G1
Eu, Fr. 110/A3
'Eua (isl.), Tonga 175/H7
Eubeanangee Swamp NP, Austl. 172/D2
Euclid, Oh, US 188/D3
Euclides da Cunha, Braz. 212/C3
Eudora, Ar, US 187/K4
Eudunda, Austl. 173/A2
Euerbach, Ger. 112/D2
Eufaula, Al, US 191/G4
Eufaula (lake), Ok, US 185/J4
Eugendorf, Aus. 113/G7
Eugene, Or, US 184/C4
Eugene O'Neill NHS, Ca, US 193/L11
Eugenia (pt.), Mex. 200/B3
Eugenia, Austl. 173/D2
Eungella NP, Austl. 172/C3
Eunice, La, US 187/J5
Eunice, NM, US 187/G4
Eupen, Belg. 111/F2
Euphrates (riv.), Iraq,Syria 148/E3
Eura, Fin. 97/K1
Eurajoki, Fin. 97/J1
Eure (riv.), Fr. 100/D2
Eure (dept.), Fr. 110/A5
Eure-et-Loir (dept.), Fr. 110/A6

Eureka (sound), Nun., Can. 181/S7
Eureka, Ca, US 184/B5
Eureka, Mo, US 195/F9
Eureka, Mt, US 184/E3
Eureka, Nv, US 186/D3
Eureka, SD, US 185/J4
Euroa, Austl. 173/C3
Eurodisney, Fr. 88/L5
Euron (riv.), Fr. 114/C1
Europa (pt.), Gib. 102/C4
Europabrücke, Aus. 115/H3
Europe (cont.) 27
Europoort, Neth. 108/B5
Euskirchen, Ger. 111/F2
Eussenheim, Ger. 112/C3
Eustis, Fl, US 191/H4
Euston, Austl. 173/B2
Eutin, Ger. 96/D4
Eutini, Malw. 162/B5
Euville, Fr. 111/E6
Eutsuk (lake), BC, Can. 184/B2
Evain, Qu, Can. 188/E1
Evans (mt.), Co, US 187/F3
Evans (lake), Qu, Can. 188/E1
Evans, Co, US 195/C2
Evans (str.), Nun., Can. 181/H2
Evans Head, Austl. 173/E1
Evanston, Wy, US 184/F5
Evanston, Il, US 188/C4
Evansville, In, US 188/C4
Evansville, Wy, US 187/F2
Evaporation (basin), Ut, US 184/E5
Evart, Mi, US 188/C3
Evaton, SAfr. 164/D2
Evaz, Iran 146/F3
Eve, Fr. 88/L4
Even Yehuda, Isr. 149/F7
Evenkiyskiy Aut. Okrug, Rus. 122/K3
Everard (cape), Austl. 173/D3
Everard (lake), Austl. 170/A1
Everard (mt.), Austl. 171/G3
Everest (peak), China,Nepal 140/E2
Everest (Sagarmatha) (mtn.), China,Nepal 143/F2
Everett, Wa, US 184/C4
Evergem, Belg. 110/C1
Everglades (swamp), Fl, US 191/H5
Everglades NP, Fl, US 191/H5
Evergreen, Al, US 191/G4
Evergreen, Co, US 195/B3
Evergreen Park, Il, US 193/Q16
Everswinkel, Ger. 109/E5
Evesham, Eng, UK 91/E2
Evesham, Vale of (valley), Eng, UK 90/D2
Évian-les-Bains, Fr. 114/C5
Évinos (riv.), Gre. 105/G3
Evje, Nor. 96/B2
Evolène, Swi. 114/D5
Évora, Port. 102/B3
Évora (dist.), Port. 102/A3
Évreux, Fr. 100/D2
Évron, Fr. 100/C2
Évrótas (riv.), Gre. 105/H4
Evry, Fr. 88/J6
Evvoia (gulf), Gre. 105/H3
Evvoia (isl.), Gre. 105/H3
Evxinoúpolis, Gre. 105/H3
Ewa Beach, Hi, US 182/V13
Ewa Villages, Hi, US 182/V13
Ewan, NJ, US 196/C4
Ewarton, Jam. 203/G2
Ewaso Ng'iro (riv.), Kenya 162/C2
Ewell, Eng, UK 88/C3
Ewing, NJ, US 196/D3
Exaplátanos, Gre. 105/H2
Excelsior Springs, Mo, US 195/E5
Excursion Inlet, Ak, US 192/L4
Exe (riv.), Eng, UK 90/C4
Exeter, NH, US 189/G3
Exmoor (upland), Eng, UK 90/C4
Exmoor NP, Eng, UK 90/C4
Exmouth, Austl. 170/A3
Exmouth, Eng, UK 90/C4
Exmouth (gulf), Austl. 170/B2
Exmouth (pen.), Austl. 173/A2
Extrema, Braz. 213/G7
Extremadura (reg.), Sp. 102/B3
Exu, Braz. 212/B2
Exuma (sound), Bahm. 199/F3
Eyak, Ak, US 192/J3
Eyasi (lake), Tanz. 163/F1
Eyb (riv.), Ger. 112/C5
Eydehamn, Nor. 96/C2
Eyemouth, Sc, UK 94/D5
Eyguières, Fr. 100/F5
Eyn Hemed (ruin) Isr. 149/G8
Eyre (pen.), Austl. 167/C4
Eyre North (lake), Austl. 167/C3
Eyre South (lake), Austl. 167/C3
Ézanville, Fr. 88/K4

Ezequiel Ramos Mexía (res.), Arg. 216/C3
Ezhou, China 137/B1
Ezine, Turk. 105/K3
Ezzane (well), Alg. 154/H3

F

F.E. Walter (res.), Pa, US 196/C1
Fabbrico, It. 117/D3
Fabens, Tx, US 190/B4
Fabero, Sp. 102/B1
Faches-Thumesnil, Fr. 110/C2
Facatativá, Col. 208/D3
Fabriano, It. 101/K5
Fada (lake), Sc, UK 94/A1
Fada-N'Gourma, Burk. 161/F3
Faenza, It. 117/E4
Fafa (riv.), CAfr. 155/J6
Fafe, Port. 102/A2
Fafen Shet' (riv.), Eth. 155/P6
Fägäraş, Rom. 107/G3
Fagersta, Swe. 96/F2
Faggiola (peak), It. 117/E4
Fagnano (lake), Arg. 217/D7
Fagnano Olona, It. 116/B1
Fagnières, Fr. 111/D6
Faguibine (lake), Mali 154/D4
Fahl (well), Alg. 157/F3
Fahrenzhausen, Ger. 113/E6
Faial (isl.), Azor. 103/S12
Faido, Swi. 115/E5
Failsworth, Eng, UK 93/F4
Fains-Véel, Fr. 111/E6
Fair Haven, Mi, US 193/G6
Fair Haven, Vt, US 188/F3
Fair Hill, Md, US 196/C4
Fair Lawn, NJ, US 197/J8
Fair Oaks, Ca, US 193/M9
Fairbanks, Ak, US 192/J3
Fairfax, Va, US 196/A6
Fairfax (co.), Va, US 196/A6
Fairfield, Ct, US 197/E1
Fairfield (co.), Ct, US 197/L7
Fairfield, Mt, US 184/F4
Fairfield, Pa, US 196/A4
Fairfield, Tx, US 187/H5
Fairfield, Ut, US 195/J13
Fairland, Md, US 196/B5
Fairlee, Md, US 196/B5
Fairlie, Sc, UK 94/B5
Fairmont, WV, US 188/D4
Fairmont City, Il, US 195/G8
Fairmount, Ks, US 195/U8
Fairplay, Co, US 190/B2
Fairton, NJ, US 196/C5
Fairview, NJ, US 197/K8
Fairview, Ok, US 187/H3
Fairview Heights, Il, US 195/G8
Fairway, Ks, US 195/D5
Fairweather (mt.), Ak, US 192/L4
Fairweather (cape), Ak, US 192/L4
Faisalābād, Pak. 144/B4
Faistós (ruin), Gre. 105/J5
Faizābād, India 142/D2
Fajardo, PR 199/M8
Fakahina (isl.), FrPol. 159/M6
Fakaofo (isl.), Tok. 175/J5
Fakarava (isl.), FrPol. 159/L6
Fako (peak), Camr. 154/G7
Fakse, Den. 96/E4
Fakse Ladeplads, Den. 96/E4
Faku, China 130/E2
Fal (riv.), Eng, UK 90/B6
Fālākāta, India 143/G2
Falāmah, WBnk. 149/G7
Fálanna, Gre. 105/H3
Falcon (riv.), Mex.,US 190/D5
Falcon (cape), Alg. 158/D2
Falcón (state), Ven. 210/D2
Falconara Marittima, It. 117/G5
Falémé (riv.), Mali 154/C5
Falfurrias, Tx, US 190/D5
Falher, Ab, Can. 184/D2
Falkenberg, Swe. 96/E3
Falkensee, Ger. 98/Q6
Falkenstein, Ger. 113/G6
Falkenstein, Ger. 113/G4
Falkirk, Sc, UK 94/C5
Falkirk (pol. reg.), Sc, UK 94/C5
Falkland, Sc, UK 94/C4
Falkland Sound (str.), UK 217/E7
Falköping, Swe. 96/E2
Fall City, Wa, US 193/D2
Fall River, Ma, US 189/G3
Fallbrook, Ca, US 194/C4
Fallere (peak), It. 114/D6

Falling Spring, Il, US 195/G8
Fallingbostel, Ger. 109/G3
Fallis, Ok, US 195/N14
Fallon, Nv, US 186/C3
Falls Church, Va, US 196/A6
Fallston, Md, US 196/B4
Falmouth, Anti. 199/N8
Falmouth, Eng, UK 90/A6
Falmouth (bay), Eng, UK 90/A6
False Pass, Ak, US 192/F5
Falshöft (pt.), Ger. 96/C4
Falso (cape), Hon. 203/F3
Falso, Cabo (cape), Mex. 200/C4
Falso Cabo de Hornos (cape), Chile 217/C7
Falster (isl.), Den. 95/E5
Falterona (peak), It. 117/E5
Fălticeni, Rom. 107/H2
Falun, Swe. 96/F1
Famagusta (bay), Cyp. 149/C2
Famagusta (dist.), Cyp. 149/C2
Famagusta, Cyp. 149/C2
Fameck, Fr. 111/F5
Famenne (reg.), Belg. 111/E3
Fammau, Moel (peak), Wal, UK 93/E5
Fan Si Pan (peak), Viet. 141/H3
Fana, Nor. 96/A1
Fanchang, China 130/D5
Fandriana, Madg. 165/H8
Fang Xian, China 130/B4
Fangatau (isl.), FrPol. 159/L6
Fangataufa (isl.), FrPol. 159/L7
Fangcheng, China 130/C4
Fangcheng Gezu Zizhixian, China 141/J3
Fangshan, China 130/B3
Fanjing (peak), China 141/J2
Fannich (lake), Sc, UK 94/A1
Fanning (Tabuaeran) (isl.), Kiri. 159/K4
Fano (isl.), Den. 96/C4
Fano, It. 117/G5
Fanø (isl.), Den. 96/C4
Fanshi, China 130/C3
Fanwood, NJ, US 197/H9
Faradje, D.R. Congo 162/A2
Farafangana, Madg. 165/H8
Farāfirah, Wāḥāt al (oasis), Egypt 159/A3
Farāh, Afg. 147/H2
Farāh (riv.), Afg. 147/H2
Farallon (isls.), Ca, US 186/B3
Farallon de Medinilla (isl.), NMar. 174/D3
Farallon de Pajaros (isl.), NMar. 174/D2
Farallones de Cali, PN, Col. 208/C3
Faranah (pol. reg.), Gui. 160/C4
Faranah, Gui. 160/C4
Farángi Samariás NP, Gre. 105/H5
Faraony (riv.), Madg. 165/H8
Faraulep (isl.), Micr. 174/D4
Farciennes, Belg. 111/D3
Fareham, Eng, UK 91/E5
Faremoutiers, Fr. 110/C6
Farewell, Ak, US 192/H3
Farewell (cape), NZ 159/E5
Färgelanda, Swe. 96/D2
Farghona (pol. reg.), Uzb. 145/F4
Farghona, Uzb. 145/F4
Faribault, Mn, US 185/K4
Farīdābād, India 144/C5
Farīdkot, India 144/C4
Farīdpur, Bang. 143/G4
Farīdpur (pol. reg.), Bang. 143/G4
Farīdpur, India 142/C2
Färiskür, Egypt 149/B4
Färjestaden, Swe. 96/G3
Farkadhón, Gre. 105/H3
Farkasgyepű, Hun. 106/C2
Farley, Mo, US 195/D5
Farmers, Co, US 195/C2
Farmingdale, NJ, US 196/D3
Farmingdale, NY, US 197/M9
Farmington, De, US 196/C5
Farmington, Me, US 189/G2
Farmington, Mo, US 187/K3
Farmington, NM, US 186/E3
Farmington, Ut, US 195/K12
Farmington Hills, Mi, US 193/E6
Farnborough, Eng, UK 91/F4
Farnham, Eng, UK 88/B2
Farnham Royal, Eng, UK 88/B2
Farnworth, Eng, UK 93/F4
Faro, Yk, Can. 192/M3
Faro (int'l arpt.), Port. 102/B4
Faro, Port. 102/B4
Faro (dist.), Port. 102/A4
Faro, PN du, Camr. 154/H6
Faroe (isls.), Den. 218/G2
Fáron (isl.), Swe. 97/H3
Fårösund, Swe. 97/H3

Farquhar (cape), Austl. 170/B2
Farr West, Ut, US 195/J11
Farroupilha, Braz. 213/B4
Farrukhābād, India 142/B2
Fársala, Gre. 105/H3
Farsø, Den. 96/B4
Farson, Wy, US 184/F5
Farsund, Nor. 96/B2
Fartak, Ras (pt.), Yem. 146/F5
Farwell, Tx, US 187/G4
Fasā, Iran 146/F3
Fasano, It. 105/E2
Faşikan (pass), Turk. 149/C1
Fassberg, Ger. 109/H3
Fast Castle (pt.), Sc, UK 94/D5
Fastiv, Ukr. 120/D2
Fatagar Tuting (cape), Indo. 139/H4
Fatahjang, Pak. 144/A3
Fatehābād, India 144/C5
Fatehpur, India 142/C2
Fatehpur, India 142/B2
Fatehpur, India 147/K3
Fatick (pol. reg.), Sen. 160/A3
Fatick, Sen. 160/A3
Fátima, Port. 102/A3
Fatsa, Turk. 148/D1
Fatu Hiva (isl.), FrPol. 159/M6
Faucille, Col de la (pass), Fr. 114/C5
Faucilles (mts.), Fr. 98/C4
Faughan (riv.), NI, UK 92/A2
Fauglia, It. 116/D5
Fauldhouse, Sc, UK 94/C5
Faulkton, SD, US 185/J4
Faulquemont, Fr. 111/F5
Faure (isl.), Austl. 170/B3
Fäurei, Rom. 107/H3
Fauske, Nor. 95/E2
Faust, Ut, US 195/J13
Fauvillers, Belg. 111/E4
Faux, Tête de (peak), Fr. 114/D1
Favalto (peak), It. 117/F6
Favara, It. 104/C4
Fave (riv.), Fr. 114/C1
Faverges, Fr. 114/C6
Faverney, Fr. 114/C2
Faversham, Eng, UK 91/G4
Favignana, It. 104/C4
Favara Novarese, It. 116/B1
Favria, It. 116/A2
Favrieux, Fr. 88/G5
Fawn (riv.), On, Can. 185/L2
Fawn Grove, Pa, US 196/B4
Faxaflói (bay), Ice. 95/M7
Faxinal, Braz. 213/B2
Faya-Largeau, Chad 155/J4
Fayette, Al, US 191/G3
Fayette, Ms, US 187/K5
Fayetteville, Tn, US 191/G3
Fayetteville, Ga, US 191/G3
Fayetteville, NC, US 191/J3
Fayl-la-Forêt, Fr. 114/B2
Fazao, Monts du (mts.), Togo 161/F4
Fazao, PN du, Togo 161/F4
Fdérik, Mrta. 156/B5
Feale (riv.), Ire. 89/P10
Fear (cape), NC, US 191/J3
Feasterville-Trevose, Pa, US 196/D3
Feather (riv.), Ca, US 186/B3
Featherstone, Eng, UK 93/G4
Fécamp, Fr. 100/D2
Fecht (riv.), Fr. 114/D1
Federal Hall Nat'l Mem., NY, US 197/K9
Federal Heights, Co, US 195/B3
Federally Admin. Tribal Areas, Pak. 144/A2
Federsee (lake), Ger. 112/C6
Fedje, Nor. 96/A1
Feeny, NI, US 92/A2
Fegersheim, Fr. 112/A6
Fehérgyarmat, Hun. 106/F2
Fehmarn (isl.), Den. 96/D4
Fehmarn Belt (str.), Den. 98/F1
Fei Huang (riv.), China 130/D4
Fei Xian, China 130/D4
Feia, Lagoa (lake), Braz. 213/D2
Feicheng, China 130/D3
Feidong, China 130/D5
Feignies, Fr. 110/C3
Feijó, Braz. 214/D2
Feilans, It. 114/A5
Feira, Port. 102/A2
Feira de Santana, Braz. 212/C4
Feistritz (riv.), Aus. 113/H6
Feixi, China 130/D5
Feixian, China 130/D3
Fejér (co.), Hun. 106/D2
Fejø (isl.), Ger. 96/D4
Feketić, Serb. 106/D3
Felanitx, Sp. 103/G3
Feldafing, Ger. 115/H2
Feldberg (peak), Ger. 114/E2
Feldbach, Aus. 115/F3
Feldkirchen an der Donau, Aus. 113/H6
Feldkirchen bei Graz, Aus. 106/B2

Feldkirchen in Kärnten, Aus. 101/L3
Feletto, It. 116/D2
Feletto Umberto, It. 117/C2
Felino, It. 116/D3
Felipe Carillo Puerto, Mex. 202/D2
Felixdorf, Aus. 106/C2
Felixlândia, Braz. 213/C1
Felixstowe, Eng, UK 91/H3
Felizzano, It. 116/B3
Fell, Ger. 111/F4
Fellbach, Ger. 112/C5
Felling, Eng, UK 93/G2
Felsberg, Ger. 109/G6
Felsberg, Swi. 115/F4
Felton, Pa, US 196/B4
Felton, De, US 196/C5
Fema (peak), It. 101/K5
Femø (isl.), Den. 96/D4
Femundsmarka NP, Nor. 95/D3
Fénay, Fr. 114/B3
Fene, Sp. 102/A1
Fener (pt.), Turk. 149/D1
Fénérive, Madg. 163/K10
Feng Xian, China 130/C1
Fengári (peak), Gre. 105/J2
Fengcheng, China 129/L6
Fengcheng, China 131/C2
Fenghuang, China 141/F2
Fengle (riv.), China 130/D5
Fengnan, China 130/C2
Fengning, China 130/D2
Fengqing, China 141/G3
Fengqiu, China 130/C4
Fengrun, China 130/D2
Fengshan, Tai. 137/D3
Fengtai, China 130/H7
Fengxian, China 130/D4
Fengyang, China 130/D4
Fengyüan, Tai. 137/D3
Fengzhen, China 130/C1
Fenimore Pass (chan.), Ak, US 192/C3
Fenoarivo Atsinanana, Madg. 165/J7
Fens (phys. reg.), Eng, UK 91/G1
Fensmark, Den. 96/D4
Fensterbach (riv.), Ger. 113/F4
Fenton, Mi, US 188/D3
Fenton, Mo, US 195/G8
Fenton (lake), Mi, US 193/E7
Fenxi, China 130/B3
Feodosiya, Ukr. 120/E3
Fer, Cap de (cape), Alg. 158/K6
Ferbane, Ire. 89/Q10
Ferdinandshof, Ger. 99/G2
Fère-Champenoise, Fr. 110/C6
Fère-en-Tardenois, Fr. 110/C5
Ferento (ruin), It. 104/C2
Fergus Falls, Mn, US 185/J4
Ferguson, Mo, US 195/G8
Ferguson (lake), Nun., Can. 180/F2
Ferihegy (int'l arpt.), Hun. 106/D2
Ferkéssédougou, C.d'Iv. 160/D4
Ferlach, Aus. 101/L3
Fermanagh (dist.), NI, UK 92/A3
Fermi National Accelerator Laboratory, Il, US 193/P16
Fermignano, It. 117/F5
Fermin (pt.), Ca, US 194/F8
Fermo, It. 101/K5
Fermoselle, Sp. 102/B2
Fermoy, Ire. 89/P10
Fernán-Núñez, Sp. 102/C4
Fernandina (isl.), Ecu. 214/E7
Fernandina Beach, Fl, US 191/H4
Fernando de Noronha (isl.), Braz. 205/F3
Fernandópolis, Braz. 213/B2
Ferndale, Md, US 196/B5
Ferndale, Mi, US 193/F6
Ferney-Voltaire, Fr. 114/C5
Fernie, BC, Can. 184/E3
Fernpass (pass), Aus. 115/G3
Ferntree Gully NP, Austl. 173/G6
Ferrandina, It. 104/E2
Ferrara (prov.), It. 117/E3
Ferrara, It. 117/E3
Ferrat (cape), Alg. 158/E5
Ferreira do Alentejo, Port. 102/A3
Ferrelview, Mo, US 195/D5
Ferreñafe, Peru 214/B2
Ferret (cape), Fr. 100/C4
Ferrette, Fr. 114/D3
Ferriday, La, US 187/K5
Ferriere, It. 116/C3
Ferrière-la-Grande, Fr. 110/D3
Ferrières, Belg. 111/E3
Ferryden, Sc, UK 94/D3
Ferryfield (int'l arpt.), Eng, UK 91/G5
Ferryhill, Eng, UK 93/G2
Fertö (Neusiedler See) (lake), Aus. 101/M3
Ferté-Bernard, Fr. 100/D2
Fértil (valley), Arg. 215/C3
Ferwerd, Neth. 108/C2
Fès, Mor. 158/B2
Fès (prov.), Mor. 158/B3

Fesches-le-Châtel, Fr. 114/C2
Feshie (riv.), Sc, UK 94/C2
Fessenheim, Fr. 114/D2
Festival Centre, Austl. 171/M8
Fetesti, Rom. 107/H3
Fethaland (pt.), Sc, UK 89/W13
Fethiye, Turk. 148/B2
Feucherolles, Fr. 88/H5
Feucht, Ger. 112/E4
Feuchtwangen, Ger. 112/D4
Feuilles (lake), Qu, Can. 181/J3
Feuilles, Rivière aux (riv.), Qu, Can. 181/J3
Feuquières, Fr. 110/A4
Feuquières-en-Vimeu, Fr. 110/A3
Feurs, Fr. 100/F4
Fevzipasa, Turk. 149/E1
Feyzäbäd, Afg. 147/K1
Fez (Saiss) (int'l arpt.), Mor. 158/B3
Fezzan (reg.), Libya 154/F2
Fferna, Moel (peak), Wal, UK 93/E6
Ffestiniog, Wal, UK 92/E6
Fianarantsoa (prov.), Madg. 165/H8
Fianarantsoa, Madg. 165/H8
Fianga, Chad 154/J6
Ficarolo, It. 117/E3
Fichtelberg (peak), Ger. 113/F2
Fichtelgebirge (mts.), Ger. 113/F3
Fichtelnaab (riv.), Ger. 113/E3
Ficksburg, SAfr. 164/D3
Fidenza, It. 116/D3
Fié (riv.), Gui. 160/C4
Field (riv.), Austl. 171/M9
Fieldon, Il, US 195/G7
Fieni, Rom. 107/G3
Fier (riv.), Fr. 114/B6
Fierzë (lake), Alb. 105/G1
Fiesch, Swi. 114/E5
Fiesole, It. 117/E5
Fiesso, It. 117/F2
Fiesso Umbertiano, It. 117/E3
Fiesta Texas, Tx, US 195/T20
Fife, Wa, US 193/C3
Fife (pol. reg.), Sc, UK 94/C4
Fife Ness (pt.), Sc, UK 94/D4
Fifth Cataract (falls), Sudan 159/C5
Figalo (cape), Alg. 158/D2
Figari, Fr. 104/A2
Figeac, Fr. 100/E4
Figline Valdarno, It. 117/E5
Figueira da Foz, Port. 102/A2
Figueres, Sp. 103/G1
Figuig, Mor. 157/E2
Figuig (prov.), Mor. 158/C3
Fiherenana (riv.), Madg. 165/G8
Fiji (ctry.) 174/G6
Filadelfia, Par. 215/D1
Filadélfia, Braz. 212/A2
Filattiera, It. 116/C4
Filchner Ice Shelf, Ant. 218/Y
Filey (bay), Eng, UK 93/H3
Fili, Gre. 105/N8
Filiasi, Rom. 107/F3
Filiatá, Gre. 105/G3
Filiatrá, Gre. 105/G4
Filicudi (isl.), It. 104/D3
Filingué, Niger 161/F3
Filippiás, Gre. 105/G3
Filippoi (ruin), Gre. 105/J2
Filipstad, Swe. 96/F2
Filisur, Swi. 115/F4
Fillière (riv.), Fr. 114/C6
Fillmore, Ca, US 194/B2
Fillmore, Ut, US 186/D3
Filomeno Mata, Mex. 201/M6
Filótion, Gre. 105/J4
Filottrano, It. 117/G6
Fils (riv.), Ger. 112/C5
Filsum, Ger. 109/E2
Fimi (riv.), D.R. Congo 155/J8
Fina, Forêt Classée de (forest), Mali 160/C3
Finale Emilia, It. 117/E3
Finale Ligure, It. 116/B4
Fiñana, Sp. 102/D4
Finch Hatton, Austl. 172/C3
Findel (int'l arpt.), Lux. 111/F4
Findhorn, Sc, UK 94/C1
Findhorn (riv.), Sc, UK 94/B2
Findlay, Oh, US 188/D3
Findochty, Sc, UK 94/D1
Finesville, NJ, US 196/C2
Fingal, Austl. 173/C4
Finger (lake), On, Can. 185/K2
Finhaut, Swi. 114/C5
Finike, Turk. 149/B1
Finisterre (cape), Sp. 102/A1
Finke (riv.), Austl. 171/G3
Finke Gorge NP, Austl. 171/G3
Finkenstein, Aus. 101/K3
Finksburg, Md, US 196/B5
Finland (ctry.) 95/H2
Finland (gulf), Eur. 95/H2
Finlay (mts.), BC, Can. 180/D3
Finlay (mts.), Tx, US 190/B4
Finn (riv.), Ire. 89/Q9
Finnentrop, Ger. 109/E6
Finnigan (mt.), Austl. 172/B1
Finnis (cape), Austl. 171/G5

Finnmark (co.), Nor. 95/G1
Fino Mornasco, It. 116/C1
Finsing, Ger. 113/E6
Finspång, Swe. 96/F2
Finsteraarhorn (peak), Swi. 114/E4
Finström, Fin. 97/H1
Fintel, Ger. 109/G2
Fintona, NI, UK 92/A3
Fintry, Sc, UK 94/A1
Fiora (riv.), It. 101/J5
Fiorano, It. 117/D3
Fiordland NP, NZ 159/R12
Fiorenzuola d'Arda, It. 116/C3
Fircrest, Wa, US 193/C3
Fire Island Nat'l Seashore, NY, US 197/E2
Firenze (prov.), It. 117/E5
Firenze (Florence), It. 117/E5
Firenzuola, It. 117/E4
Firestone, Co, US 195/C2
Firmat, Arg. 216/E2
Firmi, Fr. 100/E4
Firminy, Fr. 100/F4
Firozābād, India 142/B2
Firozpur, India 144/C4
First Cataract (falls), Egypt 159/C3
Firüz Küh, Iran 146/F1
Firüzābād, Iran 146/F3
Fischa (riv.), Aus. 107/P7
Fischach, Ger. 115/G1
Fischamend Markt, Aus. 107/P7
Fischbacher Alpen (mts.), Aus. 101/L3
Fischen im Allgäu, Ger. 115/F3
Fischer, Tx, US 195/U20
Fish (riv.), Namb. 163/C5
Fish (bay), Mb, Can. 185/J3
Fish (str.), Nun., Can. 181/H2
Fisher (bay), Mb, Can. 185/J3
Fisher (str.), Nun., Can. 181/H2
Fisher Branch, Mb, Can. 185/J3
Fishermen (isl.), Austl. 172/F6
Fishers (isl.), NY, US 197/G1
Fishguard, Wal, UK 90/B3
Fisht (peak), Rus. 120/F4
Fismes, Fr. 110/C5
Fitful Head (pt.), Sc, UK 89/W14
Fitjar, Nor. 96/A2
Fitton (mt.), Yk, Can. 192/L2
Fitzgerald, Ga, US 191/H4
Fitzgerald (riv.), Austl. 167/B2
Fitzgerald River NP, Austl. 170/C5
Fitzroy (peak), Arg. 217/B6
Fitzroy (riv.), Austl. 167/B2
Fitzwilliam (str.), NW, Can. 181/R7
Fiume Veneto, It. 117/F1
Fiumicino, It. 104/C2
Five Sisters (peak), Sc, UK 94/A2
Fivemiletown, NI, UK 92/A3
Fivizzano, It. 116/D4
Fjell, Nor. 96/A1
Fjerritslev, Den. 96/C3
Fjugesta, Swe. 96/F2
Flå, Nor. 96/C1
Flachslanden, Ger. 112/D4
Fladungen, Ger. 112/D1
Flagler, Co, US 190/C2
Flagler Beach, Fl, US 191/H4
Flagstaff, Az, US 186/E4
Flambeau (riv.), Wi, US 185/L4
Flamborough, On, Can. 189/Q9
Flamborough Head (pt.), Eng, UK 93/H3
Fläming (hills), Ger. 98/G2
Flaming Gorge (res.), Ut,Wy, US 184/F5
Flaming Gorge Nat'l Rec. Area, Ut,Wy, US 186/E2
Flamingo Field (int'l arpt.), NAnt. 210/D1
Flanagan (riv.), On, Can. 185/K2
Flanders (reg.), Fr. 100/E1
Flanders, NY, US 197/F2
Flat Holm (isl.), Eng, UK 90/C4
Flat River, Mo, US 187/K3
Flathead (riv.), Mt, US 184/E4
Flathead (lake), Mt, US 184/E4
Flathead, South Fork (riv.), Mt, US 184/E3
Flattery (cape), Austl. 172/B1
Flattery (cape), Wa, US 184/B3
Flavio Alfaro, Ecu. 210/B5
Flawil, Swi. 115/F3
Flaxlanden, Fr. 114/D2
Fleet, Eng, UK 91/F4
Fleetwood, Pa, US 196/C3
Fleetwood, Eng, UK 93/E4
Flekkefjord, Nor. 96/B2
Flemington, NJ, US 196/D2
Flemington Racecourse, Austl. 173/F5
Flemish Brabant (prov.), Belg. 111/D2
Flensburg, Ger. 96/C4
Fleron, Belg. 111/E2
Flers, Fr. 100/C2
Flesland (int'l arpt.), Nor. 96/A1
Fleschhorn (peak), Swi. 114/E5

Fleurance, Fr. 100/D5
Fleurier, Swi. 114/C4
Fleurus, Belg. 111/D3
Fleury-les-Aubrais, Fr. 100/D3
Flevoland (prov.), Neth. 108/C4
Flevoland (isl.), Neth. 98/C2
Flexenpass (pass), Aus. 115/G3
Flieden, Ger. 112/C2
Flieden (riv.), Ger. 112/C2
Fliess, Aus. 115/G3
Flims, Swi. 115/F4
Flin Flon, Mb, Can. 185/H2
Flinders (bay), Austl. 170/B5
Flinders (ranges), Austl. 171/H4
Flinders (reef), Austl. 167/D2
Flinders (reefs), Austl. 167/D2
Flinders (riv.), Austl. 167/D2
Flinders Chase NP, Austl. 171/H5
Flinders Ranges NP, Austl. 171/H4
Flinders Reefs (isls.), Austl. 172/C2
Flines-lez-Raches, Fr. 110/C3
Flint (lake), Nun., Can. 181/J2
Flint (isl.), Kiri. 159/K6
Flint, Wal, UK 93/E5
Flint (hills), Ks, US 187/H3
Flint, Ga, US 191/H4
Flint, Mi, US 104/A2
Flint, South Branch (riv.), Mi, US 193/F5
Flintbek, Ger. 96/D4
Flintshire (co.), Wal, UK 93/E5
Flisa, Nor. 96/E1
Flix, Sp. 103/F2
Flixecourt, Fr. 110/B3
Flize, Fr. 111/D4
Floby, Swe. 96/E2
Floda, Swe. 96/E3
Flögelner See (riv.), Ger. 109/F1
Flöha (riv.), Ger. 113/F2
Floing, Fr. 111/D4
Flonheim, Ger. 112/B3
Flora (mt.), Austl. 170/C2
Flora, Nor. 95/C3
Flora, Il, US 187/K3
Floral Park, NY, US 197/L9
Florange, Fr. 111/F5
Florânia, Braz. 212/C2
Floraville, Il, US 195/G9
Floreffe, Belg. 111/D3
Florence, Al, US 191/G3
Florence, Az, US 186/E4
Florence, SC, US 191/J3
Florence (Firenze), It. 101/J5
Florence-Graham, Ca, US 194/F8
Florencia, Col. 210/C4
Florennes, Belg. 111/D3
Florenville, Belg. 111/E4
Flores (isl.), Indo. 139/F5
Flores (sea), Indo. 139/E5
Flores, Guat. 202/D2
Flores (dept.), Uru. 217/F2
Flores do Piauí, Braz. 212/B2
Floresta, Braz. 212/C3
Florham Park, NJ, US 197/H8
Floriano, Braz. 212/B2
Florianópolis, Braz. 213/B3
Florida, Col. 210/B4
Florida, Cuba 203/G1
Florida (str.), Cuba,US 203/K7
Florida, Hon. 202/D3
Florida, Peru 214/B2
Florida, Uru. 217/K11
Florida (dept.), Uru. 217/F2
Florida (state), US 191/H4
Florida (bay), Fl, US 191/H5
Florida, NY, US 196/D1
Florida Keys (isls.), Fl, US 191/H5
Floridablanca, Col. 210/C3
Floridia, It. 104/D4
Florin, Ca, US 193/M10
Flórina, Gre. 105/G2
Florissant, Mo, US 195/G8
Florissant Fossil Beds Nat'l Mon., Co, US 190/B2
Flörsbachtal, Ger. 112/C2
Flörsheim am Main, Ger. 112/B3
Flörsheim-Dalsheim, Ger. 112/B3
Florstadt, Ger. 112/B2
Flossenbürg, Ger. 113/F3
Floyd, Mo, US 195/E5
Floydada, Tx, US 187/G4
Fluchthorn (peak), Aus. 115/G4
Flüelapass (pass), Swi. 115/F4
Flüelen, Swi. 115/E4
Fluessen (lake), Neth. 108/C3
Flums, Swi. 115/F3
Flushing, Mi, US 188/D3
Fly (riv.), PNG 174/D5
Flying Fish (cape), Ant. 218/T
Fnjóská (riv.), Ice. 95/P6
Foam Lake, Sk, Can. 185/H3
Foča, Bosn. 106/D4
Fochabers, Sc, UK 94/D1
Fochville, SAfr. 164/P13
Fockbek, Ger. 96/C4
Focşani, Rom. 107/H3
Fogang, China 141/K3

Foggia, It. 104/D2
Foglia (riv.), It. 117/F5
Foglizzo, It. 116/A2
Fögló (isl.), Fin. 97/J3
Fogo (isl.), CpV. 151/J10
Fogo (riv.), Braz. 209/J6
Föhnsdorf, Aus. 101/L3
Föhren, Ger. 111/F4
Foix, Fr. 100/D5
Folarskardnuten (peak), Nor. 96/B1
Folda (inlet), Nor. 95/E2
Földeák, Hun. 106/E2
Folégandros (isl.), Gre. 105/J4
Folembray, Fr. 110/C4
Foley (isl.), Nun., Can. 181/J2
Folgaria, It. 115/H6
Foligno, It. 101/K5
Folkestone, Eng, UK 91/H4
Folkston, Ga, US 191/H4
Follainville-Dennemont, Fr. 88/H4
Follonica, Golfo di (gulf), It. 101/J5
Follonica, It. 101/J5
Folschviller, Fr. 111/F5
Folsom, NJ, US 196/D4
Fomboni, Com. 165/G6
Fond du Lac, Wi, US 185/L5
Fond du Lac, Sk, Can. 180/F3
Fond du Lac (riv.), Sk, Can. 180/F3
Fondi, It. 104/C2
Fondo, It. 115/H5
Fongen (peak), Nor. 95/D3
Fonni, It. 104/A2
Fonsagrada, Sp. 102/B1
Fonseca, Col. 210/C2
Fonseca (gulf), Nic. 182/D5
Font Sancte, Pic de la (peak), Fr. 101/G4
Fontaine, Fr. 100/F4
Fontaine-Châalis, Fr. 88/L4
Fontaine-lès-Dijon, Fr. 114/A3
Fontaine-lès-Luxeuil, Fr. 114/C2
Fontaine-L'Évêque, Belg. 111/D3
Fontainebleau, Fr. 100/E2
Fontana, Ca, US 194/C2
Fontanarossa (int'l arpt.), It. 104/D4
Fontanella, It. 116/C2
Fontanellato, It. 116/D3
Fontaniva, It. 117/E1
Fonte Boa, Braz. 211/E5
Fontenais, Swi. 114/D3
Fontenay-en-Parisis, Fr. 88/K4
Fontenay-le-Comte, Fr. 100/C3
Fontenay-le-Fleury, Fr. 88/J5
Fontenay-Saint-Père, Fr. 88/H4
Fontenay-sous-Bois, Fr. 88/K5
Fontenay-Trésigny, Fr. 88/L5
Fontenelle (res.), Wy, US 184/F5
Fontoy, Fr. 111/F5
Fontur (pt.), Ice. 95/P6
Foping, China 128/J5
Foraker (mt.), Ak, US 192/H3
Forbach, Fr. 111/F5
Forbach, Ger. 112/B5
Forbes, Austl. 173/D2
Forbesganj, India 143/F2
Forcarey, Sp. 102/A1
Forchheim, Ger. 112/E3
Forclaz, Col de la (pass), Swi. 114/D5
Forde, Nor. 95/C3
Fords, NJ, US 197/H9
Foreland (pt.), Eng, UK 90/C4
Foreland, The (pt.), Eng, UK 91/E5
Foremost, Ab, Can. 184/F3
Foreness (pt.), Eng, UK 91/H4
Forest, Ms, US 191/G3
Forest Hill, Md, US 196/B4
Forest Park, NY, US 197/N14
Forestier (pen.), Austl. 173/D4
Forestville, Qu, Can. 189/G1
Forestville, Md, US 196/B6
Forez, Monts du (mts.), Fr. 100/E4
Forfar, Sc, UK 94/D3
Forges-les-Bains, Fr. 88/J6
Forggensee (lake), Ger. 115/G3
Forillon NP, Qu, Can. 189/H1
Forked River, NJ, US 196/D4
Forkill, NI, UK 92/B3
Forks, Wa, US 184/B4
Forlì-Cesena (prov.), It. 117/F4
Forlimpopoli, It. 117/F4
Formartine (reg.), Sc, UK 94/D2
Formby, Eng, UK 93/E4
Formby (pt.), Eng, UK 93/E4
Formentera, Isla de (isl.), Sp. 103/F3
Formentor (cape), Sp. 103/G3
Formerie, Fr. 110/A4
Formia, It. 104/C2
Formiga, Braz. 213/B2
Formigine, It. 117/D3
Formignana, It. 117/E3
Formosa, Arg. 215/E2
Formosa, Braz. 212/A4
Formosa (peak), SAfr. 164/C4
Formosa (isl.), GBis. 160/B4

Formosa do Rio Prêto, Braz. 212/A3
Formosa, Serra (mts.), Braz. 209/G6
Formoso (riv.), Braz. 209/J6
Fornacelle, It. 117/E5
Fornaci di Barga, It. 116/D4
Fornæs (cape), Den. 96/D3
Fornebu (int'l arpt.), Nor. 96/D2
Fornovo di Taro, It. 116/D3
Forres, Sc, UK 94/C1
Forrest City, Ar, US 187/K4
Forsand, Nor. 96/B2
Forshaga, Swe. 96/E2
Forssa, Fin. 97/K1
Forst, Ger. 113/E6
Forstern, Ger. 113/E6
Forstinning, Ger. 113/E6
Forsyth, Mt, US 184/G4
Forsyth, NY, US 197/J9
Forsyth (range), Austl. 172/A3
Forsythe NWR, NJ, US 196/D5
Fort Abbās, Pak. 144/B5
Fort Augustus, Sc, UK 94/B2
Fort Beaufort, SAfr. 164/D4
Fort Belvoir, Va, US 196/A6
Fort Benton, Mt, US 184/F4
Fort Bragg, Ca, US 184/C6
Fort Chambly Nat'l Hist. Park, Qu, Can. 189/P7
Fort Chipewyan, Ab, Can. 180/E3
Fort Cobb (res.), Ok, US 187/H4
Fort Collins, Co, US 195/B1
Fort Collins Museum, Co, US 195/B1
Fort Davis, Tx, US 187/G5
Fort de Douaumont, Fr. 111/E5
Fort-de-France, Guad. 199/N9
Fort de Vaux, Fr. 111/E5
Fort Desaix, Mil. Res., Mart., Fr. 199/N9
Fort Dodge, Ia, US 185/K5
Fort Erie, On, Can. 189/S10
Fort Frances, On, Can. 185/K3
Fort Frederica Nat'l Mon., Ga, US 191/H4
Fort George Nat'l Hist. Park, On, Can. 189/R9
Fort Gibson (lake), Ok, US 190/E3
Fort Good Hope, NW, Can. 180/D2
Fort Hancock, Tx, US 190/C5
Fort Howard, Md, US 196/B5
Fort Kent, Me, US 189/G2
Fort Lauderdale, Fl, US 191/H5
Fort Lauderdale-Hollywood (int'l arpt.), Fl, US 191/H5
Fort Lee, NJ, US 197/K8
Fort Lewis, Wa, US 193/B3
Fort Liard, NW, Can. 180/D2
Fort Liberté, Haiti 203/J2
Fort Lupton, Co, US 195/C2
Fort Macleod, Ab, Can. 184/E3
Fort Madison, Ia, US 185/L5
Fort-Mahon-Plage, Fr. 110/A3
Fort Malden Nat'l Hist. Park, On, Can. 193/F7
Fort-Mardyck, Fr. 110/B2
Fort Matanzas Nat'l Mon., Fl, US 191/H4
Fort McDowell Ind. Res., Az, US 195/S18
Fort McHenry Nat'l Mon., Md, US 196/B5
Fort McMurray, Ab, Can. 180/E3
Fort McPherson, NW, Can. 192/M2
Fort Meade, Md, US 196/B5
Fort Morgan, Co, US 187/G3
Fort Myers, Fl, US 191/H5
Fort Nelson, BC, Can. 180/D3
Fort Nelson (riv.), BC, Can. 180/D3
Fort Nottingham, SAfr. 165/E3
Fort Payne, Al, US 191/G3
Fort Peck (dam), Mt, US 185/G4
Fort Peck (lake), Mt, US 184/G4
Fort Pierce, Fl, US 191/H5
Fort Portal, Ugan. 162/A2
Fort Providence, NW, Can. 180/E2
Fort Qu'Appelle, Sk, Can. 185/H3
Fort Randall (dam), SD, US 185/J5
Fort Resolution, NW, Can. 180/E2
Fort Saint James, BC, Can. 184/B2
Fort Saint John, BC, Can. 180/D3
Fort Saskatchewan, Ab, Can. 184/E2
Fort Scott, Ks, US 187/J3

Fort-Shevchenko, Kaz. 121/J3
Fort Simpson, NW, Can. 180/D2
Fort Smith, Ar, US 187/J4
Fort Smith, NW, Can. 180/E2
Fort Stanwix Nat'l Mon., NY, US 188/F3
Fort Stockton, Tx, US 187/G5
Fort Sumner, NM, US 187/F4
Fort Sumter, SC, US 191/J3
Fort Tilden, NY, US 197/K9
Fort Totten, ND, US 185/J4
Fort Vasquez Museum, Co, US 195/C2
Fort Vermilion, Ab, Can. 180/E3
Fort Wadsworth, NY, US 197/J9
Fort Walton Beach, Fl, US 191/G4
Fort Wayne, In, US 188/C3
Fort Wellington Nat'l Hist. Park, On, Can. 188/F2
Fort William, Sc, UK 94/A3
Fort Yates, ND, US 185/H4
Fort Yukon, Ak, US 192/J2
Fortaleza, Braz. 212/C1
Fortaleza dos Nogueiras, Braz. 212/A2
Fortaleza Santa Teresa, Uru. 217/G2
Forte dei Marmi, It. 116/D5
Fortescue (riv.), Austl. 170/C2
Fortescue, NJ, US 196/C5
Forth, Sc, UK 94/C5
Forth (riv.), Sc, UK 94/B4
Forth, Firth of (inlet), Sc, UK 94/C4
Fortín, Mex. 201/N8
Fortore (riv.), It. 104/D2
Fortrose, Sc, UK 94/B1
Fortuna, Braz. 212/A2
Fortuna, It. 216/D2
Fortuna Ledge, Ak, US 192/F3
Fortune (bay), Nf, Can. 189/L2
Fortune, Nf, Can. 189/L2
Forty Fort, Pa, US 196/C1
Forty Mile Scrub NP, Austl. 172/B2
Fosheim (pen.), Nun., Can. 181/S7
Foss (riv.), Eng, UK 93/G3
Fossalta di Piave, It. 117/F1
Fossalta di Portogruaro, It. 117/F1
Fossano, It. 116/A3
Fosses, Fr. 88/K4
Fosses-la-Ville, Belg. 111/D3
Fossil, Or, US 184/C4
Fossil Creek (res.), Co, US 195/B2
Fossombrone, It. 117/F5
Foster, Austl. 173/C3
Foster Pond, Il, US 195/G9
Fosterburg, Il, US 195/G8
Fostoria, Oh, US 188/D3
Fót, Hun. 107/P7
Foucarmont, Fr. 110/A4
Foucherans, Fr. 114/B3
Fougères, Fr. 100/C2
Fougerolles, Fr. 114/C2
Fouilloy, Fr. 110/B4
Foul (bay), Egypt, Sudan 155/N3
Foula (isl.), Sc, UK 89/V13
Foulness (pt.), Eng, UK 91/G3
Foulness (isl.), Eng, UK 91/G3
Foum Zguid, Mor. 156/D2
Foumban, Camr. 154/H6
Foundiougne, Sen. 160/B3
Fountain, Il, US 195/G9
Fountain Hill, Pa, US 196/C2
Fountain Hills, Az, US 195/S18
Fountain Valley, Ca, US 194/F9
Fountains Abbey, Eng, UK 93/G3
Fourchambault, Fr. 100/E3
Fourche La Fave (riv.), Ar, US 187/J4
Fourges, Fr. 88/F4
Fourmies, Fr. 110/D4
Fourth Cataract (falls), Sudan 159/C5
Fouta Djallon (phys. reg.), Gui. 160/C3
Foveaux (str.), NZ 159/R12
Fowey (riv.), Eng, UK 90/B6
Fowey, Eng, UK 90/B6
Fowler, Iran 146/E1
Fox (isls.), Ak, US 192/C5
Fox (mtn.), Yk, Can. 192/M3
Fox (mtn.), Il,Wi, US 185/L5
Fox (riv.), Il, US 193/P15
Fox Creek, Ab, Can. 184/D2
Fox Glacier, NZ 159/S11
Fox Lake, Il, US 193/P15
Fox River Grove, Il, US 193/P15
Fox Valley, Sk, Can. 184/F3

Foxe (pen.), Nun., Can. 181/J2
Foxe (chan.), Nun., Can. 181/H2
Foxe Basin (chan.), Nun., Can. 181/J2
Foxen (lake), Swe. 96/D2
Foyle (riv.), NI, UK 92/A2
Foz, Sp. 102/B1
Foz do Iguaçu, Braz. 215/F2
Frackville, Pa, US 196/B2
Fraga, Sp. 103/F2
Fragosa, Cayo (isl.), Cuba 203/G1
Fraiburgo, Braz. 213/B3
Frailes, Cordillera de los (mts.), Ven. 208/E7
Fraisans, Fr. 114/B3
Fraize, Fr. 114/D1
Frameries, Belg. 110/C3
Framlingham, Eng, UK 91/H2
Frammersbach, Ger. 112/C2
Franca, Braz. 213/C2
Francavilla al Mare, It. 104/D1
Francavilla Fontana, It. 105/F2
Francavilla in Sinni, It. 104/E2
France (ctry.) 100/D3
Frances (cape), Cuba 203/F1
Frances (lake), Yk, Can. 180/C2
Francés Viejo (cape), DRep. 199/H4
Franceville, Gabon 154/H8
Franche-Comté (pol. reg.), Fr. 114/B5
Franche-Comteé (pol. reg.), Fr. 101/G3
Francis Case (lake), SD, US 185/J5
Francisco de Orellana, Peru 214/C1
Francisco Escárcega, Mex. 202/D2
Francisco Javier Mina, Mex. 202/D2
Francisco Sá, Braz. 212/B5
Francisco Zarco, Mex. 200/A1
Francistown, Bots. 163/E5
Franco da Rocha, Braz. 213/G8
Francolino, It. 117/E3
Franconville, Fr. 88/J5
Franeker, Neth. 108/C2
Frangy, Fr. 114/B5
Frank Hahn NP, Austl. 170/C3
Franken Wald (for.), Ger. 113/E2
Frankenau, Ger. 109/F6
Frankenberg-Eder, Ger. 109/F6
Frankenburg am Hausruck, Aus. 113/G6
Frankenhöhe (mts.), Ger. 98/F4
Frankenmarkt, Aus. 113/G7
Frankenmuth, Mi, US 188/D3
Frankenthal, Ger. 112/B3
Frankfort (cap.), Ky, US 188/C4
Frankfort, SAfr. 164/E2
Frankfort, Ger. 99/H2
Frankfurt (int'l arpt.), Ger. 112/B2
Frankfurt am Main, Ger. 112/B2
Fränkische Alb (mts.), Ger. 98/F4
Fränkische Rezat (riv.), Ger. 112/D3
Fränkische Saale (riv.), Ger. 98/E3
Fränkische Schweiz (reg.), Ger. 101/G2
Fränkische Schweiz (reg.), Ger. 98/F3
Frankland (cape), Austl. 173/C4
Franklin (pt.), Ak, US 192/G1
Franklin, NC, US 191/H3
Franklin, Ky, US 188/C5
Franklin, In, US 188/C4
Franklin, Tn, US 188/C5
Franklin, WV, US 196/D1
Franklin, NJ, US 196/D1
Franklin (mts.), NW, Can. 180/D2
Franklin (bay), NW, Can. 180/D2
Franklin, NW, Can. 180/D2
Franklin, Il, US 193/Q16
Franklin D. Roosevelt (lake), Wa, US 184/D3
Franklin Lakes, NJ, US 197/J7
Franklin-Lower Gordon Wild Rivers NP, Austl. 173/C4
Franklin Mineral Museum, NJ, US 196/D1
Franklin Park, Il, US 193/Q14
Franklin Square, NY, US 197/L9
Franksville, Wi, US 193/Q14
Franois, Fr. 114/B3
Franschhoek, SAfr. 164/L10
Fransico Beltrão, Braz. 215/F2
Francisco Morato, Braz. 213/G8
Františkovy Lázně, Czh. 113/F2

Franz Josef Land (isls.), Rus. 218/C
Franz Joseph Strauss (int'l arpt.), Ger. 113/E6
Franzburg, Ger. 96/E4
Fraser (isl.), Austl. 167/E3
Fraser (mt.), Austl. 170/C3
Fraser (riv.), BC, Can. 184/C2
Fraser, Mi, US 193/G6
Fraser Lake, BC, Can. 184/B2
Fraser NP, Austl. 173/D4
Fraserburg, SAfr. 164/C4
Fraserburgh, Sc, UK 94/D1
Frasne, Fr. 114/C4
Frassine (riv.), It. 117/E2
Frassino, It. 117/D2
Frastanz, Aus. 115/F3
Frati, Monte dei (peak), It. 117/F5
Frauenfeld, Swi. 115/E2
Fraunberg, Ger. 113/F6
Fray Bentos, Uru. 217/J10
Fray Marcos, Uru. 217/L11
Frazier Park, Ca, US 186/C4
Frechen, Ger. 111/F2
Freckenfeld, Ger. 112/B4
Fred (mt.), Les. 164/E3
Frederica, De, US 196/C6
Fredericia, Den. 96/C4
Frederick (reef), Austl. 167/E3
Frederick, Co, US 195/C2
Frederick, Md, US 188/E4
Frederick (co.), Md, US 196/A5
Frederick, Oh, US 187/H4
Fredericksburg, Pa, US 196/B3
Fredericksburg, Tx, US 187/H5
Frederickton, Austl. 173/E1
Fredericton (cap.), NB, Can. 189/H2
Frederik Willem IV (falls), Sur. 211/G4
Frederiks, Den. 96/C3
Frederiksborg (co.), Den. 96/E4
Frederiksborg Slot (Frederiksborg Castle), Den. 96/E4
Frederikshavn, Den. 96/D3
Frederiksted, USVI 199/M8
Fredersdorf bei Berlin, Ger. 98/Q7
Fredonia, Az, US 186/D3
Fredonia, NY, US 188/E3
Fredriksberg, Swe. 96/F1
Fredrikstad, Nor. 96/D2
Free State (prov.), SAfr. 164/P13
Freeburg, Il, US 195/H9
Freeburg, Pa, US 196/B2
Freedom, Ok, US 190/D2
Freehold, NJ, US 196/D3
Freeland, Pa, US 196/C1
Freeland, Md, US 196/B4
Freeland, Wa, US 193/B1
Freeling (mt.), Austl. 171/G2
Freeling Heights (peak), Austl. 171/H4
Freemansburg, Pa, US 196/C2
Freeport, Bahm. 199/F2
Freeport, Il, US 185/L5
Freeport, NY, US 197/L9
Freeport, Tx, US 187/J5
Freer, Tx, US 190/D5
Freetown (cap.), SLeo. 160/B4
Fregenal de la Sierra, Sp. 102/B3
Fréhel (cape), Fr. 100/B2
Frei Inocêncio, Braz. 213/D1
Freib Mulde (riv.), Ger. 98/G3
Freiberg, Ger. 99/G3
Freiburg, Ger. 109/G1
Freiburg, Ger. 114/D2
Freienbach, Swi. 115/E3
Freihung, Ger. 113/F3
Freilassing, Ger. 113/F7
Freinsheim, Ger. 112/B3
Freire, Chile 216/B3
Freisen, Ger. 111/G4
Freising, Ger. 113/E6
Freistadt, Aus. 113/H5
Freital, Ger. 99/G3
Freixo de Espada à Cinta, Port. 102/B2
Frejorgues (int'l arpt.), Fr. 100/C5
Fréjus, Fr. 101/G5
Frekhaug, Nor. 96/A1
Frémainfille, Fr. 88/H4
Fremdingen, Ger. 112/D5
Frémécourt, Fr. 88/J4
Fremont (riv.), Ut, US 186/E3
Fremont, Oh, US 188/D3
Fremont, Mi, US 188/C4
Fremont, Ca, US 186/B3
Fremont (mt.), Ut, US 195/J11
French (riv.), On, Can. 188/D2
French Creek State Park, Pa, US 196/C3
French Frigate Shoals (bar), Hi, US 159/J2
French Guiana (dpcy.), Fr. 209/H3
French Polynesia (terr.), Fr. 159/L6

Frenchman (riv.), Can.,US 180/F4
Frenchman's (bay), On, Can. 189/R8
Frenchmans Cap (peak), Austl. 173/C4
Frenchtown, NJ, US 196/C2
Frenda, Alg. 158/F5
Frépillon, Fr. 88/J4
Freren, Ger. 109/E4
Fresco (riv.), Braz. 209/H5
Fresco, C.d'Iv. 160/D5
Fresia, Chile 216/B4
Fresnes, Fr. 88/J5
Fresnes-en-Woëvre, Fr. 111/F4
Fresnillo, Mex. 200/E4
Fresno, Ca, US 186/C3
Fresnoy-le-Grand, Fr. 110/C4
Fressenneville, Fr. 110/A3
Fretin, Fr. 110/C2
Freuchie (lake), Sc, UK 94/C3
Freudenberg, Ger. 113/E4
Freudenberg, Ger. 111/G2
Freudenburg, Ger. 111/F4
Freudenstadt, Ger. 115/E1
Frévent, Fr. 110/B3
Freycinet (har.), Austl. 170/B3
Freycinet NP, Austl. 173/D4
Freyming-Merlebach, Fr. 111/F5
Freystadt, Ger. 113/E4
Freyung, Ger. 113/G5
Fria (cape), Namb. 163/B4
Frías, Arg. 215/C2
Frías, Peru 214/B2
Fribourg, Swi. 114/D4
Fribourg (canton), Swi. 114/E3
Frick, Swi. 114/E3
Frickenhausen am Main, Ger. 112/D3
Fridingen an der Donau, Ger. 115/E1
Fridolfing, Ger. 113/F6
Friedberg, Ger. 112/B2
Friedberg, Ger. 112/D6
Friedeburg, Ger. 109/E2
Friedrichsdorf, Ger. 112/B2
Friedrichshafen, Ger. 115/F2
Friedrichstadt, Ger. 96/C4
Friedrichsthal, Ger. 111/G5
Frielendorf, Ger. 112/C2
Friesenheim, Ger. 114/D1
Friesland (prov.), Neth. 108/C2
Friesoythe, Ger. 109/E2
Frignicourt, Fr. 111/D6
Frio (riv.), Tx, US 187/H5
Friockheim, Sc, UK 94/D3
Friol, Sp. 102/B1
Frisange, Lux. 111/F4
Fristad, Swe. 96/E3
Fritsla, Swe. 96/E3
Fritzlar, Ger. 109/G6
Friuli-Venezia Giula (prov.), It. 101/A3
Friville-Escarbotin, Fr. 110/A3
Frobisher (bay), Nun., Can. 181/K2
Frogmore, Eng, UK 88/A3
Frohavel (inlet), Nor. 95/D3
Frohnleiten, Aus. 101/L3
Froid-Chapelle, Belg. 111/D3
Froideconche, Fr. 114/C2
Froissy, Fr. 110/B4
Froland, Nor. 96/C2
Frolovo, Rus. 121/G2
Frome (lake), Austl. 167/D4
Frome (riv.), Austl. 171/H4
Frome, Eng, UK 90/D4
Frome (riv.), Eng, UK 90/D5
Froncles, Fr. 114/B1
Front (range), Co, US 187/F2
Frontera, Port. 102/B3
Frontenhausen, Ger. 113/F5
Frontera, Mex. 202/C2
Frontera Comalapa, Mex. 202/C3
Frontier Army Museum, Ks, US 195/D5
Frontignan, Fr. 100/E5
Fronton, Fr. 100/D5
Frosinone, It. 104/C2
Fröso, Swe. 95/E3
Frotey-lès-Vesoul, Fr. 114/C2
Frouard, Fr. 111/F6
Frövi, Swe. 96/F2
Frøya (isl.), Nor. 95/D3
Frozen (str.), Nun., Can. 181/H2
Fruges, Fr. 110/B2
Fruit Heights, Ut, US 195/K11
Fruška Gora NP, Cro. 106/D3
Frutal, Braz. 213/B1
Frutigen, Swi. 114/D4
Frutillar, Chile 216/B4
Fryazino, Rus. 119/X9
Frýdek-Místek, Czh. 99/K4
Fu Xian, China 130/B4
Fu'an, China 137/C2
Fucecchio, It. 117/D5
Fucheng, China 130/D3
Fuchskaute (peak), Ger. 111/H1
Fuchū, Japan 135/L7
Fuchū, Japan 132/C2
Fuchuan, China 137/B3
Fuchun (riv.), China 130/D5
Fuding, China 137/D2
Fuengirola, Sp. 102/C4
Fuenlabrada, Sp. 103/N9
Fuensalida, Sp. 102/C2

Fuente, Sp. 103/N8
Fuente de Cantos, Sp. 102/B3
Fuente del Maestre, Sp. 102/B3
Fuente Obejuna, Sp. 102/C3
Fuentelapeña, Sp. 102/C2
Fuentes de Oñoro, Sp. 102/B2
Fuentesaúco, Sp. 102/C2
Fuerte (riv.), Mex. 200/C3
Fuerte Olimpo, Par. 208/G8
Fuerteventura (isl.) Canl., Sp. 156/B3
Fuga (isl.), Phil. 137/D4
Fuglebjerg, Den. 96/D4
Fugong, China 141/G2
Fugou, China 130/C4
Fuhai, China 128/E2
Fuhne (riv.), Ger. 98/F3
Fuhse (riv.), Ger. 109/H4
Fuji, Japan 133/F3
Fuji (riv.), Japan 133/F3
Fuji-san (peak), Japan 133/F3
Fuji-Hakone-Izu NP, Japan 133/F3
Fujian (prov.), China 129/L6
Fujieda, Japan 133/F3
Fujihashi, Japan 135/K4
Fujiidera, Japan 135/J6
Fujimi, Japan 135/C2
Fujino, Japan 135/C2
Fujinomiya, Japan 133/F3
Fujioka, Japan 133/F2
Fujioka, Japan 135/M5
Fujisawa, Japan 133/F3
Fujishiro, Japan 135/E2
Fujiyoshida, Japan 133/F3
Fukagawa, Japan 134/C2
Fukang, China 128/E3
Fukaya, Japan 135/C1
Fukiage, Japan 135/C1
Fukuchiyama, Japan 135/H5
Fukue, Japan 132/A4
Fukue (isl.), Japan 132/A4
Fukui, Japan 132/E2
Fukui (pref.), Japan 132/E3
Fukui, Japan 132/C2
Fukuoka, Japan 132/B4
Fukuoka, Japan 135/M4
Fukuoka (int'l arpt.) Japan 132/B4
Fukuoka (pref.), Japan 132/B4
Fukuroi, Japan 133/G2
Fukushima, Japan 133/G2
Fukushima (pref.), Japan 133/F2
Fukushima, Japan 134/B3
Fukuyama, Japan 132/C4
Fülädi (mtn.), Afg. 147/J2
Fulda (riv.), Ger. 98/E3
Fulda, Ger. 112/C1
Fullerton, Ca, US 194/G8
Fullerton (Whitehall), Pa, US 196/C2
Fully, Swi. 114/D5
Fulpmes, Aus. 115/H3
Fulton, Mo, US 187/K3
Fulton, NY, US 188/E3
Fulton, Ky, US 188/B4
Fulufjället (peak), Swe. 96/E1
Fumaiolo (peak), It. 117/F5
Fumay, Fr. 111/D4
Fumel, Fr. 100/D4
Fumin, China 141/H2
Funabashi, Japan 135/D2
Funafuti (cap.), Tuv. 174/G5
Funafuti (isl.), Tuv. 174/G5
Funan, China 130/C4
Funchal, Port. 156/A2
Funchal (int'l arpt.) Port. 156/A2
Fundación, Col. 210/C2
Fundão, Port. 102/B2
Fundy (bay), US,Can. 189/H2
Fundy NP, NB, Can. 189/H2
Funhalouro, Moz. 163/F4
Funing, China 141/J3
Funing, China 130/D3
Fuorn, Pass dal (Ofenpass) (pass), Swi. 115/G4
Fuping, China 130/C3
Fuqing, China 137/C2
Fuquan, China 141/J2
Fur (riv.), China 131/C2
Furano, Japan 134/C2
Fürfeld, Ger. 112/B3
Furmanov, Rus. 118/J4
Furnas (res.), Braz. 209/J8
Furneaux Group (isls.), Austl. 167/D4
Fürstenau, Ger. 109/E3
Fürstenfeld, Aus. 101/M3
Fürstenfeldbruck, Ger. 112/E6
Fürstenwalde, Ger. 99/H2
Fürth, Ger. 112/D3
Fürth, Ger. 112/D4
Furth, Ger. 113/F5
Furth im Wald, Ger. 113/F4
Furtwangen im Schwarzwald, Ger. 114/E1
Furudal, Swe. 96/F1
Furukawa, Japan 134/B3
Fury and Hecla (str.), Nun., Can. 181/H2
Fushan, China 130/D3
Fushan, China 130/E4
Fushun, China 131/B2
Fushun, China 141/J2
Fusignano, It. 117/E4

Fusio, Swi. 115/E5
Fuso, Japan 135/L5
Fussa, Japan 135/C2
Füssen, Ger. 115/G2
Fusui, China 136/D1
Futaba, Japan 135/A2
Futami, Japan 135/L7
Futog, Serb. 106/D3
Futrono, Chile 216/B4
Futtsu, Japan 135/D2
Futuna (isl.), Wall., Fr. 174/H6
Fuwah, Egypt 149/B4
Fuxian (lake), China 141/H3
Fuxin, China 130/E2
Fuxin Monggolzu Zizhixian, China 130/E2
Fuyang, China 130/C4
Fuyang (riv.), China 137/B2
Fuyu, China 129/M2
Fuyu, China 129/M2
Fuyuan, China 141/H2
Fuyun, China 128/E2
Füzesabony, Hun. 106/E2
Fuzhou, China 137/C2
Fyn (co.), Den. 96/D4
Fyn (isl.), Den. 95/D5
Fyne, Loch (inlet), Sc, UK 94/A5
Fyresdal, Nor. 96/C2

G

Ga Vache (isl.), Haiti 203/H2
Gaast, Neth. 108/C2
Gabas (riv.), Fr. 100/C5
Gabela, Ang. 163/B3
Gabes (gov.), Tun. 157/H2
Gabes (gulf), Tun. 157/H2
Gabicce Mare, It. 117/F5
Gablingen, Ger. 112/D6
Gablitz, Aus. 107/N7
Gabon (ctry.) 154/H7
Gaborone (cap.), Bots. 163/E5
Gabriel Leyva Solano, Mex. 200/C3
Gabrovo, Bul. 105/J1
Gaby, Ir. 116/A1
Gacko, Bosn. 105/F1
Gādarwāra, India 142/B4
Gaddy, Ok, US 195/N15
Gadmen, Swi. 115/E4
Gadsden, Al, US 191/G3
Gǎești, Rom. 107/G3
Gaeta, It. 104/C2
Gaeta, Golfo di (gulf), It. 104/C2
Gaferut (isl.), Micr. 174/D4
Gaffney, SC, US 191/H3
Gafsa, Tun. 157/H2
Gafsa (gov.), Tun. 157/H2
Gagarin, Rus. 118/G5
Gaggenau, Ger. 112/B5
Gaggio Montano, It. 117/D4
Gaglianico, It. 116/B1
Gagnoa, C.d'Iv. 160/D5
Gagny, Fr. 88/K5
Gagra, Geo. 120/G4
Gagret, India 144/D4
Gai Xian, China 131/B2
Gaïchtpass (pass), Aus. 115/G3
Gail (riv.), Aus. 101/K3
Gaildorf, Ger. 112/C5
Gaillac, Fr. 100/D5
Gailtaler (mts.), Aus. 101/K3
Gaiman, Arg. 216/D4
Gaimersheim, Ger. 113/E5
Gainesville, Tx, US 187/H4
Gainesville, Ga, US 191/H3
Gainesville, Fl, US 191/H4
Gainsborough, Eng, UK 93/H5
Gairdner (lake), Austl. 167/C4
Gairloch, Sc, UK 94/C2
Gais, Swi. 115/F3
Gaiserwald, Swi. 115/F3
Gaizina (peak), Lat. 97/L3
Gakarosa (peak), SAfr. 164/C2
Gakona, Ak, US 192/J3
Galana (riv.), Kenya 162/C2
Galand, Iran 147/G1
Galapagar, Sp. 103/M8
Galápagos (isls.), Ecu. 214/E6
Galápagos (dept.), Ecu. 214/E7
Galápagos, PN, Ecu. 214/E7
Galashiels, Sc, UK 94/D5
Galați (prov.), Rom. 107/H3
Galați, Rom. 105/J2
Galatina, It. 105/F2
Galátista, Gre. 105/H2
Galatone, It. 105/F2
Galb Azefal (hill), WSah. 156/B5
Galbiate, It. 116/C1
Galdácano, Sp. 102/D1
Gáldar, Sp. 156/B3
Galeana, Mex. 201/E3
Galela, Indo. 139/G3
Galena, Ak, US 192/G3
Galena, Md, US 196/C5
Galeota (pt.), Trin. 211/F2
Galeota (pt.), Ecu. 210/A4
Galera (pt.), Trin. 211/F2
Galera (pt.), Chile 216/B3

Galesburg, Il, US 185/L5
Galey (riv.), Ire. 89/P10
Galga (riv.), Hun. 107/R9
Galgamácsa, Hun. 107/R9
Galgorm, NI, UK 92/B2
Galich, Rus. 118/J4
Galicia (aut. comm.), Sp. 102/A1
Galičica NP, FYROM 105/G2
Galiléia, Braz. 213/D1
Galileo Galilei (int'l arpt.), It. 116/C3
Galinakopf (peak), Aus. 115/F3
Galion, Oh, US 188/D3
Gallan Head (pt.), Sc, UK 89/Q7
Gallarate, It. 116/B1
Gallatin, Tn, US 188/C4
Galle, SrL. 161/E3
Gallegos (riv.), Arg. 215/B9
Galliate, It. 116/B2
Gallicano, It. 116/D5
Galliera Veneta, It. 117/E1
Gallinas (mts.), NM, US 190/B3
Gallipoli (pt.), Col. 210/D1
Gallipoli, It. 105/F2
Gallipoli (pen.), Turk. 107/H5
Gällivare, Swe. 95/G2
Gallneukirchen, Aus. 113/H6
Gallo (cape), It. 104/C3
Gallo (lake), It. 115/G4
Gallspach, Aus. 113/G6
Galluis, Fr. 88/H5
Gallup, NM, US 186/E4
Gallur, Sp. 102/E2
Gally (riv.), Fr. 88/H5
Galston, Sc, UK 94/C5
Galten, Den. 96/C3
Galtymore (peak), Ire. 89/P10
Galva, La, US 195/P16
Galvarino, Chile 216/B3
Gálvez, Sp. 102/C3
Galveston, Tx, US 187/J5
Galveston (bay), Tx, US 187/J5
Galveston (isl.), Tx, US 187/J5
Gálvez, Sp. 102/C3
Galway, Ire. 89/P10
Galway (bay), Ire. 89/P10
Gam (riv.), Viet. 141/J3
Gamaches, Fr. 110/A4
Gamagara (riv.), SAfr. 164/C2
Gamagōri, Japan 135/M6
Gamarra, Col. 210/C2
Gamba, China 143/G1
Gamba, Gabon 161/E4
Gambaga Scarp (cliff), Gha. 161/E4
Gambais, Fr. 88/H5
Gambara, It. 116/D2
Gambat, Pak. 140/A2
Gambela NP, Eth. 155/M6
Gambell, Ak, US 192/D3
Gambellara, It. 117/E2
Gamber, Md, US 196/B5
Gambettola, It. 117/F4
Gambia, The (ctry.) 160/B3
Gambia (riv.), Gam. 160/A3
Gambier (isls.), FrPol. 159/M7
Gámbita, Col. 210/C3
Gambo, Nf, Can. 189/L1
Gambolò, It. 116/B2
Gambsheim, Fr. 112/A5
Gaming, Aus. 101/L3
Gamleby, Swe. 96/G3
Gammelstad, Swe. 95/G2
Gammertingen, Ger. 115/F1
Gammon Ranges NP, Austl. 171/H4
Gamo, Japan 135/K5
Gampern, Aus. 113/G7
Gamud (peak), Eth. 162/C1
Gan (riv.), China 129/L6
Gan, Fr. 100/C5
Gananoque, On, Can. 188/E2
Gǎncǎ, Azer. 121/H4
Ganda, Ang. 163/B3
Gandajika, D.R. Congo 163/D2
Gandaki (zone), Nepal 142/D1
Gander (lake), Nf, Can. 189/L1
Gander, Nf, Can. 189/L1
Ganderkesee, Ger. 109/F2
Gandesa, Sp. 103/F2
Gāndhī Sāgar (res.), India 140/D3
Gandhīdhām, India 147/K4
Gandhinagar, India 147/K4
Gandino, It. 116/C1
Gandoca-Manzanillo NWR, CR 203/F4
Gandu, Braz. 212/C4
Ganeb (well), Mrta. 156/C5
Ganesh (mtn.), China 143/F1
Gangānagar, India 144/D3
Gangapur, India 142/B1
Gangaw, Myan. 141/F3
Gangca, China 128/H4
Gangdisê (mts.), China 128/D5
Gangelt, Ger. 111/F2
Ganges, Fr. 100/E5
Ganges (riv.), Asia 128/E7

Ganges (Ganga) (riv.), India 142/B1
Ganges, Mouths of the (delta), Bang. 143/G5
Gangi, It. 104/D4
Gangkofen, Ger. 113/F6
Ganluo, China 141/H2
Gangoh, India 144/D3
Gannan, China 130/B3
Gannat, Fr. 100/E3
Ganquan, China 130/B3
Gansbaai, SAfr. 164/L11
Gänserndorf, Aus. 107/P7
Gansu (prov.), China 128/H4
Ganyu, China 130/D4
Ganzhou, China 137/B2
Ganzi, Ger. 98/G2
Ganzourgou (prov.), Burk. 161/E3
Gao (pol. reg.), Mali 161/F2
Gao, Mali 161/E2
Gao'an, China 137/C2
Gaocheng, China 130/C3
Gaochun, China 130/D5
Gaomi, China 130/D3
Gaoping, China 130/C3
Gaoqing, China 130/D3
Gaor Bheinn (Gulvain) (peak), Sc, UK 94/A3
Gaotai, China 128/G4
Gaotang, China 130/D3
Gaoua, Burk. 160/E4
Gaoyang, China 130/C3
Gaoyou, China 130/D4
Gaozhou, China 141/K3
Gap, Fr. 101/G4
Gap, Pa, US 196/B4
Gar (riv.), China 128/C5
Garabogazköl Aylagy (gulf), Trkm. 121/K4
Garamba, PN de la, D.R. Congo 155/L7
Garancières, Fr. 110/A6
Garanhuns, Braz. 212/C3
Garça, Braz. 213/B2
Garbsen, Ger. 109/G4
Garching an der Alz, Ger. 113/F6
Garcia de Sota, Embalse de (res.), Sp. 102/C3
Gard (riv.), Fr. 100/F4
Garda (lake), It. 101/J4
Garda, It. 117/D1
Garde, Cap de (cape), Alg. 158/K6
Gardelegen, Ger. 98/F2
Garden (isl.), Austl. 170/K7
Garden City, Ga, US 191/H4
Garden City, NY, US 197/L9
Garden City, Mi, US 193/F7
Garden City Park, NY, US 197/L9
Garden Grove, Ca, US 194/G8
Garden Ridge, Tx, US 195/U20
Garden View, Neth. 108/C4
Gardena, Col. 210/C3
Gardenstown, Sc, UK 94/D1
Gardēz, Afg. 147/J2
Gardiner, Mt, US 184/F4
Gardiner, Me, US 189/G2
Gardiner, Wa, US 193/B1
Gardiners (isl.), NY, US 197/F1
Gardiners (bay), NY, US 197/F1
Gardner (lake), Ks, US 195/D6
Gardner, Ks, US 195/D6
Gardone val Trompia, It. 116/D1
Gare Loch (inlet), Sc, UK 94/B4
Gareat el Tarf (salt pan), Alg. 158/K7
Garelochhead, Sc, UK 94/B4
Garessio, It. 116/B4
Garet el Djenoun (peak), Alg. 157/D4
Garfield, Ut, US 195/J12
Garfield, NJ, US 197/J8
Garfield (peak), Nepal 143/F2
Garforth, Eng, UK 93/G4
Gargaliánoi, Gre. 105/G4
Gargan (peak), Fr. 100/D4
Gargenville, Fr. 88/G5
Gargnano, It. 117/D1
Garh Mahārāja, Pak. 144/B2
Garhākotā, India 142/B4
Garhbeta, India 143/F4
Garhmuktesar, India 142/B1
Garibaldi, Braz. 213/B4
Garies, SAfr. 164/B3
Garioch (ranges), Austl. 167/C4
Garissa, Kenya 162/C2
Garland, Tx, US 187/H4
Garlasco, It. 116/B2
Garmisch-Partenkirchen, Ger. 115/G3
Garmsār, Iran 146/F1

Garnpung (lake), Austl. 173/B2
Garonne (riv.), Fr. 100/D4
Garopaba, Braz. 213/B4
Garou (lake), Mali 161/E2
Garoua, Camr. 154/H6
Garphyttan, Swe. 96/F2
Garraf (mts.), Sp. 103/K7
Garrel, Ger. 109/F3
Garrison (dam), ND, US 185/H4
Garrison, ND, US 185/H4
Garron (pt.), NI, UK 92/C1
Garrovillas, Sp. 102/B3
Garry (bay), Nun., Can. 181/H2
Garry (lake), Nun., Can. 181/F2
Garry (riv.), Sc, UK 94/A2
Gars am Inn, Ger. 113/F6
Garsten, Aus. 113/H6
Garte (riv.), Ger. 109/H6
Gartempe (riv.), Fr. 100/D3
Gärtringen, Ger. 112/B5
Garut, Indo. 138/C5
Garwa, India 142/D3
Garvagh, NI, UK 92/B2
Garwolin, Pol. 99/L3
Garwood, NJ, US 197/H9
Gary, In, US 188/C3
Garza García, Mex. 201/E3
Garzê, China 128/H5
Garzón, Col. 210/C4
Gas, Fr. 88/G6
Gas City, In, US 188/C3
Gas-san (peak), Japan 134/B4
Gæsafjöll (peak), Ice. 95/P6
Gaschurn, Aus. 115/G4
Gasconade (riv.), Mo, US 187/J3
Gascony (reg.), Fr. 100/C5
Gascoyne (riv.), Austl. 167/A3
Gascoyne (mt.), Austl. 170/C3
Gaspar (str.), Indo. 138/C4
Gaspar, Braz. 213/B3
Gaspé, Qu, Can. 189/H1
Gaspé (pen.), Qu, Can. 189/H1
Gaspé, Cap de (cape), Qu, Can. 189/H1
Gaspoltshofen, Aus. 113/G6
Gasport, NY, US 189/S9
Gassino Torinese, It. 116/A2
Gastins, Fr. 88/M6
Gaston (lake), NC, US 191/J2
Gastonia, NC, US 191/H3
Gastoúni, Gre. 105/G4
Gata (cape), Sp. 102/D4
Gata (cape), Cyp. 149/C2
Gata de Gorgos, Sp. 103/F3
Gata, Sierra de (mts.), Sp. 102/B2
Gatchina, Rus. 97/P2
Gatehouse-of-Fleet, Sc, UK 94/C6
Gates of the Arctic NP and Prsv., Ak, US 192/G2
Gateshead (isl.), Nun., Can. 180/F1
Gateshead, Eng, UK 93/G2
Gateshead (co.), Eng, UK 93/G2
Gatesville, Tx, US 190/D4
Gateway Arch (arch), Mo, US 195/G8
Gateway NRA, NJ,NY, US 197/K9
Gatineau, Qu, Can. 188/F2
Gatineau (riv.), Qu, Can. 188/F2
Gatow, Ger. 98/Q7
Gattaran, Phil. 137/D4
Gattendorf, Aus. 101/M2
Gattinara, It. 116/B1
Gatton, Austl. 172/D4
Gatún (dam), Pan. 203/G4
Gatún (lake), Pan. 203/G4
Gatwick (int'l arpt.), Eng, UK 88/C3
Gau Algesheim, Ger. 112/B3
Gau Bischofsheim, Ger. 112/B3
Gaubickelheim, Ger. 111/H4
Gauchy, Fr. 110/C4
Gaucín, Sp. 102/C4
Gauja (riv.), Est.,Lat. 97/L3
Gauja NP, Lat. 97/L3
Gaukönigshofen, Ger. 112/C3
Gaunless (riv.), Eng, UK 93/G2
Gaupne, Nor. 95/C3
Gaur (riv.), Sc, UK 94/B3
Gauri Sankar (peak), Nepal 143/F2
Gauripur, India 143/G2
Gausta (peak), Nor. 96/C2
Gauting, Ger. 113/E6
Gává, Sp. 103/L7
Gávdhos (isl.), Gre. 105/J5
Gavere, Belg. 110/C2
Gavi, It. 116/B3
Gavião, Port. 102/B3
Gavirate, It. 116/B1
Gävle, Swe. 96/G1
Gävleborg (co.), Swe. 95/E3
Gawler (ranges), Austl. 167/C4
Gawler, Austl. 171/H5
Gay (peak), WV, US 188/D4
Gay, Rus. 121/L2
Gaya, India 143/E3
Gaya, Niger 161/F4
Gayaza, Ugan. 162/A3
Gaylord, Mi, US 188/C2
Gayndah, Austl. 172/C4

Gaza Strip, Isr. 148/C4
Gazeran, Fr. 88/H6
Gaziantep (prov.), Turk. 148/D2
Gaziantep, Turk. 148/D2
Gaziköy, Turk. 107/H5
Gazipaşa, Turk. 149/C1
Gazon de Faing (peak), Fr. 114/D1
Gazzaniga, It. 116/C1
Gbadolite, D.R. Congo 155/K7
Gbarnga, Libr. 160/C5
Gbongan, Nga. 161/G5
Gdansk (gulf), Pol. 99/K1
Gdansk, Pol. 96/H4
Gdynia, Pol. 96/H4
Ge (lake), China 130/D5
Geal Charn (peak), Sc, UK 94/C2
Geal Charn (peak), Sc, UK 94/A3
Gebaberg (peak), Ger. 112/D1
Gebe (isl.), Indo. 139/G3
Gebhardshain, Ger. 111/G2
Gebiz, Turk. 149/B1
Gebze, Turk. 107/J5
Gede (peak), Indo. 138/C5
Gedern, Ger. 112/C2
Gedi Ruins Nat'l Mon., Kenya 162/D3
Gedikbulak, Turk. 148/E2
Gedinne, Belg. 111/D4
Gediz, Turk. 148/B2
Gediz (riv.), Turk. 148/A2
Gedser (cape), Den. 96/D4
Gedser, Den. 96/D4
Gedsted, Den. 96/C3
Geel, Belg. 111/E1
Geelong, Austl. 173/C3
Geelvink (chan.), Austl. 167/A3
Geertruidenberg, Neth. 108/B5
Geeste (riv.), Ger. 109/F2
Geeste, Ger. 109/E3
Geesthacht, Ger. 109/H2
Geeveston, Austl. 173/C4
Gefrees, Ger. 113/E2
Gē'gyai, China 128/D5
Gehrde, Ger. 109/F3
Gehrden, Ger. 109/G4
Geifas (peak), Wal, UK 90/C2
Geikie (isl.), Ont. Can. 180/F3
Geilenkirchen, Ger. 111/F2
Geilo, Nor. 96/C1
Geinö, Japan 135/K6
Geiselhöring, Ger. 113/F5
Geiselwind, Ger. 112/D3
Geisenfeld, Ger. 113/E5
Geisenhausen, Ger. 113/F6
Geisenheim, Ger. 111/G4
Geislingen, Ger. 115/E1
Geislingen an der Steige, Ger. 112/C5
Geita, Tanz. 162/A3
Gejiu, China 141/H3
Gela, It. 104/D4
Gela, Golfo di (gulf), It. 104/D4
Gelai (peak), Tanz. 162/C3
Gelderland (prov.), Neth. 108/C4
Geldermalsen, Neth. 108/C5
Geldern, Ger. 108/D5
Geldersheim, Ger. 112/D2
Geldrop, Neth. 108/C6
Geleen, Neth. 111/E2
Gelendost, Turk. 148/C2
Gelendzhik, Rus. 120/F3
Gelibolu (Gallipoli), Turk. 105/K2
Gelibolu Yarımadas NP, Turk. 105/K2
Gelincik (peak), Turk. 148/E2
Gelligaer, Wal, UK 90/C3
Gelnhausen, Ger. 112/C2
Gelsenkirchen, Ger. 108/E5
Geltendorf, Ger. 115/H1
Gelterkinden, Swi. 114/D3
Gelting, Ger. 96/C4
Gemas, Malay. 138/B3
Gembloux, Belg. 111/D2
Gemena, D.R. Congo 155/J7
Gemert, Neth. 108/C5
Gemlik (gulf), Turk. 107/J5
Gemlik, Turk. 107/J5
Gemona del Friuli, It. 101/K3
Gemsbok NP, Bots. 163/D6
Gemuk (mtn.), Ak, US 192/G3
Gemünden am Main, Ger. 112/C2
Genalē Wenz (riv.), Eth. 155/N6
Genappe, Belg. 111/D2
Genay, Fr. 114/A6
Genç, Turk. 148/...
Gendringen, Neth. 108/D5
Gendt, Neth. 108/C5
Genemuiden, Neth. 108/D3
General Abelardo L. Rodríguez (int'l arpt.), Mex. 200/A1
General Acha, Arg. 216/D3
General Alfredo Vasquez Cobo (int'l arpt.), Col. 214/D2
General Alvear, Arg. 216/D2
General Alvear, Arg. 216/E3
General Arenales, Arg. 216/E2

General Belgrano, Arg. 216/F2
General Belgrano II, Arg., Ant. 218/X
General Cabrera, Arg. 216/E2
General Carrera (lake), Chile 215/B6
General Cepeda, Mex. 201/E3
General Conesa, Arg. 216/D4
General Deheza, Arg. 216/E2
General Edward Lawrence Logan (Logan Int'l) (int'l arpt.), Ma, US 189/G3
General Enrique Godoy, Arg. 216/D3
General Francisco Villa, Mex. 201/F3
General Galarza, Arg. 217/J10
General Grant Nat'l Mem., NY, US 197/K8
General Juan Álvarez, PN, Mex. 201/F5
General Juan José Ríos, Mex. 200/C3
General Juan Madariaga, Arg. 217/F3
General La Madrid, Arg. 216/E3
General Lagos, Chile 214/D5
General Las Heras, Arg. 217/J11
General Lavalle, Arg. 217/K12
General Martín Miguel de Güemes, Arg. 215/C1
General Pico, Arg. 216/E2
General Pinedo, Arg. 215/D2
General Pinto, Arg. 216/E2
General Roca, Arg. 216/D3
General San Martín, Arg. 216/E3
General San Martín, Arg. 217/J11
General San Martín, Arg., Ant. 218/V
General Santiago Marino (int'l arpt.),Ven. 211/F2
General Terán, Mex. 201/F3
General-Toshevo, Bul. 107/J4
General Viamonte, Arg. 216/E2
General Villalobas (int'l arpt.), Mex. 200/D2
General Villegas, Arg. 216/E2
General Zaragoza, Mex. 201/F4
Generoso (peak), Swi. 115/F6
Genesee (co.), Mi, US 193/E6
Genesee (riv.), NY, US 188/E3
Genesee, Wi, US 193/P14
Genesee Depot, Wi, US 193/P14
Geneseo, Il, US 185/L5
Geneseo, NY, US 188/E3
Geneva (Léman) (lake), Fr. 101/G3
Geneva (Genève), Swi. 101/G3
Geneva (int'l arpt.), Swi. 114/C5
Geneva, Al, US 191/G4
Geneva, Ne, US 187/H2
Geneva, NY, US 188/E3
Geneva, Ut, US 195/K13
Genève (canton), Swi. 114/C5
Genève, Swi. 114/C5
Gengenbach, Ger. 114/E1
Génicourt, Fr. 88/J4
Genk, Belg. 111/E2
Genlis, Fr. 114/B3
Gennach (riv.), Ger. 115/G2
Gennargentu (mts.), It. 104/A2
Gennep, Neth. 108/C5
Gennevilliers, Fr. 88/J5
Genoa (Genova), It. 101/H4
Genoa City, Wi, US 193/P14
Genova (prov.), It. 116/C4
Genova (Genoa), It. 116/B4
Genova, Golfo di (gulf), It. 101/H4
Genovesa (isl.), Ecu. 214/F6
Gensingen, Ger. 111/G4
Gent-Brugge Kanaal (canal), Belg. 110/C1
Gent (Ghent), Belg. 110/C1
Genteng (cape), Indo. 138/C5
Genteng, Indo. 138/D5
Geographe (bay), Austl. 170/B5
Geographe (chan.), Austl. 170/B3
Georg von Neumayer, Ger., Ant. 218/Z
George (lake), Austl. 171/D2
George (pt.), Austl. 172/C3
George (riv.), Qu, Can. 181/K3
George, SAfr. 164/C4
George (lake), Ugan. 162/A3
George (lake), Fl, US 191/H4
George Land (isl.), Rus. 122/E2
George Town, Austl. 173/C4
George Town (cap.), Cay. 203/F2
George Town, Malay. 138/B2
George V (coast), Ant. 218/L
George Washington Birthplace Nat'l Mon., Va, US 191/J2
George West, Tx, US 190/D4
Georgensmünd, Ger. 112/E4
Georges (riv.), Austl. 172/G9
Georgetown, Austl. 172/A2
Georgetown, Gam. 160/B3
Georgetown (cap.), Guy. 211/G3
Georgetown, StV. 199/N9
Georgetown, Ct, US 197/E1
Georgetown, Ga, US 191/H4
Georgetown, Ky, US 188/C4
Georgetown, SC, US 191/J3
Georgetown, Tx, US 187/H5
Georgi Traykov, Bul. 107/H4
Georgia (ctry.) 121/G4
Georgia, Strait of (str.), BC, Can. 184/B3
Georgia (state), US 191/G3
Georgian (bay), On, Can. 181/H4
Georgian Bay Islands NP, On, Can. 188/D2
Georgina (riv.), Austl. 167/C3
Georgsmarienhütte, Ger. 109/F4
Gepatsch (lake), Aus. 115/G4
Gera, Ger. 98/G3
Geraardsbergen, Belg. 110/C2
Geral de Goiás, Serra (mts.), Braz. 209/J6
Geral, Serra (mts.), Braz. 215/F2
Geraldine, NZ 159/S11
Geraldton, Austl. 170/B4
Gérardmer, Fr. 114/C1
Gerasdorf bei Wien, Aus. 107/N7
Gerbéviller, Fr. 114/C1
Gerbier de Jonc (peak), Fr. 100/F4
Gerbrunn, Ger. 112/C3
Gerdau (riv.), Ger. 109/H3
Gerdine (mt.), Ak, US 192/H3
Gerede, Turk. 107/L5
Geretsried, Ger. 115/H2
Gérgal, Sp. 102/D4
Gerger, Turk. 148/D2
Gerlach, Nv, US 184/D5
Gerlachovský Štít (peak), Slvk. 99/L4
Gerlafingen, Swi. 114/D3
Germantown, Tn, US 187/K4
Germantown, Md, US 196/A5
Germany (ctry.) 98/E3
Germering, Ger. 113/E6
Germersheim, Ger. 112/B4
Germigny-l'Evêque, Fr. 88/L5
Germinaga, It. 115/E6
Germiston, SAfr. 164/E2
Gernsbach, Ger. 112/B5
Geroldsgrün, Ger. 113/E2
Gerolsbach, Ger. 113/E5
Gerolstein, Ger. 111/F3
Gerolzhofen, Ger. 112/D3
Gerpinnes, Belg. 111/D3
Gerra (Verzasca), Swi. 115/E5
Gerringong, Austl. 173/D2
Gers (riv.), Fr. 100/D5
Gersau, Swi. 115/E4
Gersfeld, Ger. 112/C2
Gersheim, Ger. 111/G5
Gerspenz (riv.), Ger. 112/B3
Gerstetten, Ger. 112/E5
Gerstheim, Fr. 114/D1
Gersthofen, Ger. 112/D6
Gerstungen, Ger. 109/H7
Gërzë, China 128/D5
Gerze, Turk. 120/E4
Gescher, Ger. 108/E5
Geseke, Ger. 109/F5
Gespunsart, Fr. 111/D4
Gessertshausen, Ger. 112/D6
Gestro Wenz (riv.), Eth. 155/P6
Gesves, Belg. 111/E3
Geta, Fin. 97/H1
Getafe, Sp. 103/N9
Gete (riv.), Belg. 111/E2
Getinge, Swe. 96/E3
Gettorf, Ger. 96/C4
Gettysburg, SD, US 185/J4
Gettysburg, Pa, US 188/E4
Gettysburg Nat'l Mil. Park, Pa, US 196/A4
Getúlio Vargas, Braz. 213/A3
Geul (riv.), Neth. 111/E2
Geureudong (peak), Indo. 138/A3
Geurie, Austl. 173/D2
Gevaş, Turk. 148/E2
Gevelsberg, Ger. 109/E6
Gevgelija, FYROM 105/H2
Gex, Fr. 114/C5
Geyer, Ger. 113/F1
Geyersberg (peak), Ger. 112/C3
Geyikli, Turk. 105/K3
Geyser (reef), Madg. 165/H6
Geyve, Turk. 107/K5
Gez (riv.), China 145/F5
Ghadāmis, Libya 157/H3
Ghaggar (riv.), India 144/C5
Ghaghara (riv.), India 142/C2
Ghakhar, Pak. 144/C3
Ghana (ctry.) 161/E4
Ghanzi, Bots. 163/D5
Gharaunda, India 144/D5
Ghardaïa, Alg. 157/F2
Ghardaïa (prov.), Alg. 157/F3
Ghardimaou, Tun. 158/L6
Gharghoda, India 142/D4
Gharyān, Libya 154/H1
Ghāt, Libya 157/H4
Ghātāl, India 143/F4
Ghātampur, India 142/C2
Ghātsīla, India 143/F4
Ghazal, Bahr el (riv.), Chad 154/J5
Ghazaouet, Alg. 158/D2
Ghāzīpur, India 142/D3
Ghaznī, Afg. 147/J2
Ghedi, It. 116/D2
Gheens, La, US 195/P17
Ghemme, It. 116/B1
Ghenghis Khan, Wall of, Mong. 129/K2
Gheorghe Gheorghiu-Dej, Rom. 107/H2
Gheorgheni, Rom. 107/G2
Gherla, Rom. 107/F2
Ghilarza, It. 104/A2
Ghinda (Gīnda), Erit. 146/C5
Ghio (lake), Arg. 216/C5
Ghirārah (gulf), Tun. 157/H2
Ghisalba, It. 116/C1
Ghisonaccia, Fr. 104/A1
Ghotki, Pak. 140/A2
Ghugri (riv.), India 143/F3
Ghūriān, Afg. 147/H2
Ghuzayyil, Bi'r al (well), Libya 154/H2
Giannutri (isl.), It. 104/B1
Giant's Castle (peak), SAfr. 164/E3
Giant's Causeway, NI, UK 92/B1
Giant Sequoia Nat'l Mon., Ca, US 186/C4
Giarre, It. 104/D4
Gibbons, Ab, Can. 184/E2
Gibbstown, NJ, US 196/C4
Gibloux (peak), Swi. 114/D4
Gibraleón, Sp. 102/B4
Gibraltar (pt.), Eng, UK 93/J5
Gibraltar (cap.), Gib. 102/C4
Gibraltar (str.), Mor.,Sp. 102/B5
Gibraltar (res.), Ca, US 194/A1
Gibraltar, Mi, US 193/F7
Gibraltar, Ven. 199/G6
Gibraltar Range NP, Austl. 173/E1
Gibson (des.), Austl. 167/B3
Gibson Desert Nature Reserve, Austl. 170/E3
Giddarbāha, India 144/C4
Giddings, Tx, US 187/H5
Giddings, Co, US 195/B1
Gidi (pass), Egypt 149/C4
Giebelstadt, Ger. 112/C3
Gieboldehausen, Ger. 109/H5
Gien, Fr. 100/E3
Giengen an der Brenz, Ger. 112/D5
Gier (riv.), Fr. 100/F4
Giessbachfälle (falls), Swi. 114/E4
Giessen (riv.), Fr.,Ger. 114/D1
Giessen, Ger. 112/B1
Giessendam, Neth. 108/B5
Gieten, Neth. 108/D2
Gif-sur-Yvette, Fr. 88/J5
Gīfān, Iran 121/L5
Gifford, Fl, US 191/H5
Gifford (riv.), Nun., Can. 181/H1
Giffre (riv.), Fr. 114/C5
Gifhorn, Ger. 109/H4
Gifu, Japan 135/L5
Giganta, Sierra de la (mts.), Mex. 200/C3
Gigante, Col. 210/C4
Giglio (isl.), It. 104/B1
Gijón, Sp. 102/C1
Gil de Vilches, PN, Chile 216/C2
Gila (riv.), Az, US 186/D4
Gila Bend, Az, US 186/D4
Gila Cliff Dwellings Nat'l Mon., NM, US 186/E4
Gila River Ind. Res., Az, US 195/R19
Gilbert, Mn, US 188/A2
Gilbert (riv.), Austl. 167/D2
Gilbert, Az, US 195/S19
Gilbert (isls.), Kiri. 174/G5
Gilberts, Il, US 193/P15
Gilbués, Braz. 212/A3
Gilching, Ger. 112/E6
Gilcrest, Co, US 195/C2
Gilford, NI, UK 92/B3
Gilford Park, NJ, US 196/D4
Gilgandra, Austl. 173/D1
Gilgil, Kenya 162/C3
Gilgit (riv.), Pak. 145/F5
Gilles (lake), Austl. 171/H5
Gillette, Wy, US 185/G4
Gillies Bay, BC, Can. 184/B3
Gillingham, Eng, UK 91/G4
Gillot (int'l arpt.), Reun., Fr. 165/S15
Gilly, Swi. 114/C5
Gilman Hot Springs, Ca, US 194/D3
Gilmer, Tx, US 187/J4
Gilpin, Co, US 195/A3
Gilgit (riv.), Pak. 147/K1
Gilze, Neth. 108/B5
Gīmbī, Eth. 155/N6
Gimbsheim, Ger. 112/B3
Gimel, Swi. 114/C4
Gimie (mt.), StL. 199/N9
Gimli, Mb, Can. 185/J3
Gimo, Swe. 96/H1
Gin Gin, Austl. 172/C4
Ginan, Japan 135/L5
Gingelom, Belg. 111/E2
Gingin, Austl. 170/B4
Gingindlovu, SAfr. 165/E3
Gingoog, Phil. 137/E6
Gingst, Ger. 96/E4
Ginosa, It. 104/E2
Ginowan, Japan 133/J7
Gioia (gulf), It. 104/D3
Gioia del Colle, It. 104/E2
Gioia Tauro, It. 104/D3
Giornico, Swi. 115/E5
Gioūra (isl.), Gre. 105/J3
Gioveretto (peak), It. 115/G5
Giovi (peak), It. 117/E5
Gipping (riv.), Eng, UK 91/G2
Girardot, Col. 208/D3
Girardville, Pa, US 196/B2
Giraumont, Fr. 111/E5
Girdle Ness (pt.), Sc, UK 94/D2
Giresun (prov.), Turk. 148/D1
Giresun, Turk. 148/D1
Girgnasco, It. 116/B1
Girīdīh, India 143/F3
Girifalco, It. 104/E3
Girling (res.), Eng, UK 88/C2
Giromagny, Fr. 114/C2
Girón, Ecu. 210/B5
Girón, Col. 210/C3
Girona, Sp. 103/G2
Gironcourt-sur-Vraine, Fr. 114/B1
Gironde (riv.), Fr. 100/C4
Gironella, Sp. 103/F1
Girraween NP, Austl. 173/D1
Giru, Austl. 172/B2
Girvan, Sc, UK 92/D1
Gisborne, NZ 159/T10
Gisenyi, Rwa. 162/A3
Gislaved, Swe. 96/E3
Gisors, Fr. 110/A5
Gistel, Belg. 110/B1
Gistrup, Den. 96/D3
Gitega, Buru. 162/A3
Gittsfjället (peak), Swe. 95/E2
Giubiasco, Swi. 115/F5
Giugliano in Campania, It. 106/B5
Giulianova, It. 101/K5
Giurgiu (prov.), Rom. 107/G3
Giurgiu, Rom. 107/G4
Giussano, It. 116/C1
Giv'at Brenner, Isr. 149/F8
Giv'at Hayyim, Isr. 149/F7
Giv'atayim, Isr. 149/F7
Give, Den. 96/C4
Givet, Fr. 111/D3
Givors, Fr. 100/F4
Givrine, Col de la (pass), Swi. 114/C5
Giyani, SAfr. 163/F5
Gizhiga (bay), Rus. 123/R3
Gizo, Sol. 174/E5
Giżycko, Pol. 97/J4
Gjerdrum, Nor. 96/D1
Gjerlev, Den. 96/D3
Gjerstad, Nor. 96/C2
Gjirokastër, Alb. 105/G2
Gjoa Haven, Nun., Can. 180/G2
Gjøvik, Nor. 96/D1
Glabbeek, Belg. 111/E2
Glace Bay, NS, Can. 189/K2
Glacier (peak), Wa, US 184/C3
Glacier Bay NP and Prsv., Ak, US 192/L4
Glacier NP, BC, Can. 184/D3
Gladbeck, Ger. 108/D5
Gladewater, Tx, US 187/J4
Gladstone, Mo, US 195/D5
Gladstone, Austl. 172/C3
Gladstone, Austl. 171/H5
Gladwin, Mi, US 188/C3
Glafsfjorden (lake), Swe. 96/D2
Glåma (riv.), Nor. 95/D3
Glamis, Sc, UK 94/D3
Glamsbjerg, Den. 96/D4
Glan, Phil. 137/E6
Glan (riv.), Ger. 98/D4
Glanamman, Wal, UK 90/C3
Gland, Swi. 114/C5
Gland (riv.), Fr. 111/D4
Glandorf, Ger. 109/F4
Glärnisch (range), Swi. 115/E3
Glarus, Swi. 115/F3
Glarus (canton), Swi. 115/E4
Glarus Alps (range), Swi. 101/H3
Glas Maol (peak), Sc, UK 94/C3
Glasgow, Mt, US 184/G3
Glasgow, Ky, US 188/C4
Glasgow, De, US 196/C4
Glasgow, Sc, UK 94/B5
Glashütten, Ger. 112/B2
Glaslyn (riv.), Wal, UK 92/D6
Glass (mts.), Ok, US 190/D2
Glass (lake), Sc, UK 94/B1
Glass (riv.), Sc, UK 94/B2
Glassboro, NJ, US 196/C4
Glastonbury, Eng, UK 90/D4
Glatt (riv.), Ger. 112/B6
Glattbach, Ger. 112/C3
Glattfelden, Swi. 115/E2
Glavinitsa, Bul. 107/H4
Glazoué, Ben. 161/F5
Glazov, Rus. 119/M4
Glems (riv.), Ger. 112/C5
Glen (riv.), Eng, UK 93/H6
Glen Burnie, Md, US 196/B5
Glen Canyon (dam), Az, US 186/E3
Glen Canyon Nat'l Rec. Area, US 186/E3
Glen Carbon, Il, US 195/H8
Glen Coe (pass), Sc, UK 94/B3
Glen Cove, NY, US 197/L8
Glen Gardner, NJ, US 196/D2
Glen Haven, Co, US 195/B2
Glen Innes, Austl. 173/D1
Glen Lyon, Pa, US 196/B1
Glen Mòr (valley), Sc, UK 94/B2
Glen Park, Mo, US 195/G9
Glen Ridge, NJ, US 197/J8
Glen Rock, Pa, US 196/B4
Glen Rock, NJ, US 197/J8
Glen Ullin, ND, US 185/H4
Glenaire, Mo, US 195/E5
Glenan, Îles de (isls.), Fr. 100/A3
Glenarm, NI, UK 92/C2
Glenarm (riv.), NI, UK 92/C2
Glenavy, NI, UK 92/B2
Glenbawn (dam), Austl. 173/D2
Glenboro, Mb, Can. 185/J3
Glencoe, SAfr. 165/E3
Glencoe, Mo, US 195/F8
Glencoe, Il, US 193/Q15
Glencoe, Sc, UK 94/A3
Glendale, Or, US 184/C5
Glendale, Az, US 195/R18
Glendale, Ca, US 194/F7
Glendale Heights, Il, US 193/P16
Glenden, Austl. 172/C3
Glendive, Mt, US 185/G4
Glendo (res.), Wy, US 185/G5
Glendora, Ca, US 194/C2
Glendun (riv.), NI, UK 92/B1
Glenealy, Ire. 92/B6
Glenelg (riv.), Austl. 173/B3
Glenelg, Md, US 196/B5
Glenelg, Sc, UK 89/R8
Glenelly (riv.), NI, UK 92/A2
Glengarry (range), Austl. 170/C3
Glenluce, Sc, UK 92/D2
Glenmere (lake), NY, US 196/D1
Glennallen, Ak, US 192/J3
Glenolden, Pa, US 196/C4
Glenorie, Austl. 172/H8
Glenpool, Ok, US 187/H4
Glenrothes, Sc, UK 94/C4
Glens Falls, NY, US 188/F3
Glenshane (pass), NI, UK 92/B2
Glenside, Pa, US 196/C3
Glenties, Ire. 89/P9
Glenveagh NP, Ire. 89/Q9
Glenview, Il, US 193/Q15
Glenwood, NJ, US 196/D1
Glenwood Springs, Co, US 186/F3
Gleouraich (peak), Sc, UK 94/A2
Glifádha, Gre. 105/N9
Glimåkra, Swe. 96/F3
Glina, Cro. 106/C3
Glinde, Ger. 109/H1
Glindow, Ger. 98/P7
Gliwice, Pol. 99/K3
Globe, Az, US 186/E4
Glockturm (peak), Aus. 115/G4
Gloggnitz, Aus. 99/H5
Głogów, Pol. 99/J3
Głogówek, Pol. 99/J3
Glonn (riv.), Ger. 112/E6
Gloria (bay), Cuba 203/G1
Glorieuses, Îles (isls.), Reun., Fr. 165/H5
Glorious (mt.), Austl. 172/E6
Glory of Russia (cape), Ak, US 192/D3
Glossop, Eng, UK 93/G5
Gloster, Ms, US 187/K5
Gloucester, Austl. 173/D1
Gloucester, On, Can. 188/F2
Gloucester, Eng, UK 90/D3
Gloucester (co.), NJ, US 196/C4
Gloucester City, NJ, US 196/C4
Gloucestershire (co.), Eng, UK 90/D3
Glovers (reef), Belz. 202/E2
Glovertown, Nf, Can. 189/L1
Głowno, Pol. 99/K3
Głubczyce, Pol. 99/J3
Głuchołazy, Pol. 99/J3
Glücksburg, Ger. 96/C4
Glückstadt, Ger. 109/G1
Glyndon, Md, US 196/B5
Glyngøre, Den. 96/C3
Glynn, NI, UK 92/C2
Gmünd, Aus. 99/H4
Gmunden, Aus. 113/G7
Gnagna (prov.), Burk. 161/E3
Gnarrenburg, Ger. 109/G2
Gniew, Pol. 97/H5
Gniezno, Pol. 99/J2
Gnjilane, Kos. 106/E4
Gnowangerup, Austl. 170/C5
Gō (riv.), Japan 132/C3
Go Cong, Viet. 136/D4
Goa (state), India 140/B4
Goālpāra, India 143/H2
Goat Fell (peak), Sc, UK 94/A5
Goba, Eth. 155/N6
Gobabis, Namb. 163/C5
Gobardānga, India 143/G4
Gobernador Castro, Arg. 216/F2
Gobernador Costa, Arg. 216/C5
Gobernador Gregores, Arg. 217/C6
Gobernador Mansilla, Arg. 217/J10
Gobi (des.), China,Mong. 128/H4
Göblberg (peak), Aus. 113/G6
Gobō, Japan 132/D4
Goch, Ger. 108/D5
Gochsheim, Ger. 112/D2
Godalming, Eng, UK 91/F4
Godāvari (riv.), India 140/C4
Goddā, India 143/F3
Godeanu (peak), Rom. 106/F3
Godech, Bul. 105/H1
Goderich, On, Can. 188/D3
Godfrey, Il, US 195/G8
Gōdo, Japan 135/L5
Gödöllő, Hun. 99/K5
Godoy Cruz, Arg. 216/C2
Gods (riv.), Mb, Can. 180/G3
Gods (lake), Mb, Can. 180/G3
Gods Mercy (bay), Nun., Can. 181/H2
Godthåb (Nuuk), Grld. 177/M3
Godwin Austen (K2) (peak), Pak. 144/D2
Goéland (lake), Qu, Can. 188/E1
Goeree (isl.), Neth. 108/A5
Goes, Neth. 108/A5
Gogebic (range), Mi, US 185/L4
Göggingen, Ger. 112/D6
Gogland (isl.), Rus. 97/M1
Gogōme, Japan 134/B4
Gogounou, Ben. 161/F4
Gogra (riv.), India 140/D2
Gohad, India 142/B2
Gohāna, India 144/D5
Gohbach (riv.), Ger. 109/G3
Goiana, Braz. 212/D2
Goiandira, Braz. 213/B1
Goiânia, Braz. 209/J7
Goianinha, Braz. 212/D2
Goiás, Braz. 209/H7
Goiás (state), Braz. 212/A5
Goiatuba, Braz. 213/B1
Goil (lake), Sc, UK 94/B4
Goirle, Neth. 108/C5
Góis, Port. 102/A2
Goito, It. 117/D2
Gojō, Japan 132/D3
Gojra, Pak. 144/B4
Gok (riv.), Turk. 120/E4
Goka, Japan 135/D1
Gokase (riv.), Japan 132/B4
Gokashō, Japan 135/K5
Gokasho (bay), Japan 135/L7
Gökçeada (isl.), Turk. 148/A1
Gökçebey, Turk. 107/L5
Gökçekaya (dam), Turk. 148/B1
Göksu (riv.), Turk. 148/D2
Göksun, Turk. 148/D2
Göktepe, Turk. 149/C1
Gol, Nor. 96/C1
Gola Gokarannāth, India 142/C1
Golan Hts. (reg.), Syria 149/D3
Golasecca, It. 116/B1
Gölbaşı, Turk. 148/D2
Golbey, Fr. 114/C1
Golborne, Eng, UK 93/F5
Gölcük, Turk. 107/J5
Gold (coast), Gha. 154/E7
Gold (mtn.), Wa, US 193/B2
Gold Bar, Wa, US 193/D2
Gold Beach, Or, US 184/B5
Gold Coast, Austl. 172/D5
Gold Hill, Co, US 195/B2
Gold River, BC, Can. 184/B3
Goldach, Swi. 115/F3
Gołdap, Pol. 97/K4
Goldbach, Ger. 112/C3
Goldberg, Ger. 96/E5
Golden, BC, Can. 184/D3
Golden, Co, US 195/B3
Golden Eagle, Il, US 195/F8
Golden Gate (chan.), Ca, US 193/J11
Golden Gate Highlands NP, SAfr. 164/D3
Golden Hinde (peak), BC, Can. 184/B3
Golden Temple, India 144/C4
Goldendale, Wa, US 184/C4
Goldene Aue (reg.), Ger. 98/F3
Goldenstedt, Ger. 109/F3
Goldkronach, Ger. 113/E2
Goldman, Mo, US 195/F9
Goldmine (mtn.), Az, US 195/S19
Goldsboro, NC, US 191/J3
Goldsboro, Md, US 196/C5
Goldsby, Ok, US 195/N15
Goldsworthy, Austl. 170/C2
Goldthwaite, Tx, US 190/D4
Göle, Turk. 148/E1
Goleniów, Pol. 96/F5
Golfito NWR, CR 203/F4
Golfo Aranci, It. 104/A2
Golfo de Santa Clara, Mex. 200/B2
Gölhisar, Turk. 149/A1
Goliad, Tx, US 187/H5
Gölköy, Turk. 148/D1
Gollach (riv.), Ger. 112/D3
Göllheim, Ger. 112/B3
Gölmarmara, Turk. 148/A2
Golmud, China 128/F4
Golovin, Ak, US 192/F3
Golovnina (peak), Rus. 134/D2
Golpāyegān, Iran 146/F2
Gölpazarı, Turk. 107/K5
Gols, Aus. 101/M3
Golts, Md, US 196/C5
Golub-Dobrzyń, Pol. 99/K2
Golubovci (int'l arpt.), Mont. 106/D4
Golyam Perelik (peak), Bul. 105/J2
Golyama Kamchiya (riv.), Bul. 107/H4
Golyama Syutkya (peak), Bul. 105/J2
Goma, D.R. Congo 162/A3
Goma (int'l arpt.), D.R. Congo 162/A3
Gomaringen, Ger. 112/C6
Gomati (riv.), India 142/C2
Gombe (state), Nga. 161/H4
Gombe (riv.), Tanz. 162/A4
Gombe NP, Tanz. 162/A4
Gomera (isl.), Canl., Sp. 156/A4
Gómez Farías, Mex. 200/D2
Gómez Palacio, Mex. 200/E3
Gomīshān, Iran 146/F1
Gommern, Ger. 98/F2
Gomoh, India 143/F4
Goms (valley), Swi. 114/E5
Gonābād, Iran 147/G2
Gonaïves, Haiti 203/H2
Gonarezhou NP, Zim. 163/F5
Gonâve (gulf), Haiti 199/G4
Gonâve (isl.), Haiti 203/H2
Gonbad-e Qābūs, Iran 147/G1
Gonbadlī, Iran 145/D5
Gönc, Hun. 99/L4
Gonçalves Dias, Braz. 212/A2
Gondelsheim, Ger. 112/B4
Gonder, Eth. 155/N5
Gondia, India 140/D3
Gondomar, Sp. 102/A1
Gondomar, Port. 102/A2
Gondrecourt-le-Château, Fr. 114/B1
Gondreville, Fr. 111/E6
Gondrexange (lake), Fr. 111/F6
Gönen, Turk. 107/H5
Gonesse, Fr. 88/K5
Gong Xian, China 131/C4
Gong Xian, China 130/C4
Gong'an, China 141/K3
Gongbo'gyamda, China 141/F2
Gongcheng, China 137/B3
Gongga (peak), China 141/H2
Gonggar, China 143/H1
Gonghe, China 128/H4
Gongliu, China 128/D3
Gongola (riv.), Nga. 154/H5
Gongshan Drungzu Nuzu Zizhixian, China 141/G2
Gongzhuling, China 130/F2
Goñi, Uru. 217/K10
Gonjo, China 128/G5
Gónnoi, Gre. 105/H3
Gonohe, Japan 134/B3
Gonubie, SAfr. 164/D4
Gonyű, Hun. 106/C2
Gonzaga, It. 117/D3
Gonzales, Tx, US 187/H5
González, Mex. 201/F4
Good Hope, La, US 195/P17
Good Hope, Cape of (cape), SAfr. 164/L11
Goodenough (cape), Ant. 218/J
Goodnews Bay, Ak, US 192/F4
Goodooga, Austl. 173/C1
Goodrich, Mi, US 193/F6
Goodwick, Wal, UK 90/B2
Goodwood, SAfr. 164/L10
Goodyear, Az, US 195/R19
Gooimeer (lake), Neth. 108/C4
Goole, Eng, UK 93/H4
Goolgowi, Austl. 173/C2
Gooloogong, Austl. 173/D2
Goolwa, Austl. 171/H5
Goomalling, Austl. 170/C4
Goombungee, Austl. 172/C4
Goondiwindi, Austl. 172/C5
Goongarrie NP, Austl. 170/D4
Goor, Neth. 108/D4
Goose (lake), Mb, Can. 185/H2
Goose (lake), Ca,Or, US 184/C5
Goose (pt.), De, US 196/C5
Goose (pt.), La, US 195/Q16
Gopālganj, India 143/E2
Gopālpur, Bang. 143/G3
Gopat (riv.), India 142/D3
Göppingen, Ger. 112/C5
Góra, Pol. 99/J3
Góra Kalwaria, Pol. 99/L3
Goražde, Bosn. 106/D4
Gorczański NP, Pol. 99/L4
Gorda (pt.), Cuba 203/F1
Gorda (pt.), Nic. 203/F3
Gorda (pt.), Nic. 203/F4
Gordevio, Swi. 115/E5
Gørding, Den. 96/C4
Gordola, Swi. 115/E5
Gordon, Austl. 173/C4
Gordon (lake), Austl. 167/D5
Gordonsbaai, SAfr. 164/L11
Gordonvale, Austl. 172/B2
Gore (pt.), Ak, US 192/H4
Goré, Chad 154/J6
Gorē, Eth. 155/N6
Gore, NZ 159/R12
Gorebridge, Sc, UK 94/C5
Görele, Turk. 148/D1
Goresbridge, Ire. 89/Q10
Gorey, Chl, UK 100/B2
Gorey, Ire. 89/Q10
Gorgān, Iran 147/F1
Gorge du Loup, Lux. 111/F4
Gorges du Ziz, Mor. 156/D2
Gorgol (pol. reg.), Mrta. 160/B3
Gorgol (riv.), Mrta. 160/B2
Gorgona, Isola di (isl.), It. 116/C6
Gorgonzola, It. 116/C1
Gori, Geo. 121/H4
Gorinchem, Neth. 108/B5
Gorizia, It. 117/G1
Gorizia (prov.), It. 117/G1
Gorj (prov.), Rom. 107/F3
Gorki, Bela. 120/D1
Gor'kiy (res.), Rus. 118/J4
Gorlice, Pol. 99/L4
Görlitz, Ger. 99/H3
Gorllwyn (peak), Wal, UK 90/C2
Gorman, Tx, US 187/H4
Gormanstown, Ire. 92/B4
Gormī, India 142/B2
Gorner (glacier), Swi. 114/D6
Gornji Milanovac, Serb. 106/E3
Gornji Vakuf, Bosn. 106/C4
Gorno-Altay Aut. Rep., Rus. 122/J4
Goro, It. 117/F3
Gorodets, Rus. 119/J4
Gorom Gorom, Burk. 161/E3
Gorong (isl.), Indo. 139/H4
Gorongoza, Moz. 163/F4
Gorontalo, Indo. 139/F3
Gorssel, Neth. 108/D4
Gorst, Wa, US 193/B2
Gortin, NI, UK 92/A2
Görwihl, Ger. 114/E2
Goryn' (riv.), Ukr. 120/C2
Gorzano (peak), It. 101/K5
Gorzów Wielkopolski, Pol. 99/H2
Gosainganj, India 142/D2
Göschenen, Swi. 115/E4
Gōse, Japan 135/J7
Gosen, Japan 133/F2
Gosford, Austl. 173/D2
Gosforth, Eng, UK 93/G2
Goshen, NJ, US 196/D5
Goshogawara, Japan 134/B3
Goslar, Ger. 109/H5
Gospić, Cro. 106/B3
Gosport, Eng, UK 91/E5
Gossas, Sen. 160/A3
Gossau, Swi. 115/F3
Gossersweiler-Stein, Ger. 111/G5
Gostivar, FYROM 105/G2
Gostyń, Pol. 99/J3
Gostynin, Pol. 99/K2
Göta (riv.), Swe. 96/G2

Götaland (reg.), Swe. 96/E3
Göteborg, Swe. 96/D3
Göteborg Och Bohus (co.), Swe. 95/D4
Gotel (mts.), Nga. 154/H6
Gotemba, Japan 133/F3
Gotène, Swe. 96/E2
Gotha, Ger. 109/H7
Gotland (co.), Swe. 95/F4
Gotland, Swe. 95/F4
Gotse Delchev, Bul. 105/H2
Gotska Sandön (isl.), Swe. 97/H2
Gotska Sandön NP, Swe. 97/H2
Götsu, Japan 132/C3
Gottenheim, Ger. 114/D1
Göttingen, Ger. 109/G5
Gottmadingen, Ger. 115/E2
Gottolengo, It. 116/D2
Götzis, Aus. 115/F3
Gouda, Neth. 108/B4
Gouda, SAfr. 164/L10
Gough (isl.), StH 80/J7
Gouin (res.), Qu, Can. 181/J4
Goulais (riv.), On, Can. 188/C2
Goulburn (riv.), Austl. 173/D2
Goulburn, Austl. 173/D2
Goulburn (isls.), Austl. 167/C2
Gould, Ar, US 190/F3
Gould (mt.), Austl. 170/C3
Gouldsboro, Pa, US 196/C1
Goulimine, Mor. 156/C3
Goulmima, Mor. 156/D3
Goundam, Mali 160/E2
Goupillières, Fr. 88/H5
Gourdon, Fr. 100/D4
Gouré, Niger 161/H3
Gourin, Fr. 100/B2
Gourits (riv.), SAfr. 164/C4
Gourma (phys. reg.), Burk. 161/F3
Gourma (prov.), Burk. 161/F3
Gourma Rharous, Mali 161/E2
Gournay-en-Bray, Fr. 110/A5
Gourock, Sc, UK 94/B5
Goussainville, Fr. 88/K4
Gouvêa, Braz. 213/D1
Gouveia, Port. 102/B2
Gouvieux, Fr. 88/K4
Gouvy, Belg. 111/E4
Gouyave, Gren. 199/N9
Govardhan, India 142/A2
Goverla (peak), Ukr. 107/G1
Governador Archer, Braz. 212/A2
Governador Dix-Sept Rosado, Braz. 212/C2
Governador Eugênio Barros, Braz. 212/A2
Governador Valadares, Braz. 213/D1
Governor Generoso, Phil. 137/E6
Governors (isl.), NY, US 197/J9
Govi-Altay (prov.), Mong. 128/F2
Govi Altayn (mts.), Mong. 128/G3
Govind Sāgar (res.), India 144/D4
Govindgarh, India 142/C3
Gower (pen.), Wal, UK 90/B3
Goya, Arg. 215/E2
Goyllarisquizga, Peru 214/B3
Göynük, Turk. 107/K5
Goyt (riv.), Eng, UK 93/F5
Gozaisho-yama (peak), Japan 135/K5
Gözeli, Turk. 148/D2
Gozo (isl.), Malta 116/B1
Gozzano, It. 116/B1
Graaff-Reinet, SAfr. 164/D4
Graafschap (phys. reg.), Neth. 108/D4
Graben, Ger. 115/G1
Graberberg (peak), Namb. 164/B2
Grabouw, SAfr. 164/L11
Grabow, Ger. 98/F2
Graça Aranha, Braz. 212/A2
Gračac, Cro. 106/B3
Gračanica, Bosn. 106/D3
Gracemere, Austl. 172/C3
Graceville, Fl, US 191/G4
Grächen, Swi. 114/D5
Gracias, Hon. 202/D3
Gracias a Dios (cape), Hon. 203/F3
Graciosa (isl.), Azor., Port. 103/S12
Grad Sofiya (prov.), Bul. 105/H1
Gradačac, Bosn. 106/D3
Gradisca d'Isonzo, It. 117/G1
Grado, It. 117/G1
Grado, Sp. 102/C2
Grady (co.), Ok, US 195/M15
Gräfelfing, Ger. 113/E6
Grafenau, Ger. 113/G6
Gräfenberg, Ger. 112/E3
Grafenrheinfeld, Ger. 112/D3
Gräfentonna, Ger. 109/H6
Grafenwöhr, Ger. 113/E3
Graffignana, It. 116/C2

Grafing bei München, Ger. 113/E6
Gråfjell (peak), Nor. 96/C1
Grafrath, Ger. 115/H1
Grafton, Austl. 173/E1
Grafton, ND, US 185/J3
Grafton, WV, US 188/D4
Grafton, Il, US 195/G8
Grafton Passage, Austl. 172/B2
Graham, Tx, US 187/H4
Graham (isl.), Nun., Can. 181/S7
Graham (isl.), BC, Can. 180/C3
Graham Bell (isl.), Rus. 122/G1
Graham Land (phys. reg.), Ant. 218/V
Grahamstown, SAfr. 164/D4
Graian Alps (range), It. 101/G4
Grain (coast), Libr. 154/D4
Grain Valley, Mo, US 195/E5
Grainau, Ger. 115/H3
Grajaú (riv.), Braz. 209/J5
Grajaú, Braz. 212/A2
Grajewo, Pol. 97/K5
Gram, Den. 96/C4
Gramada, Bul. 106/F4
Gramastetten, Aus. 113/H6
Gramat, Fr. 100/D4
Gramat, Causse de (plat.), Fr. 100/D4
Gramatneusiedl, Aus. 107/N7
Grampian (pol. reg.), Sc, UK 94/C2
Grampian (mts.), Sc, UK 94/B3
Grampians NP, Austl. 173/B3
Grampians, The (phys. reg.), Austl. 173/B3
Gramsbergen, Neth. 108/D3
Gramsh, Alb. 105/G2
Gran, Nor. 96/D1
Gran Altiplanicie Central (plat.), Arg. 215/C6
Gran Bajo de San Julián (plain), Arg. 217/C6
Gran Bajo Oriental (plain), Arg. 215/C6
Gran Canaria (isl.), Canl., Sp. 156/B4
Gran Canaria (int'l arpt.), Canl., Sp. 156/B4
Gran Chaco (plain), SAm. 205/C5
Gran Isla del Maíz (isl.), Nic. 203/F3
Gran Laguna Salada (lag.), Arg. 216/D5
Gran Paradiso, PN del, It. 101/G4
Gran Piedra (hill), Cuba 203/H2
Gran Pilastro (peak), It. 101/J3
Gran Vilaya (ruin), Peru 214/B2
Granada, Col. 210/C4
Granada, Nic. 202/E4
Granada, Sp. 102/D4
Granadilla de Abona, Canl., Sp. 156/A3
Granados, Mex. 200/C2
Granard, Ire. 89/Q10
Granby, Tx, US 187/H4
Grand (lake), Nf, Can. 181/L4
Grand (canal), China 130/D4
Grand (falls), Kenya 162/C3
Grand (canal), Az, US 195/R18
Grand (isl.), NY, US 185/M4
Grand (riv.), Mo, US 195/L3
Grand (riv.), SD, US 185/H4
Grand Bahama (isl.), Bahm. 199/F2
Grand Bank, Nf, Can. 189/L2
Grand Bassa (co.), Libr. 160/C5
Grand-Bassam, C.d'Iv. 160/E5
Grand Bay, NB, Can. 189/H2
Grand Canal d'Alsace (canal), Fr. 114/D2
Grand Canyon, Az, US 186/D3
Grand Canyon Nat'l Park, Az, US 186/D3
Grand Canyon-Parashant Nat'l Mon., Az, US 186/D3
Grand Cape Mount (co.), Libr. 160/C5
Grand Cayman (isl.), Cay. 182/E4
Grand Centre, Ab, Can. 184/F2
Grand-Charmont, Fr. 114/C2
Grand Colombier (peak), Fr. 114/B6
Grand Combine (peak), Swi. 114/D6
Grand Coulee, Wa, US 184/D4
Grand Coulee (dam), Wa, US 184/D4
Grand Drumont (peak), Fr. 114/C2
Grand Erg de Bilma (des.), Niger 154/H4
Grand Erg Occidental (des.), Alg. 157/E3

Grand Erg Oriental (des.), Alg. 157/G3
Grand Falls, NB, Can. 189/H2
Grand Falls, Nf, Can. 189/L1
Grand Forks, ND, US 185/J4
Grand Forks, BC, Can. 184/D3
Grand-Fort-Philippe, Fr. 110/B2
Grand Gabes, Tun. 157/H2
Grande-Baie, Haiti 203/H2
Grand Haven, Mi, US 188/C3
Grand Isle, La, US 191/F4
Grand Jide (co.), Libr. 160/D5
Grand Junction, Co, US 186/E3
Grand-Iahou, C.d'Iv. 160/D5
Grand Lake o' the Cherokees (lake), Ok, US 187/J3
Grand Manan (isl.), NB, Can. 189/H2
Grand-Mère, Qu, Can. 189/F2
Grand Mont Ruan (peak), Fr. 114/C6
Grand Muveran (peak), Swi. 114/D5
Grand-Popo, Ben. 161/F5
Grand Portage Nat'l Mon., Mn, US 185/L4
Grand Rapids, Mb, Can. 185/J2
Grand Rapids, Mi, US 188/C3
Grand Rhône (riv.), Fr. 100/F5
Grand Saint-Bernard, Col du (pass), Swi. 114/D6
Grand Staircase-Escalante Nat'l Mon., Ut, US 186/E3
Grand Taureau (peak), Fr. 114/C4
Grand Teton NP, Wy, US 186/E2
Grandcour, Swi. 114/C4
Grande (bay), Arg. 217/C6
Grande (isl.), Braz. 213/C2
Grande (isl.), Braz. 211/H5
Grande (riv.), Braz. 208/J7
Grande (peak), It. 104/C1
Grande (peak), It. 104/C4
Grande (pt.), Pan. 203/G4
Grande Cache, Ab, Can. 184/D2
Grande Comore (isl.), Com. 165/G5
Grande de Gurupá, Ilha (isl.), Braz. 209/H4
Grande de Manacapuru, Lago (lake), Braz. 208/F4
Grande de Matagalpa (riv.), Nic. 182/D5
Grande de Santiago (riv.), Mex. 200/D4
Grande de Tierra del Fuego (isl.), Arg., Chile 215/C7
Grande Dixence, Barrage de la (dam), Swi. 114/D5
Grande do Curuaí (lake), Braz. 211/H5
Grande Miquelon (isl.), StP, Fr. 189/K2
Grande Prairie, Ab, Can. 184/D2
Grande Saline, Haiti 203/H2
Grande, Serra (mts.), Braz. 211/F4
Grande-Synthe, Fr. 110/B1
Grande-Terre (isl.), Guad. 199/J4
Grandes Jorasses (peak), It. 114/D6
Grandfresnoy, Fr. 110/B5
Grândola, Port. 102/A3
Grandpuits-Bailly-Carrois, Fr. 88/L6
Grandson, Swi. 114/C4
Grandview, Wa, US 184/D4
Grandview, Mb, Can. 185/J3
Grandview, Tx, US 187/H4
Grandview, Mo, US 195/D6
Grandvillars, Fr. 114/C2
Grandvilliers, Fr. 110/A4
Graneros, Chile 216/N9
Granfjället (peak), Swe. 96/E1
Grange, Mont de (peak), Fr. 114/C5
Grangemouth, Sc, UK 94/C4
Granges-sur-Vologne, Fr. 114/C1
Grängesberg, Swe. 96/F1
Grangeville, Id, US 184/D4
Granisle, BC, Can. 184/B2
Granite (riv.), Mt, US 184/F4
Granite, Ut, US 195/K12
Granite City, Il, US 195/G8
Granite Reef Aqueduct, Az, US 195/S18
Granites, The (peak), Az, US 171/F2
Granja, Braz. 212/B1
Granollers, Sp. 103/L6
Grantham, Eng, UK 93/H6
Grantown-on-Spey, Sc, UK 94/C2
Grants, NM, US 186/F4
Grants Pass, Or, US 184/C5
Granville, Fr. 100/C2
Granville (lake), Mb, Can. 180/F3

Grão Mogol, Braz. 212/B5
Grapeview, Wa, US 193/B3
Gras-Ellenbach, Ger. 112/B3
Grasberg, Ger. 109/F2
Grasbrunn, Ger. 113/E6
Grasø (isl.), Swe. 96/H1
Grasonville, Md, US 196/B6
Grass (lake), Il, US 193/P15
Grasse, Fr. 101/G5
Grassie, On, Can. 189/Q9
Grasslands NP, Sk, Can. 184/G3
Grassy, Austl. 173/C4
Grassy Park, SAfr. 164/L11
Grästorp, Swe. 96/E2
Gratkorn, Aus. 101/L3
Gratz, Pa, US 196/B2
Graubünden (canton), Swi. 115/F4
Graulhet, Fr. 100/E5
Graus, Sp. 103/F1
Gravatá, Braz. 212/D3
Grave, Neth. 108/C5
Gravedona, It. 115/F4
Gravelbourg, Sk, Can. 184/G3
Gravelines, Fr. 110/B2
Gravellona Toce, It. 115/E6
Gravenhurst, On, Can. 188/E2
Grävenwiesbach, Ger. 112/B2
Gravesend, Eng, UK 88/E2
Gravina di Puglia, It. 104/C2
Gravois (pt.), Haiti 203/H2
Gray, Fr. 114/B3
Grayling, Ak, US 192/F3
Grayling, Mi, US 188/C2
Grays (har.), Wa, US 184/B4
Grays (lake), Id, US 184/F5
Grays, Eng, UK 88/C2
Grayslake, Il, US 193/P15
Grayson, Sk, Can. 185/H3
Graz, Aus. 101/L3
Grazalema, Sp. 102/C4
Great (lake), Austl. 173/C4
Great (plain), Can.,US 185/G3
Great (basin), Nv, US 182/C4
Great (falls), NJ, US 197/J8
Great Abaco (isl.), Bahm. 199/F2
Great Alfold (plain), Serb. 106/D2
Great America, Indo. 138/C4
Great Australian Bight (bay), Austl. 167/B4
Great Barrier (reef), Austl. 167/D2
Great Barrier (isl.), NZ 159/T10
Great Basin NP, Nv, US 186/D3
Great Bear (lake), NW, Can. 180/D2
Great Bend, Ks, US 187/H3
Great Bitter (lake), Egypt 149/C4
Great Brak (riv.), SAfr. 164/C3
Great Britain (isl.), Br. 89/T9
Great Cedar (swamp), NJ, US 196/D5
Great Coco (isl.), Myan. 141/F5
Great Cumbrae (isl.), Sc, UK 94/B5
Great Divide (basin), Wy, US 184/F5
Great Dividing (range), Austl. 167/D2
Great Egg (har.), NJ, US 196/D5
Great Egg Harbor (riv.), NJ, US 196/D4
Great Exuma (isl.), Bahm. 199/F3
Great Falls, Mt, US 184/F4
Great Fish (riv.), SAfr. 164/D4
Great Fish (pt.), SAfr. 164/D4
Great Guana Cay (isl.), Bahm. 199/F2
Great Harwood, Eng, UK 93/F4
Great Himalaya (range), Asia 128/D6
Great Inagua (isl.), Bahm. 199/G3
Great Indian (des.), India, Pak. 140/B2
Great Karoo (plat.), SAfr. 163/D7
Great Kei (riv.), SAfr. 164/D4
Great Mis Tor (hill), Eng, UK 90/B5
Great Missenden, Eng, UK 91/F3
Great Neck, NY, US 197/L8
Great Nicobar (isl.), India 141/F6
Great Ouse (riv.), Eng, UK 91/G2
Great Oyster (bay), Austl. 173/D4
Great Palace, Rus. 119/S7
Great Palace, Rus. 119/T7
Great Peconic (bay), Austl. 170/B4
Great Pee Dee (riv.), NY, US 191/J3
Great Piece Meadows (swamp), NJ, US 197/H8
Great Rift (valley), Afr. 163/F1
Great Ruaha (riv.), Tanz. 163/F2
Great Salt (lake), Ut, US 186/D2
Great Salt Lake (des.), Ut, US 186/D2

Great Sand Dunes Nat'l Park Co, US 187/F3
Great Sand Sea (des.), Egypt, Li 155/K2
Great Sandy (des.), Austl. 167/B2
Great Scarcies (riv.), SLeo. 160/B4
Great Shunner Fell (peak), Eng, UK 93/D3
Great Slave (lake), NW, Can. 180/E2
Great Smoky Mountains NP, NC,Tn, US 191/H3
Great South (bay), NY, US 197/E2
Great Stour (riv.), Eng, UK 88/D2
Great. Tenasserim (riv.), Myan. 136/B3
Great Victoria (lake), Austl. 167/B3
Great Victoria Desert Nature Rsv., Austl. 171/C4
Great Wall, China 128/J4
Great Western Tiers (mts.), Austl. 173/C4
Great Winterhoek (peak), SAfr. 164/L10
Great Yarmouth, Eng, UK 91/H1
Great Zab (riv.), Iraq 148/E2
Great Zimbabwe (ruin), Zim. 163/F5
Greater Accra (pol. reg.), Gha. 161/F5
Greater Antilles (isls.), NAm. 199/F3
Greater Buffalo (int'l arpt.), NY, US 189/S10
Greater Cincinnati (int'l arpt.), Ky, US 188/C4
Greater London (co.), Eng, UK 88/C2
Greater Manchester (co.), Eng, UK 93/F4
Greater Pittsburgh (int'l arpt.), Pa, US 188/D3
Greater Rochester (int'l arpt.), NY, US 188/E3
Greater Sunda (isls.), Indo. 138/C4
Grebenhain, Ger. 112/C2
Grebenstein, Ger. 109/G6
Grébon (peak), Niger 161/H2
Grecco, Uru. 217/K10
Greco (peak), It. 104/C2
Greco (cape), Cyp. 149/D2
Greding, Ger. 113/E4
Gredos, Sierra de (mts.), Sp. 102/C2
Greece (ctry.) 105/G3
Greeley, Co, US 195/C2
Greeley Number 2 (canal), Co, US 195/C2
Greely (fjord), Nun., Can. 181/S6
Green (cape), Austl. 173/D3
Green (riv.), Ky, US 188/C4
Green (bay), Mi,Wi, US 185/M4
Green (isl.), Ut,Wy, US 186/E3
Green (riv.), Ut,Wy, US 186/E3
Green Bay, Wi, US 185/M4
Green Cove Springs, Fl, US 191/H4
Green Creek, NJ, US 196/D5
Green Haven, Md, US 196/B5
Green Lane (res.), Pa, US 196/C3
Great Lowther (peak), Sc, UK 94/C6
Green River, NJ, US 196/D1
Green River, Wy, US 184/F5
Green Valley, Az, US 186/E5
Green Valley, Ca, US 194/B1
Green Valley Lake, Ca, US 194/B1
Green Village, NJ, US 197/H9
Greenbelt, Md, US 196/B6
Greenbushes, Austl. 170/C5
Greencastle, In, US 188/C4
Greencastle, Ire. 92/B1
Greendale, Wi, US 193/Q14
Greeneville, Tn, US 188/D4
Greenfield, In, US 188/C4
Greenfield, Ma, US 189/F3
Greenfield, Wi, US 193/P14
Greenfield Park, Qu, Can. 189/P7
Greenisland, NI, UK 92/C2
Greenland (sea) 177/R2
Greenmount, Md, US 196/B4
Greenock, Sc, UK 94/B5
Greenough, Austl. 170/B4
Greenough (mt.), Ak, US 192/K2
Greenport, NY, US 197/F1
Greensboro, Al, US 191/G3
Greensboro, Md, US 196/C6
Greensboro, NC, US 191/J2
Greensburg, In, US 188/C4
Greensburg, Pa, US 188/E3
Greenvale, Austl. 172/B2
Greenville, Libr. 160/C5
Greenville, Al, US 191/G4
Greenville, Ca, US 184/C5
Greenville, Mi, US 188/C3

Greenville, Ms, US 187/K4
Greenville, NC, US 191/J3
Greenville, Oh, US 188/C3
Greenville, SC, US 191/H3
Greenville, Tx, US 187/H4
Greenwater (riv.), Wa, US 193/D3
Greenwell Point, Austl. 173/D2
Greenwich, Ct, US 197/L7
Greenwich (bor.), Eng, UK 88/D2
Greenwich (pt.), Ct, US 197/L8
Greenwich Observatory, Eng, UK 88/D2
Greenwood (lake), SC, US 191/H3
Greenwood, SC, US 191/H3
Greenwood, Ms, US 187/K4
Greenwood, Mo, US 195/E6
Greenwood, De, US 196/C6
Greenwood Lake, NY, US 196/D1
Greers Ferry (lake), Ar, US 187/J4
Grefrath, Ger. 108/D6
Gregório (riv.), Braz. 208/D5
Gregory, SD, US 185/J5
Gregory (range), Austl. 167/D2
Gregory (lake), Austl. 167/B3
Greifswald, Ger. 96/E4
Greifswalder Bodden (bay), Ger. 99/G1
Greimberg (peak), Aus. 101/L3
Greiz, Ger. 101/K1
Gremyachinsk, Rus. 119/N4
Grená, Den. 96/D3
Grenada (ctry.) 199/N10
Grenada, Ms, US 187/K4
Grenade, Fr. 100/D5
Grenade, Fr. 110/B3
Grenchen, Swi. 114/D3
Grenfell, Austl. 173/D2
Grenfell, Sk, Can. 185/H3
Grennach (riv.), Ger. 112/D6
Grenoble, Fr. 100/F4
Grenzach-Wyhlen, Ger. 114/D2
Gressåmoen NP, Nor. 95/E2
Gretna (riv.), Eng, UK 93/E2
Gretna, Mb, Can. 185/J3
Gretna, La, US 195/P17
Gretna, Sc, UK 93/E2
Grettstadt, Ger. 112/D3
Gretz-Armainvilliers, Fr. 88/L5
Greve (riv.), It. 117/E5
Greve in Chianti, It. 117/E5
Grevelingendam (dam), Neth. 108/B5
Greven, Ger. 109/E4
Grevená, Gre. 105/G2
Grevenbroich, Ger. 111/F1
Grevenmacher (dist.), Lux. 111/F4
Grevenmacher, Lux. 111/F4
Grevesmühlen, Ger. 98/F2
Grevlingen (chan.), Neth. 108/A5
Grey (range), Austl. 167/D3
Grey (riv.), Nf, Can. 189/K2
Grey (pt.), NI, UK 92/C2
Grey Abbey, NI, UK 92/C2
Grey Hunter (peak), Yk, US 192/L3
Grey Peaks NP, Austl. 172/B2
Greybull, Wy, US 184/F4
Greylingstad, SAfr. 164/E2
Greymouth, NZ 159/S11
Greystones, Ire. 92/B5
Greytown, SAfr. 165/E3
Grez-Doiceau, Belg. 111/D2
Grezzana, It. 117/E1
Gribbin (pt.), Eng, UK 90/B6
Griefensee (lake), Swi. 115/E4
Griekwastad, SAfr. 164/C3
Gries am Brenner, Aus. 115/H3
Griesheim, Ger. 112/B3
Grieskirchen, Aus. 113/G6
Griessbach (riv.), Ger. 113/F5
Griesskogel (peak), Aus. 115/H3
Griesstätt, Ger. 113/F7
Griffin, Ga, US 191/G3
Griffith, Austl. 173/C2
Griffith, In, US 193/R16
Griffith Park, Ca, US 194/F7
Grigna (peak), It. 115/F6
Grignano Polesine, It. 117/E2
Grigny, Fr. 88/K6
Grijalva (riv.), Mex. 202/C2
Grim (cape), Austl. 173/C4
Grimberg, Belg. 111/D2
Grimisuat, Swi. 114/D5
Grimmen, Ger. 96/E4
Grimsby, On, Can. 189/Q9
Grimsby, Eng, UK 93/H4
Grimselpass (pass), Swi. 115/E4
Grimstad, Nor. 96/C2
Grindavík, Ice. 95/M7
Grindsted, Den. 96/C4
Grindelwald, Swi. 114/E4
Grinnell (pen.), Nun., Can. 181/S7
Grintavec (peak), Slov. 101/L3

Griqualand East (reg.), SAfr. 164/E3
Griqualand West (reg.), SAfr. 164/C2
Gris-Nez (cape), Fr. 110/A2
Grise Fiord, Nun., Can. 181/S7
Grisslehamn, Swe. 97/H1
Grisy-les-Plâtres, Fr. 88/J4
Grisy-Suisnes, Fr. 88/L5
Grivette (riv.), Fr. 88/L4
Grizzly (bay), Ca, US 193/K10
Grmeč (mts.), Bosn. 106/C3
Groaíras, Braz. 212/B1
Grobbendonk, Belg. 108/B6
Gröbenzell, Ger. 113/E6
Gröblershoop, SAfr. 164/C3
Grodków, Pol. 99/J3
Grodzisk Wielkopolski, Pol. 99/J2
Groenlo, Neth. 108/D5
Groesbeck, Tx, US 190/D4
Groesbeek, Neth. 108/C5
Groix (isl.), Fr. 100/B3
Grójec, Pol. 99/L3
Grombalia, Tun. 158/M6
Grömitz, Ger. 96/D4
Gromo, It. 115/F6
Gronau, Ger. 108/D4
Gronau, Ger. 109/G4
Groningen (prov.), Neth. 108/D2
Groningen, Neth. 108/D2
Grønlait (peak), It. 115/H5
Grono, Swi. 115/F5
Groot (riv.), SAfr. 163/D7
Groot-Marico (riv.), SAfr. 164/D2
Grootdraaidam (res.), SAfr. 164/Q13
Groote Eylandt (isl.), Austl. 167/C2
Grootegast, Neth. 108/D2
Grootfontein, Namb. 163/C4
Grootvloer (salt pan), SAfr. 164/C3
Gropello Cairoli, It. 116/B2
Gros Islet, StL. 199/N9
Gros Morne (peak), Nf, Can. 189/K1
Gros Morne NP, Nf, Can. 189/K1
Grosbliederstroff, Fr. 111/G5
Grosio, It. 115/G5
Grosne (riv.), Fr. 100/F3
Grosrouvre, Fr. 88/H5
Grossaitingen, Ger. 115/G1
Grossalmerode, Ger. 109/G6
Grossbeeren, Ger. 98/Q7
Grossbottwar, Ger. 112/C5
Grossbreitenbach, Ger. 112/D1
Grosse (isl.), Mi, US 193/F7
Grosse Aue (riv.), Ger. 109/F4
Grosse Ile, Mi, US 193/F7
Grosse Laber (riv.), Ger. 113/F5
Grosse Mühl (riv.), Aus. 113/G6
Grosse Münzenberg (peak), Namb. 164/A2
Grosse Nister (riv.), Ger. 111/G2
Grosse Pointe, Mi, US 193/G7
Grosse Pointe Farms, Mi, US 193/G7
Grosse Pointe Park, Mi, US 193/G7
Grosse Pointe Shores, Mi, US 193/G7
Grosse Pointe Woods, Mi, US 193/G7
Grosse Rodl (riv.), Aus. 113/H6
Grossenbrode, Ger. 96/E4
Grossengottern, Ger. 109/H6
Grossenkneten, Ger. 109/F3
Grossenlüder, Ger. 112/C1
Grossenwiehe, Ger. 96/C4
Grosser Ahrensberg (peak), Ger. 109/G5
Grosser Aletsch (glacier), Swi. 114/D5
Grosser Arber (peak), Ger. 113/G4
Grosser Beer-Berg (peak), Ger. 109/F1
Grosser Bösenstein (peak), Aus. 101/L3
Grosser Daumen (peak), Ger. 115/G3
Grosser Feldberg (peak), Ger. 112/B2
Grosser Gleichberg (peak), Ger. 112/D2
Grosser Heuberg (mts.), Swi. 115/E4
Grosser Knechtsand (isl.), Ger. 109/F1
Grosser Peilstein (peak), Aus. 99/H4
Grosser Plessower (lake), Ger. 98/P7
Grosser Priel (peak), Aus. 101/L3

Grosser Rachel (peak), Ger. 113/G5
Grosser Seddiner (lake), Ger. 98/P7
Grosser Selchower (lake), Ger. 98/Q7
Grosses Meer (lake), Ger. 109/E2
Grosses Moor (swamp), Ger. 109/H1
Grosseto, It. 101/J5
Grossgerau, Ger. 112/B3
Grossglienicke, Ger. 98/Q7
Grossglockner (peak), Aus. 101/K3
Grosshansdorf, Ger. 109/H1
Grossheubach, Ger. 112/C3
Grosskrotzenburg, Ger. 112/B2
Grossmaischeid, Ger. 111/G3
Grosso (cape), Fr. 101/H5
Grossrosseln, Ger. 111/F5
Grosssiegharts, Aus. 99/H4
Grosswallstadt, Ger. 112/C3
Grosswangen, Swi. 114/E3
Grosuplje, Slov. 101/L4
Grote Gete (riv.), Belg. 111/D2
Groton, SD, US 185/J4
Grotta Gigante, It. 117/G1
Grottaglie, It. 104/F2
Grottammare, It. 101/K5
Grotte de Han, Belg. 111/E3
Grouard Mission, Ab, Can. 184/D1
Groundhog (riv.), On, Can. 188/D1
Grouw, Neth. 108/C2
Grovdageaidnu-Kautokeino, Nor. 95/G1
Grove, Ok, US 187/J3
Grove (pt.), Md, US 196/B5
Grover, Mo, US 195/F8
Grover City, Ca, US 186/B4
Groveton, Va, US 196/A6
Groznyy, Rus. 121/H4
Grudovo, Bul. 107/H4
Grudziądz, Pol. 99/K2
Grumeti (riv.), Tanz. 162/B3
Grums, Swe. 96/E2
Grünau im Almtal, Aus. 113/G7
Grünburg, Aus. 113/H7
Gründau, Ger. 112/C2
Grune (pt.), Eng, UK 93/E2
Grünsfeld, Ger. 112/C3
Grünstadt, Ger. 112/B3
Grünwald, Ger. 113/E6
Gruyères, Swi. 114/D4
Gryazi, Rus. 120/F1
Grycksbo, Swe. 96/F1
Gryfice, Pol. 96/F5
Gryfino, Pol. 99/H2
Gryon, Swi. 114/D5
Gschwandt, Ger. 113/G7
Gschwend, Ger. 112/C5
Gsteig, Swi. 114/D5
Gua, India 143/E4
Guabún (pt.), Chile 216/B4
Guaca, Col. 210/C3
Guacanayabo (gulf), Cuba 199/F3
Guacarí, Col. 210/B4
Guachochi, Mex. 200/D3
Guácimo, CR 203/F4
Guaçuí, Braz. 213/D2
Guadalajara, Mex. 200/E4
Guadalajara, Sp. 102/D2
Guadalcanal, Sp. 102/C3
Guadalcanal (isl.), Sol. 174/E6
Guadalentín (riv.), Sp. 102/D4
Guadalimar (riv.), Sp. 103/N8
Guadalope (riv.), Sp. 103/E2
Guadalquivir (riv.), Sp. 102/D4
Guadalupe, Braz. 212/B2
Guadalupe, Col. 210/C4
Guadalupe, Mex. 200/E4
Guadalupe, Mex. 201/E3
Guadalupe (isl.), Mex. 177/E7
Guadalupe, Pan. 203/G4
Guadalupe, Peru 214/C4
Guadalupe, Peru 214/B2
Guadalupe, Sp. 102/C3
Guadalupe (mts.), NM,Tx, US 190/D4
Guadalupe (co.), Tx, US 195/U20
Guadalupe (peak), Tx, US 187/F5
Guadalupe, Mex. 200/D4
Guadalupe Mountains NP, Tx, US 187/F5
Guadalupe, Sierra de (mts.), Sp. 102/C3
Guadalupe Victoria, Mex. 200/B1
Guadalupe Victoria, Mex. 200/D3
Guadalupe Victoria, Mex. 201/M7
Guadarrama (riv.), Sp. 102/C3
Guadarrama, Ven. 210/D2

Guadarrama, Sp. 103/M8
Guadarrama, Sierra de (mts.), Sp. 102/C2
Guadeloupe (isl.), Guad., Fr. 199/N8
Guadeloupe NP, Guad., Fr. 199/N8
Guadeloupe Passage (chan.), Guad., Fr. 199/J4
Guadiana (riv.), Port.,Sp. 102/B3
Guadiana Menor (riv.), Sp. 102/D4
Guadix, Sp. 102/D4
Guafo (isl.), Chile 216/B4
Guafo, Boca del (mouth), Chile 216/B4
Guagua Pichincha (peak), Ecu. 210/B3
Guaíba, Braz. 213/B4
Guaíba (riv.), Braz. 213/B4
Guáimaro, Cuba 203/G1
Guainía (riv.), Col. 208/E3
Guainía (dept.), Col. 210/D4
Guaiquinima (peak), Ven. 211/F3
Guaíra, Braz. 215/F1
Guaíra, Braz. 213/B2
Guaiteca (isl.), Chile 216/B4
Guajará-Mirim, Braz. 208/E6
Guajira (pen.), Col. 210/D1
Gualaceo, Ecu. 210/B5
Gualaco, Hon. 202/E3
Gualán, Guat. 202/D3
Gualaquiza, Ecu. 214/B1
Gualeguay, Arg. 217/J10
Gualeguaychú, Arg. 217/J10
Gualtieri, It. 116/D3
Guam (isl.), Pac., US 174/D4
Guamal, Col. 210/C2
Guamblin, Isla (isl.), Chile 216/A5
Guamote, Ecu. 214/B1
Guamúchil, Mex. 200/C3
Gu'an, China 130/H7
Guan Xian, China 128/H5
Guan Xian, China 130/B4
Guanabacoa, Cuba 203/F1
Guanabara (bay), Braz. 213/K7
Guanahacabibes (gulf), Cuba 203/E1
Guanahacabibes (pen.), Cuba 203/E1
Guanaja, Hon. 202/E2
Guanaja (isl.), Hon. 202/E2
Guanajay, Cuba 203/F1
Guanajuato, Mex. 201/E4
Guanajuato (state), Mex. 182/A3
Guanambi, Braz. 212/B4
Guanape, Ven. 211/E2
Guanare, Ven. 210/D2
Guanare (riv.), Ven. 208/E2
Guanarito, Ven. 210/D2
Guanay (peak), Ven. 211/E3
Guandi (mtn.), China 130/C3
Guangchang, China 137/C2
Guangde, China 130/D5
Guangdong (prov.), China 129/K7
Guangfeng, China 137/C2
Guangling, China 130/C3
Guanglu (isl.), China 131/B3
Guangnan, China 141/J3
Guangping, China 137/C3
Guangping, China 130/D3
Guangrao, China 130/D3
Guangshan, China 130/C4
Guangxi Zhuangzu (aut. reg.), China 128/J7
Guangyuan, China 128/J5
Guangze, China 137/C2
Guangzhou, China 141/K3
Guanhães, Braz. 213/D1
Guanipa (riv.), Ven. 208/F2
Guannan, China 130/D4
Guantánamo, Cuba 203/H1
Guantánamo Bay U.S. Naval Base, Cuba 203/H2
Guantao, China 130/C3
Guanting (res.), China 130/G6
Guanujo, Ecu. 210/B5
Guanyun, China 130/D4
Guapi, Col. 210/B4
Guaporé, Braz. 213/B4
Guaporé (riv.), Braz. 205/C2
Guaqui, Bol. 214/D5
Guarabira, Braz. 212/D2
Guaraci, Braz. 213/B2
Guaraciaba do Norte, Braz. 212/D3
Guaraí, Braz. 209/J5
Guaramirim, Braz. 213/B3
Guaranda, Ecu. 210/B5
Guarani, Braz. 213/K6
Guarapari, Braz. 213/D2
Guarapuava, Braz. 213/B3
Guarará, Braz. 213/K6
Guararapes (int'l arpt.), Braz. 212/D3
Guararapes, Braz. 213/B2
Guaratinga, Braz. 212/C5
Guaratinguetá, Braz. 213/H7
Guaratuba, Braz. 213/B3
Guarda (dist.), Port. 102/B2
Guarda, Port. 102/B2
Guardamar, Sp. 103/E3
Guardamiglio, It. 116/C2
Guardarrama (riv.), Sp. 103/N8
Guardia Alta (peak), It. 115/H4
Guardia Mitre, Arg. 216/E4

Guardia Sanframondi, It. 106/B5
Guardiagrele, It. 104/D1
Guareña, Sp. 102/B3
Guarico (pt.), Cuba 203/H1
Guárico (riv.), Ven. 211/E2
Guárico (state), Ven. 211/E2
Guárico, Embalse de (res.), Ven. 211/E2
Guarujá, Braz. 213/G8
Guarulhos, Braz. 213/G8
Guarulhos (int'l arpt.), Braz. 213/G8
Guarumal, Pan. 203/F5
Guasave, Mex. 200/C3
Guasdualito, Ven. 210/D3
Guasimal, Cuba 203/G1
Guasipati, Ven. 211/F3
Guastalla, It. 116/D3
Guatemala (ctry.) 202/D3
Guatemala (cap.), Guat. 202/D3
Guateque, Col. 210/C4
Guaviare (dept.), Col. 210/C4
Guaviare (riv.), Col. 208/E3
Guaxupé, Braz. 213/G6
Guayabero (riv.), Col. 210/C4
Guayabo, Cayo (isl.), Cuba 203/G1
Guayalejo (riv.), Mex. 201/F4
Guayama, PR 199/M8
Guayama (riv.), Hon. 202/E3
Guayaquil, Ecu. 210/B5
Guayaquil (gulf), Ecu.,Peru 205/A3
Guayaquil, Gulf of (gulf), Ecu.,Peru 214/A1
Guayaramerín, Bol. 208/E6
Guayas (prov.), Ecu. 210/B5
Guayas (riv.), Col. 210/C4
Guaymas, Mex. 200/C3
Gubakha, Rus. 119/N4
Gubbio, It. 117/F6
Guben, Ger. 99/H3
Gubin, Pol. 99/H3
Gubkin, Rus. 120/F2
Gucheng, China 130/B4
Gucheng, China 130/C3
Gúdar, Sierra de (range), Sp. 103/E2
Gudenå (riv.), Den. 96/D3
Gudensberg, Ger. 109/G6
Gudermes, Rus. 121/H4
Gudivāda, India 140/D4
Gudow, Ger. 109/H1
Güdül, Turk. 107/L5
Gūdūr, India 140/C5
Guebli (lake), Mrta. 156/B5
Guebwiller, Fr. 114/D2
Guecho, Sp. 102/D1
Guelb Azefal (hill), Mrta. 156/B5
Guelma, Alg. 158/K6
Guelma (prov.), Alg. 158/K6
Guelph, On, Can. 188/D3
Guémené-Penfao, Fr. 100/C3
Guénange, Fr. 111/F5
Guérande, Fr. 100/B3
Guérara, Alg. 157/G2
Guérard, Fr. 88/C3
Guercif, Mor. 158/C2
Guéret, Fr. 100/D3
Guernes, Fr. 88/G4
Guernsey (int'l arpt.), Chl, UK 100/B2
Guernsey (isl.), Chl, UK 100/B2
Guerrero (state), Mex. 100/B2
Guerrero, Mex. 200/D2
Guerrero Negro, Mex. 200/B3
Guerville, Fr. 88/H5
Guesle (riv.), Fr. 88/H6
Gueugnon, Fr. 100/F3
Gueux, Fr. 110/C5
Gugé (peak), Eth. 155/N6
Guggisberg, Swi. 114/D4
Gugielmo Marconi (int'l arpt.), It. 117/E3
Güglingen, Ger. 112/B4
Guguan (isl.), NMar. 174/D3
Guguletu, SAfr. 164/L11
Gui (riv.), China 137/B3
Guiana Highlands (uplands), SAm. 205/C2
Guichen, Fr. 100/C3
Guichón, Uru. 217/K10
Guidel, Camr. 154/H6
Guidimaka (pol. reg.), Mrta. 160/B3
Guiding, China 141/J2
Guidizzolo, It. 116/D2
Guidonia, It. 104/C2
Guignes-Rabutin, Fr. 88/L6
Guignicourt, Fr. 110/C4
Guihulngan, Phil. 139/F1
Guija, Moz. 163/F5
Guijuelo, Sp. 102/C2
Guilder (riv.), Al, US 191/G3
Guilderton, Austl. 170/B4
Guildford, Eng, UK 88/B3
Guilherand, Fr. 100/F4
Guilin (int'l arpt.), China 137/B2
Guilin, China 141/K2
Guillaume-Delisle (lake), Qu, Can. 181/J3
Guillena, Sp. 102/B3
Guimarães, Braz. 212/A1
Guimarães, Port. 102/A2

Guimba, Phil. 137/D4
Guimeng (mtn.), China 130/D4
Guinan, China 128/H4
Guinard (riv.), Sc, UK 94/A1
Guinea (ctry.) 160/C4
Guinea (gulf), Afric. 151/C4
Guinea-Bissau (ctry.) 160/B3
Guînes, Fr. 110/A2
Guingamp, Fr. 100/B2
Guinguinéo, Sen. 160/B3
Guiones (pt.), CR 202/E4
Guipavas, Fr. 100/A2
Guipavas (int'l arpt.), Fr. 100/A2
Guir, Oued (riv.), Alg. 156/E2
Guiratinga, Braz. 209/H7
Güiria, Ven. 211/F2
Guisborough, Eng, UK 93/G2
Guiscard, Fr. 110/C4
Guise, Fr. 110/C4
Guitiriz, Sp. 102/B1
Guitrancourt, Fr. 88/H4
Guiuan, Phil. 137/E5
Güixa (riv.), Col. 210/B4
Guizhou (prov.), China 128/J6
Gujan-Mestras, Fr. 100/C4
Gūjar Khān, Pak. 144/B3
Gujarāt (state), India 140/B3
Gujrānwāla, Pak. 144/C3
Gujrāt, Pak. 144/C3
Gukovo, Rus. 120/F2
Gulaothi, India 142/A1
Gulargambone, Austl. 173/D1
Gulbarga, India 140/C4
Guldenbach (riv.), Ger. 111/G3
Güldüzü, Turk. 149/E1
Gulen, Nor. 96/A1
Gulf Coastal (plain), Tx, US 187/G4
Gulf Islands Nat'l Seashore, US 191/F4
Gulf Shores, Al, US 191/G4
Gulfport, Ms, US 191/F4
Gulgong, Austl. 173/D2
Guliston, Uzb. 145/C4
Gulkana, Ak, US 192/J3
Gull Lake, Sk, Can. 184/F3
Gulladuff, NI, UK 92/B2
Gullane, Sc, UK 94/D4
Gullane (pt.), Sc, UK 94/D4
Gullspång, Swe. 96/F2
Güllükdağı (Termessos) NP, Turk. 149/B1
Gülnar, Turk. 149/C1
Gulpen, Neth. 111/E2
Gülpınar, Turk. 105/K3
Gulu, Ugan. 162/B2
Gulyantsi, Bul. 107/G4
Gumal (riv.), Pak. 144/A4
Gumare, Bots. 163/D4
Gumbrechtshoffen, Fr. 111/G6
Gumdag, Trkm. 121/K5
Gumeracha, Austl. 171/M8
Gumia, India 143/E4
Gumla, India 143/E4
Gumma (pref.), Japan 133/F2
Gummersbach, Ger. 111/G1
Gumpoldskirchen, Aus. 107/N7
Gumti (riv.), India 143/H4
Gümüşhacıköy, Turk. 120/E4
Gümüşhane, Turk. 148/D1
Gümüşhane (prov.), Turk. 148/D1
Guna (peak), Eth. 155/N5
Gunbower, Austl. 173/C2
Gundagai, Austl. 173/D2
Gundelfingen, Ger. 114/D1
Gundelfingen an der Donau, Ger. 112/D5
Gundelsheim, Ger. 112/C4
Gundersheim, Ger. 111/G3
Gundershoffen, Fr. 111/G6
Gündoğmuş, Turk. 149/C1
Güneydogu Toroslar (mts.), Turk. 148/D2
Gunisao (riv.), Mb, Can. 185/J2
Gunisao (lake), Mb, Can. 185/J2
Gunja, Cro. 106/D3
Gunn City, Mo, US 195/E6
Gunnar, India 142/B1
Gunnebo, Swe. 96/G3
Gunnedah, Austl. 173/D1
Gunning, Austl. 173/D2
Gunnison (riv.), Co, US 186/F3
Gunnison, Ut, US 186/E3
Gunpowder (riv.), Md, US 196/B5
Gunpowder Falls State Park, Md, US 196/B4
Günt (riv.), India 140/D4
Güntür, India 140/D4
Günz (riv.), Ger. 98/F4
Günzburg, Ger. 112/D6
Gunzenhausen, Ger. 112/D4
Guoyang, China 130/D4
Gura Humorului, Rom. 107/G2
Guragē (peak), Eth. 155/N6

Gurbantünggut (des.), China 128/E2
Gurdāspur, India 144/C3
Gurgaon, India 144/D5
Gürgentepe, Turk. 148/D1
Gurguéia (riv.), Braz. 209/K6
Guri (dam), Ven. 211/F3
Guri (res.), Ven. 211/F3
Gurk (riv.), Aus. 101/K3
Gurkthaler Alpen (mts.), Aus. 101/K3
Gurnee, Il, US 193/Q15
Guro, Moz. 163/F4
Gürpınar, Turk. 148/E2
Gursarai, India 142/B3
Gürsu, Turk. 148/B1
Guru Sikhar (peak), India 147/K4
Gürün, Turk. 148/D2
Gurupi, Braz. 209/J6
Gurupi (riv.), Braz. 209/J4
Gurupi, Serra do (mts.), Braz. 209/J4
Gus'-Khrustal'nyy, Rus. 118/J5
Gusau, Nga. 161/G3
Gushi, China 130/C4
Gushikawa, Japan 133/J7
Gusinje, Serb. 106/D4
Guskhara, India 143/F4
Guspini, It. 104/A3
Gussola, It. 116/D3
Gustavo Díaz Ordaz, Mex. 200/C3
Gustavo Díaz Ordaz, Mex. 200/B3
Gusterath, Ger. 111/F4
Güstrow, Ger. 96/E5
Gusum, Swe. 96/G2
Gutau, Aus. 113/H6
Gütersloh, Ger. 109/F5
Guthrie, Tx, US 187/G4
Guthrie, Ok, US 195/N14
Gutiérrez Zamora, Mex. 201/M6
Guttannen, Swi. 115/E4
Guttenberg, NJ, US 197/K8
Guttingen, Swi. 115/F2
Gutulia NP, Nor. 95/E3
Guwāhāti, India 141/F2
Guxhagen, Ger. 109/G6
Guxian, China 130/B3
Guy Fawkes River NP, Austl. 173/E1
Guyana (ctry.) 211/G3
Guyancourt, Fr. 88/J5
Guyandotte (riv.), WV, US 191/H2
Guyang, China 130/B2
Guyenne (reg.), Fr. 100/C4
Guymon, Ok, US 187/G3
Guyra, Austl. 173/D1
Guyuan, China 128/J4
Güzelbağ, Turk. 149/B1
Güzelsu, Turk. 149/B1
Guzhang, China 141/J2
Guzhen, China 130/D4
Guzmán (lake), Mex. 200/D2
Gwadar, Pak. 147/H3
Gwaii Haanas NP, BC, Can. 180/C3
Gwalia, Austl. 170/C3
Gwalior, India 142/B2
Gwanda, Zim. 163/E5
Gwandalan, Austl. 173/D2
Gwash (riv.), Eng, UK 93/F1
Gwaunceste (peak), Wal, UK 90/C2
Gwda (riv.), Pol. 99/J2
Gwersyllt, Wal, UK 93/E5
Gweru, Zim. 163/E4
Gwydir (riv.), Austl. 173/D1
Gwynedd (co.), Wal, UK 92/D5
Gwyrfai (riv.), Wal, UK 92/D5
Gy, Fr. 114/B3
Gya (pass), China 143/E1
Gyaca, China 141/G2
Gyál, Hun. 107/R10
Gyasikan, Gha. 161/F5
Gyda (pen.), Rus. 125/G2
Gyhum, Ger. 109/G2
Gyirong, China 143/E1
Gyldenløveshøj (peak), Den. 96/D4
Gympie, Austl. 172/D4
Gyōda, Japan 135/C1
Gyoma, Hun. 106/F2
Gyömrő, Hun. 107/R10
Győr, Hun. 106/C2
Győr-Moson-Sopron (co.), Hun. 99/J5
Győrújbarát, Hun. 106/C2
Gyöngyös, Arm. 121/G4
Gyzylarbat, Trkm. 121/L5
Gżira, Malta 104/L7

H

Hå, Nor. 96/A2
Ha Giang, Viet. 141/H3
Ha Noi (Hanoi) (cap.), Viet. 141/J3
Haacht, Belg. 111/D2
Haag, Aus. 113/H6
Haag am Hausruck, Aus. 113/G6
Haag an der Amper, Ger. 113/E6
Haag in Oberbayern, Ger. 113/F6

Haaksbergen, Neth. 108/D4
Haaltert, Belg. 110/D2
Haamstede, Neth. 108/A5
Haan, Ger. 108/E6
Ha'apai Group (isl.), Tonga 175/H7
Haapavesi, Fin. 95/H2
Haapsalu, Est. 97/K2
Haar, Ger. 113/F2
Haardt (mts.), Ger. 101/G2
Haarlem, Neth. 108/B4
Haast, NZ 175/R11
Haasts Bluff Abor. Land, Austl. 171/F2
Hab (riv.), Pak. 147/J3
Habahe, China 128/E2
Habartov, Czh. 113/F2
Habbānīyah, Iraq 146/D3
Habicht (peak), Aus. 115/H3
Habiganj, Bang. 143/H3
Habikino, Japan 135/J6
Habomai (isls.), Rus. 134/D2
Haboro, Japan 134/B1
Hābra, India 143/G4
Habsheim, Fr. 114/D2
Hacha (falls), Ven. 211/F3
Hache (riv.), Ger. 109/F3
Hachenburg, Ger. 111/G2
Hachijō, Japan 133/F4
Hachikai, Japan 135/L5
Hachimori, Japan 134/B3
Hachinohe, Japan 133/G3
Hachiōji, Japan 135/C2
Hacıbektaş, Turk. 148/C2
Hacienda Heights, Ca, US 194/G8
Hacılar, Turk. 148/C2
Hack (mt.), Austl. 171/H4
Hackensack, NJ, US 197/J8
Hackensack (riv.), NJ, US 197/J8
Hackettstown, NJ, US 196/D2
Hackney (bor.), Eng, UK 88/C2
Haḍabat al Jilf al Kabīr (plat.), Egypt 159/A4
Hadāli, Pak. 144/B3
Hadamar, Ger. 112/B2
Hadano, Japan 133/F3
Hadarba (cape), Sudan 159/D4
Hadd, Ra's al (pt.), Oman 147/G4
Haddenham, Eng, UK 91/F3
Haddington, Sc, UK 94/D5
Haddonfield, NJ, US 196/C4
Hadejia (riv.), Nga. 161/H3
Hadelner (canal), Ger. 109/F1
Hadera, Isr. 149/F7
Haderslev, Den. 96/C4
Hadhramaut (reg.), Yem. 146/E6
Hadim, Turk. 148/C2
Hadjout, Alg. 158/G4
Hadleigh, Eng, UK 88/E2
Hadley (bay), Nun., Can. 180/F1
Hadlow, Eng, UK 88/E3
Hadrian's Wall, Eng, UK 93/F1
Hadselfjorden (inlet), Nor. 95/E1
Hadsten, Den. 96/D3
Hadsund, Den. 96/D3
Haeju (bay), NKor. 131/C4
Haeju, NKor. 131/C4
Haena (pt.), Hi, US 182/S9
Haenam, SKor. 131/D5
Hafik, Turk. 148/D2
Hāfizābād, Pak. 144/B3
Haflong, India 141/F2
Hafnarfjördhur, Ice. 95/N7
Hafnarhreppur, Ice. 95/P7
Haft Gel, Iran 146/E2
Hafun (pt.), Som. 155/R5
Hagåtña (cap.), Guam 174/D3
Hagelstadt, Ger. 113/F5
Hagemeister (isl.), Ak, US 192/F4
Hagen, Ger. 109/E6
Hagen am Teutoburger Wald, Ger. 109/F4
Hagen im Bremischen, Ger. 109/F2
Hagenow, Ger. 99/D5
Hagerman, NM, US 190/B3
Hagerstown, Md, US 188/E4
Hagetmau, Fr. 100/C5
Hagfors, Swe. 96/E1
Hagi, Japan 132/B3
Hagnau am Bodensee, Ger. 115/F2
Hagondange, Fr. 111/F5
Hags (pt.), Ire. 89/P10
Haguenau, Fr. 111/G6

Hai (riv.), China 130/D3
Hai Duong, Viet. 136/D1
Hai Phong, Viet. 141/J3
Hai Van (pass), Viet. 136/E2
Hai'an, China 130/E4
Haibach, Ger. 112/C3
Haibara, Japan 135/J6
Haicheng, China 131/B3
Haidenaab (riv.), Ger. 113/E3
Haidershofen, Aus. 113/H6
Haifeng, China 137/C3
Haifa (dist.), Isr. 149/D3
Haiger, Ger. 101/H1
Haikou (int'l arpt.), China 137/B3
Hailākāndi, India 141/F3
Hailar, China 129/L2
Hailar (riv.), China 129/M2
Haileybury, On, Can. 188/E2
Hailsham, Eng, UK 91/G5
Hailun, China 129/N2
Haimen, China 130/E5
Haimhausen, Ger. 113/E6
Haiming, Aus. 115/G3
Haiming, Ger. 113/F6
Haina, Ger. 109/G6
Hainan (isl.), China 129/B4
Hainan (prov.), China 128/J8
Hainan (str.), China 137/B3
Hainaut (prov.), Belg. 110/D2
Hainburg, Ger. 112/C1
Haines, Ak, US 192/L3
Haines City, Fl, US 191/H4
Haines Junction, Yk, Can. 192/L3
Hainesville, Il, US 193/P15
Hainich (mts.), Ger. 109/G6
Hainichen, Ger. 113/F1
Haining, China 130/L9
Haiti (ctry.) 203/H2
Haixia (str.), China 129/K7
Haixing, China 130/D3
Haiyan, China 137/B3
Haiyan, China 128/H4
Haiyang (isl.), China 131/B3
Haiyang, China 130/E3
Haiyang, China 130/D4
Haizhou (bay), China 130/D4
Hāj (peak), Czh. 113/F2
Hajdúböszörmény, Hun. 99/L5
Hajdúdorog, Hun. 99/L5
Hajdúhadház, Hun. 106/E2
Hajdúnánás, Hun. 99/L5
Hajdúszoboszló, Hun. 99/L5
Hājīpur, India 143/E3
Hajjah, Yem. 146/D5
Hajdout, Alg. 158/G4
Hajnówka, Pol. 99/M2
Hajós, Hun. 106/D2
Haka, Myan. 141/F3
Hakee (pt.), Austl. 171/H3
Hakkari (prov.), Turk. 148/E2
Hakken-san (peak), Japan 132/D3
Hakkōda-san (peak), Japan 134/B3
Hakodate, Japan 134/B3
Hakone, Japan 135/C3
Hakone-yama (peak), Japan 135/C3
Haku-san (peak), Japan 133/F2
Hakui, Japan 133/E2
Hakusan, Japan 135/K6
Hakusan NP, Japan 133/E2
Hakushū, Japan 135/B2
Hāla, Pak. 147/J3
Halab (prov.), Syria 149/E1
Halab (Aleppo), Syria 149/E1
Halabjah, Iraq 146/E2
Halachó, Mex. 201/M6
Halawa, Hi, US 182/T10
Halcon (mt.), Phil. 139/F1
Halden, Nor. 96/D2
Haldensleben, Ger. 109/E4
Haldenwang, Ger. 115/G2
Haldia, India 143/G4
Haldībāri, India 143/G2
Haldimand, On, Can. 189/Q10
Haldimand-Norfolk (co.), On, Can. 189/Q10
Hale (riv.), Austl. 171/G3
Hale, Eng, UK 93/G5
Hale, Eng, UK 93/F5
Haledon, NJ, US 197/J8
Haleiwa, Hi, US 182/V12
Halen, Belg. 111/E2
Hales Corners, Wi, US 193/P14
Halesowen, Eng, UK 90/D2
Haleyville, Al, US 191/G3
Half Assini, Gha. 160/E5
Half Falls (mtn.), Pa, US 196/A3
Half Moon Bay, Ca, US 193/K12
Half Tide Beach, Austl. 172/C3
Halfing, Ger. 113/F7
Halfway, WBnk. 149/D4

Haliburton Highlands (uplands), On, Can. 188/E2
Halifax (cap.), NS, Can. 189/J2
Halifax (int'l arpt.), NS, Can. 189/J2
Halifax (bay), Austl. 167/D2
Halifax, Austl. 172/B2
Halifax, Eng, UK 93/G4
Haliun, Mong. 128/G2
Hall, Austl. 173/C2
Hall (pen.), Nun., Can. 181/K2
Hall (isls.), Micr. 174/E4
Hall (co.), Ak, US 192/H1
Hall Beach, Nun., Can. 181/H2
Hall Park, Ok, US 195/N15
Halladale (riv.), Sc, UK 89/S7
Hallam (Hellam), Pa, US 196/B4
Halland (co.), Swe. 95/E4
Hällbybrunn, Swe. 96/G2
Halle, Ger. 109/F4
Halle, Ger. 99/G3
Halle, Belg. 111/D2
Halle-Neustadt, Ger. 98/F3
Hällefors, Swe. 96/F2
Halleforsnäs, Swe. 96/G2
Hallein, Aus. 101/K3
Hallenberg, Ger. 109/F6
Hallertau (reg.), Ger. 113/E5
Hallettsville, Tx, US 187/H5
Halley, UK, Ant. 218/Y
Hallingdalselvi (riv.), Nor. 96/C1
Hallock, Mn, US 185/J3
Hallsberg, Swe. 96/F2
Hallstahammar, Swe. 96/G2
Hallstavik, Swe. 96/H1
Hallu (riv.), Fr. 98/D4
Halluin, Fr. 110/C2
Hallwang, Aus. 113/G7
Hallwilersee (lake), Swi. 114/E3
Hallyŏ Haesang NP, SKor. 131/E5
Halmahera (sea), Indo. 139/G2
Halmahera (isl.), Indo. 139/G3
Halmstad, Swe. 96/C3
Hals, Den. 96/D3
Halsteren, Neth. 108/B5
Haltern, Ger. 109/E5
Halton (co.), Eng, UK 93/F5
Halton Hills, On, Can. 189/Q9
Halver, Ger. 109/E6
Halverder Aa (riv.), Ger. 109/E4
Ham, Fr. 110/C4
Ham, Oued El (riv.), Alg. 158/G5
Ham-sous-Varsberg, Fr. 111/F5
Hamada, Japan 132/C3
Hamada de Tinrhert (plat.), Alg. 157/G3
Hamada du Drâa (plat.), Alg. 156/D3
Hamada du Tinrhert (plat.), Alg. 157/G2
Hamada Safia (plat.), Mali 156/D3
Hamadān, Iran 146/E2
Hamadat Marzūq (plat.), Libya 157/H3
Hamadat Tinghert (uplands), Libya 154/H2
Hamadat Tinghert (uplands), Libya 157/H3
Hamāh (prov.), Syria 149/E2
Hamāh, Syria 149/E2
Hamajima, Japan 135/L7
Hamakita, Japan 133/E3
Hamam, Turk. 149/E1
Hamamatsu, Japan 133/E3
Hamami (reg.), Mrta. 156/C5
Hamanaka, Japan 134/D2
Hamāţah (peak), Egypt 159/C3
Hamath Tiberias NP, Isr. 149/D3
Hamatombetsu, Japan 134/C1
Hambantota, SrL. 140/D6
Hambergen, Ger. 109/F2
Hambleton (hills), Eng, UK 93/G3
Hambühren, Ger. 109/G3
Hamburg, NY, US 188/E3
Hamburg (state), Ger. 109/G2
Hamburg, Pa, US 196/B4
Hamburg (Fuhlsbüttel) (int'l arpt.), Ger. 109/G1

Hamford Water (inlet), Eng, UK 91/H3
Hamgyŏng-bukto (prov.), NKor. 131/E2
Hamgyŏng-namdo (prov.), NKor. 131/D2
Hamh, Syria 148/D3
Hamhŭng, NKor. 131/D3
Hamhŭng-si (prov.), NKor. 131/D3
Hami, China 128/F3
Hamilton, Austl. 173/B3
Hamilton, Mt, US 184/E4
Hamilton, Al, US 191/G3
Hamilton, Tx, US 187/H5
Hamilton (har.), On, Can. 189/Q9
Hamilton (inlet), Nf, Can. 181/L3
Hamilton (mt.), Ca, US 193/L12
Hamilton, Sc, UK 94/B5
Hamilton Mil. Res., NY, US 197/J9
Hamilton-Wentworth (co.), On, Can. 189/Q9
Hamina, Fin. 97/M1
Hamīrpur, India 142/C3
Hamīrpur, India 144/D4
Hamm, Ger. 109/E5
Hamm, Belg. 111/E2
Hamm, Ger. 112/B3
Hamm, Ger. 111/G2
Hamma-Bouziane, Alg. 158/K6
Hammam Lif, Tun. 158/M6
Hammamat (gulf), Tun. 158/M6
Hammamet, Tun. 158/M6
Hammarland, Fin. 97/H1
Hammarön (isl.), Swe. 96/E2
Hammarstrand, Swe. 95/F3
Hamme, Ger. 109/F2
Hamme, Belg. 111/D1
Hammel, Den. 96/C3
Hammelburg, Ger. 112/C2
Hammerfest, Nor. 95/G1
Hammershus, Den. 96/F4
Hammersmith and Fulham (bor.), Eng, UK 88/A1
Hamminkeln, Ger. 108/D5
Hammonasset (pt.), Ct, US 197/F1
Hammond, In, US 188/C4
Hammond, La, US 191/F4
Hammonton, NJ, US 196/D4
Hamnvik, Nor. 95/F1
Hamont-Achel, Belg. 108/C6
Hampshire Downs (hills), Eng, UK 91/E4
Hampstead, Md, US 196/B4
Hampton Bays, NY, US 197/J9
Hampton Court, Eng, UK 88/C2
Hampton Nat'l Hist. Site, Md, US 196/B5
Hamp'yŏng, SKor. 131/D5
Hamtramck, Mi, US 193/F7
Hamura, Japan 135/C2
Hamyang, SKor. 131/D4
Hamyŏl, SKor. 131/D4
Han (riv.), China 125/M6
Hana (riv.), India 142/C5
Hana, Hi, US 182/U10
Hanak, Turk. 148/E1
Hanamaki, Japan 134/B4
Hanamalo (pt.), Hi, US 182/U11
Hanang (peak), Tanz. 162/B4
Hanau, Ger. 112/B2
Hanazono, Japan 135/C1
Hancocks Bridge, NJ, US 196/C5
Handa, Japan 135/L6
Handan, China 130/C3
Handeloh, Ger. 109/G2
Handiã, India 142/C3
Hanford Reach Nat'l Mon., Wa, US 184/C4
Hangayn (mts.), Mong. 128/G2
Hangingstone (hill), Eng, UK 90/B2
Hangklip (cape), SAfr. 164/L11
Hangu, Pak. 144/A2
Hangzhou (bay), China 130/L9
Hanhöhiy (mts.), Mong. 128/G2
Hani, Turk. 148/E2
Haningfield (res.), Eng, UK 88/E2
Hannō, Japan 135/C2
Hannover (int'l arpt.), Ger. 109/G4
Hannover, Ger. 109/G4
Hannover, Belg. 111/E2
Hannut, Belg. 111/E2
Hanöbukten (bay), Swe. 95/E4
Hanover, NH, US 189/F3

Hanover, On, Can. 188/D2
Hanover, SAfr. 164/D3
Hanover, Pa, US 196/B6
Hanover (isl.), Chile 217/B6
Hanover Park, Il, US 193/P16
Hansen (dam), Ca, US 194/F7
Hanshan, China 130/D5
Hanshou, China 137/B2
Hänsi, India 144/C5
Hanstedt, Ger. 109/H2
Hansville, Wa, US 193/B2
Hantzsch (riv.), Nun., Can. 181/J2
Hanumängarh, India 144/C5
Hanwood, Austl. 173/C2
Hanyü, Japan 135/H2
Hanyuan, China 141/H2
Hanzhong, China 128/J5
Hao (isl.), FrPol. 175/L6
Hapch'ŏn, SKor. 131/E5
Happy Valley (res.), Austl. 171/M9
Happy Valley-Goose Bay, Nf, Can. 181/K3
Haptŏk, SKor. 131/D4
Häpur, India 142/A1
Haquira, Peru 214/C4
Har-Ayrag, Mong. 129/J2
Har Karmel (Mount Carmel) (peak), Isr. 149/G6
Har Meron (peak), Isr. 149/D3
Har Ramon (peak), Isr. 149/D4
Hara, Japan 135/A2
Harahan, La, US 195/P17
Haramachi, Japan 133/G2
Harappa (ruin), Pak. 144/B4
Harare (cap.), Zim. 163/F4
Harash, Bi'r al (well), Libya 155/K2
Haravilliers, Fr. 88/J4
Harbel, Libr. 160/C5
Harbeson, De, US 196/C6
Harbin, China 129/N2
Harbiye, Turk. 149/E1
Harbonnières, Fr. 110/B4
Harbour Breton, Nf, Can. 189/L2
Harbour Grace, Nf, Can. 189/L2
Hårby, Den. 96/D4
Hard, Aus. 115/F3
Hardä, India 147/L4
Hardangervidda NP, Nor. 96/B3
Hardau (riv.), Ger. 109/H3
Hardegsen, Ger. 109/G5
Hardenberg, Neth. 108/D3
Harderwijk, Neth. 108/C4
Hardheim, Ger. 112/C3
Hardin, Mt, US 184/G4
Harding, SAfr. 165/K3
Hardoi, India 142/C2
Hardoi Branch (riv.), India 142/C2
Hardricourt, Fr. 88/H4
Hardy (pen.), Chile 217/C7
Hare (bay), Nf, Can. 189/L1
Hare Dimona (peak), Isr. 149/D4
Harefield, Eng, UK 88/B2
Harelbeke, Belg. 110/C2
Haren, Ger. 109/E3
Haren, Neth. 108/D2
Härer, Eth. 155/P6
Harford (co.), Md, US 196/B4
Hargesheim, Ger. 111/G4
Hargeville, Fr. 88/H5
Hargeysa, Som. 155/P6
Harghita (prov.), Rom. 107/G2
Harghita (peak), Rom. 107/G2
Hari (riv.), Indo. 138/B4
Hari (str.), Est. 97/K2
Harihar, India 147/L6
Härim, Syria 149/E1
Harima (sea), Japan 132/D3
Harimä, Jor. 149/D3
Harima, Japan 135/G6
Harima (bay), Japan 135/G6
Haringey (bor.), Eng, UK 88/C2
Haringhäta (riv.), Bang. 143/G4
Haringvliet (chan.), Neth. 108/B5
Haringvlietdam (dam), Neth. 108/B5
Haripur, Pak. 144/B3
Harirüd (riv.), Afg. 147/H2
Häris, WBnk. 149/G7
Harjavalta, Fin. 97/K1
Harlan, Ky, US 188/D4
Harlech, Wal, UK 92/D6
Harlingen, Tx, US 190/D5
Harlingen, Neth. 108/C2
Harlow, Eng, UK 88/D1
Harlowton, Mt, US 184/F4
Harmannsdorf, Aus. 107/N7
Harmelen, Neth. 108/B4
Harnes, Fr. 110/B3
Harney (basin), Or, US 186/C2
Harney (lake), Or, US 184/D5
Harney (peak), SD, US 185/H5
Harney (valley), Or, US 184/D5
Harney, Md, US 196/A4
Harnöli, Pak. 144/A3
Haro (cape), Mex. 200/C3

Haro, Sp. 102/D1
Harold, Ca, US 194/B1
Harpenden, Eng, UK 91/F3
Harper (mt.), Yk, Can. 192/L3
Harper (mt.), Ak, US 192/K3
Harper, Ks, US 187/H3
Harper, Libr. 160/D5
Harper, Wa, US 193/F7
Harper Woods, Mi, US 193/F7
Harpstedt, Ger. 109/F3
Harqin Zuoyi Monggolzu Zizhixian, China 130/D2
Harrah, Ok, US 195/N15
Harrai, India 142/B4
Harran, Turk. 148/D2
Harricana (riv.), Qu, Can. 181/J4
Harriman, Tn, US 188/C5
Harriman, NY, US 196/D1
Harriman, Austl. 173/E1
Harrington, De, US 196/C6
Harrington Park, NJ, US 197/K8
Harris (mt.), Austl. 171/F3
Harris (lake), Austl. 171/G4
Harris (isl.), Sc, UK 89/C3
Harris Park, Co, US 195/B4
Harrisburg, Ne, US 185/H5
Harrisburg, Il, US 188/B4
Harrisburg (cap.), Pa, US 196/B3
Harrislee, Ger. 96/C4
Harrismith, SAfr. 164/E3
Harrison (bay), Ak, US 192/H1
Harrison, Ar, US 188/B3
Harrison, Mi, US 188/C2
Harrison, NY, US 197/L8
Harrison, NJ, US 197/J9
Harrison (cape), Nf, Can. 181/L3
Harrison (lake), BC, Can. 184/C3
Harrisonville, Il, US 195/G9
Harrisonville, Mo, US 195/E6
Harrisville, Ut, US 195/K11
Harrodsburg, Ky, US 188/C4
Harrogate, Eng, UK 93/G4
Harrow (bor.), Eng, UK 88/B2
Harry S Truman (res.), Mo, US 187/J3
Harsefeld, Ger. 109/F2
Harsewinkel, Ger. 109/F5
Harson's Island, Mi, US 193/G6
Hart (lake), Or, US 186/C2
Hart, Mi, US 188/C3
Hart (riv.), Yk, Can. 180/C2
Hart (riv.), Ky, US 188/C4
Hart (isl.), NY, US 197/K8
Hart Fell (peak), Sc, UK 94/C6
Hartbeesrivier (riv.), SAfr. 164/C3
Härteigen (peak), Nor. 96/B1
Hartelkanaal (riv.), Neth. 108/B5
Hartford (cap.), Ct, US 189/F3
Hartford, Il, US 195/G8
Hartford, NJ, US 196/D4
Hartford City, In, US 188/C3
Hartheim, Ger. 114/D2
Hartington, Ne, US 187/H2
Hartkirchen, Aus. 113/H6
Hartland (pt.), Eng, UK 90/C3
Hartland, Mi, US 193/E6
Hartlepool, Eng, UK 93/G2
Hartlepool, Eng, UK 93/G2
Hartleton, Pa, US 196/A2
Hartley Wintney, Eng, UK 88/A3
Hartly, De, US 196/C5
Hartney, Mb, Can. 185/H3
Hartsdale, NY, US 197/K7
Hartselle, Al, US 191/G3
Hartshill, Eng, UK 91/E1
Hartstene (isl.), Wa, US 193/B3
Hartwell, Ga, US 191/H3
Hartwell (lake), Ga,SC, US 191/H3
Hartz Mountain NP, Austl. 173/C4
Haruhi, Japan 135/L5
Harun (peak), Indo. 139/E3
Härünäbäd, Pak. 144/B5
Härüt (riv.), Afg. 147/H2
Harvey, ND, US 185/J4
Harvey, La, US 195/P17
Harvey, Austl. 170/B5
Harvey, Il, US 193/Q16
Harveys (lake), Pa, US 196/B1
Harwich, Eng, UK 91/H3
Haryana (state), India 140/C2
Harz (mts.), Ger. 98/F3
Hasan, Turk. 148/C2
Hasan Abdäl, Pak. 144/B3
Hasanpur, India 142/B1
Hasbrouck Heights, NJ, US 197/J8
Hasdo (riv.), India 143/E3
Hase (riv.), Ger. 98/D2
Hasel, Ger. 112/D1
Haselünne, Ger. 109/E3

Hasenmatt (peak), Swi. 114/D3
Hashima, Japan 135/L5
Hashimoto, Japan 132/D3
Hasi el Farsia (well), WSah. 156/C4
Häsilpur, Pak. 144/B5
Haskell, Tx, US 187/H4
Haslach an der Mühl, Aus. 113/H5
Haslach im Kinzigtal, Ger. 114/E1
Hasle bei Burgdorf, Swi. 114/D3
Haslemere, Eng, UK 91/F4
Haslingden, Eng, UK 93/F4
Hasloh, Ger. 109/G1
Haspres, Fr. 110/C3
Hassa, Turk. 149/E1
Hassan, India 140/C5
Hassan (El Aaiún) (int'l arpt.), WSah. 156/B4
Hassberge (hills), Ger. 112/D2
Hassel, Ger. 109/G3
Hassel Sound (str.), Nun., Can. 181/S7
Hasselt, Neth. 108/D3
Hasselt, Belg. 111/E2
Hassfurt, Ger. 112/D2
Hassi Bahbah, Alg. 158/G5
Hassi bou Zid (well), Alg. 157/F3
Hassi el Hadjar (well), Alg. 157/G3
Hassi el Mislane (well), Alg. 157/H4
Hassi er Rebib (well), Alg. 157/G2
Hässleholm, Swe. 96/E3
Hasslo (int'l arpt.), Swe. 96/G2
Hassloch, Ger. 112/B4
Haste, Ger. 109/G4
Hastings, Austl. 173/C3
Hastings, Ne, US 187/H2
Hastings, Mi, US 188/C3
Hastings, NZ 175/T10
Hastings, Eng, UK 91/G5
Hastings Battlesite, Eng, UK 91/G5
Hastings-On-Hudson, NY, US 197/K7
Hasuda, Japan 135/D2
Hasunuma, Japan 135/E2
Hasvik, Nor. 95/G1
Hat Chao Mai NP, Thai. 136/B5
Hat Head, Austl. 173/E1
Hat Head NP, Austl. 173/E1
Hat Nai Yang NP, Thai. 136/B5
Hat Yai, Thai. 136/C5
Hat Yai (int'l arpt.), Thai. 136/C5
Hatashō, Japan 135/K5
Hatavch, Mong. 129/K2
Hatay (prov.), Turk. 148/C2
Hatboro, Pa, US 196/C3
Hatch, NM, US 186/F4
Hatcher (peak), Arg. 217/B6
Hateg, Rom. 107/F3
Hatfield, Pa, US 196/C3
Hatfield, Eng, UK 88/C1
Hatfield Peverel, Eng, UK 88/E1
Hatgal, Mong. 128/H1
Hāthras, India 142/B2
Hātia (riv.), Bang. 143/H4
Hatia North (isl.), Bang. 143/H4
Hātia, South (isl.), Bang. 143/H4
Hatibah, Ras (pt.), SAr. 146/C4
Hato (int'l arpt.), NAnt. 210/D1
Hato Corozal, Col. 210/D1
Hato Mayor, DRep. 199/H4
Hatogaya, Japan 135/D2
Hatoyama, Japan 135/C2
Hatsu (isl.), Japan 135/T10
Hatta, India 142/B3
Hattah-Kulkyne NP, Austl. 171/J5
Hattem, Neth. 108/D4
Hatten, Ger. 109/F2
Hatten, Fr. 111/G6
Hatteras, NC, US 191/K3
Hatteras (cape), NC, US 191/K3
Hattfjelldal, Nor. 96/E2
Hattersheim am Main, Ger. 112/B2
Hattiesburg, Ms, US 191/F4
Hattieville, Belz. 202/D2
Hattingen, Ger. 109/E6
Hattula, Fin. 97/L1
Hatvan, Hun. 106/E2
Hatzenbühl, Ger. 112/B4
Hatzfeld, Ger. 109/F6
Hau Giang (riv.), Viet. 136/D4
Haud (reg.), Eth. 155/Q6
Haugesund, Nor. 96/A2
Haukipudas, Fin. 95/H2
Haune (riv.), Ger. 112/C1
Haunsberg (peak), Aus. 113/F7
Hauppauge, NY, US 197/E2
Hauraki (gulf), NZ 175/S10
Häus, Nor. 96/A1

Hausach, Ger. 114/E1
Hausjärvi, Fin. 97/L1
Hausleiten, Aus. 107/N7
Hausstock (peak), Swi. 115/F4
Haut Atlas (mts.), Mor. 154/D1
Haut-Rhin (dept.), Fr. 114/D2
Haut-Normandie (pol. reg.), Fr. 100/D2
Haute-Saône (dept.), Fr. 114/B2
Haute-Savoie (dept.), Fr. 114/C5
Hautefeuille, Fr. 88/L5
Hautes Fagnes (uplands), Belg. 111/E3
Hauteville de Gâtine (uplands), Fr. 100/C3
Hauteville-Lompnes, Fr. 114/B6
Hautmont, Fr. 110/C3
Hauts (plat.), Alg.,Mor. 157/E2
Havant, Eng, UK 91/F5
Havasu (lake), Az,Ca, US 186/D4
Havdhem, Swe. 96/H3
Havel (canal), Ger. 98/P6
Havel (riv.), Ger. 99/G2
Havelange, Belg. 111/E3
Haveli, Pak. 144/B4
Havelian, Pak. 144/B3
Havelländischer Grosser Hauptkanal (canal), Ger. 98/P6
Havelock, NC, US 191/J3
Havelte, Neth. 108/D3
Havencore (isl.), Eng, UK 91/G3
Haverfordwest, Wal, UK 90/B3
Haverhill, Ma, US 189/G3
Haverhill, Eng, UK 91/G2
Havering (bor.), Eng, UK 88/D2
Havířov, Czh. 99/K4
Havixbeck, Ger. 109/E5
Havlíčkuv Brod, Czh. 99/H4
Havneby, Den. 96/C4
Havre, Mt, US 184/F3
Havre de Grace, Md, US 196/B4
Havre-Saint-Pierre, Qu, Can. 189/J1
Havsa, Turk. 105/K2
Havza, Turk. 148/C1
Haw (riv.), NC, US 191/J3
Hawaii (state), US 182/S10
Hawaii (isl.), US 182/U11
Hawaiian (isls.), Hi, US 175/H2
Hawaii Kai, Hi, US 182/W13
Hawaii Volcanoes NP, Hi, US 182/U11
Hawaiian Gardens, Ca, US 194/F8
Hawalli, Kuw. 146/E3
Hawarden, Wal, UK 93/E5
Hawera, NZ 175/S10
Haweswater (res.), Eng, UK 93/F2
Hawi, Hi, US 182/U10
Hawick, Sc, UK 94/D6
Hawke (cape), Austl. 173/E2
Hawke (bay), NZ 167/H6
Hawker, Austl. 171/H4
Hawkesbury (isl.), BC, Can. 184/A2
Hawkesbury, On, Can. 188/F2
Hawkesbury (riv.), Austl. 172/G8
Hawks Nest, Austl. 173/E2
Haworth, NJ, US 197/K8
Hawston, SAfr. 164/L11
Hawthorn Woods, Il, US 193/P15
Hawthorne, Nv, US 186/C3
Hawthorne, Ca, US 194/F8
Hawthorne, NJ, US 197/J8
Hawthorne, NJ, US 197/K8
Hawwärah, Jor. 149/D3
Haxby, Eng, UK 93/G3
Hay, Austl. 173/C2
Hay (pt.), Austl. 172/C3
Hay (riv.), Ab,BC, Can. 180/E2
Hay River, NW, Can. 180/E2
Hayachine-san (peak), Japan 134/B4
Hayakawa, Japan 135/A3
Hayama, Japan 135/D3
Hayange, Fr. 111/F5
Haybes, Fr. 111/D4
Haycock, Ak, US 192/F2
Haydock, Eng, UK 93/F5
Hayes (mt.), Ak, US 192/J3
Hayes (pen.), Grld. 181/T7
Hayes (riv.), Mb, Can. 180/G3
Hayingen, Ger. 115/F1
Haylaastay, Mong. 129/J2
Hayle (riv.), Eng, UK 90/A6
Hayling (isl.), Eng, UK 91/F5
Haymana, Turk. 148/C2
Haynesville, La, US 187/J4
Hayrabolu, Turk. 107/H5
Hays, Ks, US 187/H3
Hays (co.), Tx, US 195/U20
Haysyn, Ukr. 120/D2
Hayward, Wi, US 185/L4

Hazär (mtn.), Iran 147/G3
Hazard, Ky, US 188/D4
Hazäribag, India 143/E4
Hazebrouck, Fr. 110/B2
Hazel Park, Mi, US 193/F7
Hazelwood, Mo, US 195/G8
Hazen (bay), Ak, US 192/E3
Hazen (str.), NW,Nun., Can. 181/R7
Hazlehurst, Ms, US 191/F3
Hazlemere, Eng, UK 88/A2
Hazlet, NJ, US 197/J10
Hazleton (mts.), BC, Can. 184/A2
Hazleton, Pa, US 196/C2
Hazlett (lake), Austl. 171/F2
Hazratbal Mosque, India 144/C2
Hazro, Pak. 144/B3
Hazu, Japan 135/M6
He (riv.), China 137/B3
Headcorn, Eng, UK 91/G4
Heads of Ayr (pt.), Sc, UK 94/B6
Healdsburg, Ca, US 186/B3
Healesville, Austl. 173/C3
Healy, Ak, US 192/J3
Heanor, Eng, UK 93/G6
Heard (isl.), Austl. 218/E
Hearst, On, Can. 188/D1
Heart (riv.), ND, US 185/H4
Heart Law (hill), Sc, UK 94/D5
Heath (pt.), Qu, Can. 189/J1
Heathcote, Austl. 173/C3
Heathcote NP, Austl. 172/G9
Heathrow (int'l arpt.), Eng, UK 88/B2
Hebbronville, Tx, US 190/D5
Hebei (prov.), China 129/K4
Hebertshausen, Ger. 113/E6
Hebrides (isls.), UK 89/Q8
Hebrides (sea), Sc, UK 89/Q8
Hebron, Ne, US 187/H2
Hebron, Il, US 193/P15
Heby, Swe. 96/G2
Hecate (str.), BC, Can. 184/F3
Hecelchakán, Mex. 202/D1
Hechi, China 141/J3
Hechingen, Ger. 112/B6
Hechtel, Belg. 111/E1
Hechthausen, Ger. 109/G1
Hecker, Il, US 195/H9
Hecla, SD, US 185/J4
Hecla and Griper (bay), NW,Nun., Can. 181/R7
Hector (mt.), Ab, Can. 184/D3
Heddal, Nor. 96/C2
Hedel, Neth. 108/C5
Hedemora, Swe. 96/F1
Hedensted, Den. 96/C4
Hedmark (co.), Nor. 95/D3
Hedo-misaki (cape), Japan 133/K7
Hédouville, Fr. 88/J4
Heede, Ger. 109/E3
Heek, Ger. 109/E4
Heemskerk, Neth. 108/B3
Heemstede, Neth. 108/B4
Heerde, Neth. 108/D4
Heerenveen, Neth. 108/C3
Heerhugowaard, Neth. 108/B3
Heerlen, Neth. 111/E2
Heers, Belg. 111/E2
Heesch, Neth. 108/C5
Heeslingen, Ger. 109/G2
Heeze, Neth. 108/C5
Hefa (Haifa), Isr. 149/F6
Hefei, China 130/D5
Hefeng Tujiazu Zizhixian, China 137/B2
Hegang, China 129/P2
Hegau (mts.), Ger. 101/H3
Hegau (reg.), Ger. 98/E5
Heggenes, Nor. 96/C1
Hegins, Pa, US 196/B2
Hegura (isl.), Japan 135/J6
Hei (riv.), Japan 134/B4
Heidberg, Ger. 96/C4
Heideck, Ger. 112/E4
Heidelberg, SAfr. 164/L10
Heidelberg, SAfr. 164/E3
Heidelberg, Ger. 112/B4
Heiden, Ger. 108/D5
Heiden, Swi. 115/F3
Heidenheim, Ger. 112/D4
Heidenreichstein, Aus. 99/H4
Heiderscheid, Lux. 111/E4
Heigenbrücken, Ger. 112/C2
Heihe, China 129/N1
Heikendorf, Ger. 96/C4
Heilbron, SAfr. 164/D3
Heilbronn, Ger. 112/C4
Heiligenberg, Ger. 115/F2
Heiligenblut, Aus. 101/K3
Heiligenhafen, Ger. 96/D4
Heiligenberg, Ger. 108/D6
Heiligenstadt, Ger. 109/H6
Heilong (Amur) (riv.), China,Rus. 123/N5
Heilongjiang (prov.), China 129/N2
Heiloo, Neth. 108/D4

Heimaey (isl.), Ice. 95/N7
Heimbach, Ger. 111/F2
Heimberg, Swi. 114/D4
Heimsheim, Ger. 112/B5
Heinola, Fin. 97/M1
Heinsberg, Ger. 111/F1
Heishan, China 131/B2
Heist-op-den-Berg, Belg. 111/D1
Heitersheim, Ger. 114/D2
Heiwa, Japan 135/L5
Hejian, China 130/D3
Hejin, China 130/B4
Hejing, China 128/E3
Hekimhan, Turk. 148/D2
Hekinan, Japan 135/L6
Hekla (vol.), Ice. 95/N7
Hekou, China 141/H3
Hel, Pol. 97/H4
Helan (mts.), China 128/J4
Helbe (riv.), Ger. 109/H6
Helden, Neth. 108/D6
Helena (cap.), Mt, US 184/E4
Helena (riv.), Austl. 170/L6
Helensburgh, Sc, UK 94/B4
Helgasjön (lake), Swe. 96/F3
Helgoland (isl.), Ger. 96/B4
Helgoländer (bay), Ger. 96/C5
Helgoländer (bay), Wa, US 193/B3
Heliodora, Braz. 213/H7
Heliport (int'l arpt.), Swe. 96/E3
Hellas (see Greece) 105/G3
Helleh (riv.), Iran 146/F3
Hellendoorn, Neth. 108/D4
Hellenthal, Ger. 111/F3
Hellertown, Pa, US 196/C2
Hellevoetsluis, Neth. 108/B5
Hellin, Sp. 102/E3
Hells (canyon), Id, US 184/D4
Hells Canyon Nat'l Rec. Area, US 184/D4
Hell's Gate NP, Kenya 162/C3
Helmand (riv.), Afg. 147/H2
Helmbrechts, Ger. 113/E2
Helmet (mtn.), Ak, US 192/K2
Helmetta, NJ, US 197/H10
Helmond, Neth. 108/C6
Helmstadt, Ger. 112/C3
Helmstedt, Ger. 98/F2
Helong, China 129/N3
Helotes, Tx, US 195/T20
Helper, Ut, US 186/E3
Helsenhorn (peak), Swi. 114/C5
Helsingør, Den. 96/E3
Helsinki (Helsingfors) (cap.), Fin. 95/H3
Helsinki-Vantaa (int'l arpt.), Fin. 97/L1
Hem (riv.), Fr. 110/B2
Hemau, Ger. 113/E4
Hemel Hempstead, Eng, UK 88/B1
Hemer, Ger. 109/E6
Hemet, Ca, US 194/D3
Hemmingen, Ger. 109/G4
Hemmoor, Ger. 109/G1
Hemphill, Tx, US 190/E4
Hempstead, Tx, US 187/H5
Hempstead (har.), NY, US 197/L8
Hempstead, NY, US 197/L9
Hemse, Swe. 96/H3
Hemsedal, Nor. 96/C1
Hemsworth, Eng, UK 93/G4
Henan (prov.), China 129/K5
Henån, Swe. 96/D2
Henares (riv.), Sp. 102/D2
Henashi-zaki (pt.), Japan 134/A3
Hendaye, Fr. 100/C5
Hendek, Turk. 107/K5
Henderson, NC, US 188/E4
Henderson, Nv, US 186/D3
Henderson, Tn, US 188/B5
Henderson, Ky, US 188/C4
Henderson, Co, US 195/C3
Henderson (isl.), Pitc. 175/N7
Hendersonville, NC, US 191/H3
Hendersonville, Tn, US 188/C4
Hendrik-Ido-Ambacht, Neth. 108/B5
Hendrik Verwoerd (res.), SAfr. 164/D3
Hendrina, SAfr. 165/E2
Henefer, Ut, US 195/J12
Heng (mtn.), China 130/L8
Heng (isl.), China 130/L8
Hengduan (mts.), China 128/G6
Hengelo, Neth. 108/D4
Hengoed, Wal, UK 90/C3
Hengshan, China 137/B2
Hengshan, China 130/C3
Hengshui, China 130/C3
Hengyang, China 137/B2
Heniches'k, Ukr. 120/E3

Hénin-Beaumont, Fr. 110/B3
Henley-on-Thames, Eng, UK 91/F3
Henlopen (cape), De, US 196/C6
Henndorf am Wallersee, Aus. 113/G7
Henne, Den. 96/C4
Hennebont, Fr. 100/B3
Hennenman, SAfr. 164/D2
Hennigsdorf, Ger. 98/Q6
Henrietta, Tx, US 187/H4
Henrietta Maria (cape), On, Can. 181/H3
Henry (cape), BC, Can. 192/M5
Henry (mts.), Ut, US 186/E3
Henry Ford Museum and Greenfield Village Historical Site, Mi, US 193/E7
Henryetta, Ok, US 187/J4
Henryville, Pa, US 196/C1
Hensies, Belg. 110/C3
Hentiy (prov.), Mong. 129/J2
Hentiyn (mts.), Mong. 128/J2
Henty, Austl. 173/C2
Henzada, Myan. 141/G4
Heppenheim an der Bergstrasse, Ger. 112/B3
Hepu, China 141/J3
Heqing, China 141/H2
Hequ, China 130/B3
Heradhsvötn (riv.), Ice. 95/N6
Herät, Afg. 147/H2
Herbert, Sk, Can. 184/G3
Herbert River (falls), Austl. 172/B2
Herbert River Falls NP, Austl. 172/B2
Herberton, Austl. 172/B2
Herbeumont, Belg. 111/E4
Herblay, Fr. 88/J5
Herbolzheim, Ger. 114/D1
Herbrechtingen, Ger. 112/D5
Herbstein, Ger. 112/C1
Hercegnovi, Mont. 106/D4
Herculaneum, Mo, US 195/G9
Herculaneum (ruin), It. 104/D2
Hercules, Ca, US 193/K10
Herdecke, Ger. 109/E6
Hereford, Eng, UK 90/D2
Hereford, Md, US 196/B4
Hereford (inlet), NJ, US 196/D5
Hereford, Pa, US 196/C2
Hereford, Tx, US 187/G4
Herefordshire (co.), Eng, UK 90/D2
Hereheretue (isl.), FrPol. 175/L7
Hereke, Turk. 107/J5
Herend, Hun. 106/D2
Herentals, Belg. 108/B6
Herford, Ger. 109/F4
Hergiswil, Swi. 115/E4
Héricourt, Fr. 114/C2
Hérimoncourt, Fr. 114/C3
Herington, Ks, US 187/H3
Herisau, Swi. 115/F3
Herk (riv.), Belg. 111/E2
Herk-de-Stad, Belg. 111/E2
Hèrlen Gol (Kerulen) (riv.), Mong. 129/K2
Herleshausen, Ger. 109/H6
Herma Ness (cape), Sc, UK 89/W13
Hermannsburg, Austl. 171/G2
Hermannsburg Abor. Land, Austl. 171/G2
Hermansverk, Nor. 96/B1
Hermanus, SAfr. 164/L11
Hermeray, Fr. 88/G6
Hermersberg, Ger. 111/G4
Hermes, Fr. 110/B5
Hermeskeil, Ger. 111/F4
Hermiston, Or, US 184/D4
Hermitage, Rus. 119/T7
Hermosa Beach, Ca, US 194/F8
Hermosillo, Mex. 200/C2
Hernández, Mex. 200/B2
Hernani, Sp. 102/E1
Herndon, Pa, US 196/B2
Herne, Ger. 109/E5
Herne, Belg. 110/D2
Herne Bay, Eng, UK 91/H4
Herning, Den. 96/C3
Heroes de la Independencia, Mex. 200/B2
Heroica Caborca, Mex. 200/B2
Heroica Ciudad de Tlaxiaco, Mex. 200/B2
Heroica Nogales, Mex. 200/C2
Heroldsberg, Ger. 112/E3
Hérouville-Saint-Clair, Fr. 100/C2
Hérouville, Fr. 88/J4
Herpf (riv.), Ger. 112/D1
Herre, Nor. 96/C2
Herrenberg, Ger. 112/B5
Herrera, Sp. 102/C4

Herrera de Pisuerga, Sp. 102/C1
Herrera del Duque, Sp. 102/C3
Herrero (pt.), Mex. 196/C6
Herrestad, Swe. 96/D2
Herrieden, Ger. 112/D4
Herriman, Ut, US 195/J12
Herrlisheim, Fr. 111/G6
Herrljunga, Swe. 96/E2
Herrsching am Ammersee, Ger. 115/H2
Hers (riv.), Fr. 100/D5
Herschbach, Ger. 111/G2
Hersbruck, Ger. 113/E3
Herscheid, Ger. 109/E6
Herselt, Belg. 111/D1
Hershey, Pa, US 196/B3
Hersheypark, Pa, US 196/B3
Herstal, Belg. 111/E2
Herten, Ger. 109/E5
Hertford, NC, US 191/J2
Hertford, Eng, UK 91/F3
Herval d'Oeste, Braz. 213/B3
Hervás, Sp. 102/C2
Herve, Belg. 111/E2
Hervey (bay), Austl. 167/E3
Hervey Bay, Austl. 172/D4
Hervey Bay (reef), Austl. 172/D3
Herxheim bei Landau, Ger. 112/B4
Herzberg am Harz, Ger. 109/H5
Herzebrock-Clarholz, Ger. 109/F5
Herzele, Belg. 110/C2
Herzliyya, Isr. 149/F7
Herzogenaurach, Ger. 112/D3
Herzogenbuchsee, Swi. 114/D3
Herzogenburg, Aus. 106/B1
Herzogenrath, Ger. 111/F2
Hesbaye (plat.), Belg. 98/C3
Hesdin, Fr. 110/B3
Hesel, Ger. 109/E2
Heshui, China 128/J4
Heshun, China 130/C3
Hésingue, Fr. 114/D2
Hesperange, Lux. 111/F4
Hesperia, Ca, US 194/C2
Hess (riv.), Yk, Can. 180/C2
Hessel (riv.), Ger. 109/F5
Hessen (state), Ger. 101/H1
Hessen, Ger. 109/H4
Hessisch Lichtenau, Ger. 109/G6
Hessisch Oldendorf, Ger. 109/G4
Hetaüdä, Nepal 143/E2
Heteren, Neth. 108/C5
Hettenleidelheim, Ger. 112/B3
Hettinger, ND, US 185/H4
Hetton-le-Hole, Eng, UK 93/G2
Hettstadt, Ger. 112/C3
Hetzerath, Ger. 111/F4
Heubach (riv.), Ger. 109/E5
Heubach, Ger. 112/D5
Heuchelheim, Ger. 112/B1
Heukuppe (peak), Aus. 99/H5
Heusden, Neth. 108/C5
Heusden-Zolder, Belg. 111/E1
Heusenstamm, Ger. 112/B2
Heusweiler, Ger. 111/F5
Hève, Cap de la (cape), Fr. 100/D2
Heves, Hun. 106/E2
Heves (co.), Hun. 106/E2
Hewitt, NJ, US 197/H7
Hewlett (pt.), NY, US 197/K9
Hewlett, NY, US 197/L9
Hex River (mts.), SAfr. 164/L10
Hex River (pass), SAfr. 164/L10
Hexenkopf (peak), Aus. 115/G3
Heyerode, Ger. 109/H6
Heythuysen, Neth. 108/C6
Heywood, Austl. 173/B3
Heywood, Eng, UK 93/F4
Heze, China 130/C4
Hialeah, Fl, US 191/H5
Hiawatha, Ks, US 187/J3
Hibbing, Mn, US 185/L4
Hibbs (pt.), Austl. 173/C4
Hicacos (pt.), Cuba 199/E3
Hichisō, Japan 135/M4
Hickman (mt.), BC, Can. 192/M4
Hickory, NC, US 191/H3
Hickory, La, US 195/Q16
Hickory Run State Park, Pa, US 196/C1
Hicksville, NY, US 197/L8
Hico, Tx, US 187/H5
Hida (riv.), Japan 133/E3
Hidaka, Japan 134/C2
Hidaka, Japan 134/C2
Hidaka (mts.), Japan 134/C2
Hidalgo, Mex. 201/F3
Hidalgo (state), Mex. 182/B3
Hidalgo del Parral, Mex. 200/D3
Hidden Hills, Ca, US 194/B2
Hidrolândia, Braz. 212/B2
Hierapolis (ruin), Turk. 148/B2
Hieroglyphic (mts.), Az, US 195/R18
Hierro (isl.), Canl., Sp. 156/A4

Hieve (lake), Ger. 109/E2
Higashi-Chichibu, Japan 135/C1
Higashi-Matsuyama, Japan 135/C1
Higashi-Ōsaka, Japan 135/J6
Higashikurume, Japan 135/D2
Higashimurayama, Japan 135/C2
Higashine, Japan 134/B4
Higashiura, Japan 135/G6
Higashiura, Japan 135/L6
Higashiyoshino, Japan 135/J7
High (des.), Or, US 184/C5
High (hill), Pa, US 196/C1
High (isl.), China 129/V10
High Bridge, NJ, US 196/D2
High Island, Tx, US 190/E4
High Level, Ab, Can. 180/E3
High Point, NC, US 191/H3
High Ridge, Mo, US 195/F9
High River, Ab, Can. 184/E3
High Street (peak), Eng, UK 93/F3
High Willhays (hill), Eng, UK 90/B5
High Wycombe, Eng, UK 91/F3
Higham, Eng, UK 88/E2
Higham Ferrers, Eng, UK 91/F2
Highland, Ca, US 194/C2
Highland, Ut, US 195/K13
Highland, In, US 193/R16
Highland (pol. reg.), Sc, US 94/A2
Highland Lakes, NJ, US 196/D1
Highland Park, Co, US 195/A4
Highland Park, Mi, US 193/F7
Highland Park, NJ, US 197/H10
Highlands, NJ, US 197/K10
Highrock (lake), Mb, Can. 185/H2
Highspire, Pa, US 196/B3
Hightstown, NJ, US 196/D3
Highwood, Il, US 193/Q15
Higley, Az, US 195/S19
Higuera de Zaragoza, Mex. 200/C3
Hihyā, Egypt 149/B4
Hiidenportin NP, Fin. 95/J3
Hiiumaa (isl.), Est. 97/K2
Híjar, Sp. 103/E2
Hijāz, Jabal al (mts.), SAr. 146/C3
Hiji, Japan 132/B4
Hijuelas de Conchali, Chile 216/N8
Hikami, Japan 135/H5
Hikari, Japan 135/F2
Hikone, Japan 135/K5
Hikueru (isl.), FrPol. 175/L6
Hikurangi (peak), NZ 175/T10
Hildburghausen, Ger. 112/D2
Hilden, Ger. 111/F1
Hilders, Ger. 112/C1
Hildesheim, Ger. 109/G4
Hilgermissen, Ger. 109/G3
Hill (isl.), Pa, US 196/B3
Hill City, Ks, US 187/H3
Hill of Fare (hill), Sc, UK 94/D2
Hill of Stake (hill), Sc, UK 94/B5
Hillaby (mt.), Bar. 199/P9
Hillburn, NY, US 197/J7
Hillcrest, NY, US 197/J7
Hille, Ger. 109/F4
Hillegom, Neth. 108/B4
Hillerød, Den. 96/E4
Hillesheim, Ger. 111/F3
Hillingdon (bor.), Eng, UK 88/B2
Hillsboro, Md, US 196/C6
Hillsboro, ND, US 185/J4
Hillsboro, Oh, US 188/D4
Hillsboro, Or, US 184/C4
Hillsboro, Tx, US 187/H4
Hillsborough (chan.), Austl. 172/C3
Hillsborough, Ca, US 193/K11
Hillsborough, NJ, US 196/D3
Hillsdale, Mi, US 188/C3
Hillsdale, Ks, US 195/D6
Hillsdale (lake), Ks, US 195/D6
Hillsdale, NJ, US 197/J7
Hillside, NJ, US 197/J9
Hillside, Sc, UK 94/D3
Hillston, Austl. 173/C2
Hillswick, Sc, UK 89/W13
Hilltop, Co, US 195/C4
Hilltown, NI, UK 92/B3
Hilo, Hi, US 182/U11
Hilongos, Phil. 137/D5
Hilpoltstein, Ger. 112/E4
Hilpsford (pt.), Eng, UK 93/E3
Hilsa, India 143/E3
Hilterfingen, Swi. 114/D4
Hilton Head (isl.), SC, US 191/H3
Hilton Head Island, SC, US 191/H3
Hilvarenbeek, Neth. 108/C5
Hilversum, Neth. 108/C4
Hilzingen, Ger. 115/E2
Himāchal Pradesh (state), India 144/D3
Himalaya (range), Asia 125/G6
Himālchuli (peak), Nepal 143/E1
Himamaylan, Phil. 137/D5
Himanka, Fin. 95/G2
Himberg, Aus. 107/N7
Himeji, Japan 132/D3
Himeji Castle, Japan 132/D3
Himi, Japan 133/E2
Himmelpforten, Ger. 109/G1
Ḩimş (prov.), Syria 148/D3
Ḩimş, Syria 149/E2
Hinche, Haiti 203/H2
Hinchinbrook (isl.), Austl. 167/D2
Hinchinbrook Entrance (chan.), Ak., US 192/J3
Hinchinbrook Island NP, Austl. 172/B2
Hinckley, Eng, UK 91/E1
Hincks Conservation Park, Austl. 171/H5
Hindan (riv.), India 142/A1
Hindaun, India 142/A2
Hindelang, Ger. 115/G3
Hindeloopen, Neth. 108/C3
Hindley, Eng, UK 93/F4
Hindmarsh (lake), Austl. 173/B3
Hindu Kush (mts.), Asia 125/F6
Hindupur, India 140/C5
Hinesville, Ga, US 191/H4
Hinganghāt, India 140/C3
Hingol (riv.), Pak. 147/J3
Hingoli, India 140/C4
Hingorja, Pak. 147/J3
Hınıs, Turk. 148/E2
Hino, Japan 135/K5
Hino, Japan 135/C2
Hino (riv.), Japan 135/K5
Hino-misaki (cape), Japan 132/C3
Hinode, Japan 135/C2
Hinohara, Japan 135/C2
Hinojosa del Duque, Sp. 102/C3
Hinsdale, Il, US 193/Q16
Hinte, Ger. 109/E2
Hinterbrühl, Aus. 107/N7
Hinterrhein (riv.), Swi. 115/F4
Hinterrugg (peak), Swi. 115/F3
Hinterweidenthal, Ger. 111/G5
Hinton, Ab, Can. 184/D2
Hinton, WV, US 188/D4
Hinwil, Swi. 115/E3
Hipólito Bouchard, Arg. 216/E2
Hippolytushoef, Neth. 108/B3
Hipswell, Eng, UK 93/G3
Hira Highlands (uplands), Japan 135/J5
Hirado, Japan 132/A4
Hirakata, Japan 135/J6
Hirakud (res.), India 140/D3
Hiraman (riv.), Kenya 162/C3
Hiran (riv.), India 142/B4
Hiranai, Japan 134/B3
Hirara, Japan 133/H8
Hirata, Japan 133/C3
Hirata, Japan 135/L5
Hiratsuka, Japan 135/C3
Hirfanlı (dam), Turk. 148/C2
Hîrlău, Rom. 107/H2
Hiro'o, Japan 134/C2
Hirosaki, Japan 134/B3
Hiroshima, Japan 132/C3
Hiroshima (pref.), Japan 132/C3
Hirschaid, Ger. 112/D3
Hirschau, Ger. 113/E3
Hirschhorn, Ger. 112/B4
Hirson, Fr. 111/D4
Hîrşova, Rom. 107/H3
Hirtshals, Den. 96/C3
Hirukawa, Japan 135/M4
Hisai, Japan 135/K6
Hisarcık, Turk. 148/B2
Ḩisbān, Jor. 149/D4
Ḩişn al 'Abr, Yem. 146/E5
Hispaniola (isl.), DRep.,Haiti 199/G4
Historic Houses of Odessa, De, US 196/C5
Historic Towne of Smithville, NJ, US 196/D5
Hisua, India 143/E3
Hīt, Iraq 148/E3
Hitachi, Japan 133/G2
Hitachi-Ōta, Japan 133/G2
Hitchin, Eng, UK 91/F3
Hitoyoshi, Japan 132/B4
Hitra (isl.), Nor. 95/C3
Hittisau, Aus. 115/F3
Hitzacker, Ger. 98/F2
Hitzkirch, Swi. 115/E3
Hiyoshi, Japan 135/J5
Hizan, Turk. 148/E2
Hjälmaren (lake), Swe. 96/G2
Hjartfjellet (peak), Nor. 95/E2
Hjelmeland, Nor. 96/B2
Hjerm, Den. 96/C3
Hjo, Swe. 96/F2
Hjørring, Den. 96/C3
Hka (riv.), Myan. 136/B1
Hkakabo (peak), Myan. 141/G2
Hlabisa, SAfr. 165/E3
Hlohovec, Slvk. 106/C1
Hluboká nad Vltava, Czh. 113/H4
Hluhluwe, SAfr. 165/F3
Hlukhiv, Ukr. 120/E2
Hmawbi, Myan. 141/G4
Ho, Gha. 161/F5
Hoa Binh, Viet. 136/D1
Hoare (bay), Nun., Can. 181/K2
Hobara, Japan 133/G2
Hobart, Austl. 173/C4
Hobart (int'l arpt.), Austl. 173/C4
Hobart, Wa, US 193/D3
Hobbs, NM, US 187/G4
Hoboken, Belg. 108/B6
Hoboken, NJ, US 197/J9
Hoboksar Monggol Zizhixian, China 128/E2
Hobro, Den. 96/C3
Hochalmspitze (peak), Aus. 101/K3
Höchberg, Ger. 112/C3
Hochdorf, Ger. 115/F1
Hochfelden, Fr. 111/G6
Hochfinsler (peak), Swi. 115/F3
Hochgrat (peak), Ger. 115/G3
Hochheim am Main, Ger. 112/B2
Hochkönig (peak), Aus. 101/K3
Hŏch'ŏn (riv.), NKor. 131/D2
Hochschwab (peak), Aus. 101/L3
Hochsimmer (peak), Ger. 111/G3
Hochspeyer, Ger. 111/G5
Höchst, Aus. 115/F3
Höchst im Odenwald, Ger. 112/B3
Hochstadt am Main, Ger. 112/E2
Höchstadt an der Aisch, Ger. 112/D3
Hochstädt an der Donau, Ger. 112/D5
Hochstetten-Dhaun, Ger. 111/G4
Hochvogel (peak), Aus. 115/G3
Hochwang (peak), Swi. 115/F4
Hockenheim, Ger. 112/B4
Hockessin, De, US 196/C4
Hockley, Eng, UK 88/F2
Hod Hasharon, Isr. 149/F7
Hodal, India 142/A2
Hodder (riv.), Eng, UK 93/F4
Hoddesdon, Eng, UK 88/D1
Hodenhagen, Ger. 109/G3
Hodges (lake), Ca, US 194/C4
Hodgeville, Sk, Can. 184/G3
Hodh (phys. reg.), Mrta. 160/C2
Hodh El Gharbi (pol. reg.), Mrta. 160/C2
Hódmezővásárhely, Hun. 106/E2
Hodonín, Czh. 99/J4
Hoekse Waard (isl.), Neth. 108/B5
Hoensbroek, Neth. 111/E2
Hoeselt, Belg. 111/E2
Hoevelaken, Neth. 108/C4
Hoeven, Neth. 108/B5
Hoeybuktmoen (int'l arpt.), Nor. 95/J1
Hof, Ger. 113/E2
Hofbieber, Ger. 112/C1
Höfdhakaupstadhur, Ice. 95/N6
Hoffman Estates, Il, US 193/P15
Hofgeismar, Ger. 109/G6
Hofheim am Taunus, Ger. 112/B2
Hofheim in Unterfranken, Ger. 112/D2
Hofmeyr, SAfr. 164/D3
Hofong Qagan Salt (lake), China 130/B3
Hofors, Swe. 96/G1
Hofsá (riv.), Ice. 95/P6
Hofsjökull (glacier), Ice. 95/N7
Hōfu, Japan 132/B3
Hogarth (mt.), Austl. 171/H2
Hogyész, Hun. 106/D2
Hoh Xil (mts.), China 128/E4
Höhbürd, Mong. 128/H2
Hohe Acht (peak), Ger. 111/G3
Hohe Geige (peak), Aus. 115/G4
Hohe Tauern (mts.), Aus. 101/K3
Hohe Tauern NP, Aus. 101/K3
Hohegrass (peak), Ger. 109/G6
Hohen Neuendorf, Ger. 98/Q6
Hohenbrunn, Ger. 113/E6
Hohenems, Aus. 115/F3
Hohenhameln, Ger. 109/H4
Hohenlinden, Ger. 113/F6
Hohenlockstedt, Ger. 98/E2
Hohenloher Ebene (plain), Ger. 98/E4
Hohenpeissenberg, Ger. 115/G2
Hohenroth, Ger. 112/D2
Hoher Dachstein (peak), Aus. 101/K3
Hoher Ifen (peak), Ger. 115/G3
Hoher Randen (peak), Ger. 115/E2
Hohgant (peak), Swi. 114/D4
Hohhot, China 129/K3
Höhn, Ger. 111/G2
Hohneck (peak), Fr. 114/D1
Hohnstorf, Ger. 109/H2
Hohokam Pima Nat'l Mon., Az, US 186/E4
Höhr-Grenzhausen, Ger. 111/G3
Hoi An, Viet. 136/E3
Hoima, Ugan. 162/A2
Hoisington, Ks, US 187/H3
Højby, Den. 96/D4
Højer, Den. 96/C4
Hōjō, Japan 132/C4
Hokitika, NZ 175/S11
Hokkaidō (isl.), Japan 134/B2
Hokksund, Nor. 96/C2
Hokota, Japan 133/G2
Hokudan, Japan 135/G6
Hokusei, Japan 135/L5
Hol, Nor. 96/C1
Holbox, Mex. 202/E1
Holbrook, Austl. 173/C2
Holbrook, Az, US 186/E4
Holbrook, NY, US 197/E2
Holderness (pen.), Eng, UK 93/H4
Holdorf, Ger. 109/F3
Holdrege, Ne, US 187/H2
Holeby, Den. 96/D4
Holguín, Cuba 203/G1
Holiday Hills, Il, US 193/P15
Holitna (riv.), Ak, US 192/G3
Höljes, Swe. 96/E1
Holladay-Cottonwood, Ut, US 195/K12
Holland, Mi, US 188/C3
Holland (pt.), Md, US 196/B6
Hollandale, Ms, US 187/K4
Hollandse IJssel (riv.), Neth. 108/B5
Hollandstoun, Sc, UK 89/V14
Hollenstedt, Ger. 109/G2
Hollfeld, Ger. 112/E3
Holliday, Ks, US 195/D5
Hollis, Ok, US 187/H4
Hollis, Ak, US 192/M4
Hollister, Ca, US 186/B3
Hollister (mt.), Austl. 170/B2
Hollogne-aux-Pierres, Belg. 111/E2
Hollola, Fin. 97/L1
Höllviksnäs, Swe. 96/E4
Holly, Wa, US 193/B2
Holly Springs, Ms, US 191/F3
Hollywood, Fl, US 191/H5
Hollywood Bowl, Ca, US 194/F7
Hollywood Park, Tx, US 195/U20
Holm, Ger. 109/G1
Holman, NW, Can. 180/E1
Hólmavík, Ice. 95/N6
Holmdel, NJ, US 196/D3
Holmes (reefs), Austl. 167/D2
Holmesdale (valley), Eng, UK 88/C3
Holmestrand, Nor. 96/D2
Holmfirth, Eng, UK 93/G4
Holmsjön (lake), Swe. 95/F3
Holmsund, Swe. 95/G3
Ḩolon, Isr. 149/F7
Holstebro, Den. 96/C3
Holston (riv.), Tn, US 191/H2
Holt, Mo, US 195/E5
Holt, Ca, US 193/M11
Holtålen, Nor. 95/D3
Holten, Neth. 108/D4
Holtland, Ger. 109/E2
Holton, Ks, US 187/J3
Holtsville, NY, US 197/E2
Holy (isl.), Sc, UK 94/A5
Holy Cross, Ak, US 192/G3
Holyhead, Wal, UK 92/D5
Holyoke, Co, US 187/G2
Holyoke, Ma, US 189/F3
Holywell, Wal, UK 93/E5
Holywood, NI, UK 92/C2
Holzkirchen, Ger. 101/J3
Holzminden, Ger. 109/G5
Holzwickede, Ger. 109/E5
Hom (riv.), Namb. 164/B3
Homberg, Ger. 109/G6
Homberg, Ger. 108/D6
Hombori Tondo (peak), Mali 161/E3
Hombourg-Haut, Fr. 111/F5
Homburg, Ger. 111/G5
Home (bay), Nun., Can. 181/K2
Home Hill, Austl. 172/B2
Homécourt, Fr. 111/E5
Homeland, Ca, US 194/C3
Homer, Ak, US 192/H4
Homer, La, US 187/J4
Homestead, Fl, US 191/H5
Homestead Nat'l Mon. of America, Ne, US 187/H2
Homewood, Al, US 191/G3
Homewood, Il, US 193/Q16
Homib (riv.), Erit. 146/C5
Hommersåk, Nor. 96/A2
Homochitto (riv.), Ms, US 190/F4
Homyel', Bela. 120/D1
Homyel'skaya Voblasts Bela. 120/D1
Hon Quan, Viet. 136/D4
Honaunau-Napoopoo, Hi, US 182/U11
Honbetsu, Japan 134/C2
Honddu (riv.), Wal, UK 90/C2
Hondeklipbaai, SAfr. 164/B3
Hondo (riv.), Belz. 202/D2
Hondo, Japan 132/B4
Hondo, Tx, US 187/H5
Hondschoote, Fr. 110/B2
Hondsrug (reg.), Neth. 108/D3
Hondsrug (hills), Neth. 98/D2
Honduras (gulf), NAm. 202/E2
Honduras (ctry.) 202/E3
Honey (lake), Ca, US 184/C5
Honey Brook, Pa, US 196/C3
Honey Creek, Wi, US 193/P14
Hong (isl.), SKor. 131/C5
Hong (lake), China 130/C5
Hong (riv.), China 130/C4
Hong Gai, Viet. 141/J3
Hong Kong (dpcy.), China 137/B3
Hong Kong (isl.), China 137/B3
Hong'an, China 130/C5
Hongch'ŏn, SKor. 131/D4
Hongdu (riv.), China 141/J2
Honghu, China 137/B2
Hongjiang, China 141/J2
Hongqiao (int'l arpt.), China 130/L8
Hongshui (riv.), China 128/J6
Hongsŏng, SKor. 131/D4
Hongtong, China 130/B3
Honguedo (passg.), Qu, Can. 189/H1
Hongwŏn, NKor. 131/D2
Hongze, China 130/D4
Hœnheim, Fr. 111/G6
Honiara (cap.), Sol. 174/E5
Honjō, Japan 134/B4
Honjō, Japan 135/C1
Honolulu (cap.), Hi, US 182/T10
Honolulu (co.), Hi, US 182/V13
Honolulu (int'l arpt.), Hi, US 182/W13
Honouliuli, Hi, US 182/V13
Hönow, Ger. 98/Q6
Honshū (isl.), Japan 129/Q5
Hood (pt.), Austl. 170/C5
Hood, Ca, US 193/L10
Hood (mt.), Ca, US 193/J10
Hood (mt.), Or, US 184/C4
Hood Canal (str.), Wa, US 184/C4
Hoofddorp, Neth. 108/B4
Hoogeloon, Neth. 108/C6
Hoogeveen, Neth. 108/D3
Hoogeveense Vaart (canal), Neth. 108/D3
Hoogezand, Neth. 108/D2
Hooghly (riv.), India 143/F5
Hooghly-Chinsura, India 143/G4
Hoogkarspel, Neth. 108/C3
Hooglede, Belg. 110/C2
Hoogstraten, Belg. 108/B6
Hook (pt.), Ire. 89/Q10
Hook (sound), Austl. 172/C3
Hookena, Hi, US 182/U11
Hoonah, Ak, US 192/L4
Hooper, Ut, US 195/J11
Hooper Bay, Ak, US 192/E3
Hoopeston, Il, US 188/C3
Hoopstad, SAfr. 164/D2
Höör, Swe. 96/E4
Hoorn, Neth. 108/C3
Hoornse Hop (bay), Neth. 108/C3
Hoover (dam), Az, US 186/D3
Hoover, Mo, US 195/D5
Hopa, Turk. 148/E1
Hopatcong, NJ, US 196/D2
Hopatcong (lake), NJ, US 196/D2
Hope (lake), Austl. 167/A4
Hope, BC, Can. 184/C3
Hope, Ak, US 192/J3
Hope, NJ, US 196/D2
Hope Vale Aboriginal Community, Austl. 172/B1
Hopedale, Nf, Can. 181/K3
Hopelchén, Mex. 202/D2
Hopeman, Sc, UK 94/C1
Hopes Advance (cape), Qu, Can. 181/K2
Hope's Nose (pt.), Eng, UK 90/C6
Hopetown, SAfr. 164/D3
Hopewell, NJ, US 196/D3
Hopewell Furnace NHS, Pa, US 196/C3
Hopkins (riv.), Austl. 173/B3
Hopkins (lake), Austl. 167/B3
Hopkinsville, Ky, US 188/C4
Hoppecke (riv.), Ger. 109/F6
Hoppegarten, Ger. 98/Q6
Hoppstädten-Weiersbach, Ger. 111/G4
Hopsten, Ger. 109/E4
Hoquiam, Wa, US 184/C4
Horace (mtn.), Ak, US 192/J2
Horado, Japan 135/L4
Hōrai-san (peak), Japan 135/J5
Horasan, Turk. 148/E1
Horažďovice, Czh. 113/G4
Horb am Neckar, Ger. 112/B6
Horbourg-Wihr, Fr. 114/D1
Hörbranz, Aus. 115/F2
Horche, Sp. 102/D2
Horconcitos, Pan. 203/F4
Hordaland (co.), Nor. 95/C3
Hördt, Ger. 112/B4
Hœrdt, Fr. 111/G6
Horezu, Rom. 107/G3
Horgau, Ger. 112/D6
Horgen, Swi. 115/E3
Horine, Mo, US 195/G9
Horinger, China 130/B2
Horley, Eng, UK 88/C3
Horlivka, Ukr. 120/F2
Hormigüeros, PR 199/M8
Hormuz (str.), Oman 147/G3
Horn, Aus. 101/L2
Horn (pt.), Ice. 218/H
Horn-Bad Meinberg, Ger. 109/F5
Hornachuelos, Sp. 102/C4
Hornád (riv.), Slvk. 99/L4
Hornavan (lake), Swe. 95/F2
Hornbach, Ger. 111/G5
Hornberg, Ger. 115/E1
Horndal, Swe. 96/G1
Horneburg, Ger. 109/G1
Hornell, NY, US 188/E3
Horní Bříza, Czh. 113/G3
Horní Slavkov, Czh. 113/F2
Hornisgrinde (peak), Ger. 112/B5
Hornos (cape), Chile 217/D7
Hornoy-le-Bourg, Fr. 110/A4
Hornslet, Den. 96/D3
Hörnum (cape), Ger. 96/C4
Horoshiri-dake (peak), Japan 134/C2
Hořovice, Czh. 113/G3
Horqin Zuoyi Houqi, China 130/E2
Horqin Zuoyi Zhongqi, China 130/E1
Hörsching, Aus. 113/H6
Horse Cave, Ky, US 188/C4
Horsefly (lake), BC, Can. 184/C2
Horsens, Den. 96/C4
Horseshoe (lake), Il, US 195/G8
Horseshoe (lake), Co, US 195/B2
Horsetooth (res.), Co, US 195/B1
Horsey (isl.), Eng, UK 91/H3
Horsforth, Eng, UK 93/G4
Horsham, Austl. 173/B3
Horsham, Eng, UK 91/F4
Horsham, Pa, US 196/C3
Horšovský Týn, Czh. 113/F3
Horst, Neth. 108/D6
Hörstel, Ger. 109/E4
Horstmar, Ger. 109/E4
Horta, Azor., Port. 103/S12
Horten, Nor. 96/D2
Hortes, Fr. 114/B2
Hortobágyi NP, Hun. 106/E2
Horton (pt.), NY, US 197/F1
Horton (riv.), NW, Can. 180/D2
Horuphav, Den. 96/C4
Horusický Rybník (lake), Czh. 113/H4
Hørve, Den. 96/D4
Ḩorvot Dor, Isr. 149/F6
Horw, Swi. 115/E3
Horwich, Eng, UK 93/F4
Horwood (lake), On, Can. 188/D2
Hösbach, Ger. 112/C2
Hosenfeld, Ger. 112/C1
Hoshiārpur, India 144/C4
Hosingen, Lux. 111/F3
Hospental, Swi. 115/E4
Hosszúpereszteg, Hun. 106/C2
Hoste (isl.), Chile 217/C7
Hot Springs, SD, US 185/H5
Hot Springs NP, Ar, US 187/J4
Hotaka, Japan 133/E2
Hotaka-dake (peak), Japan 133/E2
Hotan, China 128/C4
Hotan (riv.), China 128/D4
Hotazel, SAfr. 164/C2
Hotont, Mong. 128/H2
Hottah (lake), NW, Can. 180/E2
Hottentot (bay), Namb. 164/A2
Hotton, Belg. 111/E3
Houari Boumedienne (int'l arpt.), Alg. 158/G4
Houdain, Fr. 110/B3
Houdan, Fr. 88/G5
Houet (prov.), Burk. 160/D4
Houffalize, Belg. 111/E3
Houghton Lake, Mi, US 188/C2
Houghton-le-Spring, Eng, UK 93/G2
Houilles, Fr. 88/J5
Houlton, Me, US 189/H2
Houma, China 130/B4
Houplines, Fr. 110/B2
Hourdel (pt.), Fr. 110/A3
Hourn, Loch (inlet), Sc, UK 94/A2
Hourtin, Fr. 100/C4
Housatonic (riv.), Ct, US 197/E1
House (range), Ut, US 186/D3
House Springs, Mo, US 195/F9
Housesteads Roman Fort, Eng, UK 93/F1
Houssen, Fr. 114/D1
Houston, BC, Can. 184/B2
Houston, Ak, US 192/J3
Houston, De, US 196/C6
Houston, Mo, US 187/K3
Houston, Ms, US 191/F3
Houston, Tx, US 187/J5
Houtbaai, SAfr. 164/L11
Houten, Neth. 108/C4
Houthulst, Belg. 110/B2
Houtman Abrolhos (isl.), Austl. 170/B4
Houtribdijk (dam), Neth. 108/C3
Houtskär (isl.), Fin. 97/J1
Houyet, Belg. 111/E3
Hov, Nor. 96/D1
Hova, Swe. 96/F2
Hovd, Mong. 128/F2
Hovd (prov.), Mong. 128/F2
Hövelhof, Ger. 109/F5
Hovenweep Nat'l Mon., Ut, US 186/E3
Hovfjället (peak), Swe. 96/E1
Hovmantorp, Swe. 96/F3
Hövsgöl (prov.), Mong. 128/G1
Hovsta, Swe. 96/F2
Howard, Austl. 172/D4
Howard (hill), Ak, US 192/H2
Howard (pass), Ak, US 192/G2
Howard (co.), Md, US 196/B5
Howard Hanson (res.), Wa, US 193/D3
Howard Hanson (dam), Wa, US 193/D3
Howe (cape), Austl. 173/D3
Howe of the Mearns (reg.), Sc, UK 94/D3
Howell, Mi, US 188/D3
Howell, NJ, US 196/D3
Howick, SAfr. 165/E3
Howland (isl.), Pac., US 175/H4
Höxter, Ger. 109/G5
Hoxud, China 128/E3
Hoy (isl.), Sc, UK 89/V14
Hoya, Ger. 109/G3
Hōya, Japan 135/D2
Høyanger, Nor. 96/B1
Hoyerswerda, Ger. 99/H3
Hoylake, Eng, UK 93/E5
Hoyland Nether, Eng, UK 93/G4
Hoyo de Manzanares, Sp. 103/N8
Hoyos, Sp. 102/B2
Hoyoux (riv.), Belg. 111/E3
Hozumi, Japan 135/L5
Hracholusky (res.), Czh. 113/F3
Hradec Králové, Czh. 99/H3
Hradište (peak), Czh. 113/G2
Hrasnica, Bosn. 106/D4
Hrastnik, Slov. 101/L3
Hrazdan, Arm. 121/H4
Hrodna, Bela. 97/K5
Hrodzyenskaya Voblasts Bela. 118/E5
Hrolleifsborg (peak), Ice. 95/M6
Hron (riv.), Slvk. 99/K4
Hronov, Czh. 99/J3
Hrubieszów, Pol. 99/M3
Hrubý Jeseník (mts.), Czh.,Pol. 99/J3
Hrútafjöll (peak), Ice. 95/P6
Hsinchu, Tai. 137/D3
Hua (peak), China 130/B4
Hua Hin, Thai. 136/B3
Hua Xian, China 130/C4
Hua'an, China 137/C2
Huacaybamba, Peru 214/B3
Huachi, China 128/J4
Huacho, Peru 214/B3
Huachón, Peru 214/C3
Huachuca City, Az, US 186/E5
Huacrachuco, Peru 214/B3
Huade, China 129/K3
Huahine (isl.), FrPol. 175/K6
Huai (riv.), China 130/C4
Huai'an, China 130/D4
Huai'an, China 130/D4
Huaibei, China 129/L5
Huaibin, China 130/C4
Huaiji, China 141/K3
Huailai, China 130/G6
Huainan, China 130/D4
Huairen, China 130/C3
Huairou, China 130/H6
Huaiyang, China 130/C4
Huaiyin, China 130/D4
Huaiyin, China 130/D4
Huaiyuan, China 130/D4
Huajicori, Mex. 200/D4
Huajuapan de León, Mex. 202/B2
Hualahuises, Mex. 201/F3
Hualañé, Chile 216/C2
Hualgayoc, Peru 214/B2
Hualien, Tai. 137/D3
Hualla, Peru 214/C4
Huallaga (riv.), Peru 214/B3
Huallanca, Peru 214/B3
Huallanca, Peru 214/B3
Huamachuco, Peru 214/B2
Huamantanga, Peru 214/B3
Huamantla, Mex. 201/M7
Huambo, Ang. 163/C3
Huambos, Peru 214/B2
Huan (riv.), China 130/B4
Huan Xian, China 128/J4
Huancané, Peru 214/D4
Huancapi, Peru 214/C4
Huancaspata, Peru 214/B3
Huancavelica (dept.), Peru 214/C4
Huancavelica, Peru 214/C4
Huancayo, Peru 214/C4
Huanchaca (peak), Bol. 208/E8
Huang (riv.), China 125/L6
Huangchuan, China 130/C4
Huanggang (peak), China 137/C2
Huanghua, China 130/D3
Huangling, China 130/B4
Huanglong, China 130/B4
Huangping, China 141/J2
Huangqi (lake), China 130/C2
Huangshan, China 137/C2
Huangtang (lake), China 130/C5
Huangtu (plat.), China 130/B4
Huanguelén, Arg. 216/E3
Huangyan, China 137/D2
Huangzhong, China 128/H4
Huanren, China 131/C2
Huanta, Peru 214/C4
Huantai, China 130/D3
Huántar, Peru 214/B3
Huánuco (dept.), Peru 214/C3
Huánuco, Peru 214/B3
Huanuni, Bol. 208/E7
Huapi (mts.), Nic. 203/E3
Huaquechula, Mex. 201/L8
Huaquillas, Ecu. 214/A1
Huaral, Peru 214/B3
Huaraz, Peru 214/B3
Huari, Peru 214/B3
Huaricolca, Peru 214/C3
Huarina, Bol. 214/D5
Huarmey, Peru 214/B3
Huarochirí, Peru 214/B4
Huarocondo, Peru 214/C4
Huarong, China 137/B2
Huásabas, Mex. 200/C2
Huasahuasi, Peru 214/C3
Huascarán (peak), Peru 214/B3
Huatabampo, Mex. 200/C3
Huatunas (lake), Bol. 208/E6
Huatuxco, Mex. 201/N7
Huauchinango, Mex. 201/L6
Huaura, Peru 214/B3
Huautla de Jiménez, Mex. 202/B2
Huayacocotla, Mex. 201/L6
Huaying, China 137/A1
Huaylas, Peru 214/B3
Huayllay, Peru 214/B3
Huayopata, Peru 214/C4
Huayuan, China 141/J2
Huazhou, China 141/K3
Hubbard (mt.), Ak, US 192/L3
Hubbard Creek (res.), Tx, US 187/H4
Hubei (prov.), China 129/K5
Hubei (pass), China 130/B4
Hubli-Dhārwār, India 147/L5
Huch'ang, NKor. 131/D2
Hückelhoven, Ger. 111/F1
Hückeswagen, Ger. 111/G1
Hucknall, Eng, UK 93/G5
Huddersfield, Eng, UK 93/G4
Huddinge, Swe. 96/G2
Hude, Ger. 109/F2
Hudiksvall, Swe. 96/G1
Hudson (cape), Ant. 218/L
Hudson (bay), Can. 181/H2
Hudson (str.), Nun.,Qu, Can. 181/J2
Hudson, Qu, Can. 189/M7
Hudson, Co, US 195/C2
Hudson (co.), NJ, US 197/J9
Hudson (riv.), NJ,NY, US 188/F3
Hudson, NY, US 188/F3
Hudson Bay, Sk, Can. 185/H2
Hudson's Hope, BC, Can. 180/D3
Hue, Viet. 136/D2
Huedin, Rom. 107/F2
Huehuetenango, Guat. 202/D3
Huehuetla, Mex. 201/L6
Huehuetlán, Mex. 201/L8
Huejotzingo, Mex. 201/L7
Huejuquilla el Alto, Mex. 200/E4
Huejutla de Reyes, Mex. 202/B1
Huelma, Sp. 102/D4
Huelva, Sp. 102/B4
Huelva (riv.), Sp. 102/B4
Huequi (vol.), Chile 216/B4
Huercal-Overa, Sp. 102/E4
Huerfano (riv.), Co, US 187/F3
Huesca, Sp. 103/E1
Huéscar, Sp. 102/D4
Huetamo de Nuñez, Mex. 201/E5
Huete, Sp. 102/D2
Huexoculco, Mex. 201/R10
Hüfingen, Ger. 115/E2
Hugh Town, Eng, UK 89/Q12
Hughenden, Austl. 172/B3
Hughenden Valley, Eng, UK 88/A2
Hughes, Ak, US 192/H2
Hughes, Arg. 216/E2
Hughesville, Pa, US 196/B1
Huglfing, Ger. 115/H2
Hugli (riv.), India 140/E3
Hugo, Ok, US 187/J4
Huguan, China 130/C3
Hui Xian, China 130/C4
Hui'an, China 137/C2
Huib-Hock (plat.), Namb. 164/B2
Huichang, China 137/C2
Huichapan, Mex. 201/K6
Hŭich'ŏn, NKor. 131/D2
Huila (dept.), Col. 210/C4
Huila, Nevado del (peak), Col. 210/C4

Huilai, China 137/C3
Huilango, Mex. 201/Q9
Huili, China 141/H2
Huimanguillo, Mex. 202/C2
Huimin, China 130/D3
Huinca Renancó,
Arg. 216/D2
Huining, China 128/J4
Hüisaek-pong (peak),
NKor. 131/D2
Huishui, China 141/J2
Huisne (riv.), Fr. 100/D2
Huissen, Neth. 108/C5
Huitong, China 141/J2
Huittinen, Fin. 97/K1
Huitzilan, Mex. 201/M7
Huitzuco, Mex. 201/K8
Huixcolotla, Mex. 201/M8
Huixquilucan, Mex. 201/Q10
Huixtla, Mex. 202/C3
Huize, China 141/H2
Huizen, Neth. 108/C4
Hujra, Pak. 144/B4
Hulan, China 129/N2
Hulett, Wy, US 185/G4
Hullbridge, Eng, UK 88/E2
Hüllhorst, Ger. 109/F4
Hulst, Neth. 108/B6
Hultsfred, Swe. 96/F3
Huma, China 129/N1
Huma (riv.), China 129/M1
Humahuaca, Arg. 215/C1
Humaitá, Braz. 208/F5
Humansdorp, SAfr. 164/D4
Humay, Peru 214/C4
Humber (riv.), Nf, Can. 189/K1
Humber (bay),
On, Can. 189/R8
Humber (riv.), Eng, UK 93/H4
Humberto de Campos,
Braz. 212/B1
Humble, Tx, US 187/J5
Humboldt, Sk, Can. 185/G2
Humboldt (bay), 203/G5
Humboldt (range),
Nv, US 186/C2
Humboldt (riv.),
Nv, US 186/C2
Humboldt, Tn, US 188/B5
Hume (lake), Austl. 173/C2
Húmeda, Pampa (plain),
Arg. 216/D2
Humenné, Slvk. 99/L4
Humida, Pampa (plain),
Arg. 215/D4
Humlum, Den. 96/C3
Hummels Wharf,
Pa, US 196/B2
Hummelstown,
Pa, US 196/B3
Humphrey (pt.), Ak, US 192/K2
Humphreys (peak),
Az, US 186/E4
Hün, Libya 154/J2
Húnaflói (bay), Ice. 95/N6
Hunan (prov.), China 129/K6
Hundsangen,
Ger. 111/G3
Hunedoara, Rom. 106/F3
Hunedoara (prov.),
Rom. 106/F3
Hünenberg, Swi. 115/E2
Hünfeld, Ger. 101/H1
Hung Yen, Viet. 136/D1
Hungaroring, Hun. 107/R9
Hungary (ctry.) 106/D2
Hungen, Ger. 112/B2
Hüngnam, NKor. 131/D3
Hunjiang, China 131/D2
Hunnebostrand, Swe. 96/D2
Hunsel, Neth. 108/C6
Hunsrück (mts.), Ger. 98/D4
Hunte (riv.), Ger. 98/E2
Hunter (isl.), Austl. 167/D5
Hunter (riv.), Austl. 173/D2
Hunter (mt.), Ak, US 192/H3
Hunter, Tx, US 195/U20
Hunterdon (co.),
NJ, US 196/C2
Huntingdon, In, US 188/C4
Huntingdon, Eng, UK 91/F2
Huntington, In, US 188/C3
Huntington, NY, US 197/M8
Huntington (bay),
NY, US 197/M8
Huntington, WV, US 188/D4
Huntington Bay,
NY, US 197/M8
Huntington Beach,
Ca, US 194/G8
Huntington Park,
Ca, US 194/F8
Huntington Station,
NY, US 197/M8
Huntington Woods,
Mi, US 193/F7
Huntley, II, US 193/P15
Huntly, NZ 175/T10
Huntly, Sc, UK 94/D2
Hunts Inlet, BC, Can. 192/M4
Hunts Point, Wa, US 193/C2
Huntsville, Al, US 191/G3
Huntsville, On, Can. 188/E2
Huntsville, Ut, US 195/K11
Huntsville (riv.),
Pa, US 196/B1
Hunucmá, Mex. 202/D1
Hünxe, Ger. 108/D5
Hunyuan, China 130/C3
Huo (mtn.), China 130/B3
Huo (mtn.), China 130/D5
Huocheng, China 128/D3
Huojia, China 130/C4
Huolin Gol, China 129/L2
Huoqiu, China 130/D4

Huoshan, China 130/D5
Huozhou, China 130/B3
Hurdal, Nor. 96/D1
Hure Qi, China 130/E2
Hurepoix (reg.), Fr. 88/H6
Hurley, NM, US 186/E4
Hurley, Eng, UK 88/A2
Hurley (riv.), Ire. 92/B4
Hurlford, Sc, UK 94/B5
Huron (lake), Can.,US 188/D2
Huron (mts.), Mi, US 188/B2
Huron (pt.), Mi, US 193/G6
Huron (riv.), Mi, US 193/E7
Hurricane, WV, US 188/D4
Hurtaut (riv.), Fr. 110/D4
Hürtgenwald (reg.),
Ger. 111/F2
Hürth, Ger. 111/F2
Hurup, Den. 96/C3
Husainābād, India 143/E3
Húsavík, Ice. 95/P6
Husher, Wi, US 193/Q14
Huşi, Rom. 107/J2
Huskisson, Austl. 173/D2
Huslia, Ak, US 192/G2
Husnes, Nor. 96/A2
Husum, Ger. 96/C4
Husum, Swe. 95/F3
Hutag, Mong. 128/H2
Hutchinson, Mn, US 185/K4
Hutchinson, Ks, US 187/H3
Hüttisheim, Ger. 115/F1
Hüttlingen, Ger. 112/D5
Hüttschlag, Aus. 113/H3
Huttwil, Swi. 114/D3
Hutuo (riv.), China 130/C3
Huwwārah, WBnk. 149/G2
Huy, Belg. 111/E2
Huyton-with-Roby,
Eng, UK 93/F5
Huzhou, China 130/L9
Hvammstangi, Ice. 95/N6
Hvannadalshnúkur
(peak), Ice. 95/P7
Hvar (isl.), Cro. 104/E1
Hvide Sande, Den. 96/C4
Hvítá, Ice. 95/N7
Hvolsvöllur, Ice. 95/N7
Hwange, Zim. 163/E4
Hwange (Wankie) NP,
Zim. 163/E4
Hwanghae-bukto (prov.),
NKor. 131/D3
Hwanghae-namdo (prov.),
NKor. 131/C3
Hwangju, NKor. 131/C3
Hwangju (riv.), NKor. 131/C3
Hwasun, SKor. 131/D5
Hyades (peak), Chile 216/B5
Hyattstown, Md, US 196/A5
Hyattsville, Md, US 196/A6
Hydaburg, Ak, US 192/M4
Hyde, Eng, UK 93/F5
Hyder, Ak, US 192/M4
Hyderabad, India 140/C4
Hyderābād, Pak. 147/J3
Hyères, Fr. 101/G5
Hyères, Îles d' (isls.),
Fr 101/G5
Hyesan, NKor. 131/E2
Hygiene, Co, US 195/B2
Hyland (riv.), Yk, Can. 180/D2
Hyllestad, Nor. 96/A1
Hyltebruk, Swe. 96/E3
Icó, Braz. 212/C2
Hylton (hill), Ky, US 188/D4
Hyō-no-sen (peak),
Japan 132/D3
Hyōgo (pref.), Japan 132/D3
Hyŏndŭng-san (peak),
SKor. 131/G6
Hyrum, Ut, US 186/E2
Hythe, Eng, UK 91/H4
Hyūga, Japan 132/B4
Hyvinkää, Fin. 97/L1
Hywel, Moel (peak),
Wal, UK 90/C2

I

I-n-Amenas, Alg. 157/H3
I-n-Azaoua, Oued (riv.),
Niger 157/H5
I-n-Dagouber (well),
Mali 157/E5
I-n-Echaï (well), Mali 161/E1
I-n-Gall, Niger 161/G2
I-n-Guezzam, Alg. 161/G2
I-n-Milach (well),
Mali 161/E2
I-n-Sâkâne, 'Erg (des.),
Mali 161/E1
I-n-Salah, Alg. 157/F4
I-n-Tassik (well),
Mali 161/E2
Iacanga, Braz. 213/B2
Iaciara, Braz. 212/A4
Iaco (riv.), Braz. 208/E6
Iaçu, Braz. 212/B4
Iáf di Montasio (peak),
It. 101/K3
Iakora, Braz. 165/H8
Ialomiţa (prov.), Rom. 107/H3
Ialomiţa (riv.), Rom. 107/H2
Iaşi, Rom. 107/H2
Iaşi (prov.), Rom. 107/H2
Iasmos, Gre. 105/J2
Iatan, Mo, US 195/D5

Iba, Phil. 137/C4
Ibadan, Nga. 161/F5
Ibagué, Col. 208/C3
Ibaiti, Braz. 213/B2
Ibajay, Phil. 137/D5
Ibanda, Ugan. 162/A3
Ibans (lake), Hon. 203/E3
Ibapabana, Serra da
(range), Braz. 212/B1
Ibar (riv.), Kos., Serb. 106/E4
Ibara, Japan 132/C3
Ibaraki (pref.), Japan 133/F2
Ibaraki, Japan 135/J6
Ibaraki, Japan 135/E1
Ibaraté, Braz. 213/G8
Ibarra, Ecu. 210/B4
Ibarreta, Arg. 215/E2
Ibb, Yem. 146/D6
Ibba (riv.), Sudan 155/L6
Ibbenbüren, Ger. 109/E4
Ibdekkene (riv.), Mali 161/F2
Iberia, Peru 214/D3
Iberia, Peru 214/C2
Ibérico, Sistema (range),
Sp. 102/D2
Iberville, Qu, Can. 189/P7
Ibi, Sp. 103/E2
Ibiá, Braz. 213/C1
Ibiapina, Braz. 212/B1
Ibicaraí, Braz. 212/C4
Ibicuy, Arg. 217/J10
Ibigawa, Japan 135/L5
Ibimirim, Braz. 212/C3
Ibiraçu, Braz. 213/D1
Ibirapuã, Braz. 212/B5
Ibitinga, Braz. 213/B2
Ibiúna, Braz. 213/F8
Ibiza (isl.), Sp. 103/F3
Ibiza, Sp. 103/F3
Ibo, Moz. 163/H3
Ibo (riv.), Japan 132/D3
Iboro, Nga. 161/F5
Ibotirama, Braz. 212/B4
Iboundji (peak),
Gabon 154/H8
Ibrány, Hun. 99/L4
Ibshawāy, Egypt 149/B5
Ibuki, Japan 135/K5
Ibuki-yama (peak),
Japan 135/K5
Ica (dept.), Peru 214/C4
Ica, Peru 214/C4
Iça (riv.), Braz. 208/E4
Içana (riv.), Braz. 208/E3
Icel (riv.), Turk. 148/C2
Iceland (ctry.) 95/N7
Icém, Braz. 213/B2
Ichalkaranji, India 147/K5
Ichāmati (riv.), India 143/G4
Ichchāpuram, India 140/D4
Ichenhausen, Ger. 112/D6
Ichhāwar, India 142/A4
Ichihara, Japan 135/E3
Ichijima, Japan 135/H5
Ichikawa, Japan 135/D2
Ichikawada, Japan 135/E3
Ichinohe, Japan 134/B3
Ichinomiya, Japan 135/D2
Ichinomiya, Japan 135/E3
Ichinomiya, Japan 135/G7
Ichinomiya, Japan 135/L5
Ichinoseki, Japan 134/B4
Ichishi, Japan 135/K6
Ichkeul (lake), Tun. 158/L6
Ich'ŏn, SKor. 131/D4
Ichtegem, Belg. 110/C1
Ickesburg, Pa, US 196/A3
Icod de los Vinos,
Canl., Sp. 156/A3
Icy (bay), Ak, US 192/K4
Icy (cape), Ak, US 192/F1
Icy (pt.), Ak, US 192/L4
Icy (str.), Ak, US 192/L4
Idabel, Ok, US 187/J4
Idaho (state), US 184/E5
Idaho Springs,
Co, US 195/A3
Idanha-a-Nova, Port. 102/B3
Idar, India 140/B3
Idar-Oberstein, Ger. 111/G4
Idarkopf (peak), Ger. 111/G4
Idaville, Pa, US 196/A3
Ide, Japan 135/J6
Ideles, Alg. 157/G5
Idfū, Egypt 159/C3
Idhi (well), Gre. 105/H4
Idhra, Gre. 105/H4
Idice (riv.), It. 117/E4
Idjwe, Ile (isl.),
D.R. Congo 162/A3
Idku, Egypt 149/B4
Idle (riv.), Eng, UK 93/H5
Idlib (prov.), Syria 105/H1
Idlib, Syria 149/E2
Idnah, WBnk. 101/L4
Idrija, Slov. 101/L4
Idriss I (dam), Mor. 158/B2
Idriss I, Barrage (res.),
Mor. 158/B2
Idro, Lago d' (lake),
It. 116/D1
Idstein, Ger. 111/H3
Ie (isl.), Japan 133/J7
Ieper, Belg. 110/B2
Ierápetra, Gre. 105/J5
Ierissós, Gre. 105/H2
Ifakara, Tanz. 162/C5
Ifalik (isl.), Micr. 174/D4
Ifanadiana, Madg. 165/H8
Ife, Nga. 161/G5
Iferfes (well), Libya 157/H3
Iffeldorf, Ger. 115/H2
Iffezheim, Ger. 112/B5

Iforas, Adrar des (upland),
Alg.,Mali 154/F4
Ifrane, Mor. 156/D2
Iga (riv.), Japan 135/K6
Iga, Japan 135/K6
Igal, Hun. 106/C2
Iganga, Ugan. 162/B2
Igaporã, Braz. 212/B4
Igara Paraná (riv.),
Col. 210/C5
Igarapava, Braz. 213/C2
Igarapé Grande, Braz. 212/A2
Igarapé-Miri, Braz. 209/J4
Igaratá, Braz. 213/G8
Igarka, Rus. 122/J3
Igatpuri, India 140/B4
Igdet (peak), Mor. 156/C3
Iğdır, Turk. 148/F2
Igel, Ger. 111/F4
Iggesund, Swe. 96/G1
Ightham, Eng, UK 88/D3
Igikpak (mt.), Ak, US 192/H2
Iglesias, It. 104/A3
Igli, Alg. 157/F3
Igling, Ger. 115/G1
Igloolik, Nun., Can. 181/H2
Ignace, On, Can. 185/L3
Ignacio, Ca, US 193/J10
Ignacio de la Llave,
Mex. 201/P8
Ignacio Zaragoza,
Mex. 200/D2
Iğneada Burnu (cape),
Turk. 105/L4
Igney, Fr. 114/C1
Ignon (riv.), Fr. 114/A2
Igny, Fr. 88/J5
Igombe (riv.), Tanz. 162/B4
Igora Paraná (riv.),
Col. 214/C1
Igoumenitsa, Gre. 105/G3
Igra, Rus. 119/M4
Igreja, Morro da
(peak), Braz. 213/B4
Iguaçu (riv.), Braz. 205/D5
Iguaçu, PN do, Braz. 213/A4
Iguaí, Braz. 212/B4
Iguala, Mex. 201/K8
Igualada, Sp. 103/F2
Iguape, Braz. 213/C3
Iguape (riv.), Braz. 213/B3
Iguatu, Braz. 212/C2
Iguazú, PN del, Arg. 215/F2
Iguetti (lake), Mrta. 156/C5
Iheya (isl.), Japan 133/J7
Ihhayrhan, Mong. 128/J2
Ihosy, Madg. 165/H8
Ihotry (lake), Madg. 165/G8
Ihuari, Peru 214/B3
Ii, Fin. 95/H2
Iida, Japan 135/F3
Iide-san (peak), Japan 133/F2
Iijoki (riv.), Fin. 95/H2
Iinan, Japan 135/K7
Iisalmi, Fin. 95/H2
Iitaka, Japan 135/K7
Iitti, Fin. 97/M1
Iiyama, Japan 133/F2
Iizuka, Japan 132/B4
Ijebu Ode, Nga. 161/F5
Ijill, Mrta. 156/B5
Ijill (lake), Mrta. 156/B5
Ijira, Japan 135/L4
IJmeer (bay), Neth. 108/C4
IJmuiden, Neth. 108/B4
Ijnaoun (well), Mrta. 160/B2
Ijoki (riv.), Fin. 95/H2
IJssel (riv.), Neth. 108/C3
IJsselmeer (lake), Neth. 98/C2
IJsselmuiden, Neth. 108/C3
IJsselstein, Neth. 108/C4
Ijuí, Braz. 215/F2
Ijûin, Japan 132/B5
Ijzer (riv.), Belg. 98/B3
Ik (riv.), Rus. 119/M5
Ikahavo (plat.), Madg. 165/H7
Ikalamavony, Madg. 165/H8
Ikare, Nga. 161/G5
Ikaría, Gre. 148/A2
Ikaría (isl.), Gre. 105/J4
Ikaruga, Japan 135/J6
Ikeda, Japan 132/C3
Ikeda, Japan 134/C2
Ikeda, Japan 135/H6
Ikeda, Japan 135/L4
Ikeja, Nga. 161/F5
Ikenokoya-yama (peak),
Japan 135/K7
Ikerre, Nga. 161/G5
Ikhtiman, Bul. 105/H1
Iki (isl.), Japan 132/A4
Iki (chan.), Japan 132/A4
Ikire, Nga. 161/G5
Ikirun, Nga. 161/G5
Ikizce, Turk. 148/C2
Ikoma, Japan 135/J6
Ikongo, Madg. 165/H8
Ikopa (riv.), Madg. 165/H7
Ikorodu, Nga. 161/F5
Ikuno, Japan 132/D3
Ila Orangun, Nga. 161/G4
Ilabaya, Peru 214/D5
Ilagan, Phil. 137/D4
Ilām, Iran 146/E2
Ilan, Tai. 137/D3
Ilanz, Swi. 115/F4
Ilaro, Nga. 161/F5
Ilave (riv.), Peru 214/D5
Ilave, Peru 214/D5
Iława, Pol. 99/K2

Ilawe-Ekiti, Nga. 161/G5
Ile (riv.), China.,Kaz. 128/C3
Ile-à-la-Crosse,
Sk, Can. 184/G2
Ile-a-la-Crosse (lake),
Sk, Can. 184/G2
Ile-de-France (pol. reg.),
Fr. 110/A4
Ilek (riv.), Rus. 121/K2
Ilek (riv.), Rus. 121/K2
Iles Ehotilés, PN des,
C.d'Iv. 160/E5
Iles Tristao, Îles (isls.),
Gui. 160/B4
Ilesha, Nga. 161/G5
Ilfis (riv.), Swi. 114/D4
Ilgaz, Turk. 120/E4
Ilgın, Turk. 148/B2
Ilha Grande (bay),
Braz. 213/J8
Ilha Grande, Baía de
(bay), Braz. 213/C2
Ilha Solteira, Reprêsa
(res.), Braz. 209/H7
Ilhabela, Braz. 213/H8
Ilhavo, Port. 102/A2
Ilhéus, Braz. 212/C4
Iliamna, Ak, US 192/H4
Iliamna (lake),
Ak, US 192/G4
Iliamna (vol.), Ak, US 192/H3
Iliç, Turk. 148/D2
Ilıca, Turk. 121/G5
Ilıca, Turk. 148/B2
Ilijaš, Bosn. 106/D4
Iliniza (peak), Ecu. 210/B5
Illbille (mt.), Austl. 171/G3
Illéla, Niger 161/G3
Iller (riv.), Ger. 101/J2
Illertissen, Ger. 115/G1
Illescas, Sp. 102/D2
Illiers-Combray, Fr. 100/D2
Illimani (peak), Bol. 208/E7
Illingen, Ger. 111/G5
Illinois (riv.), Il, US 188/B3
Illinois (state), US 188/B4
Illizi, Alg. 157/H4
Illizi (prov.), Alg. 157/G4
Illkirch-Graffenstaden,
Fr. 114/D1
Illmensee, Ger. 115/F2
Illora, Sp. 102/D4
Illovo, SAfr. 165/E3
Ilm (riv.), Ger. 98/F4
Ilmajoki, Fin. 95/G3
Ilme (riv.), Ger. 109/G5
Il'men (lake), Rus. 122/D4
Ilo, Peru 214/D5
Ilobu, Nga. 161/G5
Ilorin, Nga. 161/G4
Ilovlya (riv.), Rus. 121/H2
Ilpendam, Neth. 108/B4
Ilse (riv.), Ger. 109/H5
Ilsede, Ger. 109/H4
Ilsenburg, Ger. 109/H5
Ilsfeld, Ger. 112/C4
Ilshofen, Ger. 112/D4
Ilulissat, Grld. 181/S2
Ilyas Burnu (pt.), Turk. 107/H5
Ilych (riv.), Rus. 119/N3
Ilz (riv.), Ger. 99/G4
Imabari, Japan 132/C3
Imaichi, Japan 133/F2
Imaloto (riv.), Madg. 165/H8
Imamoğlu, Turk. 148/C2
Imandra (lake), Rus. 95/J2
Imari, Japan 132/A4
Imatra, Fin. 97/N1
Imazu, Japan 135/K5
Imba (lake), Japan 135/E2
Imba, Japan 135/E2
Imbabura (prov.),
Ecu. 210/B4
Imbituba, Braz. 213/B4
Imbituva, Braz. 213/B3
Imeni Moskvy (canal),
Rus. 119/W9
Imerimandroso, Madg. 165/H7
Imi n'tanout, Mor. 156/C3
Imishli, Azer. 121/H5
Imittós (peak), Gre. 105/N9
Imja (isl.), SKor. 131/C5
Imlay, Nv, US 186/C2
Immendingen, Ger. 115/E2
Immenhausen, Ger. 109/G6
Immenstaad am Bodensee,
Ger. 115/F2
Immenstadt im Allgäu,
Ger. 115/G2
Immingham, Eng, UK 93/H4
Immokalee, Fl, US 191/H5
Imnavait (mtn.),
Ak, US 192/J2
Imola, It. 117/E4
Imotski, Cro. 104/E2
Imouzzèr-Kandar,
Mor. 158/B2
Imperatriz, Braz. 212/A2
Imperia, It. 116/B2
Imperial, Sk, Can. 185/G3
Imperial, Peru 214/B4
Imperial, Ne, US 187/F2

Imperial, Mo, US 195/G9
Imperial Beach,
Ca, US 194/C5
Imperial Palace,
Japan 135/D2
Impero (riv.), It. 116/B3
Impfondo, Congo 155/J7
Imphal, India 141/F3
Imphy, Fr. 100/E3
Impruneta, It. 117/E5
Imrali (isl.), Turk. 107/J5
Imranlı, Turk. 148/D2
Imroz, Gre. 105/J2
Imshil, SKor. 131/D5
Imst, Aus. 115/G3
Imuris, Mex. 200/C2
Ina (riv.), Swi. 114/D4
Ina, Japan 133/E3
Ina, Japan 135/E2
Ina, Japan 135/D2
Ina (riv.), Pol. 96/F5
Inabe, Japan 135/L5
Inabu, Japan 135/M5
Inagawa, Japan 135/H6
Inagi, Japan 135/D2
Inambari (riv.), Peru 214/D4
Inami, Japan 135/J6
Inaouene (riv.), Mor. 158/B2
Inapari, Peru 214/D4
Inarijärvi (lake), Fin. 95/H1
Inau (peak), Rom. 107/G2
Inawashiro (lake),
Japan 133/F2
Inazawa, Japan 135/L5
Inca, Sp. 103/G3
Incekum (pt.), Turk. 149/C1
Incheville, Fr. 110/A3
Inchinnan, Sc, UK 94/B5
Inchkeith (isl.), 94/C4
Inchnadamph, Sc, UK 89/F7
Inch'ŏn, SKor. 131/D4
Inch'on-Gwangyŏksi
(prov.), SKor. 131/D4
Incirliova, Turk. 148/A2
Incisa in Val d'Arno,
It. 117/E5
Inconfidentes, Braz. 213/G7
Incudine, Mont l' (peak),
Fr. 104/A2
Indaiá (riv.), Braz. 213/C1
Indaiatuba, Braz. 213/B2
Indalsälven (riv.), Swe. 95/E3
Indanan, Phil. 139/F2
Inde (riv.), Ger. 111/F2
Inden, Ger. 111/F2
Independence (mts.),
Nv, US 184/E5
Independence,
Ks, US 187/J3
Independence,
Ca, US 186/C3
Independence,
Mo, US 195/E5
Independence, Belz. 202/D2
Independence Nat'l Hist.
Park,
Pa, US 196/C4
Independência,
Braz. 212/B2
Independencia, Peru 214/B4
Index, Wa, US 193/D2
Inönü, Turk. 148/B2
India (ctry.) 125/G7
Indian (ocean) 81/N6
Indian Echo Caverns,
Pa, US 196/B3
Indian Head, Sk, Can. 185/H3
Indian Hills, Co, US 195/B3
Indian Peaks Wilderness
Area, Co, US 195/A2
Indiana (state), US 188/C3
Indiana, Pa, US 188/E3
Indianapolis (int'l arpt.),
In, US 188/C4
Indianapolis (cap.),
In, US 188/C4
Indianola, Ms, US 187/K4
Indianola, Wa, US 193/B2
Indiantown, Fl, US 191/H5
Indiga, Rus. 119/N1
Indigirka (riv.), Rus. 123/P3
Indija, Serb. 106/E3
Indio, Ca, US 186/C4
Indira Gandhi (int'l arpt.),
India 144/D3
Indo. 138/D5
Indochina (reg.), Laos 141/H4
Indonesia (ctry.) 139/E4
Indore, India 147/L4
Indragiri (riv.), Indo. 138/B4
Indramayu (cape),
Indo. 139/E4
Indrāvati (riv.), India 140/D4
Indre (riv.), Fr. 100/D3
Indre Arna, Nor. 96/A1
Indrois (riv.), Fr. 100/D3
Induno Olona, It. 115/E6
Indus (riv.), Asia 147/J4
Industry, Ca, US 194/G7
Inebolu, Turk. 148/C1
Inece, Turk. 107/H5
Inecik, Turk. 107/H5
Inedbirrene (int'l arpt.),
Alg. 157/H4
Inegöl, Turk. 148/B1
Iner (riv.), Col. 112/C3
Ineu, Rom. 106/F2
Inezgane, Mo. 156/C3
Inezgane (Agadir)
(int'l arpt.), Mor. 156/C3
Infanta (cape), SAfr. 164/C4
Infiernillo (res.),
Mex. 182/A4
Infiernillo, Presa del
(dam), Mex. 200/E5
Infiesto, Sp. 102/C1

Ingapirca (ruin), Ecu. 210/B5
Ingatestone, Eng, UK 88/E2
Ingelmunster, Belg. 110/C2
Ingeniero Jacobacci,
Arg. 216/C4
Ingeniero Luiggi,
Arg. 216/D2
Ingersheim, Fr. 114/D1
Ingettolgoy, Mong. 128/H2
Ingham, Austl. 172/B2
Ingleside, Md, US 196/C5
Inglewood, Austl. 173/B3
Inglewood, Ca, US 194/F8
Inglis, Fl, US 191/H4
Ingoda (riv.), Rus. 123/M4
Ingolstadt, Ger. 113/E5
Ingrid Christianson
(coast), Ant. 218/F
Ingushetia, Resp.,
Rus. 121/H4
Ingwavuma, SAfr. 165/E2
Ingwiller, Fr. 111/G6
Inhambane, Moz. 163/G5
Inhambupe, Braz. 212/C3
Inharrime, Moz. 163/G5
Inhumas, Braz. 212/B2
Inhumas, Braz. 209/J7
Iniesta, Sp. 102/E3
Inifel (well), Alg. 157/F3
Inini (riv.), FrG. 211/H4
Inírida (riv.), Col. 208/E3
Inishbofin (isl.), Ire. 88/N10
Inishowen (pen.), Ire. 92/A1
Inishowen (pt.), Ire. 92/B1
Inje, SKor. 131/E3
Injune, Austl. 172/C4
Inkster, Mi, US 193/F7
Inland (sea), Japan 132/C4
Inle (lake), Myan. 141/G3
Inn (riv.), Aus. 101/J3
Inn (riv.), Ger. 101/K2
Inn (riv.), Swi. 101/J3
Innbach (riv.), Aus. 113/H6
Innellan, Sc, UK 94/B5
Inner (chan.), Belz. 202/D2
Inner (sound), Sc, UK 89/R8
Inner Hebrides (isls.),
Sc, UK 89/Q8
Inner Mongolia (reg.),
China 125/L5
Innerdouny (hill),
Sc, UK 94/C4
Innerleithen, Sc, UK 94/C5
Innerste (riv.), Ger. 109/G4
Innerkirchen, Swi. 115/E4
Innichen (San Candito),
It. 101/K3
Innisfail, BC, Can. 184/E2
Innisfail, Austl. 172/B2
Innoko (riv.), Ak, US 192/G3
Innsbruck, Aus. 115/H3
Innviertel (reg.), Aus. 113/G6
Inny (riv.), Eng, UK 90/B5
Ino, Japan 132/C4
Inocência, Braz. 213/B1
Inongo, D.R. Congo 155/J8
Inönü, Turk. 148/B2
Inowrocław, Pol. 99/K2
Insch, Sc, UK 94/D2
Inscription (cape),
Austl. 170/B3
Insein, Myan. 141/G4
Inside (passg.),
BC, Can. 184/A2
Insjön, Swe. 96/F1
Inta, Rus. 119/N2
Intendente Alvear,
Arg. 216/E2
Intepe, Turk. 105/K2
Intercourse, Pa, US 196/B3
Interior (plat.),
BC, Can. 184/B2
Interlaken, Swi. 114/D4
Internacional (int'l arpt.),
Braz. 214/D2
Internacional (int'l arpt.),
Mex. 201/E5
International Peace Garden,
ND, US 185/H3
Inthanon (peak), Thai. 141/G4
Intorsura Buzăului,
Rom. 107/H3
Intracoastal Waterway,
La, US 195/P17
Intragna, Swi. 115/E5
Introbio, It. 115/F6
Inubō-zaki (pt.), Japan 133/G3
Inukjuak, Qu, Can. 181/J3
Inutil (bay), Chile 217/C7
Inuvik, NW, Can. 192/M2
Inuyama, Japan 135/L5
Inver (bay), Sc, UK 94/C1
Inveraray, Sc, UK 94/B4
Inverbervie, Sc, UK 94/D3
Invercargill, NZ 175/R12
Inverclyde (pol. reg.),
Sc, UK 94/B5
Inverell, Austl. 173/D1
Invergordon, Sc, UK 94/B1
Inverie, Sc, UK 89/R8
Inverigo, It. 116/C1
Inverkeithing, Sc, UK 94/C4
Inverloch, Austl. 173/C3
Invermay, Sk, Can. 185/H3
Inverness, Sc, UK 94/B2
Inverness, Al, US 191/G3
Inverness, Fl, US 191/H4
Inverno, It. 116/B1
Inverurie, Sc, UK 94/D2

Investigator (str.),
Austl. 167/C4
Invorio, It. 116/B1
Inwood, NY, US 197/L9
Inyanga, Zim. 163/F4
Inyangani (peak), Zim. 163/F4
Inymney (peak), Rus. 192/D2
Inyo (mts.), Ca, US 186/C3
Inza, Rus. 121/H1
Inzai, Japan 135/E2
Inzigkofen, Ger. 115/F1
Inzing, Aus. 115/H3
Iō-shima (isl.), Japan 132/A5
Ioánnina (int'l arpt.),
Gre. 105/G3
Ioánnina, Gre. 105/G3
Iolotan', Trkm. 147/H1
Iona (isl.), Sc, UK 89/G8
Iona, PN da, Ang. 163/B4
Ione, Co, US 195/C2
Ione, Ca, US 186/B3
Ionian (sea), Gre. 105/F3
Ionian (isls.), Gre. 105/F3
Ios (isl.), Gre. 105/J4
Iowa (state), US 187/J2
Iowa (riv.), Ia, US 185/K5
Iowa Falls, Ia, US 185/K5
Ipameri, Braz. 213/B1
Ipanema, Braz. 212/B2
Iparia, Peru 214/C3
Ipatinga, Braz. 213/D1
Ipel' (riv.), Slvk. 99/K4
Iphofen, Ger. 112/D3
Ipiales, Col. 208/C3
Ipiaú, Braz. 212/C4
Ipil, Phil. 137/D6
Ipirá, Braz. 212/C4
Ipirá, Braz. 213/B3
Ipoh, Malay. 138/B3
Ipoly (riv.), Hun. 99/K4
Iporá, Braz. 209/H7
Iporanga, Braz. 213/B3
Ipsala, Turk. 105/K2
Ipsheim, Ger. 112/D3
Ipswich, SD, US 185/J4
Ipswich, Eng, UK 91/H2
Ipu, Braz. 212/B2
Ipuã, Braz. 213/B2
Ipubi, Braz. 212/B2
Ipueiras, Braz. 212/B2
Ipuiúna, Braz. 213/G7
Ipumba (hill), Tanz. 162/A4
Ipun, Isla (isl.), Chile 216/B5
Ipupiara, Braz. 212/B3
Iqaluit (cap.), Nun.,
Can. 181/K2
Iquique, Chile 208/D8
Iquitos, Peru 214/C1
Irago (chan.), Japan 135/L6
Irago-misaki (cape),
Japan 135/M6
Iráklia, Gre. 105/H2
Iráklia (isl.), Gre. 105/J4
Iráklion, Gre. 105/J5
Iráklion (int'l arpt.),
Gre. 105/J5
Iramaia, Braz. 212/B4
Iran (mts.),
Indo.,Malay. 138/D3
Iran (ctry.) 125/E6
Irapa, Ven. 211/F2
Irapuato, Mex. 201/E4
Iraq (ctry.) 146/D2
Irará, Braz. 212/C3
Irati, Braz. 213/B3
Iraucuba, Braz. 212/C1
Irbid (gov.), Jor. 149/D3
Irbid, Jor. 149/D3
Irbil, Iraq 148/E2
Irecê, Braz. 212/B3
Ireland (riv.), 89/P10
Ireland's Eye (isl.), Ire. 92/B5
Iremel' (peak), Rus. 119/N4
Iretama, Braz. 213/A3
Irfon (riv.), Wal, UK 90/C2
Irharhar, Oued (riv.),
Alg. 157/G4
Irhazer Oua-n-Agadez
(riv.), Niger 161/G2
Iri, SKor. 131/D5
Irian Jaya (reg.), Indo. 139/H4
Iricoume (mts.), Braz. 211/G4
Irig, Serb. 106/D3
Irígui (phys. reg.),
Mali 160/D2
Iriklinskiy (res.), Rus. 121/L2
Iringa (prov.), Tanz. 162/B5
Iringa, Tanz. 162/B4
Iriomote (isl.), Japan 133/G7
Iriri (riv.), Braz. 209/H4
Irish (sea), Ire.,UK 92/C4
Irlam, Eng, UK 93/F5
Irō-zaki (pt.), Japan 133/F3
Iroise (bay), Fr. 100/A2
Iron Baron, Austl. 171/H5
Iron Knob, Austl. 171/H5
Iron Mountain, Mi, US 185/L4
Irondale, Co, US 195/B3
Ironton, Oh, US 188/D4
Ironton, Ut, US 195/K13
Ironwood, Mi, US 185/L4
Ironwood Forest Nat'l Mon.,
Az, US 186/E4
Irpin' (riv.), Rus. 120/E1
Irrawaddy (Ayeyarwady)
(riv.), Myan. 141/G4
Irrawaddy, Mouths of the
(delta), Myan. 141/F4
Irsch, Ger. 111/F4
Irsen (riv.), Ger. 111/F3
Irsina, It. 104/E2
Irt (riv.), Eng, UK 93/E3
Irthing (riv.), Eng, UK 93/F1
Irthlingborough,
Eng, UK 91/F2

Irtysh (riv.), Rus. 125/G4
Iruma, Japan 135/C2
Irumu, D.R. Congo 162/A2
Irún, Sp. 102/E1
Irvine, Ca, US 194/G8
Irvine, Sc, UK 94/B5
Irvine (bay), Sc, UK 94/B5
Irvine (riv.), Sc, UK 94/B5
Irving, Tx, US 190/D3
Irvington, NJ, US 197/J9
Irvington, NY, US 197/K7
Is (peak), Sudan 159/C4
Is-sur-Tille, Fr. 114/B2
Īsa Khel, Pak. 144/A3
Isaac (riv.), Austl. 167/D3
Isabela (isl.), Ecu. 214/E7
Isabela, Phil. 139/F2
Isabela, PR 199/M8
Isabelia (mts.), Nic. 202/E3
Isabella (bay), Nun., Can. 181/K2
Isaccea, Rom. 107/J3
Isachsen (cape), Nun., Can. 181/R7
Ísafjardhardjúp (inlet), Ice. 95/M6
Ísafjördhur, Ice. 95/M6
Isahaya, Japan 132/B4
Isalo, PN de l', Madg. 165/H8
Isalo Ruiniform (mass.), Madg. 165/H8
Isana (riv.), Col. 210/D4
Isandhlwana Battlesite, SAfr. 165/E3
Isangano NP, Zam. 162/A5
Isaouanne-n-Irarraren (des.), Alg. 157/G4
Isaouanne-n-Tifernine (des.), Alg. 157/G4
Isarco (riv.), It. 101/J3
Isarco (Eisack) (riv.), It. 115/H4
Isaszeg, Hun. 107/R9
Isawa, Japan 135/B2
Isbergues, Fr. 110/B2
Iscar, Sp. 102/C2
Ischgl, Aus. 115/G3
Ischia, It. 106/A5
Ise (bay), Japan 133/E3
Ise (riv.), Eng, UK 91/E1
Ise, Japan 135/L7
Ise-Shima NP, Japan 133/E3
Isehara, Japan 133/F3
Iselin, NJ, US 197/H9
Isen, Ger. 113/F6
Isen (riv.), Ger. 98/G4
Isenthal, Swi. 115/E4
Iseo (lake), It. 101/J4
Iseo, It. 116/D1
Iseo, Lago d' (lake), It. 116/C1
Isère (riv.), Fr. 100/F4
Isère (dept.), Fr. 114/B6
Iserlohn, Ger. 109/E6
Isernia, It. 104/D2
Isesaki, Japan 133/F2
Iset' (riv.), Rus. 145/D1
Iseyin, Nga. 161/F5
'Isfiyā, Isr. 149/G6
Ishi (riv.), Japan 135/J7
Ishibashi, Japan 133/F2
Ishibe, Japan 135/K5
Ishidoriya, Japan 134/B4
Ishigaki (isl.), Japan 137/D3
Ishige, Japan 133/F2
Ishikari, Japan 134/B2
Ishikari (bay), Japan 134/B2
Ishikari (mts.), Japan 134/C2
Ishikari (riv.), Japan 134/B2
Ishikawa (pref.), Japan 133/E2
Ishikawa, Japan 133/G2
Ishiki, Japan 135/M6
Ishim (riv.), Rus. 122/H4
Ishim, Rus. 119/R4
Ishimbay, Rus. 121/L1
Ishinomaki, Japan 134/B4
Ishioka, Japan 133/G2
Ishizuchi-san (peak), Japan 132/C4
Isiboro Sécure, PN, Bol. 208/E7
Isigny-sur-Mer, Fr. 100/C2
Isil'kul', Rus. 145/F2
Isiolo, Kenya 162/C2
Isiro, D.R. Congo 155/L7
Isisford, Austl. 172/B4
Iskenderun, Turk. 149/E1
Iskenderun, Gulf of (gulf), Turk. 149/D1
Iskilip, Turk. 148/C1
Iskŭr (riv.), Aus. 107/G4
Iskŭr (res.), Bul. 107/F4
Iskŭr (riv.), Bul. 105/H1
Isla, Mex. 202/C2
Isla (riv.), Sc, UK 94/C3
Isla Aguada, Mex. 202/D2
Isla Cabritos, PN, DRep. 203/J2
Isla Cedros, Mex. 200/B2
Isla Cristina, Sp. 102/B4
Isla de Maipo, Chile 216/N8
Isla de Salamanca, PN, Col. 210/C2
Isla de San Andrés (int'l arpt.), Col. 203/F3
Isla Gorge NP, Austl. 172/C4
Isla Guamblin, PN, Chile 216/B5
Isla Isabela, PN, Mex. 200/D4
Isla Magdalena, PN, Chile 215/B5
Isla Mujeres, Mex. 202/E1
Islāhiye, Turk. 149/E1
Islām Kot, Pak. 147/K4
Islāmābād (cap. terr.), Pak. 144/B3
Islāmābād (cap.), Pak. 144/B3
Islāmābād/Rāwalpindi (int'l arpt.), Pak. 144/B3
Islāmnagar, India 142/B1
Islamorada, Fl, US 191/H5
Islāmpur, India 143/G2
Islāmpur, India 143/E3
Island (lake), Mb, Can. 180/G3
Island (co.), Wa, US 193/B2
Island Beach State Park, NJ, US 196/D4
Island Lagoon (lake), Austl. 171/H4
Island Lake, Mb, Can. 185/K2
Island Lake, Il, US 193/P15
Island Park, NY, US 197/L9
Islands (bay), Nf, Can. 189/K1
Islay, Peru 214/C5
Islay (isl.), Sc, UK 89/Q9
Isle (riv.), Fr. 100/D4
Isle of Anglesey (co.), Wal, UK 92/D5
Isle of Ely (phys. reg.), Eng, UK 91/G2
Isle of Portland (pen.), Eng, UK 90/D5
Isle of Thanet (phys. reg.), Eng, UK 91/H4
Isle of Wight (co.), Eng, UK 91/E5
Isle Royale NP, Mi, US 188/B2
Isleton, Ca, US 193/L10
Islington (bor.), Eng, UK 88/A1
Islip, NY, US 197/E2
Ismailovo Park, Rus. 119/W9
Ismaning, Ger. 113/E6
Isny, Ger. 115/G2
Isoanala, Madg. 165/H8
Isobe, Japan 135/L7
Isojärven NP, Fin. 97/L1
Isojärvi (lake), Fin. 97/J1
Isoka, Zam. 162/B5
Isola del Liri, It. 104/C2
Isola della Scala, It. 117/D2
Isola di Capo Rizzuto, It. 104/E3
Isola Vicentina, It. 117/E1
Isonzo (riv.), It. 117/G1
Isorella, It. 116/D2
Isparta, Turk. 148/B2
Isparta (prov.), Turk. 148/B2
Isperikh, Bul. 107/H4
Ispir, Turk. 121/G4
Israel (ctry.) 149/C3
Issaquah, Wa, US 193/C2
Issel (riv.), Ger. 108/D5
Isselburg, Ger. 108/D5
Issenheim, Fr. 114/D2
Issia, C.d'Iv. 160/D5
Issoire, Fr. 100/E4
Issou, Fr. 88/H5
Issoudun, Fr. 100/E3
Issum, Ger. 108/D5
Issy-les-Moulineaux, Fr. 88/J5
Istállós-kó (peak), Hun. 106/E1
Istanbul (prov.), Turk. 107/J5
Istanbul, Turk. 107/J5
Istead Rise, Eng, UK 88/E2
Istiaía, Gre. 105/H3
Istmina, Col. 210/B3
Istok, Kos. 106/E4
Istra (riv.), Rus. 119/W9
Istrana, It. 117/F1
Istranca (mts.), Turk. 107/H5
Istres, Fr. 100/F5
Istrina (pen.), Cro. 106/A3
Isulan, Phil. 139/F2
Isumi, Japan 135/E3
Itabaiana, Braz. 212/C3
Itabaiana, Braz. 212/D3
Itabaianinha, Braz. 212/C3
Itabapoana (riv.), Braz. 213/D2
Itaberaba, Braz. 212/B4
Itabira, Braz. 213/D1
Itabirito, Braz. 213/D2
Itaboraí, Braz. 213/L7
Itabuna, Braz. 212/C4
Itacaiunas (riv.), Braz. 209/H5
Itacarambi, Braz. 212/A4
Itacoatiara, Braz. 208/G4
Itacuaí (riv.), Braz. 208/D5
Itacuruba, Braz. 212/C3
Itaguaí, Braz. 213/K7
Itaguara, Braz. 213/C2
Itaguatins, Braz. 212/A2
Itagüí, Col. 208/C2
Itaí, Braz. 213/B2
Itaíba, Braz. 212/C3
Itaiçaba, Braz. 212/C2
Itainópolis, Braz. 212/B3
Itaiópolis, Braz. 213/B3
Itaipú (dam), Par. 215/F2
Itaipu (res.), Braz.,Par. 215/F1
Itaituba, Braz. 209/G4
Itajá, Braz. 213/B1
Itajaí, Braz. 213/B3
Itajaí (riv.), Braz. 213/B3
Itajubá, Braz. 213/H7
Itajuípe, Braz. 212/C4
Itako, Japan 133/G3
Itakura, Japan 135/D1
Italy (ctry.) 85/F4
Italy, Tx, US 187/H4
Itamaraju, Braz. 212/C5
Itamarandiba, Braz. 212/B5
Itambacuri, Braz. 212/B5
Itambé, Braz. 212/B4
Itambé, Pico de (peak), Braz. 212/B5
Itami, Japan 135/H6
Itamonte, Braz. 213/J7
Itampolo, Madg. 165/G9
Itanhaém, Braz. 213/G9
Itanhandu, Braz. 213/C2
Itanhém, Braz. 212/B5
Itanhém (riv.), Braz. 213/D1
Itanhomi, Braz. 213/D1
Itaobim, Braz. 212/B5
Itaocara, Braz. 213/D2
Itapagé, Braz. 212/C1
Itaparica (isl.), Braz. 212/C4
Itapé, Braz. 212/C4
Itapebi, Braz. 212/C4
Itapecerica, Braz. 213/C2
Itapecuru-Mirim, Braz. 212/A1
Itapemirim, Braz. 213/D2
Itaperuna, Braz. 213/D2
Itapetim, Braz. 212/C2
Itapetinga, Braz. 212/B4
Itapetininga, Braz. 213/B2
Itapeva, Braz. 213/B2
Itapevi, Braz. 213/G8
Itapicuri (riv.), Braz. 212/C3
Itapicuru (riv.), Braz. 209/K5
Itapipoca, Braz. 212/C1
Itapira, Braz. 213/G7
Itapitanga, Braz. 212/C4
Itaporanga, Braz. 213/B2
Itaquaquecetuba, Braz. 213/G8
Itarantim, Braz. 212/B4
Itararé, Braz. 213/B3
Itariri, Braz. 213/F9
Itārsi, India 142/A4
Itatiaia, PN de, Braz. 213/J7
Itatiba, Braz. 213/G7
Itaueira (riv.), Braz. 209/K5
Itaueira, Braz. 212/B2
Itaúna, Braz. 213/C2
Itayanagi, Japan 134/B3
Itbayat, Phil. 137/D3
Itbayat (isl.), Phil. 137/D3
Itchen (riv.), Eng, UK 91/E4
Itéa, Gre. 105/H3
Iténez (riv.), Bol. 205/C4
Itezhi-Tezhi (dam), Zam. 163/E4
Ith (hills), Ger. 109/G4
Ithaca, NY, US 188/E3
Ithaca, (Itháki) (isl.), Gre. 105/G3
Itháki, Gre. 105/G3
Ithon (riv.), Wal, UK 90/C2
Itimbiri (riv.), D.R. Congo 155/K7
Itinga, Braz. 212/B5
Itiruçu, Braz. 212/B4
Itō, Japan 133/F3
Itogon, Phil. 137/D4
Itoigawa, Japan 133/E2
Itoman, Japan 133/J7
Iton (riv.), Fr. 100/D2
Itonuki, Japan 135/L5
Itororó, Braz. 212/B4
Itsukaichi, Japan 135/C2
Itter (riv.), Ger. 109/F6
Itterbeck, Ger. 108/D3
Ittiri, It. 104/A2
Itu, Braz. 213/C2
Ituango, Col. 210/C3
Ituberá, Braz. 212/C4
Ituí (riv.), Braz. 208/D5
Ituiutaba, Braz. 213/B1
Itumbiara, Braz. 213/B1
Itumbiara, Barragem (res.), Braz. 213/B1
Itumirim, Braz. 213/J6
Ituna, Sk, Can. 185/H3
Itupiranga, Braz. 209/J5
Ituporanga, Braz. 213/B3
Iturama, Braz. 213/B1
Ituri (riv.), D.R. Congo 162/A2
Itutinga, Reprêsa de (res.), Braz. 213/C2
Ituverava, Braz. 213/C2
Ituxi (riv.), Braz. 208/E5
Ituzaingó, Uru. 217/K11
Ityāy al Bārūd, Egypt 149/B4
Itz (riv.), Ger. 98/F3
Iul'tin (peak), Rus. 192/C2
Iúna, Braz. 213/D2
Ivaí (riv.), Braz. 213/B3
Ivaiporã, Braz. 213/B3
Ivalojoki (riv.), Fin. 95/H1
Ivančice, Czh. 101/M2
Ivanec, Cro. 101/M3
Ivanhoe, Austl. 173/C2
Ivanhoe (riv.), On, Can. 188/D1
Ivanjica, Serb. 106/E4
Ivanjska, Bosn. 106/C3
Ivankovo, Cro. 106/D3
Ivano-Frankivs'k, Ukr. 120/C2
Ivano-Frankivs'ka Oblasti, Ukr. 120/C2
Ivanof Bay, Ak, US 192/G4
Ivanovo, Rus. 118/J4
Ivanovovskaya Oblast, Rus. 118/J4
Ivato, Madg. 165/H8
Ivato (int'l arpt.), Madg. 165/H7
Ivaylovgrad (res.), Bul. 105/J2
Ivaylovgrad, Bul. 105/K2
Ivdel, Rus. 122/G3
Iveragh (pen.), Ire. 88/P11
Iverny, Fr. 88/L5
Ivindo (riv.), Gabon 154/H7
Ivohibe, Madg. 165/H8
Ivondro (riv.), Madg. 165/J7
Ivory (coast), C.d'Iv. 154/D7
Ivösjön (lake), Swe. 96/F3
Ivrea, It. 116/A2
Ivrindi, Turk. 148/A2
Ivry-sur-Seine, Fr. 88/K5
Ivujivik, Qu, Can. 181/J2
Ivvavik NP, Yk, Can. 180/B2
Iwafune, Japan 135/D1
Iwai, Japan 133/F2
Iwaizumi, Japan 134/B4
Iwaki, Japan 133/G2
Iwaki-san (peak), Japan 134/B3
Iwakuni, Japan 132/C3
Iwakura, Japan 135/L5
Iwama, Japan 135/E1
Iwami, Japan 132/D3
Iwamizawa, Japan 134/B2
Iwamura, Japan 135/M5
Iwanai, Japan 134/B2
Iwanuma, Japan 133/G1
Iwasaki, Japan 134/A3
Iwata, Japan 133/E3
Iwataki, Japan 135/H4
Iwate (pref.), Japan 134/B4
Iwate, Japan 134/B4
Iwate-san (peak), Japan 134/B4
Iwatsuki, Japan 135/D2
Iwere Ile, Nga. 161/F5
Iwo, Nga. 161/G5
Iwo Jima (isl.), Japan 174/D2
Iwŏn, NKor. 131/E2
Iwuy, Fr. 110/C3
Ixcán (riv.), Guat. 202/D3
Ixelles, Belg. 111/D2
Ixmiquilpan, Mex. 201/K6
Ixopo, SAfr. 165/E3
Ixtapaluca, Mex. 201/L7
Ixtapan de la Sal, Mex. 201/K8
Ixtlán del Río, Mex. 200/D4
Iyo (sea), Japan 132/C4
Iyo, Japan 132/C4
Izabal (lake), Guat. 198/D4
Īzad Khvāst, Iran 146/F2
Izamal, Mex. 202/D1
Izberbash, Rus. 121/H4
Izegem, Belg. 110/C2
Izhevsk, Rus. 119/M4
Izhma (riv.), Rus. 119/M2
Izhora (riv.), Rus. 119/T7
Izi (well), Alg. 157/F3
Izigan (cape), Ak, US 192/E5
Izkī, Oman 147/G4
Izmayil, Ukr. 107/J3
Izmir, Turk. 148/A2
Izmir (prov.), Turk. 148/A2
Izmit (gulf), Turk. 107/J5
Izmit, Turk. 107/J5
Iznájar, Sp. 102/C4
Iznik, Turk. 107/J5
Iznik (lake), Turk. 107/J5
Izola, Slov. 117/G1
Izra', Syria 149/E3
Izsák, Hun. 106/D2
Iztaccíhuatl-Popocatépetl, PN, Mex. 201/L7
Izu (pen.), Japan 133/F3
Izu (isls.), Japan 133/F4
Izúcar de Matamoros, Mex. 201/L8
Izuhara, Japan 132/A3
Izumi, Japan 132/B4
Izumi, Japan 134/B4
Izumi, Japan 135/H7
Izumi-Ōtsu, Japan 135/H7
Izumi-Sano, Japan 135/H7
Izumo, Japan 132/C3
Izunagaoka, Japan 135/B3
Izushi, Japan 135/G5
Izyum, Ukr. 120/F2

J

J. Paul Getty Museum, Ca, US 194/E7
Jääsjärvi (lake), Fin. 97/M1
Jaba', WBnk. 149/G7
Jabal 'Abd al 'Azīz (mts.), Syria 148/D2
Jabal Abu Rujmayn (mts.), Syria 148/D3
Jabal Abyad (plat.), Sudan 159/B5
Jabal al 'Arab (mts.), Syria 149/E3
Jabal an Nuṣayriyah (mts.), Syria 149/E2
Jabal ar Ruwāq (mts.), Syria 149/D3
Jabal as Sawdā' (hills), Libya 154/H2
Jabal ash Shaykh (peak), Leb. 149/D3
Jabal Lubnān (gov.), Leb. 149/D2
Jabal Ramm (peak), Jor. 149/D5
Jabal 'Unāzah (peak), SAr. 148/D3
Jabalí (pt.), Pan. 203/F5
Jabalón (riv.), Sp. 102/D3
Jabalpur, India 142/B4
Jabālyah, Gaza 149/D4
Jabbeke, Belg. 110/C1
Jablah, Syria 149/D2
Jablanica (mts.), Alb. 105/G2
Jablonec nad Nisou, Czh. 99/H3
Jaboatão dos Guararapes, Braz. 212/D3
Jaboticabal, Braz. 213/B2
Jabuka, Serb. 106/E3
Jabung (cape), Indo. 138/B4
Jaca, Sp. 103/E1
Jacaré (riv.), Braz. 212/B3
Jacareí, Braz. 213/H8
Jaceel (riv.), Som. 155/Q5
Jáchymov, Czh. 113/F2
Jacinto, Braz. 212/B5
Jacinto Arauz, Arg. 216/E3
Jackman, Me, US 189/G2
Jackpot, Nv, US 184/E5
Jacks Mountain (ridge), Pa, US 196/A2
Jacksboro, Tx, US 187/H4
Jackson, Al, US 191/G4
Jackson, Ca, US 186/B3
Jackson, La, US 187/K5
Jackson, Mi, US 188/C3
Jackson, Mo, US 187/K3
Jackson (co.), Mo, US 195/E5
Jackson (cap.), Ms, US 187/K4
Jackson (mts.), Nv, US 184/D5
Jackson, Tn, US 188/B5
Jackson, Wy, US 184/F5
Jackson (lake), Wy, US 186/E2
Jacksonville, Al, US 191/G3
Jacksonville, Ar, US 187/J4
Jacksonville, Fl, US 191/H4
Jacksonville (int'l arpt.), Fl, US 191/H4
Jacksonville, Il, US 187/K3
Jacksonville, NC, US 191/J3
Jacksonville Beach, Fl, US 191/H4
Jacktown, Ok, US 195/N14
Jacmel, Haiti 203/H2
Jacobābād, Pak. 147/J3
Jacobina, Braz. 212/B3
Jacobsdal, SAfr. 164/D3
Jacobstown, NJ, US 196/D3
Jacobus, Pa, US 196/B4
Jacomo (lake), Mo, US 195/E6
Jacona de Plancarte, Mex. 200/E5
Jacques-Cartier (riv.), Qu, Can. 189/G2
Jacques Cartier (peak), Qu, Can. 189/H1
Jacuí (riv.), Braz. 215/F2
Jacuípe (riv.), Braz. 209/L6
Jacupiranga, Braz. 213/B3
Jacura, Ven. 210/D2
Jadacaquiva, Ven. 210/D2
Jaddi (pt.), Pak. 147/H3
Jade, Ger. 109/F2
Jade (riv.), Ger. 109/F1
Jade (bay), Ger. 98/E2
Jadebusen (bay), Ger. 109/F2
Jaén, Peru 214/B2
Jaén, Sp. 102/D4
Jaffa (cape), Austl. 173/A3
Jaffna, SrL. 140/C6
Jagādhri, India 144/D4
Jagdīspur, India 143/E3
Jagersfontein, SAfr. 164/D3
Jægerspris, Den. 96/D4
Jagna, Phil. 137/D6
Jagraon, India 144/C4
Jagst (riv.), Ger. 101/J2
Jagtiāl, India 140/C4
Jaguaquara, Braz. 212/C4
Jaguarão, Braz. 215/F3
Jaguarão (riv.), Braz. 217/G2
Jaguarari, Braz. 212/B3
Jaguaretama, Braz. 212/C2
Jaguariaíva, Braz. 213/B3
Jaguaribara, Braz. 212/C2
Jaguaribe (riv.), Braz. 209/L5
Jaguaribe, Braz. 212/C2
Jaguariúna, Braz. 213/G7
Jaguaruana, Braz. 212/C2
Jagungal (mt.), Austl. 173/D3
Jahānābād, India 143/E3
Jahāngīra, Pak. 144/B3
Jahāngīrābād, India 142/B1
Jahrom, Iran 146/F3
Jaicós, Braz. 212/B2
Jailolo, Indo. 139/G3
Jailu (riv.), China 130/C4
Jainca, China 128/H4
Jāis, India 142/C2
Jaisalmer, India 147/K3
Jaisinghnagar, India 142/C4
Jājapur, India 140/E3
Jājarm, Iran 147/G1
Jajce, Bosn. 106/C3
Jakarta (cap.), Indo. 138/C5
Jakobstad (Pietarsaari), Fin. 118/D3
Jal, NM, US 187/G4
Jala, Mex. 200/D4
Jalacingo, Mex. 201/M7
Jalaid Qi, China 129/M2
Jalal-Abad, Kyr. 145/F4
Jalal-Abad (obl.), Kyr. 145/E4
Jalālābād, Afg. 144/A2
Jalālābād, India 142/B2
Jalālābād, India 144/C4
Jalālābād, India 144/D5
Jalāli, India 142/B2
Jalālpur, India 142/D2
Jalālpur, Pak. 144/B3
Jalālpur Pīrwāla, Pak. 144/A5
Jalamah, WBnk. 149/G6
Jalangi (riv.), India 143/G3
Jalapa, Guat. 202/D3
Jalapa, Mex. 201/N7
Jalapa, Mex. 202/C2
Jalatlaco, Mex. 201/Q10
Jālaun, India 142/B2
Jaldhāka (riv.), India 143/G2
Jales, Braz. 213/B2
Jalesar, India 142/B2
Jalingo, Nga. 154/H6
Jalisco, Mex. 200/D4
Jallouvre, Pic de (peak), Fr. 114/C6
Jalon (riv.), Sp. 102/E2
Jalostotitlán, Mex. 200/E4
Jalpa, Mex. 200/E4
Jalpa de Méndez, Mex. 202/C2
Jalpan de Serra, Mex. 201/F4
Jaltenango de la Paz, Mex. 202/C3
Jaltepec (riv.), Mex. 202/C2
Jáltipan de Morelos, Mex. 202/C2
Jālūd, WBnk. 149/G7
Jaluit (isl.), Mrsh. 174/F4
Jalūlā', Iraq 148/F3
Jam, Iran 146/F3
Jamaame, Som. 155/P7
Jamaare (riv.), Nga. 154/H5
Jamaica (ctry.) 203/G2
Jamaica (chan.), Jam. 203/H2
Jamaica (bay), NY, US 196/K9
Jamālpur, Bang. 143/G3
Jamanxim (riv.), Braz. 209/G5
Jamapa, Mex. 201/N7
Jamari (riv.), Braz. 208/F5
Jambi, Indo. 138/B4
Jambuair (cape), Indo. 138/A2
James (pt.), Chile 216/B5
James (bay), Qu, Can. 181/H3
James (peak), Ut, US 195/K11
James (riv.), Va, US 185/J4
James Campbell NWR, Hi, US 182/V12
James M. Cox Dayton (int'l arpt.), Oh, US 188/C4
James Ross (str.), Nun., Can. 180/G1
Jamesburg, NJ, US 196/D3
Jamestown, Austl. 171/H5
Jamestown, Co, US 195/B2
Jamestown, ND, US 185/J4
Jamestown, NY, US 188/E3
Jamestown, Tn, US 188/C4
Jamīrāpāt (range), India 142/D4
Jāmke, Pak. 144/C3
Jammerbugt (bay), Den. 96/C3
Jammu and Kashmīr (state), India 144/C3
Jāmpur, Pak. 144/A5
Jāmtāra, India 143/F4
Jämtland (co.), Swe. 95/E3
Jamūi, India 143/F3
Jamuna (riv.), Bang. 143/G3
Jan (lake), Sk, Can. 185/H2
Jan Kempdorp, SAfr. 164/D2
Jan Mayen (isl.), Nor. 218/G
Jan Smuts (Johannesburg) (int'l arpt.), SAfr. 164/E2
Janakkala, Fin. 97/L1
Janakpur, Nepal 143/E2
Janakpur (zone), Nepal 143/E2
Janaúba, Braz. 212/B4
Janaucu, Ilha (isl.), Braz. 209/H3
Jandaia do Sul, Braz. 213/B2
Jandaq, Iran 147/F2
Jandowae, Austl. 172/C4
Jándula (riv.), Sp. 102/C4
Jangaon, India 140/C4
Jangipur, India 143/G3
Janikowo, Pol. 99/K2
Janīn, WBnk. 149/G7
Janja, Bosn. 106/D3
Janjevo, Kos. 106/E4
Janos, Mex. 200/C2
Jánoshalma, Hun. 106/D2
Jánosháza, Hun. 106/C2
Janów Lubelski, Pol. 99/M3
Jansenville, SAfr. 164/D4
Januária, Braz. 212/A4
Janvry, Fr. 88/J6
Janzé, Fr. 100/C3
Japan (ctry.) 129/Q4
Japan, Sea of (sea), Asia 129/P3
Japanese Alps NP, Japan 133/E2
Japurá (riv.), Braz. 205/C3
Jaqué, Pan. 203/G5
Jarābulus, Syria 148/D2
Jaraíz de la Vera, Sp. 102/C2
Jarama (riv.), Sp. 102/D2
Jaramānah, Syria 149/E3
Jarandilla de la Vera, Sp. 102/C2
Jaranwāla, Pak. 144/B4
Jarash, Jor. 149/D3
Järbo, Swe. 96/G1
Jarby (pt.), IM, UK 92/D3
Jardim, Braz. 212/C2
Jardín América, Arg. 215/E2
Jardines de la Reina (arch.), Cuba 203/G1
Jardinópolis, Braz. 213/C2
Jargalant, Mong. 128/G2
Jari (riv.), Braz. 205/D2
Jaridih, India 143/F4
Jarmen, Ger. 96/E5
Järna, Swe. 96/G2
Jarny, Fr. 111/E5
Jarocin, Pol. 99/J3
Jaroměř, Czh. 99/H3
Jarosław, Pol. 99/M3
Jarrettsville, Md, US 196/B4
Jarrow, Eng, UK 93/G2
Jars (plain), Laos 136/C2
Jarud Qi, China 130/E1
Järvenpää, Fin. 97/L1
Jarville-la-Malgrange, Fr. 111/F6
Jarvis (isl.), Pac., US 175/J5
Järvsö, Swe. 96/G1
Jáse-Nagykun-Szolnok (prov.), Hun. 106/E2
Jashpurnagar, India 143/E4
Jasidih, India 143/F3
Jāsk, Iran 147/G3
Jasło, Pol. 99/L4
Jason (isl.), Mald. 217/E6
Jasper, Ab, Can. 184/D2
Jasper, Al, US 191/G3
Jasper, Fl, US 191/H4
Jasper, Tx, US 187/J5
Jasper, Ga, US 191/G3
Jasper, In, US 188/C4
Jasper NP, Ab, Can. 184/D2
Jaspur, India 142/B1
Jastrebarsko, Cro. 106/B3
Jastrowie, Pol. 99/J2
Jastrzębie Zdrój, Pol. 99/K4
Jaswantnagar, India 142/B2
Jászapáti, Hun. 99/L5
Jászárokszállás, Hun. 106/D2
Jászberény, Hun. 99/K5
Jataí, Braz. 213/B1
Jatapu (riv.), Braz. 208/G3
Jatāra, India 142/B3
Jataté (riv.), Mex. 202/D2
Jāti, Pak. 147/J4
Jatibonico, Cuba 203/G1
Játiva, Sp. 103/E3
Jatoi Janūbi, Pak. 144/A5
Jaú (riv.), Braz. 208/F4
Jaú, Braz. 213/B2
Jaua Sarisariñama, PN, Ven. 208/F3
Jauaperi (riv.), Braz. 208/F3
Jauaperi (riv.), Braz. 211/F5
Jauaru, Serra (mts.), Braz. 209/H4
Jaudon, Mo, US 195/D6
Jauharābād, Pak. 144/B3
Jauja, Peru 214/C3
Jaumave, Mex. 201/F4
Jaun, Swi. 114/D4
Jaunay-Clan, Fr. 100/D3
Jaunpass (pass), Swi. 114/D4
Java (isl.), Indo. 138/C5
Java (sea), Indo. 138/D5
Javari (riv.), Braz. 208/D5
Jávea, Sp. 103/F3
Javier (isl.), Chile 217/B5
Javorie (peak), Slvk. 106/D1
Javornice (riv.), Czh. 113/G2
Javorník (peak), Czh. 113/G4
Javorová Skála (peak), Czh. 113/H3
Jawāla Mukhi, India 144/D4
Jawor, Pol. 99/J3
Jayanca, Peru 214/B2
Jayapura, Indo. 139/K4
Jaynagar, India 143/F2
Jaynagar, India 143/G4
Jayton, Tx, US 187/G4
Jbel Bani (mts.), Mor. 156/D3
Jean Lafitte, La, US 195/P17
Jeberos, Peru 214/B2
Jebjerg, Den. 96/C3
Jed Water (riv.), Sc, UK 94/D6
Jedburgh, Sc, UK 94/D6
Jedlicze, Pol. 99/L4
Jędrzejów, Pol. 99/L3
Jeetze (riv.), Ger. 98/F2
Jefferson (co.), Co, US 195/B3
Jefferson (parish), La, US 195/P17
Jefferson (riv.), La, US 195/P17
Jefferson (co.), Mo, US 195/F9
Jefferson (mt.), Or, US 184/C4
Jefferson, Tx, US 187/J4
Jefferson (co.), Wi, US 193/N14
Jefferson City (cap.), Mo, US 187/J3
Jeffersonville, In, US 188/C4
Jeffrey City, Wy, US 186/F2
Jeffreys Bay, SAfr. 164/D4
Jegenstorf, Swi. 114/D3
Jeinemeni (peak), Chile 216/B5
Jēkabpils, Lat. 97/L3
Jelcz-Laskowice, Pol. 99/J3
Jelenia Góra, Pol. 99/H3
Jelep (pass), China 140/E2
Jelgava, Lat. 97/K3
Jemaa Sahim, Mor. 156/C2
Jemappes, Belg. 110/C3
Jember, Indo. 138/D5
Jemez Pueblo, NM, US 186/F4
Jeminay, China 128/E2
Jemmal, Tun. 158/M7
Jempang (lake), Indo. 139/E4
Jena, La, US 187/J5
Jena, Ger. 98/F3
Jenaz, Swi. 115/F4
Jenbach, Aus. 101/J3
Jendouba, Tun. 158/L6
Jendouba (gov.), Tun. 158/L6
Jeneponto, Indo. 139/E5
Jengen, Ger. 115/G2
Jenkintown, Pa, US 196/C3
Jennings, La, US 187/J5
Jennings, Mo, US 195/G8
Jenny Lind (isl.), Nun., Can. 180/F2
Jens Muck (isl.), Nun., Can. 181/H2
Jeppener, Arg. 217/J11
Jequetepeque, Peru 214/B2
Jequié, Braz. 212/B4
Jequitaí, Braz. 212/A5
Jequitinhonha, Braz. 212/B5
Jequitinhonha (riv.), Braz. 205/E4
Jerada, Mor. 158/C2
Jerba (isl.), Tun. 155/H2
Jérémie, Haiti 203/H2
Jeremoabo, Braz. 212/C3
Jerez de García Salinas, Mex. 200/E4
Jerez de la Frontera, Sp. 102/B4
Jerez de los Caballeros, Sp. 102/B3
Jericho, Austl. 172/B3
Jericho, NY, US 197/L8
Jericho (Arīḥā), Isr. 149/D4
Jericó, Braz. 212/C2
Jerilderie, Austl. 173/C2
Jerissa, Tun. 158/L7
Jerramungup, Austl. 170/C5
Jersey (isl.), Chl, UK 100/B2
Jersey (co.), Il, US 195/G7
Jersey City, NJ, US 197/J9
Jersey City (res.), NJ, US 197/H8
Jersey Shore, Pa, US 196/A1
Jerumenha, Braz. 212/B2
Jerusalem (dist.), Isr. 149/D4
Jerusalem (Yerushalayim) (cap.), Isr. 149/G8
Jervis (inlet), BC, Can. 184/C3
Jervis Bay, Austl. 173/D2
Jerzu, It. 104/A3
Jesberg, Ger. 109/G6
Jesenice, Slov. 101/L3
Jesenice (res.), Czh. 113/F2
Jesi, It. 117/G5
Jessheim, Nor. 96/D1
Jessore (pol. reg.), Bang. 143/G4
Jesuânia, Braz. 213/H6
Jesup, Ga, US 191/H4
Jésus (isl.), Qu, Can. 189/N6
Jesús Carranza, Mex. 202/C2
Jesús de Machaca, Bol. 214/D5
Jesús María, Arg. 215/D3
Jesús Menéndez, Cuba 203/G1
Jeta, Ilha de (isl.), GBis. 160/A4
Jetmore, Ks, US 187/H3
Jetpur, India 147/K4
Jettingen-Scheppach, Ger. 112/D6
Jetzendorf, Ger. 113/E6
Jeumont, Fr. 111/D3
Jevenstedt, Ger. 98/E1
Jever, Ger. 109/E1
Jevnaker, Nor. 96/D1
Jewar, India 142/A1
Jewel Cave Nat'l Mon., SD, US 185/H5
Jezerce (peak), Alb. 105/F1
Jezerní Stěna (peak), Czh. 113/G4
Jeziorak (lake), Pol. 99/K2
Jhā Jhā, India 143/F3
Jhajjar, India 144/D5
Jhālawār, India 147/L4
Jhalida, India 143/E4
Jhālū, India 142/B1
Jhang Sadar, Pak. 144/B4
Jhanjhārpur, India 143/F2
Jhānsi, India 142/B3
Jhārgrām, India 143/F4
Jharia, India 143/F4
Jharkhand (state), India 143/E4
Jharsuguda, India 143/E5
Jhawāriān, Pak. 144/B3
Jhelum, Pak. 144/B3
Jhelum (riv.), Pak. 147/K2
Jhenida, Bang. 143/G4
Jhumra, Pak. 144/B4
Ji-Paraná, Braz. 208/F6
Ji Xian, China 130/C4
Ji Xian, China 130/H6
Jia Xian, China 130/B4
Jiading, China 130/L8
Jiahe, China 141/K2
Jialing (riv.), China 125/K6
Jiamusi, China 129/P2
Jian (riv.), China 137/B3
Jianchang, China 130/D2
Jiang (riv.), China 136/E1
Jiang Xian, China 130/B4
Jiang'an, China 141/J2
Jiangcheng Hanizu Yizu Zizhixian, China 141/H3
Jiangchuan, China 141/H3
Jiangdu, China 130/D4
Jianghua Yaozu Zizhixian, China 141/K3
Jiangjin, China 141/J2
Jiangmen, China 141/K3
Jiangning, China 130/D5
Jiangsu (prov.), China 129/L5
Jiangxi (prov.), China 129/K6
Jiangyin, China 130/E5
Jiangyong, China 141/K2
Jiangyou, China 128/H5

Jianhe, China 141/J2
Jianhu, China 130/D4
Jianli, China 137/E2
Jian'ou, China 137/C2
Jianshi, China 129/J5
Jianshui, China 141/H3
Jianyang, China 137/C2
Jiaocheng, China 130/C3
Jiaohe, China 129/N3
Jiaojiang, China 137/H2
Jiaokou, China 130/C3
Jiaoling, China 137/C3
Jiaonan, China 130/D4
Jiaozuo, China 130/C4
Jiashan, China 130/D4
Jiashan, China 130/L9
Jiashi, China 145/G5
Jiaxiang, China 130/D4
Jiaxing, China 130/L9
Jiayin, China 129/P2
Jiayu, China 137/E2
Jiayuguan, China 128/G4
Jibou, Rom. 107/F2
Jibsh, Ra's (pt.),
Oman 147/G4
Jicarón (isl.), Pan. 203/F5
Jičín, Czh. 99/H3
Jiddah, SAr. 146/C4
Jieshou, China 130/C4
Jiexiu, China 130/C3
Jieyang, China 137/C3
Jifnā, Isr. 149/G8
Jigalong Abor. Land,
Austl. 170/D2
Jigawa (prov.), Nga. 161/H4
Jiguani, Cuba 203/G1
Jigzhi, China 128/H5
Jihlava (riv.), Czh. 101/L2
Jihlava, Czh. 99/H4
Jihlavský (pol. reg.),
Czh. 99/H4
Jijel (prov.), Alg. 158/H4
Jijel, Alg. 158/H4
Jijia (riv.), Rom. 107/H2
Jijiga, Eth. 155/P6
Jijona, Sp. 103/E3
Jilhã, Reprêsa (res.),
Braz. 213/B2
Jilhava (riv.), Czh. 99/H4
Jilib, Som. 155/P7
Jilin, China 129/N3
Jilin, China 129/N3
Jilin (prov.), China 129/N3
Jiloca (riv.), Sp. 102/E2
Jilotepec, Mex. 201/K7
Jílové u Prahy, Czh. 113/H3
Jim Thorpe, Pa, US 196/C2
Jíma, Eth. 155/N6
Jimaní, DRep. 203/J2
Jimbolia, Rom. 106/E3
Jimboomba, Austl. 172/D4
Jimena de la Frontera,
Sp. 102/C4
Jiménez, Mex. 200/D3
Jiménez, Mex. 201/E2
Jimo, China 130/E3
Jimokuji, Japan 135/L6
Jimsar, China 128/E3
Jin (riv.), China 141/K2
Jin Xian, China 130/C3
Jinan, China 130/D3
Jinchang, China 128/H4
Jincheng, China 130/C4
Jinchuan, China 128/H5
Jinci Temple, China 130/C3
Jīnd, India 144/D3
Jindabyne (dam),
Austl. 173/D3
Jindabyne, Austl. 173/D3
Jindřichuv Hradec,
Czh. 99/H4
Jing Xian, China 129/L5
Jing Xian, China 141/J2
Jingde, China 130/B3
Jingdezhen, China 141/H3
Jingdong, China 141/H3
Jinggangshan, China 141/K2
Jinghai, China 130/H7
Jinghe, China 145/H2
Jinghong, China 141/H3
Jingjiang, China 130/E4
Jingle, China 130/B3
Jingmen, China 130/C5
Jingshan, China 130/C5
Jingxi, China 141/J3
Jingyuan, China 128/H4
Jinhu, China 130/D4
Jinhua, China 137/C2
Jining, China 130/C2
Jining, China 130/D4
Jinja, Ugan. 162/B2
Jinkou, China 141/H2
Jinotega, Nic. 202/E4
Jinotepe, Nic. 202/E4
Jinping, China 141/J2
Jinsha, China 141/J2
Jinsha (riv.), China 125/J7
Jinshan, China 130/L9
Jinshi, China 141/K2
Jintan, China 130/D4
Jintotolo (chan.), Phil. 137/D5
Jintür, India 147/L5
Jinxi, China 137/C2
Jinxi, China 130/E2
Jinxiang, China 130/D4
Jinyun, China 137/H2
Jinzhai, China 130/C5
Jinzhou (bay), China 131/A3
Jinzhou, China 130/E2
Jiparaná (riv.), Braz. 208/F5
Jipijapa, Ecu. 210/A5
Jiquilpan de Juárez,
Mex. 200/E5
Jiquipilco, Mex. 201/Q9

Jiřkov, Czh. 113/G1
Jishan, China 130/B4
Jishou, China 141/K2
Jishui, China 137/C2
Jisr ash Shughūr,
Syria 149/E2
Jiu (riv.), Rom. 107/F3
Jiujiang, China 137/C2
Jiujiang, China 130/D4
Jiulong, China 141/H2
Jiutai, China 129/N3
Jiutepec, Mex. 201/K8
Jiuwan (mts.), China 128/J6
Jixi, China 129/P2
Jixi, China 137/C1
Jiyang, China 130/D3
Jiyuan, China 130/C4
Jīzān, SAr. 146/D5
Jize, China 130/C3
Jizera (riv.), Czh. 99/H3
Jizō-zaki (pt.), Japan 132/D3
Jizzakh, Uzb. 145/E4
Jizzakh (pol. reg.),
Uzb. 145/E4
Joaçaba, Braz. 213/B3
Joachín, Mex. 201/N8
Joaíma, Braz. 212/B5
João Câmara, Braz. 212/D2
João Lisboa, Braz. 212/A2
João Monlevade,
Braz. 213/D1
João Pessoa, Braz. 212/D2
João Pinheiro, Braz. 212/A5
Joaquín V. González,
Arg. 215/D2
Jobabo, Cuba 203/G1
Jockgrim, Ger. 112/B4
Jocón, Hon. 202/E3
Jodar, Sp. 102/D4
Jodhpur, India 147/K3
Jodoigne, Belg. 111/D2
Joensuu, Fin. 95/J3
Jõetsu, Japan 133/F2
Jogbani, India 143/F2
Johannesberg, Ger. 112/C2
Johannesburg, SAfr. 164/E2
Johanngeorgenstadt,
Ger. 113/F2
Johilla (riv.), India 142/C4
John Day, Or, US 184/D4
John Day, Or, US 184/D4
John Day Fossil Beds Nat'l
Mon., Or, US 184/D4
John Day, Middle Fork
(riv.), Or, US 184/D4
John Day, North Fork
(riv.), Or, US 184/D4
John F. Kennedy
(int'l arpt.), NY, US 197/K9
John Forrest NP,
Austl. 170/L6
John H. Kerr (res.),
NC,Va, US 191/G2
John Martin (res.),
Co, US 190/C2
John Wayne/Orange County
(int'l arpt.), Ca, US 194/G8
Johnson (co.), Ks, US 195/D6
Johnson City, Tn, US 188/D4
Johnsonburg, NJ, US 196/D2
Johnsons Crossing,
Yk, Can. 192/M3
Johnston (falls), Zam. 162/A5
Johnston (lake),
Austl. 167/B4
Johnston Atoll (isl.),
Pac., US 175/J3
Johnstone, Sc, UK 94/B5
Johnstown, Pa, US 188/E3
Johnstown, Pa, US 195/C2
Johnsville, Md, US 196/A4
Johor Baharu, Malay. 138/B3
Jöhstadt, Ger. 113/G1
Joigny, Fr. 100/C2
Joinville, Braz. 213/B3
Joinville, Fr. 100/C2
Jojutla, Mex. 201/K8
Jokioinen, Fin. 97/K1
Jokkmokk, Swe. 95/F2
Jökulsárgljúfur NP,
Ice. 95/P6
Jolanda di Savoia, It. 117/E3
Joliette, Qu, Can. 188/F2
Jollyville, Tx, US 187/H5
Jolo (isl.), Phil. 139/F2
Jolo, Phil. 139/F2
Jomala, Fin. 97/H1
Jombang, Indo. 138/D5
Jomda, China 128/G5
Jomo Kenyatta
(int'l arpt.), Kenya 162/C3
Jona, Swi. 115/E3
Jonacatepec, Mex. 201/L8
Jonava, Lith. 97/L4
Jonchery-sur-Vesle,
Fr. 111/D5
Jones, Ok, US 195/N14
Jones (inlet), NY, US 197/L9
Jones (mtn.), Pa, US 196/A2
Jones (sound),
Nun., Can. 181/S7
Jones Beach State Park,
NY, US 197/L9
Jonesboro, Ar, US 187/L3
Jonesboro, La, US 187/L4
Jönköping, Swe. 96/F3
Jönköping (co.), Swe. 96/F3
Jonquière, Qu, Can. 189/G1
Jonuta, Mex. 198/C4
Joondalup, Austl. 170/K6
Joplin, Mo, US 187/J3
Joppatowne (Joppa),
Md, US 196/B5
Jora, India 142/A2

Jordan, Mt, US 184/G4
Jordan, On, Can. 189/R9
Jordan (riv.), Isr.,Jor. 149/D4
Jordan (ctry.) 146/C2
Jordan Valley, Or, US 184/D5
Jordânia, Braz. 212/B4
Jorge (cape), Chile 217/B6
Jorge Chavez
(int'l arpt.), Peru 214/B4
Jork, Ger. 109/G1
Jornada del Muerto
(valley), NM, US 190/B3
Jørpeland, Nor. 96/B2
Jos (plat.), Nga. 161/H4
Jos, Nga. 161/H4
Jose Abad Santos,
Phil. 139/G2
José Batlle y Ordóñez,
Uru. 217/G2
José Bonifácio,
Braz. 213/B2
José Cardel, Mex. 201/N7
José de Freitas,
Braz. 212/B2
José de San Martín,
Arg. 215/B5
José Enrique Rodó,
Uru. 217/K10
José María Morelos,
Mex. 202/D2
Jose Marti (int'l arpt.),
Cuba 203/F1
José Pedro Varela,
Uru. 217/G2
José, South (dept.),
Uru. 217/F2
Josefa Camejo
(int'l arpt.), Ven. 210/D2
Joseph Bonaparte
(gulf), Austl. 167/B2
Joshin-Etsu Kogen NP,
Japan 133/F2
Joshua, Tx, US 187/H5
Joshua (riv.), Ct, US 197/F1
Joshua Tree NP,
Ca, US 186/D4
Jossa (riv.), Ger. 112/C2
Jotunheimen NP, Nor. 96/C1
Jouanne (riv.), Fr. 100/C2
Jouarre, Fr. 88/M5
Joué-lès-Tours, Fr. 100/D3
Jœuf, Fr. 111/F5
Jourama Falls NP,
Austl. 172/B2
Jourdanton, Tx, US 187/H5
Joure, Neth. 108/C3
Joutseno, Fin. 97/N1
Joux (lake), Swi. 114/B4
Jouy-en-Josas, Fr. 88/J5
Jouy-le-Châtel, Fr. 88/M6
Jouy-le-Moutier, Fr. 110/C6
Jouy-sur-Morin, Fr. 88/N6
Jovellanos, Cuba 203/F1
Joveyn (riv.), Iran 147/G1
Jowai, India 141/F2
Joy (mt.), Yk, Can. 192/M3
Jōyō, Japan 135/J6
Jozankei Spa, Japan 134/B2
Ju Xian, China 130/D4
Juan Aldama, Mex. 200/E3
Juan de Fuca, Strait of
(str.), US,Can. 184/B3
Juan de Nova (isl.),
Reun., Fr. 165/G7
Juan Fernández (isls.),
Chile 205/A6
Juan Fernández, Arg. 216/F3
Juan José Paso, Arg. 216/E2
Juan L. Lacaze, Uru. 217/K11
Juan Santamaria
(int'l arpt.), CR 203/E4
Juancheng, China 130/C4
Juangriego, Ven. 211/F2
Juanjui, Peru 214/B2
Juarez, Sierra de
(mts.), Mex. 186/D4
Juatinga, Ponta de
(pt.), Braz. 213/J8
Juazeirinho, Braz. 212/C2
Juazeiro, Braz. 212/B3
Juazeiro do Norte,
Braz. 212/C2
Juba, Sudan 155/M7
Jubany, Arg., Ant. 218/W
Jubba (riv.), Som. 155/P7
Júbek, Ger. 98/E1
Jubones (riv.), Ecu. 214/B1
Juby (cape), Mor. 156/B4
Júcar (riv.), Sp. 103/E3
Jucás, Braz. 212/C2
Jüchen, Ger. 111/F1
Juchipila, Mex. 200/E4
Juchique de Ferrer,
Mex. 201/N7
Juchitán de Zaragoza,
Mex. 202/C2
Juchitepec, Mex. 201/R10
Jucurutu, Braz. 212/D2
Judaberg, Nor. 96/A2
Judenburg, Aus. 101/L3
Judith
(riv.), Mt, US 184/F4
Juelsminde, Den. 96/D4
Jughaynah, Egypt 159/B3
Juigalpa, Nic. 203/E4
Juilly, Fr. 88/L4
Juine (riv.), Fr. 100/B2
Juist (isl.), Ger. 108/D1
Juiz de Fora, Braz. 213/K6
Jujurieux, Fr. 114/B5
Juiz (mt.), Yk, Can. 192/M3
Jujuy, Peru 214/D5
Julia Creek, Austl. 172/A3

Juliaca, Peru 214/D4
Julian Alps (mts.), It. 101/K3
Juliana Top (peak),
Sur. 209/G3
Jülich, Ger. 111/F2
Julio A. Mella, Cuba 203/H1
Juliustown, NJ, US 196/D3
Jullundur, India 144/C4
Julu, China 130/C3
Jumbilla, Peru 214/B2
Jumilla, Sp. 102/E3
Juminda (pt.), Est. 97/L2
Jumla, Nepal 142/D1
Jümme (riv.), Ger. 109/C2
Jūmonji, Japan 134/B4
Junāgadh, India 147/K4
Junan, China 130/D4
Juncal (peak), Chile 216/N8
Juncos (riv.), Chile 216/N8
Junction, Tx, US 187/H5
Junction City, Or, US 184/C4
Jundiaí, Braz. 213/G8
Jundu (mts.), China 130/H6
Juneda, Sp. 103/F2
Junee, Austl. 173/C2
Jungar Qi, China 130/B3
Jungfrau (peak), Swi. 114/D4
Jungfraujoch, Swi. 114/D4
Jungingen, Lux. 111/F4
Juniata (co.), Pa, US 196/A2
Juniata (riv.), Pa, US 188/E3
Junik, Kos. 106/E4
Junín, Peru 214/B3
Junín (dept.), Peru 214/C3
Junín, Ecu. 214/B1
Junín, Arg. 216/C2
Junín, Arg. 216/E2
Junín de los Andes,
Arg. 216/C3
Juniper Hills, Ca, US 194/C2
Junji (pass), China 130/C3
Juno Beach, Fl, US 191/H5
Junqueirópolis, Braz. 213/B2
Junsele, Swe. 95/F3
Juparanã, Lagoa (lake),
Braz. 213/D1
Jupiter (riv.), Qu, Can. 189/J1
Jupiter, Fl, US 191/H5
Jupiter (mt.), Wa, US 193/A2
Juquiá, Braz. 213/C3
Juquitiba, Braz. 213/F8
Jur (riv.), Sudan 155/L6
Jur pri Bratislave,
Slvk. 106/C1
Jura (mts.), Fr. 114/B4
Jura (dept.), Fr. 114/B4
Jura (pen.), Sc, UK 89/R8
Jura (isl.), Sc, UK 89/Q9
Jurado, Col. 210/B3
Jurançon, Fr. 100/C5
Jurbise, Belg. 110/C2
Jurf al Kannā, Isr. 149/G6
Jūrmala, Lat. 97/K3
Juruá (riv.), Braz. 205/D4
Juruena (riv.), Braz. 205/D4
Juruti, Braz. 209/G4
Jussey, Fr. 114/B2
Jussy, Swi. 114/C5
Justo Daract, Arg. 216/D2
Jutaí, Braz. 208/E5
Jutaí (riv.), Braz. 208/E4
Jutiapa, Guat. 202/D3
Juticalpa, Hon. 202/E3
Jutland, NJ, US 196/D2
Jutland (pen.), Den. 95/D4
Juventud, La (isl.),
Cuba 203/F1
Juye, China 130/D4
Juzhang (riv.), China 130/C5
Juziers, Fr. 88/H4
Južna Morava (riv.),
Serb. 106/E4
Jyderup, Den. 96/D4

K

Ka (riv.), Nga. 154/F5
Ka (isl.), NKor. 131/C3
Ka Lae (cape), Hi, US 182/T11
Kaaawa, Hi, US 182/W12
Kaabong, Ugan. 162/B2
Kaala (peak), Hi, US 182/V12
Kaalualu, Hi, US 182/U11
Kaap Plato (plat.),
SAfr. 164/C3
Kaarina, Fin. 97/K1
Kaarst, Ger. 108/D6
Kabadak (riv.), Bang. 143/G4
Kabaena (isl.), Indo. 139/F5
Kabah (ruin), Mex. 202/D1
Kabala, SLeo. 160/C4
Kabale, Ugan. 162/A3
Kabalega (falls), Ugan. 155/M7
Kabalega NP, Ugan. 155/M7
Kabalo, D.R. Congo 163/E2
Kabamba, Lac (lake),
D.R. Congo 163/E2
Kabara, D.R. Congo 162/A3
Kabarai, Indo. 139/H4
Kabardino-Balkaria,
Resp., Rus. 121/G4
Kabare, D.R. Congo 162/A3
Kabinakagani
On, Can. 188/C1
Kabinda, D.R. Congo 163/D2
Kabīr, Oued el
(riv.), Alg. 158/H4
Kabīrwāla, Pak. 144/A4

Kableshkovo, Bul. 107/H4
Kābol (Kabul) (cap.),
Afg. 147/J2
Kabompo (riv.), Zam. 163/D3
Kabongo, D.R. Congo 163/E2
Kabrai, India 142/C3
Kabul (riv.), Afg. 147/J2
Kabul (Kābol) (cap.),
Afg. 147/J2
Kaburuang
(isl.), Indo. 139/G3
Kačanik, Kos. 106/E4
Kachalola, Zam. 163/F3
Kachemak (bay),
Ak, US 192/H4
Kachin (div.), Myan. 141/G2
Kadaianallur, India 140/C6
Kadam (peak), Ugan. 162/B2
Kadam (isl.), Myan. 141/G5
Kadan (isl.), Myan. 136/B3
Kadan, Czh. 113/G2
Kadavu (isl.), Fiji 174/G6
Kadaï (riv.), Myan. 136/B3
Kadina, Austl. 171/H5
Kadınhanı, Turk. 148/C1
Kadiogo
(prov.), Burk. 161/E3
Kadiolo, Mali 160/D4
Kadiri, India 140/C5
Kadirli, Turk. 148/D2
Kadışehri, Turk. 148/C1
Kadnja, Bosn. 106/D3
Kadoka, SD, US 185/H5
Kadoma, Zim. 163/E4
Kadoma, Japan 135/J6
Kaduna, Nga. 161/G4
Kaduna (riv.), Nga. 161/G4
Kaduna (state), Nga. 161/G4
Kaduqli, Sudan 155/L5
Kaedi, Mrta. 160/B2
Kaech'ŏn, NKor. 131/C3
Kaes○ng, NKor. 131/C4
Kaesŏng (mt.), Wa, US 193/A2
Kaesŏng-si (prov.),
NKor. 131/D4
Kafar Jar Ghar (mts.),
Afg. 147/J2
Kalaa Kbira, Tun. 158/M7
Kaffraria (reg.), SAfr. 164/D4
Kaffrine, Sen. 160/B3
Kafirévos (cape), Gre. 105/J3
Kafr Ash Shaykh (gov.),
Egypt 159/B1
Kafr ash Shaykh,
Egypt 159/B1
Kafr az Zayyāt, Egypt 149/B4
Kafr Kannā, Isr. 149/G6
Kafr Mandā, Isr. 149/G6
Kafr Qari', Isr. 149/G6
Kafr Qāsim, Isr. 149/G7
Kafu (riv.), Ugan. 162/A2
Kafue, Zam. 163/E4
Kafue (riv.), Zam. 163/E4
Kafue NP, Zam. 161/F4
Kaga, Japan 132/E2
Kaga Bandoro, CAfr. 155/J6
Kagan, Uzb. 145/D5
Kağan (valley), Pak. 144/B2
Kagawa (pref.), Japan 132/D3
Kağızman, Turk. 148/E1
Kagoshima (int'l arpt.),
Japan 132/B5
Kagoshima, Japan 132/B5
Kagoshima (bay),
Japan 132/B5
Kagoshima (dept.),
Japan 133/G3
Kahaluu, Hi, US 182/W13
Kahama, Tanz. 162/B3
Kahayan (riv.), Indo. 138/D4
Kahiu (pt.), Hi, US 182/T10
Kahl am Main, Ger. 112/C2
Kāhna, Pak. 144/C4
Kahoka, Mo, US 185/L5
Kahoolawe (isl.),
Hi, US 182/T10
Kahperusvaara
(peak), Fin. 95/G1
Kahramanmaraş, Turk. 148/D2
Kahror Pakka, Pak. 144/B3
Kāhta, Turk. 148/D2
Kahuku, Hi, US 182/W12
Kahuku (pt.), Hi, US 182/W12
Kahului, Hi, US 182/T10
Kahuzi-Biega, PN de,
D.R. Congo 163/E1
Kai Besar (isl.), Indo. 139/H5
Kai Kecil (isl.), Indo. 139/H5
Kaiapoi, NZ 175/S11
Kaibab
(plat.), Az, US 186/D3
Kaibara, Japan 135/H5
Kaieteur (falls), Guy. 211/G3
Kaieteur NP, Guy. 211/G3
Kaifeng, China 130/C4
Kaifeng, China 130/C4
Kaikohe, NZ 175/S10
Kaikoura, NZ 175/S11
Kaili, China 141/J2
Kailu, China 130/E2
Kailua, Hi, US 182/W13
Kailua, Hi, US 182/W13
Kaimanawa
(riv.), Alg. 158/H4
Kaimganj, India 142/B2

Kaimur (range),
India 142/C3
Kainab (riv.), Namb. 164/B2
Kainach (riv.), Aus. 106/B2
Kainan, Japan 132/D3
Kainji (dam), Nga. 161/G4
Kainji (lake), Nga. 161/G4
Kainji Lake NP, Nga. 161/F4
Kainóuryion, Gre. 105/G3
Kaipara (har.), NZ 175/S10
Kairāna, India 144/D5
Kairi, Austl. 172/B2
Kairouan, Tun. 158/L7
Kairouan (gov.), Tun. 158/L7
Kaisei, Japan 135/C3
Kaiseregg (peak),
Swi. 114/D4
Kaiserslautern, Ger. 111/G3
Kaisersesch, Ger. 111/G3
Kaitaia, NZ 175/S10
Kaithal, India 144/D5
Kaiwi (chan.), Hi, US 182/T10
Kaiyang, China 141/J2
Kaiyuan, China 141/H3
Kaiyuan, China 130/F2
Kaizu, Japan 135/L5
Kaizuka, Japan 135/H7
Kajaani, Fin. 95/H2
Kaji-san (peak), SKor. 131/E5
Kajiado, Kenya 162/C3
Kajikazawa, Japan 135/A2
Kakadu NP, Austl. 167/E1
Kakamas, SAfr. 164/C3
Kakamega, Kenya 162/B2
Kakamigahara, Japan 135/L5
Kakanj, Bosn. 106/D3
Kake, Ak, US 192/M4
Kaketsa (mtn.),
BC, Can. 192/M4
Kaduna (riv.), Nga. 161/G4
Kakhovka, Ukr. 107/L2
Kakhovs'ke
Vodoskhovyshche
(res.), Ukr. 120/E3
Kālūr Kot, Pak. 144/A3
Kalush, Ukr. 120/C2
Kalutara, SrL. 140/C6
Kaluzhskaya Oblast
Rus. 118/G5
Kalyān, India 147/K5
Kāmā, D.R. Congo 163/E1
Kakrāla, India 142/B2
Kakrima (riv.), Gui. 160/B4
Kaktovik, Ak, US 192/K1
Kakuda, Japan 133/G2
Kakunodate, Japan 134/B4
Kakuma (peak),
Hi, US 182/T10
Kala (riv.), Namb. 164/C2
Kalabahi, Indo. 139/G5
Kalabo, Zam. 163/D3
Kalach, Rus. 121/G2
Kalach-na-Donu, Rus. 121/G2
Kalachinsk, Rus. 145/F1
Kaladan (riv.), Myan. 141/F3
Kālāgarh, India 142/B1
Kalahari
(des.), Namb. 164/C2
Kalahari-Gemsbok NP,
SAfr. 163/C6
Kalaheo, Hi, US 182/S10
Kalaiya, Nepal 143/E2
Kalale, Ben. 161/F4
Kalam, China 141/H3
Kalamákion, Gre. 105/N8
Kalamariá, Gre. 105/H2
Kalamáta, Gre. 105/H4
Kalamazoo, Mi, US 188/C3
Kalampáka, Gre. 105/G3
Kalandy, Madg. 165/J6
Kalaoa, Hi, US 182/U11
Kalasin, Thai. 136/C2
Kalāswāla, Pak. 144/C3
Kalāt, Pak. 147/J3
Kalaupapa, Hi, US 182/T10
Kalávryta, Gre. 105/H3
Kalbach, Ger. 112/B2
Kalbar, Austl. 172/D4
Kalbarri, Austl. 170/B3
Kalbarri NP, Austl. 170/B3
Kaldakvísl (riv.), Ice. 95/N7
Kale, Turk. 120/F6
Kale, Turk. 149/A1
Kalecik, Turk. 148/C1
Kalefeld, Ger. 109/H5
Kalemie (int'l arpt.),
D.R. Congo 162/A4
Kalemie, D.R. Congo 162/A4
Kalemyo, Myan. 141/F3
Kalety, Pol. 99/K3
Kalewa, Myan. 141/F3
Kaleya, Zam. 163/E4
Kāli (riv.), India 142/B1
Kāli (riv.), India 142/B2
Kāli (riv.), Nepal 142/D1
Kalianda, Indo. 138/C5
Kalima, D.R. Congo 155/L8
Kalimantan (reg.),
Indo. 138/D4
Kálimnos (isl.), Gre. 148/A2
Kalimpong, India 143/G2
Kalinadi (riv.), India 140/B4
Kaliningrad, Rus. 97/J4
Kaliningradskaya Oblast,
Rus. 118/D5
Kalinkavichy, Bela. 120/D1
Kaliro, Ugan. 162/A2
Kalisizo, Ugan. 162/A3
Kalispell, Mt, US 184/E3
Kalisz, Pol. 99/K3
Kalix, Swe. 95/G2
Kalixälven
(riv.), Swe. 95/G2

Kāliyāganj, India 143/G3
Kalkaska, Mi, US 188/C2
Kallham, Aus. 113/G6
Kallinge, Swe. 96/F3
Kallinge
(int'l arpt.), Swe. 96/F3
Kallithéa, Gre. 105/N9
Kallsjön (lake), Swe. 95/E3
Kalmar, Swe. 96/G3
Kalmar (co.), Swe. 95/F4
Kalmar
(int'l arpt.), Swe. 96/G3
Kalmarsund (sound),
Swe. 96/G3
Kalmthout, Belg. 108/B6
Kalmykia, Resp., Rus. 122/G5
Kālna, India 143/G4
Kalni (riv.), Bang. 143/H3
Kalocsa, Hun. 106/D2
Kalofer, Bul. 107/G4
Kalohi (chan.), Hi, US 182/T10
Kalokhórion, Gre. 105/H2
Kalol, India 147/K4
Kalomo, Zam. 163/E4
Kalomo, Ugan. 162/B2
Kālpi, India 142/B2
Kalpin, China 128/C3
Kalsdorf bei Graz,
Aus. 101/L3
Kaltag, Ak, US 192/G3
Kaltbrunn, Swi. 115/F3
Kaltenleutgeben,
Aus. 107/N7
Kaltennordheim,
Ger. 112/D1
Kaltern (Caldaro), It. 101/J3
Kaluga, Rus. 118/G5
Kalungu, Ugan. 162/A3
Kalungwishi
(riv.), Zam. 162/A5
Kamagaya, Japan 135/E2
Kamaishi, Japan 134/B4
Kamakou (peak),
Hi, US 182/T10
Kamakura, Japan 135/D3
Kamália, Pak. 144/B4
Kamalo, Hi, US 182/T10
Kāman, India 142/A2
Kaman, Turk. 148/C2
Kamango (lake), Mali 160/E2
Kamanjab, Namb. 163/B4
Kamarang, Guy. 211/F3
Kāmāreddi, India 140/C4
Kāmārhāti, India 143/G4
Kamaria (falls), Guy. 211/G3
Kambalda, Austl. 170/D4
Kambar, Pak. 140/A2
Kambara, Japan 135/B3
Kambove, D.R. Congo 163/E3
Kamchatka
(pen.), Rus. 125/Q4
Kamchatskaya Oblast,
Rus. 123/R4
Kamchiya (riv.), Bul. 107/H4
Kamen, Ger. 109/E5
Kamen'-na-Obi, Rus. 145/H2
Kamenka, Rus. 121/H1
Kameno, Bul. 107/H4
Kamensk-Shakhtinskiy,
Rus. 120/G2
Kamensk-Ural'skiy,
Rus. 119/P4
Kameoka, Japan 135/J5
Kameyama, Japan 135/K6
Kami (isl.), Japan 135/M6
Kami-koshiki (isl.),
Japan 132/A5
Kamiah, Id, US 184/D4
Kamień Pomorski, Pol. 96/F5
Kamienna (isls.), Indo. 139/E5
Kamieskroon, SAfr. 164/B3
Kamifukuoka, Japan 135/D2
Kamiiso, Japan 134/B3
Kamiishizu, Japan 135/C1
Kamiizumi, Japan 135/C2
Kamikawa, Japan 135/C2
Kamikuishiki, Japan 135/B2
Kamilo (pt.), Hi, US 182/U11
Kamina, D.R. Congo 163/E2
Kaminak (riv.), NKor. 131/E4
Kaminoyama, Japan 134/B4
Kaminuriak (riv.),
Nf, Can. 181/K3
Kamishak (bay),
Ak, US 192/H4
Kamiyahagi, Japan 135/M5
Kamiyaku, Japan 133/G3
Kamla (riv.), India 143/F3
Kamloops, BC, Can. 184/C3
Kammaki, Slov. 101/L3
Kamnik, Slov. 101/L3
Kamo, Japan 133/G3
Kamoenai, Japan 134/B2
Kamogawa, Japan 135/F3
Kamojima, Japan 132/D3
Kamp (riv.), Aus. 99/H4
Kamp-Bornhofen, Ger. 111/G3
Kamp-Lintfort, Ger. 108/D5
Kampala
(cap.), Ugan. 162/B2

Kampar, Malay. 138/B3
Kampar (riv.), Indo. 138/B3
Kampen, Neth. 108/C3
Kampen, Ger. 96/C4
Kamphaeng Phet, Thai. 136/C5
Kamphaeng Phet (ruin),
Thai. 136/B2
Kamp'o, SKor. 131/E5
Kampong Kuala Besut,
Malay. 138/B2
Kampong Saom (bay),
Camb. 138/B1
Kampong Saom,
Camb. 136/C4
Kampville, Mo, US 195/F8
Kamsack, Sk, Can. 185/H3
Kamsdorf, Ger. 203/F4
Kamuchawie (lake),
Mb,Sk, Can. 185/H1
Kamui-misaki (cape),
Japan 134/B2
Kámuk (mtn.), CR 203/F4
Kamuli, Ugan. 162/B2
Kam'yanets'-Podil's'kyy,
Ukr. 120/C2
Kamyshin, Rus. 121/H2
Kanaaupscow (riv.),
Qu, Can. 181/J3
Kanab, Ut, US 186/D3
Kanaga (vol.), Ak, US 192/C6
Kanairiktok (riv.),
Nf, Can. 181/K3
Kanan, Japan 135/J7
Kananga, D.R. Congo 163/D2
Kanangra-Boyd NP,
Austl. 173/D2
Kanash, Rus. 119/K5
Kanasin, Mex. 202/D1
Kanawake Ind. Res.,
Qu, Can. 189/N7
Kanawha (riv.),
WV, US 191/H2
Kanazawa, Japan 133/E2
Kanchanaburi, Thai. 136/B3
Kānchenjunga (peak),
Nepal 140/F2
Kānchipuram, India 140/C5
Kandahār, Afg. 147/J2
Kandalaksha, Rus. 118/G2
Kandalaksha (gulf),
Rus. 95/K2
Kándanos, Gre. 105/H5
Kandé, Togo 161/F4
Kandel (peak), Ger. 114/E1
Kandel, Ger. 112/B4
Kander (riv.), Swi. 114/D2
Kandern, Ger. 114/D2
Kandersteg, Swi. 114/D5
Kandhkot, Pak. 147/J3
Kāndhla, India 144/D5
Kāndi, Ben. 161/F4
Kāndi, India 143/F3
Kandi (cape), Indo. 139/F3
Kandira, Turk. 107/K5
Kandos, Austl. 173/D2
Kandukūr, India 140/C5
Kandy, SrL. 140/D6
Kane (basin), Grld. 181/T7
Kane (co.), Il, US 193/P16
Kanem (reg.), Chad 154/H5
Kaneohe, Hi, US 182/W13
Kaneohe (bay),
Hi, US 182/W13
Kaneohe Marine Air Corps
Station, Hi, US 182/W13
Kaneville, Il, US 193/N16
Kaneyama, Japan 134/B4
Kang, Bots. 163/D5
Kanga (riv.), Bang. 143/G5
Kangaba, Mali 160/D4
Kangal, Turk. 148/D2
Kangan, Iran 146/F3
Kangan Abor. Land,
Austl. 170/C2
Kanganpur, Pak. 144/C4
Kangar, Malay. 136/C5
Kangaroo (isl.), Austl. 167/C4
Kangāsala, Fin. 97/L1
Kangāvar, Iran 146/F2
Kangbao, China 129/K3
Kangding, China 128/H5
Kangean (isls.), Indo. 139/E5
Kanggye, NKor. 131/D2
Kanggyŏng, SKor. 131/F6
Kanghwa, SKor. 131/D4
Kangiqsualujjuaq,
Qu, Can. 181/K3
Kangiqsujuaq,
Qu, Can. 181/J2
Kangirsuk, Qu, Can. 181/K2
Kangjin, SKor. 131/D5
Kangmar, China 143/G1
Kangnam, (mts.), NKor. 131/C3
Kangnŭng, SKor. 131/E4
Kangra, India 144/D3
Kangrinboqê (peak),
China 128/D5
Kangshan, Tai. 137/K9
Kangto (peak), China 141/F2
Kangwŏn-do (prov.),
SKor. 131/E4
Kanha NP, India 142/C4
Kani, Japan 135/M5
Kanie, Japan 135/L6
Kanin (pen.), Rus. 218/C
Kanin Nos (pt.), Rus. 118/J2
Kaniva, Austl. 173/B3
Kanjiza, Serb. 106/E2
Kankakee, Il, US 193/Q17
Kankan (pol. reg.),
Gui. 160/C4

Kankan, Gui. 160/C4
Kanmuri-yama (peak), Japan 132/C3
Kannami, Japan 135/B3
Kannapolis, NC, US 191/H3
Kannauj, India 142/B2
Kannon-zaki (pt.), Japan 135/D3
Kannus, Fin. 95/G3
Kano, Nga. 161/H4
Kano (state), Nga. 161/H4
Kan'onji, Japan 132/C3
Kanouse (mtn.), NJ, US 197/H7
Kanoya, Japan 132/B5
Kanra, Japan 135/B1
Kansai (int'l arpt.), Japan 135/C3
Kansai (isl.), Japan 135/H7
Kansas (state), US 187/H3
Kansas (riv.), Ks, US 195/D5
Kansas City (int'l arpt.), Mo, US 187/J3
Kansas City, Ks, US 195/D5
Kansas City, Mo, US 195/D5
Kansasville, Wi, US 193/P14
Kansk, Rus. 122/K4
Kansŏng, SKor. 131/E3
Kantábanji, India 140/D3
Känth, India 142/B1
Kantó (prov.), Japan 133/F2
Kantunilkin, Mex. 202/E3
Kanuku (mts.), Guy. 208/G3
Kanuma, Japan 133/F2
Kanye, Bots. 163/E5
Kaohsiung, Tai. 137/D3
Kaohsiung (int'l arpt.), Tai. 137/D3
Kaokoveld (mts.), Namb. 163/B4
Kaolack, Sen. 160/A3
Kaolack (pol. reg.), Sen. 160/B3
Kaolinovo, Bul. 107/H4
Kaoma, Zam. 163/D3
Kapaa, Hi, US 182/S9
Kapaahu, Hi, US 182/U11
Kapaau, Hi, US 182/U10
Kapalong, Phil. 137/E6
Kapan, Arm. 121/H5
Kapchorwa, Ugan. 162/B2
Kapellen, Belg. 108/C1
Kapenguria, Kenya 162/B2
Kapidaği (pen.), Turk. 107/H5
Kapingamarangi (isl.), Micr. 174/E4
Kapiri Mposhi, Zam. 163/E3
Kapiskau (riv.), On, Can. 181/H3
Kaplice, Czh. 113/H6
Kapos (riv.), Hun. 106/C2
Kaposvár, Hun. 106/C2
Kappl, Aus. 115/G3
Kapsan, NKor. 131/E2
Kapuas (riv.), Indo. 138/C4
Kapuas Hulu (mts.), Indo.,Malay. 138/D3
Kapunda, Austl. 171/H5
Kapürthala, India 144/C4
Kapuskasing, On, Can. 188/D1
Kapuskasing (riv.), On, Can. 188/D1
Kapuvár, Hun. 101/M3
Kapydzhik (peak), Azer. 121/H5
Kap'yŏng, SKor. 131/D4
Kara (riv.), Rus. 119/Q1
Kara (sea), Rus. 218/A3
Kara, Togo 161/F4
Kara-saki (pt.), Japan 132/A3
Karaali, Turk. 148/C2
Karabiğa, Turk. 107/H5
Karabük, Turk. 148/C1
Karaburun, Turk. 107/J5
Karaca (peak), Turk. 148/D2
Karacabey, Turk. 148/B1
Karacaköy, Turk. 107/J5
Karaçal (peak), Turk. 149/C1
Karacaoğlan, Turk.
Karachayevo-Cherkesiya, Resp., Rus. 121/G4
Karachev, Rus. 120/E1
Karāchi, Pak. 147/J4
Karadere, Turk. 107/K5
Karaginskiy (isl.), Rus. 125/R4
Karaj, Iran 146/F1
Karakax (riv.), China 147/L1
Karakaya (dam), Turk. 148/D2
Karakelong (isl.), Indo. 139/G3
Karakhoto (ruin), China 128/H3
Karakol, Kyr. 145/G4
Karakoram (range), India 144/D2
Karakoram (pass), India 144/D2
Karakoro (riv.), Mali 160/B3
Karakorum (ruin), Mong. 128/H2
Karakorum (ruin), Mong. 145/G5
Karakorum (pass), China 147/L1
Karaköse, Turk. 148/E2
Karakul' (lake), Taj. 145/F3
Karakumy (des.), Trkm. 122/F5

Karakyon (peak), Trkm. 145/B4
Karakyr (peak), Trkm. 147/H1
Karam (riv.), Indo. 139/E4
Karaman (prov.), Turk. 148/C2
Karaman, Turk. 148/C2
Karamay, China 128/D2
Karamea Bight (bay), NZ 175/S11
Kárpathos (prov.), Gre. 148/A3
Karamoja (prov.), Ugan. 162/B2
Karamürsel, Turk. 107/J5
Karangasem, Indo. 139/E5
Karratha, Austl. 170/C2
Karanginskiy (isl.), Rus. 123/S4
Karanginskiy (bay), Rus. 123/S4
Käranja, India 140/C3
Karanpur, India 144/B5
Karapınar, Turk. 148/C2
Karasabai, Guy. 211/G3
Karaşar, Turk. 107/L5
Karasburg, Namb. 164/B3
Karasjohka-Karasjok, Nor. 95/H1
Karasu, Turk. 107/K5
Karasu, Japan 135/L6
Karasuk, Rus. 145/G2
Karatá (lag.), Nic. 203/F3
Karataş, Turk. 149/D1
Karatoya (riv.), Bang. 143/G3
Karauli, India 142/A2
Karaurgan, Turk. 148/E1
Karáva (peak), Gre. 105/G3
Karawang, Indo. 138/C5
Karayaka, Turk. 120/F4
Karayazı, Turk. 148/E2
Karazhal, Kaz. 145/F3
Karbalā' (gov.), Iraq 148/E3
Karbalā', Iraq 148/F3
Karben, Ger. 112/B2
Karcag, Hun. 106/E2
Kardhámila, Gre. 105/K3
Kardhítsa, Gre. 105/G3
Kardhitsomagoúla, Gre. 105/G3
Kareha (riv.), India 143/E3
Karelí, India 142/B4
Karelia (reg.), Rus. 95/J2
Karelia, Resp., Rus. 122/D3
Karera, India 142/B3
Karesuando, Swe. 95/G1
Karêt (reg.), Mrta. 156/D4
Karf Ash Shaykh (gov.), 148/B4
Kargı, Turk. 148/C1
Kargil, India 144/D2
Karhijärvi (lake), Fin. 97/K1
Karhula, Fin. 97/M1
Kariá, Gre. 105/G3
Karia Ba Mohammed, Mor. 158/B2
Kariaí, Gre. 105/J2
Kāshīpur, India 142/B1
Karianga, Madg. 165/H8
Kariba (dam), Zam. 163/E4
Kariba (lake), Zam., Zim. 151/E6
Kariba, Zim. 163/E4
Kariba-yama (peak), Japan 134/A2
Karibib, Namb. 163/C5
Karimama, Ben. 161/F3
Karimata (isl.), Indo. 138/D4
Karimata (str.), Indo. 138/C4
Karīmnagar, India 140/C4
Karimunjawa (isls.), Indo. 138/D5
Kariótissa, Gre. 105/H2
Karise, Den. 96/E4
Karisimbi (vol.), D.R. Congo 162/A3
Karisimbi (vol.), Rwa. 163/E1
Káristos, Gre. 105/J3
Kariya, Japan 135/L6
Karkaar (mts.), Som. 155/C6
Kärkäl, India 140/B5
Karkar (isl.), PNG 174/D5
Karkinits'ka Zatoka (gulf), Ukr. 120/D3
Karkkila, Fin. 97/L1
Karkonoski NP, Pol. 99/H3
Karla Marksa (peak), Taj. 147/K1
Karlholmsbruk, Swe. 96/G1
Karlino, Pol. 96/F4
Karlovarský (pol. reg.), Czh. 113/F2
Karlovo, Bul. 105/J1
Karlovy Vary, Czh. 113/F2
Karlsdorf-Neuthard, Ger. 112/B4
Karlsfeld, Ger. 113/E6
Karlshamn, Swe. 96/F3
Karlshuld, Ger. 112/E5
Karlskoga, Swe. 96/F2
Karlskron, Ger. 113/E6
Karlskrona, Swe. 96/F3
Karlsruhe, Ger. 112/B4
Karlstad, Swe. 96/E2
Karlstadt, Ger. 112/C3
Karlstein am Main, Ger. 112/C2
Karluk, Ak, US 192/H4
Karmāla, India 147/L5
Karnali (riv.), Nepal 142/C1
Karnali (zone), Nepal 142/C1
Karnaphuli (res.), Bang. 143/H4
Karnataka (state), India 140/C4

Karnes City, Tx, US 187/H5
Karnobat, Bul. 105/K1
Kärnten (prov.), Aus. 101/K3
Karonga, Malw. 162/B5
Karoo NP, SAfr. 164/D4
Karoo NP, SAfr. 164/C4
Karoonda, Austl. 173/A2
Karor, Pak. 144/A4
Karoso (cape), Indo. 139/E5
Kárpathos, Gre. 148/A3
Kárpathos (isl.), Gre. 148/A3
Karpatskiy NP, Ukr. 107/G1
Karpenision, Gre. 105/G3
Karratha, Austl. 170/C2
Kars, Turk. 148/E1
Kars (prov.), Turk. 148/E1
Kars (riv.), Turk. 121/G4
Kärsämäki, Fin. 118/E3
Karsantı, Turk. 148/C2
Karshi (int'l arpt.), Uzb. 145/E5
Kārthmāndu (cap.), Nepal 143/E2
Kartárpur, India 144/C4
Kartuzy, Pol. 96/H4
Karuah, Austl. 173/D2
Karuma (falls), Ugan. 162/B2
Karumba, Austl. 172/A2
Karūn (riv.), Iran 146/E2
Karup, Den. 96/C3
Karvinná, Czh. 99/K4
Karwár, India 149/A1
Kaş, Den. 96/C3
Kasaan, Ak, US 192/M4
Kasabonika (lake), On, Can. 185/L2
Kasagi, Japan 135/J6
Kasahara, Japan 135/M5
Kasai (riv.), India 143/F4
Kasai, Japan 132/D3
Kasai (riv.), D.R. Congo 163/C1
Kasama, Zam. 163/G2
Kasamatsu, Japan 135/L5
Kasane, Bots. 163/E4
Kasaoka, Japan 132/C3
Kasar (cape), Sudan 159/D5
Kāsaragod, India 140/C5
Kasartori-yama (peak), Japan 135/K6
Kasba (lake), NW,Nun., Can. 180/F2
Kasba Tadla, Mor. 156/D2
Kaseda, Japan 132/B5
Kasese, Ugan. 162/A2
Kashaf (riv.), Iran 147/H1
Käshän, Iran 146/F2
Kashi, China 145/G5
Kashiba, Japan 135/J6
Kashihara, Japan 135/J6
Kashima, Japan 132/B4
Kashima, Japan 133/G3
Kashima (bay), Japan 135/F1
Kashin, Rus. 118/H4
Kashipur, India 142/B1
Kashiwa, Japan 135/D2
Kashiwara, Japan 135/J6
Kashiwazaki, Japan 133/F2
Kashmir (reg.), India,Pak. 145/G5
Kashmüng Ghar (range), Afg. 144/A2
Kasigau (peak), Kenya 162/C3
Kasigluk, Ak, US 192/F3
Kasilof, Ak, US 192/H3
Kasimov, Rus. 118/J5
Kasiruta (isl.), Indo. 139/G4
Kasiui (isl.), Indo. 139/H4
Kaskaskia (riv.), Il, US 187/K3
Kaslo, BC, Can. 184/D3
Kasongo, D.R. Congo 163/E1
Kásos (isl.), Gre. 148/A3
Kaspichan, Bul. 107/H4
Kaspiysk, Rus. 121/H4
Kassala, Sudan 146/C5
Kassándra (pen.), Gre. 105/H2
Kassándra (pen.), Gre. 105/H3
Kassel, Ger. 109/G6
Kasserine, Tun. 158/L7
Kasserine (gov.), Tun. 158/L7
Kassikaityu (riv.), Guy. 211/G4
Kassler, Co, US 195/B4
Kasson, Mn, US 185/K4
Kastamonu, Turk. 148/C1
Kastamonu (prov.), Turk. 148/C1
Kastanéai, Gre. 105/K2
Kaštel Stari, Cro. 106/C4
Kaštel Sućurac, Cro. 106/C4
Kastéllaun, Ger. 111/G3
Kastéllion, Gre. 105/J5
Kasterlee, Belg. 108/B6
Kastl, Ger. 113/E4
Kastoria, Gre. 105/G2
Kastrakíou (lake), Gre. 105/G3
Kasuga, Japan 135/H5
Kasuga, Japan 135/D2
Kasugai, Japan 135/L5
Kasukabe, Japan 133/F3
Kasumiga (lake), Japan 133/G2
Kasungu, Malw. 163/F3
Kaşūr, Pak. 144/C4
Kat O Chau (isl.), China 129/V9
Katahdin (mt.), Me, US 189/G2

Katákolon, Gre. 105/G4
Katanga (reg.), D.R. Congo 163/D2
Katanga (pol. reg.), D.R. Congo 162/A5
Katangi, India 142/B4
Katanning, Austl. 170/C5
Katano, Japan 135/J6
Katastárion, Gre. 105/G4
Katavi NP, Tanz. 162/A4
Katavi NP, Tanz. 163/C1
Katchall (isl.), India 141/F6
Katerini, Gre. 105/H2
Kates Needle (peak), Ak, US 192/M4
Katete, Zam. 163/F3
Katghora, India 142/B1
Käthgodām, India 142/B1
Kathiawar (pen.), India 147/K4
Kathleen (mt.), Austl. 171/G2
Kathu, India 141/G3
Kati, Mali 160/C3
Katiola, C.d'Iv. 160/D4
Katlehong, SAfr. 164/E2
Katlenburg-Lindau, Ger. 109/H5
Katmai (vol.), Ak, US 192/H4
Katmai NP, Ak, US 192/G4
Káto Akhaïa, Gre. 105/G3
Katokhí, Gre. 105/G3
Katonah, NY, US 197/E1
Katonga (riv.), Ugan. 162/A2
Katoúna, Gre. 105/G3
Katowice, Pol. 99/K3
Katra, India 143/F4
Käträs, India 143/F4
Katrine (lake), Sc, UK 94/B4
Katrineholm, Swe. 96/G2
Katsikás, Gre. 105/G3
Katsina (state), Nga. 161/G3
Katsina, Nga. 161/G3
Katsina Ala (riv.), Nga. 161/H5
Katsunuma, Japan 135/B2
Katsura (riv.), Japan 135/J5
Katsuragi, Japan 132/D3
Katsuragi (prov.), Turk. 148/C2
Katsuragi-san (peak), Japan 135/H7
Katsuta, Japan 133/G3
Katsuura, Japan 133/G3
Katsuyama, Indo. 138/B4
Katsuyama, Japan 135/B3
Kattakurgan, Uzb. 145/E5
Kattegat (str.), Den. 96/D3
Katumbi, Malw. 162/B5
Kätwa, India 143/G4
Katwe-Kabatooro, Ugan. 162/A3
Katwijk aan Zee, Neth. 108/B4
Katy, Tx, US 187/J5
Katzenbach (riv.), Ger. 112/B4
Katzenelnbogen, Ger. 111/G3
Katzhütte, Ger. 112/D1
Katzwinkel, Ger. 111/F3
Kau-ye (isl.), Myan. 136/B4
Kauai (chan.), Hi, US 182/S10
Kauai (isl.), Hi, US 182/S9
Kaufbeuren, Ger. 115/G1
Kaufering, Ger. 115/G1
Kaufungen, Ger. 109/G6
Kauhava, Fin. 118/D3
Kauhola (pt.), Hi, US 182/U10
Kauiki (pt.), Hi, US 182/U10
Kaukaveld (uplands), Namb. 163/C5
Kaukura (isl.), FrPol. 175/L6
Kaulakahi (chan.), Hi, US 182/R9
Kaulsdorf, Ger. 113/E1
Kaumalapau, Hi, US 182/T10
Kauna (pt.), Hi, US 182/T10
Kaunakakai, Hi, US 182/T10
Kaunas (int'l arpt.), Lith. 97/K4
Kaunas (res.), Lith. 97/L4
Kaunas, Lith. 97/K4
Kaupanger, Nor. 96/B1
Kauttua, Fin. 97/K1
Kavadarci, FYROM 105/H2
Kavajë, Alb. 105/F2
Kavála, Gre. 105/J2
Kavalerovo, Rus. 129/Q3
Kävali, India 140/C5
Kavangel (isls.), Palau 174/C4
Kavaratti, India 140/B5
Kavarna, Bul. 107/J4
Kavgolovskoye (lake), Rus. 119/T6
Kavieng, PNG 174/E5
Kavîr-e Namak (dry lake), Iran 145/C6
Kävlinge, Swe. 96/E4
Kaw (lake), Ok, US 187/J8
Kawa (ruin), Sudan 159/B2
Kawabe, Japan 134/B3
Kawachi, Japan 135/E2
Kawachi-Nagano, Japan 135/J7

Kawaihoa (pt.), Hi, US 182/R10
Kawaikini (peak), Hi, US 182/S9
Kawajima, Japan 135/C2
Kawakami, Japan 135/B2
Kawakami, Japan 133/G2
Kawamata, Japan 133/G2
Kawambwa, Zam. 162/A5
Kawanishi, Japan 135/H6
Kawanishi, Japan 135/J6
Kawardha, India 142/C4
Kawarau (lakes), On, Can. 188/D2
Kawasaki, Japan 133/F3
Kawasato, Japan 135/D1
Kawashima, Japan 135/L5
Kawaue, Japan 135/M4
Kawela (Kawela Bay), Hi, US 182/V12
Kawerau, NZ 175/T10
Kawlin, Myan. 141/G3
Kawthaung, Myan. 136/B4
Kax (riv.), China 128/D3
Kay (pt.), Yk, Can. 192/L2
Kaya, SKor. 131/E5
Kaya, Japan 135/H5
Kaya-san (peak), SKor. 131/D4
Kayadibi, Turk. 148/C2
Kayagangiri (peak), CAfr. 154/J6
Kayah (state), Myan. 141/G4
Kayan (riv.), Indo. 139/E3
Kayanga (riv.), Sen. 160/B3
Kaycee, Wy, US 184/G5
Kayenta, Az, US 186/E3
Kayes, Mali 160/C3
Kayes (pol. reg.), Mali 160/C3
Kayin (state), Myan. 141/G4
Kayl, Lux. 111/F5
Kaymaz, Turk. 107/K5
Kaynarca, Turk. 107/K5
Kayoa (isl.), Indo. 139/G3
Kayrakkum (lake), Kayser (mts.), Sur. 211/G3
Kayseri, Turk. 148/C2
Kayseri (prov.), Turk. 148/C2
Kaysersberg, Fr. 114/D1
Kaysville, Ut, US 195/K11
Kayuagung, Indo. 138/B4
Kazakhstan (ctry.) 122/G5
Kazan', Rus. 119/L5
Kazan (int'l arpt.), Rus. 119/L5
Kazan (riv.), Nun., Can. 180/F2
Kazancı, Turk. 149/C1
Kazanlı, Turk. 149/D1
Kazanlŭk, Bul. 105/J1
Kazbek (peak), Geo. 121/H4
Käzerūn, Iran 146/F3
Kazgan (riv.), China 128/C4
Kazımkarabekir, Turk. 148/C2
Kazincbarcika, Hun. 99/L3
Kazo, Japan 135/D1
Kazuno, Japan 134/B3
Ke Ga (cape), Viet. 136/E4
Ké Macina, Mali 160/D3
Kéa (isl.), Gre. 105/J4
Kéa, Gre. 105/J4
Keaau, Hi, US 182/U11
Keady, NI, UK 92/B3
Keahole (pt.), Hi, US 182/T11
Keansburg, NJ, US 197/J10
Kearney, Mo, US 187/H2
Kearney, Ne, US 187/H3
Kearns, Ut, US 195/E5
Kearny, NJ, US 197/J8
Kearny (pt.), NI, UK 92/C3
Keawakapu, Hi, US 182/T10
Keawekaheka (pt.), Hi, US 182/U11
Keban (dam), Turk. 148/D2
Kebbi (state), Nga. 161/G4
Kébémer, Sen. 160/A3
Kebili, Tun. 158/M6
Kebnekaise (peak), Swe. 95/F2
Kebumen, Indo. 138/C5
Kecel, Hun. 106/D2
Keçiborlu, Turk. 148/B2
Kecskemét, Hun. 106/D2
Kedah (state), Malay. 136/C5
Kedainiai, Lith. 97/K4
Kédougou, Sen. 160/B3
Kédougou (prov.), Burk. 160/B3
Keego Harbor, Mi, US 193/F6
Keele (riv.), NW, Can. 180/D2
Keelung, Tai. 137/D2
Keelung, Japan 133/G8
Keen (mt.), Sc, UK 94/D3
Keepit (dam), Austl. 173/D1
Keer-Weer (cape), Austl. 172/A1
Keetmanshoop, Namb. 164/B2
Keewatin, Ire. 89/H1
Kefallinía (isl.), Gre. 105/G3
Kefar Sava, Isr. 149/F7
Kefar Vitkin, Isr. 149/F7

Keflavík, Ice. 95/M7
Keflavík (int'l arpt.), Ice. 95/M7
Kehl, Ger. 114/D1
Kehrsatz, Swi. 114/D4
Keighley, Eng, UK 93/G4
Keihoku, Japan 135/J5
Keimoes, SAfr. 164/C3
Kéita (riv.), Chad 155/J6
Keith, Austl. 173/B3
Keith, Sc, UK 94/D1
Kejimkujik NP, NS, Can. 189/H2
Kekaha, Hi, US 182/S10
Kékes (peak), Hun. 99/K5
Kelan, China 130/B3
Kelang (isl.), Indo. 139/G4
Kelang, Malay. 138/B3
Kelberg, Ger. 111/F3
Kelbra, Ger. 109/H5
Kelheim, Ger. 113/E5
Kelkheim, Ger. 112/B2
Kelkıt, Turk. 120/F4
Kelkıt (riv.), Turk. 148/D1
Kell, Ger. 111/F4
Kellenhusen, Ger. 96/D4
Keller (peak), Ca, US 194/C2
Keller (lake), Wi, US 193/P14
Kellerberrin, Austl. 170/C4
Kellogg, Id, US 184/D4
Kells, NI, UK 92/B2
Kélo, Chad 154/J6
Kelowna, BC, Can. 184/D3
Kelsey (pt.), Eng, UK 90/A6
Kelso, Wa, US 184/C4
Kelso, Sc, UK 94/D5
Kelsterbach, Ger. 112/B2
Keluang, Malay. 138/B3
Kelvington, Sk, Can. 185/H2
Kem', Rus. 118/G2
Kemah, Turk. 120/F5
Kemaliye, Turk. 148/D2
Kemalpaşa, Turk. 148/E1
Kemasik, Malay. 138/B3
Kematen an der Ybbs, Aus. 113/H6
Kematen in Tirol, Aus. 115/H3
Kembs, Fr. 114/D2
Kemena (riv.), Malay. 138/D2
Kemence, Hun. 99/K4
Kemer, Turk. 149/B1
Kemer i Gjuhëzës (cape), Alb. 105/F2
Kemerovo, Rus. 122/J4
Kemerovskaya Oblast, Rus. 122/J4
Kemi, Fin. 95/H2
Kemijärvi, Fin. 118/E2
Kemijoki (riv.), Fin. 95/H2
Kemmerer, Wy, US 184/F5
Kemnath, Ger. 113/E3
Kemnay, Austl. 173/B2
Kemp (lake), Tx, US 187/H4
Kempele, Fin. 118/E2
Kempen, Ger. 108/D6
Kempenich, Ger. 111/F3
Kempenland (phys. reg.), Belg. 108/C6
Kempisch Kanaal (canal), Belg. 111/E1
Kempsey, Austl. 173/E1
Kempston, Eng, UK 91/F2
Kempt (res.), Qu, Can. 188/F2
Kempten, Ger. 115/G2
Kempton, Austl. 173/C4
Kempton Park, SAfr. 164/Q13
Kemptown, Md, US 196/A5
Kemri, India 142/B1
Kemul (peak), Indo. 139/E3
Ken (riv.), India 142/C3
Ken (lake), Sc, UK 94/C5
Ken-zaki (pt.), Japan 135/B3
Kenadsa, Alg. 157/F3
Kenai, Ak, US 192/H3
Kenai Fjords NP, Ak, US 192/H4
Kendal, Eng, UK 93/F3
Kendal, Indo. 138/J14
Kendalia, NZ 175/T20
Kendall, Austl. 173/E1
Kendall (co.), Il, US 193/P16
Kendall (co.), Tx, US 195/T20
Kendall Park, NJ, US 196/D3
Kendallville, In, US 188/C3
Kéndavros, Gre. 105/J2
Kéndari, Indo. 139/F4
Kenedy, Tx, US 187/H5
Kenge, D.R. Congo 163/C1
Kenhardt, SAfr. 164/C3
Kenhorst, Pa, US 196/C3
Kenié-Baoulé, Réserve de, Mali 160/C3
Kenilworth, Eng, UK 91/E2
Kenilworth, NJ, US 197/H9
Kenli, China 130/D3
Kenmare, ND, US 185/H3
Kenmare, Ire. 89/H1
Kenmare (riv.), Ire. 89/H1
Kenmore, NY, US 189/S10
Kenmore, Wa, US 195/C2
Kenmore, Austl. 172/A1
Kenn (reef), Austl. 167/E4

Kenn, Ger. 111/F4
Kennebec (riv.), Me, US 189/G2
Kennebunk, Me, US 189/G3
Kennedy (chan.), Grld.,Nun., Can. 181/T6
Kennedy (range), Austl. 170/B3
Kennedy Entrance (chan.) 192/H4
Kennedyville, Md, US 196/C5
Kettering, Eng, UK 91/F2
Kennelbach, Aus. 115/F3
Kennemerduinen, NP de, Neth. 108/B4
Kenner, La, US 195/P17
Kenner and Avon (canal), Eng, UK 90/C4
Kenneth, Ks, US 195/D6
Kenneth, Mo, US 187/K3
Kennett Square, Pa, US 196/C4
Kennewick, Wa, US 184/D4
Kennewick, Wa, US 184/D4
Kenogami (riv.), On, Can. 181/H3
Kenora, On, Can. 185/K3
Kenosha, Wi, US 193/Q14
Kenosha (co.), Wi, US 193/P14
Kensico (res.), NY, US 197/K7
Kensington and Chelsea (bor.), Eng, UK 88/A1
Kent (pen.), Nun., Can. 180/G2
Kent (co.), On, Can. 193/G6
Kent (riv.), Eng, UK 93/F3
Kent, Oh, US 188/D3
Kent (lake), Mi, US 193/E7
Kent, Wa, US 195/C3
Kent County (int'l arpt.), Mi, US 188/C3
Kent Group (isls.), Austl. 173/C3
Kentaü, Kaz. 145/E4
Kenton, De, US 196/C5
Kenton, Oh, US 188/D3
Kentucky (state), US 191/G2
Kentucky (riv.), Ky, US 188/C4
Kentucky (lake), Ky, US 191/F2
Kentville, NS, Can. 189/H2
Kenya (ctry.) 162/C2
Kenzingen, Ger. 114/D1
Keonjhar, India 140/E3
Keppel Sands, Austl. 172/C3
Kerala (state), India 140/C5
Keran, PN de la, Togo 161/F4
Kerang, Austl. 173/B2
Keratéa, Gre. 105/N9
Kerava, Fin. 97/L1
Kerch' (str.), Rus.,Ukr. 120/F3
Kerch, Ukr. 120/F3
Keremeos, BC, Can. 184/D3
Kerempe Burnu (cape), Turk. 148/C1
Keren, Erit. 146/C5
Kerepestarcsa, Hun. 99/J4
Kergüelen (isl.), Fr. 81/N8
Kericho, Kenya 162/B3
Kerikeri (cape), NZ 175/S9
Kerinci (mt.), Indo. 138/B4
Kerio (riv.), Kenya 162/C2
Kerio Valley Nat'l Rsv., Kenya 162/B3
Kerkdriel, Neth. 108/C5
Kerkenah (isl.), Tun. 157/H2
Kerki, Trkm. 145/E5
Kerkinis (lake), Gre. 105/H2
Kerkrade, Neth. 111/F2
Kerkwijk, Neth. 108/C5
Kermadec (isls.), NZ 174/G8
Kermān, Iran 147/G2
Kermānshāh, Iran 146/E2
Kermit, Tx, US 186/D4
Kern, South Kern (riv.), Ca, US 194/C4
Kerns, Swi. 115/E4
Kéros (isl.), Gre. 105/J4
Kérou, Ben. 161/F4
Kerr (lake), Ok, US 187/J4
Kerr (res.), NC,Va, US 191/J2
Kerrobert, Sk, Can. 184/F3
Kerrville, Tx, US 187/H5
Kert (riv.), Mor. 158/C2
Kerulen (riv.), Mong. 129/K3
Kerzaz, Alg. 157/F3
Kerzenheim, Ger. 111/H4
Kerzers, Swi. 114/D3
Kesagami (riv.), On, Can. 188/D1
Keşan, Turk. 105/K2
Kesen'numa, Japan 134/B4
Keshod, India 140/B3
Keshan, China
Keski-Suomi (prov.), Fin. 95/H3
Keskin, Turk. 148/C1
Kessel, Neth. 108/D5
Kesselbach (riv.), Ger. 112/C4
Kestel, Turk. 148/B1
Kesteren, Neth. 108/C5

Keszthely, Hun. 106/C2
Keť (riv.), Rus. 122/J4
Keta, Gha. 161/F5
Keta (riv.), Rus. 122/K3
Ketchikan, Ak, US 192/M4
Kete Krachi, Gha. 161/E5
Ketelmeer (lake), Neth. 108/C3
Kétou, Ben. 161/F5
Kętrzyn, Pol. 97/K2
Ketsch, Ger. 112/B4
Kettering, Eng, UK 91/F2
Kettle (riv.), Mn, US 184/D3
Kettle Moraine State Forest, Wi, US 193/P14
Ketzin, Ger. 98/P7
Keukenhof, Neth. 108/B4
Kevelaer, Ger. 108/D5
Kewaunee, Wi, US 188/C2
Keweenaw (pen.), Mi, US 185/L4
Keweenaw (pt.), Mi, US 185/M4
Keweenaw (bay), Mi, US 185/L4
Key Largo, Fl, US 191/H5
Key West, Fl, US 191/H5
Keymar, Md, US 196/A4
Keyport, NJ, US 197/J10
Keyser, WV, US 193/B2
Keystone (lake), Ok, US 187/H3
Kežmarok, Slvk. 99/L4
Khaanziir (cape), Som. 155/Q5
Khabarovsk, Rus. 129/Q2
Khabarovskiy Kray, Rus. 123/P4
Khagaria, India 143/F3
Khair, India 142/A2
Khairābād, India 142/C2
Khairpur, Pak. 144/B5
Khairpur, Pak. 147/J3
Khakasiya, Resp., Rus. 123/P6
Khalándrion, Gre. 105/N8
Khalīlābād, India 142/D2
Khalkhāl, Iran 146/E1
Khalkhidhikhi (pen.), Gre. 105/H2
Khalkidhón, Gre. 105/H3
Khalkís, Gre. 105/H3
Khamar-Daban (mts.), Rus. 128/H1
Khambhāliya, India 147/J4
Khambhat, India 147/K4
Khamīs Mushayt, SAr. 146/D5
Khammam, India 140/D4
Khamr, Yem. 146/D5
Khān Yūnus, Gaza 149/D4
Khānābād, Afg. 147/J1
Khānaqīn, Iraq 148/F3
Khandwa, India 147/L4
Khanem (well), Alg. 157/F3
Khānewāl, Pak. 144/A4
Khāngāh Dogrān, Pak. 144/B4
Khāngarh, Pak. 144/A4
Khaniá, Gre. 105/J5
Khanka (lake), China,Rus. 129/P3
Khanna, India 144/C4
Khānpur, Pak. 144/A5
Khanty-Mansiysk, Rus. 122/G3
Khanty-Mansiyskiy Aut. Okrug, Rus. 122/G3
Khao Chamao-Khao Wong NP, Thai. 136/C3
Khao Khitchakut NP, Thai. 136/C3
Khao Laem (res.), Thai. 141/G4
Khao Sam Roi Yot NP, Thai. 136/B3
Khao Yai NP, Thai. 136/C3
Kharagpur, India 143/F4
Kharagpur, India 143/F3
Kharak, Pak. 144/A3
Khārān, Pak. 147/J3
Kharar, India 143/F4
Kharar, India 144/C4
Kharbatā, Isr. 149/G8
Khargon, India 144/B3
Khārīān, Pak. 144/B3
Kharkiv, Ukr. 120/F2
Kharkiv (int'l arpt.), Ukr. 120/F2
Kharkivs'ka Oblasti, Ukr. 120/F2
Kharmanli, Rus. 105/J2
Kharovsk, Rus. 118/J4
Kharrour (riv.), Mor. 158/B2
Kharsia, India 142/C4
Khartoum (Kharṭūm) (cap.), Sudan 146/B5
Khartoum (Kharṭūm) (prov.), Sudan 146/B5
Khasavyurt, Rus. 121/H4
Khāsh (riv.), Afg. 147/H2
Khāsh, Iran 147/H3
Khasi (hills), India 143/H3
Khaskovo (pol. reg.), Bul.
Khaskovo (prov.), Bul. 105/J2
Khatanga, Rus. 218/J2
Khatanga (gulf), Rus. 123/J2
Khatauli, India 144/D5
Khātegaon, India 142/B1
Khatma, India 142/B1
Khatlon (obl.), Taj. 145/E2
Khatmia (pass), Egypt 149/C4

Khātra, India 143/F4
Khatt Atoui (riv.), Mrta. 154/B3
Khaur, Pak. 144/B3
Khaybar (pass), Afg. 144/A2
Khazzān Dūkān (res.), Iraq 148/F3
Khazzān Jabal Al Awliyā (dam), Sudan 155/M4
Khekra, India 144/D5
Khemis el Khechna, Alg. 158/G4
Khemis Miliana, Alg. 158/G4
Khémisset (prov.), Mor. 158/A3
Khémisset, Mor. 158/A3
Khenchela (prov.), Alg. 157/K2
Khenchela, Alg. 158/K7
Khénifra, Mor. 156/D2
Khepoyarvi (lake), Rus. 119/T6
Kheri, India 142/C2
Khersān (riv.), Iran 146/F2
Kherson, Ukr. 107/L2
Kherson (int'l arpt.), Ukr. 107/L2
Khersons'ka Oblasti, Ukr. 120/E3
Khilok, Rus. 129/K1
Khimki, Rus. 119/W9
Khios, Gre. 105/K3
Khios (isl.), Gre. 105/J3
Khirpai, India 143/F4
Khisarya, Bul. 105/J1
Khiva, Uzb. 145/D4
Khlebarovo, Bul. 107/H4
Khmel'nyts'ka Oblasti, Ukr. 120/C2
Khmel'nytskyy, Ukr. 120/C2
Kho Sawai (plat.), Thai. 141/H4
Khodzheyli, Uzb. 145/C4
Khojak (pass), Pak. 147/J2
Kholm, Afg. 147/J1
Kholmsk, Rus. 129/R2
Khomeynishahr, Iran 146/F2
Khon Kaen, Thai. 136/C2
Khopër (riv.), Rus. 122/F4
Khor (riv.), Rus. 123/P5
Khóra Sfakíon, Gre. 105/J3
Khorazm (pol. reg.), Uzb. 145/D4
Khoríon, Gre. 148/A2
Khorramābād, Iran 146/F3
Khorramshahr, Iran 146/E2
Khorugh, Taj. 145/D5
Khotol (mtn.), Ak, US 192/G3
Khouribga, Mor. 156/D2
Khowai, India 141/F3
Khrisoúpolis, Gre. 105/J2
Khromtaū, Kaz. 121/J2
Khrysi (isl.), Gre. 105/J5
Khuan Ubon Ratana (lake), Thai. 136/C2
Khudian, Pak. 144/C4
Khuis, Bots. 164/C2
Khujand, Taj. 145/E4
Khulna (pol. div.), Bang. 143/G4
Khünjeräb (pass), Pak. 147/L1
Khunjerab NP, Pak. 145/G5
Khunti, India 143/B3
Khurai, India 142/B3
Khurda, India 140/E3
Khurja, India 142/A1
Khushāb, Pak. 144/B3
Khust, Ukr. 99/M4
Khūtär, India 142/C1
Khuzdār, Pak. 147/J3
Khvalynka, Rus. 129/P3
Khvonsār, Iran 146/F2
Khvor, Iran 147/G2
Khvoy, Iran 121/H5
Khwaja Rawash (int'l arpt.), Afg. 145/K6
Khyber (pass), Pak. 144/A2
Kia, Sol. 174/E5
Kiama, Austl. 173/D2
Kiamichi (mts.), Ok, US 190/E3
Kiana, Ak, US 192/F2
Kibæk, Den. 96/C3
Kibali (riv.), D.R. Congo 162/A2
Kibergneset (pt.), Nor. 95/J2
Kibo (Kilimanjaro) (peak), Tanz. 162/C3
Kiboga, Ugan. 162/A1
Kibrişcik, Turk. 107/K5
Kibwezi, Kenya 162/C3
Kičevo, FYROM 105/G2
Kichha, India 142/B1
Kickapoo, Ks, US 195/D5
Kidal, Mali 161/F2
Kidal (pol. reg.), Mali 161/F2
Kidapawan, Phil. 139/G2
Kidderminster, Eng, UK 90/D2
Kidepo Valley NP, Ugan. 155/M7
Kidsgrove, Eng, UK 93/F5
Kiel (bay), Den. 95/D5
Kiel, Ger. 96/D4
Kielce, Pol. 99/L3
Kielder (res.), Eng, UK 93/F1
Kien An, Viet. 136/D1
Kierspe, Ger. 111/G4

Kiev (Kyyiv) (cap.), Ukr. 120/D2
Kiffa, Mrta. 160/C2
Kifisiá, Gre. 105/N8
Kigali (cap.), Rwa. 162/A3
Kigali (Gregoire Kayibanda) (int'l arpt.), Rwa. 162/A3
Kiği, Turk. 148/E2
Kigoma (pol. reg.), Tanz. 162/A4
Kigoma, Tanz. 162/A4
Kigye, SKor. 131/E4
Kihei, Hi, US 182/T10
Kihnu (isl.), Est. 97/L2
Kiholo, Hi, US 182/U11
Kihti (str.), Fin. 97/J1
Kii (chan.), Japan 132/D4
Kii (mts.), Japan 132/D4
Kijang, SKor. 131/E5
Kikai (isl.), Japan 133/L6
Kikepa (pt.), Hi, US 182/R9
Kikiktat (mtn.), Ak, US 192/H2
Kikinda, Serb. 106/E3
Kikonai, Japan 134/B3
Kikwit, D.R. Congo 163/C2
Kil, Swe. 96/E2
Kilafors, Swe. 96/G1
Kilauea, Hi, US 182/S9
Kilbarchan, Sc, UK 94/B5
Kilberry, Ire. 89/Q10
Kilbirnie, Sc, UK 94/B5
Kilbrannan (sound), Sc, UK 94/A5
Kilchoan, Sc, UK 89/Q8
Kilchu, NKor. 131/E2
Kilcoole, Ire. 92/B5
Kilcormac, Ire. 89/Q10
Kilcoy, Austl. 172/D4
Kildare, Ire. 89/Q10
Kildeer, Il, US 193/P15
Kil'den (isl.), Rus. 118/G1
Kilembe Estates, Ugan. 162/A2
Kilgarvan, Ire. 89/P11
Kilgore, Tx, US 187/J4
Kilian (isl.), Nun., Can. 180/E1
Kilifi, Kenya 162/C3
Kilimanjaro (pol. reg.), Tanz. 162/C3
Kilimanjaro (int'l arpt.), Tanz. 162/C3
Kilimanjaro NP, Tanz. 162/C3
Kilimli, Turk. 107/K5
Kilinochchi, SrL. 140/D6
Kilis, Turk. 149/E1
Kiliya, Ukr. 107/J3
Kilkee, Ire. 89/N10
Kilkeel, NI, UK 92/B3
Kilkenny (co.), Ire. 92/A6
Kilkenny, Ire. 92/A6
Kilkis, Gre. 105/H2
Kilkivan, Austl. 172/D4
Kill, Ire. 89/Q10
Kill Van Kull (riv.), NJ,NY, US 197/J9
Killam, Ab, Can. 184/F2
Killarney, Austl. 173/E1
Killarney, Mb, Can. 185/J3
Killarney, Ire. 89/P10
Killarney NP, Ire. 89/P10
Killdeer, ND, US 185/H4
Killearn, Sc, UK 94/B4
Killeen, Tx, US 187/H5
Killenaule, Ire. 89/Q10
Killiecrankie, Pass of (pass), Sc, UK 94/C3
Killin, Sc, UK 94/B4
Killinchy, NI, UK 92/C3
Killinek (isl.), Nun., Can. 181/K2
Killini (peak), Gre. 105/H4
Killini, Gre. 105/G4
Killorglin, Ire. 89/N10
Killough, NI, UK 92/C3
Killybegs, Ire. 89/P9
Killyclogher, NI, UK 92/A2
Killyleagh, NI, UK 92/C3
Kilmacanogue, Ire. 92/B5
Kilmacolm, Sc, UK 94/B5
Kilmacow, Ire. 89/Q10
Kilmallock, Ire. 89/P10
Kilmar Tor (hill), Eng, UK 90/B5
Kilmarnock, Sc, UK 94/B5
Kilmaurs, Sc, UK 94/B5
Kilmichael (pt.), Ire. 92/B6
Kilmore, Austl. 173/C3
Kilmore Quay, Ire. 89/Q10
Kilombero (riv.), Tanz. 162/C5
Kilosa, Tanz. 162/C4
Kilraghts, NI, UK 92/B1
Kilrea, NI, UK 92/B2
Kilrush, Ire. 89/P10
Kilsyth, Sc, UK 94/B5
Kilwa Kivinje, Tanz. 162/C5
Kilwinning, Sc, UK 94/B5
Kimba, Austl. 171/H5
Kimball, SD, US 185/J5
Kimbe, PNG 174/E5
Kimberley (cape), Austl. 172/B2
Kimberley (plat.), Austl. 167/B2
Kimberley, BC, Can. 184/E3
Kimberley, SAfr. 164/D3
Kimch'aek, NKor. 131/E2
Kimch'ŏn, SKor. 131/E4
Kimhae, SKor. 131/E5
Kimhae (int'l arpt.), SKor. 131/E5
Kimi, Gre. 105/J3
Kimina, Gre. 105/H2

Kimitsu, Japan 133/F3
Kimje, SKor. 131/D5
Kimméria, Gre. 105/J2
Kimmirut, Nun., Can. 181/K2
Kimolos (isl.), Gre. 105/J4
Kimp'o, SKor. 131/F6
Kimp'o (int'l arpt.), SKor. 131/F6
Kimpō-zan (peak), Japan 135/B2
Kimry, Rus. 118/H4
Kinabalu (peak), Malay. 139/E2
Kinabatangan (riv.), Malay. 139/E2
Kinango, Kenya 162/C4
Kinbasket (lake), BC, Can. 184/D2
Kinbrace, Sc, UK 89/S7
Kincaid, Sk, Can. 184/G3
Kincardine, On, Can. 188/D2
Kincardine, Sc, UK 94/C4
Kinchega NP, Austl. 173/B2
Kinder Scout (peak), Eng, UK 93/G5
Kindersley, Sk, Can. 184/F3
Kindia, Gui. 160/B4
Kindia (pol. reg.), Gui. 160/B4
Kinding, Ger. 113/E5
Kindsbach, Ger. 111/G5
Kindu, D.R. Congo 163/C1
Kinel', Rus. 121/J1
Kineshma, Rus. 118/J4
King (lake), Austl. 170/C5
King (mt.), Austl. 172/B4
King (sound), Austl. 167/B2
King (riv.), BC, Can. 184/B2
King (mt.), BC, Can. 192/N4
King (peak), Yk, Can. 192/K3
King (co.), Wa, US 193/D2
King Christian (isl.), Nun., Can. 181/R7
Kingling, Sk, Can. 185/H3
King Christian IX Land (reg.), Grld. 177/P3
King Christian X Land (reg.), Grld. 177/Q2
King City, Ca, US 186/B3
King Cove, Ak, US 192/F4
King Frederik VI Coast (reg.), Grld. 177/N3
King Frederik VIII Land (reg.), Grld. 177/Q2
King George (isls.), FrPol. 175/L6
King George Is. (isls.), Qu, Can. 181/J3
King George's (res.), Eng, UK 88/C2
King Leopold (ranges), Austl. 167/B2
King of Prussia, Pa, US 196/C3
King Salmon, Ak, US 192/G4
King William (isl.), Nun., Can. 180/G2
King William's Town, SAfr. 164/D4
Kingaroy, Austl. 172/C4
Kingfisher, Ok, US 187/H4
Kingfisher (co.), Ok, US 195/M14
Kinghorn, Sc, UK 94/C4
Kinglake NP, Austl. 173/G5
Kingman, Ks, US 187/H3
Kingman, Az, US 186/D4
Kingman (reef), Pac., US 175/J4
Kings (riv.), Ca, US 186/C3
Kings (co.), NY, US 197/K9
Kings (peak), Ut, US 186/E2
Kings Canyon NP, Ca, US 186/C3
Kings Langley, Eng, UK 88/B1
King's Lynn, Eng, UK 91/G1
Kings Park, Austl. 170/K6
Kings Point, NY, US 197/L8
King's Seat (hill), Sc, UK 94/C4
Kingsbridge, Eng, UK 90/C6
Kingscote, Austl. 171/H5
Kingscourt, Ire. 89/Q10
Kingsford, Mi, US 188/B2
Kingsport, Tn, US 188/D4
Kingston, Austl. 173/C4
Kingston, Austl. 174/F7
Kingston, On, Can. 188/E2
Kingston, NY, US 188/F3
Kingston (cap.), Jam. 203/G2
Kingston, Pa, US 196/C1
Kingston, Wa, US 193/B2
Kingston S.E., Austl. 173/A3
Kingston upon Hull, Eng, UK 93/H4
Kingston upon Hull (co.), Eng, UK 93/H4
Kingston upon Thames, Eng, UK 88/C2
Kingston upon Thames (bor.), Eng, UK 88/C2
Kingstown (cap.), StV. 199/N9
Kingstree, SC, US 191/H3
Kingsville, Tx, US 190/D5
Kingsville, Md, US 196/B5
Kingswood, Eng, UK 90/D4
Kingussie, Sc, UK 94/B2
Kınık, Turk. 148/A2

Kinkaid (mt.), Ak, US 192/L4
Kinkala, Congo 163/B1
Kinki (prov.), Japan 132/D3
Kinlochewe, Sc, UK 94/A1
Kinlochleven, Sc, UK 94/B3
Kinloss, Sc, UK 94/C1
Kinna, Swe. 96/E3
Kinnairds (pt.), Sc, UK 94/D1
Kinnelon, NJ, US 197/H8
Kinnelon (lake), NJ, US 197/H8
Kinnitty, Ire. 89/Q10
Kino (riv.), Japan 132/D3
Kinoje (riv.), On, Can. 188/D1
Kinomoto, Japan 135/K5
Kinrooi, Belg. 111/E1
Kinross, Sc, UK 94/C4
Kinsach (riv.), Ger. 113/F4
Kinsale, Ire. 89/P11
Kinsarvik, Nor. 96/B1
Kinshasa (cap.), D.R. Congo 163/C1
Kinston, NC, US 191/J3
Kintampo, Gha. 161/E4
Kinto (riv.), Japan 132/D3
Kintore, Sc, UK 94/D2
Kintyre (pt.), Sc, UK 89/R8
Kintzheim, Fr. 114/D1
Kinu (riv.), Japan 133/F2
Kinvarra, Ire. 89/P10
Kinyeti (peak), Sudan 155/M7
Kinzig (riv.), Ger. 98/E4
Kipahulu, Hi, US 182/T10
Kiparissía (gulf), Gre. 105/G4
Kiparissia, Gre. 105/G4
Kipawa (lake), Qu, Can. 188/E2
Kipkarren (riv.), Kenya 162/B2
Kipling, Sk, Can. 185/H3
Kipnuk, Ak, US 192/F4
Kippel, Swi. 114/D5
Kippen, Sc, UK 94/B4
Kippure (peak), Ire. 92/B5
Kipushi, D.R. Congo 163/E3
Kira, Japan 135/M6
Kira Panayía (isl.), Gre. 105/H3
Kirakira, Sol. 174/F6
Kiranomena, Madg. 165/H7
Kīratpur, India 142/B1
Kirazlı, Turk. 105/K2
Kirby, Tx, US 195/U21
Kirchberg, Swi. 114/D3
Kirchberg, Swi. 115/F3
Kirchberg, Ger. 111/G4
Kirchberg an der Iller, Ger. 115/G1
Kirchberg an der Jagst, Ger. 112/C4
Kirchdorf, Ger. 109/F3
Kirchdorf an der Krems, Aus. 113/H7
Kirchenlamitz, Ger. 113/F2
Kirchenthumbach, Ger. 113/E3
Kirchheim, Ger. 115/G1
Kirchheim bei München, Ger. 113/E6
Kirchheim unter Teck, Ger. 112/C5
Kirchheimbolanden, Ger. 112/B3
Kirchhundem, Ger. 109/F6
Kirchlengern, Ger. 109/F4
Kirchlinteln, Ger. 109/G3
Kirchsee (lake), Ger. 115/H2
Kirchseeon, Ger. 113/E6
Kirchweidach, Ger. 113/F6
Kirchzarten, Ger. 115/B1
Kirchzell, Ger. 112/C3
Kircudbright (bay), Sc, UK 92/D2
Kirensk, Rus. 123/L4
Kirgiz Steppe (upland), Kaz. 122/F5
Kirgizskiy (mts.), Kyr. 145/H4
Kiriákion, Gre. 105/H3
Kiribati (ctry.) 174/H5
Kırık, Turk. 148/E1
Kırıkhan, Turk. 135/D1
Kırıkkale, Turk. 148/C2
Kırıkkale (prov.), Turk. 148/C2
Kirishi, Rus. 97/Q2
Kirishima-Yaku NP, Japan 132/B5
Kirishima-yama (peak), Japan 132/B5
Kiritimati (Christmas) (isl.), Kiri. 175/K4
Kırkağaç, Turk. 148/A2
Kirkby, Eng, UK 93/F5
Kirkby in Ashfield, Eng, UK 93/G5
Kirkcaldy, Sc, UK 94/C4
Kirkcudbright, Sc, UK 92/D2
Kirkee, India 147/K5
Kirkenær, Nor. 96/E1
Kirkintilloch, Sc, UK 94/B5
Kirklees (co.), Eng, UK 93/G4
Kirkland, Me, US 189/G3
Kirkkonummi (Kyrkslätt), Fin. 97/L1
Kirkland, Qu, Can. 189/N7

Kirkland (hill), Sc, UK 94/C6
Kirkland Lake, On, Can. 188/D1
Kirklar (peak), Turk. 148/A2
Kirklareli, Turk. 107/H5
Kirklareli (prov.), Turk. 107/H5
Kirkliston, Sc, UK 94/C5
Kirkstone (pass), Eng, UK 93/F3
Kirkwall, Sc, UK 89/V14
Kirkwood, SAfr. 164/D4
Kirkwood, De, US 196/C4
Kirn, Ger. 111/G4
Kirov, Rus. 120/E1
Kirov, Rus. 119/L4
Kirovskaya Oblast, Rus. 119/L4
Kirovo-Chepetsk, Rus. 119/L4
Kirovohrad, Ukr. 120/E2
Kirovohrads'ka Oblasti, Ukr. 120/D2
Kirovsk, Rus. 118/G2
Kirriemuir, Sc, UK 94/D3
Kirrweiler, Ger. 112/B4
Kirsanov, Rus. 121/G1
Kirşehir (prov.), Turk. 148/C2
Kirşehir, Turk. 148/C2
Kirtizkuri, Japan 134/B3
Kiruna, Swe. 95/G2
Kiryū, Japan 133/F2
Kisa, Swe. 96/F3
Kisai, Japan 135/D1
Kisakata, Japan 134/A4
Kisangani, D.R. Congo 155/L8
Kisarazu, Japan 133/F3
Kisber, Hun. 99/K5
Kisei, Japan 135/K7
Kiselevsk, Rus. 122/J4
Kishanganj, India 143/F2
Kishangarh, India 147/K3
Kishiwada, Japan 135/H7
Kishorganj, Bang. 143/H3
Kishtwar, India 144/C3
Kishwaukee (riv.), Il, US 193/N15
Kisigo (riv.), Tanz. 162/B3
Kisii, Kenya 162/B3
Kiska (vol.), Ak, US 192/B5
Kiska (isl.), Ak, US 192/B6
Kiskatinnaw (riv.), BC, Can. 184/C2
Kiskitto (lake), Mb, Can. 185/J2
Kiskőrös, Hun. 106/D2
Kiskunfélegyháza, Hun. 106/D2
Kiskunhalas, Hun. 106/D2
Kiskunmajsa, Hun. 106/D2
Kiskunsági Nemzeti NP, Hun. 106/D2
Kislovodsk, Rus. 121/G4
Kismaayo (Chisimayu), Som. 155/P8
Kiso (riv.), Japan 133/E3
Kisogawa, Japan 135/L5
Kisozaki, Japan 135/L5
Kissamos, Gre. 105/H5
Kissimmee, Fl, US 191/H4
Kissimmee (lake), Fl, US 191/H4
Kissimmee, Fl, US 191/H4
Kisújszállás, Hun. 106/E2
Kisvárda, Hun. 99/M4
Kita, Mali 160/C3
Kita-Ibaraki, Japan 133/G2
Kitaaiki, Japan 135/J5
Kitadaitō (isl.), Japan 133/L8
Kitagata, Japan 135/L5
Kitakami (mts.), Japan 134/B4
Kitakami (riv.), Japan 134/B4
Kitakami, Japan 134/B4
Kitakata, Japan 133/F2
Kitakawabe, Japan 135/A1
Kitakyūshū, Japan 132/B4
Kitale, Kenya 162/B2
Kitami, Japan 134/C2
Kitamimaki, Japan 135/A1
Kitamoto, Japan 135/C2
Kitan (str.), Japan 135/G7
Kitangiri (lake), Tanz. 162/B4
Kitchener, On, Can. 188/D3
Kitgum, Ugan. 162/B2
Kithira, Gre. 105/H4
Kithira (isl.), Gre. 105/J4
Kithnos, Gre. 105/J4
Kithnos (isl.), Gre. 105/J4
Kitimat Arm (lake), BC, Can. 184/A2
Kitsap (co.), Wa, US 193/B2
Kitsuki, Japan 132/B4
Kitt Peak, Az, US 186/D4
Kittanning, Pa, US 196/A3
Kittatinny (mts.), NJ, US 196/C1
Kittery, Me, US 189/G3
Kittredge, Co, US 195/B3
Kitui, Kenya 162/C3

Kitumbeine (peak), Tanz. 162/C3
Kitwe, Zam. 163/B3
Kitzbühel, Aus. 101/K3
Kitzingen, Ger. 112/D3
Kiunga Marine Nat'l Rsv., Kenya 162/D3
Kiuruvesi, Fin. 118/E3
Kiuyu (int'l arpt.), Tanz. 162/C4
Kivalina, Ak, US 192/F2
Kivalo (mts.), Fin. 95/H2
Kivijärvi (lake), Fin. 97/M1
Kiviöli, Est. 97/M2
Kivu (lake), D.R. Congo 162/A3
Kıyıköy, Turk. 107/J5
Kiyokawa, Japan 135/C3
Kiyosu, Japan 135/L5
Kizel, Rus. 119/N4
Kizil (riv.), China 122/H6
Kızılcadağ, Turk. 149/A1
Kızılcahamam, Turk. 148/C1
Kızıldag NP, Turk. 148/B2
Kızılhisar, Turk. 148/B2
Kızılırmak (riv.), Turk. 148/C1
Kızıltepe, Turk. 148/E2
Kızılyaka, Turk. 149/C1
Kızlyar, Rus. 121/H4
Kizu (riv.), Japan 132/E3
Kizukuri, Japan 134/B3
Kizu, Japan 135/J6
Kjerkestinden (peak), Nor. 95/F1
Kjevik (int'l arpt.), Nor. 96/C2
Kjølen (mts.), Nor. 95/E2
Kladanj, Bosn. 106/D3
Kladno, Czh. 113/H2
Kladovo, Serb. 106/F3
Klagenfurt, Aus. 101/L3
Klaipėda, Lith. 97/J4
Klamath (mts.), Ca,Or, US 184/C5
Klamath (riv.), Or, US 184/C5
Klamath Falls, Or, US 184/C5
Klangenan, Indo. 138/H4
Klarälven (riv.), Swe. 95/E3
Klarup, Den. 96/D3
Klášterec nad Ohří, Czh. 113/G2
Klatovy, Czh. 113/G4
Klaus, Aus. 115/F4
Klausen (Chiusa), It. 115/H4
Klausenpass (pass), Swi. 115/F4
Klawock, Ak, US 192/M4
Klaza (mtn.), Yk, Can. 192/J4
Klazienaveen, Neth. 108/E3
Kleinblittersdorf, Ger. 111/G5
Kleine Elster (riv.), Ger. 99/G3
Kleine Emme (riv.), Swi. 114/E4
Kleine Gete (riv.), Belg. 111/D2
Kleine Laber (riv.), Ger. 113/F5
Kleine Nete (riv.), Belg. 111/D1
Kleinheubach, Ger. 112/C3
Kleinlützel, Swi. 114/D3
Kleinmachnow, Ger. 98/Q7
Kleinmond, SAfr. 164/L11
Kleinolifants (riv.), SAfr. 164/Q12
Kleinrinderfeld, Ger. 112/C3
Kleinsee, SAfr. 164/B3
Kleinwallstadt, Ger. 112/C3
Kleinwinterheim, Ger. 112/B3
Kleppe, Nor. 96/A1
Kleppestø, Nor. 96/A1
Klerksdorp, SAfr. 164/D2
Kleve, Ger. 108/D5
Klin, Rus. 118/H4
Klina, Kos. 106/E4
Klingenberg am Main, Ger. 112/C3
Klingenmünster, Ger. 112/B4
Klingenthal, Ger. 113/F2
Klinovec (peak), Czh. 113/F2
Klintsy, Rus. 120/E1
Klip (riv.), SAfr. 164/P12
Klippan, Swe. 96/E3
Klisura, Bul. 105/H4
Klitmøller, Den. 96/C3
Kljajićevo, Serb. 106/D3
Kljuc, Bosn. 106/C3
Kłodawa, Pol. 99/K2
Kłodzko, Pol. 99/J3
Klöntaler-See (lake), Swi. 115/F4
Klosterbach (riv.), Ger. 109/F3
Klosterlechfeld, Ger. 115/G2
Klosterneuburg, Aus. 101/M2
Klosters, Swi. 115/F4
Klosterwappen (peak), Aus. 99/H5
Kloten, Swi. 115/E3
Klötze, Ger. 98/F2
Kluane NP, Yk, Can. 192/K3
Kluane (lake), Yk, Can. 192/K3
Kluczbork, Pol. 99/K3
Klukwan, Ak, US 192/L4
Klütz, Ger. 96/E4
Klyaz'ma (riv.), Rus. 118/H4
Klyuchevskaya, Rus. 99/L4
Klyuchevskaya (peak), Rus. 123/S4
Kok (riv.), Myan. 136/B1

Knäred, Swe. 96/E3
Knaresborough, Eng, UK 93/G3
Knee (lake), Mb, Can. 185/K2
Knetzgau, Ger. 112/D3
Knezha, Bul. 107/G4
Knight (inlet), BC, Can. 184/B3
Knighton, Wal, UK 90/C2
Knightsen, Ca, US 193/L11
Knin, Cro. 106/C3
Knittelfeld, Aus. 101/L3
Knittlingen, Ger. 112/B4
Knivsta, Swe. 96/G2
Knjaževac, Serb. 106/F4
Knob (cape), Austl. 170/C5
Knob (peak), Phil. 139/F1
Knobby (pt.), Austl. 170/B4
Knoch (hill), Sc, UK 94/D1
Knockcloghrim, NI, UK 92/B2
Knösen (pt.), Swe. 96/E4
Knesen (peak), Den. 96/D3
Knosós (Knossos) (ruin), Gre. 105/J5
Knottingley, Eng, UK 93/G4
Knott's Berry Farm, Ca, US 194/G8
Knowsley (co.), Eng, UK 93/F3
Knox (coast), Ant. 218/G
Knox (cape), BC, Can. 192/M4
Knox City, Tx, US 187/H4
Knoxville, Tn, US 188/D5
Knutsford, Eng, UK 93/F5
Knysna, SAfr. 164/C4
Ko (riv.), Sen. 160/B3
Ko-saki (pt.), Japan 132/A3
Ko Samut NP, Thai. 136/C3
Koali, Hi, US 182/T10
Koani, Tanz. 162/C4
Koáth, India 143/E3
Kobayashi, Japan 132/B5
Kōbe, Japan 135/H6
København (int'l arpt.), Den. 96/E4
Kobern-Gondorf, Ger. 111/G3
Kobipato (peak), Indo. 139/G4
Koblach, Aus. 115/F3
Koblenz, Swi. 115/E2
Koblenz, Ger. 111/G3
Kobryn, Bela. 99/N2
Kobuchizawa, Japan 135/A2
Kobuk, Ak, US 192/G2
Kobuk (riv.), Ak, US 192/G2
Kobuk Valley NP, Ak, US 192/G2
Kobushi-ga-take (peak), Japan 133/F3
Kocába (riv.), Czh. 113/H3
Kocaeli (prov.), Turk. 107/J5
Koçalı, Turk. 148/D2
Kočani, FYROM 105/H2
Kocapınar, Turk. 148/E2
Kočevje, Slov. 101/L4
Koch (isl.), Nun., Can. 181/J2
Koch'ang, SKor. 131/D5
Koch'ang, SKor. 131/D5
Kochel am See, Ger. 115/H2
Kochelsee (lake), Ger. 115/H2
Kocher (riv.), Ger. 101/H2
Kocherinovo, Bul. 105/H1
Kōchi, Japan 132/C4
Kōchi (pref.), Japan 132/C4
Kodaira, Japan 135/C2
Kodala, India 140/E4
Kodama, Japan 135/C1
Kodarmā, India 143/E3
Kodiak, Ak, US 192/H4
Kodiak (isl.), Ak, US 192/H4
Kodinār, India 147/K4
Kodomari, Japan 134/B3
Kodry (hills), Mol. 107/H2
Koekelare, Belg. 110/B1
Koel (riv.), India 140/D3
Koes, Namb. 164/B2
Koesan, SKor. 131/D4
Koetari (riv.), Sur. 211/G4
Kofa (mts.), Az, US 186/D4
Kofarnihon (riv.), Taj. 145/E5
Kofçaz, Turk. 107/H5
Koffiefontein, SAfr. 164/D3
Kofiau (isl.), Indo. 139/G4
Koforidua, Gha. 161/E5
Kōfu, Japan 133/F3
Koga, Japan 135/D1
Koganei, Japan 135/D2
Kogon (riv.), Gui. 154/C5
Kogum (isl.), SKor. 131/D5
Kōgum (isl.), SKor. 131/D5
Kohāt, Pak. 144/A3
Kohīma, India 141/F2
Kohoku, Japan 135/L5
Kohout (peak), Cz. 113/J3
Kohtla-Järve, Est. 97/M2
Kohunlich (ruin), Mex. 202/D2
Koimisis, Gre. 105/H2
Koito (riv.), Japan 135/D3
Koiva (riv.), Lat. 97/M3
Kōje (isl.), SKor. 131/E5
Kojōnup, Austl. 170/C5
Kojšovská (peak), Slvk. 99/L4
Kok (riv.), Myan. 136/B1

Kōka, Japan 135/K6
Kokai (riv.), Japan 135/E2
Kōkar (isl.), Fin. 97/J3
Kokemäenjoki (riv.), Fin. 97/J1
Kokhonak, Ak, US 192/H4
Kokkola (Karleby), Fin. 118/D3
Koko Head (pt.), Hi, US 182/W13
Kokomo, In, US 188/C3
Kokrajhar, India 143/H2
Kokrines, Ak, US 192/H3
Koksan, NKor. 131/D3
Kökshetaū, Kaz. 145/E2
Kökshetaū (obl.), Kaz. 145/E2
Koksijde, Belg. 110/B1
Koksoak (riv.), Qu, Can. 181/K3
Kokstad, SAfr. 164/D3
Kokubu, Japan 132/B5
Kola (pen.), Rus. 218/C
Kola (riv.), Rus. 118/G1
Kolaka, Indo. 139/F4
Kolār, India 140/C5
Kolāras, India 142/A3
Kolašin, Mont. 106/D4
Kolbäck, Swe. 96/G2
Kol'bay (peak), Kaz. 145/E2
Kolbermoor, Ger. 101/K3
Kolbuszowa, Pol. 99/L3
Kolda (pol. reg.), Sen. 160/B3
Kolding, Den. 96/C4
Kölen (mts.), Swe. 95/E2
Kolgompya (cape), Rus. 97/N2
Kolguyev (isl.), Rus. 218/C
Kolhāpur, India 147/K5
Koliba (riv.), Gui. 160/B3
Koliganek, Ak, US 192/G4
Kolín, Czh. 99/H3
Kolkasrags (pt.), Lat. 97/K3
Kolkata (Calcutta), India 143/G4
Kolkata (Calcutta) (int'l arpt.), India 143/G4
Kollbach (riv.), Ger. 113/F5
Kollnburg, Ger. 113/F4
Kollum, Neth. 108/D2
Köln (Cologne), Ger. 111/F2
Kolno, Pol. 99/L2
Koło, Pol. 120/A1
Koloa, Hi, US 182/S10
Kołobrzeg, Pol. 96/F4
Kolokani, Mali 160/C3
Kolomna, Rus. 118/H5
Kolomyya, Ukr. 107/G1
Kolondiéba, Mali 160/D4
Kolossa (riv.), Mali 160/D3
Kolpashevo, Rus. 122/J4
Kolpino, Rus. 119/T7
Kolsva, Swe. 96/F2
Kolubara (riv.), Serb. 106/D3
Koluszki, Pol. 99/K3
Kolva (riv.), Rus. 119/N2
Kolwezi, D.R. Congo 163/E3
Kolyma (riv.), Rus. 125/Q3
Kolyma (range), Rus. 125/Q3
Kolyma Lowland (plain), Rus. 123/R2
Kom (peak), Bul. 105/H1
Komádi, Hun. 106/E2
Komadugu Gana (riv.), Niger.,Nga. 154/H5
Komadugu Yobe (riv.), Nga. 161/H3
Komae, Japan 135/D2
Komagane, Japan 135/L5
Komaki, Japan 135/L5
Komandorskiye (isls.), Rus. 125/R4
Komárno, Slvk. 106/D2
Komárom, Hun. 106/D2
Komárom-Esztergom (prov.), Hun. 106/D2
Komatiirivier (riv.), SAfr. 164/Q13
Komatke, Az, US 195/R19
Komatsu, Japan 132/E2
Komatsu (int'l arpt.), Japan 132/E2
Komatsushima, Japan 132/D4
Kombissiri, Burk. 161/E3
Kome (isl.), Tanz. 162/B3
Komi, Resp., Rus. 119/M2
Komi-Permyatskiy Aut. Okrug, Rus. 119/M2
Komló, Hun. 106/D2
Kommetjie, SAfr. 164/L11
Kommunizma (peak), Taj. 145/F5
Komodo (isl.), Indo. 139/E5
Komodo Island NP, Indo. 139/E5
Komoé (riv.), C.d'Iv. 154/E6
Komono, Japan 135/L5
Komoran (isl.), Indo. 139/K5
Komoro, Japan 135/A1
Komotini, Gre. 105/J2
Kompasberg (peak), SAfr. 164/D3
Komsomolets (isl.), Rus. 125/J1
Komsomol'skiy, Rus. 119/P2
Komür (pt.), Turk. 105/K3
Kon Tum, Viet. 136/D3
Konakovo, Rus. 118/H4
Konan, Japan 135/C1
Kōnan, Japan 135/L5

Kōnan, Japan 135/K6
Konār (riv.), India 143/E4
Konār (res.), India 143/E4
Konar (riv.), Afg. 144/A2
Konaweha (riv.), Indo. 139/F4
Konda, Japan 135/H6
Kondagaon, India 140/D4
Kondinin, Austl. 170/C5
Kondoa, Tanz. 162/B4
Kondopoga, Rus. 118/G3
Kondūz, Afg. 145/E5
Kong, C.d'Iv. 160/D4
Kong (riv.), Laos 136/D3
Kong (isl.), Camb. 136/C4
Kong Miao, China 130/D4
Kongiganak, Ak, US 192/F4
Kongju, SKor. 131/D4
Kongō-zan (peak), Japan 135/J7
Kongolo, D.R. Congo 163/E2
Kongoussi, Burk. 161/E3
Kongsberg, Nor. 96/C2
Kongsvinger, Nor. 96/F1
Kongur (peak), China 145/G3
Koniecpol, Pol. 99/K3
Königs Wusterhausen, Ger. 98/Q7
Königsberg in Bayern, Ger. 112/D2
Königsberg-Stein, Ger. 112/B5
Königsbronn, Ger. 112/D5
Königsbrunn, Ger. 115/G1
Königsdorf, Ger. 115/H2
Königsfeld im Schwarzwald, Ger. 115/E1
Königslutter am Elm, Ger. 109/H4
Königstein im Taunus, Ger. 112/B2
Königswinter, Ger. 111/G2
Konin, Pol. 99/K2
Kónitsa, Gre. 105/G2
Köniz, Swi. 114/D4
Konjic, Bosn. 106/C4
Könkämäeno (riv.), Fin. 118/D1
Konkouré (riv.), Gui. 160/B4
Konnevesi, Fin. 118/E3
Konolfingen, Swi. 114/D4
Konosu, Japan 135/D1
Konotop, Ukr. 120/E2
Konqi (riv.), China 122/J5
Konsen (plat.), Japan 134/D2
Końskie, Pol. 99/L3
Konstancin-Jeziorna, Pol. 99/L2
Konstantynów Łódzki, Pol. 99/K3
Konstanz, Ger. 115/F2
Kontich, Belg. 111/D1
Kontiolahti, Fin. 118/F3
Konuralp, Turk. 107/K5
Kóny, Hun. 106/C2
Konya, Turk. 148/C2
Konya (prov.), Turk. 148/C2
Konz, Ger. 111/F4
Koondrook, Austl. 173/C2
Koorawatha, Austl. 173/D2
Koorda, Austl. 170/C4
Kootenai (riv.), Id, US 184/D3
Kootenay (lake), BC, Can. 180/E3
Kootenay NP, BC, Can. 184/D3
Kootingal, Austl. 173/D1
Kop-Gejdi (pass), Turk. 148/E2
Kopäganj, India 142/D2
Kopargaon, India 147/K5
Kópavogur, Ice. 95/N7
Kope (peak), C.d'Iv. 160/D5
Köpenick, Ger. 98/Q7
Koper, Slov. 101/K4
Kopervik, Nor. 96/A2
Kopeysk, Rus. 119/P5
Kopfing im Innkreis, Aus. 113/G6
Köping, Swe. 96/G2
Kopondei (cape), Indo. 139/F5
Koporskiy (bay), Rus. 97/N2
Koppang, Nor. 96/D1
Kopparberg, Swe. 96/F2
Kopparberg (co.), Swe. 95/E3
Koppies, SAfr. 164/Q2
Koprivnica, Cro. 106/C2
Koprivshtitsa, Bul. 105/J1
Köprü (riv.), Turk. 149/B1
Köprülü, Turk. 149/C1
Köprülü Kanyon NP, Turk. 148/B2
Kor (riv.), Iran 146/F2
Kora, India 142/C2
Kōra, Japan 135/K5
Kora NP, Kenya 162/C3
Korab (peak), Alb. 105/G2
Koráb (peak), Czh. 113/G4
Korakuen Garden, Japan 132/C3
Koraluk (riv.), Nf, Can. 181/K3
Korana (riv.), Cro. 101/L4
Koraput, India 140/D4
Korba, India 140/D4
Korba, Tun. 158/M6
Korbach, Ger. 109/F6
Korçë, Alb. 105/G2
Korčula (isl.), Cro. 104/E1
Korčulanski Kanal (chan.), Cro. 104/E1
Kord Küy, Iran 146/F1

Kordel, Ger. 111/F4
Korea (bay), China,NKor. 131/B3
Korea (str.), Japan,SKor. 132/A4
Korea, North (ctry.) 131/D2
Korea, South (ctry.) 131/D4
Korean Folk Village, SKor. 131/G7
Korenovsk, Rus. 120/F3
Korhogo, C.d'Iv. 160/D4
Korinós, Gre. 105/H2
Kórinthos (Corinth), Gre. 105/H4
Kóris-hegy (peak), Hun. 106/C2
Kōriyama, Japan 133/G2
Korizo, Passe de (pass), Chad 154/J3
Korkodon (riv.), Rus. 123/R3
Korkuteli, Turk. 149/B1
Korla, China 128/E3
Kormakiti (cape), Cyp. 149/C2
Körmend, Hun. 101/M3
Kornat (isl.), Cro. 106/B4
Körner, Ger. 109/H6
Korneuburg, Aus. 107/N7
Korntal-Münchingen, Ger. 112/C5
Kornwestheim, Ger. 112/C5
Köröglu (peak), Turk. 107/K5
Korogwe, Tanz. 162/C4
Koroit, Austl. 173/B3
Koronadal, Phil. 137/D6
Korónia (lake), Gre. 105/H2
Koronowo, Pol. 99/J2
Koropion, Gre. 105/N9
Koror (cap.), Palau 174/C4
Körös (riv.), Hun. 106/E2
Korosten', Ukr. 120/D2
Korostyshiv, Ukr. 120/D2
Korotaikha (riv.), Rus. 119/P1
Korovin (vol.), Ak, US 192/D5
Korpo (Korppoo), Fin. 97/J1
Korsakov, Rus. 129/R2
Korschenbroich, Ger. 108/D6
Korsør, Den. 96/D4
Korsze, Pol. 97/J4
Kortemark, Belg. 110/C1
Kortenaken, Belg. 111/E2
Kortenberg, Belg. 111/D2
Kortessem, Belg. 111/E2
Kortrijk, Belg. 110/C2
Korup, PN de, Camr. 161/H5
Koryak (range), Rus. 125/R3
Koryakskiy Aut. Okrug, Rus. 123/S3
Koryazhma, Rus. 119/K3
Koryōng, Japan 135/J6
Koryŏng, SKor. 131/E5
Kós (isl.), Gre. 148/A2
Kós, Gre. 148/A2
Kosai, Japan 133/E3
Kosai, Japan 135/A2
Kösching, Ger. 113/E5
Kościan, Pol. 99/J2
Kościerzyna, Pol. 96/G4
Kosciusko (mt.), Austl. 173/D3
Kosciusko, Ms, US 191/F3
Kosciusko NP, Austl. 173/D3
Köse, Turk. 148/D1
Kosei, Japan 135/K6
Koshigaya, Japan 133/F3
Koshim (riv.), Kaz. 145/B3
Koshiki (isls.), Japan 133/K5
Kosi, India 142/A2
Kosi (zone), Nepal 143/F2
Kosi (riv.), India 140/E2
Košice, Slvk. 99/L4
Košický (pol. reg.), Slvk. 99/L4
Koskinoú, Gre. 148/B2
Kosoba (peak), Kaz. 145/G3
Kosŏng, SKor. 131/E3
Kosŏng, NKor. 131/E3
Kosovo (ctry.) 106/E4
Kosovo Polje, Kos. 106/E4
Kosovska Kamenica, Kos. 106/E4
Kosovska Mitrovica, Kos. 106/E4
Kosový (riv.), Czh. 113/F3
Kosrae (isl.), Micr. 174/F4
Kossi (prov.), Burk. 160/D3
Kossou, Barrage de (dam), C.d'Iv. 160/D5
Kossou, Lac de (lake), C.d'Iv. 154/D6
Kosta, Swe. 96/F3
Kostelec nad Černými Lesy, Czh. 113/H3
Koster, SAfr. 164/P4
Kostinbrod, Bul. 105/H1
Kostopil', Ukr. 120/C2
Kostroma (riv.), Rus. 118/J4
Kostroma, Rus. 118/J4
Kostromskaya Oblast, Rus. 118/J4
Kostrzyn, Pol. 99/H2
Kostrzyn, Pol. 99/J2
Kostyantynivka, Ukr. 120/F2
Koszalin, Pol. 96/G4
Kőszeg, Hun. 101/M3

Kot Kapūra, India 144/C4
Kot Mūmin, Pak. 144/B3
Kot Rādha Kishan, Pak. 144/C4
Kot Samāba, Pak. 144/A5
Kota, India 142/D4
Kota, India 147/L3
Kōta, Japan 135/M6
Kota Baharu, Malay. 141/H6
Kota Kinabalu, Malay. 139/E2
Kotaagung, Indo. 138/B5
Kotabaru, Indo. 139/E4
Kotabumi, Indo. 138/B4
Kotapad, India 140/D4
Kotdwāra, India 142/B1
Kotel, Bul. 105/K1
Kotel'nich, Rus. 119/L4
Kotel'nikovo, Rus. 121/G3
Kotel'nyy (isl.), Rus. 123/P7
Kothagūdem, India 140/D4
Köthen, Ger. 98/F3
Kotido, Ugan. 162/B2
Kotka, Fin. 97/M1
Kotlas, Rus. 119/K3
Kotli Lohārān, Pak. 144/C3
Kotlik, Ak, US 192/F3
Kotlin (isl.), Rus. 119/S7
Kotō, Japan 135/K5
Kotoka (int'l arpt.), Gha. 161/E5
Kotor, Mont. 106/D4
Kotor Varoš, Bosn. 106/C3
Kotovo, Rus. 121/H2
Kotovsk, Rus. 121/G1
Kotri, Pak. 147/J4
Kottayam, India 140/C6
Kotto (riv.), CAfr. 155/K6
Kotuy (riv.), Rus. 125/K3
Kotzebue, Ak, US 192/F2
Kotzebue (sound), Ak, US 192/E2
Kötzting, Ger. 113/F4
Kouandé, Ben. 161/F4
Kouchibouguac NP, NB, Can. 189/H2
Koudougou, Burk. 161/E3
Koufonision (isl.), Gre. 105/J5
Kougarok (mtn.), Ak, US 192/E2
Koukdjuak (riv.), Nun., Can. 181/J2
Koula-Moutou, Gabon 154/H8
Kouliko, Mali 160/C3
Koulikoro (pol. reg.), Mali 160/C3
Kouloutou (riv.), Sen. 160/B3
Koumbi Saleh (ruin), Mrta. 160/D3
Koumi, Japan 135/A1
Koumra, Chad 155/J6
Koundara, Gui. 160/B3
Kounradskiy, Kaz. 145/G3
Kountze, Tx, US 187/J5
Koupela, Burk. 161/E3
Kouritenga (prov.), Burk. 161/F3
Kourou, FrG. 209/H2
Koussi (peak), Chad 155/J4
Koutiala, Mali 160/D3
Kouvola, Fin. 97/M1
Kovada Gölü NP, Turk. 148/B2
Kovashi (riv.), Rus. 119/S7
Kovdozero (lake), Rus. 95/J2
Kovel', Ukr. 120/C2
Kovilj, Serb. 106/E3
Kovilpatti, India 140/C6
Kovrov, Rus. 118/J4
Kovür, India 140/C5
Kovylkino, Rus. 121/G1
Kowanana Aboriginal Community, Austl. 172/A1
Kowkcheh (riv.), Afg. 147/J1
Kowl-e Namaksār (riv.), Afg. 145/D6
Kowloon, China 137/B3
Kowt-e Ashrow, Afg. 147/J2
Kōyaguchi, Japan 135/J7
Kōyama, Japan 132/B5
Koynare, Bul. 107/G4
Koyuk, Ak, US 192/F3
Koyukuk (riv.), Ak, US 192/G3
Koyukuk, Ak, US 192/G3
Koyukuk, South Fork (riv.), Ak, US 192/H2
Kozakai, Japan 135/M6
Kōzaki, Japan 135/A2
Kozaklı, Turk. 148/C2
Kozan, Turk. 148/C2
Kozáni, Gre. 105/G2
Kozara NP, Bosn. 106/C3
Kozhikode (Calicut), India 140/C5
Kozhozero (lake), Rus. 118/H3
Kozhva (riv.), Rus. 119/M2
Kozienice, Pol. 99/L3
Kozloduy, Bul. 105/H1
Kozlu, Turk. 107/K5
Kozluk, Turk. 148/E2
Koźmin, Pol. 99/J3
Kōzu (isl.), Japan 133/F3
Kozyatyn, Ukr. 120/D2
Kos'va (riv.), Rus. 119/N3
Kos'yu (riv.), Rus. 119/N2
Kpalimé, Togo 161/F5
Kpandu, Gha. 161/F5
Kpémé, Togo 161/F5
Kra (isth.), Myan. 141/G6

Kraai (riv.), SAfr. 164/D3
Kraaifontein, SAfr. 164/L10
Krabi, Thai. 136/B4
Kragerø, Nor. 96/C2
Kragujevac, Serb. 106/E3
Kraiburg am Inn, Ger. 113/F6
Kraichbach (riv.), Ger. 112/B4
Kraichgau (reg.), Ger. 101/H2
Krailling, Ger. 113/E6
Krakatau (vol.), Indo. 138/C5
Kraków, Pol. 99/K3
Kralendijk, NAnt. 210/D1
Kraljevo, Serb. 106/E4
Kralkızı (dam), Turk. 148/E2
Královéhradecký (pol. reg.), Czh. 99/H3
Kralovice, Czh. 113/G3
Kralupy nad Vltavou, Czh. 113/H2
Kramators'k, Ukr. 120/F2
Kramfors, Swe. 95/F3
Kranéa Elassónos, Gre. 105/G3
Kranebitten (int'l arpt.), Aus. 115/H3
Kranenburg, Ger. 108/D5
Kranidhion, Gre. 105/H4
Kranj, Slov. 101/L3
Kranskop, SAfr. 165/E3
Krapkowice, Pol. 99/J3
Kraslice, Czh. 113/F2
Kraśnik, Pol. 99/M3
Kraśnik Fabryczny, Pol. 99/M3
Krasnoarmeysk, Rus. 121/H2
Krasnodar, Rus. 120/F3
Krasnodar (int'l arpt.), Rus. 120/F3
Krasnodarskiy Kray, Rus. 122/D5
Krasnogorsk, Rus. 119/W9
Krasnohrad, Ukr. 120/F2
Krasnokamensk, Rus. 129/L1
Krasnokamsk, Rus. 119/M4
Krasnolobodsk, Rus. 121/H2
Krasnotur'insk, Rus. 122/G4
Krasnoural'sk, Rus. 119/P4
Krasnovodsk (int'l arpt.), Trkm. 121/K5
Krasnoyarsk, Rus. 119/W9
Krasnoyarskiy Kray, Rus. 122/J4
Krasnyy Kut, Rus. 121/H2
Krasnyy Luch, Ukr. 120/F3
Krasnyy Sulin, Rus. 120/G3
Kratovo, FYROM 105/H1
Krautheim, Ger. 112/C4
Kravanh (mts.), Camb. 141/H5
Kreb en Nâga (cliff), Mali 156/D5
Kreck (riv.), Ger. 112/D2
Krefeld, Ger. 108/D6
Kreiensen, Ger. 109/G5
Kremastón (lake), Gre. 105/G3
Kremenchuk, Ukr. 120/E2
Kremenchuts'ke Vodoskhovyshche (res.), Ukr. 120/E2
Kremlin, Rus. 119/W9
Kremmen, Ger. 98/Q6
Kremmling, Co, US 186/F2
Krempe, Ger. 109/G1
Krems an der Donau, Aus. 99/H4
Kremsmünster, Aus. 113/H6
Krenglbach, Aus. 113/G6
Kresgeville, Pa, US 196/C2
Kresna, Bul. 105/H2
Kressbronn am Bodensee, Ger. 115/F2
Kresta (gulf), Rus. 123/T3
Kréstena, Gre. 105/G4
Kretinga, Lith. 97/J4
Kreuzau, Ger. 111/F2
Kreuzberg (peak), Ger. 112/C2
Kreuzlingen, Swi. 115/F2
Kreuztal, Ger. 111/G2
Kreuzwertheim, Ger. 112/C3
Kría Vrísi, Gre. 105/H2
Kribi, Camr. 154/G7
Krieglach, Aus. 101/L3
Kriens, Swi. 115/E3
Kriftel, Ger. 112/B2
Kril'on (pen.), Rus. 134/B1
Kril'on (cape), Rus. 134/C1
Krimpen aan de IJssel, Neth. 108/B5
Krinídhes, Gre. 105/J2
Kriós (cape), Gre. 105/H5
Krishna (riv.), India 140/C5
Krishnagiri, India 140/C5
Krishnanagar, India 143/G4
Kristdala, Swe. 96/G3
Kristiansand, Nor. 96/B2
Kristianstad (co.), Swe. 95/E4
Kristianstad (int'l arpt.), Swe. 96/F4
Kristiansund, Nor. 95/B3
Kristinehamn, Swe. 96/F2

Kriva Palanka, FYROM 105/H1
Krk (isl.), Cro. 106/B3
Krk, Cro. 106/B3
Krnov, Czh. 99/J3
Krokom, Swe. 95/E3
Krókos, Gre. 105/G2
Krolevets', Ukr. 120/E2
Krombach, Ger. 112/C2
Kroměříž, Czh. 99/J4
Kronach, Ger. 113/E2
Kronberg im Taunus, Ger. 112/B2
Kronoberg (co.), Swe. 95/E4
Kronshtadt, Rus. 119/S6
Kronstorf, Aus. 113/H6
Kroombit Tops NP, Austl. 172/C4
Kroonstad, SAfr. 164/D2
Kropotkin, Rus. 121/G3
Kropp, Ger. 96/C4
Krosno, Pol. 99/L4
Krosno Odrzańskie, Pol. 99/H2
Krotoszyn, Pol. 99/J3
Krottenkopf (peak), Aus. 115/G3
Krousón, Gre. 105/J5
Kröv, Ger. 111/G4
Krško, Slov. 101/L4
Kruckau (riv.), Ger. 109/G1
Kruger NP, SAfr. 165/E2
Krugersdorp, SAfr. 164/P13
Kruglitsa (peak), Rus. 119/N5
Kruibeke, Belg. 108/B6
Kruisfontein, SAfr. 164/D4
Krujë, Alb. 105/F2
Krumbach, Ger. 115/G1
Krummenau, Swi. 115/F3
Krummovgrad, Bul. 105/J2
Krün, Ger. 115/H3
Krupina, Slvk. 106/D1
Kruså, Den. 96/C4
Kruševac, Serb. 106/E4
Kruševo, FYROM 105/G2
Krušné Hory (Erzgebirge) (mts.), Czh.,Ger. 101/K1
Kruzof (isl.), Ak, US 192/L4
Krychaw, Bela. 120/D1
Krym, Aut. Rep., Ukr. 120/E3
Krymsk, Rus. 121/K1
Krynica, Pol. 99/L4
Kryvyy Rih, Ukr. 107/L2
Krzna (riv.), Pol. 99/M3
Krzyż, Pol. 99/J2
Ksar el Kebir, Mor. 158/B2
Ksar Hellal, Tun. 158/M7
Ksel (peak), Alg. 157/F2
Ksour Essef, Tun. 158/M7
Ktima, Cyp. 149/C2
Ku-Ring-Gai NP, Austl. 172/H8
Ku Sathan (peak), Thai. 136/C2
Kuah, Malay. 136/B5
Kuala Belait, Bru. 138/D3
Kuala Dungun, Malay. 138/B3
Kuala Kerai, Malay. 141/H6
Kuala Lipis, Malay. 138/B3
Kuala Lumpur (cap.), Malay. 138/B3
Kuala Pilah, Malay. 138/B3
Kuala Selangor, Malay. 138/B3
Kuala Terengganu, Malay. 141/H6
Kualapuu, Hi, US 182/T10
Kuancheng, China 130/D2
Kuandian, China 131/C2
Kuantan, Malay. 138/B3
Kuban' (riv.), Rus. 120/F3
Kubaysah, Iraq 148/E3
Kubenskoye (lake), Rus. 118/H4
Kubokawa, Japan 132/C4
Kubrat, Bul. 107/H4
Kučevo, Serb. 106/E3
Kuchen (peak), Aus. 115/F3
Kuchen, Ger. 112/C5
Kuching, Malay. 138/D3
Kuchino (isl.), Japan 133/K6
Kuchinoerabu (isl.), Japan 132/A5
Kuchl, Aus. 101/K3
Küçükbahçe, Turk. 105/K3
Küçükkuyu, Turk. 105/K3
Kudamatsu, Japan 132/B4
Kudat, Malay. 139/E2
Kudus, Indo. 138/D5
Kudymkar, Rus. 119/M4
Kufra (oasis), Libya 155/K3
Kufstein, Aus. 115/H3
Kugaaruk, Nun., Can. 180/E2
Kugluktuk, Nun., Can. 180/C2
Kühbach, Ger. 112/E6
Kuhmo, Fin. 97/L1
Kuhmoinen, Fin. 97/L1
Kuhn, Il, US 195/H8
Kühpäyeh, Iran 146/F2
Kuito, Ang. 163/D3
Kuiu (isl.), Ak, US 192/L4
Kujang, Indo. 139/F4
Kujawsko-Pomorskie (prov.), Pol. 99/K2
Kujawy (reg.), Pol. 99/K2

Kuji, Japan 134/B3
Kuju-san (peak), Japan 132/B4
Kukalaya (riv.), Nic. 203/E3
Kuki, Japan 133/F2
Kukizaki, Japan 135/E2
Kukkia (lake), Fin. 97/L1
Kūl (riv.), Iran 146/F2
Kula, Bul. 106/F4
Kula, Serb. 106/D3
Kula Kangri (peak), Bhu. 143/H1
Kulachi, Pak. 144/A4
Kulai, Malay. 138/B3
Kulal (mt.), Kenya 162/C2
Kulalsville, Pa, US 196/C3
Kulandag (mts.), Kaz. 145/B4
Kuldīga, Lat. 97/J3
Kulebaki, Rus. 118/J5
Kulgām, India 144/C3
Kuli, Rus. 145/D1
Kulin, Austl. 170/C5
Kullen (cape), Swe. 96/E3
Kullu, India 144/D3
Kulmbach, Ger. 113/E2
Kulob, Taj. 147/J1
Kuloy (riv.), Rus. 119/J2
Kulpahār, India 142/B3
Kulpmont, Pa, US 196/B2
Kulpsville, Pa, US 196/C3
Kul'sary, Kaz. 121/K3
Kulsheim, Ger. 112/C3
Kulsi (riv.), India 143/H2
Kültepe, Turk. 148/C1
Kulti, India 143/F4
Kulunda (lake), Rus. 145/G2
Kulunda, Rus. 145/G2
Kum (riv.), SKor. 131/D4
Kumagaya, Japan 133/F2
Kumaishi, Japan 134/A2
Kumamoto (int'l arpt.), Japan 132/B4
Kumamoto (pref.), Japan 132/B4
Kumamoto, Japan 132/B4
Kumano, Japan 132/E4
Kumanovo, FYROM 105/G1
Kumār (riv.), Bang. 143/G4
Kumasi, Gha. 161/E5
Kumatori, Japan 135/H7
Kumba, Camr. 154/G7
Kumbia, Austl. 172/C4
Kumbo, Camr. 154/H6
Kumch'on, Kor. 131/F6
Kumé (isl.), Japan 137/E2
Kumertau, Rus. 121/K1
Kumgang-san (peak), NKor. 131/E3
Kumi, Ugan. 162/B2
Kumi, SKor. 131/E4
Kumihama, Japan 135/G4
Kumkale, Turk. 105/K3
Kumköy, Turk. 107/H6
Kumla, Swe. 96/F2
Kumluca, Turk. 149/B1
Kümmersbruck, Ger. 113/E4
Kumo, Nga. 154/H5
Kumon (range), Myan. 141/G2
Kümsan, SKor. 131/D4
Kumta, India 147/K6
Kunashiri (isl.), Rus. 123/Q5
Kunch, India 142/B3
Kunda, India 142/C3
Kundarkhi, India 142/B1
Kundelungu, PN de, D.R. Congo 163/E3
Kundian, Pak. 144/A3
Kundla, India 147/K4
Kundu, SKor. 131/D5
Kungälv, Swe. 96/D3
Kungsangen (int'l arpt.), Swe. 96/G2
Kungsbacka, Swe. 96/D3
Kungshamn, Swe. 96/D2
Kungur, Rus. 119/N4
Kunhegyes, Hun. 106/E2
Kunimi-dake (peak), Japan 132/B4
Kuningan, Indo. 138/C5
Kunisaki (isl.), Japan 132/C5
Kunitachi, Japan 135/C2
Kunjah, Pak. 144/C2
Kunjirap (pass), China 147/L1
Kunkletown, Pa, US 196/C2
Kunlun (mts.), China 128/C4
Kunmadaras, Hun. 99/L5
Kunming, China 141/H2
Kunsan, SKor. 131/D5
Kunshan, China 130/E4
Kuntia, Bang. 143/G4
Kunwāri (riv.), India 142/A2
Kunwi, SKor. 131/E4
Kunya, China 130/E3
Künzell, Ger. 112/C1
Künzvartské (pass), Czh. 113/G5
Kuocang (peak), China 129/M6
Kuohijärvi (lake), Fin. 97/L1
Kupa (riv.), Cro. 106/B3
Kupang, Indo. 139/F6
Kupino, Rus. 145/G2
Kuppenheim, Ger. 112/B5
Kupreanof (isl.), Ak, US 192/L4

Kup'yans'k, Ukr. 120/F2
Kuqa, China 129/L3
Kür (riv.), Azer. 121/J5
Kürāli, India 144/D4
Kurama-yama (peak), Japan 135/J5
Kuranda, Austl. 172/B2
Kurashiki, Japan 132/C3
Kurayoshi, Japan 132/C3
Kurdistan (reg.), Asia 122/E6
Kürdzhali, Bul. 105/J2
Kürdzhali (res.), Bul. 105/J2
Kure (mts.), Turk. 148/C1
Kure, Japan 132/C3
Küre, Turk. 148/C1
Kure (isl.), Hi, US 174/H2
Kuressaare, Est. 97/K2
Kureyka (riv.), Rus. 122/K3
Kurgan, Rus. 119/O5
Kurganskaya Oblast, Rus. 119/O5
Kuri, SKor. 131/G6
Kuria (isl.), Kiri. 174/G4
Kuria Muria (isls.), Oman 147/G5
Kurihashi, Japan 135/D1
Kurikoma-yama (peak), Japan 134/B3
Kuril (isls.), Rus. 125/O5
Kurima (riv.), Nic. 203/E3
Kurimoto, Japan 135/F2
Kurinwas (riv.), Nic. 203/E3
Kurisawa, Japan 134/B2
Kuriyama, Japan 134/B2
Kürkçü, Turk. 149/C1
Kurla, India 140/D4
Kurnool, India 140/C4
Kuro-shima (isl.), Japan 132/A5
Kurodashō, Japan 135/G5
Kuroishi, Japan 134/B3
Kuroiso, Japan 133/G2
Kuroso-yama (peak), Japan 135/K6
Kurotaki, Japan 135/J7
Kurrajong, Austl. 172/G8
Kurram (riv.), Afg.,Pak. 147/J2
Kurrimine Beach, Austl. 172/B2
Kuršėnai, Lith. 97/K3
Kurseong, India 143/G3
Kursiu Nerija NP, Lith. 97/J4
Kursk, Rus. 120/F2
Kurskaya Oblast, Rus. 120/F2
Kurskaya Spit (bar), Lith.,Rus. 97/J4
Kurskiy (lag.), Lith.,Rus. 97/J4
Kurtalan, Turk. 148/E2
Kürten, Ger. 111/G1
Kuru (riv.), Sudan 155/L6
Kuruca (pass), Turk. 148/E2
Kurucay, Turk. 148/D2
Kuruçay (riv.), Turk. 121/G4
Kuruktag (mts.), China 128/E3
Kuruman, SAfr. 164/C2
Kurumansrivier (riv.), SAfr. 164/C2
Kurume, Japan 132/B4
Kurunegala, SrL 140/D6
Kurupukari, Guy. 211/G3
Kurur (riv.), Sudan 159/B4
Kurye, SKor. 131/D5
Kuryong (riv.), NKor. 131/C3
Kuş Cenneti NP, Turk. 148/B1
Kuşadası, Turk. 148/A2
Kusatsu, Japan 135/J5
Kusel, Ger. 111/G4
Kushalgarh, India 147/K4
Kushida (riv.), Japan 135/K7
Kushigata, Japan 135/J3
Kushihara, Japan 135/M5
Kushikino, Japan 132/B5
Kushima, Japan 132/C5
Kushimoto, Japan 132/D4
Kushiro (riv.), Japan 134/D2
Kushiro, Japan 134/D2
Kushiro-Shitsugen NP, Japan 134/D2
Kushtia (pol. reg.), Bang. 143/G4
Kushtia, Bang. 143/G4
Kusiyana (riv.), Bang. 143/H3
Kuskokwim (bay), Ak, US 192/F4
Kuskokwim (mts.), Ak, US 192/G3
Kuskokwim, North Fork (riv.), Ak, US 192/H3
Kuskokwim, South Fork (riv.), Ak, US 192/H3
Küsnacht, Swi. 115/E3
Kusŏng, NKor. 131/C3
Kussharo (lake), Japan 134/C2
Küssnacht am Rigi, Swi. 115/E3
Küstenkanal (canal), Ger. 109/E3
Kusterdingen, Ger. 112/C5
Kūstī, Sudan 155/M5

Kusu, Japan 135/L6
Kut (isl.), Thai. 141/H5
Kūtahya, Turk. 148/B2
K'ut'aisi (int'l arpt.), Geo. 121/G2
K'ut'aisi, Geo. 121/G4
Kutch (reg.), India 147/J4
Kutch, Gulf of (gulf), India 147/J4
Kutchan, Japan 134/B1
Kutcharo (lake), Japan 134/C1
Kutenholz, Ger. 109/G2
Kutná Hora, Czh. 99/H4
Kutno, Pol. 99/K2
Kutsuki, Japan 135/J5
Küttigen, Swi. 114/E3
Kutu, D.R. Congo 155/H8
Kutzenhausen, Ger. 112/D6
Kutztown, Pa, US 196/C2
Kuujjua (riv.), NW, Can. 180/E1
Kuujjuaq, Qu, Can. 181/K3
Kuusamo, Fin. 95/J2
Kuusankoski, Fin. 97/M1
Kuutse (hill), Est. 97/M2
Kuvandyk, Rus. 121/L2
Kuwait (ctry.) 146/E3
Kuwait (cap.), Kuw. 146/E3
Kuwānā (riv.), India 140/D2
Kuwana, Japan 135/L5
Kuybyshev (res.), Rus. 122/E4
Kuyto (lake), Rus. 95/J2
Kuytun, China 128/E3
Kuyuwini (riv.), Guy. 211/G4
Kuze, Japan 135/K4
Kuzitrin (riv.), Ak, US 192/E2
Kuznetsk, Rus. 121/H1
Kuzucubelen, Turk. 149/D1
Kuzumaki, Japan 134/B3
Kvaløy (isl.), Nor. 95/F1
Kværndrup, Den. 96/D4
Kvarner (gulf), Cro. 106/B3
Kvarnerić (chan.), Cro. 106/B3
Kvigtinden (peak), Nor. 95/E2
Kvinesdal, Nor. 96/B2
Kvinnherad, Nor. 96/B2
Kviteseid, Nor. 96/C2
Kwa (riv.), D.R. Congo 163/C1
Kwach'ŏn, SKor. 131/F7
Kwajalein (isl.), Mrsh. 174/F4
Kwale, Kenya 165/E3
KwaMashu, SAfr. 165/E3
Kwanak-san (peak), SKor. 131/F7
Kwangch'ŏn, SKor. 131/D4
Kwangju, SKor. 131/D5
Kwangju-Gwangyŏksi (prov.), SKor. 131/D5
Kwangmyŏng, SKor. 131/F7
Kwango (riv.), D.R. Congo 163/C2
Kwangyang, SKor. 131/D5
Kwania (lake), Ugan. 155/M7
Kwansan, SKor. 131/D5
Kwara (state), Nga. 161/G4
Kwaraha (riv.), Tanz. 162/B4
Kwataboahegan (riv.), On, Can. 188/D1
Kwazulu Natal (prov.), SAfr. 165/E3
Kwekwe, Zim. 163/E4
Kwethluk, Ak, US 192/F3
Kwidzyn, Pol. 97/H5
Kwigillingok, Ak, US 192/F4
Kwili (riv.), D.R. Congo 163/C1
Kwilu (riv.), D.R. Congo 163/C2
Kwinana, Austl. 170/K7
Kyabé, Chad 155/J6
Kyabram, Austl. 173/C3
Kyaiktiyo Pagoda, Myan. 136/B2
Kyaikto, Myan. 141/G4
Kyakhta, Rus. 128/J1
Kyan-zaki (cape), Japan 137/J7
Kyangin, Myan. 141/G4
Kyaukpadaung, Myan. 141/G3
Kyaukpyu, Myan. 141/F4
Kyaukse, Myan. 141/G3
Kyenjojo, Ugan. 162/A2
Kyeryong-san NP, SKor. 131/D4
Kyjov, Czh. 99/J4
Kyle, Sk, Can. 180/F3
Kyle (reg.), Sc, UK 94/B5
Kyll (riv.), Ger. 111/F3
Kymi (riv.), Fin. 97/M1
Kymijoki (riv.), Fin. 97/M1
Kymore, India 142/B3
Kyneton, Austl. 173/C3
Kynšperk nad Ohří, Czh. 113/F2
Kyōga (lake), Ugan. 155/M7
Kyōga-misaki (cape), Japan 132/D3
Kyogle, Austl. 173/D5
Kyonan, Japan 133/D3
Kyŏngbok Palace, SKor. 131/F6
Kyŏnggi (bay), SKor. 131/C4
Kyŏnggi-do (prov.), SKor. 131/D4

INDEX SECTION

254 Kyŏng – Laoan

Kyŏngju, SKor. 131/E5
Kyŏngju NP, SKor. 131/E5
Kyŏngsan, SKor. 131/E5
Kyŏngsang-bukto (prov.), SKor. 131/E4
Kyŏngsang-namdo (prov.), SKor. 131/E5
Kyōto (pref.), Japan 132/D3
Kyōto, Japan 135/J5
Kyōtō Imperial Palace, Japan 135/J6
Kyōwa, Japan 135/E1
Kyrenia (dist.), Cyp. 149/C2
Kyrenia, Cyp. 149/C2
Kyrgyzstan (ctry.) 145/F4
Kyritz, Ger. 98/G2
Kyrösjärvi (lake), Fin. 97/K1
Kythrea, Cyp. 149/C2
Kyūshū (isl.), Japan 132/B5
Kyūshū Highlands (uplands), Japan 132/B4
Kyustendil, Bul. 105/H1
Kywebwe, Myan. 141/F4
Kyyivs'ka Oblasti, Ukr. 120/D2
Kyyivs'ke Vodoskhovyshche (res.), Ukr. 120/D2
Kyzyl, Rus. 128/F1

L

La Algaba, Sp. 102/B4
La Almunia de Doña Godina, Sp. 102/E2
La Amistad Int'l Park, CR 198/E6
La Araucanía (pol. reg.), Chile 216/B3
La Ascensión, Mex. 201/F3
La Asunción, Ven. 211/F2
La Aurora (int'l arpt.), Guat. 202/D3
La Babia, Mex. 190/C4
La Baie, Qu, Can. 189/G1
La Banda, Arg. 215/D2
La Bañeza, Sp. 102/C1
La Bassée, Fr. 110/B2
La Baule-Escoublac, Fr. 100/B3
La Belle, Fl, US 191/H5
La Birse (riv.), Swi. 114/D3
La Blanquilla (isl.), Ven. 211/E2
La Bocana, Mex. 200/B3
La Bresse, Fr. 114/C2
La Broque, Fr. 114/D1
La Calera, Chile 216/N8
La Campana, Sp. 102/C4
La Cañada (peak), Cuba 203/F1
La Canada-Flintridge, Ca, US 194/F7
La Capelle, Fr. 110/C4
La Carlota, Sp. 102/C4
La Carlota, Arg. 216/E2
La Carolina, Sp. 102/D3
La Catedral (peak), Mex. 201/Q9
La Ceiba, Hon. 202/E3
La Ceiba (int'l arpt.), Hon. 202/E3
La Celle-les-Bordes, Fr. 88/H6
La Celle-Saint-Cloud, Fr. 88/J5
La Celle-sur-Morin, Fr. 88/L5
La Chapelle-de-Guinchay, Fr . 114/A5
La Chapelle-Saint-Luc, Fr. 100/F2
La Chaux-de-Bonds, Swi. 114/C3
La Chinita (int'l arpt.), Ven. 210/D2
La Chorrera, Pan. 203/G4
La Cienega, NM, US 187/F4
La Ciotat, Fr. 100/F5
La Clusaz, Fr. 114/C6
La Concepción, Nic. 202/E4
La Concepción, Pan. 203/F4
La Concepcíon, Ven. 210/D2
La Coronilla, Uru. 217/G2
La Coruña, Sp. 102/A1
La Couronne, Fr. 100/D4
La Crèche, Fr. 100/C3
La Crescenta-Montrose, Ca, US 194/F7
La Croix-en-Brie, Fr. 88/M6
La Croix, Lac (lake), On, Can. 185/L3
La Cruz, Chile 216/N8
La Cruz, Col. 210/B4
La Cruz, CR 202/E4
La Cruz, Mex. 200/D4
La Cruz, Uru. 217/K10
La Cumbre (vol.), Ecu. 214/E7
La Dôle (peak), Swi. 114/C5
La Dorada, Col. 208/D2
La Dormida, Arg. 216/D2
La Esperanza, Hon. 202/D3
La Estrada, Sp. 102/A1
La Estrella, Chile 216/N9
La Falda, Arg. 215/D3
La Fayette, Ga, US 191/G3
La Fère, Fr. 110/C4
La Ferté-Gaucher, Fr. 110/C6
La Ferté-Macé, Fr. 100/C2
La Ferté-Milon, Fr. 88/M7
La Ferté-Sous-Jouarre, Fr. 110/C6
La Flèche, Fr. 100/C3
La Fría, Ven. 210/C2
La Galite (isl.), Tun. 158/L6
La Garamba NP, D.R. Congo 162/A2
La Garita (mts.), Co, US 190/B2
La Garriga, Sp. 103/L6
La Gineta, Sp. 102/E3
La Gloria, Col. 210/C2
La Goulette, Tun. 158/M6
La Gran Sabana (plain), Ven. 208/F2
La Grande, Or, US 184/D4
La Grande (riv.), Qu, Can. 181/J3
La Grande Ruine (peak), Fr. 101/G4
La Grange, Ga, US 191/G3
La Grange, Tx, US 187/H5
La Grita, Ven. 203/J4
La Gruyère (lake), Swi. 114/D4
La Guajira (dept.), Col. 210/C2
La Guajira (pen.), Col. 210/D1
La Guardia, Sp. 102/A2
La Guardia (int'l arpt.), NY, US 197/K8
La Habana (Havana) (cap.), Cuba 198/E3
La Habra, Ca, US 194/G8
La Have (riv.), NS, Can. 189/H2
La Higuera, Chile 215/B2
La Honda, Ca, US 193/K12
La Houssaye-en-Brie, Fr. 88/L5
La Huaca, Peru 214/A2
La Huacana, Mex. 201/E5
La Huerta, Mex. 200/D5
La Isla, Mex. 201/Q10
La Jalca, Peru 214/B2
La Joya, Peru 214/D5
La Joya de los Sachas, Ecu. 210/B5
La Junta, Co, US 187/G3
La Junta, Mex. 200/D2
La Laguna, Canl., Sp. 156/A3
La Libertad, Ecu. 210/A5
La Libertad, Guat. 202/D2
La Libertad, Hon. 202/E3
La Libertad (dept.), Peru 214/B3
La Ligua, Chile 216/C2
La Línea de la Concepción, Sp. 102/C4
La Llagosta, Sp. 103/L6
La Loche, Sk, Can. 184/F1
La Loggia, It. 116/A3
La Louvière, Belg. 111/D3
La Luisiana, Sp. 102/C4
La Luz, NM, US 187/F4
La Machine, Fr. 100/E3
La Maddalena, It. 104/A2
La Madeleine, Fr. 110/C2
La Malbaie, Qu, Can. 189/G2
La Marsá, Tun. 158/M6
La Martre (lake), NW, Can. 180/E2
La Masica, Hon. 202/E3
La Mauricie NP, Qu, Can. 188/F2
La Mensura (peak), Col. 210/C4
La Merca, Sp. 102/B1
La Merced, Peru 214/C3
La Mesa, Ca, US 194/C5
La Mesa (int'l arpt.), Hon. 202/E3
La Mesa, Ven. 210/D2
La Mira, Mex. 200/E5
La Mirada, Ca, US 194/F8
La Moine (riv.), Il, US 188/B3
La Montaña (phys. reg.), Peru 214/C3
La Moure, ND, US 185/J4
La Neuveville, Swi. 114/D3
La Norville, Fr. 88/J6
La Orchila (isl.), Ven. 199/H5
La Orotava, Canl., Sp. 156/A3
La Oroya, Peru 214/C3
La Palma, Pan. 203/G4
La Palma (isl.), Sp. 156/A3
La Paloma, Uru. 217/G2
La Pampa (prov.), Arg. 216/D3
La Paz, Arg. 215/E3
La Paz, Arg. 216/D2
La Paz (cap.), Bol. 208/E7
La Paz (dept.), Bol. 214/D4
La Paz, Col. 210/C2
La Paz, Col. 210/C3
La Paz, Hon. 202/E3
La Paz, Mex. 200/C3
La Paz (bay), Mex. 200/C3
La Paz, Uru. 217/K11
La Pêche, Qu, Can. 188/F2
La Peña, Pan. 198/E6
La Perla, Mex. 200/D2
La Pérouse (str.), Japan,Rus 129/R2
La Perouse (str.), Japan,Rus. 125/P5
La Petite-Raon, Fr. 114/C1
La Piedad Cavadas, Mex. 200/E4
La Plata, Md, US 188/E4
La Plata, Col. 210/C4
La Plata, Arg. 217/K11
La Pobla de Lillet, Sp. 103/F1
La Pocatière, Qu, Can. 189/G2
La Pola de Gordón, Sp. 102/C1
La Ponge (lake), Sk, Can. 184/G2
La Porte, In, US 188/C3
La Prairie, Qu, Can. 189/P7
La Pryor, Tx, US 187/H5
La Puebla, Sp. 103/G3
La Puebla de Almoradiel, Sp. 102/D3
La Puebla de Cazalla, Sp. 102/C4
La Puebla de Montalbán, Sp. 102/C3
La Puente, Ca, US 194/G7
La Puntilla (pt.), Ecu. 210/A5
La Quebrada, Ven. 210/D2
La Queue-les-Yvelines, Fr . 110/A6
La Quiaca, Arg. 208/E8
La Rambla, Sp. 102/C4
La Reforma, Mex. 200/C3
La Rinconada, Sp. 102/C4
La Rioja, Arg. 215/C2
La Rioja (aut. comm.), Sp. 102/D1
La Rioja (prov.), Sp. 102/D1
La Robla, Sp. 102/C1
La Roche (lake), Sk, Can. 184/F1
La Roche, Swi. 114/D4
La Roche-en-Ardenne, Belg. 111/E3
La Roche-sur-Foron, Fr. 114/C5
La Roche-sur-Yon, Fr. 100/C3
La Rochelle, Fr. 100/C3
La Roda, Sp. 102/D3
La Romana, DRep. 199/H4
La Ronge, Sk, Can. 185/G2
La Rúa, Sp. 102/B1
La Salle, Co, US 195/C2
La Sarraz, Swi. 114/C4
La Sarre, Qu, Can. 188/E1
La Sauvette (peak), Fr. 101/G5
La Scie, Nf, Can. 189/L1
La Serena, Chile 215/B2
La Seu d'Urgell, Sp. 103/F1
La Seyne-sur-Mer, Fr. 100/F5
La Sierpe, Cuba 203/G1
La Sila (mts.), It. 104/E3
La Silueta (peak), Chile 217/B7
La Solana, Sp. 102/D3
La Souterraine, Fr. 100/D3
La Spezia (prov.), It. 116/C4
La Spezia, It. 116/C4
La Tabatière, Qu, Can. 189/K1
La Teste, Fr. 100/C4
La Tête à l'Ane (peak), Fr. 114/C6
La Tigra, PN, Hon. 202/E3
La Toma, Arg. 216/D2
La Tortue (isl.), Haiti 203/H1
La Tortuga (isl.), Ven. 211/E2
La Tortuga, Isla (isl.), Ven. 208/E1
La Tour-de-Peilz, Swi. 114/C5
La Tour-de-Trême, Swi. 114/D4
La Tremblade, Fr. 100/C4
La Trinitaria, Mex. 202/C2
La Troncal, Ecu. 210/B5
La Tuque, Qu, Can. 189/F2
La Turbie, Fr. 116/H8
La Unión, Chile 216/B4
La Unión, Col. 210/B4
La Unión, ESal. 202/E3
La Unión, Mex. 201/E5
La Unión, Peru 214/A2
La Unión, Peru 214/B3
La Unión, Sp. 103/E4
La Uníon, Ven. 210/E2
La Vecilla, Sp. 102/C1
La Verna, It. 117/E5
La Verne, Ca, US 194/C2
La Vernia, Tx, US 195/U21
La Verrière, Fr. 88/H5
La Víbora, Mex. 190/C5
La Victoria, Ven. 208/E1
La Victoria, Ven. 210/D3
La Wantzenau, Fr. 111/G6
Laa an der Thaya, Aus. 101/M2
Laaber, Ger. 113/E4
Laage, Ger. 96/E5
Laakirchen, Aus. 113/G7
Laarne, Belg. 110/C1
Laas Caanood, Som. 155/Q6
Laas Qoray, Som. 155/Q5
Laatzen, Ger. 109/G4
Laax, Swi. 115/F4
Labason, Phil. 137/D6
L'Abbaye, Swi. 114/C4
Labdah (Leptis Magna) (ruin), Libya 154/H1
Labé, Gui. 160/B4
Labé (pol. reg.), Gui. 160/B4
Labe (Elbe) (riv.), Czh. 101/L1
Laberweinting, Ger. 113/F5
Labian (cape), Malay. 139/E2
Labin, Cro. 106/B3
Labinsk, Rus. 121/G3
Labná (ruin), Mex. 202/D1
Laborde, Arg. 216/E2
Laborec (riv.), Slvk. 99/L4
Laboulaye, Arg. 216/E2
Labrador (reg.), Nf, Can. 181/K3
Labrador (sea), Can.,Grld. 177/M4
Labrador City, Nf, Can. 181/K3
Lábrea, Braz. 208/F5
Labruguière, Fr. 100/E5
Labry, Fr. 111/E5
Labuk (riv.), Malay. 139/E2
Labuk (bay), Malay. 139/E2
Labuništa, FYROM 105/G2
Labutta, Myan. 141/F4
Laç, Alb. 105/F2
Lac Afwein (riv.), Kenya 162/C2
Lac du Bonnet, Mb, Can. 185/J3
Lac La Biche, Ab, Can. 184/F2
Lac-Mégantic, Qu, Can. 189/G2
L'Acadie, Qu, Can. 189/P7
Lacantum (riv.), Mex. 202/D2
Lacaune, Fr. 100/E5
Laccadive (sea), India 140/B5
Lacchiarella, It. 116/C2
Lacepede (bay), Austl. 173/A3
Lach Dera (riv.), Som. 155/P7
Lacha (lake), Rus. 118/H3
Lachapelle-aux-Pots, Fr. 110/A5
Lachay (pt.), Peru 214/B3
Lachen, Swi. 115/E3
Lachenaie, Qu, Can. 189/N6
Lachendorf, Ger. 109/H3
Lāchi, Pak. 144/A3
L'Achigan (riv.), Qu, Can. 189/N6
Lachine, Qu, Can. 189/N7
Lachlan (riv.), Austl. 173/C2
Lachte (riv.), Ger. 109/H3
Lackawanna, NY, US 189/S10
Lackawanna (co.), Pa, US 196/C1
Läckö, Swe. 96/E2
Lacombe, Ab, Can. 184/E2
Lacombe, La, US 195/Q16
Laconia, NH, US 189/G3
Lacroix-Saint-Ouen, Fr. 110/B5
Ladainha, Braz. 212/B5
Ladakh (mts.), India 147/L2
Ladbergen, Ger. 109/E4
Ladder (hills), Sc, UK 94/C2
Lądek-Zdrój, Pol. 99/J3
Ladenburg, Ger. 112/B4
Ladera Heights, Ca, US 194/F8
Ladismith, SAfr. 164/C4
Ladispoli, It. 104/C2
Ladoga (lake), Rus. 218/D
Ladoix-Serrigny, Fr. 114/A3
Ladrillero (mtn.), Chile 217/B7
Ladue, Mo, US 195/G8
Lādwa, India 144/D5
Lady Isle (isl.), Sc, UK 94/B5
Ladybank, Sc, UK 94/C4
Ladybower (res.), Eng, UK 93/G5
Ladybrand, SAfr. 164/D3
Ladysmith, SAfr. 165/E3
Lae (isl.), Mrsh. 174/F4
Laer, Ger. 109/E4
Lafayette, Ca, US 193/K11
Lafayette, Co, US 195/B3
Lafayette, In, US 188/C3
Lafayette, La, US 187/J5
Lafayette, NJ, US 196/D1
Lafia, Nga. 161/H4
Lafitte, La, US 195/P17
Laflamme (riv.), Qu, Can. 188/E1
Lafnitz (riv.), Aus. 101/L3
Lafontaine, Qu, Can. 189/M6
Lafourche (parish), La, US 195/T17
Laga Balal (riv.), Kenya 162/C2
Laga Mado Gali (riv.), Kenya 162/C2
Laga Merille (riv.), Kenya 162/C2
Lagan, Swe. 96/E3
Lagan (riv.), Swe. 96/E3
Lagarto, Braz. 212/C3
Lagawe, Phil. 137/D4
Lagdo, Lac de (lake), Camr. 154/H6
Lage, Ger. 109/F5
Lage Vaart (canal), Neth. 108/C4
Lågen (riv.), Nor. 96/C1
Lages, Braz. 213/B3
Laggan (lake), Sc, UK 94/B3
Lagh Bogal (riv.), Kenya 162/C2
Lagh Bor (riv.), Kenya 155/N7
Lagh Kutulo (riv.), Kenya 162/D2
Laghouat (prov.), Alg. 157/F2
Laghouat, Alg. 157/F2
Lagnieu, Fr. 114/B6
Lagny-le-Sec, Fr. 88/L4
Lagny-sur-Marne, Fr. 88/L5
Lago da Pedra, Braz. 212/A2
Lago de Atitlán, PN, Guat. 202/D3
Lago Puelo, PN, Arg. 216/C4
Lago Verde, Chile 216/C5
Lagoa, Port. 102/A4
Lagoa da Prata, Braz. 213/C2
Lagoa Formosa, Braz. 213/C1
Lagoa Vermelha, Braz. 213/B4
Lagoda (lake), Rus. 95/J3
Lagonegro, It. 104/D2
Lagord, Fr. 100/C3
Lagos, Nga. 161/F5
Lagos (state), Nga. 161/F5
Lagos, Port. 102/A4
Lagos de Moreno, Mex. 200/E4
Lagosanto, It. 117/F3
Laguardia, Sp. 102/D1
Laguna, Braz. 213/B4
Laguna Beach, Ca, US 194/C3
Laguna Blanca, PN, Arg. 216/C3
Laguna de Duero, Sp. 102/C2
Laguna de la Restinga, PN, Ven. 211/E2
Laguna del Laja, PN, Chile 216/C3
Laguna del Rey, Mex. 200/E3
Laguna Hills, Ca, US 194/C3
Laguna San Rafael, PN, Chile 215/B6
Lagunas, Peru 214/C2
Lagunas, Peru 214/B2
Lagunas de Chacahua, PN, Mex. 202/B2
Lagunas de Montebello, Mex. 198/C4
Lagunas de Zempoala, PN, Mex. 201/Q10
Lagunillas, Ven. 210/D2
Laguntara (lag.), Hon. 203/E3
Lahad Datu, Malay. 139/E2
Lahār, India 142/B2
Lāharpur, India 142/C2
Lahat, Indo. 138/B4
Lāhījān, Iran 146/F1
Lahn (riv.), Ger. 98/E3
Lahnstein, Ger. 111/G3
Laholm, Swe. 96/E3
Laholms (bay), Den. 96/F3
Lahore, Pak. 144/C4
Lahore (int'l arpt.), Pak. 144/C4
Lahr, Ger. 114/D1
Lahti, Fin. 97/L1
Laï, Chad 154/J6
Lai Chau, Viet. 136/C1
Lai'an, China 130/D4
Laibin, China 137/A3
Laichingen, Ger. 112/C5
Laidon (lake), Sc, UK 94/B3
Laie, Hi, US 182/W12
Laifeng Tujiazu Zizhixian, China 137/A2
L'Aigle, Fr. 100/D2
Laigueglia, It. 116/B5
Laihia, Fin. 95/G3
Lainate, It. 116/C1
Laingsburg, SAfr. 164/C4
Lainioälven (riv.), Swe. 95/G1
Laishui, China 130/G7
Laisvall, Swe. 95/F2
Laitila, Fin. 97/J1
Laives (Leifers), It. 115/H5
Laiwu, China 130/D3
Laixi, China 130/E3
Laiyuan, China 130/C3
Laizhou (bay), China 130/D3
Laja (lake), Chile 216/C3
Lajas, Peru 214/B2
Laje, Braz. 212/B3
Lajeado, Braz. 213/B4
Lajedo, Braz. 212/C3
Lajes, Braz. 212/C2
Lajes, Azor., Port. 103/S12
Lajes (int'l arpt.), Azor., Port. 103/S12
Lajing (pass), Nepal 143/E1
Lajinha, Braz. 213/D2
Lajosmizse, Hun. 106/D2
L'Akagera, PN de, Rwa. 162/A3
Lakato, Madg. 165/J7
Lake (co.), Il, US 193/P15
Lake Aluma, Ok, US 195/N14
Lake Amadeus Abor. Land, Austl. 171/F3
Lake Arrowhead, Ca, US 194/C2
Lake Barrington, Il, US 193/P15
Lake Beulah, Wi, US 193/P14
Lake Bluff, Il, US 193/Q15
Lake Boga, Austl. 173/B2
Lake Bogoria Nat'l Rsv., Kenya 162/C2
Lake Bolac, Austl. 173/B3
Lake Cargelligo, Austl. 173/C2
Lake Catherine, Il, US 193/P15
Lake Chany (lake), Rus. 145/G2
Lake Charles, La, US 187/J5
Lake Chelan Nat'l Rec. Area, Wa, US 184/C3
Lake City, Fl, US 191/H4
Lake Clark NP and Prsv., Ak, US 192/G3
Lake District NP, Eng, UK 93/E2
Lake Elsinore, Ca, US 194/C3
Lake Forest, Il, US 193/Q15
Lake Forest Park, Wa, US 193/C2
Lake Fork (res.), Tx, US 190/E3
Lake Grace, Austl. 170/C5
Lake Havasu City, Az, US 186/D4
Lake Hiwassee, Ok, US 195/N14
Lake in the Hills, Il, US 193/P15
Lake Jackson, Tx, US 187/J5
Lake Lotawana, Mo, US 195/E6
Lake Louise, Ab, Can. 184/D3
Lake Malawi NP, Malw. 163/F3
Lake Manyara NP, Tanz. 162/B3
Lake Mburo NP, Ugan. 162/A3
Lake Mead Nat'l Rec. Area, US 186/D4
Lake Meredith Nat'l Rec. Area, Tx, US 190/C3
Lake Minchumina, Ak, US 192/H3
Lake Mohawk, NJ, US 196/D1
Lake Nakuru NP, Kenya 162/C3
Lake of the Woods (lake), US,Can. 185/K3
Lake Orion, Mi, US 193/F6
Lake Point Junction, Ut, US 195/J12
Lake Providence, La, US 187/K4
Lake Ronkonkoma, NY, US 197/E2
Lake Shore, Md, US 196/B5
Lake Station, In, US 193/R16
Lake Success, NY, US 197/L8
Lake Villa, Il, US 193/P15
Lake Wales, Fl, US 191/H5
Lake Winnebago, Mo, US 195/E6
Lake Worth, Fl, US 191/H5
Lake Zurich, Il, US 193/P15
Lakehurst, NJ, US 196/D3
Lakehurst Naval Air Eng. Ctr., NJ, US 196/D3
Lakeland, Fl, US 191/H4
Lakeland Village, Ca, US 194/C3
Lakemoor, Il, US 193/P15
Lakeport, Ca, US 186/B3
Lakes Entrance, Austl. 173/D3
Lakes NP, The, Austl. 173/C3
Lakesfjorden (inlet), Nor. 95/H1
Lakeside, Ca, US 194/D5
Lakeview, Or, US 184/C5
Lakeview, Ut, US 195/K13
Lakeview, Ca, US 194/C3
Lakeville (lake), Mi, US 193/F6
Lakeway, Tx, US 187/H5
Lakewood, Wa, US 184/C3
Lakewood, Co, US 195/B3
Lakewood, NJ, US 196/D3
Lakewood, Ca, US 194/F8
Lakewood, Il, US 193/P15
Lakhemaa NP, Est. 97/L2
Lakhīmpur, India 142/C2
Lakhnādon, India 142/B4
Laki (vol.), Ice. 95/N7
Lakki, Pak. 144/A3
Lakkíon, Gre. 148/A2
Lakonía (gulf), Gre. 105/H4
Lakshadweep (isls.), India 140/B5
Lakshadweep (terr.), India 140/B6
Lal Suhanra NP, Pak. 144/B5
Lāla Mūsa, Pak. 144/B3
Lalana (riv.), Madg. 165/H8
Lalang (riv.), Indo. 138/B4
Lālganj, India 143/E3
Lālgola, India 143/G3
Lāliān, Pak. 144/B4
Lalín, Sp. 102/A1
Lalinde, Fr. 100/D4
Lalitpur, India 142/B3
Lalitpur (Pāṭan), Nepal 143/E2
Lalla Rookh Abor. Land, Austl. 170/C2
Lamachan (peak), Sc, UK 92/D1
Lamadrid, Mex. 190/C5
Lamanai (ruin), Belz. 202/D2
Lamandau (riv.), Indo. 138/D4
Lamar, Co, US 187/G3
Lamarche, Fr. 114/B1
Lamarche-sur-Saône, Fr . 114/B3
Lamarque, Arg. 216/D3
Lamas, Peru 214/B2
Lambach, Aus. 113/G6
Lamballe, Fr. 100/B2
Lambaré, Par. 215/E2
Lambaréné, Gabon 154/H8
Lambari, Braz. 213/H6
Lambay (isl.), Ire. 89/Q10
Lambayeque (dept.), Peru 214/A2
Lambayeque, Peru 214/B2
Lambé Coba (riv.), Mali 160/C3
Lambert-St. Louis (int'l arpt.), Mo, US 187/K3
Lambert's Bay, SAfr. 164/B4
Lambertville, Mi, US 188/D3
Lambertville, NJ, US 196/D3
Lambesc, Fr. 100/F5
Lambeth (bor.), Eng, UK 88/C2
Lambrama, Peru 214/C4
Lambrecht, Ger. 112/B4
Lambro (riv.), It. 116/C2
Lambsheim, Ger. 112/B3
Lambton (co.), On, Can. 193/H6
Lambunao, Phil. 137/D5
Lamego, Port. 102/B2
Lamèque (isl.), NB, Can. 189/H2
Lameroo, Austl. 171/J5
Lamesa, Tx, US 187/G4
Lamía, Gre. 105/H3
Lamington (riv.), NJ, US 196/D2
Lamington NP, Austl. 172/D5
Lamitan, Phil. 137/D6
Lamlash, Sc, UK 94/A5
Lamma (isl.), China 129/U11
Lammermuir (hills), Sc, UK 94/D5
Lammhult, Swe. 96/F3
Lammi, Fin. 97/L1
Lamone (riv.), It. 101/J4
Lamont, Ca, US 186/C4
Lamorlaye, Fr. 88/K4
Lamotrek (isl.), Micr. 174/D4
Lampa, Chile 216/N8
Lampa, Peru 214/D4
Lampang, Thai. 136/B2
Lampasas, Tx, US 187/H5
Lampasas (riv.), Tx, US 190/D4
Lampazos de Naranjo, Mex. 201/E3
Lampedusa, It. 104/C5
Lampedusa (isl.), It. 104/C5
Lampertheim, Ger. 112/B3
Lampeter, Pa, US 196/B4
Lamphun, Thai. 136/B2
Lampman, Sk, Can. 185/H3
Lamporecchio, It. 117/D5
Lamstedt, Ger. 109/G1
Lamu, Kenya 162/D3
Lamud, Peru 214/B2
Lamwa (peak), Ugan. 162/B2
Lan Sang NP, Thai. 136/B2
Lana, It. 115/H4
Lana, Río de la (riv.), Mex. 202/C2
Lanai (isl.), Hi, US 182/T10
Lanaihale (peak), Hi, US 182/T10
Lanaken, Belg. 111/E2
Lanark, Sc, UK 94/C5
Lanbi (isl.), Myan. 141/G5
Lancang Lahuzu Zizhixian, China 141/G3
Lancashire (co.), Eng, UK 93/F4
Lancashire (plain), Eng, UK 93/E4
Lancaster (sound), Nun., Can. 181/H1
Lancaster, Eng, UK 93/F3
Lancaster, Ca, US 186/C4
Lancaster, NY, US 189/S10
Lancaster, Pa, US 196/B3
Lancaster (co.), Pa, US 196/B4
Lancaster, SC, US 191/H3
Lancelin, Austl. 170/B4
Lanciano, It. 104/D1
L'Ancienne-Lorette, Qu, Can. 189/G2
Lanco, Chile 216/B3
Łańcut, Pol. 99/M3
Lancy, Swi. 114/C5
Land Kehdingen (reg.), Ger. 109/G1
Landau an der Isar, Ger. 113/F5
Landau in der Pfalz, Ger. 112/B4
Landeck, Aus. 115/G3
Landen, Belg. 111/E2
Lander, Wy, US 184/F5
Landerneau, Fr. 100/A2
Landes (reg.), Fr. 100/C4
Landes de Lanvaux (mts.), Fr. 100/B3
Landesbergen, Ger. 109/G3
Landis, Sk, Can. 184/F2
Landis Valley Museum, Pa, US 196/B3
Landisburg, Pa, US 196/A3
Landivisiau, Fr. 100/A2
Landrecies, Fr. 110/C3
Landri Sales, Braz. 212/B2
Landriano, It. 116/C2
Land's End (pt.), Eng, UK 90/A6
Landsberg, Ger. 115/G1
Landser, Fr. 114/D2
Landshut, Ger. 113/F5
Landskrona, Swe. 96/E4
Landsmeer, Neth. 108/B4
Landstuhl, Ger. 111/G5
Landvetter (int'l arpt.), Swe. 96/E3
Lane End, Eng, UK 88/A2
Lanester, Fr. 100/B3
Lanett, Al, US 191/G3
Lang Craig (pt.), Sc, UK 94/D3
Lang Kha Tuk (peak), Thai. 136/B4
Lang Son, Viet. 141/J3
Lang Suan, Thai. 136/B4
Langadhás, Gre. 105/H2
Langdon, ND, US 185/J3
Langeac, Fr. 100/E4
Langebaanweg, SAfr. 164/L10
Langeberg (mts.), SAfr. 164/L10
Langeland (isl.), Ger. 96/D4
Langelsheim, Ger. 109/H5
Langen, Ger. 109/F1
Langen, Ger. 112/B3
Langenaltheim, Ger. 112/D5
Langenargen, Ger. 115/F2
Langenau, Ger. 112/D5
Langenbach, Ger. 113/E6
Langenberg, Ger. 109/E6
Langenburg, Sk, Can. 185/H3
Längenfeld, Aus. 115/G3
Langenfeld, Ger. 111/F1
Langenhagen, Ger. 109/G4
Langenhorn, Ger. 96/C4
Langenlois, Aus. 99/H4
Langenpreising, Ger. 113/E6
Langenselbold, Ger. 112/C2
Langenstein, Aus. 113/H6
Langenthal, Swi. 114/D3
Langenzenn, Ger. 112/D3
Langenzersdorf, Aus. 107/N7
Langeoog, Ger. 109/E1
Langeoog (isl.), Ger. 109/E1
Langerringen, Ger. 115/G1
Langeskov, Den. 96/D4
Langesund, Nor. 96/C2
Langeten (riv.), Swi. 114/D3
Langfang, China 130/H7
Langfurth, Ger. 112/D4
Langham, Sk, Can. 184/G2
Langhirano, It. 116/D3
Langholm, Sc, UK 93/F1
Langhorne, Pa, US 196/D3
Langjökull (glacier), Ice. 95/N7
Langkawi (isl.), Malay. 141/G6
Langley, Wa, US 193/C1
Langnau im Emmental, Swi. 114/D4
Langney (pt.), Eng, UK 91/G5
Langogne, Fr. 100/E4
Langon, Fr. 100/C4
Langøya (isl.), Nor. 95/E1
Langquaid, Ger. 113/F5
Langres, Fr. 114/B2
Langres, Plateau de (plat.), Fr. 100/F3
Langsa, Indo. 138/A3
Langshyttan, Swe. 96/G1
Langtang Lirung (peak), Nepal 143/E1
Langtang NP, Nepal 143/E1
Langtry, Tx, US 190/C4
Languedoc (reg.), Fr. 100/E5
Languedoc-Roussillon (pol. reg.), Fr. 100/E5
Langwedel, Ger. 109/G3
Langweid an Lech, Ger. 112/E6
Langwies, Swi. 115/F4
Langxi, China 130/D5
Lanham-Seabrook, Md, US 196/B6
Lanigan, Sk, Can. 185/G3
Laniloa (pt.), Hi, US 182/W12
Lanin (vol.), Arg. 216/C3
Lanin, PN, Arg. 215/B4
Länkäran, Azer. 121/J5
Lanlacuni Bajo, Peru 214/D4
Lannemezan (plat.), Fr. 100/D5
Lannion (bay), Fr. 100/B2
Lannion, Fr. 100/B2
Lansdale, Pa, US 196/C3
Lansdowne, India 142/B1
Lansdowne, Pa, US 196/C4
Lansdowne-Baltimore Highlands, Md, US 196/B5
Lansford, Pa, US 196/C2
Lanshan, China 141/K2
Lansing (cap.), Mi, US 188/C3
Lansing, Ks, US 195/D5
Lansing, Il, US 193/Q16
Lanta (isl.), Thai. 141/G6
Lantau (chan.), China 129/T11
Lantau (peak), China 129/T11
Lantau (isl.), China 129/T10
Lanterne (riv.), Fr. 114/C2
Lanús, Arg. 217/J11
Lanusei, It. 104/A3
Lanxi, China 137/C2
Lanzarote (int'l arpt.), Canl., Sp. 156/B3
Lanzarote (isl.), Canl., Sp. 156/B3
Lanžhot, Czh. 99/J4
Lanzhou, China 128/H4
Lao (mts.), China 131/D2
Lao (peak), China 130/E3
Lao Cai, Viet. 136/C1
Laoag, Phil. 137/D4
Laoang, Phil. 137/E5

Laohekou, China 130/B4
Laojun (mtn.), China 130/B4
Laon, Fr. 110/C4
Laos (ctry.) 136/C2
Laoshan, China 130/E3
Laotuding (peak), China 131/C2
Laou (riv.), Mor. 158/B2
Lapa, Braz. 213/B3
Lapeer, Mi, US 188/D3
Lapeer (co.), Mi, US 193/F6
Lapinlahti, Fin. 118/E3
Lapithos, Cyp. 149/C2
Lapland (reg.), Swe. 218/D
Laporte, Co, US 195/B1
Lappeenranta, Fin. 97/K1
Lappersdorf, Ger. 113/F4
Lappi (prov.), Fin. 95/F2
Laptev (sea), Rus. 125/M2
Lapua, Fin. 118/D3
Lapy, Pol. 99/M2
L'Aquila, It. 104/C1
Lär, Iran 147/F3
Lara, Alg. 173/C3
Lara (state), Ven. 210/D2
Laracha, Sp. 102/B1
Larache (prov.), Mor. 158/B2
Larache, Mor. 158/A2
Laragne-Montéglin, Fr. 100/M1
Laramie (riv.), Wy, US 185/G5
Laramie, Wy, US 185/G5
Laramie (mts.), Wy, US 185/G5
Laranjeiras do Sul, Braz. 213/A3
Larat (isl.), Indo. 139/H5
Larba, Alg. 158/G4
Larchmont, NY, US 197/K8
Lærdalsøyri, Nor. 96/B1
Laredo, Peru 214/B3
Laredo (int'l arpt.), Tx, US 190/D5
Laredo, Tx, US 190/D5
Laredo, Sp. 102/D1
Laren, Neth. 108/C4
Lares, Peru 214/C4
Largo, Fl, US 191/H5
Largo, Md, US 196/B6
Largo (bay), Sc, UK 94/D4
Largo, Cayo (isl.), Cuba 203/F1
Largs, Sc, UK 94/B5
Largue (riv.), Fr. 114/C2
Lariang (riv.), Indo. 139/E4
Larino, It. 104/D2
Lárisa, Gre. 105/H3
Lark (riv.), Eng, UK 91/G2
Lärkäna, Pak. 147/J3
Larkhall, Sc, UK 94/C5
Larkspur, Ca, US 193/J11
Larmor-Plage, Fr. 100/B3
Larnaca (int'l arpt.), Cyp. 149/C2
Larnaca (dist.), Cyp. 149/C2
Larnaca, Cyp. 149/C2
Larne, NI, UK 92/C2
Larne (dist.), NI, UK 92/C2
Larne Lough (inlet), NI, UK 92/C2
Larned, Ks, US 187/H4
Larochette, Lux. 111/F4
Laroque-d'Olmes, Fr. 100/D5
Larose, La, US 191/F4
Larreynaga, Nic. 202/E3
Larroque, Arg. 217/J10
Larsen Bay, Ak, US 192/H4
Larsen Ice Shelf, Ant. 218/V
Larsen Sound (bay), Nun., Can. 180/G1
L'Artois, Collines de (hills), Fr. 98/A3
Laruns, Fr. 100/C5
Larvik, Nor. 96/D2
Las Animas, Co, US 187/G3
Las Aves (isls.), Ven. 199/H5
Las Breñas, Arg. 216/D3
Las Cabezas de San Juan, Sp. 102/C4
Las Cabras, Chile 216/N9
Las Cruces, NM, US 186/F4
Las Delicias, Mex. 210/C3
Las Eutimias, Mex. 190/C4
Las Flores, Arg. 216/F3
Las Guacamayas, Mex. 200/E5
Las Hermosas, PN, Col. 210/C4
Las Higueras, Arg. 216/D2
Las Lajas, Arg. 216/C3
Las Lajas (peak), Arg. 216/C3
Las Lomas, Peru 214/A2
Las Lomitas, Arg. 215/D1
Las Margaritas, Mex. 202/D2
Las Martinas, Cuba 203/E1
Las Mercedes, Ven. 211/E2
Las Minas (peak), Hon. 202/D3
Las Nieves, Mex. 200/D4
Las Orquídeas, PN, Col. 210/B3
Las Palmas, Pan. 203/G4
Las Palmas de Cocalán, PN, Chile 216/N9
Las Palmas de Gran Canaria, Canl., Sp. 156/B3
Las Pedroñeras, Sp. 102/D3
Las Perdices, Arg. 216/C2
Las Perlas (arch.), Pan. 203/G4

Las Piedras, Peru 214/D4
Las Piedras, Ven. 210/C2
Las Piedras, Uru. 217/K11
Las Pipinas, Arg. 217/F2
Las Rosas, Mex. 202/C2
Las Rozas de Madrid, Sp. 103/N9
Las Tablas, Pan. 203/F5
Las Varas, Mex. 200/D4
Las Varillas, Arg. 215/D3
Las Vegas, NM, US 187/F4
Las Vegas, Nv, US 186/D3
Lasalle, Qu, Can. 189/N7
Lasberg, Aus. 113/H6
Lascano, Uru. 217/G2
Lashio, Myan. 141/G3
Lashkar Gāh, Afg. 147/H2
Lasne-Chapelle-Saint-Lambert, Belg. 111/D2
Læsø (isl.), Den. 96/D3
Lasolo (riv.), Indo. 139/F4
Lassen (peak), Ca, US 184/C5
Lassen Volcanic NP, Ca, US 186/B2
L'Assomption, Qu, Can. 189/P6
L'Assomption (co.), Qu, Can. 189/N6
L'Assomption (riv.), Qu, Can. 189/P6
Last Mountain (lake), Sk, Can. 185/G3
Lastovo (isl.), Cro. 104/E1
Lastovski (chan.), Cro. 106/C4
Lastovski Kanal (chan.), Cro. 104/E1
Lastra a Signa, It. 117/E5
Lastrup, Ger. 109/E3
Lata, Sol. 174/F6
Latacunga, Ecu. 210/B5
Latady (isl.), Ant. 218/U
L'Atakora (prov.), Ben. 161/F4
Lātehār, India 143/E4
Latemar (peak), It. 115/H5
Laterza, It. 104/E2
Lathan (riv.), Fr. 100/C3
Lathrop, Ca, US 193/M11
Latina, It. 104/C2
Latisana, It. 117/G1
Latorica (riv.), Slvk.,Ukr. 99/M4
Latrobe, Austl. 173/C4
Latrobe (mt.), Austl. 173/C3
Latrobe (riv.), Austl. 173/C3
Lattes, Fr. 100/E5
Lattingtown, NY, US 197/L8
Lātūr, India 147/L5
Latvia (ctry.) 97/L3
Lau Group (isl.), Fiji 174/H6
Laubach, Ger. 112/B1
Lauca, PN, Chile 208/D7
Lauch (riv.), Fr. 101/G3
Lauchert (riv.), Ger. 112/C6
Lauchheim, Ger. 112/D5
Lauda-Königshofen, Ger. 112/C3
Lauder, Sc, UK 94/D5
Lauderdale (lakes), Wi, US 193/N14
Lauenbrück, Ger. 109/G2
Lauenburg, Ger. 109/H2
Lauenen, Swi. 114/D5
Lauenförde, Ger. 109/H5
Lauer (riv.), Ger. 112/D2
Lauf, Ger. 112/E3
Laufach, Ger. 112/C2
Laufen, Swi. 114/D3
Laufen, Ger. 113/F7
Laufenburg, Swi. 114/E2
Lauffen am Neckar, Ger. 112/C4
Laughlen (mt.), Austl. 171/G2
Lauhanvuoren NP, Fin. 118/D3
Lauingen, Ger. 112/D5
Launceston, Austl. 173/C4
Launette (riv.), Fr. 88/L4
Laupahoehoe, Hi, US 182/U11
Laupen, Swi. 114/D4
Lauperswil, Swi. 114/D4
Laupheim, Ger. 115/F1
Laura, Austl. 171/H5
Laureana di Borrello, It. 104/E3
Laurel, Mt, US 184/F4
Laurel, Ms, US 191/F4
Laurel, Md, US 196/B5
Laurel Springs, NJ, US 196/C4
Laureldale, Pa, US 196/C3
Laurelton, Pa, US 196/A2
Laurence Harbor, NJ, US 197/J10
Laurencekirk, Sc, UK 94/D3
Laurens, SC, US 191/H3
Laurentian (plat.), On, Can. 180/G3
Laurentides, Qu, Can. 189/N6
Laurinburg, NC, US 191/J3
Laurium, Mi, US 185/L4
Lausanne, Swi. 114/C4
Lauscha, Ger. 112/E2
Laut (isl.), Indo. 139/E4
Lautaro, Chile 216/B3
Lauter, Ger. 113/F1
Lauter (riv.), Ger. 98/E3
Lauterach (riv.), Ger. 113/E4
Lauterbach (riv.), Ger. 112/E2

Lauterbach, Ger. 112/C1
Lauterbourg, Fr. 112/B5
Lauterbrunnen, Swi. 114/D4
Lauterecken, Ger. 111/G4
Lauve, Nor. 96/D2
Lauwers (chan.), Neth. 108/D1
Lauwersmeer (lake), Neth. 108/D2
Lava Beds Nat'l Mon., Ca, US 184/C5
Lavagna (riv.), It. 116/C4
Lavagna, It. 116/C4
Laval, Fr. 100/C2
Laval, Qu, Can. 189/N6
Lavalleja (dept.), Uru. 217/G2
Lavallette, NJ, US 196/D4
Lavans-lès-Saint-Claude, Fr. 114/B5
Lavant (riv.), Aus. 101/L3
Lavapié (pt.), Chile 216/B3
Lavaur, Fr. 100/D4
Laveen, Az, US 195/R19
Lavelanet, Fr. 100/D5
Lavello, It. 104/D2
Laveno, It. 115/E6
Laverton, Austl. 170/D4
Lavey, Swi. 114/D5
Lavezzola, It. 117/E3
Lavino (riv.), It. 117/E4
Lavis, It. 115/H5
Lavos, Port. 102/A2
Lavras, Braz. 213/C2
Lavras da Mangabeira, Braz. 212/C2
Lávrion, Gre. 105/J4
Lawa (riv.), FrG. 211/H4
Lāwar Khās, India 142/A1
Lawarai (pass), Pak. 144/A2
Lawit (mtn.), Indo. 138/D3
Lawit (peak), Malay. 141/H6
Lawndale, Ca, US 194/F8
Lawnhill, BC, Can. 192/M5
Lawra, Gha. 160/E4
Lawrence, Ks, US 187/J3
Lawrence, Ma, US 189/G3
Lawrence, NY, US 197/L9
Lawrenceburg, In, US 188/C4
Lawrenceburg, Ky, US 191/G2
Lawrence Water (riv.), Sc, UK 94/D5
Lawrenceburg, Tn, US 191/G3
Lawrencetown, NI, UK 92/B3
Lawrenceville, Ga, US 191/H3
Lawrenceville, NJ, US 196/D3
Lawson, Mo, US 195/E5
Lawu (peak), Indo. 138/D5
Lawz, Jabal al (peak), SAr. 146/C3
Laxá, Swe. 96/F2
Laxey, IM, UK 92/D3
Laxou, Fr. 111/F6
Lay (riv.), Fr. 100/C3
Lay-Saint-Christophe, Fr. 111/F6
Laya (riv.), Rus. 119/N2
Layar (cape), Indo. 139/E4
Laylān, Iraq 148/F3
Layon (riv.), Fr. 100/C3
Laysan (isl.), Hi, US 175/M2
Layton, NJ, US 196/D1
Layton, Ut, US 195/K11
Lazarevac, Serb. 106/E3
Lázaro Cárdenas, Mex. 200/B2
Lázaro Cárdenas, Mex. 200/E5
Lbrtktepe, Turk. 105/K2
Le Ban-Saint-Martin, Fr. 111/F5
Le Blanc, Fr. 100/D3
Le Blanc-Mesnil, Fr. 88/K5
Le Breuil, Fr. 100/F3
Le Cannet, Fr. 101/G5
Le Cateau-Cambrésis, Fr. 110/C3
Le Chasseral (peak), Swi. 114/D3
Le Chasseron (peak), Swi. 114/C4
Le Chesnay, Fr. 88/J5
Le Chesne, Fr. 110/D5
Le Cheval Blanc (peak), Fr. 114/C5
Le Cheylard, Fr. 100/F4
Le Cornate (peak), It. 101/J3
Le Creusot, Fr. 100/F3
Le Crotoy, Fr. 98/A3
Le Gore, Md, US 196/A4
Le Grammont (peak), Swi. 114/C5
Le Grand (cape), Austl. 170/D5
Le Grand Ballon (peak), Fr. 114/C2
Le Grau-du-Roi, Fr. 100/F5
Le Grazie, It. 116/C4
Le Havre, Fr. 100/D2
Le Landeron, Swi. 114/D3
Le Lavandou, Fr. 101/G5
Le Locle, Swi. 114/C3
Le Luc, Fr. 101/G5
Le Mans, Fr. 100/D2
Le Mée-sur-Seine, Fr. 88/K6
Le Mesnil-Amelot, Fr. 88/K4
Le Mesnil-Esnard, Fr. 110/A5
Le Mesnil-le-Roi, Fr. 88/J5

Le Mesnil-Saint-Denis, Fr. 88/H5
Le Mesnil-sur-Oger, Fr. 110/D6
Le Môle (peak), Fr. 114/C5
Le Morond (peak), Fr. 114/C4
Le Moure de la Gardille (peak), Fr. 100/E4
Le Murge (mts.), It. 104/E2
Le Noirmont (peak), Fr. 114/C4
Le Noirmont (peak), Swi. 114/C5
Le Noirmont, Swi. 114/C3
Le Nouvion-en-Thiérache, Fr. 52/C3
Le Palais, Fr. 100/B3
Le Palais-sur-Vienne, Fr. 100/D4
Le Passage, Fr. 100/D4
Le Perray-en-Yvelines, Fr. 88/H5
Le Petit Ballon (peak), Fr. 114/D2
Le Plessis-Belleville, Fr. 88/L4
Le Plessis-Feu-Aussoux, Fr. 88/M5
Le Plessis-Placy, Fr. 88/L4
Le Port, Reun., Fr. 165/S15
Le Portel, Fr. 110/A2
Le Puy-en-Velay, Fr. 100/E4
Le Russey, Fr. 114/C3
Le Suchet (peak), Swi. 114/C4
Le Tampon, Reun., Fr. 165/S15
Le Teil, Fr. 100/F4
Le Tholy, Fr. 114/C1
Le Touquet-Paris-Plage, Fr. 110/A2
Le Tréport, Fr. 110/A3
Le Val-d'Ajol, Fr. 114/C2
Le Vésinet, Fr. 88/J5
Le Vigan, Fr. 100/E5
Lea (riv.), Eng, UK 91/F3
Leach (lake), Ca, US 185/K4
Leach (riv.), Eng, UK 91/E3
Leacock-Leola-Bareville, Pa, US 196/B3
Lead, SD, US 187/G3
Leader, Sk, Can. 184/F3
Leader Water (riv.), Sc, UK 94/D5
Leadon (riv.), Eng, UK 90/D3
Leadville, Co, US 187/F2
Leaf (riv.), Ms, US 191/F4
Leaghur (lake), Austl. 173/B2
League City, Tx, US 187/H5
Leakey, Tx, US 187/H5
Leam (riv.), Eng, UK 91/E2
Leamington, On, Can. 188/D3
Le'an, China 137/C2
Leander (pt.), Austl. 170/B4
Leaota (peak), Rom. 107/G3
Learmonth, Austl. 170/B2
Leatherhead, Eng, UK 88/C3
Leavenworth, Ks, US 195/D5
Leavenworth (co.), Ks, US 195/D5
Leavenworth, Wa, US 184/C4
Leawood, Ks, US 195/D6
Leba, Pol. 99/J1
Lebach, Ger. 111/F5
Lebak, Phil. 137/D6
Lebane, Serb. 106/E4
Lebanon (ctry.) 149/D3
Lebanon (mts.), Leb. 149/D3
Lebanon, In, US 188/C3
Lebanon, Ky, US 188/C4
Lebanon, Mo, US 187/J3
Lebanon, NH, US 189/F3
Lebanon, NJ, US 196/D2
Lebanon, Or, US 184/C4
Lebanon, Pa, US 196/B3
Lebanon, Tn, US 188/C4
Lebbeke, Belg. 111/D2
Lebel-sur-Quévillon, Qu, Can. 188/E1
Lebene (riv.), Mor. 158/B2
Lébény, Hun. 106/C2
Lębork, Pol. 96/G4
Lebrija, Sp. 102/B4
Lebu, Chile 216/B3
Lebu, Chile 216/B3
Leça da Palmeira, Port. 102/A2
Lecce, It. 105/F2
Lecco, It. 116/C1
Lecco (prov.), It. 116/C1
Lecco, Lago di (lake), It. 116/C1
Lech, Aus. 115/G3
Lech (riv.), Ger. 101/K2
Lechang, China 137/B3
Lechbruck, Ger. 115/G2
Leck, Ger. 96/C4
Lectoure, Fr. 100/D5
Łęczna, Pol. 99/M3
Leda (riv.), Ger. 109/E2
Ledang (peak), Malay. 138/B3
Lede, Belg. 110/C2
Ledegem, Belg. 110/C2
Ledesma, Sp. 102/B2
Lelai (cape), Indo. 139/G3
Ledge Point, Austl. 170/B4
Ledong, China 141/J4

Ledro (lake), It. 115/G6
Ledu (peak), It. 115/F5
Leduc, Ab, Can. 184/E2
Lee (riv.), Ire. 89/P11
Lee (mtn.), Pa, US 196/B1
Leech (lake), Mn, US 185/K4
Leeds, Eng, UK 93/G4
Leeds (co.), Eng, UK 93/G4
Leeds and Bradford (int'l arpt.), Eng, UK 93/G4
Leeds and Liverpool (canal), Eng, UK 93/G4
Leeds Point, NJ, US 196/D5
Leegebruch, Ger. 98/Q6
Leek, Neth. 108/D2
Leek, Eng, UK 93/F5
Leeman, Austl. 170/B4
Leer, Ger. 109/E2
Leerdam, Neth. 108/C4
Leersum, Neth. 108/C4
Lees Summit, Mo, US 195/E6
Leesburg, Fl, US 191/H4
Leesburg, NJ, US 196/D5
Leese, Ger. 109/G3
Leesport, Pa, US 196/C3
Leesville, La, US 187/J5
Leeton, Austl. 173/C2
Leeu (riv.), SAfr. 164/L10
Leeudoringstad, SAfr. 164/D2
Leeuwarden, Neth. 108/C2
Leeuwin (cape), Austl. 170/B5
Leeuwin-Naturaliste NP, Austl. 170/B5
Leeward (isls.), NAm. 199/J4
Leff (riv.), Fr. 100/B2
Lefka, Cyp. 149/C2
Lefo (peak), Camr. 161/H5
Lefroy (lake), Austl. 170/D4
Legana, Austl. 173/C4
Leganés, Sp. 103/N9
Legaspi, Phil. 137/D5
Legau, Ger. 115/G2
Legazpia, Sp. 102/D1
Legges Tor (peak), Austl. 173/C4
Legionowo, Pol. 99/L2
Léglise, Belg. 111/E4
Legnago, It. 117/E2
Legnano, It. 101/H4
Legnaro, It. 117/E2
Legnica, Pol. 99/J3
Legnone (peak), It. 115/F5
Leh, India 144/D2
Leh Palace, India 144/D2
Lehi, Ut, US 195/K13
Lehigh (co.), Pa, US 196/C2
Lehigh Acres, Fl, US 191/H5
Lehighton, Pa, US 196/C2
Lehinch, Ire. 89/P10
Lehrberg, Ger. 112/D4
Lehrte, Ger. 109/G4
Lei (riv.), China 141/K2
Leiah, Pak. 144/A4
Leiblfing, Ger. 113/F5
Leibo, China 141/H4
Leicester, Eng, UK 91/E1
Leicester (co.), Eng, UK 91/E1
Leicestershire (co.), Eng, UK 93/H6
Leichhardt (dam), Austl. 171/H2
Leichhardt (riv.), Austl. 167/C2
Leichlingen, Ger. 111/G1
Leiden, Neth. 108/B4
Leiderdorp, Neth. 108/B4
Leidschendam, Neth. 108/B4
Leie (riv.), Belg. 110/C2
Leifers (Laives), It. 101/J3
Leigh, Eng, UK 93/F5
Leigh Creek, Austl. 171/H4
Leimebamba, Peru 214/B2
Leimen, Ger. 112/B4
Leimersheim, Ger. 112/B4
Leinefelde, Ger. 109/H6
Leinfelden-Echterdingen, Ger. 112/C5
Leinster (mt.), Ire. 89/Q10
Leinster, Austl. 170/D3
Leinster (reg.), Ire. 92/A5
Leipsic, De, US 196/C5
Leipzig, Ger. 98/G3
Leiria, Port. 102/A3
Leiria (dist.), Port. 102/A3
Leisler (mt.), Austl. 171/F2
Leith (hill), Eng, UK 88/B3
Leitha (riv.), Aus. 99/J5
Leixlip, Ire. 92/B5
Leizhou (pen.), China 141/J3
Lek (riv.), Neth. 98/C3
Le Kef, Tun. 158/L6
Le Kef (gov.), Tun. 158/L6
Lekhainá, Gre. 105/G4
Lekki (lag.), Nga. 161/G5
Leksands-Noret, Swe. 96/F1
Leksozero (lake), Rus. 118/G2
Leland, Ms, US 187/K4

Leling, China 130/D3
Lelystad, Neth. 108/C3
Lem, Den. 96/C3
Lema (peak), It. 115/E5
Léman (Geneva) (lake), Fr. 101/G3
Lemberg, Ger. 111/G5
Lembu (peak), Indo. 138/A3
Leme, Braz. 213/C2
Lemenjoen NP, Fin. 95/H1
Lemgo, Ger. 109/F4
Lemland (isl.), Fin. 97/H2
Lemland, Fin. 97/J1
Lemmer, Neth. 108/C3
Lemmon, SD, US 185/H4
Lemon Grove, Ca, US 194/C5
Lempa (riv.), ESal. 202/D3
Lempäälä, Fin. 97/K1
Lempdes, Fr. 100/E4
Lemoos, Aus. 115/G3
Lemva (riv.), Rus. 119/P2
Lemvig, Den. 96/C3
Lemwerder, Ger. 109/F2
Lena (riv.), Rus. 125/M3
Lena, Nor. 96/D1
Léry, Qu, Can. 189/N7
Lenape (lake), NJ, US 196/D5
Lençóis Maranhenses, PN dos, Braz. 209/K4
Lençóis Paulista, Braz. 213/B2
Lenina (peak), Taj. 145/F5
Leninabad (int'l arpt.), Swi. 114/C4
Leningradskaya Oblast, Rus. 118/G3
Leninobod (obl.), Taj. 145/E4
Leninogorsk, Rus. 119/M5
Leninsk-Kuznetskiy, Rus. 122/J4
Leninváros, Hun. 99/L5
Lenk, Swi. 114/D5
Lenne (riv.), Ger. 111/G1
Lennestadt, Ger. 109/F6
Lenningen, Ger. 112/C5
Lennox (isl.), Chile 217/D7
Lennox, Ca, US 194/F8
Lennox (hills), Sc, UK 94/B5
Lennoxtown, Sc, UK 94/B5
Leno, It. 116/D2
Lenoir, NC, US 191/H3
Lenoir City, Tn, US 191/G3
Lenora, Czh. 113/G5
Lens, Fr. 110/C3
Lens, Belg. 110/C2
Lensahn, Ger. 96/D4
Lensk, Rus. 123/M3
Lenting, Ger. 113/E5
Lentini, It. 104/D4
Lenvik, Nor. 95/F1
Leny, Pass of (pass), Sc, UK 94/B4
Lenzburg, Swi. 114/E3
Lenzkirch, Ger. 115/E2
Léo, Burk. 161/E4
Leoben, Aus. 101/L3
Leográ (riv.), It. 115/E5
Leola, SD, US 185/J4
León, Mex. 201/E4
León (int'l arpt.), Mex. 200/C3
León, Nic. 202/E3
León, Sp. 102/C1
León (riv.), Tx, US 190/D3
Leon, Etang de (lake), Fr. 100/C4
León-Guanajuato (int'l arpt.), Mex. 201/E4
Leon Springs, Tx, US 195/T20
Leon Valley, Tx, US 195/T21
Leona Valley, Ca, US 194/B1
Leonard, Mi, US 193/F6
Leonard, Tx, US 187/H4
Leonardo, NJ, US 197/J10
Leonardo da Vinci (int'l arpt.), It. 104/C2
Leonberg, Ger. 112/C5
Leonding, Aus. 113/H6
Leone (riv.), It. 115/E6
Leones, Arg. 216/E2
Leonforte, It. 104/D4
Leongatha, Austl. 173/C4
Leonia, NJ, US 197/K8
Leonidhion, Gre. 105/H4
Leonora, Austl. 170/D4
Leopoldkanaal (riv.), Belg. 110/C2
Leopoldsburg, Belg. 111/E1
Leopoldsdorf im Marchfelde, Aus. 107/P7
Leopoldshöhe, Ger. 109/F4
Leopoldina, Braz. 213/J7
Leoville, Sk, Can. 184/G2
Lepaera, Hon. 202/D3

Lépanges-sur-Vologne, Fr. 114/C2
Lepe, Sp. 102/B4
L'Épiphanie, Qu, Can. 189/P6
Lepontine Alps (mts.), Swi. 101/H3
Léraba (riv.), 160/D4
Lercara Friddi, It. 104/C4
Lerdo de Tejada, Mex. 202/C2
Leribe, Les. 164/E3
Lerici, It. 116/C4
Lerín, Sp. 102/E1
Lerma, Sp. 102/D1
Lerma, Mex. 201/Q10
Lerma (riv.), Mex. 201/K7
Lerma (isl.), Gre. 105/G3
Lérouville, Fr. 111/E6
Lerwick, Sc, UK 89/W13
Les Alluets-le-Roi, Fr. 88/H5
Les Bois, Swi. 114/C3
Les Breuleux, Swi. 114/D3
Les Bréviaires, Fr. 88/H5
Les Cayes, Haiti 203/H2
Les Cèdres, Qu, Can. 189/M7
Les Clayes-sous-Bois, Fr. 88/H5
Les Contamines-Montjoie, Fr. 114/C6
Les Diablerets (range), Swi. 114/D5
Les Essarts-le-Roi, Fr. 88/H5
Les Gets, Fr. 114/C5
Les Hautes-Rivières, Fr. 111/D4
Les Herbiers, Fr. 100/C3
Les Islettes, Fr. 111/E5
Les Mesnuls, Fr. 88/H5
Les Molières, Fr. 88/J6
Les Mureaux, Fr. 110/A6
Les Ponts-de-Martel, Swi. 114/C4
Les Sables-d'Olonne, Fr. 100/C3
Les Salines (int'l arpt.), Alg. 158/K6
Les Ulis, Fr. 88/J5
Les Verrières, Swi. 114/C4
Lesa, It. 116/B1
Leshan, China 141/H2
Lésigny, Fr. 88/K5
Lesima (peak), It. 116/C3
Lesjöfors, Swe. 96/F2
Leskovac, Serb. 106/E4
Leslie, Sc, UK 94/C4
Lesmahagow, Sc, UK 94/C5
Lesneven, Fr. 100/A2
Lešnica, Rus. 106/D3
Lesosibirsk, Rus. 122/J4
Lesotho (ctry.) 164/E6
Lesozavodsk, Rus. 129/P2
Lesparre-Médoc, Fr. 100/C4
Lesquin (int'l arpt.), Fr. 110/C2
Lesse (riv.), Belg. 98/C3
Lessebo, Swe. 96/F3
Lesser Antilles (isls.), NAm. 199/M8
Lesser Caucasus (mts.), Asia 121/G4
Lesser Slave (lake), Ab, Can. 180/E3
Lesser Sunda (isls.), Indo. 139/E5
Lessines, Belg. 110/C2
Lésvos (isl.), Gre. 99/J3
Leszno, Pol. 99/J3
Létavértes, Hun. 106/F2
Letchworth, Eng, UK 91/F3
Letham, Sc, UK 94/D3
Lethbridge, Ab, Can. 184/E3
Lethe (riv.), Ger. 109/F2
Lethem, Guy. 211/G4
Leti (isls.), Indo. 139/G5
Leticia, Col. 214/D2
Leting, China 130/D3
Letlhakane, Bots. 163/E5
Letlhakeng, Bots. 163/D5
Letnitsa, Bul. 107/G4
L'Étoile, Fr. 110/B3
Letpadan, Myan. 141/G4
Letschin, Ger. 99/H2
Letsók-Aw (isl.), Myan. 138/A1
Letterkenny, Ire. 89/Q9
Leucate, Fr. 100/E5
Leuk, Swi. 114/D5
Leun, Ger. 112/B1
Leusden-Zuid, Neth. 108/C4
Leuser (peak), Indo. 138/A3
Leuterhausen, Ger. 112/D4
Leutkirch im Allgäu, Ger. 115/G2
Leuze-en-Hainaut, Belg. 110/C2
Levádhia, Gre. 105/H3
Levallois-Perret, Fr. 88/J5
Levante, Riviera di (coast), It. 116/C4
Levanto, It. 116/C4
Levanger, Nor. 95/D3
Levasy, Mo, US 195/F5
Level (isl.), Chile 216/B5
Level, Md, US 196/B4

Levelland, Tx, US 187/G4
Levelock, Ak, US 192/G4
Leven (pt.), SAfr. 165/F2
Leven, Sc, UK 94/D4
Leven (lake), Sc, UK 94/A3
Leven, Sc, UK 94/C4
Leveque (cape), Austl. 167/B2
Leverburgh, Sc, UK 89/Q8
Leverkusen, Ger. 111/F1
Levice, Slvk. 106/D1
Levico Terme, It. 115/H5
Levier, Fr. 114/C4
Levin, NZ 175/T11
Lévis, Qu, Can. 189/G2
Lévis-Saint-Nom, Fr. 88/H5
Levittown, Pa, US 196/D3
Levittown, NY, US 197/L9
Levkás, Gre. 105/G3
Levkás (isl.), Gre. 105/G3
Levkímmi, Gre. 105/G3
Levoča, Slvk. 99/L4
Levrier (bay), Mrta. 156/A5
Levski, Bul. 107/G4
Lewes, Eng, UK 91/G5
Lewin Brzeski, Pol. 99/J3
Lewis (riv.), Wa, US 184/C4
Lewis (range), Mt, US 184/E3
Lewis (hills), Nf, Can. 189/K1
Lewis (pass), NZ 175/S11
Lewis, Sc, UK 89/Q7
Lewis and Clark (lake), Ne,SD, US 185/J5
Lewis Smith (lake), Al, US 191/G3
Lewisburg, Tn, US 191/G3
Lewisburg, WV, US 188/D4
Lewisburg, Pa, US 196/B2
Lewisham (bor.), Eng, UK 88/C2
Lewisporte, Nf, Can. 189/L1
Lewiston, Id, US 184/D4
Lewiston, Me, US 189/G2
Lewiston, NY, US 189/R9
Lewistown, Mt, US 184/F4
Lewistown, Pa, US 188/E3
Lewotobi (peak), Indo. 139/F5
Lexington, Ky, US 188/C4
Lexington, NC, US 191/H3
Lexington, Ne, US 185/J5
Lexington, Tn, US 188/B5
Lexington Park, Md, US 188/E4
Leyburn, Eng, UK 93/G3
Leyden, Co, US 195/B3
Leye, China 141/J3
Leyland, Eng, UK 93/F4
Leysin, Swi. 114/D5
Leyton, Swi. 114/D5
Lez (riv.), Fr. 100/F4
Leżajsk, Pol. 99/M3
Lezhë, Alb. 105/F2
Lézignan-Corbières, Fr. 100/E5
Lezuza, Sp. 102/D3
L'gov, Rus. 120/E2
Lhanbryd, Sc, UK 94/C1
Lhari, China 128/F5
Lhasa, China 140/F2
Lhazê, China 143/F1
L'Hongrin (lake), Swi. 114/D5
Lhorong, China 128/G5
L'Hospitalet de Llobregat, Sp. 103/L7
Lhozhag, China 143/H1
Lhünzê, China 141/G2
Li (riv.), China 137/B2
Li (riv.), China 141/K2
Li (mtn.), China 130/B4
Li Xian, China 137/B2
Lian (riv.), China 137/C2
Lian Xian, China 141/K3
Liancheng, China 137/C2
Liancourt, Fr. 110/B5
Liancourt Rocks (isl.), Asia 132/B2
Liangcheng, China 130/C2
Liangpran (peak), Indo. 138/D3
Liangzi (lake), China 130/C5
Lianhua, China 141/K2
Lianjiang, China 141/K3
Liannan Yaozu Zizhixian, China 137/B3
Lianshui, China 130/D4
Lianyuan, China 130/C5
Lianyungang, China 130/D4
Liao (riv.), China 131/A2
Liao (mtn.), China 130/B4
Liaocheng, China 130/D3
Liaodong (pen.), China 131/A3
Liaodong (isls.), China 130/E3
Liaodong, Gulf of (gulf), China 129/M3
Liaoning (prov.), China 129/N3
Liaoyang, China 131/B2
Liaoyuan, China 129/N3
Liaozhong, China 131/B2
Liāqatpur, Pak. 144/A5
Liard (riv.), NW, Can. 180/D2
Libby, Mt, US 184/E3
Libenge, D.R. Congo 155/C3
Libercourt, Fr. 110/C3
Liberdade (riv.), Braz. 209/H6
Liberdade, Braz. 213/J7
Liberec, Czh. 99/H3
Liberecký (pol. reg.), Czh. 99/H3

Liberia, CR 203/E4
Liberia (ctry.) 160/C5
Libertad, Belz. 202/D2
Libertad, Ven. 210/D2
Libertad, Uru. 217/K11
Libertador General
San Martín, Arg. 215/D1
Liberty, Ky, US 188/C4
Liberty (res.), Md, US 196/B5
Liberty, Ms, US 187/K6
Liberty, Mo, US 195/C5
Liberty, Tx, US 187/J5
Liberty, Ut, US 195/K11
Liberty Grove,
Md, US 196/B4
Libertyville, Il, US 193/P15
Libin, Belg. 111/E4
Libo, China 141/J2
Libobo (cape), Indo. 139/G4
Liboc (riv.), It. 99/G3
Libochovice, Czh. 113/H2
Libon, Phil. 137/D5
Librazhd, Alb. 105/G2
Libres, Mex. 201/M7
Libreville (cap.),
Gabon 154/C4
Libya (ctry.) 154/J2
Libyan (plat.), Libya 155/K1
Libyan (des.),
Egypt,Libya 155/K2
Licantén, Chile 216/B2
Licata, It. 104/C4
Lice, Turk. 148/E2
Lich, Ger. 112/B1
Licheng, China 130/C3
Licheng, China 130/D3
Lichfield, Eng, UK 91/F1
Lichinga, Moz. 163/G3
Lichtenau, Ger. 109/F5
Lichtenau, Ger. 112/D4
Lichtenau, Ger. 112/B5
Lichtenburg, SAfr. 164/D2
Lichtenfels, Ger. 112/D2
Lichtenrade, Ger. 98/O7
Lichtensteig, Swi. 115/F3
Lichtenvoorde, Neth. 108/D5
Lichtervelde, Belg. 110/C1
Lichuan, China 137/A1
Licinio de Almeida,
Braz. 212/B4
Lick Observatory,
Ca, US 193/L12
Licking (riv.),
Ky, US 188/C4
Licosa (cape), It. 104/D2
Licques, Fr. 110/A2
Lida, Bela. 97/L3
Liddell Water (riv.),
Sc, UK 93/F1
Liddes, Swi. 114/D6
Liddon (gulf),
NW, Can. 181/R7
Lidhoríkion, Gre. 105/H3
Lidingö, Swe. 96/H2
Lidköping, Swe. 96/E2
Lido, It. 117/F2
Lido di Iesolo, It. 117/F1
Lido di Ostia, It. 104/C2
Lidzbark, Pol. 99/K2
Lidzbark Warmiński,
Pol. 97/J4
Liebenau, Aus. 113/H6
Liebenbergsvlei (riv.),
SAfr. 164/E2
Liebig (mt.), Austl. 171/F2
Liechtenstein (ctry.) 115/F3
Liedekerke, Belg. 111/D2
Liège, Belg. 111/E2
Liège (prov.), Belg. 111/E3
Lieksa, Fin. 118/F3
Lienden, Neth. 108/C5
Lienen, Ger. 109/E4
Lienz, Aus. 101/K3
Liepāja, Lat. 97/J3
Lier, Belg. 111/D1
Lierneux, Belg. 111/E3
Lieser (riv.), Ger. 111/F3
Liesjärven NP, Fin. 97/K1
Liesse-Notre-Dame,
Fr. 110/C4
Liestal, Swi. 114/D3
Lieto, Fin. 97/K1
Liévin, Fr. 110/B3
Lièvre (riv.), Qu, Can. 188/F2
Liez (lake), Fr. 114/B2
Liezen, Aus. 101/L3
Liffey (riv.), Ire. 92/B5
Liffol-le-Grand, Fr. 114/B1
Lifford, Ire. 89/O9
Ligao, Phil. 139/F1
Lightning Ridge, Austl. 173/C1
Lightwater, Eng, UK 88/D6
Lignano Sabbiadoro,
It. 117/G2
Ligny-en-Barrois, Fr. 111/E6
Ligoncio (peak), It. 115/F5
Ligourión, Gre. 105/H4
Liguori, Mo, US 195/G9
Liguria (pol. reg.), It. 116/B4
Liguria (prov.), 101/H5
Ligurian (sea), Fr.,It. 101/H5
Lihou (reefs), Austl. 167/E2
Lihue, Hi, US 182/U10
Lijiang Naxizu Zizhixian,
China 141/H2
Lijin, China 130/D3
Likasi, D.R. Congo 163/E3
Likely, BC, Can. 184/C2
Likoma (isl.), Malw. 163/F3
Likouala, D.R. Congo 154/H7
Likova (riv.), Rus. 119/W9
L'Île-Perrot, Qu, Can. 189/N7
Lilani, Pak. 144/B3
Lilienthal, Ger. 109/F2

Liling, China 141/K2
Lilla Edet, Swe. 96/E2
Lille, Belg. 108/B6
Lille, Fr. 110/C2
Lille Bælt (chan.), Ger. 96/C4
Lillehammer, Nor. 96/D1
Lillers, Fr. 110/B2
Lillesand, Nor. 96/C2
Lillestrøm, Nor. 96/D2
Lilliwaup, Wa, US 193/A3
Lillo, Sp. 102/D3
Lillooet, BC, Can. 184/C3
Lillooet (riv.), BC, Can. 184/C3
Lilongwe (cap.),
Malw. 163/F3
Liloy, Phil. 137/D6
Lim (riv.), Serb. 106/D4
Lima, Arg. 217/J11
Lima, It. 116/C4
Lima (riv.), It. 117/D4
Lima (cap.), Peru 214/B4
Lima (dept.), Peru 214/B3
Lima (riv.), Port. 103/A2
Lima, Oh, US 188/C3
Lindi, Tanz. 162/C5
Lindlar, Ger. 111/G1
Lindley, SAfr. 164/D2
Lindome, Swe. 96/E3
Lindon, Ut, US 195/K13
Lindre (lake), Fr. 111/F6
Lindsay, Ca, US 186/C3
Lindsay, On, Can. 188/E2
Lindsay (mt.), Austl. 170/C5
Lindsay (mt.), Austl. 171/F3
Lindsdal, Swe. 96/G3
Line (isls.), Kiri. 175/J4
Line Mountain (mtn.),
Pa, US 196/B2
Lineboro, Md, US 196/B4
Linen, Ger. 109/E6
Linfen, China 130/B3
Ling (riv.), Sc, UK 94/A2
Ling Xian, China 141/K2
Ling Xian, China 130/D3
Lingbao, China 130/B4
Lingchuan, China 141/K2
Lingchuan, China 130/C4
Linge (riv.), Neth. 108/C5
Lingen, Ger. 109/E3
Lingfield, Eng, UK 88/C3
Lingga (isls.), Indo. 138/B3
Linglestown, Pa, US 196/B3
Lingolsheim, Fr. 114/D1
Lingqiu, China 130/C2
Lingshan, China 141/J3
Lingshan, China 130/C3
Lingshi, China 130/B3
Lingshui, China 141/K4
Linguère, Sen. 160/B3
Lingyin Si, China 130/L9
Lingyuan, China 131/H3
Lingyun, China 141/J3
Linhai, China 141/L2
Linhares, Braz. 213/D1
Linhe, China 128/J3
Linköping, Swe. 96/F2
Linli, China 137/B2
Linlithgow, Sc, UK 94/C5
Linosa (isl.), It. 158/N7
Linqing, China 130/C3
Linqu, China 130/D3
Linru, China 130/C4
Lins, Braz. 213/B2
Linschoten, Neth. 108/B4
Linshu, China 130/D3
Linta (riv.), Madg. 165/H9
Linthal, Swi. 115/F4
Linton, ND, US 185/H4
Linwood, Eng, UK 94/B5
Linxi, China 130/C3
Linyi, China 130/D3
Linyi, China 130/D3
Linyi, China 130/C4
Linying, China 130/C4
Linz (int'l arpt.),
Aus. 113/H6
Linz, Aus. 113/H6
Linz am Rhein, Ger. 111/G2
Linzhang, China 130/C3
Lion (gulf), Fr.,Sp. 103/G1
Lipa, Phil. 137/D5
Lipari (isl.), It. 104/D3
Lipari (isls.), It. 104/D3
Lipari, It. 104/D3
Liperi, Fin. 118/F3
Lipetsk, Rus. 120/F1
Lipetsk (int'l arpt.),
Rus. 120/F1
Lipetskaya Oblast,
Rus. 120/F1
Lipez (riv.), Bol. 208/E8
Lipez, Cordillera de
(mts.), Bol. 208/E8
Liping, China 141/J2
Lipljan, Kos. 106/E4
Lipno (res.), Czh. 113/H5
Lipno, Pol. 99/K2
Lipno, Udolní nádrž
(lake), Czh. 101/L2
Lipova, Rom. 106/E2
Lippe (riv.), Ger. 111/G1
Lippstadt, Ger. 109/F5
Liptovský Svätý Mikuláš,
Slvk. 99/K4
Liptrap (cape), Austl. 173/C3
Lira, Ugan. 162/B2
Lircay, Peru 214/C4

Liri (riv.), It. 104/C2
Liria, Sp. 103/E3
Liro (riv.), It. 115/F5
Lisboa (dist.), Port. 102/A3
Lisboa (int'l arpt.),
Port. 103/P10
Lisboa (Lisbon)
(cap.), Port. 103/P10
Lisbon, ND, US 185/J4
Lisbon, Me, US 189/G2
Lisbon, Md, US 196/A5
Lisburn (dist.), NI, UK 92/B2
Lisburn, NI, UK 92/B2
Lisburne (cape),
Ak, US 192/C2
Lisdoonvarna, Ire. 89/P10
Liselund (cape),
Nor. 96/D3
Liselje, Den. 96/D3
Lisha (riv.), China 141/H2
Lishu, China 131/H2
Lishui, China 137/C2
Lisianski (isl.), Hi, US 175/H2
Lisieux, Fr. 100/C4
Liski, Rus. 120/F2
Lisle, Il, US 193/P16
L'Isle-Adam, Fr. 88/J4
L'Isle-en-Dodon, Fr. 100/D5
L'Isle-sur-la-Sorgue, Fr. 100/F5
L'Isle-sur-le-Doubs, Fr. 114/C3
Lisle-sur-Tarn, Fr. 100/D5
Lismore, Austl. 173/E1
Lisnacree, NI, UK 92/B3
Lišov, Czh. 113/H4
Lispeszentadorján,
Hun. 106/C2
Lisse, Neth. 108/B4
Lisses, Fr. 88/K6
List, Ger. 96/C4
Lister (riv.), Ger. 109/E6
Listowel, On, Can. 188/D3
Listowel, Ire. 89/P10
Lit. Scarcies (riv.),
SLeo. 160/B4
Litang, China 128/H6
Litang (riv.), China 141/H2
Lițāni (riv.), Leb. 149/D3
Litavka (riv.), Czh. 113/H3
Litchfield, Mn, US 185/M4
Litchfield, Il, US 187/K3
Litchfield Park,
Az, US 195/R19
Lith, Neth. 108/C5
Litherland, Eng, UK 93/F5
Lithgow, Austl. 173/D2
Lithuania (ctry.) 97/K4
Litija, Slov. 101/L3
Litin, Ukr. 120/E2
Litókhoron, Gre. 105/H2
Litoměřice, Czh. 113/H1
Littabella NP, Austl. 172/D4
Littau, Swi. 115/F3
Little (riv.), Ar, US 187/J4
Little (riv.), Ga, US 191/H4
Little (riv.), Tx, US 190/D4
Little (riv.), NC, US 191/J3
Little Abitibi (riv.),
On, Can. 188/D1
Little Andaman (isl.),
India 141/F5
Little Belt (mts.),
Mt, US 184/F4
Little Bighorn Battlefield
Nat'l Mon., Mt, US 184/G4
Little Bitter (lake),
Egypt 149/C2
Little Blue (riv.),
Ks,Ne, US 187/H2
Little Calumet (riv.),
Il, US 193/Q16
Little Cayman (isl.),
Cay. 199/E4
Little Colorado (riv.),
Az, US 195/R19
Little Creek, De, US 196/C5
Little Cumbrae (isl.),
Sc, UK 94/A5
Little Current (riv.),
On, Can. 185/M3
Little Current,
On, Can. 188/D2
Little Desert NP,
Austl. 173/B3
Little Diomede (isl.),
Ak, US 192/E2
Little Egg (har.),
NJ, US 196/D4
Little Falls, Mn, US 185/M4
Little Falls, NJ, US 197/J8
Little Ferry, NJ, US 197/J8
Little Fork (riv.),
Mn, US 185/K3
Little Inagua (isl.),
Bahm. 199/G3
Little Karoo (valley),
SAfr. 164/C4
Little Lehigh (riv.),
Pa, US 196/C3
Little Minch (str.),
Sc, UK 89/Q8
Little Missouri (riv.),
Ar, US 187/J4
Little Neck (bay),
NY, US 197/K8
Little Nicobar (isl.),
India 141/F6
Little Para (res.),
Austl. 171/M8
Little Para (riv.),
Austl. 171/M8
Little Patuxent (riv.),
Md, US 196/B5
Little Peconic (bay),
NY, US 197/F2
Little Platte (riv.),
Mo, US 195/D5

Little Prairie, Wi, US 193/N14
Little Red (riv.),
Ar, US 187/J4
Little Rock (cap.),
Ar, US 187/J4
Little Schuylkill (riv.),
Pa, US 196/B2
Little Sioux (riv.),
Ia, US 185/K5
Little Smoky (riv.),
Ab, Can. 184/D2
Little Snake (riv.),
Co, US 186/C2
Little Stour (riv.),
Eng, UK 91/H4
Little Wabash (riv.),
Il, US 187/K4
Little White (riv.),
SD, US 187/G2
Little Wood (riv.),
Id, US 184/E5
Little Zab (riv.), Iraq 148/E3
Littleborough,
Eng, UK 93/F4
Littlefield, Tx, US 187/G4
Littlehampton,
Eng, UK 91/F5
Littlerock, Ca, US 194/C1
Littlestown, Pa, US 196/A4
Littleton, NH, US 189/G2
Littleton, Co, US 195/B3
Liuba, China 137/A1
Liucheng, China 141/J3
Liuzhou, China 141/J3
Livádhion, Gre. 105/H2
Livanátai, Gre. 105/H3
Live Oak, Fl, US 191/H4
Live Oak, Tx, US 195/U20
Livengood, Ak, US 192/J2
Livenza (riv.), It. 117/F2
Liverdun, Fr. 111/F6
Liverdy-en-Brie, Fr. 88/L5
Livermore (mt.),
Tx, US 187/F5
Livermore, Ca, US 193/L12
Liverpool (cape),
Nun., Can. 181/J1
Liverpool, NS, Can. 189/H2
Liverpool (bay),
NW, Can. 181/J1
Liverpool, Eng, UK 93/F5
Liverpool (co.), Eng, UK 93/F5
Liverpool (bay),
Wal, UK 93/E5
Livingston, Guat. 202/D3
Livingston, Sc, UK 94/C5
Livingston (co.),
Mi, US 193/E6
Livingston, Mt, US 184/F4
Livingston, NJ, US 197/H8
Livingston, Tx, US 187/J5
Livingston (lake),
Tx, US 187/J5
Livingston, Zam. 163/E4
Livingstone (falls),
Congo 163/B2
Livingstone
(range), Ab, Can. 184/E3
Livno, Bosn. 106/C4
Livny, Rus. 120/F1
Livojoki (riv.), Fin. 95/H2
Livonia, Mi, US 188/D3
Livorno (prov.), It. 116/D6
Livorno, It. 116/C4
Livorno Ferraris, It. 116/B2
Livramento do Brumado,
Braz. 212/B4
Livron-sur-Drôme, Fr. 100/F4
Livry-Gargan, Fr. 88/K5
Lixin, China 130/D4
Lixnaw, Ire. 89/P10
Lixoúrion, Gre. 105/G3
Lixus (ruin), Mor. 124/D6
Liyang, China 130/D5
Lizard (pt.), Eng, UK 90/A7
Lizard, The (pen.),
Eng, UK 90/A7
Lizy-sur-Ourcq, Fr. 110/C5
Ljubic, Serb. 106/E4
Ljubija, Bosn. 106/C3
Ljubljana (cap.),
Slov. 101/L3
Ljubuški, Bosn. 105/E1
Ljugarn (riv.), Swe. 96/E3
Ljungby, Swe. 96/E3
Ljungskile, Swe. 96/D2
Ljusne, Swe. 96/G1
Ljustero (isl.), Swe. 97/H2
Lkst (peak), Mor. 156/C3
Llabanere
(int'l arpt.), Fr. 100/E5
Llaillay, Chile 216/N8
Llanada (vol.), Chile 216/C3
Llallagua, Bol. 208/E7
Llanberis, Pass of
(pass), Wal, UK 92/D5
Llancañelo (lake),
Arg. 216/C2
Llandovery, Wal, UK 90/C3
Llandrindod Wells,
Wal, UK 90/C2
Llandudno, Wal, UK 92/E5

Llanes, Sp. 102/C1
Llanfairfechan,
Wal, UK 92/E5
Llangansport, In, US 188/C3
Llangollen, Wal, UK 93/E6
Llanidloes, Wal, UK 90/C2
Llano (riv.), Tx, US 187/H5
Llano, Tx, US 187/H5
Llano Estacado
(plain), US 187/G4
Llanos (plain),
Col.,Ven. 210/D3
Lleida, Sp. 103/F2
Llera de Canales,
Mex. 201/F4
Llerena, Sp. 102/C3
Lleyn (pen.), Wal, UK 92/D6
Llívia, Sp. 103/F1
Llobregat (riv.), Sp. 103/F1
Llodio, Sp. 102/D1
Lloret de Mar, Sp. 103/G2
Llorona (pt.), CR 198/E6
Lloyd (pt.), NY, US 197/M8
Lloyd Harbor,
NY, US 197/M8
Lloydminster, Sk, Can. 184/F2
Lloyds (riv.), Nf, Can. 189/K1
Lluchmayor, Sp. 103/G3
Llullaillaco (vol.),
Arg.,Chile 215/C1
Llwchwr (riv.),
Wal, UK 90/B3
Llwchwr, Wal, UK 90/C3
Llynfi (riv.), Wal, UK 90/C3
Lo (riv.), China 130/B3
Loa, Ut, US 186/E3
Loa (riv.), Chile 208/E8
Loa (riv.), Chile 216/C4
Loaca (canal), Sp. 103/N8
Loange (riv.),
D.R. Congo 155/K8
Loano, It. 116/B4
Loaoya (canal), Sp. 103/N8
Lobbes, Belg. 111/D3
Loberia, Arg. 216/F3
Lobethal, Austl. 171/M8
Lobito, Ang. 163/B3
Lökösháza, Hun. 106/E2
Lobos, Peru 214/A2
Lobos (isl.), Nun., Can. 181/K2
Lobos (riv.), Mex. 202/B4
Lobos de Tierra, Isla
(isl.), Peru 208/B5
Lobos, Punta de (pt.),
Chile 216/M9
Lobos, Punta de (pt.),
Mt, US 184/C4
Locarno, Swi. 115/E5
Loch na Sealga (lake),
Sc, UK 94/A1
Loch Raven (res.),
Md, US 196/B5
Lochaber (reg.),
Sc, UK 94/A3
Locharbriggs,
Sc, UK 92/E1
Lochau, Aus. 115/F2
Lochboisdale, Sc, UK 89/O8
Lochbuie, Co, US 195/C2
Lochem, Neth. 108/D4
Loches, Fr. 100/D3
Lochgelly, Sc, UK 94/C4
Lochgilphead, Sc, UK 94/A4
Lochindorb (lake),
Sc, UK 94/C2
Lochmaben, Sc, UK 92/E1
Lochmaddy, Sc, UK 89/O8
Lochów, Pol. 99/L2
Lochristi, Belg. 110/C1
Lochwinnoch,
Sc, UK 94/B5
Lochy (lake), Sc, UK 94/B3
Lochy (riv.), Sc, UK 94/B3
Lock, Austl. 171/G5
Lock Haven, Pa, US 188/E3
Lockerbie, Sc, UK 93/E1
Lockhart, Austl. 173/C2
Lockington, Austl. 173/C3
Locknitz (riv.), Ger. 98/F2
Lockport, NY, US 188/E3
Lockport, Il, US 193/P16
Lockwood (res.),
NJ, US 197/H8
Locon, Fr. 110/B2
Locri, It. 104/E3
Locumba, Peru 214/D6
Locust Fork (riv.),
Al, US 191/G3
Lod, Isr. 149/F8
Lod (riv.), Ger. 112/C5
Loddon (riv.), Austl. 173/C1
Loddon (riv.),
Eng, UK 91/E4
Lodève, Fr. 100/E5
Lodge Pole, Rus. 118/G3
Lodi, It. 116/C2
Lodi (prov.), It. 116/C2
Lodi, Ca, US 186/B3
Lodi, Oh, US 197/J8
Lodi, D.R. Congo 163/D1
Lodosa, Sp. 102/D2
Lodrino, Swi. 115/E5
Łódź, Pol. 99/K3
Lodzkie (prov.), Pol. 99/K3
Loei, Thai. 141/G3
Loen (riv.), Ger. 112/C4
Loenen, Neth. 108/C4
Loeriesfontein, SAfr. 164/C3
Lofa (riv.), Libr. 160/C5
Löffingen, Ger. 115/F2
Lofoten (isl.), Nor. 95/E2
Lofty (range), Austl. 170/C4
Lofty (mt.), Austl. 171/M8
Logan, NM, US 190/C3
Logan, Oh, US 188/D4
Logan (co.), US 195/N14

Logan, Ut, US 184/F5
Logan, WV, US 188/D4
Logansport, In, US 188/C3
Loganton, Pa, US 196/A1
Loganville, Pa, US 196/B4
Logatec, Slov. 101/L4
Logone (riv.), Chad 154/J6
Lograto, It. 116/D2
Logroño, Sp. 102/D1
Logrosán, Sp. 102/C3
Løgstør, Den. 96/C3
Løgten, Den. 96/D3
Lohals, Den. 96/D4
Lohärdaga, India 143/E4
Lohfelden, Ger. 109/G6
Lohja, Fin. 97/L1
Lohjanjärvi
(lake), Fin. 97/K1
Lohmar, Ger. 111/G2
Lohmen, Ger. 113/H1
Löhnberg, Ger. 112/B1
Löhne, Ger. 109/F3
Löhne, Ger. 109/F4
Lohr, Ger. 112/C3
Loi-kaw, Myan. 141/G4
Loi Lun (range),
China,Myan. 128/G7
Loing (riv.), Fr. 98/B5
Loir (riv.), Fr. 100/D3
Loire (riv.), Fr. 100/C3
Loisin (riv.), Fr. 111/E5
Loita (hills), Kenya 155/N8
Loja (prov.), Ecu. 214/B2
Loja, Ecu. 214/B2
Loja, Sp. 102/C4
Løjt Kirkeby, Den. 96/C4
Lokeren, Belg. 110/D1
Lokitaung, Kenya 162/B1
Løkken, Den. 96/C3
Løkken, Nor. 95/D2
Lokoja, Nga. 161/G5
Lokolo (riv.),
D.R. Congo 155/K8
Lokomby, Madg. 165/H8
Lokoro (riv.),
D.R. Congo 155/J8
Loks (isl.), Nun., Can. 181/K2
Lol (riv.), Sudan 155/L6
Lolland (isl.), Den. 95/D5
Lollar, Ger. 112/B3
Lolo (peak), Mt, US 184/E4
Lolui (isl.), Ugan. 162/B3
Lom, Nor. 95/D3
Lom Sak, Thai. 136/C2
Loma (mts.), SLeo. 154/C6
Loma (pt.), Ca, US 194/C5
Loma Bonita, Mex. 202/C2
Loma Linda, Ca, US 194/C2
Loma Mansa
(peak), SLeo. 160/C4
Loma Negra, Arg. 216/E3
Lomami (riv.),
D.R. Congo 157/K8
Lomas de Zamora,
Arg. 217/J11
Lomazzo, It. 116/C1
Lombard, Il, US 193/P16
Lombardia, Mex. 200/E5
Lombardia
(pol. reg.), It. 101/H4
Lomblen (isl.), Indo. 139/F5
Lombok (isl.), Indo. 139/E5
Lomé (int'l arpt.),
Togo 161/F5
Lomé (cap.), Togo 161/F5
Lomello, It. 116/B2
Lomita, Ca, US 194/F8
Lomma, Swe. 96/E4
Lommel, Belg. 108/C6
Lomnice (riv.), Czh. 113/G4
Lomnice nad Lužnicí,
Czh. 113/H4
Lomond (lake),
Sc, UK 94/B4
Lomond (hills),
Sc, UK 94/C4
Lomone (riv.), It. 117/E4
Lomonosov, Rus. 119/S7
Lompobatang (peak),
Indo. 139/E5
Lompoc, Ca, US 186/B4
Łomża, Pol. 99/M2
Loni, India 144/D5
Lonigo, It. 117/E2
Löningen, Ger. 109/E3
Loncoche, Chile 216/B3
Loncopué, Arg. 216/C3
Londerzeel, Belg. 111/D2
London, On, Can. 188/D3
London (cap.), UK 88/C2
London, Ky, US 188/D4
London, City of (bor.),
Eng, UK 88/A1
Londonderry (cape),
Austl. 167/B2
Londonderry (isl.),
Chile 217/C7
Londonderry (dist.),
NI, UK 92/A2
Londonderry,
NI, UK 92/A2
Londrina, Braz. 213/B2
Lone (riv.), Ger. 112/C5
Lone Grove, Ok, US 187/H4
Lone Jack, Mo, US 195/E6
Lone Pine Sanctuary,
Austl. 172/E1
Lonesome NP,
Austl. 172/C3
Long, Ak, US 192/G3
Long (lake), On, Can. 185/M3
Long (lake), Sc, UK 94/A2

Long (riv.), China 137/A3
Long (isl.), Bahm. 199/F3
Long (isl.), NY, US 189/F3
Long (mtn.),
Wal, UK 90/C1
Long Beach,
Wa, US 184/B4
Long Beach,
On, Can. 189/R10
Long Beach (isl.),
NJ, US 196/D4
Long Beach, Ca, US 194/C4
Long Beach, NY, US 197/L9
Long Branch, NJ, US 196/E3
Long Cay (isl.),
Bahm. 199/G3
Long Crag (hill),
Eng, UK 94/C6
Long Eaton, Eng, UK 93/G6
Long Grove, Il, US 193/P15
Long Hill, Ct, US 197/E1
Long, Loch (inlet),
Sc, UK 94/B4
Long Mynd, The (hill),
Eng, UK 90/D1
Long Neck (pt.),
Eng, UK 90/D1
Long Range (mts.),
Nf, Can. 189/K2
Long Valley, NJ, US 196/D2
Long Xuyen, Viet. 136/D4
Longá (riv.), Braz. 212/B1
Longare, It. 117/E2
Longaví, Chile 216/C2
Longboat Key, Fl, US 191/H5
Longbranch,
Wa, US 193/B3
Longchang, China 141/J2
Longchuan, China 137/C3
Longchuan, China 141/G3
Longde, China 128/J4
Longeau (riv.), Fr. 111/E5
Longeville-en-Barrois,
Fr. 111/E6
Longeville-lès-Metz,
Fr. 111/F5
Longeville-lès-Saint-Avold,
Fr. 111/F5
Longfellow (mts.),
Me, US 189/G2
Longfield, Eng, UK 88/D2
Longford, Austl. 173/C4
Longford, Ire. 89/Q10
Longhua, China 131/H3
Longhui, China 141/K2
Longjumeau, Fr. 88/J5
Longkou, China 131/H3
Longlac, On, Can. 185/M3
Longli, China 141/J2
Longmen, China 137/B3
Longmen Shiyao,
China 141/J2
Longmont, Co, US 195/B2
Longnan, China 137/B3
Longniddry, Sc, UK 94/D5
Longonot (peak),
Kenya 162/C3
Longperrier, Fr. 88/K4
Longport-sur-Orge, Fr. 88/J6
Longport, NJ, US 196/D5
Longpré-les-Corps-Saints,
Fr. 110/A3
Longquan, China 137/C2
Longreach, Austl. 172/B3
Longshan, China 137/A2
Longshou (mts.),
China 128/H4
Longueau, Fr. 110/B4
Longuenesse, Fr. 110/B2
Longuesse, Fr. 88/H4
Longueuil, Qu, Can. 189/P6
Longuyon, Fr. 111/E4
Longvic, Fr. 114/B3
Longview, Wa, US 184/C4
Longview, Tx, US 187/J4
Longwood Gardens,
Pa, US 196/C4
Longwy, Fr. 111/E4
Longyan, China 137/C3
Longyearbyen, Nor. 122/B2
Longyou, China 137/C2
Longzhou, China 136/D1
Loni, India 144/D5
Lonigo, It. 117/E2
Löningen, Ger. 109/E3
Lonquimay, Arg. 216/E3
Lons, Fr. 100/C5
Lons-le-Saunier, Fr. 114/B4
Lönsboda, Swe. 96/F3
Lontzen, Belg. 111/F2
Lonza (riv.), Swi. 114/D5
Looe (isl.), Eng, UK 90/B6
Lookout (cape),
NC, US 191/J3
Lookout (pt.),
Austl. 172/B1
Loolmalasin (peak),
Tanz. 162/B3
Loon Lake, Sk, Can. 184/F2
Loon op Zand, Neth. 108/C5
Loop Head (pt.), Ire. 88/P10
Loos, Fr. 110/C2
Lop Buri, Thai. 136/C3
Lopary, Madg. 165/H8
Lopez (cape), Gabon 154/G8
López Mateos,
Mex. 201/Q9
Lopik, Neth. 108/B5
Lopori (riv.),
D.R. Congo 155/K7
Lopphavet (bay),
Nor. 95/G1
Loppi, Fin. 97/L1

Lora del Río, Sp. 102/C4
Lorain, Oh, US 188/D3
Loralai, Pak. 147/J2
Lorca, Sp. 102/E4
Lord Howe (isl.), Austl. 174/E8
Lordsburg, NM, US 186/E4
Lorelei, Ger. 111/G3
Lorena, Braz. 213/H7
Lorengau, PNG 174/D5
Lorenskog, Nor. 96/D2
Lorentz (riv.), Indo. 139/J5
Lorentzsluizen (dam), Neth. 108/C2
Loreo, It. 117/F2
Loreto, Braz. 212/A2
Loreto, It. 117/G6
Loreto, Mex. 200/C3
Loreto (int'l arpt.), Mex. 200/C3
Loreto, Mex. 200/E4
Loreto, Ecu. 210/B5
Loreto (state), Peru 210/C5
Lorette, Mb, Can. 185/J3
Lorgues, Fr. 101/G5
Lorian (swamp), Kenya 155/N7
Lorica, Col. 210/C2
Lorient, Fr. 100/B3
L'Oriental (pol. reg.), Mor. 157/E2
Lorillard (riv.), Nun., Can. 180/G2
Lorinci, Hun. 99/K5
Loring, Ks, US 195/D5
Loriol-sur-Drôme, Fr. 100/F4
Lorn, Firth of (inlet), Sc, UK 89/Q8
Lorne, Austl. 173/B3
Lorosuk (peak), Kenya 162/B2
Lorquin, Fr. 111/G6
Lörrach, Ger. 114/D2
Lorrain (plat.), Fr. 98/C4
Lorraine, Qu, Can. 189/P6
Lorraine (pol. reg.), Fr. 101/G2
Lorraine (reg.), Fr. 111/E5
Lorsch, Ger. 112/B3
Lorup, Ger. 109/E3
Los Alamitos, Ca, US 194/F8
Los Alamos, NM, US 187/F4
Los Alerces, PN, Arg. 215/B5
Los Altos, Ca, US 193/K12
Los Amates, Guat. 202/D3
Los Andes, Chile 216/N8
Los Andes, Col. 210/B4
Los Angeles, Chile 216/B3
Los Angeles, Ca, US 194/F7
Los Angeles (co.), Ca, US 194/B2
Los Angeles (int'l arpt.), Ca, US 194/E8
Los Angeles, Ca, US 194/B2
Los Angeles Outer (har.), Ca, US 194/F8
Los Aquijes, Peru 214/C4
Los Aztecas, Mex. 201/F4
Los Banos, Ca, US 186/B3
Los Barrios, Sp. 102/C4
Los Canarreos (arch.), Cuba 203/F1
Los Cardales, Arg. 217/J11
Los Cerrillos, Uru. 217/K11
Los Chonos (arch.), Chile 216/B5
Los Corrales de Buelna, Sp. 102/C1
Los Glaciares, PN, Arg. 215/B6
Los Katios, PN, Col. 210/B3
Los Lagos, Chile 216/B3
Los Lagos (pol. reg.), Chile 216/B3
Los Llanos de Aridane, Canl., Sp. 156/A3
Los Lunas, NM, US 186/F4
Los Mármoles, PN, Mex. 202/B1
Los Menucos, Arg. 216/C4
Los Mochis, Mex. 200/C3
Los Mosquitos (gulf), Pan. 203/F4
Los Muermos, Chile 216/B5
Los Navalmorales, Sp. 102/C3
Los Navalucillos, Sp. 102/C3
Los Órganos, Peru 214/B1
Los Padres National Forest, Ca, US 194/A1
Los Palacios y Villafranca, Sp. 102/C4
Los Pingüinos, PN, Chile 217/C7
Los Planes, Mex. 200/C3
Los Reyes, Mex. 201/R10
Los Reyes de Salgado, Mex. 200/D4
Los Ríos (prov.), Ecu. 214/B1
Los Roques, Islas (isls.), Ven. 208/E1
Los Santos, Pan. 203/F5
Los Santos de Maimona, Sp. 102/B3
Los Sauces, Chile 216/B3
Los Taques, Ven. 210/D2
Los Teques, Ven. 208/E1
Los Testigos (isls.), Ven. 211/F2
Los Vilos, Chile 216/C1
Los Yébenes, Sp. 102/C3
Losai Nat'l Rsv., Kenya 162/C4
Losheim, Ger. 111/F4
Losice, Pol. 99/M2
Lošinj (isl.), Cro. 106/B3

Losne, Fr. 114/B3
Losone, Swi. 115/E5
Losoya, Tx, US 195/U13
Lossburg, Ger. 115/E1
Losser, Neth. 108/E4
Lossie (riv.), Sc, UK 94/C1
Lössnitz, Ger. 113/F1
Lossoganeu (hill), Tanz. 162/C4
Lost River (range), Id, US 186/D1
Lost River Caverns, Pa, US 196/C2
Lostallo, Swi. 115/F5
Lot (riv.), Fr. 100/D4
Lota, Chile 216/B3
Lotawana (lake), Mo, US 195/E6
Løten, Nor. 96/D1
Lotte, Ger. 109/E4
Lotukei (peak), Sudan 162/B1
Lotung, Tai. 137/D3
Lou (riv.), China 130/B5
Louang Namtha, Laos 141/H3
Louangphrabang, Laos 141/H4
Loubomo, Congo 163/B1
Loudéac, Fr. 100/B2
Loudi, China 141/K2
Loudun, Fr. 100/D3
Loue (riv.), Fr. 100/F3
Loufan, China 130/B3
Louga (pol. reg.), Sen. 160/B3
Louga, Sen. 160/B2
Lough Foyle (lake), UK 92/A1
Loughborough, Eng, UK 91/E1
Loughbrickland, NI, UK 92/B3
Lougheed (isl.), Nun., Can. 181/R7
Loughrea, Ire. 89/P10
Loughton, Eng, UK 88/D2
Louhans, Fr. 114/B4
Louis Botha (Durban) (int'l arpt.), SAfr. 165/E3
Louisiade (arch.), PNG 174/E6
Louisiana (state), US 190/E4
Louisville, Co, US 195/B3
Louisville, Ky, US 188/C4
Louisville, Ms, US 191/F3
Loukkos (riv.), Mor. 158/A2
Louny, Czh. 113/G2
Loup, Middle (riv.), Ne, US 185/J5
Loup, North (riv.), Ne, US 185/H5
Loup, South (riv.), Ne, US 185/J5
Lourches, Fr. 110/C3
Lourdes, Fr. 100/C5
Lourdes/Tarbes (int'l arpt.), Fr. 100/D5
Loures, Port. 103/P10
Louriçal, Port. 102/A3
Lourinhã, Port. 102/A3
Lousã, Port. 102/A2
Lousa, Port. 103/Q10
Louth, Eng, UK 93/H5
Louth (co.), Ire. 92/B4
Louth, Ire. 92/B3
Loutrá Aidhipsoú, Gre. 105/H3
Loutrákion, Gre. 105/H4
Loútsa, Gre. 105/P9
Louvain (Leuven), Belg. 111/D2
Louveira, Braz. 213/G8
Louviers, Fr. 100/D2
Louviers, Co, US 195/B2
Louvigné-du-Désert, Fr. 100/C2
Louvres, Fr. 88/K4
Louvroil, Fr. 110/C3
Lovaart (riv.), Belg. 110/B1
Lovat' (riv.), Rus. 118/F5
Lovat' (riv.), Bela.,Rus. 97/P3
Lovćen NP, Mont. 106/D4
Love Point, Md, US 196/B5
Lovech (prov.), Bul. 105/J1
Loveland, Co, US 195/B2
Loveland (lake), Co, US 195/B2
Lovell, Wy, US 184/F4
Lovelock, Nv, US 186/C2
Lovere, It. 116/D1
Loving, NM, US 187/F4
Lovington, NM, US 187/G4
Lóvö, Hun. 101/M3
Lovosice, Czh. 113/H1
Lovozero (lake), Rus. 118/G2
Low (cape), Nun., Can. 181/H2
Lowa (riv.), D.R. Congo 157/L8
Lowell, Ma, US 189/G3
Löwen (riv.), Namb. 164/B2
Löwenstein, Ger. 112/C4
Lower (bay), Sc, UK 94/B4
Lower (dam), Wa, US 193/D3
Lower Arrow (lake), BC, Can. 184/D3
Lower Engadine (valley), Swi. 115/G4
Lower Ganges (canal), India 142/B2

Lower Glenelg NP, Austl. 173/B3
Lower Hutt, NZ 175/S11
Lower Kalskag, Ak, US 192/F3
Lower Latham (res.), Co, US 195/C2
Lower Otay (lake), Ca, US 194/D5
Lower Red (lake), Mn, US 185/K4
Lower Rhine (riv.), Neth. 108/C5
Lower Rouge (riv.), Mi, US 193/E7
Lower Trajan's Wall, Mol.,Ukr. 120/D3
Lower Tunguska (riv.), Rus. 125/J3
Lower Zambezi NP, Zam. 163/E2
Lowestoft, Eng, UK 91/H2
Lowicz, Pol. 99/K2
Lowther (hills), Sc, UK 94/C6
Loxstedt, Ger. 109/F2
Loxton, SAfr. 164/C3
Loxton, Austl. 171/J5
Loyalton, Pa, US 196/B2
Loyalty (isls.), NCal., Fr. 174/F7
Loyettes, Fr. 114/B6
Loyne (lake), Sc, UK 94/A2
Loysville, Pa, US 196/A3
Loznica, Serb. 106/D3
Loznitsa, Bul. 107/H4
Lozova, Ukr. 120/F2
Lozovaya, Ukr. 120/F2
Lozovik, Serb. 106/E3
Lügde, Ger. 109/G5
Lu (mtn.), China 130/D3
Lu (riv.), China 130/C5
Lu Xian, China 141/J2
Lualaba (riv.), D.R. Congo 163/E1
Luan (riv.), China 130/D3
Luan Xian, China 130/D3
Luanchuan, China 130/B4
Luanda (cap.), Ang. 163/B2
Luang (peak), Thai. 136/B4
Luang Lagoon (lag.), Thai. 141/H6
Luangwa (riv.), Zam. 163/F2
Luangwe, Zam. 162/A5
Luanping, China 130/D2
Luanshya, Zam. 163/E3
Luapula (prov.), Zam. 163/E3
Luarca, Sp. 102/B1
Luba, EqG. 154/G7
Lubaantun (ruin), Belz. 202/D2
Lubaczów, Pol. 99/M3
Lubań, Pol. 99/H3
Lubango, Ang. 163/B3
Lubansenshi (riv.), Zam. 163/E3
Lubartów, Pol. 99/M3
Lubawa, Pol. 99/K2
Lübbecke, Ger. 109/F4
Lübbeek, Belg. 111/D2
Lubbock, Tx, US 187/G4
Lubelska (uplands), Pol. 99/M3
Lubelskie (prov.), Pol. 99/M3
Lubero (riv.), D.R. Congo 162/A4
Lubień Kujawski, Pol. 99/K2
Lubin, Pol. 99/J3
Lublin, Pol. 99/M3
Lubliniec, Pol. 99/K3
Lubmin, Ger. 96/E4
Lubnaig (lake), Sc, UK 94/B4
Lubny, Ukr. 120/E2
Luboń, Pol. 99/J2
Lubrín, Sp. 102/D4
Lubsko, Pol. 99/H3
Lubudi, D.R. Congo 163/E2
Lubuklinggau, Indo. 138/B4
Lubuksikaping, Indo. 138/B3
Lubumbashi, D.R. Congo 163/E3
Lubuskie (prov.), Pol. 99/H2
Lucan, Ire. 92/B5
Lucania (mt.), Yk, Can. 192/K3
Lucas González, Arg. 217/J10
Lucca (prov.), It. 116/D5
Lucca, It. 116/D5
Lucciana, Fr. 104/A1
Luce (bay), Sc, UK 92/D2
Lucedale, Ms, US 191/F4
Lucélia, Braz. 213/B2
Lucena, Phil. 137/D5
Lucena, Sp. 102/C4
Lucena del Cid, Sp. 103/E2
Lučenec, Slvk. 99/K4
Lucens, Swi. 114/C4
Lucerne, Co, US 195/C2
Lucerne (lake), Swi. 101/H3
Lucerne (Vierwaldstättersee) (lake), Swi. 115/E3
Lucheng, China 130/C3
Lüchow, Ger. 98/F2
Lucinda, Austl. 172/B2
Luckeesarai, India 143/F3
Luckenwalde, Ger. 99/G2
Lucknow, India 142/C2
Luco dei Marsi, It. 104/C2
Lucomagno, Passo del (pass), Swi. 115/E4

Lucrecia (cape), Cuba 203/H1
Lucrezia, It. 117/F5
Luda Kamchiya (riv.), Bul. 105/K1
Lüdenscheid, Ger. 109/E6
Lüderitz, Namb. 164/A2
Ludesch, Aus. 115/F3
Ludhiāna, India 144/C4
Ludian, China 141/H2
Ludinghausen, Ger. 109/E5
Ludington, Mi, US 188/C3
Ludogorie (reg.), Bul. 107/H4
Ludvika, Swe. 96/F1
Ludwigs (canal), Ger. 113/E4
Ludwigsburg, Ger. 112/C5
Ludwigsfelde, Ger. 98/G7
Ludwigshafen, Ger. 115/F2
Ludwigshafen, Ger. 112/B4
Ludwigslust, Ger. 98/F2
Ludwigsstadt, Ger. 113/E2
Ludza, Lat. 97/M4
Luebo, D.R. Congo 163/D2
Luena, Ang. 163/C3
Lufeng, China 137/C3
Lufkin, Tx, US 187/J5
Luga (bay), Rus. 97/N2
Luga, Rus. 97/N2
Luga (riv.), Rus. 97/N2
Lugagnano, It. 117/D2
Lugagnano Val d'Arda, It. 116/C3
Lugano, Swi. 115/E6
Lugano (lake), It. 115/E6
Luganville, Van. 174/F6
Lugards (falls), Kenya 162/C3
Lugavčina, Serb. 106/E3
Lugenda (riv.), Moz. 163/G3
Lugg (riv.), Eng, UK 90/D2
Lugg (riv.), Wal, UK 90/C2
Lugnaquillia (peak), Ire. 92/B6
Lugo, It. 117/E4
Lugo, Sp. 102/B1
Lugogo (riv.), Ugan. 162/B2
Lugoj, Rom. 106/E3
Lugrin, Fr. 114/C5
Lugunga (peak), Tanz. 162/C4
Lugungwa (riv.), D.R. Congo 163/D1
Lühe (riv.), Ger. 109/H2
Luhe, China 130/D4
Luhe-Wildenau, Ger. 113/F3
Luhombero (peak), Tanz. 162/C4
Luino, It. 115/E6
Luis B. Sánchez, Mex. 200/B1
Luís Correia, Braz. 212/B1
Luján, Arg. 217/J11
Lujiang, China 130/D5
Lukácsháza, Hun. 101/M3
Lukang, Tai. 137/D3
Lukavac, Bosn. 106/D3
Luke (mt.), Austl. 170/C3
Lukenie (riv.), D.R. Congo 163/C1
Lukovit, Bul. 105/J1
Luków, Pol. 99/M3
Lukuga (riv.), D.R. Congo 162/A4
Lukulu (riv.), Zam. 163/D3
Lukulu (riv.), Zam. 162/A5
Lukunor (isl.), Micr. 174/E4
Luleå, Swe. 118/D2
Luleälven (riv.), Swe. 95/G2
Luliang, China 141/H2
Luling, La, US 195/P17
Luling (pass), China 130/B4
Lulong, China 130/D3
Lulonga (riv.), D.R. Congo 151/E4
Lulsgate (int'l arpt.), Eng, UK 90/D4
Lulua (riv.), D.R. Congo 163/D2
Lumangwe (falls), Zam. 162/A5
Lumberton, Tx, US 187/J6
Lumberton, NC, US 191/J3
Lumberton, NJ, US 196/D4
Lumbini (zone), Nepal 142/D2
Lumbo, Moz. 163/H3
Lumbrales, Sp. 102/B2
Lumbres, Fr. 110/B2
Lumby, BC, Can. 184/D3
Lumding, India 141/J3
Lumigny-Nesles-Ormeaux, Fr. 88/L5
Luminárias, Braz. 213/J6
Lummen, Belg. 111/E2
Lumparland, Fin. 97/J1
Lumsden, Sk, Can. 185/G3
Lumsden, NZ 175/R12
Lumut, Malay. 138/B3
Luna (mtn.), It. 117/D3
Lunahuaná, Peru 214/B4
Lund, Swe. 96/E4
Lundazi, Zam. 163/F3
Lundby, Den. 96/D4
Lundi (riv.), Zim. 163/F5
Lundy (isl.), Eng, UK 90/B4
Lune (riv.), Ger. 109/F2
Lune (riv.), Eng, UK 93/F2
Lüneburg, Ger. 109/H2
Lüneburger Heide (reg.), Ger. 98/F2
Lunel, Fr. 100/F5

Lünen, Ger. 109/E5
Lunenburg, NS, Can. 189/H2
Lunestedt, Ger. 109/F2
Lüneville, Fr. 101/G2
Lung Kwu Chau (isl.), China 129/T10
Lunga (riv.), Zam. 163/E3
Lungern, Swi. 114/E4
Lungi, SLeo. 160/B4
Lungi (Freetown) (int'l arpt.), SLeo. 160/B4
Lunglei, India 141/F3
Lungue-Bungo (riv.), Ang. 163/C3
Luni (riv.), India 147/K3
Lünne, Ger. 109/E4
Luocheng, China 141/J3
Luodian, China 141/J2
Luoding, China 141/K3
Luohe, China 130/C4
Luoma (lake), China 130/D4
Luongo (riv.), Zam. 162/A5
Luoning, China 130/B4
Luoshan, China 130/C4
Luoshuikan, China 137/A1
Luoyang, China 130/C4
Luoyuan, China 137/C2
Luozi, D.R. Congo 163/B1
Lupanshui, China 141/H2
Luqa (int'l arpt.), Malta 104/L7
Luqu, China 128/H5
Luqu, China 130/B4
Lūrah (riv.), Afg. 147/J2
Lure, Fr. 114/C2
Lurgan, NI, UK 92/B3
Lurin, Peru 214/B4
Lúrio, Moz. 163/H3
Lúrio (riv.), Moz. 163/G3
Lurnfeld, Aus. 101/K3
Lurøy, Nor. 95/E2
Lusaka (cap.), Zam. 163/E4
Lusambo, D.R. Congo 163/D1
Lusen (peak), Ger. 113/G5
Lusenga NP, Zam. 162/A5
Lushan, China 130/C4
Lushi, China 130/B4
Lushnja, Alb. 105/F2
Lushoto, Tanz. 162/C4
Lushui, China 141/G2
Lusignan, Fr. 100/D3
Luhans'k, Ukr. 120/F2
Luhans'ka Oblasti, Ukr. 120/F2
Lusk, Wy, US 185/G5
Lusk, Ire. 92/B4
Lustenau, Aus. 115/F3
Lutanga (riv.), D.R. Congo 155/J7
Luther, Ok, US 195/N14
Luthern, Swi. 114/D3
Lutherville, Md, US 196/B5
Lütjehorn (isl.), Ger. 108/D1
Lütjenburg, Ger. 96/D4
Luton, Eng, UK 91/F3
Luton, Eng, UK 91/F3
Luton (int'l arpt.), Eng, UK 91/F3
Lutry, Swi. 114/C5
Lutselk'e, NW, Can. 180/E2
Luts'k, Ukr. 120/C2
Lutter, Ger. 109/F5
Lutterbach, Fr. 114/D2
Lutz (riv.), Aus. 115/F3
Lützelholm (bay), Ant. 218/C
Luumäki, Fin. 97/M1
Luverne, Mn, US 185/J5
Luvua (riv.), D.R. Congo 162/A4
Luwego (riv.), Tanz. 163/G2
Luwero, Ugan. 162/B2
Luwingu, Zam. 162/A5
Lux, Fr. 114/A4
Luxembourg (ctry.), Belg 111/E4
Luxembourg (prov.), Belg 111/E4
Luxembourg (cap.), Lux. 111/F4
Luxeuil-les-Bains, Fr. 114/C2
Luxi, China 141/K2
Luxi, China 141/G3
Luxor (int'l arpt.), Egypt 159/C3
Luyi, China 130/C4
Luz, Braz. 213/C1
Luz (coast), Port. 102/B4
Luza (riv.), Rus. 119/L3
Luzein, Swi. 115/F4
Luzern, Swi. 115/E3
Luzern (canton), Swi. 114/E3
Luzerne (co.), Pa, US 196/B1
Luzhai, China 141/J3
Luzhi, China 141/J2
Luzhou, China 141/J2
Luziânia, Braz. 212/A5
Luzilândia, Braz. 212/B1
Lužnice (riv.), Czh. 99/H4
Luzon (isl.), Phil. 137/D4
Luzon (str.), Phil. 174/A3
Lužuice (riv.), Czh. 99/J3
Luzzara, It. 117/D3
Luzzi, It. 104/E3
L'viv, Ukr. 120/B2
L'vivs'ka Oblasti, Ukr. 120/B2
Lwala (peak), Ugan. 162/B2
Lwi (riv.), Myan. 136/C1
Lyantonde, Ugan. 162/B2
Lyapin (riv.), Rus. 119/P2
Lycksele, Swe. 95/F2
Lycoming (co.), Pa, US 196/A1
Lyell Brown (mt.), Austl. 171/F2

Lykens, Pa, US 196/B2
Lyman, Wy, US 184/F5
Lyme (bay), Eng, UK 90/C5
Lymington, Eng, UK 91/E5
Lymm, Eng, UK 93/F5
Lyna (riv.), Pol. 99/L1
Lynas (pt.), Wal, UK 92/D5
Lynbrook, NY, US 197/L9
Lynch, Md, US 196/B5
Lynches (riv.), SC, US 191/H3
Lyndhurst, NJ, US 197/J8
Lynn (riv.), Eng, UK 93/F1
Lynn, Ma, US 189/G3
Lynn Haven, Fl, US 191/G4
Lynn Lake, Mb, Can. 180/F3
Lynwood, Ca, US 194/F8
Lyon, Fr. 100/F4
Lyon (riv.), Sc, UK 94/B3
Lyon, Sc, UK 94/B3
Lyon (Satolas) (int'l arpt.), Fr. 114/B6
Lyons, Ks, US 187/H3
Lyons, Co, US 195/B2
Lyons (riv.), Austl. 170/C3
Lyons, Wi, US 193/P14
Lype (hill), Eng, UK 90/C4
Lyra (reef), PNG 174/E5
Lys (riv.), It. 116/A1
Lys (riv.), Fr. 100/E1
Lys-lez-Lannoy, Fr. 110/C2
Lysá nad Labem, Czh. 113/H2
Lysaker, Nor. 96/D2
Lysá (peak), Czh. 113/F2
Lysekil, Swe. 96/C2
Lysina (peak), Czh. 113/F2
Lys'va, Rus. 119/N4
Lysychans'k, Ukr. 120/F2
Lytham Saint Anne's, Eng, UK 93/E4
Lytle, Tx, US 187/H5
Lytle Creek, Ca, US 194/C2
Lytton, BC, Can. 184/C3
Lyubertsy, Rus. 119/W9
Lyubotyn, Ukr. 120/E2
Lyudinovo, Rus. 120/E1
Lywd (riv.), Wal, UK 90/C2

M

M. Aleman (res.), Mex. 198/B4
Ma-Ubin, Myan. 141/G4
Ma'alot-Tarshiha, Isr. 149/D3
Ma'an, Jor. 149/D4
Ma'an (prov.), Jor. 149/D4
Ma'anshan, China 130/D5
Maarheeze, Neth. 108/C5
Maarianhamina (Mariehamn), Fin. 97/H1
Ma'arrat an Nu'mān, Syria 149/E2
Maarssen, Neth. 108/C4
Maartensdijk, Neth. 108/C4
Maas (riv.), Belg. 108/C5
Maasbracht, Neth. 111/E1
Maasbree, Neth. 108/D6
Maaseik, Belg. 111/E1
Maassluis, Neth. 108/B5
Maastricht, Neth. 111/E2
Maastricht (int'l arpt.), Neth. 111/E2
Mabalacat, Phil. 137/D4
Mabalane, Moz. 163/F5
Mabaruma, Guy. 211/G2
Mabechi (riv.), Japan 134/B3
Mabian, China 141/H2
Mabinay, Phil. 137/D6
Mabopane, SAfr. 164/Q12
Mabote, Moz. 163/F5
Mabule, Bots. 164/D2
Mac Robertson Land (phys. reg.), Ant. 218/D
Macá (peak), Chile 216/B5
Macachín, Arg. 216/E3
Macaé, Braz. 213/D2
Macael, Sp. 102/D4
Macaíba, Braz. 212/D2
Mação, Port. 102/A3
Macapá, Braz. 209/H3
Macará, Ecu. 214/B2
Macarani, Braz. 212/B4
Macari, Peru 214/D4
Macarthur, Austl. 173/B3
Macas, Ecu. 210/B5
Macau, Braz. 212/C2
Macau, China 137/B3
Macau (dpcy.), China 137/B3
Macaúbas, Braz. 212/B4
Macauley (isl.), NZ 174/G7
Macuira, PN, Col. 210/D1
Macaya, Pic de (peak), Haiti 203/H2

Macdona, Tx, US 195/T21
MacDonald (lake), Austl. 171/F2
Macdonnell (ranges), Austl. 167/G3
Macduff, Sc, UK 94/D1
Maceda, Sp. 102/B1
Macedonia (reg.), Gre. 105/G2
Macedonía (int'l arpt.), Gre. 105/H2
Macedonia (Former Yugoslav Republic of Macedonia) (ctry.) 105/G2
Maceió (pt.), Braz. 212/C2
Maceió, Braz. 212/D3
Macerata (prov.), It. 117/G6
Macerata, It. 101/K5
Macfarlane (lake), Austl. 171/H5
Machacalis, Braz. 212/B5
Machacamarca, Bol. 208/E7
Machache (peak), Les. 164/D3
Machachi, Ecu. 210/B5
Machado, Braz. 213/H6
Machado (swamp), Col. 210/C2
Machadodorp, SAfr. 165/E2
Machakos, Kenya 162/C3
Machala, Ecu. 214/B1
Machalí, Chile 216/N9
Machalilla, PN, Ecu. 214/A1
Machanga, Moz. 163/F5
Machaquilá (riv.), Guat. 202/D2
Machars, The (pen.), Sc, UK 92/D2
Machattie (lake), Austl. 171/H3
Machaze, Moz. 163/F5
Machecoul, Fr. 100/C3
Machemma (ruin), SAfr. 165/E1
Macheng, China 130/C5
Machens, Mo, US 195/G8
Machichaco (cape), Sp. 102/D1
Machida, Japan 135/C2
Machilipatnam, India 140/D4
Machiques, Ven. 210/C2
Machovo Jezero (lake), Czh. 113/H1
Machu Picchu (ruin), Peru 214/C4
Machupo (riv.), Bol. 208/F6
Machynlleth, Wal, UK 90/C1
Macina (phys. reg.), Mali 154/E4
Macintyre (riv.), Austl. 173/C1
Mackay, Austl. 172/C3
Mackay (lake), Austl. 171/F2
Mackenzie, Austl. 172/C3
Mackenzie, BC, Can. 184/C2
Mackenzie (bay), NW,Yk, Can. 180/C2
Mackenzie (mts.), NW, Can. 180/C2
Mackenzie (riv.), NW, Can. 180/E2
Mackenzie King (isl.), NW, Can. 181/R7
Mackinac Island, Mi, US 188/C2
Mackinaw City, Mi, US 188/C2
Macklin, Sk, Can. 184/F2
Macknade, Austl. 172/B2
Macksville, Austl. 173/E1
Maclean, Austl. 173/E1
Maclear, SAfr. 164/E3
Macleay (riv.), Austl. 172/F7
Macleod (lake), Austl. 170/B3
Macmillan (riv.), Yk, Can. 192/L3
Macomb, Il, US 185/L6
Macomb (co.), Mi, US 193/G6
Macomb, Ok, US 195/N15
Macomer, It. 104/A2
Mâcon, Fr. 100/F3
Macon, Ga, US 191/H3
Macon, Mo, US 187/J3
Macondes, Planalto dos (plat.), Moz. 162/C5
Macosquin, NI, UK 92/B1
Macotera, Sp. 102/C2
Macoupin (co.), Il, US 195/G7
Macquarie (har.), Austl. 173/C4
Macquarie (isl.), 81/S8
Macquarie (riv.), Austl. 173/C1
Macquarie (riv.), Austl. 171/H3
Macroom, Ire. 89/P11
Macujer, Col. 210/C3
Maculizo (riv.), Braz. 208/F5
Macumba (riv.), Austl. 171/H3
Macungie, Pa, US 196/C2
Macusani, Peru 214/D4
Macuspana, Mex. 202/C2
Macuzari, Presa (dam), Mex. 200/C3

Madan, Bul. 105/J2
Madanapalle, India 140/C5
Madaoua, Niger 161/G3
Madaras, Hun. 106/D2
Madauk, Myan. 141/G4
Madawaska, Me, US 189/G2
Madawaska (riv.), On, Can. 188/E2
Madeira (dam), Pan. 208/E2
Madeira (aut. reg.), Port. 103/U34
Madeira (riv.), Braz. 208/F5
Mädelegabel (peak), 115/G3
Madeleine, Îles de la (isls.), Qu, Can. 189/J2
Madeline (isl.), Wi, US 185/L4
Maden, Turk. 148/D2
Mäder, Aus. 115/F3
Madera, Mex. 200/C2
Madera, Ca, US 186/B3
Madgaon (Margao), India 147/K5
Madhipura, India 143/F2
Madhubani, India 143/F2
Madhumati (riv.), Bang. 143/G4
Madhupur, India 143/F3
Madhya Pradesh (state), India 140/C3
Madidi (riv.), Bol. 208/E6
Madīnat ath Thawrah, Syria 148/D3
Madirovalo, Madg. 165/H3
Madison, Ca, US 193/K9
Madison, Ct, US 197/F1
Madison, Fl, US 191/H4
Madison, Il, US 195/G8
Madison, In, US 188/C4
Madison, Ms, US 191/F3
Madison (riv.), Mt, US 184/F4
Madison, Ne, US 185/J5
Madison, NJ, US 197/J8
Madison (co.), Oh, US 195/G8
Madison, SD, US 185/J4
Madison Heights, Mi, US 193/F6
Madisonville, Tx, US 187/J5
Madisonville, Ky, US 188/C4
Madisonville, La, US 195/P16
Madiun, Indo. 138/D5
Mado Gashi, Kenya 162/C2
Madoi, China 128/G5
Madon (riv.), Fr. 98/D4
Madrakah, Ra's al (pt.), Oman 147/G5
Madre (lag.), Mex. 201/F3
Madre (lag.), Mex. 190/D5
Madre de Deus de Minas, Braz. 213/J6
Madre de Dios (riv.), Bol. 208/E6
Madre de Dios (isl.), Chile 217/A6
Madre de Dios (dept.), Peru 214/C4
Madre del Sur, Sierra (mts.), Mex. 198/A4
Madre Occidental, Sierra (mts.), Mex. 200/D3
Madre Oriental, Sierra (mts.), Mex. 201/F4
Madrid (aut. comm.), Sp. 102/C2
Madrid (cap.), Sp. 103/N9
Madridejos, Sp. 102/D3
Madrigal, Peru 214/D4
Madrigal de las Altas Torres, Sp. 102/C2
Madrigalejo, Sp. 102/C3
Madrisahorn (peak), Swi. 115/F4
Madroñera, Sp. 102/C3
Madugula, India 140/D4
Madura (isl.), Indo. 138/D5
Madurai, India 140/C6
Mae Hong Son, Thai. 141/G4
Mae Ping NP, Thai. 136/B2
Mae Tho (peak), Thai. 136/B2
Mae Ya (mtn.), Thai. 136/B2
Maebashi, Japan 133/F2
Maella, Sp. 103/F2
Maep'o, SKor. 131/E4
Maerne, It. 117/F1
Maestra, Sierra (mts.), Cuba 203/G2
Maevatanana-Ambanivohitra, Madg. 165/H7
Maewo (isl.), Van. 174/D3
Mafeteng, Les. 164/D3
Mafia (chan.), Tanz. 162/C5
Mafia (isl.), Tanz. 162/C4
Mafikeng, SAfr. 164/D2
Mafou (riv.), Gui. 160/C4
Mafra, Braz. 213/B3
Mafra, Port. 103/P10
Magadan, Rus. 123/R4
Magadino, Swi. 115/E5
Magaliesberg (mts.), SAfr. 164/P12
Magaliesburg, SAfr. 164/P12
Magallanes y Antártica Chilena (prov.), Chile 217/C7

Magangué, Col. 210/C2
Mağara, Turk. 149/C1
Magaria, Niger 161/H3
Magat (riv.), Phil. 137/D4
Magazine (mtn.), Ar, US 187/K11
Magdalena, Arg. 217/K11
Magdalena, Bol. 208/F6
Magdalena (riv.), Col. 210/C2
Magdalena (dept.), Col. 210/C2
Magdalena (peak), Malay. 139/E3
Magdalena de Kino, Mex. 200/C2
Magdeburg, Ger. 98/F2
Magdelaine Cays (isls.), Austl. 167/E2
Magé, Braz. 213/K7
Mage-shima (isl.), Japan 132/B5
Magee, Ms, US 191/F4
Magee (isl.), NI, UK 92/C2
Magelang, Indo. 138/D5
Magellan (str.), Arg.,Chile 217/C7
Magenta, It. 116/B2
Magenta (lake), Austl. 170/C5
Magerøya (isl.), Nor. 95/H1
Maggia, Swi. 115/C5
Maggia (riv.), Swi. 115/C5
Maggio (peak), It. 117/E6
Maggiorasca (peak), It. 116/C3
Maggiore (lake), It. 101/H4
Maghāghah, Egypt 159/B2
Maghar, India 142/D2
Maghera, NI, UK 92/B2
Magherafelt (co.), NI, UK 92/B2
Magherafelt, NI, UK 92/B2
Maghīla (peak), Tun. 158/D2
Maghnia, Alg. 158/D2
Magilligan (pt.), NI, UK 92/B1
Maglaj, Bosn. 106/D3
Maglić (peak), Mont. 106/D4
Maglie, It. 105/F2
Maglod, Hun. 107/R10
Magna, Ut, US 195/J12
Magnac-Laval, Fr. 100/D3
Magnetawan (riv.), On, Can. 188/D2
Magnetic Passage, Austl. 172/B2
Magnitogorsk, Rus. 119/N5
Magnitogorsk (int'l arpt.), Rus. 119/N5
Magnolia, Ar, US 187/J4
Magnolia, De, US 196/C5
Magny-en-Vexin, Fr. 110/A5
Magny-les-Hameaux, Fr. 88/J3
Mago NP, Eth. 155/N6
Mágoè, Moz. 163/F4
Magog, Qu, Can. 189/F2
Magpie (riv.), Qu, Can. 189/H1
Magpie (lake), Qu, Can. 189/H1
Magpie Ouest (riv.), Qu, Can. 189/H1
Magra (riv.), It. 116/C4
Magreta, It. 117/D3
Maguan, China 136/D1
Magude, Moz. 163/F6
Magugnano, It. 117/D1
Magway (Magwe), Myan. 141/F3
Magway (div.), Myan. 141/F3
Maha Sarakham, Thai. 136/C2
Mahābād, Iran 146/E1
Mahabe, Madg. 165/H8
Mahābhārat (range), Nepal 142/C1
Mahabo, Madg. 165/H8
Mahaboboka, Madg. 165/H9
Mahād, India 147/K5
Mahadeo (range), India 142/A4
Mahaica, Guy. 211/G3
Mahaica-Berbice (pol. reg.), Guy. 211/G3
Mahaicony Village, Guy. 211/G3
Mahajamba (riv.), Madg. 165/H7
Mahajamba (bay), Madg. 165/H6
Mahajanga (prov.), Madg. 165/H6
Mahajanga, Madg. 165/H6
Mahajilo (riv.), Madg. 165/H7
Mahakali (zone), Nepal 142/C1
Mahakam (riv.), Indo. 139/E3
Mahalapye, Bots. 163/E5
Mahale Mountains NP, Tanz. 162/A4
Mahallāt, Iran 146/F2
Maham, India 144/D5
Māhān (riv.), India 142/D1
Māhān, Iran 147/G2
Mahānadī (riv.), India 140/D3
Mahananda (riv.), India 143/F3
Mahandiabani (riv.), C.d'Iv. 160/D4

Mahanoro, Madg. 165/J7
Mahanoy City, Pa, US 196/B2
Mahantango (mtn.), Pa, US 196/B2
Mahārājganj, India 143/E2
Mahārājganj, India 142/D2
Mahārajpur, India 140/C2
Mahārāshtra (state), India 140/B4
Mahāshān (ruin), Bang. 143/G3
Mahasoabe, Madg. 165/H8
Mahavavy (riv.), Madg. 165/H7
Mahawa (riv.), India 142/B1
Mahazoarivo, Madg. 165/H8
Mahazoma, Madg. 165/H7
Mahbubnagar, India 140/C4
Mahdia, Guy. 211/G3
Mahdia, Tun. 158/M7
Mahdia (prov.), Tun. 158/M7
Mahébourg, Mrts. 165/T15
Mahendranagar, Nepal 142/C1
Mahesāna, India 147/K4
Mahgawān, India 142/B2
Mahia (pen.), NZ 175/T10
Mahilyow (int'l arpt.), Bela. 97/P5
Mahilyow, Bela. 97/P5
Mahilyowskaya Voblasts Bela. 118/F5
Mahīshādal, India 143/F4
Mahitsy, Madg. 165/H7
Mahlaing, Myan. 141/G3
Mahlberg, Ger. 114/D1
Mahuva, India 147/K4
Mahlow, Ger. 98/Q7
Mahmel (peak), Alg. 154/G1
Mahmūdābād, India 142/C2
Mahroni, India 142/B3
Mahukona, Hi, US 182/U10
Mahuva, India 147/K4
Mahwah, India 142/A2
Mahwah, NJ, US 197/J7
Mai-Ndombe (lake), D.R. Congo 155/J8
Maia, Port. 102/A2
Maiala NP, Austl. 172/E6
Maicao, Col. 210/C2
Maïche, Fr. 114/C3
Maicuru (riv.), Braz. 209/H3
Maidenhead, Eng, UK 91/F3
Maidens, Sc, UK 94/B6
Maidstone, Sk, Can. 184/F2
Maidstone, Eng, UK 91/G4
Maidstone, On, Can. 193/G7
Maiduguri, Nga. 154/H5
Maienfeld, Swi. 115/F4
Maigue (riv.), Ire. 89/P10
Maihar, India 142/C3
Maihara, Japan 135/M5
Maikala (range), India 142/C4
Maiko, PN de la, D.R. Congo 155/L8
Mailani, India 142/C1
Maili, Hi, US 182/V13
Mailly-le-Camp, Fr. 111/D6
Mailsi, Pak. 144/B5
Main (riv.), NI, UK 92/B2
Main (riv.), Ger. 98/E4
Main-Donau (canal), Ger. 112/D3
Main Range NP, Austl. 172/C6
Mainaguri, India 143/G2
Mainbernheim, Ger. 112/D3
Maincy, Fr. 88/L6
Maine (state), US 189/G2
Maine (riv.), Ire. 89/P10
Maine (reg.), Fr. 100/C2
Maine, Collines du (hills), Fr. 100/C2
Maine, Gulf of (gulf), Me, US 189/G3
Mainhardt, Ger. 112/C4
Mainhausen, Ger. 112/B2
Mainland (isl.), Sc, UK 89/V14
Mainling, China 141/F2
Mainpuri, India 142/B2
Mainstockheim, Ger. 112/D3
Maintirano, Madg. 165/H7
Mainz, Ger. 112/B2
Maio (isl.), CpV. 151/K10
Maipo (vol.), Chile 216/P9
Maipo (riv.), Chile 216/N8
Maipú, Arg. 216/F3
Maipú, Chile 216/N8
Maira (riv.), It. 101/G4
Maira (str.), Arg. 217/D7
Mairwa, India 143/E2
Mais Gate (int'l arpt.), Haiti 203/H2
Maisach, Ger. 112/E6
Maisí (cape), Cuba 203/H2
Maison-Rouge, Fr. 88/M6
Maisons-Alfort, Fr. 88/J5
Maisons-Laffitte, Fr. 88/J5
Maithon (res.), India 143/F4
Maitland, Austl. 173/D2

Maitland (riv.), On, Can. 188/D3
Maitland, Austl. 171/H5
Maitri, India, Ant. 218/A
Maizhokunggar, China 141/F2
Maizières-lès-Metz, Fr. 111/F5
Maizuru, Japan 135/H5
Maizuru (bay), Japan 135/H4
Maja e Zezë (peak), Alb. 105/G2
Majadahonda, Sp. 103/N9
Majagual, Col. 210/C2
Majardah (mts.), Alg. 158/K6
Majāz Al Bāb, Tun. 158/L6
Majdanpek, Serb. 106/E3
Majene, Indo. 139/E4
Majia (riv.), China 130/D3
Majiang, China 137/A2
Majorca (isl.), Sp. 103/G3
Majur, Serb. 106/D3
Makabe, Japan 135/E1
Makaha, Hi, US 182/V13
Makakilo City, Hi, US 182/V13
Makālu (peak), China 143/F2
Makālu (peak), Nepal 140/E2
Makarska, Cro. 105/E1
Makassar (str.), Indo. 139/E4
Makatea (isl.), FrPol. 175/L6
Makawao, Hi, US 182/T10
Makaw (mass.), Madg. 165/H8
Makemo (isl.), FrPol. 175/L6
Makena, Hi, US 182/T10
Makeni, SLeo. 160/B4
Makgadikgadi (salt pans), Bots. 163/D5
Makhachkala, Rus. 121/H4
Makhdūmpur, Pak. 144/B4
Makhfar al Busayyah, Iraq 146/E2
Makhmūr, Iraq 148/E3
Makian (isl.), Indo. 139/G3
Makin (isl.), Kiri. 174/G4
Makinohara, Japan 135/K5
Makinsk, Kaz. 145/F2
Makioka, Japan 135/B2
Makiyivka, Ukr. 120/F2
Makkah, SAr. 146/C4
Makkovik, Nf, Can. 181/L3
Makó, Hun. 106/E2
Makokou, Gabon 154/H7
Makonde (plat.), Tanz. 162/C5
Maków Mazowiecki, Pol. 99/L2
Makrákómi, Gre. 105/H3
Makran (coast), Iran 147/G3
Makran (reg.), Iran 147/H3
Makrokhórion, Gre. 105/H2
Maksutlu, Turk. 105/K2
Makteir (riv.), Mrta. 156/C5
Makthar, Tun. 158/L7
Makurazaki, Japan 132/B5
Makurdi, Nga. 161/H5
Makushin (vol.), Ak, US 192/E5
Mal Abrigo, Uru. 217/K11
Mala (pt.), CR 202/E4
Mala (pt.), Pan. 203/G5
Mala, Peru 214/B4
Malabar (coast), India 140/B5
Malabata (pt.), Mor. 158/B2
Malabo (cap.), EqG. 154/G7
Malacacheta, Braz. 212/B5
Malacca (str.), Asia 138/A3
Malacky, Slvk. 99/J4
Maladers, Swi. 115/F4
Maladzyechna, Bela. 97/M4
Málaga (int'l arpt.), Sp. 102/C4
Málaga, Sp. 102/C4
Malaga, NJ, US 196/C4
Malaga Cove (bay), Ca, US 194/F8
Malagarasi (riv.), Tanz. 162/A4
Malagón, Sp. 102/D3
Malagueta (bay), Cuba 203/G1
Malahide, Ire. 92/B5
Malaimbandy, Madg. 165/H8
Malaita (isl.), Sol. 174/F5
Malakāl, Sudan 155/M6
Malakangiri, India 140/D4
Malakwāl, Pak. 144/B3
Malambo, Col. 210/C2
Malang, Indo. 138/D5
Malanga, Nepal 143/E2
Malange, Ang. 163/C2
Malartic, Qu, Can. 188/E1
Malasoro (pt.), Indo. 139/E5
Malatya (riv.), Turk. 148/D2
Malatya, Turk. 148/D2
Malavalli, Swi. 115/E5
Malavi, India 144/C4
Malaveira, Port. 103/P10
Malawi (ctry.) 163/F3
Malawi (Nyasa) (lake), Malw. 162/B5
Malay (pen.), Thai. 141/G6
Malaya (reg.), Malay. 138/B3
Malaybalay, Phil. 137/E6
Malāyer, Iran 146/E2
Malaysia (ctry.) 111/F6
Malazemel'skaya (tundra), Rus. 119/L2
Malazgirt, Turk. 148/E2

Malbaie (riv.), Qu, Can. 189/G1
Malbork, Pol. 97/H4
Malcesine, It. 117/D1
Malchin, Ger. 96/E5
Malcontenta, It. 117/F2
Maldegem, Belg. 110/C1
Malden, Mo, US 187/K3
Malden (isl.), Kiri. 175/K5
Maldive (isls.), Mald. 140/B6
Maldives (ctry.) 125/G9
Maldon, Austl. 173/C3
Maldon, Eng, UK 91/G3
Maldonado (peak), Uru. 217/G2
Maldonado, Uru. 217/G2
Maldonado (dept.), Uru. 217/G2
Male (cap.), Mald. 125/G9
Maléa (cape), Gre. 105/H4
Malegaon, India 147/K4
Malekula (isl.), Van. 174/F6
Malemort-sur-Corrèze, Fr. 100/D4
Malente, Ger. 96/D4
Maleny, Austl. 172/D4
Maleo, It. 116/C2
Malesina, Gre. 105/H3
Malfa, It. 104/D3
Malgobek, Rus. 121/H4
Malgrat de Mar, Sp. 103/G2
Malgrate, It. 116/C1
Malheur (lake), Or, US 186/C2
Malheur (riv.), Or, US 184/D5
Malheureux (cape), Mrts. 165/T14
Mali (riv.), Myan. 141/G2
Mali (riv.), Myan. 136/B3
Mali (ctry.) 154/E4
Mali Lošinj, Cro. 106/B3
Mália, Gre. 105/J5
Malibu, Ca, US 194/B2
Malīhābād, India 142/C2
Malila, Swe. 96/F3
Malin Head (pt.), Ire. 89/Q9
Malinao, Indo. 139/F3
Malindi, Kenya 162/D3
Maling (pass), China 130/C3
Malio (riv.), Madg. 165/H8
Malipo, China 136/D1
Malir Cantonment, Pak. 147/J4
Malka Mari NP, Kenya 155/P7
Malkara, Turk. 107/H5
Malko Tŭrnovo, Bul. 107/H5
Mallacoota, Austl. 173/D3
Mallaig, Sc, UK 89/R8
Mallānwān, India 142/C2
Mallavesi (lake), Fin. 97/K1
Mallee Cliffs NP, Austl. 173/B2
Mallén, Sp. 103/E2
Malleray, Swi. 114/D3
Mallero (riv.), It. 115/F5
Mallersdorf-Pfaffenberg, Ger. 113/F5
Malles (Mals), It. 115/G4
Malloa, Chile 216/N9
Mallow, Ire. 89/P10
Malmberget, Swe. 95/G2
Malmédy, Belg. 111/F3
Malmesbury, SAfr. 164/L10
Malmköping, Swe. 96/G2
Malmö, Swe. 96/E4
Malmöhus (co.), Swe. 95/E5
Malmslätt, Swe. 96/F2
Malnate, It. 116/B1
Malo, It. 117/E1
Maloelap (isl.), Mrsh. 174/G4
Malone, NY, US 188/F2
Malong, China 141/H2
Malonje (peak), Tanz. 162/A5
Malonno, It. 115/G5
Małopolska (uplands), Pol. 99/K3
Małopolskie (prov.), Pol. 99/K4
Malpartida de Cáceres, Sp. 102/B3
Malpartida de Plasencia, Sp. 102/B3
Malpelo (isl.), Col. 208/B3
Malpensa (int'l arpt.), It. 116/B1
Malpica, Sp. 102/A1
Malš (riv.), Aus. 113/G5
Malsch, Ger. 112/B5
Malše (riv.), Czh. 99/H4
Målstek (peak), Czh. 113/G4
Malta, Mt, US 184/G3
Malta, Braz. 212/C2
Malta (chan.), Malta 104/L7
Malta (ctry.) 104/L7
Maltahöhe, Namb. 163/C5
Maltby, Eng, UK 93/G5
Malters, Swi. 114/E4
Maltorne (riv.), Fr. 88/G6
Malung, Swe. 96/E1
Malvaglia, Swi. 115/E5
Malvan, India 147/K5
Malveira, Port. 103/P10
Malvern, Pa, US 196/C3
Malvern, NY, US 197/L9
Malvinas (Falkland) (isls.), UK 217/W
Malvy Uzen' (riv.), Rus. 121/H2
Malyn, Ukr. 120/D2
Malyy Yenisey (riv.), Rus. 128/G1
Malžéville, Fr. 111/F6
Mamanguape, Braz. 212/D2

Mamaroneck, NY, US 197/L8
Mamba, Zam. 163/E4
Mamba, Japan 135/B1
Mambajao, Phil. 137/D6
Mambasa, D.R. Congo 162/A2
Mamberamo (riv.), Indo. 139/J4
Mambéré (riv.), CAfr. 154/J7
Mambij, Syria 148/D2
Mamburao, Phil. 137/D5
Mamer, Lux. 111/F4
Mamers, Fr. 100/D2
Mamfé, Camr. 161/H5
Mamming, Ger. 113/F5
Mammoth, Az, US 186/E4
Mammoth Cave NP, Ky, US 191/G2
Mamoré (riv.), Braz. 208/E6
Mamou, La, US 187/J5
Mamoutzou, May. 165/H6
Mampikony, Madg. 165/H7
Mampong, Gha. 161/E5
Mamry (lake), Pol. 97/J4
Mamuju, Indo. 139/E4
Mamuru (riv.), Braz. 209/G4
Mamwera (peak), Tanz. 162/C4
Man, C.d'Iv. 160/D5
Man, Isle of (isl.), IM, UK 92/D3
Man Mia (riv.), Thai. 136/B4
Mana, FrG. 211/H3
Manabī (prov.), Ecu. 210/A5
Manacapuru, Braz. 208/F4
Manacle (pt.), Eng, UK 90/A6
Manado, Indo. 139/F3
Manage, Belg. 111/D3
Managua (cap.), Nic. 202/E3
Managua (lake), Nic. 202/E3
Manahawkin, NJ, US 196/D4
Manakambahiny, Madg. 165/J7
Manakara, Madg. 165/J8
Manalapan, NJ, US 196/D3
Manali, India 144/D3
Manambaho (riv.), Madg. 165/H7
Manambolo (riv.), Madg. 165/H7
Mananantanana (riv.), Madg. 165/H8
Mananara, Madg. 165/J7
Mananara (riv.), Madg. 165/H8
Mananjary (isl.), Madg. 165/J8
Mananjary, Madg. 165/J8
Manara (pt.), It. 116/C4
Manaratsandry, Madg. 165/H7
Manas, China 128/E3
Manas (int'l arpt.), Kyr. 145/F4
Manas (peak), Kyr. 145/F4
Manas (riv.), India 143/H2
Manas, China 128/E2
Manaslu (peak), Nepal 143/E1
Manasquan, NJ, US 196/D3
Manasquan (riv.), NJ, US 196/D3
Manassa, Co, US 190/B2
Manastir Dečani, Kos. 105/G1
Manastir Gračanica, Kos. 106/E4
Manastir Sopoćani, Serb. 106/E4
Manatsuru, Japan 135/C3
Manaus, Braz. 208/F4
Manawatu (riv.), NZ 175/T11
Mañazo, Peru 214/D4
Manazuru-misaki (cape), Japan 135/C3
Mance (riv.), Fr. 114/B2
Mancha Real, Sp. 102/D4
Mancheng, China 130/G7
Mancherāl, India 140/C4
Manchester (lake), Austl. 172/E7
Manchester (bay), NY, US 197/L8
Manchester, Eng, UK 93/F5
Manchester (co.), Eng, UK 93/F5
Manchester (Ringway) (int'l arpt.), Eng, UK 93/F5
Manchester, Ky, US 188/D4
Manchester, Mo, US 195/P9
Manchester, Md, US 196/B4
Manchester, NH, US 189/G3
Manchester, Pa, US 196/B3
Manchester, Wa, US 193/B2
Manchuria (reg.), China 129/M3
Mancieulles, Fr. 111/E5
Máncora, Peru 214/A2
Mand (riv.), Iran 147/F3
Manda, PN de, Chad 155/K5
Mandabe, Madg. 165/H8
Mandaguari, Braz. 213/H1
Mandal, India 140/B3
Mandal, Nor. 96/B2
Mandal-Ovoo, Mong. 128/H3
Mandala (peak), Indo. 139/K4
Mandalay, Myan. 141/G3
Mandalay (div.), Myan. 141/G3
Mandalgovĭ, Mong. 128/J2

Mandalī, Iraq 146/E2
Mandan, ND, US 185/H4
Mandasavu (peak), Indo. 139/F5
Mandaue, Phil. 137/D5
Mandeb (str.), D.R. Congo 162/A2
Mandello del Lario, It. 115/F6
Mandera, Kenya 155/P7
Mandeure, Fr. 114/C3
Mandeville, La, US 195/P16
Mandeville, Jam. 203/G2
Mandi Bahāuddīn, Pak. 144/B3
Mandi Dabwāli, India 144/C3
Mandī Sādiqganj, Pak. 144/B4
Mandié, Moz. 163/F4
Mandiola (isl.), Indo. 139/G4
Mandira (res.), India 143/E4
Mandla, India 142/C4
Mandø (isl.), Den. 96/C4
Mándok, Hun. 99/M4
Mandoto, Madg. 165/H7
Mandoúdhion, Gre. 105/H3
Mándra, Gre. 105/N8
Mandrare (riv.), Madg. 165/H9
Mandritsara, Madg. 165/J6
Mandsaur, India 147/L4
Mandurah, Austl. 170/C5
Manduria, It. 105/F2
Māndvi, India 147/J4
Mandya, India 140/C5
Mané (pass), Nepal 142/D1
Manéngouba, Massif du (peak), Camr. 161/H5
Maner, India 143/E3
Manerbio, It. 116/C2
Manfalūt, Egypt 146/B3
Manfredonia, It. 104/D2
Manfredonia, Golfo di (gulf), It. 104/D2
Mang (riv.), China 130/B4
Manga, Braz. 212/B4
Manga, Burk. 161/E4
Mangabeiras, Chapada das (hills), Braz. 209/J6
Mangai, D.R. Congo 163/C1
Mangaia (isl.), Cooks. 175/L7
Mangaldai, India 141/F2
Mangaldan, Phil. 137/D4
Mangalia, Rom. 107/J4
Mangalisa (peak), Madg. 165/H7
Mangalore, India 140/B5
Mangaratiba, Braz. 213/J7
Mangareva (isl.), FrPol. 175/M7
Manger, Nor. 96/A1
Mangghystaŭ (obl.), Kaz. 122/F5
Mangghystaŭ Tübegi (pen.), Kaz. 121/J3
Mangghystaŭ Üstirti (plat.), Kaz. 121/K4
Mangkalihat (cape), Indo. 139/E3
Mangla (dam), Pak. 144/B3
Mangla, Pak. 144/B3
Mangla (res.), Pak. 144/B3
Manglaralto, Ecu. 214/A1
Manglares (pt.), Col. 210/B4
Manglaur, India 142/A1
Mangles (bay), Austl. 170/K7
Mango, Togo 161/F4
Mangoche, Malw. 163/F3
Mangoky (riv.), Madg. 163/J11
Mangole (isl.), Indo. 139/G4
Mangoro (riv.), Madg. 165/J7
Mangotsfield, Eng, UK 90/D4
Mángrol, India 147/K4
Manguarde, Port. 102/B2
Mangueira (lake), Braz. 217/G2
Mangum, Ok, US 187/H4
Manhasset, NY, US 197/L8
Manhasset (bay), NY, US 197/L8
Manhattan, Mt, US 184/F4
Manhattan (isl.), NY, US 197/K9
Manhattan Beach, Ca, US 194/F8
Manhay, Belg. 111/E3
Manheim, Pa, US 196/B3
Manhiça, Moz. 163/F6
Manhuaçu, Braz. 213/D2
Manhuaçu (riv.), Braz. 213/K8
Maniago, It. 117/E1
Maniamba, Moz. 163/F3
Maniāri (riv.), India 142/C4
Manicoré (riv.), Braz. 208/F5
Manicoré, Braz. 208/F5
Manicouagan (res.), Qu, Can. 189/G1
Manifold (cape), Austl. 172/C3
Manigotagan, Mb, Can. 185/J3
Manihāri, India 143/F3
Manihi (isl.), FrPol. 175/L6

Manihiki (isl.), Cooks. 175/J6
Manikarchar, India 143/G3
Manila (cap.), Phil. 137/D5
Manila, Austl. 173/D1
Manipa (str.), Indo. 139/G4
Manipat (hills), India 142/D4
Manipur (state), India 141/F3
Manisa (prov.), Turk. 148/B2
Manistee, Mi, US 188/C2
Manistee (riv.), Mi, US 188/C2
Manistique, Mi, US 188/C2
Manitoba (prov.), Can. 180/D2
Manitoba (lake), Mb, Can. 185/J3
Manitou (riv.), Qu, Can. 189/H1
Manitou Springs, Co, US 187/F3
Manitoulin (isl.), On, Can. 188/D2
Manitowoc, Wi, US 185/M4
Maniwaki, Qu, Can. 188/F2
Manizales, Col. 208/C2
Manja, Madg. 165/H8
Manjakandriana, Madg. 165/J7
Manjimup, Austl. 170/C5
Mankono, C.d'Iv. 160/D4
Manley Hot Springs, Ak, US 192/H2
Manlleu, Sp. 102/D1
Manlyutka, Rus. 119/R4
Manmād, India 147/K4
Mannar, SrL. 140/C6
Mannar (gulf), India,SrL. 140/C6
Mannedorf, Swi. 115/E3
Mannheim, Ger. 112/B4
Manning, SC, US 191/H3
Manning (cape), NW, Can. 181/Q7
Manning, Ab, Can. 180/E3
Mannington Meadow (lake), NJ, US 196/C4
Mannum, Austl. 171/H5
Mano (riv.), Libr. 160/C5
Manokotar, Ak, US 192/G4
Manolo Fortich, Phil. 137/D6
Manombo, Madg. 165/G8
Manono, D.R. Congo 163/E2
Manorville, NY, US 197/F2
Manosque, Fr. 100/F5
Manouane (riv.), Qu, Can. 189/G1
Manouane (lake), Qu, Can. 189/G1
Manp'o, NKor. 131/D2
Manra (Sydney) (isl.), Kiri. 175/H5
Manresa, Sp. 103/K6
Mansa, Zam. 162/A5
Mānsa, India 144/C5
Mansa Konko, Gam. 160/B3
Mansalay, Phil. 139/F1
Mānsehra, Pak. 144/B2
Mansel (isl.), Nun., Can. 181/H2
Mansfield, Austl. 173/C3
Mansfield, Eng, UK 93/G5
Mansfield, La, US 187/J4
Mansfield, Oh, US 188/D3
Mansfield Woodhouse, Eng, UK 93/G5
Mansilla de las Mulas, Sp. 102/C1
Manta, Ecu. 210/A5
Mantalingajan (mt.), Phil. 139/E2
Mantaro (riv.), Peru 208/C6
Manteca, Ca, US 186/B3
Mantecal, Ven. 210/D3
Manteigas, Port. 102/B2
Mantena, Braz. 213/D1
Manthani, India 140/C4
Manti, Ut, US 186/E3
Mantiqueira, Serra da (mts.), Braz. 209/K8
Mantorp, Swe. 96/F2
Mantova (prov.), It. 116/C2
Mäntsälä, Fin. 97/L1
Mantua, Cuba 203/E1
Mantua, NJ, US 196/C3
Mantua, Ut, US 195/K11
Manturovo, Rus. 119/K4
Mäntyharju, Fin. 97/M1
Manú, Peru 214/D4
Manú, PN, Peru 214/D4
Manua Atoll (atoll), Cooks. 175/K6
Manuel Alves da Natividade (riv.), Braz. 209/J6
Manuel Benavides, Mex. 200/C2
Manuel J. Cobo, Arg. 217/K11
Manui (isl.), Indo. 139/F4
Manuk (riv.), Indo. 138/C5
Manukau, NZ 175/S10
Manumuskin (riv.), NJ, US 196/D5

Manuripe (riv.), Bol. 208/E6
Manuripe Heath Amazonica, Reserva Nacional, Bol. 214/D4
Manus (isl.), PNG 174/D5
Manville, NJ, US 196/D2
Many, La, US 187/J5
Many Farms, Az, US 186/E3
Manyara (lake), Tanz. 162/B3
Manych-Gudilo (lake), Rus. 121/G3
Manzanares, Sp. 102/D3
Manzanares (riv.), Sp. 103/N8
Manzanares el Real, Sp. 103/N8
Manzanillo, Mex. 200/D5
Manzanillo (int'l arpt.), Mex. 200/D5
Manzanillo, Cuba 203/G1
Manzano (mts.), NM, US 190/B3
Manzano, It. 117/G1
Manzhouli, China 129/L2
Manzilah, Buhayrat al (lake), Egypt 149/B4
Manzini, Swaz. 165/E2
Mao, Chad 154/J5
Maoke (mts.), Indo. 139/J4
Maoming, China 141/K3
Mapastepec, Mex. 202/C3
Mapi (riv.), Indo. 139/J5
Mapimí, Bolsón de (depr.), Mex. 200/D3
Mapire, Ven. 211/E3
Maple (riv.), ND, US 185/J4
Maple Creek, Sk, Can. 184/D3
Maple Grove, Qu, Can. 189/N7
Maple Park, Il, US 193/N16
Maple Shade, NJ, US 196/D4
Maple Valley, Wa, US 193/C3
Mapleton, Ut, US 195/K13
Maplewood, Mo, US 195/G8
Maplewood, NJ, US 197/H9
Maporal, Ven. 210/D3
Mapuera (riv.), Braz. 208/G3
Maputo (int'l arpt.), Moz. 165/F2
Maputo (cap.), Moz. 165/F2
Maqdam (cape), Sudan 159/D5
Maqên Gangri (peak), China 128/G5
Maquan (Damqog) (riv.), China 142/E1
Maquinchao, Arg. 216/C4
Maquoketa (riv.), Ia, US 187/K2
Mar (mts.), Braz. 205/E5
Mar (reg.), Sc, UK 94/D2
Mar Chiquita (lake), Arg. 215/D3
Mar de Ajó, Arg. 217/F3
Mar del Plata, Arg. 216/F3
Mar del Tuyú, Arg. 217/F3
Mara (pol. reg.), Tanz. 162/B3
Mara (riv.), Tanz. 162/B3
Marabá, Braz. 209/J5
Maracá, Ilha de (isl.), Braz. 209/H3
Maracaibo, Ven. 210/D2
Maracaibo (lake), Ven. 210/D2
Maracaju, Serra de (mts.), Braz. 209/G8
Maracás, Braz. 212/B4
Maracás, Chapada de (hills), Braz. 212/B4
Maracay, Ven. 208/E1
Maracena, Sp. 102/D4
Marādah, Libya 154/J2
Maradi, Niger 161/G3
Maradi (dept.), Niger 161/G3
Marāgheh, Iran 146/E1
Mārahra, India 142/B2
Marahuaca (peak), Ven. 211/E3
Marais de St-Gond (swamp), Fr. 110/C6
Marais des Cygnes (riv.), Ks,Mo, US 187/J3
Marajó (bay), Braz. 209/J4
Marajó, Ilha de (isl.), Braz. 209/H4
Maralal, Kenya 162/C2
Maralinga-Tjarutja Abor. Land, Austl. 171/F4
Marambaia, Ilha (isl.), Braz. 213/K8
Maramureş (co.), Rom. 99/M5
Marana, Az, US 186/E4
Marand, Iran 121/G1
Marang, Malay. 138/B2
Maranguape, Braz. 212/C1
Maranhão (riv.), Braz. 209/J6
Maranhão (state), Braz. 212/A2
Marano sul Panaro, It. 117/D2
Marano Vicentino, It. 117/E1
Maranoa (riv.), Austl. 167/G3
Marañón (riv.), Peru 214/B2
Marans, Fr. 100/C3

Maraoue, PN de la, C.d'Iv. 160/D5
Marapi (peak), Indo. 138/B4
Maras (peak), Indo. 138/C4
Mărăşeşti, Rom. 107/H3
Marathon, On, Can. 185/M3
Marathon, Fl, US 191/H5
Marathon, Tx, US 190/C4
Marathón, Gre. 105/N8
Marau, Braz. 213/A4
Maraulīānwāla, Pak. 144/B3
Maravatío de Ocampo, Mex. 201/E5
Marawi, Phil. 137/D6
Marbach, Swi. 114/D4
Marbach am Neckar, Ger. 112/C5
Marbache, Fr. 111/F6
Marbella, Sp. 102/C4
Marble Bar, Austl. 170/C2
Marbleton, Wy, US 184/F5
Marburg, Ger. 101/H1
Marburg (lake), Pa, US 196/B4
Marca, Ponta da (pt.), Ang. 163/B4
Marcali, Hun. 106/C2
Marcallo, It. 116/B2
Marcapata, Peru 214/D4
March, Eng, UK 91/G1
Marche (prov.), It. 101/K5
Marche (mts.), Fr. 100/D3
Marche-en-Famenne, Belg. 111/E3
Marchémoret, Fr. 88/L4
Marchena, Sp. 102/C4
Marchena (isl.), Ecu. 214/E6
Marcheno, It. 116/D1
Marchiennes, Fr. 110/C3
Marchin, Belg. 111/E3
Marchtrenk, Aus. 113/H6
Marciana Marina, It. 104/B1
Marcilly, Fr. 88/L4
Marcilly-sur-Tille, Fr. 114/B2
Marck, Fr. 110/A2
Marckolsheim, Fr. 114/D1
Marco, Braz. 212/B1
Marco, Fl, US 191/H5
Marco Polo (int'l arpt.), It. 117/F2
Marcoing, Fr. 110/C3
Marcon, It. 117/F1
Marcona, Peru 214/C4
Marconi (mt.), BC, Can. 184/E3
Marcos Juárez, Arg. 216/E2
Marcoussis, Fr. 88/J6
Marcovia, Hon. 202/E3
Marcq-en-Barœul, Fr. 110/C2
Marcus Baker (mt.), Ak, US 192/J3
Marcy (mt.), NY, US 188/F2
Mardān, Pak. 144/B2
Marden, Eng, UK 88/E3
Mardeuil, Fr. 110/C5
Mardin (town), Turk. 148/E2
Marecchia (riv.), It. 117/F5
Maree (lake), Sc, UK 89/R8
Mareeba, Austl. 172/B2
Mareil-sur-Mauldre, Fr. 88/H5
Marengo, Il, US 193/N15
Marennes, Fr. 100/C4
Mareuil-sur-Ourcq, Fr. 88/M4
Marfa, Tx, US 187/F5
Margalla Hills NP, Pak. 144/B3
Marganets', Ukr. 120/E3
Margao (Madgaon), India 147/K5
Margaret (mt.), Austl. 170/C2
Margaret River, Austl. 170/B5
Margarita (peak), Ca, US 194/C4
Margarita, Isla de (isl.), Ven. 208/F1
Margaritión, Gre. 105/G3
Margate, SAfr. 165/E3
Margate, Eng, UK 91/H4
Margate City, NJ, US 196/D5
Margeride, Monts de la (mts.), Fr. 100/E4
Margherita (peak), Ugan. 162/A2
Marghilon, Uzb. 145/F4
Marghita, Rom. 106/F2
Margny-lès-Compiègne, Fr. 110/B5
Margos, Peru 214/B3
Margosatubig, Phil. 137/D6
Margraten, Neth. 111/E2
Mari, Braz. 212/D2
Maria (mt.), Austl. 173/D4
María Cleófas (isl.), Mex. 200/D4
Maria da Fé, Braz. 213/H7
Maria Island NP, Austl. 173/D4
María Madre (isl.), Mex. 200/D4
María Magdalena (isl.), Mex. 200/D4
Maria van Diemen (cape), NZ 175/S9
Mariāhū, India 142/D3
Marian, Austl. 172/C3
Marianao, Cuba 203/F1
Marianna, Fl, US 191/G4
Marianna, Ar, US 187/J4
Mariano Comense, It. 116/C1
Mariano Marcos, Phil. 137/D6
Mariánské Lázně, Czh. 113/F3
Marias (riv.), Mt, US 184/F3
Mariato (pt.), Pan. 203/F5
Maribo, Den. 96/D4
Maribor, Slov. 101/L3
Maricá, Braz. 213/L7
Maricopa (co.), Az, US 195/R18
Marié (riv.), Braz. 208/E4
Marie Byrd Land (phys. reg.), Ant. 218/S
Marie-Galante (isl.), Dom. 199/J4
Mariehamn (int'l arpt.), Fin. 97/H1
Mariel, Cuba 203/F1
Marienhafe, Ger. 109/E1
Marienheide, Ger. 111/G1
Mariental, Namb. 163/C5
Mariestad, Swe. 96/E2
Marietta, Ok, US 187/H4
Marietta, Ga, US 191/G3
Marietta, Pa, US 196/B3
Marignane, Fr. 100/F5
Marigot, Dom. 199/N9
Marijampolė, Lith. 97/K4
Marília, Braz. 213/B2
Marín, Sp. 102/A1
Marin (co.), Ca, US 193/J10
Marin-Epagnier, Swi. 114/D3
Marina, It. 104/D3
Marina del Rey, Ca, US 194/F8
Marina del Rey (har.), Ca, US 194/F8
Marina di Andora, It. 116/B5
Marina di Montemarciano, It. 117/G5
Marina di Ravenna, It. 117/F4
Marine Nat'l Rsv., Kenya 162/D3
Marine World Africa USA, Ca, US 193/K10
Marineland, Austl. 171/M8
Marines, Fr. 88/H4
Marinette, Wi, US 185/M4
Maringá, Braz. 213/B2
Marinha Grande, Port. 102/A3
Marinhas, Port. 102/A2
Marion (reef), Austl. 167/E2
Marion, Al, US 191/G3
Marion, In, US 188/C3
Marion, Ky, US 188/B4
Marion, Mi, US 188/C2
Marion, Oh, US 188/D3
Marion (lake), SC, US 191/H3
Maripa, Ven. 211/E3
Mariposa, Ca, US 186/C3
Mariscal Estigarribia, Par. 208/F8
Mariscal Sucre (int'l arpt.), Ecu. 210/B5
Maritime Alps (mts.), Fr. 101/G4
Maritsa (riv.), Bul. 107/H5
Mariupol', Ukr. 120/F3
Mariupol' (int'l arpt.), Ukr. 120/F3
Mariy-El, Resp., Rus. 122/G6
Marj 'Uyūn, Leb. 149/D3
Mark (riv.), Belg. 108/B6
Mark Twain NWR, Il, US 195/F7
Mark Twain (lake), Mo, US 187/J3
Mark Twain NWR, Mo, US 195/G8
Marka (riv.), Ger. 109/E3
Marka (Merca), Som. 155/P7
Markam, China 141/G2
Markaryd, Swe. 96/E3
Markdorf, Ger. 115/F2
Markelsdorfer (pt.), Ger. 96/D4
Marken (isl.), Neth. 108/C4
Markerwaard (polder), Neth. 108/C3
Market Harborough, Eng, UK 91/F2
Markgroningen, Ger. 112/C5
Markham, On, Can. 189/R8
Markham (bay), Nun., Can. 181/J2
Marki, Pol. 99/L2
Markinch, Sc, UK 94/C4
Markit, China 145/G5
Markleeville, Ca, US 186/C3
Markneukirchen, Ger. 113/F2
Markópoulon, Gre. 105/N9
Markovac, Serb. 106/E3
Marks, Rus. 121/H2
Marksville, La, US 187/J5
Markt Bibart, Ger. 112/D3
Markt Erlbach, Ger. 112/D4
Markt Indersdorf, Ger. 113/E6
Markt Rettenbach, Ger. 115/G2
Markt Sankt Florian, Aus. 113/H6
Markt Schwaben, Ger. 113/E6
Marktbreit, Ger. 112/D3
Marktheidenfeld, Ger. 112/C3
Marktl, Ger. 113/F6
Marktoberdorf, Ger. 115/G2
Marktredwitz, Ger. 113/F3
Marl, Ger. 109/E5
Marla, Austl. 171/G3
Marlboro, NJ, US 196/D3
Marlboro (Upper Marlboro), Md, US 196/B6
Marle, Fr. 110/C4
Marlengo (Marling), It. 115/H4
Marlenheim, Fr. 111/G6
Marles-en-Brie, Fr. 88/L5
Marles-les-Mines, Fr. 110/B3
Marlow, Eng, UK 91/F3
Marlow, Ger. 96/E4
Marlton, NJ, US 196/D4
Marly, Fr. 111/F5
Marly, Fr. 110/C3
Marly-la-Ville, Fr. 88/K4
Marly-le-Roi, Fr. 88/J5
Marmagão, India 147/K5
Marmande, Fr. 100/D4
Marmara, Turk. 107/H5
Marmara (isl.), Turk. 107/H5
Marmara (sea), Turk. 107/J5
Marmaraereğlisi, Turk. 107/H5
Marmaris, Turk. 148/B2
Marmelos (riv.), Braz. 208/F5
Marmion (lake), Austl. 170/D4
Marmirolo, It. 117/D2
Marmolada (peak), It. 101/J3
Marmolejo, Sp. 102/C3
Marmontana (peak), It. 115/F5
Marmora, NJ, US 196/D5
Marmoutier, Fr. 111/G6
Marnay, Fr. 114/B3
Marnaz, Fr. 114/C5
Marne (riv.), Fr. 100/F2
Marne, Ger. 96/C5
Marne (dept.), Fr. 110/C6
Marne au Rhin, Canal de la (canal), Fr. 111/D6
Maro (reef), Hi, US 175/H2
Maroa, Ven. 211/E4
Maroantsetra, Madg. 165/J6
Marokau (isl.), FrPol. 175/L6
Marolambo, Madg. 165/J8
Maroldsweisach, Ger. 112/D2
Marolles-en-Brie, Fr. 88/M5
Marolles-en-Hurepoix, Fr. 88/J6
Maromokotro (peak), Madg. 165/J6
Marondera, Zim. 163/F4
Marone, It. 116/D1
Maroni (riv.), FrG.,Sur. 209/H3
Maroochydore-Mooloolaba, Austl. 172/D4
Maroon Town, Jam. 203/G2
Marostica, It. 117/E1
Marotandrano, Madg. 165/J7
Marotiri (Bass Is.) (isls.), FrPol. 175/L7
Marotta, It. 117/G5
Maroua, Camr. 154/H5
Marouini (riv.), FrG. 211/H4
Marovato, Madg. 165/J6
Marovoay, Madg. 165/H7
Marowijne (dist.), Sur. 211/H3
Marpingen, Ger. 111/G5
Marple, Eng, UK 93/F5
Marquan (riv.), China 140/E2
Marquard, SAfr. 164/D3
Marquarie (riv.), Austl. 173/C1
Marquesas (isls.), FrPol. 175/M5
Marquise, Fr. 110/A2
Marracuene, Moz. 165/F2
Marradi, It. 117/E4
Marrah (mts.), Sudan 155/K5
Marrah (peak), Sudan 155/K5
Marrakech, Mor. 156/D3
Marrero, La, US 195/P17
Marromeu, Moz. 163/G4
Marrupa, Moz. 163/G3
Mars (peak), It. 116/A1
Marsá al Burayqah, Libya 155/J1
Marsá Maţrūḩ (cap.), Egypt 159/A2
Marsabit, Kenya 162/C2
Marsabit Nat'l Rsv., Kenya 162/C2
Marsala, It. 104/C4
Marsange (riv.), Fr. 88/L5
Marsannay, Fr. 114/A3
Marsberg, Ger. 109/F6
Marsciano, It. 101/K5
Marsdiep Texelstroom (chan.), Neth. 108/B3
Marseille, Fr. 100/F5
Marseille-en-Beauvaisis, Fr. 110/A4
Marsh (isl.), La, US 190/E4
Marshall (riv.), Austl. 171/H2
Marshall, Sk, Can. 184/F2
Marshall, Co, US 195/B3
Marshall, Mn, US 185/K4
Marshall, Mo, US 187/J3
Marshall, Tx, US 187/J4
Marshall, Ut, US 195/J12
Marshall Islands (ctry.) 174/G3
Marshallton, De, US 196/C4
Marshalltown, Ia, US 185/K5
Marshdale, Co, US 195/B3
Marshfield, Mo, US 187/J3
Märsta, Swe. 96/G2
Marston (lake), Co, US 195/B3
Marsyandi (riv.), Nepal 143/E1
Marta, It. 104/B1
Martaban, Myan. 136/B2
Martaban (gulf), Myan. 136/B2
Martapura, Indo. 138/D4
Marte R. Gomez, Mex. 200/C3
Martelange, Belg. 111/E4
Martellago, It. 117/F1
Martensville, Sk, Can. 184/G2
Martfeld, Ger. 109/G3
Martha's Vineyard (isl.), Ma, US 189/G3
Martignacco, It. 117/G1
Martigny, Swi. 114/D5
Martigny-les-Bains, Fr. 114/B1
Martigues, Fr. 100/F5
Martil, Mor. 158/B2
Martin, Tn, US 188/B4
Martin (lake), Al, US 191/G3
Martin, Slvk. 99/K4
Martin Vaz (isls.), Braz. 209/N8
Martina Franca, It. 105/E2
Martinengo, It. 116/C1
Martinez, Ga, US 191/H3
Martínez de la Torre, Mex. 201/M6
Martinho Campos, Braz. 213/C1
Martinique (isl.), Fr. 199/N9
Martinique Passage (chan.), Dom.,Mart. 199/J4
Martinon, Gre. 105/H3
Martinópole, Braz. 212/B1
Martinópolis, Braz. 213/B2
Martins, Braz. 212/C2
Martins Creek, Pa, US 196/C2
Martinsburg, WV, US 188/E4
Martinsville, Va, US 188/E4
Martorell, Sp. 103/K7
Martos, Sp. 102/D4
Martre (riv.), Qu, Can. 188/F1
Martres-Tolosane, Fr. 100/D5
Marty, SD, US 185/J5
Marugame, Japan 132/C3
Maruim, Braz. 212/C3
Maruko, Japan 133/F2
Marum, Neth. 108/D2
Maruoka, Japan 132/E2
Marutea (isl.), FrPol. 175/M7
Marv Dasht, Iran 146/F3
Marxheim, Ger. 112/D5
Mary, Trkm. 147/H1
Mary Anne Passage, Austl. 170/B2
Mary Esther, Fl, US 191/G4
Mary-sur-Marne, Fr. 88/M4
Maryborough, Austl. 173/B3
Maryborough, Austl. 172/D4
Marydale, SAfr. 164/C3
Marydel, Md, US 196/C5
Maryfield, Sk, Can. 185/H3
Maryland (co.), Libr. 160/C5
Maryland (state), US 188/E4
Maryland City, Md, US 196/B5
Maryland Heights, Mo, US 195/G8
Maryland Line, Md, US 196/B4
Marystown, Nf, Can. 189/L2
Marysville, Ks, US 187/H3
Marysville, Pa, US 196/B3
Maryville, Tn, US 191/H3
Maryville, Il, US 195/H8
Marzabotto, It. 117/E4
Marzano (peak), It. 104/D2
Marzo (pt.), Col. 210/B3
Marzūq, Libya 154/H2
Masada (ruin), Isr. 149/D4
Masai Mara Nat'l Rsv., Kenya 163/F1
Masai Steppe (grsld.), Tanz. 162/C4
Masaka, Ugan. 162/A3
Masamagrell, Sp. 103/E3
Masamba, Indo. 139/F4
Masan, SKor. 131/E5
Masangwe (hill), Tanz. 162/A4
Masaya, Nic. 202/E4
Masbate (isl.), Phil. 137/D5
Mascara, Alg. 158/F5
Mascarene (isls.), Mrts 165/T15
Mascota, Mex. 200/D4
Mascouche, Qu, Can. 189/N6
Maselheim, Ger. 115/F1
Maserà di Padova, It. 117/E2
Maseru (cap.), Les. 164/D3
Masevaux, Fr. 114/D2
Masfjorden, Nor. 96/A1
Mashan, China 137/A3
Mashhad (int'l arpt.), Iran 145/C5
Mashike, Japan 134/B2
Māshkīd (riv.), Iran 147/H3
Mashtūl as Sūq, Egypt 149/B4
Mashū (lake), Japan 134/D2
Masiaca, Mex. 200/C3
Maside, Sp. 102/A1
Masim (peak), Rus. 121/L1
Masindi, Ugan. 162/A2
Maşīrah, Jazīrat (isl.), Oman 147/G4
Masisea, Peru 214/C3
Masjed-e Soleymān, Iran 146/E2
Mask (lake), Ire. 89/P10
Masker (peak), Mor. 156/D2
Masnou, Sp. 103/L7
Masoala (cape), Madg. 165/J6
Masoala (pen.), Madg. 163/L10
Masoarivo, Madg. 165/H7
Mason, Mi, US 188/C3
Mason, Tx, US 187/H5
Mason (co.), Wa, US 193/A3
Mason (lake), Wa, US 193/B3
Mason and Dixon Line, Pa, US 196/B4
Masone, It. 116/B4
Masonville, Co, US 195/B2
Masquefa, Sp. 103/K6
Massa, It. 116/D4
Massa-Carrara (prov.), It. 116/C4
Massa Finalese, It. 117/E3
Massa Fiscaglia, It. 117/F3
Massa Lombarda, It. 117/E4
Massa Marittima, It. 101/J5
Massa Martana, It. 101/K5
Massachusetts (state), US 189/F3
Massachusetts (bay), Ma, US 189/G3
Massaciuccoli, Lago di (lake), It. 116/D5
Massafra, It. 105/E2
Massangena, Moz. 163/F5
Massapê, Braz. 212/B1
Massapequa, NY, US 197/M9
Massapequa Park, NY, US 197/M9
Massarosa, It. 116/D5
Massbach, Ger. 112/D2
Massena, NY, US 188/F2
Masset, BC, Can. 192/M4
Massey (sound), Nun., Can. 181/S7
Massey, Md, US 196/C5
Massillon, Oh, US 188/D3
Massy, Fr. 88/J5
Masterton, NZ 175/T11
Mastgat (chan.), Neth. 108/B5
Mastic, NY, US 197/F2
Mastic Beach, NY, US 197/F2
Mastník (riv.), Czh. 113/H3
Mastūj (riv.), Pak. 144/A2
Mastung, Pak. 147/J3
Masuda, Japan 132/B3
Masuho, Japan 135/A2
Masurai (peak), Indo. 138/B4
Masvingo, Zim. 163/F5
Maswa Game Rsv., Tanz. 162/B3
Maşyāf, Syria 149/E2
Mat (riv.), Alb. 105/F2
Mata Grande, Braz. 212/C3
Mata Utu, Fr. 175/H6
Matābhānga, India 143/G2
Matadi, D.R. Congo 163/B2
Matador, Tx, US 187/G4
Matagalpa, Nic. 202/E3
Matagami (lake), Qu, Can. 188/E1
Matagorda (bay), Tx, US 190/D4
Matagorda (isl.), Tx, US 190/D4
Matale, SrL. 140/D6
Matam, Sen. 160/B3
Matamoros, Pa, US 196/D1
Matamoros, Mex. 200/E3
Ma'ţan as Sarra (well), Libya 155/K3
Matandu (riv.), Tanz. 162/C5
Matane (riv.), Qu, Can. 189/H1
Matane, Qu, Can. 189/H1
Matanga, Madg. 165/H8
Matanzas, Cuba 198/E3
Matão, Braz. 213/B2
Matape (riv.), Mex. 200/C2
Matapedia (riv.), Qu, Can. 189/H1
Mataquito (riv.), Chile 216/C2
Matara (ruin), Erit. 146/C6
Matara, SrL. 140/D6
Mataram, Indo. 139/E5
Mataránga, Gre. 105/G3
Mataró, Sp. 103/L6
Matatiele, SAfr. 164/E3
Mataura (riv.), NZ 175/R12
Matawan, NJ, US 197/J10
Matehuala, Mex. 201/E4
Matéri, Ben. 161/F4
Maternillos (pt.), Cuba 199/F3
Mátészalka, Hun. 99/M5
Mateur, Tun. 158/L6
Mathay, Fr. 114/C3
Matheniko Game Rsv., Ugan. 162/B2
Mathew's (peak), Kenya 162/C2
Mathews (lake), Ca, US 194/C3
Mathis, Tx, US 190/D4
Mathoura, Austl. 173/C2
Mathurā, India 142/A2
Mati, Phil. 137/E6
Matías Barbosa, Braz. 213/K6
Matias Olímpio, Braz. 212/B1
Matías Romero, Mex. 202/C2
Matíguas, Nic. 203/E3
Matilija (dam), Ca, US 194/A2
Matinha, Braz. 212/A2
Matinhos, Braz. 213/B3
Matinicock (pt.), NY, US 197/L8
Matiyuri (riv.), Ven. 210/D3
Mātla (riv.), India 143/G5
Matlock, Eng, UK 93/G5
Mato Grosso (plat.), Braz. 209/G6
Mato Grosso do Sul (state), Braz. 213/A1
Mato Grosso, Planalto do (plat.), Braz. 209/H6
Mato Verde, Braz. 212/B4
Matopos, Zim. 163/E5
Matosinhos, Port. 102/A2
Matoya (bay), Japan 135/L7
Maţraḩ, Oman 147/G4
Matrei am Brenner, Aus. 115/H3
Matrei in Osttirol, Aus. 101/K3
Matriz de Camaragibe, Braz. 212/D3
Matroosberg (peak), SAfr. 164/L10
Matsalu (gulf), Est. 97/K2
Matsapa (Manzini) (int'l arpt.), Swaz. 165/E2
Matsiatra (riv.), Madg. 165/H8
Matsoandakana, Madg. 165/J6
Matsubara, Japan 135/J6
Matsubushi, Japan 135/D2
Matsuda, Japan 135/C3
Matsudo, Japan 135/D2
Matsue, Japan 132/C3
Matsuida, Japan 135/B1
Matsumae, Japan 134/B3
Matsumoto, Japan 133/E2
Matsuo, Japan 135/E2
Matsusaka, Japan 135/L6
Matsushima, Japan 134/B4
Matsutō, Japan 132/E2
Matsuyama, Japan 132/C4
Matt, Swi. 115/F4
Mattagami (riv.), On, Can. 188/D1
Mattarello, It. 115/H6
Mattawa, On, Can. 188/E2
Matterhorn (peak), It.,Swi. 114/D6
Mattertal (valley), Swi. 114/D5
Mattese, Mo, US 195/G9
Matthews (mtn.), Ak, US 192/H2
Mattig (riv.), Aus. 113/G6
Mattighofen, Aus. 113/G6
Mattituck, NY, US 197/F2
Mattmarksee (lake), Swi. 114/D5
Mattō, Japan 132/E2
Mattock (riv.), Ire. 92/B4
Mattsee, Aus. 113/G7
Matucana, Peru 214/B3
Maturín, Ven. 211/F2
Matusadona NP, Zim. 163/E4
Matzen, Aus. 107/P7
Maú (riv.), Guy. 208/G3
Mau (peak), Kenya 162/B3
Mau Aimma, India 142/C3
Mau Rānīpur, India 142/B3
Mauá, Braz. 213/C2
Maubert-Fontaine, Fr. 111/D4
Maubeuge, Fr. 110/C3
Maubourguet, Fr. 100/D5
Mauchline, Sc, UK 94/B5
Maud (pt.), Austl. 170/B2
Maud, Sc, UK 94/D1
Maudaha, India 142/C3
Mauerbach, Aus. 107/N7
Mauerkirchen, Aus. 113/G6
Maués, Braz. 208/G4
Maués Açu (riv.), Braz. 208/G4
Maug (isls.), NMar. 174/D2
Mauganj, India 142/C3
Maughold, IM, UK 92/D3
Maughold (pt.), IM, UK 92/D3
Mauguio, Fr. 100/F5
Maui (isl.), Hi, US 182/T10
Mauke (isl.), Cookls. 175/K7
Maulbronn, Ger. 112/B5
Mauldre (riv.), Fr. 110/A6
Maule (pol. reg.), Chile 216/B2
Maule (riv.), Chile 216/C2
Maule, Fr. 88/H5
Mauléon, Fr. 100/C3
Maullín, Chile 216/B4
Maumee (riv.), In,Oh, US 188/C3
Maun, Bots. 163/D4
Mauna Kea (peak), Hi, US 182/U11
Mauna Loa (peak), Hi, US 182/U11
Maunath Bhanjan, India 142/D3
Maungdaw, Myan. 141/F3
Mauperthuis, Fr. 88/M5
Maupertus (int'l arpt.), Fr. 100/C2
Maupiti (isl.), FrPol. 175/K6
Maur, Swi. 115/E3
Maurāwān, India 142/C2
Maurecourt, Fr. 88/J5
Maurepas (lake), La, US 195/P16
Maurepas, Fr. 110/A6
Mauriac, Fr. 100/E4
Maurice (lake), Austl. 171/F4
Maurice (riv.), NJ, US 196/C5
Mauricetown, NJ, US 196/C5
Maurienne (valley), Fr. 101/G4
Maurilândia, Braz. 213/B1
Mauritania (ctry.) 154/C4
Mauriti, Braz. 212/C2
Mauritius (ctry.) 165/T15
Mauston, Wi, US 185/L5
Mauthausen, Aus. 113/H6
Mauvoisin, Barrage de (dam), Swi. 114/D6
Mavrommátion, Gre. 105/H3
Mavrovo NP, FYROM 105/G2
Maw Daung (pass), Thai. 136/B4
Mawāna, India 142/A1
Mawlaik, Myan. 141/F3
Mawlamyine (Moulmein), Myan. 136/B2
Mawson, Austl., Ant. 218/E
Maxaranguape, Braz. 212/D2
Maxcanú, Mex. 202/D1
Maxdorf, Ger. 112/B4
Maxéville, Fr. 111/F6
Maxhütte-Haidhof, Ger. 113/F4
May (cape), NJ, US 196/D5
May-en-Multien, Fr. 88/M4
May, Isle of (isl.), Sc, UK 94/D4
May Pen, Jam. 203/G2
Maya (isl.), Indo. 138/C4
Maya (riv.), Rus. 125/N4
Maya (mts.), Guat. 202/D2
Maya-san (peak), Japan 135/H6
Mayaguana (isl.), Bahm. 199/G3
Mayaguana Passage (chan.), Bahm. 203/H1
Mayagüez, PR 199/M8
Mayakovskogo (peak), Taj. 147/K1
Mayang, China 141/J2
Mayarí, Cuba 203/H1
Maybee, Mi, US 193/E8
Maybole, Sc, UK 94/B6
Maydān, Iraq 146/E2
Mayen, Ger. 111/G3
Mayenne, Fr. 100/C2
Mayenne (riv.), Fr. 100/C3
Mayerthorpe, Ab, Can. 184/E2
Mayfield, Ky, US 188/B4
Mayfield, Sc, UK 94/C5
Maykop, Rus. 120/G3
Maymyo, Myan. 141/G3
Maynooth, Ire. 89/Q10
Mayo (riv.), Arg. 215/B6
Mayo, Yk, Can. 192/L3
Mayo, Md, US 196/B6
Mayotte (isl.), May. 165/H6
Mays Landing, NJ, US 196/D5
Maysville, Ky, US 188/D4
Maythalūn, WBnk. 149/G7
Mayville, ND, US 185/J4
Maywood, NJ, US 197/J8
Maywood, Il, US 193/Q16
Maywood, Ca, US 194/F8
Mazabuka, Zam. 163/E4
Mazagão, Braz. 209/H4
Mazamet, Fr. 100/E5
Mazán, Peru 214/C1
Mazār-e Sharīf, Afg. 147/J1
Mazara del Vallo, It. 104/C4
Mazara, Val di (valley), It. 104/C4
Mazarrón, Sp. 102/E4
Mazaruni (riv.), Guy. 208/G2
Mazatán, Mex. 200/C2
Mazatenango, Guat. 202/D3
Mazatlán, Mex. 200/D4
Mažeikiai, Lith. 97/K3
Mazeppa NP, Austl. 172/B3
Mazgirt, Turk. 148/D2
Mazıkıran (pass), Turk. 148/D2
Mazingarbe, Fr. 110/B3
Mazocruz, Peru 214/D5
Mazong (peak), China 128/G3
Mazowieckie (prov.), Pol. 99/L2
Mazury (reg.), Pol. 99/L2
Mazyr, Bela. 120/D1
Mbabala (isl.), Zam. 162/A5
Mbabane (cap.), Swaz. 165/E2
Mbabo (peak), Camr. 154/H6
Mbacké, Sen. 160/B3
Mbaïki, CAfr. 155/J7
Mbakaou, Lac de (lake), Camr. 154/H6
Mbala, Zam. 162/A5
Mbale, Ugan. 162/B2
Mbalmayo, Camr. 154/H7
Mbandaka, D.R. Congo 155/J7
Mbarangandu (riv.), Tanz. 162/C5
Mbarara, Ugan. 162/A3
Mbata, CAfr. 155/J7
Mbeya (peak), Tanz. 162/B5
Mbeya (range), Tanz. 163/F2
Mbeya, Tanz. 162/B5
Mbeya (pol. reg.), Tanz. 162/B5
Mbini, EqG. 154/G7
Mbini (riv.), EqG.,Gabon 154/H7
Mbirizi, Ugan. 162/A3
Mbomou (riv.), CAfr. 155/L6
M'Bour, Sen. 160/A3
Mbuji-Mayi, D.R. Congo 163/D2
Mbwemburu (riv.), Tanz. 162/C5
McAdoo, Pa, US 196/C2
McAfee, NJ, US 196/D1
McAlester, Ok, US 187/J4
McAlisterville, Pa, US 196/A2
McAllen, Tx, US 190/D5
McBride, BC, Can. 184/C2
McCall, Id, US 184/D4
McCarran (int'l arpt.), Nv, US 186/D3
McCarthy, Ak, US 192/K3
McClain (co.), Ok, US 195/M15
McClure, Pa, US 196/A2
McClusky, Il, US 195/G7
McClusky, ND, US 185/H4
McComb, Ms, US 187/K5
McConaughy (lake), Ne, US 185/H5
McCook, Ne, US 187/G2
McCormick, SC, US 191/H3
McCreary, Mb, Can. 185/J3
McCullom Lake, Il, US 193/P15
McDaniel, Md, US 196/B6
McDermitt, Nv, US 184/D5
McDonald (mt.), Ak, US 192/F3
McDonald (isls.), Austl. 81/N8
McDonnell (mt.), Austl. 171/H5
McDougall (pass), NW,Yk, Can. 192/L2
McDowell (mts.), Az, US 195/S18
McElhattan, Pa, US 196/A1
McGhee Tyson (int'l arpt.), Tn, US 191/H3
McGrath, Ak, US 192/G3
McGregor (riv.), BC, Can. 184/C2
McGregor, On, Can. 193/G7
McHenry (co.), Il, US 193/N15
McKean (isl.), Kiri. 175/H5
McKeand (riv.), Nun., Can. 181/K2
McKee City, NJ, US 196/D5
McKeesport, Pa, US 188/E3
McKenzie, Tn, US 188/B4
McKinlay, Austl. 172/A3
McKinley (mt.), Ak, US 192/H3
McKinleyville, Ca, US 184/B5
McLaughlin, SD, US 185/H4
McLean, Va, US 196/A6
McLennan, Ab, Can. 184/D2
McLeod (lake), Austl. 170/B3
McLeod (riv.), BC, Can. 184/D2
McLeod (bay), NW, Can. 180/E2
McLeod Lake, BC, Can. 184/C2
M'Clintock (chan.), Nun., Can. 180/F1
McLoud, Ok, US 195/N15
M'Clure (str.), NW, Can. 181/Q7
McMinnville, Or, US 184/C4
McMinnville, Tn, US 188/C5
McMurdo, US, Ant. 218/M
McNeil (isl.), Wa, US 193/B3
McPherson, Ks, US 187/H3
McQueeney, Tx, US 195/U20
Mdantsane, SAfr. 164/D4
M'diq, Mor. 158/B2
Me-akan-dake (peak), Japan 134/C2
Mead, Co, US 195/C2
Mead (lake), Az,Nv, US 186/D3
Meade (riv.), Ak, US 192/G2
Meadow Lake, Sk, Can. 184/F2
Meadow Valley Wash (riv.), Nv, US 186/D3

Meadowbrook, Il, US 195/G8
Meadowlands Sports Complex, NJ, US 197/J8
Meadows, Md, US 196/B6
Meadville, Ms, US 191/F4
Meadville, Pa, US 188/D3
Mealhada, Port. 102/A2
Meall a' Bhuiridh (peak), Sc, UK 94/B3
Meall Buidhe (peak), Sc, UK 94/B3
Meall Dearg (peak), Sc, UK 94/C3
Meall Dubh (peak), Sc, UK 94/B2
Meall nam Fuaran (peak), Sc, UK 94/C4
Meall Tairneachan (peak), Sc, UK 94/C3
Mearim (riv.), Braz. 209/J5
Meat (mtn.), Ak, US 192/F2
Meath (co.), Ire. 92/B4
Meath Park, Sk, Can. 185/G2
Méaulte, Fr. 110/B4
Meaux, Fr. 88/C5
Mecapalapa, Mex. 201/M6
Mècatina,Rivière du Petit (riv.), Nf,Qu, Can. 181/K3
Mecca, Mo, US 195/D5
Mechanicsburg, Pa, US 196/A4
Mechanicsburg Naval Rsv., Pa, US 196/B3
Mecheria, Alg. 157/F2
Mechi (zone), Nepal 143/F7
Mechra-Bel-Ksiri, Mor. 158/B2
Mecidiye, Turk. 105/K2
Mecitözü, Turk. 148/C1
Meckenbeuren, Ger. 115/F2
Meckenheim, Ger. 111/G2
Mecklenburg-Vorpommern (state), Ger. 96/E5
Mecklenburger (bay), Ger. 98/F1
Mecuia (peak), Moz. 163/G3
Meda, It. 116/C1
Medak, India 140/C4
Medan, Indo. 138/A3
Médanos, Arg. 216/E3
Medanos de Coro, PN, Ven. 210/D2
Medanosa (pt.), Arg. 217/D6
Mede Lomellina, It. 116/B2
Médéa, Alg. 158/G4
Médéa (prov.), Alg. 158/G4
Medebach, Ger. 109/F6
Medeiros Neto, Braz. 212/B5
Medel (peak), Swi. 115/E4
Medemblik, Neth. 108/B3
Meden (riv.), Eng, UK 93/G5
Medenine, Tun. 157/H2
Medenine (gov.), Tun. 157/H2
Medesano, It. 116/D3
Medetsiz (peak), Turk. 148/C2
Medford, Or, US 184/C5
Medford, NY, US 197/E2
Medford Lakes, NJ, US 196/D4
Medgidia, Rom. 107/J3
Media, Pa, US 196/C4
Media Luna, La (isls.), Hon. 203/F3
Medias, Rom. 107/G2
Medical Lake, Wa, US 184/D4
Medicine Bow, Wy, US 185/G5
Medicine Bow (range), Wy, US 186/F2
Medicine Hat, Ab, Can. 184/F3
Medina (riv.), Tx, US 187/H5
Medina, Braz. 212/B5
Medina, Col. 210/C3
Medina, ND, US 185/J4
Medina, Oh, US 188/D3
Medina, Wa, US 193/C2
Medina de Pomar, Sp. 102/D1
Medina de Rioseco, Sp. 102/C2
Medina del Campo, Sp. 102/C2
Medina-Sidonia, Sp. 102/C4
Medinaceli, Sp. 102/D2
Medinipur, India 143/F4
Mediouna, Mor. 156/C2
Mediterranean (sea) 85/E5
Mednogorsk, Rus. 121/L2
Medole, It. 116/D2
Medolla, It. 117/E3
Medugorje, Bosn. 106/C4
Medveditsa (riv.), Rus. 122/E5
Medvezh'i (isls.), Rus. 123/S2
Medvezh'yegorsk, Rus. 118/G3
Medvode, Slov. 101/L3
Medway (co.), Eng, UK 91/G4
Meekatharra, Austl. 170/C4
Meeker, Co, US 186/F2
Meeker Park, Co, US 195/A2
Meerbusch, Ger. 108/D6
Meerhout, Belg. 111/E1
Meersburg, Ger. 115/F2
Meerssen, Neth. 111/E2

Meerut, India 142/A1
Meeteetse, Wy, US 184/F4
Megála Kalívia, Gre. 105/G3
Megáli Panayía, Gre. 105/H2
Megalópolis, Gre. 105/H4
Megantic (peak), Qu, Can. 189/G2
Mégara, Gre. 105/H3
Megève, Fr. 114/C6
Meghālaya (state), India 141/F2
Meghna (riv.), Bang. 143/H4
Megiddo, Isr. 149/G6
Mégiscane (lake), Qu, Can. 188/E1
Mégiscane (riv.), Qu, Can. 188/E1
Megista (isl.), Greece 149/A1
Mehaigne (riv.), Belg. 111/E2
Mehamn, Nor. 95/H1
Meharry (mt.), Austl. 170/C2
Mehdia, Alg. 158/F5
Mehdiya-Plage, Mor. 158/B2
Mehe (riv.), Ger. 109/G1
Mehedinți (prov.), Rom. 106/F3
Mehlingen, Ger. 111/G4
Mehlville, Mo, US 195/G9
Mehrān (riv.), Iran 147/F3
Mehring, Ger. 111/F4
Mehrnbach, Aus. 113/G6
Mehtar Lām, Afg. 144/A2
Mehtar Lām, Afg. 144/A2
Mei (riv.), China 137/C3
Meia Ponte (riv.), Braz. 213/B1
Meiganga, Camr. 154/H6
Meighen (isl.), Nf, Can. 181/R7
Meigu, China 141/H2
Meihekou, China 129/N3
Meikle Bin (peak), Sc, UK 94/B4
Meikle Black Law (hill), Sc, UK 94/D5
Meikle Says Law (peak), Sc, UK 94/D5
Meiktila, Myan. 141/G3
Meilen, Swi. 115/E3
Meine, Ger. 109/H4
Meiners Oaks, Ca, US 194/A2
Meinersen, Ger. 109/H4
Meinerzhagen, Ger. 111/G1
Meiningen, Ger. 112/D1
Meiringen, Swi. 114/E4
Meisenheim, Ger. 111/G4
Meishan (res.), China 130/C5
Meishan, Ger. 99/G3
Meissner (peak), Ger. 109/G6
Meitan, China 137/A2
Meitingen, Ger. 112/D5
Meiwa, Japan 135/L6
Meix-devant-Virton, Belg. 111/E4
Meizhou, China 137/C3
Mejaniga, It. 117/E2
Mejaouda (well), Mrta. 156/D5
Mejorada del Campo, Sp. 103/N9
Mek'elē, Eth. 155/N5
Meknès (prov.), Mor. 158/B3
Meknès, Mor. 158/B3
Mekong (riv.), Asia 128/G5
Mekong, Mouths of the (delta), Viet. 141/J6
Mekongga (peak), Indo. 138/D4
Mekoryuk, Ak, US 192/E3
Melaka, Malay. 138/B3
Melanesia (reg.) 174/E5
Melappālaiyam, India 140/C6
Melawi (riv.), Indo. 138/D4
Melbeck, Ger. 109/H2
Melbourne, Fl, US 191/H4
Melbourne (isl.), Nun., Can. 180/F2
Melbourne, Austl. 173/G5
Melbu, Nor. 95/E1
Melchor (isl.), Chile 216/B5
Melchor Múzquiz, Mex. 190/C3
Melchor Ocampo, Mex. 201/Q9
Meldola, It. 117/F4
Meldorf, Ger. 96/C4
Mele (cape), It. 116/B3
Melenci, Serb. 106/E3
Melenki, Rus. 118/J5
Melesse, Fr. 100/C2
Meleuz, Rus. 121/K1
Melfi, It. 104/D2
Melfort, Sk, Can. 185/H2
Melgar de Fernamental, Sp. 102/C1
Melhus, Nor. 95/D3
Melibocus (peak), Ger. 112/B3
Melida, Swi. 115/E6
Melígalas, Gre. 105/G4
Melíki, Gre. 105/H2
Melilli, (peak), Kenya 162/C3
Melilla, Sp. 158/D2
Melimoyu (peak), Chile 216/B5

Melipilla, Chile 216/N8
Mélisey, Fr. 114/C2
Melissano, It. 105/F3
Melita, Mb, Can. 185/H3
Melito di Porto Salvo, It. 104/D4
Melitopol', Ukr. 120/E3
Melitota, Md, US 196/B5
Melkbosstrand, SAfr. 164/L10
Melksham, Eng, UK 90/D4
Mella (riv.), It. 116/D2
Mellan Fryken (lake), Swe. 96/E2
Melle, Ger. 109/F4
Melle, Belg. 110/C2
Mellea (riv.), It. 116/A3
Mellègue, Oued (riv.), Alg. 158/K7
Mellerud, Swe. 96/E2
Mellieha, Malta 104/L7
Mellingen, Swi. 115/E3
Mellizo Sur (peak), Chile 217/B6
Mellrichstadt, Ger. 112/D2
Mellum (isl.), Ger. 109/F1
Melmoth, SAfr. 165/E3
Melnik, Bul. 105/H2
Mělník, Czh. 113/H2
Melo, Uru. 215/F3
Melocheville, Qu, Can. 189/N7
Melrose, Md, US 196/B4
Melrose, Sc, UK 94/D5
Melrose Abbey, Sc, UK 94/D5
Melrose Park, Il, US 193/Q16
Mels, Swi. 115/F3
Melsungen, Ger. 109/G6
Meltham, Eng, UK 93/G4
Melton, Austl. 173/C3
Melton Mowbray, Eng, UK 91/F1
Melun, Fr. 88/K6
Melville (cape), Phil. 139/E2
Melville, Sk, Can. 185/H3
Melville (isl.), Austl. 167/C2
Melville (bay), Austl. 167/C2
Melville, Il, US 195/G8
Melville (cape), Austl. 172/B1
Melville (lake), Nf, Can. 181/L3
Melville (pen.), Nun., Can. 181/K2
Melville, NY, US 197/M8
Melvindale, Mi, US 193/F7
Mélykút, Hun. 106/D2
Melzo, It. 116/C2
Memāri, India 143/G4
Memmert (isl.), Ger. 108/D1
Memmingen, Ger. 115/G2
Memphis, Mo, US 185/K5
Memphis, China 137/A2
Memphis (int'l arpt.), Tn, US 187/K4
Memphis, Tx, US 187/G4
Memphis, Tn, US 187/K4
Memphis (ruin), Egypt 149/B5
Memphis, Mi, US 193/G6
Mena, Ar, US 187/J4
Menaggio, It. 115/F5
Menai (str.), Wal, UK 92/D5
Menai Bridge, Wal, UK 92/D5
Ménaka, Mali 161/F3
Menaldum, Neth. 108/C2
Menarandra (riv.), Madg. 165/H9
Menard, Tx, US 187/H5
Menasalbas, Sp. 102/C3
Menavava (riv.), Madg. 165/H7
Mendawai (riv.), Indo. 138/D4
Mende, Fr. 100/C4
Menden, Ger. 109/E6
Mendenhall (cape), Ak, US 192/E4
Mendes, Braz. 213/K7
Mendez, Mex. 201/F3
Mendham, NJ, US 196/D2
Mendig, Ger. 111/G3
Mendocino, Ca, US 186/B3
Mendocino (cape), Ca, US 140/A3
Mendooran, Austl. 173/D1
Mendota (lake), Wi, US 193/C2
Mendoza, Arg. 216/C2
Mendoza (prov.), Arg. 216/C2
Mendoza, Cuba 203/E1
Mendoza, Peru 214/B2
Mendoza (El Plumerillo) (int'l arpt.), Arg. 216/C2
Mene Grande, Ven. 210/D2
Menemen, Turk. 120/C5
Menen, Belg. 110/C2
Menengai Crater, Kenya 162/C3
Menengiyn (plain), Mong. 129/L2
Menfi, It. 104/C4
Meng Xian, China 130/C4
Mengcheng, China 130/D4
Mengen, Ger. 115/F2
Mengen, Turk. 148/B1
Mengersgereuth-Hämmern, Ger. 112/D2
Mengerskirchen, Ger. 112/B1
Menges, Slov. 101/L3
Menggala, Indo. 138/C4

Menghai, China 136/C1
Mengibar, Sp. 102/D4
Mengkofen, Ger. 113/F5
Mengla, China 136/C1
Menglian Daizu Lahuzu Vazu Zizhixian, China 141/G3
Mengyin, China 130/D4
Mengzi, China 141/H3
Menindee, Austl. 173/B2
Menindee (dam), Austl. 173/B2
Menindee (lake), Austl. 171/J5
Meningie, Austl. 173/A2
Menlo Park, Ca, US 193/K12
Menlo Park, NJ, US 197/H9
Menlolat (peak), Chile 216/B5
Mennecy, Fr. 88/K6
Menominee Falls, Wi, US 188/B3
Menomonie, Wi, US 185/L4
Menongue, Ang. 163/C4
Menorca (int'l arpt.), Sp. 103/H3
Menorca (Minorca) (isl.), Sp. 103/H2
Mentasta Lake, Ak, US 192/K3
Mentawai (isls.), Indo. 138/A4
Mentawai (str.), Indo. 138/A4
Menteroda, Ger. 109/H6
Menthon-Saint-Bernard, Fr. 114/C6
Mentone, Tx, US 187/G5
Mentone, Ca, US 194/C2
Mentone, Oh, US 188/D3
Mentue (riv.), Swi. 114/C4
Menucourt, Fr. 88/H4
Menuma, Japan 135/C1
Menyapa (peak), Indo. 139/E3
Menzel Bou Zelafa, Tun. 158/M6
Menzel Bourguiba, Tun. 158/L6
Menzel Temime, Tun. 158/M6
Menzie (mt.), Yk, Can. 192/M3
Menzies, Austl. 170/C4
Menzingen, Swi. 115/E3
Menznau, Swi. 114/D4
Meolo, It. 117/F1
Meon (riv.), Eng, UK 91/E5
Meoquí, Mex. 200/D2
Mepistskaro (peak), Geo. 121/G4
Meppel, Neth. 108/D3
Meppen, Ger. 109/E4
Meppen, Il, US 195/F8
Mequinenzo, Embalse de (res.), Sp. 103/E2
Mer, It. 100/D3
Mera (riv.), It. 115/F5
Meramec (riv.), Mo, US 187/K3
Merano, It. 115/H4
Merate, It. 116/C1
Meratus (mts.), Indo. 138/D4
Meraux, La, US 195/O17
Merbein, Austl. 173/B2
Mercaderes, Col. 210/B4
Mercantour, PN du, Fr. 101/G4
Mercatello sul Metauro, It. 117/F5
Mercato Saraceno, It. 117/F5
Merced (riv.), Ca, US 186/B3
Merced, Ca, US 186/B3
Mercedario (peak), Arg. 215/B3
Mercedes, Arg. 215/E2
Mercedes, Arg. 216/D2
Mercedes, Arg. 217/J11
Mercedes, Uru. 217/J10
Mercer (co.), NJ, US 196/D3
Mercer (isl.), Wa, US 193/C2
Mercer Island, Wa, US 193/C2
Mercerville-Hamilton Square, NJ, US 196/D3
Merchtem, Belg. 111/D2
Mercier, Qu, Can. 189/N7
Mercoal, Ab, Can. 184/D2
Mercy (cape), Nun., Can. 181/K2
Mercy-le-Bas, Fr. 111/E5
Merdith (cape), UK 217/E7
Merefa, Ukr. 120/F2
Merelbeke, Belg. 110/C2
Merenberg, Ger. 112/B1
Mergozzo, It. 115/E6
Mergui (arch.), Myan. 141/G5
Mergui (Myeik), Myan. 136/B3
Meriç, Turk. 107/H5
Méricourt, Fr. 88/C4
Méricourt, Fr. 110/B3
Mérida, Ven. 210/D2
Mérida (state), Ven. 210/D2
Mérida, Mex. 202/D1
Mérida, Cordillera de (mts.), Ven. 208/D2
Metán, Arg. 215/D2

Merimbula, Austl. 173/D3
Merinda, Austl. 172/C3
Mering, Ger. 112/D6
Merinos, Uru. 217/K10
Merja Zerga (lake), Mor. 158/A2
Mérk, Hun. 106/F2
Merkendorf, Ger. 112/D4
Merksem, Belg. 108/B6
Merksplas, Belg. 108/B6
Merlimont, Fr. 110/A3
Merlo, Arg. 217/J11
Meroe (ruin), Sudan 146/B5
Merone, It. 116/C1
Merredin, Austl. 170/C4
Merriam, Ks, US 195/D5
Merrick, NY, US 197/L9
Merrick (peak), Sc, UK 92/D1
Merrill, Wi, US 185/L4
Merrill Creek (res.), NJ, US 196/C2
Merrimack, NH, US 189/G3
Merritt, BC, Can. 184/C3
Merritt Island, Fl, US 191/H4
Merriwa, Austl. 173/D2
Mers-les-Bains, Fr. 110/A3
Mersch, Lux. 111/F4
Merse (riv.), Sc, UK 94/D5
Mersey (riv.), Eng, UK 93/F5
Merseyside (co.), Eng, UK 93/F5
Mersing, Malay. 138/B3
Mertert, Lux. 111/F4
Mertesdorf, Ger. 111/F4
Merthyr Tydfil, Wal, UK 90/C3
Merthyr Tydfil (co.), Wal, UK 90/C3
Mértola, Port. 102/B4
Merton (bor.), Eng, UK 88/C2
Mertzon, Tx, US 187/G5
Mertzwiller, Fr. 111/G6
Meru (mt.), Tanz. 162/C3
Meru, Kenya 162/C2
Méru, Fr. 110/B5
Meru NP, Kenya 162/C2
Merville, Fr. 110/B2
Merwedekanaal (riv.), Neth. 108/C5
Méry-sur-Oise, Fr. 88/J4
Merzen, Ger. 109/F4
Merzenich, Ger. 111/F2
Merzifon, Turk. 148/C1
Merzig, Ger. 111/F5
Mesa (mtn.), Ak, US 192/G3
Mesa, Az, US 195/S19
Mesa (peak), Arg. 217/C6
Mesa Verde NP, Co, US 186/E3
Mesabi (range), Mn, US 185/K4
Mesach Mellet (hills), Libya 157/H4
Mesagne, It. 105/E2
Mesarás (gulf), Gre. 105/J5
Mescalero (ridge), NM, US 190/C3
Meschede, Ger. 109/F6
Mesco, Punta di (pt.), It. 116/C4
Mescolino (peak), It. 117/F5
Meseta de Montemayor (plat.), Arg. 216/D5
Mesgouez (lake), Qu, Can. 188/F1
Mesola, It. 117/F3
Mesolóngion, Gre. 105/G3
Mesomeloka, Madg. 165/J8
Mesopotamia (reg.), Arg. 215/E3
Mesoraca, It. 104/E3
Mespelbrunn, Ger. 112/C3
Mesquite, Tx, US 187/H4
Mesrouh (peak), Mor. 156/C2
Messaad, Alg. 154/F1
Messancy, Belg. 111/E4
Messel, Ger. 112/B3
Messina, SAfr. 163/F5
Messina (str.), It. 104/D3
Messina, It. 104/D3
Messini (gulf), Gre. 105/H4
Messini, Gre. 105/H4
Messkirch, Ger. 115/E2
Messstetten, Ger. 115/E1
Messy, Fr. 88/L5
Mesta (riv.), Bul. 105/H2
Mestre, It. 117/F2
Mestrino, It. 117/E2
Mesudiye, Turk. 120/F4
Mesumba (peak), Tanz. 162/C4
Mesurado (cape), Libr. 160/C5
Meta (dept.), Col. 210/C4
Meta (riv.), Col.,Ven. 210/D3
Meta Incognita (pen.), Nun., Can. 181/K2
Metabetchouan, Qu, Can. 189/G1
Métabetchouane (riv.), Qu, Can. 189/G1
Metairie, La, US 195/P17
Metaline, Colline (mts.), It. 117/D6
Metamora, Mi, US 193/F6
Metán, Arg. 215/D2
Metapontum (ruin), It. 104/E2
Metauro (riv.), It. 117/F5
Metelen, Ger. 109/E4
Metéora, Gre. 105/G3
Metepec, Mex. 201/Q10

Methven, Sc, UK 94/C4
Metica (riv.), Col. 210/C4
Metković, Cro. 105/E1
Metlakatla, Ak, US 192/M4
Metlatonoc, Mex. 202/B2
Metlili Chaamba, Alg. 157/F2
Metnitz, Aus. 101/L3
Metro Toronto Zoo, On, Can. 189/R8
Metropolis, Il, US 188/B4
Metropolitan Oakland (int'l arpt.), Ca, US 186/B3
Metropolitana de Santiago (pol. reg.), Chile 216/N8
Métsovon, Gre. 105/G3
Mettawa, Il, US 193/Q15
Mettenheim, Ger. 113/F6
Mettet, Belg. 111/D3
Mettingen, Ger. 109/E4
Mettlach, Ger. 111/F4
Mettmach, Aus. 113/G6
Mettmann, Ger. 108/D6
Metu, Eth. 155/N6
Metuchen, NJ, US 197/H9
Metula, Isr. 149/D3
Metz, Fr. 111/F5
Metz-Nancy-Lorraine (int'l arpt.), Fr. 111/F6
Meudon, Fr. 88/J5
Meudt, Ger. 111/G3
Meulan, Fr. 88/H4
Meulebeke, Belg. 110/C2
Meung, Fr. 100/D3
Meurthe-et-Moselle (dept.), Fr. 111/E6
Meuse (dept.), Fr. 111/E6
Meuse (riv.), Fr. 98/C4
Meuzin (riv.), Fr. 114/A3
Mévasseret Ziyyon, Isr. 149/G8
Mexborough, Eng, UK 93/G5
Mexia, Tx, US 187/H5
Mexiana, Ilha (isl.), Braz. 209/J3
Mexicalcingo, Mex. 201/Q10
Mexicali, Mex. 200/B1
Mexico (ctry.) 200/D4
Mexico (cap.), Mex. 201/Q10
México (state), Mex. 198/A5
Mexico (gulf), NAm. 198/C2
Mexico, Mo, US 187/K3
Meximieux, Fr. 114/B6
Meybod, Iran 146/F2
Meyers Chuck, Ak, US 192/M4
Meyerton, SAfr. 164/Q13
Meymaneh, Afg. 147/H1
Meyrin, Swi. 114/C6
Meythet, Fr. 114/C6
Meyzieu, Fr. 114/A6
Mezdra, Bul. 105/H1
Mèze, Fr. 100/E5
Mezen' (riv.), Rus. 122/E3
Mezen' (bay), Rus. 119/J2
Mezha (riv.), Bela. 97/P4
Mezhdurechensk, Rus. 122/J4
Mezhdusharskiy (isl.), Rus. 122/F2
Midi (canal), Fr. 100/D5
Mézières-sur-Seine, Fr. 88/H5
Mezoberény, Hun. 106/E2
Mezőkovácsháza, Hun. 106/E2
Mezőkövesd, Hun. 99/L5
Mezőtúr, Hun. 106/E2
Mezquital (riv.), Mex. 200/D4
Mezzana (peak), It. 115/G5
Mezzocorona, It. 115/H5
Mezzogoro, It. 117/F3
Mezzolombardo, It. 115/H5
Mfangano (isl.), Kenya 162/B3
Mga (riv.), Rus. 119/U7
M'goun (peak), Mor. 156/D3
Mhamdia Fouchana, Tun. 158/M6
Mhòr (lake), Sc, UK 94/B3
Mhow, India 147/L4
Mi (riv.), China 137/B2
Mi-shima (isl.), Japan 132/B3
Mianchi, China 130/C4
Miandrivazo, Madg. 165/H7
Mīāneh, Iran 146/E1
Miāni, India 147/H5
Mianning, China 141/H2
Mianyang, China 128/H5
Miao'er (peak), China 137/B2
Miarinarivo, Madg. 165/H7
Miary, Madg. 165/G8
Miass, Rus. 119/P5
Migori (riv.), Kenya 162/B3

Miass (riv.), Rus. 119/P5
Miastko, Pol. 96/G4
Mica Creek, BC, Can. 184/D2
Michalovce, Slvk. 99/L4
Michelfeld, Ger. 113/E3
Michelson (mt.), Ak, US 192/K2
Michelstadt, Ger. 112/C3
Michendorf, Ger. 98/Q7
Michigan (state), US 188/C2
Michigan (lake), US 188/C2
Michigan City, In, US 188/C3
Michipicoten (isl.), On, Can. 188/C2
Michoacán de Ocampo (state), Mex. 198/A4
Michurin, Bul. 107/H4
Michurinsk, Rus. 121/G1
Mico (riv.), Nic. 198/E5
Micoud, StL. 199/N9
Micronesia (reg.) 174/E3
Micronesia, Federated States of (ctry.) 174/D4
Mid Yell, Sc, UK 89/W13
Midal (well), Niger 161/G2
Midal (riv.), Sp. 103/E2
Middelburg, SAfr. 164/D3
Middelburg, SAfr. 165/E2
Middelburg, Neth. 108/A5
Middelharnis, Neth. 108/B5
Middelkerke, Belg. 110/B1
Middle (bay), Japan 135/M6
Middle Alkali (lake), Ca, US 186/C2
Middle Andaman (isl.), India 141/F5
Middle Caicos (prov.), Fin. 95/H3
Middle Concho (riv.), Tx, US 190/C4
Middle Raccoon (riv.), Ia, US 187/J2
Middle River, Md, US 196/B5
Middle Sister (peak), Or, US 184/C4
Middleberg, Md, US 196/A4
Middleberg, Ok, US 195/M15
Middleburg, Pa, US 196/A2
Middlebury, Vt, US 188/F2
Middlemount, Austl. 172/C3
Middleport, Pa, US 196/B2
Middlesboro, Ky, US 188/D4
Middlesbrough, Eng, UK 93/G2
Middlesbrough (co.), Eng, UK 93/G2
Middlesex (co.), Eng, UK 88/B2
Middlesex, NJ, US 196/D2
Middleton, Eng, UK 93/F4
Middleton (bay), Austl. 172/B1
Middletown, De, US 196/C5
Middletown, NJ, US 197/J10
Middletown, Pa, US 196/B3
Midelt, Mor. 156/D2
Midi (canal), Fr. 100/D5
Midi-Pyrénées (pol. reg.), Fr. 100/D4
Midland, On, Can. 188/E2
Midland, Mi, US 188/C3
Midland, Tx, US 187/G5
Midland, Wa, US 193/C3
Midland Park, NJ, US 197/K8
Midleton, Ire. 89/P11
Midlothian, Il, US 193/Q16
Midlothian (pol. reg.), Sc, UK 94/C5
Midlum, Ger. 109/F1
Midongy Atsimo, Madg. 165/H8
Midu, China 141/H2
Midvale, Ut, US 195/K12
Midway (isls.), Pac., US 174/J3
Midway, De, US 196/C6
Midway, Il, US 195/H8
Midway, Ut, US 195/N15
Midyan (reg.), SAr. 146/C3
Midyat, Turk. 120/F4
Mie, Japan 132/B4
Mie (pref.), Japan 132/B4
Miechów, Pol. 120/B2
Miechucino, Pol. 99/K1
Międzychód, Pol. 99/H2
Mięndzyrzecz, Pol. 99/M3
Międzyzdroje, Pol. 96/F5
Miehlen, Ger. 111/G3
Mielec, Pol. 99/M3
Miena, Austl. 173/C4
Miercurea Cluc, Rom. 107/G2
Mieres, Sp. 102/C1
Miesbach, Ger. 101/A3
Miesville, Mn, US 185/K5
Miesso, Eth. 155/N6
Mifflin, Pa, US 196/A2
Mifflinburg, Pa, US 196/A2
Migdal Ha'emeq, Isr. 149/G6
Migennes, Fr. 100/E3
Migmanong, It. 116/B3
Mignovillard, Fr. 114/C4
Migori (riv.), Kenya 162/B3

Migori, Kenya 162/B3
Miguel Alemán, Mex. 200/C2
Miguel Aleman, Presa (dam), Mex. 201/M8
Miguel Alves, Braz. 212/B2
Miguel Auza, Mex. 200/E3
Miguel Calmon, Braz. 212/B3
Miguel Hidalgo (int'l arpt.), Mex. 200/E4
Miguel Hidalgo (res.), Mex. 200/C3
Miguel Pereira, Braz. 213/K7
Miguel Riglos, Arg. 216/E3
Miguelete, Uru. 217/K11
Miguelópolis, Braz. 213/B2
Miguelturra, Sp. 102/D3
Migūm, SKor. 131/G6
Mihama, Japan 132/D3
Mihama, Japan 135/L6
Mihara, Japan 132/C3
Mihara, Japan 135/J4
Miharu, Japan 133/G2
Mihla, Ger. 109/H6
Miho, Japan 135/E2
Mihrābpur, Pak. 147/J3
Mijares (riv.), Sp. 103/E2
Mijas, Sp. 102/C4
Mijdrecht, Neth. 108/B4
Mikasa, Japan 134/B2
Mikata, Japan 135/J4
Mikata (lake), Japan 135/J4
Mikawa (bay), Japan 135/M6
Mikhaylovka, Rus. 121/G2
Mikhmoret, Isr. 149/F7
Miki, Japan 135/G6
Mikinai, Gre. 105/H4
Mikínai (Mycenae) (ruin), Gre. 105/H4
Mikkeli (prov.), Fin. 95/H3
Mikonos, Gre. 105/J4
Mikonos (isl.), Gre. 105/J4
Mikri Prespa (lake), Alb.,Gre. 105/G2
Mikri Prespa NP, Gre. 105/G2
Mikuma, Japan 135/L6
Mikumi NP, Tanz. 163/G2
Mikuni, Japan 132/E2
Mikuni-tōge (pass), Japan 133/G2
Mikura (riv.), Japan 133/F4
Mila (prov.), Alg. 158/M4
Milagro, Ecu. 210/B5
Milak, India 142/B1
Milan (Milano), It. 101/H4
Milano, Austl. 173/A2
Milano (prov.), It. 116/C2
Milano (Milan), It. 101/H4
Milas, Turk. 148/A2
Milazzo, It. 104/D3
Milbank, SD, US 185/J4
Mildura, Austl. 173/B2
Miles, Tx, US 190/C4
Miles, Austl. 172/C4
Miles City, Mt, US 185/G4
Milešovka (peak), Czh. 113/G1
Milestone, Sk, Can. 185/G3
Miletto (peak), It. 104/D2
Milevsko, Czh. 113/H4
Milford, Ct, US 197/E1
Milford, De, US 196/C6
Milford (lake), Ks, US 190/D2
Milford, Mi, US 193/E6
Milford, NJ, US 196/C2
Milford, Ut, US 186/D3
Milford Haven, Wal, UK 90/A3
Milford Haven (inlet), Wal, UK 90/A3
Milgis (riv.), Kenya 162/C2
Mili (isl.), Mrsh. 174/G4
Miliana, Alg. 158/G4
Milicz, Pol. 99/J3
Milidong Town, Hi, US 182/V13
Milk (hill), Eng, UK 91/E4
Milk (riv.), Can.,US 180/F4
Milk River, Ab, Can. 184/E3
Mill (isl.), Nun., Can. 181/J2
Mill (riv.), Ct, US 197/E1
Mill Neck, NY, US 197/L8
Millaa Millaa, Austl. 172/B2
Millau, Fr. 100/E4
Millbrae, Ca, US 193/K11
Millbrook (res.), Austl. 171/M8
Millburn, NJ, US 197/K9
Millcreek, Ut, US 195/K12
Mille Iles, Fr.
Mille Lacs (lake), Mn, US 185/K4
Milledgeville, Ga, US 191/H3
Miller, SD, US 185/J4
Millerovo, Rus. 121/G2
Millers Ferry (dam), Al, US 191/G3
Millersburg, Pa, US 196/B2
Millerstown, Pa, US 196/A2
Millersville, Pa, US 196/B3
Millesimo, It. 116/B4
Millicent, Austl. 173/B3
Milliken, Co, US 195/C2
Millingen aan de Rijn, Neth. 108/D5

Millington, Md, US 196/C5
Millinocket, Me, US 189/G2
Millisle, NI, UK 92/C2
Millmerran, Austl. 172/C4
Millmont, Pa, US 196/A2
Millport, Sc, UK 94/B5
Mills Junction, Ut, US 195/J12
Millstadt, Il, US 195/G9
Millstone (riv.), NJ, US 196/D3
Millstream-Chichester NP, Austl. 170/C2
Millthorpe, Austl. 173/D2
Milltown, NJ, US 197/H10
Milltown Malbay, Ire. 89/P10
Millville, Pa, US 196/B1
Millville, NJ, US 196/C5
Millwood (lake), Ar, US 190/E3
Milmay, NJ, US 196/D5
Milnathort, Wal, UK 93/E5
Milne (bay), PNG 174/E5
Milngavie, Sc, UK 94/B5
Milnrow, Eng, UK 93/F4
Milo, Me, US 189/G2
Milo (riv.), Gui. 160/C4
Milolii, Hi, US 182/U11
Milos (isl.), Gre. 105/J4
Milos, Gre. 105/J4
Milseburg (peak), Ger. 112/C1
Miltenberg, Ger. 112/C3
Milton, Austl. 173/D2
Milton, On, Can. 189/Q8
Milton, NZ 175/R12
Milton (res.), Co, US 195/C2
Milton, Fl, US 191/G4
Milton, NH, US 189/G3
Milton, Pa, US 196/B1
Milton, Ut, US 195/K11
Milton, Wa, US 193/C3
Milton-Freewater, Or, US 184/D4
Milton Keynes, Eng, UK 91/F2
Milton Keynes (co.), Eng, UK 91/F2
Milton Ness (pt.), Sc, UK 94/D3
Milton of Campsie, Sc, UK 94/B5
Milwaukee, Wi, US 185/M5
Milwaukee (co.), Wi, US 193/P14
Milz (riv.), Ger. 112/D2
Mimi (riv.), Japan 132/B4
Mimizan, Fr. 100/C4
Mimmaya, Japan 134/B3
Min (riv.), China 128/H5
Min Xian, China 128/H5
Mina (riv.), Alg. 158/F5
Mīnāb, Iran 147/G3
Minahasa (pen), Indo. 139/F3
Minakuchi, Japan 135/K6
Minamata, Japan 132/B4
Minami Alps NP, Japan 133/F3
Minami-tori-shima (isl.), Japan 174/E2
Minamiaiki, Japan 135/B1
Minamiashigara, Japan 135/C3
Minamichita, Japan 135/L6
Minamidaitō (isl.), Japan 133/L8
Minamiiō (isl.), Japan 174/D2
Minamikawara, Japan 135/C1
Minamimaki, Japan 135/A2
Minamiyamashiro, Japan 135/J6
Minano, Japan 135/C1
Minas, Cuba 203/G1
Minas (peak), Ecu. 210/B5
Minas, Uru. 217/G2
Minas de Matahambre, Cuba 203/F1
Minas de Ríotinto, Sp. 102/B4
Minas Gerais (state), Braz. 212/A5
Minas Novas, Braz. 212/B5
Minatitlán, Mex. 202/C2
Minbu, Myan. 141/F3
Minbya, Myan. 141/F3
Minch, The (North Minch) (str.), UK 89/Q8
Minchinābād, Pak. 144/B3
Minchinmávida (vol.), Chile 216/B4
Mincio (riv.), It. 117/D2
Mindanao (isl.), Phil. 139/F2
Mindanao (sea), Phil. 139/F2
Mindel (riv.), Ger. 98/F4
Mindelheim, Ger. 115/G1
Mindelo, CpV. 151/J10
Minden, Ger. 109/F4
Minden, La, US 187/J4
Minden, Ne, US 187/H4
Mindoro (isl.), Phil. 137/D5
Mindoro (str.), Phil. 137/C5
Mine (pt.), Ire. 89/Q10
Mineiros, Braz. 209/H7
Mineola, Tx, US 187/J4
Mineola, NY, US 197/L8
Mineral del Monte, Mex. 201/L6
Mineral Wells, Tx, US 187/H4
Mineral'nye Vody (int'l arpt.), Rus. 121/G3

Mineral'nye Vody, Rus. 121/G3
Minerbe, It. 117/E2
Minerbio, It. 117/E3
Minerbio (pt.), Fr. 101/H5
Minersville, Pa, US 196/B2
Minfeld, Ger. 112/B4
Minfeng, China 128/D4
Ming (riv.), China 141/J3
Mingãçevir, Azer. 121/H4
Mingãçevir Su Anbari (res.), Azer. 121/H4
Mingan (riv.), Qu, Can. 189/J1
Mingãora, Pak. 144/B2
Mingenew, Austl. 170/B4
Minglanilla, Sp. 102/E3
Mingshui, China 129/N2
Mingxi, China 137/C2
Minhe, China 128/H4
Minhla, Myan. 141/G4
Minho (riv.), Sp. 102/A1
Minidoka Internment Nat'l Mon., Id, US 184/E6
Minigwal (lake), Austl. 170/D4
Minitonas, Mb, Can. 185/H2
Minlaton, Austl. 171/H5
Minle, China 128/H4
Minna, Nga. 161/G4
Minneapolis, Mn, US 185/K4
Minneapolis-St. Paul (Wold-Chamberlain) (int'l arpt.), Mn, US 185/K4
Minnedosa, Mb, Can. 185/J3
Minnesota (state), US 185/K4
Minnesota (riv.), Mn, US 185/K4
Minnigaff, Sc, UK 92/D2
Minnis (lake), On, Can. 188/B1
Minnitaki (lake), On, Can. 185/K3
Miño (riv.), Port.,Sp. 102/A1
Mino, Japan 135/L4
Minobu, Japan 133/F3
Minokamo, Japan 135/M5
Mino'o, Japan 135/H6
Mino'o (riv.), Japan 135/H6
Minori, Japan 135/E1
Minot, ND, US 185/H3
Minqin, China 128/H4
Minqing, China 137/C2
Minquan, China 130/C4
Minsener Oog (isl.), Ger. 109/F1
Minsk (cap.), Bela. 97/M5
Minsk (int'l arpt.), Bela. 97/M5
Mińsk Mazowiecki, Pol. 99/L2
Minskaya Voblasts Bela. 120/C1
Mintaka (pass), China 147/K1
Mintaka (pass), Pak. 145/F5
Mintlaw, Sc, UK 94/E1
Minto, Ak, US 192/J2
Minto, NB, Can. 189/H2
Minto (inlet), NW, Can. 180/E1
Minūf, Egypt 149/B4
Minusinsk, Rus. 122/K4
Minusio, Swi. 115/E5
Minya al Qamh, Egypt 149/B4
Minyip, Austl. 173/B3
Miquan, China 128/E3
Mira, Port. 102/A2
Mira (riv.), Col. 210/B4
Mira Loma, Ca, US 194/C2
Mira Monte, Ca, US 194/A2
Mira Taglio, It. 117/F2
Mirabel (int'l arpt.), Qu, Can. 189/M6
Mirabel, Qu, Can. 189/M6
Mirabela, Braz. 212/A5
Mirabello, It. 117/E3
Miracema, Braz. 213/D2
Miracema do Norte, Braz. 209/J5
Miradolo Terme, It. 116/C2
Mirador, Braz. 212/A2
Mirador (pass), Chile 216/C4
Miraflores, Col. 210/C4
Miraflores, Col. 210/C3
Miraflores, Mex. 200/D4
Miraflores, Peru 214/B3
Miragoâne, Haiti 203/H2
Miraj, India 147/K5
Miramar, Arg. 216/F3
Miramar Naval Air Station, Ca, US 194/C4
Mirambéllou (gulf), Gre. 105/J5
Miramichi, NB, Can. 189/H2
Miramont-de-Guyenne, Fr. 100/D4
Miranda (vol.), Peru 214/D5
Miranda, Braz. 209/G8
Miranda de Ebro, Sp. 102/D1
Miranda do Corvo, Port. 102/A2
Miranda do Douro, Port. 102/B2
Mirandela, Port. 102/B2
Mirandola, It. 101/J4
Mirandópolis, Braz. 213/B2
Mirano, It. 117/F2
Mīrānpur, India 142/A1

Mirante do Paranapanema, Braz. 213/B2
Mirassol, Braz. 213/B2
Miravalles (peak), Sp. 102/B1
Miravalles (vol.), CR 203/E4
Mirebalais, Haiti 203/H2
Mirebeau, Fr. 114/B3
Mirecourt, Fr. 114/C1
Mirfield, Eng, UK 93/G4
Miri, Malay. 138/D3
Miriam Vale, Austl. 172/C4
Mirim (lake), Braz. 215/F3
Mirimire, Ven. 210/D2
Mirina, Gre. 105/J3
Miritiparaná (riv.), Col. 210/D5
Mirna (riv.), Cro. 117/G2
Mirnyy, Rus. 123/M3
Mirnyy, Rus., Ant. 218/G
Mirond (lake), Sk, Can. 185/H2
Mirow, Ger. 98/G2
Mirror (lake), Wi, US 196/D4
Mirtóōn (sea), Gre. 105/H4
Miryang, SKor. 131/E5
Mirzāpur, India 142/D3
Misa (riv.), It. 117/G5
Misāha (well), Egypt 159/A4
Misaka, Japan 135/B2
Misaki, Japan 132/D3
Misaki, Japan 135/E3
Misano Adriatico, It. 117/F5
Misantla, Mex. 201/N1
Misato, Japan 135/C1
Misato, Japan 135/D2
Misato, Japan 135/K6
Misawa, Japan 134/B3
Mishan, China 129/P2
Mishawaka, In, US 188/C3
Misheguk (mtn.), Ak, US 192/F2
Mishima, Japan 133/F3
Misilmeri, It. 104/C3
Misiones, Sierra de (mts.), Arg. 215/E2
Miskolc, Hun. 99/L4
Misono, Japan 135/L6
Misool (isl.), Indo. 139/H4
Misquah (hills), Mn, US 185/L4
Mission, Tx, US 190/D5
Mission (bay), Ca, US 194/C5
Mission, Ks, US 195/D5
Mission Beach, Austl. 172/B2
Mission Hills, Ks, US 195/D5
Mission Ind. Res., Ca, US 194/C4
Mission San Buenaventura Ca, US 194/A2
Mission San Jose, Ca, US 193/L12
Mission San Juan Capistrano, Ca, US 194/C3
Mission Viejo, Ca, US 194/C3
Missisa (lake), On, Can. 185/M2
Missiscabi (riv.), Qu, Can. 188/E1
Mississauga, On, Can. 189/Q8
Mississippi (pt.), Austl. 170/D5
Mississippi (state), US 191/F4
Mississippi (delta), La, US 191/F4
Mississippi River Gulf Outlet (canal), La, US 195/O17
Missoula, Mt, US 184/D4
Missouri (riv.), US 183/G3
Missouri (state), US 187/J3
Missouri City, Mo, US 195/E5
Missouri City, Tx, US 187/J5
Mistaken (pt.), Nf, Can. 189/L2
Mistassibi (riv.), Qu, Can. 189/F1
Mistassibi Nord-Est (riv.), Qu, Can. 189/F1
Mistassini, Qu, Can. 189/F1
Mistassini (riv.), Qu, Can. 189/F1
Mistassini (lake), Qu, Can. 181/J3
Mistelbach an der Zaya, Aus. 101/M2
Misti (vol.), Peru 214/D5
Mistissini, Qu, Can. 189/F1
Mistrás (ruin), Gre. 105/H4
Mistretta, It. 104/D4
Misty Fjords Nat'l Mon., Ak, US 192/M4
Misugi, Japan 135/K6
Mita, Punta de (pt.), Mex. 200/D4
Mitaka, Japan 135/D2
Mitake, Japan 135/M5
Mitama, Japan 135/B2
Mitare, Ven. 210/D2
Mitchell, Austl. 172/B4

Mitchell (riv.), Austl. 172/A1
Mitchell, Il, US 195/G8
Mitchell (mt.), NC, US 191/H3
Mitchell, SD, US 185/J5
Mitchell River NP, Austl. 173/C3
Mitha Tiwāna, Pak. 144/B3
Mithankot, Pak. 144/A5
Mithi, Pak. 147/J4
Mithimna, Gre. 105/K3
Mitiaro (isl.), Cookls. 175/K6
Mitilíni, Gre. 105/K3
Mitla (pass), Egypt 149/C4
Mitla (ruin), Mex. 202/B2
Mito, Japan 133/G2
Mito, Japan 135/M6
Mitomi, Japan 135/B2
Mitra (peak), EqG. 154/G7
Mitre (pen.), Arg. 215/C7
Mitry-Mory, Fr. 88/K5
Mitsamiouli, Com. 165/G6
Mitsinjo, Madg. 165/H7
Mitsio, Nosy (isl.), Madg. 165/J6
Mits'iwa, Erit. 155/N4
Mitsue, Japan 135/K7
Mitsukaidō, Japan 135/D1
Mitsuke, Japan 133/F2
Mittagong, Austl. 173/D2
Mittagspitze (peak), Aus. 115/F3
Mittainville, Fr. 88/G5
Mittelberg, Aus. 115/G3
Mittelland (canal), Ger. 109/F4
Mittelradde (riv.), Ger. 109/E3
Mittenwald, Ger. 115/H3
Mittersill, Aus. 101/K3
Mitterteich, Ger. 113/F4
Mittlere-Isar (canal), Ger. 113/E6
Mittweida, Ger. 98/G3
Mitú, Col. 210/D4
Mitumba, Monts (mts.), D.R. Congo 163/E1
Mitwitz, Ger. 112/E2
Miura (pen.), Japan 135/D3
Miura, Japan 135/D3
Miwa, Japan 135/H5
Miwa, Japan 135/L5
Mixco Viejo (ruin), Guat. 202/D3
Mixquiahuala, Mex. 201/K6
Mixteco (riv.), Mex. 202/B2
Miya (riv.), Japan 135/K7
Miyagawa, Japan 135/K7
Miyagi (pref.), Japan 134/B4
Miyake (isl.), Japan 133/F3
Miyako, Japan 134/B4
Miyako (isls.), Japan 133/H8
Miyakonojō, Japan 132/B5
Miyama, Japan 135/J5
Miyama, Japan 135/L4
Miyanojō, Japan 132/B5
Miyashiro, Japan 135/D2
Miyazaki (pref.), Japan 132/K12
Miyazaki, Japan 132/B5
Miyazu (lake), Japan 135/H4
Miyazu (bay), Japan 135/H4
Miyi, China 141/H2
Miyoshi, Japan 132/C3
Miyoshi, Japan 135/D2
Miyoshi, Japan 135/M5
Miyota, Japan 135/C1
Miyun, China 130/H6
Miyun (res.), China 130/H6
Mizen (pt.), Ire. 92/B6
Miziya, Bul. 107/F4
Mizoram (state), India 141/F3
Mizpah, NJ, US 196/D5
Mizpe Ramon, Isr. 149/D4
Mizuho, Japan 135/D2
Mizuho, Japan 135/H5
Mizunami, Japan 135/M5
Mizusawa, Japan 134/B4
Mjölby, Swe. 96/F2
Mjøndalen, Nor. 96/D2
Mjörn (lake), Swe. 96/E3
Mjøsa (lake), Nor. 95/D3
Mkata (plain), Tanz. 162/C4
Mkokotoni, Tanz. 162/C4
Mkomazi (riv.), Tanz. 162/C4
Mkomazi Game Rsv., Tanz. 162/C4
Mkombo (riv.), Tanz. 162/A4
Mkondoa (riv.), Tanz. 162/C4
Mkorn (peak), Mor. 156/D3
Mkumbi (pt.), Tanz. 162/C4
Mkushi, Zam. 163/F3
Mkuze (riv.), SAfr. 165/F2
Mlada Boleslav, Czh. 113/H2
Mladá Vožice, Czh. 113/H3
Mladenovac, Serb. 106/E3
Mlawk (lake), NJ, US 196/D2
Mława, Pol. 99/L2
Mljet (isl.), Cro. 105/E1
Mljet NP, Cro. 105/E1
Mmabatho, SAfr. 164/D2
Mnyera (riv.), Tanz. 162/B5
Mo Duc, Viet. 136/E3
Moa, Cuba 203/H1
Moa (isl.), Indo. 139/G5
Moa (riv.), SLeo. 160/C5
Moab, Ut, US 186/D3

Moala Group (isl.), Fiji 174/G6
Moama, Austl. 173/C1
Moamba, Moz. 165/F2
Moaña, Sp. 102/A1
Moanda, Gabon 154/H8
Moate, Ire. 89/Q10
Mobara, Japan 135/E3
Mobaye, CAfr. 155/K7
Moberly, Mo, US 187/J3
Moberly Lake, BC, Can. 184/C2
Mobile, Al, US 191/F4
Mobridge, SD, US 185/H4
Moca (pass), Turk. 149/C1
Mocache, Ecu. 210/B5
Mocajuba, Braz. 209/J4
Mocha (riv.), Rus. 119/W9
Mochima, PN, Ven. 211/G2
Mochizuki, Japan 135/A1
Mochudi, Bots. 163/E5
Mochumí, Peru 214/B2
Mocímboa da Praia, Moz. 162/D5
Möckeln (lake), Swe. 96/E3
Mockfjärd, Swe. 96/F1
Möckmühl, Ger. 112/C4
Moclín, Sp. 102/D4
Mocoa, Col. 210/B4
Mococa, Braz. 213/F6
Mocorito, Mex. 200/D3
Moctezuma, Mex. 201/E4
Moctezuma, Mex. 200/C2
Moctezuma (riv.), Mex. 201/E4
Mocuba, Moz. 163/G4
Modāsa, India 147/K4
Modderrivier (riv.), SAfr. 164/D3
Modena (prov.), It. 117/D3
Modena, It. 117/D3
Moder (riv.), Fr. 101/G2
Modesto, Ca, US 186/B3
Modica, It. 104/D4
Modigliana, It. 117/E4
Modjeska, Ca, US 194/C3
Modjigo (reg.), Niger 154/H4
Mödling, Aus. 107/N7
Modot, Mong. 129/J2
Modřica, Bosn. 106/D3
Modugno, It. 104/E2
Moe, Austl. 173/C3
Moeb (bay), Namb. 164/A2
Moël-y-Llyn (peak), Wal, UK 90/C2
Moelfre (peak), Wal, UK 90/C1
Moen, Nor. 95/F1
Moenkopi (riv.), US 186/E3
Moerai (isl.), FrPol. 175/K7
Moerbeke, Belg. 110/C1
Moers, Ger. 108/D6
Moervaart (riv.), Belg. 110/C1
Moesa (riv.), Swi. 115/F5
Moffett Field Naval Air Sta., Ca, US 193/K12
Moga, India 144/C4
Mogadouro, Port. 102/B2
Mogami (riv.), Japan 134/B4
Mogami, Japan 134/B4
Mogaung, Myan. 141/G2
Mogent (riv.), Sp. 103/L6
Moghul Gardens, India 144/C3
Mogi das Cruzes, Braz. 213/G8
Mogi-Guaçu, Braz. 213/G7
Mogi-Guaçu (riv.), Braz. 213/G7
Mogi-Mirim, Braz. 213/G7
Mogilno, Pol. 99/J2
Moglia, It. 117/D3
Mogliano Veneto, It. 117/F1
Möglingen, Ger. 112/C5
Mogoro, It. 104/A3
Mogotes (pt.), Arg. 216/F3
Mogotón (peak), Nic. 202/E3
Moguer, Sp. 102/B4
Mohács, Hun. 105/F3
Mohaeli (isl.), Com. 165/G6
Mohales Hoek, Les. 164/D3
Mohall, ND, US 185/H3
Mohamed V (dam), Mor. 158/C2
Mohamed V, Barrage (res.), Mor. 158/C2
Mohamed V (Casablanca) (int'l arpt.), Mor. 158/C2
Mohammadia, Alg. 158/F5
Mohammedia-Znata (prov.), Mor. 158/A2
Mohammedia, Mor. 158/A3
Mohawk (lake), NJ, US 196/D2
Moheda, Swe. 96/F3
Mohembo, Bots. 163/D4
Mohican (cape), Ak, US 192/E3
Möhlin, Swi. 115/G5
Möhne (riv.), Ger. 109/F6
Möhnestausee (lake), Ger. 109/F5
Mohnton, Pa, US 196/B2
Moho, Peru 214/D4
Mohrsville, Pa, US 196/C2

Mohyliv-Podil's'kyy, Ukr. 107/H1
Moi (int'l arpt.), Kenya 162/C4
Moi, Nor. 96/B2
Moie, It. 117/G5
Moinești, Rom. 107/H2
Moinkum (des.), Kaz. 122/H5
Moinsi (hills), Gha. 161/E5
Moira, Fr. 100/F4
Moira (riv.), On, Can. 196/B1
Moirans, Fr. 100/F4
Moirans-en-Montagne, Fr. 114/B2
Moisie (riv.), Qu, Can. 181/K3
Moislains, Fr. 110/B4
Moissac, Fr. 100/D4
Moisselles, Fr. 88/J4
Moita, Port. 103/Q10
Moitaco, Ven. 211/E3
Mojácar, Sp. 102/E4
Mojave (riv.), Ca, US 186/C4
Mojave (des.), Ca, US 186/C4
Mojave, Ca, US 186/C4
Mojiang Hanizu Zizhixian, China 141/H3
Mojijit (lake), On, Can. 185/L3
Mojkovac, Mont. 106/D4
Mojos, Llanos de (plain), Bol. 208/E6
Moju (riv.), Braz. 209/J4
Mōka, Japan 133/F2
Mokameh, India 143/E3
Mokapu (pt.), Hi, US 182/W13
Mokau (riv.), NZ 175/S10
Mokelumne (riv.), Ca, US 186/B3
Mokelumne (aqueduct), Ca, US 193/M11
Mokena, Il, US 193/O16
Mokil (isl.), Micr. 174/E4
Mokochu (peak), Thai. 136/B3
Mokohinau (isls.), NZ 175/S9
Mokohshūng, India 141/F2
Mokolo, Camr. 154/H5
Mokp'o, SKor. 131/D5
Mokrin, Serb. 106/E3
Mokuleia, Hi, US 182/V12
Mol, Serb. 106/E3
Mol, Belg. 108/C6
Moláoi, Gre. 105/H4
Molare, It. 116/B3
Molas, Punta (pt.), Mex. 202/E1
Molat (isl.), Cro. 106/B3
Molatón (peak), Sp. 102/E3
Mold, Wal, UK 93/E5
Moldavia (reg.), Rom. 107/H2
Moldavian Carpathians (range), Rom. 107/G2
Moldova (ctry.) 107/H2
Moldova (riv.), Rom. 107/G2
Moldova Nouă, Rom. 106/E3
Moldoveanu (peak), Rom. 107/G3
Mole (riv.), Eng, UK 90/C2
Mole NP, Gha. 161/E4
Môle Saint-Nicolas, Haiti 203/H2
Molepolole, Bots. 163/E5
Molina, Sp. 102/E2
Molina, Chile 216/C2
Molina de Segura, Sp. 102/E3
Moline, Il, US 185/L5
Molinella, It. 117/E3
Molínicos, Sp. 102/D3
Molino de Flores, PN, Mex. 201/R9
Molins de Rei, Sp. 103/L7
Molise (reg.), It. 104/D2
Molkom, Swe. 96/E2
Möll (riv.), Aus. 101/K3
Mollendo, Peru 214/C5
Mollerussa, Sp. 103/F2
Molles (pt.), Chile 216/C2
Mollet del Vallès, Sp. 103/L6
Mölln, Ger. 98/F2
Molln, Aus. 101/L3
Molo (riv.), Togo 154/F6
Molodezhnaya, Rus., Ant. 218/D
Mologa (riv.), Rus. 118/G4
Molokai (isl.), Hi, US 182/T10
Moloma (riv.), Rus. 119/L4
Molong, Austl. 173/D2
Mólos, Gre. 105/H3
Molsheim, Fr. 114/D1
Molteno, SAfr. 164/D3
Molu (isl.), Indo. 139/G4
Molucca (sea), Asia 139/G4
Molucca Islands (arch.), Indo. 139/G3
Molveno, It. 115/G5
Molvena, It. 117/E1
Mombaça, Braz. 212/C4
Mombasa, Kenya 162/C4
Mombetsu, Japan 134/C1
Mombetsu, Japan 134/C1
Mömbris, Ger. 112/C2
Momchilgrad, Bul. 107/G5

Momfafa (cape), Indo. 139/H4
Momignies, Belg. 111/D3
Mömlingen, Ger. 112/C3
Momo, It. 116/B1
Momoishi, Japan 134/B3
Mompós, Col. 210/C2
Mon (state), Myan. 141/G4
Mon (riv.), Myan. 141/F3
Møn (isl.), Den. 95/E5
Mona (isl.), PR 199/M8
Mona (passg.), NAm. 199/L8
Monaco (ctry.) 116/J8
Monaco, Ca, US 194/G7
Monaco, Port of (har.), Mona. 116/J8
Monadhliath (mts.), Sc, UK 94/B2
Monagas (state), Ven. 211/F2
Monaghan (co.), Ire. 92/A3
Monaghan, Ire. 92/A3
Monar (lake), Sc, UK 94/A2
Monarch (peak), Swi. 114/D4
Monashee (mts.), BC, Can. 184/D3
Monastir, Tun. 158/M7
Moncada, Sp. 103/E3
Moncalieri, It. 101/G4
Moncalvo, It. 116/B2
Monção, Braz. 212/A1
Moncayo, Sierra del (range), Sp. 102/E2
Mönch (peak), Swi. 114/D4
Mönchegorsk, Rus. 118/G2
Mönchengladbach, Ger. 108/D6
Monchique, Serra de (mts.), Port. 102/A4
Monchique, Port. 102/A4
Moncks Corner, SC, US 191/H3
Monclova, Mex. 201/E3
Moncton, NB, Can. 189/H2
Mondego (cape), Port. 102/A2
Mondego (riv.), Port. 102/A2
Mondéjar, Sp. 102/D2
Mondolfo, It. 117/G5
Mondoñedo, Sp. 102/B1
Mondorf-les-Bains, Lux. 111/F4
Mondoví, It. 116/A4
Mondovi, Wi, US 185/L4
Mondragón, Sp. 102/D1
Mondragone, It. 104/C2
Mondsee (lake), Aus. 113/G7
Monéglia, It. 116/C4
Monemvasia, Gre. 105/H4
Mones Cazón, Arg. 216/E3
Monesterio, Sp. 102/B3
Money (riv.), Sc, UK 92/C2
Moneyreagh, NI, UK 92/C2
Monferrato (reg.), It. 101/G4
Monforte, Sp. 102/B1
Monforte, Port. 102/B3
Mongaguá, Braz. 213/G9
Mongers (lake), Austl. 170/C4
Monghidoro, It. 117/E4
Mongo, Chad 155/J5
Mongo (riv.), Gui. 160/C4
Mongolia (ctry.) 128/G2
Mönh Hayrhan (peak), Mong. 128/F2
Mönh Sarĭdag (peak), Mong. 128/H1
Monheim, Ger. 112/D5
Monifieth, Sc, UK 94/D4
Moniquirá, Col. 210/C3
Monistrol de Montserrat, Sp. 103/K6
Monistrol-sur-Loire, Fr. 100/F4
Monitor (range), Nv, US 186/C3
Monkayo, Phil. 137/E6
Mońki, Pol. 99/M2
Monks (isl.), Nic. 202/F3
Monmouth, Il, US 185/L5
Monmouth, Or, US 184/C4
Monmouth Beach, NJ, US 196/E3
Monmouth Junction, NJ, US 196/D3
Monmouth Mil. Res., NJ, US 196/D3
Monmouthshire (co.), Wal, UK 90/D3
Monnow (riv.), Eng, UK 90/C2
Monnickendam, Neth. 108/C4
Mono (riv.), Togo 154/F6
Mono (lake), Ca, US 186/C3
Mono (prov.), Ben. 161/G4
Monocacy (riv.), Md, US 196/A4
Monor, Hun. 106/D2
Monóvar, Sp. 103/E3
Monreal del Campo, Sp. 102/E2
Monreale, It. 104/C3
Monroe (lake), Fl, US 191/G3
Monroe, Ga, US 191/H3
Monroe, La, US 187/J4

Monroe, Mi, US 188/D3
Monroe, NC, US 191/H3
Monroe, NY, US 196/C1
Monroe, Ut, US 186/D3
Monroe, Wa, US 193/C2
Monroe, Wi, US 185/L5
Monroe City, Il, US 195/G9
Monroeville, Al, US 191/G4
Monroeville, NJ, US 196/C4
Monrovia (cap.), Libr. 160/C5
Monrovia, Ca, US 194/G7
Mons, Belg. 110/C3
Monsanto, Port. 102/B2
Monschau, Ger. 111/F2
Monsefú, Peru 214/B2
Monselice, It. 101/J4
Monsenhor Tabosa, Braz. 212/B2
Monsey, NY, US 197/J7
Monsheim, Ger. 112/B3
Monster, Neth. 108/B4
Mönsteras, Swe. 96/G3
Monsummano Terme, It. 117/D5
Montabaur, Ger. 111/G3
Montagnana, It. 117/E2
Montagne d'Ambre NP, Madg. 165/J6
Montagny-Sainte-Félicité, Fr. 88/L4
Montagu, SAfr. 164/M10
Montague (str.), Ak, US 192/J4
Montague, Tx, US 187/H4
Montague, PE, Can. 189/J2
Montague, NJ, US 196/D1
Montaigu, Fr. 100/C3
Montaione, It. 117/D5
Montalbán, Sp. 103/E2
Montalbano Jonico, It. 104/E2
Montale, It. 117/E5
Montale, It. 117/D3
Montalieu-Vercieu, Fr. 114/B6
Montalvão, Port. 102/B3
Montalvo, Ca, US 194/A2
Montana (prov.), Bul. 106/F4
Montana, Swi. 114/D5
Montana (state), US 184/F4
Montanaro, It. 116/A2
Montanha, Braz. 212/B5
Montara, Ca, US 193/J11
Montargis, Fr. 100/E2
Montataire, Fr. 110/B4
Montauban, Fr. 100/D4
Montauk, NY, US 197/G1
Montauk (pt.), NY, US 197/G1
Montbard, Fr. 100/F3
Montbéliard, Fr. 114/C2
Montblanc, Sp. 103/F2
Montcada i Reixac, Sp. 103/L7
Montceau-les-Mines, Fr. 100/F3
Montclair, Ca, US 194/C2
Montclair, NJ, US 197/J8
Montcornet, Fr. 110/D4
Montdidier, Fr. 110/B4
Monte Albán (ruin), Mex. 202/B2
Monte Alegre, Braz. 209/H4
Monte Alegre de Goiás, Braz. 212/A4
Monte Alegre de Minas, Braz. 213/B1
Monte Alegre do Piauí, Braz. 212/A3
Monte Alto, Braz. 213/B2
Monte Azul, Braz. 212/B4
Monte Carmelo, Braz. 213/C1
Monte Carmelo, Ven. 210/D2
Monte Caseros, Arg. 215/E3
Monte Común, Arg. 216/D2
Monte Escobedo, Mex. 200/E4
Monte Maíz, Arg. 216/E2
Monte Pascoal, PN de, Braz. 209/L7
Monte Pascoal, PN de, Braz. 212/C5
Monte Rosa (peak), It. 114/D5
Monte San Savino, It. 117/E5
Montealegre, Sp. 102/E3
Montebello (isls.), Austl. 170/B3
Montebello, Ca, US 194/F7

Montebello Vincentino, It. 117/E2
Montebelluna, It. 117/F1
Montebruno, It. 116/C3
Montecarlo, Arg. 215/F2
Montecassiano, It. 117/G6
Montecatini Terme, It. 117/D5
Montecavolo, It. 116/D3
Montecchio, It. 117/F5
Montechiaro d'Asti, It. 116/B2
Montecito, Ca, US 194/A2
Montecristo (isl.), It. 104/B1
Montecristo, PN, ESal. 202/D3
Montefeltro (reg.), It. 117/F5
Monteforte d'Alpone, It. 117/E2
Montefrío, Sp. 102/C4
Montego Bay, Jam. 203/G2
Montegranaro, It. 117/G5
Montegrotto Terme, It. 117/E2
Montehermoso, Sp. 102/B2
Monteiro, Braz. 212/C2
Montelavar, Port. 103/P10
Montélimar, Fr. 100/F4
Montellano, Sp. 102/C4
Montello, Nv, US 184/E6
Montelupo Fiorentino, It. 117/E5
Montemagno, It. 116/B3
Montemarciano, It. 117/G5
Montemor-o-Novo, Port. 102/A3
Montemor-o-Velho, Port. 102/A2
Montemorelos, Mex. 201/E3
Montemuro (peak), Port. 102/A2
Montendre, Fr. 100/C4
Montenegro, Braz. 213/B4
Montenero di Bisaccia, It. 104/D2
Montepulciano, It. 117/F5
Montereau-Faut-Yonne, Fr. 100/E2
Montereau-sur-le-Jard, Fr. 88/L6
Monterey, Ca, US 186/B3
Monterey (bay), Ca, US 186/B3
Monterey Park, Ca, US 194/F7
Montería, Col. 210/C2
Montero, Bol. 208/F7
Monteros, Arg. 215/C2
Monterosso (peak), It. 115/G4
Monterosso al Mare, It. 116/C4
Monterotondo, It. 104/C1
Monterrey, Mex. 201/E3
Monterrey, Sp. 102/B2
Montes (pt.), Arg. 217/C6
Montes Altos, Braz. 212/A2
Montes Claros, Braz. 212/B5
Montescaglioso, It. 104/E2
Montese, It. 117/D4
Montespertoli, It. 117/E5
Montesson, Fr. 88/J5
Monteux, Fr. 100/F4
Montevarchi, It. 117/E5
Montevideo, Mn, US 185/K4
Montevideo (cap.), Uru. 217/K11
Montevideo (dept.), Uru. 217/K11
Montévrain, Fr. 88/L5
Montezuma (peak), Az, US 195/R19
Montezuma Castle Nat'l Mon., Az, US 186/E4
Montfermeil, Fr. 88/K5
Montferrand-le-Château, Fr. 114/B3
Montfoort, Neth. 108/B4
Montfort-L'Amaury, Fr. 110/C4
Montgeron, Fr. 88/K5
Montgomery, Wal, UK 90/C1
Montgomery (cap.), Al, US 191/G3
Montgomery, Il, US 193/P16
Montgomery (co.), Md, US 196/A5
Montgomery, Pa, US 196/B1
Montgomery, WV, US 188/D4
Montgomery Village, Md, US 196/A5
Montgomeryville, Pa, US 196/C3
Montgrand (peak), Fr. 100/F5
Monthermé, Fr. 111/D4
Monthey, Swi. 114/C6
Monthureux-sur-Saône, Fr. 114/B1
Monthyon, Fr. 88/L4
Monti Sabini (mts.), It. 104/C1
Monticelli d'Ongina, It. 116/C2
Monticelli Terme, It. 116/D2
Monticello, Mo, US 185/L5
Monticello, Ky, US 188/C4
Monticello, In, US 188/C3
Monticello, La, US 187/K4
Monticello, Fl, US 191/H4
Monticello, Va, US 191/J2

Monticello Conte Otto, It. 117/E1
Montichiari, It. 116/D2
Montier-en-Der, Fr. 114/A1
Montignies-le-Tilleul, Belg. 111/D3
Montigny-en-Gohelle, Fr. 52/B3
Montigny-le-Bretonneux, Fr. 30/J5
Montigny-le-Roi, Fr. 114/B2
Montijo, Sp. 102/B3
Montijo, Port. 103/Q10
Montilla, Sp. 102/C4
Montivilliers, Fr. 100/D2
Montlebon, Fr. 114/C3
Montléry, Fr. 88/J6
Montluçon, Fr. 100/E3
Montluel, Fr. 114/B6
Montmagny, Qu, Can. 189/G2
Montmédy, Fr. 111/E4
Montmerle-sur-Saône, Fr. 114/A5
Montmirail, Fr. 110/C6
Montmorency, Fr. 88/J5
Montmorillon, Fr. 100/D3
Montmorot, Fr. 114/B4
Monto, Austl. 172/C4
Montoir-de-Bretagne, Fr. 42/B3
Montois-la-Montagne, Fr. 111/F5
Montone (riv.), It. 117/E4
Montopoli, It. 117/D5
Montorio Veronese, It. 117/E2
Montoro, Sp. 102/C3
Montour (ridge), Pa, US 196/B2
Montour, Pa, US 196/B1
Montoursville, Pa, US 196/B1
Montpelier (cap.), Vt, US 189/F2
Montpellier, Fr. 100/E5
Montreal (lake), Sk, Can. 185/G2
Montreal (riv.), On, Can. 188/C2
Montréal, Qu, Can. 189/N6
Montréal-Est, Qu, Can. 189/N6
Montréal-la-Cluse, Fr. 114/A5
Montréal-Nord, Qu, Can. 189/N6
Montréjeau, Fr. 100/D5
Montreuil, Fr. 88/K5
Montreuil-Bellay, Fr. 100/C3
Montreuil-sur-Epte, Fr. 88/G4
Montreux, Swi. 114/C5
Montrevel-en-Bresse, Fr. 114/B5
Montricher, Swi. 114/C4
Montrose, Co, US 186/F3
Montrose (basin), Sc, UK 94/D3
Montrose, Sc, UK 94/D3
Montrouge, Fr. 88/J5
Montry, Fr. 88/L5
Monts, Fr. 100/D3
Montseny, PN, Sp. 103/L6
Montserrado (co.), Libr. 160/C5
Montserrat (peak), Sp. 103/F2
Montserrat (dpcy.), UK 199/N8
Montsoult, Fr. 88/J4
Montvale, NJ, US 197/J7
Montville, NJ, US 197/H8
Monywa, Myan. 141/G3
Monza, It. 116/C2
Monze, Zam. 163/E4
Monzingen, Ger. 111/G4
Monzón, Peru 214/B3
Monzón, Sp. 103/F2
Mooirivier, SAfr. 165/E3
Mool (riv.), SAfr. 164/P13
Moonta, Austl. 171/H5
Moora, Austl. 170/C4
Moorcroft, Wy, US 185/G4
Moordrecht, Neth. 108/B5
Moore (lake), Austl. 170/C4
Moore, Ok, US 195/N15
Moore Haven, Fl, US 191/H5
Moore River NP, Austl. 170/B4
Moorea (isl.), FrPol. 175/K6
Moorenweis, Ger. 115/H1
Moorestown, NJ, US 196/D4
Mooresville, NC, US 191/H3
Mooretown, On, Can. 193/H6
Moorfoot (hills), Sc, UK 94/C5
Moorhead, Mn, US 185/J4
Moorpark, Ca, US 194/B2
Mooreesburg, SAfr. 164/L10
Moorslede, Belg. 110/C2
Moosburg, Ger. 113/E6
Moose (mtn.), Sk, Can. 185/H3
Moose (riv.), On, Can. 188/D1
Moose Creek, On, Can. 193/H6
Moose Jaw, Sk, Can. 185/G3

Moose Pass, Ak, US 192/J3
Moosehead (lake), Me, US 189/G2
Mooseheart (mtn.), Ak, US 192/H3
Mooseheart, Il, US 193/P16
Moosomin, Sk, Can. 185/H3
Moosonee, On, Can. 188/D1
Moosseedorf, Swi. 114/D3
Moosthenning, Ger. 113/F5
Mopti (pol. reg.), Mali 160/E3
Mopti, Mali 160/D3
Moquegua (dept.), Peru 214/D5
Moquegua, Peru 214/D5
Moquehuà, Arg. 217/J11
Mor (riv.), India 143/F4
Mór, Hun. 106/D2
Mora, Camr. 154/H5
Mora (riv.), NM, US 187/F4
Mora, NM, US 187/F4
Mora, Port. 102/A3
Mora, Swe. 96/F1
Mora de Rubielos, Sp. 103/E2
Morača (riv.), Mont. 106/C4
Morada Nova, Braz. 212/C2
Morada Nova de Minas, Braz. 213/C1
Morādābād, India 142/B1
Morado, PN, Chile 216/B3
Morafenobe, Madg. 165/H7
Moragg, Pol. 97/H5
Moraga, Ca, US 193/K11
Mórahalom, Hun. 106/D2
Morainvilliers, Fr. 88/H5
Moral de Calatrava, Sp. 102/D3
Moraleja, Sp. 102/B2
Morales, Guat. 202/D3
Moramanga, Madg. 165/J7
Moranbah, Austl. 172/C3
Morane (isl.), FrPol. 175/M7
Morangis, Fr. 88/K5
Morano Calabro, It. 104/E3
Morant Bay, Jam. 203/G2
Morar (lake), Sc, UK 89/R8
Moraro Chrome, Madg. 165/J7
Morata de Tajuña, Sp. 103/N9
Moratalla, Sp. 102/E3
Moratuwa, SrL. 140/C6
Morava (riv.), Czh. 99/J4
Moravia (riv.), Czh. 99/J4
Moravská Třebová, Czh. 99/J4
Moravské Budějovice, Czh. 99/H4
Morawa, Austl. 170/C4
Morawhanna, Guy. 208/G2
Moray (pol. reg.), Sc, UK 94/E2
Moray Firth (inlet), Sc, UK 94/B1
Morbach, Ger. 111/G4
Morbegno, It. 115/F5
Morbier, Fr. 114/C4
Morbio Inferiore, Swi. 115/F6
Morbras (riv.), Fr. 88/K5
Mörbylånga, Swe. 96/G3
Moroto (riv.), Ugan. 162/B2
Moroyama, Japan 135/C2
Morpará, Braz. 212/B3
Morpeth, Eng, UK 93/G1
Morphou, Cyp. 149/C2
Morphou (bay), Cyp. 149/C2
Morra (lake), Neth. 108/C3
Morrinhos, Braz. 213/B1
Morris (pt.), Austl. 171/F3
Morris, Mb, Can. 185/J3
Morris (res.), Ca, US 194/C2
Morris, Mn, US 185/K4
Morris (co.), NJ, US 196/D2
Morris Jesup (cape), Grld 218/J
Morris Plains, NJ, US 197/H8
Morrison, Co, US 195/B3
Morristown, NJ, US 196/D2
Morristown NHP, NJ, US 196/D2
Morrisville, Pa, US 196/D3
Morro Bay, Ca, US 186/B4
Morro de Môco (peak), Ang. 163/C3
Morro de Puercos (pt.), Pan. 203/F5
Morro do Chapéu, Braz. 212/B3
Morro, Punta del (pt.), Mex. 201/N7
Morrocoy, PN, Ven. 210/D2
Mórrope, Peru 214/A2
Morros, Braz. 212/A1
Morrosquillo (gulf), Col. 203/G4
Mörrum, Swe. 96/F3
Mørs (isl.), Den. 96/C3
Morsang-sur-Orge, Fr. 88/K6
Morsbach, Ger. 111/G2
Morsbach, Fr. 111/F5

Morschwiller-le-Bas, Fr. 114/D2
Morse, Ks, US 195/D6
Morse Mill, Mo, US 195/F9
Morshansk, Rus. 121/G1
Morskoy (isl.), Kaz. 121/J3
Morsum, Ger. 109/G3
Mortagne (riv.), Fr. 114/C1
Mortagne-sur-Sèvre, Fr. 100/C3
Mortara, It. 116/B2
Mortcerf, Fr. 88/L5
Morte (pt.), Eng, UK 90/B4
Morte (riv.), Fr. 114/C3
Morteau, Fr. 114/C3
Mortefontaine, Fr. 88/K4
Mortegliano, It. 117/G1
Mortes, Rio das (riv.), Braz. 209/H6
Mortlake, Austl. 173/B3
Morton, Wa, US 184/C4
Morton, Il, US 187/K2
Morton Grove, Il, US 193/Q15
Morton NP, Austl. 173/D2
Morton NWR, NY, US 197/F2
Mortsel, Belg. 108/B6
Morungaba, Braz. 213/G7
Moruya, Austl. 173/D2
Morvan (plat.), Fr. 100/E3
Morven, Austl. 172/B4
Morven (peak), Sc, UK 94/C2
Morvi, India 147/K4
Morvillars, Fr. 114/C2
Morwell, Austl. 173/C3
Morzine, Fr. 114/C5
Moriya, Japan 135/D2
Mos, Sp. 102/A1
Mosbach, Ger. 112/C4
Mosby, Mo, US 195/E5
Moscavide, Port. 103/P10
Moscow (Moskva) (cap.), Rus. 119/W9
Moscow (upland), Rus. 118/F5
Moscow, Id, US 184/D4
Moscow University Ice Shelf, Ant. 218/J
Moselle (riv.), Fr. 101/G2
Moselle (dept.), Fr. 111/F5
Moselotte (riv.), Fr. 114/C2
Moses Lake, Wa, US 184/D4
Mosfellsbær, Ice. 95/N7
Mosgiel, NZ 175/S12
Moshaweng (riv.), SAfr. 164/C2
Moshchnyy (isl.), Rus. 97/M2
Moshi, Tanz. 162/C4
Moshoeshoe (Maseru) (int'l arpt.), Les. 164/D3
Mosina, Pol. 99/J2
Moskovskaya Oblast, Rus. 118/H5
Moskva (riv.), Rus. 118/G5
Moskva (Moscow) (cap.), Rus. 120/F1
Mosonmagyaróvár, Hun. 106/C2
Mosquera, Col. 210/B4
Mosquero, NM, US 187/G4
Mosquitia (phys. reg.), Hon. 203/E3
Mosquito (pt.), Pan. 203/G4
Mosquitos, Golfo de los (gulf), Pan. 203/F4
Moss, Nor. 96/D2
Moss Beach, Ca, US 193/J11
Moss Bluff, La, US 187/J5
Moss Point, Ms, US 191/F4
Moss-Side, NI, UK 92/B1
Moss Vale, Austl. 173/D2
Mosselbaai, SAfr. 164/C4
Mosses, Col des (pass), Swi. 114/D5
Mossi Highlands (uplands), Burk. 160/E4
Mössingen, Ger. 112/C6
Mossman, Austl. 172/B2
Mossoró, Braz. 212/C2
Most, Czh. 113/G1
Mostaganem (prov.), Alg. 158/F4
Mostaganem, Alg. 158/F5
Mostar, Bosn. 105/E1
Mostardas, Braz. 213/B4
Móstoles, Sp. 103/N9
Mota del Cuervo, Sp. 102/D3
Motagua (riv.), Guat. 198/D4
Motala, Swe. 96/F2
Motherwell, Sc, UK 94/C5
Motian (mtn.), China 130/E2
Motīhāri, India 143/E2
Motilla del Palancar, Sp. 102/E3
Motobu, Japan 133/J7
Motomiya, Japan 133/G2
Motono, Japan 135/E2
Motosu (lake), Japan 135/B3
Motosu, Japan 135/L5
Motovskiy (gulf), Rus. 95/K1
Motoyoshi, Japan 134/B4

Motozintla de Mendoza, Mex. 202/C3
Moy, NI, UK 92/B3
Motril, Sp. 102/D4
Motsuta-misaki (cape), Japan 134/A2
Motta di Livenza, It. 117/F1
Motta Visconti, It. 116/B2
Mottarone (peak), It. 116/B1
Motul de Carrillo Puerto, Mex. 202/D1
Motupe, Peru 214/B2
Motygino, Rus. 122/K4
Mouchard, Fr. 114/B4
Mouchoir Passage (chan.), 203/J1
Moúdhros, Gre. 105/J3
Moudon, Swi. 114/C4
Mougris (well), Mrta. 160/B2
Mouhoun (prov.), Burk. 160/E3
Mouïla, Gabon 154/H8
Mouïna (well), Alg. 157/F3
Moul (well), Niger 154/H4
Moulamein (riv.), Austl. 173/C2
Moulamein, Austl. 173/C2
Moulay Idriss, Mor. 158/B2
Moulins, Fr. 100/E3
Moulouya (riv.), Mor. 158/C2
Moultrie, Ga, US 191/H4
Moultrie (lake), SC, US 191/J3
Moundou, Chad 154/J6
Moundsville, WV, US 188/D4
Mount Aberdeen NP, Austl. 172/B3
Mount Abu, India 147/K4
Mount Airy, NC, US 188/D4
Mount Airy, Md, US 196/A5
Mount Allan Abor. Land, Austl. 171/G2
Mount Aspiring NP, NZ 175/R11
Mount Baker-Snoqualmie, Wa, US 193/D1
Mount Baker-Snoqualmie Nat'l For., Wa, US 193/D3
Mount Baldy, Ca, US 194/C2
Mount Barker, Austl. 170/C5
Mount Barker, Austl. 171/M9
Mount Barkly Abor. Land, Austl. 171/G2
Mount Beauty, Austl. 173/C3
Mount Bold (res.), Austl. 171/M9
Mount Buffalo NP, Mo, US 187/J3
Mount Carmel, Il, US 188/C4
Mount Carmel, Pa, US 196/B3
Mount Darwin, Zim. 163/F4
Mount Diablo State Park, Ca, US 193/L11
Mount Eccles NP, Austl. 173/B3
Mount Elgon NP, Ugan. 162/B2
Mount Elliot NP, Austl. 172/B3
Mount Everard, Guy. 211/G3
Mount Field NP, Austl. 173/C4
Mount Gambier, Austl. 173/B3
Mount Garnet, Austl. 172/B2
Mount Holly, NJ, US 196/D4
Mount Holly Springs, Pa, US 196/A3
Mount Imlay NP, Austl. 173/D3
Mount Isa, Austl. 171/H2
Mount Joy, Pa, US 196/B3
Mount Kaputar NP, Austl. 173/D1
Mount Kenya NP, Kenya 162/C3
Mount Kisco, NY, US 197/E1
Mount Larcom, Austl. 172/C3
Mournai, Gre. 105/J4
Mount Laurel, NJ, US 196/D4
Mount Lofty (ranges), Austl. 171/M9
Mount Magnet, Austl. 170/C4
Mount Mistake NP, Austl. 172/D4
Mount Morgan, Austl. 172/C3
Mount Morris, Mi, US 188/D3
Mount Nebo, Austl. 172/E6
Mount Olive, NC, US 191/J3
Mount Pearl, Nf, Can. 189/L2
Mount Penn, Pa, US 196/C3

Mount Pleasant, Ia, US 185/L5
Mount Pleasant, Mi, US 188/C3
Mount Pleasant, Ut, US 186/E3
Mount Pleasant, De, US 196/C6
Mount Pleasant (int'l arpt.), UK 217/F6
Mount Pleasant, Austl. 171/N8
Mount Pocono, Pa, US 196/C1
Mount Prospect, Il, US 193/P15
Mount Rainier, Md, US 196/B6
Mount Rainier NP, Wa, US 184/C4
Mount Remarkable NP, Austl. 171/H5
Mount Revelstoke NP, BC, Can. 184/D3
Mount Richmond NP, Austl. 173/B3
Mount Rushmore Nat'l Mem., SD, US 187/G2
Mount Spec NP, Austl. 172/B2
Mount St. Helens Nat'l Volcanic Mon., Wa, US 184/C4
Mount Sterling, Ky, US 188/D4
Mount Torrens, Austl. 171/M8
Mount Vernon, Il, US 188/D4
Mount Vernon, NY, US 197/K8
Mount Vernon, Oh, US 188/D3
Mount Vernon, Tx, US 187/J4
Mount Vernon, Va, US 196/A6
Mount Vernon, Wa, US 184/C3
Mount Walsh NP, Austl. 172/C4
Mount Warning NP, Austl. 172/D5
Mount Welcome Abor. Land, Austl. 170/C2
Mount William NP, Austl. 173/D4
Mount Wolf, Pa, US 196/B3
Mountain (riv.), NW, Can. 180/D2
Mountain Ash, Wal, UK 90/C3
Mountain Green, Ut, US 195/K11
Mountain Grove, Mo, US 187/J3
Mountain Home, Id, US 184/E5
Mountain Lakes, NJ, US 197/H8
Mountain Point, Ak, US 192/M4
Mountain Top, Pa, US 196/C1
Mountain View, Ar, US 187/J4
Mountain View, Ca, US 193/K12
Mountain View, Hi, US 182/U11
Mountain View, NJ, US 197/H9
Mountain Village, Ak, US 192/F3
Mountain Zebra NP, SAfr. 164/D4
Mountainhome, Pa, US 196/C1
Mountainside, NJ, US 197/H9
Mountlake Terrace, Wa, US 193/C2
Mountmellick, Ire. 89/Q10
Mountrath, Ire. 89/Q10
Mount's (bay), Eng, UK 90/A6
Mountville, Pa, US 196/B3
Moura, Port. 102/B3
Moura, Austl. 172/C4
Mourão, Port. 102/B3
Mourenx, Fr. 100/C5
Mourmelon-le-Grand, Fr. 111/D5
Mourmelon-le-Petit, Fr. 111/D5
Mourne (mts.), NI, UK 92/B3
Mouroux, Fr. 88/M5
Mouscron, Belg. 110/C2
Mousseaux-sur-Seine, Fr. 88/G4
Moussoro, Chad 154/J5
Moussy-le-Neuf, Fr. 88/K4
Moussy-le-Vieux, Fr. 88/K4
Mouths of the Niger, Nga. 154/G6
Moutier, Swi. 114/D3
Mouvaux, Fr. 110/C2
Mouy, Fr. 110/B5
Mouydir (plat.), Alg. 157/G4
Mouzákion, Gre. 105/G3
Mouzon, Fr. 111/E4
Moville, Ire. 92/A1

Moxotó (riv.), Braz. 212/C3
Moy, NI, UK 92/B3
Moyamba, SLeo. 160/B4
Moye (isl.), China 131/B4
Moyen Atlas (mts.), Mor. 154/D1
Moyenmoutier, Fr. 114/C1
Moyeuvre-Grande, Fr. 111/F5
Moyle (dist.), NI, UK 92/B1
Moyo (isl.), Indo. 139/E5
Moyo, Ugan. 162/A2
Moyobamba, Peru 214/B2
Moyowosi (riv.), Tanz. 162/A3
Moyu, China 128/C4
Moyuta, Guat. 202/D3
Mozambique (ctry.), Afr. 163/G4
Mozambique (chan.), Afr. 163/G5
Mozhaysk, Rus. 118/H5
Mozhga, Rus. 119/M4
Mozzanica, It. 116/C2
Mozzecane, It. 117/D2
Mpanda, Tanz. 162/A4
Mpigi, Ugan. 162/B2
Mpika, Zam. 162/A5
Mporokoso, Zam. 162/A5
Mpraeso, Gha. 161/E5
Mpulungu, Zam. 162/A5
Mpumalanga (prov.), SAfr. 165/E2
Mpwapwa, Tanz. 162/C4
Mragowo, Pol. 97/J5
Mrkonjić Grad, Bosn. 106/C3
Msaken, Tun. 158/M7
M'Sila (prov.), Alg. 157/F2
M'sila, Alg. 158/H5
M'sila (riv.), Alg. 158/H5
Msoun (riv.), Mor. 158/C2
Msta (riv.), Rus. 118/G3
Mszana Dolna, Pol. 99/L4
Mtorwi (peak), Tanz. 162/B5
Mtsensk, Rus. 120/F1
Mtubatuba, SAfr. 165/F3
Mtunzini, SAfr. 165/F3
Mtwara, Tanz. 162/D5
Mtwara (pol. reg.), Tanz. 162/C5
Mu-kawa (riv.), Japan 134/C2
Mu Ko Similan NP, Thai. 136/B4
Mu Ko Surin NP, Thai. 136/B4
Mualama, Moz. 163/G4
Muan, SKor. 131/D5
Muang Hinboun, Laos 136/D2
Muang Khammouan, Laos 136/D2
Muang Khong, Laos 136/D3
Muang Khongxedon, Laos 136/D3
Muang Pak-lay, Laos 136/C2
Muang Pakxan, Laos 136/C2
Muang Sing, Laos 141/H3
Muang Viang, Laos 136/C2
Muang Xaignabouri, Laos 136/C2
Muang Xay, Laos 141/H3
Muar, Malay. 138/B3
Muarabungo, Indo. 138/B4
Muāri (pt.), Pak. 147/J4
Mubārakpur, India 142/D2
Mubende, Ugan. 162/A2
Mucajaí (riv.), Braz. 208/F3
Much, Ger. 111/G2
Muchinga (mts.), Zam. 163/F3
Muck (isl.), Sc, UK 89/Q8
Muckleshoot Ind. Res., Wa, US 193/C3
Mucojo, Moz. 163/H3
Mucupina (mtn.), Hon. 202/E3
Mucur, Turk. 148/C2
Mucuri (riv.), Braz. 209/K7
Mud Mountain (dam), Wa, US 193/D3
Mud Mountain (lake), Wa, US 193/D3
Mudanjiang, China 129/N3
Mudanya, Turk. 112/C3
Mudau, Ger. 112/C3
Mudbach (riv.), Ger. 129/N2
Muddan (riv.), China 129/N2
Muddas NP, Swe. 95/G2
Muddy Run (res.), Pa, US 196/B4
Müden, Ger. 109/H3
Mudersbach, Ger. 111/G2
Mudgee, Austl. 173/D2
Mudjatik (riv.), Sk, Can. 180/F3
Mudon, Myan. 136/B2
Mudurnu (riv.), Turk. 107/K5
Muela (peak), Chile 217/B7
Muerte, Cerro de la (peak), CR 203/F4
Muff, Ire. 92/A1
Mufulira, Zam. 163/E3
Mugardos, Sp. 102/A1
Mugganj, Japan 135/L4
Mughal Sarai, India 142/D3
Mugi, Japan 135/L6
Mugia, Sp. 102/A1
Muğla, Turk. 148/B2

Muğla (prov.), Turk. 148/B2
Mughalzhar Taüy (mts.), Kaz. 145/C3
Muhamdi, India 142/C2
Muḥammad (pt.), Egypt 159/C3
Muhammadābād, India 142/D3
Muhavura (vol.), Rwa. 162/A3
Muhila, Monts (mts.), D.R. Congo 163/E3
Mühlacker, Ger. 112/B5
Mühldorf, Ger. 113/F6
Mühleberg, Swi. 114/D4
Mühlenbeck, Ger. 98/Q6
Mühlhausen, Ger. 113/E4
Mühlheim am Main, Ger. 112/B2
Mühlheim an der Donau, Ger. 115/E1
Mühltroff, Ger. 113/E1
Mühlviertel (reg.), Aus. 99/G4
Muhos, Fin. 118/E2
Muhu (isl.), Est. 97/K2
Muiden, Neth. 108/C4
Muir of Ord, Sc, UK 94/B1
Muir Woods Nat'l Mon., Ca, US 193/J11
Muirkirk, Sc, UK 94/B5
Muizon, Fr. 110/C5
Muju, SKor. 131/D4
Mukacheve, Ukr. 99/H4
Mukawa, Japan 134/B2
Mukawwar (isl.), Sudan 159/D4
Mukden, Bol. 214/D3
Mukeriãn, India 144/C4
Mukhayyam al Yarmūk, Syria 149/E3
Mukhmãs, Isr. 149/G8
Mukinbudin, Austl. 170/C4
Mukō, Japan 135/J6
Mukono, Ugan. 162/B2
Mukoshima (isls.), Japan 174/D2
Muktsar, India 144/C4
Mukwonago, Wi, US 193/P14
Mula, Sp. 102/E3
Mulanje, Malw. 163/G4
Mulchatna (riv.), Ak, US 192/G4
Mulchén, Chile 216/B3
Mulde (riv.), Ger. 98/G3
Mulegé, Mex. 200/C3
Muleshoe, Tx, US 187/G4
Mulhacén, Cerro de (peak), Sp. 102/D4
Mülhausen, Ger. 109/H6
Mülheim an der Ruhr, Ger. 108/D4
Mulhouse, Fr. 114/D2
Muli (riv.), Indo. 139/J5
Muli Zangzu Zizhixian, China 141/H2
Muling (pass), China 130/D4
Mull (isl.), Sc, UK 89/R8
Mull of Galloway (pt.), Sc, UK 92/D2
Mull of Kintyre (pt.), Sc, UK 92/C1
Mull of Logan (pt.), Sc, UK 92/D2
Mullach Coire Mhic Fhearchair (peak), Sc, UK 94/A1
Mullaghcleevaun (peak), Ire. 92/B5
Mullaghmore (peak), NI, UK 92/B2
Mullaittivu, SrL. 140/D6
Mullardoch (lake), Sc, UK 94/A2
Muller (mts.), Indo. 138/D4
Mullewa, Austl. 170/B4
Müllheim, Ger. 114/D2
Müllheim, Swi. 115/F2
Mullica (riv.), NJ, US 196/D4
Mullica Hill, NJ, US 196/C4
Mullingar, Ire. 89/Q10
Mullins, SC, US 191/H3
Mullumbimby, Austl. 173/E1
Mulobezi, Zam. 163/E4
Multai, India 142/B3
Multãn, Pak. 144/A4
Multnomah (falls), Or, US 184/C4
Mulu (peak), Malay. 138/D3
Mulwala, Austl. 173/C2
Mum Nauk (pt.), Thai. 136/B5
Mumbai (Bombay), India 147/K5
Mumbwa, Zam. 163/E4
Mümling (riv.), Ger. 112/B3
Mumoni (peak), Kenya 162/C3
Mun (riv.), Thai. 141/H4
Muna (isl.), Indo. 139/F4
Muna, Mex. 202/D1
Munamägi (hill), Est. 97/M3
Muñani, Peru 214/D4
Muncar, Indo. 138/D5
Münchberg, Ger. 113/E3
München (Munich), Ger. 113/E6
Münchenstein, Swi. 114/D2

Munchique (peak), Col. 210/B4
Munchique, PN, Col. 210/B4
Münchmünster, Ger. 113/E5
Muncie, In, US 188/C3
Muncy, Pa, US 196/B1
Mundaring, Austl. 170/L6
Munday, Tx, US 187/H4
Mundelein, Il, US 193/Q15
Münden, Ger. 109/G6
Munderfing, Aus. 113/G6
Munderkingen, Ger. 115/F1
Mundo (riv.), Sp. 102/D3
Mundo Novo, Braz. 215/F1
Mundo Novo, Braz. 212/B3
Mundubbera, Austl. 172/C4
Munera, Sp. 102/D3
Mungaoli, India 142/B3
Mungeli, India 142/C4
Munger, India 143/F3
Mungo NP, Austl. 173/B2
Mun'gyŏng, SKor. 131/E4
Munising, Mi, US 185/M4
Munkebo, Den. 96/D4
Munkedal, Swe. 96/D2
Munkfors, Swe. 96/E2
Munku-Sardyk (peak), Rus. 128/H1
Munsan, SKor. 131/F6
Münsingen, Swi. 114/D4
Münsingen, Ger. 112/C6
Munster (reg.), Ire. 89/P10
Munster, Ger. 109/H3
Munster, Fr. 114/D1
Münster, Swi. 115/C5
Munster, In, US 193/R16
Münster, Ger. 112/B3
Münster/Osnabrück (int'l arpt.), Ger. 109/E4
Münstereifel, Ger. 111/F2
Münsterhausen, Ger. 112/D6
Münsterland (reg.), Ger. 98/C2
Münstermaifeld, Ger. 111/G3
Muntele Mare (peak), Rom. 107/F2
Muntendam, Neth. 108/D2
Muntok, Indo. 138/C4
Müntschemier, Swi. 114/D4
Münzenberg, Ger. 112/B2
Münzkirchen, Aus. 113/G6
Munzur Vadisi NP, Turk. 148/D2
Muonio, Fin. 95/G2
Muonioälven (riv.), Swe. 95/G1
Muotathal, Swi. 115/E4
Mupa, PN da, Ang. 163/C4
Muping, China 130/D4
Muqdisho (Mogadishu) (cap.), Som. 155/H7
Muqeibila, Isr. 149/G6
Mur (riv.), Aus. 101/L3
Mura (riv.), Hun.,Slov. 106/C2
Muradnagar, India 144/D5
Murakami, Japan 133/F1
Murallón (peak), Chile 217/B6
Murano, It. 117/F2
Murat (peak), Turk. 148/E2
Muratlı, Turk. 148/C2
Muratlı, Turk. 107/H5
Murayama, Japan 134/B4
Murchison (riv.), Austl. 170/B4
Murchison (mt.), Austl. 170/C3
Murchison, NZ 175/S11
Murcia, Sp. 103/E4
Murcia (aut. comm.), Sp. 102/E4
Murderkill (riv.), De, US 196/C6
Murdochville, Qu, Can. 189/J1
Murdock (pt.), Austl. 172/B1
Mürefte, Turk. 107/H5
Mureş (prov.), Rom. 107/G2
Mureş (riv.), Rom. 107/E2
Muret, Fr. 100/D5
Murfreesboro, Ar, US 187/J4
Murgab (riv.), Turk. 145/G3
Murgap (riv.), Trkm. 122/G6
Murgon, Austl. 172/C4
Muri, Swi. 115/E3
Muri bei Bern, Swi. 114/D4
Muria (riv.), Indo. 138/D5
Muriaé, Braz. 213/D2
Murias de Paredes, Sp. 102/C1
Murici, Braz. 212/C4
Mürİdke, Pak. 144/C4
Müritz (lake), Ger. 98/G2
Murlİganj, India 143/F3
Murmansk, Rus. 118/G1
Murmansk (int'l arpt.), Rus. 118/G1

Murmanskaya Oblast, Rus. 95/J1
Murnau, Ger. 115/H2
Muro, Sp. 103/G3
Muro, Japan 135/K6
Muro Lucano, It. 104/D2
Muros, Sp. 102/A1
Muroto, Japan 132/D4
Muroto-zaki (pt.), Japan 132/D4
Murowana Goślina, Pol. 99/J2
Murphy, NC, US 191/G3
Murphy, Mo, US 195/G9
Murr (riv.), Ger. 112/C5
Murra, Nic. 202/E3
Murramarang NP, Austl. 173/D2
Murray (riv.), Austl. 173/B2
Murray, Ky, US 188/B4
Murray (lake), SC, US 191/H3
Murray, Ut, US 195/K12
Murray Bridge, Austl. 171/H5
Murraysburg, SAfr. 164/C3
Murrayville, Austl. 173/B2
Murree, Pak. 144/B3
Murrieta, Ca, US 194/C3
Murrieta Hot Springs, Ca, US 194/C3
Murrumbidgee (riv.), Austl. 173/C2
Murrumburrah, Austl. 173/C2
Murrurundi, Austl. 173/D1
Murshidābād, India 143/G3
Murtala Muhammed (int'l arpt.), Nga. 161/F5
Murtaröl (peak), Swi. 115/G4
Murten, Swi. 114/D4
Murtoa, Austl. 173/B3
Murud (peak), Malay. 138/D3
Murupara, NZ 175/T10
Mururoa (isl.), FrPol. 175/M7
Murwāra, India 142/C4
Murwillumbah, Austl. 172/D5
Mürz (riv.), Aus. 99/H5
Mürzzuschlag, Aus. 99/H5
Muş (riv.), Turk. 148/E2
Muş, Turk. 148/E2
Musabeyli, Turk. 149/E1
Musāfirkhāna, India 142/C2
Musala (peak), Bul. 107/F4
Musan, NKor. 131/E1
Musashino, Japan 135/D2
Musconetcong (riv.), NJ, US 196/C2
Muscoot (res.), NY, US 197/E1
Muscoy, Ca, US 194/C2
Musekwapoort (pass), SAfr. 163/E5
Museum of Flight, Wa, US 193/C2
Musgrave (ranges), Austl. 171/F3
Musgrave Harbour, Nf, Can. 189/L1
Mushābani, India 143/F4
Mushie, D.R. Congo 154/J8
Mushin, Nga. 161/F5
Mushkī (riv.), Indo. 138/B4
Musile di Piave, It. 117/F1
Musinga (peak), Col. 210/B3
Muskego, Wi, US 193/P14
Muskegon, Mi, US 188/C3
Muskegon (riv.), Mi, US 188/C3
Muskingum (riv.), Oh, US 188/D4
Muskoka (lake), On, Can. 188/E2
Musoma, Tanz. 162/B3
Musone (riv.), It. 117/G6
Musquaro (lake), Qu, Can. 189/J1
Musselburgh, Sc, UK 94/C5
Musselshell (riv.), Mt, US 184/F4
Mussomeli, It. 104/C4
Musson, Belg. 111/E4
Mussoorie, India 142/D2
Mustafakemalpaşa, Turk. 148/B1
Mustang, Ok, US 195/M15
Müstair, Swi. 115/G4
Musters (lake), Arg. 216/C3
Musu-dan (pt.), NKor. 131/E2
Müt, Egypt 159/B3
Mut, Turk. 149/C1
Mutá, Ponta do (pt.), Braz. 212/C4
Mutare, Zim. 163/F4
Muthill, Sc, UK 94/C4
Mutis (peak), Indo. 139/F5
Mutsamudu, Com. 165/H6
Mutsu (bay), Japan 134/B3
Mutsu, Japan 134/B3

Mutsuzawa, Japan 135/E3
Muttekopf (peak), Aus. 115/G3
Muttenz, Swi. 114/D2
Mutters, Aus. 115/H3
Mutterstadt, Ger. 112/B4
Muttler (peak), Swi. 115/G4
Muttonville, Mi, US 193/G6
Mutum, Braz. 213/D1
Mutsu, Japan 132/D4
Müynoq, Uzb. 121/L4
Muzaffargarh, Pak. 144/A4
Muzaffarnagar, India 144/D5
Muzaffarpur, India 143/E2
Muzambinho, Braz. 213/G6
Muzon (cape), Ak, US 192/M4
Muztag (peak), China 128/D4
Muztagata (peak), China 145/G5
Muzzana del Turgnano, It. 117/G1
Mwadui, Tanz. 162/B3
Mwana (cape), Kenya 162/D3
Mwanza (pol. reg.), Tanz. 162/B3
Mwanza, Tanz. 162/B3
Mweelrea (peak), Ire. 89/P10
Mweka, D.R. Congo 163/D1
Mwene-Ditu, D.R. Congo 163/D2
Mwense, Zam. 162/A5
Mweru (lake), D.R. Congo 163/E2
Mweru-Wantipa NP, Zam. 162/A5
Mwesi (mtn.), Tanz. 162/A4
My Son Temples (ruin), Viet. 136/E3
My Tho, Viet. 136/D4
Myall Lakes NP, Austl. 173/E2
Myanaung, Myan. 141/G4
Myanmar (Burma) (ctry.) 141/G3
Myebon, Myan. 141/F3
Myerstown, Pa, US 196/B3
Myggenäs, Swe. 96/D2
Myingyan, Myan. 141/G3
Myitkyinā, Myan. 141/G2
Myjava, Slvk. 99/J4
Mykolayiv, Ukr. 107/L2
Mykolayiv (int'l arpt.), Ukr. 107/L2
Mykolayivs'ka Oblasti, Ukr. 120/D3
Mylau, Ger. 113/F1
Mymensingh (pol. reg.), Bang. 143/H3
Mynämäki, Fin. 97/J1
Mynydd Eppynt (mts.), Wal, UK 90/C2
Mynydd Pencarreg (peak), Wal, UK 90/B2
Mynydd Preseli (mtn.), Wal, UK 90/B3
Myŏgi, Japan 135/B1
Myohaung, Myan. 141/F3
Myŏkō-san (peak), Japan 133/F2
Myŏngch'ŏn, NKor. 131/E2
Myrhorod, Ukr. 120/E2
Myrtle Beach, SC, US 191/J3
Myrtle Creek, Or, US 184/C5
Myrtleford, Austl. 173/C3
Mysen, Nor. 96/D2
Myślenice, Pol. 99/K4
Myślibórz, Pol. 99/H2
Myslivna (peak), Czh. 113/H5
Mysore, India 140/C5
Mystery Bay Rec. Area, NJ, US 196/D4
Mystic Island, NJ, US 196/D4
Myszków, Pol. 99/K3
Mytishchi, Rus. 119/W9
Mže (riv.), Czh. 98/G4
Mzimba, Malw. 162/B5
Mzuzu, Malw. 162/B5

N

Na (riv.), Viet. 136/C1
Naab (riv.), Ger. 101/J2
Naaldwijk, Neth. 108/B4
Naalehu, Hi, US 182/U11
Naama (prov.), Alg. 157/E2
Naantali, Fin. 97/K1
Naarden, Neth. 108/C4
Narim im Machlande, Aus. 113/H6
Naas, Ire. 89/Q10
Nababeep, SAfr. 164/B3
Nabari, Japan 135/K6
Nabari (riv.), Japan 135/K6
Nabberu (lake), Austl. 170/C3
Nabburg, Ger. 113/F4
Naberezhnye Chelny, Rus. 119/M5
Nabeul, Tun. 104/B4
Nabeul (gov.), Tun. 104/B4
Nābha, India 144/D4
Nabiac, Austl. 173/E2
Nabisipi (riv.), Qu, Can. 189/J1
Nabón, Ecu. 214/B1
Nabua, Phil. 137/D5

Nacala, Moz. 163/H3
Nacaome, Hon. 202/E3
Nachi-Katsuura, Japan 132/D4
Nachingwea, Tanz. 162/C5
Nāchod, Czh. 99/J3
Nachrodt-Wiblingwerde, Ger. 109/E6
Nacimiento, Chile 216/B3
Naco, Mex. 200/C2
Nacogdoches, Tx, US 187/J5
Nácori Chico, Mex. 200/C2
Nacozari de García, Mex. 200/C2
Nādbai, India 142/A2
Nadder (riv.), Eng, UK 90/D4
Nadiād, India 147/K4
Nādlac, Rom. 106/E2
Nador (prov.), Mor. 158/C2
Nador, Mor. 158/C2
Nadur, Malta 104/L6
Nadvirna, Ukr. 107/G1
Nærbø, Nor. 96/B2
Næstved, Den. 96/D4
Nafada, Nga. 161/H4
Nafels, Swi. 115/F3
Nafüsah, Jabal (mts.), Libya 157/H3
Naga, Phil. 137/D5
Nagagami (riv.), On, Can. 188/C1
Nagahama, Japan 132/C4
Nagahama, Japan 135/K5
Nagai, Japan 133/G1
Nagaizumi, Japan 135/B3
Nagakute, Japan 135/M5
Nāgāland (state), India 141/F2
Nagambie, Austl. 173/C3
Nagano, Japan 133/F2
Nagano (pref.), Japan 133/E3
Nagaoka, Japan 133/F2
Nagaokakyō, Japan 135/J6
Nagaon (Nowgong), India 141/F2
Nagar, India 142/A2
Nagara (riv.), Japan 133/E3
Nagara, Japan 135/D3
Nagareyama, Japan 135/D2
Nāgārjuna Sāgar (res.), India 140/C4
Nagarote, Nic. 198/D5
Nagarzê, China 143/H1
Nagas (pt.), BC, Can. 192/M5
Nagasaki, Japan 132/A4
Nagasaki (int'l arpt.), Japan 132/A4
Nagasaki (pref.), Japan 132/A4
Nagasaki Peace, Japan 132/A4
Nagashima, Japan 135/L5
Nagato, Japan 132/B3
Nagato, Japan 135/A1
Nagatoro, Japan 135/C1
Nagaur, India 147/K3
Nāgercoil, India 140/C6
Nagina, India 142/B1
Nago, Japan 133/J7
Nago-Torbole, It. 115/G6
Nagod, India 142/C3
Nagold (riv.), Ger. 112/B5
Nagold, Ger. 112/B5
Nagorno-Karabakh (prov.), Azer. 121/H5
Nagoya, Japan 135/L5
Nagoya Castle, Japan 135/L5
Nagpula (pass), China 143/F1
Nāgpur, India 147/K4
Nags Head, NC, US 191/K3
Naguri, Japan 135/C2
Nagy-Milic (peak), Hun. 99/L4
Nagyatád, Hun. 106/C2
Nagyecsed, Hun. 99/M5
Nagyhalász, Hun. 106/E1
Nagykanizsa, Hun. 106/C2
Nagykáta, Hun. 73/E1
Nagykőrös, Hun. 106/D2
Naha, Japan 133/J7
Nahal Shillo (riv.), Isr.,WBnk. 149/G7
Nahan, India 144/D4
Nahanni NP, NW, Can. 180/D2
Nahariyya, Isr. 149/D3
Nahāvand, Iran 146/E2
Nahe (riv.), Ger. 101/G2
Nahel Soreq (riv.), Isr. 149/F8
Nahouri (prov.), Burk. 161/E4
Nahr 'Atbarah (riv.), Sudan 155/M4
Nahr Mufjir (riv.), Isr.,WBnk. 149/G7
Nahr Ouassel (riv.), Alg. 158/F5
Nahuel Huapi (lake), Arg. 216/C4
Nahuel Huapi, PN, Arg. 216/C4
Nahuelbuta, PN, Chile 216/A3
Naica, Mex. 200/D3
Naihāti, India 143/G4
Naila, Ger. 113/E3
Naiman Qi, China 130/C2
Nā'īn, Iran 146/F2
Nainital, India 142/B1
Nainpur, India 142/C4

Naintré, Fr. 100/D3
Nairn (riv.), Sc, UK 94/B2
Nairn, Sc, UK 94/C1
Nairne, Austl. 171/M9
Nairobi NP, Kenya 162/C3
Nairobi (cap.), Kenya 162/C3
Naivasha, Kenya 162/C3
Naives-Rosières, Fr. 111/E6
Najafābād, Iran 146/F2
Nájera, Sp. 102/D1
Naju, SKor. 131/D5
Naka, Japan 135/G5
Naka (riv.), Japan 132/D4
Nakadōri (isl.), Japan 132/A4
Nakai, Japan 135/C3
Nakajō, Japan 133/F1
Nakalele (pt.), Hi, US 182/T10
Nakamichi, Japan 135/B2
Nakaminato, Japan 133/G2
Nakamura, Japan 132/C4
Nakano, Japan 133/F2
Nakano (lag.), Japan 132/D4
Nakasato, Japan 134/B3
Nakashibetsu, Japan 134/D2
Nakasongola, Ugan. 162/B2
Nakatane, Japan 133/L5
Nakatomi, Japan 135/A3
Nakatsu, Japan 132/B4
Nakatsugawa, Japan 133/E3
Nakazato, Japan 135/B3
Nakfa, Japan 135/M5
Nakhodka, Rus. 129/P3
Nakhon Nayok, Thai. 136/C3
Nakhon Pathom, Thai. 136/C3
Nakhon Phanom, Thai. 136/D2
Nakhon Ratchasima, Thai. 136/D2
Nakhon Sawan, Thai. 136/C3
Nakhon Si Thammarat, Thai. 136/B4
Nakkila, Fin. 97/J1
Nakło nad Notecią, Pol. 99/J2
Naknek, Ak, US 192/G4
Nakodar, India 144/C4
Nakonde, Zam. 162/B5
Naksan-sa, SKor. 131/E3
Nakskov, Den. 96/D4
Naktong, SKor. 131/E4
Naktong (riv.), SKor. 131/E4
Nakūr, India 144/D5
Nakuru, Kenya 162/C3
Nakusp, BC, Can. 184/D3
Nāl (riv.), Pak. 147/J3
Nalayh, Mong. 128/J2
Nalbach, Ger. 111/F5
Nalbāri, India 143/F2
Nalbaugh NP, Austl. 173/D3
Nal'chik (int'l arpt.), Rus. 121/G4
Nal'chik, Rus. 121/G4
Nalgonda, India 140/C4
Nalhāti, India 143/F3
Naliya, India 147/J4
Nallıhan, Turk. 107/K5
Nalón (riv.), Sp. 102/C1
Nālūt, Libya 157/H3
Nam (riv.), NKor. 131/D3
Nam Dinh, Viet. 141/J3
Nam Nao NP, Thai. 136/C2
Nam Un (res.), Thai. 136/C2
Namakzār-e Shadād (salt pan), Iran 147/G2
Namangan (pol. reg.), Uzb. 145/F4
Namangan, Uzb. 145/F4
Namaqualand (reg.), SAfr. 164/B3
Namaripi (cape), Indo. 139/J4
Namasagali, Ugan. 162/B2
Namatanai, PNG 174/E5
Namborn, Ger. 111/G4
Nambour, Austl. 172/D4
Nambucca Heads, Austl. 173/E1
Nambung NP, Austl. 170/B4
Namdae (riv.), NKor. 131/E2
Namdalseid, Nor. 95/D2
Namegawa, Japan 135/C1
Namekagon (riv.), Wi, US 185/L4
Namentenga (prov.), Burk. 161/E4
Namerikawa, Japan 133/F2
Nametil, Moz. 163/G4
Namhae, SKor. 131/D5
Namhae (isl.), SKor. 131/D5
Namib (des.), Namb. 163/B5
Namibe, Ang. 163/B4
Namibia (ctry.) 163/C5
Namie, Japan 133/G2
Namioka, Japan 134/B3
Namja (pass), Nepal 140/D2
Namjagbarwa (peak), China 141/G2
Namling, China 140/D2
Namloser Wetterspitze (peak), Aus. 115/G3
Nammoku, Japan 135/B1
Namnoi (peak), Myan. 136/B4
Namonuito (isl.), Micr. 174/D4
Namorik (isl.), Mrsh. 174/F4
Namp'o, NKor. 131/D3
Namp'o, Ecu.,Peru 210/B5
Nampula, Moz. 163/G4
Namsê (pass), China 140/D2
Namsos, Nor. 95/D2

Namu (isl.), Mrsh. 174/F4
Namur (prov.), Belg. 111/D3
Namur, Belg. 111/D3
Namwŏn, SKor. 131/D5
Namysłów, Pol. 99/J3
Nan (riv.), Thai. 141/H4
Nan, Thai. 136/C2
Nanae, Japan 134/B3
Nanango, Austl. 172/D4
Nanao, Japan 133/E2
Nanauta, India 144/D5
Nancha, China 129/N2
Nanchang, China 137/C2
Nanchang, China 137/C2
Nancheng, China 137/C3
Nanchong, China 128/J5
Nancy, Fr. 111/F6
Nanda Devi (peak), India 128/C5
Nandan, China 141/J3
Nānded, India 140/C4
Nanding (riv.), China 141/G3
Nandrin, Belg. 111/E3
Nandu (riv.), China 137/A4
Nandurbār, India 147/K4
Nandyāl, India 140/C4
Nanfeng, China 137/C2
Nang Xian, China 141/F2
Nanga Parbat (peak), Pak. 144/C2
Nangapinoh, Indo. 138/D4
Nangis, Fr. 88/M6
Nangnim (mts.), NKor. 131/D2
Nangong, China 130/C3
Nangtud (mt.), Phil. 139/F1
Nangwarry, Austl. 173/B3
Nanhui, China 130/L8
Nanjian Yizu Zizhixian, China 141/H2
Nanjing, China 130/L8
Nankāna Sāhib, Pak. 144/B4
Nankang, China 137/B2
Nankoku, Japan 132/C4
Nanle, China 130/C3
Nanliu (riv.), China 141/J3
Nannestad, Nor. 96/D1
Nanning, China 141/J3
Nannup, Austl. 170/B5
Nanpi, China 130/D3
Nanping, China 137/C2
Nansei (riv.), Japan 135/L7
Nansen (sound), Nun., Can. 181/T6
Nant (lake), Sc, UK 94/A4
Nantai-san (peak), Japan 133/F2
Nanterre, Fr. 88/J5
Nanteuil-le-Haudouin, Fr. 88/K4
Nanteuil-lès-Meaux, Fr. 88/L6
Nanticoke, On, Can. 188/D3
Nanticoke, Pa, US 196/B1
Nanton, Ab, Can. 184/E3
Nantong, China 137/D1
Nantua, Fr. 114/B4
Nantucket (isl.), Ma, US 189/G3
Nantwich, Eng, UK 93/F5
Nanuet, NY, US 197/J9
Nanumanga (isl.), Tuv. 174/G5
Nanumea (isl.), Tuv. 174/G5
Nanuque, Braz. 212/B5
Nanxi, China 130/C4
Nanxiong, China 137/B3
Nanyang, China 130/C4
Nanyuki, Kenya 162/C3
Nanzhang, China 130/C5
Nao, Cabo de la (cape), Sp. 103/F3
Naococane (lake), Qu, Can. 181/J3
Naogaon, Bang. 143/G3
Naokot, Pak. 140/A3
Naolinco, Mex. 201/N7
Naoua (falls), C.d'Iv. 161/E4
Naousa, Gre. 105/H2
Náoussa, Gre. 105/J4
Napa, Ca, US 193/K10
Napa (co.), Ca, US 193/K10
Napa (riv.), Ca, US 193/K10
Napa (valley), Ca, US 193/K10
Napa Junction, Ca, US 193/K10
Napak (peak), Ugan. 162/B2
Napanee, On, Can. 188/E2
Napaskiak, Ak, US 192/F3
Napf (peak), Swi. 114/D4
Napier, NZ 175/T10
Napier, SAfr. 164/L11
Naples (Napoli), It. 104/D2
Napo (prov.), Ecu. 210/B5
Napo (riv.), Ecu.,Peru 210/B5
Napoléon, ND, US 185/J4
Napoleon, Oh, US 188/D3
Napoleonville, La, US 187/K5

Napoli, Golfo di (gulf), It. 104/C2
Napuka (isl.), FrPol. 175/L6
Naqil Sumārah (pass), Yem. 146/D6
Nara, Mali 160/D3
Nāra (riv.), Pak. 147/J4
Nara, Japan 135/J6
Nara (riv.), Japan 132/D4
Naracoorte, Austl. 173/B3
Naraini, India 142/C3
Naranbulag, Mong. 128/F2
Naranjal, Ecu. 214/B1
Naranjito, Ecu. 214/B1
Naranjos, Mex. 202/B1
Narāq, Iran 146/F2
Narasannapeta, India 140/D4
Narashino, Japan 135/E2
Narathiwat, Thai. 136/C5
Nārāyanganj, Bang. 143/H4
Nārāyani (zone), Nepal 143/E2
Nārāyani, Nepal 143/E2
Nārāyanpet, India 140/C4
Narbonne, Fr. 100/E5
Narceo (riv.), Sp. 102/B1
Nardò, It. 105/F2
Nare (pt.), Eng, UK 90/B6
Narellan, Austl. 172/G9
Narembeen, Austl. 170/C5
Nares (str.), Can.,Grld. 181/T6
Narew (riv.), Pol. 118/D5
Narganá, Pan. 203/G4
Narinda (bay), Madg. 165/H6
Nariño (dept.), Col. 210/B4
Narita (int'l arpt.), Japan 133/G3
Narita, Japan 135/E2
Nariz (peak), Chile 217/C7
Narkatiāganj, India 143/E2
Narmada (riv.), India 140/C3
Narman, Turk. 121/G4
Narni, It. 104/C1
Narodnaya (peak), Rus. 119/P2
Narok, Kenya 162/B3
Narón, Sp. 102/A1
Narooma, Austl. 173/D3
Nārowāl, Pak. 144/C3
Nærøy, Nor. 95/D2
Narra, Phil. 139/E2
Narrabri, Austl. 173/C1
Narrandera, Austl. 173/C2
Narrogin, Austl. 170/C5
Narromine, Austl. 173/C2
Narva (res.), Est.,Rus. 118/F4
Narva (riv.), Est.,Rus. 97/M2
Narvacan, Phil. 137/D4
Narvik, Nor. 95/F1
Narwāna, India 144/D5
Nar'yan-Mar, Rus. 119/M2
Naryn (obl.), Kyr. 145/G4
Naryn (riv.), Kyr. 145/G4
Naryn, Kyr. 122/H5
Naryn Qum (plain), Kaz. 121/J2
Narzole, It. 116/A3
Näsäud, Rom. 107/G2
Naschel, Arg. 216/D2
Nash (pt.), Wal, UK 90/C4
Nashua, NH, US 189/G3
Nashville (int'l arpt.), Tn, US 188/C4
Nashville (cap.), Tn, US 188/C4
Našice, Cro. 106/D3
Nasielsk, Pol. 99/L2
Nasijärvi (lake), Fin. 97/K1
Naso (pt.), Phil. 139/F1
Nāsirābād, India 147/K3
Näsriganj, India 143/E3
Nass (riv.), BC, Can. 192/N4
Nassarawa (state), Nga. 161/G4
Nassau (cap.), Bahm. 199/F2
Nassau (bay), Chile 217/D7
Nassau (isl.), Cooks. 175/J6
Nassau, Ger. 111/G3
Nassau, De, US 196/C6
Nassau (co.), NY, US 197/E2
Nasser (lake), Egypt 159/C4
Nässereith, Aus. 115/G3
Nässjö, Swe. 96/F3
Nassogne, Belg. 111/E3
Nastapoka (isls.), Qu, Can. 181/J3
Nastätten, Ger. 111/G3
Næstved, Den. 96/D4
Nasu-dake (peak), Japan 133/F2
Nata, Bots. 163/E5
Natá, Pan. 210/A2
Natagaima, Col. 210/B4

Natal, Braz. 212/D2
Naţanz, Iran 146/F2
Natashō, Japan 135/J5
Natashquan (riv.), Qu, Can. 181/K3
Natchez, Ms, US 187/K5
Natchez Trace Nat'l Parkway, US 188/D2
Natchitoches, La, US 187/J5
Naters, Swi. 114/D5
Näthdwāra, India 147/K4
Natimuk, Austl. 173/B3
Nation (riv.), BC, Can. 184/B2
National Agriculture Research Center, Md, US 196/B6
National Aquarium, Md, US 196/B5
National Archaeological Museum, Gre. 105/N8
National City, Ca, US 194/C5
National Cowboy Hall of Fame and Western Heritage Center, Ok, US 195/N14
National Exhibition Centre, Eng, UK 91/E2
National Institutes of Health, Md, US 196/A6
National Museum, Mona. 116/J8
National Security Agency, Md, US 196/B5
Natitingou, Ben. 161/F4
Natl, Jor. 149/D4
Natron (lake), Tanz. 162/B3
Natternbach, Aus. 113/G6
Nattheim, Ger. 112/D5
Nättraby, Swe. 96/F3
Natuna (isls.), Indo. 138/C3
Natural Bridge Caverns, Tx, US 195/U20
Natural Bridges Nat'l Mon., Ut, US 186/E3
Naturaliste (cape), Austl. 173/D4
Naturaliste (chan.), Austl. 170/B3
Naturaliste (cape), Austl. 170/B5
Naturno (Naturns), It. 115/G4
Naucalpan, Mex. 201/Q10
Naucelle, Fr. 100/E4
Nauders, Aus. 115/G4
Naudesnek (pass), SAfr. 164/E3
Nauen, Ger. 98/P6
Naugachhia, India 143/F3
Naugaon Sādāt, India 142/B1
Nauhcampatépetl (vol.), Mex. 201/M7
Nauheim, Ger. 112/B3
Naujan, Phil. 137/D5
Naujoji-Akmenė, Lith. 97/K3
Naumburg, Ger. 109/G6
Naumburg, Ger. 98/F3
Nauort, Ger. 111/G3
Naʿūr, Jor. 149/D4
Nauru (ctry.) 174/F5
Nāushahra, India 144/C3
Naushahra Virkhan, Pak. 144/B4
Nauta, Peru 214/C2
Nautla, Mex. 201/N6
Nauvo (Nagu), Fin. 97/J1
Nava, Mex. 201/E2
Nava, Colle di (pass), It. 116/A4
Nava del Rey, Sp. 102/C2
Navajo (res.), NM, US 186/F3
Navajo Nat'l Mon., Az, US 186/E3
Navalcarnero, Sp. 103/M9
Navalmoral de la Mata, Sp. 102/C2
Navalvillar de Pela, Sp. 102/C3
Navapolatsk, Bela. 97/N4
Navarin (cape), Rus. 123/T3
Navarino (isl.), Chile 215/C8
Navarra (aut. comm.), Sp. 102/D1
Navarro, Arg. 217/J11
Navàs, Sp. 103/F2
Navas de San Juan, Sp. 102/D3
Navasota (riv.), Tx, US 201/F2
Navassa (isl.), Myan. 203/H2
Navax (pt.), Eng, UK 90/A6
Nave, It. 116/D1
Navenne, Fr. 114/C2
Navia, Sp. 102/B1
Navia (riv.), Sp. 102/B1
Navidad, Chile 216/N8
Navina, Ok, US 195/N14
Naviraí, Braz. 215/F1
Nävodari, Rom. 107/J3
Navojoa, Mex. 200/C3
Navolato, Mex. 200/D4
Návpaktos, Gre. 105/G3
Návplion, Gre. 105/H4
Navsāri, India 147/K4
Navy Board (inlet), Nun., Can. 181/H1
Navy Yard City, Wa, US 193/B2
Nawābganj, India 142/B1
Nawābganj, India 142/C2
Nawābganj, Bang. 143/F3
Nawābshāh, Pak. 147/J3
Nawāda, India 143/E3

Nawān Jandānwāla, Pak. 144/A3
Nawāshahr, India 144/D4
Nawāshahr, Pak. 144/B2
Nawoiy, Uzb. 145/E4
Nawoiy (pol. reg.), Uzb. 145/D4
Nawş, Ra's (pt.), Oman 147/G5
Naxçivan, Azer. 121/H5
Naxçivan Aut. Rep., Azer. 121/H5
Naxi, China 141/J2
Náxos, Gre. 105/J4
Náxos (isl.), Gre. 105/J4
Nay Pyi Taw (cap.), Myan. 141/G4
Nayarit (state), Mex. 200/D4
Nayong, China 141/J2
Nayoro, Japan 134/C1
Nayramadlin (peak), Mong. 128/G2
Nayzatash (pass), Taj. 145/F5
Nazaré, Braz. 212/G4
Nazaré, Port. 102/A3
Nazaré do Piauí, Braz. 212/B2
Nazaré Paulista, Braz. 213/G8
Nazareth, Pa, US 196/C2
Nazareth, Belg. 110/C2
Nazas (riv.), Mex. 200/D3
Nazas, Mex. 200/D3
Nazca, Peru 214/C4
Naze, Japan 133/K6
Naze, The (pt.), Eng, UK 91/J4
Nazerat (Nazareth), Isr. 149/G6
Nazilli, Turk. 148/B2
Nazrēt, Eth. 155/N6
Nazyvayevsk, Rus. 145/F1
Nchelenge, Zam. 162/A5
Ncheu, Malw. 163/F3
Ndalatando, Ang. 163/B2
Ndali, Ben. 161/F4
Ndele, CAfr. 155/K6
Ndende (isl.), Sol. 174/F6
N'Djamena (cap.), Chad 154/J5
Ndola, Zam. 163/E3
Ndrhamcha (lake), Mrta. 160/B2
Né (riv.), Fr. 100/C4
Néa Alikarnassós, Gre. 105/J5
Néa Ankhíalos, Gre. 105/H3
Néa Artáki, Gre. 105/H3
Néa Ionía, Gre. 105/H3
Néa Ionía, Gre. 105/N8
Néa Ionía, Gre. 105/H2
Néa Kallikrátia, Gre. 105/H2
Néa Kíos, Gre. 105/H4
Néa Mikhanióna, Gre. 105/H2
Néa Moudhaniá, Gre. 105/H2
Néa Potídhaia, Gre. 105/H2
Néa Tríglia, Gre. 105/H2
Néa Zíkhni, Gre. 105/H2
Neagh (lake), NI, UK 92/B2
Neale (lake), Austl. 171/F3
Neales (riv.), Austl. 171/G3
Neamţ (prov.), Rom. 107/H2
Neaophli-le-Château, Fr. 88/H5
Neápolis, Gre. 105/H4
Neápolis, Gre. 105/G4
Neápolis, Gre. 105/J5
Near (isls.), Ak, US 192/A5
Neath, Wal, UK 90/C3
Neath (riv.), Wal, UK 90/C3
Neath Port Talbot (co.), Wal, UK 90/C3
Neavitt, Md, US 196/B6
Nebbi, Ugan. 162/A2
Nebel-Horn (peak), Ger. 115/G3
Nebikon, Swi. 114/D3
Nebitdag, Trkm. 121/K5
Neblina (peak), Braz. 211/E4
Nebo (mt.), Austl. 172/E6
Nebraska (state), US 187/G2
Nebrodi (mts.), It. 104/C4
Nechako (riv.), BC, Can. 180/D3
Neches (riv.), Tx, US 190/E4
Nechisar NP, Eth. 155/N6
Nechranice (res.), Czh. 113/G2
Neckar (riv.), Ger. 98/D4
Neckarbischofsheim, Ger. 112/B4
Neckargemünd, Ger. 112/B4
Neckarsteinach, Ger. 112/B4
Neckarsulm, Ger. 112/B4
Necker (isl.), Hi, US 175/J2
Necochea, Arg. 216/F3
Necoclí, Col. 210/C2
Necrópoli (ruin), It. 104/C1
Neda, Sp. 102/A1
Nedelino, Bul. 105/J2
Nedelišće, Cro. 101/M3
Nederland, Tx, US 195/A3
Nederland, Co, US 195/B3
Nederweert, Neth. 108/C6
Neede, Neth. 108/D4
Needles, Ca, US 186/D4
Needles, The, Eng, UK 91/E5
Needmore, Ok, US 195/N15

Neepawa, Mb, Can. 185/J3
Neerabup NP, Austl. 170/K6
Neerpelt, Belg. 108/C6
Neetze (riv.), Ger. 109/H2
Neetze, Ger. 109/H2
Neffelbach (riv.), Ger. 111/F2
Neftekamsk, Rus. 119/M4
Nefud (des.), SAr. 146/D3
Nefyn, Wal, UK 92/D6
Negēlē, Eth. 155/N6
Negev (reg.), Isr. 148/C4
Negoiu (peak), Rom. 107/G3
Negombo, SrL. 140/C6
Negotin, Serb. 106/F3
Negotino, FYROM 105/H2
Negra (pt.), Peru 214/A2
Negra (range), Braz. 212/A3
Negra (pt.), Belz. 202/D2
Negrais (cape), Myan. 141/F4
Negrar, It. 117/D1
Negreira, Sp. 102/A1
Negreşti, Rom. 107/H2
Negritos, Peru 214/A2
Negro (riv.), Arg. 215/D5
Negro (peak), Arg. 216/C3
Negro (riv.), Uru. 215/E3
Negros (isl.), Phil. 137/D6
Nehbandān, Iran 147/H2
Nei Monggol (aut. reg.), China 129/K3
Nei Monggol (plat.), China 129/J3
Neiafu, Tonga 175/H6
Neiba, DRep. 199/G4
Neiba (mts.), DRep. 203/J2
Neiderösterreich (prov.), Aus. 101/L2
Neige, Crêt de la (peak), Fr. 114/B5
Neihuang, China 130/C4
Neijiang, China 128/J6
Neilston, Sc, UK 94/B5
Neiqiu, China 130/C3
Neisse (riv.), Ger. 99/H3
Neiva, Col. 210/C4
Neixiang, China 130/B4
Nejanilini (lake), Mb, Can. 180/G3
Nejdek, Czh. 113/F2
Nejrab (int'l arpt.), Syria 149/E1
Nek'emtē, Eth. 155/N6
Nekso, Den. 96/F4
Nelas, Port. 102/B2
Nelidovo, Rus. 118/G4
Nellingen, Ger. 112/C5
Nellore, India 140/C5
Nelson (cape), Austl. 173/B3
Nelson (isl.), Ak, US 192/E3
Nelson (str.), Chile 215/A7
Nelson, BC, Can. 184/D3
Nelson, NZ 175/S11
Nelson (riv.), Mb, Can. 180/G3
Nelson, Eng, UK 93/F4
Nelson-Atkins Museum of Fine Art, Mo, US 195/D5
Nelson Bay, Austl. 173/E2
Nelson Lagoon, Ak, US 192/F4
Nelson Lakes NP, NZ 175/S11
Nelspruit, SAfr. 163/F6
Néma, Mrta. 160/D2
Néma, Dhar (cliff), Mrta. 160/D2
Neman, Rus. 99/M1
Nembro, It. 116/C1
Neméa, Gre. 105/H4
Nemingha, Austl. 173/D1
Nemira (peak), Rom. 107/H2
Nemours, Fr. 100/E2
Nemunas (riv.), Lith. 97/K4
Nemuro, Japan 134/D2
Nemuro (pen.), Japan 134/D2
Nen (riv.), China 129/M2
Nenagh, Ire. 89/P10
Nenana, Ak, US 192/J3
Nendaz, Swi. 114/D5
Nene (riv.), Eng, UK 93/J6
Nenetskiy Aut. Okrug, Rus. 119/L2
Nenjiang, China 129/N2
Nentershausen, Ger. 109/G6
Nentershausen, Ger. 111/G3
Nenzing, Aus. 115/F3
Neo Volcanica, Cordillera (mts.), Mex. 201/Q10
Néon Petrítsion, Gre. 105/H2
Neoria Husainpur, India 142/B1
Néos Marmarás, Gre. 105/H2
Neosho (riv.), Ks,Ok, US 187/J3
Nepal (ctry.) 142/D1
Nepālganj, Nepal 142/C1
Nepanagar, India 147/L4
Nepean, On, Can. 188/F2
Nepean (riv.), Austl. 172/G8
Nepean, Peru 214/B3
Nepessina (lake), Mi, US 193/F6
Nephi, Ut, US 186/D4
Nepisiguit (riv.), NB, Can. 189/H2
Nepomuk, Czh. 113/G4

Neptune City, NJ, US 196/D3
Nera (riv.), It. 101/K5
Nérac, Fr. 100/D4
Neratovice, Czh. 113/H2
Nerekhta, Rus. 118/J4
Neresheim, Ger. 112/D5
Neretva (riv.), Bosn. 106/D4
Neris (riv.), Lith. 97/L4
Nerja, Sp. 102/D4
Nermete (pt.), Peru 214/A2
Nerokoúros, Gre. 105/J5
Nerone (peak), It. 117/F5
Nerpio, Sp. 102/D3
Nersingen, Ger. 112/D6
Nerva, Sp. 102/B4
Nervesa della Battaglia, It. 117/F1
Nerviano, It. 116/B1
Nes, Neth. 108/C2
Nes, Nor. 96/D1
Nes Ziyyona, Isr. 149/F8
Nesbyen, Nor. 96/C1
Nesebŭr, Bul. 105/K1
Nesher, Isr. 149/G6
Neskaupstadhur, Ice. 95/Q6
Nesle, Fr. 110/B4
Nesles-la-Vallée, Fr. 88/J4
Nesquehoning, Pa, US 196/C2
Nehbandān, Iran 147/H2
Nei Monggol (aut. reg.), China 129/K3
Nei Monggol (plat.), China 129/J3
Ness (lake), Sc, UK 94/B2
Ness (riv.), Sc, UK 94/B2
Nesselrode (mt.), Ak, US 192/M4
Nesselwang, Ger. 115/G2
Nesslau, Swi. 115/F3
Neston, Eng, UK 93/E5
Nestório, Gre. 105/G2
Néstos (riv.), Gre. 107/G5
Netanya, Isr. 149/F7
Netarhāt, India 143/E4
Netcong, NJ, US 196/D2
Nethe (riv.), Ger. 109/G5
Netherlands (ctry.) 98/C3
Netherlands Antilles (dpcy.), Neth. 199/N8
Netolice, Czh. 113/H4
Netphen, Ger. 111/H2
Netstal, Swi. 96/D4
Nette (riv.), Ger. 108/D6
Nettebach (riv.), Ger. 111/G3
Nettersheim, Ger. 111/F3
Nettetal, Ger. 108/D6
Nettilling (lake), Nun., Can. 181/J2
Nettuno, It. 104/C2
Netzschkau, Ger. 113/F1
Neu Darchau, Ger. 109/H2
Neu-Isenburg, Ger. 112/B2
Neu-Ulm, Ger. 112/D6
Neu Zittau, Ger. 98/O7
Neubiberg, Ger. 113/E6
Neubrandenburg, Ger. 99/G2
Neubulach, Ger. 112/B5
Neuburg, Ger. 112/B5
Neuburg an der Donau, Ger. 112/E5
Neuburg an der Kammel, Ger. 115/G1
Neuchâtel, Swi. 114/C1
Neuchâtel (canton), Swi. 114/C1
Neuchâtel, Lac de (lake), Swi. 101/L3
Neuenbürg, Ger. 112/B5
Neuenburg am Rhein, Ger. 114/D2
Neuendettelsau, Ger. 112/D4
Neuenhagen, Ger. 98/O6
Neuenhaus, Ger. 108/D3
Neuenkirchen, Ger. 109/F3
Neuenkirchen, Ger. 109/F3
Neuenkirchen, Ger. 109/H2
Neuenrade, Ger. 109/E6
Neuenstadt am Kocher, Ger. 112/C4
Neuenstein, Ger. 112/C4
Neuerburg, Ger. 111/F3
Neuf-Brisach, Fr. 114/D1
Neufahrn bei Freising, Ger. 113/E6
Neufchâteau, Fr. 114/B1
Neufchâteau, Belg. 111/E4
Neufchâtel-en-Bray, Fr. 100/D2
Neufchâtel-Hardelot, Fr. 110/A2
Neufchelles, Fr. 88/M4
Neufmanil, Fr. 111/D4
Neufmoutiers-en-Brie, Fr. 88/L5
Neuhaus am Inn, Ger. 113/G6
Neuhaus am Rennweg, Ger. 112/E1
Neuhaus-Schierschnitz, Ger. 112/E1
Neuhäusel, Ger. 111/G3
Neuhausen am Rheinfall, Swi. 115/E2
Neuhof, Ger. 112/C2
Neuhof an der Zenn, Ger. 112/D4
Neuhofen, Ger. 112/B4
Neuhofen an der Krems, Aus. 113/H6
Neuilly-en-Thelle, Fr. 110/B5
Neuilly-l'Evêque, Fr. 114/B2
Neuilly-sur-Marne, Fr. 88/K5
Neuilly-sur-Seine, Fr. 88/J5
Neukirchen, Ger. 96/C4

Neukirchen an der Vöckla, Aus. 113/G6
Neukirchen vorm Wald, Ger. 113/G5
Neumarkt (Enga), It. 115/H5
Neumarkt im Mühlkreis, Aus. 113/H6
Neumarkt in der Oberpfalz, Ger. 113/E4
Neumarkt-Sankt Veit, Ger. 113/F6
Neumünster, Ger. 96/C4
Neunkirch, Swi. 115/E2
Neunkirchen, Aus. 101/M3
Neunkirchen, Ger. 111/H2
Neunkirchen, Ger. 111/H2
Neunkirchen, Ger. 111/G5
Neunkirchen-Seelscheid, Ger. 111/G2
Neupotz, Ger. 112/B4
Neuquén (riv.), Arg. 215/C4
Neuquén, Arg. 216/C3
Neuquén (prov.), Arg. 216/C3
Neuruppin, Ger. 98/G2
Neusäss, Ger. 112/D6
Neuse (riv.), NC, US 191/J3
Neusiedl am See, Aus. 101/M3
Neusiedler (lake), Aus. 99/J5
Neusiedler See (lake), Aus. 106/C2
Neuss, Ger. 108/D6
Neustadt am Rübenberge, Ger. 109/G3
Neustadt an der Aisch, Ger. 112/D3
Neustadt an der Donau, Ger. 113/E5
Neustadt an der Waldnaab, Ger. 113/F3
Neustadt an der Weinstrasse, Ger. 112/B4
Neustadt bei Coburg, Ger. 112/E2
Neustadt in Holstein, Ger. 96/D4
Neustift im Stubaital, Aus. 115/H3
Neustrelitz, Ger. 98/G2
Neutraubling, Ger. 113/F5
Neuves-Maisons, Fr. 100/F4
Neuvic, Fr. 100/E4
Neuville-sur-Saône, Fr. 114/A6
Neuwied, Ger. 111/G3
Neuzelle, Ger. 99/H2
Neva (riv.), Rus. 97/P2
Nevada (state), US 186/C3
Nevada, Mo, US 187/J3
Nevada (mts.), Col. 210/C2
Nevada, Sierra (mts.), Sp. 102/D4
Nevado de Colima PN, Mex. 200/D5
Nevado de Toluca, PN, Mex. 201/K7
Nevado del Huila, PN, Col. 208/C3
Nevado, Sierra del (mts.), Arg. 216/C3
Nevel', Rus. 97/N3
Nevele, Belg. 110/C1
Nevel'sk, Rus. 129/R2
Nevers, Fr. 100/E3
Nevinnomyssk, Rus. 121/G3
Nevis (isl.), StK. 199/N8
Nevis (peak), StK. 199/N8
Nevola (riv.), It. 117/G5
Nevşehir (prov.), Turk. 148/C2
Nevşehir, Turk. 148/C2
New (riv.), Guy. 208/G3
New, WV, US 188/D4
New Albany, In, US 188/C4
New Albany, Ms, US 191/F3
New Amsterdam, Guy. 211/G3
New Ancholme (riv.), Eng, UK 93/G5
New Athens, Il, US 195/N14
New Baltimore, Mi, US 193/G6
New Bataan, Phil. 137/E6
New Bedford, Ma, US 189/G3
New Berlin, Tx, US 195/U21
New Berlin, Pa, US 196/B2
New Berlin, Wi, US 193/P14
New Berlinville, Pa, US 196/C3
New Bern, NC, US 191/J3
New Braunfels, Tx, US 195/U20
New Britain, Ct, US 189/F3
New Britain (isl.), PNG 174/D5
New Britain, Pa, US 196/C3
New Brunswick (prov.), Can. 189/H2
New Brunswick, NJ, US 197/H10
New Buffalo, Pa, US 196/B3
New Buildings, NI, UK 92/A2
New Caledonia (isl.), NCal., Fr. 174/F7
New Caledonia (terr.), NCal., Fr. 174/F6

New Canaan, Ct, US 197/M7
New Castle, De, US 196/C4
New Castle (co.), De, US 196/C4
New Castle, In, US 188/D4
New Castle, Pa, US 188/D3
New Chicago, In, US 193/R16
New City, NY, US 197/K7
New Columbia, Pa, US 196/B1
New Columbus, Pa, US 196/B1
New Cumberland, Pa, US 196/B3
New Cumnock, Sc, UK 94/B6
New Delhi (cap.), India 144/D5
New Denver, BC, Can. 184/D3
New Egypt, NJ, US 196/D3
New England NP, Austl. 173/E1
New Freedom, Pa, US 196/B4
New Galloway, Sc, UK 92/D1
New Georgia (isls.), Sol. 174/E5
New Georgia (sound), Sol. 174/E5
New Glasgow, NS, Can. 189/J2
New Glasgow, Qu, Can. 189/N6
New Gretna, NJ, US 196/D4
New Guinea (isl.), Indo.,PNG 174/C5
New Hampshire (state), US 189/G2
New Hanover, SAfr. 165/E2
New Hanover, Il, US 195/G9
New Hanover (isl.), PNG 174/D5
New Haven, Ct, US 189/F3
New Haven, Mi, US 193/G6
New Hebrides (isls.), Van. 174/F6
New Holland, Pa, US 196/B3
New Hope, Pa, US 196/D3
New Hyde Park, NY, US 197/L9
New Iberia, La, US 187/K5
New Ireland (isl.), PNG 174/E5
New Jersey (state), US 196/D3
New Kensington, Pa, US 188/E3
New Kowloon, China 129/U10
New Lenox, Il, US 193/Q16
New Lisbon, NJ, US 196/D4
New Liskeard, On, Can. 188/E2
New London, Ct, US 189/F3
New Madrid, Mo, US 187/K3
New Market, Md, US 196/A5
New Meadows, Id, US 184/D4
New Mexico (state), US 186/G4
New Milford, NJ, US 197/J8
New Mills, Eng, UK 93/F5
New Norfolk, Austl. 173/C4
New Orleans, La, US 195/P17
New Orleans (Moisant Field), La, US 195/P17
New Oxford, Pa, US 196/A4
New Philadelphia, Oh, US 188/D3
New Philadelphia, Pa, US 196/B2
New Pitsligo, Sc, UK 94/D1
New Plymouth, NZ 175/S10
New Port Richey, Fl, US 191/H4
New Providence (isl.), Bahm. 199/F3
New Providence, NJ, US 197/H9
New Richmond, Qu, Can. 189/H1
New River (mts.), Az, US 195/R18
New River, Az, US 195/R18
New Rochelle, NY, US 197/K8
New Rockford, ND, US 185/J4
New Romney, Eng, UK 91/G5
New Ross, Ire. 89/Q10
New Rossington, Eng, UK 93/G5
New Sarpy, La, US 195/P17
New Schwabenland (phys. reg.), Ant. 218/Z
New Siberian (isls.), Rus. 125/N2
New Smyrna Beach, Fl, US 191/H4
New South Wales, Austl. 173/D1
New South Wales (state), Austl. 173/C2

New Stuyahok, Ak, US 192/G4
New Town, ND, US 185/H4
New Tripoli, Pa, US 196/C2
New Ulm, Mn, US 185/K4
New Waterford, NS, Can. 189/J2
New Westminster, BC, Can. 184/C3
New Windsor, Md, US 196/A4
New York (state), US 188/G3
New York, NY, US 197/K9
New Zealand (ctry.) 175/S10
Newark, Oh, US 188/D3
Newark, De, US 196/C4
Newark (int'l arpt.), NJ, US 197/J9
Newark, NJ, US 197/J9
Newark, Ca, US 193/K11
Newark (bay), NJ, US 197/J9
Newark-on-Trent, Eng, UK 93/H5
Newberry, In, US 195/G8
Newberry, SC, US 191/H3
Newberry, Mi, US 188/C2
Newberry Nat'l Volcanic Mon., Or, US 184/C5
Newburgh, Sc, UK 94/C4
Newburgh, Eng, UK 91/E4
Newburn, Eng, UK 93/G2
Newcastle, Austl. 173/D2
Newcastle, SAfr. 165/E2
Newcastle, Ire. 92/B5
Newcastle, Indo. 139/H5
Newcastle, Ok, US 195/M15
Newcastle, NI, UK 92/C3
Newcastle (int'l arpt.), Eng, UK 93/G1
Newcastle, Wy, US 185/G5
Newcastle-under-Lyme, Eng, UK 93/F6
Newcastle upon Tyne, Eng, UK 93/G2
Newcastle upon Tyne (co.), Eng, UK 93/G1
Newcastleton, Sc, UK 93/F1
Newe Yam, Isr. 149/F6
Newel, Ger. 111/F4
Newell, Austl. 172/B2
Newenham (cape), Ak, US 192/F4
Newfane, NY, US 189/S9
Newfield, NJ, US 196/C4
Newfoundland (isl.), Can. 189/L1
Newfoundland, NJ, US 197/H7
Newfoundland, Pa, US 196/C1
Newfoundland and Labrador (prov.), Can. 181/K3
Newhalen, Ak, US 192/H4
Newham (bor.), Eng, UK 88/D2
Newhaven, Eng, UK 91/F5
Newington, Eng, UK 88/F3
Newkirk, Ok, US 187/H3
Newllano, La, US 187/J5
Newmains, Sc, UK 94/C5
Newman (mt.), Austl. 170/C2
Newman, Austl. 170/C2
Newmarket, On, Can. 188/E2
Newmarket, Eng, UK 91/G2
Newmill, Sc, UK 94/D1
Newnan, Ga, US 191/G3
Newport, Eng, UK 90/D1
Newport, Wal, UK 90/D3
Newport (co.), Wal, UK 90/D3
Newport, Ar, US 187/K4
Newport (bay), Ca, US 194/C3
Newport, De, US 196/C4
Newport, Ky, US 188/C4
Newport, Or, US 184/B4
Newport, RI, US 189/G3
Newport, Tn, US 188/D5
Newport, Vt, US 189/F2
Newport, Wa, US 184/D3
Newport Beach, Ca, US 194/G8
Newport Meadows (lake), NJ, US 196/D3
Newport-on-Tay, Sc, UK 94/D4
Newport Pagnell, Eng, UK 91/F2
Newquay, Eng, UK 90/A6
Newry (dist.), NI, UK 92/B3
Newry (canal), NI, UK 92/B3
Newton, Tx, US 187/J5
Newton, Ma, US 189/G3
Newton, NJ, US 196/D1
Newton Abbot, Eng, UK 90/C5
Newton-le-Willows, Eng, UK 93/F5
Newton Mearns, Sc, UK 94/B5
Newton Stewart, Sc, UK 92/D2
Newton Tors (hill), Eng, UK 94/D5

Newtonmore, Sc, UK 94/B2
Newtonville, NJ, US 196/D4
Newtown, Austl. 173/B3
Newtown, Wal, UK 90/D1
Newtown, Pa, US 196/D3
Newtown Mount Kennedy, Ire. 92/B5
Newtown Saint Boswells, Sc, UK 94/D5
Newtown Square, Pa, US 196/C4
Newtownabbey, NI, UK 92/C2
Newtownards, NI, UK 92/C2
Newtownhamilton, NI, UK 92/B3
Newtownstewart, NI, UK 92/A2
Newtyle, Sc, UK 94/C3
Nextlalpan, Mex. 201/Q9
Neyagawa, Japan 135/J6
Neyriz, Iran 147/F3
Neyshābūr, Iran 147/G1
Neyva (riv.), Rus. 119/P4
Neyveli, India 140/C5
Neyyāttinkara, India 140/C6
Nezahualcóyotl, Mex. 201/Q10
Neznayka (riv.), Rus. 119/W9
Nezperce, Id, US 184/D4
Ngabang, Indo. 138/C3
Ngabordamlu (cape), Indo. 139/H5
Ngai-Ndethya Nat'l Rsv., Kenya 162/C3
Ngamring, China 143/F1
Nganda (peak), Malw. 162/B5
Ngangerabeli (plain), Kenya 162/C3
Ngaoundéré, Camr. 154/H6
Ngarkat Conservation Park, Austl. 171/J5
Ngatik (isl.), Micr. 174/E4
Ngoan Muc (pass), Viet. 136/E4
Ngoc Linh (peak), Viet. 141/J4
Ngomeni (cape), Kenya 162/D3
Ngong, Kenya 162/C3
Ngonye (falls), Zam. 163/D4
Ngorongoro Consv. Area, Tanz. 162/B3
Ngounié (riv.), Gabon 154/H8
Nguigmi, Niger 154/H5
Ngulu (isl.), Micr. 174/C4
Ngumbe Sukani (pt.), Tanz. 162/C5
Nguru (mts.), Tanz. 162/C4
Ngwenya (peak), Swaz. 165/E2
Nha Trang, Viet. 136/E3
Nhamunda (riv.), Braz. 205/D3
Nhill, Austl. 173/B3
Nhlangano, Swaz. 165/E2
Niagara (falls), Can.,US 189/R9
Niagara (riv.), Can.,US 189/R9
Niagara (co.), On, Can. 189/R9
Niagara Falls, On, Can. 189/R9
Niagara Falls, NY, US 189/R9
Niagara-on-the-Lake, On, Can. 189/R9
Niamey (dept.), Niger 161/F3
Niamey (cap.), Niger 161/F3
Niamey (int'l arpt.), Niger 161/F3
Niamtougou, Togo 161/F3
Niandan (riv.), Afr. 161/G5
Niangara, D.R. Congo 155/L7
Niangay (lake), Mali 154/E4
Niangzi (pass), China 130/C3
Nias (isl.), Indo. 138/A3
Niassa (prov.), Moz. 162/B5
Nicaragua (ctry.) 203/E3
Nicaragua (lake), Nic. 203/E4
Nicastro-Sambiase, It. 104/E3
Nice, Fr. 101/G5
Niceville, Fl, US 191/G4
Nichinan, Japan 132/B5
Nichlaul, India 142/D2
Nicholas (chan.), Bang. 203/F1
Nichols Hills, Ok, US 195/M14
Nicholson (range), Austl. 170/C2
Nickerie (dist.), Sur. 211/G3
Nickerie (riv.), Sur. 211/G3
Nickol (bay), Austl. 170/C2
Nicobar (isls.), India 141/F6
Nicolás Bravo, Mex. 202/D2
Nicolás Romero, Mex. 201/Q9
Nicolet, Qu, Can. 189/F2
Nicolls (pt.), NY, US 197/F2

Nicoma Park, Ok, US 195/N15
Nicosia, It. 104/D4
Nicosia (cap.), Cyp. 149/C2
Nicosia (dist.), Cyp. 149/C2
Nicotera, It. 104/D3
Nicoya, CR 203/E4
Nicoya (gulf), CR 203/E4
Nicoya, Peninsula de (pen.), CR 203/E4
Nidau, Swi. 114/D3
Nidd (riv.), Eng, UK 93/G3
Nidda, Ger. 112/B2
Nidda (riv.), Ger. 98/E3
Niddatal, Ger. 112/B2
Nidder (riv.), Ger. 112/C2
Nideggen, Ger. 111/F2
Nidge (prov.), Turk. 148/C2
Nidwalden (canton), Swi. 115/E4
Nidzica, Pol. 99/L2
Niebüll, Ger. 96/C4
Nied (riv.), Fr. 101/G2
Niedenstein, Ger. 109/G6
Nieder-Olm, Ger. 111/H4
Niederanven, Lux. 111/F4
Niederbipp, Swi. 114/D3
Niederbronn-les-Bains, Fr. 111/G6
Niedere Tauern (mts.), Aus. 101/K3
Niederfischbach, Ger. 111/G2
Niederlausitz (reg.), Ger. 99/G3
Niedernhausen, Ger. 112/B2
Niederösterreich (prov.), Aus. 106/B2
Niedersachsen (state), Ger. 96/C5
Niedersächsisches Wattenmeer NP, Ger. 109/E1
Niedersachswerfen, Ger. 109/H5
Niederstetten, Ger. 112/C4
Niederstotzingen, Ger. 112/D5
Niederurnen, Swi. 115/F3
Niederwerrn, Ger. 112/D2
Niederwinkling, Ger. 113/F5
Niederzier, Ger. 111/F2
Niederzissen, Ger. 111/G3
Niefern-Öschelbronn, Ger. 112/B5
Niegocin (lake), Pol. 97/J5
Nieheim, Ger. 109/G5
Niemodlin, Pol. 99/J3
Nienburg, Ger. 109/G3
Nienhagen, Ger. 109/H3
Niénokoué (peak), C.d'Iv. 160/D5
Nieppe, Fr. 110/B2
Niéri (riv.), Sen. 160/B3
Niers (riv.), Ger. 111/F1
Nierstein, Ger. 112/B3
Niet Ban Tinh Xa, Viet. 136/D4
Nieuw-Amsterdam, Sur. 209/G2
Nieuw-Bergen, Neth. 108/D5
Nieuw-Loosdrecht, Neth. 108/C4
Nieuw-Nickerie, Sur. 211/G3
Nieuw-Schoonebeek, Neth. 108/D3
Nieuw-Vossemeer, Neth. 108/B5
Nieuwe Pekela, Neth. 108/D2
Nieuwegein, Neth. 108/C4
Nieuwerkerk aan de IJssel, Neth. 108/B5
Nieuweschans, Neth. 109/E2
Nieuwkoop, Neth. 108/B4
Nieuwleusen, Neth. 108/D3
Nieuwoudtville, SAfr. 164/B3
Nieuwpoort, Belg. 110/B1
Nieves, Mex. 200/E3
Niğde, Turk. 148/C2
Nigel, SAfr. 164/E2
Niger (ctry.) 154/G4
Niger (delta), Nga. 161/G5
Niger (riv.), Afr. 154/F5
Nigeria (ctry.) 154/G6
Nigg (bay), Sc, UK 94/B1
Nighthawk (lake), On, Can. 188/D1
Nightmute, Ak, US 192/F3
Nigrán, Sp. 102/A1
Nigríta, Gre. 105/H2
Nihoa (isl.), Hi, US 175/J2
Nihonmatsu, Japan 133/G2
Nihtaur, India 142/B1
Nii (isl.), Japan 133/F3
Niigata (int'l arpt.), Japan 133/F2
Niigata, Japan 133/F2
Niigata (pref.), Japan 134/A4
Niihama, Japan 132/C4
Niihari, Japan 135/E1
Niihau (isl.), Hi, US 182/R10
Niimi, Japan 132/C3
Niitsu, Japan 133/F2
Niiza, Japan 135/D2
Níjar, Sp. 102/D4
Nijkerk, Neth. 108/C4
Nijlen, Belg. 111/D1
Nijmegen, Neth. 108/C5
Níkaia, Gre. 105/H3
Nikel', Rus. 95/J1
Nikishka, Ak, US 192/H3
Nikísiani, Gre. 105/J2
Nikki, Ben. 161/F4
Nikkō, Japan 133/F2
Nikkō NP, Japan 133/F2
Niklasdorf, Aus. 101/L3
Nikolai, Ak, US 192/H3
Nikolayevsk-na-Amure, Rus. 123/Q4
Nikol'sk, Rus. 121/H1
Nikolski, Ak, US 192/E5
Nikonga (riv.), Tanz. 162/A3
Nikopol', Ukr. 120/E3
Nikopol, Bul. 107/G4
Niksar, Turk. 120/F4
Nīkshahr, Iran 147/H3
Nikšić, Mont. 106/D4
Nikumaroro (Gardner) (isl.), Kiri. 175/H5
Nikunau (isl.), Kiri. 174/G5
Nile (delta), Egypt 149/B4
Nile (riv.), Afr. 155/M2
Niles, Mi, US 188/C3
Niles, Oh, US 188/D3
Niles, Il, US 193/Q15
Ni'līn, Isr. 149/G8
Nilópolis, Braz. 213/K7
Nilsiä, Fin. 118/F3
Nilvange, Fr. 111/F5
Nīmāj, India 140/B2
Nimba (peak), C.d'Iv. 160/C5
Nimba (co.), Libr. 160/C5
Nîmes, Fr. 100/F5
Nimsbach (riv.), Ger. 111/F4
Nimule NP, Sudan 162/A2
Nin, Cro. 106/B3
Nīnawā (gov.), Iraq 148/E3
Nīnawá (Nineveh) (ruin), Iraq 148/E2
Ninepin Group (isls.), China 129/V11
Ninfas (pt.), Arg. 216/D4
Ning'an, China 129/N3
Ningbo, China 130/E5
Ningde, China 137/C2
Ningdu, China 137/C2
Ninggang, China 141/K2
Ninghua, China 137/C2
Ningjin, China 130/C3
Ningjin, China 130/D3
Ninglang Yizu Zizhixian, China 141/H2
Ningling, China 130/C4
Ningming, China 141/J3
Ningwu, China 130/C3
Ningxia Huizu (aut. reg.), China 128/J4
Ningxiang, China 137/B2
Ningyang, China 130/D4
Ningyuan, China 141/K2
Ninh Binh, Viet. 136/D1
Ninilchik, Ak, US 192/H3
Niningo (isls.), PNG 174/D5
Ninohe, Japan 134/B3
Ninomiya, Japan 135/C3
Ninove, Belg. 110/D2
Ninoy Aquino (int'l arpt.), Phil. 137/D5
Niobara (riv.), Ne, US 182/F3
Niobrara (riv.), Ne, US 185/H5
Niokolo-Koba, PN du, Sen. 160/B3
Niono, Mali 160/D3
Nioro-du-Rip, Sen. 160/B3
Nioro du Sahel, Mali 160/C3
Niort, Fr. 100/C3
Nipawin, Sk, Can. 185/H2
Nipe (bay), Cuba 203/H1
Nipigon, On, Can. 185/L3
Nipigon (lake), On, Can. 180/G3
Nipissing (lake), On, Can. 181/J4
Ñiquén, Chile 216/C3
Niquero, Cuba 203/G1
Nirasaki, Japan 133/F3
Nirayama, Japan 135/B3
Nirimba Army Afld., Austl. 172/G8
Nirmal, India 140/C4
Nirmāli, India 143/F2
Niš, Serb. 106/E4
Niš (int'l arpt.), Serb. 106/E4
Nišava (riv.), Serb. 105/H1
Niscemi, It. 104/D4
Nishiazai, Japan 135/K5
Nishibiwajima, Japan 135/L5
Nishiharu, Japan 135/L5
Nishikatsura, Japan 135/B2
Nishiki (riv.), Japan 132/B3
Nishiki, Japan 135/H5
Nishinomiya, Japan 135/H6
Nishino'omote, Japan 132/B5
Nishio, Japan 135/M6
Nishiwaki, Japan 135/G6
Nisko, Pol. 99/M3
Nisqually, Wa, US 193/B3
Nisqually (riv.), Wa, US 193/B3
Nisqually Ind. Res., Wa, US 193/B3
Nisqually Reach (str.), Wa, US 193/B3
Nissan (isl.), PNG 174/E5
Nisser (lake), Nor. 96/C2
Nisshin, Japan 135/M5
Nissum (bay), Den. 96/C3
Nisswa, Mn, US 185/K4
Nistru (riv.), Mol. 107/H1
Niterói, Braz. 213/K7
Nith (riv.), Sc, UK 94/C6
Nith (riv.), Sc, UK 92/E1
Nithsdale (valley), Sc, UK 92/E1
Nitra, Slvk. 106/D1
Nitra (riv.), Slvk. 99/K4
Nitriansky (pol. reg.), Slvk. 99/K4
Nitsa (riv.), Rus. 119/P4
Nitta, Japan 135/C1
Nittedal, Nor. 96/D1
Nittel, Ger. 111/F4
Nittenau, Ger. 113/F4
Niuafo'ou (isl.), Tonga 175/H6
Niuatoputapu Group (isls.), Tonga 175/H6
Niue (terr.), NZ 175/H7
Niue (isl.), Niue 175/J6
Niulakita (isl.), Tuv. 174/G6
Niulan (riv.), China 141/H2
Niut (peak), Indo. 138/C3
Niutao (isl.), Tuv. 174/G5
Nivelles, Belg. 111/D2
Nivernais, Collines de (hills), Fr. 100/E3
Niverville, Mb, Can. 185/J3
Niwot, Co, US 195/B2
Niyazov (int'l arpt.), Trkm. 145/C5
Niyodo (riv.), Japan 132/C4
Nizāmābād, India 140/C4
Nizhegorodskaya Oblast, Rus. 121/G1
Nizhnekama (res.), Rus. 119/M4
Nizhnekamsk, Rus. 119/L5
Nizhneudinsk, Rus. 123/K4
Nizhnevartovsk, Rus. 122/H3
Nizhniy Lomov, Rus. 121/G1
Nizhniy Novgorod, Rus. 119/K4
Nizhniy Tagil, Rus. 119/N4
Nizhyn, Ukr. 120/D2
Nizip, Turk. 148/D2
Nízke Tatry NP, Slvk. 120/A2
Nizza Monferrato, It. 116/B3
Nizzanim, Isr. 149/F8
Njardhvík, Ice. 95/M7
Njombe (riv.), Tanz. 162/B4
Nkandla, SAfr. 165/E3
Nkayi, Congo 163/B1
Nkhata Bay, Malw. 162/B5
N'kongsamba, Camr. 154/G7
Nkululu (riv.), Tanz. 162/B4
Nkusi (riv.), Ugan. 162/A2
Nmai (riv.), Myan. 141/G2
Noailles, Fr. 110/B5
Noākhāli (pol. reg.), Bang. 143/H4
Noale, It. 117/F1
Noāmundi, India 143/E4
Noank, Ct, US 197/F1
Noatak, Ak, US 192/F2
Noatak (riv.), Ak, US 192/F2
Noatak Nat'l Prsv., Ak, US 192/F2
Nobeoka, Japan 132/B4
Noble, Ok, US 195/N15
Noboa, Ecu. 210/A5
Noboribetsu, Japan 134/B2
Noce (riv.), It. 115/G5
Noceto, It. 116/D3
Noci, It. 105/E2
Nockamixon State Park, Pa, US 196/C3
Noda, Japan 135/D2
Nodagawa, Japan 135/H4
Noé (cape), Alg. 158/D2
Nogales, Az, US 186/E5
Nogales, Mex. 201/M8
Nogara, It. 117/E2
Nogaro, Fr. 100/C5
Nogat (riv.), Pol. 97/H4
Nogata, Japan 132/B4
Nogent, Fr. 114/B1
Nogent-l'Artaud, Fr. 110/C6
Nogent-le-Rotrou, Fr. 100/D2
Nogent-sur-Oise, Fr. 110/B5
Nogent-sur-Seine, Fr. 100/E2
Nogi, Japan 135/D1
Noginsk, Rus. 119/X9
Nogoa (riv.), Austl. 172/B4
Nogodan-san (peak), SKor. 131/D5
Nogoonnuur, Mong. 128/F2
Nogoyá, Arg. 215/E3
Nógrád (co.), Hun. 99/K5
Nogwak-san (peak), SKor. 131/E4
Nohar, India 144/C5
Noheji, Japan 134/B3
Nohfelden, Ger. 111/G4
Nohkú (pt.), Mex. 202/E2
Noi (riv.), Viet. 141/J5
Noidans-lès-Vesoul, Fr. 114/C2
Noire (riv.), Qu, Can. 188/E2
Noires, Montagnes (mts.), Fr. 100/B2
Noirmoutier, Île de (isl.), Fr. 100/B3
Noisiel, Fr. 110/B6
Noisy-le-Grand, Fr. 88/K5
Noisy-le-Mec, Fr. 88/K5
Noisy-le-Roi, Fr. 88/J5
Nojima-zaki (pt.), Japan 133/F3
Nokia, Fin. 97/K1
Nokilalaki (peak), Indo. 139/F4
Nola, CAfr. 154/J7
Noli, It. 116/B4
Noli, Capo di (cape), It. 116/B4
Nomadgi NP, Austl. 173/D2
Nombre de Dios, Mex. 200/D4
Nombre de Dios (mts.), Hon. 202/E3
Nome, Ak, US 192/E3
Nome (cape), Ak, US 192/F3
Noměny, Fr. 111/F6
Nomexy, Fr. 114/C1
Nomo-misaki (cape), Japan 132/B5
Nomo-zaki (pt.), Japan 132/A4
Nonacho (lake), NW, Can. 180/F2
Nonantola, It. 117/E3
Nondalton, Ak, US 192/H4
None, It. 101/G4
Nonette (riv.), Fr. 110/B5
Nong Han (res.), Thai. 136/D2
Nong Khai, Thai. 136/C2
Nong'an, China 129/N3
Nongoma, SAfr. 165/E2
Nongstoin, India 143/H3
Nonnweiler, Ger. 111/F4
Nonoava, Mex. 200/D3
Nonouti (isl.), Kiri. 174/G5
Nonri (isl.), China 130/E5
Nonsan, SKor. 131/D4
Nontron, Fr. 100/D4
Noord-Brabant (prov.), Neth. 108/C5
Noord Holland (prov.), Neth. 108/B3
Noordbeveland (isl.), Neth. 108/A5
Noorderhaaks (isl.), Neth. 108/B3
Noordhollandsch Kanaal (riv.), Neth. 108/B3
Noordostpolder (polder), Neth. 108/C3
Noordwijk aan Zee, Neth. 108/B4
Noordwijkerhout, Neth. 108/B4
Noordzeekanaal (canal), Neth. 108/B4
Noormarkku, Fin. 97/J1
Noorvik, Ak, US 192/F2
Nootka (isl.), BC, Can. 184/B3
Nora, Swe. 96/F2
Norala, Phil. 139/F2
Norberg, Swe. 96/F1
Norberto de la Riestra, Arg. 217/J11
Norchia (ruin), It. 104/B1
Norco, Ca, US 194/C3
Norco, La, US 195/P16
Nord (riv.), Qu, Can. 189/M6
Nord (canal), Fr. 110/B4
Nord (prov.), Fr. 110/C3
Nord-Kivu (pol. reg.), D.R. Congo 162/A3
Nord-Ostsee (Kiel) (canal), Ger. 109/G1
Nord-Ouest (prov.), Camr. 161/H5
Nord-Ouest (pol. reg.), Mor. 158/B2
Nord-Pas-de-Calais (pol. reg.), Fr. 100/D1
Nord-Radde (riv.), Ger. 109/E3
Nord-Sud Kanal (canal), Ger. 109/E3
Nord-Trøndelag (co.), Nor. 95/E2
Nordborg, Den. 96/C4
Nordby, Den. 96/D4
Norddeich, Ger. 109/E1
Nordela (int'l arpt.), Azor., Port. 103/T13
Norden, Ger. 109/E1
Nordenham, Ger. 109/F1
Nordenskjöld (arch.), Rus. 122/J2
Norderney, Ger. 109/E1
Norderney (isl.), Neth. 109/E1
Norderstedt, Ger. 109/G1
Nordhausen, Ger. 98/F3
Nordholz, Ger. 109/F1
Nordhorn, Ger. 109/E4
Nordhouse, Fr. 114/D1
Nordjylland (co.), Den. 96/C3
Nordkapp (cape), Nor. 95/H1
Nordkapp, Nor. 95/H1
Nordkinn (pt.), Nor. 95/H1
Nordkirchen, Ger. 109/E5
Nordland (co.), Nor. 95/E2
Nördlingen, Ger. 112/D5
Nordmaling, Swe. 95/F3
Nordreisa, Nor. 95/G1
Nordrhein-Westfalen (state), Ger. 98/E3
Nords Wharf, Austl. 173/D2
Nordwalde, Ger. 109/E4
Nore (riv.), Ire. 89/Q10
Noresund, Nor. 96/C1
Norfolk (mt.), Austl. 173/C4
Norfolk (lake), Ar,Mo, US 187/J3
Norfolk, Ne, US 185/J5
Norfolk (isl.), Austl. 174/F7
Norfolk Broads (swamp), Eng, UK 91/H1
Norg, Neth. 108/D2
Norheimsund, Nor. 96/B1
Norikura-dake (peak), Japan 133/E2
Noril'sk, Rus. 122/J3
Normal, Il, US 185/L5
Norman, Ok, US 195/N15
Norman Manley (int'l arpt.), Jam. 203/G2
Norman Wells, NW, Can. 180/D2
Normanby (isl.), PNG 174/E6
Normandie, Collines de (hills), Fr. 100/C2
Normandy (reg.), Fr. 100/C2
Normandy Beach, NJ, US 196/D4
Normandy Park, Wa, US 193/C3
Normanton, Austl. 172/A2
Normanton South, Eng, UK 93/G4
Norotshama (peak), Namb. 164/B3
Norquay, Sk, Can. 185/H3
Ñorquinco, Arg. 216/C4
Norrbotten (co.), Swe. 95/F2
Nørre Alslev, Den. 96/D4
Nørre Nebel, Den. 96/C4
Nørre Vorupør, Den. 96/C3
Norridge, Il, US 193/Q16
Norris (lake), Tn, US 191/G2
Norristown, Pa, US 196/C3
Norrköping, Swe. 96/G2
Norrland (reg.), Swe. 95/F2
Norrsundet, Swe. 96/G1
Norrtälje, Swe. 97/H2
Nors, Den. 96/C3
Norseman, Austl. 170/D5
Norsjö, Swe. 95/F2
Norte (pt.), Arg. 217/F3
Norte (pt.), Arg. 216/E4
Norte, Cabo do (cape), Braz. 209/J3
Norte de Santander (dept.), Col. 210/C2
Norte Los Rodeos (int'l arpt.), Sp. 156/A3
Norte, Serra do (mts.), Braz. 208/G6
Nortelândia, Braz. 209/G6
Nörten-Hardenberg, Ger. 109/G5
North (pt.), Austl. 173/C3
North (pt.), Austl. 173/C4
North (pt.), Austl. 170/B4
North (cape), PE, Can. 189/J2
North (sea), Eur. 94/D4
North (cape), NZ 175/S9
North (isl.), NZ 175/S10
North (sound), Sc, UK 89/V14
North (chan.), UK 92/C1
North (cape), Ak, US 192/D5
North (pt.), Md, US 196/B5
North Albanian Alps (mts.), Alb.,Mont. 106/D4
North America (cont.) 119
North Andaman (isl.), India 141/F5
North Arlington, NJ, US 197/J8
North Aulatsivik (isl.), Nf, Can. 181/K3
North Aurora, Il, US 193/P16
North Ayrshire (pol. reg.), Sc, UK 94/A5
North Battleford, Sk, Can. 184/F2
North Bay, On, Can. 188/E2
North Bay, Wi, US 193/Q14
North Beach, Md, US 196/B6
North Beach Haven, NJ, US 196/D4
North Bellmore, NY, US 197/L9
North Bend, Or, US 184/B5
North Bend, Wa, US 193/D3
North Bergen, NJ, US 197/J8
North Berwick, Sc, UK 94/D4
North Branch (riv.), Md, US 196/B5
North Branch, NJ, US 196/D2
North Branford, Ct, US 197/F1
North Brunswick, NJ, US 196/D3
North Buganda (prov.), Ugan. 162/B2
North Caicos (isl.), UK 203/J1
North Caldwell, NJ, US 197/J8
North Canadian (riv.), Ok, US 187/H3
North Cape May, NJ, US 196/D6
North Caribou (lake), On, Can. 185/L2
North Carolina (state), US 191/H3
North Cascades NP, Wa, US 184/C3
North Central (plain), Tx, US 201/F1
North Charleston, SC, US 191/J3
North Cowichan, BC, Can. 184/C3
North Dakota (state), US 185/H4
North Dorset Downs (uplands), Eng, UK 90/D5
North Down (dist.), NI, UK 92/C2
North East, Pa, US 188/E3
North East (pt.), Austl. 172/C3
North East, Md, US 196/C4
North Eastern (prov.), Kenya 162/C2
North Esk (riv.), Sc, UK 94/C5
North Foreland (pt.), Eng, UK 91/H4
North Fork Crow (riv.), Mn, US 185/K4
North Fort Myers, Fl, US 191/H5
North French (riv.), On, Can. 188/D1
North Frisian (isls.), Ger. 98/D1
North Front (int'l arpt.), UK 156/D1
North Gauhāti, India 143/H2
North Haledon, NJ, US 197/J8
North Hero, Vt, US 188/F2
North Highlands, Ca, US 193/L9
North Kansas City, Mo, US 195/D5
North Kitui Nat'l Rsv., Kenya 162/C3
North Korea (ctry.) 131/D2
North Lakhimpur, India 141/F2
North Lanarkshire (pol. reg.), Sc, UK 94/C5
North Las Vegas, Nv, US 186/D3
North Lincolnshire (co.), Eng, UK 93/H4
North Lindenhurst, NY, US 197/M9
North Little Rock, Ar, US 187/J4
North Luangwa NP, Zam. 163/F3
North Magnetic Pole 181/R7
North Minch (The Minch) (str.), Sc, UK 89/Q8
North Moose (lake), Mb, Can. 185/J2
North Mountain (mtn.), Pa, US 196/B1
North Myrtle Beach, SC, US 191/J3
North Ogden, Ut, US 195/K11
North Ossetian Aut. Rep., Rus. 121/G4
North Pacific (ocean) 80/A4
North Pine (riv.), Austl. 172/E6
North Plainfield, NJ, US 197/H9
North Platte, Ne, US 185/H5
North Platte (riv.), Ne,Wy, US 187/G2
North Pole, Ak, US 192/J3
North Pole 218/G
North Potomac, Md, US 196/A5
North Prairie, Wi, US 193/P14
North Puyallup, Wa, US 193/C3
North Raccoon (riv.), Ia, US 185/K5
North Ronaldsay (isl.), Sc, UK 89/V14
North Salt Lake, Ut, US 195/K12
North Saskatchewan (riv.), Ab,Sk, Can. 180/E3
North Shields, Eng, UK 93/G2
North Siberian Lowland (plain), Rus. 122/K2
North Skunk (riv.), Ia, US 187/J2
North Somerset (co.), Eng, UK 90/D4
North Stadbroke (isl.), Austl. 172/D4
North Taranaki Bight (bay), NZ 175/S10
North Thompson (riv.), BC, Can. 184/D3
North Tolsta, Sc, UK 89/Q7
North Tonawanda, NY, US 189/S9
North Tyne (riv.), Eng, UK 93/F1
North Tyneside (co.), Eng, UK 93/G1
North Uist (isl.), Sc, UK 89/Q8
North Umpqua (riv.), Or, US 186/B2
North Valley Stream, NY, US 197/L9
North Vancouver, BC, Can. 180/D4
North Wales, Pa, US 196/C3
North Weald Bassett, Eng, UK 88/D1
North West (cape), Austl. 170/B2
North-West Frontier (co.), India 144/A3
North West Highlands (uplands), Sc, UK 89/R8
North Wildwood, NJ, US 196/D6
North Wilton, Ct, US 197/E1
North York, Can. 189/Q8
North York Moors NP, Eng, UK 93/G3
North Yorkshire (co.), Eng, UK 93/G3
Northallerton, Eng, UK 93/G3
Northam, Austl. 170/C4
Northampton, Austl. 170/B4
Northampton, Eng, UK 91/F2
Northampton, Ma, US 189/F3
Northampton, Pa, US 196/C2
Northampton (co.), Pa, US 196/C2
Northampton Uplands (uplands), Eng, UK 91/E2
Northamptonshire (co.), Eng, UK 91/E2
Northbrook, Il, US 193/Q15
Northeast (cape), Ak, US 192/E3
Northeast (pt.), Bahm. 203/H1
Northeast (pt.), Jam. 203/G2
Northeast Land (isl.), Sval. 218/E
Northeast Lincolnshire (co.), Eng, UK 93/H4
Northeim, Ger. 109/G5
Northern (pol. reg.), Gha. 161/E4
Northern (dist.), Isr. 149/D3
Northern (pol. reg.), Malw. 162/B5
Northern (prov.), SLeo. 160/B4
Northern (prov.), Ugan. 162/B2
Northern Areas (terr.), Pak. 145/F5
Northern Cape (prov.), SAfr. 164/C3
Northern Cook (isls.), CookIs. 175/J6
Northern Dvina (riv.), Rus. 85/J2
Northern Light (lake), On, Can. 188/B1
Northern Mariana Islands (dpcy.), US 174/D3
Northern Province (prov.), SAfr. 164/E2
Northern Sporades (isls.), Gre. 105/J3
Northern Territory (terr.), Austl. 167/C2
Northern Ural (mts.), Rus. 119/N3
Northern Uvals (hills), Rus. 119/K4
Northfield, Mn, US 185/K4
Northfleet, Eng, UK 88/D2
Northglenn, Co, US 195/C3
Northport, Al, US 191/G3
Northport (Old Northport), NY, US 197/E2
Northumberland (str.), Can. 189/J2
Northumberland, Pa, US 196/B2
Northumberland NP, Eng, UK 94/D6
Northvale, NJ, US 197/K7
Northville, Mi, US 193/E7
Northway, Ak, US 192/K3
Northwest Gander (riv.), Nf, Can. 189/L1
Northwest Territories (terr.), Can. 180/D2
Northwich, Eng, UK 93/F5
Northwood, ND, US 185/J4
Norton (bay), Ak, US 192/F3
Norton (sound), Ak, US 192/E3
Norton Shores, Mi, US 188/C3
Nortorf, Ger. 96/C4
Norvegia (cape), Ant. 218/Y
Nörvenich, Ger. 111/F2
Norwalk, Oh, US 188/D3
Norwalk, Ca, US 194/F8
Norwalk, Ct, US 197/M7
Norwalk (riv.), Ct, US 197/M7
Norway (ctry.) 95/C3
Norwegian (bay), Nun., Can. 181/S7
Norwegian (sea), Eur. 85/D2
Norwich, NY, US 188/F3
Norwich, Eng, UK 91/H1
Norwich (int'l arpt.), Eng, UK 91/H1
Norwood, NJ, US 197/K8
Nos Emine (cape), Bul. 107/H4
Nos Kaliakra (pt.), Bul. 107/J4
Nos Maslen Nos (pt.), Bul. 107/H4
Nosappu-misaki (cape), Japan 134/D2
Nose, Japan 135/H6
Noshappu-misaki (cape), Japan 134/B1
Noshaq (peak), Afg. 147/K1
Noshiro, Japan 134/B3
Nosivka, Ukr. 120/D2
Nosong (cape), Malay. 139/E2
Noşratābād, Iran 147/G3
Noss Head (pt.), Sc, UK 89/S7
Nossa Senhora da Glória, Braz. 212/C3
Nossa Senhora das Dores, Braz. 212/C3
Nossebro, Swe. 96/E2
Nosy-Varika, Madg. 165/J8
Notch (cape), Chile 217/B6
Notec (riv.), Pol. 99/J2
Noto (pen.), Japan 133/E2
Noto, It. 104/D4
Noto Antica (ruin), It. 104/D4
Noto, Golfo di (gulf), It. 104/D4
Noto, Val di (valley), It. 104/D4
Notodden, Nor. 96/C2
Notogawa, Japan 135/K5
Notoro (lake), Japan 134/C1
Notre Dame (mts.), On, Can. 181/J4
Notre Dame (bay), Nf, Can. 181/L4
Notre Dame, Fr. 88/K5
Notre-Dame-de-l'Île-Perrot, Qu, Can. 189/N7
Notsé, Togo 161/F5
Nott (mt.), Austl. 171/G5
Nottaway (riv.), Qu, Can. 181/J3
Nøtterøy, Nor. 96/D2
Nottingham (isl.), Nun., Can. 181/H2
Nottingham, Eng, UK 93/G6
Nottingham (co.), Eng, UK 93/G6
Nottinghamshire (co.), Eng, UK 93/G5
Nottuln, Ger. 109/E5
Nouâdhibou, Mrta. 156/A5
Nouâdhibou (int'l arpt.), Mrta. 156/A5
Nouakchott (cap.), Mrta. 160/B2
Nouakchott (int'l arpt.), Mrta. 160/B2
Nouna, Burk. 160/E3
Noupoort, SAfr. 164/D3
Nouvion-sur-Meuse, Fr. 111/D4
Nœux-les-Mines, Fr. 110/B3
Nouzonville, Fr. 111/D4
Nova Andradina, Braz. 209/H8
Nova Cruz, Braz. 212/D2
Nová Dubnica, Slvk. 99/K4
Nova Friburgo, Braz. 213/D2
Nova Gorica, Slov. 117/G1
Nova Gradiška, Cro. 106/C3
Nova Iguaçu, Braz. 213/K7
Nova Kakhovka, Ukr. 107/L2
Nova Olinda, Braz. 212/C2
Nova Olinda do Norte, Braz. 208/G4
Nova Pazova, Serb. 106/E3
Nova Prata, Braz. 213/B4
Nova Russas, Braz. 212/B2
Nova Scotia (prov.), Can. 189/J2
Nova Sintra, CpV. 151/J11
Nova Soure, Braz. 212/C3
Nova Varoš, Serb. 106/D4
Nova Venécia, Braz. 213/D1
Nova Xavantina, Braz. 209/H6
Nova Zagora, Bul. 107/H4
Novaci, Rom. 107/F3
Novafeltria, It. 117/F5
Novara, It. 116/B2
Novate Mezzola, It. 115/F5
Novaya Sibir' (isl.), Rus. 123/R2
Novaya Zemlya (isl.), Rus. 218/C
Nove, It. 117/E1
Nové Hrady, Czh. 113/H5
Nové Město nad Váhom, Slvk. 99/J4
Nové Strašecí, Czh. 113/G2
Nové Zámky, Slvk. 106/D2
Novelda, Sp. 103/E3
Novellara, It. 117/D3
Noventa, It. 117/E2
Noventa di Piave, It. 117/F1
Noventa Vicentina, It. 117/E2
Novgorod, Rus. 97/P2
Novgorodskaya Oblast, Rus. 118/G4
Novi, Mi, US 193/E7
Novi Bečej, Serb. 106/E3
Novi di Modena, It. 117/D3
Novi Iskŭr, Bul. 107/F4
Novi Ligure, It. 101/H4
Novi Pazar, Serb. 106/E4
Novi Pazar, Bul. 107/H4
Novi Sad, Serb. 106/D3
Novi Vinodolski, Cro. 106/B3
Novillars, Fr. 114/C3
Nóvita, Col. 210/B3
Novo (riv.), Braz. 213/K6
Novo Alexeyevka (int'l arpt.), Geo. 121/H4

Novo Aripuanã, Braz. 208/F5
Novo Hamburgo, Braz. 213/B4
Novo Horizonte, Braz. 213/B2
Novo Miloševo, Serb. 106/E3
Novo Oriente, Braz. 212/B2
Novoanninskiy, Rus. 121/G2
Novocheboksarsk, Rus. 119/K4
Novocherkassk, Rus. 120/G3
Novogrudok, Bela. 97/L5
Novohrad-Volyns'kyy, Ukr. 120/C2
Novohradské Hory (mts.), Czh. 113/H5
Novokuybyshevsk, Rus. 121/J1
Novokuznetsk, Rus. 122/J4
Novolazarevskaya, Rus., Ant. 218/A9
Novomoskovsk, Rus. 120/F1
Novorossiysk, Rus. 120/F3
Novoshakhtinsk, Rus. 120/F3
Novosibirsk (res.), Rus. 145/H2
Novosibirsk, Rus. 145/H1
Novosibirsk (Tolmachevo) (int'l arpt.), Rus. 145/H1
Novosibirskaya Oblast, Rus. 145/G1
Novotroitsk, Rus. 121/L2
Novoukrayinka, Ukr. 120/D2
Novovolyns'k, Ukr. 120/C2
Novovyatsk, Rus. 119/L4
Novozybkov, Rus. 120/D1
Novska, Cro. 106/C3
Nový Jičín, Czh. 99/K4
Nowa Dęba, Pol. 99/L3
Nowa Ruda, Pol. 99/J3
Nowa Sarzyna, Pol. 99/M3
Nowa Sól, Pol. 99/H3
Nowata, Ok, US 187/J3
Nowe, Pol. 99/K2
Nowe Miasto Lubawskie, Pol. 99/K2
Nowgong, India 142/B3
Nowitna (riv.), Ak, US 192/G3
Nowogard, Pol. 96/F5
Nowood (riv.), Wy, US 186/F1
Nowshāk (peak), Afg. 145/F5
Nowshera, Pak. 144/A2
Nowy Dwór Gdański, Pol. 97/H4
Nowy Sącz, Pol. 99/L4
Nowy Staw, Pol. 97/H4
Nowy Targ, Pol. 99/L4
Nowy Tomyśl, Pol. 99/J2
Noya, Sp. 102/A1
Noye (riv.), Fr. 110/B4
Noyon, Fr. 110/C4
Nsanje, Malw. 163/G4
Nsawam, Gha. 161/E5
Nsumbu NP, Zam. 162/A5
Nsuta, Gha. 161/E5
Ntoroko, Ugan. 162/A2
Ntungamo, Ugan. 162/A3
Ntusi, Ugan. 162/A2
Nu, Crêt du (peak), Fr. 114/B5
Nuangola, Pa, US 196/C1
Nūbah, Jibāl an (mts.), Sudan 155/M5
Nubian (des.), Sudan 159/C4
Nucet, Rom. 107/F2
Nucla, Co, US 190/A2
Nucourt, Fr. 88/H4
Nüdlingen, Ger. 112/C1
Nueces (riv.), Tx, US 190/D4
Nueltin (lake), Mb,Nun., Can. 180/G2
Nuenen, Neth. 108/C6
Nueva Alejandría, Peru 214/C2
Nueva Concepción, Guat. 202/D3
Nueva Esparta (state), Ven. 211/E2
Nueva Florida, Ven. 210/D2
Nueva Gerona, Cuba 203/F1
Nueva Helvecia, Uru. 217/K11
Nueva Imperial, Chile 216/B3
Nueva Italia de Ruiz, Mex. 200/E5
Nueva Loja, Ecu. 210/B4
Nueva Ocotepéque, Hon. 202/D3
Nueva Palmira, Uru. 217/J10
Nueva Rosita, Mex. 201/E3
Nueva Villa de Padilla, Mex. 201/F3
Nueve de Julio, Arg. 216/E2
Nuevitas, Cuba 203/G1
Nuevo, Ca, US 194/C3
Nuevo Balsas, Mex. 201/F5
Nuevo Berlín, Uru. 217/J10
Nuevo Casas Grandes, Mex. 200/D2
Nuevo Chagres, Pan. 203/F4
Nuevo, Gulfo (gulf), Arg. 215/D5
Nuevo Ideal, Mex. 200/D3
Nuevo Ixcatlán, Mex. 202/C2
Nuevo Laredo, Mex. 201/F3

Nuevo Leon (state), Mex. 198/A2
Nuevo Rocafuerte, Ecu. 210/C5
Nufenen, Swi. 115/F4
Nufenenpass (pass), Swi. 115/E5
Nuguria (isls.), PNG 174/F5
Nuhne (riv.), Ger. 109/F6
Nui (isl.), Tuv. 174/G5
Nuiqsut, Ak, US 192/H1
Nuits-Saint-Georges, Fr. 114/A3
Nukata, Japan 135/M6
Nuku'alofa (cap.), Tonga 174/H7
Nukufetau (isl.), Tuv. 174/G5
Nukulaelae (isl.), Tuv. 174/H5
Nukumanu (atoll), PNG 174/E5
Nukunonu (isl.), Tok. 175/H5
Nukuoro (isl.), Micr. 174/E4
Nukus (int'l arpt.), Uzb. 145/C4
Nukus, Uzb. 145/C4
Nukutavake (isl.), FrPol. 175/M6
Nulato, Ak, US 192/G3
Nules, Sp. 103/E3
Nullarbor (plain), Austl. 170/E5
Nullarbor NP, Austl. 171/F4
Numana, It. 117/G5
Numansdorp, Neth. 108/B5
Numata, Japan 133/F2
Numazu, Japan 133/F3
Nümbrecht, Ger. 111/G2
Numfoor (isl.), Indo. 139/H4
Nummi, Fin. 97/K1
Numurkah, Austl. 173/C3
Nunapitchuk, Ak, US 192/F3
Nunchia, Col. 210/C3
Nundle, Austl. 173/D1
Nuneaton, Eng, UK 91/E1
Nungarin, Austl. 170/C4
Nungatta NP, Austl. 173/D3
Nunivak (isl.), Ak, US 192/E4
Nunningen, Swi. 114/D3
Nuñoa, Peru 214/D4
Nunspeet, Neth. 108/C4
Nuon (riv.), Libr. 160/C5
Nuoro, It. 104/A2
Nuquí, Col. 210/B3
Nur (mts.), Turk. 149/E1
Nura (riv.), Kaz. 145/F2
Nürburgring, Ger. 111/F3
Nure (riv.), It. 116/C3
Nuremberg, Pa, US 196/B2
Nurhak, Turk. 148/D2
Nuri (ruin), Sudan 159/B5
Nuriootpa, Austl. 171/H5
Nurmijärvi, Fin. 97/L1
Nürnberg (int'l arpt.), Ger. 112/E3
Nürnberg, Ger. 112/E4
Nürpur, Pak. 144/B3
Nurri (mt.), Austl. 173/C1
Nürtingen, Ger. 112/C5
Nushagak (riv.), Ak, US 192/F3
Nushki, Pak. 147/J3
Nutberry (hill), Sc, UK 94/C5
Nuth, Neth. 111/E2
Nuthe-Graben (riv.), Ger. 98/Q7
Nutley, NJ, US 197/J8
Nutwood, Il, US 195/F7
Nuuk (Godthåb), Grld. 177/M3
Nuvolento, It. 115/F3
Nuy (riv.), SAfr. 164/L10
Nüziders, Aus. 115/F3
Nxai Pan NP, Bots. 163/C3
Nyabisindu, Rwa. 162/A3
Nyack, NY, US 197/K7
Nyah, Austl. 173/B2
Nyah West, Austl. 173/B2
Nyainqêntanglha (peak), China 128/F5
Nyaki NP, Malw. 163/F3
Nyala, Sudan 155/K5
Nyalam, China 143/E1
Nyandoma, Rus. 118/J3
Nyanza (prov.), Kenya 162/B3
Nyasa (lake), Malw. 163/F3
Nybro, Swe. 96/F3
Nyêmo, China 143/H1
Nyeri, Kenya 162/C3
Nyima, China 128/E5
Nyírábrány, Hun. 106/C2
Nyíradony, Hun. 99/M5
Nyírbátor, Hun. 99/M5
Nyíregyháza, Hun. 106/C2
Nyírmada, Hun. 99/M4
Nyiru (mt.), Kenya 162/C2
Nykøbing, Den. 96/D4
Nykøbing, Den. 96/D4
Nyköping, Swe. 96/G2
Nylstroom, SAfr. 164/D2
Nynäshamn, Swe. 96/G2
Nyngan, Austl. 173/C2
Nyoman (riv.), Bela. 120/B1
Nyon, Swi. 114/C5
Nyons, Fr. 100/F4
Nýřany, Czh. 113/G3
Nýrsko, Czh. 113/G4
Nýrsko (res.), Czh. 113/G4
Nysa, Pol. 99/J3
Nyssa, Or, US 184/D5

Nysted, Den. 96/D4
Nyūdo-zaki (pt.), Japan 134/A4
Nyuk (lake), Rus. 118/F2
Nyúl, Hun. 106/C2
Nyunzu, D.R. Congo 162/C3
Nyūzen, Japan 133/E2
Nzega, Tanz. 162/B4
Nzérékoré (pol. reg.), Gui. 160/C4
Nzérékoré, Gui. 160/C5
Nzi (riv.), C.d'Iv. 154/E6

O

Ō-shima (isl.), Japan 134/A3
Oa, Mull of (pt.), Sc, UK 89/Q9
Oahe (dam), SD, US 185/H4
Oahe (lake), ND,SD, US 185/H4
Oahu (isl.), Hi, US 182/V13
Oak Forest, Il, US 193/Q16
Oak Grove, Mo, US 195/E6
Oak Hill, WV, US 188/D4
Oak Park, Il, US 193/Q16
Oak Park, Mi, US 193/F7
Oak Ridge, Tn, US 188/C3
Oak Ridge, NJ, US 196/D1
Oak View, Ca, US 194/A2
Oakbank, Mb, Can. 185/J3
Oakdale, La, US 187/J5
Oakes, ND, US 185/J4
Oakey, Austl. 172/C4
Oakham, Eng, UK 91/F1
Oakhurst, Ca, US 186/C3
Oakland, Ca, US 186/B3
Oakland, Md, US 196/B5
Oakland (co.), Mi, US 193/E6
Oakland (lake), Mi, US 193/F6
Oakland, NJ, US 197/J7
Oakland (bay), Wa, US 193/A3
Oaklands, Austl. 173/C2
Oakley, Ca, US 193/L10
Oakover (riv.), Austl. 170/D2
Oakridge, Or, US 184/C5
Oakville, La, US 195/P17
Oakville, Mo, US 195/G9
Oakville, On, Can. 189/Q9
Oakwood Hills, Il, US 193/P15
Oamaru, NZ 175/S12
Ōamishirasato, Japan 135/E2
Oat (mtn.), Ca, US 194/B2
Oatlands, Austl. 173/C4
Oaxaca (state), Mex. 198/B4
Oaxaca de Juárez, Mex. 202/B2
Ob' (gulf), Rus. 125/G3
Ob' (riv.), Rus. 125/F3
Ob Luang Gorge, Thai. 136/B2
Obama, Japan 135/J4
Obama (bay), Japan 135/J4
Och'amch'ire, Geo. 121/G4
Oban (hills), Nga. 161/H5
Oban, Sc, UK 89/R8
Obanazawa, Japan 134/B4
Obara, Japan 135/M5
Obata, Japan 135/L7
Ober-Olm, Ger. 112/B3
Ober Ramstadt, Ger. 112/B3
Oberá, Arg. 215/E2
Oberalppass (pass), Swi. 115/E4
Oberalpstock (peak), Swi. 115/E4
Oberammergau, Ger. 115/H2
Oberasbach, Ger. 112/D4
Oberau, Ger. 115/H2
Oberburg, Swi. 114/D3
Oberderdingen, Ger. 112/B4
Oberdiessbach, Swi. 114/D4
Oberding, Ger. 113/E6
Oberdorf, Swi. 114/D3
Oberdorla, Ger. 109/H6
Oberelsbach, Ger. 112/D2
Oberentfelden, Swi. 114/D3
Oberglatt, Swi. 115/E3
Obergünzburg, Ger. 115/G2
Oberhaching, Ger. 113/E6
Oberhausen, Ger. 108/D6
Oberkirch, Ger. 114/E1
Oberkochen, Ger. 112/D4
Oberkotzau, Ger. 113/E2
Oberlausitz (reg.), Ger. 99/H3
Oberlin, Ks, US 187/G3
Obernai, Fr. 114/D1
Obernburg am Main, Ger. 112/C3
Oberndorf am Neckar, Ger. 115/E1
Oberndorf bei Salzburg, Aus. 113/F7
Oberneukirchen, Aus. 113/H6
Obernkirchen, Ger. 109/G4
Oberon, Austl. 173/D2
Oberösterreich (prov.), Aus. 99/G4
Oberpfälzer Wald (for.), Ger. 113/F3
Oberrieden, Ger. 112/D5
Oberriet, Swi. 115/F3
Obersaxen, Swi. 115/F4
Oberschleissheim, Ger. 113/E6
Oberschneiding, Ger. 113/E6
Obersiggenthal, Swi. 115/F3
Oberstammheim, Swi. 115/E2

Oberstaufen, Ger. 115/G2
Oberstdorf, Ger. 115/G3
Oberthal, Ger. 111/G4
Obertrum am See, Aus. 113/G7
Obertshausen, Ger. 112/B2
Oberursel, Ger. 112/B2
Oberuzwil, Swi. 115/F3
Oberviechtach, Ger. 113/F4
Oberwald, Swi. 115/E4
Oberwart, Aus. 106/C2
Oberwesel, Ger. 111/G3
Oberwil, Swi. 114/D4
Obfelden, Swi. 115/E3
Obi (str.), Indo. 139/G4
Obi (isls.), Indo. 139/G4
Óbidos, Braz. 209/G4
Óbidos, Port. 102/A3
Obihiro, Japan 134/C2
Obilić, Kos. 106/E4
Obing, Ger. 113/F6
Obira, Japan 134/B1
Óbitsu (riv.), Japan 135/D3
Obluch'ye, Rus. 129/P2
Obninsk, Rus. 118/H5
Obo, CAfr. 155/L6
Oborniki, Pol. 99/J2
Oborniki Śląskie, Pol. 99/J3
Obra (riv.), Pol. 99/J2
Obrenovac, Serb. 106/E3
Obrež, Serb. 106/E4
Obrigheim, Ger. 112/C4
Obrigheim, Ger. 112/B4
Observatory, Austl. 173/G5
Obtrumer (lake), Aus. 113/G7
Ōbu, Japan 135/L6
Obuasi, Gha. 161/E5
Obw. (canton), Swi. 115/E4
Obzor, Bul. 107/H4
Ocala, Fl, US 191/H4
Ocampo, Mex. 200/E3
Ocaña, Sp. 102/D3
Ocaña, Col. 210/C2
Occhieppo Inferiore, It. 116/B1
Occhieppo Superiore, It. 116/A1
Occhiobello, It. 117/E3
Occidental, Cordillera (mts.), Ecu. 208/C3
Occimiano, It. 116/B2
Ocean (cape), Ak, US 192/C3
Ocean (co.), NJ, US 196/D4
Ocean (riv.), It. 104/D2
Ocean Beach, NY, US 197/E2
Ocean City, Md, US 188/F4
Ocean City, NJ, US 196/D5
Ocean Falls, BC, Can. 184/B2
Ocean Gate, NJ, US 196/D4
Ocean Grove, NJ, US 196/D3
Ocean View, NJ, US 196/D5
Oceanographic Museum, Mona. 116/J8
Oceanside, Ca, US 194/C4
Oceanside, NY, US 197/L9
Ocean Springs, Ms, US 191/G5
Och'amch'ire, Geo. 121/G4
Ocheltree, Ks, US 195/D6
Ochiishi-misaki (cape), Japan 134/D2
Ochil (hills), Sc, UK 94/C4
Ocho Rios, Jam. 203/G2
Ochsenfurt, Ger. 112/D3
Ochsenhausen, Ger. 115/F1
Ochsenkopf (peak), Aus. 115/F3
Ochtendung, Ger. 111/G3
Ochtrup, Ger. 109/E4
Ochtum (riv.), Ger. 109/F2
Ockelbo, Swe. 96/G1
Ockenheim, Ger. 111/G4
Ocmulgee (riv.), Ga, US 191/H3
Ocmulgee Nat'l Mon., Ga, US 191/H3
Ocna Mureş, Rom. 107/F2
Ocna Sibiului, Rom. 107/G3
Ocoña (riv.), Peru 208/D6
Ocoña, Peru 214/C5
Oconee (lake), Ga, US 191/H3
Oconee (riv.), Ga, US 191/H3
Oconto, Wi, US 185/M4
Ocosingo, Mex. 202/C2
Ocotal, Nic. 202/E3
Ocotlán, Mex. 200/E4
Ocotlán de Morelos, Mex. 202/B2
Ocoyoacac, Mex. 201/Q10
Ocozocoautla de Espinosa, Mex. 202/C2
Ocracoke, NC, US 191/K3
Ocros, Peru 214/B3
Octeville, Fr. 100/C2
October Revolution (isl.), Rus. 125/H2
Oda (peak), Sudan 159/D4
Oda, Japan 132/C4
Odaesan NP, SKor. 131/E4
Ōdai, Japan 135/K7
Ōdaigahara-san (peak), Japan 132/E4
Ōdate, Japan 134/B3
Odawara, Japan 133/F3
Odda, Nor. 96/B1
Odde (peak), Eth. 159/D6
Odder, Den. 96/D4
Odeborn (riv.), Ger. 109/F6
Odelzhausen, Ger. 112/E6
Odemira, Port. 102/A4
Odemiş, Turk. 148/B2
Ödendaalsrus, SAfr. 164/D2
Odense, Den. 96/D4

Odense (int'l arpt.), Den. 96/D4
Odenthal, Ger. 111/G1
Odenton, Md, US 196/B5
Odenwald (reg.), Ger. 112/B3
Oder (Odra) (riv.), Ger.,Pol. 99/H2
Oder-Spree Kanal (canal), Ger. 98/Q7
Oderen, Fr. 114/C2
Oderhaff (lag.), Ger. 99/H2
Oderzo, It. 117/F1
Ödeshög, Swe. 96/F2
Odesa, Turk. 148/B1
Odes'ka Oblasti, Ukr. 120/D3
Odessa, De, US 196/C5
Odessa, Ukr. 107/K2
Odessa, Wa, US 184/D4
Odessa, Tx, US 187/G5
Odet (riv.), Fr. 100/B2
Odienné, C.d'Iv. 160/D4
Odiongan, Phil. 137/D5
Odintsovo, Rus. 119/W9
Odivelas, Port. 103/P10
Odobeşti, Rom. 107/H3
Odoorn, Neth. 108/D3
Odorheiu Secuiesc, Rom. 107/G2
Ödražaci, Serb. 106/D3
Ōe, Japan 135/H6
Ōe-yama (peak), Japan 135/H5
Oegstgeest, Neth. 108/B4
Oeiras, Braz. 212/B2
Oelde, Ger. 109/F5
Oelsnitz, Ger. 113/F2
Oelwein, Ia, US 185/L5
Oenpelli, Austl. 170/F2
Oensingen, Swi. 114/D3
Oer-Erkenschwick, Ger. 109/E5
Oestrich-Winkel, Ger. 112/B2
Oetz, Aus. 115/G3
Of, Turk. 148/E1
O'Fallon, Mo, US 195/F8
O'Fallon, Il, US 195/H8
Ofanto (riv.), It. 104/D2
Ofaqim, Isr. 149/D4
Offa, Nga. 161/G4
Offaly (co.), Ire. 92/A5
Offanengo, It. 116/C2
Offement, Fr. 114/C2
Offenbach, Ger. 112/B2
Offenbach an der Queich, Ger. 112/B4
Offenburg, Ger. 114/D1
Offingen, Ger. 112/D6
Offstein, Ger. 112/B4
Oftersheim, Ger. 112/B4
Oftringen, Swi. 114/D3
Oga, Japan 134/A4
Oga (pen.), Japan 134/A4
Ogachi, Japan 134/B4
Ogaden (maj.), Eth. 155/P6
Ōgaki, Japan 135/L5
Ogano, Japan 135/C2
Ogasawara, Japan 174/D2
Ogatsu, Japan 134/B4
Ogawa, Japan 134/B3
Ogawa, Japan 135/C1
Ogawara (lake), Japan 134/B3
Ogbomosho, Nga. 161/G4
Ogden, Ut, US 195/K11
Ogden Bay (bay), Ut, US 195/J11
Ogden, South Fork (riv.), Ut, US 195/K11
Ogdensburg, NY, US 188/F2
Ogdensburg, NJ, US 196/D1
Ogeechee (riv.), Ga, US 191/H4
Oggiono, It. 116/C1
Ogi, Japan 133/F2
Ogino, Fl, US 191/H5
Ogles, Il, US 195/G8
Oglesby, Tx, US 201/F2
Oglio (riv.), It. 116/C2
Ognon (riv.), Fr. 114/B2
Ogoamas (peak), Indo. 139/F3
Ogoki (lake), On, Can. 185/M3
Ogoki (res.), On, Can. 185/M3
Ogooué (riv.), Gabon 154/H8
Ogose, Japan 135/C2
Ogosta (riv.), Bul. 107/F4
Ogre, Lat. 97/L3
Oguchi, Japan 135/L5
Ogulin, Cro. 106/B3
Ogun (riv.), Nga. 154/F6
Ogurjaly (isl.), Trkm. 145/B5
Oh Me Edge (hill), Eng, UK 94/D6
Oka, Nga. 161/G5
Okabaji (lakes), Ia, US 185/K5
Okok (riv.), Ugan. 162/B2
Okolona, Ms, US 191/F3

O'Higgins (pol. reg.), Chile 216/B1
O'Higgins (lake), Chile 217/B6
Ohio (riv.), US 188/B4
Ohio (state), US 188/D3
Ōhira, Japan 135/D1
Ohlsdorf, Aus. 113/G7
Ohlstadt, Ger. 115/H2
Ohm (riv.), Ger. 112/C1
Ōho, Japan 135/E1
Ohoopee (riv.), Ga, US 191/H4
Ohře (riv.), Czh. 98/H3
Ohre (riv.), Ger. 98/F2
Ohrid, FYROM 105/G2
Ohrid (lake), Alb., Mac. 105/G2
Oi (riv.), China 141/G2
Ōi, Japan 135/J5
Ōi, Japan 135/M7
Ōi (riv.), Japan 135/D2
Oich (lake), Sc, UK 94/B2
Oieras, Port. 103/P10
Oignies, Fr. 110/B3
Oignon (riv.), Fr. 114/B5
Oil City, Pa, US 188/E3
Oildale, Ca, US 194/C3
Oil Crow, Yk, Can. 192/L2
Oirschot, Neth. 108/C5
Oise (dept.), Fr. 110/B5
Oise (riv.), Fr. 98/B4
Oise à l'Aisne, Canal de l' (canal), Fr. 110/C4
Oiseaux du Djoudj, PN des, Sen. 160/A2
Ōiso, Japan 135/C3
Oisterwijk, Neth. 108/C5
Ōita (mts.), Lux. 111/E4
Ōita, Japan 132/B4
Ōita (pref.), Japan 132/B4
Ōita (riv.), Japan 132/B4
Ōizumi, Japan 135/C1
Ōizumi, Japan 135/M2
Ojai, Ca, US 194/A2
Ojcowski NP, Pol. 99/K3
Ojebyn, Swe. 95/G2
Ōji, Japan 135/J6
Ojima, Japan 135/C1
Ojinaga, Mex. 200/D2
Ojiya, Japan 133/F2
Ojo de Agua, Mex. 201/Q9
Ojo de Liebre (lag.), Mex. 200/B3
Ojocaliente, Mex. 200/E4
Ojos del Salado (peak), Chile 215/C2
Ojos Negros, Sp. 102/E2
Ojuelos de Jalisco, Mex. 201/E4
Oka, Qu, Can. 189/M7
Oka, Nga. 161/G5
Oka (riv.), Rus. 123/L4
Okabe, Japan 135/C1
Okahandja, Namb. 163/C5
Okak (isl.), Nf, Can. 181/K3
Okanagan (lake), BC, Can. 180/D4
Okanagan Falls, BC, Can. 184/D3
Okanda, PN de l', Gabon 163/B1
Okano (riv.), Gabon 163/B1
Okanogan, Wa, US 184/D3
Okanogan (riv.), Wa, US 184/D3
Ōkawa, Japan 132/B4
Ōkawa, Japan 134/B3
Okaya, Japan 133/F2
Okayama (pref.), Japan 132/C3
Okayama, Japan 132/C3
Okazaki, Japan 135/M6
Okch'ǒn, SKor. 131/D4
Okęcie (int'l arpt.), Pol. 99/L2
Okeechobee, Fl, US 191/H5
Okeechobee (lake), Fl, US 191/H5
Okement (riv.), Eng, UK 90/B6
Okha, Rus. 123/Q4
Okhi Óros (peak), Gre. 105/J3
Okhotsk, Sea of (sea), Japan,Rus. 125/P4
Okhta (riv.), Rus. 119/T6
Okhtyrka, Ukr. 120/E2
Oki (isls.), Japan 132/C3
Okidaitō (isl.), Japan 133/L8
Okigwi, Nga. 161/G5
Okinawa (isl.), Japan 133/J7
Okinawa (pref.), Japan 133/J8
Okinawa (state), US 187/H4
Okino-shima (isl.), Japan 132/C4
Okinoerabu (isl.), Japan 133/K7
Okitipupa, Nga. 161/G5
Okkan, Myan. 141/G4
Okku, SKor. 131/D5
Oklahoma (state), US 187/H4
Oklahoma City (cap.), Ok, US 195/M15
Okmulgee, Ok, US 187/J4
Oko, Nga. 161/G5
Okobaji (lakes), Ia, US 185/K5
Okok (riv.), Ugan. 162/B2
Okolona, Ms, US 191/F3

Okoppe, Japan 134/C1
Okotoks, Ab, Can. 184/E3
Okovango (riv.), Namb. 151/E6
Oksbøl, Den. 96/C4
Oksskolten (peak), Nor. 95/E2
Oktyabr'sk, Rus. 121/J1
Oktyabr'skiy, Rus. 119/M5
Okuchi, Japan 132/B4
Okulovka, Rus. 118/G4
Okushiri, Japan 134/A2
Okutama (lake), Japan 135/C2
Okutama, Japan 135/C2
Ola, La, US 187/J5
Ōlafsfjördhur, Ice. 95/N6
Ōlafsvik, Ice. 95/M7
Olalla, Wa, US 193/B3
Olanchito, Hon. 202/E3
Öland (isl.), Swe. 95/F4
Ölands södra udde (pt.), Swe. 96/G3
Olathe, Ks, US 195/D6
Olavarría, Arg. 216/E3
Oława, Pol. 99/J3
Olberg, Az, US 195/S19
Olbia, It. 104/A2
Olching, Ger. 113/E6
Olcott, NY, US 189/S9
Old (riv.), Ca, US 193/L11
Old Bahama (chan.), Cuba 203/G1
Old Bar, Austl. 173/E1
Old Bedford (canal), Eng, UK 91/G2
Old Bethpage, NY, US 197/M9
Old Bridge, NJ, US 197/H10
Old City, Isr. 149/G8
Old Crow, Yk, Can. 192/L2
Old Faithful Geyser, Wy, US 184/F4
Old Field (pt.), NY, US 197/E2
Old Fort Niagara, NY, US 189/R9
Old Harbor, Ak, US 192/H4
Old Man of Hoy, Sc, US 89/V14
Old Mill Creek, Il, US 193/Q15
Old Nene (riv.), Eng, UK 91/F2
Old Rhine (riv.), Neth. 108/B4
Old Saybrook, Ct, US 197/F2
Old Tappan, NJ, US 197/K8
Old Town, Me, US 189/G2
Old Windsor, Eng, UK 88/B2
Old Wives (lake), Sk, Can. 185/G3
Oldeani (peak), Tanz. 162/B3
Oldebroek, Neth. 108/C4
Oldemarkt, Neth. 108/C3
Oldenburg, Ger. 109/F2
Oldenburg, Ger. 109/G1
Oldenzaal, Neth. 108/D4
Oldham, Eng, UK 93/F4
Oldham (co.), Eng, UK 93/F4
Oldman (riv.), Ab, Can. 184/E3
Oldmeldrum, Sc, UK 94/D2
Oldoog (isl.), Ger. 109/E1
Olds, Ab, Can. 184/E3
Olduvai Gorge, Tanz. 162/B3
Oldwick, NJ, US 196/D2
Olean, NY, US 188/E3
Olecko, Pol. 97/K4
Oleggio, It. 116/C1
Oleiros, Port. 102/B3
Oleiros, Sp. 102/A1
Olekma (riv.), Rus. 123/N4
Oleksandriya, Ukr. 120/E2
Olele (pt.), Wa, US 193/B2
Olema, Ca, US 193/K10
Olenegorsk, Rus. 118/G1
Olenek, Rus. 123/M2
Olenek (bay), Rus. 123/M2
Oléron, Île (isl.), Fr. 100/C4
Olesa de Montserrat, Sp. 103/K6
Oleśnica, Pol. 99/J3
Olesno, Pol. 99/K3
Olfen, Ger. 109/E5
Olga (mt.), Austl. 171/F3
Olginate, It. 116/C1
Ölgiy, Mong. 128/F2
Ólhão, Port. 102/B4
Oli Qoltyq Sory (swamp), Kaz. 145/B3
Oliena, It. 104/A2
Olifantshoek, SAfr. 164/P12
Olifantsrivier (riv.), SAfr. 163/E5
Olimarao (isl.), Micr. 174/D4
Olimbia (Olympia) (ruin), Gre. 105/G4
Olimbos NP (Olympos NP), Gre. 105/H2
Olímpia, Braz. 213/B2
Olímpos Beydağları NP, Turk. 148/B2

Olinda, Braz. 212/D3
Olindina, Braz. 212/C3
Oliva, Sp. 103/E3
Oliva de la Frontera, Sp. 102/B3
Olivais, Port. 103/P10
Olivenza, Sp. 102/B3
Oliveira, Braz. 213/C2
Oliver, BC, Can. 184/D3
Olivet, Fr. 100/D3
Olivone, Swi. 115/E4
Olla, La, US 187/J5
Ollachea, Peru 214/D4
Ollagüe (vol.), Chile 208/E8
Ollainville, Fr. 88/J6
Olleros, Peru 214/B3
Ollon, Swi. 114/D5
Olofström, Swe. 96/F3
Olomane (riv.), Qu, Can. 189/J1
Olomouc, Czh. 99/J4
Olomoucký (pol. reg.), Czh. 99/J4
Olongapo, Phil. 137/D5
Olonne-sur-Mer, Fr. 100/C4
Olorgasailie Nat'l Mon., Kenya 162/C3
Oloron-Sainte-Marie, Fr. 100/C5
Olot, Sp. 103/G1
Oloy (range), Rus. 123/S3
Olpe, Ger. 111/G1
Olsberg, Ger. 109/F6
Olst, Neth. 108/D4
Olsztyn, Pol. 97/J5
Olsztynek, Pol. 99/L2
Olt (prov.), Rom. 107/G3
Olt (riv.), Rom. 107/G3
Olten, Swi. 114/D3
Olteniţa, Rom. 107/H3
Olteţ (riv.), Rom. 107/F3
Oltre il Colle, It. 115/F6
Oltu, Turk. 148/E1
Oltu (riv.), Turk. 148/E1
Olur, Turk. 148/E1
Olvera, Sp. 102/C4
Olympia (cap.), Wa, US 184/C4
Olympic (mts.), Wa, US 184/C4
Olympic Dam, Austl. 171/H4
Olympic Game Farm, Wa, US 193/A1
Olympic National Forest, Wa, US 193/A2
Olympic NP, Wa, US 184/B4
Olympic Park, SKor. 131/G6
Olympos (Mount Olympus) (peak), Gre. 105/H2
Olympus (mt.), Gre. 105/H2
Olympus (peak), Cyp. 149/C2
Olyutorskiy (bay), Rus. 123/S3
Oma (riv.), Rus. 119/K2
Ōma, Japan 134/B3
Ōma-zaki (pt.), Japan 134/B3
Ōmachi, Japan 133/E2
Omae-zaki (pt.), Japan 135/C3
Ōmagari, Japan 134/B4
Omagh (dist.), NI, UK 92/A2
Omagh, NI, UK 92/A2
Omak, Wa, US 184/D3
Oman (gulf), Asia 147/H4
Omar Torrijos Herrera (int'l arpt.), Pan. 203/G4
Ølen, Nor. 96/A2
Omaruru, Namb. 163/C5
Omas, Peru 214/B4
Omatako (riv.), Namb. 163/C4
Omate, Peru 214/D5
Ombai (str.), Indo. 139/F5
Ombrone (riv.), It. 101/J5
Omeath, Ire. 92/B3
Omegna, It. 101/H4
Ōme, Japan 135/C2
Omeo, Austl. 173/C3
Ōmerli, Turk. 148/E2
Ometepec, Mex. 202/B2
Ōmi, Japan 135/K5
Ōmihachiman, Japan 135/K5
Omiš, Cro. 104/E1
Omitlán (riv.), Mex. 202/B2
Ōmiya, Japan 133/G2
Ōmiya, Japan 135/K7
Ommaney (cape), Ak, US 192/M4
Ommen, Neth. 108/D4
Omnögovi (prov.), Mong. 128/H3
Omo NP, Eth. 155/N6
Omo Wenz (riv.), Eth. 155/N6
Omodeo (lake), It. 104/A2
Omolon, Rus. 125/Q3

Omono (riv.), Japan 134/B4
Omsk, Rus. 145/F1
Omsk (int'l arpt.), Rus. 145/F2
Omskaya Oblast, Rus. 145/F1
Ōmu, Japan 134/C1
Omul (peak), Rom. 107/G3
Ōmura, Japan 132/A4
Ōmutag, Bul. 107/H4
Ōmuta, Japan 132/B4
Omutninsk, Rus. 119/M4
Onagawa, Japan 134/B4
Onalaska, Tx, US 190/E4
Onaping (lake), On, Can. 188/D2
Oñate, Sp. 102/D1
Onaway, Mi, US 188/C2
Onchan, IM, UK 92/D3
Onda, Sp. 103/E3
Ondava (riv.), Slvk. 99/L4
Ondjiva, Ang. 163/C4
Ondo, Nga. 161/G5
Ondo (state), Nga. 161/G5
Ondörhaan, Mong. 129/K2
Onè, It. 117/E1
Onega, Rus. 118/H3
Onega (bay), Rus. 118/G2
Onega (lake), Rus. 218/D
Onega (pen.), Rus. 118/H2
Onega (riv.), Rus. 122/D3
Oneida, NY, US 188/F3
Oneida, Pa, US 196/B2
Oneonta, NY, US 188/F3
Onex, Swi. 114/C5
Ongjin, NKor. 131/C4
Ongole, India 140/D4
Ongtüstik Qazaqstan, Kaz. 122/G5
Onhaye, Belg. 111/D3
Onida, SD, US 185/H4
Onil, Sp. 103/E3
Onilahy (riv.), Ang. 165/G8
Onishi, Japan 135/C1
Onitsha, Nga. 161/G5
Onjuku, Japan 135/E3
Onkaparinga (riv.), Austl. 171/M8
Onnaing, Fr. 110/C3
Onny (riv.), Eng, UK 90/D2
Ōno, Japan 132/D3
Ōno, Japan 132/D3
Ōno, Japan 135/L5
Onoda, Japan 132/B4
Onomichi, Japan 132/C3
Onon, Mong. 129/K2
Onon (riv.), Rus. 129/K1
Onoto, Ven. 211/E2
Onotoa (isl.), Kiri. 174/G5
Onrusrivier, SAfr. 164/L11
Onslow, Austl. 170/B2
Ontake-san (peak), Japan 133/E3
Ontario, Or, US 184/D4
Ontario, Ca, US 194/C2
Ontario (prov.), Can. 180/H3
Ontario (lake), Can.,US 188/E3
Ontelaunee (lake), Pa, US 196/C3
Onteniente, Sp. 103/E3
Ontonagon, Mi, US 185/L4
Ontong Java (isl.), Sol. 174/E5
Onyang, SKor. 131/D4
Onzaga, Col. 210/C3
Oologah (lake), Ok, US 190/D2
Oona River, BC, Can. 192/M5
Oost-Vlaanderen (prov.), Belg. 110/C2
Oost-Vlieland, Neth. 110/C1
Oostburg, Neth. 110/C1
Oostelijk Flevoland (polder), Neth. 108/C3
Oostende (Ostend), Belg. 110/B3
Oosterhout, Neth. 108/B5
Oosterscheidedam (dam),Neth. 108/A6
Oosterwolde (riv.), Neth. 98/B3
Oosterwolde, Neth. 108/D3
Oosterzele, Belg. 110/C2
Oostkamp, Belg. 110/C1
Oostvaarderplassen (lake),Neth. 108/C3
Oostzaan, Neth. 108/B4
Ootmarsum, Neth. 108/D4
Opaka, Bul. 107/H4
Opalenica, Pol. 99/J2
Opasatika (riv.), On, Can. 188/D1
Opatija, Cro. 106/B3
Opatów, Pol. 99/L3
Opava, Czh. 99/J4
Opelika, Al, US 191/G3
Opelousas, La, US 187/J5
Opera, It. 116/C2
Opfingen, Ger. 115/F1
Opglabbeek, Belg. 111/E1
Ophir, Ak, US 192/G3
Ophir, Ut, US 195/J13
Ophthalmia (range), Austl. 170/C2
Oploo, Neth. 108/C5
Opmeer, Neth. 108/B3
Opoczno, Pol. 99/L3
Opole, Pol. 99/J3
Opole Lubelskie, Pol. 99/L3
Opolskie (prov.), Pol. 99/J3
Opovo, Serb. 106/E3
Opp, Al, US 191/G4
Oppdal, Nor. 95/D3

Oppeano, It. 117/E2
Oppenau, Ger. 114/E1
Oppenheim, Ger. 112/B3
Oppland (co.), Nor. 95/D3
Opportunity, Wa, US 184/D4
Opwijk, Belg. 111/D2
Oquirrh (mts.), Ut, US 195/J12
Or, 'Aqiva, Isr. 149/F6
Or Yehuda, Isr. 149/F7
Ora, Japan 135/C2
Öra, Japan 135/C1
Oradell, NJ, US 197/J8
Oradell (res.), NJ, US 197/J8
Orahovac, Kos. 106/E4
Orahovica, Cro. 106/C3
Orai, India 142/B3
Oraison, Fr. 114/B4
Orange, Austl. 173/D2
Orange (cape), Braz. 209/H3
Orange, Fr. 100/F4
Orange (riv.), Nam.,SAfr. 163/C6
Orange, Ca, US 194/G8
Orange, Ct, US 197/E1
Orange, NJ, US 197/J8
Orange (co.), NY, US 196/D1
Orange, Tx, US 187/J5
Orange, Va, US 188/E4
Orange Park, Fl, US 191/H4
Orange Walk, Belz. 202/D2
Orangeburg, SC, US 191/H3
Orangeburg, NY, US 197/K7
Orangeville, On, Can. 188/D3
Orangeville, Pa, US 196/B3
Orango (isl.), GBis. 160/A4
Oranienburg, Ger. 98/G6
Oranje (mts.), Sur. 211/H4
Oranjekanaal (riv.), Neth. 108/D3
Oranjemund, Namb. 164/B3
Oranjestad, Aruba. 210/D1
Oranmore, Ire. 89/P10
Orapa, Bots. 163/E5
Oras, Phil. 137/E5
Orăştie, Rom. 107/F3
Oravița, Rom. 106/E3
Orb (riv.), Fr. 100/E5
Orba (riv.), It. 116/B3
Orbe, Swi. 114/C4
Orbe (riv.), Swi. 114/C4
Orbetello, It. 116/D1
Orbigo (riv.), Sp. 102/C1
Orbost, Austl. 173/D3
Orbyhus, Swe. 96/G1
Orcemont, Fr. 88/H6
Orcera, Sp. 102/D3
Orchamps, Fr. 114/B3
Orchamps-Vennes, Fr. 114/C3
Orchard (lake), Mi, US 193/F6
Orchard City, Co, US 186/F3
Orchard Farm, Mo, US 195/G8
Orchard Homes, Mt, US 184/E4
Orchard Lake Village, Mi, US 193/F6
Orchid (isl.), Tai. 137/D5
Orchies, Fr. 110/C3
Orciano di Pesaro, It. 117/F5
Orco (riv.), It. 101/G4
Orcopampa, Peru 214/C4
Orcotuna, Peru 214/C3
Ord, Ne, US 185/J5
Ordaz (int'l arpt.), Mex. 200/D4
Ordes, Sp. 102/A1
Ordesa y Monte Perdido, PN de, Sp. 103/F1
Ordos (des.), China 128/J4
Ordos (Mu Us Shamo) (des.), China 128/J4
Ordu, Turk. 148/D1
Ordu (prov.), Turk. 148/D1
Ore, Nga. 161/G5
Orealla, Guy. 211/G3
Örebro, Swe. 96/F2
Örebro (prov.), Swe. 95/E4
Örebro (int'l arpt.), Swe. 96/F2
Oregon (state), US 184/C5
Oregon Caves Nat'l Mon., Or, US 184/C5
Oregon City, Or, US 184/C4
Öregrund, Swe. 96/H1
Orekhovo-Zuyevo, Rus. 118/H5
Orël, Rus. 120/F1
Orellana, Peru 214/C4
Orellana la Vieja, Sp. 102/C3
Orem, Ut, US 195/K13
Orenberg (int'l arpt.), Rus. 121/K2
Orenburg, Rus. 121/K2
Orenburgskaya Oblast, Rus. 145/B2
Orense, Sp. 102/B1

Orestiás, Gre. 105/K2
Øresund (sound), Swe. 96/E4
Oreti (riv.), NZ 175/R12
Orford, Austl. 173/C4
Orford (pt.), Eng, UK 91/H2
Organ Pipe Cactus Nat'l Mon., Az, US 186/D4
Orgãos, Serra dos (mts.), Braz. 213/K7
Orgaz, Sp. 102/D3
Orgelet, Fr. 114/B4
Orgeurs, Fr. 88/H5
Orgeval, Fr. 88/H5
Orgosolo, It. 104/A2
Orhaneli, Turk. 120/D5
Orhangazi, Turk. 107/J5
Orhei, Mol. 107/J2
Orhon (riv.), Mong. 128/J2
Oria, Sp. 102/D4
Orient (pt.), NY, US 197/F1
Orient (riv.), Fr. 114/B4
Oriental, Mex. 201/M7
Oriental, Cordillera (mts.), SAm. 208/C5
Orientale (prov.), D.R. Congo 162/A3
Oriente, Árg. 216/E3
Origny-Sainte-Benoîte, Fr. 110/C4
Orihuela, Sp. 103/E3
Orillia, On, Can. 188/E2
Orimattila, Fin. 97/L1
Orinda, Ca, US 193/K11
Orinoco (delta), Ven. 211/F2
Orinoco (riv.), Col.,Ven. 211/F2
Orio al Serio (int'l arpt.), It. 116/C2
Oriolo, It. 104/E2
Orion (lake), Mi, US 193/F6
Orissa (state), India 140/D3
Orissa Coast (canal), India 143/F5
Oristano, It. 104/A3
Oristano, Golfo di (gulf), It. 104/A3
Orivesi, Fin. 97/L1
Oriximiná, Braz. 209/G4
Orizaba, Mex. 201/M8
Orizona, Braz. 212/A5
Orjen (peak), Mont. 106/D4
Örjiva, Sp. 102/D4
Orke (riv.), Ger. 109/F6
Örkelljunga, Swe. 96/E3
Orkhomenós, Gre. 105/H3
Orkney, SAfr. 164/D2
Orkney (isls.), UK 218/G
Orla, Tx, US 190/C4
Orland Park, Il, US 193/Q16
Orlândia, Braz. 213/C2
Orlando (int'l arpt.), Fl, US 191/H4
Orlando, Fl, US 191/H4
Orlando, Capo d' (cape), It. 104/D3
Orléanais (reg.), Fr. 100/D2
Orleans, Ca, US 184/C5
Orleans (parish), La, US 195/P16
Orlenbach, Ger. 111/G2
Orlík (res.), Czh. 113/H3
Orlová, Czh. 99/K4
Orlovskaya Oblast, Rus. 120/F1
Orly (int'l arpt.), Fr. 88/K5
Orly, Fr. 88/K5
Ormanli, Turk. 107/K5
Ormea, It. 116/A4
Ormília, Gre. 105/H2
Ormiston, Sc, UK 94/D5
Ormoc, Phil. 137/D5
Ormond Beach, Fl, US 191/H4
Ormskirk, Eng, UK 93/F4
Ornain (riv.), Fr. 100/F2
Ornans, Fr. 114/C3
Ornavasso, It. 115/E6
Orne (riv.), Fr. 98/C4
Ørnes, Nor. 95/E2
Orneta, Pol. 97/J4
Örnsköldsvik, Swe. 95/F3
Oro (riv.), Mex. 212/C2
Oro Grande, Ca, US 194/C1
Oro, Monte d' (peak), Fr. 104/A1
Oro Valley, Az, US 186/E4
Orocó, Braz. 212/C3
Orocué, Col. 210/D3
Orodara, Burk. 160/D4
Orofino, Id, US 184/D4
Orolo (riv.), It. 117/E1
Oroluk (isl.), Micr. 174/E4
Oron-la-Ville, Swi. 114/C4
Orono, Me, US 189/G2
Oronsay (isl.), Sc, UK 89/P8
Orontes (riv.), Syria 148/D3
Oropesa, Sp. 102/C3
Oroqen Zizhiqi, China 129/M1
Orós, Braz. 212/C2
Orosei, It. 104/A2
Orosei, Golfo di (gulf), It. 104/A2
Orosháza, Hun. 106/E2
Oroszlány, Hun. 106/D2
Orovada, Nv, US 184/D5
Oroville, Wa, US 184/D3
Oroville, Ca, US 186/B3
Orphin, Fr. 88/H6
Orpund, Swi. 114/D3
Orrefors, Swe. 96/F3
Orrell, Eng, UK 93/F4
Orrick, Mo, US 195/E5

Orrin (riv.), Sc, UK 94/B2
Orrin (res.), Sc, UK 94/B2
Orroli, It. 104/A3
Orroroo, Austl. 171/H5
Orrtanna, Pa, US 196/A4
Orry-la-Ville, Fr. 88/K4
Orsa, Swe. 96/F1
Orsago, It. 117/F1
Orsay, Fr. 88/J5
Orsett, Eng, UK 88/E2
Orsha, Bela. 97/P4
Orsk, Rus. 121/L2
Orsonnens, Swi. 114/C4
Orșova, Rom. 106/F3
Ørsta, Nor. 95/C3
Orsundsbro, Swe. 96/G2
Orta (lake), It. 101/H4
Orta, Turk. 120/E4
Orta Nova, It. 104/D2
Ortaca, Turk. 148/B2
Ortaköy, Turk. 148/C1
Ortaköy, Turk. 148/C2
Ortega, Col. 210/C4
Ortegal (cape), Sp. 102/B1
Ortenberg, Ger. 112/C2
Orth an der Donau, Aus. 107/P7
Orthez, Fr. 100/C5
Ortigara (peak), It. 115/H5
Ortigueira, Sp. 102/B1
Orting, Wa, US 193/C3
Ortiz, Mex. 200/C2
Ortles (mts.), It. 101/J3
Ortles (peak), It. 115/G4
Ortón (riv.), Bol. 208/E6
Ortona, It. 104/D1
Ortonville, Mn, US 185/J4
Ortonville, Mi, US 193/F6
Örtze (riv.), Ger. 109/H3
Orümiyeh, Iran 148/F2
Orurillo, Peru 214/D4
Oruro, Bol. 208/E7
Orust (isl.), Swe. 96/D2
Orvieto, It. 101/K5
Orvilliers, Fr. 88/G5
Orwell (riv.), Eng, UK 91/H2
Orwigsburg, Pa, US 196/B2
Oryakhovo, Bul. 107/F4
Orzinuovi, It. 116/C2
Orzysz, Pol. 97/J5
Os, Nor. 96/A1
Osa, Rus. 119/M4
Osa, Peninsula de (pen.), CR 208/B2
Osage (riv.), Mo, US 187/J3
Osage Beach, Mo, US 187/J3
Ōsaka (pref.), Japan 132/D3
Ōsaka, Japan 135/J6
Ōsaka Castle, Japan 135/H6
Osan, SKor. 131/D4
Osasco, Braz. 213/G8
Ōsato, Japan 135/C1
Osborn (mt.), Ak, US 192/E3
Osburg, Ger. 111/F4
Osby, Swe. 96/E3
Osceola, Ar, US 188/B5
Oschersleben, Ger. 98/F2
Oschiri, It. 104/A2
Oscura (mts.), NM, US 190/B3
Osdorf, Ger. 109/G1
Osh, Kyr. 145/F4
Oshamambe, Japan 134/B2
Oshawa, On, Can. 189/S8
Oshino, Japan 135/B3
Oshkosh, Wi, US 185/H5
Oshnovīyeh, Iran 148/F2
Oshogbo, Nga. 161/G5
Osijek, Cro. 106/D3
Osio Sotto, It. 116/C1
Osipaonica, Serb. 106/E3
Oskarshamn, Swe. 96/G3
Oskarström, Swe. 96/E3
Oskol (riv.), Rus.,Ukr. 120/F2
Oslo (cap.), Nor. 96/D2
Osmānābād, India 147/L5
Osmancık, Turk. 148/C1
Osmaneli, Turk. 107/K5
Osmaniye, Turk. 149/E1
Osnabrück, Ger. 109/F4
Osnago, It. 116/C1
Oso (riv.), D.R. Congo 162/A3
Oso (mt.), La, US 193/M12
Osogna, Swi. 115/E3
Osório, Braz. 213/B4
Osorno, Sp. 102/C1
Osorno, Chile 216/B4
Osoyoos, BC, Can. 184/D3
Ospedaletti, It. 116/A5
Ospedaletto Euganeo, It. 117/E2
Ospitaletto, It. 116/D1
Osprey (reef), Austl. 167/D2
Oss, Neth. 108/C5
Ossa (riv.), Austl. 173/C4
Ossa, Sierra de (mts.), Port. 102/B3
Osse (riv.), Nga. 161/G5
Osséja, Fr. 100/D5
Ossett, Eng, UK 93/G4
Ossi, It. 104/A2
Ossining, NY, US 197/K7
Ossora, Rus. 118/G4
Ostashkov, Rus. 118/G4
Ostbevern, Ger. 109/E4
Ostellato, It. 117/E3
Osten, Ger. 109/G1
Osterburg, Ger. 98/F2

Osterburken, Ger. 112/C4
Osterbybruk, Swe. 96/G1
Osterbymo, Swe. 96/F3
Ostercappeln, Ger. 109/F4
Osterdalälven (riv.), Swe. 96/F1
Osterems (chan.), Ger. 108/D1
Östergötland (co.), Swe. 95/E4
Osterhofen, Ger. 113/G5
Osterholz-Scharmbeck, Ger. 109/F2
Osteria Grande, It. 117/E4
Ostermiething, Aus. 113/F6
Osterode am Harz, Ger. 109/H5
Östersund, Swe. 95/E3
Östervåla, Swe. 96/G1
Ostfildern, Ger. 112/C5
Østfold (co.), Nor. 95/D4
Ostfriesland (reg.), Ger. 109/E2
Osthammar, Swe. 96/H1
Ostheim vor der Rhön, Ger. 112/D3
Osthofen, Ger. 112/B3
Ostia Antica (ruin), It. 104/C2
Ostiano, It. 116/D2
Ostiglia, It. 117/E2
Ostional NWR, CR 202/E4
Östra Silen (lake), Swe. 96/E2
Östra Vetere, It. 117/G5
Ostrach (riv.), Ger. 112/C6
Ostrava, Czh. 99/K4
Ostravský (pol. reg.), Czh. 99/J4
Ostrhauderfehn, Ger. 109/E2
Öśtri Rt (cape), Mont. 106/D4
Ostricourt, Fr. 110/C3
Ostróda, Pol. 97/H5
Ostrołęka, Pol. 99/L2
Ostrov, Czh. 113/F2
Ostrov, Rus. 97/N3
Ostrów Mazowiecka, Pol. 99/L2
Ostrów Wielkopolski, Pol. 99/J3
Ostrowiec Świętokrzyski, Pol. 99/L3
Ostrzeszów, Pol. 99/J3
Ostseebad Binz, Ger. 96/E4
Ostseebad Göhren, Ger. 96/E4
Ostseebad Prerow, Ger. 96/E4
Oststeinbek, Ger. 109/H1
Ostuni, It. 105/E2
Ostwald, Fr. 112/A5
Osum (riv.), Bul. 107/G4
Osum (riv.), Slvk. 106/E5
Osumi (isls.), Japan 132/B5
Ōsumi (pen.), Japan 132/B5
Osun (state), Nga. 161/G5
Osuna, Sp. 102/C4
Osvaldo Cruz, Braz. 213/B2
Oswaldtwistle, Eng, UK 93/F4
Oswego, NY, US 188/E3
Oswego, Il, US 193/P16
Oswestry, Eng, UK 93/E6
Oświęcim (Auschwitz), Pol. 99/K3
Ōta (riv.), Japan 132/C3
Ōta, Japan 135/C2
Otake, Japan 132/C3
Ōtaki, Japan 135/D3
Ōtaki, Japan 135/B2
Ōtaki-yama (peak), Japan 133/G2
Otava (riv.), Czh. 101/K2
Otavalo, Ecu. 210/B4
Otavi, Namb. 163/C4
Ōtawara, Japan 135/D1
Otay, Ca, US 194/C5
Otelu de Rey, Sp. 102/B1
Oteros (riv.), Mex. 200/C3
Otgon Tenger (peak), Mong. 128/G2
Othello, Wa, US 184/D4
Othis, Fr. 88/L4
Othonoí (isl.), Gre. 105/F3
Oti (riv.), Gha. 161/F4
Otjiwarongo, Namb. 163/C5
Otley, Eng, UK 93/G4
Otočac, Cro. 106/B3
Otofuke, Japan 134/C2
Otog Qi, China 128/J4
Otok, Cro. 106/D3
Ōtone, Japan 135/D1
Otopeni (int'l arpt.), Rom. 107/H3
Otoskwin (riv.), On, Can. 185/L3
Otowa, Japan 135/M6
Otra (riv.), Nor. 96/C2
Otradnyy, Rus. 121/J1
Otranto, It. 105/F2
Otranto, Strait of (str.), It. 105/F2
Otrokovice, Czh. 99/J4
Otse, Bots. 164/D2
Ōtsu, Japan 135/J6
Otsuchi, Japan 134/B4
Ōtsuki, Japan 135/C2
Otta, Nga. 161/F5
Otta (riv.), Nor. 95/D3
Ottawa (cap.), On, Can. 188/F2
Ottawa, Oh, US 188/C3
Ottawa, Ks, US 187/J3

Ottawa (int'l arpt.), On, Can. 188/F2
Ottawa (isls.), Nun., Can. 181/H3
Ottawa (riv.), On, Can. 188/E2
Ottensheim, Aus. 113/H6
Otter (riv.), Eng, UK 90/C5
Otterbach, Ger. 111/G5
Otterberg, Ger. 111/G4
Otterndorf, Ger. 109/F1
Ottersberg, Ger. 109/G2
Ottershaw, Eng, UK 88/B2
Otterville, Il, US 195/G7
Ottignies-Louvain-la-Neuve, Belg. 111/D2
Öttingen im Bayern, Ger. 112/D5
Ottmarsheim, Fr. 114/D2
Ottnang am Hausruck, Aus. 113/G6
Otto, Mo, US 195/F9
Ottobeuren, Ger. 115/G2
Ottobrunn, Ger. 113/E6
Ottone, It. 116/C3
Ottosdal, SAfr. 164/D2
Ottsville, Pa, US 196/C3
Ottumwa, Ia, US 185/K5
Otukpo, Nga. 161/G5
Otumba de Gómez Farías, Mex. 201/L7
Ouro Preto, Braz. 213/D2
Otuzco, Peru 214/B2
Otway (cape), Austl. 173/B3
Otway (bay), Chile 217/B3
Otway NP, Austl. 173/B3
Otwock, Pol. 99/L2
Ötztal Alps (mts.), Aus. 101/J3
Ötztaler Ache (riv.), Aus. 115/G3
Ou (mts.), Japan 134/B4
Ōu, Japan 134/B4
Ouachita (mts.), 187/J4
Ouachita (riv.), Ar,La, US 187/J4
Ouadda, CAfr. 155/K6
Ouaddaï (reg.), Chad 155/J5
Ouadi Haddad (riv.), Chad 155/J4
Ouadi Rimé (riv.), Chad 155/J4
Ouagadougou (int'l arpt.), Burk. 161/E3
Ouagadougou (cap.), Burk. 161/E3
Ouahigouya, Burk. 161/E3
Ouaka (riv.), CAfr. 155/K6
Oualâta, Dhar (cliff), Mrta. 160/D2
Ouallam, Niger 161/F3
Ouanda Djallé, CAfr. 155/K6
Ouanne (riv.), Fr. 100/E3
Ouarane (pol. reg.), Mrta. 154/C3
Ouarane (reg.), Mrta. 154/C3
Ouargla (prov.), Alg. 157/G3
Ouargla, Alg. 157/G3
Ouarkziz, Jebel (mts.), Mor. 156/C3
Ouarzazate (int'l arpt.), Mor. 156/D3
Ouarzazate, Mor. 156/D3
Ouasiemsca (riv.), Qu, Can. 188/F1
Oubangui (riv.), CAfr. 155/J7
Oubritenga (prov.), Burk. 161/E3
Ouche (riv.), Fr. 114/B3
Oud-Beijerland, Neth. 108/B5
Oud-Turnhout, Belg. 108/B6
Ōuda, Japan 135/J7
Oudalan (prov.), Burk. 161/E3
Ouddorp, Neth. 108/A5
Oude IJssel (riv.), Neth. 108/D5
Oude Pekela, Neth. 108/E2
Oude Westereems (chan.), Neth. 108/D1
Oudenaarde, Belg. 110/C2
Oudenbosch, Neth. 108/B5
Oudenburg, Belg. 110/C1
Oudewater, Neth. 108/B4
Oudon, Fr. 100/C3
Oudtshoorn, SAfr. 164/C4
Oued el Hadjar (well), Mali 160/D2
Oued Moulouyadeu (riv.), Mor. 154/E1
Oued Sous (riv.), Mor. 154/D1
Oued Zem, Mor. 154/D1
Ouémé (riv.), Ben. 154/F6
Ouémé (prov.), Ben. 161/F4
Ouenza, Alg. 158/L7
Ouerrha (riv.), Mor. 158/K7
Ouessa, Ben. 161/F4
Ouesso, Congo 154/J8
Ouest (prov.), Camr. 161/H5
Ouest (pt.), Haiti 203/H1
Ouezzane, Mor. 158/K7
Oughterard, Ire. 89/P10
Ouham (riv.), CAfr. 154/J6
Ouidah, Ben. 161/F5
Oujda, Mor. 158/D2
Oujda (Angads), (int'l arpt.), Mor. 158/D2
Oujeft, Mrta. 156/C5
Oulad Teïma, Mor. 154/D1
Oulangan NP, Fin. 118/F2
Ould Birni (well), Alg. 157/H4

Oulnina (peak), Austl. 171/H5
Oulu, Fin. 118/E2
Oulu (prov.), Fin. 95/H2
Oulujärvi (lake), Fin. 95/H2
Oulujoki (riv.), Fin. 95/H2
Oum El Bouaghi, Alg. 158/K7
Oum er Rbia, Oued (riv.), Mor. 156/D2
Oum er Rhia, Mor. 154/D1
Ounasjoki (riv.), Fin. 95/H2
Oupeye, Belg. 111/E2
Our (riv.), Eur. 111/E4
Ource (riv.), Fr. 100/F3
Ourcq (riv.), Fr. 98/B4
Ourcq, Canal de l' (canal), Fr. 88/K5
Øure Anarjokka NP, Nor. 95/H1
Øure Dividal NP, Nor. 95/F1
Ouricuri, Braz. 212/C3
Ourinhos, Braz. 213/B2
Ourique, Port. 102/A4
Ouro Fino, Braz. 213/G7
Ouro, Ponta do (pt.), Moz. 165/F2
Ouro Preto, Braz. 213/D2
Ouroux-sur-Saône, Fr. 114/A4
Ourthe Occidentale (riv.), Belg. 111/E3
Ourthe Orientale (riv.), Belg. 111/E3
Ouse (riv.), Eng, UK 93/H4
Oust (riv.), Fr. 100/B3
Outaouais (riv.), Qu, Can. 188/F2
Outardes (riv.), Qu, Can. 189/G1
Outardes Quatre (lake), Qu, Can. 189/G1
Outeïd Arkas (well), Mali 160/D2
Outer Hebrides (isls.), Sc, UK 89/P8
Outes, Sp. 102/A1
Outjo, Namb. 163/C5
Outlook, Sk, Can. 184/G3
Outreau, Fr. 110/A2
Outremont, Qu, Can. 189/N6
Ouvéze (riv.), Fr. 100/F4
Ouyen, Austl. 173/B2
Ouzinkie, Ak, US 192/H4
Ovada, It. 116/B3
Ovalle, Chile 215/B3
Ovana (peak), Ven. 211/E3
Ovar, Port. 102/A2
Overath, Ger. 111/G2
Overflakkee (isl.), Neth. 108/A5
Overhalla, Nor. 95/D2
Overholser (lake), Ok, US 195/M14
Overijse, Belg. 111/D2
Overijssel (prov.), Neth. 108/D3
Overijssels (riv.), Neth. 108/D4
Overkalix, Swe. 95/G2
Overland, Mo, US 195/G8
Overland Park, Ks, US 195/D6
Overlea, Md, US 196/B5
Overo (peak), Arg. 216/C5
Overpelt, Belg. 111/E1
Overton, Nv, US 186/D3
Overtorneå, Swe. 118/D2
Overum, Swe. 96/G3
Oviedo, Sp. 102/C1
Ovoca, Ire. 92/B6
Övörhangay (prov.), Mong. 128/H2
Övre Fryken (lake), Swe. 96/E1
Øvre Pasvik NP, Nor. 95/J1
Ovriá, Gre. 105/G3
Owando, Congo 154/J8
Owani, Japan 134/B3
Owariasahi, Japan 135/M5
Owase, Japan 132/E3
Owassa (lake), NJ, US 196/D1
Owasso, Ok, US 187/J3
Owego, NY, US 188/E3
Owen (mt.), NZ 175/S11
Owen, Austl. 171/H5
Owen Falls (dam), Ugan. 162/B2
Owen Roberts (int'l arpt.), UK 203/F2
Owen Sound, On, Can. 188/D2
Owenkillew (riv.), NI, UK 92/A2
Owens (riv.), Ca, US 186/C3
Owensboro, Ky, US 188/C4
Owenton, Ky, US 188/C4
Owingen, Ger. 115/F2
Owings, Md, US 196/B6
Owings Mills, Md, US 196/B5
Owl Creek (mts.), Wy, US 184/F4
Owo, Nga. 161/G5
Owosso, Mi, US 188/C3
Owyhee (riv.), Id,Or, US 184/D5
Owyhee, South Fork (riv.), Nv, US 184/D5
Owyhee (lake), Or, US 184/D4
Owyhee (mts.), Id, US 186/C2

Oulnina (peak), Austl. 171/H5
Owyhee (riv.), Id,Or, US 184/D5
Oxapampa, Peru 214/C3
Oxbow (lake), Mi, US 193/F6
Oxbow, Sk, Can. 185/H3
Oxelösund, Swe. 96/G2
Oxford (lake), Mb, Can. 185/K2
Oxford, Eng, UK 91/E3
Oxford (canal), Eng, UK 91/E3
Oxford, Mi, US 193/F6
Oxford, Ms, US 191/F3
Oxfordshire (co.), Eng, UK 91/E3
Oxie, Swe. 96/E4
Oxkutzcab, Mex. 202/D1
Oxnard, Ca, US 194/A2
Oxnard Beach, Ca, US 194/A2
Oxon Hill (farm), Md, US 196/A6
Oxon Hill-Glassmanor, Md, US 196/B6
Oxted, Eng, UK 88/C2
Oyabe, Japan 133/F2
Oyama, Japan 133/F2
Oyama, Japan 135/B3
Ōyama, Japan 135/K6
Oyamazaki, Japan 135/J6
Oyapock (riv.), Fr. 209/H3
Oye-Plage, Fr. 110/B2
Oyem, Gabon 154/H7
Oyen, Ab, Can. 184/F3
Øyer, Nor. 96/D1
Oykell (riv.), Sc, UK 89/R8
Oyo (state), Nga. 161/F4
Oyo, Nga. 161/F5
Oyodo (riv.), Japan 132/B5
Oyodo, Japan 135/J7
Oyón, Peru 214/B3
Oyonnax, Fr. 114/B5
Oyster Bay, NY, US 197/L8
Oyster Bay (har.), NY, US 197/L8
Oyster Bay Cove, NY, US 197/L8
Oyster Bay NWR, NY, US 197/L8
Oyten, Ger. 109/G2
Oyu (riv.), Kaz. 145/B3
Ozamiz, Phil. 137/D6
Ozanne (riv.), Fr. 100/D2
Ozark (plat.), Mo, US 187/J3
Ozark, Ar, US 187/J4
Ozark, Al, US 191/G4
Ozark (mts.), Ar,Mo, US 183/H4
Ozarks, Lake of the (lake), Mo, US 190/E2
Ozd, Hun. 99/L4
Ozernoy (cape), Rus. 123/S4
Ozette (lake), Wa, US 184/B3
Ozhiski (lake), On, Can. 185/L3
Ozieri, It. 104/A2
Özkonak, Turk. 148/C2
Ozoir-la-Ferrière, Fr. 88/L5
Ozona, Tx, US 187/D5
Ozora, Hun. 106/D2
Ozorków, Pol. 99/K3
Özouer-le-Voulgis, Fr. 88/L6
Ozuluama de Mascareñas, Mex. 202/B1
Ozzano dell'Emilia, It. 117/E4

P

P. K. Le Rouxdam (res.), SAfr. 164/D3
Pa-an, Myan. 136/B2
Pa Sak (riv.), Thai. 141/H4
Paar (riv.), Ger. 98/F4
Paarl, SAfr. 164/L10
Paauilo, Hi, US 182/U10
Pabbi, Pak. 144/A2
Pabellón de Arteaga, Mex. 200/E4
Pabianice, Pol. 99/K3
Pābna, Bang. 143/G3
Pābna (pol. reg.), Bang. 143/G3
Pacaás Novos, PN dos (mts.), Braz. 208/F6
Pacaás Novos, Serra dos (mts.), Braz. 208/F6
Pacajá (riv.), Braz. 209/H4
Pacajus, Braz. 212/C2
Pacaltsdorp, SAfr. 164/C4
Pacaraimã (mts.), Braz. 208/F3
Pacaya Samiria, Reserva Nacional, Peru 214/C2
Paccha, Peru 214/C3
Paceco, It. 104/C4
Pachacamac (ruin), Peru 214/B3
Pachaconas, Peru 214/C4
Pachamarca (riv.), Peru 214/C3
Pachino, It. 104/D4
Pachitea (riv.), Peru 214/C3
Pachiza, Peru 214/C3
Pachmarhī, India 142/B4
Pachuca, Mex. 201/L6
Pacific (ocean) 125/N8

Pacific (range), BC, Can. 184/B3
Pacific, Wa, US 193/C3
Pacific Palisades, Hi, US 182/W13
Pacifico (mtn.), Ca, US 194/B2
Pacinan (cape), Indo. 138/D5
Pacitan, Indo. 138/D5
Paço de Arcos, Port. 103/P10
Pad Idan, Pak. 147/J3
Padampur, India 140/D3
Padang, Indo. 138/B4
Padangpanjang, Indo. 138/B4
Padangsidempuan, Indo. 138/A3
Paddock Lake, Wi, US 193/P14
Paddock Wood, Eng, UK 88/E3
Paderborn, Il, US 195/G9
Paderborn, Ger. 109/F5
Paderno, It. 117/F1
Padiham, Eng, UK 93/F4
Padilla, Bol. 208/F7
Padina, Serb. 106/E3
Padjelanta NP, Swe. 95/F2
Padova (prov.), It. 117/E2
Padova, It. 117/E2
Padrão, Ponta do (pt.), Ang. 163/B2
Padrauna, India 142/D2
Padre (isl.), Tx, US 190/D5
Padre Island Nat'l Seashore, Tx, US 190/D5
Padrón, Sp. 102/A1
Paducah, Ky, US 188/B4
Paducah, Tx, US 187/G4
Padul, Sp. 102/D4
Padula, It. 104/D2
Paektŏk-san (peak), SKor. 131/E4
Paektu-san (peak), NKor. 131/E2
Paese, It. 117/F1
Páez, Col. 210/C3
Páez, Col. 210/C4
Pafúri, Moz. 163/F5
Pag, Cro. 106/B3
Pag (isl.), Cro. 106/B3
Pagadian, Phil. 139/F2
Pagai Selatan (isl.), Indo. 138/B4
Pagai Utara (isl.), Indo. 138/B4
Pagan, Myan. 141/F3
Pagan (isl.), NMar. 174/D1
Paganica, It. 104/C1
Page, Az, US 186/E3
Pager (riv.), Ugan. 162/B2
Pagny-sur-Moselle, Fr. 111/F6
Pagosa Springs, Co, US 186/F3
Pagwachuan (riv.), On, Can. 188/C1
Pahala, Hi, US 182/U11
Pahang (riv.), Malay. 138/B3
Páhara (lag.), Nic. 203/F3
Pahárpur, Pak. 144/A3
Pahāsu, India 142/B1
Pahlgãm, India 144/C2
Pahrump, Nv, US 186/D3
Pahuatlán, Mex. 201/L6
Pahute (mesa), Nv, US 186/C3
Pai (lake), China 130/C3
Paia, Hi, US 182/T10
Paignton, Eng, UK 90/C6
Paiján, Peru 214/B2
Päijänne (lake), Fin. 95/H3
Paikü (lake), China 143/E1
Pailolo (chan.), Hi, US 182/T10
Paimio, Fin. 97/K1
Paine (peak), Chile 216/B8
Paine, Chile 216/N8
Painesville, Oh, US 188/D3
Paint (lake), Mb, Can. 185/J2
Paint Rock, Tx, US 190/D4
Painted (des.), Az, US 186/E4
Paipa, Col. 210/C3
País Vasco (aut. comm.), Sp. 102/D1
Paisley, Sc, UK 94/B5
Paita, Peru 214/A2
Paithan, India 140/C4
Pajala, Swe. 95/G2
Paján, Ecu. 210/A5
Pajęczno, Pol. 99/K3
Pakanbaru, Indo. 138/B4
Pakch'ŏn, NKor. 131/C3
Pakenham, Austl. 173/G6
Pakenham (cape), Chile 217/B6
Pákhnes (peak), Gre. 105/J5
Pakhra (riv.), Rus. 119/W9
Pakistan (ctry.) 147/H3
Paklenica NP, Cro. 106/B3
Pakokku, Myan. 141/G3
Pakowki (lake), Ab, Can. 184/F3
Pakrac, Cro. 106/C2
Paks, Hun. 106/D2
Pakwach, Ugan. 162/A2
Pakxe, Laos 136/D3
Pala, Chad 154/H6
Pala (riv.), US 194/C4
Pala Ind. Res., Ca, US 194/C4
Palace, Mona. 116/J8
Palafrugell, Sp. 103/G2
Palagonia, It. 104/D4

Palagruža (isls.), Cro. 104/E1
Pálairos, Gre. 105/G3
Palaiseau, Fr. 88/J5
Pālakollu, India 140/D4
Palamás, Gre. 105/H3
Palamós, Sp. 103/G2
Palana, Rus. 123/R4
Palangkaraya, Indo. 138/D4
Pālanpur, India 147/K4
Palaoa (pt.), Hi, US 182/T10
Palapye, Bots. 163/E5
Palar (riv.), India 140/C5
Palas de Rey, Sp. 102/B1
Pālāsbāri, India 143/H2
Palatine, Il, US 193/P15
Palatka, Fl, US 191/H4
Palau (ctry.) 174/C4
Palau We (isl.), Indo. 138/A2
Palaw, Myan. 136/B3
Palawan (isl.), Phil. 137/C6
Palawan Passage (chan.), Phil. 137/C6
Pālayankottai, India 140/C6
Palazzolo Acreide, It. 104/D4
Palazzolo dello Stella, It. 117/G1
Palazzolo sull'Oglio, It. 116/C1
Palé, EqG. 154/G8
Pale, Bosn. 106/D4
Paleleh, Indo. 139/F3
Palembang, Indo. 138/B4
Palena (riv.), Chile 216/B4
Palena, Chile 216/C4
Palencia, Sp. 102/C1
Palenque, Mex. 202/D2
Palenque, PN, Mex. 202/C2
Palermo, It. 104/C3
Palermo, NJ, US 196/D5
Palese (int'l arpt.), It. 104/E2
Palestine (lake), It. 116/B2
Palestro, It. 116/B2
Pālghar, India 147/K5
P'algong-san (peak), SKor. 131/D5
P'algong-san (peak), SKor. 131/E4
Palgrave (mt.), Austl. 170/B2
Palhano, Braz. 212/D1
Palhoça, Braz. 213/B3
Pāli, India 147/K3
Paliã Kalãn, India 142/C1
Palić, Serb. 106/D2
Palikea (peak), Hi, US 182/V13
Palikir (cap.), Micr. 174/E4
Paliouórion (cape), Gre. 105/H3
Palisades (cliff), NJ, NY, US 197/K8
Palisades, NY, US 197/K8
Palisades Interstate Park, NJ, US 196/D1
Palisades Park, NJ, US 197/K8
Paliseul, Belg. 111/F4
Pālitāna, India 147/K4
Palizada, Mex. 198/C4
Paljenik (peak), Bosn. 106/C3
Palk (str.), India 140/C6
Pallamallawa, Austl. 173/D1
Pallarenda, Austl. 172/B2
Pallas-Ounastunturin NP, Fin. 95/H1
Pallasca, Peru 214/B2
Pallastunturi (peak), Fin. 95/H1
Palliser (cape), NZ 175/T11
Palm Bay, Fl, US 191/H4
Palm Beach (int'l arpt.), Fl, US 191/H5
Palm City, Ca, US 194/C5
Palm Harbor, Fl, US 191/H4
Palm Island Aboriginal Settlement, Austl. 172/B2
Palm Springs, Ca, US 186/C4
Palma, Moz. 163/H3
Palma, Sp. 103/G3
Palma del Río, Sp. 102/C4
Palma di Montechiaro, It. 104/C4
Palma Mallorca (int'l arpt.), Sp. 103/G3
Palma Soriano, Cuba 203/H1
Palmácia, Braz. 212/C2
Palmanova, It. 117/G1
Palmar (riv.), Ven. 203/H4
Palmares, Braz. 212/D3
Palmarito, Ven. 210/D3
Palmas, Braz. 213/A3
Palmas (cape), Libr. 160/D5
Palmdale, Ca, US 194/B1
Palmeira, Braz. 213/B3
Palmeira, CpV. 151/K10
Palmeira dos Índios, Braz. 212/C3
Palmeirais, Braz. 212/B2
Palmeiras (riv.), Braz. 212/A4
Palmeiras, Braz. 212/B4
Palmeirinha, Ponta da (pt.), Ang. 163/B2
Palmela, Port. 103/Q10
Palmer, US, Ant. 218/V
Palmer, Wa, US 193/D3

Palmer Land (phys. reg.), Ant. 218/V
Palmerston, NZ 175/S12
Palmerston (cape), Austl. 172/C3
Palmerston Atoll (atoll), Cooks. 175/J6
Palmerston North, NZ 175/T11
Palmerston NP, Austl. 172/B2
Palmerton, Pa, US 196/C2
Palmetto, Fl, US 191/H5
Palmi, It. 104/D3
Palmilla, Chile 216/C2
Palmillas (pt.), Cuba 203/F1
Palmira, Col. 210/B4
Palmital, Braz. 213/B2
Palmitas, Uru. 217/K10
Palmyra (isl.), Hi, US 182/R10
Palmyra, India 143/G4
Palmyra, Ut, US 195/K13
Palmyra (isl.), 175/J4
Palmyra, Pa, US 196/B3
Palmyra (Tadmur) (ruin), Syria 148/D3
Palmyras (pt.), India 140/E3
Palni, India 140/C5
Palo, Phil. 137/D5
Palo Alto, Ca, US 186/B3
Palo Alto, Pa, US 196/B2
Palo Pinto, Tx, US 187/H4
Palo Verde, PN, CR 198/D5
Palomeu (riv.), Sur. 211/H4
Palon (peak), It. 117/E1
Palos (cape), Sp. 103/E4
Palos de la Frontera, Sp. 102/B4
Palos Hills, Il, US 193/Q16
Palos Verdes (hills), Ca, US 194/F8
Palos Verdes (pt.), Ca, US 194/F8
Palos Verdes Estates, Ca, US 194/F8
Palosco, It. 116/C1
Palpalá, Arg. 215/C1
Palpetu (cape), Indo. 139/G4
Palu, Indo. 139/F4
Palu, Turk. 148/D2
Paluan, Phil. 137/D5
Palwal, India 142/A1
Pamangkat, Indo. 138/C3
Pambula, Austl. 173/D3
Pamiers, Fr. 100/D5
Pamir (reg.), China,Taj. 122/H6
Pamlico (riv.), NC, US 191/J3
Pamlico (sound), NC, US 191/J3
Pampa, Tx, US 187/G4
Pampachiri, Peru 214/C4
Pampacolca, Peru 214/C4
Pampas (plain), Arg. 216/E3
Pampas, Peru 214/C4
Pampas, Peru 214/C4
Pampilhosa da Serra, Port. 102/B2
Pamplona, Sp. 102/E1
Pamplona, Col. 210/C3
Pampulha (int'l arpt.), Braz. 213/D1
Pāmpur, India 144/C2
Pamukova, Turk. 107/K5
Pan de Azúcar, PN, Chile 215/B2
Panaba, Mex. 202/D1
Panabo, Phil. 137/E6
Pānāgar, India 142/B4
Panagyurishte, Bul. 107/G4
Panaitan (isl.), Indo. 138/B5
Panaji, India 147/K5
Panama (ctry.) 203/F4
Panamá (bay), Pan. 203/G4
Panamá (cap.), Pan. 203/G4
Panama (canal), Pan. 203/G4
Panama (gulf), Pan. 212/A5
Panama City, Fl, US 191/G4
Panama, Isthmus of (isth.), Pan. 203/F4
Panamá Viejo (ruin), Pan. 210/B2
Panamint (range), Ca, US 186/C3
Panao, Peru 214/B3
Panaro (riv.), It. 101/J4
Panay (isl.), Phil. 137/D5
Pancake (range), Nv, US 186/C3
Pančevo, Serb. 106/E3
Pančicev vrh (peak), Serb. 106/E4
Pancilet (res.), India 143/F4
Panciu, Rom. 107/H3
Pandamatenga, Bots. 163/E4
Pandharpur, India 147/L5
Pandino, It. 116/C2
Pando, Uru. 217/L11
Pāndoh, India 144/D4
Pandrup, Den. 96/C3
Pandua, India 143/G4
Panevėžys, Lith. 97/L4
Panfilov, Kaz. 122/J5
Pangai, Tonga 175/H6
Pangaion (peak), Gre. 105/J2
Pangani, Tanz. 162/C4
Pangani (riv.), Tanz. 162/C3

Pangkalanberandan, Indo. 138/A3
Pangkalaseang (cape), Indo. 139/F4
Pangkalpinang, Indo. 138/C4
Pangnirtung, Nun., Can. 181/K2
Panguipulli, Chile 216/B3
Panguitch, Ut, US 186/D3
Pangutaran, Phil. 139/F2
Pangutaran (isl.), Phil. 137/C6
Paniai (lake), Indo. 139/J4
Paniau (peak), Hi, US 182/R10
Pānīhāti, India 143/G4
Pānīpat, India 144/D5
Paniqui, Phil. 137/D4
Panj (riv.), Afg. 147/K1
Panjwīn, Iraq 146/E1
Panke (riv.), Ger. 98/Q6
Panna, India 142/C3
Pannawonica, Austl. 170/C2
Pannikin (isl.), Austl. 172/F7
Pano Lefkara, Cyp. 149/C2
Panorama, Braz. 213/B2
Panshan, China 130/C3
Pantanal (lowland), Braz. 209/G7
Pantanal Matogrossense, PN, Braz. 209/G7
Pantelleria, It. 104/B4
Pantelleria (isl.), It. 104/C4
Pantigliate, It. 116/C2
Pantin, Fr. 88/K5
Pantoja, Peru 210/C5
Pantin, Sp. 102/B1
Pantukan, Phil. 137/E6
Pánuco (riv.), Mex. 198/B3
Pánuco, Mex. 202/B1
Panzhihua, China 141/H2
Panzós, Guat. 202/D3
Pão de Açúcar, Braz. 212/C3
Paola, It. 104/E3
Paola, Malta 104/M7
Paoli, Pa, US 196/C3
Paonia, Co, US 186/F3
Paonta Sahib, India 144/D4
Paoua, CAfr. 154/J6
Pápa, Hun. 106/C2
Papa Westray (isl.), Sc, UK 89/V14
Papagayo (gulf), CR 198/D5
Papaikou, Hi, US 182/U11
Papanduva, Braz. 213/B3
Papantla, Mex. 201/M6
Papaplaya, Peru 214/C2
Papenburg, Ger. 109/E2
Papendrecht, Neth. 108/B5
Paphos, Cyp. 149/C2
Paphos (dist.), Cyp. 149/C2
Papingut (peak), Alb. 105/G2
Papisoi (cape), Indo. 139/H4
Pappenheim, Ger. 112/D5
Papua New Guinea (ctry.) 174/D5
Papudo, Chile 216/C2
Papunya, Austl. 171/F2
Pará (riv.), Braz. 209/H4
Pará (state), Braz. 212/A1
Para (dist.), Sur. 211/H3
Pará (falls), Ven. 211/E3
Pará de Minas, Braz. 213/C1
Para, South (riv.), Austl. 171/M8
Para Wirra NP, Austl. 171/M8
Paraburdoo, Austl. 170/C2
Paracambi, Braz. 213/K7
Paracas (pen.), Peru 214/B4
Paracas, Reserva Nacional, Peru 214/B4
Paracatu, Braz. 212/A5
Paracatu (riv.), Braz. 212/A5
Paracel (isls.), 137/E3
Paracho de Verduzco, Mex. 200/E5
Paracín, Serb. 106/E4
Paradhísion (int'l arpt.), Gre. 148/B2
Paradip, India 140/E3
Paradis, La, US 195/P17
Paradise (valley), Az, US 195/R18
Paradise, Mo, US 195/D5
Paradise, Nf, Can. 189/R8
Paradise Valley, Az, US 195/S18
Paragominas, Braz. 212/A1
Paraguá (riv.), Bol. 208/F6
Paraguá (riv.), Ven. 208/F2
Paraguaçu, Braz. 213/H6
Paraguaçu (riv.), Braz. 205/E4
Paraguaçu Paulista, Braz. 213/B2
Paraguaipoa, Ven. 210/C1
Paraguaná, Península de (pen.), Ven. 208/D1
Paraguarí, Par. 215/E2
Paraguay (ctry.) 205/C5
Paraguay (riv.), Par. 215/E1
Paraíba (state), Braz. 212/C2

Paraíba do Sul, Braz. 213/K7
Paraíba do Sul (riv.), Braz. 213/H8
Paraibano, Braz. 212/B2
Paraibuna, Braz. 213/H8
Paraim (riv.), Braz. 212/A3
Parainen (Pargas), Fin. 97/K1
Paraíso, Mex. 202/C2
Paraíso, CR 203/F4
Paraíso do Norte de Goiás, Braz. 209/J6
Parakou, Ben. 161/F4
Paramaribo (cap.), Sur. 209/G2
Paramaribo (dist.), Sur. 211/H3
Parambu, Braz. 212/C2
Paramillo (peak), Col. 210/C3
Paramillo, PN, Col. 208/C2
Paramirim (riv.), Braz. 209/K6
Paramirim, Braz. 212/B4
Paramithía, Gre. 105/G3
Paramount, Ca, US 194/F8
Paramus, NJ, US 197/J8
Paramushir (isl.), Rus. 125/Q5
Paraná, Arg. 215/D3
Paraná (riv.), It. 116/D3
Paraná (state), Braz. 213/B3
Paraná, It. 116/D3
Paraná (riv.), SAm. 215/E3
Paraná Ibicuy (riv.), Arg. 217/J10
Paraná Uraríá (riv.), Braz. 205/E3
Paranaíba, Braz. 212/A4
Paranaíba, Braz. 213/B1
Paranapanema (riv.), Braz. 215/F1
Paranapiacaba, Serra do (mts.), Braz. 205/H4
Paranatinga (riv.), Braz. 205/D4
Paranavaí, Braz. 215/F1
Parang, Phil. 139/F2
Paraopeba, Braz. 213/C1
Parapetí (riv.), Bol. 208/F7
Parati, Braz. 213/J8
Paratico, It. 116/C1
Paratinga, Braz. 212/B4
Paratinga (riv.), Braz. 213/H8
Parral, Chile 216/C3
Parras de la Fuente, Mex. 212/D2
Parrita, CR 203/E4
Pārbati (riv.), India 147/L4
Parbhani, India 147/L5
Parchim, Ger. 98/F2
Pardes Hanna-Karkur, Isr. 149/F7
Pārdi, India 147/K4
Pardo (riv.), Braz. 209/J8
Pardone (cape), SAfr. 164/D4
Pardubice, Czh. 99/H3
Pardubický (pol. reg.), Czh. 99/J4
Pare, Indo. 138/D5
Pare (mts.), Tanz. 162/C3
Parecis (mts.), Braz. 205/C4
Paredes de Nava, Sp. 102/C1
Paredón, Mex. 212/A5
Paredones, Chile 216/C2
Parelhas, Braz. 212/C2
Parempuyre, Fr. 100/C4
Parenda, India 140/C4
Parent (lake), Qu, Can. 188/E1
Parentis-en-Born, Fr. 100/C4
Parepare, Indo. 139/F4
Parera, Arg. 216/D2
Parets del Valles, Sp. 103/L6
Pargny-sur-Saulx, Fr. 111/D6
Paria (riv.), Ut, US 186/E3
Paria (gulf), Trin.,Ven. 211/F2
Paria, Peninsula de (pen.), Ven. 208/F1
Pariaco, Peru 214/B3
Pariaguán, Ven. 211/E2
Pariaman, Indo. 138/B4
Parikkala, Fin. 95/N3
Parima, Serra (mts.), Braz. 208/F3
Parinacota (peak), Bol. 214/D5
Parinari, Peru 214/B2
Pariñas (pt.), Peru 214/A2
Paríngu Mare (peak), Rom. 107/F3
Parintins, Braz. 209/G4
Paris, Tx, US 187/J4
Paris, Ar, US 187/J4
Paris (cap.), Fr. 88/K5
Paris (dept.), Fr. 110/B6
Parita (bay), Pan. 203/F4
Pariti, Indo. 139/F5
Park (range), Co, US 186/F2
Park (pt.), Eng, UK 90/A5

Park City, Ut, US 195/L12
Park City, Il, US 193/Q15
Park Falls, Wi, US 185/L4
Park Rapids, Mn, US 185/K4
Park Ridge, Il, US 193/Q16
Park Ridge, NJ, US 197/J7
Park River, ND, US 185/J3
Parkano, Fin. 95/G3
Parker, Tx, US 187/H4
Parker, Az, US 186/D4
Parker, Co, US 195/C3
Parkersburg, WV, US 188/D4
Parkes, Austl. 173/D2
Parkesburg, Pa, US 196/C4
Parkgate, NI, UK 92/B2
Parkdale, Mo, US 195/F9
Parkside, Pa, US 196/C4
Parkstetten, Ger. 113/F5
Parkton, Md, US 196/B4
Parkville, Mo, US 195/D5
Parkville, Md, US 196/B5
Parkway-Sacramento, Ca, US 193/L9
Parla, Sp. 103/N9
Parlakhemundi, India 140/D4
Parli, India 147/L5
Parma, Oh, US 188/D3
Parma (prov.), It. 116/C3
Parma (riv.), It. 116/D3
Parma, It. 116/D3
Parmain, Fr. 88/J4
Parnaíba, Braz. 212/B2
Parnaguá, Braz. 212/B3
Parnaíba, Braz. 212/B1
Parnaíba (riv.), Braz. 205/E3
Parnamirim, Braz. 212/C3
Parnamirim, Braz. 209/L5
Parnarama, Braz. 212/B2
Parnassós (peak), Gre. 105/H3
Parnassós NP, Gre. 105/H3
Párnis (peak), Gre. 105/N8
Párnis Óros NP, Gre. 105/N8
Párnon (mts.), Gre. 105/H4
Pärnu (bay), Est. 97/L3
Pärnu, Est. 97/L2
P'aro-ho (lake), SKor. 131/D3
Paron, Fr. 100/E2
Parona di Valpolicella, It. 117/D2
Paroo (riv.), Austl. 173/C1
Páros (isl.), Gre. 105/J4
Páros, Gre. 105/J4
Parow, SAfr. 164/L10
Parowan, Ut, US 186/D3
Parpan, Swi. 115/F4
Parral, Chile 216/C3
Parras de la Fuente, Mex. 212/D2
Parrett (riv.), Eng, UK 90/D4
Parrita, CR 203/E4
Parry (isls.), NW,Nun., Can. 181/R7
Parry (bay), Nun., Can. 181/H2
Parry (chan.), Nun., Can. 180/F1
Parry Sound, On, Can. 188/D2
Parsberg, Ger. 113/E4
Parseierspitze (peak), Aus. 115/G3
Parshall, ND, US 185/H4
Parsippany-Troy Hills, NJ, US 197/H8
Parsnip (riv.), BC, Can. 184/C2
Partenstein, Ger. 112/C2
Parthenay, Fr. 100/C3
Partille, Swe. 96/E3
Partinico, It. 104/C3
Partizansk, Rus. 129/P3
Partizánske, Slvk. 99/K4
Partridge (riv.), On, Can. 188/C1
Partūr, India 147/L5
Paru (riv.), Braz. 209/H4
Paru de Oeste (riv.), Braz. 205/D2
Paruro, Peru 214/D4
Parvatipuram, India 140/D4
Parys, SAfr. 164/D2
Pas-de-Calais (dept.), Fr. 110/A3
Pas de Morgins (pass), Fr. 114/C5
Pasadena, Tx, US 187/J5
Pasadena, Nf, Can. 189/K1
Pasadena, Md, US 196/B5
Pasadena, Ca, US 194/F7
Pasado (cape), Ecu. 210/A5
Pasaje, Ecu. 214/B1
Pasaman (peak), Indo. 138/B3
Pasān, India 142/D4
Pascagoula, Ms, US 191/F4
Pascani, Rom. 107/H2
Pasching, Aus. 113/H6
Pasco, Wa, US 184/D4
Pasco (dept.), Peru 214/C3
Pascua (riv.), Chile 217/B6

Pascua, Isla de (Easter) (isl.), Chile 175/Q7
Pascuales, Ecu. 214/B1
Pasewalk, Ger. 96/F5
Pasian di Prato, It. 117/G1
Pasiano, It. 117/F1
Pasig, Phil. 137/D5
Pasinler, Turk. 148/E2
Pasión, Río de la (riv.), Guat. 202/D2
Paslęk, Pol. 97/H4
Paslęka (riv.), Pol. 99/L2
Pasley (cape), Austl. 170/D5
Pašman (isl.), Cro. 106/B4
Pasni, Pak. 147/H3
Paso de Indios, Arg. 216/C4
Paso de los Libres, Arg. 215/E2
Paso de los Toros, Uru. 217/K10
Paso de Ovejas, Mex. 201/N7
Paso del Macho, Mex. 201/N8
Paso del Planchón (peak), Chile 216/C2
Paso Robles (El Paso de Robles), Ca, US 186/B4
Pasrūr, Pak. 144/C3
Pass (peak), Yk, Can. 192/M3
Passa Quatro, Braz. 213/J7
Passagem Franca, Braz. 212/B2
Passaic (riv.), NJ, US 196/D2
Passaic, NJ, US 197/J8
Passau, Ger. 113/G5
Passero (pt.), It. 104/D4
Passo Fundo, Braz. 213/A4
Passo Fundo, Barragem do (res.), Braz. 213/A3
Passons, It. 117/G1
Passoré (prov.), Burk. 161/E3
Passos, Braz. 213/C2
Passwang (peak), Swi. 114/D3
Passy, Fr. 114/C6
Pastavy, Bela. 97/M4
Pastaza (riv.), Ecu.,Peru 214/B2
Pastaza (dept.), Ecu. 210/B5
Pastek (riv.), Pol. 97/J5
Pasto, Col. 210/B4
Pastoriza, Sp. 102/B1
Pastos Bons, Braz. 212/A2
Pasuruan, Indo. 138/D5
Pásztó, Hun. 99/K5
Pata, Bol. 208/E6
Patagonia (phys. reg.), Arg. 216/D4
Patah (peak), Indo. 138/B4
Patan, India 142/B4
Pātan, India 147/K4
Pataná (peak), Braz. 213/B3
Patapsco (riv.), Md, US 196/A5
Patapsco, Md, US 196/B4
Pataudi, India 144/D5
Pataz, Peru 214/B2
Patchogue, NY, US 197/E2
Paternò, It. 104/D4
Paterna, Sp. 103/E3
Paterson, NJ, US 197/J8
Pathalgaon, India 142/D4
Pathānkot, India 144/C3
Pathein (Bassein), Myan. 141/F4
Pathfinder (res.), Wy, US 184/G5
Pati, Indo. 138/D5
Patía (riv.), Col. 210/B4
Patiāla, India 144/D4
Patikul, Phil. 139/F2
Patna, India 143/F3
Patna, Sc, UK 94/B6
Patnongon, Phil. 139/F1
Patnos, Turk. 148/E2
Pato Branco, Braz. 213/A3
Patoka (riv.), In, US 191/G2
Patos, Braz. 212/C2
Patos, Alb. 105/F2
Patos de Minas, Braz. 213/C1
Patos, Lagoa dos (lake), Braz. 215/G3
Patrai (gulf), Gre. 105/G3
Pātrasāer, India 143/F4
Patrātu, India 143/F4
Patricia (mt.), Austl. 171/F2
Patricio Lynch (isl.), Chile 217/A6
Patrocínio, Braz. 213/C1
Patscherkofel (peak), Aus. 115/H3
Pattani, Thai. 136/C5
Patti, India 144/C3
Patti, It. 104/D3
Pattoki, Pak. 144/B4
Pattukkottai, India 140/C5
Pattullo (mt.), BC, Can. 192/N4
Patuākhāli (pol. reg.), Bang. 143/G4
Patuākhāli, Bang. 143/H4

Patuca (riv.), Hon. 198/D5
Patuca (mts.), Hon. 202/E3
Patuca (pt.), Hon. 203/E3
Patuxent, Md, US 196/B5
Patuxent NWR, Md, US 196/B5
Patuxent River State Park, Md, US 196/A5
Páty, Hun. 107/Q9
Pátzcuaro, Mex. 201/E5
Pau Brasil, Braz. 212/C4
Pau, Fr. 100/C5
Pau dos Ferros, Braz. 212/C2
Paucarbamba, Peru 214/C4
Paucartambo, Peru 214/C4
Pauillac, Fr. 100/C4
Pauini (riv.), Braz. 208/E5
Paulaya (riv.), Hon. 203/E3
Paulinia, Braz. 213/F7
Paulins Kill (riv.), NJ, US 196/D2
Paulistana, Braz. 212/B3
Paullo, It. 116/C2
Paulo Afonso, Braz. 212/C3
Paulo Afonso, PN de, Braz. 212/C3
Paulo Ramos, Braz. 212/A2
Paulpietersburg, SAfr. 165/E2
Pauls Valley, Ok, US 187/H4
Paulsboro, NJ, US 196/C4
Pauma Valley, Ca, US 194/D4
Paungde, Myan. 141/M4
Pavão, Braz. 212/B5
Pavel Banya, Bul. 105/J1
Pavia (prov.), It. 116/C2
Pavia, It. 116/C2
Pavie, Fr. 100/D5
Pavlikeni, Bul. 107/G4
Pavlodar (obl.), Kaz. 145/G3
Pavlodar, Kaz. 145/G2
Pavlof (vol.), Ak, US 192/F4
Pavlohrad, Ukr. 120/E2
Pavlovo, Rus. 118/J5
Pavone Canavese, It. 116/A2
Pavone del Mella, It. 116/D2
Pavullo nel Frignano, It. 117/D4
Paw Paw, Mi, US 188/C3
Pawan (riv.), Indo. 138/D4
Pawãyan, India 142/C1
Pawhuska, Ok, US 187/H3
Pawnee (riv.), Ks, US 187/G3
Pawtucket, RI, US 189/G3
Paxoí (isl.), Gre. 105/F3
Paxson, Ak, US 192/J3
Paxton, Austl. 173/D2
Pay-Khoy (mts.), Rus. 122/G3
Payakumbuh, Indo. 138/B4
Payerne, Swi. 114/C4
Payette (riv.), Id, US 184/D5
Payne (lake), Qu, Can. 181/J3
Paynesville, Austl. 173/C3
Pays de Caux (reg.), Fr. 100/D2
Pays de France (reg.), Fr. 88/K4
Pays de la Loire (reg.), Fr. 100/C3
Paysandú, Uru. 217/J10
Payson, Az, US 186/E4
Payson, Ut, US 186/E2
Payún (peak), Arg. 216/C3
Paz (riv.), Guat. 202/D3
Paz de Ariporo, Col. 210/D3
Paz de Río, Col. 210/C3
Pazar, Turk. 148/D1
Pazar, Turk. 121/G4
Pazarcık, Turk. 148/D2
Pazardzhik, Bul. 107/G4
Pazaryeri, Turk. 107/G4
Pazin, Cro. 106/A3
Peabiru, Braz. 213/A2
Peace (riv.), BC, Can. 180/D3
Peace Memorial Park, Japan 132/C3
Peaceful Valley, Co, US 195/B2
Peachland, BC, Can. 184/D3
Peachtree City, Ga, US 191/G3
Peak Charles NP, Austl. 170/D5
Peak District NP, Eng, UK 93/G5
Peak Hill, Austl. 170/C3
Peal de Becerro, Sp. 102/D4
Peapack-Gladstone, NJ, US 196/D2
Pearblossom, Ca, US 194/C1
Pearl (har.), Hi, US 182/W13
Pearl, Ms, US 191/F3
Pearl and Hermes (reef), Hi, US 175/H2
Pearl Beach, Mi, US 193/G6
Pearl City, Hi, US 182/W13
Pearl River (estu.), China
Pearl River, La, US 195/Q16
Pearl River, NY, US 197/J7
Pearland, Tx, US 194/B1
Pearsall, Tx, US 187/H5
Pearson (int'l arpt.), On, Can. 189/Q8
Pearston, SAfr. 164/D4
Peary (chan.), Nun., Can. 181/R7
Pease (riv.), Tx, US 187/G4

Pebane, Moz. 163/G4
Pebas, Peru 214/D1
Pebble (isl.), Mald. 217/E6
Peć, Kos. 106/E4
Peccia, Swi. 115/E5
Peccioli, It. 117/D5
Pécel, Hun. 107/R10
Pech de Guillaument (peak), Fr. 100/E5
Pechanga Ind. Res., Ca, US 194/C4
Pechora, Rus. 119/N2
Pechora (bay), Rus. 119/M1
Pechora (riv.), Rus. 125/C3
Peckham, Co, US 195/C2
Peconic (riv.), NY, US 197/F2
Pecos, Tx, US 190/C4
Pecos (riv.), Tx, US 190/C4
Pecq, Belg. 110/C2
Pecquencourt, Fr. 110/C3
Pécs, Hun. 106/D2
Peculiar, Mo, US 195/E6
Pecy, Fr. 88/M6
Pedder (lake), Austl. 173/C4
Pedemonte, It. 117/D2
Pedernales (riv.), Tx, US 201/F2
Pedley, Ca, US 194/C3
Pedra Azul, Braz. 212/B5
Pedra Lume, CpV. 151/K10
Pedralva, Braz. 213/H7
Pedregal, Ven. 210/D2
Pedreguer, Sp. 103/F3
Pedreira, Braz. 213/G7
Pedreiras, Braz. 212/A2
Pedricktown, NJ, US 196/C4
Pedro (pt.), SrL. 140/D6
Pedro Avelino, Braz. 212/C2
Pedro Betancourt, Cuba 203/F1
Pedro Carbo, Ecu. 210/A5
Pedro Cays (isl.), Jam. 199/F4
Pedro li, Braz. 212/B2
Pedro IV (isl.), Braz. 211/E4
Pedro Juan Caballero, Par. 215/E1
Pedro Leopoldo, Braz. 213/C1
Pedro Luro, Arg. 216/E3
Pedro Osório, Braz. 213/A4
Peebles, Sc, UK 94/C5
Peedamulla Abor. Land, Austl. 170/B2
Peekskill, NY, US 196/E1
Peel (inlet), Austl. 170/B5
Peel (isl.), Austl. 172/F6
Peel (sound), Nun., Can. 180/G1
Peel (co.), On, Can. 189/Q8
Peel (riv.), Yk, Can. 180/C2
Peel, IM, UK 92/D3
Peel Fell (peak), Eng, UK 94/D6
Peene (riv.), Ger. 96/E5
Peer, Belg. 111/E1
Pegasus (bay), NZ 175/S11
Pegnitz, Ger. 113/E3
Pegnitz (riv.), Ger. 98/F4
Pego, Sp. 103/F3
Pego do Altar, Barragem de (res.), Port. 102/A3
Pegognaga, It. 117/D2
Pegwell (bay), Eng, UK 91/H4
Pehlivanköy, Turk. 107/H5
Pehowa, India 144/C4
Pehuajó, Arg. 216/E2
Pehuenche (pass), Chile 216/C2
Pei Xian, China 130/D4
Peine, Ger. 109/H4
Peipus (lake), Est.,Rus. 97/M2
Peiting, Ger. 115/G2
Peixe (riv.), Braz. 213/B2
Peixoto, Reprêsa de (res.), Braz. 213/C2
Pekalongan, Indo. 138/C5
Pekan, Malay. 138/B3
Pekan Nanas, Malay. 138/B3
Pekhora (riv.), Rus. 119/W9
Pekin, Il, US 185/L5
Pelada, Pampa (plain), Arg. 216/C3
Pelado (vol.), Mex. 201/Q10
Pelagie (isls.), It. 116/C3
Peleaga (peak), Rom. 106/F3
Pelee (isl.), On, Can. 181/H4
Pelée (pt.), On, Can. 181/H4
Pelée (peak), Mart., Fr. 199/N9
Pelham, On, Can. 189/Q9
Pelham, Al, US 191/G3
Pelham, NY, US 197/K8
Pelham Bay Park, NY, US 197/K8
Pelham Manor, NY, US 197/K8
Pelhřimov, Czh. 99/H4
Pelican (isl.), Ab, Can. 184/E2
Pelican (lake), Sk, Can. 185/H2
Pelican, Ak, US 192/L4
Pelican Narrows, Sk, Can. 185/H2
Pelindaba, Ponta de (pt.), GBis. 160/A4
Pelister (peak), FYROM 105/G2

Pelister NP, FYROM 105/G2
Peljekaise NP, Swe. 95/F2
Peljesac (pen.), Cro. 105/E1
Peljesac (pen.), Cro. 106/C4
Pell Lake, Wi, US 193/P14
Pélla, Gre. 105/H2
Pella (ruin), Gre. 105/H2
Pellegrini, Arg. 216/E3
Pellestrina, It. 117/F2
Pello, Fin. 118/E2
Pelly (riv.), Yk, Can. 180/C2
Pelly (bay), Nun., Can. 180/N2
Pelly Bay, Nun., Can. 180/N2
Peloponnesus (reg.), Gre. 105/G3
Peloritani, Monti (mts.), It. 104/D4
Pelotas (riv.), Braz. 215/F2
Pelotas, Braz. 213/A4
Pelplin, Pol. 97/H5
Pemali (cape), Indo. 139/F5
Pemali (cape), Indo. 139/F4
Pematangsiantar, Indo. 138/A3
Pemba, Moz. 163/H3
Pemba (isl.), Tanz. 163/G2
Pemba North (prov.), Tanz. 162/C4
Pemba South (prov.), Tanz. 162/C4
Pemberton, Austl. 170/C6
Pemberton, BC, Can. 184/C3
Pemberton, NJ, US 196/D4
Pembina (riv.), ND, US 184/F2
Pembina, ND, US 185/J3
Pembroke, On, Can. 188/E2
Pembroke, Wal, UK 90/B3
Pembrokeshire (co.), Wal, UK 90/A3
Pembrokeshire Coast NP, Wal, UK 90/A3
Pembury, Eng, UK 91/G4
Pemuco, Chile 216/B3
Pen Argyl, Pa, US 196/C2
Pen, The (lake), La, US 195/P17
Pen-y-Ghent (peak), Eng, UK 93/F3
Pen-y-Gogarth (pt.), Wal, UK 92/E5
Pen y Gurnos (peak), Wal, UK 90/C2
Peña Blanca (mtn.), Pan. 203/F4
Peña de Cerredo (mtn.), Sp. 102/C1
Peñafiel, Sp. 102/C2
Penafiel, Port. 102/A2
Peñaflor, Chile 216/N8
Penalva, Braz. 212/A1
Penamacor, Port. 102/B2
Peñápolis, Braz. 213/B2
Peñaranda de Bracamonte, Sp. 102/C2
Peñarroya (peak), Sp. 103/E2
Peñarroya-Pueblonuevo, Sp. 102/C3
Penarth, Wal, UK 90/C4
Peñas (cape), Sp. 102/C1
Peñas (cape), Arg. 217/D2
Penas, Golfo de (gulf), Chile 215/A6
Peñasco (riv.), NM, US 187/F4
Pench (riv.), India 142/B5
Penchard, Fr. 88/C3
Penco, Chile 216/B3
Pend Oreille (lake), Id, US 184/D4
Pendelikón (peak), Gre. 105/N8
Pendembu, SLeo. 160/C4
Pendências, Braz. 212/C2
Pendjar (riv.), Burk. 161/F3
Pendjari, PN de la, Ben. 154/F5
Pendle (hill), Eng, UK 93/F4
Pendleton, Or, US 184/D4
Peneda-Gerês NP, Port. 102/A2
Penedo, Braz. 212/C4
Penetanguishene, On, Can. 188/E2
Penglai, China 130/E3
Penguin, Austl. 173/C4
Penha, Braz. 213/B3
Penhold, Ab, Can. 184/E2
Peníbético, Sistema (range), Sp. 102/C4
Penicuik, Sc, UK 94/C5
Península de Paria, PN, Ven. 211/F2
Peñíscola, Sp. 103/F2
Penitente, Serra do (mts.), Braz. 209/J5
Penmaenmawr, Wal, UK 92/D5
Penmarc'h, Pointe de (pt.), Fr. 100/A3
Penn Forest (res.), Pa, US 196/C3
Penn Hills, Pa, US 188/E3
Penna, Punta della (cape), It. 104/D1
Penne (pt.), It. 105/E2
Penne, It. 104/C1
Penner (riv.), India 140/C5

Pennine Alps (mts.), Swi. 101/G4
Pennine Chain (mts.), Eng, UK 93/F2
Pennington, NJ, US 196/D3
Penns Creek (mtn.), Pa, US 196/A2
Penns Grove, NJ, US 196/C4
Penns Park, Pa, US 196/D3
Pennsauken, NJ, US 196/C4
Pennsburg, Pa, US 196/C3
Pennsville, NJ, US 196/C4
Pennsylvania (state), US 188/E3
Penny (str.), Nun., Can. 181/S7
Penobscot (riv.), Me, US 189/G2
Penola, Austl. 173/B3
Peñón Blanco, Mex. 200/D3
Penon de Al Hoceima (isl.), Sp. 158/C2
Penonomé, Pan. 203/F4
Penrhyn Mawr (pt.), Wal, UK 92/D6
Penrhyn Mawr (pt.), IM, UK 92/D5
Penrith, Eng, UK 93/F2
Pensacola, Fl, US 191/G4
Pensacola (mts.), Ant. 218/X
Pense, Sk, Can. 185/G3
Penshurst, Austl. 173/B3
Pentagon Fed. Govt. Res., Va, US 196/A6
Pentecost (isl.), Van. 174/F6
Pentecoste, Braz. 212/C1
Penteleu (peak), Rom. 107/H3
Penthalaz, Swi. 114/C4
Penticton, BC, Can. 184/D3
Pentire (pt.), Eng, UK 90/B5
Pentland, Austl. 172/B3
Pentland (hills), Sc, UK 94/C5
Pentland Firth (inlet), Sc, UK 89/V14
Peñuelas, PN, Chile 216/N8
Penwith (pen.), Eng, UK 90/A6
Penza, Rus. 121/H1
Penzance, Eng, UK 90/A6
Penzberg, Ger. 115/H2
Penzenskaya Oblast, Rus. 121/G1
Penzhina (riv.), Rus. 123/S3
Penzhina (bay), Rus. 123/S3
Penzing, Ger. 115/G1
Penzlin, Ger. 98/G2
Peoria, Az, US 195/R18
Pepe (lake), Cuba 203/F1
Pepeekeo, Hi, US 182/U11
Pepeekeo (pt.), Hi, US 182/U11
Pepel, SLeo. 160/B4
Pepinster, Belg. 111/E2
Pequannock, NJ, US 197/H8
Pequeña Isla del Maíz (isl.), Nic. 203/F3
Pequest (riv.), NJ, US 196/D2
Perabumulih, Indo. 138/B4
Perales (riv.), Sp. 103/M9
Peralta, Sp. 102/E1
Pérama, Gre. 105/J5
Pérama, Gre. 105/N9
Percé, Qu, Can. 189/H1
Percée (peak), Fr. 114/C6
Perch (lake), On, Can. 188/E2
Perchtoldsdorf, Aus. 107/N7
Percival (lakes), Austl. 170/E2
Percy (isls.), Austl. 172/C3
Percy Isles (chan.), Austl. 172/C3
Perdekop, SAfr. 165/E2
Pérdhika, Gre. 105/H4
Perdida (riv.), Braz. 212/A3
Perdido (mtn.), Sp. 103/F1
Peregian Beach, Austl. 172/D4
Pereira, Col. 208/C3
Pereira Barreto, Braz. 213/B2
Pereiro, Braz. 212/C2
Perelló, Sp. 103/F2
Perelló, Sp. 102/C4
Perenjori, Austl. 170/B5
Peretola (int'l arpt.), It. 117/E5
Perg, Aus. 113/H6
Pergamino, Arg. 216/E2
Pergamum (ruin), Turk. 148/A2
Pergine Valsugana, It. 115/H3
Pergola, It. 105/G3
Péribonca (riv.), Qu, Can. 189/G1
Perico, Cuba 203/F1
Pericos, Mex. 200/D3
Pericos, Mex. 200/D3
Périgueux, Fr. 100/D4
Perijá, Sierra de (mts.), Col. 208/D2
Peristéra (isl.), Gre. 105/H3
Peristéri, Gre. 105/N8
Perito Moreno, Arg. 216/C5
Perito Moreno, PN, Arg. 215/B6
Perkasie, Pa, US 196/C3

Perl, Ger. 111/F5
Perlas (lag.), Nic. 198/E5
Perlas (pt.), Nic. 203/F3
Perleberg, Ger. 98/F2
Perlez, Serb. 106/E3
Perlis (state), Malay. 136/B5
Perm', Rus. 119/N4
Permskaya Oblast, Rus. 119/N4
Përmet, Alb. 105/G2
Pernambuco (state), Braz. 212/C3
Pernate, It. 116/B2
Pernes-les-Fontaines, Fr. 100/F4
Pernik, Bul. 106/F4
Perniö, Fin. 97/K1
Peron (pen.), Austl. 170/B3
Péronne, Fr. 110/B4
Perote, Mex. 201/M7
Pérouges, Fr. 114/B6
Perpignan, Fr. 100/E5
Perray (riv.), Fr. 88/H6
Perrigny, Fr. 114/B4
Perris, Ca, US 194/C3
Perris, Ca, US 194/C3
Perris State Rec. Area, Ca, US 194/C3
Perros-Guirec, Fr. 100/B2
Perrot, Ile (isl.), Qu, Can. 189/N7
Perry, Fl, US 191/H4
Perry, Ga, US 191/H3
Perry, Ok, US 187/H3
Perry, Ut, US 195/J11
Perry Hall, Md, US 196/B5
Perry, Mont, US 196/B5
Perryton, Tx, US 187/G3
Perryville, Ak, US 192/G4
Perryville, Md, US 196/B4
Persan, Fr. 88/J4
Persian (gulf), Asia 146/E3
Perstorp, Swe. 96/E3
Perth, Austl. 170/K6
Perth, Austl. 173/C4
Perth (int'l arpt.), Austl. 170/K6
Perth, On, Can. 188/E2
Perth, Sc, UK 94/C4
Perth Amboy, NJ, US 197/H9
Perth nd Kinross (pol. reg.), Sc, UK 94/C4
Perth Zoo, Austl. 170/K6
Pertuis, Fr. 100/F5
Pertuis Breton (inlet), Fr. 100/C3
Pertusato (cape), Fr. 104/A2
Peru (ctry.) 214/C3
Peru, Il, US 185/L5
Peru, In, US 188/C3
Perucácko (lake), Bosn. 106/D4
Perugia, It. 101/K5
Peruíbe, Braz. 213/G9
Peruque, Mo, US 195/F8
Perushtitsa, Bul. 107/G4
Péruwelz, Belg. 110/C2
Pervari, Turk. 148/E2
Pervomays'k, Ukr. 107/K1
Pervomays'k, Rus. 119/J5
Pervoural'sk, Rus. 119/N4
Perwez, Belg. 111/D2
Péry, Swi. 114/D3
Pesa (riv.), It. 117/E5
Pesagi (peak), Indo. 138/B4
Pésaro, It. 117/F5
Pesaro e Urbino (prov.), It. 117/F5
Pescadores (Penghu) (isls.), China 137/C3
Pescantina, It. 117/D2
Pescara, It. 104/D1
Pescara (riv.), It. 104/C6
Pescasseroli, It. 104/C1
Pescia, It. 117/D5
Peseux, Swi. 114/C4
Pesha (riv.), Rus. 119/L2
Peshawar, Pak. 144/A2
Peshawar (int'l arpt.), Pak. 144/A2
Peshtera, Bul. 107/G4
Peshtigo, Wi, US 185/M4
Peshtigo (riv.), Wi, US 188/B2
Pesmes, Fr. 114/B3
Peso da Régua, Port. 102/B2
Pesqueira, Braz. 212/C3
Pessac, Fr. 100/C4
Pest (co.), Hun. 106/D2
Pestovo, Rus. 119/V9
Pestovo, Rus. 119/V9
Petah Tiqwa, Isr. 149/F7
Petal, Ms, US 191/F4
Petalión (gulf), Gre. 105/J4
Petaluma (ruin), Mex. 200/C2
Petaluma, Ca, US 193/J10
Pétange, Lux. 111/E4
Petare, Ven. 208/E1
Pétas, Gre. 105/G3
Petatlán (riv.), Mex. 200/C2
Petatlán, Mex. 201/E5
Petauke, Zam. 163/F3
Petawawa (riv.), On, Can. 188/E2
Petawawa, On, Can. 188/E2
Peten Itzá (lake), Guat. 202/D2
Petenwell (lake), Wi, US 185/L4
Peter (isl.), Nor. 218/U
Peterborough, Austl. 171/H5

Peterborough, On, Can. 188/E2
Peterborough, Eng, UK 91/F1
Peterborough (co.), Eng, UK 91/F1
Peterhead, Sc, UK 94/E1
Peterlee, Eng, UK 93/G2
Petermann Abor. Land, Austl. 171/F3
Peteroa (vol.), Chile 216/C2
Petersaurach, Ger. 112/D4
Petersberg, Ger. 112/C1
Petersfield, Eng, UK 91/F4
Petershagen, Ger. 109/F4
Petershagen, Ger. 98/D6
Petershausen, Ger. 113/E6
Peterson, Ut, US 195/K11
Pétervására, Hun. 99/L4
Petilia Policastro, It. 104/E3
Pétionville, Haiti 203/H2
Petit Goâve, Haiti 203/H2
Petit Lac Manicouagan (lake), Qu, Can. 189/H1
Petit Loango, PN du, Gabon 163/A1
Petit-Noir, Fr. 114/B4
Petite Miquelon (isl.), 188/D5
Petite Rivière de l'Artibonite, Haiti 203/H2
Petite Rivière Noire (peak), Mrts. 165/T15
Petite-Rosselle, Fr. 111/F5
Petitcodiac, NB, Can. 189/H2
Petitt Morin (riv.), Fr. 100/E2
Petkeljärven NP, Fin. 118/F3
Petlād, India 147/K4
Petlalcingo, Mex. 202/B2
Peto, Mex. 202/D1
Petorca, Chile 216/C2
Petoskey, Mi, US 188/C2
Petra (Batrâ) (ruin), Jor. 149/D4
Petra (isls.), Rus. 123/M2
Petrel, Sp. 103/E3
Petrella (peak), It. 104/C2
Petrich, Bul. 107/F4
Petrified Forest NP, Az, US 186/E4
Petrila, Rom. 107/F3
Petrodvorets, Rus. 119/S7
Petrokhanski Prokhod (pass), Bul. 105/H1
Petrokrepost' (bay), Rus. 119/U7
Petrolândia, Braz. 212/C3
Petrolina, Braz. 212/B3
Petropavlovsk-Kamchatskiy, Rus. 123/R4
Petrópolis, Braz. 213/K7
Petrovaradin, Serb. 106/D3
Petrovsk, Rus. 121/G1
Petrovsk-Zabaykal'skiy, Rus. 128/J1
Petrozavodsk, Rus. 118/G3
Petrus Steyn, SAfr. 164/E2
Petrusburg, SAfr. 164/D3
Petrusville, SAfr. 164/D3
Pettenbach, Aus. 113/H6
Petteril (riv.), Eng, UK 93/F2
Petzeck (peak), Aus. 101/K3
Peuerbach, Aus. 113/G6
Peulik (mt.), Ak, US 192/G4
Peumo, Chile 216/N9
Pevely, Mo, US 195/G9
Pewaukee (lake), Wi, US 193/X13
Pewaukee, Wi, US 193/P13
Peyrehorade, Fr. 100/C5
Peza (riv.), Rus. 119/L2
Pézenas, Fr. 100/E5
Pfaffenhofen, Ger. 115/G1
Pfaffenhofen an der Ilm, Ger. 112/D6
Pfaffenhofen an der Ilm, Ger. 113/E5
Pfaffenhoffen, Fr. 111/G6
Pfäffikon, Swi. 115/E3
Pfaffing, Ger. 113/F7
Pfaffnau, Swi. 114/D3
Pfahl (ridge), Ger. 113/F4
Pfälzer Wald (mts.), Ger. 111/G5
Pfälzerwald (mts.), Ger. 112/A4
Pfalzgrafenweiler, Ger. 112/B5
Pfarrhof Esternberg, Aus. 113/G5
Pfarrkirchen, Ger. 113/F5
Pfatter, Ger. 113/F5
Pfeffenhausen, Ger. 113/E5
Pfettrach, Ger. 113/E5
Pfieffe (riv.), Ger. 109/G6
Pfinztal, Ger. 112/B5
Pforzheim, Ger. 112/B5
Pfreimd, Ger. 113/F3
Pfronstetten, Ger. 112/C6
Pfronten, Ger. 115/G2
Pfullendorf, Ger. 115/F2
Pfunds, Aus. 115/G4
Pfungstadt, Ger. 112/B3
Phagwāra, India 144/C4
Phalaudia, India 144/D5
Phalempin, Fr. 110/C2
Phalia, Pak. 144/B3
Phalodi, India 147/K3

Phalsbourg, Fr. 111/G6
Phan Rang, Viet. 136/E4
Phan Thiet, Viet. 136/E4
Phanat Nikhom, Thai. 136/C3
Phang Hoei (range), Thai. 136/C3
Phangnga, Thai. 136/B4
Phanom Dongrak (mts.), Thai. 141/H5
Pharr, Tx, US 190/B1
Phatthalung, Thai. 136/C5
Phaya Fo (peak), Thai. 136/B2
Phayao, Thai. 136/B2
Phelan, Ca, US 194/C2
Phenix City, Al, US 191/G3
Phet Buri, Thai. 136/B3
Phetchabun, Thai. 136/C2
Phichit, Thai. 136/C2
Philadelphia, Ms, US 191/F3
Philadelphia, Pa, US 196/C4
Philadelphia (int'l arpt.), Pa, US 196/C4
Philip, SD, US 185/H4
Philip S.W. Goldson (int'l arpt.), Belz. 202/D2
Philippeville, Belg. 111/D3
Philippi, WV, US 188/D4
Philippine (sea), Asia 137/D4
Philippines (ctry.) 137/D5
Philippsburg, Ger. 112/B4
Philipsburg, Mt, US 184/E4
Philipsdam (dam), Neth. 108/B5
Philipstown, SAfr. 164/D3
Phillaur, India 144/C4
Phillipsburg, NJ, US 196/C2
Phillott, Austl. 172/B4
Phimai (ruin), Thai. 136/C2
Phitsanulok, Thai. 136/C2
Phnom Penh (Phnum Pénh) (cap.), Camb. 136/D4
Phnum Penh (int'l arpt.), Camb. 136/D4
Pho (pt.), Thai. 136/C5
Phoenix (cap.), Az, US 195/R19
Phoenix, La, US 195/Q17
Phoenix (isls.), Kiri. 175/H5
Phoenix Park, Ire. 92/B5
Phoenix Sky Harbor (int'l arpt.), Az, US 195/S19
Phoenixville, Pa, US 196/C3
Phongsali, Laos 141/H3
Phou Bia (peak), Laos 136/C2
Phou Huatt (peak), Viet. 141/H4
Phou Xai Lai Leng (peak), Laos 136/D2
Phra Nakhon Si Ayutthaya, Thai. 136/C3
Phra Thong (isl.), Thai. 136/B4
Phrae, Thai. 136/C2
Phu Hin Rong Kla NP, Thai. 136/C2
Phu Kradung NP, Thai. 136/C2
Phu Luong (peak), Viet. 141/H3
Phu Phan NP, Thai. 136/C2
Phu Quoc (isl.), Viet. 141/H5
Phu Rua NP, Thai. 136/C2
Phu Tho, Viet. 141/J3
Phuket, Thai. 136/B5
Phuket (isl.), Thai. 136/B5
Phularwan, Pak. 144/B3
Phulpur, India 142/D3
Piaçabuçu, Braz. 212/C3
Piacenza (prov.), It. 116/C2
Piacenza, It. 116/C2
Piádena, It. 116/D2
Pian di Serra (peak), It. 117/F6
Pian-Upe Game Rsv., Ugan. 162/B2
Piancastagnaio, It. 104/B1
Piancó, Braz. 212/C2
Pianello val Tidone, It. 116/C2
Pianezza, It. 116/A1
Piangipane, It. 117/F4
Pianoro, It. 117/E4
Pianosa (isl.), It. 104/A1
Piarco (int'l arpt.), Trin. 211/F2
Piaseczno, Pol. 99/L2
Piatra Neamţ, Rom. 107/H2
Piauí (riv.), Braz. 212/B3
Piauí (state), Braz. 212/B3
Piave (riv.), It. 101/K3
Piazza, It. 116/D1
Piazza, It. 116/D1
Piazza al Serchio, It. 116/D4
Piazza Armerina, It. 104/D4
Piazza Brembana, It. 115/F6
Piazzola sul Brenta, It. 117/E1
Pic de Nore (peak), Fr. 100/E5
Pic d'Orhy (peak), Fr. 100/C5
Pic du Canigou (peak), Fr. 100/E5
Pica, Chile 208/E8
Picacho del Centinela (peak), Mex. 200/D2
Picachos, Cerro Dos (peak), Mex. 200/B2
Picardie (pol. reg.), Fr. 100/E2
Picardy (reg.), Fr. 110/B4
Picatinny Arsenal, NJ, US 196/D2
Picayune, Ms, US 191/F4
Piccolo (lag.), It. 105/E2

Pichacani, Peru 214/D5
Pichanal, Arg. 215/D1
Pichidegua, Chile 216/N9
Pichilemu, Chile 216/B2
Pichincha (dept.), Ecu. 210/B4
Pichincha, Ecu. 210/A5
Pichl bei Wels, Aus. 113/G6
Pichor, India 142/B3
Pichucalco, Mex. 202/C2
Pickens, Ms, US 187/K4
Pickering, On, Can. 189/R8
Pickering, Vale of (valley), Eng, UK 93/H3
Pickle Lake, On, Can. 185/L3
Picnic Bay, Austl. 172/B2
Pico (isl.), Azor., Port. 103/S12
Pico da Neblina, PN do, Braz. 208/F3
Pico de Orizaba, PN, Mex. 201/M7
Pico Rivera, Ca, US 194/F8
Pico Truncado, Arg. 216/D5
Picos, Braz. 212/B2
Picota, Peru 214/B2
Picsi, Peru 214/B2
Picton, On, Can. 188/E3
Pictou, NS, Can. 189/J2
Picture Rocks, Pa, US 196/B2
Pictured Rocks Nat'l Lakeshore, Mi, US 185/M4
Pictured Rocks Nat'l Lakeshore, Mi, US 188/C2
Piddle (riv.), Eng, UK 90/D5
Pidurutagala (peak), SrL. 140/D6
Piedade, Port. 103/P10
Piedade do Rio Grande, Braz. 213/K6
Piedecuesta, Col. 210/C3
Piedimulera, It. 115/E5
Piedmont (upland), US 191/H3
Piedmont, Ok, US 195/M14
Piedmont, Ca, US 193/K11
Piedra Grande, Ven. 210/D2
Piedrabuena, Sp. 102/C3
Piedrahita, Sp. 102/C2
Piedras (pt.), Arg. 217/K11
Piedras Coloradas, Uru. 217/K10
Piedras Negras, Mex. 202/C2
Piedras Negras, Mex. 201/N8
Piedras, Rio de las (riv.), Peru 208/D2
Piedritas, Arg. 216/E2
Piekary Śląskie, Pol. 99/K3
Piekenierskloof (pass), SAfr. 164/L10
Pieksämäki, Fin. 118/E3
Pielinen (lake), Fin. 95/J3
Piemonte (prov.), It. 101/G4
Pieniński NP, Pol. 99/L4
Piennes, Fr. 111/E5
Piera, Sp. 103/K6
Pierce, Ne, US 185/J5
Pierce, Co, US 195/C1
Pierceland, Sk, Can. 184/F2
Pieris, It. 117/G1
Piermont, NY, US 197/K7
Pierowall, Sc, UK 89/V14
Pierre (cap.), SD, US 185/H4
Pierre-de-Bresse, Fr. 114/B4
Pierre-Levée, Fr. 88/M5
Pierrefitte-sur-Seine, Fr. 88/K5
Pierrefonds, Qu, Can. 189/N7
Pierrelatte, Fr. 100/F4
Pierrelaye, Fr. 88/J4
Pierrevert, Fr. 100/F5
Pierry, Fr. 110/C5
Piešťany, Slvk. 99/J4
Piesting (riv.), Aus. 107/P7
Piet Retief, SAfr. 165/E2
Pieterlen, Swi. 114/D3
Pietermaritzburg, SAfr. 165/E3
Pietersburg, SAfr. 163/E5
Pietra Ligure, It. 116/B3
Pietralunga, It. 117/F6
Pietramelara, It. 104/D2
Pietravecchia (peak), It. 116/A5
Pietrosul, It. 107/G2
Pietrosul (peak), Rom. 107/G2
Pieve del Cairo, It. 116/B2
Pieve di Cento, It. 117/E3
Pieve di Soligo, It. 117/F1
Pieve di Teco, It. 116/B3
Pieve Emanuele, It. 116/C1
Pieve Ligure, It. 116/C3
Pieve Porto Morone, It. 116/C2
Pieve Santa Stefano, It. 117/F5
Pieve Vergonte, It. 115/E6
Pievepelago, It. 116/D4
Pigeon (riv.), Mn, US 185/L3
Pigeon, Mi, US 188/D2
Pigeon Bay, Qu, Can. 188/E2
Pigeon Forge, Tn, US 191/H3
Pigs (bay), Cuba 198/E3
Pigüé, Arg. 216/E2

Pigüm (isl.), SKor. 131/C5
Pihāni, India 142/C2
Pijijiapan, Mex. 202/C3
Pijnacker, Neth. 108/B4
Pijol (peak), Hon. 202/E3
Pike (co.), Pa, US 196/C1
Pikes Creek (res.), Pa, US 196/B1
Piketberg, SAfr. 164/L10
Pikeville, Ky, US 188/D4
Pikit, Phil. 137/D6
Pila, Arg. 217/J12
Pila, Pol. 99/J2
Pilanesberg (range), SAfr. 164/P12
Pilani, India 144/C5
Pilão Arcado, Braz. 212/B3
Pilar, Arg. 216/E1
Pilar, Braz. 212/D3
Pilar, Par. 215/E2
Pilar, Phil. 137/D5
Pilatus (peak), Swi. 115/E4
Pilaya (riv.), Bol. 208/F8
Pilchuck (riv.), Wa, US 193/C3
Pilcomayo (riv.), SAm. 213/D1
Pili, Phil. 137/D5
Pilica (riv.), Pol. 99/L3
Pilion (peak), Gre. 105/H3
Pilis, Hun. 106/D2
Pilis (peak), Hun. 107/Q9
Pilismarót, Hun. 107/R9
Piliscsaba, Hun. 107/Q9
Pilisvörösvár, Hun. 107/Q9
Pilkhua, India 144/C4
Pillar (cape), Austl. 173/C4
Pillar (peak), SrL. 140/D6
Pillar, Eng, UK 93/E3
Pillar (pt.), Ca, US 193/J12
Pillau (ruin), Thai. 173/D1
Pillon, Col du (pass), Swi. 114/D5
Pillow, Pa, US 196/B2
Pilões, Serra dos (mtn.), Braz. 212/A5
Pílos, Gre. 105/G4
Pilot (mtn.), Tn, US 188/C4
Pilot Point, Ak, US 192/G4
Pilot Station, Ak, US 192/F3
Pilsting, Ger. 113/F5
Pima, Az, US 186/E4
Pimpri-Chinchwad, India 147/K5
Pináculo (peak), Arg. 217/B6
Pinamar, Arg. 217/F3
Pinang (cape), Malay. 138/A2
Pinang (isl.), Malay. 138/A2
Pinar del Río, Cuba 203/F1
Pinarbaşı, Turk. 148/D2
Pınarhisar, Turk. 107/H5
Pinatubo, Ecu. 214/B1
Pinawa, Mb, Can. 185/K3
Pincher Creek, Ab, Can. 184/E3
Pinconning, Mi, US 188/D2
Pincota, Rom. 106/E2
Pincourt, Qu, Can. 189/N7
Pińczów, Pol. 99/L3
Pind Dādan Khān, Pak. 144/B3
Pindamonhangaba, Braz. 213/H7
Pindaré (riv.), Braz. 209/J4
Pindaré-Mirim, Braz. 212/A1
Pindhos NP, Gre. 105/G3
Pindi Bhattiān, Pak. 144/B4
Pindi Gheb, Pak. 144/B3
Pindobaçu, Braz. 212/B3
Pindus (mts.), Gre. 105/G2
Pindwāra, India 147/K4
Pine Barrens (phys. reg.), NJ, US 196/C4
Pine Bluff, Ar, US 187/J4
Pine Bluffs, Wy, US 185/G5
Pine Creek (pt.), Ct, US 197/E1
Pine Falls, Mb, Can. 185/J3
Pine Grove, Pa, US 196/B2
Pine Hill, NJ, US 196/D4
Pine Island, Mn, US 188/A2
Pine Island Bay (flat), Ant. 218/S
Pine Lawn, Mo, US 195/G8
Pine Point, NW, Can. 180/E2
Pine Ridge, SD, US 185/H5
Pine, South Branch (riv.), Mi, US 193/G6
Pine, The (hills), US 185/G4
Pinecliff (lake), NJ, US 197/H1
Pinecliffe, Co, US 195/B3
Pinedale, Wy, US 184/F5
Pinega (riv.), Rus. 122/G3
Pineimuta (riv.), On, Can. 185/L2

INDEX SECTION

270 Pinel – Port H

Pinelands, SAfr. 164/L10
Piñera, Uru. 217/K10
Pinerolo, It. 101/G4
Pinetown, SAfr. 165/E3
Pineuilh, Fr. 100/D4
Pineview (res.), Ut, US 195/K11
Pineville, La, US 187/J5
Pinewood Springs, Co, US 195/B2
Ping (riv.), Thai. 141/G4
Ping Chau (isl.), China 129/V9
Pingbian Miaozu Zizhixian, China 141/H3
Pingding, China 130/C3
Pingdingshan, China 130/C4
Pingdu, China 130/D3
Pingelap (isl.), Micr. 174/F4
Pingelly, Austl. 170/C5
Pinggu, China 130/H6
Pingguo, China 141/J3
Pinghe, China 137/C3
Pinghu, China 130/L9
Pingjiang, China 137/B2
Pingjing (pass), China 130/C5
Pingle, China 141/K3
Pinglu, China 130/B4
Pinglu, China 130/C3
Pingnan, China 137/B3
Pingquan, China 130/D2
Pingshan, China 130/C3
Pingshun, China 130/C3
Pingtan, China 137/C2
Pingtang, China 141/J2
P'ingtung, Tai. 137/D3
Pingxiang, China 141/K2
Pingxiang, China 141/J3
Pingxing Guan (pass), China 130/C3
Pingyao, China 130/C3
Pingyi, China 130/D4
Pingyin, China 130/D3
Pingyu, China 130/C4
Pingyuan, China 130/D3
Pinhal, Braz. 213/G7
Pinhal Novo, Port. 103/Q10
Pinhão, Braz. 213/B3
Pinheiro, Braz. 212/A1
Pinheiros, Braz. 212/B5
Pinhel, Port. 102/B2
Piniós (riv.), Gre. 105/G4
Pinjar (lake), Austl. 170/K6
Pinjarra, Austl. 170/B5
Pink, Ok, US 195/N15
Pinkafeld, Aus. 106/C2
Pinkawillinie Conservation Park, Austl. 171/G5
Pinkegat (chan.), Neth. 108/C2
Pinnacles Nat'l Mon., Ca, US 186/B3
Pinnaroo, Austl. 171/J5
Pinnau (riv.), Ger. 109/G1
Pinneberg, Ger. 109/G1
Pino Hachado (pass), Arg. 216/C3
Pino Torinese, It. 116/A2
Pinole, Ca, US 193/K10
Pinon Hills, Ca, US 194/C2
Pinos (mt.), Ca, US 186/C4
Pinos, Mex. 201/E4
Pinos, Isla de (Isla de la Juventud) (isl.), Cuba 198/E3
Pinos-Puente, Sp. 102/D4
Pinoso, Sp. 103/E3
Pins, Île des (isl.), NCal., Fr. 174/F7
Pinsdorf, Aus. 113/G7
Pinsk, Bela. 120/C1
Pinta, Isla (isl.), Ecu. 214/E6
Pinto, Sp. 103/N9
Pinto, Chile 216/C3
Pinzolo, It. 115/G5
Pio Ix, Braz. 212/B2
Pio Xii, Braz. 212/A1
Piobbico, It. 117/F5
Pioche, Nv, US 186/D3
Piombino, It. 101/J5
Piombino Dese, It. 117/F1
Pioneer World, Austl. 170/L7
Pioner (isl.), Rus. 122/J2
Pionki, Pol. 99/L3
Piorini (riv.), Braz. 208/F4
Piorini (lake), Braz. 211/F5
Piota (riv.), It. 116/B3
Piotrków Trybunalski, Pol. 99/K3
Piove di Sacco, It. 117/F2
Piovene-Rocchette, It. 117/E1
Pipariā, India 142/B4
Pipe Spring Nat'l Mon., Az, US 186/D3
Piper, Ks, US 195/D5
Pipersville, Pa, US 196/C3
Pipestone (riv.), On, Can. 180/G3
Piplān, Pak. 144/A3
Pipmuacan (res.), Qu, Can. 181/J4
Pippingarra Abor. Land, Austl. 170/C2
Pipra, India 142/D3
Pipraich, India 142/D2
Piqua, Oh, US 188/C3
Piquet Carneiro, Braz. 212/C2
Piquete, Braz. 213/H7
Piquiri (riv.), Braz. 209/H7
Pīr Mahal, Pak. 144/B4
Pir Panjal (range), India 144/C3
Piracanjuba, Braz. 213/B1
Piracicaba, Braz. 213/C2
Piracuruca, Braz. 212/B1
Pirae-bong (peak), NKor. 131/C2
Piraí, Braz. 213/K7
Piraí do Sul, Braz. 213/B3
Piraiévs, Gre. 105/N9
Piraju, Braz. 213/B2
Pirajuí, Braz. 213/B2
Pirámide (peak), Chile 217/B6
Piran, Slov. 117/G1
Pirané, Arg. 215/E2
Piranga (riv.), Braz. 213/D2
Piranhas (riv.), Braz. 209/L5
Piranji (riv.), Braz. 212/C2
Pirapemas, Braz. 212/A1
Pirapora, Braz. 212/A5
Pirapòzinho, Braz. 213/B2
Pirarajá, Uru. 217/G2
Pirássununga, Braz. 213/C2
Pires do Rio, Braz. 213/B1
Pírgos, Gre. 105/G4
Pírgos, Gre. 105/J5
Piriápolis, Uru. 217/G2
Pirin (mts.), Bul. 107/F5
Pirin (peak), Bul. 107/F5
Pirin NP, Bul. 107/F5
Piripiri, Braz. 212/B2
Piritiba, Braz. 212/B3
Píritu, Ven. 210/D2
Pirkkala, Fin. 97/K1
Pirmasens, Ger. 111/G5
Pirna, Ger. 99/G3
Piro, India 143/E3
Pirot, Serb. 106/F4
Pirre (mtn.), Pan. 203/G5
Pirthīpur, India 142/B3
Piru (lake), Ca, US 194/B1
Piru, Ca, US 194/B2
Piryíon, Gre. 105/J3
Pisa, It. 116/D5
Pisa (prov.), It. 117/D6
Pisac, Peru 214/D4
Pisanino (peak), It. 116/D4
Pisau (cape), Malay. 139/E2
Pisba, PN, Col. 210/C3
Piscataway, Md, US 196/B6
Piscataway, NJ, US 196/D2
Pisco (riv.), Peru 208/C6
Pisco, Peru 214/B4
Piscobamba, Peru 214/B3
Písek (peak), Czh. 113/H3
Písek, Czh. 113/H4
Pishan, China 128/C4
Pishīn, Pak. 147/J2
Pīshīn, Iran 147/H3
Piskavica, Bosn. 106/C3
Pisoc (peak), Swi. 115/G4
Pisogne, It. 116/D1
Pissis (peak), Arg. 215/C2
Pistakee (lake), Il, US 193/P15
Pisticci, It. 104/E2
Pistoia (prov.), It. 117/D5
Pistoia, It. 117/D5
Pisuerga (riv.), Sp. 102/C1
Pisz, Pol. 99/L2
Pit (riv.), Ca, US 186/B2
Pitalito, Col. 210/B4
Pitanga, Braz. 213/B3
Pitcairn (isl.), Pitc. 175/N7
Pitcairn Islands (dpcy.), UK 175/N7
Piteå, Swe. 95/G2
Piteälven (riv.), Swe. 95/F2
Pitești, Rom. 107/G3
Píthion, Gre. 105/K2
Pithiviers, Fr. 100/E2
Pithoragarh, India 142/C1
Pitigliano, It. 104/B1
Pitiquito, Mex. 200/B2
Pitjantjatjara Abor. Lands, Austl. 171/F3
Pitkas Point, Ak, US 192/F3
Pitlochry, Sc, UK 94/C3
Pitman, NJ, US 196/C4
Pitmedden, Sc, UK 94/D2
Pitomača, Cro. 106/C3
Piton de la Fournaise (peak), Reun., Fr. 165/S15
Piton des Neiges (peak), Reun., Fr. 165/S15
Pitrufquén, Chile 216/B3
Pitt Water (bay), Austl. 172/H8
Pittenweem, Sc, UK 94/D4
Pittsburg, Ks, US 187/J3
Pittsburgh, Pa, US 188/E3
Pittsfield, Me, US 189/G2
Pittsfield, Ma, US 188/F3
Pittston, Pa, US 188/F3
Pittstown, NJ, US 196/D2
Pittsworth, Austl. 172/C4
Pitzbach (riv.), Aus. 115/G4
Piuí, Braz. 213/C2
Piumazzo, It. 117/E3
Piura, Peru 214/A2
Piura (dept.), Peru 214/A2
Pivdenny Buh (riv.), Ukr. 120/D2
Pivijay, Col. 210/C2
Pixoyal, Mex. 198/C4
Piz d'Err (peak), Swi. 115/F4
Pizacoma, Peru 214/D5
Pizarra, Sp. 102/C4
Pizhma (riv.), Rus. 119/K4
Pizol (peak), Swi. 115/F4
Pizzighettone, It. 116/C2
Pizzo, It. 104/E3
Pizzo dei Tre Signori (peak), It. 115/F6
Pizzo della Presolana (peak), It. 115/G6
Pizzo di Coca (peak), It. 115/G5
Pizzo di Vogorno (peak), Swi. 115/E5
Pizzuto (peak), It. 104/C1
Placentia, Nf, Can. 189/L2
Placentia (bay), Nf, Can. 189/L2
Placentia, Ca, US 194/G8
Placer, Phil. 137/E6
Placer (co.), Ca, US 193/M9
Placetas, Cuba 203/G1
Plachkovtsi, Bul. 107/G4
Plaffeien, Swi. 114/D4
Plai Mat (riv.), Thai. 136/C3
Plaidt, Ger. 111/G3
Plailly, Fr. 88/K4
Plain City, Ut, US 195/J11
Plain Dealing, La, US 187/J4
Plaine (riv.), Fr. 114/C1
Plainfield, NJ, US 197/H9
Plainfield, Il, US 193/P16
Plains, Tx, US 187/G4
Plains, Pa, US 196/C1
Plainsboro, NJ, US 196/D3
Plainview, Tx, US 187/G4
Plainview, Mn, US 188/A2
Plainview, NY, US 197/M8
Plaisir, Fr. 88/H5
Plan-les-Ouates, Swi. 114/C5
Planá, Czh. 113/F3
Plana Cays (isls.), Bahm. 203/H1
Planaltina, Braz. 212/A4
Plancher-Bas, Fr. 114/C2
Plancher-les-Mines, Fr. 114/C2
Plandište, Serb. 106/E3
Planeta Rica, Col. 210/C2
Planken, Lcht. 115/F3
Plant City, Fl, US 191/H4
Plantation, Fl, US 191/H5
Plaquemines (parish), La, US 195/Q17
Plasencia, Sp. 102/B2
Plasy, Czh. 113/G3
Plata (estu.), Arg.,Uru. 217/K11
Platani (riv.), It. 104/C4
Plate Taile, Barrage de la (dam), Belg. 111/D3
Plateau (state), Nga. 161/H4
Platí, Gre. 105/H2
Platinum, Ak, US 192/F4
Plato, Col. 210/C2
Platón Sánchez, Mex. 202/B1
Platte (riv.), Ne, US 187/H2
Platte City, Mo, US 195/D5
Platte, North (riv.), Ne,Wy, US 187/G2
Platte, South (riv.), Co, US 187/G2
Platteville, Co, US 195/C2
Plattling, Ger. 113/F5
Plattsburgh, NY, US 188/F2
Plauen, Ger. 113/F1
Plav, Serb. 106/D4
Plavna Dadaint (peak), Swi. 115/G4
Playa de los Muertos (ruin), Hon. 202/E3
Playa del Carmen, Mex. 202/E1
Playa Noriega (lake), Mex. 200/C2
Playa Vicente, Mex. 202/C2
Playas (lake), NM, US 186/E5
Playas, Ecu. 210/A5
Playgreen (lake), Mb, Can. 185/J2
Pleasant (lake), Az, US 195/R18
Pleasant Grove, Ut, US 195/K13
Pleasant Hill, Ca, US 193/K11
Pleasant Hill, Mo, US 195/E6
Pleasant Hills, Md, US 196/B5
Pleasant Valley, Mo, US 195/E5
Pleasant View, Co, US 195/B3
Pleasant View, Ut, US 195/K11
Pleasanton, Ca, US 193/L11
Pleasanton, Tx, US 187/H5
Pleasantville, NJ, US 196/D5
Pleasantville, NY, US 197/K7
Pleaux, Fr. 100/E4
Pleiku, Viet. 136/D3
Pleinfeld, Ger. 112/D4
Pleisse (riv.), Ger. 98/G3
Plenty (riv.), Austl. 173/G5
Plenty (bay), NZ 175/T10
Plentywood, Mt, US 185/G3
Plérin, Fr. 100/B2
Plesná (riv.), Czh. 113/F2
Pleso (int'l arpt.), Cro. 106/C3
Pleszew, Pol. 99/J3
Plétipi (lake), Qu, Can. 189/G1
Plettenberg, Ger. 109/E6
Pleurtuit (int'l arpt.), Fr. 100/B2
Pleven, Bul. 107/G4
Pliska, Bul. 107/H4
Plitvice Lakes NP, Cro. 106/B3
Pljevlja, Mont. 106/D4
Plobsheim, Fr. 114/D1
Plöcckenstein (peak), Ger. 113/G5
Ploče, Cro. 105/E1
Plochingen, Ger. 112/C5
Płock, Pol. 99/K2
Pločno (peak), Bosn. 106/C4
Ploemeur, Fr. 100/B3
Ploiești, Rom. 107/H3
Plomárion, Gre. 105/K3
Plombières, Belg. 111/E2
Plombières-lès-Dijon, Fr. 114/A3
Plön, Ger. 96/D4
Płońsk, Pol. 99/L2
Plouay, Fr. 100/B3
Ploučnice (riv.), Czh. 99/H3
Ploufragan, Fr. 100/B2
Plougastel-Daoulas, Fr. 100/A2
Plouguernével, Fr. 100/B2
Plouzané, Fr. 100/A2
Plovdiv, Bul. 107/G4
Plovdiv (pol. reg.), Bul. 107/G4
Plover Cove (res.), China 129/U10
Pluguffan (int'l arpt.), Fr. 100/A3
Plum (isl.), NY, US 197/F1
Plumridge Lakes Nature Rsv., Austl. 170/E4
Plumsteadville, Pa, US 196/C3
Plungė, Lith. 97/J4
Plymouth, Eng, UK 90/B6
Plymouth (co.), Eng, UK 90/B6
Plymouth (sound), Eng, UK 90/B6
Plymouth (cap.), Monts., UK 199/N8
Plymouth, In, US 188/C3
Plymouth, NC, US 191/J3
Plymouth, NH, US 189/G3
Plymouth, Pa, US 196/C1
Plymouth, Wi, US 188/C3
Plynlimon (peak), Wal, UK 90/C2
Plzeň, Czh. 113/G3
Plzeňský (pol. reg.), Czh. 113/G4
PNC Bank Arts Center, NJ, US 197/J10
Pniel, SAfr. 164/L10
Pniewy, Pol. 99/J2
Pô, Burk. 161/E4
Po (riv.), It. 101/J4
Po di Venezia (riv.), It. 117/F2
Po di Volano (riv.), It. 117/E3
Po Klong Garai Cham Towers, Viet. 136/E4
Po, Mouths of the (delta), It. 101/K4
Pô, PN de, Burk. 161/E4
Po Toi Group (isls.), China 129/V11
Po, Valle del (valley), It. 101/J4
Poá, Braz. 213/G8
Poa (riv.), Ven. 211/E2
Poag, Il, US 195/G8
Pobé, Ben. 161/F5
Pobedy (peak), Kyr. 128/D3
Pobiedziska, Pol. 99/J2
Pobla de Segur, Sp. 103/F1
Pocahontas, Ar, US 187/K3
Poção de Pedra, Braz. 212/A2
Pochep, Rus. 120/E1
P'och'ŏn, SKor. 131/G6
Pocinhos, Braz. 212/C2
Pöcking, Ger. 115/H2
Pöcking, Ger. 113/G6
Pocklington (reef), PNG 174/E6
Poço Fundo, Braz. 213/H6
Poções, Braz. 212/B4
Pocola, Ok, US 187/J4
Poconé, Braz. 209/G7
Pocono (mts.), Pa, US 196/C1
Pocono (lake), Pa, US 196/C1
Pocono Lake, Pa, US 196/C1
Pocono Pines, Pa, US 196/C1
Poços de Caldas, Braz. 213/G6
Pocrí, Pan. 203/F4
Podbořany, Czh. 113/G2
Poddębice, Pol. 99/K3
Podenzano, It. 116/C3
Podgorica (cap.), Mont. 106/D4
Podkarpackie (prov.), Pol. 99/L4
Podlasie (reg.), Bela.,Pol. 99/M3
Podlaskie (prov.), Pol. 99/M2
Podol'sk, Rus. 119/W9
Podor, Sen. 160/B2
Podporozh'ye, Rus. 118/G3
Podravska Slatina, Cro. 106/C3
Podujevo, Kos. 106/E4
Pofadder, SAfr. 164/B3
Poggibonsi, It. 117/E6
Poggio Renatico, It. 117/E3
Poggio Rusco, It. 117/E3
Poggiola, It. 117/E6
Pogromni (vol.), Ak, US 192/F5
P'ohang, SKor. 131/E4
Pohénégamook, Qu, Can. 189/G2
Pohja (Pojo), Fin. 97/K1
Pohjanmaa (reg.), Fin. 95/G3
Pohjois-Karjala (prov.), Fin. 118/F3
Pohnpei (isl.), Micr. 174/E4
Pohoiki, Hi, US 182/U11
Pohopoco Mtn. (mtn.), Pa, US 196/C2
Poigny-la-Forêt, Fr. 88/H5
Poing, Ger. 113/E6
Poinsett (cape), Ant. 218/H
Point (lake), NW, Can. 180/E2
Point au Fer (isl.), La, US 187/K5
Point Baker, Ak, US 192/M4
Point Fortin, Trin. 211/F2
Point Hope, Ak, US 192/E2
Point Lay, Ak, US 192/F2
Point Lookout (peak), Austl. 173/E1
Point Mugu Naval Air Sta., Ca, US 194/A2
Point Mugu State Park, Ca, US 194/A2
Point of Aire (pt.), Wal, UK 93/E5
Point of Ayre (pt.), IM, UK 92/D3
Point Pelee NP, On, Can. 188/D3
Point Pleasant, NJ, US 196/D3
Point Pleasant, Pa, US 196/C3
Point Pleasant, WV, US 188/D4
Point Pleasant Beach, NJ, US 196/D3
Point Salines (int'l arpt.), Gren. 211/F1
Point Salvation Abor. Rsv., Austl. 170/D4
Pointe-à-Pitre, Guad., Fr. 199/N8
Pointe à Raquette, Haiti 203/H2
Pointe-aux-Trembles, Qu, Can. 189/P6
Pointe-Calumet, Qu, Can. 189/N6
Pointe-Claire, Qu, Can. 189/N7
Pointe de Chassiron (pt.), Fr. 100/C3
Pointe de l'Arcouest (pt.), Fr. 100/B2
Pointe des Verres (peak), Fr. 114/C6
Pointe-du-Lac, Qu, Can. 189/F2
Pointe du Sablon (pt.), Fr. 100/F5
Pointe-Noire, Congo 163/B1
Poirino, It. 116/A3
Poissonier (pt.), Austl. 170/C1
Poissy, Fr. 88/J5
Poitiers, Fr. 100/D3
Poitou (reg.), Fr. 100/C3
Poitou-Charentes (reg.), Fr. 100/C3
Poix-de-Picardie, Fr. 110/A4
Poix-Terron, Fr. 111/D4
Pojuca, Braz. 212/C4
Pok Liu Chau (isl.), China 129/U11
Pokaran, India 147/K3
Pokharā, Nepal 142/D1
Pokhvistnevo, Rus. 121/K1
Pol-e Khomrī, Afg. 147/J1
Pola de Laviana, Sp. 102/C1
Pola de Lena, Sp. 102/C1
Pola de Siero, Sp. 102/C1
Polabská Nížina (phys. reg.), Czh. 101/L1
Pol'ana (peak), Slvk. 120/A2
Poland (ctry.) 99/K2
Połaniec, Pol. 99/L3
Polatlı, Turk. 132/C2
Polatsk, Bela. 97/N4
Polch, Ger. 111/G3
Połczyn-Zdrój, Pol. 96/G5
Pole of Inaccessability, Ant. 218/E
Polesella, It. 117/E3
Polesine (reg.), It. 117/E3
Poleski NP, Pol. 99/M3
Polgár, Hun. 106/E2
Pŏlgyo, SKor. 131/D5
Políaigos (isl.), Gre. 105/J4
Policastro, Golfo di (gulf), It. 104/D3
Police, Pol. 96/F5
Policoro, It. 104/E2
Poligny, Fr. 114/B4
Políkastron, Gre. 105/H2
Políkhni, Gre. 105/H2
Polikhnítos, Gre. 105/K3
Polillo (isl.), Phil. 137/D4
Polis, Cyp. 149/C2
Polistena, It. 104/E3
Políyiros, Gre. 105/H2
Polje, Slov. 101/L3
Polkowice, Pol. 99/J3
Polla, It. 104/D2
Pollença, Sp. 103/G3
Polochic (riv.), Guat. 202/D3
Polomolok, Phil. 137/E6
Polonia (cape), Uru. 217/G2
Polonnaruwa, SrL. 140/D6
Polonne, Ukr. 120/C2
Polski Trŭmbesh, Bul. 107/G4
Polson, Mt, US 184/E4
Poltava, Ukr. 120/E2
Poltavs'ka Oblasti, Ukr. 120/E2
Poluostrov Barsakel'mes (isl.), Kaz. 145/C3
Poluška (peak), Czh. 113/H5
Polvijärvi, Fin. 118/F3
Polyarnyy, Rus. 118/G1
Polynesia (reg.) 174/G6
Pomabamba, Peru 214/B3
Pomarance, It. 101/J5
Pomarico, It. 104/E2
Pomáz, Hun. 107/R9
Pomba (riv.), Som. 213/D2
Pombal, Braz. 212/C2
Pombal, Port. 102/A3
Pombas, CpV. 151/J9
Pomerania (reg.), Pol. 96/F4
Pomeranian (bay), Ger.,Pol. 96/F4
Pomerode, Braz. 213/B3
Pomeroon-Supenaam (pol. reg.), Guy. 211/G3
Pomeroy, Wa, US 184/D4
Pomeroy, NI, UK 92/B2
Pommersfelden, Ger. 112/D3
Pomona, Ca, US 194/C2
Pomona, NJ, US 196/D5
Pomona, Md, US 196/B5
Pomorie, Bul. 107/H4
Pomorskie (prov.), Pol. 99/J1
Pomos (pt.), Cyp. 149/C2
Pompano Beach, Fl, US 191/H5
Pompei (ruin), It. 104/D2
Pompeu, Braz. 213/C1
Pompey, Fr. 111/F6
Pompeys Pillar Nat'l Mon., Mt, US 184/G4
Pompiano, It. 116/C2
Pompton (riv.), NJ, US 197/H8
Pompton Lakes, NJ, US 197/H8
Poncarale, It. 116/D2
Ponce, PR 199/M8
Ponchatoula, La, US 195/P16
Poncheville (lake), Qu, Can. 188/E1
Pond, Mo, US 195/F8
Pond (inlet), Nun., Can. 181/J1
Pond (pt.), Ct, US 197/E1
Pond Inlet, Nun., Can. 181/J1
Pondicherry, India 140/C5
Pondicherry (terr.), India 140/C5
Ponente, Riviera di (coast), Fr. 116/B5
Ponferrada, Sp. 102/B1
Pongdong, SKor. 131/D5
Ponghwa, SKor. 131/E4
Pongolo (riv.), SAfr. 165/E2
Poni (prov.), Burk. 160/E4
Poniatowa, Pol. 99/M3
Ponnaiyar (riv.), India 140/C5
Ponoka, Ab, Can. 184/E2
Ponoy (riv.), Rus. 122/D3
Pons, Fr. 100/C4
Ponsacco, It. 116/D5
Pont-à-Celles, Belg. 111/D3
Pont-à-Marcq, Fr. 110/C2
Pont-D'Ain, Fr. 114/B5
Pont-de-Chéruy, Fr. 114/B6
Pont-de-Roide, Fr. 114/C3
Pont-de-Vaux, Fr. 114/A5
Pont-de-Veyle, Fr. 114/A5
Pont-du-Château, Fr. 100/E4
Pont-Remy, Fr. 110/A3
Pont-Saint-Esprit, Fr. 100/F4
Pont-Saint-Martin, It. 116/A1
Pont-Sainte-Maxence, Fr. 110/B5
Ponta Delgada, Azor., Port. 103/T13
Ponta do Pico (peak), Azor., Port. 103/S12
Ponta Grossa, Braz. 213/B3
Ponta Porã, Braz. 215/E1
Pontalina, Braz. 213/B1
Pontarlier, Fr. 114/C4
Pontarmé, Fr. 88/K4
Pontassieve, It. 117/E5
Pontault-Combault, Fr. 88/K5
Pontax (riv.), Qu, Can. 188/E1
Pontcarré, Fr. 88/L5
Pontchartrain (lake), La, US 191/F4
Pontchâteau, Fr. 100/B3
Ponte Alta do Bom Jesus, Braz. 212/A4
Ponte Alta do Tocantins, Braz. 212/A3
Ponte Buggianese, It. 117/D5
Ponte de Sor, Port. 102/A3
Ponte dell'Olio, It. 116/C3
Ponte di Legno, It. 115/G5
Ponte di Piave, It. 117/F1
Ponte do Lima, Port. 102/A2
Ponte Lambro, It. 116/C1
Ponte Nova, Braz. 213/D2
Ponte San Nicolò, It. 117/E2
Pontecagnano, It. 104/D2
Pontecorvo, It. 104/C2
Pontecurone, It. 116/B3
Pontedera, It. 116/D5
Pontefract, Eng, UK 93/G4
Ponteland, Eng, UK 93/G1
Pontelongo, It. 117/F2
Pontenure, It. 116/C3
Pontes e Lacerda, Braz. 208/G7
Pontestura, It. 116/B2
Pontevedra, Sp. 102/A1
Pontevico, It. 116/D2
Ponthévrard, Fr. 88/H6
Ponthieu (reg.), Fr. 110/A3
Pontiac, Il, US 185/L5
Pontiac, Mi, US 188/D3
Pontiac (lake), Mi, US 193/E6
Pontianak, Indo. 138/C4
Pontivy, Fr. 100/B2
Pontoise, Fr. 88/J4
Pontoon Beach, Il, US 195/G8
Pontotoc, Ms, US 191/F3
Pontpoint, Fr. 110/B5
Pontremoli, It. 116/C4
Pontresina, Swi. 115/F5
Pontypool, Wal, UK 90/C3
Ponza, It. 104/C2
Ponziane, Isole (isls.), It. 104/C2
Poole, Eng, UK 90/E5
Poole (bay), Eng, UK 91/E5
Poole (co.), Eng, UK 90/D5
Poolewe, Sc, UK 89/R8
Poona (Pune), India 147/K5
Poondarrie (peak), Austl. 170/C3
Poondinna (mt.), Austl. 171/F3
Poopó (lake), Bol. 208/E7
Poortugaal, Neth. 108/B5
Põõsapää (pt.), Est. 97/K2
Poosepatuck Ind. Res., NY, US 197/F2
Popayán, Col. 210/B4
Poperinge, Belg. 110/B2
Popigochic (riv.), Mex. 200/C2
Popilta (lake), Austl. 171/J5
Popio (lake), Austl. 173/B2
Poplar (riv.), Mb,On, Can. 180/G3
Poplar (isl.), Md, US 196/B6
Poplar, Mt, US 185/G3
Poplar Bluff, Mo, US 187/K3
Poplarville, Ms, US 191/F4
Popocatépetl (vol.), Mex. 201/L7
Popoli, It. 104/C1
Popovo, Bul. 107/H4
Poppberg (peak), Ger. 113/E4
Poppenhausen, Ger. 112/D2
Poppenhausen, Ger. 112/C2
Poppi, It. 117/E5
Poprad, Slvk. 99/L4
Poprad (riv.), Slvk. 99/L4
Poranga, Braz. 212/B2
Porangatu, Braz. 209/J6
Porbandar, India 147/J4
Porcari, It. 116/D5
Porce (riv.), Col. 210/C3
Porcheville, Fr. 88/H5
Porcia, It. 117/F1
Porcuna, Sp. 102/C4
Porcupine (riv.), Can.,US 192/K2
Porcupine Gorge NP, Austl. 172/B3
Porcupine Plain, Sk, Can. 185/H2
Pordenone (prov.), It. 117/F2
Pordenone, It. 117/F1
Pordim, Bul. 107/G4
Pore, Col. 210/D3
Poreč, Cro. 117/G2
Poretta (int'l arpt.), Fr. 104/A1
Pori (int'l arpt.), Fin. 97/J1
Pori, Fin. 97/J1
Porirua, NZ 175/S11
Porlezza, It. 115/F5
Pornic, Fr. 100/B3
Porongurup NP, Austl. 170/C5
Póros, Gre. 105/H4
Porpoise (bay), Ant. 218/J
Porrentruy, Swi. 114/D3
Porretta Terme, It. 117/D4
Porriño, Sp. 102/A1
Porsangen (inlet), Nor. 95/H1
Porsgrunn, Nor. 96/C2
Porsuk (riv.), Turk. 148/B2
Port (isl.), Japan 135/H6
Port Alberni, BC, Can. 184/B3
Port Albert, Austl. 173/C3
Port Alexander, Ak, US 192/M4
Port Alfred, SAfr. 164/D4
Port Alice, BC, Can. 184/B3
Port Angeles, Wa, US 184/C3
Port Antonio, Jam. 203/G2
Port Appin, Sc, UK 94/A3
Port Arthur, Tx, US 187/J5
Port au Choix, Nf, Can. 189/K1
Port-au-Prince (cap.), Haiti 203/H2
Port Augusta, Austl. 171/H5
Port Bannatyne, Sc, UK 94/A5
Port Blair, India 141/F5
Port Blakely, Wa, US 193/C2
Port Bolivar, Tx, US 190/E4
Port-Bouët, C.d'Iv. 160/E5
Port Bouet (Abidgan) (int'l arpt.), C.d'Iv. 160/E5
Port Broughton, Austl. 171/H5
Port Canning, India 143/G4
Port Carbon, Pa, US 196/B2
Port Charlotte, Fl, US 191/H5
Port Chester, NY, US 197/L8
Port Clements, BC, Can. 192/M5
Port Clinton, Oh, US 188/D3
Port Clinton, Pa, US 196/B2
Port Colborne, On, Can. 189/R10
Port Columbus (int'l arpt.), Oh, US 188/D4
Port Davey (har.), Austl. 173/C4
Port-de-Paix, Haiti 203/H2
Port Deposit, Md, US 196/B4
Port Dickson, Malay. 138/B3
Port Discovery (bay), Wa, US 193/B1
Port Douglas, Austl. 172/B2
Port Edward, BC, Can. 192/M4
Port Elgin, On, Can. 188/D2
Port Elizabeth, SAfr. 164/D4
Port Elizabeth, NJ, US 196/D5
Port Ellen, Sc, UK 89/Q9
Port Elliot, Austl. 171/H5
Port Erin, IM, UK 92/D3
Port-Eynon (pt.), Wal, UK 90/B3
Port Fairy, Austl. 173/B3
Port Gamble, Wa, US 193/B2
Port Gamble Ind. Res., Wa, US 193/B2
Port-Gentil, Gabon 154/G8
Port Gibson, Ms, US 187/K5
Port Glasgow, Sc, UK 94/B5
Port Graham, Ak, US 192/H4
Port Harcourt, Nga. 161/G5
Port Harcourt (int'l arpt.), Nga. 161/G5
Port Hardy, BC, Can. 184/B3
Port Hawkesbury, NS, Can. 189/J2
Port Hedland, Austl. 170/C2
Port Hedland (int'l arpt.), Austl. 170/C2
Port Heiden, Ak, US 192/G4
Port Hueneme, Ca, US 194/A2
Port Huron, Mi, US 188/D3
Port Isaac (bay), Eng, UK 90/B5
Port Jefferson, NY, US 197/E2
Port-la-Nouvelle, Fr. 100/E5
Port Lambton, On, Can. 193/H6
Port Lavaca, Tx, US 187/H5
Port Lincoln, Austl. 171/G5
Port Lions, Ak, US 192/H4
Port Loko, SLeo. 160/B4
Port-Louis, Guad., Fr. 199/N8
Port Louis (cap.), Mrts. 165/T15
Port Macdonnell, Austl. 173/B3
Port Macquarie, Austl. 173/E1
Port Madison Ind. Res., Wa, US 193/B2
Port Maria, Jam. 203/G2
Port McNeill, BC, Can. 184/B3
Port-Menier, Qu, Can. 189/H1
Port Monmouth, NJ, US 197/J10
Port Nolloth, SAfr. 164/B3
Port Norris, NJ, US 196/C5
Port of Ness, Sc, UK 89/Q7
Port-of-Spain (cap.), Trin. 211/F2
Port Orange, Fl, US 191/H4
Port Penn, De, US 196/C4
Port Phillip (bay), Austl. 173/C3
Port Pirie, Austl. 171/H5
Port Elizabeth, SAfr. 164/D4
Port Elizabeth, NJ, US 196/D5
Port Ellen, Sc, UK 89/Q9
Port Elliot, Austl. 171/H5
Port Erin, IM, UK 92/D3
Port-Eynon (pt.), Wal, UK 90/B3
Port Fairy, Austl. 173/B3
Port Gamble, Wa, US 193/B2
Port Gamble Ind. Res., Wa, US 193/B2
Port-Gentil, Gabon 154/G8
Port Gibson, Ms, US 187/K5
Port Glasgow, Sc, UK 94/B5
Port Graham, Ak, US 192/H4
Port Harcourt, Nga. 161/G5
Port Harcourt (int'l arpt.), Nga. 161/G5
Port Hardy, BC, Can. 184/B3
Port Hawkesbury, NS, Can. 189/J2
Port Hedland, Austl. 170/C2
Port Hedland (int'l arpt.), Austl. 170/C2
Port Heiden, Ak, US 192/G4

Port Hueneme, Ca, US 194/K2
Port Huron, Mi, US 188/D3
Port Isaac (bay), Eng, UK 90/B5
Port Jefferson, NY, US 197/E2
Port-la-Nouvelle, Fr. 100/E5
Port Lambton, On, Can. 193/H6
Port Lavaca, Tx, US 187/H5
Port Lincoln, Austl. 171/G5
Port Lions, Ak, US 192/H4
Port Loko, SLeo. 160/B4
Port-Louis, Guad., Fr. 199/N8
Port Louis (cap.), Mrts. 165/T15
Port Macdonnell, Austl. 173/B3
Port Macquarie, Austl. 173/E1
Port Madison Ind. Res., Wa, US 193/B2
Port Maria, Jam. 203/G2
Port McNeill, BC, Can. 184/B3
Port-Menier, Qu, Can. 189/H1
Port Monmouth, NJ, US 197/J10
Port Nolloth, SAfr. 164/B3
Port Norris, NJ, US 196/C5
Port of Ness, Sc, UK 89/Q7
Port-of-Spain (cap.), Trin. 211/F2
Port Orange, Fl, US 191/H4
Port Penn, De, US 196/C4
Port Phillip (bay), Austl. 173/C3
Port Pirie, Austl. 171/H5
Port Reading, NJ, US 197/J9
Port Republic, NJ, US 196/D4
Port Royal, Pa, US 196/A2
Port Saint Joe, Fl, US 191/G4
Port-Saint-Louis-du-Rhône, Fr. 100/F5
Port Saint Lucie, Fl, US 191/H5
Port Saint Mary, IM, UK 92/D3
Port Shepstone, SAfr. 165/E3
Port Stephens (bay), Austl. 173/E1
Port-sur-Saône, Fr. 114/C2
Port Townsend, Wa, US 184/C3
Port-Vendres, Fr. 100/E5
Port Victoria, Austl. 210/D2
Port-Vila (cap.), Van. 174/F4
Port Wakefield, Austl. 171/H5
Port Washington, NY, US 197/K8
Port Weld, Malay. 138/B3
Porta Westfalica (pass), Ger. 109/F4
Porta Westfalica, Ger. 109/F4
Portachuelo, Bol. 208/F7
Portadown, NI, UK 92/B2
Portaferry, NI, UK 92/C3
Portage, Mi, US 188/C3
Portage Des Sioux, Mo, US 195/G8
Portage la Prairie, Mb, Can. 185/J4
Portalegre (dist.), Port. 102/B3
Portalegre, Port. 102/B3
Portales, NM, US 187/G4
Portarlington, Ire. 89/Q10
Portbou, Sp. 103/G1
Porteirinha, Braz. 212/B4
Portel, Braz. 209/H4
Porters (lake), Pa, US 196/C1
Portglenone, NI, UK 92/B2
Portimão, Port. 102/B4
Portishead, Eng, UK 90/D4
Portknockie, Sc, UK 94/D1
Portland, Austl. 173/C4
Portland, Austl. 173/E1
Portland (cape), Austl. 173/C4
Portland, In, US 188/D3
Portland, Me, US 189/G3
Portland, Or, US 184/C4
Portland (int'l arpt.), Or, US 184/C4
Portland, Tn, US 188/C3
Portland Canal (inlet), BC, Can. 192/M4
Portland Jetport (int'l arpt.), Me, US 189/G3
Portlaoise, Ire. 89/Q10
Portlaw, Ire. 89/Q10
Portlethen, Sc, UK 94/D2
Portmarnock, Ire. 92/B5
Portmore, Jam. 203/G2
Portneuf (riv.), Qu, Can. 189/G1
Porto (gulf), Fr. 104/A1
Porto, Port. 102/A2
Porto (dist.), Port. 102/A2
Porto (int'l arpt.), Port. 102/A2

Porto Azzurro, It. 101/J5
Porto Belo, Braz. 213/B3
Porto Calvo, Braz. 212/D3
Porto Ceresio, It. 115/E6
Pôrto da Fôlha, Braz. 212/C3
Porto de Mós, Port. 102/A3
Porto Empedocle, It. 104/C4
Porto Ercole, It. 104/B1
Porto Ferreira, Braz. 213/C2
Porto Franco, Braz. 212/A2
Porto Garibaldi, It. 117/F3
Porto Inglês, CpV. 151/K10
Porto Nacional, Braz. 209/J6
Porto-Novo (cap.), Ben. 161/F5
Porto Potenza Picena, It. 117/G6
Porto Recanati, It. 117/G6
Porto Sant'Elpidio, It. 101/K5
Porto Santo (isl.), Port. 156/A2
Porto Santo Stefano, It. 104/B1
Porto Seguro, Braz. 212/C5
Porto Tolle, It. 117/F3
Porto Torres, It. 104/A2
Porto União, Braz. 213/B3
Porto Valtravaglia, It. 115/E6
Porto-Vecchio, Fr. 104/A2
Porto Velho, Braz. 208/F5
Portobelo, PN, Pan. 203/G4
Portocannone, It. 104/D2
Portocivitanova, It. 101/K5
Portoferraio, It. 101/J5
Portofino, It. 116/C4
Portogruaro, It. 117/F1
Portomaggiore, It. 117/E3
Portovenere, It. 116/C4
Portoviejo, Ecu. 210/A5
Portpatrick, Sc, UK 92/C2
Portree, Sc, UK 89/Q8
Portrush, NI, UK 92/B1
Portsea (isl.), Eng, UK 91/E5
Portslade-by-Sea, Eng, UK 91/F5
Portsmouth, Dom. 199/N9
Portsmouth, Eng, UK 91/E5
Portsmouth (co.), Eng, UK 91/E5
Portsmouth, NH, US 189/G3
Portsoy, Sc, UK 94/D1
Portstewart, NI, UK 92/B1
Portugal (ctry.), 102/A3
Portugalete, Sp. 102/D1
Portuguesa (riv.), Ven. 210/D2
Portuguesa (state), Ven. 210/D2
Portumna, Ire. 89/P10
Porvenir, Chile 217/C7
Porvenir, Uru. 217/K10
Porzuna, Sp. 102/C3
Posada, It. 104/A2
Posadas, Arg. 215/E2
Posadas, Sp. 102/C4
Posavina (valley), Bosn. 106/C3
Poschiavo, Swi. 115/G5
Poso, Fin. 118/F2
Poso (lake), Indo. 139/F4
Posof, Turk. 148/E1
Posŏng, SKor. 131/D5
Posŏng (riv.), SKor. 131/D5
Posorja, Ecu. 210/A5
Posse, Braz. 212/A4
Possession (pt.), Wa, US 193/C2
Possession (sound), Wa, US 193/C2
Post, Tx, US 187/G4
Post Falls, Id, US 184/D4
Poste Maurice Cortier (ruin), Alg. 157/F3
Postmasburg, SAfr. 164/C3
Postojna, Slov. 101/L4
Postoloprty, Czh. 113/G2
Potam, Mex. 200/C3
Potaro-Siparuni (pol. reg.), Guy. 211/G3
Potchefstroom, SAfr. 164/D2
Poteau, Ok, US 187/J4
Potenza (riv.), It. 104/C1
Potenza, It. 104/D2
Potenza Picena, It. 117/G6
Potes, Sp. 102/C1
Potholes (res.), Wa, US 184/D4
Poti, Ga., Braz. 209/K5
Po'ti, Geo. 121/G4
Potiraguá, Braz. 212/C5
Potomac (riv.), It. 191/F4
Potomac, Md, US 196/A5
Potosí, Bol. 208/E7
Potosí, Mo, US 187/K3
Potrerillos, Chile 215/C2
Potsdam, NY, US 188/F2
Potsdam, Ger. 98/G7
Pottawatomie (co.), Ok, US 195/N15
Pottendorf, Aus. 101/M3
Pottenstein, Ger. 113/E3
Potters Bar, Eng, UK 88/C1
Pöttmes, Ger. 112/E5
Pottstown, Pa, US 196/C3
Pottsville, Pa, US 196/B2
Pottuvil, SrL. 140/D6
Poudre d'Or, Mrts. 165/T15
Poughkeepsie, NY, US 188/F3

Pouilley-les-Vignes, Fr. 114/B3
Poulaphoucha (res.), Ire. 92/B5
Poulton-le-Fylde, Eng, UK 93/G5
Poŭn, SKor. 131/D4
Pourri (peak), Fr. 101/G4
Pouru-Saint-Remy, Fr. 111/E4
Pouso Alegre, Braz. 213/H7
Pouthisat (riv.), Camb. 141/H5
Pouzauges, Fr. 100/C3
Považská Bystrica, Slvk. 99/K4
Povegliano Veronese, It. 117/D2
Poverty Point Nat'l Mon., La, US 187/K4
Poviglio, It. 116/D3
Póvoa de Varzim, Port. 102/A2
Povoação, Azor., Port. 103/T13
Povorino, Rus. 121/G2
Povungnituk (riv.), Qu, Can. 181/J2
Povungnituk, Qu, Can. 181/J2
Poway, Ca, US 194/C5
Powder (riv.), Mt,Wy, US 185/G4
Powell (lake), Az,Ut, US 186/E3
Powell, Wy, US 184/F4
Powell River, BC, Can. 184/B3
Power (res.), NY, US 189/R9
Powers (lake), Wi, US 193/P14
Powys (co.), Wal, UK 93/E6
Powys, Vale of (valley), Wal, UK 90/C1
Poxoreo, Braz. 209/H7
Poyang (lake), China 137/C2
Poynton, Eng, UK 93/F5
Poyo, Sp. 102/A1
Poysdorf, Aus. 99/J4
Poza Rica, Mex. 201/M6
Požarevac, Serb. 106/E3
Požega, Serb. 106/E4
Poznań, Pol. 99/J2
Pozo Alcón, Sp. 102/D4
Pozoblanco, Sp. 102/C3
Pozohondo, Sp. 102/E3
Pozuelo de Alarcón, Sp. 103/N9
Pozuelos, Ven. 211/E2
Pozuzo, Peru 214/C3
Pozza, It. 117/D3
Pozzallo, It. 104/D4
Pozzo Formigaro, It. 116/B3
Pozzonovo, It. 117/E2
Ppa. de Salamanca (plain), Arg. 216/F1
Pracham Hiang (pt.), Thai. 136/B4
Prachatice, Czh. 113/H4
Prachin Buri (riv.), Thai. 136/C3
Prachin Buri, Thai. 136/C3
Prachuap Khiri Khan, Thai. 136/B4
Praděd (peak), Czh. 99/J3
Pradera, Col. 210/B4
Prades, Fr. 100/E5
Prado, Braz. 212/C5
Prado del Rey, Sp. 102/C4
Prado Flood Control (basin), Ca, US 194/C3
Pragelpass (pass), Swi. 115/E4
Praha (Prague) (cap.), Czh. 113/H2
Praha (peak), Czh. 99/J3
Praha (pol. reg.), Czh. 113/H2
Prahova (prov.), Rom. 107/G3
Praia (cap.), CpV. 151/K11
Praia (int'l arpt.), CpV. 151/K11
Praia da Vitória, Azor., Port. 103/S12
Praia Grande, Braz. 213/G9
Prairie Dog Town Fk. (riv.), Tx, US 187/G4
Prairie du Chien, Wi, US 185/L5
Prairie Grove, Il, US 193/P15
Prairie View, Tx, US 187/J5
Prairie Village, Ks, US 195/D6
Prairies (riv.), Qu, Can. 189/N6
Prairietown, Il, US 195/H4
Pralboino, It. 116/D2
Pralungo, It. 116/B1
Pram (riv.), Aus. 113/G6
Prambachkirchen, Aus. 113/G6
Pran Buri (res.), Thai. 141/G5
Prangins, Swi. 114/C4
Prānhita (riv.), India 140/C4
Prapat, Indo. 138/A3
Præstø, Den. 96/E4
Praszka, Pol. 99/K4
Prat, Chile, Ant. 218/W4
Prata, Braz. 213/B1
Prata (riv.), Braz. 212/A5
Prata di Pordenone, It. 117/F1
Prathersville, Mo, US 195/E4
Prato, It. 117/E5
Prato (prov.), It. 117/E5

Prato allo Stelvio (Prad am Stilfserjoch), It. 115/G4
Prato (Leventina), Swi. 115/E5
Pratola Peligna, It. 117/B6
Pratomagno (mts.), It. 117/E5
Pratovecchio, It. 117/E5
Pratt (isl.), Chile 217/B6
Pratt, Ks, US 187/H3
Pratteln, Swi. 114/D2
Prattville, Al, US 191/G3
Prauthoy, Fr. 114/B2
Pravets, Bul. 105/H1
Pravia, Sp. 102/B1
Prawle (pt.), Eng, UK 90/C6
Praxedis G. Guerrero, Mex. 200/D2
Praya, Indo. 139/E5
Pré-Saint-Didier, It. 114/C6
Preah Vihear (ruin), Camb. 136/D3
Précy-sur-Oise, Fr. 110/B5
Predappio, It. 117/E4
Predazzo, It. 101/J3
Predeal, Rom. 107/G3
Predosa, It. 116/B3
Preeceville, Sk, Can. 185/H3
Preetz, Ger. 96/D4
Preganziol, It. 117/F1
Pregarten, Aus. 113/H6
Pregolya (riv.), Pol. 97/J4
Pregolya (riv.), Rus. 99/L1
Pregonero, Ven. 210/D2
Preissac (lake), Qu, Can. 188/F1
Premana, It. 115/F6
Prémery, Fr. 100/E3
Premià de Mar, Sp. 103/L7
Prenzlau, Ger. 99/G2
Přerov, Czh. 99/J4
Presanella (peak), It. 115/G5
Prescot, Eng, UK 93/F5
Prescott, Az, US 186/D4
Prescott, On, Can. 188/F2
Preševo, Serb. 106/E4
Presidencia Roque Sáenz Peña, Arg. 215/D2
Presidente Dutra, Braz. 212/A2
Presidente Epitácio, Braz. 213/A2
Presidente Olegário, Braz. 213/A2
Presidente Venceslau, Braz. 213/B2
Presidential Lake Estates, NJ, US 196/D4
Presidio, Tx, US 187/F5
Presidio (riv.), Mex. 200/D4
Preslav, Bul. 107/H4
Presles, Fr. 88/J4
Presles-en-Brie, Fr. 88/L5
Prešov, Slvk. 99/L4
Prešovský (pol. reg.), Slvk. 99/L4
Prespa (lake), Eur. 105/G2
Presque Isle, Me, US 189/G2
Pressath, Ger. 113/E3
Pressbaum, Aus. 107/N7
Prestatyn, Wal, UK 93/E5
Prestea, Gha. 161/E5
Prestfoss, Nor. 96/C1
Preston (cape), Austl. 170/C2
Preston, Md, US 196/C6
Preston, Wa, US 193/D2
Preston, Eng, UK 93/F4
Prestonpans, Sc, UK 94/D5
Prestonsburg, Ky, US 188/D4
Prestwick (int'l arpt.), Sc, UK 94/B5
Prestwick, Sc, UK 94/B6
Prêto (riv.), Braz. 209/J6
Pretoria (cap.), SAfr. 164/E2
Pretty Boy (res.), Md, US 196/B4
Preussisch Olendorf, Ger. 109/F4
Prevalje, Slov. 101/L3
Prévéza, Gre. 105/G3
Prévost, Qu, Can. 189/M6
Prey Veng, Camb. 136/D4
Pribilof (isls.), Ak, US 192/D4
Priboj, Serb. 106/D4
Příbram, Czh. 113/H3
Price (riv.), Ut, US 186/E3
Price, Ut, US 186/E3
Price, Md, US 196/C5
Prichard, Al, US 191/F4
Prichsenstadt, Ger. 112/D3
Priego, Sp. 102/D2
Priego de Córdoba, Sp. 102/C4
Prien am Chiemsee, Ger. 113/F7
Prieska, SAfr. 164/C3
Priest (lake), Id, US 184/D3
Priest River, Id, US 184/D3
Prieta (mtn.), Sp. 102/C1
Prievidza, Slvk. 99/K4
Prignitz (reg.), Ger. 98/F2
Prijedor, Bosn. 106/C3
Prijepolje, Serb. 106/D4
Prikaspian (plain), Kaz.,Rus. 122/E5
Prilep, FYROM 105/G2
Prilly, Swi. 114/C4
Prima Porta, It. 104/C1
Prima Tapia, Mex. 200/A1

Prime Hook NWR, De, US 196/C6
Primeira Cruz, Braz. 212/B1
Primero (cape), Chile 217/B6
Primorskiy Kray, Rus. 123/P5
Primorsko, Bul. 107/H4
Primorsko-Akhtarsk, Rus. 120/F3
Prims (riv.), Ger. 111/F4
Prince Albert, Sk, Can. 185/G2
Prince Albert (pen.), NW, Can. 180/E1
Prince Albert (sound), NW, Can. 180/E1
Prince Albert NP, SAfr. 164/C4
Prince Alfred (cape), NW, Can. 180/D1
Prince Charles (isl.), Nun., Can. 181/J2
Prince Edward (isl.), Can. 177/L5
Prince Edward Island (prov.), Can. 189/J2
Prince Edward Island NP, PE, Can. 189/J2
Prince Edward (isls.), SAfr. 81/L7
Prince George, BC, Can. 184/C2
Prince Georges (co.), Md, US 196/B6
Prince Gustav Adolf (sea), Nun., Can. 181/R7
Prince Leopold (isl.), Nun., Can. 180/G1
Prince of Wales (str.), NW, Can. 180/E1
Prince of Wales (isl.), Ak, US 180/C3
Prince Olav (coast), Ant. 218/D7
Prince Patrick (isl.), NW, Can. 181/R7
Prince Regent (inlet), Nun., Can. 180/G1
Prince Rupert, BC, Can. 192/M4
Prince William (sound), Ak, US 180/B2
Princenhof (lake), Neth. 108/C2
Princes Risborough, Eng, UK 91/F3
Princes Town, Trin. 199/J5
Princesa Isabel, Braz. 212/C2
Princess Charlotte (bay), Austl. 172/A1
Princess Margaret (range), Nun., Can. 181/S6
Princess Royal (isl.), BC, Can. 180/C3
Princeton, Mn, US 185/K4
Princeton, BC, Can. 184/C3
Princeton, In, US 188/C4
Princeton, Ky, US 188/C4
Princeton, NJ, US 196/D3
Princeton Junction, NJ, US 196/D4
Princeville, Hi, US 182/S9
Príncipe (isl.), SaoT. 154/G7
Prindle (vol.), Ak, US 192/K3
Prineville, Or, US 184/C4
Pringsewu, Indo. 138/B5
Pringy, Fr. 114/C4
Prinsenbeek, Neth. 108/B5
Prinses Margriet (canal), Neth. 108/C2
Prinzapolka, Nic. 203/F3
Prinzapolka (riv.), Nic. 203/E3
Priolo di Gargallo, It. 104/D4
Prior (cap.), Sp. 102/A1
Priore (peak), It. 101/K5
Priozersk, Rus. 97/P1
Pripet Marshes (swamp), Bela.,Ukr. 120/C2
Pripyat' (riv.), Ukr. 120/C2
Prisdorf, Ger. 109/G1
Priština (cap.), Kos. 106/E4
Prittriching, Ger. 115/G1
Pritzwalk, Ger. 98/G2
Privas, Fr. 100/F4
Privolzhskiy, Rus. 121/H3
Privolzhskiy, Rus. 121/K1
Priyutovo, Rus. 121/K1
Prizren, Kos. 106/E4
Prnjavor, Serb. 106/D3
Prnjavor, Bosn. 106/D3
Probištip, FYROM 105/H1
Probolinggo, Indo. 138/D5
Probstzella, Ger. 113/E1
Proctor (lake), Tx, US 187/H4
Proctor (pt.), La, US 195/Q17
Proddatūr, India 140/C5
Proença-a-Nova, Port. 102/B3
Profondeville, Belg. 111/D3
Progreso, Mex. 201/K6
Progreso, Mex. 202/D1
Progreso, Pan. 203/F4
Progreso, Uru. 217/K11
Progress, Rus. 117/E3
Progresso, Braz. 213/B2

Promissão, Reprêsa (res.), Braz. 213/B2
Promissão, Braz. 213/B2
Propriá, Braz. 212/C3
Propriano, Fr. 104/A2
Proserpine, Austl. 172/C3
Prosna (riv.), Pol. 99/J2
Prospect Park, NJ, US 197/J8
Prospector (mtn.), Yk, Can. 192/J3
Prosperidad, Phil. 139/G4
Prosperous, Ire. 89/Q10
Prostějov, Czh. 99/J4
Proston, Austl. 172/C4
Proszowice, Pol. 99/L3
Protivín, Czh. 113/H4
Provadiya, Bul. 107/H4
Provence (reg.), Fr. 100/F5
Provence (int'l arpt.), Fr. 101/G4
Provence-Alpes-Côte-d'Azur, Fr. 101/G4
Providence (cap.), RI, US 189/G3
Providencia, Isla de (isl.), Col. 198/E5
Providência, Serra de (mts.), Braz. 208/F6
Providenciales (isl.), Bahm. 203/H1
Provins, Fr. 100/E2
Provo (riv.), Ut, US 195/K13
Provo, Ut, US 195/K13
Provo (peak), Ut, US 195/K13
Provost, Ab, Can. 184/F2
Prozor, Bosn. 106/D4
Prudentópolis, Braz. 213/B3
Prudhoe (bay), Ak, US 192/J1
Prudhoe Bay, Ak, US 192/J1
Prudnik, Pol. 99/J3
Prüm (riv.), Ger. 98/D4
Prüm, Ger. 111/F3
Prunay-en-Yvelines, Fr. 88/H6
Prunelli-di-Fiumorbo, Fr. 104/A1
Pruszcz Gdański, Pol. 96/H4
Pruszków, Pol. 99/L2
Prut (riv.), Eur. 107/J2
Pryor, Ok, US 187/J3
Pryluky, Ukr. 120/E2
Prymors'k, Ukr. 120/F3
Prypyats' (riv.), Bela. 120/C2
Przasnysz, Pol. 99/L2
Przemków, Pol. 99/H3
Przemyśl, Pol. 99/M4
Przeworsk, Pol. 99/M3
Przylądek Rozewie (cape), Pol. 96/H4
Przysucha, Pol. 99/L3
Psará (isl.), Gre. 105/J3
Psárion, Gre. 105/G4
Psël (riv.), Rus.,Ukr. 120/E2
Pskov (lake), Rus. 118/E5
Pskov, Rus. 97/N3
Pskovskaya Oblast, Rus. 118/F4
Psˇovka (riv.), Czh. 113/H2
Pszczyna, Pol. 99/K4
Ptolemaïs, Gre. 105/G2
Ptuj, Slov. 101/L3
Pu Xian, China 130/B3
Puan, SKor. 131/D5
Pubei, China 137/A3
Pucacaca, Peru 214/B2
Pucallpa, Peru 214/C2
Pucará, Ecu. 214/B1
Pucará, Peru 214/D4
Pucarani, Bol. 214/D5
Pucaurco, Peru 210/D5
Puchenau, Aus. 113/H6
Pucheng, China 137/C2
Pucheng, China 130/B4
Puchheim, Ger. 113/E6
Puch'on, SKor. 131/F7
Puchuncaví, Chile 216/N8
Pucioasa, Rom. 107/G3
Puck, Pol. 96/H4
Pucking, Aus. 113/H6
Pucón, Chile 216/C4
Pucusana, Peru 214/B4
Pudasjärvi, Fin. 118/E2
Puderbach, Ger. 111/G2
Pudsey, Eng, UK 93/G4
Pudu (riv.), China 141/F1
Pudukkottai, India 140/C6
Puebla (state), Mex. 198/B4
Puebla, Mex. 201/L7
Puebla de Alcocer, Sp. 102/C3
Puebla de Don Fadrique, Sp. 102/D4
Puebla de la Calzada, Sp. 102/B3
Puebla de Sanabria, Sp. 102/B1
Puebla de Trives, Sp. 102/B1
Puebla del Caramiñal, Sp. 102/A1
Pueblito, Col. 210/C2
Pueblo, Co, US 186/F3
Pueblo Nuevo, Nic. 202/E3
Pueblo Nuevo, Ven. 210/D1
Pueblo Yaqui, Mex. 200/C3
Puente, India 140/D5
Puente Alto, Chile 216/N8
Puente Caldelas, Sp. 102/A1
Puente-Ceso, Sp. 102/A1
Puente de Ixtla, Mex. 201/K8

Puente del Inca, Arg. 216/C2
Puente-Genil, Sp. 102/C4
Puente Nacional, Col. 210/C3
Puente Piedra, Peru 214/B3
Puenteareas, Sp. 102/A1
Puentedeume, Sp. 102/A1
Puentes de García Rodríguez, Sp. 102/A1
Pueo (pt.), Hi, US 182/R10
Puerco (riv.), NM, US 186/E4
Puerto Acosta, Bol. 214/D4
Puerto Aisén, Chile 217/B6
Puerto América, Peru 214/B2
Puerto Ángel, Mex. 202/B3
Puerto Armuelles, Pan. 203/F4
Puerto Asís, Col. 210/B4
Puerto Ayacucho, Ven. 211/E3
Puerto Ayora, Ecu. 214/B1
Puerto Baquerizo Moreno, Ecu. 214/B1
Puerto Barrios, Guat. 202/D3
Puerto Bermúdez, Peru 214/C3
Puerto Berrío, Col. 210/C2
Puerto Cabello, Ven. 210/D1
Puerto Cabezas, Nic. 203/F3
Puerto Carreño, Col. 210/E2
Puerto Cisnes, Chile 216/B5
Puerto Cortés, Mex. 200/C3
Puerto Cortés, Hon. 202/E3
Puerto Cumarebo, Ven. 210/D2
Puerto de la Cruz, Sp. 156/A3
Puerto de la Libertad, Mex. 200/B2
Puerto de Navacerrada (pass), Sp. 103/M8
Puerto del Rosario, Sp. 156/B3
Puerto del Son, Sp. 102/A1
Puerto Deseado, Arg. 217/C6
Puerto El Carmen, Ecu. 210/C4
Puerto Escondido, Col. 210/B2
Puerto Escondido, Mex. 202/B3
Puerto Heath, Bol. 214/D3
Puerto Iguazú, Arg. 215/F2
Puerto Inca, Peru 214/C3
Puerto Ingeniero Ibáñez, Chile 216/C5
Puerto Inírida, Col. 210/D3
Puerto La Cruz, Ven. 211/E2
Puerto Leguízamo, Col. 210/C4
Puerto Lempira, Hon. 203/F3
Puerto López, Col. 210/C3
Puerto Lumbreras, Sp. 102/E4
Puerto Madero, Mex. 202/C3
Puerto Madryn, Arg. 216/C4
Puerto Magdalena, Mex. 200/B3
Puerto Maldonado, Peru 200/D2
Puerto Montt, Chile 216/B5
Puerto Morazán, Nic. 202/E3
Puerto Morelos, Mex. 198/D3
Puerto Napo, Ecu. 210/C4
Puerto Natales, Chile 217/B6
Puerto Obaldía, Pan. 203/G4
Puerto Ocopa, Peru 214/C3
Puerto Padre, Cuba 203/G1
Puerto Páez, Ven. 211/E3
Puerto Pirítu, Ven. 211/E2
Puerto Portillo, Peru 214/C3
Puerto Prado, Peru 214/C3
Puerto Princesa, Phil. 139/E2
Puerto Quellón, Chile 216/B5
Puerto Real, Sp. 102/B4
Puerto Rico, Col. 210/C4
Puerto Rico, Col. 210/C4
Puerto Rico (dpcy.), US 199/M8
Puerto Rondón, Col. 210/D3
Puerto San Carlos, Mex. 200/B3
Puerto San Julián, Arg. 217/D6
Puerto Santa Cruz, Arg. 217/C7
Puerto Serrano, Sp. 102/C4
Puerto Suárez, Bol. 208/G7
Puerto Supe, Peru 214/B3
Puerto Tejada, Col. 210/B4
Puerto Vallarta, Mex. 200/C4
Puerto Varas, Chile 216/B5
Puerto Viejo, CR 203/E4
Puerto Villamil, Ecu. 214/E2
Puerto Wilches, Col. 210/C2
Puerto Williams, Chile 217/D8
Puertollano, Sp. 102/C3
Pueyrredón (lake), 216/B6
Puffin (isl.), Wal, UK 92/D5
Pugachev, Rus. 121/J1
Puget (sound), Wa, US 193/C2
Puigcerdà, Sp. 103/F1

Pujut (cape), Indo. 138/C5
Pukalani, Hi, US 182/T10
Puk'an-san (peak), SKor. 131/F6
Puk'an-san NP, SKor. 131/D4
Pukapuka (isl.), Cookis. 175/J6
Pukarua (isl.), FrPol. 175/M6
Pukaskwa NP, On, Can. 188/D1
Pukch'ŏng, NKor. 131/E2
Pukdae (riv.), NKor. 131/E2
Pukhan (riv.), NKor.,SKor. 131/D3
Pukhrāyān, India 142/B2
Pukovac, Serb. 106/E4
Pukp'ot'ae-san (peak), NKor. 131/E2
Pula, Cro. 106/A3
Pulacayo, Bol. 208/E8
Pulandian (bay), China 131/A3
Pulanduta (pt.), Phil. 139/F1
Pulap (isl.), Micr. 174/D4
Pulaski, Va, US 188/D4
Pulaski, Tn, US 191/G3
Pulau (riv.), Indo. 139/J5
Puławy, Pol. 99/L3
Pulguk-sa, SKor. 131/E5
Pulheim, Ger. 111/F2
Pulisan (cape), Indo. 139/G3
Pulkovo (int'l arpt.), Rus. 119/T7
Pullach im Isartal, Ger. 115/H1
Pullman, Wa, US 184/D4
Pully, Swi. 114/C5
Pulsnitz (riv.), Czh. 99/G3
Pułtusk, Pol. 99/L2
Pülümür, Turk. 148/D2
Pum (riv.), China 143/F1
Pulversheim, Fr. 114/D2
Puma (lake), China 143/H1
Pumu (pass), China 143/G2
Puná de Atacama (plat.), Arg. 215/C2
Puná, Isla (isl.), Ecu. 208/B4
Punākha, Bhu. 143/G2
Punata, Bol. 208/E7
Pūnch, India 144/C3
Pūnch (riv.), India 144/C3
Pūndri, India 144/D5
Pune (Poona), India 147/K5
Punggal (cape), Malay. 138/B3
P'unggi, SKor. 131/E4
P'ungsan, NKor. 131/E2
Pungwe (falls), Zim. 163/F4
Punjab (plain), Pak. 147/K2
Punjab (state), Pak. 140/B2
Puno (dept.), Peru 214/D4
Puno, Peru 214/D4
Pünpün (riv.), India 143/E3
Punta, Ca, US 194/A2
Punta Alta, Arg. 216/E3
Punta Arena (pt.), Mex. 200/C4
Punta Arenas, Chile 217/C7
Punta Banda (cape), Mex. 200/A1
Punta Cardón, Ven. 210/D2
Punta Celarain (pt.), Mex. 202/E1
Punta Colnett (pt.), Mex. 200/A2
Punta Colonet, Mex. 200/A2
Punta de Bombón, Peru 214/D5
Punta de Mata, Ven. 211/F2
Punta del Este, Uru. 217/G2
Punta del Este (Capitán Curbelo) (int'l arpt.), Uru. 217/G2
Punta Gorda, Fl, US 191/H5
Punta Gorda, Belz. 202/D2
Punta Marina, It. 117/F4
Punta Raisi (int'l arpt.), It. 104/C4
Punta Umbría, Sp. 102/B4
Puntarenas, CR 203/E4
Puolo (pt.), Hi, US 182/S10
Pupiales, Col. 210/B4
Pupuya (peak), Bol. 214/D4
Puquio, Peru 214/C4
Pur (riv.), Rus. 122/H3
Puracé (vol.), Col. 210/B4
Puracé, PN, Col. 208/C2
Pūranpur, India 142/B2
Purbeck (isl.), Eng, UK 90/D5
Purcell (mts.), BC, 184/D4
Purcell, Ok, US 187/H4
Puré (riv.), Col. 210/C4
Purén, Chile 216/B3
Purgatoire (riv.), Co, US 187/G3
Pürgen, Ger. 115/G1
Purgstall an der Erlauf, Aus. 101/L2
Purī, India 140/D3
Purification, Col. 210/C4
Puri (riv.), India 143/E3
Purkersdorf, Aus. 107/N7
Purmerend, Neth. 108/B3
Pūrna (riv.), India 140/C4
Pūrna, India 143/F3
Puruni (riv.), Guy. 211/G3
Purranque, Chile 215/B5
Purué (riv.), Braz. 210/D4
Purūlia, India 143/F4
Purús (riv.), Braz. 205/C3

Purushottampur, India 140/D4
Pürvomay, Bul. 107/G4
Purwa, India 142/C2
Purwokerto, Indo. 138/C5
Pusad, India 140/C4
Pusan, SKor. 131/E5
Pusan-Gwangyŏksi (prov.), SKor. 131/E5
Pusat Gayo (mts.), Indo. 138/A3
Puschendorf, Ger. 112/D3
Pushkin, Rus. 119/T7
Püspökladány, Hun. 106/E2
Pusur (riv.), Bang. 143/G4
Putaendo, Chile 216/C2
Putian, China 137/C2
Putina, Peru 214/D4
Puting (cape), Indo. 138/D4
Putla de Guerrero, Mex. 202/B2
Putomayo (dept.), Col. 210/C4
Putorana (mts.), Rus. 122/K3
Putrachoique (peak), Arg. 216/C4
Putre, Chile 214/D5
Puttalam, SrL. 140/C6
Putte, Belg. 111/D1
Puttelange-aux-Lacs, Fr. 111/F3
Putten, Neth. 108/C4
Putten (isl.), Neth. 108/B5
Püttlach (riv.), Ger. 113/E3
Püttlingen, Ger. 111/F5
Putu (range), Libr. 160/C5
Putumayo (riv.), SAm. 210/C5
Putussibau, Indo. 138/D3
Puu Kukui (peak), Hi, US 182/T10
Puu Moaulanui (peak), Hi, US 182/T10
Puu o Mahuka Heiau State Mon., Hi, US 182/V12
Puuanahulu, Hi, US 182/U11
Puuiki, Hi, US 182/T10
Puula (lake), Fin. 97/M1
Puurs, Belg. 111/D1
Puuwai, Hi, US 182/R10
Puy de Sancy (peak), Fr. 100/E4
Puyallup, Wa, US 184/C4
Puyallup (riv.), Wa, US 193/C3
Puyallup Ind. Res., Wa, US 193/C3
Puyang, China 130/D3
Puyehué (lake), Chile 216/B4
Puyehue (vol.), Chile 216/B4
Puylaurens, Fr. 100/D5
Puymorens, Col de (pass), Fr. 100/D5
Puyŏ, SKor. 131/D4
Puyo, Ecu. 210/B5
Puzal, Sp. 103/E3
Pwani (pol. reg.), Tanz. 162/C4
Pwllheli, Wal, UK 92/D6
Pyandzh (riv.), Taj. 145/F5
Pyaozero (lake), Rus. 95/J2
Pyapon, Myan. 141/G4
Pyasina (riv.), Rus. 122/J2
Pyatigorsk, Rus. 121/G3
Pyfara (peak), Fr. 100/F4
Pyhä-Häkin NP, Fin. 118/E3
Pyhäjärvi, Fin. 118/E3
Pyhäjärvi (lake), Fin. 97/K1
Pyhäntä, Fin. 118/E2
Pyhätunturi (peak), Fin. 118/E2
Pyinmana, Myan. 141/G4
P'yŏngan-bukto (prov.), NKor. 131/C2
P'yŏngan-namdo (prov.), NKor. 131/C3
P'yŏngch'ang, SKor. 131/E4
P'yŏnggang, NKor. 131/D3
P'yŏnghae, SKor. 131/E4
P'yŏngsan, NKor. 131/C3
P'yŏngsong, NKor. 131/C3
P'yŏngt'aek, SKor. 131/D4
P'yŏngyang (int'l arpt.), NKor. 131/C3
P'yŏngyang (cap.), NKor. 131/C3
P'yŏngyang-si (prov.), NKor. 131/C3
Pyŏnsanbando NP, SKor. 131/D5
Pyramid (lake), Nv, US 186/B3
Pyramid (mtn.), BC, Can. 192/M4
Pyramids of Jīzah, Egypt 149/B5
Pyrenees (mts.), Fr.,Sp. 85/D4
Pyrénées Occidental, PN des, Fr. 100/C5
Pyryatyn, Ukr. 120/E2
Pyrzyce, Pol. 99/H2
Pyshma (riv.), Rus. 119/Q4
Pyu, Myan. 141/G4
Pyuthän, Nepal 142/D1

Q

Qâ 'al Jafr (salt pan), Jor. 149/E4
Qabalān, WBnk. 149/G7
Qabāţiyah, WBnk. 149/G7
Qadima, Isr. 149/F7
Qādirpur Rān, Pak. 144/A4
Qā'en, Iran 147/G2
Qafa e Malit (pass), Alb. 105/G1
Qaffīn, WBnk. 149/G7
Qahar Youyi Qianqi, China 130/C2
Qahar Youyi Zhongqi, China 130/C2
Qaidam (basin), China 128/F4
Qalansuwa, Isr. 149/F7
Qal'at Dizah, Iraq 148/F2
Qal'eh-ye Now, Afg. 145/D6
Qalqīlyah, WBnk. 149/F7
Qamdo, China 128/G5
Qamīnis, Libya 154/K1
Qapshagay Bögeni (res.), Kaz. 145/G4
Qapshaghay, Kaz. 145/G4
Qaraghandy, Kaz. 145/F3
Qaraghandy (obl.), Kaz. 145/F3
Qarataū, Kaz. 145/F4
Qarataū Zhotasy (mts.), Kaz. 145/E4
Qareh Chāy (riv.), Iran 146/E2
Qareh Sū (riv.), Iran 121/H5
Qarqan (riv.), China 128/F4
Qarrit (pass), Alb. 105/G2
Qarshi, Uzb. 145/E5
Qarūn (lake), Egypt 159/B2
Qashqadaryo (pol. reg.), Uzb. 145/D5
Qasr-e Qand, Iran 147/H3
Qasr-e-Shīrīn, Iran 146/E2
Qa'tabah, Yem. 146/D6
Qatar (ctry.) 146/F3
Qattara (depr.), Egypt 148/A4
Qaţţīnah, Buḩayrat (lake), Syria 149/E2
Qaydaq Sory (swamp), Kaz. 121/K3
Qayyārah, Iraq 148/E3
Qazaqtyng Usaqshoqylyghy (uplands), Kaz. 122/H5
Qāzi Ahmad, Pak. 140/A2
Qazvīn, Iran 146/F1
Qedma, Isr. 149/F8
Qendrevica (peak), Alb. 105/F2
Qezel Owzan (riv.), Iran 146/E1
Qi Xian, China 131/B2
Qian (mts.), China 131/D2
Qian (riv.), China 130/D5
Qian'an, China 129/M3
Qianxi, China 130/J6
Qianyang, China 137/B2
Qiaojia, China 141/H2
Qibyā, Isr. 149/G8
Qidong, China 131/C3
Qidong, China 130/L8
Qiemo, China 128/E4
Qihe, China 130/D3
Qijiang, China 137/A2
Qikiqtarjuaq, Nun., Can. 181/K2
Qila Didar Singh, Pak. 144/C3
Qila Sobha Singh, Pak. 144/C3
Qilian (mts.), China 128/G4
Qilian (peak), China 128/G4
Qimantag (mts.), China 128/F4
Qimen, China 137/C2
Qin (mts.), China 130/B4
Qing (riv.), China 137/B1
Qing'an, China 129/N2
Qingdao, China 130/E3
Qingfeng, China 130/C3
Qinghai (mts.), China 128/G4
Qinghai (prov.), China 128/G4
Qinghe, China 130/C3
Qinglong, China 130/D2
Qingpu, China 130/L8
Qingshui (riv.), China 137/A2
Qingshuihe, China 130/B3
Qingyuan, China 141/K3
Qingyun, China 130/D3
Qingzhou, China 130/D3
Qinhuangdao, China 130/D3
Qinshui, China 130/C4
Qinyang, China 130/C3
Qinyuan, China 130/C3
Qinzhou, China 141/J3
Qionglai (mts.), China 128/H5
Qiongshan, China 141/K4
Qiongzhong, China 141/K4
Qiqihar, China 129/M2
Qira, China 128/D4
Qiryat Ata, Isr. 149/G6
Qiryat Gat, Isr. 149/G8
Qiryat Mal'akhi, Isr. 149/G8
Qiryat Motzkin, Isr. 149/F6
Qiryat Shemona, Isr. 149/D3
Qiryat Tiv'on, Isr. 149/G6
Qiryat Yam, Isr. 149/G6
Qitai, China 128/F3
Qitaihe, China 129/P2
Qixia, China 130/E3
Qixing (riv.), China 123/P5
Qizilqum (des.), Kaz. 122/G5
Qogir (peak), China 147/L2
Qom (riv.), Iran 146/F2
Qom, Iran 146/F2
Qomsheh, Iran 146/F2

Qonduz (riv.), Afg. 147/J1
Qonggyai, China 143/H1
Qongqirat Aut. Rep., Uzb. 121/L3
Qormi, Malta 104/L7
Qorveh, Iran 146/E1
Qostanay (obl.), Kaz. 145/D2
Qostanay (int'l arpt.), Kaz. 119/P5
Qostanay, Kaz. 119/P5
Qoţūr, Iran 148/F2
Qu (riv.), China 129/L6
Quabbin (res.), Ma, US 189/H3
Quairading, Austl. 170/C5
Quakenbrück, Ger. 109/E3
Quakertown, Pa, US 196/C3
Quambatook, Austl. 173/B2
Quanah, Tx, US 187/H4
Quanbao (mtn.), China 130/B4
Quang Ngai, Viet. 136/E3
Quang Tri, Viet. 136/D2
Quanjiao, China 130/D4
Quannan, China 137/B3
Quantocks, The (hills), Eng, UK 90/C4
Quanzhou, China 137/C3
Qu'appelle (dam), Sk, Can. 185/G3
Qu'appelle (riv.), Sk, Can. 185/G3
Quaqtaq, Qu, Can. 181/K2
Quaregnon, Belg. 110/C3
Quarles (mts.), Indo. 139/E4
Quarona, It. 116/B1
Quarrata, It. 117/D5
Quarryville, Pa, US 196/B4
Quarto d'Altino, It. 117/F1
Quartu Sant'Elena, It. 104/A3
Quartz Hill, Ca, US 194/B6
Quatre Bornes, Mrts. 165/T15
Quattervals (peak), Swi. 115/G4
Quba, Azer. 121/J4
Qūchān, Iran 147/G1
Queanbeyan, Austl. 173/D2
Québec (int'l arpt.), Qu, Can. 189/G2
Québec (cap.), Qu, Can. 189/G2
Québec (prov.), Can. 181/J3
Quebra-Cangalha, Serra (mts.), Braz. 213/H4
Quecholac, Mex. 201/M8
Quechutenango, Mex. 201/F5
Quedal (pt.), Chile 216/B4
Queen Alia (int'l arpt.), Jor. 149/E4
Queen Anne, Md, US 196/C6
Queen Annes (co.), Md, US 196/C5
Queen Charlotte, BC, Can. 192/M5
Queen Charlotte (isls.), BC, Can. 180/C3
Queen Charlotte (str.), BC, Can. 184/B3
Queen Charlotte (sound), BC, Can. 180/C4
Queen City, Tx, US 187/J4
Queen Creek, Az, US 195/S19
Queen Elizabeth (isls.), NW, Can. 181/Q7
Queen Mary (coast), Ant. 218/G
Queen Mary, Ca, US 194/F8
Queen Mary (res.), Eng, UK 88/B2
Queen Maud (mts.), Ant. 218/P
Queen Maud (gulf), Nun., Can. 180/F2
Queen Maud Land (phys. reg.), Ant. 218/Z
Queen Victoria Spring Nature Reserve, Austl. 170/D4
Queens (chan.), Nun., Can. 181/Q7
Queens (co.), NY, US 197/E2
Queensberry (peak), Sc, UK 94/C6
Queensferry, Sc, UK 94/C5
Queensland, Austl. 173/B1
Queensland (state), Austl. 167/G3
Queenstown, Austl. 173/C4
Queenstown, SAfr. 164/D3
Queenstown, NZ 175/R12
Queenstown, Md, US 196/B6
Queich (riv.), Ger. 111/H5
Queidersbach, Ger. 111/G4
Queilén, Chile 216/B4
Queimada, Ilha (isl.), Braz. 209/H4
Queimadas, Braz. 212/D2
Queimadas, Braz. 212/C3
Quelimane, Moz. 163/G4
Queluz, Port. 103/P10
Quemado, Punta del (pt.), Cuba 203/H1
Quemú Quemú, Arg. 216/E3
Quepos, CR 203/E4
Quequén, Arg. 216/F3
Quequén Grande (riv.), Arg. 216/F3
Querecotillo, Peru 214/A2
Querétaro, Mex. 201/E4
Querétaro de Arteaga (state), Mex. 198/A5

Querimbas, Arquipélago das (arch.), Moz. 163/H3
Quero, It. 117/E1
Querobabi, Mex. 200/C2
Quesada, CR 203/E4
Quesada, Sp. 102/D4
Queshan, China 130/C4
Quesnel, BC, Can. 184/C2
Quesnel (lake), BC, Can. 180/D3
Quesnoy-sur-Deūle, Fr. 110/C2
Questa, NM, US 187/F3
Questembert, Fr. 100/B3
Quetigny, Fr. 114/B3
Quetta, Pak. 147/J2
Queulat, PN, Chile 216/B5
Quevedo, Ecu. 208/C4
Quevedo (riv.), Ecu. 210/B5
Quezaltenango, Guat. 202/D3
Quezon, Phil. 139/E2
Quezon City, Phil. 137/D5
Qufu, China 130/D4
Qui Nhon, Viet. 136/E3
Quibdó, Col. 210/B3
Quiberon, Fr. 100/B3
Quiberon (bay), Fr. 100/B3
Quibor, Ven. 210/D2
Quicacha, Peru 214/C4
Quiçama, PN da, Ang. 163/B2
Quickborn, Ger. 109/G1
Quiers, Fr. 88/L6
Quierschied, Ger. 111/G5
Quila, Mex. 200/D3
Quilán (cape), Chile 216/B4
Quilca, Peru 214/C5
Quilcene, Wa, US 193/B2
Quiliano, It. 116/B2
Quilicura, Chile 216/N8
Quill (lakes), Sk, Can. 185/G2
Quillabamba, Peru 214/C4
Quillacollo, Bol. 208/E7
Quillagua (pt.), Chile 216/B3
Quillan, Fr. 100/E5
Quilleco, Chile 216/C3
Quillota, Chile 216/N8
Quilmaná, Peru 214/B4
Quilon, India 140/C6
Quilpie, Austl. 172/B4
Quilpué, Chile 216/N8
Quimili, Arg. 215/D2
Quimper, Fr. 100/A2
Quimperlé, Fr. 100/B3
Quincey, Fr. 114/C2
Quincy, Wa, US 184/D4
Quincy, Fl, US 191/G4
Quincy, Ma, US 189/G3
Quincy-sous-Sénart, Fr. 88/K5
Quincy-Voisins, Fr. 88/L5
Quindío (dept.), Col. 210/A4
Quinhagak, Ak, US 192/F4
Quinn (riv.), Nv, US 186/C2
Quinns Rocks, Austl. 170/K6
Quinta de la Serena, Sp. 102/C3
Quintana Roo (state), Mex. 198/D4
Quintanar de la Orden, Sp. 102/D3
Quintanar del Rey, Sp. 102/E3
Quintero, Chile 216/N8
Quinto (riv.), Arg. 216/D2
Quinto, Sp. 102/E2
Quinto, Swi. 115/E4
Quinto di Treviso, It. 117/F1
Quinto di Valpantena, It. 117/E2
Quinton, NJ, US 196/C4
Quinzano d'Oglio, It. 116/C2
Quionga, Moz. 163/H2
Quipapá, Braz. 212/C3
Quirihue, Chile 216/B3
Quirindi, Austl. 173/D1
Quirinópolis, Braz. 213/B1
Quiriquire, Ven. 211/F2
Quiroga, Mex. 201/E5
Quiroga, Sp. 102/B1
Quiruvilca, Peru 214/B3
Quisiro, Ven. 210/D2
Quispamsis, NB, Can. 189/H2
Quissico, Moz. 163/F5
Quistello, It. 117/D3
Quitilipi, Arg. 215/D2
Quitman, Ga, US 191/H4
Quitman, Ms, US 191/G3
Quito (cap.), Ecu. 210/B4
Quixeramobim, Braz. 212/C2
Qujiang, China 141/K3
Qujing, China 141/H3
Quoque, NY, US 197/F2
Quoich (riv.), Nun., Can. 180/G2
Quoich (lake), Sc, UK 94/A2
Quoile (riv.), NI, UK 92/C3
Quoin (pt.), SAfr. 164/L11
Qurayyat, Oman 147/G4
Quron, Uzb. 145/F4
Qurghonteppa, Taj. 147/J1
Qurnat as Sawdā' (peak), Leb. 149/E2
Qūş, Egypt 159/C3
Qusmuryn Köli (lake), Kaz. 119/P5
Qusum, China 128/F6
Quttinirpaaq NP, Nun., Can. 181/T6
Quwo, China 130/M4
Quwu (mts.), China 128/H4
Quyang, China 130/C3
Quyghonteppa, Taj. 147/J1
Quzhou, China 130/C3
Quzhou, China 130/C3

Qyzylorda, Kaz. 145/E4
Qyzylorda (obl.), Kaz. 145/D4

R

Raab (riv.), Aus. 101/L3
Raab, Aus. 113/G6
Raabs an der Thaya, Aus. 99/H4
Raahe, Fin. 118/E2
Raalte, Neth. 108/D4
Raamsdonk, Neth. 108/B5
Ra'ananna, Isr. 149/F7
Raanes (pen.), Nun., Can. 181/S7
Raasay (isl.), Sc, UK 94/A3
Rab (isl.), Cro. 106/B3
Rab, Cro. 106/B3
Rāba (riv.), Hun. 106/C2
Rāba (pt.), Indo. 138/A3
Rábahidvég, Hun. 101/M3
Rabat (cap.), Mor. 158/A2
Rabat, Malta 104/C5
Rabat (Sale) (int'l arpt.), Mor. 158/A2
Rabat (Victoria), Malta 104/L6
Rabigh, SAr. 146/C4
Rabgala (pass), China 143/F2
Rabil, CpV. 151/K10
Rabinal, Guat. 202/D3
Rabiusa (riv.), Swi. 115/F4
Rabka, Pol. 99/K4
Rabkavi-Banhatti, India 147/L5
Raby (pt.), On, Can. 189/S8
Racconigi, It. 116/A2
Raccoon (pt.), La, US 187/K5
Rach Gia (bay), Viet. 136/D4
Rach Gia, Viet. 136/D4
Raciborz, Pol. 99/K3
Racine (peak), Swi. 114/C3
Racine, Wi, US 185/M5
Racine (co.), Wi, US 193/P14
Rada Tilly, Arg. 216/D5
Radama (isl.), Madg. 144/D4
Rădăuți, Rom. 107/G2
Radebeul, Ger. 113/F3
Radeče (peak), Czh. 113/G3
Rakamaz, Hun. 106/E1
Radevormwald, Ger. 109/E6
Radisson, Qu, Can. 184/G2
Radlett, Eng, UK 88/C2
Radnice, Czh. 113/G3
Radolfzell, Ger. 115/E2
Radom, Bul. 106/F4
Radomir, Bul. 106/F4
Radomsko, Pol. 99/K3
Radoviš, FYROM 105/H2
Radovljica, Slov. 101/L3
Radøy (isl.), Nor. 96/A1
Radstadt, Aus. 101/K3
Radviliškis, Lith. 97/K4
Radwā, Jabal (peak), SAr. 146/C4
Raldon, It. 117/E2
Raleigh (cap.), NC, US 191/J3
Raleigh-Durham (int'l arpt.), NC, US 191/J3
Ralik Chain (isls.), Mrsh. 174/F4
Ralingen, Ger. 111/F4
Ralston, Ab, Can. 184/F3
Ram Allāh, Isr. 149/G8
Rāmallāh, Isr. 149/G8
Ramalho, Serra do (mts.), Braz. 209/K6
Ramapo (riv.), NJ, US 196/J7
Ramapo (mts.), NJ, US 197/H7
Ramat Gan, Isr. 149/F7
Ramat Hasharon, Isr. 149/F7
Ramatlabama (peak), SAfr. 164/D4
Rambervillers, Fr. 114/C1
Rame (pt.), Eng, UK 90/B5
Ramenskoye, Rus. 119/X9
Rāmeswaram, India 140/C6
Rāmgangā (riv.), India 142/C1
Ramgarh, India 143/E5
Rāmgarh, India 143/F4
Rāmhormoz, Iran 146/E2
Ramior (lake), Mex. 190/B5
Rāmjībanpur, India 143/F4
Ramla, Isr. 149/G8
Ramlu (peak), Erit. 146/D6
Ramme, Den. 96/C3
Rammūn, Isr. 149/G8
Rāmnagar, India 142/B1
Rāmnagar, India 144/C1
Rāmnagar, India 144/C5
Rāmnagar, India 142/D2
Rahatgarh, India 142/B3
Ramon (lake), Mex. 190/B5
Ramonchamp, Fr. 114/C2
Ramor (lake), Ire. 92/A4
Ramos (riv.), Mex. 190/B5
Ramosch, Swi. 115/G4
Rampart, Ak, US 192/H2
Rampillon, Fr. 88/M6
Rāmpur, India 144/D4
Rāmpur, India 142/C2
Rāmpur Phūl, India 144/C2
Rāmpura, India 142/B2
Ramree (isl.), Myan. 141/F4
Rāmsanehī ghāt, India 142/C2
Ramsbottom, Eng, UK 93/F4
Ramseur, NC, US
Ramsden Heath, Eng, UK 88/C2
Ramsen, Swi. 115/E2
Ramsey (lake), On, Can. 188/D2
Ramsey (isl.), Wal, UK 90/A3
Ramsey, NJ, US 197/J7
Ramsey, IM, UK 92/D3

Ramsey (bay), IM, UK 92/D3
Ramsgate, Eng, UK 91/H4
Ramstein-Miesenbach, Ger. 111/G5
Ramu (riv.), PNG 174/D5
Rana, Nor. 95/E2
Rānāghāt, India 143/G4
Rancagua, Chile 216/N9
Rance (riv.), Fr. 100/C2
Rancharia, Braz. 213/B2
Rancheria (riv.), Col. 210/C2
Rānchī, India 143/E4
Rancho Palos Verdes, Ca, US 194/F8
Rancho Santa Fe, Ca, US 194/C4
Ranchos, Arg. 216/F2
Ranchos de Taos, NM, US 187/F3
Rancocas, NJ, US 196/D4
Rancul, Arg. 216/D2
Randaberg, Nor. 96/A2
Randallstown, Md, US 196/B5
Randalstown, NI, UK 92/B2
Randazzo, It. 104/D4
Randburg, SAfr. 164/P13
Randers, Den. 96/D3
Randolph, NJ, US 196/D2
Randow (riv.), Ger. 99/H2
Randsfjorden (lake), Nor. 96/D1
Raneå, Swe. 118/D2
Rang (peak), Thai. 136/C2
Rang-du-Fliers, Fr. 110/A3
Rāngāmāti (pol. reg.), Bang. 143/H4
Rāngāmāti, Bang. 141/F3
Rangasa (cape), Indo. 139/E4
Rangely, Co, US 186/E2
Ranger, Tx, US 187/H4
Rangia, India 143/H2
Rangiora, NZ 175/S11
Rangiroa (isl.), FrPol. 175/L6
Rangoon (Yangon) (cap.), Myan. 141/G4
Rangpur, Bang. 143/G3
Rangpur (pol. reg.), Bang. 143/G3
Rangsdorf, Ger. 98/Q7
Rānī bennur, India 147/L6
Rānīganj, India 143/F4
Rānīkhet, India 142/B1
Rānīpur, India 142/B3
Rānī pura, India 144/B4
Ranibennur ...
Ranikhet ...
Ranong, Thai. 136/B4
Ranotsara, Madg. 165/H8
Ransbach-Baumbach, Ger. 111/G3
Ranst, Belg. 108/B6
Ranstadt, Ger. 112/B2
Rantabe, Madg. 165/J6
Rantekombola (peak), Indo. 139/F4
Rantigny, Fr. 110/B5
Rantis, WBnk. 149/G7
Rantoul, Il, US 185/L5
Rantsila, Fin. 118/E2
Ranzan, Japan 135/C1
Raon Co (peak), Laos 136/D2
Raon-l'Étape, Fr. 114/C1
Raoping, China 137/C3
Rāvi (riv.), Ind.,Pak. 147/K2
Ravne na Koroškem, Slov. 101/L3
Rawa Mazowiecka, Pol. 99/L3
Rāwah, Iraq 148/E3
Raoyang, China 130/C3
Rapa (isl.), FrPol. 175/L7
Rapallo, It. 116/C4
Rapel (lake), Chile 216/N9
Rapid City, SD, US 185/H4
Rappahannock (riv.), Va, US 188/E4
Rapper (cape), Chile 216/B5
Rāpti (zone), Nepal 142/D1
Rāpti (riv.), India 142/D1
Rara NP, Nepal 142/D1
Raritan (bay), NJ, US 196/D3
Raritan (riv.), NJ, US 196/D2
Raritan, South Branch (riv.), NJ, US 196/D2
Rarotonga (isl.), Cooks. 175/J7
Ra's al 'Ayn, Syria 148/E2
Ra's al Basīt (pt.), Syria 149/D1
Ra's al Khaymah, UAE 147/G3
Ra's an Naqb, Jor. 149/D5
Ra's aţ Ţīb (Cape Bon) (cape), Tun. 158/M6
Ras Dashen (peak), Eth. 155/N5
Râs el Ma, Alg. 158/D2
Râs el Oued, Alg. 158/H5
Ras San Dimitri (pt.), Malta 104/L6
Ra's Ṣawqirah (pt.), Oman 147/G5

Rasa (pt.), Arg. 216/E4
Raschau, Ger. 113/F1
Rashaant, Mong. 128/F2
Rasharkin, NI, UK 92/B2
Rāshayyā, Leb. 149/D3
Rashīd, Egypt 149/B4
Rasht, Iran 146/E1
Raška, Serb.
Rasmussen (basin), Nun., Can. 180/G2
Raso (cape), Port. 103/P10
Rason (lake), Austl. 170/D4
Rasrā, India 142/D3
Rassina, It. 117/E5
Rasskazovo, Rus. 121/G1
Rastatt, Ger. 112/B5
Rastede, Ger. 109/F2
Rasūlnagar, Pak. 144/B3
Rat (isls.), Ak, US 192/B6
Rat Buri, Thai. 136/B3
Rata (cape), Indo. 138/B5
Ratak Chain (isls.), Mrsh. 174/F3
Ratangarh, India 147/K3
Ratangarh, India 142/D4
Rāth, India 142/C2
Rathbun (lake), Ia, US 185/K5
Rathcoole, Ire. 92/B5
Rathdowney, Ire. 89/Q10
Rathdrum, Ire.
Rathenow, Ger. 98/G2
Rathfriland, NI, UK 89/P10
Rathkeale, Ire.
Rathlin (isl.), NI, UK 92/B1
Rathlin (sound), NI, UK 92/B1
Rathluirc, Ire. 89/P10
Rathmore, Ire. 89/P10
Rathnew, Ire. 92/B6
Ratia, India 144/C5
Ratingen, Ger. 108/D6
Ratlām, India 147/L4
Ratnagiri, India 147/K5
Ratnapura, SrL. 140/D6
Ratoath, Ire. 92/B4
Raton, NM, US 187/F3
Rattray (pt.), Sc, UK 94/E1
Rättvik, Swe. 96/F1
Raub, Malay. 138/B3
Rauch, Arg. 216/F3
Raudales Malpaso, Mex. 202/C2
Raudhinúpur (pt.), Ice. 95/P6
Raufarhöfn, Ice. 95/P6
Raufoss, Nor. 96/D1
Rauhe Ebrach (riv.), Ger. 112/D3
Raul Soares, Braz. 213/D2
Rauma, Fin. 97/J1
Raunheim, Ger. 112/B2
Raurkela, India 143/E4
Rausu, Japan 134/D1
Rautjärvi, Fin. 97/N1
Ravanusa, It. 104/C4
Rāvar, Iran 147/G2
Ravels, Belg. 108/B6
Ravenna, It. 117/F4
Ravenna (prov.), It. 117/F4
Ravenna, Ca, US 194/B2
Ravensburg, Ger. 115/F2
Ravensdale, Wa, US 193/D3
Ravenshoe, Austl. 172/B2
Ravensthorpe, Austl. 170/D5
Ravenswood, WV, US 188/D4
Rawmarsh, Eng, UK 93/G5
Rawson, Arg. 216/D4
Rawtenstall, Eng, UK
Raxaul Bazar, India 143/E2
Ray (cape), Nf, Can. 189/K2
Raya (peak), Indo. 138/D4
Rāyadrug, India
Raychikhinsk, Rus. 129/N2
Rayleigh, Eng, UK 91/G3
Raymond, Ab, Can. 184/E3
Raymond, Wa, US 184/C4
Raymond, Co, US 195/B2
Raymond, Wi, US 193/P14
Raymondville, Tx, US 190/D5
Raymore, Mo, US 195/E6
Rayón, Mex. 200/C2
Rayón, Mex. 201/Q10
Rayón, PN, Mex. 200/C2
Rayong, Thai. 136/C3
Raytown, Mo, US 195/E6
Rayville, La, US 187/K4
Raz, Pointe de (pt.), Fr. 100/A2
Razlel (lake), Rom. 107/J3
Razgrad, Bul. 107/H4
Razlog, Bul.
Re di Castello (peak), It. 115/G5
Ré, Île de (isl.), Fr. 100/C3

Rea (riv.), Eng, UK 90/D1
Reading, Eng, UK 91/F4
Reading (co.), Eng, UK 91/E4
Reading, Pa, US 196/C3
Realicó, Arg. 216/D2
Realp, Swi. 115/E4
Reamstown, Pa, US 196/B3
Reao (isl.), FrPol. 175/M6
Réau, Fr. 88/K6
Rebais, Fr. 110/C6
Rebecca (lake),
Austl. 170/D4
Rębiechowo (int'l arpt.),
Pol. 96/H4
Rebouças, Braz. 213/B3
Rebstein, Swi. 115/F3
Rebun, Japan 134/B1
Recanati, It. 117/G6
Recco, It. 116/C4
Recherche (arch.),
Austl. 170/D5
Rechnitz, Aus. 101/M3
Rechthalten, Swi. 114/C4
Rechytsa, Bela. 120/D1
Recife (cape), SAfr. 164/D4
Recke, Ger. 109/E4
Reckingen, Swi. 115/E5
Recklinghausen,
Ger. 109/E5
Recknitz (riv.), Ger. 98/G2
Réclère, Swi. 114/C3
Recoaro Terme, It. 117/E1
Reconvilier, Swi. 114/D3
Recuay, Peru 214/B3
Red (sea), Afr.,Asia 146/C4
Red (riv.), Mb, Can. 185/J3
Red (riv.), China,Viet. 128/H7
Red (riv.), US 190/E4
Red (riv.), Mn, US 183/G2
Red (lakes), Mn, US 183/H2
Red (riv.), Viet. 141/H3
Red Bank, NJ, US 196/D3
Red Bluff (lake),
Tx, US 187/G5
Red Bluff, Ca, US 186/B2
Red Cliffs, Austl. 173/B2
Red Cloud, Ne, US 187/H2
Red Deer, Ab, Can. 184/E2
Red Deer (riv.),
Sk, Can. 180/E3
Red Devil, Ak, US 192/G3
Red Hill (peak),
Hi, US 182/T10
Red Hill, Pa, US 196/C3
Red Indian (lake),
Nf, Can. 189/K1
Red Lake (lake),
Mn, US 185/K3
Red Lake, On, Can. 185/K3
Red Lion, De, US 196/C4
Red Lion, Pa, US 196/B4
Red Lodge, Mt, US 184/F4
Red, North Fork (riv.),
US 187/G4
Red River of the North
(riv.), US,Can. 185/J3
Red Rock (lake),
Ia, US 185/K5
Red Rocks (pt.), Austl. 171/G6
Red Sea (hills), Sudan 159/D2
Red Volta (riv.), Burk. 161/E4
Red Wing, Mn, US 185/K4
Reda, Pol. 96/H4
Redange-sur-Attert,
Lux. 111/E4
Redbridge (bor.),
Eng, UK 88/D2
Redcar, Eng, UK 93/G2
Redcar and Cleveland (co.),
Eng, UK 93/G2
Redcliff, Ab, Can. 184/F2
Redcliffe (mt.),
Austl. 170/D4
Redden, De, US 196/C6
Reddersburg, SAfr. 164/D3
Redding, Ca, US 186/B2
Redding, Ct, US 197/E1
Redditch, Eng, UK 91/E2
Rede (riv.), Eng, UK 93/F1
Redenção do Gurguéia,
Braz. 212/A3
Redfield, SD, US 185/J4
Redford, Mi, US 193/F7
Redhill, Eng, UK 88/C2
Rédics, Hun. 106/C2
Redkey, In, US 188/C3
Redland, Md, US 196/A5
Redlands, Ca, US 194/C2
Redmond, Or, US 184/C4
Rednitz (riv.), Ger. 112/D4
Redon, Fr. 100/B3
Redondela, Sp. 102/A1
Redondo, Port. 102/B3
Redondo, Wa, US 193/C3
Redondo Beach,
Ca, US 194/F8
Redoubt (vol.),
Ak, US 192/H3
Redstone (riv.),
NW, Can. 180/D2
Redvers, Sk, Can. 185/H3
Redwater, Ab, Can. 184/E2
Redway, Ca, US 184/C5
Redwood Falls,
Mn, US 185/K4
Redwood NP,
Ca, US 186/A2
Ree, Lough (lake),
Ire. 89/P10
Reed City, Mi, US 188/C3
Reeding, Ok, US 195/M14
Reedley, Ca, US 186/C3
Reeds
(bay), NJ, US 196/D4

Reedsburg, Wi, US 185/L5
Reef (pt.), Belz. 201/L5
Reef (isls.), Sol. 174/F6
Reefton, NZ 175/S11
Rees, Ger. 108/D5
Reese (riv.), Nv, US 186/C3
Reñala Khurd, Pak. 144/B4
Renan, Swi. 114/C4
Renarde (riv.), Fr. 88/J6
Renazzo, It. 117/E3
Renca, Chile 216/N8
Reforma, Mex. 202/C2
Rench (riv.), Ger. 112/A5
Renchen, Ger. 114/E1
Rend (lake), Il, US 191/F2
Rendeux, Belg. 111/E3
Rendsburg, Ger. 96/C4
Renens, Swi. 114/B5
Renfrew, On, Can. 188/E2
Renfrew, Sc, UK 96/D1
Renfrewshire (pol. reg.),
Sc, UK 94/B5
Rengam, Malay. 138/B3
Rengat, Indo. 138/B4
Rengo, Chile 216/N9
Rengsdorf, Ger. 111/G3
Renhua, China 141/K2
Reni, Ukr. 107/J3
Renish (pt.), Sc, UK 89/G8
Renkum, Neth. 108/C5
Renmark, Austl. 171/J5
Rennell (isl.), Sol. 174/F6
Rennerod, Ger. 111/H2
Rennertshofen, Ger. 112/D5
Rennes, Fr. 100/C2
Renningen, Ger. 112/B6
Reno, Nv, US 186/C3
Reno (riv.), It. 101/J4
Renoster (riv.), SAfr. 164/C3
Renqiu, China 130/D3
Rensselaer, In, US 188/C3
Rentchler, Il, US 195/H9
Rentería, Sp. 102/E1
Renton, Wa, US 184/C4
Renton, Sc, UK 94/B5
Renwez, Fr. 111/D4
Réo, Burk. 161/E3
Reoti, India 143/E3
Répcelak, Hun. 101/M3
Repelón, Col. 203/H4
Repentigny, Qu, Can. 189/P6
Republic, Wa, US 184/D3
Republican (riv.),
Ks,Ne, US 187/H2
Repulse (bay), Austl. 172/C3
Repulse Bay (isl.),
Ca, US 172/C3
Repulse Bay,
Nun., Can. 181/H2
Requena, Peru 214/C2
Requena, Sp. 103/E3
Requinoa, Chile 216/N9
Reriutaba, Braz. 212/B2
Reşadiye, Turk. 148/D1
Reschensee (Resia)
(lake), It. 115/G4
Rescue (pt.), Chile 216/B5
Resegone (peak), It. 116/C1
Resen, FYROM 105/G2
Resende, Braz. 213/J7
Resende, Port. 102/B2
Reserve, NM, US 186/E4
Resia, Passo di (pass),
It. 115/G4
Resia (Reschensee)
(lake), It. 115/G4
Resistencia, Arg. 215/E2
Reşiţa, Rom. 106/E3
Res Jebel, Tun. 158/M6
Resolution (isl.),
Nun., Can. 181/K2
Respenda de la Peña,
Sp. 102/C1
Resplendor, Braz. 213/D1
Restigouche (riv.),
NB, Can. 189/H2
Reston, Mb, Can. 185/H3
Reston, Va, US 196/A6
Reszel, Pol. 97/J4
Retalhuleu, Guat. 202/D3
Rethel, Fr. 111/D4
Rethem, Ger. 109/G3
Réthimnon, Gre. 105/J5
Retie, Belg. 108/C6
Retrezap NP, Rom. 106/F3
Rétság, Hun. 106/D2
Rettenberg, Ger. 115/G2
Retz, Aus. 99/H4
Réunion (dpcy.), Fr. 165/S15
Reus, Sp. 103/F2
Reusel, Neth. 108/C6
Reuss (riv.), Swi. 115/E3
Reuterstadt Stavenhagen,
Ger. 96/F5
Reutlingen, Ger. 112/C6
Reutov, Rus. 119/W9
Reutte, Aus. 115/G3
Revadim, Isr. 149/F8
Réveillon (riv.), Fr. 114/D1
Revel, Fr. 100/D5
Revelstoke, BC, Can. 184/D3
Revere, It. 117/E2
Revfülöp, Hun. 106/C2
Revigny-sur-Ornain, Fr. 111/D6
Revillagigedo (isls.),
Mex. 200/B5
Revin, Fr. 111/D3
Revolyutsii (peak),
Taj. 145/F3
Revúca, India 147/G5
Revsbotn (inlet), Nor. 95/G1
Rewa, India 143/C3
Rewari, India 143/C2
Rex (mtn.), Ak, US 192/J3
Rey, Isla del (isl.),
Pan. 203/G4
Reyes, Bol. 208/E6

Reyes (pt.), Ca, US 186/B3
Reyhanlı, Turk. 149/E1
Reykjanestá (cape),
Ice. 95/M7
Reykjavik (int'l arpt.),
Ice. 95/N7
Reykjavik (cap.),
Ice. 95/N7
Reynosa, Mex. 201/F3
Reyssouze (riv.), Fr. 114/B5
Rezé, Fr. 100/C3
Rēzekne, Lat. 97/M3
Rezzato, It. 116/D1
Rhaetian Alps (mts.),
Swi., Aus 101/H3
Rhallamane (reg.),
Mrta. 156/D3
Rhallamane (lake),
Mrta. 156/C3
Rhart (peak), Mor. 156/D3
Rhat (peak), Mor. 156/D3
Rhätikon (mts.),
Aus.,Swi. 115/F3
Rheda-Wiedenbrück,
Ger. 109/D5
Rhede, Ger. 108/D5
Rhede, Ger. 108/D4
Rheden, Neth. 108/D4
Rheidol (riv.), Wal, UK 90/C2
Rheinau, Swi. 115/E3
Rheinbach, Ger. 111/F2
Rheinberg, Ger. 108/D5
Rheinbreitbach, Ger. 111/G2
Rheinbrohl, Ger. 111/G3
Rheine, Ger. 109/E4
Rheinfall, Swi. 115/E3
Rheinfelden, Ger. 114/D2
Rheinland-Pfalz (state),
Ger. 112/A3
Rheinwaldhorn (peak),
Swi. 115/F5
Rheinzabern, Ger. 112/B4
Rhemiles (well), Alg. 156/E3
Rhenen, Neth. 108/C5
Rheris, Oued (riv.),
Mor. 156/D3
Rhinau, Fr. 114/D1
Rhine (riv.), Eur. 85/E4
Rhine-Herne (canal),
Ger. 109/E5
Rhinns (pt.), Sc, UK 89/Q9
Rhinns, The (pt.),
Sc, UK 92/C2
Rhino Camp, Ugan. 162/A2
Rhiou (riv.), Alg. 158/F5
Rhiou (riv.), Alg. 158/F5
Rhir (cape), Mor. 156/C3
Rhisnes, Belg. 111/D3
Rhiw (riv.), Wal, UK 90/C1
Rho, It. 116/C1
Rhode Island (state),
US 189/G3
Rhodes (isl.), Gre. 148/A3
Rhön (mts.), Ger. 112/D1
Rhondda, Wal, UK 90/C3
Rhondda Cynon Taff
(co.), Wal, UK 90/C3
Rhône (dept.), Fr. 114/A6
Rhône (riv.), Fr. 100/F4
Rhône (glacier), Swi. 115/E4
Rhône-Alpes (pol. reg.),
Fr. 114/B5
Rhône au Rhin (canal),
Fr. 114/B3
Rhonelle (riv.), Fr. 110/C3
Rhosllanerchrugog,
Wal, UK 93/E6
Rhum (isl.), Sc, UK 89/Q8
Rhume (riv.), Ger. 109/H5
Rhumel, Oued el (riv.),
Alg. 158/J4
Rhyddhywel (peak),
Wal, UK 90/C2
Rhyl, Wal, UK 92/E5
Riachão, Braz. 212/A2
Riachão das Neves,
Braz. 212/A3
Riachão do Jacuípe,
Braz. 212/C3
Riacho de Santana,
Braz. 212/B4
Riachuelo, Braz. 212/D2
Rialto, Ca, US 194/C2
Rianjo, Sp. 102/A1
Riaño, Sp. 102/C1
Riāsi, India 144/C1
Riau (isls.), Indo. 138/B3
Riaza, Sp. 102/D2
Ribadeo, Sp. 102/B1
Ribadesella, Sp. 102/C1
Riban'i Manamby (mts.),
Madg. 165/H9
Ribble (riv.), Eng, UK 93/F4
Ribblesdale (valley),
Eng, UK 93/F3
Ribe, Den. 96/C4
Ribe (co.), Den. 96/C4
Riese Pio X, It. 117/E2
Ribécourt-Dreslincourt,
Fr. 110/B4
Ribeira (riv.), Braz. 213/B3
Ribeira Brava, CpV. 151/J10
Ribeira de Pena,
Port. 102/B2
Ribeira do Pombal,
Braz. 212/C3
Ribeira Grande,
Azor., Port. 103/T13
Ribeirão, Braz. 212/E2
Ribeirão do Pinha,
Braz. 213/B2
Ribeiro Gonçalves,
Braz. 212/A2
Ribera, It. 104/C4
Ribérac, Fr. 100/D4

Riberalta, Bol. 208/E6
Ribniţa, Mol. 107/J2
Ribnitz-Damgarten,
Ger. 96/E4
Ričany u Prahy, Czh. 113/H3
Ricaurte, Col. 210/B4
Riccia, It. 104/D2
Riccione, It. 117/F5
Ricco'del Golfo, It. 116/C4
Rice (lake), On, Can. 188/E2
Richard Toll, Sen. 160/B2
Richards (lakes),
NW, Can. 180/C2
Richard's Bay, SAfr. 165/F3
Richardson (lakes),
Me, US 189/G2
Richboro, Pa, US 196/C3
Riche (cape), Austl. 170/C5
Richebourg, Fr. 88/C5
Richel (isl.), Neth. 108/C2
Richelieu, Qu, Can. 189/P7
Richfield, Ut, US 186/D3
Richfield, Pa, US 196/A2
Richhill, NI, UK 92/B3
Richland, NJ, US 196/D5
Richland, Ok, US 195/M14
Richland, Pa, US 196/B3
Richland, Wa, US 184/D4
Richland Balsam (peak),
NC, US 191/H3
Richland Center,
Wi, US 185/L5
Richland Creek (res.),
Tx, US 187/H5
Richlandtown,
Pa, US 196/C3
Richmond, Austl. 172/A3
Richmond, BC, Can. 184/C3
Richmond, Qu, Can. 189/F2
Richmond, SAfr. 165/E3
Richmond, SAfr. 164/C3
Richmond, Il, US 193/P15
Richmond, Ky, US 188/C4
Richmond (co.),
NY, US 196/D2
Richmond Beach-Innis
Arden,
Wa, US 193/B2
Richmond Heights,
Mo, US 195/G8
Richmond Hill,
On, Can. 189/R8
Richmond Park (bor.),
Eng, UK 88/C2
Richmond Upon Thames
(bor.), Eng, UK 88/B2
Richmond-Windsor,
Austl. 172/G8
Richtersveld NP,
SAfr. 164/B3
Richterswil, Swi. 115/E3
Richwiller, Fr. 114/D2
Rickets Glen State Park,
Pa, US 196/B1
Rickmansworth,
Eng, UK 88/B2
Ricla, Sp. 102/E2
Ricse, Hun. 99/L4
Ridder, Aus. 146/D6
Ridderkerk, Neth. 108/B5
Rideau (riv.), On, Can. 188/E2
Ridgecrest, Ca, US 186/C4
Ridgefield, Ct, US 197/E1
Ridgefield, NJ, US 197/K8
Ridgefield Park,
NJ, US 197/J8
Ridgeland, Ms, US 187/K4
Ridgely, Mo, US 195/D5
Ridgely, Md, US 196/C6
Ridgewood State Park,
NJ, US 196/D2
Rideau (riv.), Fr. 110/A2
Riding Mountain NP,
Mb, Can. 185/H3
Ridlees Cairn (hill),
Eng, UK 94/D6
Riecito (riv.), Col. 210/D3
Ried im Innkreis,
Aus. 113/G6
Ried im Traunkreis,
Aus. 113/H6
Riede, Ger. 109/F3
Riedisheim, Fr. 114/D2
Riedlingen, Ger. 115/F1
Riegelsberg, Ger. 111/F5
Riegsee (lake), Ger. 115/H2
Riehen, Swi. 114/D2
Riemst, Belg. 111/E2
Rieneck, Ger. 112/C2
Riesa, Ger. 96/F3
Rieschweiler-Mühlbach,
Ger. 111/G5
Riesco (isl.), Chile 216/B7
Riesi, It. 104/D4
Rieti, It. 104/C1
Riffe (lake), Wa, US 184/C4
Rifle, Co, US 186/F3
Rifsnes (pt.), Ice. 95/N6
Rift Valley (prov.),
Kenya 162/B2
Riga (gulf), Eur. 97/K2
Riga (Riga) (cap.),
Lat. 97/L3
Rigby, Id, US 184/F5
Rigestan (pol. reg.),
Afg. 147/H2
Riggins, Id, US 184/D4
Rigi (peak), Swi. 115/E3
Rignano sull'Arno, It. 117/E5

Rigolet, Nf, Can. 181/L3
Rihand (dam), India 142/D3
Rihand (riv.), India 142/D3
Rihand Sāgar (res.),
India 140/D3
Riihimäki, Fin. 97/L1
Riiser-Larsen (pen.),
Ant. 218/C
Riiser-Larsen Ice Shelf,
Ant. 218/Y
Riisitunturin NP,
Fin. 118/F2
Rijeka, Cro. 106/B3
Rijksmuseum Kröller Müller,
Neth. 108/C4
Rijnsburg, Neth. 108/B4
Rijsbergen, Neth. 108/B5
Rijssen, Neth. 108/D4
Rijswijk, Neth. 108/B4
Rikers (isl.),
NY, US 197/K8
Rikitea, FrPol. 175/M7
Rikuchū-Kaigan NP,
Japan 134/C4
Rikuzentakata, Japan 134/B4
Rila, Bul. 105/H1
Rila (mts.), Bul. 107/F4
Rillieux-la-Pape, Fr. 114/A6
Rilski Manastir, Bul. 105/H1
Rimatara (isl.), FrPol. 175/K7
Rimbach, Ger. 112/B3
Rimbey, Ab, Can. 184/E2
Rimini, It. 117/F4
Rimnicu Sărat, Rom. 107/H3
Rimnicu Vilcea, Rom. 107/G3
Rimogne, Fr. 111/D4
Rimouski, Qu, Can. 189/G1
Rimpar, Ger. 112/C2
Rimpfischhorn (peak),
Swi. 114/D5
Rinas (int'l arpt.), Alb. 105/F2
Rinbung, China 143/G1
Rinchnach, Ger. 113/G5
Rincón de la Vieja, PN,
CR 198/D5
Rincón de Romos,
Mex. 200/E4
Ringarooma, Austl. 173/C4
Ringas, NJ, US 196/D3
Ringboy (pt.), NI, UK 92/C3
Ringebu, Nor. 96/D1
Ringelspitz (peak),
Swi. 115/F4
Ringgold, La, US 187/J4
Ringkøbing (fjord),
Den. 96/B3
Ringkøbing, Den. 96/B3
Ringkøbing (co.), Den. 96/B3
Ringoes, NJ, US 196/D3
Ringsend, NI, UK 92/B1
Ringstedt, Den. 96/D4
Ringtown, Pa, US 196/B2
Ringvassøy (isl.),Nor. 95/F1
Ringvassøy (isl.),Nor. 95/F1
Ringwood, Eng, UK 91/E5
Ringwood, NJ, US 197/J7
Ringwood State Park,
NJ, US 196/D1
Rinia (isl.), Gre. 105/J4
Rintein, Ger. 109/G4
Rio Abiseo, PN,
Peru 208/C5
Rio Azul, Braz. 213/B3
Rio Blanco, Mex. 201/M8
Rio Bonito, Braz. 213/L7
Rio Branco, Braz. 208/E5
Rio Branco do Sul,
Braz. 213/B3
Rio Bravo, Mex. 201/F3
Rio Bueno, Chile 216/B4
Rio Casca, Braz. 213/D2
Rio Cauto, Cuba 203/G1
Rio Clarillo, PN,
Chile 216/N8
Rio Claro, Braz. 213/J7
Rio Claro, Trin. 211/F2
Rio Colorado, Arg. 216/D2
Rio Cuarto, Arg. 216/D2
Rio de Janeiro, Braz. 213/K7
Rio de Janeiro (state),
Braz. 213/E5
Rio de Janeiro (int'l arpt.),
Braz. 213/K7
Rio Dell, Ca, US 184/B5
Rio Gallegos, Arg. 217/C6
Rio Grande, Arg. 217/C7
Rio Grande, Braz. 213/A5
Rio Grande, NJ, US 196/D5
Rio Grande (plain),
Tx, US 198/B2
Rio Grande City,
Tx, US 190/D5
Rio Grande (riv.),
SAfr. 164/D3
Rio Grande da Serra,
Braz. 213/G8
Rio Grande Do Norte,
(state) Braz. 212/C2
Rio Grande do Piauí,
Braz. 212/B2
Rio Grande Valley
(int'l arpt.), Tx, US 190/D5
Rio Jaú, PN do, Braz. 208/F4
Rio Lagartos, Mex. 202/D1
Rio Largo, Braz. 212/D3
Rio Maior, Port. 102/A3
Rio Mayo, Arg. 216/C5
Rio Negrinho, Braz. 213/B3
Rio Negro (prov.), Arg. 216/D3
Rio Negro, NJ, US 195/D5
Rio Negro, Chile 216/B4

Rio Negro, Embalse de
(res.), Uru. 215/E3
Rio Paranaíba, Braz. 213/C1
Rio Pardo, Braz. 213/A4
Río Pilcomayo, PN,
Arg. 215/E2
Rio Prêto (range),
Braz. 212/A5
Rio Rancho, NM, US 186/F4
Rio Real, Braz. 212/C3
Rio Saliceto, It. 117/D3
Rio Simpson, PN,
Chile 216/B5
Riversonderendreeks
(mts.), SAfr. 164/L11
Rivignano, It. 117/G1
Rivne, Ukr. 120/C2
Rivnens'ka Oblasti,
Ukr. 120/C2
Rio Tercero, Arg. 215/D3
Rio Tigre, Ecu. 210/B5
Rio Tinto, Braz. 212/D2
Rio Verde, Braz. 213/B1
Rio Verde, Chile 217/C7
Rio Verde, Mex. 201/E4
Rio Verde de Mato Grosso,
Braz. 209/H7
Rio Vista, Ca, US 193/L10
Riobamba, Ecu. 210/C2
Riohacha, Col. 210/C2
Rioja, Peru 214/B2
Riolândia, Braz. 213/B1
Riolo Terme, It. 117/E4
Riom, Fr. 100/E4
Riom-ès-Montagne,
Fr. 100/E4
Riomaggiore, It. 116/C4
Rion-des-Landes,
Fr. 100/C5
Rivoli, It. 116/A2
Rivolta d'Adda, It. 116/C2
Rixensart, Belg. 111/D2
Rixheim, Fr. 114/D2
Riyāq, Leb. 149/D3
Rize, Turk. 148/E1
Rize (prov.), Turk. 148/E1
Rizhao, China 130/D4
Rizokarpasso, Cyp. 149/D2
Rizzuto (cape), It. 105/E3
Rjukan, Nor. 96/C2
Rkîz (lake), Mrta. 160/B2
Roa, Sp. 102/D2
Roa, Nor. 96/D1
Road Town (cap.),
BVI 199/M8
Roan (plat.), Co, US 186/E3
Roan Fell (hill), Sc, UK 93/F1
Roanne, Fr. 100/F3
Roanoke, Al, US 191/G3
Roanoke (riv.), Va, US 188/E4
Roanoke (pt.), NY, US 197/F2
Roatán (isl.), Hon. 198/D4
Roatán, Hon. 202/E2
Robāt Karīm, Iran 146/F1
Robbiate, It. 116/C1
Robbins (isl.), Austl. 173/C4
Robbio, It. 116/B2
Robe (mt.), Austl. 173/A3
Robe, Austl. 173/A3
Robe (riv.), Ire. 89/P10
Robecchetto con Induno,
It. 116/B1
Röbel, Ger. 96/F4
Robert (peak), Fr. 114/B5
Robert Lee, Tx, US 187/G5
Roberts (mtn.),
Ak, US 192/E4
Roberts (Monrovia)
(int'l arpt.), Libr. 160/C5
Robertsfors, Swe. 95/G2
Robertsganj, India 142/D3
Robertson, SAfr. 164/L10
Robertsport, Libr. 160/C5
Robertstown, Ire. 89/Q10
Roberval, Qu, Can. 189/F1
Robesonia, Pa, US 196/B3
Robinson (ranges),
Austl. 170/C3
Robinson Crusoe (isl.),
Chile 205/B3
Robinson Gorge NP,
Austl. 172/C4
Robinvale, Austl. 173/B2
Roblin, Mb, Can. 185/H3
Robore, Bol. 208/G7
Robson (mt.),
BC, Can. 184/D2
Robstown, Tx, US 190/D5
Roby, Tx, US 187/G4
Roc du Haut du Faite
(peak), Fr. 114/D2
Roca, Cabo da (cape),
Port. 103/P10
Roca Partida (isl.),
Mex. 200/B5
Roca Partida, Punta (pt.),
Mex. 202/C2
Rocafuerte, Ecu. 210/A5
Rocas (isl.), Braz. 209/M4
Rocca San Casciano,
It. 117/E4
Roccabianca, It. 116/D2
Roccastrada, It. 101/J5
Rocciamelone (peak),
It. 101/G4
Rocha, Uru. 217/G2
Rocha (dept.), Uru. 217/G2
Rochdale, Eng, UK 93/F4
Rochdale (co.), Eng, UK 93/F4
Roche, Swi. 114/C5
Roche du Sapin Sec
(peak), Fr. 114/C1
Roche-lez-Beaupré,
Fr. 114/C3
Rochefort, Fr. 100/C4
Rochefort, Belg. 111/E3
Rochelle Park, NJ, US 197/J8
Rochers du Bourbet
(peak), Fr. 114/C3
Rochester, Austl. 173/C3
Rochester, Eng, UK 88/D2
Rochester, Mn, US 185/K4
Rochester, NY, US 188/E3
Rochester, NH, US 189/G3
Rochester, Eng, UK 91/G4
Rochester, Wi, US 193/P14
Rochford, Eng, UK 88/F2
Rochfordbridge, Ire. 89/P10
Rock (co.), Wi, US 193/P15
Rock (riv.), Ia,Mo, US 187/H2
Rock Creek, Yk, Can. 192/L3
Rock Forest, Qu, Can. 189/G2
Rock Glen, Pa, US 196/B2
Rock Hall, Md, US 196/B5
Rock Hill, SC, US 191/H3
Rock Island, Il, US 185/L5

Rock S – Sādri

Rock Springs, Wy, US 184/F5
Rockall (isl.), UK 85/C3
Rockaway, NJ, US 196/D2
Rockaway (riv.), NJ, US 196/D2
Rockaway (inlet), NY, US 197/K9
Rockaway (pt.), NY, US 197/K9
Rockdale, Il, US 193/P17
Rockefeller (plat.), Ant. 218/R
Rockenhausen, Ger. 111/G4
Rockford, Il, US 185/L5
Rockglen, Sk, Can. 185/G3
Rockhampton, Austl. 172/C3
Rockingham, NC, US 191/J3
Rockingham, Austl. 170/K7
Rockland, On, Can. 188/F2
Rockland, Me, US 189/G2
Rockland (co.), NY, US 196/D1
Rockland Lake, NY, US 197/K7
Rocklands (res.), Austl. 173/B3
Rockledge, Fl, US 191/H4
Rockledge, Pa, US 196/C3
Rockport, Tx, US 190/D4
Rocks, Md, US 196/B4
Rocksprings, Tx, US 187/G5
Rockstone, Guy. 211/G3
Rockville, Md, US 188/E4
Rockville Centre, NY, US 197/L9
Rockwall, Tx, US 187/H4
Rockwood, Tn, US 191/G3
Rocky (mtn.), Ky, US 188/D4
Rocky (mts.), Can.,US 177/E4
Rocky (pt.), NY, US 197/F1
Rocky Cape NP, Austl. 173/C4
Rocky Harbour, Nf, Can. 189/K1
Rocky Island (lake), On, Can. 188/D2
Rocky Mount, NC, US 191/J3
Rocky Mountain House, Ab, Can. 184/E2
Rocky Mountain NP, Co, US 186/F2
Rocroi, Fr. 111/D4
Rodach (riv.), Ger. 113/E2
Rodach bei Coburg, Ger. 112/D2
Rodalben, Ger. 111/G5
Rødberg, Nor. 96/C1
Rødbyhavn, Den. 96/D4
Roddickton, Nf, Can. 189/K1
Rødding, Den. 96/C4
Roden (riv.), Eng, UK 93/F6
Rodenbach, Ger. 112/C3
Rodeo, Mex. 200/D3
Rodeo, Ca, US 193/K10
Rödermark, Ger. 112/B3
Rodewisch, Ger. 113/F1
Rodez, Fr. 100/E4
Rodholívos, Gre. 105/H2
Ródhos (ruin), Gre. 148/B2
Ródhos (Rhodes), Gre. 148/B2
Rodigo, It. 116/D2
Roding (riv.), Eng, UK 88/D2
Roding, Ger. 113/F4
Rodinga (mt.), Austl. 171/G3
Rödinghausen, Ger. 109/F4
Rodoč, Bosn. 105/E1
Rodolfo Sánchez Toboada, Mex. 200/A2
Rodríguez, Uru. 217/K11
Roe (riv.), NI, UK 92/B2
Roebourne, Austl. 170/C2
Roebuck (bay), Austl. 167/B2
Roeland Park, Ks, US 195/D5
Roen (peak), It. 115/H5
Roer (riv.), Neth. 108/D6
Roermond, Neth. 108/C6
Roes Welcome Sound (str.), Nun., Can. 181/H2
Roeselare, Belg. 110/C2
Roesiger (lake), Wa, US 193/D2
Rogachev, Bela. 120/D1
Rogaland (co.), Nor. 95/C4
Rogaška Slatina, Slov. 101/L3
Rogatica, Bosn. 106/D4
Rogers (mt.), Va, US 188/D4
Rogers, Ar, US 187/J3
Rogers City, Mi, US 188/D2
Rogersville, Tn, US 188/D4
Roggwil, Swi. 114/D3
Rogliano, Fr. 101/H5
Roglio (riv.), It. 117/D5
Rognon (riv.), Fr. 100/F2
Rogoźno, Pol. 99/J2
Rogue (riv.), Or, US 186/B2
Rohl (riv.), Sudan 155/L6
Rohr, Ger. 113/E5
Rohrbach bei Mattersburg, Aus. 101/M3
Rohrbach in Oberösterreich, Aus. 113/G5
Rohrbach-lès-Bitche, Fr. 111/G5
Rohri, Pak. 147/J3
Röhrmoos, Ger. 113/E6
Rohtak, India 144/D5
Roi Et, Thai. 136/C2
Roine (lake), Fin. 97/L1
Roissy, Fr. 88/K5
Roissy-en-France, Fr. 88/K4
Rojas, Arg. 216/E2
Rojo (cape), PR 199/M8
Rojo, Cabo (cape), Mex. 202/B1
Rokan (riv.), Indo. 138/B3
Rokeby Croll Creek NP, Austl. 172/A1
Rokel (riv.), SLeo. 160/C4
Rokkasho, Japan 134/B3
Rokkō-san (peak), Japan 135/H6
Rokugō, Japan 135/A3
Rokycany, Czh. 113/G3
Rokytka (riv.), Czh. 113/H2
Rolampont, Fr. 114/B2
Rolândia, Braz. 213/B2
Rolava (riv.), Czh. 113/F2
Rolde, Neth. 108/D3
Rolla, ND, US 185/J3
Rolla, BC, Can. 184/C2
Rolla, Mo, US 187/K3
Rolle, Swi. 114/C5
Rolling Fork, Ms, US 187/K4
Rolling Hills Estates, Ca, US 194/F8
Rolling Meadows, Il, US 193/P15
Rollingbay, Wa, US 193/B2
Rollinsville, Co, US 195/A3
Rolo, It. 117/D3
Rom (peak), Ugan. 162/B2
Roma, Austl. 172/C4
Roma, Swe. 96/H3
Roma (Rome) (cap.), It. 104/C2
Romagnano Sesia, It. 116/B1
Romagnat, Fr. 100/E4
Romain (cape), SC, US 191/J3
Romaine (riv.), Qu, Can. 181/K3
Roman, Bul. 107/F4
Roman, Rom. 107/H2
Romang (str.), Indo. 139/G5
Romang (isl.), Indo. 139/G5
Romania (ctry.) 107/F3
Romano Canavese, It. 116/A2
Romano, Cayo (isl.), Cuba 203/G1
Romano d'Ezzelino, It. 117/E1
Romano di Lombardia, It. 116/C1
Romans d'Isonzo, It. 117/G1
Romans-sur-Isère, Fr. 100/F4
Romanshorn, Swi. 115/F2
Romanzof (cape), Ak, US 192/E3
Rombas, Fr. 111/F5
Romblon, Phil. 137/D5
Rome (cap.), It. 104/C2
Rome, Ga, US 191/G3
Rome, NY, US 188/F3
Rome, Wi, US 193/N14
Romenay, Fr. 114/B4
Romeoville, Il, US 193/P16
Römhild, Ger. 112/D2
Romilly-sur-Seine, Fr. 100/E2
Rommani, Mor. 156/D2
Rommerskirchen, Ger. 111/F1
Romney Marsh (phys. reg.), Eng, UK 91/G4
Romny, Ukr. 120/E2
Rømø (isl.), Den. 96/C4
Romoland, Ca, US 194/C3
Romont, Swi. 114/C4
Romorantin-Lanthenay, Fr. 100/D3
Romsey, Eng, UK 91/E5
Rømskog, Nor. 96/D2
Ronald Reagan Washington National (int'l arpt.), DC, US 196/A6
Ronan, Mt, US 184/E4
Roncade, It. 117/F1
Roncador Cay (isl.), Col. 203/G3
Roncador, Serra do (mts.), Braz. 209/H6
Ronchamp, Fr. 114/C2
Ronchi dei Legionari (int'l arpt.), It. 117/G1
Ronchi dei Legionari, It. 117/G1
Ronciglione, It. 104/C1
Ronco (riv.), It. 117/F5
Ronco All'Adige, It. 117/E2
Ronco Scrivia, It. 116/B3
Roncoferraro, It. 117/D2
Roncq, Fr. 110/C2
Ronda, Sp. 102/C4
Rondane NP, Nor. 95/D3
Ronde, Tête (peak), Swi. 114/D5
Rondonópolis, Braz. 209/H7
Rong (riv.), China 141/J2
Rong Xian, China 141/K3
Rongcheng, China 131/B4
Rongcheng, China 130/G7
Ronge (lake), Sk, Can. 180/F3
Rongelap (isl.), Mrsh. 174/F3
Rongerik (isl.), Mrsh. 174/F3
Ronkonkoma, NY, US 197/E2
Rønne, Den. 96/F4
Ronne Ice Shelf, Ant. 218/W
Ronneby, Swe. 96/F3
Ronnenberg, Ger. 109/G4
Ronquerolles, Fr. 88/J4
Ronsard (cape), Austl. 170/B3
Ronsberg, Ger. 115/G2
Ronse, Belg. 110/C2
Ronuro (riv.), Braz. 209/H6
Roodeport, SAfr. 164/P13
Rooiberg (peak), Namb. 164/B2
Roorkee, India 140/C2
Roosendaal, Neth. 108/B5
Roosevelt, Ut, US 186/E2
Roosevelt (canal), Az, US 195/S19
Roosevelt (riv.), Braz. 205/C4
Roosevelt (mt.), BC, Can. 180/D3
Roosevelt, NJ, US 196/D3
Roosevelt (isl.), Ant. 218/N
Roosevelt, NY, US 197/L9
Root (mt.), Ak, US 192/L4
Root (riv.), Wi, US 193/P14
Root, West Branch (riv.), Wi, US 193/P14
Roque Pérez, Arg. 217/J11
Roquetas de Mar, Sp. 102/D4
Roraima (peak), Braz. 208/F2
Roraima (peak), Ven. 211/F3
Roraima (state), Braz. 211/F4
Rorke's Drift, SAfr. 165/E3
Rorke's Drift Battlesite, SAfr. 165/E3
Rorketon, Mb, Can. 185/J3
Røros, Nor. 95/D3
Rorschach, Swi. 115/F3
Rosa (cape), Alg. 158/L6
Rosà, It. 117/E1
Rosa (lake), Bahm. 203/H1
Rosa Punta (pt.), Mex. 200/C3
Rosa Zárate, Ecu. 210/B4
Rosablanche (peak), Swi. 114/D5
Rosal, Sp. 102/A2
Rosales, Mex. 200/D2
Rosamorada, Mex. 200/D4
Rosanna (riv.), Aus. 115/G3
Rosario, Arg. 216/E2
Rosário, Braz. 212/A1
Rosario, Mex. 200/C3
Rosario, Mex. 200/D4
Rosario, Uru. 217/K11
Rosario de la Frontera, Arg. 215/D2
Rosario del Tala, Arg. 217/J10
Rosário do Sul, Braz. 215/F3
Rosarito, Mex. 200/A1
Rosarno, It. 104/D3
Rosas, Col. 210/B4
Rosas, Golfo di (gulf), Sp. 103/G1
Rosate, It. 116/C2
Rosay, Fr. 88/G5
Rosbach vor der Höhe, Ger. 112/B2
Rosche, Ger. 109/H3
Roscoff, Fr. 100/B2
Roscommon, Ire. 89/P10
Roscrea, Ire. 89/Q10
Rosdorf, Ger. 109/G5
Rose (isl.), ASam. 175/J6
Rose (pt.), BC, Can. 192/M4
Rose Belle, Mrts. 165/T15
Roseau, Mn, US 185/K3
Roseau (riv.), Mn, US 185/J3
Roseau (cap.), Dom. 199/N9
Roseaux, Haiti 203/H2
Rosebery, Austl. 173/C4
Roseburg, Or, US 184/C5
Rosedale, Ms, US 187/K4
Rosedale, Il, US 195/F7
Rosedale, Md, US 196/B5
Rosehearty, Sc, UK 94/D1
Roseira, Braz. 213/H7
Roseland, NJ, US 197/H8
Roselette, Aiguille de (peak), Fr. 114/C6
Roselle, NJ, US 197/H9
Roselle, Il, US 193/P16
Roselle Park, NJ, US 197/H9
Rosemead, Ca, US 194/F7
Rosemère, Qu, Can. 189/N6
Rosenberg, Tx, US 187/J5
Rosenberg, Ger. 112/D4
Rosenfeld, Ger. 115/E1
Rosenhayn, NJ, US 196/C5
Rosenheim, Ger. 101/K3
Roses, Sp. 103/G1
Roseto, Pa, US 196/C2
Roseto degli Abruzzi, It. 101/L5
Rosetown, Sk, Can. 184/G3
Rosetta (riv.), Egypt 149/B4
Roseville, Mi, US 193/G6
Rosewood Heights, Il, US 195/G8
Rosh Ha'ayin, Isr. 149/F7
Rosh Hakarmel (pt.), Isr. 149/F6
Rosh Haniqra (pt.), Isr. 149/D3
Rosheim, Fr. 114/D1
Rosières-en-Santerre, Fr. 110/B4
Rosignano Marittimo, It. 116/D6
Roşiori de Vede, Rom. 107/G3
Roskilde, Den. 96/E4
Roskilde (co.), Den. 96/D4
Roslavl', Rus. 120/E1
Roslev, Den. 96/C3
Rosmalen, Neth. 108/C5
Rosmaninhal, Port. 102/B3
Rosneath, Sc, UK 94/B4
Rosny-sous-Bois, Fr. 88/K5
Rosolina, It. 117/F2
Rosolini, It. 104/D4
Rosporden, Fr. 100/B3
Rösrath, Ger. 111/G2
Ross (isl.), Ant. 218/M
Ross (sea), Ant. 218/P
Ross, Austl. 173/C4
Ross (isl.), Mb, Can. 185/J2
Ross (pt.), On, Can. 189/S8
Ross (dist.), Sc, UK 94/C1
Ross Ice Shelf, Ant. 218/N
Rossa (peak), It. 101/K3
Rossa, Swi. 115/F5
Rossall (pt.), Eng, UK 93/E4
Rossano Stazione, It. 104/E3
Rossano Veneto, It. 117/E1
Rossbach, Ger. 113/F5
Rossberg (peak), Fr. 114/D2
Rossdorf, Ger. 112/B3
Rossel (isl.), PNG 174/E6
Rosselange, Fr. 111/F5
Rosshaupten, Ger. 115/G2
Rossiglione, It. 116/B3
Rossignol (lake), NS, Can. 189/H2
Rosskeeragh (pt.), Ire. 89/P9
Rossland, BC, Can. 184/D3
Rosso, Mrta. 160/B2
Rossosh', Rus. 120/F2
Rossstock (peak), Swi. 115/E4
Rosstal, Ger. 112/D4
Rossville, Ok, US 195/N14
Røst, Nor. 95/E2
Rosthern, Sk, Can. 185/G2
Rostock, Ger. 96/E4
Rostov, Rus. 120/F3
Rostov, Rus. 118/H4
Rostov (int'l arpt.), Rus. 120/F3
Rostovskaya Oblast, Rus. 121/G2
Rostrenen, Fr. 100/B2
Rostrevor, NI, UK 92/B3
Roswell, NM, US 187/F4
Rot (riv.), Ger. 98/E4
Rota, Sp. 102/B4
Rota (isl.), NMar. 174/D3
Rote Wand (peak), Aus. 115/F3
Rotenburg, Ger. 109/G2
Rotenburg an der Fulda, Ger. 109/G7
Roter Main (riv.), Ger. 98/F3
Rötgen, Ger. 111/F2
Roth (riv.), Ger. 115/G1
Roth bei Nürnberg, Ger. 112/E4
Rothaargebirge (mts.), Ger. 109/F6
Rothau, Fr. 114/D1
Röthenbach an der Pegnitz, Ger. 112/E4
Rothenberg, Ger. 112/B3
Rothenburg, Swi. 115/E3
Rothenburg ob der Tauber, Ger. 112/D4
Rothera, UK, Ant. 218/V
Rotherham, Eng, UK 93/G5
Rotherham (co.), Eng, UK 93/G5
Rothes, Sc, UK 94/C1
Rothesay, Sc, UK 94/A5
Rotheux-Rimière, Belg. 111/E2
Rothschild, Wi, US 185/L4
Rothwell, Eng, UK 91/F2
Rothwell, Eng, UK 93/G4
Roti (isl.), Indo. 139/F6
Rotorua, NZ 175/T10
Rotselaar, Belg. 111/D2
Rott (riv.), Ger. 98/G4
Rott am Inn, Ger. 113/F7
Rottach-Egern, Ger. 98/F5
Rotte (riv.), Fr. 111/F6
Rotten (riv.), Swi. 114/E5
Rottenacker, Ger. 115/F1
Röttenbach, Ger. 112/E4
Rottenberg, Ger. 112/C2
Rottenburg am Neckar, Ger. 112/B6
Rottenburg an der Laaber, Ger. 113/F5
Rotterdam (int'l arpt.), Neth. 108/B5
Rotterdam, Neth. 108/B5
Rotthalmünster, Ger. 113/G6
Röttingen, Ger. 112/C3
Rottne, Swe. 96/F3
Rottnest (isl.), Austl. 170/B5
Rottofreno, It. 116/C2
Rottum (riv.), Ger. 115/F1
Rottumeroog (isl.), Neth. 108/D1
Rottumerplaat (isl.), Neth. 108/D1
Rottweil, Ger. 115/E1
Rotuma (isl.), Fiji 174/G6
Rötz, Ger. 113/F4
Roubaix, Fr. 110/C2
Roubion (riv.), Fr. 100/F4
Roudnice nad Labem, Czh. 113/H2
Rouen, Fr. 100/D2
Rouffach, Fr. 114/D2
Rouge (riv.), Qu, Can. 181/J4
Rouge, Middle (riv.), Mi, US 193/F7
Rougemont, Fr. 114/C3
Rougemont-le-Château, Fr. 114/C2
Rough (riv.), Ky, US 191/G2
Roullet-Saint-Estèphe, Fr. 100/D4
Round (hill), Pa, US 196/B3
Round Hill (pt.), Austl. 172/C4
Round Lake, Il, US 193/P15
Round Lake Beach, Il, US 193/P15
Round Lake Park, Il, US 193/P15
Round Rock, Tx, US 187/H5
Round Valley (res.), NJ, US 196/D2
Roundup, Mt, US 184/F4
Roundway (hill), Eng, UK 90/E4
Rousay (isl.), Sc, UK 89/V14
Rousies, Fr. 110/D3
Rousinov, Czh. 99/J4
Roussillon, Fr. 100/F4
Rouvres, Fr. 88/M4
Rouvroy, Belg. 111/E4
Rouxville, SAfr. 164/D3
Rouyn-Noranda, Qu, Can. 188/E1
Rovaniemi, Fin. 118/E2
Rovaniemi (int'l arpt.), Fin. 118/E2
Rovasenda, It. 116/B1
Rovato, It. 116/C1
Roverbella, It. 117/D2
Rovereto, It. 117/D3
Rovereto, It. 115/H6
Rovigo (prov.), It. 117/E2
Rovigo, It. 117/E2
Rovinj, Cro. 117/G2
Rovuma (riv.), Moz. 162/B5
Rowley (isl.), Nun., Can. 139/J2
Rowley Shoals (isl.), Austl. 167/A2
Roxa (isl.), GBis. 160/B4
Roxana, Il, US 195/G8
Roxas, Phil. 137/C5
Roxas, Phil. 137/D4
Roxas, Phil. 137/D5
Roxboro, NC, US 188/E4
Roxen (lake), Swe. 96/F2
Roxo (cape), Sen. 160/A3
Roy, NM, US 190/B3
Roy, Ut, US 195/J11
Roy, Wa, US 193/B3
Roya (riv.), Fr. 101/G5
Royal (canal), Ire. 93/B3
Royal Botanical Garden, On, Can. 189/Q9
Royal Chitwan NP, Nepal 143/E2
Royal Lakes, Il, US 195/H7
Royal Natal NP, SAfr. 164/E3
Royal NP, Austl. 173/D2
Royal NP, The, Austl. 172/H9
Royal Oak, Mi, US 193/F7
Royal Paekje Tombs, SKor. 131/D4
Royal Tombs, Viet. 136/D2
Royal Tunbridge Wells, Eng, UK 91/G4
Royale, Isle (isl.), Mi, US 185/L4
Royalton, Pa, US 196/B3
Royan, Fr. 100/C4
Roye, Fr. 114/C2
Roye, Fr. 110/B4
Royersford, Pa, US 196/C3
Røyken, Nor. 96/D2
Royston, Eng, UK 91/F2
Royston, Eng, UK 93/G4
Royton, Eng, UK 93/F4
Rožaje, Mont. 106/E4
Rozay-en-Brie, Fr. 110/B6
Rozenburg, Neth. 108/B5
Rozhaya (riv.), Rus. 119/W9
Rožmberk (lake), Czh. 113/H4
Rožmital pod Třemšínem, Czh. 113/G3
Rožňava, Slvk. 99/L4
Roztoczański PN, Pol. 99/M3
Roztoky, Czh. 113/H2
Rozzano, It. 116/C2
Rrëshen, Alb. 105/F2
Rt Kamenjak (cape), Cro. 106/A3
Rt Ploča (pt.), Cro. 106/B4
Rtishchevo, Rus. 121/G1
Ruacana (falls), Ang. 163/B4
Ruaha NP, Tanz. 162/B4
Ruapehu (vol.), NZ 175/T10
Rub' al Khali (des.), SAr. 146/E5
Rubelles, Fr. 88/L6
Rubeshibe, Japan 134/C2
Rubí, Sp. 103/L7
Rubidoux, Ca, US 194/C3
Rubiera, It. 117/D3
Rubigen, Swi. 114/D4
Rubim, Braz. 212/B5
Rubizhne, Ukr. 120/F2
Rubondo NP, Tanz. 162/A3
Ruby, Ak, US 192/G3
Ruby (lake), Nv, US 186/D2
Ruby (mts.), Nv, US 186/D2
Rubyvale, Austl. 172/B3
Rucheng, China 137/B2
Rucphen, Neth. 108/B5
Ruda Woda (lake), Pol. 99/K2
Rudall River NP, Austl. 170/D2
Rūdarpur, India 142/D2
Rudauli, India 142/C2
Rüdersdorf, Ger. 98/Q7
Rüdesheim, Ger. 112/A3
Rudiano, It. 116/C2
Rudkøbing, Den. 96/D4
Rudnik, Pol. 99/M3
Rūdnyy, Kaz. 119/P5
Rudolf (isl.), Rus. 122/F1
Rudolstadt, Ger. 101/J1
Rudong, China 130/E4
Rūdsar, Iran 146/F1
Rue, Swi. 114/C4
Rue (pt.), NI, UK 92/B1
Rue, Fr. 110/A3
Rueda, Sp. 102/C2
Rueil-Malmaison, Fr. 88/J5
Ruell (riv.), Sc, UK 94/A4
Ruelle-sur-Touvre, Fr. 100/D4
Ruen (peak), Bul. 106/F4
Ruetzbach (riv.), Aus. 115/H3
Ruffano, It. 105/F3
Ruffec, Fr. 100/D3
Rufiji (riv.), Tanz. 162/C4
Rufina, It. 117/E5
Rufino, Arg. 216/E2
Rufisque, Sen. 160/A3
Rugao, China 130/E4
Rugby, ND, US 185/J3
Rugby, Eng, UK 91/E2
Rugeley, Eng, UK 91/E1
Rügen (isl.), Ger. 96/E4
Ruggell, Lcht. 115/F3
Ruhmannsfelden, Ger. 113/F5
Ruhnu saar (isl.), Lat. 97/K3
Ruhr (riv.), Ger. 98/D3
Ruhr (reg.), Ger. 98/E3
Ruhrgebiet (phys. reg.), Ger. 108/D6
Ruhstorf an der Rott, Ger. 113/F5
Rui'an, China 137/D2
Ruicheng, China 130/B4
Ruidoso, NM, US 187/F4
Ruinen, Neth. 108/D3
Ruiselede, Belg. 110/C1
Ruiz, Mex. 200/D4
Rujen (peak), FYROM 105/H1
Ruki (riv.), D.R. Congo 155/J8
Rukwa (lake), Tanz. 162/B4
Rukwa (pol. reg.), Tanz. 162/B4
Rulles (riv.), Belg. 111/E4
Rülzheim, Ger. 112/B4
Rum, Aus. 115/H3
Rum Cay (isl.), Bahm. 199/G3
Ruma, Serb. 106/D3
Ruma NP, Kenya 162/B3
Rumbek, Sudan 155/L6
Rumes, Belg. 110/C2
Rumford, Me, US 189/G2
Rumia, Pol. 96/H4
Rumilly, Fr. 114/B6
Rümlang, Swi. 115/E3
Rumoi, Japan 134/B2
Rumphi, Malw. 162/B5
Rumson, NJ, US 196/E3
Rumst, Belg. 111/D1
Rumuruti, Kenya 162/C2
Runabay (pt.), NI, UK 92/B1
Runan, China 130/C4
Runcorn, Eng, UK 93/F5
Runding, Ger. 113/F4
Rundu, Namb. 163/C4
Rungwa (riv.), Tanz. 162/B4
Rungwa Game Rsv., Tanz. 162/B4
Rungwe (peak), Tanz. 162/B5
Runkel, Ger. 112/B2
Runn (lake), Swe. 96/F1
Runnemede, NJ, US 196/C4
Running Springs, Ca, US 194/C2
Ruo (riv.), China 123/K5
Ruokolahti, Fin. 97/N1
Ruoqiang, China 128/E4
Rupat (isl.), Indo. 138/B3
Rupea, Rom. 107/G2
Rupel (riv.), Belg. 111/D1
Rupert (riv.), Qu, Can. 139/J3
Rūpnagar, India 144/D4
Ruppichteroth, Ger. 111/G2
Rupt-sur-Moselle, Fr. 114/C2
Rupununi (riv.), Guy. 211/G4
Rur (riv.), Ger. 98/D3
Rur-Strasse (lake), Ger. 111/F2
Rurrenabaque, Bol. 208/E6
Rurutu (isl.), FrPol. 175/K7
Rusape, Zim. 163/F4
Rüschegg, Swi. 114/D4
Rüschlikon, Swi. 115/E3
Ruscom (riv.), On, Can. 193/G7
Ruse, Bul. 107/G4
Ruse (pol. reg.), Bul. 107/G4
Rusera, India 143/F3
Rush (lake), Ut, US 195/J13
Rush, Ire. 92/B4
Rushan, China 130/E3
Rushden, Eng, UK 91/F2
Rushville, In, US 188/C4
Rusk, Tx, US 187/J5
Russ, Fr. 114/D1
Russ Lake Nat'l Rec. Area, Wa, US 184/C3
Russbach (riv.), Aus. 107/N7
Russell (isls.), Austl. 172/F7
Russell, Mb, Can. 185/H3
Russell (lake), Mb, Can. 185/H1
Russell (isl.), Nun., Can. 180/F1
Russell (lake), Ga,SC, US 191/H3
Russell Gulch, Co, US 195/A3
Russellville, Al, US 191/G3
Russellville, Ar, US 187/J4
Russellville, Ky, US 188/C4
Rüsselsheim, Ger. 112/B3
Russi, It. 117/F4
Russia (ctry.) 122/H3
Russian (riv.), Ca, US 186/B3
Russian Mission, Ak, US 192/F3
Russkaya, Rus., Ant. 218/Q
Rust'avi, Geo. 121/H4
Rustenburg, SAfr. 163/E6
Ruston, La, US 187/J4
Ruston, Wa, US 193/C3
Rute, Sp. 102/C4
Ruteng, Indo. 139/F5
Rüthen, Ger. 109/F6
Rutherford, NJ, US 197/J8
Rutherglen, Sc, UK 94/B5
Rüthi, Swi. 115/F3
Ruthin, Wal, UK 93/E5
Ruthven, On, Can. 193/G7
Rüti, Swi. 115/E3
Rüti, Swi. 115/F4
Rutland (co.), Eng, UK 91/F1
Rutland, Vt, US 188/F3
Rutland Water (res.), Eng, UK 91/F1
Rutog, China 128/C5
Rutshuru (riv.), D.R. Congo 162/A3
Ruukki, Fin. 118/E2
Ruurlo, Neth. 108/D4
Ruvo di Puglia, It. 104/E2
Ruvu (riv.), Tanz. 162/C4
Ruvubu (riv.), Buru. 162/A3
Ruvuma (pol. reg.), Tanz. 162/C5
Ruvuma (riv.), Moz.,Tanz. 162/B5
Ruwāndūz, Iraq 148/F2
Ruwenzori (range), Ugan. 162/A2
Ruwenzori NP, Ugan. 162/A3
Ruy Barbosa, Braz. 212/B4
Ruyang, China 130/C4
Ruzayevka, Rus. 121/H1
Ruzizi (riv.), D.R. Congo 162/A3
Ružomberok, Slvk. 99/K4
Ruzyně (int'l arpt.), Czh. 113/H2
Rwanda (ctry.) 162/A3
Ryan (mt.), Austl. 173/D2
Ryan (mt.), Austl. 172/A1
Ryan (inlet), Sc, UK 92/C2
Ryazan', Rus. 121/G1
Ryazanskaya Oblast, Rus. 121/G1
Ryazhsk, Rus. 120/G1
Rybachiy (pen.), Rus. 95/K1
Rybinsk, Rus. 118/H4
Rybinsk (res.), Rus. 118/H4
Rybnik, Pol. 99/K3
Rycroft, Ab, Can. 184/D2
Ryd, Swe. 96/F3
Rydaholm, Swe. 96/F3
Ryde, Eng, UK 91/E5
Ryde, Ca, US 193/L10
Rydet, Swe. 96/D3
Rye (bay), Eng, UK 91/G5
Rye, Eng, UK 91/G5
Rye, NY, US 197/L8
Rye (riv.), Eng, UK 93/H3
Rye Brook, NY, US 197/L7
Rye Patch (res.), Nv, US 186/C2
Rygge, Nor. 96/D2
Ryki, Pol. 99/L3
Rylstone, Austl. 173/D2
Ryōkami, Japan 135/B2
Ryōtsu, Japan 133/F1
Ryōzen-yama (peak), Japan 135/K5
Rypin, Pol. 99/K2
Rysy (peak), Pol. 99/L4
Ryton, Eng, UK 93/G2
Rytterknægten (peak), Den. 96/F4
Ryūgasaki, Japan 133/G3
Ryukyu (isls.), Japan 133/H7
Ryūō, Japan 135/B2
Ryūō, Japan 135/K5
Rzeszów, Pol. 99/M3
Rzhev, Rus. 118/G4

S

's-Graveland, Neth. 108/C4
's Gravendeel, Neth. 108/B5
's Heerenberg, Neth. 108/D5
's Hertogenbosch, Neth. 108/C5
Sa Dec, Viet. 136/D4
Saab (int'l arpt.), Swe. 96/F2
Sääksjärvi (lake), Fin. 97/K1
Saal an der Donau, Ger. 113/E5
Saalbach (riv.), Ger. 112/B4
Saaldorf, Ger. 113/E2
Saale (riv.), Ger. 98/F3
Saales, Col de (pass), Fr. 114/D1
Saalfeld, Ger. 101/J1
Saalfelden am Steinernen Meer, Aus. 101/K3
Saane (riv.), Swi. 114/D5
Saanen, Swi. 114/D5
Saanta (peak), Kenya 162/C2
Saar (riv.), Ger. 111/F5
Saarbrücken, Ger. 111/F5
Saarburg, Ger. 111/F4
Saaremaa (isl.), Est. 97/K2
Saarland (state), Ger. 101/G2
Saarlouis, Ger. 111/F5
Saas, Swi. 115/F4
Saas Fee, Swi. 114/D5
Saastal (valley), Swi. 114/D5
Sab (riv.), Camb. 136/D3
Saba (isl.), NAnt. 199/N8
Šabac, Serb. 106/D3
Sabadell, Sp. 103/L6
Sabae, Japan 132/E3
Sabah (reg.), Malay. 139/E2
Sabalgarh, India 142/A2
Sabana (arch.), Bang. 203/F1
Sabana de Uchire, Ven. 211/E2
Sabanalarga, Col. 210/C3
Sabanalarga, Col. 210/C2
Sabancuy, Mex. 202/D2
Sabaneta, Ven. 210/D2
Sabang, Indo. 138/A2
Sabanita, Pan. 203/G4
Sabasṭīyah, WBnk. 149/G7
Sabat (riv.), Sudan 155/L6
Sabbio Chiese, It. 116/D1
Sabbioneta, It. 116/D3
Sabhā, Libya 154/H2
Sabie (riv.), Moz. 165/F2
Sabinal, Cayo (isl.), Cuba 203/G1
Sabiñánigo, Sp. 103/E1
Sabinas, Mex. 201/E5
Sabinas (riv.), Mex. 201/E5
Sabinas Hidalgo, Mex. 201/E5
Sabine (lake), La,Tx, US 187/J5
Sabine (riv.), La,Tx, US 187/J5
Sabinópolis, Braz. 213/D1
Sabkhat al Bardawīl (lag.), Egypt 149/C4
Sabkhat al Jabbūl (lake), Syria 148/D3
Sabkhat al Mūḩ (lake), Syria 148/D3
Sablayan, Phil. 137/D5
Sable (isl.), NS, Can. 189/K3
Sable (cape), NS, Can. 189/H3
Sablé-sur-Sarthe, Fr. 100/C3
Saboeiro, Braz. 212/C2
Sabor (riv.), Port. 102/B2
Sabra (cape), Indo. 139/H4
Sabrina (coast), Ant. 218/J
Sabugal, Port. 102/B2
Sabzevār, Iran 147/G1
Sacajawea (peak), Or, US 184/D4
Sácama, Col. 210/C3
Sacaton, Az, US 195/S19
Sacavém, Port. 103/P10
Saccarello (peak), It. 116/A4
Sacco (riv.), It. 104/C2
Sacedón, Sp. 102/D2
Săcele, Rom. 107/G3
Sachigo (lake), On, Can. 185/K2
Sachigo (riv.), On, Can. 180/G3
Sachs Harbour, NW, Can. 180/D1
Sachseln, Swi. 115/E4
Sachsen (state), Ger. 98/G3
Sachsen-Anhalt (state), Ger. 98/F3
Sachsenbrunn, Ger. 112/D2
Sachsenhagen, Ger. 109/G4
Sacile, It. 117/F1
Säckingen, Ger. 114/D2
Sackville, NB, Can. 189/H2
Saclay, Fr. 88/J5
Saco, Me, US 189/G3
Sacramento (cap.), Ca, US 186/B3
Sacramento, Braz. 213/C1
Sacramento (co.), Ca, US 193/M10
Sacramento (riv.), Ca, US 186/B2
Sacramento (valley), Ca, US 186/B3
Sacramento (mts.), NM, US 182/E5
Sacramento, Pampa del (plain), Peru 214/C2
Sacramento River Deep Water Ship Canal, Ca, US 193/L10
Sacratif (cape), Sp. 102/D4
Sacred (falls), Hi, US 182/W12
Sacro (peak), It. 104/E2
Sacro Monte, It. 116/B1
Sada, SAfr. 164/D4
Sádaba, Sp. 102/E1
Sadābād, India 142/B2
Sa'dah, Yem. 146/D5
Saddam (int'l arpt.), Iraq 148/F3
Saddle (hills), Ab,BC, Can. 184/C2
Saddle (riv.), NJ, US 197/J8
Saddle Brook, NJ, US 197/J8
Saddle River, NJ, US 197/J7
Saddle Rock, NY, US 197/K8
Saddle, The (peak), Sc, UK 94/A2
Saddleworth, Austl. 171/H5
Sādhaura, India 144/D4
Sādiqābād, Pak. 147/K3
Sado (isl.), Japan 129/Q4
Sado (riv.), Port. 102/A3
Sadovo, Bul. 107/G4
Sadowara, Japan 132/B4
Sādri, India 147/K3

Sadulshahar, India 144/C5
Saerbeck, Ger. 109/E4
Saeul, Lux. 111/E4
Safājah (well), Egypt 159/C3
Safed Koh (range), Pak. 144/A3
Saffānīyah, Ra's as (pt.), SAr. 146/E3
Saffig, Ger. 111/G3
Säffle, Swe. 96/E2
Safford, Az, US 186/E4
Saffron Walden, Eng, UK 91/G2
Safi (cape), Mor. 156/C2
Safi, Mor. 156/C2
Safīd (riv.), Afg. 147/J1
Safid Khers (mts.), Afg. 147/K1
Safīd Kūh (mts.), Afg. 147/H2
Safidon, India 144/D5
Safien, Swi. 115/F4
Safīpur, India 142/C2
Şāfītā, Syria 149/E2
Safonovo, Rus. 118/G5
Safranbolu, Turk. 148/C1
Sag Harbor, NY, US 197/F2
Saga (pref.), Japan 132/A4
Saga, China 143/E1
Saga, Japan 132/B4
Sagae, Japan 134/B4
Sagaing, Myan. 141/G3
Sagaing (div.), Myan. 141/F3
Sagami (sea), Japan 133/F3
Sagami (riv.), Japan 135/C2
Sagami (lake), Japan 135/C2
Sagami (bay), Japan 135/C3
Sagamihara, Japan 135/C2
Sagamiko, Japan 135/C2
Sagamore Hill Nat'l Hist. Site, NY, US 197/M8
Sāgar, India 142/B4
Sagard, Ger. 96/E4
Sagarmatha (zone), Nepal 143/F2
Sagarmatha (Everest) (mtn.), China,Nepal 143/F2
Sagarmatha NP, Nepal 143/F2
Sagauli, India 143/E2
Sagavanirktok (riv.), Ak, US 192/J2
Sagay, Phil. 139/F1
Saggart, Ire. 92/B5
Saghyz (riv.), Kaz. 121/K2
Saginaw, Mi, US 188/D3
Saginaw (bay), Mi, US 188/D3
Saglek (bay), Nf, Can. 139/K3
Sagone, Golfe de (gulf), Fr. 104/A1
Sagter Ems (riv.), Ger. 109/E2
Sagua de Tánamo, Cuba 203/H1
Sagua la Grande, Cuba 203/F1
Saguaro NP, Az, US 186/E4
Saguenay (riv.), Qu, Can. 189/G1
Saguia el Hamra (riv.), WSah. 154/C2
Sagunto, Sp. 103/E3
Sagy, Fr. 88/H4
Sa'gya, China 143/G1
Saḥāb, Jor. 149/D4
Sahagún, Sp. 102/C1
Sahagún, Col. 210/C2
Sahagún, Mex. 201/L7
Saḥam, Jor. 149/D3
Sahand (mtn.), Iran 146/E1
Sahara (des.), Afr. 151/B2
Sahāranpur, India 144/D5
Saharsa, India 143/F3
Sahaspur, India 142/B1
Sahaswān, India 142/B1
Sahavato, Madg. 165/J8
Sahāwar, India 142/B2
Sahel (riv.), Alg. 158/H4
Sāhibganj, India 143/F3
Şahinli, Turk. 107/H5
Sāhīwāl, Pak. 144/B4
Sahiwal, Pak. 144/B4
Şaḥrā Marzūq (des.), Libya 154/H3
Şaḥrā' Rabyānah (des.), Libya 155/K3
Sahrho, Jebel (mts.), Mor. 156/D3
Sahuaripa, Mex. 200/C2
Sahuayo de Morelos, Mex. 200/E4
Šahy, Slvk. 99/K4
Sai (canal), India 140/D2
Sai Yok NP, Thai. 136/B3
Saïda, Alg. 158/F5
Saidpur, Bang. 143/G3
Saidpur, India 142/D3
Saignelégier, Swi. 114/D3
Saigō, Japan 132/C2
Saigon, Viet. 136/D4
Saijō, Japan 132/C4
Saikai NP, Japan 132/A4
Saiki, Japan 132/B4
Sailly, Fr. 88/H4
Sailly-sur-la-Lys, Fr. 110/B2
Sailu, India 147/L5
Saimaa (lake), Fin. 95/J3
Sain Alto, Mex. 200/E4
Sainghin-en-Weppes, Fr. 110/B2
Sains-du-Nord, Fr. 110/D3
Saint Abb's (pt.), Sc, UK 94/D5
Saint-Affrique, Fr. 100/E5
Saint Agnes (pt.), Eng, UK 90/A6
Saint Albans, WV, US 188/D4
Saint Alban's, Nf, Can. 189/L2
Saint Albans, Vt, US 188/F2
Saint Albans, Eng, UK 88/C1
Saint Albert, Ab, Can. 184/E2
Saint-Amable, Qu, Can. 189/P6
Saint-Amand-les-Eaux, Fr. 110/C3
Saint-Amand-Montrond, Fr. 100/E3
Saint-Amarin, Fr. 114/D2
Saint-Ambroise, Qu, Can. 189/G1
Saint-Amé, Fr. 114/C1
Saint-André, Reun., Fr. 165/S15
Saint-André, Fr. 110/C2
Saint-André-de-Cubzac, Fr. 100/C4
Saint-André-les-Vergers, Fr. 100/F2
Saint Andrew's (bay), Sc, UK 94/D4
Saint Andrews, Sc, UK 94/D4
Saint Ann (cape), SLeo. 160/B5
Saint Anns, On, Can. 189/Q9
Saint Ann's (pt.), Wal, UK 90/A3
Saint Ann's Bay, Jam. 199/F4
Saint Anthony, Nf, Can. 189/L1
Saint-Antoine, Qu, Can. 189/N6
Saint Arnaud, Austl. 173/B3
Saint-Arnoult-en-Yvelines, Fr. 88/H6
Saint Aubin, Chl, UK 100/B2
Saint-Aubin, Swi. 114/C4
Saint-Aubin, Fr. 114/B3
Saint-Augustin, Fr. 88/M5
Saint Augustine, Fl, US 191/H4
Saint Augustine Beach, Fl, US 191/H4
Saint Austell (bay), Eng, UK 90/B6
Saint Austell, Eng, UK 90/B6
Saint-Avé, Fr. 100/B3
Saint-Avold, Fr. 111/F5
Saint-Barthélemy (isl.), Fr. 199/N8
Saint-Barthélemy-d'Anjou, Fr. 100/C3
Saint-Barthélemy, Pic de (peak), Fr. 100/D5
Saint Bees (pt.), Eng, UK 92/E2
Saint-Benoît, Qu, Can. 189/M6
Saint-Benoît, Fr. 100/D3
Saint-Benoît, Reun., Fr. 165/S15
Saint Bernard, La, US 195/Q17
Saint Bernard (parish), La, US 195/Q17
Saint-Berthevin, Fr. 100/C2
Saint-Blaise, Swi. 114/C3
Saint-Blaise, Qu, Can. 189/P7
Saint Blaize (cape), SAfr. 164/C4
Saint Boswells, Sc, UK 94/D5
Saint-Brice-Courcelles, Fr. 110/C5
Saint-Brice-sous-Forêt, Fr. 88/K5
Saint Bride's (bay), Wal, UK 90/A3
Saint-Brieuc, Fr. 100/B2
Saint-Brieuc (bay), Fr. 100/B2
Saint-Bruno-de-Montarville, Qu, Can. 189/P6
Saint-Calais, Fr. 100/D3
Saint-Canut, Qu, Can. 189/M6
Saint Catharines, On, Can. 189/R9
Saint Catherine (mt.), Gren. 211/F1
Saint Catherine's (pt.), Eng, UK 91/E5
Saint Catherine's (hill), Eng, UK 91/E5
Saint-Céré, Fr. 100/D4
Saint-Cergue, Swi. 114/C5
Saint-Cergues, Fr. 114/C5
Saint-Chamond, Fr. 100/F4
Saint Charles, Il, US 193/P16
Saint Charles (parish), La, US 195/P17
Saint Charles, Md, US 188/E4
Saint Charles, Mo, US 195/G8
Saint Charles (co.), Mo, US 195/F8
Saint-Chély-d'Apcher, Fr. 100/E4
Saint-Chéron, Fr. 88/J6
Saint Christoffel (peak), NAnt. 210/D1
Saint Clair (lake), Can.,US 193/G7
Saint Clair (peak), Az, US 195/S18
Saint Clair (co.), Il, US 195/G9
Saint Clair (co.), Mi, US 193/G6
Saint Clair, Mi, US 188/D3
Saint Clair, Pa, US 196/B2
Saint Clair Beach, On, Can. 193/G7
Saint Clair Shores, Mi, US 193/G6
Saint-Claude, Fr. 114/B5
Saint Cloud, Mn, US 185/K4
Saint-Cloud, Fr. 88/J5
Saint-Constant, Qu, Can. 189/N7
Saint Croix (riv.), US 188/A2
Saint Croix (isl.), USVI 199/M8
Saint Cyr (mt.), Yk, Can. 192/M3
Saint-Cyr-l'École, Fr. 88/J5
Saint-Cyr-sous-Dourdan, Fr. 88/J6
Saint-Cyr-sur-Morin, Fr. 88/M5
Saint David's (pt.), Wal, UK 90/A3
Saint David's, Wal, UK 90/A3
Saint-Denis, Fr. 88/K5
Saint-Denis, Reun., Fr. 165/S15
Saint-Denis-en-Bugey, Fr. 114/B6
Saint-Dié, Fr. 114/C1
Saint-Dizier, Fr. 111/D6
Saint-Doulchard, Fr. 100/E3
Saint-Édouard, Qu, Can. 189/N7
Saint Eleanors, PE, Can. 189/J2
Saint Elias (cape), Ak, US 192/K4
Saint Elias (mt.), Ak, US 192/K3
Saint Elias (mts.), Ak, US 180/B2
Saint-Éloy-les-Mines, Fr. 100/E3
Saint-Esprit, Qu, Can. 189/N6
Saint-Estève, Fr. 100/E5
Saint-Étienne, Fr. 100/F4
Saint-Étienne-au-Mont, Fr. 110/A2
Saint-Étienne-de-Baïgorry, Fr. 100/C5
Saint-Étienne-de-Tinée, Fr. 101/G4
Saint-Étienne-du-Rouvray, Fr. 100/D2
Saint-Étienne-lès-Remiremont, Fr. 114/C1
Saint-Eustache, Qu, Can. 189/N6
Saint Eustatius (isl.), NAnt. 199/N8
Saint-Fargeau-Ponthierry, Fr. 88/K6
Saint-Félicien, Qu, Can. 189/F1
Saint-Félix, Fr. 114/B6
Saint-Florent-sur-Cher, Fr. 100/E3
Saint-Florentin Fr. 100/E2
Saint-Floris, PN de, CAfr. 155/K6
Saint-Four, Fr. 100/E4
Saint Francis (riv.), Ar, US 187/K4
Saint Francis (riv.), Mo, US 191/F2
Saint Francis, Ks, US 187/G3
Saint Francis (cape), SAfr. 164/D4
Saint Francis, Wi, US 193/Q14
Saint Francisville, La, US 187/K5
Saint Francois (mts.), Mo, US 191/F2
Saint Gallen (canton), Swi. 115/F3
Saint-Gaudens, Fr. 100/D5
Saint-Genis-Pouilly, Fr. 114/C5
Saint George, Austl. 172/C5
Saint George, NB, Can. 189/H2
Saint George (cape), Nf, Can. 189/K1
Saint George (isl.), Ak, US 192/E4
Saint George, Ak, US 192/E4
Saint George (pt.), Ca, US 184/B5
Saint George, SC, US 191/H3
Saint George, Ut, US 186/D3
Saint George's, Nf, Can. 189/K1
Saint George's (bay), Nf, Can. 189/J2
Saint-Georges, Qu, Can. 189/G2
Saint George's (cap.), Gren. 211/F1
Saint George's (chan.), Ire.,UK 89/Q11
Saint Georges, De, US 196/C4
Saint-Germain, Fr. 114/C2
Saint-Germain-de-la-Grange, Fr. 88/H5
Saint-Germain-du-Bois, Fr. 114/B4
Saint-Germain-du-Corbéis, Fr. 100/D2
Saint-Germain-du-Plain, Fr. 114/A4
Saint-Germain-en-Laye, Fr. 88/J5
Saint-Germain-lès-Corbeil, Fr. 88/K6
Saint-Germain-sous Doue, Fr. 88/M5
Saint-Germain-sur-Morin, Fr. 88/L5
Saint-Germer-de-Fly, Fr. 110/A5
Saint-Gervais, Fr. 88/H4
Saint-Gervais-les-Bains, Fr. 114/C6
Saint-Ghislain, Belg. 110/C3
Saint-Gilles, Fr. 100/F5
Saint-Gilles-Croix-de-Vie, Fr. 100/C3
Saint-Gingolph, Swi. 114/C5
Saint-Girons, Fr. 100/D5
Saint-Gobain, Fr. 110/C4
Saint Govan's (pt.), Wal, UK 90/B3
Saint-Gratien, Fr. 88/J5
Saint Hedwig, Tx, US 195/U21
Saint Helena (bay), SAfr. 163/C7
Saint Helena (isl.), Austl. 172/F6
Saint Helens, Austl. 173/D4
Saint Helens (pt.), Austl. 173/D4
Saint Helens, Eng, UK 93/F5
Saint Helens (co.), Eng, UK 93/F5
Saint Helens, Or, US 184/C4
Saint Helens (mt.), Wa, US 184/C4
Saint Helier (cap.), Chl, UK 100/B2
Saint-Herblain, Fr. 100/C3
Saint-Hilarion, Fr. 88/H6
Saint-Hippolyte, Fr. 114/C3
Saint-Honoré, Qu, Can. 189/G1
Saint-Hubert, Qu, Can. 189/P6
Saint-Hubert, Belg. 111/E3
Saint-Hyacinthe, Qu, Can. 188/F2
Saint Ignace (isl.), On, Can. 185/L3
Saint Ignace, Mi, US 188/C2
Saint-Imier, Swi. 114/D3
Saint-Isidore-de-Laprairie, Qu, Can. 189/N7
Saint Ives (bay), Eng, UK 90/A6
Saint Ives, Eng, UK 91/F2
Saint Ives, Eng, UK 90/A6
Saint Jacques (int'l arpt.), Fr. 100/C2
Saint-Jacques-le-Mineur, Qu, Can. 189/P7
Saint James, NY, US 197/E2
Saint James (cape), BC, Can. 180/C3
Saint-Jean (riv.), Qu, Can. 189/H1
Saint-Jean (lake), Qu, Can. 139/J4
Saint-Jean-d'Angély, Fr. 100/C4
Saint-Jean-de-la-Ruelle, Fr. 100/D3
Saint-Jean-de-Losne, Fr. 114/B3
Saint-Jean-Port-Joli, Qu, Can. 189/G2
Saint-Jean-sur-Richelieu, Qu, Can. 188/F2
Saint-Jeoire, Fr. 114/C5
Saint-Jérôme, Qu, Can. 189/N6
Saint Joe, La, US 195/Q16
Saint Joe (riv.), Id,Wa, US 186/E4
Saint John, NB, Can. 189/H2
Saint John (isl.), USVI 199/M8
Saint John (riv.), Me, US 189/G2
Saint John The Baptist (parish), La, US 195/P16
Saint Johns, Az, US 186/E4
Saint Johns (riv.), Fl, US 191/H4
Saint John's (cap.), Anti. 199/N8
Saint John's (pt.), NI, UK 92/C3
Saint Johnsbury, Vt, US 189/F2
Saint Jones (riv.), De, US 196/C5
Saint Joseph (riv.), In,Mi, US 188/C3
Saint Joseph (isl.), On, Can. 188/C2
Saint Joseph, La, US 187/K5
Saint Joseph, Mo, US 187/J3
Saint Joseph (lake), On, Can. 180/G3
Saint-Joseph, Reun., Fr. 165/S15
Saint-Juéry, Fr. 100/E5
Saint-Julien, Fr. 114/B3
Saint-Julien-en-Genevois, Fr. 114/C5
Saint-Julien-les-Villas, Fr. 100/F2
Saint-Junien, Fr. 100/D4
Saint-Just-en-Chaussée, Fr. 110/B4
Saint Kilda (isl.), UK 89/P8
Saint Kitts (isl.), StK. 199/J4
Saint Kitts and Nevis (ctry.) 199/N8
Saint-Lambert, Qu, Can. 189/P6
Saint Laurent, Mb, Can. 185/J3
Saint-Laurent (riv.), Qu, Can. 189/G1
Saint-Laurent, Qu, Can. 189/N6
Saint-Laurent-Blangy, Fr. 110/B3
Saint-Laurent-de-Cerdans, Fr. 100/E5
Saint-Laurent du Maroni, FrG. 209/H2
Saint-Laurent-en-Grandvaux, Fr. 114/B4
Saint-Laurent-sur-Saône, Fr. 114/A5
Saint Lawrence, Nf, Can. 189/L2
Saint Lawrence (riv.), Can.,US 188/F2
Saint Lawrence, Pa, US 196/C3
Saint Lawrence (isl.), Ak, US 192/D3
Saint Lawrence (gulf), Can. 189/J1
Saint Lawrence Islands NP, On, Can. 188/E2
Saint-Lazare, Qu, Can. 189/M7
Saint-Léger, Belg. 111/E4
Saint-Léger-en-Yvelines, Fr. 88/H5
Saint-Léger-lès-Domart, Fr. 110/B3
Saint Leonard (mt.), Austl. 173/G5
Saint-Léonard, Qu, Can. 189/N6
Saint-Léonard, Fr. 114/D2
Saint-Leu, Reun., Fr. 165/S15
Saint-Leu-d'Esserent, Fr. 110/B5
Saint-Leu-la-Forêt, Fr. 88/J4
Saint Llorenç del Munt, PN, Sp. 103/K6
Saint-Lô, Fr. 100/C2
Saint Louis, Sk, Can. 185/G2
Saint Louis (riv.), Mn, US 188/A2
Saint-Louis, Sen. 160/A2
Saint-Louis (pol. reg.), Sen. 160/B3
Saint Louis, Mo, US 195/G8
Saint Louis (co.), Mo, US 195/F8
Saint-Louis, Fr. 114/D2
Saint Louis (lake), Qu, Can. 189/N7
Saint-Louis, Reun., Fr. 165/S15
Saint-Louis-de-Gonzague, Qu, Can. 189/N7
Saint-Louis-de-Kent, NB, Can. 189/H2
Saint-Louis du Nord, Haiti 203/H2
Saint-Loup-sur-Semouse, Fr. 114/C2
Saint-Lubin-des-Joncherets, Fr. 100/D2
Saint-Luc, Qu, Can. 189/P7
Saint Lucia (ctry.) 199/N9
Saint Lucia (lake), SAfr. 165/F3
Saint Lucia (cape), SAfr. 165/F3
Saint Lucia (chan.), Mart.,StL. 199/N9
Saint Lucia Estuary, SAfr. 165/F3
Saint-Lucien, Fr. 88/G6
Saint Maarten (isl.), NAnt. 199/N8
Saint Magnus (bay), Sc, UK 89/W13
Saint-Maixent l'École, Fr. 100/C3
Saint Malo, Mb, Can. 185/J3
Saint-Malo, Fr. 100/B2
Saint-Malo, Golfe de (gulf), Fr. 100/B2
Saint-Mandrier-sur-Mer, Fr. 100/F5
Saint-Marc, Haiti 203/H2
Saint-Marc-sur-Richelieu, Qu, Can. 189/P6
Saint-Marcel, Fr. 114/A4
Saint-Mard, Fr. 88/L4
Saint Maries, Id, US 184/D4
Saint Martin (lake), Mb, Can. 185/J3
Saint-Martin (isl.), Guad., Fr. 199/N8
Saint-Martin, Swi. 114/D5
Saint-Martin-Boulogne, Fr. 110/A2
Saint-Martin-d'Ablois, Fr. 110/C6
Saint-Martin-d'Hères, Fr. 100/F4
Saint-Martin-du-Tertre, Fr. 88/K4
Saint-Martin-la-Garenne, Fr. 88/H4
Saint Martinville, La, US 187/K5
Saint Mary (cape), Gam. 160/A3
Saint Mary (peak), Austl. 171/H4
Saint Mary's, Ak, US 192/F3
Saint Marys, Austl. 173/D4
Saint Marys, Ga, US 191/H4
Saint Marys, Pa, US 188/E3
Saint Mary's, On, Can. 188/D3
Saint Mary's (riv.), NS, Can. 189/J2
Saint-Mathieu-de-Beloeil, Qu, Can. 189/N7
Saint Matthew (isl.), Ak, US 192/D3
Saint Matthews, SC, US 191/H3
Saint Matthias Group (isls.), PNG 174/E5
Saint-Maur-des-Fossés, Fr. 88/K5
Saint-Maurice, Swi. 114/D5
Saint-Maurice (riv.), Qu, Can. 139/J4
Saint-Max, Fr. 111/F6
Saint-Maximin-la-Sainte-Baume, Fr. 100/F5
Saint-Memmie, Fr. 111/D6
Saint-Méry, Fr. 88/L6
Saint Michael, Ak, US 192/F3
Saint Michaels, Md, US 196/B6
Saint-Michel (bay), Fr. 100/C2
Saint-Michel, Fr. 111/D4
Saint-Michel-sur-Meurthe, Fr. 114/C1
Saint-Michel-sur-Orge, Fr. 88/J6
Saint-Mihiel, Fr. 111/E6
Saint Monance, Sc, UK 94/D4
Saint-Nabord, Fr. 114/C1
Saint-Nazaire, Fr. 100/B3
Saint Neots, Eng, UK 91/F2
Saint-Nicolas, Belg. 111/E2
Saint-Nicolas-d'Aliermont, Fr. 100/D2
Saint Niklaus, Swi. 114/D5
Saint-Nom-la-Bretèche, Fr. 88/J5
Saint-Omer, Fr. 110/B2
Saint-Omer-en-Chaussée, Fr. 110/A4
Saint-Ouen, Fr. 110/B3
Saint-Ouen-en-Brie, Fr. 88/L6
Saint-Ouen-L'Aumône, Fr. 88/J4
Saint-Pamphile, Qu, Can. 189/G2
Saint-Pascal, Qu, Can. 189/G2
Saint-Pathus, Fr. 88/L4
Saint Paul, Ab, Can. 184/F2
Saint Paul (cape), Gha. 161/F5
Saint Paul (riv.), Libr. 154/C6
Saint Paul, Reun., Fr. 165/S15
Saint Paul, Ak, US 192/D4
Saint Paul (isl.), Ak, US 192/W23
Saint Paul, Ks, US 190/E2
Saint Paul (cap.), Mn, US 185/K4
Saint-Paul-lès-Dax, Fr. 100/C5
Saint Paul Rocks (isl.), Braz. 80/H5
Saint Paul's Church Nat'l Hist. Site, NY, US 197/K8
Saint-Pé-de-Bigorre, Fr. 100/C5
Saint Peter, Mn, US 185/K4
Saint Peter (isl.), Austl. 171/G5
Saint Peter Port (cap.), Chl, UK 100/B2
Saint Peters, Mo, US 195/F8
Saint Petersburg, Fl, US 191/H5
Saint Petersburg, Rus. 119/T7
Saint-Philippe-de-Laprairie, Qu, Can. 189/P7
Saint-Pierre (isl.), StP., Fr. 189/K2
Saint-Pierre, StP., Fr. 189/K2
Saint-Pierre, Mart., Fr. 199/N9
Saint-Pierre, Reun., Fr. 165/S15
Saint Pierre and Miquelon (dpcy.), Fr. 189/K2
Saint-Pierre-des-Corps, Fr. 100/D3
Saint-Pierre-du-Mont, Fr. 100/C5
Saint-Pierre-du-Perray, Fr. 88/K6
Saint-Pierre-en-Faucigny, Fr. 114/C5
Saint Pierre-Jolys, Mb, Can. 185/J3
Saint-Pierre-sur-Dives, Fr. 100/C2
Saint-Point (lake), Fr. 114/C4
Saint-Pol-de-Léon, Fr. 100/B2
Saint-Pol-sur-Mer, Fr. 110/B1
Saint-Pol-sur-Ternoise, Fr. 110/B3
Saint-Pourçain-sur-Sioule, Fr. 100/E3
Saint-Prex, Swi. 114/C5
Saint-Prix, Fr. 88/J4
Saint-Quentin, Fr. 110/C4
Saint-Quentin, Canal de (canal), Fr. 110/C4
Saint-Rambert-en-Bugey, Fr. 114/B6
Saint-Raphaël, Fr. 101/G5
Saint-Rémi, Qu, Can. 189/N7
Saint-Rémy-de-Provence, Fr. 100/F5
Saint-Rémy-lès-Chevreuse, Fr. 88/J5
Saint-Rémy-l'Honoré, Fr. 88/H5
Saint-Roch-de-l'Achigan, Qu, Can. 189/N6
Saint Rose, La, US 195/P17
Saint Sampson's, Chl, UK 100/B2
Saint-Saulve, Fr. 110/C3
Saint-Sauveur, Fr. 114/C2
Saint-Sauveur-des-Monts, Qu, Can. 189/M6
Saint-Sever, Fr. 100/C5
Saint Simons (isl.), Ga, US 191/H4
Saint Simons Island, Ga, US 191/H4
Saint-Souplets, Fr. 88/L4
Saint Stephen, NB, Can. 189/H2
Saint-Sulpice, Fr. 100/D5
Saint Tammany, La, US 195/Q16
Saint Tammany (parish), La, US 195/P16
Saint Thomas, On, Can. 188/D3
Saint Thomas (isl.), USVI 199/H4
Saint-Timothée, Qu, Can. 189/M7
Saint-Trivier-de-Courtes, Fr. 114/B5
Saint-Tropez, Fr. 101/G5
Saint-Urbain-Premier, Qu, Can. 189/N7
Saint-Ursanne, Swi. 114/D3
Saint-Valery-en-Caux, Fr. 100/D2
Saint-Valery-sur-Somme, Fr. 110/A3
Saint-Vallier, Fr. 100/F3
Saint-Vaury, Fr. 100/D3
Saint Vincent (pt.), Austl. 173/C4
Saint Vincent (isl.), StV. 199/N9
Saint Vincent, It. 116/A1
Saint Vincent and the Grenadines (ctry.) 199/N9
Saint-Vincent-de-Tyrosse, Fr. 100/C5
Saint Vincent Passage (chan.), StL.,StV. 199/N9
Saint-Vit, Fr. 114/B3
Saint-Vith, Belg. 111/F3
Saint-Vrain, Fr. 88/K6
Saint Walburg, Sk, Can. 184/F2
Saint-Witz, Fr. 88/K4
Saint-Yrieix-la-Perche, Fr. 100/D4
Sainte-Agathe-des-Monts, Qu, Can. 188/F2
Sainte-Anne-des-Monts, Qu, Can. 189/H1
Sainte-Anne-des-Plaines, Qu, Can. 189/N6
Sainte-Aulde, Fr. 88/M5
Sainte-Croix, Swi. 114/C4
Sainte-Croix-aux-Mines, Fr. 114/D1
Sainte-Geneviève-des-Bois, Fr. 88/K6
Sainte-Julie, Qu, Can. 189/P6
Sainte-Marie, Qu, Can. 189/G2
Sainte-Marie, Mart., Fr. 199/N9
Sainte-Marie-aux-Chênes, Fr. 111/F5
Sainte Marie, Nosy (isl.), Madg. 165/J7
Sainte-Martine, Qu, Can. 189/N7
Sainte-Maxime, Fr. 101/G5
Sainte-Mesme, Fr. 88/H6
Sainte Rose du Lac, Mb, Can. 185/J3
Sainte-Sigolène, Fr. 100/F4
Sainte-Thérèse, Qu, Can. 189/N6
Sainte-Tulle, Fr. 100/F5
Saintes, Fr. 100/C4
Sainthia, India 143/F4
Saipal (peak), Nepal 142/D1
Saipan (isl.), NMar. 174/D3
Saitama (pref.), Japan 133/F2
Saito, Japan 132/B4
Saiwa Swamp NP, Kenya 162/B2
Sajama, Bol. 214/D5
Sajama, PN, Bol. 214/D5
Sajószentpéter, Hun. 99/L4
Sak (riv.), SAfr. 164/C3
Sakado, Japan 135/C2
Sakae, Japan 135/E2
Sakahogi, Japan 135/L5
Sakai, Japan 132/E2
Sakai, Japan 133/F2
Sakai (riv.), Japan 135/C3
Sakai, Japan 135/C1
Sakaide, Japan 132/C3
Sakaigawa, Japan 135/B2
Sakaiminato, Japan 132/C3
Sakakawea (lake), ND, US 185/H3
Sakami (lake), Qu, Can. 139/J3
Sakaraha, Madg. 165/H8
Sakarya (riv.), Turk. 148/B1
Sakarya (prov.), Turk. 107/K5
Sakauchi, Japan 135/K4
Sakawa, Japan 132/C4
Sakay (riv.), Madg. 165/H7
Sakçagöze, Turk. 148/D2
Sakeny (riv.), Madg. 165/H7
Sakété, Ben. 161/F5
Sakha (Yakutiya), Resp., Rus. 123/Q4
Sakhalin (gulf), Rus. 123/Q4
Sakhalin (isl.), Rus. 123/Q4
Sakhalinskaya Oblast, Rus. 123/Q4
Sakhnīn, Isr. 149/G6
Sakht Sar, Iran 146/F1
Şäki, Azer. 121/H4
Sakishima (isl.), Japan 133/G8
Sakmara (riv.), Rus. 145/C2
Sakon Nakhon, Thai. 136/D2
Sakrand, Pak. 147/J3
Sakti, India 142/D4
Saku, Japan 133/F2
Saku, Japan 135/A1
Sakura, Japan 135/E1
Sakura, Japan 135/E2
Sakuragawa, Japan 135/E2
Sakurai, Japan 135/J6
Saky, Ukr. 120/E3
Sakya Monastery, China 143/G1
Säkylä, Fin. 97/K1
Sal (isl.), CpV. 151/K10
Sal (pt.), Hon. 202/E3
Sal (riv.), Rus. 121/G3
Sal Rei, CpV. 151/K10
Šaľa, Slvk. 106/C1
Sala, Swe. 96/G2
Sala Baganza, It. 116/D3
Sala Consilina, It. 104/D2
Salada (lake), Mex. 200/B1
Saladas, Arg. 215/E2
Saladillo, Arg. 216/F2
Saladilio (riv.), Arg. 217/J11
Salado (riv.), Arg. 216/D3
Salado (riv.), Mex. 201/E3
Salado del Norte (riv.), Arg. 205/C5
Salaga, Gha. 161/E4
Şalāḩ Ad Dīn (gov.), Iraq 148/E3
Sălaj (prov.), Rom. 107/F2
Salālah, Oman 146/F5
Salamá, Guat. 202/D3
Salamajärven NP, Fin. 118/E3
Salamanca, Mex. 201/E4
Salamanca, Sp. 102/C2
Salamanca, NY, US 188/E3
Salamat (riv.), Chad 155/J6
Salamatof, Ak, US 192/H3
Salamina, Col. 210/C2
Salamís, Gre. 105/H3
Salamís (isl.), Gre. 105/N9
Salamīyah, Syria 149/E2
Salangen, Nor. 95/F1
Salas, Peru 214/B2
Salas, Sp. 102/B1
Salas de los Infantes, Sp. 102/D1
Salavat, Rus. 121/K1
Salaverry, Peru 214/B3
Salayar (isl.), Indo. 139/F5
Salbris, Fr. 100/E3
Salcantay (peak), Peru 214/C4
Saldaña, Sp. 102/C1
Saldanhabaai (bay), Safr. 164/K10
Saldus, Lat. 97/K3
Sale, Austl. 173/C3
Sale, It. 116/B3
Salé, Mor. 158/A2
Salé (prov.), Mor. 158/A3
Sale, Eng, UK 93/F5
Sale Marasino, It. 116/D1
Salebabu (isl.), Indo. 139/G3
Salekhard, Rus. 122/G3
Salem, Ger. 115/F2
Salem, India 140/C5
Salem, In, US 188/C4
Salem, Mi, US 193/E7
Salem, NH, US 189/G3
Salem, NJ, US 196/C4
Salem (co.), NJ, US 196/C4
Salem (cap.), Or, US 184/C4
Salemi, It. 104/C4
Salentina (pen.), It. 105/F2
Salerno, It. 104/D2
Salerno, Golfo di (gulf), It. 104/D2
Sales (pt.), Eng, UK 91/G2

Saleux, Fr. 110/B4
Salfit, WBnk. 149/G7
Salford, Eng, UK 93/F5
Salford (co.), Eng, UK 93/F5
Salgado Filho (int'l arpt.), Braz. 213/B4
Salgar, Col. 210/B4
Salgesch, Swi. 114/D5
Salgótarján, Hun. 99/K4
Salgueiro, Braz. 212/C3
Salhus, Nor. 96/A1
Salies-de-Béarn, Fr. 100/C5
Salies-du-Salat, Fr. 100/D5
Salīf, Yem. 146/D5
Salihli, Turk. 148/B2
Salihorsk, Bela. 120/C1
Salima, Malw. 163/F3
Salīmah (oasis), Sudan 159/B4
Salina, Ut, US 186/E3
Salina (is.), It. 104/D3
Salina (pt.), Bahm. 203/H1
Salina Cruz, Mex. 202/C2
Salinas, Y, Ca, US 186/B3
Salinas, Braz. 212/B5
Salinas, Ca, US 186/B3
Salinas (cape), Sp. 103/G3
Salinas, Ecu. 210/A5
Salinas de Hidalgo, Mex. 201/E4
Salinas Pueblo Missions Nat'l Mon., NM, US 187/F4
Salinas Y Aguada Blanca, Reserva Nacional, Peru 214/D4
Saline (riv.), Ks, US 190/D2
Saline, It. 117/D6
Saline, Sc, UK
Salinópolis, Braz. 209/J4
Salins-les-Bains, Fr. 114/B4
Salisbury, NC, US 191/H3
Salisbury (plain), Eng, UK 90/D4
Salisbury, Eng, UK 91/E4
Salisbury (isl.), Nun., Can. 139/J2
Salisbury, NY, US 197/L9
Salitre (riv.), Braz. 212/B3
Salitre, Ecu. 210/B5
Salla, Fin. 118/F2
Salladasburg, Pa, US 196/A1
Sallanches, Fr. 114/C6
Salland (phys. reg.), Neth. 108/D4
Sallatouk (pt.), Gui. 160/B3
Sallaumines, Fr. 110/B3
Sallent, Sp. 103/F2
Salliquelló, Arg. 216/E3
Sallisaw, Ok, US 187/J4
Sally (pass), Ire. 92/B5
Salm (riv.), Ger. 111/F3
Salmān Pāk, Iraq 148/F3
Salmās, Iran 148/F2
Salmon (riv.), BC, Can. 184/C2
Salmon, Id, US 184/E4
Salmon (riv.), Id, US 184/E4
Salmon Arm, BC, Can. 184/D3
Salmon Falls (riv.), Id,Nv, US 186/D2
Salmon River (mts.), Id, US 184/E4
Salmon, South Fork (riv.), US 186/C2
Salmtal, Ger. 111/F4
Salò, It. 116/D1
Salo, Fin. 97/K1
Salon, India 142/C2
Salon (riv.), Fr. 98/C5
Salon-de-Provence, Fr. 100/F5
Salonga, PN de la, D.R. Congo 155/K8
Salonta, Rom. 106/E2
Salouël, Fr. 110/B4
Salpausselkä (mts.), Fin. 97/M1
Salpo, Peru 214/B2
Salses-le-Château, Fr. 100/E5
Sal'sk, Rus. 121/G3
Salso (riv.), It. 104/C4
Salsomaggiore Terme, It. 116/C3
Salt (riv.), SAfr. 164/C4
Salt (riv.), Az, US 195/R19
Salt (range), Pak. 144/B3
Salt Cay (isl.), UK 203/J1
Salt Draw (riv.), Tx, US 190/D2
Salt Fork Arkansas (riv.), Ks,Ok, US 187/H3
Salt Fork Red (riv.), Ok,Tx, US 187/G4
Salt Lake (co.), Ut, US 195/J12
Salt Lake City (cap.), Ut, US 195/K12
Salt Meadow NWR, Ct, US 197/F1
Salt, North Fork (riv.), Mo, US 187/J2
Salt River Ind. Res., Az, US 195/S18
Salta, Arg. 215/C1
Saltaire, NY, US 197/E2
Saltash, Eng, UK 90/B6
Saltcoats, Sc, UK 94/B5
Saltdal, Nor. 95/E2
Saltee (isls.), Ire. 89/Q10
Saltfjorden (inlet), Nor. 95/E2
Saltillo, Mex. 201/E3

Salto, Uru. 215/E3
Salto, Braz. 213/C2
Salto da Divisa, Braz. 212/C5
Salto del Guairá, Par. 215/F1
Salto Grande (res.), Arg. 215/E3
Salto Santiago, Reprêsa de (res.), Braz. 213/A3
Salton Sea (lake), Ca, US 186/C4
Saltvik, Fin. 97/J1
Saluda (riv.), SC, US 191/G3
Salug, Phil. 137/D6
Saluggia, It. 116/B2
Salūr, India 140/D4
Salurn (Salorno), It. 115/H5
Salut, Îles du (isls.), FrG. 209/H2
Saluzzo, It. 116/A2
Salvación (bay), Chile 217/B6
Salvador (lake), La, US 195/P17
Salvaleón de Higüey, DRep. 199/H4
Salvaterra de Magos, Port. 102/A3
Salvatierra, Mex. 201/E4
Salvatierra de Miño, Sp. 102/A1
Salween (riv.), Asia 141/G4
Salyan, Azer. 121/J5
Salyersville, Ky, US 188/D4
Salza (riv.), Aus. 99/H5
Salzach (riv.), Ger. 98/G5
Salzano, It. 117/F1
Salzbergen, Ger. 109/E4
Salzburg, Aus. 101/K3
Salzburg (int'l arpt.), Aus.
Salzburg (prov.), Aus. 99/G5
Salzgitter, Ger. 109/H4
Salzhemmendorf, Ger. 109/G4
Salzkotten, Ger. 109/F5
Salzwedel, Ger. 98/F2
Sam Rayburn (res.), Tx, US 190/E4
Sam Sao (mts.), Laos,Viet. 136/C1
Sam Son, Viet. 193/J11
Sama, Sp. 102/C1
Samak (cape), Indo. 138/C4
Samales Group (isls.), Phil. 139/F2
Samālkha, India 144/D5
Samalkot, India 140/D4
Samana, India 144/C4
Samaná (cape), DRep. 199/H4
Samana (isl.), Bahm. 203/H1
Samandağ, Turk. 149/D1
Samani, Japan 134/C2
Samaniego, Col. 210/B4
Samannūd, Egypt 149/B4
Samaqua (riv., Qu, Can. 189/F1
Samar, Jor. 149/D3
Samar (isl.), Phil. 137/E5
Samara (riv.), Rus. 145/B2
Samara (int'l arpt.), Rus.
Samara, Rus. 121/J1
Samarai, PNG 174/E6
Samarate, It. 116/B1
Samaria (reg.), WBnk. 149/G7
Samarinda, Indo. 139/E4
Samarqand, Uzb. 145/E5
Samarqand (pol. reg.), Uzb. 145/E5
Sāmarrā', Iraq 148/E3
Samāstipur, India 143/F4
Samaxi, Azer. 121/J4
Sâmba, India 144/C2
Sambalpur, India 140/D3
Sambao (riv.), Madg. 165/H7
Sambar (cape), Indo. 138/C4
Sambas, Indo. 138/C3
Sambava, Madg. 165/J6
Sambhal, India 142/B1
Sambir, Ukr. 99/M4
Sambor Prei Kuk (ruin), Camb. 136/D3
Samborombón, Arg. 216/D4
Samborombón (bay), Arg. 217/F2
Sambre (riv.), Fr. 81/G4
Sambre à l'Oise, Canal de (canal), Fr. 110/C4
Sambriāl, Pak. 144/C3
Sambu, Japan 135/E2
Samburu Nat'l Rsv., Kenya 162/C2
Samch'ŏk, SKor. 131/E4
Samch'ŏnp'o, SKor. 131/E5
Samedan, Swi. 115/F4
Samer, Fr. 110/A2
Samfya Mission, Zam. 162/A5
Sámi, Gre. 105/G3
Samiria (riv.), Peru 214/C2
Samit (cape), Camb. 136/C4
Samkos (peak), Camb. 136/C3
Sammamish (lake), Wa, US 193/C2
Sammeron, Fr. 88/M5

Samnangjin, SKor. 131/E5
Samnaun, Swi. 115/G4
Samoa (ctry.) 175/H6
Samobor, Cro. 106/B3
Samoëns, Fr. 114/C6
Samoggia (riv.), It. 117/E4
Samokov, Bul. 107/F4
Samora (riv.), Port. 103/Q10
Samora Correia, Port. 103/Q10
Sámos (isl.), Gre. 148/A2
Sámos (isl.), Gre. 148/A2
Samothráki, Gre. 105/J2
Sampacho, Arg. 216/D2
Samper de Calanda, Sp. 103/E2
Sampit (riv.), Indo. 138/D4
Sampit, Indo. 138/D4
Samsø (isl.), Den. 96/D4
Samsø Bælt (chan.), Den. 96/D4
Samson (mt.), Austl. 172/E6
Samsonvale (lake), Austl. 172/E6
Samsun, Turk. 148/D1
Samsun (prov.), Turk. 148/C1
Samther, India 142/B3
Samugheo, It. 104/A3
Samui (isl.), Thai. 141/H6
Samukawa, Japan 135/C3
Samundri, Pak. 144/B4
Samur (riv., Azer.,Rus. 122/E5
Samut Prakan, Thai. 136/C3
Samut Sakhon, Thai. 136/C3
Samut Songkhram, Thai. 136/B3
Samye Monastery, China 143/H1
San (riv.), Camb. 136/D3
San, Mali 160/D3
San (riv.), Pol. 99/M3
San Adrián, Cabo de (cape), Sp. 102/A1
San Agustín (cape), Phil. 137/E6
San Agustín, Col. 210/B4
San Agustín de Guadalix, Sp. 103/N8
San Agustín, Parque Arqeológico, Col. 210/B4
San Ambrosio (isl.), Chile 205/B5
San Andreas (lake), Ca, US 193/J11
San Andres (mts.), NM, US 186/F4
San Andrés (lake), Mex. 202/B1
San Andrés, Col. 210/C3
San Andrés, Col. 203/F3
San Andrés Cuexcontitlán, Mex. 201/Q10
San Andrés de Giles, Arg. 217/J11
San Andrés de Machaca, Bol. 214/D5
San Andrés del Rabanedo, Sp. 102/C1
San Andrés, Isla de (isl.), Col. 198/E5
San Andrés Tuxtla, Mex. 202/C2
San Angelo, Tx, US 190/C4
San Anselmo, Ca, US 193/J11
San Antonio (cape), Arg. 217/F3
San Antonio, Chile 216/N8
San Antonio, Ecu. 210/B4
San Antonio, Mex. 200/C4
San Antonio, Peru 214/B4
San Antonio, Uru. 217/K11
San Antonio, Ven. 211/F2
San Antonio, Tx, US 194/C2
San Antonio (riv.), Tx, US 190/D4
San Antonio Abad, Sp. 103/F3
San Antonio de Areco, Arg. 217/J11
San Antonio de Caparo, Ven. 210/D3
San Antonio del Golfo, Ven. 211/F2
San Antonio del Táchira, Ven. 210/C3
San Antonio Oeste, Arg. 216/D4
San Antonio, Punta (pt.), Mex. 200/B2
San Augustine, Tx, US 190/E4
San Bartolo, Peru 214/B4
San Bartolomé de Tirajana, Canl. 103/X17
San Bartolome Tlaltelulco, Mex. 201/Q10
San Bartolomeo in Bosco, It. 117/E5
San Bartolomeo in Galdo, It. 104/D2
San Bautista, Uru. 217/L11
San Benedetto (range), It. 117/E5
San Benedetto del Tronto, It. 101/K5
San Benedetto in Alpe, It. 117/E5
San Benedetto Po, It. 117/D2
San Benedicto (isl.), Mex. 200/C5

San Bernardo, Chile 216/N8
San Bernardo (pt.), Col. 210/C2
San Bernardino, Ca, US 194/C2
San Bernardino (co.), Ca, US 194/C2
San Bernardino (mts.), Ca, US 194/C2
San Bernardino Nat'l Forest, Ca, US 194/C2
San Blas, Mex. 200/D4
San Blas, Mex. 200/C3
San Blas (cape), Fl, US 191/G4
San Bonifacio, It. 117/E2
San Borja, Bol. 208/E6
San Bruno, Mex. 200/B3
San Bruno, Ca, US 193/K11
San Buenaventura, Mex. 201/E3
San Buenaventura (Ventura), Ca, US 194/A2
San Candido (Innichen), It. 101/K3
San Carlos, Chile 216/C3
San Carlos, Mex. 201/E2
San Carlos, Mex. 201/F3
San Carlos, Nic. 203/E4
San Carlos, Pan. 210/B2
San Carlos, Phil. 137/D4
San Carlos, Uru. 217/G2
San Carlos, Ven. 210/D2
San Carlos (lake), Az, US 186/E4
San Carlos, Ca, US 193/K11
San Carlos de Bariloche, Arg. 216/C4
San Carlos de Bariloche (int'l arpt.), Arg. 216/C4
San Carlos de Río Negro, Ven. 211/E4
San Carlos del Zulia, Ven. 210/D2
San Casciano in Val di Pesa, It. 117/E5
San Cataldo, It. 105/F2
San Cayetano, Arg. 216/F3
San Cesario sul Panaro, It. 117/E3
San Ciro de Acosta, Mex. 201/F4
San Clemente (isl.), Ca, US 186/C4
San Clemente, Ca, US 194/C4
San Clemente, Sp. 102/D3
San Clemente del Tuyú, Arg. 217/F3
San Colombano al Lambro, It. 116/C2
San Cristóbal, Arg. 215/D3
San Cristóbal (isl.), Sol. 174/F6
San Cristóbal (vol.), Nic. 202/E3
San Cristóbal, Cuba 203/F1
San Cristóbal, Ven. 210/C3
San Cristóbal de las Casas, Mex. 202/C2
San Cristobal Wash (riv.), Az, US 200/B1
San Damiano d'Asti, It. 116/B3
San Diego (cape), Arg. 217/D7
San Diego, Ca, US 194/C5
San Diego (aqueduct), Ca, US 194/C4
San Diego (bay), Ca, US 194/C5
San Diego (co.), Ca, US 194/C4
San Diego, Tx, US 190/D5
San Diego International-Lindbergh Field (int'l arpt.), Ca, US 194/C5
San Diego Naval Station, Ca, US 194/C5
San Diego Wild Animal Park, Ca, US 194/C4
San Diego Zoo, Ca, US 194/C5
San Diequito (riv.), Ca, US 194/C5
San Dimas, Ca, US 194/C2
San Donà di Piave, It. 117/F1
San Donnino, It. 117/E5
San Dorligo della Valle, It. 117/G1
San Esteban de Gormaz, Sp. 102/D2
San Felice Circeo, It. 104/C2
San Felice del Benaco, It. 116/D1
San Felice sul Panaro, It. 117/E3
San Felipe, Mex. 200/B2
San Felipe, Ven. 210/D2
San Felipe, Chile 216/N8
San Felipe de Puerto Plata, DRep. 199/G4
San Felipe de Vichayal, Peru 214/A2
San Felipe Jalapa de Díaz, Mex. 201/F5
San Felipe Torres Mochas, Mex. 201/E4
San Felix (isl.), Chile 205/A5
San Fernando, Arg. 217/J11
San Fernando, Chile 216/C2
San Fernando (riv.), Mex. 190/D5

San Fernando, Phil. 137/D4
San Fernando, Phil. 137/D4
San Fernando, Sp. 102/B4
San Fernando, Trin. 211/F2
San Fernando, Ca, US 194/C2
San Fernando (valley), Ca, US 194/B2
San Fernando de Apure, Ven. 211/E3
San Fernando de Atabapo, Ven. 211/E4
San Fernando de Henares, Sp. 103/N9
San Fernando de Presas, Ca, US 193/K11
San Fior di Sopra, It. 117/F1
San Francesco al Campo, It. 116/A2
San Francisco, Arg. 215/D3
San Francisco, Col. 210/C3
San Francisco, ESal. 202/D3
San Francisco, Ven. 210/D2
San Francisco (riv.), Az,NM, US 186/E4
San Francisco, Ca, US 186/B3
San Francisco (co.), Ca, US 193/K11
San Francisco (int'l arpt.), Ca, US 193/K11
San Francisco Acuautla, Mex. 201/R10
San Francisco Bay NWR, Ca, US 193/K11
San Francisco, Cabo de (cape), Ecu. 210/A4
San Francisco Chimalpa, Mex. 201/Q10
San Francisco de la Paz, Hon. 202/E3
San Francisco de Macorís, DRep. 199/G4
San Francisco de Mostazal, Chile 216/N8
San Francisco del Mezquital, Mex. 200/D4
San Francisco del Monte de Oro, Arg. 216/D2
San Francisco del Oro, Mex. 200/D3
San Francisco del Rincón, Mex. 198/B4
San Francisco Telixtlahuaca, Mex. 202/B2
San Fratello, It. 104/D3
San Gabriel (riv.), Ca, US 194/C2
San Gabriel (pt.), Mex. 200/B2
San Gabriel (res.), Mex. 201/E3
San Gabriel, Ecu. 210/B4
San Gavino Monreale, It. 104/A3
San Germán, Cuba 203/G1
San Germano Vercellese, It. 116/B2
San Gil, Col. 210/C3
San Gimignano, It. 117/E6
San Giorgio delle Pertiche, It. 117/E1
San Giorgio di Piano, It. 116/B3
San Giorgio Ionico, It. 105/F2
San Giorgio Piacentino, It. 116/C3
San Giovanni al Natisone, It. 117/G1
San Giovanni Bianco, It. 116/C1
San Giovanni Gemini, It. 104/C4
San Giovanni in Croce, It. 116/D2
San Giovanni in Fiore, It. 104/E3
San Giovanni in Marignano, It. 117/F5
San Giovanni in Persiceto, It. 117/E3
San Giovanni Lupatoto, It. 117/E2
San Giovanni Valdarno, It. 117/E5
San Giuliano, It. 117/E5
San Giuliano Terme, It. 116/D5
San Giustino, It. 117/F5
San Giusto Canavese, It. 116/A2
San Gorgonio (mtn.), Ca, US 186/C4
San Gottardo, Passo del (pass), Swi. 115/E4
San Gregorio, Arg. 216/E2
San Gregorio, Uru. 217/L10
San Hipólito Punta (pt.), Mex. 200/B3
San Ignacio, Belz. 202/D2
San Ignacio, Bol. 208/F7
San Ignacio, Chile 216/B3
San Ignacio, Mex. 200/B3
San Ignacio, Mex. 201/E4
San Ignacio, Peru 214/B2
San Ignacio, Peru 214/B2
San Ildefonso, Sp. 102/D2
San Isidro, Nic. 202/E3

San Isidro, CR 203/F4
San Jacinto, Col. 210/C2
San Jacinto, Uru. 217/L11
San Javier, Chile 216/C2
San Javier, Sp. 103/E4
San Javier, Uru. 217/J10
San Jerónimo, Mex. 200/E3
San Joaquín, Bol. 208/F6
San Joaquin (riv.), Ca, US 186/C3
San Joaquín, Col. 210/C3
San Joaquin (hills), Ca, US 194/G8
San Joaquin (co.), Ca, US 193/L11
San Joaquín (peak), Ecu. 214/F7
San Jorge (cape), Arg. 216/D5
San Jorge (gulf), Arg. 216/D5
San Jorge (riv.), Col. 210/C3
San Jorge (bay), Mex. 200/B2
San Jorge, Golfo di (gulf), Sp. 103/F2
San José, Arg. 216/D4
San José (cap.), CR 203/E4
San José (isl.), Mex. 200/C3
San José, Peru 214/D4
San Jose, Phil. 137/D4
San Jose, Phil. 137/D5
San José, Sp. 103/F3
San José (riv.), Uru. 217/K11
San José (dept.), Uru. 217/K11
San Jose, Ca, US 186/B3
San Jose (hills), Ca, US 194/G7
San Jose (int'l arpt.), Ca, US 186/B3
San Jose de Buenavista, Phil. 137/D5
San José de Chiquitos, Bol. 208/F7
San José de Guanipa, Ven. 211/E2
San José de Guaribe, Ven. 211/E2
San José de Jáchal, Arg. 215/C3
San José de la Esquina, Arg. 216/E2
San Jose de Los Molinos, Peru 214/C4
San José de los Remates, Nic. 202/E3
San José de Maipo, Chile 216/N8
San José de Mayo, Uru. 217/K11
San José de Raíces, Mex. 201/E3
San José de Seque, Ven. 210/D2
San José del Cabo, Mex. 200/C3
San José del Guaviare, Col. 210/C4
San José Iturbide, Mex. 201/E4
San José Viejo, Mex. 200/C4
San Juan, Arg. 215/C3
San Juan (riv.), Arg. 215/C3
San Juan, Peru 214/C4
San Juan (basin), NM, US 190/A2
San Juan (riv.), NM, US 190/B2
San Juan, Phil. 137/D5
San Juan, PR 199/M8
San Juan (pt.), ESal. 202/D3
San Juan (mts.), Co, US 186/F3
San Juan (cape), Arg. 217/E7
San Juan Abajo, Mex. 200/D4
San Juan Bautista, Par. 215/E2
San Juan Bautista Coixtlahuaca, Mex. 202/B2
San Juan Bautista Tuxtepec, Mex. 202/B2
San Juan Bautista Valle Nacional, Mex. 202/B2
San Juan Capistrano, Ca, US 194/C3
San Juan de Alicante, Sp. 103/E3
San Juan de Aznalfarache, Sp. 102/B4
San Juan de la Costa, Mex. 200/C3
San Juan de Lima (pt.), Mex. 200/E5
San Juan de los Cayos, Ven. 210/D2
San Juan de los Lagos, Mex. 200/E4
San Juan de los Morros, Ven. 210/D2
San Juan del Norte, Nic. 203/F4
San Juan del Río, Mex. 201/F4
San Juan del Río, Mex. 200/D3
San Juan Guichicovi, Mex. 202/C2
San Juan Hot Springs, Ca, US 194/C3
San Juan Ixcaquixtla, Mex. 201/M8
San Juan Juquila Mixes, Mex. 202/C2

San Juan Nepomuceno, Col. 210/C2
San Juanico, Mex. 200/B3
San Juanico Punta (pt.), Mex. 200/B3
San Junito, Mex. 200/D2
San Justo, Arg. 215/D3
San Lázaro (cape), Mex. 200/B3
San Lazzaro, It. 117/E4
San Leandro, Ca, US 193/K11
San Leandro, Ca, US 193/K11
San Lorenzo (cape), Ecu. 208/B4
San Lorenzo, Bol. 208/E6
San Lorenzo (peak), Chile 217/B5
San Lorenzo, Ecu. 210/B4
San Lorenzo, Hon. 202/E3
San Lorenzo, Nic. 202/E3
San Lorenzo, Peru 214/D3
San Lorenzo (riv.), Mex. 200/D3
San Lorenzo, Arg. 217/J11
San Lorenzo al Mare, It. 116/A5
San Lorenzo de El Escorial, Sp. 103/M8
San Lorenzo in Campo, It. 117/F5
San Lucas, Nic. 202/E3
San Lucas, Cabo (cape), Mex. 200/C4
San Luís, Arg. 216/D2
San Luis, Cuba 203/H1
San Luís, Guat. 202/D2
San Luis, Peru 214/B4
San Luis, Ven. 210/D2
San Luis (valley), Co, US 190/B2
San Luis Acatlán, Mex. 202/B2
San Luis al Medio, Uru. 217/G2
San Luis de la Paz, Mex. 201/E4
San Luis Obispo, Ca, US 186/B4
San Luis Potosí (state), Mex. 198/A3
San Luis Potosí, Mex. 201/E4
San Luis Rey (riv.), Ca, US 194/C4
San Luis Rey, Ca, US 194/C4
San Luis Río Colorado, Mex. 200/B1
San Luís, Sierra de (mts.), Arg. 216/D2
San Manuel, Az, US 186/E4
San Marcello Pistoiese, It. 117/D4
San Marcos, Peru 214/B3
San Marcos, Peru 214/B2
San Marcos, Tx, US 187/H5
San Marcos, Mex. 198/B4
San Marcos, Guat. 202/D3
San Marcos, CR 203/E4
San Maria di Porto Novo, It. 117/G5
San Mariano, Phil. 137/D3
San Marino (ctry.) 117/F5
San Marino (cap.), SMar. 117/F5
San Marino, Ca, US 194/F7
San Martín (riv.), Bol. 208/F6
San Martín (dept.), Peru 214/B2
San Martín, Mex. 201/R9
San Martín, Col. 210/C3
San Martín (lake), Arg. 217/B6
San Martín, Arg. 216/C2
San Martín Cuautlalpan, Mex. 201/R10
San Martín de los Andes, Arg. 216/C4
San Martín de Valdeiglesias, Sp. 102/C2
San Martino Buon Albergo, It. 117/E2
San Martino-di-Lota, Fr. 104/A1
San Martino di Lupari, It. 117/E1
San Martino di Venezze, It. 117/E2
San Martino in Passiria (Sankt Martin in Passieir), It. 115/H4
San Martino in Rio, It. 117/D3
San Martino in Strada, It. 116/C2
San Martino Siccomario, It. 116/C2
San Mateo, Peru 214/B3
San Mateo, Sp. 103/F2
San Mateo, Mex. 201/Q10
San Mateo, Ca, US 186/B3
San Mateo (co.), Ca, US 193/K12
San Mateo Atarasquillo, Mex. 201/Q10
San Mateo Xoloc, Mex. 201/Q10
San Matías, Bol. 208/G7
San Matías, Golfo (gulf), Arg. 216/D4

San Maurizio d'Opaglio, It. 116/B1
San Mauro Pascoli, It. 117/F4
San Mauro Torinese, It. 116/A2
San Michele al Tagliamento, It. 117/F1
San Miguel (riv.), Bol. 208/F6
San Miguel, Peru 214/B4
San Miguel, Peru 214/C4
San Miguel, Mex. 200/E2
San Miguel, ESal. 202/D3
San Miguel (gulf), Pan. 203/G4
San Miguel (riv.), Col. 210/B4
San Miguel Coatlincham, Mex. 201/R10
San Miguel de Allende, Mex. 201/E4
San Miguel de los Bancos, Ecu. 210/B4
San Miguel de Tucumán, Arg. 215/C2
San Miguel del Monte, Arg. 217/J11
San Miguel Tlaixpan, Mex. 201/R9
San Miguel Totolapan, Mex. 198/A4
San Miniato, It. 117/D5
San Nicolas (isl.), Ca, US 186/B4
San Nicolás de los Arroyos, Arg. 216/E2
San Nicolò, It. 116/C2
San Onofre (mtn.), Ca, US 194/C4
San Onofre, Ca, US 194/C4
San Onofre, Col. 210/C2
San Pablo, Chile 216/B4
San Pablo, Col. 210/B4
San Pablo, Peru 214/B2
San Pablo, Phil. 137/D5
San Pablo (int'l arpt.), Sp. 102/C4
San Pablo, Ven. 211/E2
San Pablo, Ca, US 193/K11
San Pablo (res.), Ca, US 193/K11
San Pablo Bay NWR, Ca, US 193/K10
San Pablo de las Salinas, Mex. 201/Q9
San Pablo Huixtepec, Mex. 202/B2
San Pablo, It. 116/D2
San Pawl il-Baħar, Malta 104/L7
San Pedro, Arg. 217/J10
San Pedro, Arg. 215/D1
San Pedro, Belz. 202/E2
San Pedro, Chile 216/N8
San Pedro (vol.), Chile 215/C1
San Pedro, C.d'Iv. 160/D5
San Pedro (riv.), Guat. 202/D2
San Pedro, Mex. 200/E3
San Pedro (riv.), Mex. 200/D3
San Pedro Arriba, Mex. 201/Q10
San Pedro Carchá, Guat. 202/D2
San Pedro de Cajas, Peru 214/C3
San Pedro de la Cueva, Mex. 200/C2
San Pedro de Lloc, Peru 214/B2
San Pedro de Lóvago, Nic. 203/E3
San Pedro de Macorís, DRep. 199/H4
San Pedro del Pinatar, Sp. 103/E4
San Pedro Huamelula, Mex. 202/C2
San Pedro Pochutla, Mex. 202/B3
San Pedro, Sierra de (mts.), Sp. 102/B3
San Pedro Sula, Hon. 202/D2
San Pedro Tapanatepec, Mex. 202/C2
San Pedro Totoltepec, Mex. 201/Q10
San Pellegrino Terme, It. 116/C1
San Piero a Sieve, It. 117/E5
San Piero in Bagno, It. 117/E5
San Pietro (isl.), It. 104/A3
San Pietro in Casale, It. 117/E3
San Pietro in Gù, It. 117/E1
San Pietro in Vincoli, It. 117/F4
San Pietro in Volta, It. 117/F2
San Polo d'Enza, It. 116/D3
San Polo di Piave, It. 117/E1
San Possidonio, It. 117/E3
San Quentin, Ca, US 193/K11
San Quintín (cape), Mex. 200/B2
San Quintín, Mex. 200/B2
San Rafael (riv.), Ut, US 186/E3
San Rafael, Arg. 216/C2
San Rafael, Mex. 201/N6
San Rafael, Peru 214/B3
San Rafael, Peru 214/C3

San Rafael (hills), Ca, US 194/F7
San Rafael del Moján, Ven. 210/D2
San Ramón, CR 203/E4
San Ramón, Peru 214/C3
San Ramón, Uru. 217/L11
San Ramon, Ca, US 193/L11
San Ramón de la Nueva Orán, Arg. 215/D1
San Remo, It. 116/A5
San Rocco al Porto, It. 116/C2
San Romano, It. 117/D5
San Roque, Sp. 102/C4
San Rosendo, Chile 216/B3
San Saba (riv.), Tx, US 187/H5
San Salvador (cap.), ESal. 202/D3
San Salvador (riv.), Uru. 217/J10
San Salvador de Jujuy, Arg. 215/C1
San Salvador el Seco, Mex. 201/M7
San Salvador, Isla (isl.), Bahm. 199/G3
San Salvador (Watling) (isl.), Bahm. 199/G3
San Salvatore Monferrato, It. 116/B3
San Salvo, It. 104/D1
San Sebastián, Sp. 102/E1
San Sebastián de los Reyes, Sp. 103/N8
San Sebastián de Yalí, Nic. 202/E3
San Sebastiano, It. 116/D1
San Secondo Parmense, It. 116/D3
San Severo, It. 104/D2
San Telmo (pt.), Mex. 200/E5
San Timoteo, Ven. 210/D2
San Valentín (peak), Chile 216/B5
San Valentino, It. 117/G1
San Vicente (res.), Ca, US 194/D5
San Vicente, Mex. 200/A2
San Vicente, ESal. 202/D3
San Vicente, Chile 216/C2
San Vicente de Alcántara, Sp. 102/B3
San Vicente de Cañete, Peru 214/B4
San Vicente del Caguán, Col. 210/C4
San Vicente del Raspeig, Sp. 103/E3
San Vicino (peak), It. 101/K5
San Vincenzo, It. 101/J5
San Vito (cape), It. 104/C3
San Vito, CR 203/F4
San Vito al Tagliamento, It. 117/F1
San Ysidro, Ca, US 194/C5
Saña, Peru 214/B2
Sana (riv.), Bosn. 106/C3
Şan'ā' (Sanaa) (cap.), Yem. 146/D5
Sanae IV, SAfr., Ant. 218/Z
Sanaga (riv.), Camr. 151/C4
Sanak (isl.), Ak, US 192/F5
Sanana (isl.), Indo. 139/G4
Sanandaj, Iran 146/E1
Sananduva, Braz. 213/B3
Sanaur, India 144/D4
Sānāwad, India 147/L4
Sanborn, NY, US 189/S9
Sanch'ŏng, SKor. 131/D5
Sancti Spíritu, Arg. 216/E2
Sancti Spíritus, Cuba 203/G1
Sand (riv.), Ab, Can. 184/F2
Sand (riv.), SAfr. 164/D3
Sand (pt.), Eng, UK 90/D4
Sand (hills), Ne, US 187/G2
Sand, Nor. 96/B2
Sand am Main, Ger. 112/D3
Sand Point, Ak, US 192/F4
Sanda, Japan 135/H6
Sanda (isl.), Sc, UK 92/C1
Sandakan, Malay. 139/E2
Sandane, Nor. 95/C3
Sandanski, Bul. 107/F5
Sandarne, Swe. 96/G1
Sanday (isl.), Sc, UK 89/V14
Sandbach, Eng, UK 93/F5
Sandberg, Ger. 112/C2
Sande, Ger. 109/F1
Sandefjord, Nor. 96/D2
Sandersville, Ga, US 191/H3
Sandhurst, Eng, UK 91/F4
Sandia, Peru 214/D4
Sandıklı, Turk. 148/B2
Sandīla, India 142/C2
Sandino, Cuba 198/E3
Sandnes, Nor. 96/A2
Sandomierz, Pol. 99/L3
Sandoná, Col. 210/B4
Sándorfalva, Hun. 106/E2
Sandougou (riv.), Sen. 160/B3
Sandover (riv.), Austl. 171/G2
Sandoway, Myan. 141/F4
Sandpoint, Id, US 184/D3
Sandrakatsy, Madg. 165/J7
Sandrigo, It. 117/E1
Sands (pt.), NY, US 197/L8
Sands Point, NY, US 197/L8
Sandspit, BC, Can. 192/M5
Sandstedt, Ger. 109/F2
Sandstone, Austl. 170/C3
Sandu Shuizu Zizhixian, China 141/J2
Sandusky, Mi, US 188/D3
Sandusky, Oh, US 188/D3
Sandvika, Nor. 96/D2
Sandviken, Swe. 96/G1
Sandweiler, Lux. 111/F4
Sandwell (co.), Eng, UK 90/D2
Sandwich (cape), Austl. 172/B2
Sandwich, Eng, UK 91/H4
Sandwīp (isl.), Bang. 143/H4
Sandy, Ut, US 195/K12
Sandy (cape), Austl. 172/D4
Sandy (lake), On, Can. 180/G3
Sandy (pt.), RI, US 197/G1
Sandy Bay, Sk, Can. 185/H2
Sandy Hook (bay), NJ, US 196/D3
Sandy Hook (bar), NJ, US 197/J10
Sandy Hook Lighthouse, NJ, US 197/J10
Sandy Springs, Ga, US 191/G3
Sanem, Lux. 111/E4
Sånfjällets NP, Swe. 95/E3
Sanford (mt.), Ak, US 192/K3
Sanford, Me, US 189/G3
Sanford, NC, US 191/J3
Sanford, Fl, US 191/H4
Sangamner, India 147/K5
Sangamon (riv.), Il, US 187/K3
Sangān (mtn.), Afg. 147/H2
Sangaria, India 144/C5
Sangatte, Fr. 110/A2
Sangay (vol.), Ecu. 210/B5
Sangay, PN, Ecu. 208/C4
Sangenjo, Sp. 102/A1
Sanggan (riv.), China 130/C2
Sanggau, Indo. 138/D3
Sanggou (bay), China 131/B4
Sangha (riv.), Congo 154/J7
Sangihe (isl.), Indo. 139/G3
Sangihe (isls.), Phil. 125/M9
Sangju, SKor. 131/E4
Sangkulirang, Indo. 139/E3
Sāngla, Pak. 144/B4
Sāngli, India 147/K5
Sangmélima, Camr. 154/H7
Sangō, Japan 135/J6
Sangre de Cristo (mts.), US 187/F3
Sangre Grande, Trin. 211/F2
Sangri, China 143/J1
Sangro (riv.), It. 104/D2
Sangrūr, India 144/C4
Sangster (int'l arpt.), Jam. 203/G2
Sangue, Rio do (riv.), Braz. 208/G6
Sangüesa, Sp. 102/E1
Sanguie (prov.), Burk. 161/E4
Sanguinetto, It. 117/E2
Sangzhi, China 137/B2
Sanhe, China 130/H7
Sani (pass), Les. 164/E3
Sāni Bheri (riv.), Nepal 142/D1
San'in Kaigin NP, Japan 132/D3
Saniquellie, Libr. 160/C5
Sanjō, Japan 133/F2
Sankanbiriwa (peak), SLeo. 160/C4
Sankh (riv.), India 143/E4
Sankoroni (riv.), Gui. 160/C4
Sankosh (riv.), India 143/G2
Sankt Aegyd am Neuwalde, Aus. 101/L3
Sankt Agatha, Aus. 113/G6
Sankt Andrä, Aus. 101/L3
Sankt Andrä-Wördern, Aus. 107/N7
Sankt Andreasberg, Ger. 109/H5
Sankt Anton am Arlberg, Aus. 115/G3
Sankt Augustin, Ger. 111/G2
Sankt Blasien, Ger. 114/E2
Sankt Florian am Inn, Aus. 113/G6
Sankt Gallen, Swi. 115/F3
Sankt Gallenkirch, Aus. 115/F3
Sankt Georgen bei Salzburg, Aus. 113/F7
Sankt Georgen im Attergau, Aus. 113/G7
Sankt Georgen im Schwarzwald, Ger. 115/E1
Sankt Goar, Ger. 111/G3
Sankt Goarshausen, Ger. 111/G3
Sankt Ingbert, Ger. 111/G5
Sankt Johann im Pongau, Aus. 101/K3
Sankt Johann in Tirol, Aus. 101/K3
Sankt Leonhard im Pitztal, Aus. 115/G3
Sankt Leonhard in Passeier (San Leonardo in Passiria), It. 115/H4
Sankt Marien, Aus. 113/H6
Sankt Martin im Mühlkreis, Aus. 113/H6
Sankt Michael in Obersteiermark, Aus. 101/L3
Sankt Moritz, Swi. 115/F5
Sankt Oswald bei Freistadt, Aus. 113/H5
Sankt Pantaleon, Aus. 113/F6
Sankt Peter am Hart, Aus. 113/G6
Sankt Peter in der Au, Aus. 113/H6
Sankt Peter-Ording, Ger. 96/C4
Sankt Pölten, Aus. 99/H4
Sankt Stephan, Swi. 114/D4
Sankt Ulrich bei Steyr, Aus. 113/H6
Sankt Valentin, Aus. 113/H6
Sankt Veit, Aus. 106/B1
Sankt Veit an der Glan, Aus. 101/L3
Sankt Wendel, Ger. 111/G5
Sankt Wolfgang, Ger. 113/F6
Sanlúcar de Barrameda, Sp. 102/B4
Sanmatenga (prov.), Burk. 161/E3
Sanmen, China 137/D2
Sanmenxia, China 130/B4
Sanming, China 137/C2
Sannan, Japan 135/H5
Sannazzaro de'Burgondi, It. 116/B2
Sannicandro Garganico, It. 104/D2
Sannikova (str.), Rus. 123/P2
San'nohe, Japan 134/B3
Sannois, Fr. 88/J5
Sano, Japan 133/F2
Sanok, Pol. 99/M4
Sanquhar, Sc, UK 94/C6
Sanquianga, PN, Col. 208/C3
Sans Bois (mts.), Ok, US 190/E3
Sansepolcro, It. 117/F5
Sanshui, China 137/B3
Sant Adrià de Besòs, Sp. 103/L7
Sant Boi de Llobregat, Sp. 103/L7
Sant Carles de la Ràpita, Sp. 103/F2
Sant Celoni, Sp. 103/L6
Sant Cugat del Vallès, Sp. 103/L7
Sant Feliu de Guíxols, Sp. 103/G2
Sant Feliu de Llobregat, Sp. 103/L7
Sant Julia, And. 100/D5
Sant Pere de Ribes, Sp. 103/K7
Sant Sadurní d'Anoia, Sp. 103/K7
Sant Vicenç de Castellet, Sp. 103/K6
Sant Vicenç dels Horts, Sp. 103/L7
Santa (riv.), Peru 214/B3
Santa, Peru 214/B3
Santa Ana, Bol. 208/E6
Santa Ana, Ecu. 210/A5
Santa Ana, ESal. 202/D3
Santa Ana, Hon. 202/E3
Santa Ana (vol.), ESal. 202/D3
Santa Ana, Mex. 200/C2
Santa Ana, Ca, US 194/G8
Santa Ana (riv.), Ca, US 194/C3
Santa Ana (mts.), Ca, US 194/C3
Santa Ana, Ven. 210/C3
Santa Ana, Ven. 210/D2
Santa Ana del Alto Beni, Bol. 208/E7
Santa Anna, Tx, US 187/H5
Santa Bárbara, Braz. 213/D1
Santa Bárbara, Chile 216/B3
Santa Bárbara, Hon. 202/D3
Santa Bárbara, Mex. 200/D3
Santa Barbara, Ca, US 194/A2
Santa Barbara (co.), Ca, US 194/A1
Santa Bárbara, Ven. 210/D3
Santa Bárbara, Ven. 210/D2
Santa Bárbara d'Oeste, Braz. 213/C2
Santa Barbara Mountains Nat'l Rec. Area, Ca, US 194/E7
Santa Catalina, Phil. 137/D6
Santa Catalina, Ven. 210/D3
Santa Catalina, Pan. 203/F4
Santa Catalina (isl.), CA, US 186/C4
Santa Catalina, Gulf of (gulf), Ca, US 186/C4
Santa Catarina (state), Braz. 213/B3
Santa Catarina, Mex. 201/E3
Santa Catarina, Ilha de (isl.), Braz. 215/G2
Santa Cecília, Braz. 213/B3
Santa Clara, Cuba 203/G1
Santa Clara, Mex. 200/E3
Santa Clara, Ven. 211/E2
Santa Clara, Ca, US 193/L12
Santa Clara (co.), Ca, US 193/L12
Santa Clara, Barragem de (res.), Port. 102/A4
Santa Clara de Olimar, Uru. 217/G2
Santa Clarita, Ca, US 194/B2
Santa Clotilde, Peru 210/C5
Santa Coloma de Farners, Sp. 103/G2
Santa Coloma de Gramanet, Sp. 103/L7
Santa Comba, Sp. 102/A1
Santa Croce di Magliano, It. 104/D2
Santa Croce sull'Arno, It. 117/D5
Santa Cruz (riv.), Az, US 187/E5
Santa Cruz, Braz. 212/C2
Santa Cruz, Peru 214/C2
Santa Cruz, Mex. 200/C2
Santa Cruz, Phil. 137/E6
Santa Cruz, Phil. 137/D5
Santa Cruz, Ca, US 186/B3
Santa Cruz, Phil. 137/D5
Santa Cruz (isls.), Sol. 174/F6
Santa Cruz (riv.), Arg. 217/C6
Santa Cruz (mts.), Guat. 202/D3
Santa Cruz, CR 202/E4
Santa Cruz, Chile 216/C2
Santa Cruz (prov.), Arg. 216/C5
Santa Cruz (isl.), Ecu. 214/E7
Santa Cruz da Graciosa, Azor., Port. 103/S12
Santa Cruz da Vitória, Braz. 212/C4
Santa Cruz das Flores, Azor., Port. 103/R12
Santa Cruz de Bucaral, Ven. 210/D2
Santa Cruz de El Seibo, DRep. 199/H4
Santa Cruz de la Palma, Sp. 156/A3
Santa Cruz de la Sierra, Bol. 208/F7
Santa Cruz de la Zarza, Sp. 102/D3
Santa Cruz de Mudela, Sp. 102/D3
Santa Cruz de Orinoco, Ven. 211/E2
Santa Cruz de Tenerife, Sp. 156/A3
Santa Cruz del Quiché, Guat. 202/D3
Santa Cruz del Sur, Cuba 203/G1
Santa Cruz do Capibaribe, Braz. 212/C2
Santa Cruz do Piauí, Braz. 212/B2
Santa Cruz do Rio Pardo, Braz. 213/B2
Santa Cruz do Sul, Braz. 213/A4
Santa Cruz Island (isl.), Ca, US 186/C4
Santa Elena, Peru 214/C2
Santa Elena (bay), CR 202/E4
Santa Elena, Hon. 202/E3
Santa Elena (cape), CR 202/E4
Santa Elena, Ecu. 210/A5
Santa Elena (peak), Arg. 216/D5
Santa Elena de Uairén, Ven. 211/F3
Santa Eugenia de Ribeira, Sp. 102/A1
Santa Eulalia del Río, Sp. 103/F3
Santa Fe, Arg. 215/D3
Santa Fe (cap.), NM, US 187/F4
Santa Fe (riv.), Fl, US 191/H4
Santa Fé, Sp. 102/D4
Santa Fe, Cuba 203/F1
Santa Fé do Sul, Braz. 213/B2
Santa Fe Springs, Ca, US 194/F8
Santa Felicia (dam), Ca, US 194/B2
Santa Filomena, Braz. 212/A3
Santa Giustina (lake), It. 115/H5
Santa Helena, Braz. 212/A1
Santa Helena de Goiás, Braz. 213/B1
Santa Inés (isl.), Chile 215/B7
Santa Inês, Braz. 212/C4
Santa Inês, Braz. 212/A1
Santa Isabel, Braz. 213/G8
Santa Isabel, Ecu. 214/B1
Santa Isabel (isl.), Sol. 174/E5
Santa Isabel (riv.), Guat. 202/D2
Santa Isabel, Arg. 216/D3
Santa Isabel, Arg. 216/E2
Santa Isabel de Sihuas, Peru 214/C5
Santa Isabel, Pico de (peak), EqG. 154/G7
Santa Juliana, Braz. 213/C1
Santa Lucía, Canl. 103/X17
Santa Lucía, Ecu. 210/B5
Santa Lucía, Peru 214/D4
Santa Lucía, Uru. 217/K11
Santa Lucía, Ven. 210/D2
Santa Lucia di Piave, It. 117/F1
Santa Luz, Braz. 212/C3
Santa Luzia, Braz. 212/A1
Santa Luzia, Braz. 213/D1
Santa Luzia, Braz. 212/C2
Santa Luzia (isl.), CpV. 151/J10
Santa Magdalena (isl.), Mex. 200/B3
Santa Magdalena, Arg. 216/E2
Santa Margarita (isl.), Mex. 200/B3
Santa Margarita (riv.), Ca, US 194/C4
Santa Margherita Ligure, It. 116/C4
Santa Maria, Braz. 215/F2
Santa Maria, Ca, US 186/B4
Santa Maria (riv.), Mex. 190/B4
Santa María (riv.), Mex. 200/D2
Santa María (bay), Mex. 200/C3
Santa María (cape), Port. 102/B4
Santa Maria (isl.), Azor., Port. 103/T13
Santa María (isl.), Chile 216/B3
Santa Maria, CpV. 151/K10
Santa María, Chile 216/N8
Santa María, Ecu. 214/E7
Santa María (isl.), Ecu. 214/E7
Santa Maria a Monte, It. 117/D5
Santa María, Cabo de (cape), Moz. 165/F2
Santa Maria Capua Vetere, It. 104/D2
Santa Maria, Chapadão de (hills), Braz. 212/A4
Santa Maria da Boa Vista, Braz. 212/C3
Santa Maria da Vitória, Braz. 212/A4
Santa María de Cayón, Sp. 102/D1
Santa María de Ipire, Ven. 211/E2
Santa María de Nanay, Peru 214/C1
Santa María del Oro, Mex. 200/D3
Santa Maria della Versa, It. 116/C3
Santa Maria di Leuca, Capo (cape), It. 105/F3
Santa Maria do Suaçuí, Braz. 212/B5
Santa Maria Maddalena, It. 117/E3
Santa Maria Maggiore, It. 115/E5
Santa Maria Nuova, It. 117/G6
Santa María Xadani, Mex. 198/B4
Santa Marta, Col. 210/C2
Santa Marta Grande (cape), Braz. 213/B4
Santa Marta, Sierra Nevada de (mts.), Col. 210/C2
Santa Monica (bay), Ca, US 194/B3
Santa Monica (mts.), Ca, US 194/B2
Santa Monica, Ca, US 194/F7
Santa Monica Mountains Nat'l Rec. Area, Ca, US 194/B2
Santa Olalla del Cala, Sp. 102/B4
Santa Paula (peak), Ca, US 194/A2
Santa Paula, Ca, US 194/A2
Santa Pola, Sp. 103/E3
Santa Pola, Cabo de (cape), Sp. 103/E3
Santa Quitéria, Braz. 212/B2
Santa Quitéria do Maranhão, Braz. 212/B1
Santa Rita, Braz. 212/A1
Santa Rita, Braz. 212/D2
Santa Rita, Ven. 210/D2
Santa Rita de Cássia, Braz. 212/A3
Santa Rita do Sapucaí, Braz. 213/H7
Santa Rosa, Arg. 208/F8
Santa Rosa, Arg. 216/D3
Santa Rosa, Arg. 215/C3
Santa Rosa, Braz. 215/F2
Santa Rosa, PN, CR 202/E4
Santa Rosa, Ecu. 214/B1
Santa Rosa, Peru 214/D4
Santa Rosa, Uru. 217/K11
Santa Rosa, Ven. 210/D2
Santa Rosa, Ca, US 186/B3
Santa Rosa, NM, US 187/F4
Santa Rosa (range), Nv, US 186/C2
Santa Rosa and San Jacinto Mountains Nat'l Mon., Ca, US 186/C4
Santa Rosa, Bajo de (plain), Arg. 216/D4
Santa Rosa de Aguán, Hon. 202/E3
Santa Rosa de Copán, Hon. 202/D3
Santa Rosa de Osos, Col. 210/C3
Santa Rosa de Viterbo, Braz. 213/C2
Santa Rosa Island (isl.), Ca, US 186/B4
Santa Rosalía (pt.), Mex. 200/B2
Santa Rosalía, Mex. 200/B3
Santa Rosalía, Ven. 210/D2
Santa Rosalía, Ven. 211/E3
Santa Sofia, It. 117/E5
Santa Susana (mts.), Ca, US 194/B2
Santa Teresa (riv.), Braz. 209/J6
Santa Teresa, Austl. 171/G3
Santa Teresa Abor. Land, Austl. 171/G2
Santa Teresa, PN, Uru. 217/G2
Santa Teresinha, Braz. 209/H6
Santa Teresita, Arg. 217/F3
Santa Vitória, Braz. 213/B1
Santa Vitória do Palmar, Braz. 217/G2
Santa Ynez (mts.), Ca, US 194/A2
SantAantioco (isl.), It. 104/A3
Santaella, Sp. 102/C4
Sant'Agata Bolognese, It. 117/E3
Sant'Agata di Militello, It. 104/D3
Sant'Agata Feltria, It. 117/F5
Sant'Agostino, It. 117/E3
Sant'Alberto, It. 117/F3
Santan (canal), Az, US 195/S19
Santana, Braz. 212/A4
Santana (isl.), Braz. 212/B1
Santana do Acaraú, Braz. 212/B1
Santana do Ipanema, Braz. 212/C3
Santana do Livramento, Braz. 215/E3
Santander, Sp. 102/D1
Santander (dept.), Col. 210/C3
Santander de Quilichao, Col. 210/B4
Santander Jiménez, Mex. 201/F3
Sant'Angelo in Vado, It. 117/F5
Sant'Angelo Lodigiano, It. 116/C2
Sant'Antioco, It. 104/A3
Sant'Antonio, It. 117/D2
Santañy, Sp. 103/G3
Sant'Apollinare in Classe, It. 117/F4
Santarcángelo, It. 117/F4
Santarém, Braz. 209/H4
Santarém (dist.), Port. 102/A3
Santarém, Port. 102/A3
Sant'arsenio, It. 104/D2
Santee (riv.), SC, US 191/J3
Santee, Ca, US 194/D5
Sant'Eufemia (gulf), It. 104/D3
Santena, It. 116/A3
Santerno (riv.), It. 101/J4
Santeuil, Fr. 88/H4
Santhia, It. 116/B2
Santiago, Braz. 215/F2
Santiago, Peru 214/C4
Santiago, Phil. 137/D4
Santiago (res.), Ca, US 194/C3
Santiago (peak), Ca, US 194/C3
Santiago (int'l arpt.), Sp. 102/A1
Santiago, Pan. 203/F4
Santiago (mtn.), Pan. 203/F4
Santiago (riv.), Peru 210/B5
Santiago (mts.), Tx, US 190/C4
Santiago (cap.), Chile 216/N8
Santiago (cape), Chile 217/B6
Santiago Cuautlalpan, Mex. 201/R10
Santiago Cuautlalpan, Mex. 201/Q9
Santiago de Cao, Peru 214/B2
Santiago de Chocorvos, Peru 214/C4
Santiago de Chuco, Peru 214/B3
Santiago de Compostela, Sp. 102/A1
Santiago de Cuba, Cuba 203/H1
Santiago de los Caballeros, DRep. 199/G4
Santiago de Machaca, Bol. 214/D5
Santiago del Estero, Arg. 215/D2
Santiago do Cacém, Port. 102/A3
Santiago Ixcuintla, Mex. 200/D4
Santiago Jamiltepec, Mex. 202/B2
Santiago Juxtlahuaca, Mex. 202/B2
Santiago Miahuatlán, Mex. 201/M8
Santiago Papasquiaro, Mex. 200/D3
Santiago Pinotepa Nacional, Mex. 202/B2
Santiago Tilapa, Mex. 201/Q10
Santiago Tolman, Mex. 201/R9
Santiago Vázquez, Uru. 217/K11
Santiago Zacatepec, Mex. 202/C2
Sant'Ilario d'Enza, It. 116/D3
Sāntipur, India 143/G4
Säntis (peak), Swi. 115/F3
Santisteban del Puerto, Sp. 102/D3
Santō, Japan 135/G5
Santō, Japan 135/K5
Santo Amaro, Braz. 212/C4
Santo Amaro, Ilha de (isl.), Braz. 213/G8
Santo Anastácio, Braz. 213/B2
Santo André, Braz. 213/G8
Santo Ângelo, Braz. 215/F2
Santo Antão (isl.), CpV. 151/J9
Santo António, SaoT. 154/G7
Santo Antônio de Jesus, Braz. 212/C4
Santo Antônio de Pádua, Braz. 213/D2
Santo Antônio do Içá, Braz. 210/E5
Santo Antônio do Jacinto, Braz. 212/B5
Santo Antônio dos Lopes, Braz. 212/A2
Santo Domingo (cap.), DRep. 199/H4
Santo Domingo, Mex. 201/E4
Santo Domingo (pt.), Mex. 200/B3
Santo Domingo, Cuba 203/F1
Santo Domingo, Chile 216/N8
Santo Domingo de la Calzada, Sp. 102/D1
Santo Domingo de los Colorados, Ecu. 210/B5
Santo Domingo Petapa, Mex. 202/C2
Santo Domingo Tehuantepec, Mex. 202/C2
Santo Domingo Zanatepec, Mex. 202/C2
Santo Estêvão, Braz. 212/C4
Santo Onofre (riv.), Braz. 212/B4
Santo Stefano Belbo, It. 116/B3
Santo Stefano d'Aveto, It. 116/C3
Santo Stefano di Magra, It. 116/C4
Santo Stino di Livenza, It. 117/F1
Santo Tomás, Peru 214/C4
Santo Tomás, Peru 214/B2
Santo Tomás, Mex. 200/A2
Santo Tomás (pt.), Mex. 200/A2
Santo Tomás (vol.), Ecu. 214/E7
Santo Tomé, Arg. 215/E2
Santo Tomé, Arg. 215/D3
Santoña, Sp. 102/D1
Santorso, It. 117/E1
Santos, Braz. 213/G8
Santos Dumont (int'l arpt.), Braz. 213/K7
Santos Dumont, Braz. 213/K6
Santos Reyes Nopala, Mex. 202/B2
Santuario di Crea, It. 116/B2
Santuario di Oropa, It. 116/A1
Şānūr, WBnk. 149/G7
Sanwa, Japan 135/D1
São Benedito, Braz. 212/B2
São Benedito do Rio Prêto, Braz. 212/B1
São Bento, Braz. 212/C2
São Bento, Braz. 212/A1
São Bento do Sapucaí, Braz. 213/H7
São Bento do Sul, Braz. 213/B3
São Bento do Una, Braz. 212/C3
São Bernardo do Campo, Braz. 213/G8
São Borja, Braz. 215/E2
São Carlos, Braz. 213/C2
São Cristóvão, Braz. 212/C3
São Desidério, Braz. 212/A4
São Domingos (riv.), Braz. 212/A4
São Domingos, Braz. 212/A4
São Domingos do Maranhão, Braz. 212/A2
São Félix do Xingu, Braz. 209/H5
São Fidélis, Braz. 213/D2
São Filipe, CpV. 151/J11
São Francisco, Braz. 212/A4
São Francisco (riv.), Braz. 205/F3
São Francisco do Sul, Braz. 213/B3
São Francisco, Ilha de (isl.), Braz. 215/G2
São Fransisco de Paula, Braz. 213/B4
São Gabriel, Braz. 215/F3
São Gabriel da Palha, Braz. 213/D1
São Gonçalo, Braz. 213/K7
São Gonçalo do Abaeté, Braz. 212/A5
São Gonçalo do Sapucaí, Braz. 213/H6
São Gotardo, Braz. 213/C1
São Joachim da Barra, Braz. 213/C2
São João Batista, Braz. 212/A1
São João Batista, Braz. 213/B3
São João da Aliança, Braz. 212/A4
São João da Barra, Braz. 213/D2
São João da Boa Vista, Braz. 213/G6
São João da Madeira, Port. 102/A2
São João da Pesqueira, Port. 102/B2
São João da Ponte, Braz. 212/A4
São João das Lampas, Port. 103/P10
São João de Meriti, Braz. 213/K7
São João del Rei, Braz. 213/C2
São João do Paraíso, Braz. 212/B4
São João do Piauí, Braz. 212/B3
São João dos Patos, Braz. 212/B2
São João Evangelista, Braz. 213/D1
São João, Ilhas de (isl.), Braz. 209/K4
São João Nepomuceno, Braz. 213/K6
São João, Serra de (mts.), Braz. 208/F5
São Joaquim, Braz. 213/B4
São Joaquim, PN de, Braz. 213/B4
São Jorge (isl.), Azor., Port. 103/S12
São José, Braz. 213/B3
São José da Laje, Braz. 212/C3
São José de Mipibu, Braz. 212/D2
São José de Piranhas, Braz. 212/C2
São José de Ribamar, Braz. 212/A1
São José do Belmonte, Braz. 212/C2
São José do Egito, Braz. 212/C2
São José do Norte, Braz. 213/A5
São José do Peixe, Braz. 212/B2
São José do Rio Pardo, Braz. 213/G6
São José do Rio Prêto, Braz. 213/B2
São José dos Campos, Braz. 213/H8
São José dos Pinhais, Braz. 213/B3
São Julião, Braz. 212/B2
São Leopoldo, Braz. 213/B4
São Lourenço (riv.), Braz. 209/G7
São Lourenço, Braz. 213/H7
São Lourenço, Port. 103/P11
São Lourenço do Sul, Braz. 213/B4
São Luís, Braz. 212/A1
São Luís do Curu, Braz. 212/C1
São Luís do Quitunde, Braz. 212/D3
São Manoel, Braz. 213/B2
São Marcos (riv.), Braz. 212/A5
São Marcos (bay), Braz. 205/E3
São Martinho do Porto, Port. 102/A3
São Mateus, Braz. 213/E1
São Mateus (riv.), Braz. 213/D1
São Mateus do Maranhão, Braz. 212/A2
São Mateus do Sul, Braz. 213/B3
São Miguel, Braz. 212/C2
São Miguel (isl.), Azor., Port. 103/T13
São Miguel Arcanjo, Braz. 213/C2
São Miguel do Tapuio, Braz. 212/B2
São Miguel dos Campos, Braz. 212/C3
São Nicolau (isl.), CpV. 151/J10
São Paulo (state), Braz. 213/B2
São Paulo, Braz. 213/G8
São Paulo de Olivença, Braz. 208/E4
São Paulo do Potengi, Braz. 212/D2
São Pedro da Aldeia, Braz. 213/D2
São Pedro do Piauí, Braz. 212/B2
São Pedro do Sul, Port. 102/A2
São Raimundo das Mangabeiras, Braz. 212/A2
São Raimundo Nonato, Braz. 212/B3
São Romão, Braz. 212/A5

São Roque, Cabo de
(cape), Braz. 212/D2
São Roque do Pico,
Azor., Port. 103/S12
São Sebastião (pt.),
Moz. 163/G4
São Sebastião, Braz. 213/H8
São Sebastião do Paraíso,
Braz. 213/C2
São Sebastião, Ilha de
(isl.), Braz. 213/C2
São Simão, Barragem de
(res.), Braz. 213/B1
São Teotónio, Port. 102/A4
São Tiago, Port. 213/C2
São Tiago (isl.), CpV. 151/K10
São Tomé (cap.),
SaoT. 154/G7
São Tomé (isl.), SaoT. 154/G7
São Tomé and Príncipe
(ctry.) 154/F7
São Tomé, Cabo de
(cape), Braz. 213/D2
São Vicente, Braz. 213/G8
São Vicente (cape),
Port. 102/A4
São Vicente (isl.),
CpV. 151/J10
Saône (riv.), Fr. 100/F3
Saône-et-Loire (dept.),
Fr. 114/B4
Saori, Japan 135/L5
Saouru (riv.), Alg. 154/E1
Sápai, Gre. 105/J2
Sapallanga, Peru 214/C4
Sapanca, Turk. 107/K5
Sapatgrám, India 143/H2
Sapé, Braz. 212/D2
Sapele, Nga. 161/G5
Sapelo (isl.), Ga, US 191/H4
Saphane, Turk. 120/D5
Sapiéndza (isl.),
Gre. 105/G4
Sapkyo, SKor. 131/D4
Sapo (mts.), Pan. 203/G5
Sapo NP, Libr. 160/C5
Saposoa, Peru 214/B2
Sappemeer, Neth. 108/D2
Sapphire, Austl. 172/B3
Sappington, Mo, US 195/G8
Sapporo, Japan 134/B2
Sapri, It. 104/D2
Sapsi (isl.), SKor. 131/D3
Sapt Kosi (riv.), Nepal 143/F2
Sapucaí (riv.), Braz. 213/H7
Sapucaia, Braz. 213/L6
Saqqez, Iran 146/E1
Saquena, Peru 214/C2
Saquisilí, Ecu. 210/B5
Sar (mts.), Kos. 104/E3
Sar Dasht, Iran 148/F2
Sar-e Pol, Afg. 145/F5
Sara Buri, Thai. 136/C3
Sarāb, Iran 146/E1
Saraguro, Ecu. 214/B5
Sarāī Alamgir, Pak. 144/B3
Sarāī Sidhu, Pak. 144/A4
Sarajevo (cap.), Bosn. 106/D4
Saraland, Al, US 191/F4
Saramacca (dist.),
Sur. 211/H3
Saran (peak), Indo. 138/D4
Saran', Kaz. 145/F3
Saranac Lake,
NY, US 188/F2
Sarandápótamos (riv.),
Gre. 105/N8
Sarandë, Alb. 105/G3
Sarandí de Navarro,
Uru. 217/K10
Sarandí del Yi, Uru. 217/K10
Sarandí Grande, Uru. 217/K10
Sarangami
(isls.), Phil. 139/G2
Sārangpur, India 147/L4
Saransk, Rus. 121/H1
Sarapul, Rus. 119/M4
Sarare (riv.), Ven. 210/D3
Sarasota, Fl, US 191/H5
Saratoga, Wy, US 184/G5
Saratoga, Ca, US 193/K12
Saratoga Springs,
NY, US 188/F3
Saratov (res.), Rus. 121/J1
Saratov, Rus. 121/H2
Saratovskaya Oblast,
Rus. 145/A2
Saravan, Laos 136/D3
Sarawak
(reg.), Malay. 138/D3
Saray, Turk. 107/H5
Sarayacu, Ecu. 210/B5
Sarāyan (riv.), India 142/C2
Saraykôy, Turk. 148/B2
Sarayönü, Turk. 148/C2
Sárbogárd, Hun. 106/D2
Sarcelles, Fr. 88/K5
Sárda (riv.), India 142/C1
Sārda (canal), India 142/C2
Sarda (riv.), India 142/C1
Sardara, It. 104/A3
Sardārshahar, India 144/C5
Sardegna (prov.), It. 104/A2
Sardhana, India 144/D5
Sardinata, Col. 210/C2
Sardinaux, Cap des
(cape), Fr. 101/G5
Sardis (lake), Ms, US 187/K4
Sardis (lake), Ok, US 187/J4
Sareks NP, Swe. 95/F2
Sarektjåkko (peak),
Swe. 95/F2
Sarempaka (peak),
Indo. 139/E4

Sarentino, It. 115/H4
Sarezzo, It. 116/D1
Sargans, Swi. 115/F3
Sargodha, Pak. 144/B3
Sarh, Chad 155/J6
Sārī, Iran 146/F1
Sari-Solenzara, Fr. 104/A2
Sariaya, Phil. 137/D5
Saribi (cape), Indo. 139/J4
Sarigan (isl.), NMar. 174/D3
Sarikamış, Turk. 148/E1
Sarikaya, Turk. 120/E5
Sarikaya
(prov.), Turk. 148/C2
Sarikei, Malay. 138/D3
Sarina, Austl. 172/C3
Sarine (riv.), Swi. 101/G3
Sariñena, Sp. 103/E2
Sarîr Kalanshiyũ (des.),
Libya 154/K2
Sarîr Tibastî (des.),
Libya 154/J3
Sarita, Tx, US 190/D5
Sariwŏn, NKor. 131/C3
Sarju (riv.), India 142/C1
Sark (isl.), Chl, UK 100/B2
Sarkad, Hun. 106/E2
Sarkant, Kaz. 128/C2
Sarkişla, Turk. 148/D2
Sarköy, Turk. 107/H5
Sarlat-la-Canéda, Fr. 100/D4
Sarleinsbach, Aus. 113/G5
Sarmato, It. 116/C2
Sarmeola, It. 117/E2
Sarmiento, Arg. 216/C5
Sarmiento
(peak), Chile 217/C17
Särna, Swe. 96/E1
Sarnano, It. 101/K5
Sarnen, Swi. 115/E4
Sarnia, On, Can. 188/D3
Sarnico, It. 116/C1
Sarny, Ukr. 120/C2
Saroma
(lake), Japan 134/C1
Saronic (gulf), Gre. 105/H4
Saronno, It. 116/C1
Saros (gulf), Turk. 107/H5
Sárospatak, Hun. 99/L4
Sarpsborg, Nor. 96/D2
Sarralbe, Fr. 111/G6
Sarre-Union, Fr. 111/G6
Sarre, It. 105/E2
Sarre (riv.), Slov. 101/L3
Sarrebourg, Fr. 111/G6
Sarria, Sp. 102/B1
Sarroch, It. 111/D6
Sarry, Fr. 111/D6
Sarsāwa, India 144/D4
Sarsina, It. 117/F5
Sarstedt, Ger. 109/G4
Sarstún (riv.),
Guat. 202/D3
Sartang (riv.), Rus. 123/P3
Sarteano, It. 104/B1
Sartène, Fr. 104/A2
Sarthe (riv.), Fr. 100/C3
Sartrouville, Fr. 88/J5
Sarufutsu, Japan 134/C1
Saruhanlı, Turk. 148/A2
Sárvár, Hun. 101/M3
Sárviz (riv.), Hun. 106/D2
Sarysik Atgraŭ Qumy
(des.), Kaz. 128/C2
Saryshaghan, Kaz. 145/F3
Sarysu (riv.), Kaz. 122/G5
Sarzana, It. 116/C4
Sas Van Gent, Neth. 110/C1
Sasaginnigack (lake),
Mb, Can. 185/K3
Sasarām, India 143/E3
Sasayama, Japan 135/H5
Sasayama (riv.),
Japan 135/H5
Sásd, Hun. 106/D2
Sasebo, Japan 132/A4
Sashima, Japan 135/D1
Saskatchewan (prov.),
Can. 180/F3
Saskatchewan (riv.),
Can. 180/G3
Saskatoon, Sk, Can. 184/G2
Saslaya (mtn.),
Nic. 203/E3
Saslaya, PN, Nic. 203/E3
Sásni, India 142/B2
Sasolburg, SAfr. 164/D2
Sasovo, Rus. 121/G1
Saspamco, Tx, US 195/U21
Sassafras, Md, US 196/C5
Sassafras (riv.),
Md, US 196/B5
Sassandra (riv.),
C.d'Iv. 154/D6
Sassandra, C.d'Iv. 160/D5
Sassari, It. 104/A2
Sassello, It. 116/B4
Sassenberg, Ger. 109/F4
Sassenheim, Neth. 108/B4
Sassnitz, Ger. 96/E4
Sasso Marconi, It. 117/E4
Sassocorvaro, It. 117/F5
Sassoferrato, It. 117/F6
Sassuolo, It. 117/D3
Sástago, Sp. 103/E2
Sasyk (lake), Ukr. 107/J3
Sata-misaki (cape),
Japan 132/B5
Sātāra, India 147/K5
Satawan (isl.), Micr. 174/E4
Säter, Swe. 96/F1
Saticoy, Ca, US 194/B2
Satilla (riv.), Ga, US 191/H4
Satipo, Peru 214/C3

Sātkhira, Bang. 143/G4
Sátoraljaújhely, Hun. 99/L4
Satpayev, Kaz. 145/E3
Satpura (range),
India 147/K4
Satte, Japan 135/D1
Satteins, Aus. 115/F3
Satteldorf, Ger. 112/D4
Sattler, Tx, US 195/U20
Satu Mare, Rom. 99/M5
Satu Mare (co.), Rom. 99/M5
Satun, Thai. 136/C5
Sauce, Peru 214/B2
Sauce Grande (riv.),
Arg. 216/E3
Saucillo, Mex. 200/D2
Sauda, Nor. 96/B2
Saúde, Braz. 212/B3
Saudhárkrókur, Ice. 95/N6
Saudi Arabia (ctry.) 146/D3
Sauer (riv.), Ger. 109/F5
Sauerlach, Ger. 115/H2
Sauerland (reg.), Ger. 98/D3
Sauěruiná (riv.), Braz. 208/G6
Saugatuck (riv.),
Ct, US 197/E1
Saujon, Fr. 100/C4
Sauk (riv.), Mn, US 185/K4
Sauk Centre, Mn, US 185/K4
Sauk Rapids, Mn, US 185/K4
Saül, FrG. 209/H3
Sauland, Nor. 96/C2
Sauldre (riv.), Fr. 100/D3
Saulgau, Ger. 115/F1
Saulheim, Ger. 112/B3
Saulieu, Fr. 100/F3
Sault-lès-Rethel, Fr. 111/D5
Sault Sainte Marie,
On, Can. 188/C2
Sault Ste. Marie,
Mi, US 188/C2
Saulx (riv.), Fr. 114/C2
Saulx (riv.), Fr. 114/C2
Saulxures-sur-Moselotte,
Fr. 114/C2
Saumur, Fr. 100/C3
Saunders (peak),
Austl. 170/E3
Saura (riv.), India 143/F3
Saurimo, Ang. 163/D2
Sausalito, Ca, US 193/J11
Sausseron (riv.), Fr. 88/J4
Sauteurs, Gren. 211/F1
Sava, It. 105/E2
Sava (riv.), Slov. 101/L3
Savá, Hon. 202/E3
Savage (dam),
Ca, US 194/D5
Savage River,
Austl. 173/C4
Savai'i (isl.), Sam. 175/H6
Savalou, Ben. 161/F5
Savane (riv., Qu, Can. 189/G1
Savanna-la-Mar,
Jam. 203/G2
Savannah, Ga, US 191/H3
Savannah, Tn, US 191/F3
Savannah (riv.),
US 191/H3
Savannakhet, Laos 136/D2
Savant (lake), On, Can. 185/L3
Sāvantvādi, India 140/B4
Sāvar, Swe. 95/G3
Savaştepe, Turk. 148/A2
Save (riv.), Moz. 163/F5
Sāveh, Iran 146/F1
Savena (riv.), It. 117/E4
Sāveni, Rom. 107/H2
Saverdun, Fr. 100/D5
Saverne, Fr. 111/G6
Savièse, Swi. 114/D2
Savigliano, It. 101/G4
Savignano sul Panaro,
It. 117/E4
Savignano sul Rubicone,
It. 117/F4
Savigny-le-Temple,
Fr. 88/K6
Savigny-sur-Orge,
Fr. 88/K5
Savio (riv.), It. 101/K5
Sävja, Swe. 96/G2
Savognin, Swi. 115/F4
Savoie (dept.), Fr. 114/C6
Savona (prov.), It. 116/B4
Savona, It. 116/B4
Savoonga, Ak, US 192/D3
Savoy (prov.), Fr. 100/F4
Savoy Alps (mts.), Fr. 114/C6
Savsat, Turk. 148/E1
Sävsjö, Swe. 96/F3
Savu (sea), Indo. 139/F5
Savuhlntob, Indo. 138/B4
Sawankhalok, Thai. 136/B2
Sawara, Japan 133/G3
Sawasaki-bana (pt.),
Japan 133/F2
Sawda', Jabal (peak),
SAr. 146/D5
Saweba (cape), Indo. 139/H4
Sawel (mtn.), NI, UK 92/A2
Sawi, Neth. 108/C5
Sawtell, Austl. 173/E1
Sawtooth (range),
Id, US 184/E4
Sawtooth Nat'l Rec. Area,
Id, US 184/E5
Sawu (isls.), Indo. 139/F6
Sax, Sp. 103/E3
Saxman, Ak, US 192/M4
Saxon, Swi. 114/D5
Say, Niger 161/F3
Saya, Japan 135/L5
Sayama, Japan 133/F3

Sayama, Japan 135/J6
Sayán, Peru 214/B3
Saydā, Leb. 149/D3
Sayıl (ruin), Mex. 202/D1
Saynbach (riv.), Ger. 111/G2
Sayreville, NJ, US 197/H10
Sayula, Mex. 200/E5
Sayville, NY, US 197/E2
Saywūn, Yem. 146/E5
Sazan (isl.), Alb. 105/F2
Sázava (riv.), Czh. 101/L2
Sbaa, Alg. 157/E3
Scafell Pikes (peak),
Eng, UK 93/E3
Scalasaig, Sc, UK 89/Q8
Scald Law (peak),
Sc, UK 94/C5
Scalea, It. 104/D3
Scalino (peak), It. 115/F5
Scalloway, Sc, UK 89/W13
Scammon Bay,
Ak, US 192/E3
Scandia, Wa, US 193/B2
Scandiano, It. 117/D3
Scandicci, It. 117/E5
Scapa Flow (chan.),
Sc, UK 89/V14
Scar Water (riv.),
Sc, UK 92/E1
Scarborough, Can. 189/R8
Scarborough,
Eng, UK 93/H3
Scarborough Shoal (isl.),
Phil. 137/C4
Scardovari, It. 117/F3
Scarpe (riv.), Fr. 98/B3
Scarperia, It. 117/E5
Scarriff, Ire. 89/P10
Scarsdale, La, US 195/Q17
Scarsdale, NY, US 197/K7
Sceaux, Fr. 88/J5
Scenic Oaks,
Tx, US 195/T20
Scey-sur-Saône-et-St-Albin,
Fr. 114/B2
Schaefferstown,
Pa, US 196/B3
Schaerbeek, Belg. 111/D2
Schaffhausen (canton),
Swi. 115/E2
Schaffhausen, Swi. 115/E2
Schäftlarn, Ger. 115/H2
Schagen, Neth. 108/B3
Schaijk, Neth. 108/C5
Schalchen, Aus. 113/G6
Schalkau, Ger. 112/E2
Schalksmühle, Ger. 109/E6
Schanck (cape),
Austl. 173/C3
Schangnau, Swi. 114/D4
Scharans, Swi. 115/F4
Schardenberg, Aus. 113/G5
Schärding, Aus. 113/G6
Scharfreiter (peak),
Aus. 115/H3
Scharhorn (isl.), Ger. 109/F1
Scharnebeck, Ger. 109/H2
Scharnitz (pass), Aus. 115/H3
Scharnstein, Aus. 113/G7
Schashagen, Ger. 98/F1
Schattdorf, Swi. 115/E4
Schauenstein, Ger. 113/E2
Schaumburg,
Il, US 193/P15
Scheemda, Neth. 108/D2
Scheer, Ger. 115/F1
Scheessel, Ger. 109/G2
Schefferville,
Qu, Can. 139/K3
Scheibbs, Aus. 99/H4
Scheidegg, Ger. 115/F3
Scheinfeld, Ger. 112/D3
Schelde (riv.), Belg. 100/E1
Schelklingen, Ger. 112/C6
Schell Creek (range),
Nv, US 186/D3
Schellerten, Ger. 109/H4
Schellville, Ca, US 193/K10
Schenectady,
NY, US 188/F3
Schenefeld, Ger. 109/G1
Schermbeck, Ger. 108/D5
Scherpenzeel, Neth. 108/C3
Schertz, Tx, US 195/U20
Schesaplana (peak),
Aus. 115/F3
Schesslitz, Ger. 112/D3
Scheyern, Ger. 113/E5
Schiedam, Neth. 108/B5
Schieder-Schwalenberg,
Ger. 109/G5
Schiehallon (peak),
Sc, UK 94/B3
Schier Monnikoog (isl.),
Neth. 98/D2
Schierling, Ger. 113/F5
Schiermonnikoog (isl.),
Neth. 108/D1
Schiermonnikoog,
Neth. 108/D2
Schiers, Swi. 115/F4
Schifferstadt, Ger. 112/B4
Schiffweiler, Ger. 111/G5
Schijndel, Neth. 108/C5
Schilde, Belg. 108/B6
Schildmeer (lake),
Neth. 108/D2
Schillighörn (cape),
Ger. 109/F1
Schillingfürst, Ger. 112/D4
Schiltach, Ger. 115/E1
Schiltigheim, Fr. 111/G6
Schinnen, Neth. 111/E2
Schinznach-Dorf,
Swi. 114/E3

Schio, It. 117/E1
Schipbeek (riv.), Neth. 108/D4
Schirmeck, Fr. 114/D1
Schkumbin (riv.), Alb. 105/G2
Schladen, Ger. 109/H4
Schladming, Aus. 101/K3
Schlanders (Silandro),
It. 101/J3
Schlangen, Ger. 109/F5
Schlangenbad, Ger. 112/B2
Schleiden, Ger. 111/F2
Schleitheim, Swi. 115/E2
Schleiz, Ger. 113/E1
Schlema, Ger. 113/F1
Schleswig, Ger. 96/C4
Schleswig-Holstein
(state), Ger. 96/B4
Schleswig-Holsteinisches
Wattenmeer NP, Ger. 96/C4
Schleuse (riv.), Ger. 112/D2
Schleusingen, Ger. 112/D1
Schliengen, Ger. 114/D2
Schlierbach, Aus. 113/H7
Schlieren, Swi. 115/E3
Schloss Herrenchiemsee,
Ger. 113/F7
Schloss Holte-Stukenbrock,
Ger. 109/F5
Schloss Sansoucci,
Ger. 98/Q7
Schloss Wilhelmstein,
Ger. 109/G4
Schlotheim, Ger. 109/H6
Schluchsee, Ger. 114/E2
Schlüchtern, Ger. 112/C2
Schlüsselfeld, Ger. 112/D3
Schlüsslberg, Aus. 113/G6
Schmalkalden, Ger. 101/J1
Schmallenberg, Ger. 109/F6
Schmeich (riv.),
Ger. 109/F5
Schmelz, Ger. 111/F5
Schmiech (riv.), Ger. 112/C6
Schmitten, Swi. 114/D4
Schmitten, Ger. 112/B2
Schmutter (riv.), Ger. 112/D5
Schnaitsee, Ger. 113/F6
Schnaittach, Ger. 113/E3
Schnaittenbach, Ger. 113/F1
Schnecksville,
Pa, US 196/C2
Schneeberg (peak),
Ger. 113/E2
Schneeberg, Ger. 113/F1
Schneifel (upland),
Ger. 98/D3
Schneverdingen,
Ger. 109/G2
Schofield Barracks,
Hi, US 182/V12
Schöllkrippen, Ger. 112/C2
Schömberg, Ger. 115/E1
Schömberg, Ger. 112/B5
Schönaich, Ger. 112/C5
Schönau im Schwarzwald,
Ger. 114/D2
Schönberg, Ger. 96/D4
Schönberg, Ger. 113/G5
Schondorf am Ammersee,
Ger. 115/H1
Schondra (riv.),
Ger. 112/C2
Schönebeck, Ger. 98/F2
Schönecken, Ger. 111/F2
Schönefeld (int'l arpt.),
Ger. 98/Q7
Schongau, Ger. 115/G2
Schöningen, Ger. 98/F2
Schönsee, Ger. 113/F3
Schonungen, Ger. 112/D2
Schönwald, Ger. 113/E2
Schoonebeek, Neth. 108/D3
Schoonhoven, Neth. 108/B5
Schoorl, Neth. 108/B3
Schopfheim, Ger. 111/G4
Schöppenstedt, Ger. 109/H4
Schorndorf, Ger. 112/C5
Schortens, Ger. 109/E1
Schoten, Belg. 108/B6
Schotten, Ger. 112/C1
Schouten (isl.), Austl. 173/D4
Schouten (isls.), Indo. 174/D4
Schouwen (isl.), Neth. 108/A5
Schramberg, Ger. 115/E1
Schrankogel (peak),
Aus. 115/H3
Schreckhorn (peak),
Swi. 114/E4
Schriesheim, Ger. 112/B4
Schrobenhausen, Ger. 112/E5
Schroffenstein (peak),
Namb. 164/B2
Schrozberg, Ger. 112/D4
Schruns, Aus. 115/F3
Schübelbach, Swi. 115/E3
Schuby, Ger. 96/C4
Schulenburg, Tx, US 187/H5
Schulzendorf, Ger. 98/Q7
Schunter (riv.), Ger. 109/H4
Schussen (riv.), Ger. 115/F2
Schussenried, Ger. 115/F1
Schutter (riv.), Ger. 112/A6
Schutterwald, Ger. 114/D1
Schüttorf, Ger. 109/E4
Schuylkill (riv.),
Pa, US 196/C3
Schuylkill Haven,
Pa, US 196/B2

Schwabach, Ger. 112/D4
Schwabhausen bei Dachau,
Ger. 115/G4
Schwabmünchen, Ger. 115/G1
Schwäbisch Gmünd,
Ger. 112/C5
Schwäbisch Hall, Ger. 112/C4
Schwäbische Alb
(range), Ger. 98/E4
Schwaigern, Ger. 112/C4
Schwaig bei Nürnberg,
Ger. 112/C4
Schwaigern, Ger. 112/C4
Schwalbach, Ger. 111/F5
Schwalbach am Taunus,
Ger. 112/B2
Schwalm (riv.), Ger. 98/E3
Schwalmtal, Ger. 108/D6
Schwandorf im Bayern,
Ger. 113/F4
Schwanebeck, Ger. 98/Q6
Schwanenstadt, Aus. 113/G6
Schwaner (mts.), Indo. 138/D4
Schwanewede, Ger. 109/F2
Schwanfeld, Ger. 112/D3
Schwarza (riv.), Ger. 112/E1
Schwarzach, Ger. 113/E3
Schwarzach im Pongau,
Aus. 101/K3
Schwarzenbach am Wald,
Ger. 113/E2
Schwarzenbek, Ger. 109/H1
Schwarzenberg, Ger. 113/F1
Schwarzenbruck, Ger. 112/E4
Schwarzenburg, Swi. 114/D4
Schwarzenfeld, Ger. 113/F3
Schwarzer Mann
(peak), Ger. 111/F3
Schwarzhorn
(peak), Aus. 115/H3
Schwarzwald (Black Forest)
(for.), Ger. 112/C6
Schwaz, Aus. 101/J3
Schwebheim, Ger. 112/D3
Schwechat, Aus. 107/N7
Schwechat
(int'l arpt.), Aus. 107/P7
Schwedt, Ger. 99/H2
Schwegenheim, Ger. 112/B4
Schweich, Ger. 111/F4
Schweinfurt, Ger. 112/D2
Schweitenkirchen,
Ger. 113/E5
Schweizer-Reneke,
SAfr. 164/D2
Schwelm, Ger. 109/E6
Schwendi, Ger. 115/F1
Schwenksville,
Pa, US 196/C3
Schwerin, Ger. 96/D5
Schwerte, Ger. 109/E6
Schwetzingen, Ger. 112/B4
Schwinge (riv.), Ger. 109/G2
Schwörstadt, Ger. 114/D2
Schwülme (riv.), Ger. 109/G5
Schwülper, Ger. 109/H4
Schwyz (canton), Swi. 115/E3
Schwyz, Swi. 115/E3
Sciacca, It. 104/C4
Scicli, It. 104/D4
Scinawa, Pol. 99/J3
Scionzier, Fr. 114/C5
Sciota, Pa, US 196/C2
Scioto (riv.), Oh, US 188/D4
Scobey, Mt, US 185/G3
Scoglitti, It. 104/D4
Scole, Eng, UK 91/G1
Scone, Austl. 173/D2
Scopello, It. 116/B1
Scordia, It. 104/D4
Scorzè, It. 117/F2
Scotch Corner,
Eng, UK 93/G3
Scotch Plains,
NJ, US 197/H9
Scotia (sea) 218/W
Scotland (isl.), Austl. 92/D1
Scott (cape), BC, Can. 180/D3
Scott (cape), NW,
Can. 139/R7
Scott (lake),
NW,Sk, Can. 180/F2
Scott, NZ, Ant. 218/M
Scott City, Ks, US 187/G3
Scott NP, Austl. 167/B3
Scott (reef), Austl. 167/C2
Scottburgh, SAfr. 165/E3
Scotts (cr.), Austl. 171/M9
Scottish Borders
(reg.), Sc, UK 94/C5
Scotts Bluff Nat'l Mon.,
Ne, US 187/G2
Scottsboro, Al, US 191/G3
Scottsburg, In, US 188/C4
Scottsdale, Az, US 186/E4
Scottsdale, Austl. 173/C4
Scottsville, Ky, US 191/G2
Scottville, Mi, US 188/C3
Scourie, Sc, UK 89/R7
Scranton, Pa, US 188/F3
Scrivia (riv.), It. 116/B3

Scunthorpe, Eng, UK 93/H4
Scuol, Swi. 115/G4
Scuppernong
(riv.), Wi, US 193/N14
Scurdie Ness
(pt.), Sc, UK 94/D3
Scutari (lake),
Alb., Mont. 106/D4
Sea Cliff, Ca, US 194/A2
Sea Cliff, NY, US 197/L8
Sea Girt, NJ, US 196/D3
Sea Isle City, NJ, US 196/D5
Sea Lake, Austl. 173/B2
Sea-Tac, Wa, US 193/C3
Seabeck, Wa, US 193/B2
Seabra, Braz. 212/B4
Seabrook, NJ, US 196/C5
Seaford, Eng, UK 91/G5
Seaford, NY, US 197/M9
Seaforde, NI, UK 92/C3
Seaforth, Austl. 172/C3
Seagraves, Tx, US 187/G4
Seaham, Eng, UK 93/G2
Seahorse
(pt.), Nun, Can. 139/J2
Sehnde, Ger. 109/G4
Seahurst, Wa, US 193/C3
Seal, Eng, UK 88/D3
Seal (riv.), MB, Can. 180/G3
Seal (pt.), Chile 216/B5
Seal (cape), SAfr. 164/C4
Seal Beach, Ca, US 194/F8
Seale, Al, US 191/G3
Seamer, Eng, UK 93/H3
Seano, It. 117/E6
Searcy, Ar, US 187/K4
Seascale, Eng, UK 92/E3
Seaside, Or, US 184/B4
Seaside Heights,
NJ, US 196/D4
Seaside Park, NJ, US 196/D4
Seaton, Eng, UK 90/C5
Seaton (riv.), Eng, UK 90/C5
Seaton Carew, Eng, UK 93/G2
Seattle, Wa, US 184/C4
Sébaco, Nic. 202/E3
Sebaou (riv.), Alg. 158/H4
Sebastian, Fl, US 191/H5
Sebastián Vizcaíno
(bay), Mex. 200/B2
Sebayan (peak), Indo. 138/D4
Sebdou, Alg. 158/D2
Sébékoro, Mali 160/C3
Sebeş, Rom. 107/G3
Sebeş (riv.), Rom. 107/G3
Sebezh, Rus. 97/N3
Sebinkarahisar, Turk. 148/D1
Sebiş, Rom. 106/F2
Seboeis (riv.), Me, US 189/G1
Sebou, Oued (riv.), Mor. 156/D2
Sebree, Ky, US 188/C4
Sebring, Fl, US 191/H5
Sebuku (isl.), Indo. 139/E4
Secaucus, NJ, US 197/J8
Secchia (riv.), It. 101/J4
Sechura, Peru 214/A2
Sechura (bay), Peru 214/A2
Sechura, Desierto de
(des.), Peru 214/A2
Seclin, Fr. 110/C2
Seco (riv.), Arg. 217/D6
Seco (riv.), Mex.,US 200/C2
Second Mountain
(mtn.), Pa, US 196/B3
Second Watchung
(mtn.), NJ, US 197/H9
Secunda, SAfr. 164/E2
Secure (riv.), Bol. 208/E7
Sedalia, Mo, US 187/J3
Sedan, Fr. 111/D4
Sedano, Sp. 102/D1
Sedaung (mtn.),
Myan. 136/B3
Sedbergh, Eng, UK 93/F3
Seddülbahir, Turk. 105/K2
Sedeh, Iran 147/G2
Sederot, Isr. 149/D4
Sedgefield, Eng, UK 93/G2
Sedhiou, Sen. 160/B3
Sedlčany, Czh. 113/H3
Sedlo (peak), Czh. 113/H1
Sedona, Az, US 186/E4
Sedrata, Alg. 158/K6
Sedrun, Swi. 115/E4
Sędziszów, Pol. 99/L3
Seeb (int'l arpt.),
Oman 147/G4
Seeboden, Aus. 101/K3
Seefeld in Tirol, Aus. 115/H3
Seehausen, Ger. 98/F2
Seeheim-Jugenheim,
Ger. 112/B3
Seekirchen Markt,
Aus. 113/F6
Seekooi (riv.), SAfr. 164/D3
Seelow, Ger. 99/H2
Seer Green, Eng, UK 88/B2
Sées, Fr. 100/D2
Seesen, Ger. 109/H5
Seeshaupt, Ger. 115/H2
Seeve (riv.), Ger. 109/G2
Seewalchen, Aus. 113/G7
Seewis im Prättigau,
Swi. 115/F4
Sefaatlı, Turk. 148/C2
Sefrou, Mor. 158/B3

Sefton (co.), Eng, UK 93/E4
Segamat, Malay. 138/B3
Segarcea, Rom. 107/G3
Ségbana, Ben. 161/G4
Ségélo-Koro, C.d'Iv. 160/D4
Segelstad Bru, Nor. 96/D1
Seget, Indo. 139/H4
Segezha, Rus. 118/G3
Segorbe, Sp. 103/E3
Ségou, Mali 160/D3
Ségou (pol. reg.), Mali 160/D3
Segovia, Col. 210/C3
Segovia, Sp. 102/C2
Segozero (lake), Rus. 118/G3
Segrate, It. 116/C3
Segré, Fr. 100/C3
Segre (riv.), Sp. 103/F2
Seguam (isl.), Ak, US 192/D5
Séguédine, Niger 154/H3
Séguéla, C.d'Iv. 160/D5
Seguin, Tx, US 190/D4
Segura (riv.), Sp. 103/E3
Segura (riv.), Sp. 102/D3
Segusino, It. 117/F2
Sehnde, Ger. 109/G4
Sehithwa, Bots. 163/D5
Sehore, India 140/C3
Sehwän, Pak. 147/J3
Seibersdorf, Ger. 111/G4
Seiersberg, Aus. 106/B2
Seika, Japan 135/J6
Seiling, Ok, US 187/H3
Seille (riv.), Fr. 98/C5
Seinäjoki, Fin. 118/D3
Seine (riv.), On, Can. 185/L3
Seine (bay), Fr. 100/D2
Seine (riv.), Fr. 100/D2
Seine-et-Marne
(dept.), Fr. 110/B5
Seine-Maritime
(dept.), Fr. 110/A4
Seine-st-Denis
(dept.), Fr. 110/B6
Seitenstetten, Aus. 113/H6
Seiwa, Japan 135/K7
Seix, Fr. 100/D5
Seixal, Port. 103/P10
Sejaka, Indo. 139/E4
Sejerø (isl.), Den. 96/D4
Sejny, Pol. 97/K4
Sekayu, Indo. 138/B4
Seke, Tanz. 162/A2
Sekenke, Tanz. 162/A3
Seki (riv.), Japan 149/L1
Seki, Japan 135/L3
Seki, Japan 135/K6
Sekigahara, Japan 135/K5
Sekijo, Japan 135/D1
Sekiyado, Japan 135/D1
Sekondi, Gha. 161/E5
Sel, Nor. 95/D3
Selah, Wa, US 184/C4
Selaphum, Thai. 136/C2
Selargius, It. 104/A3
Selaru (isl.), Indo. 139/H5
Selatan (cape), Indo. 138/D4
Selawik (lake),
Ak, US 192/F2
Selayar (isl.), Indo. 139/F5
Selb, Ger. 113/F2
Selbitz, Ger. 113/E2
Selbitz (riv.), Ger. 113/E2
Selbu, Nor. 95/D3
Selby, SD, US 185/H4
Selby, Eng, UK 93/G4
Selby-on-the-Bay,
Md, US 196/B6
Selci, It. 117/F6
Selçuk, Turk. 148/A2
Selden, NY, US 197/E2
Sele (riv.), It. 104/D2
Selebi-Phikwe, Bots. 163/E5
Seleli (hill), Tanz. 162/B5
Selemdzha (riv.), Rus. 123/N4
Selenga (prov.), Mong. 128/J2
Selenge (riv.), Mong. 128/J2
Selenginsk, Rus. 123/L4
Selenicë, Alb. 105/F2
Sélestat, Fr. 114/D1
Selety (riv.), Kaz. 145/F2
Seleznëvo, Rus. 97/M3
Selfoss, Ice. 95/N7
Sélibabi, Mrta. 160/B3
Seligenstadt, Ger. 112/B2
Seliger (lake), Rus. 118/G4
Selimbau, Indo. 138/D3
Selimiye, Turk. 148/A2
Selinsgrove, Pa, US 196/B2
Seljord, Nor. 96/C2
Selkan (tun.), Japan 134/B3
Selkirk, Sc, UK 94/D5
Selkirk, Mb, Can. 180/G3
Selkirk (mts.), BC, Can. 184/D3
Selleck, Wa, US 193/D3
Sellersville, Pa, US 196/C3
Sellières, Fr. 114/B4
Sells, Az, US 186/E5
Selly Oak, Eng, UK 90/E2
Sellye, Hun. 106/C3
Selm, Ger. 109/E5
Selma, Al, US 191/F3
Selmer, Tn, US 191/F3
Selongey, Fr. 114/B3
Selouma, Gui. 160/C4
Selous Game Reserve,
Tanz. 162/B4
Selsey, Eng, UK 91/F5
Selsey Bill (pt.),
Eng, UK 91/F5
Selsingen, Ger. 109/G2
Sel'tso, Rus. 120/E1
Seltz, Fr. 112/B5
Sélune (riv.), Fr. 100/C2

Selvas (for.), Braz. 205/C3
Selvik, Nor. 95/R9
Selwyn, Austl. 172/A3
Selwyn (range),
 Austl. 172/A3
Selz (riv.), Ger. 101/H2
Semara, WSah. 154/C2
Semarang, Indo. 138/B5
Semarsot, India 142/D4
Sembehun, SLeo. 160/B5
Sembera (riv.), Czh. 113/H2
Semberong (riv.),
 Malay. 138/B3
Şemdinli, Turk. 148/F2
Séméac, Fr. 100/C5
Semenivka, Ukr. 120/E1
Semenivka, Ukr. 120/E2
Semenov, Rus. 119/J4
Semeru (peak), Indo. 138/D5
Semey, Kaz. 145/H2
Semikarakorsk, Rus. 121/G3
Semilovo, Rus. 121/G1
Semiluki, Rus. 120/F1
Seminole (lake),
 Ga, US 191/G4
Seminole, Tx, US 190/C3
Seminoe (res.), Wy, US 186/F2
Semitau, Indo. 138/D4
Semliki
 (riv.), D.R. Congo 162/A2
Semnän, Iran 146/F1
Semnon (riv.), Fr. 100/C3
Semois (riv.), Belg. 100/F2
Semporna, Malay. 139/E3
Semsales, Swi. 114/C4
Semskefjellet
 (peak), Nor. 95/E2
Sen (riv.), Camb. 141/H5
Sen-san (peak), Japan 135/G2
Sena, Thai. 141/H5
Senador Pompeu,
 Braz. 212/C2
Senaja, Malay. 139/E2
Senaki, Geo. 121/G4
Senanga, Zam. 163/D4
Sénas, Fr. 148/B5
Senatobia, Ms, US 191/F3
Sence (riv.), Eng, UK 91/E1
Send, Eng, UK 88/B3
Sendai (riv.), Japan 132/D3
Sendai, Japan 133/G1
Sendai, Japan 132/B5
Sendai (int'l arpt.),
 Japan 133/G1
Sendai (bay), Japan 134/B4
Sendai (riv.), Japan 132/B5
Senden, Ger. 112/D6
Senden, Ger. 109/E5
Sendenhorst, Ger. 109/E5
Senec, Slvk. 99/J4
Seneca Creek State Park,
 Md, US 196/A5
Seneffe, Belg. 111/D2
Senegal (ctry.) 160/B3
Sénégal (riv.), Afr. 160/B2
Senekal, SAfr. 163/E2
Seney NWR, Mi, US 188/C2
Senezhskoye
 (lake), Rus. 119/W8
Senfi, Gha. 161/E5
Senftenberg, Ger. 99/H3
Sengenthal, Ger. 113/E4
Sengilev, Rus. 121/J1
Sengor, Bhu. 143/H2
Senguer (riv.), Arg. 216/C3
Senhor do Bonfim,
 Braz. 212/B3
Senica, Slvk. 99/J4
Senirkent, Turk. 148/B2
Senise, It. 104/E2
Senj, Cro. 101/L4
Senja (isl.), Nor. 95/F1
Senkaku-Shotō
 (isl.), Japan 133/G8
Şenkaya, Turk. 148/E1
Şenköy, Turk. 149/E1
Senlis, Fr. 110/B5
Senmonoron, Camb. 136/D3
Sennan, Japan 135/H7
Sennar (dam), Sudan 155/M5
Senne (riv.), Belg. 111/D2
Sennecy-le-Grand, Fr. 114/A4
Sennfeld, Ger. 112/D2
Senno, Bela. 97/N4
Sennoy, Rus. 121/G2
Sennoy, Rus. 121/H1
Sennwald, Swi. 115/F3
Sennybridge, Wal, UK 90/C3
Séno (prov.), Burk. 161/F3
Senones, Fr. 114/C1
Senorbì, It. 104/A3
Senou (Bamako)
 (int'l arpt.), Mali 160/D3
Senovo, Bul. 107/H4
Sens, Fr. 100/E2
Sensuntepeque, ESal. 202/D3
Senta, Serb. 106/E3
Sentani, Indo. 139/K4
Sentery, D.R. Congo 163/E2
Senya Beraku, Gha. 161/E5
Senyavin (isls.), Micr. 174/E4
Senzig, Ger. 98/Q7
Seohara, India 142/B1
Seon, Swi. 114/E3
Seondha, India 142/B2
Seoni, India 142/B4
Seoni Mälwä, India 142/A4
Seoul (Sŏul)
 (cap.), SKor. 131/D4
Seoul Grand Park,
 SKor. 131/G7
Seoul Jikhalsi
 (prov.), SKor. 131/D4
Sepetiba (bay), Braz. 213/J8
Sepik (riv.), PNG 174/D5

Sep'o, NKor. 131/D3
Sepólno Krajeńskie,
 Pol. 99/J2
Sept-Îles, Qu, Can. 189/H2
Septemvri, Bul. 49/G4
Septeuil, Fr. 88/H5
Sepulveda
 (dam), Ca, US 194/F7
Sequeros, Sp. 102/B2
Sequoia NP, Ca, US 186/C5
Serafimovich, Rus. 121/G2
Seraincourt, Fr. 88/H4
Seraing, Belg. 111/E2
Serampore, India 143/G4
Sèran (riv.), Fr. 114/D3
Serasan
 (str.), Indo.,Malay. 138/C3
Seravezza, It. 116/D6
Serbia and Montenegro
 (ctry.) 106/D3
Serbia (reg.), Serb. 106/E4
Serchio (riv.), It. 116/D4
Serdobsk, Rus. 121/H1
Serebryansk, Kaz. 122/J5
Serebryansk, Rus. 118/H5
Seredka (riv.), Bela. 121/G2
Serednikovo, Rus. 118/H5
Seregno, It. 116/C2
Serein (riv.), Fr. 98/D4
Serémange-Erzange,
 Fr. 111/F5
Seremban, Malay. 138/B3
Serengeti NP, Tanz. 155/M8
Serenje, Zam. 163/F3
Serere, Ugan. 162/A1
Sergach, Rus. 119/K5
Sergeantsville, NJ, US 196/D3
Sergen, Turk. 107/H5
Sergeya Kirova
 (isls.), Rus. 122/J2
Sergeyevka, Kaz. 119/G5
Sergipe (state), Braz. 212/C3
Sergiyev Posad, Rus. 118/H4
Sergnano, It. 116/C3
Seria, Bru. 138/D3
Seriate, It. 116/C2
Sérifontaine, Fr. 110/A5
Sérifos, Gre. 105/J4
Sérifos (isl.), Gre. 105/J4
Sérignan, Fr. 100/E5
Serik, Turk. 148/B2
Seringa, Serra da
 (mts.), Braz. 209/H6
Serio (riv.), It. 116/C2
Serkout (peak), Alg. 157/G5
Sermaize-les-Bains,
 Fr. 111/D6
Sermide, It. 117/E4
Sermovodsk, Rus. 121/J1
Sernur, Rus. 119/L4
Serón, Sp. 102/D4
Serós, Sp. 103/F2
Serottini (peak), It. 115/G5
Serov, Rus. 122/G4
Serowe, Bots. 163/E5
Serpa, Port. 102/B4
Serpeddi (peak), It. 104/A3
Serpent's Mouth
 (str.), Trin.,Ven. 211/F2
Serpentine (dam),
 Austl. 173/C4
Serpentine Lakes,
 Austl. 171/F4
Serpukhov, Rus. 118/H5
Serra (peak), It. 116/D6
Serra, Braz. 213/K6
Serra Branca, Braz. 212/C2
Serra da Bocaina, PN da,
 Braz. 213/G3
Serra da Canastra, PN da,
 Braz. 213/D1
Serra da Capivara, PN da,
 Braz. 212/B3
Serra da Estrela
 (peak), Port. 102/B2
Serra da Estrela
 (mts.), Port. 102/A3
Serra do Cipó, PN da,
 Braz. 213/D1
Serra dos Órgãos, PN da,
 Braz. 213/K7
Serra San Bruno, It. 104/E3
Serra San Quirico, It. 117/G7
Serra Talhada, Braz. 212/C2
Serra, Gre. 105/H2
Serralta di San Vito
 (peak), It. 104/E3
Serramanna, It. 104/A3
Serramazzoni, It. 117/D5
Serrana Bank (isl.),
 Col. 203/G3
Serranía de la Cerbatana
 (mts.), Ven. 211/E3
Serranía de la Neblina, PN,
 Ven. 211/E4
Serranías del Burro
 (mts.), Mex. 200/E2
Serranilla Bank
 (isl.), Col. 203/G3
Serranópolis, Braz. 213/B1
Serrat (cape), Tun. 158/L6
Serravalle, It. 117/F4
Serravalle, SMar. 117/F4
Serravalle Scrivia, It. 116/B4
Serravalle Sesia, It. 116/B2
Serre (riv.), Fr. 98/B4
Serrenti, It. 104/A3
Serrinha, Braz. 212/C3
Serris, Fr. 88/L5
Sertã, Port. 102/A3
Sertânia, Braz. 212/C2
Sertãozinho, Braz. 213/H2
Sertavul (pass), Turk. 148/C2

Serteng (mts.), China 128/F4
Serui, Indo. 139/J4
Seruyan (riv.), Indo. 138/D4
Servance, Fr. 114/C2
Servi, Turk. 148/E2
Sérvia, Gre. 105/G2
Serviceton, Austl. 173/B3
Sesebi (ruin), Sudan 159/B4
Sese (isls.), Ugan. 162/A3
Sesepe, Indo. 139/H4
Sesheke, Zam. 163/D4
Sesia (riv.), It. 101/H4
Sesimbra, Port. 102/A3
Sesimbra, Port. 103/P11
Seskar (isl.), Rus. 97/N1
Sespe, Ca, US 194/B2
Sespe (cr.), Ca, US 194/A1
Sespe Condor Sanctuary,
 Ca, US 194/C3
Sesslach, Ger. 112/D2
Sesto Calende, It. 116/B2
Sesto Fiorentino, It. 117/E6
Sesto San Giovanni, It. 116/C2
Sesto Ulteriano, It. 116/C3
Sestola, It. 117/D5
Sestra (riv.), Rus. 118/W9
Sestri Levante, It. 116/C5
Sestroretsk, Rus. 119/S6
Setagamu, Nga. 161/F5
Setana (peak), It. 115/G4
Shah Alam, Malay. 138/B3
Setana, Japan 134/A2
Séte, Fr. 100/E5
Sete Lagoas, Braz. 213/C1
Sethärja, Pak. 147/J3
Seti (riv.), Nepal 142/C1
Seti (zone), Nepal 142/C1
Sétif, Alg. 158/H4
Sétif (wilaya), Alg. 158/H4
Seto, Japan 135/M5
Seto-Naikai NP, Japan 132/C4
Setouchi, Japan 133/K6
Settat, Mor. 156/D2
Settepani (peak), It. 116/B5
Settimo Torinese, It. 116/A2
Settimo Vittone, It. 116/A1
Settle, Eng, UK 93/F3
Settsu, Japan 135/J6
Setúbal (dist.), Port. 102/A3
Setúbal (bay), Port. 102/A3
Setúbal, Port. 103/Q10
Seubersdorf, Ger. 113/E4
Seudre (riv.), Fr. 100/C4
Seugne (riv.), Fr. 100/C4
Seuil-d'Argonne, Fr. 111/E6
Seul (lake), On, Can. 180/G3
Seulimeum, Indo. 138/A2
Seurre, Fr. 114/B4
Seuzach, Swi. 115/E2
Sevan, Arm. 121/H4
Sevana (lake), Arm. 121/H4
Sevastopol', Ukr. 120/E3
Sevelen, Swi. 115/F3
Seven (riv.), Eng, UK 93/H3
Seven Heads (pt.), Ire. 89/P11
Seven Valleys, Pa, US 196/B4
Sevenoaks, Eng, UK 88/D3
Sevenoaks Weald,
 Eng, UK 88/D3
Severn (riv.), Wal, UK 93/F6
Severn (riv.), On, Can. 180/G3
Severn (riv.), Md, US 196/B5
Severn Park, Md, US 196/B5
Severnaya Osetiya-Alaniya,
 Resp., Rus. 121/G4
Severnaya Sos'va
 (riv.), Rus. 119/N3
Severnaya Zemlya
 (isls.), Rus. 122/J2
Severnyy, Rus. 119/P4
Severo-Kuril'sk, Rus. 123/P4
Severo-Yeniseyskiy,
 Rus. 122/K3
Severobaykal'sk, Rus. 123/L4
Severodvinsk, Rus. 118/H2
Severomorsk, Rus. 118/G1
Severomuysk, Rus. 123/M4
Sha'nabī, Jabal ash
 (peak), Tun. 158/L7
Severoural'sk, Rus. 119/N3
Severskaya, Rus. 120/F3
Severukha, Rus. 119/P4
Seveso, It. 116/C2
Sevier (des.), Ut, US 186/D3
Sevierville, Tn, US 191/H3
Sevilla, Col. 210/C3
Sevilla, Sp. 102/C4
Seville, Austl. 173/G5
Sevlievo, Bul. 107/G4
Sevnica, Slov. 106/B2
Sevojno, Serb. 106/D4
Sevran, Fr. 88/L5
Sevsk, Rus. 120/E1
Sewa (riv.), SLeo. 160/C5
Seward (pen.), Ak, US 192/E2
Seward, Ak, US 187/H2
Seward, Ne, US 187/H2
Seward, NJ, US 197/J9
Sewell, Chile 216/N9
Seyah Cheshmeh, Iran 121/H5
Seybaplaya, Mex. 202/D2
Seychelles (ctry.) 81/M6
Seydhisfjördhur, Ice. 95/Q6
Seydişehir, Turk. 148/B2
Seyhan (dam), Turk. 148/C2
Seyhan (riv.), Turk. 149/D1
Seyitgazi, Turk. 148/B2
Seym (riv.), Rus. 120/E2
Seymour, Austl. 173/C3
Seymour, Tx, US 187/H4
Seynod, Fr. 114/C6

Seyssel, Fr. 114/B6
Sežana, Slov. 101/K4
Sézanne, Fr. 110/C6
Sezimovo Usti, Czh. 113/H4
Sezze, It. 104/C2
Sfax, Tun. 157/H2
Sfax (gov.), Tun. 157/H2
Sfîntu Gheorghe, Rom. 107/J3
Sfîntu Gheorghe, Rom. 107/G3
Sfîntu Gheorghe Branch
 (riv.), Rom. 107/J3
Sfizef, Alg. 158/E5
Sgurr na Lapaich (peak),
 Sc, UK 94/A2
Sha (riv.), China 130/C4
Sha Tin, China 129/U10
Shaanxi (prov.), China 128/J5
Shaba Nat'l Rsv.,
 Kenya 162/C2
Shābāzpur (riv.), Bang. 143/H4
Shabeelle (riv.), Som. 155/P7
Shabla, Bul. 107/J4
Shabqadar, Pak. 144/A2
Shabunda, D.R. Congo 155/L8
Shache, China 145/G5
Shade (mtn.), Pa, US 196/A2
Shadrinsk, Rus. 119/P4
Shafter, Tx, US 190/B4
Shagamu, Nga. 161/F5
Shagany (lake), Ukr. 107/J3
Shageluk, Ak, US 192/G3
Shah Kot, Pak. 144/B4
Shāhābād, India 142/B1
Shāhābād, India 142/B1
Shāhābād, India 147/G2
Shahdād, Iran 147/G2
Shāhdādkot, Pak. 147/J3
Shahdol, India 142/C4
Shāhganj, India 142/D2
Shāhhāt, Libya 155/K1
Shāhjahānpur, India 142/B2
Shāhpur, Pak. 144/A3
Shāhpur Chākar, Pak. 140/A2
Shāhpura, India 142/A2
Shahr-e Kord, Iran 146/F2
Shahr Sultān, Pak. 144/A5
Shāhröd (Emāmshahr),
 Iran 147/F1
Shā'ib al Banāt (peak),
 Egypt 159/C3
Shaikhpura, India 143/E3
Shājāpur, India 147/L4
Shakargarh, Pak. 144/C3
Shakaskraal, SAfr. 165/E3
Shakawe, Bots. 163/D4
Shakhrisabz, Uzb. 145/E5
Shakhtinsk, Kaz. 145/G5
Shakhty, Rus. 120/G3
Shakhun'ya, Rus. 119/K4
Shaki, Nga. 161/F4
Shakotan (pen.),
 Japan 134/B2
Shaktoolik, Ak, US 192/F3
Shalbuzdag (peak),
 Rus. 121/H4
Shallow Reach (inlet),
 Austl. 171/M8
Shalqar, Kaz. 121/L3
Shaluli (mts.), China 128/G5
Shām, Jabal ash (peak),
 Oman 147/G4
Shama (riv.), Tanz. 163/F2
Shamattawa (riv.),
 On, Can. 139/H3
Shāmgarh, India 147/L4
Shamil, Iran 147/G3
Shāmli, India 144/D5
Shammar, Jabal
 (mts.), SAr. 146/D3
Shamokin, Pa, US 196/B2
Shamokin Dam,
 Pa, US 196/B2
Shamrock (mtn.),
 Shelley (isl.), Pa, US 196/B3
Shamrock, Tx, US 187/G4
Shamsābād, India 142/B2
Shamva, Zim. 163/F4
Shan (plat.), Myan. 128/G7
Shan (state), Myan. 141/G3
Shandon, Pa, US 196/B2
Shandong (prov.),
 China 129/L4
Shandong (isl.),
 China 130/E3
Shangcai, China 130/C4
Shangcheng, China 130/C5
Shangdu, China 129/K3
Shanghai (prov.),
 China 129/M5
Shanghai, China 130/L8
Shanghang, China 137/C2
Shanghe, China 130/D3
Shangqiu, China 130/C4
Shangshui, China 130/C4
Shangyi, China 130/C2
Shangyou, China 137/B3
Shannon (riv.), Ire. 89/P10
Shanshan, China 128/F3
Shantar (isls.), Rus. 123/P4
Shantar, China 125/N4
Shantou, China 129/L7
Shanxi (prov.), China 129/K4
Shanyin, China 130/C3
Shaoguan, China 141/K3
Shaowu, China 137/D1
Shaoxing, China 137/D2
Shaoyang, China 129/K5
Shaoyang, China 141/K2
Shapkina (riv.), Rus. 119/M2
Shaqlāwah, Iraq 148/F2
Sharafkhāneh, Iran 148/F2
Sharbatāt, Ra's ash (cape),
 Oman 147/G5

Sharga, Mong. 128/G2
Shari, Japan 134/D2
Sharingol, Mong. 128/J2
Shark (bay), Austl. 170/B3
Shark River (inlet),
 NJ, US 196/D3
Sharon, Pa, US 188/D3
Sharp (mtn.), Ut, US 195/K11
Sharpe (lake),
 SD, US 185/J4
Sharqpur, Pak. 144/C4
Shar'ya, Rus. 119/K4
Shashi, China 137/B1
Shasta (lake), Ca, US 184/C5
Shasta (mt.), Ca, US 184/C5
Shatskiy NP, Ukr. 99/M3
Shatt al Arab (riv.),
 Iraq 146/E2
Shatt al Jarīd (dry lake),
 Gabon 154/G1
Shattuck, Ok, US 187/G3
Shaunavon, Sk, Can. 184/F3
Shavano Park, Tx, US 195/T20
Shaw, Eng, UK 91/F4
Shawano, Wi, US 185/L4
Shawinigan, Qu, Can. 189/F2
Shawnee, Ok, US 187/H4
Shawnee (res.),
 Ok, US 195/N15
Shawnee, Ks, US 195/D5
Shay Gap, Austl. 170/C2
Shaykhān, Iraq 148/F2
Shchara (riv.), Bela. 120/C1
Shchekino, Rus. 120/F1
Shchelkovo, Rus. 119/W9
Shchigry, Rus. 120/F2
Shchuchinsk, Kaz. 145/F2
She Xian, China 137/C2
Shea Stadium,
 NY, US 197/K9
Shebelē Wenz (riv.),
 Eth. 155/P6
Sheberghān, Afg. 147/J1
Sheboygan,
 Wi, US 185/M5
Shediac, NB, Can. 189/H2
Shee (riv.), Sc, UK 94/C3
Sheelin (lake), Ire. 92/A4
Sheep (mtn.), Ak, US 192/F2
Shefar'am, Isr. 149/G6
Shefayim, Isr. 149/F7
Sheffield, Austl. 173/C4
Sheffield, Eng, UK 93/G5
Sheffield (co.), Eng, UK 93/G5
Sheffield, Al, US 191/G3
Sheffield (isl.),
 Ct, US 197/M7
Shehuén (riv.), Arg. 215/B6
Shek Uk (mtn.), Tn, US 191/G3
Shekhun'ya, Rus. 119/K4
Shekhupura, Pak. 144/B4
Shekhüpura (cape),
 Rus. 123/S3
Shelagskiy (cape),
 Rus. 123/S3
Shelburne, NS, Can. 189/H3
Shelby, Mt, US 184/F3
Shelby, Ms, US 187/K4
Shelby, Wi, US 188/C3
Shelby, NC, US 191/H3
Shelbyville (lake),
 Il, US 191/F2
Shelbyville, Pa, US 196/B3
Shelbyville, In, US 188/C4
Sheldon Point,
 Ak, US 192/F3
Shelekhov (gulf),
 Rus. 125/Q3
Shelikof (str.), Ak, US 192/H4
Shell (pt.), Eng, UK 91/G4
Shell Lake, Wi, US 185/L4
Shell Rock (riv.),
 Ia, US 185/K5
Shellbrook, Sk, US 185/G2
Shelter (isl.), NY, US 197/F1
Shelter Island (sound),
 NY, US 197/F1
Shelton, Wa, US 184/C4
Shelton, Ct, US 197/E1
Shen Xian, China 130/C3
Shenandoah, Pa, US 196/B2
Shenandoah NP,
 Va, US 188/D4
Shenchi, China 130/C3
Sheng Xian, China 137/D2
Shenge (pt.), SLeo. 160/B5
Shengena (peak),
 Tanz. 162/C4
Shennongjia, China 130/B5
Shenqiu, China 130/C4
Shenyang, China 129/M5
Shenzhen, China 141/K3
Shepetivka, Ukr. 120/C2
Shepherd (isls.), Van. 174/F6
Sheppey, Isle of (isl.),
 Eng, UK 91/G4
Shepshed, Eng, UK 91/E1
Sheqi, China 130/C4
Sherbro (isl.), SLeo. 160/B5
Sherbrooke, Qu, Can. 189/G2
Shere (mtn.), Iran 161/G5
Sheremetyevo
 (int'l arpt.), Rus. 119/W9
Sherghāti, India 143/E3
Sheridan, Wa, US 184/G4
Sheridan, Co, US 195/B3
Sheridan, Wy, US 187/H4
Sherman, Tx, US 187/H4
Sherpur, Bang. 143/H3
Sherwood (pt.),
 Ct, US 197/E1
Sherwood-san (peak),
 Japan 133/A2
Shirane-san (peak),
 Japan 133/B2
Sheung Shui-Fanling,
 China 129/U10

Sheyang (riv.), China 130/D4
Sheyang, China 130/E4
Sheyenne (riv.),
 ND, US 185/J4
Shi (riv.), China 130/C4
Shi San Ling, China 130/H6
Shibakawa, Japan 135/B3
Shibata, Japan 133/F2
Shibayama, Japan 135/E2
Shibecha, Japan 134/D2
Shibetsu, Japan 135/E2
Shibetsu, Japan 134/D2
Shibin al Kaum,
 Egypt 149/B4
Shibin al Qanāṭir,
 Egypt 149/B4
Shibogama (lake),
 On, Can. 139/H3
Shibushi (bay), Japan 132/C5
Shicheng, China 137/C2
Shicheng (isl.),
 China 131/B3
Shithātha, Iraq 148/E3
Shickshinny, Pa, US 196/B1
Shiderty (riv.), Kaz. 145/F2
Shido, Japan 132/D3
Shiga, Japan 135/J5
Shiyan, China 130/B4
Shihezi, China 128/E3
Shijak, Alb. 105/F2
Shijiazhuang, China 130/C3
Shijōnawate, Japan 135/K6
Shikabe, Japan 134/B2
Shikarpur, India 142/B1
Shikārpur, Pak. 147/J3
Shikata, Japan 135/G6
Shikishima, Japan 135/B2
Shikohābād, India 142/B2
Shikoku (isl.), Japan 132/C4
Shikoku (mts.), Japan 132/C4
Shikotsu (lake), Japan 134/B2
Shikotsu-Tōya NP,
 Japan 134/B2
Shildon, Eng, UK 93/G2
Shilka (riv.), Rus. 125/L4
Shilla (peak), India 147/L2
Shillington, Pa, US 196/C3
Shillong, India 141/F2
Shiloh, Il, US 195/H8
Shiloh, NJ, US 196/C5
Shilou, China 130/B3
Shimabara, Japan 132/B4
Shimagahara, Japan 135/J6
Shimamoto, Japan 135/J6
Shimane (pref.),
 Japan 132/C3
Shimanovsk, Rus. 123/N4
Shimasahi, Japan 135/K5
Shimba Hills Nat'l Rsv.,
 Kenya 162/C4
Shimbara (bay), Japan 132/B4
Shimber Berris (peak),
 Som. 155/Q5
Shimizu, Japan 134/C2
Shimizu, Japan 135/B3
Shimo-Koshiki (isl.),
 Japan 132/A5
Shimobe, Japan 135/A3
Shimoda, Japan 133/F3
Shimodate, Japan 135/F2
Shimofusa, Japan 135/E2
Shimoichi, Japan 135/J7
Shimokita (pen.),
 Japan 133/B3
Shimonita, Japan 135/B2
Shimonoseki, Japan 132/B4
Shimotsuma, Japan 135/M5
Shimoyama, Japan 135/M5
Shimukappu, Japan 134/D2
Shin (lake), Sc, UK 89/R7
Shindo, SKor. 131/F6
Shingū, Japan 132/D4
Shinhyōn, SKor. 132/A3
Shinji (lake), Japan 132/C3
Shinjō, Japan 134/B4
Shinjō, Japan 135/J7
Shinkawa, Japan 135/M5
Shinminato, Japan 133/E2
Shinnecock (bay),
 NY, US 197/F1
Shinnecock Ind. Res.,
 NY, US 197/F1
Shinsei, Japan 135/L5
Shintoku, Japan 134/C2
Shintone, Japan 135/E2
Shinyanga, Tanz. 162/B2
Shinyanga (pol. reg.),
 Tanz. 162/B2
Shio-no-misaki (cape),
 Japan 132/D4
Shiogama, Japan 133/G1
Shioya-saki (pt.),
 Japan 133/G2
Ship Bottom, NJ, US 196/D4
Shipley, Eng, UK 93/G4
Shippan (pt.), Ct, US 197/L7
Shippegan, NB, Can. 189/H2
Shippo, Japan 135/L5
Shiprock, NM, US 186/E3
Shir (mtn.), Iran 147/F3
Shirakami-misaki
 (cape), Japan 134/B2
Shirakawa, Japan 135/B2
Shirakawa, Japan 135/B2
Shirakawa-tōge (pass),
 Japan 134/C2
Shirako, Japan 135/E2
Shirane, Japan 135/A2
Shirane-san (peak),
 Japan 133/F3
Shiranuka, Japan 134/D2
Shiraoi, Japan 134/B2

Shiraoka, Japan 135/D1
Shīrāz, Iran 146/F3
Shirbin, Egypt 149/B4
Shiretoko-misaki
 (cape), Japan 134/D1
Shiretoko NP, Japan 134/D1
Shiriya-zaki
 (pt.), Japan 134/B3
Shirjiu (lake), China 130/D5
Shirley, NY, US 197/F2
Shiroi, Japan 135/E2
Shiroishi, Japan 133/G1
Shirone, Japan 133/F2
Shiroyama, Japan 135/C2
Shīrvān, Iran 147/G1
Shishaldin (vol.),
 Ak, US 192/F5
Shishgarh, India 142/B1
Shishi, China 137/C3
Shishmaref, Ak, US 192/E2
Shishou, China 137/B2
Shisui, Japan 135/E2
Shivpurī, India 142/A3
Shivpurī NP, India 142/A3
Shixing, China 141/K3
Shiyan, China 130/B4
Shizhu, China 137/A2
Shizugawa, Japan 134/B4
Shizuishan, China 128/J4
Shizukuishi, Japan 134/B4
Shizunai, Japan 134/C2
Shizuoka (pref.),
 Japan 134/B2
Japan 134/B2
Shkumbin (riv.), Alb. 106/C5
Shmidta (cape), Rus. 122/C1
Shoal (pt.), Austl. 170/B4
Shoal Lake, Mb, Can. 185/H3
Shoalhaven (riv.),
 Austl. 173/D2
Shōbara, Japan 132/C3
Shōbu, Japan 135/D1
Shōdo (isl.), Japan 132/D3
Shoemakersville,
 Pa, US 196/C3
Shokanbetsu-dake (peak),
 Japan 134/B2
Sholāpur, India 147/L5
Sholl (peak), Arg. 217/D6
Shōnan, Japan 135/E2
Shorāpur, India 140/C4
Shoreham-by-Sea,
 Eng, UK 91/F5
Shorewood, Wi, US 193/Q13
Shorewood, Il, US 193/P16
Shorkot, Pak. 144/B4
Short (mtn.), Tn, US 191/G3
Shortland (isls.), Sol. 174/C5
Shoshone (riv.),
 Wy, US 184/F1
Shoshone (mts.),
 Nv, US 186/C3
Shoshoni, Wy, US 184/F5
Shostka, Ukr. 120/E2
Shotts, Sc, UK 94/C5
Shou Xian, China 130/D4
Shouguang, China 130/D3
Shouyang, China 130/C3
Show Low, Az, US 186/E4
Showa, Japan 135/B2
Shōwa, Japan 135/D2
Shpanberga (chan.),
 Rus. 134/E2
Shpola, Ukr. 120/D2
Shreveport, La, US 187/J4
Shrewsbury, Mo, US 195/G8
Shrewsbury, Eng, UK 90/D1
Shrewsbury, Pa, US 196/B4
Shropshire (co.),
 Eng, UK 93/E6
Shropshire Union (canal),
 Eng, UK 91/E4
Shū (riv.), Kaz. 123/H5
Shu (riv.), China 130/D5
Shuangbai, China 141/H3
Shuangcheng, China 129/N2
Shuangliao, China 130/E2
Shuangpai, China 141/K2
Shuangyashan,
 China 129/P2
Shu'ayb, Jabal an (peak),
 Yem. 146/D5
Shubrā al Khaymah,
 Egypt 149/B4
Shubrā Khīt, Egypt 149/B4
Shucheng, China 130/D5
Shu'fāṭ, Isr. 149/G8
Shufu, China 145/G5
Shuiyang (riv.), China 130/D5
Shujāābād, Pak. 144/A5
Shulan, China 129/N3
Shule, China 145/G5
Shule (riv.), China 128/G4
Shumagin (isls.),
 Ak, US 192/G4
Shumen, Bul. 107/H4
Shumerlya, Rus. 119/K5
Shunak (peak), Kaz. 145/F3
Shungnak, Ak, US 192/G2
Shunyi, China 130/H6
Shuo Xian, China 130/C3
Shupiyan, India 144/C3
Shūr (riv.), Iran 147/G2
Shurugwi, Zim. 163/E4
Shūshtar, Iran 146/E2
Shuswap (peak),
 BC, Can. 184/D3
Shuwaykah, WBnk. 149/G7
Shuya, Japan 118/J4
Shuyang, China 130/D4
Shwebo, Myan. 141/G3

Shwegyin, Myan. 141/G4
Shyghys Qazaqstan
 (obl.), Kaz. 122/J5
Shymkent, Kaz. 145/E4
Shyok (riv.), India 147/L2
Si Satchanalai
 (ruin), Thai. 136/B2
Si Xian, China 130/D4
Siāh Küh (mts.), Afg. 147/H2
Siak (riv.), Indo. 138/B4
Siālkot, Pak. 144/C3
Sianów, Pol. 96/G4
Siapa (riv.), Ven. 211/E4
Siargao (isl.), Phil. 137/E6
Siasi, Phil. 139/F2
Siaton (pt.), Phil. 139/F2
Siaton, Phil. 137/D6
Siau (isl.), Indo. 139/G3
Šiauliai, Lith. 97/K4
Sibalom, Phil. 137/D5
Sibay, Rus. 121/L1
Sibbo (Sipoo), Fin. 97/L1
Šibenik, Cro. 106/B4
Siberia (reg.), Rus. 125/H3
Siberut (isl.), Indo. 138/A4
Sibi, Pak. 147/J3
Sibiloi NP, Kenya 155/N7
Sibiti, Congo 163/B3
Sibiu, Rom. 107/G3
Sibiu (prov.), Rom. 107/G2
Sibley, Mo, US 195/E5
Sibolga, Indo. 138/A3
Sibu, Malay. 138/D3
Sibuco, Phil. 139/F2
Sibuguey (isl.), Phil. 139/F1
Sibut, CAfr. 155/K6
Sibuyan (isl.), Phil. 139/F1
Sibuyan (sea), Phil. 139/F1
Sicamous, BC, Can. 184/D3
Sichuan (prov.), China 128/H5
Sicilia (pol. reg.), It. 104/C4
Sicily (isl.), It. 104/C3
Sicily, Strait of
 (str.), It. 104/B3
Sico (riv.), Hon. 198/D4
Sicuani, Peru 214/D4
Šid, Serb. 106/D3
Siddipet, India 140/C4
Siderno Marina, It. 104/E3
Siderópolis, Braz. 213/B4
Sidewinder (mtn.),
 Ca, US 194/C1
Sīdhauli, India 142/C2
Sidhi, India 142/C3
Sidhirókastron, Gre. 105/H2
Sidhpur, India 147/K4
Sidi Aïssa, Alg. 158/G5
Sīdī Barrānī, Egypt 159/A2
Sidi Bel-Abbes, Alg. 158/E5
Sidi Bennour, Mor. 156/C2
Sidi Bouzid, Tun. 158/L7
Sidi Bou Zid (gov.),
 Tun. 158/L7
Sidi Kacem, Mor. 158/B2
Sidi Kacem (prov.),
 Mor. 158/B2
Sīdī Sālim, Egypt 149/B4
Sidi Slimane, Mor. 158/B2
Sidi Yahya du Rharb,
 Mor. 158/B2
Sidlaw (hills), Sc, UK 94/C3
Sidmouth, Eng, UK 90/C5
Sidney, BC, Can. 184/C3
Sidney, Mt, US 185/G4
Sidney, Oh, US 188/C3
Sidney Lanier (lake),
 Ga, US 191/H3
Sidra (gulf), Libya 154/J1
Sieci, It. 117/E5
Siedlce, Pol. 99/M2
Sieg (riv.), Ger. 101/G1
Siegburg, Ger. 111/G2
Siegen, Ger. 111/H2
Siegenburg, Ger. 113/E5
Siegendorf im Burgenland,
 Aus. 101/M3
Siemianówka (lake),
 Pol. 99/M2
Siemiatycze, Pol. 99/M2
Siemreab, Camb. 136/C3
Siena (prov.), It. 117/E6
Siena, It. 101/J5
Siene (riv.), It. 100/C2
Sieradz, Pol. 99/K3
Sieraków, Pol. 99/J2
Sierning, Aus. 113/H6
Sierpc, Pol. 99/K2
Sierra (peak), Ca, US 194/C3
Sierra Blanca,
 Tx, US 187/F5
Sierra de la Macarena, PN,
 Col. 208/D3
Sierra de San Pedro Mártir,
 Mex. 200/B2
Sierra Estrella (mts.),
 Az, US 195/R19
Sierra Grande, Arg. 216/D4
Sierra Leone (ctry.) 160/B4
Sierra Leone (cape),
 SLeo. 160/B4
Sierra Madre, Ca, US 194/C3
Sierra Mojada, Mex. 200/E3
Sierra Nevada de Santa
 Marta, PN, Col. 210/C2
Sierra Nevada, PN,
 Ven. 210/D2
Sierra Vieja (mts.),
 Mex.,US 190/B4
Sierra Vista, Az, US 186/E5
Sierras Bayas, Arg. 217/J4
Sierre, Swi. 114/D5
Siete Picos (peak),
 Sp. 103/M8

Siete Tazas, PN, Chile 216/C2
Sieve (riv.), It. 117/E5
Sif Fatima, Alg. 157/H3
Sífnos (isl.), Gre. 105/J4
Sig, Alg. 158/E5
Siga Hills (hills), Tanz. 162/B3
Sigean, Fr. 100/E5
Siġġiewi, Malta 104/L7
Sighetu Marmaţiei, Rom. 107/F2
Sighişoara, Rom. 107/G2
Sighty Crag (hill), Eng, UK 93/F1
Sigillo, It. 117/F6
Sigli, Indo. 138/A2
Sigli (cape), Alg. 158/H4
Siglufjördhur, Ice. 95/N6
Sigmaringen, Ger. 115/F1
Sigmarszell, Ger. 115/F2
Signa, It. 117/E5
Signal de la Mère Boitier (peak), Fr. 100/F3
Signal de Toussaines (peak), Fr. 100/B2
Signal d'Écouves (peak), Fr. 100/D2
Signal Hill, Ca, US 194/F8
Signau, Swi. 114/D4
Signy-L'Abbaye, Fr. 111/D4
Signy-le-Petit, Fr. 111/D4
Signy-Signets, Fr. 88/M5
Sigriswil, Swi. 114/D4
Sigtuna, Swe. 96/G2
Siguatepeque, Hon. 202/E3
Sigüenza, Sp. 102/D2
Sihl (riv.), Swi. 115/E3
Sihlsee (lake), Swi. 115/E3
Sihochac, Mex. 202/D2
Sihong, China 130/D4
Sihorā, India 142/C4
Sihuas, Peru 214/B3
Siilinjärvi, Fin. 118/E3
Siirt (prov.), Turk. 148/E2
Siirt, Turk. 148/E2
Sikandarābād, India 142/A1
Sikandarpur, India 143/E2
Sikandra Rao, India 142/B2
Sikanni Chief (riv.), BC, Can. 180/D3
Sīkar, India 147/L3
Sikasso, Mali 160/D4
Sikasso (pol. reg.), Mali 160/D4
Sikeston, Mo, US 187/K3
Sikhote-Alin' (mts.), Rus. 123/P5
Síkinos, Gre. 105/J4
Síkinos (isl.), Gre. 105/J4
Sikkim (state), India 143/G2
Siklós, Hun. 106/D3
Sikoúrion, Gre. 105/H3
Sil (riv.), Sp. 102/B1
Silai (riv.), India 143/F4
Silandro (Schlanders), It. 115/G4
Silao, India 143/E3
Silao, Mex. 201/E4
Sīlat Aẓ Ẓahr, WBnk. 149/G7
Silay, Phil. 137/D5
Silchar, India 141/F3
Şile, Turk. 107/J5
Silea, It. 117/F1
Silenen, Swi. 115/E4
Silesia (reg.), Pol. 99/H3
Siletitengiz (lake), Kaz. 145/F2
Silgadhī, Nepal 142/C1
Siliana, Tun. 158/L6
Siliana (gov.), Tun. 158/L6
Silifke, Turk. 149/C1
Silīguri, India 143/G2
Silistra, Bul. 107/H3
Silivri, Turk. 107/J5
Siljan (lake), Swe. 96/F1
Siljansnäs, Swe. 96/F1
Silkeborg, Den. 96/C3
Sill (riv.), Aus. 115/H3
Silla, Sp. 103/E3
Silla Tombs, SKor. 131/E5
Sillamäe, Est. 97/M2
Sillānwāli, Pak. 144/B4
Sillaro (riv.), It. 117/E4
Silleda, Sp. 102/A1
Sillian, Aus. 101/K3
Sillustani (ruin), Peru 214/D4
Silly-le-Long, Fr. 88/L4
Siloam Springs, Ar, US 187/J3
Silopi, Turk. 148/E2
Silsbee, Tx, US 187/J5
Silsden, Eng, UK 93/G4
Silsersee (lake), Swi. 115/F5
Siltou (well), Chad 154/J4
Šilutė, Lith. 97/J4
Silvan (dam), Turk. 148/E2
Silvaplana, Swi. 115/F5
Silvassa, India 140/B3
Silver (lake), Or, US 186/B2
Silver (riv.), Or, US 186/C2
Silver (mtn.), Ca, US 194/C1
Silver Bay, Mn, US 185/L4
Silver City, NM, US 186/E4
Silver Lake, Wi, US 193/P14
Silver Lake-Fircrest, Wa, US 193/C2
Silver Meadow (lake), NJ, US 196/C5
Silver Run, Md, US 196/A4
Silver Spring, Md, US 196/A6
Silverado, Ca, US 194/C3
Silverton, Or, US 184/C4
Silverton, Co, US 186/F3
Silverton, NJ, US 196/D3
Silverwood (lake), Ca, US 194/C2
Silves, Port. 102/A4
Silvi, It. 104/D1
Silvia, Col. 210/B4
Silvies (riv.), Or, US 186/C2
Silvretta (mts.), Aus. 115/G4
Silz, Aus. 115/G3
Sim (cape), Mor. 156/C3
Simão Dias, Braz. 212/C3
Simard (lake), Qu, Can. 188/E2
Simav, Turk. 148/B2
Simbach am Inn, Ger. 113/G6
Simcoe, On, Can. 188/D3
Simcoe (lake), Qu, Can. 139/J4
Simdega, India 143/E4
Simēn (mts.), Eth. 155/N5
Simeria, Rom. 106/F3
Simeulue (isl.), Indo. 138/A3
Simferopol', Ukr. 120/E3
Simi (hills), Ca, US 194/B2
Simi Valley, Ca, US 194/B2
Similaun (peak), It. 101/J3
Similaun (peak), Aus.,It. 115/G4
Simiti, Col. 210/C3
Simitli, Bul. 107/F5
Simiyu (riv.), Tanz. 162/B3
Simla, India 144/D4
Şimleu Silvaniei, Rom. 107/F2
Simme (riv.), Swi. 101/G3
Simmelsdorf, Ger. 113/E3
Simmerath, Ger. 111/F2
Simmerbach (riv.), Ger. 111/G4
Simmern, Ger. 111/G4
Simmertal, Ger. 111/G4
Simmszand (isl.), Neth. 108/D2
Simni (isl.), NKor. 131/C3
Simo, Fin. 118/E2
Simões, Braz. 212/B2
Simões Filho, Braz. 212/C4
Simojovel de Allende, Mex. 202/C2
Simón Bolívar (int'l arpt.), Ecu. 210/B5
Simoncello (peak), It. 117/F5
Simonstown, SAfr. 164/L11
Simpang-Kiri (riv.), Indo. 138/A3
Simpelveld, Neth. 111/E2
Simplício Mendes, Braz. 212/B2
Simplon, Swi. 114/E5
Simplonpass (pass), Swi. 114/E5
Simpson (des.), Austl. 171/H3
Simpson (pen.), Nun., Can. 180/G2
Simpson (riv.), Nun., Can. 180/G2
Simpson Desert Conservation Park, Austl. 171/H3
Simpson Desert NP, Austl. 171/H3
Simpsons Gap NP, Austl. 171/G2
Simrishamn, Swe. 96/F4
Simunul, Phil. 139/E3
Sin-le-Noble, Fr. 110/C3
Sinai (pen.), Egypt 155/M1
Sinaia, Rom. 107/G3
Sinaloa (state), Mex. 200/D3
Sinaloa de Leyva, Mex. 200/C3
Sinalunga, It. 101/J5
Sinan, China 137/A2
Sīnāwin, Libya 157/H3
Sincé, Col. 210/C2
Sincelejo, Col. 210/C2
Sinceny, Fr. 110/C4
Sinch'ŏn, NKor. 131/C3
Sinclair, Wy, US 184/G5
Sinclair (lake), Ga, US 191/H3
Sinclair (pt.), Austl. 171/G5
Sincorá, Serra do (range), Braz. 212/B4
Sind (riv.), India 140/C2
Sindal, Den. 96/D3
Sindañgan, Phil. 137/D6
Sindangbarang, Indo. 138/C5
Sindelfingen, Ger. 112/C5
Sindh (prov.), Pak. 140/A2
Sindhulimādi, Nepal 143/E2
Sındırgı, Turk. 148/B2
Sinekçi, Turk. 107/H5
Sinendé, Ben. 161/F4
Sines, Port. 102/A4
Sines (cape), Port. 102/A4
Sinfra, C.d'Iv. 160/D5
Sing Buri, Thai. 136/C3
Singapore (ctry.) 138/B3
Singapore (cap.), Sing. 138/B3
Singen, Ger. 115/E2
Şingeorz-Băi, Rom. 107/G2
Singida (pol. reg.), Tanz. 162/B4
Singida, Tanz. 162/B4
Singitic (gulf), Gre. 105/H2
Singkawang, Indo. 138/C3
Singkep (isl.), Indo. 138/B4
Singleton, Austl. 173/D2
Singleton (mt.), Austl. 170/C4
Singleton (mt.), Austl. 171/F2
Singou, Réserve Totale de Faune du, Burk. 161/F4
Sinincay, Ecu. 210/B5
Siniscola, It. 104/A2
Sinjār, Iraq 148/E2
Sinjil, WBnk. 149/G7
Sinn (riv.), Ger. 98/E3
Sinnam-dok-san (peak), NKor. 131/D2
Sinnamary, FrG. 209/H2
Sinnard, Co, US 195/C1
Sînnicolau Mare, Rom. 106/E2
Sinnūris, Egypt 149/B5
Sinnyŏng, SKor. 131/E4
Sino (co.), Libr. 160/C5
Sinoe (lake), Rom. 107/J3
Sinop, Braz. 209/G6
Sinop, Turk. 148/C1
Sinop (prov.), Turk. 148/C1
Sinop (pt.), Turk. 148/C1
Sinp'o, NKor. 131/E2
Sint-Genesius-Rode, Belg. 111/D2
Sint-Gillis-Waas, Belg. 108/B6
Sint-Katelijne-Waver, Belg. 111/D1
Sint-Laureins, Belg. 110/C1
Sint-Martens-Voeren, Belg. 111/E2
Sint-Michielsgestel, Neth. 108/C5
Sint-Niklaas, Belg. 108/B6
Sint-Oedenrode, Neth. 108/C5
Sint-Pieters-Leeuw, Belg. 111/D2
Sint-Truiden, Belg. 111/E2
Sint'aein, SKor. 131/D5
Sintang, Indo. 138/D3
Sinton, Tx, US 190/D4
Sintra, Port. 103/P10
Sintra (range), Port. 103/P10
Sinú (riv.), Col. 208/C2
Sinŭiju, NKor. 131/C2
Sinzheim, Ger. 112/B5
Sinzig, Ger. 111/G2
Sió (riv.), Hun. 106/D2
Siocon, Phil. 139/F2
Siófok, Hun. 106/D2
Sioma Ngwezi NP, Zam. 163/D4
Sion, Swi. 114/D5
Sion Mills, NI, UK 89/Q9
Sioule (riv.), Fr. 100/E4
Sioux City, Ia, US 185/J5
Sioux Lookout, On, Can. 185/L3
Sipalay, Phil. 137/D6
Sipaliwini (dist.), Sur. 211/H4
Sipaliwini (riv.), Sur. 211/G4
Sipanok (chan.), Mb,Sk, Can. 185/H2
Siparia, Trin. 211/F2
Sipí, Col. 210/B3
Siping, China 130/F2
Sipiwesk (lake), Mb, Can. 180/G3
Siple (isl.), Ant. 218/R
Siponto (ruin), It. 104/D2
Sipsey (riv.), Al, US 191/G3
Sipura (isl.), Indo. 138/A4
Siqueira Campos, Braz. 213/B2
Siquia (riv.), Nic. 198/E5
Siquisique, Ven. 210/D2
Sir Alexander (mt.), BC, Can. 184/C2
Sir Edward Pellew Group (isls.), Austl. 167/C2
Sir James Macbrien (mt.), NW, Can. 180/D2
Sir James Mitchell NP, Austl. 170/C5
Sir John (cape), Austl. 173/D4
Sir Seewoosagur Ramgoolam (int'l arpt.), Mrts. 165/T15
Sir Thomas (mt.), Austl. 171/F3
Sira (riv.), Nor. 95/C4
Siracusa (Syracuse), It. 104/D4
Sirājganj, Bang. 143/G3
Şiran, Turk. 148/D1
Sirdaryo (pol. reg.), Uzb. 145/E4
Siret, Rom. 107/H2
Siret (riv.), Rom. 107/H2
Sirha, Nepal 143/F2
Sirhind, India 144/D4
Sirik (cape), Malay. 138/D3
Sīrīk, Iran 147/G3
Sirikit (res.), Thai. 141/H4
Sirinhaém, Braz. 212/D3
Sīrīs, WBnk. 149/G7
Sirius (pt.), Ak, US 192/B5
Sirmilik Nat'l Park, Nun., Can. 139/J1
Sirmione, It. 116/D2
Sirnach, Swi. 115/F3
Şırnak, Turk. 148/E2
Şirolo, It. 117/G5
Sironj, India 142/A3
Síros (isl.), Gre. 105/J4
Siroua (peak), Mor. 156/D3
Sirsa, India 144/C5
Sirsāganj, India 142/B2
Sirsi, India 142/B1
Sirsi, India 147/K6
Sisak, Cro. 106/C3
Sisaket, Thai. 136/D3
Sishui, China 130/D4
Sisikon, Swi. 115/E4
Sisipuk (lake), Mb,Sk, Can. 185/H2
Sissach, Swi. 114/D3
Sisseton, SD, US 185/J4
Sissili (prov.), Burk. 161/E4
Sissonne, Fr. 110/C4
Sissonville, WV, US 188/D4
Sisterdale, Tx, US 195/T20
Sisteron, Fr. 100/F4
Siswā Bāzār, India 142/D2
Sitacocha, Peru 214/B2
Sītākund, Bang. 143/H4
Sītāmarhi, India 143/E2
Sītāpur, India 142/C2
Sitārganj, India 142/B1
Siteki, Swaz. 165/E2
Site of World Trade Center, NY, US 197/J9
Sitges, Sp. 103/K7
Sithoniá (pen.), Gre. 105/J2
Sitía, Gre. 105/K5
Sitidgi (lake), NW, Can. 192/M2
Sítio Novo do Grajaú, Braz. 212/A2
Sitka, Ak, US 192/L4
Sitno (peak), Slvk. 106/D1
Sittard, Neth. 111/E2
Sittensen, Ger. 109/G2
Sitter (riv.), Swi. 115/F3
Sittingbourne, Eng, UK 91/G4
Sitton (peak), Ca, US 194/C3
Sittwe (Akyab), Myan. 141/F3
Sivac, Serb. 106/D3
Sivakāsi, India 140/C6
Sīvand, Iran 146/F2
Sivas, Turk. 148/D2
Sivas (prov.), Turk. 148/D2
Siverek, Turk. 148/D2
Siviriez, Swi. 114/C4
Sivrihisar, Turk. 148/B2
Sivry-Courtry, Fr. 88/L6
Siwa Oasis (oasis), Egypt 159/A2
Sīwah, Egypt 155/L2
Siwalik (range), Nepal 140/B1
Siwān, India 143/E2
Siwāni, India 144/C5
Six Flags Great Adventure, NJ, US 196/D3
Six Flags Great America, Il, US 193/Q15
Six Flags Magic Mountain, Ca, US 194/B2
Sixmilecross, NI, UK 92/A2
Sixth (falls), Sudan 155/M4
Siyabuswa, SAfr. 163/E6
Siyāna, India 142/B1
Siyang, China 130/D4
Siziano, It. 116/C2
Siziwang, China 129/K3
Sjælland (isl.), Den. 95/D5
Sjenica, Serb. 106/E4
Sjöbo, Swe. 96/E4
Sjónfridh (peak), Ice. 95/M6
Sjuntorp, Swe. 96/E2
Skaftafell NP, Ice. 95/P7
Skagen, Den. 96/D3
Skagens (The Skaw) (cape), Den. 96/D3
Skagern (lake), Swe. 96/F2
Skagerrak (str.), Den.,Nor. 96/C3
Skaget (peak), Nor. 96/C1
Skagway, Ak, US 192/L3
Skála, Gre. 105/H4
Skälderviken (bay), Swe. 96/E3
Skálfandafljót (riv.), Ice. 95/P7
Skalica, Slvk. 99/J4
Skalice (riv.), Czh. 101/K2
Skalka (res.), Czh. 113/F2
Skælskør, Den. 96/D4
Skanderborg, Den. 96/C3
Skåne (reg.), Swe. 96/E4
Skanes (int'l arpt.), Tun. 158/M7
Skånland, Nor. 95/F1
Skänninge, Swe. 96/F2
Skanör, Swe. 96/E4
Skantzoura (isl.), Gre. 105/J3
Skara, Swe. 96/E2
Skaraborg (co.), Swe. 95/E4
Skärblacka, Swe. 96/F2
Skåre, Swe. 96/E2
Skarszewy, Pol. 96/H4
Skarżysko-Kamienna, Pol. 99/L3
Skateraw, Sc, UK 94/D5
Skattkärr, Swe. 96/E2
Skawina, Pol. 99/K4
Skeena (riv.), BC, Can. 180/D3
Skeena (mts.), BC, Can. 180/D3
Skegness, Eng, UK 93/J5
Skellefteå, Swe. 95/G2
Skellefteälven (riv.), Swe. 95/F2
Skelleftehamn, Swe. 95/G2
Skelmersdale, Eng, UK 93/F4
Skelmorlie, Sc, UK 94/B5
Skerne (riv.), Eng, UK 93/G2
Skerries, Ire. 92/B4
Skhimatárion, Gre. 105/H3
Skhirat, Mor. 158/A3
Skhirat Temara (prov.), Mor. 158/A3
Skhiza (isl.), Gre. 105/G4
Skhodnya (riv.), Rus. 119/W9
Ski, Nor. 96/D2
Skíathos, Gre. 105/H3
Skiatook, Ok, US 187/H3
Skibbereen, Ire. 89/P11
Skidegate, BC, Can. 192/M5
Skídhra, Gre. 105/H2
Skien, Nor. 96/C2
Skierniewice, Pol. 99/L3
Skikda, Alg. 158/K6
Skinári (cape), Gre. 105/G4
Skinnskatteberg, Swe. 96/F2
Skipton, Eng, UK 93/F4
Skirfare (riv.), Eng, UK 93/F3
Skíros, Gre. 105/J3
Skive, Den. 96/C3
Skjærhollen, Nor. 96/D2
Skjeberg, Nor. 96/D2
Skjelåtinden (peak), Nor. 95/E2
Skjern, Den. 96/C4
Skjern (riv.), Den. 96/C4
Škofja Loka, Slov. 101/L3
Skoghall, Swe. 96/E2
Skogstorp, Swe. 96/G2
Skokholm (isl.), Wal, UK 90/A3
Skokie (riv.), Il, US 193/Q15
Skokloster, Swe. 96/G2
Sköllersta, Swe. 96/F2
Skolniki Park, Rus. 119/W9
Skomer (isl.), Wal, UK 90/A3
Skópelos (isl.), Gre. 105/H3
Skópelos, Gre. 105/H3
Skopin, Rus. 120/F1
Skopje (cap.), FYROM 105/G1
Skopje (int'l arpt.), FYROM 106/E5
Skotterud, Nor. 96/E2
Skoútari, Gre. 105/H2
Skövde, Swe. 96/E2
Skowhegan, Me, US 189/G2
Skukum (mt.), Yk, Can. 192/L3
Skull, Ire. 89/P11
Skultorp, Swe. 96/E2
Skultuna, Swe. 96/G2
Skunk (riv.), Ia, US 188/A3
Skurup, Swe. 99/G1
Skutskär, Swe. 96/G1
Skwentna, Ak, US 192/H3
Skwierzyna, Pol. 99/H2
Skye (isl.), Sc, UK 89/Q8
Skyring (sound), Chile 217/B7
Skytop, Pa, US 196/C1
Slagelse, Den. 96/D4
Slakovský Les (for.), Czh. 113/F2
Slamannan, Sc, UK 94/C5
Slana, Ak, US 192/K3
Slaná (riv.), Slvk. 99/L4
Slane, Ire. 92/B4
Slaney (riv.), Ire. 89/Q10
Slănic, Rom. 107/G3
Slănic-Moldova, Rom. 107/H2
Slantsy, Rus. 97/N2
Slaný, Czh. 113/H2
Slapy (res.), Czh. 113/H3
Śląskie (prov.), Pol. 99/K3
Slatedale, Pa, US 196/C2
Slatina, Rom. 107/G3
Slatington, Pa, US 196/C2
Slaton, Tx, US 187/G4
Slattum, Nor. 96/D1
Slaughter Beach, De, US 196/C6
Slaughterville, Ok, US 195/N15
Slave (coast), Afr. 161/F5
Slave (riv.), NW, Can. 180/E2
Slave Lake, Ab, Can. 184/E2
Slavgorod, Rus. 145/G2
Slavkov u Brna, Czh. 101/M2
Slavonia (reg.), Cro. 106/C3
Slavonska Požega, Cro. 106/C3
Slavonski Brod, Cro. 106/D3
Slavuta, Ukr. 120/C2
Slavyanovo, Bul. 107/G4
Slavyansk-na-Kubani, Rus. 120/F3
Sławno, Pol. 96/G4
Sleen, Neth. 108/D3
Sleeper (isls.), On, Can. 139/H3
Sleeping Bear Dunes Nat'l Lakeshore, US 188/C2
Sleepy Hollow, NY, US 197/K7
Sleepy Hollow, Il, US 193/P15
Sleetmute, Ak, US 192/G3
Slidell, La, US 195/Q16
Sliedrecht, Neth. 108/B5
Sliema, Malta 104/M7
Slieve Binnian (peak), NI, UK 92/C3
Slieve Croob (peak), NI, UK 92/C3
Slieve Donard (peak), NI, UK 92/C3
Slieve Gullion (peak), NI, UK 92/B3
Slieve Snaght (peak), Ire. 92/A1
Slioch (peak), Sc, UK 94/A1
Slite, Swe. 97/H3
Sliven, Bul. 107/H4
Slivnitsa, Bul. 106/F4
Sloan, NY, US 189/S10
Sloatsburg, NY, US 197/J7
Slobodskoy, Rus. 119/L4
Slobozia, Rom. 107/H3
Slochteren, Neth. 108/D2
Slonim, Bela. 120/C1
Sloten, Neth. 108/C3
Slotermeer (lake), Neth. 108/C3
Slough, Eng, UK 88/B2
Slough (co.), Eng, UK 88/B2
Slovakia (ctry.) 99/K4
Slovenia (ctry.) 106/B3
Slovenj Gradec, Slov. 101/L3
Slovenska Bistrica, Slov. 101/L3
Slovenská L'upča, Slvk. 99/K4
Slovenske Konjice, Slov. 101/L3
Slovenské Rudohorie (mts.), Slvk. 99/L4
Slov'yans'k, Ukr. 120/F2
Słowiński PN, Pol. 96/G4
Słubice, Pol. 99/H2
Sluch' (riv.), Ukr. 120/C2
Sluderno (Schluderns), It. 115/G4
Sluis, Neth. 110/C1
Słupca, Pol. 99/J2
Słupia (riv.), Pol. 96/G4
Słupsk, Pol. 96/G4
Slutsk, Bela. 120/C1
Slyne Head (pt.), Ire. 88/F10
Smålandsstenar, Swe. 96/E3
Smallwood (res.), Nf, Can. 139/K3
Smeaton, Sk, Can. 185/G2
Smederevo, Serb. 106/E3
Smederevska Palanka, Serb. 106/E3
Smedjebacken, Swe. 96/F1
Smendou (riv.), Alg. 158/J4
Śmigiel, Pol. 99/J2
Smila, Ukr. 120/D2
Smilde, Neth. 108/D3
Smith (riv.), Mt, US 184/F4
Smith (inlet), BC, Can. 184/B3
Smith (isl.), Qu, Can. 139/J2
Smith Mountain (lake), Va, US 188/E4
Smith Village, Ok, US 195/N15
Smithburg, NJ, US 196/D3
Smithers, BC, Can. 184/B2
Smithfield, Ut, US 184/F5
Smithfield, NC, US 191/J3
Smiths Creek, Mi, US 193/G6
Smiths Falls, On, Can. 188/E2
Smithton, Austl. 173/C4
Smithton, Il, US 195/H9
Smithtown (bay), NY, US 197/E2
Smithtown, NY, US 197/E2
Smithville, Ok, US 190/E3
Smithville (lake), Mo, US 195/D5
Smithville, Mo, US 195/D5
Smoky (cape), Austl. 173/E1
Smoky (hills), Ks, US 187/H3
Smoky (riv.), Ab, Can. 180/E3
Smoky Hill (riv.), Ks, US 187/G3
Smoky Lake, Ab, Can. 184/E2
Smøla (isl.), Nor. 95/C3
Smolensk, Rus. 118/G5
Smolenskaya Oblast, Rus. 118/F5
Smólikas (peak), Gre. 105/G2
Smolyan, Bul. 107/G5
Smooth Rock Falls, On, Can. 188/D1
Smrčina (peak), Czh. 113/G5
Smutná (riv.), Czh. 113/H4
Smyadovo, Bul. 107/H4
Smyrna, Ga, US 191/G3
Smyrna (riv.), De, US 196/C5
Smyrna, De, US 196/C5
Snaefell (peak), IM, UK 92/D3
Snake (riv.), US 184/D4
Snake River (plain), Id, US 184/E5
Snares (isls.), NZ 175/R12
Snåsa, Nor. 95/E2
Snedsted, Den. 96/C3
Sneek, Neth. 108/C2
Sneekermeer (lake), Neth. 108/C2
Sneeuberg (peak), SAfr. 164/B4
Sneeuberg (mts.), SAfr. 164/D3
Sneeuwkop (peak), SAfr. 164/L11
Snejbjerg, Den. 96/C3
Sněžka (peak), Czh. 99/H3
Snežnik (peak), Slov. 101/L4
Sni Mills, Mo, US 195/E6
Śniardwy (lake), Pol. 99/L2
Snodland, Eng, UK 91/G4
Snøhetta (peak), Nor. 95/D3
Snohomish, Wa, US 193/C2
Snohomish (co.), Wa, US 193/C2
Snohomish (riv.), Wa, US 193/C2
Snoqualmie (riv.), Wa, US 193/D2
Snoqualmie (falls), Wa, US 193/D2
Snoqualmie, Wa, US 193/D2
Snoqualmie Falls, Wa, US 193/D2
Snoqualmie, Middle Fk. (riv.), Wa, US 193/D2
Snoqualmie, North Fork (riv.), Wa, US 193/D2
Snoqualmie, South Fork (riv.), Wa, US 193/D3
Snøtind (peak), Nor. 95/E2
Snowdon (peak), IM, UK 92/D5
Snowdonia NP, Wal, UK 92/D6
Snowflake, Az, US 186/E4
Snowtown, Austl. 171/H5
Snowy (peak), Ak, US 192/K2
Snowy (riv.), Austl. 173/D3
Snowy River NP, Austl. 173/D3
Snyder (co.), Pa, US 196/A2
Snydertown, Pa, US 196/B2
Snyderville, Ut, US 195/K12
Soalala, Madg. 165/H7
Soanierana-Ivongo, Madg. 165/J7
Soanindrariny, Madg. 165/H7
Soar (riv.), Eng, UK 93/G6
Soavina, Madg. 165/H8
Soavina, Madg. 165/J8
Soavinandriana, Madg. 165/H7
Sobaek (mts.), SKor. 131/D5
Soběslav, Czh. 113/H4
Sobger (riv.), Indo. 139/K4
Sobhādero, Pak. 147/J3
Sobradinho, Represa (res.), Braz. 205/E3
Sobral, Braz. 212/B1
Sobretta (peak), It. 115/G5
Sobue, Japan 135/L5
Soc Trang, Viet. 136/D4
Soča (riv.), Slov. 101/K3
Socabaya, Peru 214/D5
Sochaczew, Pol. 99/L2
Sochi, Rus. 120/F4
Soch'ŏn, SKor. 131/D4
Söchtenau, Ger. 113/F7
Soci, It. 117/E5
Society (isls.), FrPol. 175/K6
Socorro, Braz. 213/G7
Socorro, Col. 210/C3
Socorro, NM, US 186/F4
Socorro (isl.), NM, Mex. 200/C5
Socorro, Tx, US 187/F5
Socota, Peru 214/B2
Socotá, Col. 210/C3
Socotra (isl.), Yem. 125/E8
Socuéllamos, Sp. 102/D3
Soda Springs, Id, US 184/F5
Sodankylä, Fin. 118/E2
Sodegaura, Japan 135/D3
Söderbärke, Swe. 96/F1
Söderfors, Swe. 96/G1
Söderhamn, Swe. 96/G1
Söderköping, Swe. 96/G2
Södermanland (co.), Swe. 95/E4
Södertälje, Swe. 96/G2
Sodo, Eth. 155/N6
Sŏdu (riv.), NKor. 131/E2
Sodwana Bay NP, SAfr. 165/F2
Soest, Ger. 109/F5
Soest, Neth. 108/C4
Soeste (riv.), Ger. 98/D2
Sofádhes, Gre. 105/H3
Sofia (Sofiya) (cap.), Bul. 49/F4
Sofia (int'l arpt.), Bul. 107/F4
Sofiya (prov.), Bul. 107/F4
Sogamoso (riv.), Col. 210/C3
Sogamoso, Col. 210/C3
Sögel, Ger. 109/E3
Sogn Og Fjordane (co.), Nor. 95/C3
Sognafjorden (inlet), Nor. 95/C3
Sogndal, Nor. 96/B1
Søgne, Nor. 96/B2
Sogollé (well), Chad 154/J4
Söğüksu NP, Turk. 148/C1
Söğüt, Turk. 148/B1
Söğütlü, Turk. 107/K5
Sogwass (peak), Ugan. 162/B2
Sohāgpur, India 142/B4
Sohren, Ger. 111/G4
Sŏhŭng, NKor. 131/D3
Soignies, Belg. 111/D2
Soignolles-en-Brie, Fr. 88/L6
Soissons, Fr. 110/C5
Sōja, Japan 132/C3
Sojat, India 147/K3
Sŏjosŏn (bay), NKor. 131/C3
Sok (riv.), Rus. 121/J1
Sok (pt.), Thai. 136/C3
Sōka, Japan 135/D3
Sokch'o, SKor. 131/E3
Söke, Turk. 148/A2
Sokhós, Gre. 105/H2
Sokhumi, Geo. 121/G4
Sokna, Nor. 96/C1
Soko (isls.), China 129/T11
Soko Banja, Serb. 106/E4
Sokodé, Togo 161/F4
Sokol, Rus. 118/J4
Sokol (peak), Czh. 113/G4
Sokółka, Pol. 99/M2
Sokolov, Czh. 113/F2
Sokołów Podlaski, Pol. 99/M2
Sokoto (plain), Nga. 154/F5
Sokoto (riv.), Nga. 154/F5
Sokoto, Nga. 161/G3
Sokoto (state), Nga. 161/G3
Sol, Costa del (coast), Sp. 102/C4
Sol'-Iletsk, Rus. 121/K2
Sola, Nor. 96/A2
Sola (int'l arpt.), Nor. 96/A2
Solana, Phil. 137/D4
Solana Beach, Ca, US 194/C5
Solânea, Braz. 212/D2
Solano (pt.), Col. 210/B3
Solano, Phil. 137/D4
Solano (co.), Ca, US 193/L10
Solarolo, It. 117/E4
Solca, Rom. 107/G2
Sölden, Aus. 115/H4
Soldier (riv.), Ia, US 187/J2
Soldotna, Ak, US 192/H3
Soledad, Col. 210/C2
Soledad, Ven. 211/F2
Soledad Canyon (canyon), Ca, US 194/B2
Soledad de Doblado, Mex. 201/N7
Soledad de Graciano, Mex. 201/E4
Soledade, Braz. 213/A4
Solent, The (chan.), Eng, UK 91/E5
Solesino, It. 117/E2
Solesmes, Fr. 110/C3
Soleuvre (peak), Lux. 111/E4
Solferino, It. 116/D2
Solhan, Turk. 148/E2
Soliera, It. 117/D3
Soligo, It. 117/F1
Solihull, Eng, UK 91/E2
Solihull (co.), Eng, UK 91/E2
Solimões (riv.), Braz. 211/E5
Solingen, Ger. 108/E6
Sollefteå, Swe. 95/F3
Sollentuna, Swe. 96/G2
Sóller, Sp. 103/G3
Sollerön, Swe. 96/F1
Solling (mts.), Ger. 98/E3
Solmsbach (riv.), Ger. 112/B2
Søln (peak), Nor. 95/D3
Solnan (riv.), Fr. 100/F3
Solntsevo, Rus. 119/W9
Solo (riv.), Indo. 138/D5
Solok, Indo. 138/B4
Sololá, Guat. 202/D3
Solomon, Ak, US 192/F3
Solomon (riv.), Ks, US 187/H3
Solomon (sea), PNG,Sol. 174/D5
Solomon Islands (ctry.) 174/E6
Solomon, North Fork (riv.), US 187/G3
Solonchak Goklenkui (swamp), Trkm. 145/C4
Solonópole, Braz. 212/C2
Solothurn, Swi. 114/D3
Solothurn (canton), Swi. 114/D3
Solovetskiy (isls.), Rus. 118/G2
Solre-le-Château, Fr. 111/D3
Solsona, Sp. 103/F2
Solt, Hun. 106/D2
Šolta (isl.), Cro. 104/E1
Soltau, Ger. 109/G3
Soltustik Qazaqstan (obl.), Kaz. 122/G4
Soltvadkert, Hun. 106/D2
Solunska (peak), FYROM 105/G2
Solva (riv.), Wal, UK 90/A3
Solvang, Ca, US 186/B4
Sölvesborg, Swe. 96/F3
Solway Firth (inlet), Eng.,Sc, UK 92/E2
Solwezi, Zam. 163/E3
Solymár, Hun. 107/Q9
Sōma, Japan 133/G2
Soma, Turk. 148/A2
Somain, Fr. 110/C3
Somalia (ctry.) 155/Q6
Sombor, Serb. 106/D3
Sombra, On, Can. 193/H6
Sombreffe, Belg. 111/D2
Sombrerete, Mex. 200/E4
Sombrio, Braz. 213/B4
Someren, Neth. 108/C6
Somero, Fin. 97/K1
Somers, Mt, US 184/E3
Somers, Wi, US 193/Q14
Somers Point, NJ, US 196/D5
Somerset (isl.), Nun., Can. 180/G1
Somerset (co.), Eng, UK 90/D4
Somerset, Ky, US 188/C4
Somerset, NY, US 189/S9
Somerset, Pa, US 196/D3
Somerset, Tx, US 195/T21

Somerset East, SAfr. 164/D4
Somerset West, SAfr. 164/L11
Somersworth, NH, US 189/G3
Somerton, Az, US 186/D4
Somerville (lake), Tx, US 187/H5
Somerville, NJ, US 196/D2
Someş (riv.), Rom. 107/F2
Someşul Mare (riv.), Serb. 107/G2
Someswar (range), India 143/E2
Somis, Ca, US 194/B2
Sömjin (riv.), SKor. 131/D5
Somma Lombardo, It. 116/B1
Sommacampagna, It. 117/D2
Sommam (riv.), Alg. 158/H4
Sommariva del Bosco, It. 116/A3
Somme (bay), Fr. 100/D1
Somme (dept.), Fr. 110/B4
Somme (riv.), Fr. 98/B3
Somme, Canal de la (canal), Fr. 110/D4
Somme-Leuze, Belg. 111/E3
Somme-Soude (riv.), Fr.111/D6
Sommedieue, Fr. 111/E5
Sommen (lake), Swe. 96/F2
Sommet de Finiels (peak), Fr. 100/E4
Sommevoire, Fr. 111/D4
Somogy (prov.), Hun. 106/C2
Somoto, Nic. 202/E3
Son (riv.), India 140/D3
Son Servera, Sp. 103/G3
Sona, It. 117/D2
Sonāmukhi, India 143/F4
Sonāmura, India 143/H4
Sonār, India 142/B4
Sonchamp, Fr. 88/H6
Sönch'ön, NKor. 131/C3
Soncino, It. 116/C2
Sondalo, It. 115/G5
Sønder Nissum, Den. 96/C3
Sønderborg (int'l arpt.), Den. 96/C4
Sønderborg, Den. 96/C4
Sonderend (riv.), SAfr. 164/L11
Sønderjylland (co.), Den. 96/C4
Sondica (int'l arpt.), Sp. 102/D1
Sondrio, It. 115/F5
Sondrio (dept.), It. 115/F5
Sonepur, India 140/D3
Song (peak), China 130/C4
Song Xian, China 130/C4
Songea, Tanz. 162/B5
Songeons, Fr. 110/A4
Songhua (riv.), China 129/P2
Sönghwan, SKor. 131/D4
Songi (isl.), SKor. 131/C5
Songino, Mong. 128/G2
Songjiang, China 130/L8
Söngju, SKor. 131/E5
Songkhla, Thai. 136/C5
Songkhram (riv.), Thai. 141/H4
Songling, China 129/M2
Songming, China 141/H2
Söngnam, SKor. 131/D4
Songnim, NKor. 131/C3
Songololo, D.R. Congo 163/B2
Songt'an, SKor. 131/D4
Songtao Miaozu Zizhixian, China 137/A2
Songxi, China 137/C2
Songzi, China 137/B1
Songzi (pass), China 130/K6
Soni, Japan 135/K6
Sonid Youqi, China 129/K3
Sonid Zuoqi, China 129/K3
Sonipat, India 144/D5
Sonneberg, Ger. 112/E2
Sonnefeld, Ger. 112/E2
Sonnjoch (peak), Aus. 115/H3
Sonntagshorn (peak), Ger. 101/K3
Sonobe, Japan 135/J7
Sonoma (co.), Ca, US 193/J10
Sonoma (mts.), Ca, US 193/J10
Sonora (state), Mex. 200/C3
Sonora, Ca, US 186/B3
Sonora, Tx, US 187/G5
Sonoran Desert Nat'l Monument, Az, US 186/D4
Sonoyta, Mex. 200/B2
Sonoyta (riv.), Mex. 200/B2
Sonpur, India 143/E3
Sonqor, Iran 146/E2
Sönsan, SKor. 131/E4
Sonsbeck, Ger. 108/D5
Sonseca, Sp. 102/D3
Sonsonate, ESal. 202/D3
Sonsorol (isls.), Palau 174/C4
Sonta, Serb. 106/D3
Sontheim, Ger. 115/G2
Sontheim an der Brenz, Ger. 112/D5
Sonthofen, Ger. 115/G3
Sontra, Ger. 109/G6
Sonvico, Swi. 115/E5
Sopetrán, Col. 210/C3
Sopi (cape), Indo. 139/G3
Sopor, India 144/C2
Sopot, Bul. 107/G4
Sopot, Pol. 96/H4

Sopron, Hun. 101/M3
Sör (riv.), Wal, UK 90/D3
Sör Karatuley (salt pan), Kaz. 145/C4
Sör-Trøndelag (co.), Nor. 95/D3
Sör-Varanger, Nor. 95/J1
Sora, It. 104/C2
Soragna, It. 116/D3
Sörak-san (peak), SKor. 131/E3
Söraksan NP, SKor. 131/E3
Sorata, Bol. 208/E7
Sorbas, Sp. 102/D4
Sorbolo, It. 116/D3
Sorcy-Saint-Martin, Fr. 111/E6
Sorel, Qu, Can. 188/F2
Sorell-Midway Point, Austl. 173/C4
Soresina, It. 116/C2
Sörforsa, Swe. 96/G1
Sorgues, Fr. 100/F5
Sorgun, Turk. 148/C2
Sori, It. 116/C4
Soria, Sp. 102/D2
Soriano (dept.), Uru. 216/G3
Soriano, Uru. 217/J10
Sorikmerapi (peak), Indo. 138/A3
Soritor, Peru 214/B2
Sormonne (riv.), Fr. 111/D4
Sorø, Den. 96/D4
Soro, Rio do (riv.), Braz. 209/J5
Soroca, Mol. 107/J1
Sorocaba, Braz. 213/C2
Sorochinsk, Rus. 121/K1
Sorol (isl.), Micr. 174/D4
Soron, India 142/B2
Sorong, Indo. 139/H4
Soroti, Ugan. 162/B2
Söröya (isl.), Nor. 95/G1
Sørøysundet (chan.), Nor. 95/G1
Sorpestausee (lake), Ger. 109/E6
Sorraia (riv.), Port. 102/A3
Sorrento, It. 104/D2
Sorsele, Swe. 95/F2
Sorso, It. 104/A2
Sorsogon, Phil. 137/D5
Sort, Sp. 103/F1
Sörve (pt.), Est. 97/K3
Sos del Rey Católico, Sp. 102/E1
Sösan, SKor. 131/D4
Sösan Haean NP, SKor. 131/C4
Sösdala, Swe. 96/E3
Söse (riv.), Ger. 109/H5
Soshanguve, SAfr. 163/E6
Sosna (riv.), Rus. 120/F1
Sosneado (peak), Arg. 216/C2
Sosnogorsk, Rus. 119/M3
Sosnovka, Rus. 119/L4
Sosnowiec, Pol. 99/K3
Sospiro, It. 116/D2
Sos'va (riv.), Rus. 122/G3
Sot (riv.), India 142/B1
Soto del Real, Sp. 103/N8
Soto la Marina, Mex. 201/F4
Sotouboua, Togo 161/F4
Sottrum, Ger. 109/G2
Sotuta, Mex. 202/D1
Soude (riv.), Fr. 111/D6
Souderton, Pa, US 196/C3
Soúdha, Gre. 105/J5
Souffelweyersheim, Fr. 111/G6
Soufflenheim, Fr. 111/G6
Souflion, Gre. 105/K2
Soufrière (peak), StV. 199/N9
Soufrière (peak), Eng, UK 88/D2
Souillac, Fr. 199/N8
Souillac, Mrts. 165/T15
Souk Ahras, Alg. 158/K6
Souk Ahras (prov.), Alg. 158/K6
Souk el Arba du Rharb, Mor. 158/A2
Söul (Seoul) (cap.), SKor. 129/N4
Soultz-Haut-Rhin, Fr. 111/G6
Soultz-sous-Forêts, Fr. 112/A5
Soum (prov.), Burk. 161/E3
Soumagne, Belg. 111/E2
Sound, The (chan.), Den. 96/D4
Souppes-sur-Loing, Fr. 100/E2
Sour El Ghozlane, Alg. 158/G4
Sources, Mont aux (peak), Les. 164/E3
Soure, Braz. 209/J4
Soure, Port. 102/A2
Souris, Mb, Can. 185/H3
Souris, PE, Can. 189/J2
Souris (riv.), Can.,US 185/H3
Sous le Vent, Îles (isls.), FrPol. 175/K6
Sousa, Braz. 212/C2
Sousse, Tun. 158/M7
Sousse (gov.), Tun. 158/M7
Sout (riv.), SAfr. 164/C3
South (bay), Nun., Can. 181/H2
South (cape), NZ 175/R12
South (isl.), NZ 175/S11
South (mtn.), Pa, US 196/A3
South Africa (ctry.) 163/D4

South Amboy, NJ, US 197/H10
South America (cont.) 147
South Andaman (isl.), India 141/F5
South Anna (riv.), Va, US 191/J2
South Augusta, Ga, US 191/H3
South Aulatsivik (isl.), Nf, Can. 181/K3
South Australia (state), Austl. 167/C3
South Ayrshire (pol. reg.), Sc, UK 94/B6
South Bend, In, US 188/C3
South Bend, Wa, US 184/C4
South Benfleet, Eng, UK 91/G3
South Buganda (prov.), Ugan. 162/A3
South Burlington, Vt, US 188/F2
South Caicos (isl.), UK 203/J1
South Carolina (state), US 191/H3
South China (sea), Asia 125/L8
South Colby, Wa, US 193/B2
South Dakota (state), US 185/H4
South Dorset Downs (uplands), Eng, UK 90/D5
South Downs (hills), Eng, UK 91/F5
South Dum Dum, India 143/G4
South East (pt.), Austl. 173/C3
South East (cape), Austl. 173/C4
South Elgin, Il, US 193/P16
South Esk (riv.), Sc, UK 94/C3
South Esk (riv.), Sc, UK 94/C3
South Farmingdale, NY, US 197/M9
South Fork, Co, US 190/B2
South Fulton, Tn, US 188/B4
South Gate, Md, US 196/B5
South Gate, Ca, US 194/F8
South Georgia (isl.), UK 80/H8
South Gloucestershire (co.), Eng, UK 90/D3
South Hams (plain), Eng, UK 90/C6
South Holland, Il, US 193/Q16
South Island NP, SKor. 131/C4
South Jordan, Ut, US 195/K12
South Koel (riv.), India 143/E4
South Korea (ctry.) 131/D4
South Lake Tahoe, Ca, US 186/C3
South Lanarkshire (pol. reg.), Sc, UK 94/E5
South Loup (riv.), Ne, US 185/J5
South Luangwa NP, Zam. 163/F3
South Lyon, Mi, US 193/E7
South Magnetic Pole, Ant. 218/K
South Moose (lake), Mb, Can. 185/J2
South Moresby NP and Prsv., BC, Can. 192/M5
South Naknek, Ak, US 192/G4
South Normanton, Eng, UK 93/G5
South Nyack, NY, US 197/K7
South Ockenden, Eng, UK 88/D2
South Ogden, Ut, US 195/K11
South Orange, NJ, US 197/H9
South Orkney (isls.), UK 218/X
South Ossetia (reg.), Geo. 121/G4
South Oxhey, Eng, UK 88/B2
South Oyster (bay), NY, US 197/M9
South Pacific (ocean) 80/B7
South Para (res.), Austl. 171/M8
South Pasadena, Ca, US 194/F7
South Pine (riv.), Austl. 172/E6
South Plainfield, NJ, US 197/H9
South Platte (riv.), Co, US 190/C2
South Polar (plat.), Ant. 218/Y
South Pole, Ant. 218/A
South Prairie, Wa, US 193/C3
South River, NJ, US 197/H10
South Rockwood, Mi, US 193/F7
South Ronaldsay (isl.), Sc, UK 89/V14
South Roxana, Il, US 195/G8
South Salt Lake, Ut, US 195/K12
South San Francisco, Ca, US 193/K11
South Sandwich (isls.), UK 80/H8
South Saskatchewan (riv.), Sk, Can. 180/E3
South Seaville, NJ, US 196/D5

South Shetland (isls.), UK 218/W
South Shields, Eng, UK 93/G2
South Sioux City, Ne, US 185/J5
South Skunk (riv.), Ia, US 187/J2
South Taranaki Bight (bay), NZ 175/S10
South Turkana Nat'l Rsv., Kenya 162/B2
South Tyne (riv.), Eng, UK 93/F2
South Tyneside (co.), Eng, UK 93/G2
South Ubian, Phil. 139/F2
South Uist (isl.), Sc, UK 89/Q8
South Umpqua (riv.), Or, US 186/B2
South Valley Stream, NY, US 197/L9
South Weber, Ut, US 195/K11
South West (cape), Austl. 173/C4
South West NP, Austl. 173/C4
South West Rocks, Austl. 173/E1
South Whittier, Ca, US 194/F8
South Williamsport, Pa, US 196/B1
South Woodham Ferrers, Eng, UK 88/D2
South Yorkshire (co.), Eng, UK 93/G5
Southampton (cape), Nun., Can. 181/H2
Southampton (isl.), Nun., Can. 181/H2
Southampton, On, Can. 188/D2
Southampton, Eng, UK 91/E5
Southampton (co.), Eng, UK 91/E5
Southampton, NY, US 197/F2
Southampton Water (inlet), Eng, UK 91/E5
Southaven, Ms, US 187/K4
Southeast (cape), Ak, US 192/E3
Southeast (pt.), Bahm. 203/H1
Southeast (pt.), Jam. 203/G2
Southend (int'l arpt.), Eng, UK 91/G3
Southend-on-Sea, Eng, UK 91/G3
Southend-on-Sea (co.), Eng, UK 91/G3
Southern (prov.), Ugan. 162/A3
Southern (dist.), Isr. 149/D4
Southern (riv.), Austl. 170/K7
Southern Alps (mts.), NZ 175/R11
Southern Cook (isls.), CookIs. 175/J6
Southern Cross, Austl. 170/C4
Southern Indian (lake), Mb, Can. 180/G3
Southern NP, Sudan 155/L6
Southern Pines, NC, US 191/J3
Southern Uplands (hills), Sc, UK 93/D1
Southern Ural (mts.), Rus. 119/N5
Southesk Tablelands (plat.), Austl. 167/B2
Southold, NY, US 197/F1
Spooner, Wi, US 185/K4
Spotorno, It. 116/B4
Southport, NC, US 191/J3
Southport, Eng, UK 93/E4
Southport, Ct, US 195/U21
Southwark (bor.), Eng, UK 88/A1
Southwood NP, Austl. 172/C4
Southworth, Wa, US 193/C3
Sovata, Rom. 107/G2
Soverato Marina, It. 104/E3
Sovere, It. 116/D1
Sovetsk, Rus. 97/J4
Sowa, Japan 135/D1
Sowerby Bridge, Eng, UK 93/G4
Soweto, SAfr. 164/D2
Söya-misaki (cape), Japan 134/B1
Soyana (riv.), Rus. 118/J2
Soyang (lake), SKor. 131/D4
Soyaux, Fr. 100/D4
Soyen, SAfr. 164/B3
Soyhières, Swi. 114/D3
Sozh (riv.), Bela. 120/D1
Sozopol, Bul. 107/H4
Spa, Belg. 111/E3
Spada (lake), Wa, US 193/D2
Spain (ctry.) 102/C2
Spalding, Austl. 171/H5
Spalding, Eng, UK 93/H6
Spalt, Ger. 112/D4
Spanish Lake, Mo, US 195/G8
Spanish Town, Jam. 203/G2
Spannort (peak), Swi. 115/E4
Sparanise, It. 104/D2
Sparks, Nv, US 186/C3
Sparlingville, Mi, US 193/G6
Sparreholm, Swe. 96/G2
Sparta, NC, US 191/H3

Sparta, NJ, US 196/D1
Sparta, Tn, US 188/C5
Sparta, Wi, US 185/L5
Spartanburg, SC, US 191/H3
Spartel (cape), Mor. 158/B2
Spárti (Sparta), Gre. 105/H4
Spartivento (cape), It. 104/E4
Sparwood, BC, Can. 184/E3
Spassk-Dal'niy, Rus. 129/P3
Spáta, Gre. 105/N9
Spátha (cape), Gre. 105/H5
Spean (riv.), Sc, UK 94/B2
Speer (peak), Swi. 115/F3
Speer Canal (canal), Co, US 195/C2
Speicher, Swi. 115/F3
Speicher, Ger. 111/F4
Speichersdorf, Ger. 113/E3
Speke (gulf), Tanz. 162/B3
Speke (int'l arpt.), Eng, UK 93/F5
Spelle, Ger. 109/E4
Spencer (cape), Austl. 171/H5
Spencer (gulf), Austl. 171/H5
Spencer (pt.), Ak, US 192/C2
Spencer, Ia, US 185/K5
Spencer, Ok, US 195/N14
Spenge, Ger. 109/F4
Spennymoor, Eng, UK 93/G2
Spentrup, Den. 96/D3
Sperkhiás, Gre. 105/H3
Sperkhiós (riv.), Gre. 105/H3
Sperrin (mts.), NI, UK 92/A2
Spessart (range), Ger. 112/C3
Spétsai, Gre. 105/H4
Spey (riv.), Sc, UK 94/B2
Spey (bay), Sc, UK 94/C1
Speyer, Ger. 112/B4
Speyerbach (riv.), Ger. 112/B4
Spezzano Albanese, It. 104/E3
Spičák (peak), Czh. 113/F2
Spicer (isls.), Nun., Can. 181/H2
Spiekeroog (isl.), Ger. 109/E1
Spiez, Swi. 114/D4
Spigno Monferrato, It. 116/B3
Spijkenisse, Neth. 108/B5
Spike (mtn.), Ak, US 192/K2
Spilamberto, It. 117/E3
Spilion, Gre. 105/J5
Spilve (int'l arpt.), Lat. 97/L3
Spina (peak), It. 104/A2
Spinetta Marengo, It. 116/B3
Spino d'Adda, It. 116/C2
Spirano, It. 116/C1
Spirit River, Ab, Can. 184/D2
Spiritwood, Sk, Can. 184/G2
Spišská Nová Ves, Slvk. 99/L4
Spiti (riv.), India 144/D3
Spitsbergen (isl.), Sval. 218/E
Split, Cro. 106/C4
Split (int'l arpt.), Cro. 106/C4
Split (lake), Mb, Can. 180/G3
Splitrock (res.), NJ, US 197/H8
Spluga, Passo dello (pass), Swi. 115/F5
Splügen, Swi. 115/F4
Spokane, Wa, US 184/D4
Spokane (riv.), Wa, US 184/D4
Spöl (riv.), It. 115/G5
Spoleto, It. 101/K5
Spoon (riv.), Il, US 188/B3
Spotswood, NJ, US 197/H10
Spotsylvania, Va, US 191/J2
Sprague, Mb, Can. 185/K3
Spratly (isls.) 138/D2
Spree (riv.), Ger. 99/H2
Sprendlingen, Ger. 111/G4
Spresiano, It. 117/F1
Sprimont, Belg. 111/E3
Spring, Tx, US 187/J5
Spring City, Pa, US 196/C3
Spring Grove, Pa, US 196/B4
Spring Grove, Il, US 193/P15
Spring Hill, Ks, US 195/D6
Spring Lake, NJ, US 196/D3
Spring Valley, Ca, US 194/D5
Spring Valley, NY, US 197/J7
Springbok, SAfr. 164/B3
Springdale, Nf, Can. 189/K1
Springdale, Ar, US 187/J3
Springe, Ger. 109/G4
Springer, NM, US 187/F3
Springerville, Az, US 186/E4
Springfield, Ma, US 196/F3
Springfield, Mo, US 187/J3
Springfield, NJ, US 197/H9
Springfield, Oh, US 188/D4
Springfield, Tn, US 188/C4
Springfield, Vt, US 189/F3
Springfield, Va, US 196/A6
Springfontein, SAfr. 164/D3
Springhill, La, US 187/J4
Springhill, NS, Can. 189/H2
Springs, SAfr. 164/E2

Springs, NY, US 197/F1
Springside, Sk, Can. 185/H3
Springsure, Austl. 172/C4
Springville, Ut, US 195/K13
Sprockhövel, Ger. 109/E6
Spruce (peak), WV, US 188/E4
Spruce Run (res.), NJ, US 196/C2
Spui (riv.), Neth. 108/B5
Spurn (pt.), Eng, UK 93/J4
Squamish, BC, Can. 184/C3
Squaw Harbor, Ak, US 192/F4
Squaxin Island Ind. Res., Wa, US 193/A3
Squillace, Golfo di (gulf), It. 104/E3
Squinzano, It. 105/F2
Squires (mt.), Austl. 171/E3
Srbobran, Serb. 106/D3
Srebrenica, Bosn. 106/D3
Sredna (mts.), Bul. 107/G4
Srednogorie, Bul. 107/G4
Srem, Pol. 99/J2
Srīnagar, India 144/C2
Srivardhan, India 147/K5
Środa Śląska, Pol. 99/J3
Środa Wielkopolska, Pol. 99/J2
Sri Dungargarh, India 147/K3
Sri Gangānagar, India 144/B5
Sri Jayewardenepura Kotte, (cap.), SrL. 140/C6
Sri Lanka (ctry.) 140/D6
Srikākulam, India 140/D4
Staszów, Pol. 99/L3
St. Albans, Vale of (valley), Eng, UK 88/B1
St. John's (cap.), Nf, Can. 189/L2
Staten (isl.), NY, US 196/D2
Staberhuk (pt.), Ger. 96/D4
Statesboro, Ga, US 191/H3
Statesville, NC, US 191/H3
Statue of Liberty Nat'l Mon., NY, US 197/J9
Staufen im Breisgau, Ger. 114/D2
Staufenberg, Ger. 98/E3
Staveley, Eng, UK 93/G5
Stavelot, Belg. 111/E3
Staveren, Neth. 108/C3
Stavropol', Rus. 121/G3
Stavropol'skiy Kray, Rus. 122/F5
Stavrós, Gre. 105/H2
Stawell, Austl. 173/B3
Stayton, Or, US 184/C4
Ste-Marguerite (riv.), Qu, Can. 189/H1
Steamboat Slough (riv.), Ca, US 193/M10
Steamboat Springs, Co, US 186/F2
Stebbins, Ak, US 192/F3
Steckborn, Swi. 115/E2
Stederau (riv.), Ger. 109/H3
Steeg, Aus. 115/G3
Steele, ND, US 185/J4
Steele's Knowe (hill), Sc, UK 94/C4
Steelpoortrivier (riv.), SAfr. 165/E2
Steelton, Pa, US 196/B3
Steenbergen, Neth. 108/B5
Steens (mtn.), Or, US 186/C2
Steenvoorde, Fr. 110/B2
Steenwijk, Neth. 108/D3
Steep (twp.), Austl. 170/B3
Steep Holm (isl.), Eng, UK 90/D4
Steephill (lake), Wa, US 193/D2
Steeping (riv.), Eng, UK 93/J5
Steese Nat'l Conservation Area, Ak, US 192/J2
Stefansson (isl.), Nun., Can. 180/F1
Steffen (peak), Chile 216/C5
Steffisburg, Swi. 114/D4
Stege, Den. 96/E4
Steiermark (prov.), Aus. 99/H5
Steigerwald (for.), Ger. 112/D3
Steilacoom, Wa, US 193/B3
Steinbke, Ger. 109/G3
Stein, Neth. 111/E2
Stein am Rhein, Swi. 115/E2
Stein bei Nürnberg, Ger. 112/E4
Steina (riv.), Ger. 115/H3
Steinach, Ger. 113/F6
Steinach am Brenner, Aus. 115/H3
Steinbach, Mb, Can. 185/J3
Steinbach an der Steyr, Aus. 113/H7

Steinbourg, Fr. 111/G6
Steinen, Ger. 114/D2
Steiner Draper (lake), Ok, US 195/N15
Steinerkirchen an der Traun, Aus. 113/G6
Steinfeld, Ger. 109/F3
Steinfeld, Ger. 112/B4
Steinfeld, Ger. 112/B4
Steinfort, Lux. 111/E4
Steingaden, Ger. 115/G3
Steinhagen, Ger. 109/F4
Steinhausen, Swi. 115/E3
Steinhausen an der Rottum, Ger. 115/F1
Steinheim, Ger. 109/G5
Steinheim am Albuch, Ger. 112/D5
Steinheim an der Murr, Ger. 112/C5
Steinhorst, Ger. 109/H3
Steinhuder (lake), Ger. 109/G4
Steinkjer, Nor. 95/D2
Steinsland, Nor. 96/A1
Steinweiler, Ger. 112/B4
Stekene, Belg. 108/B6
Stella, SAfr. 164/D2
Stella (pass), It. 115/F5
Stellarton, NS, Can. 189/J2
Stelle, Ger. 109/H2
Stellenbosch, SAfr. 164/L10
Stello (peak), Fr. 101/H5
Stelvio, Passo di (pass), It. 115/G4
Stelvio, PN Dello, It. 101/J3
Stenay, Fr. 111/F5
Stendal, Ger. 98/F2
Steneto NP, Bul. 107/G4
Stenhousemuir, Sc, UK 94/C4
Stenungsund, Swe. 96/C2
Stephansposching, Ger. 113/F5
Stephenville, Nf, Can. 189/K1
Stephenville, Tx, US 187/H4
Sterkstroom, SAfr. 164/D3
Sterling, Ak, US 192/H3
Sterling, Co, US 187/G2
Sterlitamak, Rus. 121/K1
Sternstein (pass), Aus. 113/H5
Sterzing (Vipiteno), It. 115/H4
Stęszew, Pol. 99/J2
Štěti, Czh. 113/H2
Stettler, Ab, Can. 184/E2
Steubenville, Oh, US 188/D3
Stevenage, Eng, UK 91/F3
Stevens Village, Ak, US 192/J2
Stevenson (lake), Mb, Can. 185/J2
Stevenson Entrance (str.), Ak, US 192/H4
Stevenston, Sc, UK 94/B5
Stevensville, Mt, US 184/E4
Stevensville, Md, US 196/B6
Stevinsluizen (dam), Neth. 108/C3
Stevzing (Vipiteno), It. 101/J3
Stewart, BC, Can. 192/N4
Stewart (riv.), Yk, Can. 180/C2
Stewart (isl.), NZ 175/R12
Stewart Crossing, Yk, Can. 192/L3
Stewarton, Sc, UK 94/B5
Stewartstown, Pa, US 196/B4
Stewartstown, NI, UK 92/B2
Stewartville, Mn, US 185/K5
Steynrus, SAfr. 164/D2
Steynsburg, SAfr. 164/D3
Steyr, Aus. 113/H6
Steyr (riv.), Aus. 99/H5
Steyregg, Aus. 113/H6
Steytlerville, SAfr. 164/D4
Stia, It. 117/E5
Stiava, It. 116/D3
Stickney (mt.), Wa, US 193/D2
Stiens, Neth. 108/C2
Stigler, Ok, US 187/J4
Stigtomta, Swe. 96/G2
Stikine (riv.), Can.,US 192/M4
Stilbaai, SAfr. 164/C4
Stilfontein, SAfr. 164/D2
Stilis, Gre. 105/H3
Still Creek (res.), Pa, US 196/C2
Still Pond, Md, US 196/B5
Stilling, Den. 96/D3
Stillings, Mo, US 195/D5
Stillwater (range), Nv, US 186/C3
Stillwater, Ok, US 187/H3
Stillwater, Pa, US 196/B1
Stillwater (lake), Pa, US 196/C1
Stilo (cape), It. 104/E3
Stilwell, Ok, US 187/J4
Stilwell, Ks, US 195/D6
Stimlje, Kos. 106/E4
Stinchar (riv.), Sc, UK 92/D1
Stinnett, Tx, US 187/G4
Štip, FYROM 105/F2
Stiring-Wendel, Fr. 111/F5

Stírka (peak), Czh. 113/G4
Stirling (mt.), Austl. 170/C4
Stirling, Sc, UK 94/C4
Stirling (pol. reg.), Sc, UK 94/B4
Stirling Range NP, Austl. 170/C5
Stirone (riv.), It. 116/C3
Stjørdal, Nor. 95/D3
Stob a' Choin (peak), Sc, UK 94/B4
Stob Choire Claurigh (peak), Sc, UK 94/B3
Stochov, Czh. 113/G2
Stock, Eng, UK 88/E2
Stock (lake), Fr. 111/F6
Stockach, Ger. 115/F2
Stockerau, Aus. 107/N7
Stockertown, Pa, US 196/C2
Stockholm (cap.), Swe. 95/F4
Stockholm (co.), Swe. 96/G2
Stockhorn (peak), Swi. 114/D4
Stockport, Eng, UK 93/F5
Stockport (co.), Eng, UK 93/F5
Stocks (res.), Eng, UK 93/F4
Stocksbridge, Eng, UK 93/G5
Stockstadt am Rhein, Ger. 112/B3
Stockton, Ca, US 186/B3
Stockton (lake), Mo, US 187/J3
Stockton, NJ, US 196/D3
Stockton (plat.), Tx, US 190/C4
Stockton, Ut, US 195/J13
Stockton-on-Tees, Eng, UK 93/G2
Stockton-on-Tees (co.), Eng, UK 93/G2
Stod, Czh. 113/G3
Stoddard, Ut, US 195/K11
Stoke (pt.), Eng, UK 90/B6
Stoke-on-Trent, Eng, UK 93/F5
Stoke-on-Trent (co.), Eng, UK 93/F5
Stoke Poges, Eng, UK 88/B2
Stokenchurch, Eng, UK 88/A2
Stokes (pt.), Austl. 173/B4
Stokes NP, Austl. 170/C5
Stolac, Bosn. 105/E1
Stolberg, Ger. 111/F2
Stolbovoy (isl.), Rus. 123/P2
Stöllet, Swe. 96/E1
Stolzenau, Ger. 109/G3
Stompneuspunt (pt.), SAfr. 164/K10
Ston, Cro. 105/E1
Stone, Eng, UK 93/F6
Stone Harbor, NJ, US 196/D5
Stonehaven, Sc, UK 94/D3
Stonehenge (ruin), Eng, UK 91/E4
Stonehouse, Sc, UK 94/C5
Stonewall, Mb, Can. 185/J3
Stoney Creek, On, Can. 189/Q9
Stoney Point, On, Can. 193/Q2
Stoneyburn, Sc, UK 94/C5
Stonington, Ct, US 197/G1
Stony (pt.), Mb, Can. 185/J2
Stony Brook, NY, US 197/E2
Stony Creek (lake), Mi, US 193/E7
Stony Mountain, Mb, Can. 196/B4
Stony Point, NY, US 196/E1
Stony River, Ak, US 192/G3
Stony Tunguska (riv.), Rus. 125/J3
Stonybrook-Wilshire, Pa, US 196/B4
Stooping (riv.), Co, US 188/D1
Stor (isl.), Nun., Can. 181/S7
Stör (riv.), Ger. 109/G1
Stor-Elvdal, Nor. 96/D1
Storå, Swe. 96/F2
Stora Le (lake), Swe. 96/D2
Stora Sjöfallets NP, Swe. 95/F2
Storavan (lake), Swe. 96/A2
Stord (isl.), Nor. 96/A2
Store Bælt (chan.), Den. 96/D4
Storebø, Nor. 96/A1
Støren, Nor. 95/D3
Storfors, Swe. 96/F2
Storm (bay), Austl. 175/D4
Stormberg (mtn.), SAfr. 164/D3
Stormont, NI, UK 92/C2
Stornoway, Sc, UK 89/Q7
Storo, It. 116/D1
Storr, The (peak), Sc, UK 94/A2
Storsjön (lake), Swe. 95/E3
Storsteinsfjellet (peak), Nor. 95/F1
Storstrøm (co.), Den. 96/D4
Storvik, Swe. 96/G1
Storvreta, Swe. 96/G2
Story, Wy, US 184/G4
Stosch (isl.), Chile 217/A6

Stötten am Auerberg, Ger. 115/G2
Stoughton, Sk, Can. 185/H3
Stoumont, Belg. 111/E3
Stour (riv.), Eng, UK 90/D5
Stourbridge, Eng, UK 90/D2
Stourport-on-Severn, Eng, UK 90/D2
Stovring, Den. 96/C3
Stowe, Pa, US 196/C3
Stowmarket, Eng, UK 91/G2
Stra, It. 117/F2
Strabane (dist.), NI 92/A2
Strabane, NI, UK 89/Q9
Stradella, It. 116/C2
Straelen, Ger. 108/D6
Strahan, Austl. 173/C4
Strakonice, Czh. 113/G4
Straldzha, Bul. 107/H4
Stralsund, Ger. 96/E4
Strambino, It. 116/A2
Strand, SAfr. 164/L11
Strangford, NI, UK 92/C3
Strangford (lake), NI, UK 92/C3
Strängnäs, Swe. 96/G2
Strangways (mt.), Austl. 171/G2
Stranocum, NI, UK 92/B1
Stranraer, Sc, UK 92/C2
Strasbourg, Fr. 114/D1
Strasbourg (Entzheim) (int'l arpt.), Fr. 114/D1
Strasburg, Mo, US 195/E6
Strasburg, Pa, US 196/B4
Strassen, Lux. 111/F4
Strasshof an der Nordbahn, Aus. 107/P7
Strasswalchen, Aus. 113/G7
Stratford, Tx, US 187/G3
Stratford, On, Can. 188/D3
Stratford, NZ 175/S10
Stratford, Ct, US 197/E1
Stratford, NJ, US 196/C4
Stratford (pt.), Ct, US 197/E1
Stratford (har.), Ct, US 197/L8
Stratford and Worcester (canal), Eng, UK 90/D2
Stratford-upon-Avon, Eng, UK 91/E2
Strathalbyn, Austl. 171/H5
Strathaven, Sc, UK 94/B5
Strathbeg (bay), Sc, UK 94/E1
Strathblane, Sc, UK 94/B5
Strathearn (valley), Sc, UK 94/C4
Strathmore, Ab, Can. 184/E3
Strathmore (valley), Sc, UK 94/C3
Strathpeffer, Sc, UK 94/B1
Strathspey (valley), Sc, UK 94/C2
Straubing, Ger. 113/F5
Straumnes Horn (pt.), Ice. 95/M6
Strausberg, Ger. 98/Q6
Strausstown, Pa, US 196/B3
Strawberry (peak), Ca, US 194/C2
Strazhitsa, Bul. 107/G4
Streaky (bay), Austl. 171/G5
Streaky Bay, Austl. 171/G5
Streamwood, Il, US 193/P15
Streator, Il, US 185/L5
Středočeská Žulová Vrchovina (mts.), Czh. 99/H4
Středočeský (pol. reg.), Czh. 101/L2
Street, Md, US 196/B4
Strehaia, Rom. 107/F3
Streich (peak), Austl. 170/D4
Střela (riv.), Czh. 99/G3
Strelley Abor. Land, Austl. 170/C2
Strel'na (riv.), Rus. 118/H2
Strengberg, Aus. 113/H6
Strengelbach, Swi. 114/D3
Strengen, Aus. 115/G3
Stresa, It. 116/B1
Stretford, Eng, UK 93/F5
Strettoia, It. 116/D5
Streu (riv.), Ger. 112/D2
Strib, Den. 96/C4
Stříbro, Czh. 113/G3
Strichen, Sc, UK 94/D1
Strigno, It. 115/H5
Strijen, Neth. 108/B5
Strimón (gulf), Gre. 105/H2
Strimónas (riv.), Gre. 105/H2
Striven (lake), Sc, UK 94/A5
Strobel (lake), Arg. 217/C6
Stroeder, Arg. 216/E4
Strofádhes (isl.), Gre. 105/G4
Strom Thurmond (lake), Ga,SC, US 191/H3
Stromberg, Ger. 111/G3
Stromboli (isl.), It. 104/D3
Strömmen, Nor. 96/D1
Stromness, Sc, UK 89/V14
Stromstad, Swe. 96/D2
Strömsund, Swe. 95/E3
Strona (riv.), It. 115/G6
Strongoli, It. 105/E3
Stronie Śląskie, Pol. 99/J3
Stronsay (isl.), Sc, UK 89/V14

Stronsay Firth (inlet), Sc, UK 89/V14
Strood, Eng, UK 88/E2
Stropnice (riv.), Czh. 113/H5
Stroppiana, It. 116/B2
Stroud, Eng, UK 90/D3
Stroudsburg, Pa, US 196/C2
Struan, Sc, UK 89/Q8
Struer, Den. 96/C3
Struga, FYROM 105/G2
Struisbaai (bay), Pa, US 196/C1
SAfr. 164/C4
Strule (riv.), NI, UK 92/A2
Struma (riv.), Bul. 120/B4
Strumble (pt.), Wal, UK 90/A2
Strumica, FYROM 105/H2
Strydenburg, SAfr. 164/C3
Stryn, Nor. 95/C3
Strzegom, Pol. 99/J3
Strzelce Krajeńskie, Pol. 99/H2
Strzelce Opolskie, Pol. 120/A2
Strzelecki (mt.), Austl. 173/D4
Strzelecki (mt.), Austl. 171/G2
Strzelin, Pol. 99/J3
Strzelno, Pol. 99/K2
Strzyżów, Pol. 99/L4
Stuart (lake), BC, Can. 184/B2
Stuart (riv.), BC, Can. 184/B2
Stuart, Fl, US 191/H5
Stuarts Draft, Va, US 188/E4
Stubbekobing, Den. 96/E4
Stubbenkammer (pt.), Ger. 96/E4
Stühlingen, Ger. 115/E2
Stupava, Slvk. 101/M2
Stupino, Rus. 118/H5
Stura di Lanzo (riv.), It. 116/A2
Sturgeon (lake), On, Can. 185/L3
Sturgeon (bay), Mb, Can. 185/J3
Sturgeon (riv.), On, Can. 188/D2
Sturgeon Falls, On, Can. 188/E2
Sturgis, Mi, US 188/C4
Sturgis, SD, US 184/F4
Ŝturovo, Slvk. 99/K5
Sturt (des.), Austl. 173/B1
Sturt (mt.), Austl. 173/B1
Sturt (riv.), Austl. 171/M8
Sturt NP, Austl. 120/E1
Sturup (int'l arpt.), Swe. 96/E4
Stutterheim, SAfr. 164/D4
Stykkishólmur, Ice. 95/M6
Styr (riv.), Ukr. 120/C2
Suaçui Grande (riv.), Braz. 213/D1
Suakin (arch.), Sudan 155/N4
Suam (riv.), Kenya 162/B2
Suaqui Grande, Mex. 200/C2
Suár, India 142/B1
Suárez (riv.), Col. 210/C3
Subang, Indo. 138/C5
Subarnarekhā (riv.), India 143/E4
Sūbáṭ (riv.), Sudan 155/M6
Subaytilah, Tun. 158/L7
Subei Monggolzu Zizhixian, China 128/F4
Subi (isl.), Indo. 138/C3
Subotica, Serb. 106/D2
Succasunna-Kenvil, NJ, US 196/D2
Succiso, Alpe di (peak), It. 116/D4
Suceava, Rom. 107/H2
Suceava (prov.), Rom. 107/G2
Suchedniów, Pol. 99/L3
Suches, Bol. 214/D4
Suck (riv.), Ire. 89/P10
Sucre (cap.), Bol. 208/E7
Sucre (dept.), Col. 210/C3
Sucre, Ecu. 210/A5
Sucre (state), Ven. 211/F2
Sucúa, Ecu. 210/B5
Sucumbios (prov.), Ecu. 210/B4
Sucunduri (riv.), Braz. 208/G5
Sucupira do Norte, Braz. 212/A2
Sucuriú (riv.), Braz. 209/H7
Sucy-en-Brie, Fr. 88/K5
Sud (pol. reg.), Mor. 156/C3
Sud-Ouest (prov.), Camr. 161/H5
Suda (riv.), Rus. 118/H4
Sudama, Japan 135/A2
Sudan (ctry.), 155/L5
Sudbury, On, Can. 188/D2
Sudbury, Eng, UK 91/G2
Suddie, Guy. 211/G3
Sude (riv.), Ger. 98/F2
Suderbrarup, Ger. 96/C4
Sudeten (mts.), Czh.,Pol. 99/H3
Sudlersville, Md, US 196/C5
Südlohn, Ger. 108/D5
Sue (riv.), Sudan 155/L6
Sueca, Sp. 103/E3
Süedinenie, Bul. 107/G4
Suez (canal), Egypt 159/C2
Suez (gulf), Egypt 159/C3
Süf, Jor. 149/D3

Sufers, Swi. 115/F4
Suffern, NY, US 197/J7
Suffolk (co.), NY, US 197/F2
Suga (isl.), Japan 135/L7
Sugar Creek, Mo, US 195/E5
Sugar Grove, Il, US 193/P16
Sugar Land, Tx, US 190/E4
Sugar Loaf (peak), Wal, UK 90/C3
Sugar Notch, Pa, US 196/C1
Sugenheim, Ger. 112/D3
Sugito, Japan 135/D1
Suğla (lake), Turk. 148/C2
Suhãj, Egypt 159/B3
Suhãj (gov.), Egypt 159/B3
Sühbaatar (prov.), Mong. 129/K2
Suhl, Ger. 112/D1
Suhlendorf, Ger. 109/H3
Şuhut, Turk. 148/B2
Sui (riv.), China 137/B3
Sui (pt.), Thai. 136/B4
Sui Xian, China 130/C4
Suia-Missu (riv.), Braz. 209/H6
Suichang, China 137/C2
Suichuan, China 141/K2
Suifenhe, China 129/P3
Suihua, China 129/N2
Suijiang, China 141/H2
Suileng, China 129/N2
Suining, China 137/B2
Suipacha, Arg. 217/J11
Suiping, China 130/C4
Suippe (riv.), Fr. 98/C4
Suippes, Fr. 111/D5
Suir (riv.), Ire. 89/Q10
Suis (well), Libya 157/H4
Suishõ (isl.), Rus. 134/D2
Suita, Japan 135/J6
Suitland-Silver Hill, Md, US 196/B6
Suixi, China 141/K3
Suixi, China 130/D4
Suiyang, China 137/A2
Suize (riv.), Fr. 114/B2
Suizhong, China 130/E2
Suizhou, China 129/K5
Sūjāngarh, India 147/K3
Sukabumi, Indo. 138/C5
Sukadana (bay), Indo. 138/C4
Sukadana, Indo. 138/C4
Sukagawa, Japan 133/G2
Sukheke, Pak. 144/B4
Sukhindol, Bul. 107/G4
Sukhinichi, Rus. 120/E1
Sukhodol'skoye (lake), Rus. 97/N1
Sukhona (riv.), Rus. 122/E4
Sukhothai (ruin), Thai. 136/B2
Sukhothai, Thai. 136/B2
Sukkur, Pak. 147/J3
Sükösd, Hun. 106/D2
Sukumo, Japan 132/C4
Sula (isls.), Indo. 139/G4
Sula (riv.), Rus. 119/L2
Sulaimān (range), India 143/E4
Sulakyurt, Turk. 148/C1
Sulawesi (Celebes) (isl.), Indo. 139/E4
Sulb Temple (ruin), Sudan 159/B4
Sulby, Wal, UK 90/B4
Sulby (riv.), IM, UK 92/D3
Sulechów, Pol. 99/H2
Sulęcin, Pol. 99/H2
Sulejów, Pol. 99/K3
Sulejówek, Pol. 99/L2
Sulina, Rom. 107/J3
Sulina Branch (riv.), Rom. 107/J3
Sulingen, Ger. 109/F3
Sulitjelma (peak), Nor. 95/F2
Sullana, Peru 214/A2
Sullivan (lake), Ab, Can. 184/F3
Sullivan, Qu, Can. 188/E1
Sullivan, Wi, US 193/N13
Sully-sur-Loire, Fr. 91/F4
Sulmona, It. 104/C1
Sulphur (riv.), Tx, US 187/J4
Sulphur, Ok, US 187/H4
Sulphur Springs, Tx, US 187/J4
Sulphur Springs, Ca, US 194/A2
Sultan, Wa, US 193/D2
Sultan (riv.), Wa, US 193/D2
Sultan Kudarat, Phil. 137/D6
Sultānpur, India 142/D2
Sulu (arch.), Phil. 137/D6
Sulu (sea), Asia 137/D6
Sülüklü, Turk. 148/C2
Suluova, Turk. 120/E4
Sulūq, Libya 155/K1
Sülüsáp, Hun. 107/R10
Sulz, Swi. 114/E2
Sulz (riv.), Ger. 113/E4
Sülz (riv.), Ger. 111/G2
Sulz am Neckar, Ger. 112/B4
Sulzbach (riv.), Ger. 113/F6
Sulzbach am Main, Ger. 112/C3
Sulzbach-Rosenberg, Ger. 113/E3
Sulzberg, Ger. 115/G2

Sulzberger (bay), Ant. 218/Q
Sulzburg, Ger. 114/D2
Sulzfluh (peak), Aus. 115/F3
Sulzheim, Ger. 112/D3
Šumadija (reg.), Serb. 106/E3
Sumas, Wa, US 184/C3
Sumatra (isl.), Indo. 138/B4
Sumba (str.), Indo. 139/E5
Sumba (isl.), Indo. 139/J4
Sumbar (riv.), Trkm. 145/C5
Sumbawa (isl.), Indo. 139/E5
Sumbawa Besar, Indo. 139/E5
Sumbawanga, Tanz. 162/A4
Sumbe, Ang. 163/B3
Sumburgh Head (pt.), Sc, UK 89/W14
Sumdum (mt.), Ak, US 192/M4
Sur Reina Sofia (int'l arpt.), Sp. 156/A3
Sümeg, Hun. 106/C2
Sumenep, Indo. 138/D5
Sumiswald, Swi. 114/D3
Summerland, BC, Can. 184/D3
Summerland, Ca, US 194/A2
Summerside, PE, Can. 189/J2
Summerville, SC, US 191/H3
Summerville, Ga, US 191/G3
Summit, NJ, US 197/H9
Summit (co.), Ut, US 195/K12
Summit Bridge, De, US 196/C4
Summit Hill, Pa, US 196/C2
Sumner, Wa, US 193/C3
Sumoto, Japan 132/D3
Šumperk, Czh. 99/J4
Sumqayit, Azer. 121/J4
Sums'ka Oblasti, Ukr. 120/E2
Sumter, SC, US 191/H3
Sumy, Ukr. 120/E2
Sun (riv.), Mt, US 184/E4
Sun City, Az, US 195/R18
Sun City, Ca, US 194/C3
Sun City West, Az, US 195/R18
Sun Kosi (riv.), Nepal 143/F2
Sun Lakes, Az, US 195/S19
Sunagawa, Japan 134/B2
Sunām, India 144/C4
Sunami, Japan 135/L5
Sunbury, Pa, US 196/B2
Sunbury, Austl. 173/F5
Sunbury-on-Thames, Eng, UK 88/B2
Sunch'ang, SKor. 131/D5
Sunch'ŏn, NKor. 131/C3
Sunch'ŏn, SKor. 131/D5
Suncook, NH, US 189/G3
Sunda (isls.), Indo. 138/D4
Sunda (str.), Indo. 138/B5
Sundance, Wy, US 185/G4
Sundarbans (phys. reg.), India 143/G5
Sundargarh, India 143/E4
Sundarnagar, India 144/D4
Sundays (riv.), SAfr. 164/D4
Sunderland, Eng, UK 93/G2
Sunderland (co.), Eng, UK 93/G2
Sundern, Ger. 109/F6
Sundhouse, Fr. 114/D1
Sundown, Tx, US 187/G4
Sundown NP, Austl. 173/D1
Sundre, Ab, Can. 184/E3
Sunds, Den. 96/C3
Sungai Petani, Malay. 141/H6
Sungaipenuh, Indo. 138/B4
Sungurlare, Bul. 107/H4
Sungurlu, Turk. 148/C1
Suning, China 130/C3
Sunndal, Nor. 95/D3
Sunne, Swe. 96/E2
Sunningdale, Eng, UK 91/F4
Sütçüler, Turk. 148/B2
Sunnyside, Ca, US 194/C3
Sunnyside, Il, US 193/P15
Sunnyvale, Ca, US 186/B3
Sunomata, Japan 135/L5
Sunol, Ca, US 193/L11
Sunomata, Japan 135/L5
Sunrise (mtn.), NJ, US 196/D1
Sunset, Ut, US 195/J11
Sunset Beach, Hi, US 182/V12
Sunset Beach, Ca, US 194/F8
Sunset Crater Volcano Nat'l Mon., Az, US 186/E4
Suntar-Khayata (mts.), Rus. 123/P3
Süntel (mts.), Ger. 109/G4
Sunur (isl.), NKor. 131/C4
Sunwu, China 129/N2
Sunzu (peak), Zam. 162/A5
Suo (sea), Japan 132/B4
Suomenlinna, Fin. 97/L1
Suomenselkä (reg.), Fin. 95/H3
Supaul, India 143/F3
Supawna Meadows NWR, NJ, US 196/C4
Şuwayliḥ, Jor. 149/D3
Supŏn, SKor. 131/D5
Supe, Peru 214/B2
Superior, Mt, US 184/E4

Superior, Az, US 186/E4
Superior (upland), Wi, US 188/B2
Superior, Co, US 195/B3
Superior (lake), Can.,US 188/B2
Sür, Leb. 149/D3
Sur (pt.), Arg. 217/F3
Sura (riv.), Rus. 119/K5
Surabaya, Indo. 138/D5
Surada, India 140/D4
Surahammar, Swe. 96/G2
Sürajgarh, India 144/C5
Surak-san (peak), SKor. 131/D5
Surallah, Phil. 139/F2
Suran (riv.), Fr. 114/B5
Šurany, Slvk. 106/D1
Surat, India 147/K4
Surat, Austl. 172/C4
Surat Thani, Thai. 136/B4
Suratgarh, India 144/B5
Surčin, Serb. 106/E3
Surdulica, Serb. 106/F4
Sûre (riv.), Lux. 98/C4
Surendranagar, India 147/K4
Surgères, Fr. 114/B4
Surgut, Rus. 122/H3
Sûri, India 143/F4
Súria, Sp. 103/F2
Surigao, Phil. 137/G6
Surin, Thai. 136/C3
Suriname (ctry.), 211/G3
Surma (riv.), Bang. 143/H3
Surprise, Az, US 195/R18
Surrey, BC, Can. 184/C3
Surrey (co.), Eng, UK 91/F4
Sursee, Swi. 114/E3
Surt, Libya 154/J1
Surte, Swe. 96/E3
Surubim, Braz. 212/D2
Süruç, Turk. 148/D2
Suruga (bay), Japan 133/F3
Surumu (riv.), Braz. 211/F3
Susa, It. 116/A2
Susaki, Japan 132/C4
Susanville, Ca, US 184/C5
Susegana, It. 117/F1
Suşehri, Turk. 148/D1
Sushan (isl.), China 131/B4
Sušice, Czh. 113/G4
Susitna (riv.), Ak, US 180/A2
Susono, Japan 133/F3
Susquehanna (riv.), Md,Pa, US 188/E3
Susquehanna NWR, Md, US 196/B5
Susuman, Rus. 123/Q3
Susurluk, Turk. 148/B2
Susz, Pol. 99/K2
Sutherland, SAfr. 164/C4
Sutherland Springs, Tx, US 195/U21
Sutherlin, Or, US 184/C5
Sutjeska NP, Bosn. 106/D4
Sutlej (riv.), India 144/D4
Sütlüce, Turk. 105/K2
Sutter (co.), Ca, US 193/L9
Sutton, Ak, US 192/U3
Sutton (bor.), Eng, UK 88/C2
Sutton Coldfield, Eng, UK 91/E1
Sutton in Ashfield, Eng, UK 91/E1
Suttsu, Japan 134/B2
Suur (riv.), Est. 97/K2
Suurberge (mts.), SAfr. 164/C4
Suurbraak, SAfr. 164/C4
Suvorovo, Bul. 107/H4
Suwałki, Pol. 97/K4
Suwannee (riv.), Fl, US 191/H4
Suwanose (isl.), Japan 133/K6
Suwarrow (isls.), Cook Is. 175/J6
Suwŏn, SKor. 131/D5
Suyo, Peru 214/B2

Suze (riv.), Swi. 114/D3
Suzhou, China 130/D4
Suzhou, China 130/L8
Suzi (riv.), China 131/C2
Suzu, Japan 133/E2
Suzu-misaki (cape), Ger. 111/F2
Switzerland (ctry.) 117/G4
Suzuka, Japan 135/L6
Suzuka (riv.), Japan 135/L6
Suzuka (range), Japan 135/K6
Suzzara, It. 117/D3
Svalbard (isls.), Nor. 218/E
Svaneke, Den. 96/F4
Svängsta, Swe. 96/F3
Svanstein, Swe. 118/D2
Svatava (riv.), Czh. 113/F2
Svealand (reg.), Swe. 95/E4
Svedala, Swe. 96/E4
Sveio, Nor. 96/A2
Svelvik, Nor. 96/D2
Svendborg, Den. 96/D4
Svendsen (pen.), Nun., Can. 181/S7
Svenljunga, Swe. 96/E3
Svenstrup, Den. 96/C3
Sverdlovskaya Oblast, Rus. 122/G4
Sverdrup (chan.), Nun., Can. 181/S7
Sverdrup (isls.), Nun., Can. 181/R7
Sverdrup (isl.), Rus. 122/H2
Svetlogorsk, Bela. 120/D1
Svetlograd, Rus. 121/G3
Svetlyy, Rus. 121/M2
Svetozarevo, Serb. 106/E4
Svíahnúkar (peak), Ice. 95/P7
Svilajnac, Serb. 106/E3
Svilengrad, Bul. 107/H5
Svishtov, Bul. 107/G4
Svitavy, Czh. 99/J4
Svobodnyy, Rus. 129/N1
Svoge, Bul. 107/F4
Svratka (riv.), Czh. 101/M2
Svrljig, Serb. 106/F4
Svyatyy Nos (cape), Rus. 123/Q2
Swäbi, Pak. 144/B2
Swadlincote, Eng, UK 91/E1
Swain (reefs), Austl. 172/D3
Swains (isl.), ASam. 175/H6
Swainsboro, Ga, US 191/H3
Swakopmund, Namb. 163/B5
Swale, The (riv.), Eng, UK 91/G4
Swalmen, Neth. 108/D6
Swan (mt.), Austl. 171/G2
Swan (riv.), Austl. 170/C4
Swan (hills), Ab, Can. 180/E3
Swan (isls.), Hon. 198/E4
Swan Hill, Austl. 173/B2
Swan Hills, Ab, Can. 184/E2
Swan Reach, Austl. 171/H5
Swan River, Mb, Can. 185/H2
Swanscombe, Eng, UK 88/D2
Swansea, Austl. 173/D4
Swansea (bay), Eng, UK 90/C3
Swansea, Wal, UK 90/C3
Swansea (co.), Wal, UK 90/B3
Swansea, Il, US 195/H8
Swart Kei (riv.), SAfr. 164/D3
Swartmore, Ca, US 196/C4
Swartswood (lake), NJ, US 196/D1
Swarzędz, Pol. 99/J2

Swindon (co.), Eng, UK 91/G3
Świnoujście, Pol. 96/F5
Swinton, Eng, UK 93/G5
Swist Bach (riv.), Ger. 111/F2
Switzerland (ctry.) 117/G4
Swords, Ire. 92/B5
Swoyersville, Pa, US 196/C1
Syamozero (lake), Rus. 118/G3
Sych, Moel (peak), Wal, UK 93/E6
Syców, Pol. 99/J3
Sydney, NS, Can. 189/J2
Sydney, Austl. 172/H8
Sydney-Kingsford Smith (int'l arpt.), Austl. 172/H8
Syeverodonets'k, Ukr. 120/F2
Syke, Ger. 109/F3
Sykesville, Md, US 196/B5
Sykkylven, Nor. 95/C3
Syktyvkar, Rus. 119/L3
Sylacauga, Al, US 191/G3
Sylarna (peak), Swe. 95/E3
Sylhet (pol. reg.), Bang. 143/H3
Sylva (riv.), Rus. 119/N4
Sylvan Lake, Mi, US 193/F6
Sylvania, Oh, US 188/D3
Sylvenstein-Stausee (lake), Ger. 115/H2
Sými, Gre. 148/A2
Syntagma, Gre. 105/N8
Syosset, NY, US 197/L8
Syowa, Japan, Ant. 218/C
Syracuse, NY, US 188/E3
Syracuse, Ut, US 195/J11
Syracuse Hancock (int'l arpt.), NY, US 188/E3
Syrdariya (riv.), Kaz. 125/F5
Syria (ctry.) 148/D3
Syriam, Myan. 141/G4
Syrian (des.), Jor. 146/C2
Sysmä, Fin. 97/L1
Sysola (riv.), Rus. 119/L3
Syzran', Rus. 121/J1
Szabolcs-Szatmár-Bereg (co.), Hun. 99/L4
Szamotuły, Pol. 99/J2
Szarvas, Hun. 106/E2
Százhalombatta, Hun. 107/Q10
Szczebrzeszyn, Pol. 99/M3
Szczecin, Pol. 96/F5
Szczecinek, Pol. 96/G5
Szczytna, Pol. 99/J3
Szczytno, Pol. 99/L2
Szeged, Hun. 106/E2
Szeghalom, Hun. 106/E2
Székesfehérvár, Hun. 106/D2
Szekszárd, Hun. 106/D2
Szendro, Hun. 106/E1
Szent László-Vize (riv.), Hun. 107/Q10
Szentendre, Hun. 107/R9
Szentes, Hun. 106/E2
Szentlorinc, Hun. 106/C2
Szerencs, Hun. 99/L4
Szeskie (peak), Pol. 97/K4
Sziget-Szentmiklós, Hun. 107/R10
Szigetvár, Hun. 106/C2
Szirák, Hun. 99/K5
Szolnok, Hun. 106/E2
Szombathely, Hun. 101/M3
Szprotawa, Pol. 99/H3
Sztum, Pol. 97/H5
Szubin, Pol. 99/J2
Szydłowiec, Pol. 99/L3

T

Ta Khmau, Camb. 136/D4
Taabo, Barrage de (dam), C.d'Iv. 160/D5
Tabaco, Phil. 137/D5
Tabaquite, Trin. 211/F2
Tabarqah, Tun. 158/L6
Tabas, Iran 147/G2
Tabasará (mts.), Pan. 203/F4
Tabasco (state), Mex. 198/C4
Tabatinga, Serra da (mts.), Braz. 209/K6
Tabayama, Japan 135/B2
Tabelbala, Alg. 156/E3
Tabelbalet (well), Alg. 157/G4
Ta'benghisa, Ponta (pt.), Malta 104/L7
Taber, Ab, Can. 184/E3
Tabernes de Valldigna, Sp. 103/E3
Tabiang, Kiri. 174/F5
Tabira, Braz. 212/C2
Tabiteuea (isl.), Kiri. 174/G5
Tablas (isl.), Phil. 137/D5
Tablas de Daimiel NP, Sp. 102/D3
Table (bay), SAfr. 164/B4
Table (mtn.), SAfr. 164/L10
Table Rock (lake),
Tabligbo, Togo 161/F5
Tábor, Czh. 113/H4
Tabora (pol. reg.), Tanz. 162/B4
Tabora, Tanz. 162/B4
Tabou, C.d'Iv. 160/D5
Tabuk, Phil. 137/D4
Tabūk, SAr. 146/C3

Tabuleiro do Norte, Braz. 212/C2
Tabwemasana (peak), Van. 174/F6
Tacabamba, Peru 214/B2
Tacámbaro de Codallos, Mex. 201/E5
Tacaná (vol.), Mex. 202/C3
Tacarcuna (mtn.), Pan. 203/G4
Tacheng, China 128/D2
Tachibana (bay), Japan 132/A4
Tachikawa, Japan 133/F3
Tachinger (lake), Ger. 113/F1
Tachira (state), Ven. 210/C3
Tachov, Czh. 113/E3
Tacloban, Phil. 137/E5
Tacna, Peru 214/D5
Tacna (dept.), Peru 214/D5
Tacoma, Wa, US 184/C4
Tacora (vol.), Chile 214/D5
Tacotalpa, Mex. 202/C2
Tacuarembó, Uru. 215/E3
Tacuarembó (dept.), Uru. 217/K12
Tacutu (riv.), Braz. 211/F4
Tadaoka, Japan 135/H7
Ta'Delimara (pt.), Malta 104/M7
Tademaït, Plateau du (plat.), Alg. 154/F2
Tadepallegüdem, India 140/D4
Tadley, Eng, UK 91/E4
Tadmur, Syria 148/D3
Tadó, Col. 210/B3
Tadó, Japan 135/L5
Tadohae Hasang NP, SKor. 131/C5
Tadotsu, Japan 132/C3
Tadpatri, India 140/C5
Tadrart (mts.), Alg.,Libya 154/H2
Tadworth, Eng, UK 88/C3
T'aean, SKor. 131/D4
T'aebaek, SKor. 131/E4
Taebudo (isl.), SKor. 131/F7
Taech'ŏn, SKor. 131/D4
Taech'ŏng (isl.), SKor. 131/C4
Taedŏk, SKor. 131/D5
Taedong (riv.), NKor. 131/D3
Taegang-got (pt.), NKor. 131/D3
Taegu, SKor. 131/E5
Taegu Gwangyŏksi (prov.), SKor. 131/E5
Taehŭksan (isl.), SKor. 131/C5
Taehwa (isl.), NKor. 131/C3
T'aein, SKor. 131/D4
Taejŏn, SKor. 131/D4
Taejŏn Gwangyŏksi (prov.), SKor. 131/D4
Taeryŏng (riv.), NKor. 131/C2
Tafalla, Sp. 102/E1
Tafassasset, Oued (riv.), Alg. 157/H4
Taff (riv.), Wal, UK 90/C3
Tafi Viejo, Arg. 215/C2
Tafraout, Mor. 156/C3
Taft, La, US 195/P17
Taft, Iran 147/H3
Taftān (mtn.), Iran 147/K3
Taga, Japan 135/K5
Taganrog, Rus. 120/F3
Tagant (pol. reg.), Mrta. 160/C2
Tagarav (peak), Trkm. 121/L5
Tagawa, Japan 132/B4
Taggia, It. 116/A5
Taghit, Alg. 157/E3
Tagish, Yk, Can. 192/M3
Tagliamento (riv.), It. 101/K3
Taglio di Po, It. 117/F3
Tagolo (pt.), Phil. 139/F2
Taguasco, Cuba 203/G1
Taguatinga, Braz. 209/J7
Tagula (isl.), PNG 174/E6
Tagum, Phil. 137/E6
Tagun (riv.), Rus. 119/P4
Tagus (riv.), Port. 102/B3
Tagus Rio Tejo (lake), Port. 103/P10
Tagus (Tajo) (riv.), Sp. 102/C3
Tahan (peak), Malay. 138/C3
Tahanea (isl.), FrPol. 175/L6
Tahanroz'ka Zatoka (gulf), Rus.,Ukr. 120/F3
Tahara, Japan 135/L6
Tahat (peak), Alg. 157/G5
Tahat, Oued et (riv.), Alg. 158/F5
Tahe, China 129/M1
Tahilt, Mong. 128/G2
Tahir (pass), Turk. 148/E2
Tahiti (isl.), FrPol. 175/L6
Tahkuna (pt.), Est. 97/K2
Tahlequah, Ok, US 187/J4
Tahmoor, Austl. 173/D2
Tahneta (pass), Ak, US 192/J3
Tahoe (lake), Ca,Nv, US 186/C3
Tahoka, Tx, US 187/G4
Tahoua (dept.), Niger 161/G3
Tahoua, Niger 161/G3
Tahsis, BC, Can. 184/B3

Tahuamanu (riv.), Peru 214/D3
Tahuamanú, Peru 214/D3
Tahuata (isl.), FrPol. 175/L6
Tahulandang (isl.), Indo. 139/G3
Tahuya, Wa, US 193/A3
Tahuya (riv.), Wa, US 193/B3
Tai Long Wan (bay), China 129/V10
Tai Mo Shan (peak), China 129/U10
Taï, PN de, C.d'Iv. 154/D6
Tai Po, China 129/U10
Tai Xian, China 130/E4
Tai'an, China 131/B2
Tai'an, China 130/D3
Taiaret (well), Mor. 156/B5
Taibus, China 129/L3
Taicang, China 130/L8
Taichung, Tai. 137/E3
Taiei, Japan 135/E2
Taieri (riv.), NZ 175/S12
Taigu, China 130/C3
Taihang (mts.), China 130/C3
Taihe, China 137/B2
Taihe, China 130/C4
Taikang, China 130/C4
Taiki, Japan 134/C2
Tailem Bend, Austl. 171/H5
Taima, Japan 135/J6
Tain, Sc, UK 94/B1
T'ainan, Tai. 137/D3
Tainaron (cape), Gre. 105/H4
Taingainony, Madg. 165/H8
Tain, It. 116/B1
Taiobeiras, Braz. 212/B4
T'aipei (cap.), Tai. 137/D2
Taiping, Malay. 138/B3
Taiping, China 137/C1
Taisha, Japan 132/C3
Taishan, China 137/B3
Taishi, Japan 135/K4
Taiskirchen im Innkreis, Aus. 113/G6
Taissy, Fr. 111/D5
Taitao (pen.), Chile 216/B5
Taiti (cape), Kenya 162/B2
Taitung, Tai. 137/D3
Taiwan (ctry.) 137/D3
Taiwan (str.), China,Tai. 137/C3
Taixing, China 130/E4
Taiyetos (mts.), Gre. 105/H4
Taiyuan, China 130/C3
Taizhou, China 130/D4
Taizi (riv.), China 130/F2
Ta'izz, Yem. 146/D6
Tāj Mahal, India 142/B2
Tajikistan (ctry.) 145/E5
Tajima, Japan 133/F2
Tajimi, Japan 135/M5
Tajiri, Japan 135/H7
Tajpur, India 142/B1
Tajrish, Iran 146/F1
Tajumulco (vol.), Guat. 202/D3
Tajuña (riv.), Sp. 102/D2
Tak, Thai. 136/B2
Takahagi, Japan 133/G2
Takahama, Japan 135/J5
Takahama, Japan 135/L6
Takahashi (riv.), Japan 132/C3
Takahashi, Japan 132/C3
Takahata, Japan 133/G1
Takaishi, Japan 135/H6
Takalar, Indo. 138/D5
Takamatsu, Japan 132/D3
Takami-yama (peak), Japan 135/K7
Takanabe, Japan 132/B4
Takane, Japan 135/L2
Takanosu, Japan 134/B3
Takanosu-yama (peak), Japan 135/C2
Takaoka, Japan 133/E2
Takapuna, NZ 175/S10
Takarazuka, Japan 135/H6
Takaroa (isl.), FrPol. 175/L6
Takasaki, Japan 133/F2
Takashima, Japan 135/L5
Takatomi, Japan 135/L5
Takatori, Japan 135/J7
Takatsuki, Japan 135/J6
Takayama, Japan 133/E2
Takefu, Japan 135/L6
Takehara, Japan 132/C3
Takengon, Indo. 138/A3
Takeo, Japan 132/A4
Takestān, Iran 146/E1
Taketa, Japan 132/B4
Taketoyo, Japan 135/L6
Takhatgarh, India 140/B2
Takhatpur, India 142/C4
Takht-e Jamshīd (ruin), Iran 146/F3
Takht-i-Bhāi, Pak. 144/A2
Takijuq (lake), Nun., Can. 180/E2
Takikawa, Japan 134/B3
Takino, Japan 135/G6
Takla (lake), BC, Can. 184/B2
Takla Makan (des.), China 128/D4
Tako, Japan 135/E2
Takoradi, Gha. 161/E5
Takouch (cape), Alg. 158/K6
Takta, Mex. 200/E4
Talā, Egypt 149/B4

Tala, Uru. 217/L11
Talagang, Pak. 144/B3
Talagante, Chile 216/N8
Talāja, India 147/K4
Talak (phys. reg.), Niger 154/G4
Talamanca (mts.), CR 203/F4
Talamba, Pak. 144/B4
Talamona, It. 115/F5
Talang (peak), Indo. 138/B4
Talanga, Hon. 202/E3
Talange, Fr. 111/F5
Talant, Fr. 114/A3
Talara, Peru 214/A2
Talas (obl.), Kyr. 145/K4
Talas, Turk. 148/C2
Talas, Kyr. 145/K4
Talas (riv.), Kaz. 145/K4
Talaud (isl.), Phil. 139/G3
Talavera de la Reina, Sp. 102/C3
Talawakele, SrL. 140/D6
Talayuela, Sp. 102/C3
Talbingo, Austl. 173/D2
Talbot (mt.), Austl. 170/C3
Talbot (co.), Md, US 196/B6
Talca, Chile 216/C2
Talcahuano, Chile 216/B3
Tālcher, India 140/E3
Taldom, Rus. 118/J4
Taldyqorghan (obl.), Kaz. 145/G3
Taldyqorghan, Kaz. 145/G3
Talence, Fr. 100/C4
Talent (riv.), Swi. 114/C4
Talfer (Talvera) (riv.), It. 115/H4
Talgar, Kaz. 145/G4
Taliabu (isl.), Indo. 139/F4
Taliouine, Mor. 156/D3
Talkeetna, Ak, US 192/H3
Talkhā, Egypt 149/B4
Tall 'Afar, Iraq 148/E2
Tall al Muqayyar (ruin), Iraq 146/F2
Tall 'Asūr (peak), Isr. 149/G8
Tall Kayf, Iraq 148/E2
Talladega, Al, US 191/G3
Tallahassee (cap.), Fl, US 191/G4
Tallahatchie (riv.), Ms, US 187/K4
Tallangatta, Austl. 173/C3
Tallanstown, Ire. 92/B4
Tallering (peak), Austl. 170/B4
Talleyville, De, US 196/C4
Tallinn (cap.), Est. 97/L2
Tallman Mountain State Park, NY, US 197/K7
Talloires, Fr. 114/C6
Tallow, Ire. 89/Q10
Tallulah, La, US 187/K4
Tallulah (falls), Ga, US 191/H3
Talmassons, It. 117/G1
Talo (peak), Eth. 155/N5
Talon, Ben. 161/F5
Talodi, Sudan 155/N5
Taloga (vol.), Ak, US 192/C6
Taloga (isl.), Ak, US 192/C6
Talogan, Afg. 147/J2
Talsi, Lat. 97/K4
Talsperre Pöhl (res.), Ger. 113/F1
Taltal, Chile 215/B2
Taltson (riv.), NW, Can. 180/E2
Talumphuk (pt.), Thai. 136/C4
Talvera (Talfer) (riv.), It. 115/H4
Talwāra, India 144/C4
Tam Ky, Viet. 136/E3
Tama, Japan 135/C2
Tama (riv.), Japan 135/C2
Tamagawa, Japan 135/C2
Tamaho, Japan 135/B2
Tamaki, Japan 135/L7
Tamalameque, Col. 210/C2
Tamale, Gha. 161/E4
Tamamura, Japan 135/C1
Tamanar, Mor. 156/C3
Tamanghasset (prov.), Alg. 161/F1
Tamanghasset, Oued (riv.), Alg. 157/G5
Tamanrasset, Alg. 157/G5
Tamanrasset (prov.), Alg. 157/G5
Tamanthi, Myan. 141/G2
Tamar (riv.), Eng, UK 90/B5
Tamar (isl.), Japan 133/H8
Tamara (riv.), It. 115/G5
Tamarin, Mrts. 165/T15
Tamarindo NWR, CR 202/E4
Tamarite de Litera, Sp. 103/F2
Tamaro (peak), Swi. 115/E4
Tamási, Hun. 106/D2
Tamatsukuri, Japan 135/E1
Tamaulipas (state), Mex. 198/B3
Tamazula de Gordiano, Mex. 200/E5
Tamazunchale, Mex. 202/B1
Tamba, Japan 135/H5
Tamba (uplands), Japan 135/H5
Tambacounda (pol. reg.), Sen. 160/B3
Tambacounda, Sen. 160/B3

Tambaoura, Falaise de (cliff), Mali 160/C3
Tambelan (isls.), Indo. 138/C3
Tambellup, Austl. 170/C5
Tambo (riv.), Peru 214/C3
Tambo (peak), Swi. 115/F5
Tambo, Austl. 172/B4
Tambo Colorado (ruin), Peru 214/C4
Tambo de Mora, Peru 214/B4
Tambo Grande, Peru 214/A2
Tambobamba, Peru 214/C4
Tambohorano, Madg. 165/G7
Tambopata (riv.), Peru 214/D4
Tambora (peak), Indo. 139/E5
Tamboril, Braz. 212/B2
Tamboritha (mt.), Austl. 173/C3
Tambov, Rus. 121/G1
Tambovskaya Oblast, Rus. 121/G1
Tambre (riv.), Sp. 102/A1
Tame (riv.), Eng, UK 91/E1
Tame, Col. 210/D3
Támega (riv.), Port. 102/B2
Tamentit, Alg. 157/E4
Tameside (co.), Eng, UK 93/F5
Tamgak (peak), Niger 161/H2
Tamgue (mass.), Gui. 160/B3
Tamiahua, Mex. 202/B1
Tamiahua (lag.), Mex. 202/B1
Tamil Nādu (state), India 140/C5
Taminango, Col. 210/B4
Tāmiyah, Egypt 149/B5
Tamluk, India 143/F4
Tammany (mt.), NJ, US 196/C2
Tammela, Fin. 97/K1
Tammūn, WBnk. 149/D3
Tampa, Fl, US 191/H5
Tampa (int'l arpt.), Fl, US 191/H5
Tampere, Fin. 97/K1
Tampere-Pirkkala (int'l arpt.), Fin. 97/K1
Tampico, Mex. 202/B1
Tampoc (riv.), FrG. 211/H4
Tampon Ambohitra (peak), Madg. 165/J6
Tampulonanjing (peak), Indo. 138/C5
Tamra, Isr. 149/G6
Tamshiyacu, Peru 214/C2
Tamuin (riv.), Mex. 202/B1
Tamuín, Mex. 202/B1
Tamur (riv.), Nepal 143/F2
Tamworth, Austl. 173/D1
Tamworth, Eng, UK 91/E1
Tamyang, SKor. 131/D5
Tan (riv.), China 141/K3
Tan An, Viet. 136/D4
Tan-Tan, Mor. 156/C3
Tana (lake), Eth. 155/N5
Tana (riv.), Kenya 162/D3
Tana River Primate Nat'l Rsv., Kenya 162/D3
Tanabe, Japan 132/D4
Tanabe, Japan 135/J6
Tanabi, Braz. 213/B2
Tanacross, Ak, US 192/K3
Tanafjorden (estu.), Nor. 95/J1
Tanaga (vol.), Ak, US 192/C6
Tanaga (isl.), Ak, US 192/C6
Tanagura, Japan 133/G2
Tanah Merah, Malay. 141/M6
Tanahbala (isl.), Indo. 138/A4
Tanakpur, India 142/C1
Tanambe, Madg. 165/J7
Tanami (des.), Austl. 167/C2
Tanana, Ak, US 192/H2
Tanana (riv.), Ak, US 192/J3
Tanandava, Madg. 165/G8
Tancheng, China 130/D4
Tanch'ŏn, NKor. 131/E2
Tancítaro, Pico de (peak), Mex. 200/E5
Tancítaro, PN de, Mex. 198/A4
Tanda (lake), Mali 160/D3
Tandā, India 142/D2
Tānda, India 142/B1
Tăndărei, Rom. 107/H3
Tandil, Arg. 216/F3
Tāndliānwāla, Pak. 144/B4
Tando Ādam, Pak. 147/J4
Tando Allāhyār, Pak. 147/J3
Tando Muhammad Khān, Pak. 147/J3
Tandou (lake), Austl. 173/B2
Tandragee, NI, UK 92/B3
Tanem Taunggyi (range), Thai. 136/C2
Tanezrouft (des.), Alg. 157/E5
Tanezrouft-n-Ahenet (des), Alg. 157/F5
Tang (riv.), China 130/C4
Tanga (riv.), Rus. 145/F1
Tanga (pol. reg.), Tanz. 162/C4
Tanga, Tanz. 162/C4
Tangail, Bang. 143/G3
Tangail (pol. reg.), Bang. 143/G3
Tanganyika (lake), D.R. Congo,Tanz. 162/A4
Tangará da Serra, Braz. 208/G6

Tangent (pt.), Ak, US 192/G1
Taraklı, Turk. 107/K5
Tanger, Mor. 158/B2
Tanger (prov.), Mor. 158/A2
Tangerhütte, Ger. 98/F2
Tangermünde, Ger. 98/F2
Tanggula (mts.), China 128/E5
Tanghe, China 130/C4
Tangi, Pak. 144/A2
Tangipahoa (riv.), La, US 195/P16
Tangipahoa (parish), La, US 195/P16
Tangjin, SKor. 131/D4
Tanglewilde-Thompson Place, Wa, US 193/B3
Tangshan, China 130/J7
Tangub, Phil. 137/D6
Tangyuan, China 129/N2
Tanhaçu, Braz. 212/B4
Tanigumi, Japan 135/L4
Tanimbar (isl.), Indo. 139/H5
Taninges, Fr. 114/C5
Tanintharyi (div.), Myan. 141/B5
Tanjay, Phil. 137/D6
Tanjungbalai, Indo. 138/A3
Tanjungkarang-Telukbetung, Indo. 138/C5
Tanjungpandan, Indo. 138/C4
Tanjungpinang, Indo. 138/B3
Tanjungpura, Indo. 138/A3
Tanjungredeb, Indo. 138/A3
Tānk, Pak. 144/A3
Tankwa Karoo NP, SAfr. 164/B4
Tann, Ger. 113/F6
Tanna (isl.), Van. 174/F6
Tannan, Japan 135/H5
Tannersville, Pa, US 196/C1
Tannheim, Aus. 115/G3
Tannu-Ola (mts.), Mong.,Rus. 128/F1
Tano (riv.), Gha. 161/E5
Tānout, Niger 161/H3
Tanquian de Escobedo, Mex. 202/B1
Tansen, Nepal 142/D2
Tanță, Egypt 149/B4
Tantallon, Md, US 196/A6
Tantō, Japan 135/G5
Tantoyuca, Mex. 202/B1
Tanuku, India 140/D4
Tanumshede, Swe. 96/C2
Tanunda, Austl. 173/A2
Tanyang, SKor. 131/E4
Tanzania (ctry.) 162/B4
Tanzawa-yama (peak), Japan 135/C2
Tao (isl.), Myan. 136/B4
Tao (riv.), China 128/H3
Taolañaro, Madg. 165/H9
Taormina, It. 105/E6
Tāoru, India 144/D5
Taos, NM, US 187/F3
Taounate (town), Mor. 158/B2
Taounate, Mor. 158/B2
Taourirt, Alg. 157/H4
Taourirt, Mor. 158/C2
T'aoyüan, Tai. 137/D2
Taoyuan, China 141/K2
Tap Mun Chau (isl.), China 129/V10
Tap O'Noth (hill), Sc, UK 94/D2
Tapa, Est. 97/L2
Tapachula, Mex. 202/C3
Tapajós (riv.), Braz. 205/D3
Tapanahoni (riv.), Sur. 209/G3
Tapanti Nat'l Wild. Ref., CR 203/F4
Tapauá (riv.), Braz. 214/E3
Tapauá, Braz. 208/F5
Tapaz, Phil. 137/D5
Tapejara, Braz. 213/A4
Tapes, Braz. 213/B4
Tapeta, Libr. 160/C5
Tapia de Casariego, Sp. 102/B1
Tapiche (riv.), Peru 214/C2
Tapilula, Mex. 202/C2
Tapis (peak), Malay. 138/B3
Tapo, Peru 214/C3
Tapoa (prov.), Burk. 161/F3
Tapolca, Hun. 106/C2
Tappahannock, Va, US 188/E4
Tappan, NY, US 197/K7
Tappan Zee (lake), NY, US 197/E1
Tappan Dee (riv.), NY, US 197/K7
Tappi-zaki (pt.), Japan 134/B3
Tapps (lake), Wa, US 193/C3
Taputo NP, Thai. 136/B5
Taquara, Braz. 213/B4
Taquari, Braz. 213/B4
Taquari (riv.), Braz. 213/B4
Taquaritinga, Braz. 213/B2
Taquarituba, Braz. 213/B2
Taquil, Ecu. 214/B2
Tar (riv.), Kyr. 145/F1
Tara, Rus. 145/F1
Tara (riv.), Bosn.,Mont. 106/D4
Tara, Austl. 172/C4
Taraba (state), Nga. 161/H5
Taraba (riv.), Nga. 161/H4
Tarābulus, Leb. 149/D2
Tarābulus (Tripoli) (cap.), Libya 154/H1

Tarakan, Indo. 139/E3
Taralga, Austl. 173/D2
Taraku (isl.), Rus. 134/C2
Taralga, Austl. 173/D2
Taranaki (reg.) 144/C5
Taranagar, India 144/C5
Taranto, It. 105/E2
Taranto, Golfo di (gulf), It. 104/E2
Tarapoto, Peru 214/B2
Tarare, Fr. 100/F4
Tarariras, Uru. 217/K11
Tarascon, Fr. 100/F5
Tarascon-sur-Ariège, Fr. 100/D5
Tarata, Peru 214/D5
Tarauacá, Braz. 214/D3
Tarauacá (riv.), Braz. 214/D3
Tarawa (cap.), Kiri. 174/G4
Tarawa (isl.), Kiri. 174/G4
Tarazona, Sp. 102/E2
Tarazona, Sp. 102/E2
Tarbagatay (mts.), Kaz. 128/D2
Tarbat Ness (pt.), Sc, UK 94/C1
Tarbela (dam), Pak. 144/B2
Tarbela (res.), Pak. 144/B2
Tarbolton, Sc, UK 94/B5
Tarboro, NC, US 191/J3
Tarcento, It. 101/K3
Tarcutta, Austl. 173/C2
Tardes (riv.), Fr. 100/E3
Tardienta, Sp. 103/E2
Tardoire (riv.), Fr. 100/D4
Taree, Austl. 173/E1
Tarf Water (riv.), Sc, UK 92/D2
Tarfâwi (well), Egypt 159/B4
Tarfaya, Mor. 156/B4
Target Rock NWR, NY, US 197/M8
Targuist, Mor. 158/B2
Tarhūnah, Libya 154/H1
Tarifa, Ecu. 214/B1
Tarifa, Sp. 102/C4
Tarija, Bol. 208/F8
Tariku (riv.), Indo. 139/J4
Tarim (basin), China 128/D3
Tarim (riv.), China 128/D3
Tarin (riv.), Afg. 147/J2
Tarin (Torino), It. 101/G4
Taritatu (riv.), Indo. 139/J4
Tarkastad, SAfr. 164/D4
Tarkhankut (cape), Ukr. 107/L3
Tarkwa, Gha. 161/E5
Tarlac, Phil. 137/D4
Tarma, Peru 214/C3
Tarmstedt, Ger. 109/G2
Tarn (riv.), Fr. 100/D5
Tarn Tāran, India 144/C2
Tarnak (riv.), Afg. 147/J2
Tarnobrzeg, Pol. 99/L3
Tarnów, Pol. 99/L3
Tärnsjö, Swe. 96/G1
Taro (riv.), It. 101/J4
Tārom, Iran 147/G3
Taroom, Austl. 172/C4
Tarouca, Port. 102/B2
Taroudannt, Mor. 156/C3
Tarp, Ger. 96/C4
Tarpa, Hun. 106/F1
Tarpon Springs, Fl, US 191/H4
Tarquinia, It. 104/C1
Tarquiniyah, WBnk. 149/D4
Tarrafal, CpV. 151/K10
Tarragona, Sp. 103/F2
Tarraleah, Austl. 173/C4
Tarrega, Sp. 103/F2
Tarrenz, Aus. 115/G3
Tarrytown, NY, US 197/K7
Tarsney Lakes, Mo, US 195/E6
Tarsus, Turk. 149/D1
Tarsus (riv.), Turk. 149/D1
Tartaro (riv.), It. 117/E2
Tartas, Fr. 100/C5
Tartu (prov.), Syria 149/D4
Tartūs (prov.), Syria 149/D2
Tartūs, Syria 149/D2
Tarui, Japan 135/L5
Tarumizu, Japan 132/B5
Tarumovka, Rus. 121/H4
Tarutao NP, Thai. 136/B5
Tarvagatay (mts.), Mong. 128/G2
Tāq Kisrá (Ctesiphon) (ruin), Iraq 146/F2
Tāsch, Swi. 114/D5
Taşçı, Turk. 148/C2
Taschereau, Qu, Can. 182/E2
Tashkent (cap.), Uzb. 145/E4
Tashkent (int'l arpt.), Uzb. 145/E4
Tasikmalaya, Indo. 138/C5
Taşkent, Turk. 149/C1
Tasman (pen.), Austl. 173/C4
Tasman (sea) 174/E8
Tasman (bay), NZ 175/T10
Tasmania, Austl. 173/C4

Tasmania (state), Austl. 173/C4
Tasov, Turk. 148/D1
Taşanad, Rom. 106/F2
Taşova, Turk. 148/D1
Tasquillo, Mex. 201/K6
Tassili Oua-n Ahaggar (mts.), Alg. 157/G5
Tasu, BC, Can. 192/M5
Tașucu, Turk. 149/C1
Tata, Mor. 156/D3
Tata, Hun. 106/D2
Tatabánya, Hun. 106/D2
Tatachikapika (riv.), On, Can. 188/D2
Tatakoto (isl.), FrPol. 175/L6
Tatamy, Pa, US 196/C2
Tataouine, Tun. 157/H2
Tataouine (gov.), Tun. 157/H2
Tatar (str.), Rus. 125/P5
Tatarlar, Turk. 105/K2
Tatarsk, Rus. 145/G1
Tatarstan, Resp., Rus. 122/Q6
Tate-yama (peak), Japan 133/E2
Tatebayashi, Japan 135/C1
Tateshina, Japan 135/A1
Tateyama, Japan 133/F3
Tathlina (lake), NW, Can. 180/E2
Tathra, Austl. 173/D3
Tatitlek, Ak, US 192/J3
Tatnam (cape), Mb, Can. 180/G3
Tatry (mts.), Slvk. 99/K4
Tatsuno, Japan 133/E3
Tatsuta, Japan 135/L5
Tatura, Austl. 173/C3
Tatvan, Turk. 148/E2
Tauá, Braz. 212/B2
Tauberbischofsheim, Ger. 112/C3
Tauca, Peru 214/B3
Taufkirchen, Ger. 113/F6
Taufkirchen an der Pram, Aus. 113/G5
Taufstein (peak), Ger. 112/C1
Taulihawa, Nepal 142/D2
Taumarunui, NZ 175/T9
Taumaturgo, Braz. 214/D3
Taung, SAfr. 164/D2
Taunggyi, Myan. 141/G3
Taungup, Myan. 141/F4
Taunton, Ma, US 189/G3
Taunton, Eng, UK 90/C4
Taunus (range), Ger. 112/A2
Taunusstein, Ger. 112/B2
Taupo, NZ 175/T10
Taupo (lake), NZ 175/T10
Tauragė, Lith. 97/K4
Tauranga, NZ 175/T10
Taurianova, It. 105/E3
Taurirano, It. 105/F3
Taurus (mts.), Turk. 148/C2
Tauste, Sp. 102/E2
Tavda (riv.), Rus. 122/G4
Tavdelnyj, Fr. 116/C2
Tavernerio, It. 116/C1
Taverny, Fr. 88/J4
Taviano, It. 105/F3
Tavira, Port. 102/B4
Tavistock, Eng, UK 90/B5
Tavoy (Dawei), Myan. 136/B3
Tavoy (riv.), Myan. 136/B3
Tavşanlı, Turk. 148/B2
Taw (riv.), Eng, UK 90/B5
Tawaramoto, Japan 135/J7
Tawas City, Mi, US 188/D3
Tawau, Malay. 139/E3
Tawe (riv.), Wal, UK 90/C3
Tawern, Ger. 111/F4
Tawi (riv.), India 144/C2
Tawi-Tawi (isl.), Phil. 137/C6
Tāwūq, Iraq 148/F3
Taxco, Mex. 201/K8
Taxila (ruin), Pak. 144/B2
Taxila, Pak. 144/B2
Taxkorgan Tajik Zizhixian, China 147/K1
Tay (riv.), Sc, UK 94/C3
Tay (riv.), Sc, UK 94/C3
Tay (firth of inlet), Sc, UK 94/C4
Tay Ninh, Viet. 136/D4
Tayabamba, Peru 214/B3
Taylor, Mi, US 193/F7
Taylorsville-Bennion, Ut, US 195/K12
Taymyr (isl.), Rus. 123/K2
Taymyr (pen.), Rus. 123/K2
Taymyrskiy Aut. Okrug, Rus. 122/J2

Tayrona, PN, Col. 210/C2
Tayshet, Rus. 123/K4
Taytay, Phil. 139/E1
Taz (riv.), Rus. 125/H3
Taza (prov.), Mor. 158/C2
Taza, Mor. 158/B2
Tazawako, Japan 134/B4
Tazenakht, Mor. 156/D3
Tazewell, Tn, US 188/D4
Tāzirbū (oasis), Libya 154/K3
Tazumal (ruin), ESal. 202/D3
T'bilisi (cap.), Geo. 121/H4
T'boli, Phil. 137/D6
Tchamba, Togo 161/F4
Tchaourou, Ben. 161/F4
Tchefuncta (riv.), La, US 195/P16
Tchibanga, Gabon 154/H8
Tcholliré, Camr. 154/H6
Tczew, Pol. 97/H4
Te Anau, NZ 175/R12
Te Araroa, NZ 175/T10
Te Aroha, NZ 175/T10
Te Awamutu, NZ 175/T10
Te Kao, NZ 175/S9
Te Kuiti, NZ 175/T10
Tea (riv.), Braz. 208/E4
Teacapán, Mex. 200/D4
Teague, Tx, US 187/H5
Teaneck, NJ, US 197/J8
Teano, It. 104/D2
Teapa, Mex. 202/C2
Tearce, FYROM 105/G1
Tebak (peak), Indo. 138/B4
Tébessa (prov.), Alg. 157/G2
Tébessa, Alg. 158/L7
Tébessa (mts.), Alg. 158/L7
Tebesselamane (well), Mali 161/F2
Tebicuary (riv.), Par. 215/E2
Tebingtinggi, Indo. 138/A3
Tebourba, Tun. 104/A4
Tebulos-mta (peak), Rus. 121/H4
Tebuaté, Braz. 213/H8
Tecalitlán, Mex. 200/D5
Tecamac, Mex. 201/R9
Tecamachalco, Mex. 201/M8
Tecate, Mex. 200/A1
Tech (riv.), Fr. 100/E5
Techirghiol, Rom. 107/J3
Tecirli, It. 148/D2
Tecka, Arg. 216/C4
Tecka (riv.), Arg. 216/C4
Tecklenberg, Ger. 109/E4
Tecolutla, Mex. 201/M6
Tecomán, Mex. 200/E5
Tecozautla, Mex. 201/K6
Tecpan de Galeana, Mex. 201/E5
Tecpan (reg.), Guat. 202/D3
Tecuala, Mex. 200/D4
Tecuci, Rom. 107/H3
Tecumseh, Mi, US 188/D3
Tecumseh, Ne, US 187/H2
Tecumseh, On, Can. 193/G2
Tedjent (well), Alg. 157/H1
Tedzhen (riv.), Trkm. 122/G6
Tees (bay), Eng, UK 93/G2
Tees (riv.), Eng, UK 93/G3
Teesside (int'l arpt.), Eng, UK 93/G3
Tefé, Braz. 208/E4
Tefé (riv.), Braz. 208/F4
Teferič, Serb. 106/E4
Tega (lake), Japan 135/E2
Tegal, Indo. 138/C5
Tegel (int'l arpt.), Ger. 98/Q6
Tegelen, Neth. 108/D6
Tegeler (lake), Ger. 98/Q6
Teghri (well), Libya 157/H4
Teghra, India 143/E3
Tegid, Llyn (lake), Wal, UK 92/E4
Teglio, It. 115/G5
Tégouma (riv.), Niger 161/H3
Tegsh, Mong. 128/G2
Tegucigalpa (cap.), Hon. 202/E3
Tehek (lake), Nun., Can. 180/G2
Tehrān (cap.), Iran 146/F1
Tehuacán, Mex. 201/M8
Tehuantepec (riv.), Mex. 201/G5
Tehuantepec, Mex. 202/C2
Tehuantepec (gulf), Mex. 202/C3
Teide, Pico de (peak), Sp. 156/A3
Teifi (riv.), Wal, UK 90/B2
Teifiside (valley), Wal, UK 90/B2
Teiga (plat.), Sudan 155/L4
Teign (riv.), Eng, UK 90/C5
Teignmouth, Eng, UK 90/C5
Teisendorf, Ger. 113/F7
Teith (riv.), Sc, UK 94/B4
Tejen, Trkm. 147/H1
Tejen (riv.), Trkm. 147/H1
Tejo, Den. 96/F4
Tejupilco de Hidalgo, Mex. 201/E5
Tekamah, Ne, US 185/G4
Tekăiri, India 143/E3
Tekax de Alvaro Obregón, Mex. 202/D1
Teke, Turk. 107/J5
Teke (riv.), Kaz. 145/G4
Tekeli, Kaz. 145/G4

Tekes (riv.), China 122/J5
Tekezē Wenz (riv.), Eth. 155/N5
Tekiliktag (peak), China 128/D4
Tekirdağ, Turk. 107/H5
Tekirdağ (prov.), Turk. 107/H5
Tekit, Mex. 202/D1
Tekkali, India 140/D4
Tekke, Turk. 148/D1
Tekkeköy, Turk. 148/D1
Tekman, Turk. 148/E2
Tel Aviv (dist.), Isr. 149/G3
Tel Aviv-Yafo, Isr. 149/F7
Tel Megiddo (ruin), Isr. 149/G6
Tela, Hon. 202/E3
Télagh, Alg. 158/D2
T'elavi, Geo. 121/H4
Telde, Sp. 156/B3
Télé (lake), Mali 160/D2
Telêmaco Borba, Braz. 213/B3
Telemark (co.), Nor. 95/D4
Telen (riv.), Indo. 139/E3
Teleorman (prov.), Rom. 107/G4
Telertheba (peak), Alg. 157/G4
Teles Pires (riv.), Braz. 205/D3
Telford, Pa, US 196/C3
Telford Dawley, Eng, UK 90/D1
Telfs, Aus. 115/H3
Telgate, It. 116/C1
Telgte, Ger. 109/E5
Telica, Nic. 202/E3
Télig (well), Mali 156/E5
Telkwa, BC, Can. 184/B2
Tell City, In, US 188/C4
Teller, Ak, US 192/E2
Telli (lake), Mrta. 156/C4
Tellicherry, India 140/C5
Tellin, Belg. 111/E3
Telluride, Co, US 186/F3
Telok Anson, Malay. 138/B3
Teloloapan, Mex. 201/F5
Telšiai, Lith. 97/K4
Teltow, Ger. 98/Q7
Teltow (reg.), Ger. 99/G2
Tema, Gha. 161/E5
Temagami (lake), On, Can. 188/D2
Temax, Mex. 202/D1
Tembilahan, Indo. 138/B4
Tembisa, SAfr. 164/E2
Temblador, Ven. 211/F2
Teme (riv.), Eng, UK 90/C2
Temecula, Ca, US 194/C4
Temelkovo, Bul. 106/F4
Temerin, Serb. 106/D3
Temerloh, Malay. 138/B3
Temirtaū, Kaz. 145/F2
Témiscamie (riv.), Qu, Can. 189/F1
Témiscaming, Qu, Can. 188/E2
Temoaya, Mex. 201/Q10
Temoe (isl.), FrPol. 175/M7
Temora, Austl. 173/C2
Tempe, Az, US 195/S19
Tempio Pausania, It. 104/A2
Temple, Pa, US 196/C3
Temple City, Ca, US 194/F7
Temple of Lady Chua Xu, Viet. 136/D4
Templemore, Ire. 89/Q10
Templepatrick, NI, UK 92/B2
Templeuve, Fr. 110/C2
Templeville, Md, US 196/C5
Templin, Ger. 99/G2
Templiner (lake), Ger. 98/Q7
Tempoal de Sánchez, Mex. 202/B1
Temryuk, Rus. 120/F3
Temse, Belg. 111/D1
Temuco, Chile 216/B3
Temuka, NZ 175/S11
Ten Boer, Neth. 108/D2
Tena, Ecu. 210/B5
Tena Kourou (peak), Mali 154/D5
Tenabo, Mex. 202/D1
Tenafly, NJ, US 197/K8
Tenakee Springs, Ak, US 192/L4
Tenancingo, Mex. 201/R10
Tenango, Mex. 201/R10
Tenango de Arista, Mex. 201/Q10
Tenasserim (range), Myan. 136/B3
Tenasserim, Myan. 136/B3
Tenay, Fr. 114/B6
Tenby, Wal, UK 90/B3
Tende, Fr. 101/G4
Tende, Col de (pass), Fr. 101/G4
Tenderovsk (bay), Ukr. 107/K2
Tenderovsk Spit (isl.), Ukr. 107/K2
Tendō, Japan 134/B4
Tendre (peak), Swi. 114/C4
Ténenkou, Mali 160/D3
Ténéré (des.), Niger 154/G4
Ténéré du Tafassasset (des.), Niger 154/G3
Tenerife, Col. 210/C2
Tenerife (isl.), Sp. 156/A3

Ténès, Alg. 158/F4
Tenes (riv.), Sp. 103/L6
Teng (riv.), Myan. 141/G3
Teng Xian, China 130/D4
Tenggarong, Indo. 139/E4
Tengger (des.), China 128/H4
Tengiz Köli (lake), Kaz. 122/G4
Tenguel, Ecu. 210/B5
Tenibres (peak), It. 101/G4
Teniente Enciso, PN, Par. 215/D1
Tenja, Cro. 106/D3
Tenkodogo, Burk. 161/E4
Tenmile (riv.), Az, US 186/D4
Tennessee (state), US 191/G3
Tennessee (riv.), US 191/F3
Tenneville, Belg. 111/E3
Tennuaca (well), Mor. 156/B5
Teno, Chile 216/C2
Tenojoki (riv.), Fin. 95/H1
Tenosique de Pino Suárez, Mex. 202/D2
Tenri, Japan 135/J6
Tenryū, Japan 133/E3
Tenryū (riv.), Japan 133/E3
Tensift (pol. reg.), Mor. 156/C3
Tensift, Oued (riv.), Mor. 156/C3
Tenterfield, Austl. 173/E1
Tentolomatinan (peak), Indo. 139/F3
Tenus (peak), Kenya 162/B2
Teo, Sp. 102/A1
Teocaltiche, Mex. 198/A3
Teocelo, Mex. 201/N7
Teodelina, Arg. 216/E2
Teodoro Sampaio, Braz. 213/A2
Teófilo Otoni, Braz. 212/B5
Teopisca, Mex. 202/C2
Teotihuacán (ruin), Mex. 201/R9
Teotihuacán, Mex. 201/R9
Teotitlán del Camino, Mex. 202/B2
Tepache, Mex. 200/C2
Tepalcatepec, Mex. 200/E5
Tepalcingo, Mex. 201/L8
Tepatitlán de Morelos, Mex. 198/A3
Tepatlaxco, Mex. 201/M7
Tepeapulco, Mex. 201/L7
Tepebaşı, Turk. 149/C1
Tepehuaje, Mex. 201/F4
Tepehuanes, Mex. 200/D3
Tepeji del Río de Ocampo, Mex. 201/K7
Tepelenë, Alb. 105/F2
Tepelská Plošina (mts.), Czh. 113/F2
Tepetlaoxtoc, Mex. 201/R9
Tepexi, Mex. 201/M8
Tepexpan, Mex. 201/R9
Tepic, Mex. 200/D4
Teplá (riv.), Czh. 98/G3
Teplá Vltava (riv.), Czh. 113/G5
Teplice, Czh. 99/G3
Tepoca (cape), Mex. 200/B2
Tepoca, Cabo (cape), Mex. 200/B2
Tepoto (isl.), FrPol. 175/L6
Tepotzotlán, Mex. 201/K7
Tepoztlán, Mex. 201/K8
Tequila, Mex. 200/E4
Tequisquiapan, Mex. 201/F4
Tequixquiac, Mex. 201/K7
Ter (riv.), Sp. 103/G1
Ter Aar, Neth. 108/B4
Téra, Niger 161/F3
Tera (riv.), Sp. 102/B1
Teraina (Washington) (isl.), Kiri. 175/J4
Teramo, It. 101/K5
Terang, Austl. 173/B3
Tercan, Turk. 148/E2
Terceira (isl.), Azor., Port. 203/S12
Terek (riv.), Rus. 121/H4
Terepaima, PN, Ven. 210/D2
Teresina, Braz. 212/B2
Teresópolis, Braz. 213/L7
Terespol, Pol. 99/M2
Tergnier, Fr. 110/C4
Tergun Daba (mts.), China 128/F4
Terheijden, Neth. 108/B5
Teriberskiy (pt.), Rus. 118/G1
Terkaplesterpoelen (lake), Neth. 108/C2
Terlan (Terlano), It. 115/H4
Termas de Río Hondo, Arg. 215/D2
Termini Imerese, It. 104/C4
Términos (lag.), Mex. 202/D2
Termiz, Uzb. 147/J1
Termo, Ca, US 184/C5
Termoli, It. 104/D1
Termonfeckin, Ire. 92/B4
Termunten, Neth. 108/E2
Ternate, Indo. 139/H3
Ternberg, Aus. 113/H7
Terneuzen, Neth. 108/A6
Terni, It. 104/C1
Ternin (riv.), Fr. 100/F3
Ternoise (riv.), Fr. 110/C2
Ternopil', Ukr. 120/C2
Ternopil's'ka Oblasti, Ukr. 120/C2

Terpeniya (bay), Rus. 123/Q5
Terpni, Gre. 105/H2
Terra Nova, Braz. 212/B4
Terra Nova, Braz. 212/C3
Terra Nova NP, Nf, Can. 189/L1
Terrace, BC, Can. 184/A2
Terrace Bay, On, Can. 185/M3
Terracina, It. 104/C2
Terråk, Nor. 95/E2
Terralba, It. 104/A3
Terranuova Bracciolini, It. 117/E5
Terrassa, Sp. 103/L6
Terrasson-la-Villedieu, Fr. 100/D4
Terre Hill, Pa, US 196/B3
Terrebonne, Qu, Can. 189/N6
Terrell Hills, Tx, US 195/U21
Terri (peak), Swi. 115/F4
Terry, Mt, US 185/G4
Terry (lake), Co, US 195/B2
Terrytown, La, US 195/P17
Terschelling (isl.), Neth. 108/C2
Tertenia, It. 104/A3
Teruel, Sp. 103/E2
Terutao (isl.), Thai. 141/G6
Tervel, Bul. 107/H4
Terza Grande (peak), It. 101/K3
Terzo d'Aquileia, It. 117/G2
Tešanj, Bosn. 106/C3
Tescou (riv.), Fr. 100/D5
Tesero, It. 115/H5
Teshekpuk (lake), Ak, US 192/G1
Teshikaga, Japan 134/D2
Teshio (riv.), Japan 134/C1
Teshio, Japan 134/B1
Teshio-dake (peak), Japan 134/C2
Teslić, Bosn. 106/C3
Teslin (riv.), Yk, Can. 180/C2
Teslin (lake), BC, Can. 192/M3
Tessaoua, Niger 161/G3
Tessenderlo, Belg. 111/E1
Tessenie (Teseney), Erit. 146/C5
Test (riv.), Eng, UK 91/E4
Testa del Gargano (pt.), It. 104/E2
Tét, Hun. 106/C2
Tete, Moz. 163/F4
Tête de l'Estrop (peak), Fr. 101/G4
Teterow, Ger. 96/E5
Teteven, Bul. 107/G4
Tetiaroa (isl.), FrPol. 175/L6
Tetlin, Ak, US 192/K3
Teton (riv.), Mt, US 184/F4
Tétouan (prov.), Mor. 158/B2
Tétouan, Mor. 158/B2
Tetovo, FYROM 105/G1
Tettnang, Ger. 115/F2
Tetulia (riv.), Bang. 143/H4
Teuco (riv.), Arg. 215/D1
Teufen, Swi. 115/F3
Teúl de González Ortega, Mex. 200/E4
Teulada (cape), It. 104/A3
Teulon, Mb, Can. 185/J3
Teupasenti, Hon. 202/E3
Teuri (isl.), Japan 134/B1
Teuschnitz, Ger. 112/D3
Teutoburger Wald (for.), Ger. 109/F4
Tevere (Tiber) (riv.), It. 101/K5
Teverya, Isr. 149/D3
Teviot (riv.), Sc, UK 94/D6
Teviotdale (valley), Sc, UK 94/D6
Tewantin-Noosa, Austl. 173/D4
Tewkesbury, Eng, UK 91/E1
Texarkana, Tx, US 187/J4
Texas, Austl. 173/D1
Texas (state), US 190/C4
Texas City, Tx, US 187/J5
Texcoco, Mex. 201/R9
Texel (isl.), Neth. 98/C2
Texhoma, Ok, US 190/C2
Texmelucan, Mex. 201/L7
Texoma (lake), Ok,Tx, US 187/H4
Teyateyaneng, Les. 164/D3
Teykovo, Rus. 118/J4
Tezio (peak), It. 101/K5
Teziutlán, Mex. 201/M7
Tezonapa, Mex. 201/N8
Tezontepec de Aldama, Mex. 201/L7
Tezoyuca, Mex. 201/R9
Tezpur, India 141/G2
Tezze, It. 117/E1
Tha-Anne (riv.), Nun., Can. 180/G2
Tha Chin (riv.), Thai. 136/B3
Thabana-Ntlenyana (peak), Les. 164/E3
Thabankulu (peak), SAfr. 165/F2
Thaen (pt.), Thai. 136/B4
Thai Binh, Viet. 141/J3
Thai Nguyen, Viet. 141/J3
Thailand (gulf), Asia 136/C4

Thailand (ctry.) 136/C3
Thákurdwāra, India 142/B1
Thal, Pak. 144/A3
Thal (des.), Pak. 144/A4
Thaleban NP, Thai. 136/C5
Thaleischweiler-Fröschen, Ger. 111/G5
Thalerhof (int'l arpt.), Aus. 101/L3
Thalgau, Aus. 113/G7
Thalheim bei Wels, Aus. 113/H6
Thalmässing, Ger. 112/E4
Thalwil, Swi. 115/E3
Thamar, Jabal (peak), Yem. 146/E6
Thame (riv.), Eng, UK 91/F3
Thames (riv.), On, Can. 188/D3
Thames, NZ 175/T10
Thames (riv.), Eng., UK 91/G4
Thames Barrier, Eng, UK 88/D2
Thāna, India 147/K5
Thane Bhawan, India 144/D5
Thānesar, India 144/D5
Thangool, Austl. 172/C4
Thanh Hoa, Viet. 141/J4
Thanjavur, India 140/C5
Thann, Fr. 114/D2
Thannhausen, Ger. 115/G1
Thaon-les-Vosges, Fr. 114/C2
Thar (des.), Pak. 144/A5
Tharād, India 147/K4
Thargomindah, Austl. 172/A5
Tharrawaddy, Myan. 141/G4
Thásos, India 105/J2
Thásos (isl.), Gre. 105/J2
Thatcham, Eng, UK 91/E4
Thatcher, Az, US 186/E4
Thaton, Myan. 136/B2
Thaur, Aus. 115/H3
Thaya (riv.), Aus. 99/H4
Thayetmyo, Myan. 141/G4
Thayngen, Swi. 115/E2
Thazi, Myan. 141/G3
The Alamo, Tx, US 195/U21
The Dalles, Or, US 184/C4
The Hague ('s-Gravenhage) (cap.), Neth. 108/B4
The Oaks, Ca, US 194/B1
The Pas, Mb, Can. 185/H2
The Rock, Austl. 173/C2
The Valley (cap.), Angu. 199/N8
The Village, Ok, US 195/M14
The Woodlands, Tx, US 187/J5
The Wrekin (co.), Eng, UK 93/F6
Thebes (ruin), Egypt 159/C3
Theilheim, Ger. 112/D3
Thelma, Tx, US 195/T21
Thelon (riv.), NW,Nun., Can. 180/F2
Thémericourt, Fr. 88/H4
Theo (mt.), Austl. 171/F2
Theodore, Sk, Can. 185/H3
Theodore, Austl. 172/C4
Theodore Roosevelt (lake), Az, US 186/E4
Theodore Roosevelt NP, ND, US 185/G4
Thérain (riv.), Fr. 100/D2
Thermaic (gulf), Gre. 105/H2
Thérmi, Gre. 105/H2
Thermopílai (Thermopylae) (pass), Gre. 105/H3
Thermopolis, Wy, US 184/F5
Thérouanne (riv.), Fr. 88/L4
Thessalon, On, Can. 188/D2
Thessaloníki, Gre. 105/H2
Thessaly (reg.), Gre. 105/H3
Thet (riv.), Eng, UK 91/G2
Thetford, Eng, UK 91/G2
Thetford Mines, Qu, Can. 189/G2
Theunissen, SAfr. 164/D3
Theux, Belg. 111/E2
Thève (riv.), Fr. 88/K4
Theydon Bois, Eng, UK 88/D2
Thiais, Fr. 88/K5
Thiamis (riv.), Gre. 105/G3
Thiant, Fr. 110/C3
Thiaucourt-Regniéville, Fr. 111/E5
Thief River Falls, Mn, US 185/J3
Thielle (riv.), Swi. 114/C4
Thielsen (mt.), Or, US 184/C5
Thiene, It. 117/E1
Thiérache (reg.), Fr. 111/D4
Thierhaupten, Ger. 112/D5
Thiers, Fr. 100/E4
Thiers-sur-Thève, Fr. 88/K4
Thierville-sur-Meuse, Fr. 111/E5
Thiès (pol. reg.), Sen. 160/A3
Thiès, Sen. 160/A3
Thika, Kenya 164/E3
Thingvellir NP, Ice. 95/N7
Thionville, Fr. 111/F5
Thíra, Gre. 105/J4
Thíra (isl.), Gre. 105/J4
Third Cataract (falls), Sudan 159/B5

Third Lake, Il, US 193/Q15
Thirlmere (lake), Eng, UK 93/E2
Thirsty (mt.), Austl. 170/D5
Thirtymile (pt.), NY, US 189/V9
Thise, Fr. 114/C3
Thistilfjördhur (estu.), Ice. 95/P6
Thistle (isl.), Austl. 171/H5
Thistle (mtn.), Yk, Can. 192/L3
Thitu (isl.) 137/B5
Thivai, Gre. 105/H3
Thiverval-Grignon, Fr. 88/H5
Thjósa (riv.), Ice. 95/N7
Thlewiaza (riv.), Nun., Can. 180/G2
Thoiry, Fr. 88/H5
Tholen (isl.), Neth. 108/B5
Tholen, Neth. 108/B5
Tholey, Ger. 111/G5
Thomaston, Ga, US 191/G3
Thomastown, Ire. 89/Q10
Thomasville, Al, US 191/G4
Thomasville, Ga, US 191/H4
Thomasville, NC, US 191/H3
Thomasville, Mo, US 196/B4
Thompson, Mb, Can. 185/J2
Thompson (riv.), BC, Can. 184/C3
Thompson (lake), Austl. 170/K7
Thompson Falls, Mt, US 184/E4
Thomsen (riv.), NW, Can. 180/E1
Thomson (riv.), Austl. 172/A4
Thomson, Ga, US 191/H3
Thonance-lès-Joinville, Fr. 114/B1
Thonon-les-Bains, Fr. 114/C6
Thoreau, NM, US 186/E3
Thorens-Glières, Fr. 114/D3
Thorhild, Ab, Can. 184/E2
Thorigny-sur-Marne, Fr. 88/L5
Thorlákshöfn, Ice. 95/N7
Thornaby-on-Tees, Eng, UK 93/G2
Thornbury, Eng, UK 90/D3
Thorndale, Pa, US 196/C4
Thorne, Eng, UK 93/H4
Thorne Bay, Ak, US 192/M4
Thornhill, Sc, UK 94/B4
Thornhill, Sc, UK 92/E1
Thornhurst, Pa, US 196/C1
Thornton, Co, US 195/C3
Thornton, Ca, US 193/M10
Thornton Cleveleys, Eng, UK 93/E4
Thorold, On, Can. 189/R9
Thórshöfn, Ice. 95/P6
Thouars, Fr. 100/C3
Thouet (riv.), Fr. 100/C3
Thourotte, Fr. 110/B5
Thousand Oaks, Ca, US 194/B2
Thowa (riv.), Kenya 162/C3
Thrace (reg.), Gre.,Turk. 105/J2
Thracian (sea), Gre. 105/J2
Thredbo Village, Austl. 173/D3
Three Bridges, NJ, US 196/D2
Three Forks, Mt, US 184/F4
Three Guardsmen (mtn.), BC, Can. 192/L4
Three Hills, Ab, Can. 184/E3
Three Hummock (isl.), Austl. 173/C4
Three Kings (isls.), NZ 175/S9
Three Mile (isl.), Pa, US 196/B3
Three Pagodas (pass), Myan. 136/B3
Three Points (cape), Gha. 161/E5
Three Rivers, Mi, US 188/C3
Three Rivers, Austl. 170/C3
Three Springs, Austl. 170/B4
Thriuvananthapuram, India 140/C6
Throssell (lake), Austl. 172/E3
Thrushel (riv.), Eng, UK 90/B5
Thu Dau Mot, Viet. 136/D4
Thuin, Belg. 111/D3
Thuir, Fr. 100/E5
Thulba (riv.), Ger. 112/C3
Thule Air Base, Den. 181/T7
Thun, Swi. 114/D4
Thunder Bird (lake), Ok, US 195/N15
Thuner See (lake), Swi. 114/D4
Thung Salaeng Luang NP, Thai. 136/C2
Thüngersheim, Ger. 112/C3
Thur (riv.), Swi. 101/H3
Thurgau (canton), Swi. 115/E2
Thüringen (state), Ger. 101/J1
Thüringen, Aus. 115/F3
Thüringer Schiefergebirge (mts.), Ger. 112/E2
Thüringer Wald (for.), Ger. 101/J1
Thurles, Ire. 89/Q10
Thurnau, Ger. 112/E3
Thuró By, Den. 96/D4

Thurrock (co.), Eng, UK 91/G3
Thurso, Sc, UK 89/V14
Thurston (isl.), Ant. 218/T
Thurston (co.), Wa, US 193/A3
Thury-en-Valois, Fr. 88/M4
Thyez, Fr. 114/C5
Thyolo, Malw. 163/G4
Ti-m-Merhsoï (riv.), Niger 161/G2
Ti-n-Jedane, Oued (riv.), Alg. 157/G4
Ti-n-Zaouâten, Alg. 154/F4
Ti-Tree Abor. Land, Austl. 171/G2
Tiahuanco (ruin), Bol. 214/D5
Tian (pt.), BC, Can. 192/M5
Tian Shan (mts.), China 128/C3
Tianchang, China 130/D4
Tianguá, Braz. 212/B1
Tianjin (mun.), China 129/L4
Tianjin, China 130/H7
Tianlin, China 141/J3
Tianmen, China 137/B1
Tianmu (mts.), China 130/K9
Tianshui, China 128/J5
Tianyang, China 137/A3
Tianzhen, China 130/C2
Tianzhu, China 141/J2
Tiaret, Alg. 158/F5
Tibagi, Braz. 213/B3
Tibaji (riv.), Braz. 213/B3
Tibaná, Col. 210/C3
Tibati, Camr. 154/H6
Tibba, Pak. 144/A5
Tibé, Pic de (peak), Gui. 160/C4
Tiber (Tevere) (riv.), It. 101/J5
Tiberias (lake), Isr. 149/D3
Tibesti (mts.), Chad 154/J3
Tibet (reg.), China 125/H6
Tibet (Xizang) (aut. reg.), China 128/D5
Tibro, Swe. 96/F2
Tiburon (cape), Haiti 199/G4
Tiburon, Ca, US 193/K11
Tiburón, Isla (isl.), Mex. 200/B2
Ticao, Peru 214/D5
Tichigan (lake), Wi, US 193/P14
Tichît, Dhar (cliff), Mrta. 160/C2
Ticino (canton), Swi. 115/E5
Ticleni, Rom. 107/F3
Ticlios, Peru 214/B3
Ticonderoga, NY, US 188/F3
Ticul, Mex. 202/D1
Tidaholm, Swe. 96/F2
Tidikelt (plain), Alg. 154/F2
Tidikdja, Mrta. 160/C2
Tidone (riv.), It. 116/C3
Tidore (isl.), Indo. 139/G3
Tidra, Île (isl.), Mrta. 160/A2
Tidsit (lake), WSah. 156/B5
Tiede, PN del, Sp. 156/A3
Tiefencastel, Swi. 115/F4
Tiel, Neth. 108/C5
Tieling, China 130/E2
Tielt, Belg. 110/C2
Tielt-Winge, Belg. 111/D2
Tiemba (riv.), C.d'Iv. 160/D4
Tienen, Belg. 111/D2
Tieri, Austl. 172/C3
Tieroko (peak), Chad 155/J3
Tierp, Swe. 96/G1
Tierra Amarilla, NM, US 186/F3
Tierra Blanca, Mex. 201/N8
Tierra Colorada, Mex. 201/F5
Tierra del Fuego (isl.), Arg. 217/D7
Tierra del Fuego, Antártida e Islas del Atlántico Sur, Arg. 217/C7
Tierra del Fuego, PN, Arg. 217/D7
Tierradentro, Col. 210/B4
Tierranueva, Mex. 201/E4
Tiétar (riv.), Sp. 102/C2
Tietê, Braz. 213/L7
Tietê (riv.), Braz. 205/D5
Tiffin, Oh, US 188/D3
Tiflet, Mor. 158/A3
Tifton, Ga, US 191/H4
Tigeaux, Fr. 88/L5
Tighina (Bendery), Mol. 107/J2
Tighvein (hill), Sc, UK 94/A6
Tignère, Camr. 154/H6
Tignieu-Jameyzieu, Fr. 114/B6
Tigre (riv.), Ven. 211/F2
Tigre, Arg. 217/J11
Tigris (riv.), Iraq 146/E2
Tigui (well), Chad 155/J4
Tiguidit, Falaise de (cliff), Niger 161/G2
Tigzirt, Alg. 158/H4
Tihosuco, Mex. 202/D1
Tihuatlán, Mex. 202/B1
Tiilikajärven NP, Fin. 118/F3
Tijâra, India 142/A2
Tijuana, Mex. 194/C5
Tijuca, PN da, Braz. 213/K7
Tijucas, Braz. 213/B3

Tijuco (riv.), Braz. 213/B1
Tikamgarh, India 142/B3
Tikchik (lakes), Ak, US 192/G3
Tikehau (isl.), FrPol. 175/L6
Tikhoretsk, Rus. 118/G4
Tikhvin, Rus. 118/G4
Tikrît, Iraq 148/E3
Tikveš (lake), FYROM 105/H2
Tila, Mex. 202/C2
Tilburg, Neth. 108/C5
Tilbury, Eng, UK 88/E2
Tilden, Tx, US 190/D4
Tilghman, Md, US 196/B6
Tilghman (isl.), Md, US 196/B6
Tilhar, India 142/B2
Tilin, Myan. 141/F3
Tilisarao, Arg. 216/D2
Till (riv.), Eng, UK 94/D5
Tillabéri (dept.), Niger 161/F3
Tillaberý, Niger 161/F3
Tillamook, Or, US 184/C4
Tille (riv.), Fr. 98/C5
Tillicoultry, Sc, UK 94/C4
Tilst, Den. 96/D3
Tilt (riv.), Sc, UK 94/C3
Tiltil, Chile 216/N8
Tim, Den. 96/C3
Timan (ridge), Rus. 122/F3
Timaná, Col. 210/B4
Timanfaya, PN de, Sp. 156/B3
Timaru, NZ 175/S11
Timashevsk, Rus. 120/F3
Timbákion, Gre. 105/J5
Timbaúba, Braz. 212/D2
Timbédra, Mrta. 160/C2
Timber Lake, SD, US 185/H4
Timberlane, La, US 195/O17
Timberwood Park, Tx, US 195/U20
Timbiquí, Col. 210/B4
Timbiras, Braz. 212/B2
Timbó, Braz. 213/B3
Timboon, Austl. 173/B3
Timehri (int'l arpt.), Guy. 211/G3
Timelkam, Aus. 113/G6
Timfristós (peak), Gre. 105/G3
Timimoun, Alg. 157/F3
Timiris (cape), Mrta. 160/A2
Timiş (prov.), Rom. 106/E3
Timiş (riv.), Rom. 106/E3
Timişoara (int'l arpt.), Rom. 106/E3
Timişoara, Rom. 106/E3
Timmins, On, Can. 188/D1
Timms (hill), Wi, US 185/L4
Timnath, Co, US 195/C1
Timon, Braz. 212/B2
Timonium, Md, US 196/B5
Timor (isl.), ETim.,Indo. 139/F5
Timor (sea), Asia,Austl. 139/G5
Timóteo, Braz. 213/J6
Timpanogos Cave Nat'l Mon., Ut, US 186/E2
Timpanogos Nat'l Mon., Ut, US 195/K13
Timpson, Tx, US 187/J5
Timpton (riv.), Rus. 123/N4
Tims Ford (lake), Tn, US 191/G3
Tin Can Bay, Austl. 172/D4
Tin Shui Wai, China 129/T10
Tina (riv.), SAfr. 164/B1
Tinaca (pt.), Phil. 137/E6
Tinaco, Ven. 210/D2
Tindivanam, India 140/C5
Tindouf, Alg. 156/C4
Tindouf (prov.), Alg. 156/C4
Tineo, Sp. 102/B1
Tingalpa (res.), Austl. 172/F7
Tingaringy NP, Austl. 173/D3
Tingha, Austl. 173/D1
Tingi (mts.), SLeo. 160/C4
Tingmerkpuk (mtn.), Ak, US 192/F2
Tingo María, Peru 214/C3
Tingsryd, Swe. 96/F3
Tinguiririca (vol.), Chile 216/C2
Tinharé, Ilha de (isl.), Braz. 209/L6
Tinian (isl.), NMar. 174/D4
Tinicum Nat'l Consv. Area, Pa, US 196/C4
Tinkisso (riv.), Gui. 160/C4
Tinley Park, Il, US 193/Q16
Tinogasta, Arg. 215/C2
Tinos, Gre. 105/J4
Tinos (isl.), Gre. 105/J4
Tinqueux, Fr. 110/C5
Tinrhir, Mor. 156/C3
Tinta, Peru 214/D4
Tintagel (pt.), Eng, UK 90/B5
Tintern Abbey, Eng, UK 90/D3
Tintigny, Belg. 111/E4
Tintinara, Austl. 173/B2
Tinto (riv.), Sp. 102/B4
Tinto (peak), Sc, UK 94/C5
Tinton Falls (New Shrewsbury), NJ, US 196/D3
Tinyahuarco, Peru 214/C3
Tioga, ND, US 185/H3

Tipasa (prov.), Alg. 158/F4
Tipasa, Alg. 158/G4
Tipperary, Ire. 89/P10
Tiptür, India 140/C5
Tir Rhiwiog (peak), Wal, UK 90/C1
Tiracambu, Serra do (mts.), Braz. 209/J4
Tiran (str.), Egypt, SA 159/C3
Tiran (isl.), Egypt 159/C3
Tiran, SAr. 159/C3
Tīrān (isl.), Egypt 155/M2
Tirana (cap.), Alb. 105/F2
Tirano, It. 115/G5
Tirari (des.), Austl. 171/H4
Tiraspol, Mol. 107/J2
Tirat Karmel, Isr. 149/F6
Tire, Turk. 148/A2
Tirebolu, Turk. 120/D4
Tiree (isl.), Sc, UK 89/Q8
Tirest (well), Mali 161/F1
Tîrgovişte, Rom. 107/G3
Tîrgu Bujor, Rom. 107/H3
Tîrgu Cărbuneşti, Rom. 107/F3
Tîrgu Frumos, Rom. 107/H2
Tîrgu Jiu, Rom. 107/F3
Tîrgu Lăpuş, Rom. 107/F2
Tîrgu Mureş, Rom. 107/G2
Tîrgu Neamţ, Rom. 107/H2
Tîrgu Ocna, Rom. 107/H2
Tîrgu Secuiesc, Rom. 107/H2
Tirich Mîr (peak), Pak. 147/K1
Tiris (reg.), WSah. 156/B5
Tiris Zemmour (pol. reg.), Mrta. 156/C4
Tîrnava Mare (riv.), Rom. 107/G2
Tîrnava Mică (riv.), Rom. 107/F2
Tîrnăveni, Rom. 107/G2
Tirnavos, Gre. 105/H3
Tiros, Braz. 213/C1
Tirschenreuth, Ger. 113/F3
Tirstrup (int'l arpt.), Den. 96/D3
Tiruchchirāppalli, India 140/C6
Tiruchendūr, India 140/C6
Tiruchengodu, India 140/C6
Tirunelveli, India 140/C6
Tiruntán, Peru 214/C2
Tirupati, India 140/C5
Tiruppattūr, India 140/C5
Tiruppūr, India 140/C5
Tiruvannāmalai, India 140/C5
Tisa (riv.), Ukr. 107/G1
Tisdale, Sk, Can. 185/G2
Tista (riv.), Bang. 143/G2
Tisza (riv.), Hun. 120/B3
Tiszaföldvár, Hun. 106/E2
Tiszafüred, Hun. 106/E2
Tiszakécske, Hun. 106/E2
Tiszalök, Hun. 106/E1
Tiszavasvári, Hun. 99/L5
Titano (peak), SMar. 117/F5
Titel, Serb. 106/E3
Titicaca (lake), Bol.,Peru 214/D4
Titisee-Neustadt, Ger. 114/E2
Titlagarh, India 140/D3
Titlis (peak), Swi. 115/E4
Tito, It. 104/D2
Titov Veles, FYROM 105/G2
Titov vrh (peak), FYROM 105/G2
Titting, Ger. 112/E5
Tittmoning, Ger. 113/F6
Titu, Rom. 107/G3
Titusville, Fl, US 191/H4
Titusville, NJ, US 196/D3
Tiva (riv.), Kenya 162/C3
Tivaouane, Sen. 160/A3
Tivat, Mont. 106/D4
Tiverton, Eng, UK 90/C5
Tiwanacu, Bol. 214/D5
Tixán, Ecu. 214/B1
Tixtla de Guerrero, Mex. 201/F5
Tizayuca, Mex. 201/L7
Tizi Ouzou (prov.), Alg. 158/H4
Tizi Ouzou, Alg. 158/H4
Tizimín, Mex. 202/D1
Tiznap (riv.), China 147/L1
Tiznit, Mor. 156/C3
Tjæreborg, Den. 96/C4
Tjeldstø, Nor. 96/A1
Tjeukemeer (lake), Neth. 108/C3
Tjøme, Nor. 96/D2
Tjorn (isl.), Den. 96/D3
Tjörn (isl.), Swe. 96/D3
Tlacolula de Matamoros, Mex. 201/P8
Tlacotepec, Mex. 201/F5
Tlahualilo de Zaragoza, Mex. 200/E3
Tlalixcoyan, Mex. 201/N8
Tlalmanalco, Mex. 201/Q10
Tlalnepantla, Mex. 201/Q9
Tlaltenango de Sánchez Román, Mex. 200/E4
Tlaltizapan, Mex. 201/K8
Tlapa de Comonfort, Mex. 202/B2

Tlapacoya (ruin), Mex. 201/O10
Tlapacoyan, Mex. 201/M7
Tlapehuala, Mex. 201/E5
Tlaquepaque, Mex. 200/E4
Tlaquiltenango, Mex. 201/K8
Tlatlauquitepec, Mex. 201/M7
Tlaxcala (state), Mex. 198/A5
Tlaxcala, Mex. 201/L7
Tlaxco, Mex. 201/L7
Tlaxcoapan, Mex. 201/K6
Tlell, BC, Can. 192/M5
Tlemcen, Alg. 158/D2
Toabré, Pan. 203/F4
Toaca (peak), Rom. 107/G2
Toachi (riv.), Ecu. 210/B4
Toamasina, Madg. 165/J7
Toamasina (prov.), Madg. 165/J7
Toandos (pen.), Wa, US 193/B2
Toau (isl.), FrPol. 175/L6
Toay, Arg. 216/D3
Toba (lake), Indo. 138/A5
Toba (inlet), BC, Can. 184/B3
Toba, China 128/G5
Toba, Japan 135/L7
Toba Kākar (range), Pak. 147/J2
Toba Tek Singh, Pak. 144/B4
Tobago (isl.), Trin. 208/F1
Tobarra, Sp. 102/E3
Tobbio (peak), It. 116/B3
Tobermore, NI, UK 92/B3
Tōbetsu, Japan 134/B2
Tobias Barreto, Braz. 212/C4
Tobin (lake), Austl. 170/E2
Tobique (riv.), NB, Can. 189/H2
Tobishima, Japan 135/L5
Tobol (riv.), Rus. 119/Q5
Tobu, Japan 135/A1
Tobyhanna (lake), Pa, US 196/C1
Tobyhanna (riv.), Pa, US 196/C1
Tobyhanna, Pa, US 196/C1
Tobyhanna St. Park, Pa, US 196/C1
Tobyl (riv.), Kaz. 121/M1
Tobysh (riv.), Rus. 119/J2
Tocache, Peru 214/B3
Tocantinópolis, Braz. 212/A2
Tocantins (riv.), Braz. 205/E4
Tocantins (state), Braz. 212/A3
Toccoa, Ga, US 191/H3
Toce (riv.), It. 101/H3
Tochigi (pref.), Japan 133/F2
Tochigi, Japan 133/F2
Tochimilco, Mex. 201/L8
Tochio, Japan 133/F2
Tocina, Sp. 102/C4
Töcksfors, Swe. 96/D2
Toco, Trin. 211/F2
Tocopilla, Chile 215/B1
Tocumen, Pan. 203/G4
Tocumwal, Austl. 173/C2
Tocuyito, Ven. 210/D2
Tocuyo (riv.), Ven. 208/E1
Toda, Japan 135/D2
Toda Bhīm, India 140/C2
Todi, It. 104/C1
Tödi (peak), Swi. 115/E4
Todmorden, Eng. UK 93/F4
Todos os Santos, Baía de (bay), Braz. 212/C4
Todos Santos, Mex. 200/C4
Todtmoos, Ger. 114/C2
Todtnau, Ger. 114/D2
Toffal (hill), Mrta. 156/C5
Toffo, Ben. 161/F5
Tofield, Ab, Can. 184/E2
Tofua (isl.), Tonga 175/H6
Tōgane, Japan 135/E2
Togba (well), Mrta. 160/C2
Toggenburg (valley), Swi. 115/E3
Togher, Ire. 92/B5
Togiak, Ak, US 192/F4
Togo (ctry.) 161/F4
Tōgō, Japan 135/M5
Tōgō, Japan 135/M5
Togtoh, China 128/F2
Tōgyu-san NP, SKor. 131/D5
Tohāna, India 144/C5
Tohatchi, NM, US 190/A3
Tōhoku (prov.), Japan 133/F1
Toi, Japan 133/F3
Tōin, Japan 135/L5
Toiyabe (range), Nv, US 186/C3
Tojō, Japan 132/C3
Tojō, Japan 135/H6
Tok, Ak, US 192/K3
Tokachi (riv.), Japan 134/C2
Tōkai, Japan 135/L5
Tokaj, Hun. 99/L4
Tōkamachi, Japan 133/F2
Tokar Nat'l Rsv., Sudan 159/H3
Tokara (isls.), Japan 133/K6
Tokat, Turk. 148/D1
Tokat (prov.), Turk. 148/D1
Tŏkchŏk (isl.), NKor. 131/C4
Tŏkchŏk (arch.), NKor. 131/C4
Tokeen, Ak, US 192/M4

Tokelau (terr.), NZ 175/H5
Toki, Japan 135/M5
Toki (riv.), Japan 135/M5
Tokigawa, Japan 135/C2
Tokiname, Japan 135/L6
Tokoro (riv.), Japan 134/C2
Tokoro, Japan 134/D1
Tokorozawa, Japan 133/F3
Toksook Bay, Ak, US 192/E3
Toksun, China 128/E3
Tokuno (isl.), Japan 133/K7
Tokushima (pref.), Japan 132/C4
Tokushima, Japan 132/D3
Tokuyama, Japan 132/B3
Tōkyō (cap.), Japan 133/F3
Tōkyō (pref.), Japan 133/F3
Tōkyō (bay), Japan 135/D2
Tōkyō Disneyland, Japan 135/D2
Tola, Nic. 202/E4
Tolbo, Mong. 128/F2
Toledo, Braz. 215/F1
Toledo, Phil. 137/D5
Toledo, Oh, US 188/D3
Toledo, Sp. 102/C3
Toledo, Col. 210/C3
Toledo, Uru. 217/K11
Toledo Bend (dam), La,Tx, US 187/L6
Toledo Bend (res.), La,Tx, US 187/L6
Toledo, Montes de (mts.), Sp. 102/C3
Tolentino, It. 101/K5
Tolfa, It. 104/B1
Tolhuaca, PN, Chile 216/C3
Toli, China 128/D2
Toliara (prov.), Madg. 165/H8
Toliara, Madg. 165/G8
Tolima (dept.), Col. 210/C4
Tolitoli, Indo. 139/F3
Tolka (riv.), Ire. 92/B5
Tolleson, Az, US 195/R19
Tolmezzo, It. 101/K3
Tolna (prov.), Hun. 106/D2
Tolna, It. 106/D2
Tolo (chan.), China 129/U10
Tolo, Gulf of (gulf), Indo. 139/F4
Tolosa, Sp. 102/D1
Tolsan (isl.), SKor. 131/D5
Tolt (riv.), Wa, US 193/D2
Tolt (res.), Wa, US 193/D2
Tolt, North Fork (riv.), Wa, US 193/D2
Tolt, South Fork (riv.), Wa, US 193/D2
Toltén, Chile 216/B3
Toltén (riv.), Chile 216/B3
Toluca, Mex. 201/Q10
Tolúviejo, Col. 210/C2
Tol'yatti, Rus. 121/J1
Tom' (riv.), Rus. 122/J4
Tom Price, Austl. 170/C4
Tom White (mt.), Ak, US 192/K3
Tomakomai, Japan 134/C2
Tomamae, Japan 134/B1
Tomar, Port. 102/A3
Tómaros (peak), Gre. 105/G3
Tomarza, Turk. 148/C2
Tomás, Peru 214/C4
Tomás de Berlanga, Ecu. 214/E7
Tomaszów Lubelski, Pol. 99/M3
Tomaszów Mazowiecki, Pol. 99/L3
Tomatlán, Mex. 200/D5
Tomb of Qinshihuang, China 130/B4
Tombador, Serra do (mts.), Braz. 208/G6
Tombigbee (riv.), Al,Ms, US 191/F3
Tombouctou, Mali 160/E2
Tombstone, Az, US 186/E5
Tombua, Ang. 163/B4
Tome, Chile 216/B3
Tomé, Île (isl.), Fr. 100/B2
Tomelilla, Swe. 96/E4
Tomelloso, Sp. 102/D3
Tomini (gulf), Indo. 139/F4
Tomiño, Sp. 102/A2
Tomioka, Japan 135/C1
Tomisato, Japan 135/E2
Tomiura, Japan 135/D3
Tomiyama, Japan 133/F3
Tomiya, Japan 135/H6
Tommot, Rus. 123/N4
Tompa, Hun. 106/D2
Tompkinsville, Ky, US 188/C4
Toms (riv.), NJ, US 196/D3
Toms River, NJ, US 196/D4
Tonalá, Mex. 202/C3

Tonale, Passo del (pass), It. 115/G5
Tonasket, Wa, US 184/D3
Tonawanda, NY, US 189/S9
Tonawanda Ind. Res., NY, US 189/S9
Tonbridge, Eng. UK 88/D3
Toncontín (int'l arpt.), Hon. 202/E3
Tondabayashi, Japan 135/J7
Tondano, Indo. 139/F3
Tondou, Massif du (plat.), CAfr.,Sudan 155/K6
Tondu (peak), Fr. 114/C6
Tone (riv.), Japan 133/G3
Tone, Japan 135/E2
Tonekābon, Iran 146/F1
Tonelagee (peak), Ire. 92/B5
Tonga (ctry.) 175/H7
Tongaat, SAfr. 165/E3
Tongareva (Penrhyn) (isl.), Cookls. 175/J5
Tongariro NP, NZ 175/T10
Tongatapu (isl.), Tonga 175/H7
Tongbai, China 130/C4
Tongbu, SKor. 131/G6
Tongcheng, China 137/B2
Tongcheng, China 130/D5
Tongch'ŏn, NKor. 131/D3
Tongchuan, China 130/B4
Tongdao Dongzu Zizhixian, China 141/J2
Tongduch'on, SKor. 131/G6
Tongeren, Belg. 111/E2
Tonggu (peak), China 129/L7
Tonggu, China 141/K2
Tonghai, China 141/H3
Tonghua, China 131/C2
Tonghua, China 131/C2
Tongliao, China 130/E2
Tongling, China 137/B2
Tongling, China 129/L5
Tongno (riv.), NKor. 131/D2
Tongo (peak), Indo. 139/E5
Tongobory, Madg. 165/H8
Tongren, China 141/J2
Tongsa (riv.), Bhu. 143/H2
Tongsa Dzong, Bhu. 143/H2
Tongshan, China 137/B2
Tongue (riv.), Mt, US 184/G4
Tongue, Sc, UK 89/F7
Tongxu, China 130/C4
Tongyu, China 129/M3
Tongzi, China 137/A2
Tonino-Anivskiy (pen.), Rus. 134/C1
Tönisvorst, Ger. 108/D6
Tonk, India 147/L3
Tonkawa, Ok, US 187/H3
Tonkin (gulf) 136/D1
Tonkoui (peak), C.d'Iv. 160/D5
Tonle Sap (lake), Camb. 141/H5
Tonneins, Fr. 100/D4
Tonnerre, Fr. 100/E3
Tönning, Ger. 96/C4
Tōno, Japan 134/B4
Tonopah, Nv, US 186/C3
Tonoshō, Japan 132/D3
Tonosí, Pan. 203/F5
Tonota, Bots. 163/E5
Tons (riv.), India 142/C3
Tønsberg, Nor. 96/D2
Tonsina, Ak, US 192/J3
Tonstad, Nor. 96/B2
Tonto Nat'l For., Az, US 195/S18
Tonto Nat'l Mon., Az, US 186/E4
Tonya, Turk. 148/D1
Ton-y-Pandy, Wal, UK 90/C3
Toodyay, Austl. 170/C4
Tooele, Ut, US 195/J12
Tooele (co.), Ut, US 195/J13
Tooradin, Austl. 173/C3
Toowoomba, Austl. 172/C4
Top (mt.), Austl. 171/G2
Topanaga State Park, Ca, US 194/B2
Topanga, Ca, US 194/B2
Topanga Beach, Ca, US 194/E7
Tope de Coroa (mtn.), CpV. 151/J10
Topia, Mex. 200/D3
Topley, BC, Can. 184/B2
Toplita, Rom. 107/G2
Topocalma (cape), Chile 216/C2
Topolčany, Slvk. 99/K4
Topolobampo, Mex. 200/C3
Topolovgrad, Bul. 107/H4
Topol'noye (lake), Rus. 95/J2
Toppenish, Wa, US 184/C4
Toprakkale, Turk. 149/E1
Topton, Pa, US 196/C2
Tor (bay), Eng. UK 90/C4
Torahime, Japan 135/K5
Torata, Peru 214/D3
Torawitan (cape), Indo. 139/G3
Torbalı, Turk. 148/A2
Torbat-e Heydarīyeh, Iran 147/J1
Torbat-e Jām, Iran 145/D5
Torbay, Nf, Can. 189/L2
Torbay (co.), Eng, UK 90/C4
Torbeck, Haiti 203/H2
Torbert (mt.), Ak, US 192/H3

Torcy, Fr. 88/K5
Tordera (riv.), Sp. 103/L6
Tordesillas, Sp. 102/C2
Töreboda, Swe. 96/F2
Torelló, Sp. 103/G1
Torfaen (co.), Wal, UK 90/C3
Torzhok, Rus. 118/G4
Tosa, Japan 132/C4
Tosagua, Ecu. 210/A5
Tosashimizu, Japan 132/C4
Toscana (reg.), It. 116/D1
Toscana (prov.), It. 101/J5
Toscolano-Maderno, It. 116/D1
Toshi (isl.), Japan 135/L6
Toshibetsu (riv.), Japan 134/A2
Toshkent (pol. reg.), Uzb. 145/D3
Tosno, Rus. 97/P2
Tosontsengel, Mong. 128/G2
Toss (riv.), Swi. 101/H3
Tosson (hill), Eng, UK 94/E6
Tostado, Arg. 215/D2
Tostedt, Ger. 109/G1
Tosu, Japan 132/B4
Totana (riv.), Aus. 99/H5
Totana, Sp. 102/E4
Totness, Sur. 211/G3
Totowa, NJ, US 197/J8
Totten (inlet), Wa, US 193/A3
Tottenham, Austl. 173/C2
Tottington, Eng, UK 93/F4
Tottori, Japan 132/D3
Tottori (pref.), Japan 132/C3
Tänäs, Swe. 96/F2
Touat (reg.), Alg. 157/G5
Touba, C.d'Iv. 160/D4
Toubkal (peak), Mor. 156/D3
Toubkal, PN du, Mor. 156/D3
Touchwood (hills), Sk, Can. 185/G3
Toropets, Rus. 97/P3
Tororo, Ugan. 162/B2
Torote (riv.), Sp. 103/N8
Tougan, Burk. 160/E3
Touggourt, Alg. 157/G2
Toughkenamon, Pa, US 196/C4
Touil (riv.), Alg. 158/G3
Toul, Fr. 111/E6
Toulnustouc (riv.), Qu, Can. 189/H1
Toulon, Fr. 100/F5
Toulouse, Fr. 100/D5
Toumo (well), Niger 154/H3
Toumodi, C.d'Iv. 160/D5
Toungoo, Myan. 141/G4
Touquin, Fr. 88/M5
Toura, Monts du (mts.), C.d'Iv. 160/D5
Tourcoing, Fr. 110/C2
Tourfourine (well), Mali 156/D4
Tourlaville, Fr. 100/C2
Tournai, Belg. 110/C2
Tournan-en-Brie, Fr. 88/L5
Tournus, Fr. 114/A4
Touros, Braz. 212/D2
Tours, Fr. 100/D3
Tous, Embalse de (res.), Sp. 103/E3
Toussidé (peak), Chad 154/J3
Toussoro (peak), CAfr. 155/K6
Touws (riv.), SAfr. 164/C4
Touwsrivier, SAfr. 164/M10
Touzim, Czh. 113/G2
Tov (prov.), Mong. 128/J2
Tovar, Ven. 210/D2
Tove (riv.), Eng, UK 91/F2
Towaco, NJ, US 197/H8
Towada, Japan 133/G2
Towada (lake), Japan 133/G2
Towada-Hachimantai NP, Japan 134/B3
Towada-Hachimantai NP, Japan 134/B3
Tower City, Pa, US 196/B2
Tower Hamlets (bor.), Eng, UK 88/A1
Tower of London, Eng, UK 88/C2
Towner, ND, US 185/J3
Townridge (riv.), Eng, UK 90/B5
Townsend (mt.), Wa, US 193/A2
Townsends (inlet), NJ, US 196/D5
Townshend (cape), Austl. 172/C3
Townsville, Austl. 172/B2
Towson, Md, US 196/B4
Towuti (lake), Indo. 139/F4
Toya (lake), Japan 134/C2
Toyah, Tx, US 190/C4
Toyahvale, Tx, US 190/C4
Toyama, Japan 133/E2
Toyama (pref.), Japan 133/E2
Toyama (bay), Japan 133/E2
Toyoake, Japan 135/M5
Toyohashi, Japan 133/E3
Toyokawa, Japan 133/E3
Toyonaka, Japan 135/H6
Toyono, Japan 135/H6
Toyo'oka, Japan 132/D3

Torugart (pass), Kyr. 145/G4
Torul, Turk. 148/D1
Torun, Pol. 99/K2
Torup, Swe. 96/E3
Tory (isl.), Ire. 89/P9
Torysa (riv.), Slvk. 99/L4
Tosca (reg.), It. 116/D1
Tosaka, Japan 135/K5
Tosashimizu, Japan 132/C4
Toscana (reg.), It. 116/D1
Toshi (isl.), Japan 135/L6
Toshbetsu (riv.), Japan 134/A2
Toshkent (pol. reg.), Uzb. 145/D3
Tosno, Rus. 97/P2
Tosontsengel, Mong. 128/G2
Toss (riv.), Swi. 101/H3
Tosson (hill), Eng, UK 94/E6
Tostado, Arg. 215/D2
Tostedt, Ger. 109/G1
Tosu, Japan 132/B4
Totana (riv.), Aus. 99/H5
Totana, Sp. 102/E4
Totness, Sur. 211/G3
Totowa, NJ, US 197/J8
Totten (inlet), Wa, US 193/A3
Tottori, Japan 132/D3

Toyosato, Japan 135/E1
Toyosato, Japan 135/K5
Toyoshina, Japan 133/E2
Toyota, Japan 135/M5
Toyota, Japan 135/B2
Toyoyama, Japan 135/L5
Tozeur (gov.), Tun. 157/G2
Tozeur, Tun. 157/G2
Tozi (mt.), Ak, US 192/H2
Tra Vinh, Viet. 136/D4
Traben-Trarbach, Ger. 111/G4
Trabuco Canyon, Ca, US 194/C3
Trabzon, Turk. 148/D1
Trabzon (prov.), Turk. 148/D1
Tracadie, NB, Can. 189/H2
Trachselwald, Swi. 114/D3
Tracy, Qu, Can. 188/F2
Tracy, Mo, US 195/D5
Tracyton, Wa, US 193/B2
Tradate, It. 116/B1
Trafalgar (cape), Sp. 102/B4
Trafford (co.), Eng, UK 93/F5
Tragwein, Aus. 113/G6
Traiguén, Chile 216/B3
Trail, BC, Can. 184/D3
Traipu, Braz. 212/C3
Trairi, Braz. 212/C1
Traisen (riv.), Aus. 99/H5
Traiskirchen, Aus. 107/N7
Traismauer, Aus. 99/H4
Trakai NP, Lith. 97/L4
Traki, Lith. 97/L4
Tralee, Ire. 89/P10
Tramandaí, Braz. 213/B4
Tramelan, Swi. 114/D3
Tramin (Termeno), It. 115/H5
Tranås, Swe. 96/F2
Tranbjerg, Den. 96/D3
Trancoso, Port. 102/B2
Tranebjerg, Den. 96/D4
Tranemo, Swe. 96/E3
Tranent, Sc, UK 94/D5
Trang, Thai. 136/B5
Trangan (isl.), Indo. 139/H5
Trängsletsjön (lake), Swe. 96/E1
Trani, It. 104/E2
Tranoroa, Madg. 165/H9
Transantarctic (mts.), Ant. 218/W
Transylvania (reg.), Rom. 106/F2
Transylvanian Alps (mts.), Rom. 106/F3
Trapani, It. 104/C3
Trapper (peak), Mt, US 184/E4
Trappes, Fr. 88/J5
Traralgon, Austl. 173/C3
Trarza (pol. reg.), Mrta. 154/B4
Trasacco, It. 104/C2
Trasimeno (lake), It. 101/K5
Träslövsläge, Swe. 96/D3
Trat, Thai. 136/C3
Traun (riv.), Aus. 98/H4
Traun, Aus. 113/F6
Traunreut, Ger. 113/F7
Traunsee (lake), Aus. 113/K3
Traunstein, Ger. 113/F7
Trautmannsdorf an der Leitha, Aus. 107/P7
Travagliato, It. 116/D1
Trave (riv.), Ger. 98/F2
Travedona Monate, It. 116/B1
Travellers (lake), Austl. 173/B2
Travemünde, Ger. 98/F2
Traverse (peak), Ak, US 192/G2
Traverse (lake), Mn, SD, US 185/J4
Traverse City, Mi, US 188/C2
Traversetolo, It. 116/D3
Travis (lake), Tx, US 190/D4
Travis AFB, Ca, US 193/L10
Travnik, Bosn. 106/C3
Trawsal (peak), Eng, UK
Trawsfynydd, Llyn (lake), Wal, UK 92/D6
Trbovlje, Slov. 101/L3
Tré-la-Tête (peak), Fr. 114/C6
Treachery (mt.), Austl. 171/G2
Trebaseleghe, It. 117/E1
Trebbia (riv.), It. 101/H4
Trebel (riv.), Ger. 98/G1
Třebíč, Czh. 113/H4
Trebinje, Bosn. 105/F1
Trebišauce, It. 104/E2
Třeboň, Czh. 113/H4
Trebonne, Austl. 172/B2
Trebujena, Sp. 102/B4
Trebur, Ger. 112/B3
Trecate, It. 116/B2
Tregnago, It. 117/E1
Treig (lake), Sc, UK 94/B3
Treinta de Agosto, Arg. 216/E3
Treinta y Tres (dept.), Uru. 217/G2
Treinta y Tres, Uru. 217/G2
Trélazé, Fr. 100/C3

Trelew, Arg. 216/D4
Trélissac, Fr. 100/D4
Trelleborg, Swe. 96/F4
Tremadoc (bay), Wal, UK 92/D6
Tremblant (riv.), Ire. 92/B4
Tremblestown (riv.), Ire. 92/B4
Trembleur (lake), BC, Can. 184/B2
Tremelo, Belg. 111/D2
Tremiti (isl.), It. 104/D1
Tremont, Pa, US 196/B2
Třemošná (riv.), Czh. 113/G3
Tremp, Sp. 103/F1
Trémsin (peak), Czh. 113/G3
Trenche (riv.), Qu, Can. 188/F1
Trenčiansky (pol. reg.), Slvk. 99/J3
Trenčín, Slvk. 99/K4
Trenque Lauquen, Arg. 216/D2
Trent (riv.), Eng, UK 93/F6
Trent and Mersey (canal), Eng, UK 93/F6
Trentino-Alto Adige (pol. reg.), It. 101/J3
Trento (prov.), It. 115/G5
Trento, It. 115/H5
Trenton, On, Can. 188/E2
Trenton, Ga, US 191/G3
Trenton, Mo, US 187/K1
Trenton, NJ, US 196/D3
Trenton, Tn, US 188/B5
Trenton (cap.), NJ, US 196/D3
Trento (cap.), Nv, US 186/C2
Trenton (riv.), Tx, US 190/D4
Trinity, West Fork (riv.), Tx, US 187/H4
Trino, It. 116/B2
Triolet, Mrts. 165/T15
Tripolis, Gre. 105/H4
Tripolitania (reg.), Libya 154/H1
Trippstadt, Ger. 111/G4
Tripunittura, India 140/C6
Tripura (state), India 141/F3
Trisanna (riv.), Aus. 115/G4
Trissino, It. 117/E1
Tristan da Cunha (isl.), StH. 80/J7
Triste (peak), Arg. 216/D4
Trisuli (riv.), Nepal 143/E2
Trittau, Ger. 109/H1
Trivero, It. 116/B1
Trnava, Slvk. 99/J4
Trnavský (pol. reg.), Slvk. 99/J4
Trobriand (isls.), PNG 174/E5
Trochtelfingen, Ger. 115/F1
Troesne (riv.), Fr. 110/A3
Trofaiach, Aus. 101/L3
Trofarello, It. 116/A3
Trøgstad, Nor. 96/D2
Troia, It. 104/D2
Trois Fourches, Cap des (cape), Mor. 158/C2
Trois-Pistoles, Qu, Can. 189/G1
Trois-Ponts, Belg. 111/E3
Trois-Rivières, Qu, Can. 189/G2
Troisdorf, Ger. 111/G2
Troistorrents, Swi. 114/C5
Troisvierges, Lux. 111/F3
Troitsk, Rus. 119/P5
Trollhättan, Swe. 96/E2
Trombetas (riv.), Braz. 209/G3
Tromello, It. 116/B2
Tromie (riv.), Sc, UK 94/B3
Troms (co.), Nor. 95/F1
Tromsø, Nor. 95/F1
Tronador (peak), Arg. 216/C4
Trondheim, Nor. 95/D3
Trondheims-Fjorden (estu.), Nor. 95/D3
Tronville-en-Barrois, Fr. 111/E6
Tronzano Vercellese, It. 116/B2
Troodos (mts.), Cyp. 149/C2
Trool (lake), Sc, UK 92/D1
Troon, Sc, UK 94/B5
Trooper, Pa, US 196/C3
Tropea, It. 104/D3
Trosa, Swe. 96/G2
Trosly-Breuil, Fr. 110/B5
Trossingen, Ger. 115/E1
Trostan (peak), NI, UK 92/B1
Trostberg an der Alz, Ger. 113/G2
Trou du Nord, Haiti 203/H2
Troublaun (peak), Ire. 92/A5
Troup, Tx, US 187/J4
Trout (lake), Sc, UK 94/D1
Trout (lake), NW, Can. 180/D2
Trout Lake, Ab, Can. 184/E1
Trowbridge, Eng, UK 90/D4
Troxelville, Pa, US 196/A2
Troy, Al, US 191/G4
Troy, Mi, US 188/D3
Troy, NY, US 189/F3
Troy, Oh, US 191/G1
Troy, Il, US 195/H8

Troy Center, Wi, US 193/N14
Troyan, Bul. 107/G4
Troyanski Prokhod (pass), Bul. 107/G4
Troyes, Fr. 100/F2
Trstenik, Serb. 106/E4
Trub, Swi. 114/D4
Truitt (peak), Yk, Can. 192/M3
Trujillo, Peru 214/B3
Trujillo, Sp. 102/C3
Trujillo, Indo. 138/A3
Trujillo (state), Ven. 210/D2
Trujillo, Hon. 202/E3
Trulben, Ger. 111/G5
Truman Library and Museum, Mo, US 195/E5
Trumau, Aus. 107/N8
Trumbauersville, Pa, US 196/C3
Trumbull, Ct, US 197/E1
Trümmelbachfälle (falls), Swi. 114/D4
Trün, Bul. 106/F4
Trundle, Austl. 173/C2
Truro, NS, Can. 189/J2
Truro, Eng, UK 90/A6
Truskmore (peak), Ire. 89/P9
Trüstenik, Bul. 107/G4
Truth or Consequences, NM, US 186/F4
Trutnov, Czh. 99/H3
Truyère (riv.), Fr. 100/E4
Trwyn Cilan (pt.), Wal, UK 92/D6
Tryavna, Bul. 107/G4
Trysil, Nor. 96/E1
Trysilelva (riv.), Nor. 96/D1
Trzcianka, Pol. 99/J2
Trzebiatów, Pol. 96/F4
Trzebnica, Pol. 99/J3
Trzemeszno, Pol. 99/J2
Tsabong, Bots. 164/C2
Tsagaan Bogd (peak), Mong. 128/F2
Tsakane, SAfr. 164/Q13
Tsalgar, Mong. 128/F2
Tsant, Mong. 128/J2
Tsao, Bots. 163/D5
Tsarahonenana, Madg. 165/J6
Tsaramandroso, Madg. 165/H7
Tsaratanana, Madg. 165/H7
Tsaratanana (mass.), Madg. 165/J6
Tsast (peak), Mong. 128/F2
Tsatsana (peak), Les. 164/E3
Tsavo East NP, Kenya 163/G1
Tsavo West NP, Kenya 163/G1
Tschagguns, Aus. 115/F3
Tschierv, Swi. 115/G4
Tschlin, Swi. 115/G4
Tselfat (peak), Mor. 158/B2
Tsetserleg, Mong. 128/F2
Tsetserleg, Mong. 128/H2
Tseung Kwan O, China 129/U10
Tsévié, Togo 161/F5
Tshane, Bots. 163/D5
Tshela, D.R. Congo 163/B1
Tshikapa, D.R. Congo 163/D2
Tshuapa (riv.), D.R. Congo 155/K8
Tsiafajavona (peak), Madg. 165/H7
Tsil'ma (riv.), Rus. 119/L2
Tsimlyansk (res.), Rus. 122/E5
Tsing Yi (isl.), China 129/U10
Tsiombe, Madg. 165/H9
Tsiribihina (riv.), Madg. 165/H7
Tsiroanomandidy, Madg. 165/H7
Tsitsikamma Forest and Coastal NP, SAfr. 164/C4
Tsivory, Madg. 165/H9
Ts'khinvali, Geo. 121/G4
Tsna (riv.), Rus. 118/G4
Tsomo (riv.), SAfr. 164/D3
Tsomog, Mong. 129/J2
Tsu, Japan 135/L6
Tsu (isl.), Japan 132/A3
Tsubame, Japan 133/F2
Tsubata, Japan 133/E2
Tsuchiura, Japan 133/G2
Tsuchiyama, Japan 135/K6
Tsuen Wan, China 129/U10
Tsugaru (pen.), Japan 134/B3
Tsuge, Japan 135/J6
Tsugaru, Japan 135/L4
Tsukidate, Japan 134/B4
Tsukigase, Japan 135/K6
Tsukuba, Japan 135/E1
Tsukude, Japan 135/M6
Tsukui, Japan 135/C2
Tsukumi, Japan 132/E4
Tsumeb, Namb. 163/C4
Tsuna, Japan 135/G7
Tsuru, Japan 133/F3
Tsuruga, Japan 133/E3
Tsurugashima, Japan 135/C2
Tsurugi, Japan 133/E2
Tsurugi-san (peak), Japan 132/D4
Tsuruoka, Japan 134/A4
Tsushima, Japan 135/L5
Tsuyama, Japan 135/D3

Tua (cape), Indo. 138/C5
Tua (riv.), Port.,Sp. 102/B2
Tuam, Ire. 89/P10
Tuamapu (chan.), Chile 216/B4
Tuamotu (arch.), FrPol. 175/L6
Tuan (pt.), Indo. 138/A3
Tuan (riv.), China 130/B4
Tuangku (isl.) 138/A3
Tuao, Phil. 137/D4
Tuapse, Rus. 120/F3
Tuba City, Az, US 186/E3
Tuban, Indo. 138/D5
Tuban (riv.), Yem. 146/D6
Tubarão, Braz. 213/B4
Tubbergen, Neth. 108/D4
Tubize, Belg. 111/D2
Tubmanburg, Libr. 160/C5
Tubruq (Tobruk), Libya 155/K1
Tubuaï (isl.), FrPol. 175/K7
Tubualá, Pan. 203/G4
Tucacas, Ven. 210/D2
Tucano, Braz. 212/C2
Tuchola, Pol. 99/J2
Tuchów, Pol. 99/L4
Tuckahoe, NJ, US 196/D5
Tuckahoe (riv.), NJ, US 196/D5
Tuckahoe, NY, US 197/K8
Tuckerton, NJ, US 196/D4
Tucquegnieux, Fr. 111/E5
Tucson, Az, US 186/E4
Tucumcari, NM, US 187/G4
Tucupido, Ven. 211/E2
Tucuruí, Braz. 209/J4
Tucuruí (res.), Braz. 209/J4
Tudela, Sp. 102/E1
Tudela de Duero, Sp. 102/C2
Tuen Mun, China 129/T10
Tuenno, It. 115/H5
Tufanbeyli, Turk. 148/D2
Tug Fork (riv.), Ky,WV, US 191/H2
Tugela (riv.), SAfr. 165/E3
Tugela (falls), SAfr. 164/E3
Tugela (riv.), SAfr. 165/E3
Tughlakabad (ruin), India 144/D5
Tuguegarao, Phil. 137/D4
Tukangbesi (isls.), Indo. 139/F5
Tükh, Egypt 149/B4
Tuktoyaktuk, NW, Can. 192/M2
Tukums, Lat. 97/K3
Tukung (peak), Indo. 138/D4
Tukuyu, Tanz. 162/B4
Tukwila, Wa, US 193/C3
Tula (riv.), Kenya 162/C2
Tula, Mex. 120/F1
Tula, Rus. 120/F1
Tula (riv.), Mex. 201/K6
Tula, Mex. 201/K6
Tula, PN, Mex. 201/K6
Tulancingo, Mex. 201/L6
Tulare, Ca, US 186/C3
Tularosa (valley), NM, US 187/F4
Tularosa, NM, US 187/F4
Tulcán, Ecu. 210/B4
Tulcea, Rom. 107/J3
Tulcea (prov.), Rom. 107/J3
Tule (canal), Ca, US 193/L9
Tüledi (isls.), Rus. 145/B3
Tulia, Tx, US 187/G4
Tulik (vol.), Ak, US 192/E5
Tulin (isl.), PNG 174/E5
Tulita, NW, Can. 180/D2
Tülkarm, WBnk. 149/G7
Tulla (lake), Sc, UK 94/B3
Tullahoma, Tn, US 191/G3
Tullamarine (int'l arpt.), Austl. 173/F5
Tullamore, Austl. 173/C2
Tullamore, Ire. 89/Q10
Tulle, Fr. 100/D4
Tullibody, Sc, UK 94/C4
Tullnerbach, Aus. 107/N7
Tullow, Ire. 89/Q10
Tully, Austl. 172/B2
Tullytown, Pa, US 196/D3
Tuloma (riv.), Rus. 122/D3
Tulsa, Ok, US 187/J3
Tulsipur, Nepal 142/D1
Tulsipur, India 142/D2
Tul'skaya Oblast, Rus. 120/F1
Tultitlán, Mex. 201/Q9
Tuluá, Col. 210/C3
Tuluksak, Ak, US 192/F3
Tulum, Mex. 202/E1
Tulum (ruin), Mex. 202/E1
Tulun, Rus. 123/L4
Tumacacori Nat'l Hist. Park, Az, US 186/E5
Tumaco, Col. 210/B4
Tumatumari, Guy. 211/G3
Tumauini, Phil. 137/D4
Tumba (lake), D.R. Congo 155/J8
Tumba, Swe. 96/G2
Tumbarumba, Austl. 173/D2
Tumbes (dept.), Peru 214/A1
Tumbes, Peru 214/A1
Tumbot (peak), Camb. 136/C3
Tumby Bay, Austl. 171/H5
Tumd Youqi, China 130/B3
Tumd Zuoqi, China 130/B2

Tumen, China 129/N3
Tumen (riv.), China 131/E1
Tumeremo, Ven. 211/F3
Tumereng, Guy. 211/F3
Tumkūr, India 140/C5
Tummel (riv.), Sc, UK 94/C3
Tumpat, Malay. 141/H6
Tumpu (peak), Indo. 139/F4
Tumu, Gha. 161/E4
Tumuc-Humac (mts.), Braz. 209/H3
Tumut, Austl. 173/D2
Tunadal, Swe. 118/C3
Tunceli (prov.), Turk. 148/D2
Tunceli, Turk. 148/D2
Tunchang, China 141/K4
Tundla, India 142/B2
Tundyk (riv.), Kaz. 104/B1
Tundzha (riv.), Bul. 107/H4
Tung Chung, China 129/T10
Tung Lung (riv.), China 129/V11
Tungabhadra (res.), India 140/C4
Tungabhadra (riv.), India 140/C4
Tungamah, Austl. 173/C2
Tüngsan-got (pt.), NKor. 131/C4
Tungsten, NW, Can. 180/D2
Tungurahua (prov.), Ecu. 210/B5
Tünhel, Mong. 128/J2
Tünis (cap.), Tun. 158/M6
Tūnis (gov.), Tun. 158/M6
Tunis, Gulf of (gulf), Tun. 158/M6
Tunisia (ctry.) 157/H2
Tunjá, Col. 210/C3
Tunliu, China 130/C3
Tunnels of Vinh Moc, Viet. 136/D2
Tuntum, Braz. 212/A2
Tuolumne (riv.), Ca, US 186/C3
Tupã, Braz. 213/B2
Tupaciguara, Braz. 213/B1
Tupai (isl.), FrPol. 175/K6
Tupambaé, Uru. 217/G2
Tuparro (riv.), Col. 210/D3
Tupi Paulista, Braz. 213/B2
Tupiza, Bol. 208/E8
Tupper Lake, NY, US 188/F2
Tupungato, Arg. 216/C2
Tupungato (peak), Arg. 216/C2
Tuquan, China 141/J3
Turabah, Saud. 146/D4
Turan, Rus. 123/L4
Turangi, NZ 175/T10
Turbaco, Col. 210/C2
Turbat, Pak. 147/H3
Turbenthal, Swi. 115/E3
Turbo, Col. 210/B2
Turbotville, Pa, US 196/B1
Turčiansky Svätý Martin, Slvk. 120/A2
Turckheim, Fr. 114/D1
Turda, Rom. 107/F2
Tureia (isl.), FrPol. 175/M7
Turek, Pol. 99/K2
Turgeon (riv.), Qu, Can. 188/E1
Türgovishte, Bul. 107/H4
Turgutlu, Turk. 148/A2
Turhal, Turk. 148/D1
Turia (riv.), Sp. 103/E3
Turiaçu, Braz. 209/J4
Türkeli, Turk. 148/C1
Türkeve, Hun. 106/E2
Turkey (ctry.) 148/C2
Türkheim, Ger. 115/G1
Türkistan (riv.), Ia, US 187/K2
Türkmenbashi (Krasnovodsk), Trkm. 121/J5
Turkmenistan (ctry.) 145/C5
Türkoğlu, Turk. 148/D2
Turks and Caicos (isls.), Haiti 199/G3
Turks Island Passage (isls.), UK 199/G3
Turku (int'l arpt.), Fin. 97/K1
Turku Ja Pori (prov.), Fin. 95/G3
Turkwel (riv.), Kenya 162/B2
Turlock, Ca, US 186/B3
Turmalina, Braz. 212/B5
Turneffe (isls.), Belz. 198/D4
Turner (mt.), Austl. 170/C2
Turnersville, NJ, US 196/C4
Turnhouse (int'l arpt.), Sc, UK 94/C5
Turnhout, Belg. 108/B6

Turnor Lake, Sk, Can. 184/F1
Turnov, Czh. 99/H3
Turnu Măgurele, Rom. 107/G4
Turpan, China 128/E3
Turpan (depr.), China 128/E3
Turquino (peak), Cuba 203/G2
Turriaco, It. 117/G1
Turrialba, Bol. 138/D3
Turriff, Sc, UK 94/D1
Turt, Mong. 128/H1
Turtle (isl.), SLeo. 160/B5
Turtleford, Sk, Can. 184/F2
Turugart (pass), China 145/K4
Turukhansk, Rus. 122/J3
Tuscaloosa, Al, US 191/G3
Tuscano (arch.), It. 104/B1
Tuscarora, Nv, US 184/D1
Tuscarora (mtn.), Pa, US 196/A3
Tuscarora Ind. Res., US 189/S9
Tuskegee, Al, US 191/G3
Tustin, Ca, US 194/G8
Tuszyn, Pol. 99/K3
Tutak, Turk. 148/E2
Tutayev, Rus. 118/H4
Tutin, Serb. 106/E4
Tutóia, Braz. 212/B1
Tutong, Bru. 138/D3
Tutrakan, Bul. 107/H3
Tuttle Creek (lake), Ks, US 187/J3
Tuttlingen, Ger. 114/F1
Tutuila (isl.), ASam. 175/H6
Tutupaca (vol.), Peru 214/D5
Tututalak (mtn.), Ak, US 192/F2
Tutzing, Ger. 115/H2
Tuusula, Fin. 97/L1
Tuvalu (ctry.) 174/G5
Tuwayq, Jabal (mts.), SAr. 146/E3
Tuxpan, Mex. 200/E5
Tuxpan, Mex. 200/D4
Tuxpan de Rodríguez Cano, Mex. 202/B1
Tuxtla Gutiérrez, Mex. 202/C2
Túy, Sp. 102/A1
Tuy Hoa, Viet. 136/E3
Tuyen Quang, Viet. 136/D1
Tuymazy, Rus. 119/M5
Tüysarkän, Iran 146/E2
Tuz (lake), It. 148/C2
Tūz Khurmātū, Iraq 148/F3
Tuzigoot Nat'l Mon., Az, US 186/D4
Tuzla, Bosn. 106/D3
Tuzla, Turk. 149/D1
Tuzluca, Turk. 148/E1
Tuzlukçu, Turk. 148/B2
Tvååker, Swe. 96/E3
Tvedestrand, Nor. 96/C2
Tver', Rus. 118/G4
Tverskaya Oblast, Rus. 97/P3
Tvertsa (riv.), Rus. 118/G4
Tvürditsa, Bul. 107/G4
Twardogóra, Pol. 99/J3
Tweed (riv.), Sc, UK 94/C5
Tweed Heads, Austl. 172/D5
Twello, Neth. 108/D4
Twente (canal), Neth. 108/D4
Twente (pol. reg.), Neth. 108/D4
Twin Buttes (res.), Tx, US 187/G5
Twin Hills, Ak, US 192/F4
Twin Lakes, Wi, US 193/P14
Twin Rivers, NJ, US 196/D3
Twistringen, Ger. 109/G6
Twistringen, Ger. 109/F3
Twizel, NZ 175/S11
Two Hills, Ab, Can. 184/F2
Two Rivers, Wi, US 185/M4
Twofold (bay), Austl. 173/D3
Twyford, Eng, UK 91/F4
Twymyn (riv.), Wal, UK 90/C1
Tyatya (vol.), Rus. 134/E1
Tydeley (riv.), Sc, US 138/D3
Tyldesley, Eng, UK 93/F4
Tylersville, Pa, US 196/A2
Tylertown, Ms, US 191/F4
Tyne (riv.), Sc, UK 94/D5
Tyne and Wear (co.), Eng, UK 93/G2
Tynemouth, Eng, UK 93/G1
Tynset, Nor. 95/D3
Tyonek, Ak, US 192/H3
Tyringe, Swe. 96/E3
Tyrnavos, Gre. 105/H2
Tyrnyauz, Rus. 121/G4
Tyrrell (lake), Austl. 173/B3
Tyrrhenian (sea), It. 104/B2
Tysnes, Nor. 96/A1
Tysnesøy (isl.), Nor. 96/A2
Tysons Corner, Va, US 196/A6
Tysse, Nor. 96/A1

Tystberga, Swe. 96/G2
Tyub-Karagan (pt.), Kaz. 121/J3
Tyuleniy (isl.), Rus. 121/H3
Tyumen' (int'l arpt.), Rus. 119/Q4
Tyumen', Rus. 119/Q4
Tyumenskaya Oblast, Rus. 145/E1
Tyva, Resp., Rus. 122/K4
Tzaneen, SAfr. 163/F5
Tzucacab, Mex. 202/D1

U

U.C.-Irvine, Ca, US 194/G8
U.K. Sovereign Base Area (gov.), Cyp. 149/C2
U.S. Naval Weapons Station, Ca, US 194/F8
U.S.S. Arizona Nat'l Mem., Hi, US 182/W13
Uad Assag (riv.), WSah. 156/B5
Uad Atui (riv.), WSah. 156/B5
Uad el Jat (riv.), WSah. 156/B4
Uad Tenuaiur (riv.), WSah. 156/A5
Uamh Bheag (peak), Sc, UK 94/B4
Uatumã (riv.), Braz. 208/G4
Uauá, Braz. 212/C3
Uaupés (riv.), Braz. 208/E3
Uaxactún (ruin), Guat. 202/D2
Ubá, Braz. 213/D2
Ubach-Palenberg, Ger. 111/F2
Ubagan (riv.), Kaz. 119/Q5
Ubaitaba, Braz. 212/C4
Ubajara, Braz. 212/C4
Ubajara, PN de, Braz. 212/B1
Ubangi (riv.), D.R. Congo 151/K4
Ubatã, Braz. 212/C4
Ubatuba, Braz. 213/H8
Ubay, Phil. 137/D5
Ubaye (riv.), Fr. 101/G4
Ube, Japan 132/B4
Ubeda, Sp. 102/D3
Uberaba (lake), Braz. 208/G7
Uberaba, Braz. 213/C1
Überherrn, Ger. 111/F5
Uberlândia, Braz. 213/B1
Überlingen, Ger. 115/F2
Überlingersee (lake), Ger. 115/E2
Ubon Ratchathani, Thai. 136/D3
Ubrique, Sp. 102/C4
Ubundu, D.R. Congo 155/L8
Ucayali (dept.), Peru 214/D4
Ucayali (riv.), Peru 214/C3
Uccle, Belg. 111/D2
Ucha (riv.), Rus. 119/W9
Uchaly, Rus. 119/N5
Uchinada, India 144/D5
Uchinskoye (res.), Rus. 119/W9
Uchiza, Peru 214/B3
Uchte, Ger. 109/F3
Uchte (riv.), Ger. 98/F2
Uchumarca, Peru 214/B2
Uchumayo, Peru 214/D5
Uchur (riv.), Rus. 123/P4
Ucker (riv.), Ger. 96/E5
Uckermark (reg.), Ger. 99/G2
Uckfield, Eng, UK 91/G5
Ucluelet, BC, Can. 184/B3
Udagamandalam, India 140/C5
Udaipur, India 147/K4
Udaipura, India 142/B4
Uddevalla, Swe. 96/D2
Uddingston, Sc, UK 94/B5
Uddjaure (lake), Swe. 95/F2
Udem, Ger. 108/D5
Udenhout, Neth. 108/C5
Udgir, India 140/C4
Udhampur, India 144/C3
Udine (prov.), It. 117/G1
Udine, It. 101/K3
Udipi, India 140/D5
Udmurtia, Resp., Rus. 119/L4
Udon Thani, Thai. 136/C2
Ueckermünde, Ger. 99/P2
Ueda, Japan 133/F2
Uelsen, Ger. 108/D3
Uelzen, Ger. 109/H3
Ueno, Japan 135/E1
Ueno, Japan 135/J6
Uenohara, Japan 133/F3
Uetendorf, Swi. 114/D4
Uetersen, Ger. 109/G1
Uetze, Ger. 109/H3

Uffenheim, Ger. 112/D3
Uffing, Ger. 115/H2
Ugalla (riv.), Tanz. 162/A4
Ugalla River Game Rsv., Tanz. 162/A4
Uganda (ctry.) 162/B2
Ugento, It. 105/F3
Ugie (riv.), Sc, UK 94/E1
Ugine, Fr. 114/C6
Uglich, Rus. 118/H4
Ugod, Hun. 106/C2
Ugra (riv.), Rus. 118/G5
Ugürchin, Bul. 107/G4
Uherské Hradiště, Czh. 99/J4
Uhingen, Ger. 112/C5
Úhlava (riv.), Czh. 99/G4
Úhlava (riv.), Czh. 113/F3
Uibaí, Braz. 212/B3
Uíge, Ang. 163/C2
Üíhüng, SKor. 131/E4
Üijöngbu, SKor. 131/G6
Üiju, NKor. 131/D3
Uilkraal (riv.), SAfr. 164/L11
Uilpata (peak), Rus. 121/G4
Uinta (mts.), Ut, US 186/E2
Uintah, Ut, US 195/K11
Uiraúna, Braz. 212/C2
Üíryöng, SKor. 131/E5
Üisöng, SKor. 131/E4
Uitenhage, SAfr. 164/D4
Uitgeest, Neth. 108/B3
Uithoorn, Neth. 108/B4
Uithuizen, Neth. 108/D2
Ujae (isl.), Mrsh. 174/F4
Ujelang (isl.), Mrsh. 174/F4
Ujfehértó, Hun. 99/L5
Ujhāni, India 142/B1
Uji, Japan 135/K6
Uji (riv.), Japan 132/D3
Ujitawara, Japan 135/K6
Ujjain, India 147/L4
Ujung Pandang, Indo. 139/E5
Ukara (isl.), Tanz. 162/B3
Ukerewe (isl.), Tanz. 162/B3
Ukhta, Rus. 119/M3
Ukiah, Ca, US 186/B3
Uklāna, India 144/C5
Ukmergė, Lith. 97/L4
Ukraine (ctry.) 120/D2
Ulaanbaatar (cap.), Mong. 128/J2
Ulaangom, Mong. 128/F2
Ulaanjirem, Mong. 128/J2
Ulanhot, China 129/M2
Ulchin, SKor. 131/E4
Ulcumayo, Peru 214/C3
Ulefoss, Nor. 96/C2
Ulemiste (int'l arpt.), Est. 97/L2
Ulhäsnagar, India 147/K5
Uliastay, Mong. 128/G2
Ulindi (riv.), D.R. Congo 155/L8
Ulithi (isl.), Micr. 174/C3
Ulja, Serb. 106/E3
Ulken Borsyq Qumy (des.), Kaz. 145/C3
Ulken-Qobda (riv.), Kaz. 121/K2
Ulla (riv.), Sp. 102/A1
Ulla Ulla, Bol. 214/D4
Ulla Ulla, Reserva Nacional, Bol. 214/D4
Ulladulla, Austl. 173/D2
Ullapool, Sc, UK 89/R8
Ullared, Swe. 96/E3
Ulldecona, Sp. 103/F2
Ullensvang, Nor. 96/B1
Ulló, Hun. 107/R10
Ullsfjorden (estu.), Nor. 95/F1
Ullswater (lake), Eng, UK 93/F2
Ulm, Ger. 112/C6
Ulmarra, Austl. 173/E1
Ulmen, Ger. 111/F3
Ulricehamn, Swe. 96/E3
Ulrichen, Swi. 115/E5
Ulrichsberg, Aus. 113/G5
Ulrichstein, Ger. 112/C1
Ulrum, Neth. 108/D2
Ulsan, SKor. 131/E5
Ulsteinvik, Nor. 95/C3
Ulster (reg.), Ire. 92/A3
Ulster (riv.), Ger. 112/C1
Ulster American Folk Park, NI, UK 92/A2
Ulúa (riv.), Hon. 202/E3
Uluçınar, Turk. 149/D1
Uludağ (peak), Turk. 148/B1
Uludoruk (peak), Turk. 146/D1
Uluguru (mts.), Tanz. 162/C4
Ulukışla, Turk. 148/C2
Ulundi, SAfr. 165/E3
Uluru NP, Austl. 171/F3
Ulverston, Eng, UK 93/E3
Ulverstone, Austl. 173/C4
Ulvik, Nor. 96/B1
Ulvila, Fin. 97/J1
Ul'yanovka, Rus. 97/P2
Ul'yanovsk, Rus. 119/L5
Ul'yanovskaya Oblast, Rus. 121/H1
Ulytaū (mts.),Kaz. 145/E3
Ulytau (peak), Kaz. 145/E3
Umag, Cro. 106/A3
Uman', Ukr. 120/D2
Umán, Mex. 202/D1
Umarizal, Braz. 212/C2
Umarkot, India 140/D4
Umāsi La (pass), India 144/D3

Umbogintwini, SAfr. 165/E3
Umboi (isl.), PNG 174/D5
Umbrail (peak), Swi. 115/G4
Umbrailpass (pass), Swi. 115/G4
Umbria (prov.), It. 101/K5
Umeå (int'l arpt.), Swe. 95/G3
Umeå, Swe. 95/F2
Umeälven (riv.), Swe. 95/F2
Unter Pleichfeld, Ger. 112/D3
Umfolozi (riv.), SAfr. 165/E3
Umgeni (riv.), SAfr. 165/E3
Umhausen, Aus. 115/G3
Umiat, Ak, US 192/H2
Umkirch, Ger. 114/D1
Umkomaas, SAfr. 165/E3
Umm Durmän, Sudan 155/M4
Umm el Fahm, Isr. 149/G6
Umm Hibal (well), Egypt 159/C4
Ummendorf, Ger. 115/F1
Umnak (isl.), Ak, US 192/E5
Umnak Pass (chan.), Ak, US 192/E5
Umpqua (riv.), Or, US 184/C5
Umraniye, Turk. 148/B2
Ümsöng, SKor. 131/D4
Umtata, SAfr. 164/E3
Umurbey, Turk. 105/K2
Umziimvubu (riv.), SAfr. 164/E3
Unzen-Amakusa NP, Japan 132/A4
Unzen-dake (peak), Japan 132/B4
Unzha (riv.), Rus. 122/E4
Uozu, Japan 133/E2
Upala, CR 203/E4
Upanema, Braz. 212/C2
Upata, Ven. 211/F2
Upemba, Lac (lake), D.R. Congo 163/E2
Upemba, PN de l', D.R. Congo 163/E2
Uphall, Sc, UK 94/C5
Upington, SAfr. 164/C3
Upland, Pa, US 196/C4
Upleta, India 147/K4
Upolu (pt.), Hi, US 182/U10
Upolu (isl.), Sam. 175/H6
Upper (lake), Ca, US 186/B2
Upper (pen.), Mi, US 188/C2
Upper (bay), NY, US 196/D2
Upper Arrow (lake), BC, Can. 184/D3
Underwood, ND, US 185/H4
Upper Darby, Pa, US 196/C4
Upper Demerara-Berbice (pol. reg.), Guy. 211/G3
Upper East (pol. reg.), Gha. 161/E4
Upper Engadine (valley), Swi. 115/G4
Upper Falls, Md, US 196/B5
Upper Ganges (canal), India 142/A1
Upper Hutt, NZ 175/T11
Upper Iowa (riv.), Ia, US 187/J2
Upper Klamath (lake), Or, US 184/C5
Upper Lough Erne (lake), NI, UK 89/Q9
Upper Missouri River Breaks Nat'l Mon., Mt, US 184/F4
Upper Peoria (lake), Il, US 185/L5
Upper Red (lake), Mn, US 185/K3
Upper Rouge (riv.), Mi, US 193/F7
Upper Saddle River, NJ, US 197/J7
Upper Takutu-Upper Essequibo (pol. reg.), Guy. 211/G4
Upper Thames (valley), Eng, UK 91/E3
Upper Trajan's Wall, Mol. 120/D3
Upper West (pol. reg.), Gha. 161/E4
Upperlands, NI, UK 92/B2
Upplands-Väsby, Swe. 96/G2
Uppsala, Swe. 96/G2
Uppsala (co.), Swe. 95/F3
Upright (cape), Ak, US 192/D3
Upstart (cape), Austl. 172/B2
Upton, Wy, US 185/G4
Urabá (gulf), Col. 210/B2
Uracoa, Ven. 211/F2
Urad Qianqi, China 130/B2
Uraga (chan.), Japan 135/D3
Urahoro, Japan 134/C2
Uraim (riv.), Braz. 212/A1
Urakawa, Japan 134/C2
Ural (mts.), Rus. 85/L2
Uralla, Austl. 173/D1
Urana, Austl. 173/C2
Urandi, Braz. 212/B4
Uraricoera (riv.), Braz. 211/F4
Urasoe, Japan 133/J7
Uray, Rus. 122/G3
Urayasu, Japan 135/D3
Urbach, Ger. 112/C5
Urbana, Md, US 196/A5
Urbania, It. 117/F5
Urbano Santos, Braz. 212/B1
Urbenville, Austl. 172/D5
Urbino, It. 117/F5
Urcos, Peru 214/D4
Urda, Sp. 102/D3
Urdinarrain, Arg. 217/J10
Urdorf, Swi. 115/E3

Ure (riv.), Eng, UK 93/G3
Ures, Mex. 200/C2
Ureshino, Japan 135/K6
Urewera NP, NZ 175/T10
Urfa (prov.), Turk. 148/D2
Urfa, Turk. 148/D2
Urft (riv.), Ger. 109/G6
Urft (lake), Ger. 111/F2
Urganch, Uzb. 145/D4
Urgnano, It. 116/C1
Urho Kekkosen NP, Fin. 95/H1
Uri, India 144/C2
Uri-Rotstock (peak), Swi. 115/E4
Uriangato, Mex. 200/E5
Uribante (riv.), Ven. 210/D3
Uribia, Col. 210/D2
Urie (riv.), Sc, UK 94/D2
Uriménil, Fr. 114/C1
Urique (riv.), Mex. 200/D3
Urjala, Fin. 97/K1
Urk, Neth. 108/C3
Urla, Turk. 148/A2
Urlaţi, Rom. 107/H3
Urmar, India 144/C4
Urmia (lake), Iran 148/F2
Urmitz, Ger. 111/G3
Urmston, Eng, UK 93/F5
Urnäsch, Swi. 115/F3
Urnersee (lake), Swi. 115/E4
Uroševac, Kos. 106/E4
Urr Water (riv.), Sc, UK 92/E1
Ursensollen, Ger. 113/E4
Ursulo Galván, Mex. 201/N7
Uruaçu, Braz. 209/J6
Uruapan, Mex. 200/E5
Urubamba (riv.), Peru 208/D6
Urubamba, Peru 214/C4
Urubu (riv.), Braz. 208/G4
Uruburetama, Braz. 212/C1
Uruçuca, Braz. 212/C4
Uruçuí, Braz. 212/A2
Uruçuí Preto (riv.), Braz. 212/A3
Uruçuí, Serra do (mts.), Braz. 209/K5
Urucuia (riv.), Braz. 209/J7
Uruguaiana, Braz. 215/E2
Uruguay (ctry.) 215/E3
Uruguay (riv.), SAm. 215/G2
Urumaco, Ven. 210/D2
Ürümqi, China 128/E3
Urunga, Austl. 173/E1
Uruoca, Braz. 212/B1
Urup (isl.), Rus. 125/Q5
Ururi, Fr. 104/D2
Urussanga, Braz. 213/B4
Uryupinsk, Rus. 121/G2
Urziceni, Rom. 107/H3
Us, Fr. 88/H4
Usa, Japan 132/B4
Usa (riv.), Rus. 122/F3
Uşak, Turk. 148/B2
Uşak (prov.), Turk. 148/B2
Usakos, Namb. 163/B5
Usborne (mt.), UK 217/F6
Uscio, It. 116/C4
Usedom (isl.), Ger. 96/E4
Useldange, Lux. 111/E4
Useless Loop, Austl. 170/B3
Ushibori, Japan 135/F2
Ushibuka, Japan 132/B4
Ushiku, Japan 135/E2
Ushtobe, Kaz. 145/G3
Ushuaia, Arg. 217/C7
Usibelli, Ak, US 192/J3
Usicayos, Peru 214/D4
Usilampatti, India 140/C6
Usingen, Ger. 112/B2
Usküp, Turk. 107/H5
Uslar, Ger. 109/G5
Usman', Rus. 120/F1
Uspallata, Arg. 216/C2
Uspallata, Paso de (pass), Chile 216/N8
Usquil, Peru 214/B2
Ussel, Fr. 100/E4
Ussel, Fr. 112/D5
Usses (riv.), Fr. 114/C5
Ussuri (riv.), China,Rus. 123/P5
Ussuriysk, Rus. 129/P3
Ussy-sur-Marne, Fr. 88/M5
Ust'-Ilimsk, Rus. 123/L4
Ust'-Kamchatsk, Rus. 123/S4
Ust'-Kut, Rus. 123/L4
Ust'-Ordynskiy Buryatskiy Aut. Okrug, Rus. 123/S4
Ustěk, Czh. 113/H1
Uster, Swi. 115/E3
Ústí nad Labem, Czh. 101/L1
Ustica (isl.), It. 104/C3
Ustica, It. 104/C3
Ustka, Pol. 96/G4
Ustrzyki Dolne, Pol. 99/M4
Ust'ya (riv.), Rus. 119/K3
Ustyurt (plat.), Kaz. 125/D5
Usu, China 128/D3
Usuda, Japan 135/A1
Usuki, Japan 132/B4
Usulután, ESal. 202/D3
Usumacinta (riv.), Mex. 198/C4
Utah (state), US 195/K13
Utah (co.), Ut, US 195/K13
Utah (lake), Ut, US 186/D2
Utangan (riv.), India 142/A2
Utano, Japan 135/J7

Utashinai, Japan 134/C2
Utena, Lith. 97/L4
Uterský (riv.), Czh. 113/G3
Uthai Thani, Thai. 136/C2
Utiel, Sp. 102/E3
Utica, NY, US 188/F3
Utica, Mi, US 193/F6
Utik (lake), Mb, Can. 185/J2
Utila (isl.), Hon. 202/E2
Utinga, Braz. 212/B4
Utirik (isl.), Mrsh. 174/G3
Utiroa, Kiri. 174/G5
Utmänzai, Pak. 144/A2
Utopia Abor. Land, Austl. 171/G2
Utraulā, India 142/D2
Utrecht, SAfr. 165/E2
Utrecht, Neth. 108/C4
Utrecht (prov.), Neth. 108/C4
Utrera, Sp. 102/C4
Utsunomiya, Japan 133/F2
Uttar Pradesh (state), India 140/C2
Uttaradit, Thai. 136/C2
Uttarranchal (state), India 142/B1
Uttenweiler, Ger. 115/F1
Uttoxeter, Eng, UK 93/G6
Utuado, PR 199/M8
Utuverdeja, It. 102/C3
Utupua (isl.), Sol. 174/F6
Uturoa, FrPol. 175/K6
Utzenstorf, Swi. 114/D3
Uusikaupunki, Fin. 97/J1
Uusimaa (prov.), Fin. 95/H3
Uva (riv.), Col. 208/E3
Uvalde, Tx, US 187/H5
Uvarovo, Rus. 121/G2
Uverito, Ven. 211/E2
Uvira, D.R. Congo 162/A3
Uvongo, SAfr. 165/E3
Uvs (prov.), Mong. 128/F2
Uwajima, Japan 132/C4
Uwimmerah (riv.), Indo. 139/K5
Uxin Qi, China 130/B3
Uxmal (ruin), Mex. 202/D1
Uydzin, Mong. 128/J3
Uyo, Nga. 161/G5
Uyönch, Mong. 128/F2
Uyuni, Bol. 208/E8
Uzbekistan (ctry.) 145/D4
Uzbekistan Nat'l Park, Uzb. 145/E3
Uzein (int'l arpt.), Fr. 100/C5
Uzerche, Fr. 100/F4
Uzès, Fr. 100/F4
Uzhhorod, Ukr. 99/M4
Užice, Serb. 106/D4
Uzlovaya, Rus. 120/F1
Uznach, Swi. 115/E3
Üzümlü, Turk. 148/D2
Üzümköprü, Turk. 105/K2
Uzwil, Swi. 115/F3

V

V.P. Rosales, PN, Chile 216/N6
Vaal (riv.), SAfr. 164/D2
Vaalbos NP, SAfr. 164/D3
Vaaldam (res.), SAfr. 164/D2
Vaals, Neth. 111/F2
Vaalserberg (hill), Neth. 111/E2
Vaasa (prov.), Fin. 95/G3
Vaasa (int'l arpt.), Fin. 95/G3
Vaasa (Vasa), Fin. 95/G3
Vaassen, Neth. 108/C4
Vác, Hun. 106/D2
Vaca (mt.), Ca, US 193/K10
Vachon (riv.), Qu, Can. 181/J2
Vada, It. 116/D6
Vado Ligure, It. 116/B4
Vadsø, Nor. 95/J1
Vadstena, Swe. 96/F2
Vaduz (cap.), Lcht. 115/F3
Vaernes (int'l arpt.), Nor. 95/D3
Vaga (riv.), Rus. 118/J3
Vågå, Nor. 95/E1
Våganski vrh (peak), Cro. 106/C3
Vagney, Fr. 114/C1
Vagos, Port. 102/A2
Vågsøy, Nor. 95/C3
Vahitahi (isl.), FrPol. 175/M6
Vaiano, It. 117/E5
Vaiano Cremasco, It. 116/C1
Vaich (lake), Sc, UK 94/B1
Vaihingen an der Enz, Ger. 112/B5
Vaijāpur, India 147/K5
Vail, Co, US 187/F3
Vailate, It. 116/C1
Vaisali (riv.), India 142/B2
Vaitupu (isl.), Tuv. 174/G5
Vaivre-et-Montoille, Fr. 114/C2
Vakfıkebir, Turk. 122/F4
Vakhan (mts.), Afg. 147/K1

Vakhsh (riv.), Taj. 147/J1
Vál, Hun. 106/D2
Val-de-Marne (dept.), Fr. 110/B6
Val-d'Or, Qu, Can. 188/E1
Val Lagarina (valley), It. 117/D1
Val Marie, Sk, Can. 184/G3
Val Venosta (valley), It. 115/G4
Val Verda, Ut, US 195/K12
Val Verde, Ca, US 194/B2
Valais (canton), Swi. 114/C5
Valbo, It. 96/G1
Valburg, Neth. 108/C5
Valcheta, Arg. 216/D4
Valdagno, It. 117/E1
Valdahon, Fr. 114/C3
Valdai (hills), Rus. 118/G4
Valdarno (valley), It. 117/E5
Valdecañas, Embalse de (res.), Sp. 102/C3
Valdemarsvik, Swe. 96/G2
Valdemorillo, Sp. 103/M8
Valdense, Uru. 217/K11
Valdepeñas, Sp. 102/D3
Valderas, Sp. 102/C1
Valderrobres, Sp. 103/F2
Valdés (pen.), Arg. 216/E4
Valdeverdeja, It. 102/C3
Valdez, Ak, US 192/J3
Valdez, Ecu. 210/B4
Valdivia, Col. 210/C3
Valdivia, Chile 216/B3
Valdobbiadene, It. 117/F1
Valdoie, Fr. 114/C2
Valdosta, Ga, US 191/H4
Valdoviño, Sp. 102/A1
Vale, Or, US 184/D5
Vale of Glamorgan (co.), Wal, UK 90/C4
Valemount, BC, Can. 184/D2
Valença, Braz. 212/C4
Valença, Braz. 213/K7
Valença do Piauí, Braz. 212/B2
Valence, Fr. 100/F4
Valence, Fr. 100/F4
Valence-sur-Baïse, Fr. 100/D5
Valencia, Ven. 208/E1
Valencia (int'l arpt.), Sp. 103/E3
Valencia, Sp. 103/E3
Valencia (aut. comm.), Sp. 102/E3
Valencia, Ecu. 210/B5
Valencia (isl.), Ire. 88/P11
Valencia de Alcántara, Sp. 102/B3
Valencia de Don Juan, Sp. 102/C1
Valencia, Golfo de (gulf), Sp. 103/F3
Valenciennes, Fr. 110/C3
Valendas, Swi. 115/F4
Vălenii de Munte, Rom. 107/H3
Valente, Braz. 212/C3
Valentigney, Fr. 114/C3
Valentim (range), Braz. 212/B2
Valentine, Tx, US 190/B4
Valentines, Uru. 217/G2
Valenton, Fr. 88/K5
Valenza, It. 116/B2
Våler, Nor. 96/D1
Våler, Nor. 96/D2
Valera, Ven. 210/D2
Valff, Fr. 114/D1
Valga, Est. 97/M3
Valhalla, NY, US 197/K7
Valinco, Golfe de (gulf), Fr. 104/A2
Valinhos, Braz. 213/F7
Valkeakoski, Fin. 97/K1
Valkeala, Fin. 97/M1
Valkenburg, Neth. 111/E2
Valkenswaard, Neth. 108/C6
Vall de Uxó, Sp. 103/F3
Valladolid (int'l arpt.), Sp. 102/C2
Valladolid, Sp. 102/C2
Valladolid, Mex. 202/D1
Valle, Ecu. 210/B5
Valle d'Aosta (pol. reg.), It. 101/G4
Valle de Bravo, Mex. 201/D5
Valle de Cauca (dept.), Col. 210/B4
Valle de Guanape, Ven. 211/E2
Valle de La Pascua, Ven. 208/E2
Valle de Santiago, Mex. 201/E4
Valle de Zaragoza, Mex. 190/B5
Valle Hermoso, Mex. 201/F3
Valle Lomellina, It. 116/B2
Valle Mosso, It. 116/B1
Vallecitos de Zaragoza, Mex. 201/E5
Vallecrosia, It. 101/G5
Valledupar, Col. 210/C2
Vallée de l'Azaouak (riv.), Mali 161/G2

Vallée du Ferlo (riv.), Sen. 160/B3
Vallée du Mboune (riv.), Sen. 160/B3
Valleé du Saloum (riv.), Sen. 160/B3
Vallée du Serpent (riv.), Mali 160/C3
Vallegrande, Bol. 208/F7
Vallehermoso, Sp. 156/A3
Vallejo, Ca, US 186/B3
Vallenar, Chile 215/B2
Vallendar, Ger. 111/G3
Valleroy, Fr. 111/E5
Valletta (cap.), Malta 104/M7
Valley Brook, Ok, US 195/N15
Valley Center, Ca, US 194/C4
Valley City, ND, US 185/J4
Valley Cottage, NY, US 197/K7
Valley East, On, Can. 188/D2
Valley Forge Nat'l Hist. Park, Pa, US 196/C3
Valley of Desolation, SAfr. 164/D4
Valley of the Kings, Egypt 159/C3
Valley Park, Mo, US 195/G8
Valley Spring, Tx, US 187/H5
Valley Stream, NY, US 197/L9
Vallière (riv.), Fr. 114/B4
Vallorbe, Swi. 114/C4
Valls, Sp. 103/F2
Valluga (peak), Aus. 115/G3
Valmayor (res.), Sp. 103/M8
Valme (riv.), Ger. 109/F6
Valmeyer, Il, US 195/G9
Valmiera, Lat. 97/L3
Valmondois, Fr. 88/J4
Valognes, Fr. 100/C2
Valois (reg.), Fr. 110/B5
Valona, Bay of (bay), Alb. 105/F2
Valpaços, Port. 102/B2
Vālpārai, India 140/C5
Valparaiso, Fl, US 191/G4
Valparaiso, In, US 188/C3
Valparaiso, Mex. 200/E4
Valparaíso (pol. reg.), Chile 216/C2
Valparaíso, Chile 216/N8
Valpovo, Cro. 106/D3
Valréas, Fr. 100/F4
Vals (riv.), SAfr. 164/D2
Vals, Swi. 115/F4
Vals-les-Bains, Fr. 100/F4
Valsād, India 147/K4
Valsaquillo (res.), Mex. 201/L8
Valsbaai (bay), SAfr. 163/C7
Valserine (riv.), Fr. 114/B5
Valserrhein (riv.), Swi. 115/F4
Valsura (riv.), It. 115/G4
Valtellina (valley), It. 115/F5
Valtice, Czh. 101/M2
Valuyki, Rus. 120/F2
Valverde, Sp. 156/A4
Valverde del Camino, Sp. 102/B4
Valyermo, Ca, US 194/C2
Vâmhus, Swe. 96/F1
Vammala, Fin. 97/K1
Vámos, Gre. 105/J5
Vámosmikola, Hun. 106/D2
Vámospércs, Hun. 106/E2
Van, Turk. 148/E2
Van (lake), Turk. 148/E2
Van Buren, Me, US 189/H2
Van Buren, Ar, US 187/J4
Van Cortlandt Park, NY, US 197/K8
Van Diemen (cape), Austl. 167/C2
Van Diemen (gulf), Austl. 167/C2
Van Harinxmakanaal (riv.), Neth. 108/C2
Van Horn, Tx, US 187/F5
Van Norman Lakes, Ca, US 194/B2
Van Rees (mts.), Indo. 139/J4
Van Wert, Oh, US 188/C3
Vana-Javesi (lake), Fin. 97/K1
Vanadzor, Arm. 121/H4
Vanavaro (isl.), FrPol. 175/L7
Vancouver (mt.), Yk, Can. 192/L3
Vancouver, Wa, US 184/C4
Vancouver, BC, Can. 184/C3
Vancouver (int'l arpt.), BC, Can. 184/C3
Vancouver (cape), Austl. 170/C5
Vancouver (isl.), BC, Can. 180/D4
Vandalia, Mo, US 187/K3
Vandans, Aus. 115/F3
Vanderbijlpark, SAfr. 164/D2
Vanderbilt Museum, NY, US 197/E2
Vanderhoof, BC, Can. 184/B2
Vandœuvre-lès-Nancy, Fr. 111/F6
Vanegas, Mex. 201/E4

Vänern (lake), Swe. 96/E2
Vänersborg, Swe. 96/E2
Vangaindrano, Madg. 165/H8
Vanier (int'l arpt.), Nun., Can. 181/R7
Vanikolo (isl.), Sol. 174/F6
Vanil Noir (peak), Swi. 114/D4
Vanimo, PNG 174/D5
Vännäs, Swe. 95/F3
Vanne (riv.), Fr. 100/D2
Vannes, Fr. 100/B3
Vanoise, PN de la, Fr. 101/G4
Vanreenenpas (pass), SAfr. 164/D3
Vanrhynsdorp, SAfr. 164/B3
Vansbro, Swe. 96/F1
Vanse, Nor. 96/B2
Vansittart (isl.), Nun., Can. 181/H2
Vantaa, Fin. 97/L1
Vanua Levu (isl.), Fiji 174/G6
Vanuatu (ctry.) 174/F6
Vanwyksvlei, SAfr. 164/C3
Var (riv.), Fr. 101/G5
Vara (riv.), It. 116/C4
Vara, Swe. 96/E2
Varadero, Cuba 203/F1
Varaita (riv.), It. 116/A3
Varallo, It. 116/B1
Vārāmin, Iran 146/F1
Vārānasi, India 142/D3
Varanger-Halvøya (pen.), Nor. 95/J1
Varangerfjorden (estu.), Nor. 95/J1
Varangéville, Fr. 111/F6
Varano (lake), It. 104/D2
Varano Borghi, It. 116/B1
Varaždin, Cro. 101/M3
Varazze, It. 116/B4
Varberg, Swe. 96/E3
Vardar (riv.), FYROM 105/G2
Varde, Den. 96/C4
Várdha, Gre. 105/G3
Vardø, Nor. 95/J1
Varel, Ger. 109/F2
Varenne (riv.), Fr. 100/C2
Varennes, Qu, Can. 189/P6
Varennes-Jarcy, Fr. 88/K5
Varennes-Vauzelles, Fr. 100/E3
Vareš, Bosn. 106/D3
Varese, It. 116/B1
Varese (prov.), It. 115/E6
Varese Ligure, It. 116/C4
Vårgårda, Swe. 96/E2
Vargem do Sul, Braz. 213/G6
Vargem Grande, Braz. 212/B1
Varginha, Braz. 213/H6
Vári, Gre. 105/H4
Varilhes, Fr. 100/D5
Vārmeln (lake), Swe. 96/E2
Värmland (co.), Swe. 95/E3
Varna, Bul. 107/H4
Varna (pol. reg.), Bul. 107/H4
Värnamo, Swe. 96/F3
Varois-et-Chaignot, Fr. 114/B3
Varto, Turk. 148/E2
Vartry (riv.), Ire. 92/B5
Vartry (riv.), Ire. 92/B5
Várzea Alegre, Braz. 212/C2
Várzea da Palma, Braz. 212/A5
Várzea Grande, Braz. 209/G7
Várzea Grande, Braz. 212/B2
Varzelândia, Braz. 212/A4
Varzi, It. 116/C3
Varzo, It. 115/E5
Varzuga (riv.), Rus. 118/H2
Vas (prov.), Hun. 106/C2
Vasa Barris (riv.), Braz. 209/L5
Vásárosnamény, Hun. 99/M4
Vaşcău, Rom. 106/F2
Vashka (riv.), Rus. 119/K2
Vashon, Wa, US 193/C2
Vashon (isl.), Wa, US 193/C3
Vasilikí, Gre. 105/F3
Vasil'yevskiy (isl.), Rus. 119/S7
Vaslui (prov.), Rom. 107/H2
Vaslui, Rom. 107/H2
Vassar, Mi, US 188/D3
Vassdalsegga (peak), Nor. 96/B2
Vassouras, Braz. 213/K7
Västerås, Swe. 96/G2
Västerbotten (co.), Swe. 95/F2
Västerdalälven (riv.), Swe. 96/E1
Västernorrland (co.), Swe. 95/F3
Västervik, Swe. 96/G3
Västmanland (co.), Swe. 95/E3
Vasto, It. 104/D1
Västra Silen (lake), Swe. 96/E2

Vasvár, Hun. 106/C2
Vasyl'kiv, Ukr. 120/D2
Vaterstetten, Ger. 113/E6
Vatican City (ctry.) 104/C2
Vatnajökull (glacier), Ice. 95/P7
Vatomandry, Madg. 165/J7
Vatra Dornei, Rom. 107/G2
Vättern (lake), Swe. 95/K4
Vaucouleurs (riv.), Fr. 88/J5
Vaud (canton), Swi. 114/C4
Vaudoy-en-Brie, Fr. 88/M5
Vaudreuil-Dorion, Qu, Can. 189/M7
Vaughan, On, Can. 189/Q8
Vaughn, NM, US 187/F4
Vaughn, Wa, US 193/B3
Vaulruz, Swi. 114/C4
Vaulx-en-Velin, Fr. 114/A6
Vaupés (dept.), Col. 210/D4
Vaupés (riv.), Col. 210/D4
Vauréal, Fr. 88/J4
Vauvert, Fr. 100/F5
Vauvillers, Fr. 114/C2
Vaux (riv.), Fr. 98/C4
Vaux-sur-Seine, Fr. 88/H4
Vaux-sur-Sûre, Belg. 111/E4
Vauxhall, Ab, Can. 184/E3
Vavatenina, Madg. 165/J7
Vava'u Group (isls.), Tonga 175/H6
Vavuniya, SrL. 140/D6
Vawkavysk, Bela. 99/N2
Vaxjo (int'l arpt.), Swe. 96/F3
Växjö, Swe. 96/F3
Vaygach (isl.), Rus. 218/B
Vazante, Braz. 213/A4
Vázea Paulista, Braz. 213/G8
Vazzola, It. 117/F1
Vecchiano, It. 116/D5
Vechigen, Swi. 114/D4
Vecht (riv.), Neth. 108/D3
Vechta, Ger. 109/F3
Vechte (riv.), Ger. 108/D3
Vecsés, Hun. 106/D2
Vedano Olona, It. 116/B1
Veddige, Swe. 96/E3
Vedea (riv.), Rom. 107/G3
Vedelago, It. 117/F1
Vedia, Arg. 216/E2
Vedra, Sp. 102/A1
Veendam, Neth. 108/D2
Veenendaal, Neth. 108/C4
Veere, Neth. 108/A5
Veerse Meer (res.), Neth. 108/A5
Vefsn, Nor. 95/E2
Vega, Tx, US 187/G4
Vega (pt.), Ak, US 192/B6
Vega (isl.), Nor. 95/D2
Vega de Alatorre, Mex. 201/N6
Vegafjorden (estu.), Nor. 95/D2
Veghel, Neth. 108/C5
Végueta, Peru 214/B3
Vehkalahti, Fin. 97/M1
Vehne (riv.), Ger. 109/F3
Veigné, Fr. 100/D3
Veinticinco de Mayo, Arg. 216/E2
Veinticinco de Mayo, Arg. 217/J3
Veinticinco de Mayo, Uru. 217/K11
Veintiocho de Mayo, Ecu. 214/B1
Veintiocho de Noviembre, Arg. 217/B6
Veitsch, Aus. 106/D2
Veitshöchheim, Ger. 112/C3
Vejen, Den. 96/C4
Vejer de la Frontera, Sp. 102/C4
Vejle, Den. 96/C4
Vejle (co.), Den. 96/C4
Vejprty, Czh. 113/G2
Vela, Cabo de la (pt.), Col. 210/D1
Vela Luka, Cro. 106/C4
Velaines, Fr. 111/E6
Vélan (peak), Swi. 114/D6
Velardeña, Mex. 201/J5
Velas, Azor., Port. 103/S12
Velasco Ibarra, Ecu. 210/B5
Velázquez, Uru. 217/K11
Velbert, Ger. 109/E6
Velburg, Ger. 113/E4
Velddrif, SAfr. 164/L10
Velden, Ger. 113/F6
Velden am Wörthersee, Aus. 101/L3
Velen, Ger. 108/D5
Velenje, Slov. 101/L3
Velešta, FYROM 105/G2
Velestíno, Gre. 105/H3
Vélez, Col. 210/C3
Vélez-Blanco, Sp. 102/D4
Vélez-Málaga, Sp. 102/D4
Vélez-Rubio, Sp. 102/D4
Velhas, Rio das (riv.), Braz. 209/K7
Velika Gorica, Cro. 106/C3
Velika Kladuša, Bosn. 101/L4
Velika Plana, Serb. 106/E3
Velikaya (riv.), Rus. 118/F4
Velikiy Ustyug, Rus. 119/K3

Velikiye Luki, Rus. 97/P3
Veliko Tŭrnovo, Bul. 107/G4
Velille, Peru 214/D4
Vélingara, Sen. 160/B3
Vel'ké Kapušany, Slvk. 106/F1
Vel'ký Krtíš, Slvk. 99/K4
Velký Zvon (peak), Czh. 113/F4
Vellberg, Ger. 112/C4
Velletri, It. 104/C2
Vellinge, Swe. 96/E4
Vellmar, Ger. 109/G6
Vellore, India 140/C5
Veln, Ger. 105/H4
Velopoúla (isl.), Gre. 105/H4
Velsen, Neth. 108/B4
Velten, Ger. 98/Q6
Velva, ND, US 185/H3
Velvary, Czh. 113/H2
Velvendós, Gre. 105/H2
Vémars, Fr. 88/K4
Vemb, Den. 96/C3
Véménd, Hun. 106/D2
Venachar (lake), Sc, UK 94/B4
Venafro, It. 104/D2
Venamo (peak), Ven. 211/F3
Venancio Aires, Braz. 213/A4
Venaria, It. 101/G4
Vence, Fr. 101/G5
Venceslau Brás, Braz. 213/B2
Vendas Novas, Port. 102/A3
Vendée (riv.), Fr. 100/C3
Vendôme, Fr. 100/D3
Vendrell, Sp. 103/F2
Vendrest, Fr. 88/M4
Veneta, Laguna (lake), It. 117/F2
Venetie, Ak, US 192/J2
Veneto (pol. reg.), It. 117/E1
Venezia (prov.), It. 117/F1
Venezia, Golfo di (gulf), Eur. 117/F2
Venezia (Venice), It. 117/F2
Venezuela (gulf), Col.,Ven. 211/D2
Venezuela (ctry.) 211/E3
Vengurla, India 147/K5
Veniaminof (vol.), Ak, US 192/G4
Venice, Fl, US 191/H5
Venice, Il, US 195/G8
Venice (Venezia), It. 101/K4
Vénissieux, Fr. 100/F4
Venjansjön (lake), Swe. 96/E1
Venkatagiri, India 140/C5
Vennesla, Nor. 96/B2
Veno (bay), Den. 96/C3
Venoge (riv.), Swi. 114/C4
Venosa, It. 104/D2
Venray, Neth. 108/C5
Vent, Iles du (isls.), FrPol. 175/L6
Venta (riv.), Lat. 97/J3
Venta de Baños, Sp. 102/C2
Ventauri (riv.), Ven. 208/E3
Ventersburg, SAfr. 164/D3
Ventersdorp, SAfr. 164/D2
Venterstad, SAfr. 164/D3
Ventimiglia, It. 101/G5
Ventiseri, Fr. 104/A2
Ventnor, Eng, UK 91/E5
Ventnor City, NJ, US 196/D5
Ventspils, Lat. 97/J3
Ventuari (riv.), Ven. 211/E3
Ventura (co.), Ca, US 194/A2
Ventura (riv.), Ca, US 194/A2
Venturina, It. 116/D5
Venturosa, Braz. 212/C3
Venustiano Carranza, Mex. 198/C4
Venustiano Carranza (res.), Mex. 201/E3
Vera, Arg. 215/D3
Vera, Sp. 102/E4
Vera Cruz, Pan. 210/B2
Veracruz-Llave (state), Mex. 201/N7
Veranópolis, Braz. 213/B4
Verāval, India 147/K4
Verbania, It. 115/E6
Verberie, Fr. 110/B5
Vercelli, It. 116/B2
Vercelli (prov.), It. 116/B2
Ver-sur-Launette, Fr. 88/L4

Verde Grande (riv.), Braz. 209/K7
Verden, Ger. 109/G3
Verdhikoússa, Gre. 105/G3
Verdigris (riv.), Ks, US 187/J3
Verdinho (riv.), Braz. 213/B1
Verdon (riv.), Fr. 100/F5
Verdugo (mts.), Ca, US 194/F7
Verdun, Qu, Can. 189/N7
Vereeniging, SAfr. 164/D2
Verena (peak), It. 115/H6
Vereshchagino, Rus. 119/M4
Veretskiy (pass), Ukr. 99/M4
Verga (cape), Gui. 160/B4
Vergara, Uru. 217/G2
Vergato, It. 117/E4
Vergennes, Vt, US 188/F2
Vergiate, It. 116/B1
Vergina (ruin), Gre. 105/H2
Verigenstadt, Ger. 115/F1
Verín, Sp. 102/B2
Veríssimo, Braz. 213/B1
Vermenagna (riv.), It. 116/A4
Vermilion, Ab, Can. 184/F2
Vermilion (riv.), Ab, Can. 184/F2
Vermilion (range), Mn, US 185/K4
Vermilion Cliffs Nat'l Mon., Az, US 186/D3
Vermillion, SD, US 185/J5
Vermont (state), US 189/F2
Vernazza, It. 116/C4
Verneuil-sur-Avre, Fr. 100/D2
Verneuil-sur-Seine, Fr. 88/H5
Verneukpan (salt pan), SAfr. 164/C3
Vernier, Swi. 114/C5
Vernon, BC, Can. 184/D3
Vernon, Fr. 100/D2
Vernon Hills, Il, US 193/Q15
Vernon Valley, NJ, US 196/D1
Vernouillet, Fr. 88/H5
Vero Beach, Fl, US 191/H5
Véroia, Gre. 105/H2
Verolanuova, It. 116/D2
Verolavecchia, It. 116/D2
Verolengo, It. 116/A2
Verona (prov.), It. 117/D1
Verona, Il, US 193/P16
Verona (int'l arpt.), It. 117/D2
Verona, It. 117/D2
Verona, NJ, US 197/J8
Verónica, Arg. 217/K11
Verrès, It. 116/A1
Verret, La, US 195/Q17
Verrières-le-Buisson, Fr. 88/J5
Versa (riv.), It. 116/B3
Versailles, Ky, US 188/C4
Versailles, Fr. 88/J5
Versmold, Ger. 109/F4
Versoix, Swi. 114/C5
Vert-le-Grand, Fr. 88/K6
Vert-le-Petit, Fr. 88/K6
Vert-Saint-Denis, Fr. 88/K6
Vertana (peak), It. 115/G4
Verte (peak), It. 114/C6
Vertemate, It. 116/C1
Vertientes, Cuba 203/G1
Vertou, Fr. 100/C3
Vertova, It. 116/D1
Vertus, Fr. 110/D6
Verviers, Belg. 111/E2
Vervins, Fr. 110/C4
Verwoerdburg, SAfr. 164/Q12
Veryan (bay), Eng, UK 90/B6
Verzasca (riv.), Swi. 115/E5
Verzasca (Gerra), Swi. 115/E5
Verzuolo, It. 101/G4
Verzy, Fr. 111/D5
Vescovato, Fr. 104/A1
Vescovato, It. 116/D2
Veselí nad Lužnicí, Czh. 113/H4
Veselyy (res.), Rus. 121/G3
Vesgre (riv.), Fr. 110/A6
Vesijärvi (lake), Fin. 97/L1
Vesle (riv.), Fr. 98/C4
Vesoul, Fr. 114/C2
Vespolate, It. 116/B2
Vest-Agder (co.), Nor. 95/C4
Vest-Sjælland (prov.), Den. 96/D4
Vest-Vlaanderen (prov.), Belg. 110/B2
Vestbjerg, Den. 96/C3
Vesterålen (isls.), Nor. 95/E1
Vestfjorden (inlet), Nor. 95/D2
Vestfold (co.), Nor. 95/D3

Vestmannaeyjar, Ice. 95/N7
Vestone, It. 116/D1
Vestvågøy, Nor. 95/E1
Vestvågøya (isl.),
Nor. 95/E1
Vesuvio (Vesuvius)
(vol.), It. 104/D2
Veszprém (prov.),
Hun. 106/C2
Veszprém, Hun. 106/C2
Vészto, Hun. 106/C2
Vet (riv.), SAfr. 164/D3
Vétheuil, Fr. 88/H4
Vetlanda, Swe. 96/F3
Vetluga (riv.), Rus. 122/E4
Vetralla, It. 104/C1
Vétraz, Fr. 114/C5
Větřní, Czh. 113/H6
Vettore (peak), It. 101/K5
Veude (riv.), Fr. 100/D3
Veurne, Belg. 110/B1
Vevey, Swi. 114/C5
Vex, Swi. 114/D5
Veybach (riv.), Ger. 111/F2
Veyle (riv.), Fr. 114/B5
Veyrier-du-Lac, Fr. 114/C6
Vézelise, Fr. 114/C1
Vézère (riv.), Fr. 100/D4
Vezirköprü, Turk. 148/C2
Vezza d'Oglio, It. 115/G5
Vezzano Ligure, It. 116/C4
Viacha, Bol. 208/E7
Viadana, It. 116/D3
Viana, Braz. 212/A1
Viana del Bollo, Sp. 102/B1
Viana do Alentejo,
Port. 102/A3
Viana do Castelo,
Port. 102/A2
Viana do Castelo (dist.),
Port. 102/A2
Vianden, Lux. 111/F4
Vianen, Neth. 108/C4
Viangchan (Vientiane)
(cap.), Laos 136/C2
Viar (riv.), Sp. 102/C4
Viareggio, It. 116/D5
Viarmes, Fr. 88/K4
Viaur (riv.), Fr. 100/E4
Vibbard, Mo, US 195/E5
Vibo Valentia, It. 104/E3
Viborg, Den. 96/C3
Viborg (co.), Den. 96/C3
Vic, Sp. 103/G2
Vic-en-Bigorre, Fr. 100/D5
Vic-Fezensac, Fr. 100/D5
Vicam, Mex. 200/C3
Vícar, Sp. 102/D4
Vicarello, It. 116/D5
Vicchio, It. 117/E6
Vice, Peru 214/A2
Vicente (pt.), Ca, US 194/F8
Vicente Guerrero,
Mex. 200/E4
Vicente Guerrero,
Mex. 200/A2
Vicente López, Arg. 217/J11
Vicenza, It. 117/E1
Vicenza (prov.), It. 115/H6
Vichada (riv.), Col. 208/E3
Vichada (dept.), Col. 210/D3
Vichaya, Bol. 214/D5
Vichuga, Rus. 118/J4
Vichy, Fr. 100/E3
Vickham (cape),
Austl. 173/B3
Vicksburg, Ms, US 187/K4
Vicksburg Nat'l Mil. Park,
Ms, US 187/K4
Vico, Fr. 104/A1
Vico (lake), It. 104/C1
Vico del Gargano, It. 106/B5
Vicopisano, It. 116/D5
Viçosa, Braz. 212/C3
Viçosa, Braz. 213/D2
Viçosa do Ceará,
Braz. 212/B1
Vicosoprano, Swi. 115/F5
Vicou Gorge NP, Gre. 105/G3
Vicq, Fr. 88/H5
Victor Harbor, Austl. 171/H5
Víctor Rosales,
Mex. 200/E4
Victoria, Malay. 138/E2
Victoria (peak), Phil. 139/E2
Victoria, Austl. 173/B2
Victoria (falls), Zim. 163/E4
Victoria, Arg. 215/D3
Victoria (cap.),
BC, Can. 184/C3
Victoria (riv.), Austl. 167/C2
Victoria (state),
Austl. 173/C3
Victoria, China 141/K3
Victoria (mt.), Myan. 141/F3
Victoria, Rom. 107/G3
Victoria, Hon. 202/E3
Victoria, Chile 216/B3
Victoria (peak),
Belz. 202/D2
Victoria, Gren. 211/F1
Victoria (isl.),
NW,Nun., Can. 180/E1
Victoria (isl.),
Nun., Can. 180/F2
Victoria (lake), Afr. 162/B3
Victoria de las Tunas,
Cuba 203/G1
Victoria Land (pol. reg.),
Ant. 218/M
Victoria Nile (riv.),
Ugan. 155/M7
Victoria West, SAfr. 164/C3
Victorias, Phil. 137/D5

Victoriaville,
Qu, Can. 189/G2
Victorica, Arg. 216/D3
Victorville, Ca, US 194/C1
Victory Junction,
Ks, US 195/D5
Vicuña Mackenna,
Arg. 216/D2
Vidal (cape), SAfr. 165/F3
Vidalia, La, US 187/K5
Vidalia, Ga, US 191/H3
Vidauban, Moz. 163/G5
Vidauban, Braz. 213/B3
Videle, Rom. 107/G3
Vidhošt (peak),
Czh. 113/G4
Vidigueira, Port. 102/B3
Vidigulfo, It. 116/C2
Vidin, Bul. 107/F4
Vidisha, India 142/A4
Vidnoye, Rus. 119/W9
Vidor, Tx, US 187/J5
Vidor, Fr. 117/F1
Vidöstern (lake),
Swe. 96/F3
Vidourle (riv.), Fr. 100/E5
Vie (riv.), Fr. 100/D2
Viechtach, Ger. 113/F4
Viedma, Arg. 216/E4
Viedma (lake), Arg. 217/B6
Viehberg (peak),
Aus. 113/H5
Viejo (peak), Peru 214/B2
Viella, Sp. 103/F1
Vielsalm, Belg. 111/E3
Vienenburg, Ger. 109/H5
Vienna, WV, US 188/D4
Vienna, Va, US 196/A4
Vienne, Fr. 100/F4
Vienne (riv.), Fr. 100/D3
Vientiane (int'l arpt.),
Laos 136/C2
Vientiane (Viangchan)
(cap.), Laos 136/C2
Vieques (isl.), PR 199/M8
Viére (riv.), Fr. 111/D6
Vierlingsbeek, Neth. 108/C4
Viernheim, Ger. 112/B3
Vierre (riv.), Belg. 111/E4
Viersen, Ger. 108/D6
Vierzon, Fr. 100/E3
Viesca, Mex. 200/E3
Vieste, It. 104/E2
Viet Tri, Viet. 141/J3
Vietnam (ctry.) 136/D2
Vieux-Boucau-les-Bains,
Fr. 100/C5
Vieux Carré,
La, US 195/P17
Vieux-Charmont, Fr. 114/C2
Vieux-Condé, Fr. 110/C3
Vieux Fort, StL. 199/N9
Vieux-Thann, Fr. 114/C2
Vieze (riv.), Swi. 114/C5
Vigan, Phil. 137/D4
Vigarano Mainarda, It. 117/E3
Vigasio, It. 117/D2
Vigevano, It. 116/B2
Viggiù, It. 115/E6
Vigia, Braz. 209/J4
Vigliano Biellese, It. 116/B1
Viglio (peak), It. 104/C2
Vignacourt, Fr. 110/B3
Vignacourt, Fr. 104/C1
Vignemale (peak), Fr. 100/C5
Vigneulles-lès-Hattonchâtel,
Fr. 111/E6
Vigneux-sur-Seine, Fr. 88/K5
Vignola, It. 117/E6
Vignot, Fr. 111/E6
Vigo, Sp. 102/A1
Vigodarzere, It. 116/D4
Vigonovo, It. 117/F2
Vigonza, It. 117/E2
Vigrestad, Nor. 96/A2
Viguzzolo, It. 116/B2
Vihanti, Fin. 118/E2
Vihári, Pak. 144/B4
Vihti, Fin. 97/L1
Viitasaari, Fin. 118/E2
Vijayawada, India 140/D4
Vik, Ice. 95/N7
Vik, Nor. 96/B1
Vikersund, Nor. 96/C2
Vikeså, Nor. 96/B2
Vikhren (peak), Bul. 107/F5
Viking, Ab, Can. 184/F2
Vikmanshyttan, Swe. 96/F1
Vila Bittencourt,
Braz. 210/D5
Vila de Sena, Moz. 163/G4
Vila do Bispo, Port. 102/A4
Vila do Conde, Port. 102/A2
Vila do Porto,
Azor., Port. 103/T13
Vila Franca de Xira,
Port. 103/P10
Vila Franca do Campo,
Azor., Port. 103/T13
Vila Nova de Fozcoa,
Port. 102/B2
Vila Nova de Gaia,
Port. 102/A2
Vila Nova de Milfontes,
Port. 102/A4
Vila Pouca de Aguiar,
Port. 102/B2
Vila Real, Port. 102/B2
Vila Real (dist.),
Port. 102/B2
Vila Velha Argolas,
Braz. 213/D2

Vila Velha de Ródão,
Port. 102/B3
Vila Verde, Port. 102/A2
Vila Viçosa, Port. 102/B3
Viladecans, Sp. 103/K7
Vilafranca del Penedès,
Sp. 103/K7
Vilanandro (cape),
Madg. 165/H7
Vilanculos, Moz. 163/G5
Vieira, Braz. 213/B3
Vilanova i la Geltrú,
Sp. 103/K7
Vilar Formoso,
Port. 102/B2
Vilcabamba, Peru 214/B3
Vilcea (prov.), Rom. 107/F3
Vilches, Sp. 102/D3
Vilhelmina, Swe. 95/F2
Vilhena, Braz. 208/F6
Viliya (riv.), Bela. 118/E5
Viljandi, Est. 97/L2
Viljoenskroon,
SAfr. 164/D2
Vil'kitsogo (str.),
Rus. 123/K2
Villa Alemana,
Chile 216/N8
Villa Alhué, Chile 216/N9
Villa Ángela, Arg. 215/D2
Villa Atuel, Arg. 216/D2
Villa Bartolomea, It. 117/E2
Villa Bruzual, Ven. 210/D2
Villa Cañás, Arg. 216/E2
Villa Carcina, It. 116/D1
Villa Carlos Paz,
Arg. 215/D3
Villa Chañar Ladeado,
Arg. 216/E2
Villa Constitución,
Arg. 216/E2
Villa Corzo, Mex. 202/C2
Villa Cuauhtemoc,
Mex. 201/Q10
Villa d'Almè, It. 116/C1
Villa de Arista,
Mex. 201/E4
Villa de Cos, Mex. 200/E4
Villa de Costa Rica,
Mex. 200/D3
Villa de La Paz,
Mex. 201/E4
Villa de Reyes,
Mex. 201/E4
Villa del Carbón,
Mex. 201/Q9
Villa del Carmen,
Uru. 217/K10
Villa del Río, Sp. 102/C4
Villa di Serio, It. 116/C1
Villa Dolores, Arg. 215/C3
Villa Dolores, Arg. 216/D1
Villa Flores, Mex. 202/C2
Villa Gesell, Arg. 217/F3
Villa Guardia, It. 116/C1
Villa Hidalgo, Mex. 200/D4
Villa Hidalgo, Mex. 200/C2
Villa Huidobro,
Arg. 216/D2
Villa Iris, Arg. 216/E3
Villa Isabela, DRep. 203/J2
Villa Jaragua,
DRep. 203/J2
Villa Juárez, Mex. 203/J2
Villa Juárez, Mex. 200/D3
Villa La Angostura,
Arg. 216/C4
Villa Lázaro Cárdenas,
Mex. 201/M6
Villa López, Mex. 200/D3
Villa Mantero,
Arg. 217/J10
Villa María, Arg. 215/D3
Villa Minozzo, It. 116/D4
Villa Montes, Bol. 208/F8
Villa Nueva, Arg. 216/D2
Villa Nueva, Guat. 202/D3
Villa Nueva, Nic. 202/E3
Villa Opicina, It. 117/G1
Villa Park, II, US 193/Q16
Villa Park, Ca, US 194/G8
Villa Regina, Arg. 216/D3
Villa Rica, Peru 214/C3
Villa Rosario, Col. 210/C2
Villa Sandino, Nic. 203/E3
Villa Sarmiento,
Arg. 216/D2
Villa Serrano, Bol. 208/F7
Villa Unión, Arg. 215/C2
Villa Unión, Mex. 200/D4
Villa Valeria, Arg. 216/D2
Villa Verucchio, It. 117/F5
Villaba, Sp. 102/E1
Villablino, Sp. 102/B1
Villacañas, Sp. 102/D3
Villacarrillo, Sp. 102/D3
Villada, Sp. 102/C1
Villadiego, Sp. 102/C1
Villadose, It. 117/E2
Villafamés, Sp. 103/E2
Villafranca d'Asti, It. 116/B2
Villafranca de los Barros,
Sp. 102/B3
Villafranca del Bierzo,
Sp. 102/B1
Villafranca del Cid,
Sp. 103/E2
Villafranca di Verona,
It. 117/D2
Villafranca in Lunigiana,
It. 116/C4
Villagarcía, Sp. 102/C1
Villagrán, Mex. 201/B6

Villaguay, Arg. 215/E3
Villahermosa, Sp. 102/D3
Villahermosa, Mex. 202/C2
Villajoyosa, Sp. 103/E3
Villalba, Sp. 102/B2
Villalcampo, Embalse de
(res.), Sp. 102/B2
Villaldama, Mex. 190/C5
Villalón de Campos,
Sp. 102/C1
Villalonga, Arg. 216/E3
Villalpando, Sp. 102/C1
Villamartín, Sp. 102/C4
Villandro (peak), It. 115/H4
Villanova, It. 117/F4
Villanova, It. 117/E4
Villanova d'Asti, It. 116/B2
Villanova Mondovì, It. 116/A4
Villanterio, It. 116/C2
Villanueva, Mex. 200/E4
Villanueva, Col. 210/C2
Villanueva, Hon. 202/E3
Villanueva de Arosa,
Sp. 102/A1
Villanueva de Córdoba,
Sp. 102/C3
Villanueva de la Serena,
Sp. 102/C3
Villanueva de los Infantes,
Sp. 102/D3
Villanueva de Oscos,
Sp. 102/B1
Villanueva del Arzobispo,
Sp. 102/D3
Villanuova sul Clisi, It. 116/D1
Villány, Hun. 106/D3
Villar del Arzobispo,
Sp. 103/E3
Villarcayo, Sp. 102/D1
Villardevós, Sp. 102/B2
Villarreal de los Infantes,
Sp. 103/E3
Villarrica, Par. 215/E2
Villarrica, Chile 216/B3
Villarrica (vol.),
Chile 216/C3
Villarrica (lake),
Chile 216/B3
Villarrica, PN, Chile 216/C3
Villarrobledo, Sp. 102/D3
Villarrubia de los Ojos,
Sp. 102/D3
Villars-les-Dombes, Fr. 114/B6
Villars-sur-Glâne,
Swi. 114/D4
Villas, NJ, US 196/D5
Villasana de Mena,
Sp. 102/D1
Villasanta, It. 116/C1
Villastellone, It. 116/A3
Villaverde del Río,
Sp. 102/C4
Villaviciencio, Col. 210/C3
Villaviciosa, Sp. 102/C1
Villaviciosa de Odón,
Sp. 103/N9
Villazón, Bol. 215/C1
Villecresnes, Fr. 88/K5
Villefranche-de-Rouergue,
Fr. 100/E4
Villefranche-sur-Saône,
Fr. 100/F4
Villejuif, Fr. 88/K5
Villemur-sur-Tarn, Fr. 100/D5
Villena, Sp. 103/E3
Villeneuve, Swi. 114/C5
Villeneuve-d'Ascq, Fr. 110/C2
Villeneuve-le-Comte,
Fr. 88/L5
Villeneuve-le-Roi, Fr. 88/K5
Villeneuve-lès-Avignon,
Fr. 100/F5
Villeneuve-Saint-Denis,
Fr. 88/L5
Villeneuve-Saint-Georges,
Fr. 88/K5
Villeneuve-Saint-Germain,
Fr. 110/C5
Villeneuve-sur-Lot, Fr. 100/D4
Villeneuve-sur-Yonne,
Fr. 100/E2
Villeneuve-Tolosane,
Fr. 100/D5
Villennes-sur-Seine, Fr. 88/H5
Villeparisis, Fr. 88/K5
Villepinte, Fr. 88/K5
Villepreux, Fr. 88/J5
Villeroy, Fr. 88/L4
Villers-Bretonneux, Fr. 110/B4
Villers-Cotterêts, Fr. 111/D5
Villers-en-Arthies, Fr. 88/H4
Villers-le-Bouillet,
Belg. 111/E2
Villers-le-Lac, Fr. 111/D6
Villers-lès-Nancy, Fr. 111/F6
Villers-Saint-Genest,
Fr. 88/L4
Villers-Saint-Paul, Fr. 110/B4
Villers-Semeuse, Fr. 111/E5
Villersexel, Fr. 114/C2
Villerupt, Fr. 111/E5
Villette, Fr. 88/H5
Villeurbanne, Fr. 114/A6
Villevaudé, Fr. 88/L5
Villiers, SAfr. 164/C2
Villiers-en-Lieu, Fr. 111/D6
Villiers-le-Bel, Fr. 88/K4
Villiers-Saint-Georges,
Fr. 110/C6
Villiers-sur-Marne, Fr. 88/K5
Villiers-sur-Morin, Fr. 88/L5
Villiersdorp, SAfr. 164/L10
Villieu-Loyes-Mollon,
Fr. 114/B6

Villingen-Schwenningen,
Ger. 115/E1
Villmar, Ger. 112/B2
Villongo, It. 116/C1
Villorba, It. 117/F1
Vilnius (int'l arpt.),
Lith. 97/L4
Vilnius (cap.), Lith. 97/L4
Vils, Aus. 115/G2
Vilsbiburg, Ger. 113/F6
Vilseck, Ger. 113/E3
Vilshofen, Ger. 113/G5
Vilters, Swi. 115/F3
Vilvoorde, Belg. 111/D2
Vilyuy (riv.), Rus. 125/L3
Vilyuy (range), Rus. 123/M3
Vimercate, It. 116/C1
Vimeu (reg.), Fr. 110/A3
Vimmerby, Swe. 96/F3
Vimodrone, It. 116/C2
Vimperk, Czh. 113/G4
Vina (riv.), Camr. 154/H6
Viña del Mar, Chile 216/N8
Vinaninca, Madg. 165/J6
Vinaroz, Sp. 103/F2
Vincennes, In, US 188/C4
Vincennes (lake), It. 88/L5
Vincennes (bay),
Ant. 218/H
Vincennes, Fr. 88/K5
Vincentown,
NJ, US 196/D4
Vinces, Ecu. 210/B5
Vincey, Fr. 114/C1
Vinchos, Peru 214/C4
Vinci, It. 117/D5
Vindeby, Den. 96/D4
Vindeln, Swe. 95/F2
Vindhya (range),
India 142/A4
Vineland, NJ, US 196/C5
Vineland Station,
On, Can. 189/R9
Vineuil, Fr. 100/D3
Vingåker, Swe. 96/F2
Vinh, Viet. 136/D2
Vinh An, Viet. 137/A4
Vinh Long, Viet. 136/D4
Vinh Yen, Viet. 136/D1
Vinhais, Port. 102/B2
Vinhedo, Braz. 213/G8
Vinica, FYROM 105/H2
Viniceiro, Sp. 102/B1
Vinita, Ok, US 187/J3
Vinkovci, Cro. 106/D3
Vinnitsa, Ukr. 120/D2
Vinnyts'ka Oblasti,
Ukr. 120/D2
Vinnytsya, Ukr. 120/D2
Vinon-sur-Verdon, Fr. 100/F5
Vinson Massif (peak),
Ant. 218/U
Viola, De, US 196/C5
Viola, NY, US 197/J7
Violet Lup, US 195/Q17
Violet Town, Austl. 173/C3
Viosne (riv.), Fr. 110/A5
Vipava, Phil. 137/D5
Viracopos (int'l arpt.),
Braz. 213/F7
Viranşehir, Turk. 148/D2
Virār, India 147/K5
Virden, Mb, Can. 185/H4
Vire (riv.), Fr. 100/C2
Vire, Fr. 100/C2
Vireux-Wallerand, Fr. 111/D3
Virgem da Lapa,
Braz. 212/B5
Virgin (riv.), US 186/D3
Virgin (isls.), UK,US 199/M8
Virgin Gorda,
(isl.), UK 199/M8
Virgin Islands NP,
USVI 199/M8
Virginia, SAfr. 164/D3
Virginia (state), US 188/E4
Virginia City,
Nv, US 186/C3
Virginia Water,
Eng, UK 88/B2
Viriat, Fr. 114/B5
Virieu-le-Grand, Fr. 114/B6
Viroflay, Fr. 88/J5
Viroin (riv.), Belg. 111/D3
Viroqua, Wi, US 187/K2
Virovitica, Cro. 106/C3
Virserum, Swe. 96/F3
Virton, Belg. 111/E4
Virú, Peru 214/B3
Virudunagar, India 140/C6
Virunga, D.R. Congo 162/A3
Virunga NP,
D.R. Congo 162/A3
Viry-Châtillon, Fr. 88/K6
Vis (isl.), Cro. 106/C4
Visaginas, Lith. 97/M4
Visalia, Ca, US 186/C3
Visandre (riv.), Fr. 88/M5
Visayan (sea), Phil. 137/D5
Visbek, Ger. 109/F3
Visby, Swe. 96/H3
Visconde do Rio Branco,
Braz. 213/D2
Viscount Melville (sound),
NW,Nun., Can. 181/R7
Visé, Belg. 111/E2
Višegrad, Bosn. 106/D4
Viseu, Port. 102/B2
Viseu (dist.), Port. 102/B2
Viseu de Sus, Rom. 107/G2
Vishakhapatnam,
India 140/D4

Vishera (riv.), Rus. 119/L3
Vishoek, SAfr. 164/L11
Viskafors, Swe. 96/F3
Vislanda, Swe. 96/F3
Visnagar, India 147/K4
Višnjevac, Cro. 106/D3
Visoko, Bosn. 106/D4
Visp, Swi. 114/D5
Visperterminen, Swi. 114/D5
Visselhövede, Ger. 109/G3
Vissenbjerg, Den. 96/D4
Vissoie, Swi. 114/D5
Vista, Ca, US 194/C4
Vistonís (lake), Gre. 105/J2
Vistula (riv.), Pol. 99/K2
Vit (riv.), Bul. 107/G4
Viterbo, It. 104/C1
Viterbo (prov.), It. 104/C1
Vitez, Bosn. 106/C3
Viti Levu (isl.), Fiji 174/G6
Vitigudino, Sp. 102/B2
Vitim (plat.), Rus. 123/M4
Vitim (riv.), Rus. 121/G2
Vitkuv Kamen (peak),
Czh. 113/H5
Vitomirica, Kos. 106/E4
Vitor, Peru 214/C5
Vitória, Braz. 213/D2
Vitoria, Sp. 102/D1
Vitória da Conquista,
Braz. 212/B4
Vitória de Santo Antão,
Braz. 212/D3
Vitória do Mearim,
Braz. 212/A1
Vitorino Freire,
Braz. 212/A2
Vitosha NP, Bul. 107/F4
Vitré, Fr. 100/C2
Vitrey-sur-Mance, Fr. 114/B2
Vitrolles, Fr. 100/F5
Vitry-en-Artois, Fr. 110/B3
Vitry-le-François, Fr. 111/D6
Vitry-sur-Seine, Fr. 88/K5
Vitsebsk, Bela. 118/E5
Vitsyebskaya Voblasts
Bela. 118/E5
Vittangi, Swe. 95/G2
Vittel, Fr. 114/B1
Vittoria, It. 104/D4
Vittorio Veneto, It. 101/K4
Vivarais, Monts du
(mts.), Fr. 100/F4
Viveiro, Sp. 102/B1
Viverone (lake), It. 116/B2
Viverone, It. 116/B2
Vivian, La, US 187/J4
Vivonne, Fr. 100/D3
Vizcaíno, Sierra (mts.),
Mex. 200/B3
Vize, Turk. 107/H5
Vizhas (riv.), Rus. 119/K2
Vizianagaram, India 140/D4
Vlaardingen, Neth. 108/B5
Vlādeasa (peak),
Rom. 107/F2
Vladikavkaz, Rus. 121/H4
Vladimir, Rus. 118/J4
Vladimirskaya Oblast,
Rus. 118/J5
Vladivostok, Rus. 129/P3
Vlagtwedde, Neth. 109/E2
Vlāhița, Rom. 107/G2
Vlajna (peak), Serb. 106/E4
Vlasenica, Bosn. 106/D3
Vlašim, Czh. 101/L2
Vlasotince, Serb. 106/F4
Vlieland (isl.), Neth. 98/C2
Vliestroom (chan.),
Neth. 108/C2
Vlijmen, Neth. 108/C5
Vlissingen, Neth. 108/A6
Vlotho, Ger. 109/F4
Vltava (riv.), Czh. 99/H4
Vnukovo (int'l arpt.),
Rus. 119/W9
Vobarno, It. 116/D1
Vöcklabruck, Aus. 113/G6
Vöcklamarkt, Aus. 113/G6
Vodice, Cro. 106/B3
Vodlozero (lake),
Rus. 119/Q2
Vodňany, Czh. 113/H4
Vodskov, Den. 96/D3
Voerde, Ger. 108/D5
Vogan, Togo 161/F5
Vogelsberg (mts.),
Ger. 101/H1
Voghera, It. 115/E6
Vogogna, It. 115/E6
Vogorno (lake), Swi. 115/E5
Vogtareuth, Ger. 113/F7
Vogtland (reg.), Ger. 98/F3
Vohemar, India 140/C3
Vohibinany, India 165/H8
Vohilava, Madg. 165/H8
Vohimena (cape),
Madg. 165/H9
Vohipeno, Madg. 165/H8
Vohiposa, Madg. 165/H8
Voi, Kenya 162/C3
Void-Vacon, Fr. 111/E6
Voil (lake), Sc, UK 94/B4
Voinjama, Libr. 160/C4
Voiron, Fr. 114/B6
Voisines, Fr. 88/M5
Voise (riv.), Fr. 100/D2
Voisey (bay), Nf, Can. 181/K3
Voiteur, Fr. 114/B4
Vojens, Den. 96/C4
Vojosë (riv.), Alb. 106/D5
Vojvodina (prov.),
Serb. 106/D3
Vouga (riv.), Port. 102/A2
Völklingen, Ger. 111/F5
Volano, It. 115/H6
Volary, Czh. 113/G5

Volcán Barú, PN,
Pan. 203/F4
Volcán Poás, PN, CR 203/E4
Volcano, Hi, US 182/U11
Volcano (isls.),
Japan 174/C2
Volcans NP, Rwa. 162/A3
Volchiy Nos (cape),
Rus. 97/Q1
Volda, Nor. 95/C3
Volendam, Neth. 108/C3
Volga (riv.), Rus. 85/J3
Volga-Baltic Waterway
(canal), Rus. 118/H3
Volgelsheim, Fr. 114/C2
Volgodonsk, Rus. 121/G3
Volgograd (int'l arpt.),
Rus. 121/H2
Volgograd (res.),
Rus. 121/H2
Volgogradskaya Oblast,
Rus. 121/G2
Volkach (riv.), Ger. 112/D3
Volkach, Ger. 112/D3
Volkeradam (dam),
Neth. 108/B5
Völkermarkt, Aus. 101/L3
Volketswil, Swi. 115/E3
Volkhov, Rus. 97/Q2
Volkhov (riv.), Rus. 118/F4
Volkmarsen, Ger. 109/G6
Volksrust, SAfr. 165/E2
Volodymyr-Volyns'kyy,
Ukr. 120/C2
Vologda, Rus. 118/H4
Vologdskaya Oblast,
Rus. 118/J3
Vologne (riv.), Fr. 98/D4
Volos, Gre. 105/H3
Vólos (gulf), Gre. 105/H3
Volpago del Montello,
It. 117/F1
Volpiano, It. 116/A2
Völs, Aus. 115/H3
Vol'sk, Rus. 121/H1
Volta (riv.), Gha. 154/F6
Volta (pol. reg.), Gha. 161/F5
Volta, Gha. 161/E4
Volta Mantovana, It. 116/D2
Vóltana, It. 117/D6
Volterra, It. 117/D6
Voltage, Ger. 109/E4
V+táčnik (peak), Slvk. 99/K4
Volturino (peak), It. 104/D2
Volturno (riv.), It. 104/D2
Volubilis (ruin),
Mor. 158/B2
Vulcan, Ab, Can. 184/E3
Vulcan, Rom. 107/F3
Vulcano (isl.), It. 104/D3
Vulcano (isl.), It. 104/D3
Vulchedrŭm, Bul. 107/F4
Vŭlchi Dol, Bul. 107/H4
Vulci (ruin), It. 104/B1
Vung Tau, Viet. 136/D4
Vuohijärvi (lake), Fin. 97/M1
Vuollerim, Swe. 95/G2
Vuoska (lake), Rus. 97/S5
Vuotso, Fin. 118/E1
Vûrbitsa, Bul. 107/H4
Vuria (peak), Kenya 162/C3
Vŭrshets, Bul. 107/F4
Vyara, India 147/K4
Vyatka (riv.), Rus. 122/E4
Vyatskiye Polyany,
Rus. 119/L4
Vyazemskiy, Rus. 129/P4
Vyaz'ma, Rus. 118/G5
Vyborg, Rus. 97/N1
Vyborg (bay), Rus. 97/N1
Vychegda (riv.), Rus. 122/F3
Vygozero (lake), Rus. 118/G3
Vyhorlat (peak), Slvk. 99/M4
Výksa, Rus. 118/J3
Vym' (riv.), Rus. 119/L3
Vynohradiv, Ukr. 99/M3
Vyrnwy (riv.),
Wal, UK 90/C1
Vyshniy Volochek,
Rus. 118/G4
Vyškov, Czh. 99/J4

W

W du Benin, PN du,
Ben. 161/F4
W du Burkino Faso, PN du,
Burk. 161/F4
W du Niger, PN du,
Ben. 154/F5
W du Niger, PN du,
Niger 161/F3
W. J. van Blommestein
(lake), Sur. 209/G2
Wa, Gha. 161/E4
Waal, Ger. 115/G2
Waal (riv.), Neth. 108/C5
Waalre, Neth. 108/C6
Waalwijk, Neth. 108/C5
Waarschoot, Belg. 110/C1
Wabasca, Braz. 184/C2
Wabasca (riv.),
Ab, Can. 180/E3
Wabash, In, US 188/C3
Wabash (riv.),
Il,In, US 188/C4
Wabē Shebelē Wenz
(riv.), Eth. 155/P6
Wabern, Ger. 109/G6
Wabigoon (lake),
On, Can. 185/K3
Wabowden, Mb, Can. 185/J2
Wabrzeźno, Pol. 99/K2
Wabu (lake), China 130/D4

Wabu, SKor. 131/G6
Wachenheim an der Weinstrasse, Ger. 112/B4
Wachi, Japan 135/H5
Wachtebeke, Belg. 110/C1
Wachtendonk, Ger. 108/D6
Wächtersbach, Ger. 112/C2
Wackernheim, Ger. 112/B3
Wackersdorf, Ger. 113/F4
Waco, Tx, US 187/H5
Waconda (lake), Ks, US 187/H3
Waconia, Mn, US 185/K4
Wad Medani, Sudan 155/M5
Wada, Japan 135/E3
Wadayama, Japan 135/G5
Wadbilliga NP, Austl. 173/D3
Waddān, Libya 154/J2
Waddell, Az, US 195/R18
Waddell (dam), Az, US 195/R18
Waddenzee (sound), Neth. 98/C2
Waddington (mt.), BC, Can. 184/B3
Waddinxveen, Neth. 108/B4
Waddy (pt.), Austl. 172/D4
Wadena, Mn, US 185/K4
Wadena, Sk, Can. 185/H3
Wädenswil, Swi. 115/E3
Wadern, Ger. 111/F4
Wadersloh, Ger. 109/F5
Wadgassen, Ger. 111/F5
Wādī al Layl, Tun. 158/M6
Wādī As Sīr, Jor. 149/D4
Wādī Majardah (riv.), Tun. 158/L6
Wādī Mūsá, Jor. 149/D4
Wading (riv.), NJ, US 196/D4
Wading River, NY, US 197/F2
Wadowice, Pol. 99/K4
Wadsworth, Il, US 193/Q15
Waegwan, SKor. 131/E5
Wafangdian, China 131/A3
Wagenfeld-Hasslingen, Ger. 109/F3
Wageningen, Neth. 108/C5
Wager (bay), NW, Can. 180/G2
Wagga Wagga, Austl. 173/C2
Waggaman, La, US 195/P17
Waghäusel, Ger. 112/B4
Wagin, Austl. 170/C5
Waging am See, Ger. 113/F7
Waginger (lake), Ger. 113/F7
Wägitaler-see (lake), Swi. 115/E3
Wagna, Aus. 101/L3
Wagner, Braz. 212/B4
Wągrowiec, Pol. 99/J2
Wagstaff, Ks, US 195/D6
Wāh, Pak. 144/B3
Wah Wah (range), Ut, US 186/D3
Wahiawa, Hi, US 182/V12
Wahlern, Swi. 114/D4
Wahpeton, ND, US 185/J4
Wahrenholz, Ger. 109/H3
Wai, India 140/B4
Waialae, Hi, US 182/V12
Waialua, Hi, US 182/V12
Waianae, Hi, US 182/V13
Waiau (riv.), NZ 175/S11
Waibiamiao, China 130/D2
Waiblingen, Ger. 112/C5
Waidhaus, Ger. 113/F3
Waidhofen an der Thaya, Aus. 101/L2
Waidhofen an der Ybbs, Aus. 113/H7
Waigeo (isl.), Indo. 139/H3
Waigolshausen, Ger. 112/D3
Waihou (riv.), NZ 175/T10
Waikane, Hi, US 182/W12
Waikari, NZ 175/S11
Waikato (riv.), NZ 175/T10
Waikerie, Austl. 171/H5
Waikiki, Hi, US 182/W13
Waikoloa Village, Hi, US 182/U11
Wailuku, Hi, US 182/T10
Waimanalo, Hi, US 182/W13
Waimanalo Beach, Hi, US 182/W13
Waimate, NZ 175/S11
Waimea, Hi, US 182/S10
Waimea (falls), Hi, US 182/V12
Waimes, Belg. 111/F3
Wainfleet, On, Can. 189/R10
Waingangā (riv.), India 140/C3
Waini (riv.), Guy. 211/G2
Wainwright, Ak, US 192/F1
Wainwright, Ab, Can. 184/F2
Waipahu, Hi, US 182/V13
Waipio, Hi, US 182/U10
Waipio Acres, Hi, US 182/V13
Waipukurau, NZ 175/T10
Wairau (riv.), NZ 175/S11

Wairoa, NZ 175/T10
Waischenfeld, Ger. 113/E3
Waitaki (riv.), NZ 175/S11
Waitara, NZ 175/S10
Waizenkirchen, Aus. 113/G6
Wajima, Japan 133/E2
Waka (cape), Indo. 139/G4
Wakakusa, Japan 135/A2
Wakasa, Japan 132/D3
Wakasa (bay), Japan 135/H4
Wakaw, Sk, Can. 185/G2
Wakayama, Japan 132/D3
Wakayama (pref.), Japan 132/D4
Wake (isl.), Pac., US 174/F3
Wakefield (co.), Eng, UK 93/G4
Wakefield, Eng, UK 93/G4
Wakefield, Mi, US 188/B2
Wakema, Myan. 141/G4
Wakkanai, Japan 134/B1
Wakool, Austl. 173/C2
Wakuya, Japan 134/B4
Wakwayowkastic (riv.), On, Can. 188/D1
Wala (riv.), Tanz. 162/B4
Walachia (reg.), Rom. 107/G3
Walagunya Abor. Land, Austl. 170/D2
Wałbrzych, Pol. 99/J3
Walbury (hill), Eng, UK 91/E4
Walcha, Austl. 173/D1
Walcheren (isl.), Neth. 108/A5
Walcourt, Belg. 111/D3
Wałcz, Pol. 99/J2
Wald, Swi. 115/E3
Wald, Ger. 113/F4
Waldbillig, Lux. 111/F4
Waldbreitbach, Ger. 111/G2
Waldbröl, Ger. 111/G2
Waldbronn, Ger. 112/B5
Waldbrunn, Ger. 112/C3
Walden, Co, US 187/F2
Waldenbuch, Ger. 112/C5
Waldenburg, Swi. 114/D3
Waldenburg, Ger. 112/C4
Waldershof, Ger. 113/F3
Waldesch, Ger. 111/G3
Waldheim, Sk, Can. 184/G2
Waldighofen, Fr. 114/D2
Walding, Aus. 113/H6
Waldkirch, Ger. 114/D1
Waldmünchen, Ger. 113/F4
Waldnaab (riv.), Ger. 113/F4
Waldrach, Ger. 111/F4
Waldron, Mo, US 195/D5
Waldsassen, Ger. 113/F3
Waldshut-Tiengen, Ger. 115/E2
Waldstetten, Ger. 112/C5
Waldviertel (reg.), Aus. 99/H4
Waldwick, NJ, US 197/J8
Walea (str.), Indo. 139/F4
Waleabahi (isl.), Indo. 139/F4
Walensee (lake), Swi. 115/F3
Walenstadt, Swi. 115/F3
Wales, Ak, US 192/E2
Wales, UK 90/B3
Wales (isl.), Nun., Can. 181/H2
Wales, Wi, US 193/P14
Walferdange, Lux. 111/F4
Walgett, Austl. 173/D1
Walhalla, ND, US 185/J3
Walhalla, SC, US 191/H3
Walker (riv.), Nv, US 186/C3
Walker (lake), Nv, US 186/C3
Walker (bay), SAfr. 164/L11
Walkerston, Austl. 172/C3
Walkerton, Indo. 139/F6
Walkill (riv.), NY, US 196/D1
Walla Walla, Austl. 173/C2
Walla Walla, Wa, US 184/D4
Wallace, Id, US 184/E4
Wallaceburg, On, Can. 188/D3
Wallaroo, Austl. 171/H5
Wallasey, Eng, UK 93/E5
Walldorf, Ger. 112/B4
Walldürn, Ger. 112/C3
Walled (lake), Mi, US 193/F6
Walled City Hist. Site, SKor. 131/G7
Walled Lake, Mi, US 193/F6
Wallenhorst, Ger. 109/F4
Wallern im Burgenland, Aus. 101/M3
Wallers, Fr. 110/C2
Wallerstein, Ger. 112/D5
Wallingford, NJ, US 197/J8
Wallis (isls.), Wall., Fr. 175/H6
Wallis and Futuna (dpcy.), Fr. 174/G6
Wallisellen, Swi. 115/E3

Walloon Brabant (prov.), Belg. 111/D2
Wallowa, Japan 135/D2
Wallowa (mts.), Or, US 184/D4
Wallsend, Eng, UK 93/G2
Walney, Isle of (isl.), Eng, UK 93/E3
Walnut, Ca, US 194/G7
Walnut Canyon Nat'l Mon., Az, US 186/E4
Walnut Creek, Ca, US 193/K11
Walnut Grove, Ca, US 193/L10
Walnut Park, Ca, US 194/F8
Walnut Ridge, Ar, US 187/K3
Walnutport, Pa, US 196/D2
Walpole, Austl. 170/C5
Walpole-Nornalup NP, Austl. 170/C5
Walrus (isls.), Ak, US 192/F4
Walsall, Eng, UK 91/E1
Walsall (co.), Eng, UK 91/E1
Walsenburg, Co, US 187/F3
Walsingham (cape), Nun., Can. 181/K2
Walsrode, Ger. 109/G3
Waltenhofen, Ger. 115/G2
Walter F. George (res.),
Walter's Ash, Eng, UK 88/A2
Waltham Abbey, Eng, UK 88/D1
Waltham Forest (bor.), Eng, UK 88/A1
Walton-on-Thames, Eng, UK 88/B2
Waltrop, Ger. 109/E5
Walvis Bay, Namb. 163/B5
Walworth, Wi, US 193/N14
Walworth (co.), Wi, US 193/N14
Walyahmoning (peak), Austl. 170/C4
Walyunga NP, Austl. 170/L6
Wamba, Kenya 162/C2
Wamba, D.R. Congo 155/L7
Wamba (riv.), Ger. 96/D5
Wamel, Neth. 108/C5
Wami (riv.), Tanz. 162/C4
Wampool (riv.), Eng, UK 93/E2
Wamsutter, Wy, US 184/G5
Wanaka, NZ 175/R11
Wanamassa, NJ, US 196/D3
Wanaque (res.), NJ, US 196/D1
Wanaque, NJ, US 197/H7
Wanda (mts.), Can. 192/M2
Wanda, Il, US 195/G8
Wandering, Austl. 170/C5
Wanding, China 141/G3
Wandoan, Austl. 172/C4
Wandsworth (bor.), Eng, UK 88/C2
Wanfried, Ger. 109/H6
Wang (riv.), Thai. 141/G4
Wang Hip (peak), Thai. 136/B4
Wanganui, NZ 175/T10
Wangaratta, Austl. 173/C3
Wangdu, China 130/C3
Wangen an der Aare, Swi. 114/D3
Wangen bei Olten, Swi. 114/D3
Wangerooge (isl.), Ger. 109/E1
Wanggamet (peak), Indo. 139/F6
Wanghai Shan (peak), China 131/A2
Wangi, Swi. 115/E3
Wangjiang, China 137/C1
Wangpan (bay), China 130/E5
Wani (peak), Indo. 139/F4
Wanica (dist.), Sur. 211/H3
Wank (peak), Ger. 115/H2
Wanning, China 141/K4
Wanouchi, Japan 135/L5
Wanquan, China 130/C2
Wansbeck (riv.), Eng, UK 93/G1
Wantagh, NY, US 197/M9
Wanxian, China 128/J5
Wanze, Belg. 111/E2
Wapakoneta, Oh, US 188/D3
Wapawekka (lake), Sk, Can. 185/G2
Wapiti (riv.), Can. 184/D2
Wapoga (riv.), Indo. 139/J4
Wappapello (lake), Mo, US 187/K3
Wapsipinicon (riv.), Ia, US 185/K5

Wapwallopen, Pa, US 196/B1
Warabi, Japan 135/D2
Warangal, India 140/C4
Waratah, Austl. 173/C4
Warburg, Ger. 109/G6
Warburton, Pak. 144/B4
Warburton, Austl. 170/E3
Warburton Range Abor. Rsv., Austl. 170/E3
Warche (riv.), Belg. 111/F3
Ward, Co, US 195/A2
Ward, NZ 175/S11
Ward Cove, Ak, US 192/M4
Warden, SAfr. 164/E2
Warden (pt.), Eng, UK 91/G4
Wardenburg, Ger. 109/F2
Wardha, India 140/C3
Ward's Stone (peak), Eng, UK 93/F3
Ware, Eng, UK 91/F3
Waregem, Belg. 110/C2
Waremme, Belg. 111/E2
Waren, Ger. 96/E5
Warendorf, Ger. 109/E5
Waretown, NJ, US 196/D4
Warffum, Neth. 108/D2
Wargrave, Eng, UK 91/F4
Warialda, Austl. 173/D1
Warin Chamrap, Thai. 136/D3
Waringstown, NI, UK 92/B3
Warka, Pol. 99/L3
Warkworth, NZ 175/S10
Warlingham, Eng, UK 88/C3
Warmbad, Namb. 164/B3
Warme Bode (riv.), Ger. 109/H5
Warmebach (riv.), Ger. 109/G6
Warmenhuizen, Neth. 108/B3
Warmeriville, Fr. 111/D5
Warmia (reg.), Pol. 99/K1
Warmińsko-Mazurskie (prov.), Pol. 99/L2
Warminster, Eng, UK 90/D4
Warminster, Pa, US 196/C3
Warner (mts.), Ca, US 184/C5
Warner Robins, Ga, US 191/H3
Warnow (riv.), Ger. 96/D5
Warnsveld, Neth. 108/D4
Waroona, Austl. 170/B5
Warr Acres, Ok, US 195/N14
Warrabri, Austl. 171/G2
Warrandirinna (lake), Austl. 171/H3
Warrego (range), Austl. 172/B4
Warrego (riv.), Austl. 172/B4
Warren (pt.), NW, Can. 192/M2
Warren, Austl. 173/C1
Warren, Mn, US 185/J3
Warren, Oh, US 188/D3
Warren, Pa, US 188/E3
Warren, Ar, US 187/J4
Warren, Mi, US 188/D3
Warren, Ut, US 195/J11
Warren (riv.), Austl. 170/C5
Warren, NJ, US 196/D2
Warren (co.), NJ, US 196/C2
Warren Hill, Mo, US 195/F9
Warri, Nga. 161/G5
Warrington, Fl, US 191/G4
Warrington, Eng, UK 93/F5
Warrington (co.), Eng, UK 93/F5
Warrnambool, Austl. 173/B3
Warroad, Mn, US 185/K3
Warrumbungle NP, Austl. 173/D1
Warsaw, In, US 188/C3
Warsaw (Warszawa) (cap.), Pol. 99/L2
Warscheneck (peak), Aus. 106/B2
Warsop, Eng, UK 93/G5
Warstein, Ger. 109/F6
Warta (riv.), Pol. 99/H2
Wartberg an der Krems, Aus. 113/H7
Wartberg ob der Aist, Aus. 113/H7
Wartburg, Il, US 195/G9
Warwick, Austl. 172/D5
Warwick, Eng, UK 91/E2
Warwick, Md, US 196/C5
Warwick, NY, US 196/D1
Warwick, Ok, US 195/N14
Warwick, Me, US 189/G2
Warwick, RI, US 189/G3
Warwickshire (co.), Eng, UK 91/E2
Wasatch (co.), Ut, US 195/K12
Wasatch (range), Ut, US 186/E2
Wasbank, SAfr. 165/E3

Wasburn (riv.), Eng, UK 93/G4
Wasco, Ca, US 186/C4
Waseca, Mn, US 185/K4
Wash, The (bay), Eng, UK 93/J6
Washburn, Pak. 144/B4
Washburn (lake), Nun., Can. 180/F1
Washimiya, Japan 135/D1
Washington, Eng, UK 93/G2
Washington (cap.), US
Washington (state), US 196/A6
Washington, Il, US 185/L5
Washington, NC, US 191/J3
Washington (mt.), NH, US 189/G2
Washington, NJ, US 196/D2
Washington, Pa, US 188/D3
Washington (lake), Wa, US 193/C2
Washington (isl.), US 185/M4
Washington Dulles (int'l arpt.), Va, US 188/E4
Washington Park, Il, US 195/G8
Washington Terrace, Ut, US 195/K11
Washingtonville, Pa, US 196/B1
Washita (riv.), Ok, US 187/H4
Washtenaw (co.), Mi, US 193/E7
Wasilków, Pol. 99/M2
Wasilla, Ak, US 192/J3
Waskaganish (Rupert House), Qu, Can. 188/E1
Waskasa (bay), Japan 132/D3
Waskey (mt.), Ak, US 192/G4
Waspán, Nic. 203/F3
Wasselonne, Fr. 111/G6
Wassen, Swi. 115/E4
Wassenaar, Neth. 108/B4
Wassenberg, Ger. 111/F1
Wasserbillig, Lux. 111/F4
Wasserburg, Ger. 112/D6
Wasserburg am Inn, Ger. 113/F6
Wasserkuppe (peak), Ger. 112/C2
Wassuk (range), Nv, US 182/C4
Wassy, Fr. 114/A1
Wast Water (lake), Eng, UK 93/E3
Wasur-Rawa Biru NP, Indo. 139/K5
Waswanipi (lake), Qu, Can. 188/E1
Wat Phu, Laos 136/D3
Watampone, Indo. 139/F4
Watarai, Japan 135/L7
Watarase (riv.), Japan 133/F2
Watari, Japan 133/G1
Watch Hill (pt.), RI, US 197/G1
Watchung, NJ, US 197/H9
Watchung (mts.), NJ, US 197/H9
Water of Ae (riv.), Sc, UK 92/E1
Water of Girvan (riv.), Sc, UK 94/B6
Water of Ken (riv.), Sc, UK 92/D1
Waterbury, Ct, US 188/F3
Wateree (lake), SC, US 191/H3
Wateree (riv.), SC, US 191/H3
Waterford, Mi, US 188/D3
Waterford, Ire. 89/Q10
Waterford (co.), Ct, US 197/F1
Waterford Works, NJ, US 196/D4
Watergate (bay), Eng, UK 90/A6
Waterhen (riv.), Sk, Can. 184/F2
Waterhen (lake), Mb, Can. 185/J2
Waterloo, On, Can. 188/D3
Waterloo, Il, US 195/G9
Waterloo, Belg. 111/D2
Waterloo Battlesite, Belg. 111/D2
Waterloo Village, NJ, US 196/D2
Watermael-Boitsfort, Belg. 110/D2
Waterton Lakes Nat'l Pk., Ab, Can. 184/E3
Watertown, NY, US 188/F3
Watertown, SD, US 185/J4
Watertown, Wi, US 193/N13
Waterville, Ire. 88/N11
Waterville, Me, US 189/G2
Waterville, Wa, US 184/C4
Waterway, La, US 195/P17
Watford, Eng, UK 88/B1
Watford City, ND, US 185/H4
Wath-upon-Dearne, Eng, UK 93/G4
Watheroo NP, Austl. 170/B4
Watkins, Co, US 195/C3

Watonwan (riv.), Mn, US 187/J1
Watowato (peak), Indo. 139/G3
Watrous, Sk, Can. 185/G3
Watsa, D.R. Congo 162/A2
Watseka, Il, US 188/C3
Watson Lake, Yk, Can. 180/D2
Watsontown, Pa, US 196/B1
Watsonville, Ca, US 186/B3
Watten, Fr. 110/B2
Wattenberg, Co, US 195/C2
Wattenheim, Ger. 112/B3
Wattens, Aus. 115/H3
Wattignies, Fr. 110/C2
Wattrelos, Fr. 110/C2
Wattwil, Swi. 115/F2
Wauchope, Austl. 173/E1
Wauchula, Fl, US 191/H5
Wauconda, Il, US 193/P15
Waukarlycarly (lake), Austl. 170/D2
Waukesha, Wi, US 187/K2
Waukesha (co.), Wi, US 193/P14
Waukon, Ia, US 185/L4
Waunakee, Wi, US 193/N13
Waupaca, Wi, US 185/L4
Waupun, Wi, US 185/L5
Waurika, Ok, US 187/H4
Wauseon, Oh, US 188/D3
Waveney (riv.), Eng, UK 91/H2
Waver (riv.), Eng, UK 93/E2
Wavre, Belg. 111/D2
Wavrin, Fr. 110/B2
Wāw, Sudan 155/L6
Wawa (riv.), Nic. 203/F3
Wawagosic (riv.), Qu, Can. 188/E1
Wawasang (peak), Indo. 203/E3
Wawayanda State Park, NJ, US 196/D1
Waxahachie, Tx, US 187/H4
Waycross, Ga, US 191/H4
Wayne, Ne, US 185/J5
Wayne (co.), Pa, US 196/C3
Wayne, Pa, US 196/C3
Wayne, NJ, US 197/J8
Wayne, Mi, US 193/F7
Wayne, Il, US 193/P16
Waynesboro, Pa, US 188/E4
Waynesboro, Ms, US 191/F4
Waynesboro, Ga, US 191/H3
Waynesville, NC, US 191/H3
Waynesville, Mo, US 187/J3
Waziers, Fr. 110/C2
Wazīrābād, Pak. 144/C3
Wazuka, Japan 135/J6
Wda (riv.), Pol. 99/K2
Weald, The (grsld.), Eng, UK 91/F4
Wear (riv.), Eng, UK 93/F2
Weatherby Lake, Mo, US 195/D5
Weatherford, Tx, US 187/H4
Weatherly, Pa, US 196/C2
Weaver (riv.), Eng, UK 93/F5
Weaverville, Ca, US 186/B2
Weber (co.), Ut, US 195/J11
Weber (riv.), Ut, US 195/J11
Weber Hill, Mo, US 195/F9
Webi Jubba (riv.), Som. 155/P7
Webster, SD, US 185/J4
Webster City, Ia, US 185/K5
Webster Groves, Mo, US 195/F9
Weddell (isl.), Mald. 217/E6
Weddell (sea), 218/X
Wedderburn, Austl. 173/B3
Weddin Mountains NP, Austl. 173/D1
Wedel, Ger. 109/G1
Wedemark, Ger. 109/G3
Wee Waa, Austl. 173/D1
Weed, Ca, US 186/B2
Weehawken, NJ, US 197/J8
Weekapaug, RI, US 197/G1
Weenen, SAfr. 165/E3
Weerselo, Neth. 108/D4
Weert, Neth. 108/C6
Weesen, Swi. 115/F3
Weesp, Neth. 108/C4
Wegberg, Ger. 111/F1
Weggis, Swi. 114/D3
Wegorzewo, Pol. 97/J4
Wegrów, Pol. 99/M2
Wegscheid, Ger. 113/G5
Wehingen, Ger. 115/E2
Wehr, Ger. 114/D2
Wehre (riv.), Ger. 109/H6
Wehrheim, Ger. 112/B2
Wei Xian, China 130/C4
Wei Xian, China 130/C3
Weibersbrunn, Ger. 112/C3
Weichang, China 129/L3

Wembere (riv.), Tanz. 163/F4
Wembley, Ab, Can. 184/D2
Wembley Stadium, Eng, UK 88/C2
Wemding, Ger. 112/D5
Wemmel, Belg. 110/D1
Wemyss Bay, Sc, UK 94/B5
Wen Xian, China 130/C4
Wencheng, China 137/D2
Wenchang, China 141/K3
Wenchi, Gha. 161/E5
Wendeburg, Ger. 109/H4
Wenden, Ger. 111/G2
Wendover, Nv, US 184/E5
Wendover, Eng, UK 91/F3
Wengyuan, China 141/K3
Wenling, China 137/D2
Wenlock Edge (ridge), Eng, UK 90/D2
Wenne (riv.), Ger. 109/F6
Wennigsen, Ger. 109/G4
Wenonah, NJ, US 196/C4
Wenshan, China 141/H3
Wenshang, China 130/D4
Wenshui, China 130/C3
Wensleydale (valley), Eng, UK 93/F3
Went (riv.), Eng, UK 93/G4
Wentworth, Austl. 173/B2
Wenxi, China 130/B4
Wenzhou, China 137/D2
Wepener, SAfr. 164/D3
Wer, India 142/A2
Werdau, Ger. 101/K3
Werdohl, Ger. 109/E6
Werkendam, Neth. 108/B5
Werl, Ger. 109/E5
Werlte, Ger. 109/E3
Wermelskirchen, Ger. 111/G1
Wernberg-Köblitz, Ger. 113/F3
Werne an der Lippe, Ger. 109/E5
Werneck, Ger. 112/D3
Wernigerode, Ger. 109/H5
Werong (mt.), Austl. 173/D2
Werra (riv.), Ger. 98/E3
Werre (riv.), Ger. 98/E2
Werrikimbe NP, Austl. 173/E1
Werris Creek, Austl. 173/D1
Werse (riv.), Ger. 109/E5
Wertach, Aus. 112/D6
Wertheim, Ger. 112/C3
Wertheim NWR, NY, US 197/F2
Werther, Ger. 109/F4
Wertingen, Ger. 112/D5
Wervershoof, Neth. 108/C3
Wervik, Belg. 110/C2
Weschnitz (riv.), Ger. 112/B3
Wesefgebirge (mts.), Ger. 109/F4
Wesel, Ger. 108/D5
Wesel-Datteln (canal), Ger. 109/E5
Weser (riv.), Ger. 98/E2
Weslaco, Tx, US 190/D5
Wesley Hills, NY, US 197/J7
Wessel (isls.), Austl. 167/C2
Wesselburen, Ger. 96/C4
Wesselsbron, SAfr. 164/D3
Wessex (reg.), Eng, UK 90/D4
Wessington Springs, SD, US 185/J4
West (pt.), Austl. 173/C4
West, Tx, US 187/H5
West (cape), NZ 175/R12
West (pt.), Wa, US 193/C2
West Allis, Wi, US 187/K2
West Alton, Mo, US 195/G8
West Babylon, NY, US 197/E2
West Bank (occ. zone), Isr. 149/D3
West Bend, Wi, US 185/L5
West Bengal (state), India 143/F2
West Berkshire (co.), Eng, UK 91/E4
West Bountiful, Ut, US 195/K12
West Branch, Mi, US 188/D2
West Bridgford, Eng, UK 93/G6
West Bromwich, Eng, UK 91/E1
West Burra (isl.), UK 94/C5
West Calder, Sc, UK 94/C3
West Caldwell, NJ, US 197/H8
West Cap Howe NP, Austl. 170/C5
West Chester, Pa, US 196/C4
West Chicago, Il, US 193/P16
West Chyulu Game Consv. Area, Kenya 162/C3
West Coast NP, SAfr. 164/L10
West Columbia, SC, US 191/H3
West Covina, Ca, US 194/G7

West Creek, NJ, US 196/D4
West Dunbartonshire (pol. reg.), Sc, UK 94/B5
West Elk (mts.), Co, US 190/B2
West End, Eng, UK 88/B3
West Falkland (isl.), Falk. 215/D7
West Fargo, ND, US 185/J4
West Fayu (isl.), Micr. 174/D4
West Frisian (isls.), Neth. 98/C2
West Glen (riv.), Eng, UK 93/H6
West Grove, Pa, US 196/C4
West Haven, Ct, US 197/F1
West Haverstraw, NY, US 196/B4
West Helena, Ar, US 187/K4
West Hempstead, NY, US 197/L9
West Hills, NY, US 197/M8
West Hollywood, Ca, US 194/F7
West Humber (riv.), On, Can. 189/Q8
West Ice Shelf, Ant. 218/F
West Indies (isls.), NAm. 203/F2
West Islet (isl.), Austl. 167/E3
West Islip, NY, US 197/E2
West Jordan, Ut, US 195/K12
West Kilbride, Sc, UK 94/B5
West Kingsdown, Eng, UK 88/D3
West Knock (peak), Sc, UK 94/D3
West Lamma (chan.), China 129/U11
West Lincoln, Ne, US 187/H2
West Lothian (pol. reg.), Sc, UK 187/H2
West Lunga NP, Zam. 163/D3
West Memphis, Ar, US 187/K4
West Midlands (co.), Eng, UK 91/E1
West Milford, NJ, US 197/H7
West Milton, Pa, US 196/B1
West Monroe, La, US 187/J4
West New York, NJ, US 197/J8
West Nyack, NY, US 197/K7
West Orange, NJ, US 197/J8
West Palm Beach, Fl, US 191/H5
West Paterson, NJ, US 197/J8
West Pensacola, Fl, US 191/G4
West Plains, Mo, US 187/K3
West Point, Ne, US 185/J5
West Point (lake), Al,Ga, US 191/G3
West Point, Ms, US 191/F3
West Point (mil. res.), NY, US 197/D1
West Point, Ut, US 195/J11
West Reading, Pa, US 196/C3
West Redding, Ct, US 197/E1
West Road (riv.), BC, Can. 184/B2
West Sacramento, Ca, US 193/L9
West Sayville, NY, US 197/E2
West Seneca, NY, US 189/S10
West Siberian (plain), Rus. 122/H3
West Sussex (co.), Eng, UK 91/F4
West-Terschelling, Neth. 108/C2
West Valley City, Ut, US 195/K12
West Vancouver, BC, Can. 184/C3
West Virginia (state), US 188/D4
West Warren, Ut, US 195/J11
West Water (riv.), Sc, UK 94/D3
West Weber, Ut, US 195/J11
West Wyalong, Austl. 173/C2
West York, Pa, US 196/B4
Westall (pt.), Austl. 171/G5
Westbrook, Ct, US 197/F1
Westbury, NY, US 197/L9
Westchester (co.), NY, US 197/E1
Westcott, Eng, UK 88/B3
Westerbork, Neth. 108/D3
Westerburg, Ger. 111/G2
Westerham, Eng, UK 88/D3
Westerheim, Ger. 115/G1
Westerholt, Ger. 109/E1
Westerkappeln, Ger. 109/E4
Westerland, Ger. 96/C4
Westerlo, Belg. 111/D1

Western (prov.), Kenya 162/B2
Western (des.), Egypt 155/L2
Western (prov.), Ugan. 162/A2
Western (chan.), SKor. 131/E5
Western Area (prov.), SLeo. 160/B4
Western Australia (state), Austl. 167/B3
Western Cape (prov.), SAfr. 164/C4
Western Ghats (mts.), India 147/K5
Western Run (riv.), Md, US 196/B4
Western Sahara (reg.) 154/B3
Western Sayans (mts.), Rus. 122/J4
Westerschelde (chan.), Belg. 108/A6
Westerstede, Ger. 109/E2
Westerville, Oh, US 188/D3
Westervoort, Neth. 108/C5
Westerwald (mts.), Ger. 98/D3
Westfield, NJ, US 197/H9
Westgat (chan.), Neth. 108/D2
Westhampton, NY, US 197/F2
Westhampton Beach, NY, US 197/F2
Westheim, Ger. 112/D5
Westhill, Sc, UK 94/D2
Westhofen, Ger. 112/B3
Westhoughton, Eng, UK 93/F4
Westkapelle, Neth. 108/A5
Westlake Village, Ca, US 194/B2
Westland, Mi, US 193/F7
Westland NP, NZ 175/R11
Westminster, Co, US 195/B3
Westminster, Md, US 196/B4
Westminster, Ca, US 194/F8
Westminster, City of (bor.), Eng, UK 88/A1
Westmont, Il, US 193/P16
Westmont (Haddon), NJ, US 196/C4
Westmorland (reg.), Eng, UK 93/F3
Westmount, Qu, Can. 189/N7
Weston, Mo, US 195/D5
Weston, Ct, US 197/E1
Weston-super-Mare, Eng, UK 90/D4
Westonaria, SAfr. 164/P13
Westport, Ire. 89/P10
Westport, NZ 175/S11
Westport, Ct, US 197/E1
Westray (isl.), Sc, UK 89/V14
Westview, Il, US 195/G8
Westwego, La, US 195/P17
Westwood, Ks, US 195/D5
Westwood, NJ, US 197/J8
Westwood, Ca, US 194/B2
Westonaria, SAfr. 164/E2
Wet (mts.), Co, US 190/B2
Wetar (isl.), Indo. 139/G5
Wetar (str.), Indo. 139/G5
Wetaskiwin, Ab, Can. 184/E2
Wete, Tanz. 162/C4
Wétetnagami (riv.), Qu, Can. 188/E1
Wetherell (lake), Austl. 173/B2
Wetter, Ger. 109/E6
Wetter (riv.), Ger. 112/B2
Wetterau (reg.), Ger. 112/C2
Wetteren, Belg. 110/C2
Wetterhorn (peak), Swi. 114/E4
Wettingen, Swi. 115/E3
Wettringen, Ger. 109/E4
Wetzikon, Swi. 115/E3
Wetzlar, Ger. 112/B1
Wetzstein (peak), Ger. 113/E2
Wevelgem, Belg. 110/C2
Wewak, PNG 174/D5
Wewoka, Ok, US 187/H4
Wexford, Ire. 89/Q10
Wey (riv.), Eng, UK 88/A3
Weybridge, Eng, UK 88/B2
Weyburn, Sk, Can. 185/H3
Weygand (ruin), Alg. 157/F4
Weyland (pt.), Austl. 171/G5
Weymouth, Eng, UK 90/D5
Weymouth (bay), Austl. 171/G5
Wha Ti, NW, Can. 180/D2
Whakatane, NZ 175/T10
Whale Cove, Nun., Can. 180/G2
Whalsey (isl.), Sc, UK 89/V13
Whangarei, NZ 175/S10
Wharfe (riv.), Eng, UK 93/G3
Wheat Ridge, Co, US 195/B3

Wheatland, Wy, US 185/G5
Wheaton, Il, US 188/B3
Wheaton-Glenmont, Md, US 196/A5
Wheaton Village, NJ, US 196/C5
Wheeler (peak), Nv, US 186/D3
Wheeler (peak), NM, US 187/F3
Wheeler (lake), Al, US 191/G3
Wheeler Springs, Ca, US 194/A1
Wheeling, WV, US 188/D3
Wheeling, Il, US 193/Q15
Wheelwright, Arg. 216/E2
Whernside (peak), Eng, UK 93/F3
Whickham, Eng, UK 93/G2
Whidbey (isl.), Austl. 171/F5
Whinham (mt.), Austl. 171/F3
Whitburn, Sc, UK 94/C5
Whitby, On, Can. 189/S8
Whitby, Eng, UK 93/H3
White (lake), La, US 187/J5
White (riv.), Ar, US 187/J4
White (riv.), SD, US 185/H5
White (riv.), Tx, US 187/K2
White (lake), Austl. 171/F2
White (lake), On, Can. 188/C1
White (riv.), In, US 188/C4
White (pass), Ak, US 192/L3
White (sea), Rus. 118/H2
White (bay), Nf, Can. 181/L3
White Bear (riv.), Nf, Can. 189/K1
White City, Sk, Can. 185/G3
White Cliffs, Austl. 173/B1
White Coomb (peak), Sc, UK 94/C6
White Esk (riv.), Sc, UK 94/C6
White Fox, Sk, Can. 185/G3
White Hall, Md, US 196/B4
White Haven, Pa, US 196/C1
White Marsh, Md, US 196/B5
White Mountain, Ak, US 192/F3
White Mountains Nat'l Rec. Area, Ak, US 192/J2
White Nile (riv.), Sudan 155/M7
White Oak, Md, US 196/B5
White Otter (lake), On, Can. 185/K3
White Plains, NY, US 197/K7
White River, On, Can. 188/C1
White Rock, NM, US 190/B3
White Sands, NM, US 186/F4
White Sands Nat'l Mon., NM, US 186/F4
White Sulphur Springs, Mt, US 184/F4
White Volta (riv.), Gha. 161/E4
White, West Fork (riv.), In, US 188/C4
Whiteadder Water (riv.), Sc, UK 94/D5
Whitecourt, Ab, Can. 184/E2
Whiteface (riv.), Mn, US 185/K4
Whitefield, Eng, UK 93/F4
Whitefish, Mt, US 184/E3
Whitefish (bay), US,Can. 188/C2
Whiteford (pt.), Wal, UK 90/B3
Whiteford, Md, US 196/B4
Whitehall, Mt, US 184/E4
Whitehall, Mi, US 188/C3
Whitehaven, Eng, UK 92/E2
Whitehead, NI, UK 92/C2
Whitehills, Sc, UK 94/D1
Whitehorse (cap.), Yk, Can. 192/L3
Whitehorse (hill), Eng, UK 91/E3
Whitehouse, Tx, US 187/J4
Whitemouth (riv.), Mb, Can. 185/K3
Whiteriver, Az, US 186/E4
Whiteside (chan.), Chile 217/C7
Whitesville, NJ, US 196/D3
Whiteville, NC, US 191/J3
Whitewater (lake), On, Can. 185/L3
Whitewood, Sk, Can. 185/H3
Whithorn, Sc, UK 92/D2
Whitley Bay, Eng, UK 93/G1
Whitmore Village, Hi, US 182/V12
Whitney (lake), Tx, US 187/H4
Whitney, Tx, US 187/H5
Whitsand (bay), Eng, UK 90/B6
Whitstable, Eng, UK 91/H4
Whitsunday (isl.), Austl. 167/G3

Whittaker, Mi, US 193/E7
Whittier, Ak, US 192/J3
Whittier, Ca, US 194/F8
Whittlesea, Austl. 173/G5
Whitton, Austl. 173/C2
Whitworth, Eng, UK 93/F4
Wholdaia (lake), NW, Can. 180/F2
Whyalla, Austl. 171/H5
Wi (isl.), SKor. 131/D5
Wiang Kosai NP, Thai. 136/B2
Wiarton, On, Can. 188/D2
Wiawso, Gha. 161/E5
Wichabai, Guy. 211/G4
Wichelen, Belg. 110/C2
Wichita (riv.), Tx, US 187/H4
Wichita (mts.), Ok, US 187/H4
Wichita Falls, Tx, US 187/H4
Wick, Sc, UK 89/S7
Wickenburg, Az, US 186/D4
Wickepin, Austl. 170/C5
Wickford, Eng, UK 88/E2
Wickham, Austl. 170/C2
Wicklow (mts.), Ire. 89/Q10
Wicklow (pass), Ire. 92/B5
Wicklow, Ire. 92/B6
Wicklow (pt.), Ire. 92/B6
Wickriede (riv.), Ger. 109/F4
Wid (riv.), Eng, UK 88/E2
Widnau, Swi. 115/F3
Widnes, Eng, UK 93/F5
Więcbork, Pol. 99/J2
Wied (riv.), Ger. 101/G1
Wiedau (riv.), Ger. 109/G2
Wiefelstede, Ger. 109/F2
Wiehengebirge (ridge), Ger. 109/F4
Wiehl, Ger. 111/G2
Wielenbach, Ger. 115/H2
Wieliczka, Pol. 99/L4
Wielkopolski NP, Pol. 99/J2
Wielkopolskie (prov.), Pol. 99/J2
Wieluń, Pol. 99/K3
Wien (riv.), Aus. 107/N7
Wien (Vienna) (cap.), Aus. 107/N7
Wien (prov.), Aus. 99/J4
Wiener Neudorf, Aus. 107/N7
Wiener Neustadt, Aus. 101/M3
Wienerwald (reg.), Aus. 107/N7
Wienwald (reg.), Aus. 101/L2
Wieprz (riv.), Pol. 99/M3
Wierden, Neth. 108/D4
Wieringermeerpolder (polder), Neth. 108/B3
Wieringerwerf, Neth. 108/C3
Wieruszów, Pol. 99/K3
Wiesbaden, Ger. 112/B2
Wiese (riv.), Ger. 101/G3
Wiese (isl.), Rus. 218/A
Wieseck (riv.), Ger. 112/B1
Wiesendangen, Swi. 115/E2
Wiesensteig, Ger. 112/C5
Wiesent (riv.), Ger. 112/E4
Wiesentheid, Ger. 112/D3
Wiesloch, Ger. 112/B4
Wiesmoor, Ger. 109/E2
Wietmarschen, Ger. 109/D4
Wietze, Ger. 109/G3
Wietze (riv.), Ger. 109/G3
Wietzendorf, Ger. 109/G3
Wiezyca (peak), Pol. 96/H4
Wigan, Eng, UK 93/F4
Wigan (co.), Eng, UK 93/F4
Wiggins, Ms, US 191/F4
Wight (isl.), UK 91/E5
Wigierski NP, Pol. 99/M1
Wignehies, Fr. 110/D3
Wigry (lake), Pol. 97/K5
Wigston, Eng, UK 91/E1
Wigtown, Sc, UK 92/D2
Wigtown (bay), Sc, UK 92/D2
Wijchen, Neth. 108/C5
Wijhe, Neth. 108/D4
Wijk bij Duurstede, Neth. 108/C5
Wil, Swi. 115/F3
Wilber, Ne, US 187/H2
Wilberforce, Austl. 172/G8
Wilbur, Wa, US 184/D3
Wilburton, Ok, US 187/J4
Wilcannia, Austl. 173/B1
Wilchingen, Swi. 115/E2
Wilczek (isl.), Rus. 118/N1
Wild (coast), SAfr. 164/E4
Wild Creek (res.), Pa, US 196/C2
Wild Rice (riv.),
Wild World, Md, US 196/B6
Wildbad im Schwarzwald, Ger. 112/B5
Wildberg, Ger. 112/B5
Wildeck, Ger.
Wilders, Ks, US 195/D5
Wildeshausen, Ger. 109/F3
Wildflecken, Ger. 112/C2

Wildgrat (peak), Aus. 115/G3
Wildhaus, Swi. 115/F3
Wildhorn (peak), Swi. 114/D5
Wildomar, Ca, US 194/C3
Wildspitze (peak), Aus. 115/G4
Wildstrubel (peak), Swi. 114/D5
Wildwood, NJ, US 196/D6
Wildwood Crest, NJ, US 196/D6
Wilge (riv.), SAfr. 164/E2
Wilhelm II (coast), Ant. 218/F
Wilhelmina (mts.), Sur. 208/G3
Wilhelminakanaal (canal), Neth. 111/E4
Wilhelmshaven, Ger. 109/F1
Wilhering, Aus. 113/H6
Wilkes-Barre, Pa, US 196/C1
Wilkes Land (phys. reg.), Ant. 218/J
Wilkesboro, NC, US 188/D4
Wilkeson, Wa, US 193/C3
Wilkie, Sk, Can. 184/F2
Wilkins (sound), Ant. 218/U
Will (mt.), BC, Can. 192/N4
Will (co.), Il, US 193/P16
Willamette (riv.), Or, US 184/C4
Willandra NP, Austl. 173/C2
Willapa (bay), Wa, US 184/B4
Willard (bay), Ut, US 195/J11
Willard (lake), Wi, US 193/P14
Willard, Ut, US 195/J11
Willard, Wi, US 193/Q14
Willaura, Austl. 173/B3
Willcox, Az, US 186/E4
Willebadessen, Ger. 109/G5
Willebroek, Belg. 111/D1
Willemstad, Neth. 108/B5
Willemstad (cap.), NAnt. 210/D1
William (mt.), Austl. 173/B3
William B. Hartsfield Atlanta (int'l arpt.), Ga, US 195/P16
William Bay NP, Austl. 170/C5
Williams, Austl. 170/C5
Williams, Az, US 186/D4
Williams Lake, BC, Can. 184/C2
Williamsburg, Ky, US 188/C4
Williamsport, Pa, US 196/B1
Williamston, NC, US 191/J3
Williamstown, NJ, US 196/B2
Williamstown, NJ, US 196/D4
Williamsville, NY, US 189/S10
Willich, Ger. 108/D6
Willingboro, NJ, US 196/D3
Willingen, Ger. 109/F6
Willingham, Eng, UK 88/B2
Willis, Tx, US 187/J5
Willis Islets (isls.), Austl. 167/E2
Willisau, Swi. 114/D3
Williston, ND, US 185/H3
Williston, Fl, US 191/H4
Williston, SAfr. 164/C3
Williston (lake), BC, Can. 180/D3
Williston Park, NY, US 197/L9
Willits, Ca, US 186/B3
Willmar, Mn, US 185/K4
Willow, Ak, US 192/H3
Willow (riv.), BC, Can. 184/C2
Willow Bunch, Sk, Can. 185/G3
Willow Grove, Pa, US 196/C3
Willow Grove, De, US 196/C5
Willow Grove Naval Air Sta., Pa, US 196/C2
Willow River, BC, Can. 184/C2
Willow Street, Pa, US 196/B4
Willow Tree, Austl. 173/D1
Willowbrook, Ca, US 194/F8
Willowbrook, Il, US 193/P16
Willowmore, SAfr. 164/C4
Willows, Ca, US 186/B3
Wills (lake), Austl. 167/D3
Wills Point, La, US 195/Q17
Willstätt, Ger. 114/D1
Willunga, Austl. 171/H5
Wilmette, Il, US 193/Q15
Wilmington, NC, US 191/J3
Wilmington, Austl. 171/H5
Wilmington, De, US 196/C4
Wilmington Island, Ga, US 191/H4
Wilmslow, Eng, UK 93/F5
Wilnsdorf, Ger. 111/H2
Wilrijk, Belg. 108/B6
Wilseder (peak), Ger. 109/G2

Wilson, NC, US 191/J3
Wilson (co.), Tx, US 195/U21
Wilson, NY, US 189/S9
Wilson (mt.), Ca, US 194/B2
Wilson, Pa, US 196/C2
Wilson (cape), Nun., Can. 181/H2
Wilsons Promontory (pen.), Austl. 173/C3
Wilsons Promontory NP, Austl. 173/C3
Wilsonville, Il, US 195/H7
Wilstedt, Ger. 109/G2
Wilster, Ger. 109/G1
Wilsum, Ger. 108/D3
Wilton, Ct, US 197/E1
Wilton, Austl. 172/A3
Wiltshire (co.), Eng, UK 91/E4
Wiltz, Lux. 111/E4
Wiltz (riv.), Lux. 111/E4
Wiluna, Austl. 170/D3
Wimborne Minster, Eng, UK 90/E5
Wimereux, Fr. 110/A2
Wimmis, Swi. 114/D4
Winam (gulf), Kenya 162/B3
Winburg, SAfr. 164/D3
Winchester, Ky, US 188/C4
Winchester, Tn, US 191/G3
Winchester, Ca, US 194/C3
Winchester, Eng, UK 91/E5
Winchester Mystery House, Ca, US 193/L12
Wind (riv.), Wy, US 184/F5
Wind (lake), Wi, US 193/P14
Wind Cave NP, SD, US 187/G2
Wind Gap, Pa, US 196/C2
Wind Point, Wi, US 193/Q14
Wind River (range), Wy, US 186/E2
Windach (riv.), Ger. 115/G2
Windach, Ger. 115/G2
Winder, Ga, US 191/H3
Windermere (lake), Eng, UK 93/F3
Windermere, Eng, UK 93/F3
Windesheim, Ger. 111/G4
Windhoek (cap.), Namb. 163/C5
Windlesham, Eng, UK 88/B2
Windom, Mn, US 185/K4
Window Rock, Az, US 186/E4
Windrush (riv.), Eng, UK 91/E3
Windsbach, Ger. 112/D4
Windsor, Nf, Can. 189/L1
Windsor, NS, Can. 189/H2
Windsor, Qu, Can. 189/G2
Windsor, On, Can. 188/D3
Windsor, Eng, UK 91/F4
Windsor, Co, US 195/C2
Windsor (res.), 195/C1
Windsor, Pa, US 196/B4
Windsor and Maidenhead (co.), Eng, UK 91/F3
Windward (isls.) 199/J3
Windward Passage (passg.), Cuba,Haiti 203/H2
Winfield, BC, Can. 184/D3
Winfield, Ks, US 187/H3
Winfield, Pa, US 196/B2
Winfield, Md, US 196/A5
Wingene, Belg. 110/C1
Winger, On, Can. 189/R10
Wingham, Austl. 173/E1
Winifred (lake), Austl. 170/D2
Winifreda, Arg. 216/D3
Winisk, On, Can. 181/H3
Winkler, Mb, Can. 185/J3
Winneba, Gha. 161/E5
Winnebago (lake), Wi, US 185/L5
Winnenden, Ger. 112/C5
Winner, SD, US 185/J4
Winnetka, Il, US 193/Q15
Winnett, Mt, US 184/F4
Winnfield, La, US 187/J5
Winningen, Ger. 111/G3
Winnipeg (cap.), Mb, Can. 185/J3
Winnipeg (int'l arpt.), Mb, Can. 185/J3
Winnipeg (riv.), Mb,On, Can. 185/K3
Winnipeg (lake), Mb, Can. 185/J3
Winnipeg Beach, Mb, Can. 185/J3
Winnipegosis, Mb, Can. 185/J3
Winnipegosis (lake), Mb, Can. 185/H2
Winnsboro, La, US 187/K4
Winnsboro, SC, US 191/H3
Winnweiler, Ger. 111/G4
Winschoten, Neth. 108/E2
Winsford, Eng, UK 93/F5
Winslow, Az, US 186/E4
Winslow, Me, US 196/D4
Winslow, Wa, US 193/B2
Winsum, Neth. 108/D2

Winter Haven, Fl, US 191/H4
Winter Park, Fl, US 191/H4
Winterberg, Ger. 109/F6
Winterberge (mts.), SAfr. 164/D4
Winterlingen, Ger. 115/F1
Winters, Tx, US 187/H5
Winters Run (riv.), Md, US 196/B4
Winterstaude (peak), Aus. 115/F3
Winterswijk, Neth. 108/D5
Winterthur, Swi. 115/E3
Winterthur Museum and Gardens, De, US 196/C4
Winthrop, Me, US 189/G2
Winton, Austl. 172/A3
Wintzenheim, Fr. 114/D1
Wipper (riv.), Ger. 98/F3
Wipperau (riv.), Ger. 109/H2
Wipperfürth, Ger. 111/G1
Wirges, Ger. 111/G3
Wirrabara, Austl. 171/H5
Wirral (co.), Eng, UK 93/E5
Wirral (pen.), Eng, UK 93/E5
Wisbech, Eng, UK 91/G1
Wisch, Neth. 108/D5
Wischhafen, Ger. 109/G1
Wisconsin (riv.), Wi, US 185/L5
Wisconsin (state), US 185/L4
Wiseman, Ak, US 192/H2
Wishaw, Sc, UK 94/C5
Wishek, ND, US 185/J4
Wisła, Pol. 99/K4
Wiślany (lag.), Pol. 97/H4
Wisłoka (riv.), Pol. 99/L4
Wismar, Ger. 96/D5
Wisner, La, US 187/K5
Wissant, Fr. 110/A2
Wissembourg, Fr. 112/B3
Wissen, Ger. 111/G2
Wissey (riv.), Eng, UK 91/G1
Witbank, SAfr. 164/E2
Wit Kei (riv.), SAfr. 164/D3
Witham, Eng, UK 91/G3
Witham (riv.), Eng, UK 93/H5
Witherspoon (mt.), Ak, US 192/J3
Withlacoochee (riv.), Fl,Ga, US 191/H4
Withnell, Eng, UK 93/F4
Witjira NP, Austl. 171/G3
Witkowo, Pol. 99/J2
Witney, Eng, UK 91/E3
Witnica, Pol. 99/H2
Witry-lès-Reims, Fr. 111/D5
Wittelsheim, Fr. 114/D2
Wittem, Neth. 111/E2
Witten, Ger. 109/E6
Wittenbach, Swi. 115/F3
Wittenberg, Ger. 98/G3
Wittenberge, Ger. 98/F2
Wittenheim, Fr. 114/D2
Wittenoom, Austl. 170/C2
Wittingen, Ger. 109/H3
Wittislingen, Ger. 112/D5
Wittlich, Ger. 111/F4
Wittman, Md, US 196/B6
Wittmund, Ger. 109/E1
Wittmunder (riv.), Ger. 109/E1
Witton (pen.), Ger. 99/G1
Wittstock, Ger. 98/G2
Witu, Kenya 162/D3
Witwatersrand (reg.), SAfr. 164/P12
Witzenhausen, Ger. 109/G6
Wivenhoe (lake), Austl. 167/E3
Wixom, Mi, US 193/E6
Wkra (riv.), Pol. 99/L2
Władysławowo, Pol. 96/H4
Włocławek, Pol. 99/K2
Włocławskie (lake), Pol. 99/K2
Włodawa, Pol. 99/M3
Włoszczowa, Pol. 99/K3
Wobulenzi, Ugan. 162/B2
Wodonga, Austl. 173/C3
Wodzisław Śląski, Pol. 99/K4
Woensdrecht, Neth. 108/B6
Woerden, Neth. 108/C4
Wohlen, Swi. 115/E3
Wohlen bei Bern, Swi. 114/D4
Wohlford (lake), Ca, US 194/C4
Woippy, Fr. 111/F5
Wokam (isl.), Indo. 139/H5
Woking, Eng, UK 88/B3
Wokingham, Eng, UK 91/F4
Wokingham (co.), Eng, UK 91/F4
Wŏlch'ul-san NP, SKor. 131/D5
Wolcott, Ks, US 195/D5
Wolcottville, NY, US 189/S9
Wolczyn, Pol. 99/K3
Woleai (isl.), Micr. 174/D4
Wolf (mtn.), Ak, US 192/H2
Wolf (riv.), Wi, US 188/B2
Wolf (vol.), Ecu. 214/C7
Wolf (isl.), Ecu. 214/E6

Wolf (lake), In, US 193/Q16
Wolf Creek (mtn.), Ak, US 192/F3
Wolf Creek, Mt, US 184/E4
Wolf Point, Mt, US 185/G3
Wolfach, Ger. 115/E1
Wolfach (riv.), Ger. 112/B6
Wolfegg, Ger. 115/F2
Wolfen, Ger. 98/G3
Wolfenbüttel, Ger. 109/H4
Wolfern, Aus. 113/H6
Wölfersheim, Ger. 112/B2
Wolfhagen, Ger. 109/G6
Wolframs-Eschenbach, Ger. 112/D4
Wolfsburg, Ger. 109/H4
Wolfsegg am Hausruck, Aus. 113/G6
Wolfurt, Aus. 115/F3
Wolgast, Ger. 96/E4
Wolhusen, Swi. 114/E3
Wolin, Pol. 96/F5
Woliński PN, Pol. 99/H2
Wolkersdorf, Aus. 107/P7
Wollaston (isl.), Chile 215/C8
Wollaston (lake), Sk, Can. 180/F3
Wollaston (pen.), NW,Nun., Can. 180/E2
Wollemi NP, Austl. 173/D2
Wollerau, Swi. 115/E3
Wollongong, Austl. 173/D2
Wöllstadt, Ger. 112/B2
Wöllstein, Ger. 111/G4
Wolmaransstad, SAfr. 164/D2
Wolnzach, Ger. 113/E5
Wologizi (range), Libr. 154/C6
Wołomin, Pol. 99/L2
Wołów, Pol. 99/J3
Wolseley, SAfr. 164/L10
Wolsztyn, Pol. 99/J2
Woluwé-Saint-Lambert, Belg. 111/D2
Wolvega, Neth. 108/D3
Wolverhampton, Eng, UK 90/D1
Wolverhampton (co.), Eng, UK 90/D1
Wolverine Lake, Mi, US 193/F6
Wolziger (lake), Ger. 98/Q7
Woman (riv.), On, Can. 188/D2
Wombourne, Eng, UK 90/D1
Wombwell, Eng, UK 93/G4
Womelsdorf, Pa, US 196/B3
Wondai, Austl. 172/C4
Wonder (lake), Il, US 193/P16
Wondervu, Co, US 195/B3
Wongan Hills, Austl. 170/C4
Wŏnju, SKor. 131/D4
Wonnangatta-Moroka NP, Austl. 173/C3
Wŏnsan, NKor. 131/D3
Wonthaggi, Austl. 173/C3
Wonyulgunna (peak), Austl. 170/C3
Wood (mt.), Yk, Can. 192/K3
Wood (riv.), Sk, Can. 185/H2
Wood (mtn.), Sk, Can. 184/G3
Wood (riv.), Wi, US 195/G8
Wood Buffalo NP, NW,Ab, Can. 180/E2
Wood Dale, Il, US 193/P16
Wood-Ridge, NJ, US 197/J8
Wood River, Ne, US 185/J5
Woodbine, NJ, US 196/D5
Woodbine, Md, US 196/A5
Woodbridge, Ct, US 197/E1
Woodbridge, Ca, US 193/M10
Woodbridge, NJ, US 197/H9
Woodburn, Austl. 173/E1
Woodburn, Or, US 184/C4
Woodburn, Il, US 195/G7
Woodburn, On, Can. 189/Q9
Woodbury, NJ, US 196/C4
Woodcliff Lake, NJ, US 197/J7
Woodend, Austl. 173/B3
Woodenbong, Austl. 173/E1
Woodenbridge, Ire. 92/B6
Woodend, Austl. 172/D4
Woodgate, Austl. 172/D4
Woodgate NP, Austl. 172/D4
Woodinville, Wa, US 193/C2
Woodland, Ca, US 186/B3
Woodlark (isl.), Sol. 174/E5
Woodlawn, Md, US 196/B5
Woodlawn Park, Ok, US 195/M14
Woodmere, NY, US 197/L9
Woodmont, Ct, US 197/F1
Woodridge, Il, US 193/P16
Woodroffe (mt.), Austl. 171/F3
Woods, Ok, US 195/N15
Woods (lake), On, Can. 180/G4
Woods Cross, Ut, US 195/K12

Woods Heights, Mo, US 195/E5
Woodsboro, Md, US 196/A4
Woodside, De, US 196/C5
Woodside, Austl. 171/M8
Woodside, Ca, US 193/K12
Woodside-Drifton, Pa, US 196/C4
Woodstock, NB, Can. 189/H2
Woodstock, Il, US 187/K6
Woodstock, Eng, UK 91/E3
Woodstock, Md, US 196/B5
Woodstown, NJ, US 196/C4
Woodville, Ms, US 187/K5
Woodway, Wa, US 193/C2
Woolgoolga, Austl. 173/E1
Wooli, Austl. 173/E1
Woolrich, Pa, US 196/A1
Woomera, Austl. 171/H4
Woomera Prohibited Area, Austl. 171/G4
Woonsocket, SD, US 187/H1
Woorabinda Aboriginal Community, Austl. 172/C4
Wooramel (riv.), Austl. 170/B3
Wooster, Oh, US 188/D3
Worb, Swi. 114/D4
Worcester, Ma, US 189/G3
Worcester, Eng, UK 90/D2
Worcester, SAfr. 164/L10
Worcestershire (co.), Eng, UK 90/D2
Worcester and Birmingham (canal), Eng, UK 90/D2
Worden, Il, US 195/H8
Wörgl, Aus. 101/K3
Workington, Eng, UK 92/E2
Worksop, Eng, UK 93/G5
Workum, Neth. 108/C3
Worland, Wy, US 184/G4
World 22
Wormer, Neth. 108/B3
Wormhoudt, Fr. 110/B2
Worms (pt.), Wal, UK 90/B3
Worms, Ger. 112/B3
Wörnitz (riv.), Ger. 101/J2
Worpswede, Ger. 109/F2
Wörrstadt, Ger. 112/B3
Wörsbach (riv.), Ger. 112/B2
Worsbrough, Eng, UK 93/G4
Worth, Il, US 193/Q16
Wörth am Rhein, Ger. 112/B4
Wörth an der Donau, Ger. 113/F4
Wörth an der Isar, Ger. 113/F5
Wortham, Tx, US 187/H5
Worthing, Eng, UK 91/F5
Wörthsee (lake), Ger. 112/E6
Worton, Md, US 196/B5
Wotho (isl.), Mrsh. 174/F3
Wotje (isl.), Mrsh. 174/G4
Woudenberg, Neth. 108/C4
Woudrichem, Neth. 108/B5
Wounta (lake), Nic. 203/F3
Wouw, Neth. 108/B5
Wowoni (isl.), Indo. 139/F4
Wrangel, Ak, US 218/U
Wrangell, Ak, US 192/M4
Wrangell (mts.), Ak, US 180/D2
Wrangell-St. Elias NP and Prsv., Ak, US 192/K3
Wrath (cape), Sc, UK 89/R7
Wray, Co, US 187/G2
Wraysbury, Eng, UK 88/B2
Wraysbury (res.), Eng, UK 88/B2
Wreck (reef), Austl. 172/D3
Wreck (pt.), SAfr. 164/B3
Wrekin, The (hill), Eng, UK 90/D1
Wremen, Ger. 109/E2
Wrexham, Wal, UK 93/F5
Wrexham (co.), Wal, UK 93/E5
Wright, Wy, US 185/G5
Wrightstown, NJ, US 196/D3
Wrightwood, Ca, US 194/C2
Wrigley, NW, Can. 180/D2
Writtle, Eng, UK 91/G3
Wrocław, Pol. 99/J3
Wrzesnia, Pol. 99/J2
Wschowa, Pol. 99/J3
Wu (riv.), China 137/A2
Wu'an, China 130/C3
Wuchang, China 130/C3
Wuchang (lake), China 130/D5
Wucheng, China 130/D3
Wuchuan, China 137/A2
Wuchuan, China 137/B3
Wuchuan, China 130/B2
Wudang (mtn.), China 130/B4
Wudi, China 130/D3

Wuding (riv.), China 130/B3
Wudinna, Austl. 171/G5
Wufeng, China 137/B1
Wugang, China 137/B2
Wuhai, China 128/C4
Wuhan, China 137/B1
Wuhe (riv.), Ger. 98/O6
Wuhe, China 130/D5
Wuhu, China 130/D5
Wuhu, China 130/D5
Wuhua, China 137/C3
Wujal Wujal Aboriginal Community, Austl. 172/B1
Wujiang, China 130/L8
Wular (lake), India 144/C2
Wulfen, Ger. 109/H5
Wulften, Ger. 109/H5
Wulian, China 130/D4
Wuling (mts.), China 137/B2
Wulong, China 141/J2
Wum, Camr. 161/H6
Wumang (isl.), China 131/B3
Wümme (riv.), Ger. 109/F2
Wün, India 140/C3
Wungong (res.), Austl. 170/L7
Wuning, China 137/C2
Wünnenberg, Ger. 109/F5
Wünnewil, Swi. 114/D4
Wunsiedel, Ger. 113/F2
Wunstorf, Ger. 109/G4
Wupatki Nat'l Mon., Az, US 186/E4
Wuppertal, Ger. 109/E6
Wuqi, China 130/B3
Wuqia, China 145/C5
Wuqiang, China 130/C3
Wuqiao, China 130/D3
Würm (riv.), Ger. 111/H6
Würm K. (canal), Ger. 115/H1
Würselen, Ger. 111/F2
Würzburg, Ger. 112/C3
Wusheng (pass), China 130/C5
Wushi, China 128/C4
Wüstegarten (peak), Ger. 109/G6
Wüstenrot, Ger. 112/C4
Wusuli (riv.), China 129/P2
Wutach (riv.), Ger. 115/E2
Wutai (peak), China 130/C3
Wutai, China 130/C3
Wuteve (mt.), Libr. 160/C4
Wutha-Farnroda, Ger. 112/D1
Wutöschingen, Ger. 115/E2
Wuustwezel, Belg. 108/B6
Wuwei, China 128/H4
Wuwei, China 130/D5
Wuxi, China 130/L8
Wuxiang, China 130/C3
Wuyang, China 130/C4
Wuyi (mts.), China 137/C2
Wuyi, China 130/C3
Wuyuan, China 137/C2
Wuyuan, China 130/D4
Wuzhai, China 130/B3
Wuzhi (peak), China 141/J4
Wuzhi, China 130/C4
Wuzhi (peak), China 130/J6
Wuzhong, China 141/K3
Wyalkatchem, Austl. 170/C4
Wyandanch, NY, US 197/M8
Wyandotte (co.), Ks, US 195/D5
Wyandotte County (lake), Ks, US 195/D5
Wyandotte NWR, Mi, US 193/F7
Wyangala (dam), Austl. 173/D2
Wycheproof, Austl. 173/B3
Wyckoff, NJ, US 197/J8
Wye (riv.), Eng, UK 90/C2
Wye Mills, Md, US 196/B6
Wyee, Austl. 173/D2
Wyk, Ger. 96/C4
Wynigen, Swi. 114/D3
Wynne, Ar, US 187/K4
Wynyard, Austl. 173/C4
Wynyard, Sk, Can. 185/G3
Wyoming (state), US 184/F5
Wyoming, De, US 196/C5
Wyoming, Mi, US 188/C3
Wyoming, PN do, Braz. 209/H6
Wyoming (range), US 184/F5
Wyoming, Wy, US 186/E2
Wyomissing, Pa, US 196/C3
Wyperfeld NP, Austl. 173/B2
Wyralinu (peak), Austl. 170/D5
Wyre (riv.), Eng, UK 93/F4
Wyrzysk, Pol. 99/J2
Wysokie Mazowieckie, Pol. 99/M2
Wyszków, Pol. 99/L2

X

X-Can, Mex. 202/E1
Xa Binh Long, Viet. 136/D4
Xaçmaz, Azer. 121/J4
Xagħra, Malta 104/L6
Xai-Xai, Moz. 163/F6
Xainza, China 128/E5
Xaitongmoin, China 143/G1
Xaltianguis, Mex. 201/L8
Xan (riv.), Viet. 136/D3
Xankändi, Azer. 121/H5

Xanten, Ger. 108/D5
Xánthi, Gre. 105/J2
Xanxerê, Braz. 213/A3
Xar Moron (riv.), China 129/L3
Xarba (pass), China 143/E1
Xavantes, Reprêsa de (res.), Braz. 213/B2
Xavantes, Serra dos (mts.), Braz. 209/J6
Xayar, China 128/D3
Xenia, Oh, US 188/D4
Xerta, Sp. 103/F2
Xertigny, Fr. 114/C1
Xi (lake), China 130/E2
Xi (riv.), China 129/K7
Xiaguan, China 141/H2
Xiajin, China 130/C3
Xiamen, China 137/C3
Xiamen (int'l arpt.), China 137/C3
Xuan'en, China 137/A2
Xi'an, China 130/B4
Xiang (riv.), China 129/K6
Xiangcheng, China 141/G2
Xiangcheng, China 130/C4
Xiangcheng, China 130/C4
Xiangfan, China 130/C4
Xiangfen, China 130/B4
Xianghe, China 130/H7
Xiangkhoang, Laos 136/C2
Xiangkhoang (plat.), Laos 136/C2
Xiangning, China 130/B4
Xiangshan, China 137/D2
Xiangshui, China 130/D4
Xiangtan, China 141/K2
Xiangxiang, China 137/B2
Xiangyuan, China 130/C3
Xiangyin, China 141/H2
Xianju, China 137/D2
Xianning, China 137/B2
Xiantao, China 137/B1
Xianyang, China 128/J5
Xiao Hinggan (mts.), China 129/N2
Xiao Xian, China 130/D4
Xiaogan, China 129/K5
Xiaoqing (riv.), China 130/D3
Xiaoshan, China 130/L9
Xiaowutai (peak), China 130/C3
Xiaoyi, China 130/B3
Xiapu, China 137/C2
Xiayi, China 130/D4
Xichang, China 141/H2
Xichuan, China 141/H3
Xico, Mex. 201/N7
Xicohténcatl, Mex. 201/F4
Xicotepec, Mex. 201/M6
Xifei (riv.), China 130/C4
Xifeng, China 128/J4
Xifeng, China 141/J2
Xifeng, China 130/F2
Xigazê, China 143/G1
Xihua, China 141/H3
Xilin, China 141/J3
Xilitla, Mex. 201/B1
Xílokastron, Gre. 105/H3
Ximeng Vazu Zizhixian, China 141/G3
Xin (riv.), Hon. 202/E3
Xin Barag Zuoqi, China 129/L2
Xin'an, China 137/C2
Xin'an (riv.), China 130/D5
Xin'anjiang (res.), China 137/C2
Xin'anjiang (res.), China 130/D5
Xinbin, China 131/C2
Xincai, China 130/C4
Xinchang, China 137/D2
Xincheng, China 137/A3
Xincheng, China 130/G7
Xinfeng, China 141/K3
Xinfeng, China 141/K3
Xinfeng, China 130/C4
Xinfengjiang (res.), China 137/B3
Xing'an, China 137/B2
Xingcheng, China 130/E2
Xingcheng, China 130/D4
Xinglong, China 130/H6
Xinglong, China 130/D5
Xingtai, China 130/C3
Xingu (riv.), Braz. 209/H4
Xingyang, China 130/C4
Xingyi, China 141/H3
Xingzi, China 137/C2
Xinhe, China 128/D3
Xinhe, China 130/C3
Xinhua, China 137/B2
Xinhuang Dongzu Zizhixian, China 137/A2
Xining, China 128/H4
Xinjiang, China 130/B3
Xinjiang Uygur (reg.), China 125/H5
Xinjin, China 131/A3
Xinle, China 130/C3
Xinmin, China 131/B1
Xintai, China 130/D4
Xinxiang, China 130/C4
Xinye, China 129/K5
Xinyang, China 130/C4
Xinye, China 130/C4
Xinyi, China 141/K3
Xinyu, China 130/D4
Xinyuan, China 128/D3
Xinzo de Limia, Sp. 102/B1
Xiong Xian, China 130/H7
Xiping, China 130/C4

Xiqing (mts.), China 128/H5
Xique-Xique, Braz. 212/B3
Xitang, China 130/L9
Xitiao (riv.), China 130/K9
Xiu (riv.), China 137/B2
Xiuning, China 137/C2
Xiuwen, China 141/A2
Xiuwu, China 130/C4
Xiuyan, China 131/B2
Xixabangma (peak), China 143/E1
Xixia, China 130/B4
Xiyang (riv.), China 141/J3
Xizang (Tibet) (aut. reg.), China 128/D5
Xochicalco (ruin), Mex. 201/K8
Xonacatlán, Mex. 201/Q10
Xpujil, Mex. 202/D2
Xu (riv.), China 137/C2
Xiuwen, China 141/A2
Xuanhua, China 130/G6
Xuchang, China 130/C4
Xun (riv.), China 137/B3
Xun Xian, China 130/C4
Xunke, China 129/N2
Xunwu, China 137/C3
Xunyang, China 130/B4
Xupu, China 137/B2
Xuwen, China 141/K3
Xuyi, China 130/D4
Xuzhou, China 130/D4

Y

Y Llethr (peak), Wal, UK 92/E6
Ya'an, China 128/H6
Ya'bad, Isr. 149/G7
Yabassi, Camr. 154/G7
Yablanitsa, Bul. 107/G4
Yablonovyy (range), Rus. 125/L4
Yabrūd, Isr. 149/G9
Yabucoa, PR 199/M8
Yabuki, Japan 133/G2
Yabuzukahon, Japan 135/C1
Yachi (riv.), China 128/J6
Yachiho, Japan 135/A1
Yachimata, Japan 135/E2
Yachiyo, Japan 135/D1
Yachiyo, Japan 135/G5
Yachiyo, Japan 135/E2
Yacimiento Río Turbio, Arg. 217/B6
Yacuiba, Bol. 208/F8
Yacuma (riv.), Bol. 208/E6
Yacumbu, PN, Ven. 210/D2
Yādgīr, India 140/C4
Yadkin (riv.), NC, US 191/H2
Yaeyama (isls.), Japan 133/G8
Yāfā, Isr. 149/G6
Yağcılar, Turk. 148/B2
Yagi, Japan 135/J5
Yagorlytsk (gulf), Ukr. 107/K2
Yagoua, Camr. 155/K7
Yagradagzê (peak), China 128/G4
Yaguale (riv.), Hon. 202/E3
Yaguarón (riv.), Uru. 217/G2
Yaguas (riv.), Peru 210/D5
Yague del Sur (riv.), DRep. 203/J2
Yagur, Isr. 149/G6
Yahagi (riv.), Japan 135/M6
Yahualica de Gonzalez Gallo, Mex. 200/E4
Yahyalı, Turk. 148/C2
Yaita, Japan 133/F2
Yaizu, Japan 135/F3
Yajalón, Mex. 202/C2
Yakacık, Turk. 149/E1
Yakapınar, Turk. 149/D1
Yakima, Wa, US 184/C4
Yakima (riv.), Wa, US 184/C4
Yakishiri (isl.), Japan 134/B1
Yako, Burk. 161/E3
Yakoruda, Bul. 107/F4
Yakumo, Japan 134/B2
Yakuno, Japan 135/G5
Yakutat (bay), Ak, US 180/B3
Yakutsk, Rus. 123/N3
Yala, Thai. 136/C5
Yalahua (lag.), Mex. 202/E1
Yalangoz, Turk. 149/E1
Yalata Abor. Land, Austl. 171/F4
Yalbac (hills), Belz. 202/D2
Yalgoo, Austl. 170/B4
Yalgorup NP, Austl. 170/B5
Yalınızçam, Turk. 148/E1
Yaloké, CAfr. 155/J6
Yalong (riv.), China 128/H5
Yalova, Turk. 107/J5
Yalova, Turk. 107/H5
Yalpuh (lake), Ukr. 107/J3
Yalta, Ukr. 120/E3
Yalu (riv.), China,NKor. 131/C2
Yalutorovsk, Rus. 145/E1
Yalvaç, Turk. 148/B2
Yamada, Japan 134/B4
Yamaga, Japan 135/B4
Yamagata, Japan 129/Q4
Yamagata, Japan 133/G1
Yamagata (pref.), Japan 134/A4

Yamaguchi (pref.), Japan 132/B3
Yamaguchi, Japan 132/B3
Yamaguchi (isl.), Indo. 139/J4
Yapen (str.), Indo. 139/J4
Yamakita, Japan 135/C3
Yamal (pen.), Rus. 122/G2
Yamalo-Nenetskiy Aut. Okrug, Rus. 122/H3
Yamanaka (lake), Japan 135/B3
Yamanashi, Japan 135/B2
Yamanie (falls), Austl. 172/B2
Yamanie Falls NP, Austl. 172/B2
Yamantau (peak), Rus. 119/N5
Yamaoka, Japan 135/M5
Yamarna Abor. Rsv., Austl. 170/D4
Yamashiro, Japan 135/J6
Yamato, Japan 135/B2
Yamato, Japan 135/E1
Yamato, Japan 130/C4
Yamato (riv.), Japan 135/J6
Yamato-Kōriyama, Japan 135/J6
Yamatotakada, Japan 135/J6
Yamazoe, Japan 135/K6
Yamba, Austl. 173/E1
Yambio, Sudan 155/L7
Yambol, Bul. 107/H4
Yambrasbamba, Peru 214/B2
Yamdena (isl.), Indo. 139/H5
Yamethin, Myan. 141/G4
Yamin (riv.), Austl. 139/K4
Yamma Yamma (lake), Austl. 172/A4
Yamoto, Japan 134/B4
Yamoussoukro (cap.), C.d'Iv. 160/D5
Yampa (riv.), Co, US 186/F2
Yamuna (riv.), India 140/D2
Yamunānagar, India 144/D4
Yamzho Yumco (lake), China 140/D7
Yan (riv.), SrL. 140/D6
Yan Yean (res.), Austl. 173/G5
Yana (riv.), Rus. 125/N3
Yanagawa, Japan 132/B4
Yanahuanca, Peru 214/B3
Yanai, Japan 132/C4
Yan'an, China 130/B3
Yanaoca, Peru 214/D4
Yanaul, Rus. 119/M4
Yanbian, China 141/H2
Yancheng, China 130/C4
Yancheng, China 130/E4
Yanchep NP, Austl. 170/B4
Yanco, Austl. 173/C2
Yandeearra Abor. Rsv., Austl. 170/C2
Yandoon, Myan. 141/G4
Yanfolila, Mali 160/C4
Yangambi, D.R. Congo 155/K7
Yangbi (riv.), China 141/G2
Yangcheng, China 130/C4
Yangcheng (lake), China 130/L8
Yangchun, China 137/B3
Yangdang (mts.), China 137/C2
Yangdök, NKor. 131/D3
Yanggang-do (prov.), NKor. 131/D2
Yanggu, SKor. 131/D3
Yangiyul', Uzb. 145/E4
Yangjiang, China 141/J4
Yangma (isl.), China 131/A4
Yangon (div.), Myan. 141/G4
Yangon, SKor. 131/D3
Yangqu, China 130/C3
Yangquan, China 130/C3
Yangsan, SKor. 131/E5
Yangshuo, China 141/K3
Yangtze (Chang) (riv.), China 137/C1
Yangxin, China 130/D3
Yangxin, China 130/D3
Yangyang, SKor. 131/E3
Yangyuan, China 130/C2
Yangzhong, China 130/L8
Yangzhou, China 130/D4
Yanji, China 129/N3
Yanjin, China 130/C4
Yanjin, China 130/C4
Yankari Game Reserve, Nga. 155/H6
Yankee Stadium, NY, US 197/K8
Yanling, China 130/C4
Yanmen (pass), China 130/C3
Yanshan, China 137/C2
Yanshan, China 141/H3
Yanshi, China 130/C4
Yanshou, China 129/N2
Yantai, China 130/E3
Yanyuan, China 141/H2
Yanzhou, China 130/D4
Yao, Japan 135/J6
Yao'an, China 141/H2
Yaotsu, Japan 135/M5
Yaoundé (cap.), Camr. 154/H7
Yap (isls.), Micr. 174/C4

Yapacana, PN, Ven. 208/E3
Yapei, Gha. 161/E4
Yekaterinburg (Sverdlovsk), Rus. 119/P4
Yekateriny (chan.), Rus. 134/C1
Yelabuga, Rus. 119/M5
Yelan', Rus. 121/G2
Yelarbon, Austl. 172/C5
Yelets, Rus. 120/F1
Yélimané, Mali 160/C3
Yelizovo, Rus. 123/R4
Yell (isl.), Sc, UK 89/W13
Yellel, Alg. 158/F5
Yellow (riv.), Fl, US 191/G4
Yellow (sea), Asia 129/M5
Yellow Grass, Sk, Can. 185/G3
Yellowknife (riv.), NW, Can. 180/E2
Yellowknife (cap.), NW, Can. 180/E2
Yellowstone (lake), Wy, US 184/F4
Yellowstone (riv.), Mt, US 185/G4
Yellowstone NP, US 186/E1
Yellville, Ar, US 187/K3
Yemen (ctry.) 146/E5
Yenakiyeve, Ukr. 120/F2
Yenda, Austl. 173/C2
Yendi, Gha. 161/E4
Yengisar, China 145/G5
Yenice, Turk. 149/D1
Yenice, Turk. 107/L5
Yenice, Turk. 107/H6
Yenice (riv.), Turk. 120/E4
Yeniceoba, Turk. 148/C2
Yeniköy, Turk. 107/H5
Yenişehir, Turk. 107/J5
Yenisey (riv.), Rus. 125/H3
Yeniseysk, Rus. 122/K4
Yeo (riv.), Eng, UK 90/D4
Yeo Lake Nature Rsv., Austl. 170/D4
Yeoval, Austl. 173/D2
Yeovil, Eng, UK 90/D5
Yeppoon, Austl. 172/C3
Yeraifia (well), WSah. 156/B4
Yerakovoúni (peak), Gre. 105/H3
Yartsevo, Rus. 122/K3
Yaritagua, Ven. 210/D2
Yasato, Japan 135/E1
Yasawa Group (isls.), Fiji 174/G6
Yasel'da (riv.), Bela. 120/C1
Yashima, Japan 134/B4
Yashio, Japan 135/D2
Yashiro, Japan 135/G6
Yasnyy, Rus. 121/L2
Yasothon, Thai. 136/D3
Yass, Austl. 173/D2
Yasu (riv.), Japan 135/K6
Yasu, Japan 135/K6
Yasugi, Japan 132/C3
Yasuj, Japan 135/E1
Yasun Burnu (pt.), Turk. 148/D1
Yasuni, PN, Ecu. 208/C4
Yatabe, Japan 133/G2
Yatağan, Turk. 148/B2
Yeraifia (well), WSah. 156/B4
Yerevan (cap.), Arm. 121/H4
Yaroslavl', Rus. 118/H4
Yaroslavskaya Oblast, Rus. 118/H4
Yarpuz, Turk. 149/E1
Yarra (riv.), Austl. 173/G5
Yarra Glen, Austl. 173/G5
Yarram, Austl. 173/C3
Yarraman, Austl. 172/D4
Yarrawonga, Austl. 173/C3
Yarrow Point, Wa, US 193/C2
Yartsevo, Rus. 122/K3
Yarumal, Col. 210/C3
Yarlung Zangbo (Brahmaputra) (riv.), China 143/G1
Yarmouth, NS, Can. 189/H3
Yardımcı (pt.), Turk. 149/B1
Yardley, Pa, US 196/D3
Yardville-Groveville, NJ, US 196/D3
Yare (riv.), Eng, UK 91/H1
Yari (riv.), Col. 208/D3
Yari-ga-take (peak), Japan 133/E2
Yarımca, Turk. 107/J5
Yarloop, Austl. 170/B5
Yarkant (riv.), China 128/C4
Yatenga (prov.), Burk. 161/E3
Yateley, Eng, UK 91/F4
Yatomi, Japan 135/L5
Yatsu, Japan 135/A2
Yatsuo, Japan 133/E2
Yatsushiro, Japan 132/B4
Yatsushiro, Japan 135/B4
Yatta, WBnk. 149/D4
Yatton, Eng, UK 90/D4
Yauca, Peru 214/C4
Yauca (riv.), Peru 214/C4
Yauco, PR 199/M8
Yauli, Peru 214/B3
Yaután, Peru 214/B3
Yauyos, Peru 214/C4
Yavari (riv.), Braz.,Peru 214/C2
Yavari Mirim (riv.), Peru 214/C2
Yavaros, Mex. 200/C3
Yavay (riv.), Peru 122/H2
Yaviza, Pan. 203/G4
Yavne, Isr. 149/F8
Yavoriv, Ukr. 120/B2
Yavuzeli, Turk. 148/D2
Yawahara, Japan 135/E2
Yawata, Japan 135/J6
Yawatahama, Japan 132/C4
Yaxchilán (ruin), Guat. 202/D2
Yayladağı, Turk. 149/E2
Yayladere, Turk. 148/E2
Yazd, Iran 147/F2
Yazman, Pak. 144/A5
Yazoo (riv.), Ms, US 187/K4
Yazoo City, Ms, US 187/K4
Ybbs (riv.), Aus. 99/H4
Ybbsitz, Aus. 101/L3
Yding Skovhøj (peak), Den. 96/C3
Ye, Myan. 136/B3
Ye Xian, China 130/D3
Yeay Sen (cape), Camb. 136/C4
Yecheng, China 145/F5
Yech'ŏn, SKor. 131/E4
Yecla, Sp. 103/E3
Yécora, Mex. 200/C2
Yecuatla, Mex. 201/N7
Yedigöller Nat'l Park, Turk. 107/L5
Yeditepe, Turk. 149/E2
Yeghvard, Arm. 121/H4
Yefremov, Rus. 120/F1
Yeğirdere, Turk. 148/B2
Yegros, Par. 217/F3
Yegorlyk (riv.), Rus. 121/H3
Yehualtepec, Mex. 201/M8

Yehud, Isr. 149/F7
Yejmiadzin, Arm. 121/H4
Yilong, China 141/H2
Yima, China 130/C4
Yimen, China 141/H3
Yin (mts.), China 128/J3
Yinan, China 130/D4
Yincheng, China 130/C4
Yinchuan, China 128/J4
Yines, Rus. 118/L4
Yingde, China 141/J3
Yingkou, China 131/B2
Yingshan, China 130/D4
Yingtan, China 137/C2
Yishan, China 141/J3
Yishui, China 130/D4
Yitong (riv.), SKor. 130/C5
Yiwu, China 128/F3
Yixing, China 130/K8
Yiyang, China 130/K2
Yiyang, China 130/C4
Yiyuan, China 141/K2
Yizheng, China 130/D4
Ylöjärvi, Fin. 97/K1
Ynder (lake), Kaz. 121/J3
Yngaren (lake), Swe. 96/G2
Yobe (state), Nga. 161/H3
Yŏch'ŏn, SKor. 131/D5
Yodo, Japan 135/J6
Yoduma (riv.), Rus. 123/P4
Yoff (Dakar) (int'l arpt.), Sen. 160/A3
Yogo, Japan 135/K6
Yogoum (well), Chad 155/J4
Yŏğuntaş, Turk. 107/H5
Yogyakarta, Indo. 138/D5
Yoho NP, BC, Can. 184/D3
Yoichi, Japan 134/B2
Yojoa (lake), Hon. 202/D3
Yŏju, SKor. 131/D4
Yokadouma, Camr. 154/J7
Yōkaichi, Japan 135/K5
Yokawa, Japan 135/H6
Yokkaichi, Japan 135/L6
Yokohama, Japan 133/F3
Yokoshiba, Japan 135/E2
Yokosuka, Japan 133/F3
Yokote, Japan 134/B4
Yokoze, Japan 135/C2
Yola, Nga. 154/H6
Yolaina (mts.), Nic. 203/E4
Yolboyu, Turk. 148/D2
Yolo (co.), Ca, US 193/L9
Yolo (co.), Ca, US 193/L9
Yom (riv.), Thai. 141/H4
Yon (riv.), Fr. 100/C3
Yonago, Japan 132/C3
Yonaguni (isl.), Japan 133/G8
Yonaha-dake (peak), Japan 133/K7
Yoneshiro (riv.), Japan 134/B3
Yonezawa, Japan 133/G2
Yŏng-yang, SKor. 131/E4
Yŏngam, SKor. 131/D5
Yongamp'o, NKor. 131/C3
Yong'an, China 137/C2
Yongchang, China 128/H4
Yongcheng, China 130/D4
Yŏngch'ŏn, SKor. 131/E5
Yongchun, China 137/C2
Yongde, China 141/G3
Yongding, China 137/C3
Yongding (riv.), China 130/G6
Yŏngdŏk, SKor. 131/E4
Yongdong, China 130/C4
Yŏnggwang, SKor. 131/D5
Yŏnghae, SKor. 131/E4
Yonghe, China 130/B3
Yŏnghŭng (riv.), NKor. 131/D3
Yŏnghŭng, NKor. 131/D3
Yongji, China 130/B4
Yŏngjong (isl.), SKor. 131/F6
Yŏngju, SKor. 131/E4
Yongkang, China 137/D2
Yongmun-san (peak), SKor. 131/D4
Yongnian, China 130/C3
Yongqing, China 130/H7
Yongren, China 141/H2
Yŏngsan (riv.), SKor. 131/D5
Yongshun, China 141/J2
Yongtai, China 137/C2
Yŏngwŏl, SKor. 131/E4
Yongxing, China 137/B2
Yongxiu, China 137/C2
Yonkers, NY, US 197/K8
Yonne (riv.), Fr. 98/B5
Yono, Japan 135/D2
Yopal, Col. 210/C3
Yopurga, China 145/G5
Yoqne'am 'Illit, Isr. 149/G6
Yorba Linda, Ca, US 194/G8
Yorii, Japan 135/C1
York (cape), Austl. 167/D2
York (sound), Austl. 167/D2
York (riv.), Qu, Can. 189/H1
York (co.), Eng, UK 93/G4
York (co.), Eng, UK 93/G4
York, Ne, US 185/J5
York, Pa, US 196/B4
York (riv.), Va, US 198/B4
York, SC, US 191/H3
York (riv.), Va, US 198/E4
York Haven, Pa, US 196/B3
York Landing, Mb, Can. 185/J1
York Minster, Eng, UK 93/G4
York Springs, Pa, US 196/A4
York, Vale of (valley), Eng, UK 93/G3
Yorke (pen.), Austl. 171/H5
Yorketown, Austl. 171/H5
Yorkshire Dales NP, Eng, UK 93/F3
Yorkshire Wolds (hills), Eng, UK 93/H3
Yorkton, Sk, Can. 185/H3
Yorktown, Tx, US 187/H5
Yorktown Heights, NY, US 197/E1
Yoro, Hon. 202/E3
Yōrō (riv.), Japan 135/E3

Yorō, Japan 135/L5
Yoroi-zaki (pt.), Japan 135/L7
Yoron (isl.), Japan 133/K7
Yorosso, Mali 160/D3
Yorubaland (plat.), Nga. 154/F6
Yos Sudarso (isl.), Indo. 139/J5
Yosemite NP, Ca, US 186/C3
Yoshida, Japan 132/C4
Yoshida, Japan 135/C1
Yoshii (riv.), Japan 132/D3
Yoshii, Japan 135/B1
Yoshikawa, Japan 135/D2
Yoshima (riv.), Japan 132/D3
Yoshimi, Japan 135/C1
Yoshino (riv.), Japan 132/C4
Yoshino, Japan 135/J7
Yoshino-Kumano NP, Japan 135/J7
Yoshkar-Ola, Rus. 119/L4
Yōsu, SKor. 131/D5
Yōtei-san (peak), Japan 134/B2
Yotsukaidō, Japan 135/E2
You (riv.), China 137/A3
Young, Austl. 173/D2
Young, Uru. 217/K10
Youngs (lake), Wa, US
Youngstown, Oh, US 188/D3
Youngstown, NY, US 189/R9
Youngtown, Az, US 195/R18
Yountville, Ca, US 193/K10
Youssoufia, Mor. 156/C2
Youyang, China 141/J2
Yovi (peak), Ven. 211/E3
Yozgat, Turk. 148/C2
Ypsilanti, Mi, US 193/E7
Yr Eifl (peak), Wal, UK 92/B6
Yreka, Ca, US 186/B2
Yser (riv.), Fr. 98/B3
Ysieux (riv.), Fr. 88/K4
Ystad, Swe. 96/E4
Ysyk-Köl (lake), Kyr. 128/C3
Ysyk-Köl (obl.), Kyr. 145/H4
Ythan (riv.), Sc, UK 94/D2
Ytrac, Fr. 100/E4
Ytre Sula (isl.), Nor. 96/A1
Ytterby, Swe. 96/D3
Ytterbyn, Swe. 95/G2
Yü (peak), Tai. 137/D3
Yu (riv.), China 141/J3
Yu Xian, China 130/C3
Yu Xian, China 130/C4
Yuan (riv.), China 129/K6
Yuan (lake), China 130/C5
Yuan'an, China 130/B5
Yüanlin, Tai. 137/D3
Yuanping, China 130/C3
Yuanqu, China 130/C4
Yuanshi, China 130/C3
Yuanyang, China 130/C3
Yuba City, Ca, US 186/B3
Yūbari, Japan 134/B2
Yūbetsu, Japan 134/C1
Yūbetsu (riv.), Japan 134/C2
Yuzhno-Sakhalinsk, Rus. 129/R2
Yucaipa, Ca, US 194/C2
Yucatán (state), Mex. 202/D1
Yucatan (pen.), Mex. 202/D2
Yucatan (chan.), NAm. 202/E1
Yucca House Nat'l Mon., Co, US 186/E3
Yucheng, China 130/D3
Yucheng, China 130/C3
Yuci, China 130/C3
Yuen Long, China 129/U10
Yuendumu, Austl. 171/F2
Yuendumu Abor. Land, Austl. 171/F2
Yueqing, China 137/D2
Yueyang, China 137/B2
Yug (riv.), Rus. 122/E4
Yugan, China 137/C2
Yugawara, Japan 135/C3
Yugorskiy (pen.), Rus. 119/P1
Yuhang, China 130/L9
Yuhuan, China 137/D2
Yui, Japan 135/B3

Yujiang, China 137/C2
Yūki, Japan 133/F2
Yukon, Ok, US 195/M14
Yukon (riv.), Can.,US 192/L3
Yukon-Charley Rivers Nat'l Prsv., Ak, US 192/K2
Yukon Territory (terr.), Can. 192/L2
Yüksekova, Turk. 148/F2
Yukuhashi, Japan 132/B4
Yulara, Austl. 171/F3
Yuleba, Austl. 172/C4
Yulin, China 141/K3
Yulin, China 141/J4
Yulin, China 130/B3
Yuma, Az, US 186/D4
Yuma, Co, US 187/G2
Yumbarra Consv. Park, Austl. 171/G4
Yumbel, Chile 216/B3
Yumbo, Col. 210/B4
Yumen, China 128/G4
Yumin, China 128/D2
Yumurtalık, Turk. 149/D1
Yun Xian, China 141/H3
Yun Xian, China 130/B4
Yunak, Turk. 148/B2
Yuncheng, China 130/C4
Yuncheng, China 130/B4
Yundum (Banjul) (int'l arpt.), Gam. 160/A3
Yungang Caves, China 130/C2
Yungas (phys. reg.), Bol. 208/E7
Yungay, Chile 216/B3
Yungk'ang, Tai. 137/D3
Yunguyo, Peru 214/D5
Yunkanjini Abor. Land, Austl. 171/F2
Yunlong, China 141/G2
Yunnan (prov.), China 128/H7
Yuntai (peak), China 130/C4
Yunxi, China 130/B4
Yunxiao, China 137/C3
Yunyan (riv.), China 130/D4
Yunzhong (mtn.), China 130/C3
Yuping, China 141/J2
Yupukarri, Guy. 211/G4
Yuqiao (res.), China 130/H7
Yuracyacu, Peru 214/B2
Yurga, Rus. 122/J4
Yuri (riv.), Rus. 134/E2
Yurimaguas, Peru 214/B2
Yuruari (riv.), Ven. 211/F3
Yürük, Turk. 107/H5
Yur'yevets, Rus. 118/J4
Yuryuzan' (riv.), Rus. 119/N5
Yuscarán, Hon. 202/E3
Yushan, China 137/C2
Yushe, China 130/C3
Yushu, China 129/N3
Yusōng, SKor. 131/D4
Yusufeli, Turk. 148/E1
Yutai, China 130/D4
Yutian, China 128/D4
Yutian, China 130/H7
Yutz, Fr. 111/F3
Yuza, Japan 134/A4
Yuzawa, Japan 134/B4

Z

Za (riv.), Mor. 158/C2
Zaachila, Mex. 202/B2
Zaandam, Neth. 98/C2
Zaanstad, Neth. 108/B4
Zabbar, Malta 104/M7
Zaber (riv.), Ger. 112/C4
Ząbki, Pol. 99/L2
Ząbkowice Śląskie, Pol. 99/J3
Žabljak, Mont. 106/D4
Zábřeh, Czh. 99/J4
Zabrze, Pol. 99/K3

Zacapa, Guat. 202/D3
Zacapoaxtla, Mex. 201/M7
Zacapu, Mex. 201/E5
Zacatecas (state), Mex. 198/A3
Zacatecas, Mex. 200/E4
Zacatecoluca, ESal. 202/D3
Zacatelco, Mex. 201/L7
Zacatepec, Mex. 201/K8
Zacatlán, Mex. 201/M7
Zachary, La, US 191/F4
Zachodniopomorskie (prov.), Pol. 99/H2
Zacoalco de Torres, Mex. 200/E4
Zacualtipán, Mex. 202/B1
Zadar, Cro. 101/L4
Zadetkyi (isl.), Myan. 138/A2
Zafarwāl, Pak. 144/C3
Zafra, Sp. 102/B3
Zagań, Pol. 99/H3
Zaghouan, Tun. 158/M6
Zaghouan (gov.), Tun. 158/M6
Zagora, Mor. 156/D3
Zagorá, Gre. 105/H3
Zagorje ob Savi, Slov. 101/L3
Zagreb (cap.), Cro. 106/B3
Zagros (mts.), Iran 146/E1
Zāhedān, Iran 147/H3
Zahirābād, India 140/C4
Zaḥlah, Leb. 149/D3
Záhony, Hun. 99/M4
Zahrez Chergui (dry lake), Alg. 158/G5
Zaïdin, Sp. 103/F2
Zaidpur, India 142/C2
Zaïo, Mor. 158/C2
Zaire (see Congo, Democratic Republic of the)
Zakamensk, Rus. 128/H1
Zakarpats'ka Oblasti, Ukr. 99/L4
Zakháro, Gre. 105/G4
Zakhodnyaya Dzvina (riv.), Bela. 118/E5
Zākhū, Iraq 148/E2
Zákinthos (isl.), Gre. 105/G4
Zákinthos, Gre. 105/G4
Zakopane, Pol. 99/K4
Zakouma, PN de, Chad 155/J5
Zala (riv.), Hun. 106/C2
Zala (prov.), Hun. 106/C2
Zalaapáti, Hun. 106/C2
Zalaegerszeg, Hun. 106/C2
Zalamea de la Serena, Sp. 102/C3
Zalamea la Real, Sp. 102/B4
Zalaszentgrót, Hun. 106/C2
Zalau, Rom. 107/F2
Žalec, Slov. 101/L3
Zalţan (well), Libya 155/J2
Zaltbommel, Neth. 108/C5
Zalun, Myan. 141/G4
Zama, Japan 135/C3
Zamānia, India 142/D3
Zambezi, Zam. 163/D3
Zambezi (riv.), Afr. 163/F4
Zambia (ctry.), 163/E3
Zamboanga, Phil. 139/F2
Zambrów, Pol. 99/M2
Zamfora (riv.), Nga. 161/G3
Zami (riv.), Myan. 136/B3
Zamora (riv.), Ecu. 208/C4
Zamora, Ecu. 214/B2
Zamora, Sp. 102/C2
Zamora-Chinchipe (prov.), Ecu. 214/B2
Zamora de Hidalgo, Mex. 200/E5
Zamość, Pol. 99/M3
Zams, Aus. 115/G3
Záncara (riv.), Sp. 102/D3
Zanda, China 128/C5
Zandkreekdam (dam), Neth. 108/A5
Zandvoort, Neth. 108/B4
Zanè, It. 117/E1
Zanhuang, China 130/C3
Zanjān, Iran 146/E1
Zanjón (riv.), Mex. 186/E5
Zánka, Hun. 106/C2
Zanzibar (isl.), Tanz. 162/C4
Zanzibar (Kisauni) (int'l arpt.), Tanz. 162/C4

Zanzibar Central/South (pol. reg.),Tanz. 162/C4
Zanzibar North (prov.), Tanz. 162/C4
Zanzibar Urban/West (pol. reg.), Tanz. 162/C4
Zanzuzi (hill), Tanz. 162/B3
Zaō-san (peak), Japan 133/G1
Zaoqiang, China 130/C3
Zaouiet Kounta, Alg. 157/E4
Zaoyang, China 130/C4
Zaozhuang, China 130/D4
Zapala, Arg. 216/C3
Zapaleri (peak), SA 215/C1
Zapallar, Chile 216/C2
Zapata, Tx, US 190/D5
Zapata (pen.), Cuba 203/F1
Zapatoca, Col. 210/C2
Zápatosa (lake), Col. 210/C2
Záplatský Rybník (lake), Czh. 113/H4
Zapolyarnyy, Rus. 118/F1
Zapopan, Mex. 200/E4
Zaporizhzhya, Ukr. 120/E3
Zaporizhzhya (int'l arpt.), Ukr. 120/E3
Zaporiz'ka Oblasti, Ukr. 120/E3
Zapotal, Ecu. 210/B5
Zapotillo, Ecu. 214/A2
Zapoteta, It. 106/B3
Zaprešić, Cro. 106/B3
Zara, Turk. 148/D2
Zaragoza, Mex. 201/E2
Zaragoza (int'l arpt.), Sp. 103/E2
Zaragoza, Mex. 201/M7
Zaragoza, Col. 210/C3
Zaragoza (Saragossa), Sp. 103/E2
Zarah, Ks, US 195/D6
Zarand, Iran 147/G2
Zaranda (hill), Nga. 161/H4
Zárate, Arg. 217/J11
Zarauz, Sp. 102/D1
Zaraza, Ven. 211/E2
Zard (mtn.), Iran 146/F2
Zareh Sharan, Afg. 147/J2
Zargān, Iran 146/F3
Zaria, Nga. 161/G4
Zarmast (pass), Afg. 147/H2
Zárnești, Rom. 107/G3
Zarnovica, Slvk. 106/C2
Zarós, Gre. 105/J5
Záruby (peak), Slvk. 106/C2
Zaruma, Ecu. 214/B1
Zarumilla, Peru 214/A1
Zary, Pol. 99/H3
Zarza la Mayor, Sp. 102/B3
Zarzal, Col. 210/B3
Zarzis, Tun. 155/H2
Zāskär (range), India 144/D3
Zāskär (riv.), India 144/D3
Zastron, SAfr. 164/D3
Žatec, Czh. 113/G2
Zauche (reg.), Ger. 98/P7
Zavalla, Arg. 216/E2
Zavdi'el, Isr. 149/F8
Zaventem, Belg. 111/D2
Zavet, Bul. 107/H4
Zavidovići, Bosn. 106/D3
Zavitinsk, Rus. 129/N1
Zawadzkie, Pol. 99/K3
Zawiercie, Pol. 99/K3
Zaysan, Kaz. 128/D2
Zaysan (lake), Kaz. 128/D2
Zayü (riv.), China 141/G2
Zayu, China 203/G1
Zazárida, Ven. 210/D2
Zbąszyń, Pol. 99/H2
Žďár nad Sázavou, Czh. 99/H4
Zdice, Czh. 113/G3
Zduńska Wola, Pol. 99/K3
Zeballos (peak), Arg. 217/C5
Zebbug, Malta 104/L7
Zeddine (riv.), Alg. 158/F5
Zedelgem, Belg. 110/C1
Zeehan, Austl. 173/C4
Zeeland, Mi, US 188/C3
Zeeland (prov.), Neth. 108/A5
Zeeland, Neth. 108/A5
Zeerust, SAfr. 163/E6
Zeewolde, Neth. 108/C4
Zefat, Isr. 149/D3

Zegrzyński (res.), Pol. 99/L2
Zehdenick, Ger. 99/G2
Zeil (mt.), Austl. 171/G2
Zeil, Ger. 112/D2
Zeiselmauer, Aus. 107/N7
Zeist, Neth. 108/C4
Zeitz, Ger. 98/G3
Zejtun, Malta 104/M7
Zekharya, Isr. 149/F8
Zele, Belg. 110/D1
Zelenodol'sk, Rus. 119/L5
Zelenogorsk, Rus. 119/S6
Zelenokumsk, Rus. 121/G3
Zelhem, Neth. 108/D4
Zell, Swi. 115/E3
Zell, Swi. 114/D3
Zell am Harmersbach, Ger. 114/E1
Zell am Main, Ger. 112/C3
Zell am Moos, Aus. 113/G7
Zell am See, Aus. 101/K3
Zell an der Pram, Aus. 113/G6
Zell in Wiesental, Ger. 114/D2
Zellersee (lake), Aus. 112/G7
Zellingen, Ger. 112/C3
Zelów, Pol. 99/K3
Zeltingen-Rachtig, Ger. 111/G4
Zeltweg, Aus. 101/L3
Zemaitija NP, Lith. 97/J3
Zembra (isl.), Tun. 158/M6
Zemen, Bul. 106/F4
Zemio, CAfr. 155/L6
Zemmer, Ger. 111/F4
Zemmora, Alg. 158/F5
Zempoala, Mex. 201/N7
Zempoala (peak), Mex. 201/Q10
Zempoaltepec, Cerro (peak), Mex. 202/C2
Zemst, Belg. 111/D2
Zenica, Bosn. 106/C3
Zenith, Wa, US 193/C3
Zenn (riv.), Ger. 112/D3
Zenon Park, Sk, Can. 185/H2
Zentsūji, Japan 132/C3
Zepče, Bosn. 106/D3
Zepu, China 145/G5
Zeralda, Alg. 158/G4
Zeravshan (riv.), Taj.,Uzb. 145/G3
Zermatt, Swi. 114/D5
Zernez, Swi. 115/G4
Zernien, Ger. 109/H2
Zernograd, Rus. 120/G3
Zero Branco, It. 117/F1
Zeta (lake), Nun., Can. 180/F1
Zetel, Ger. 109/E2
Zeuthen, Ger. 98/Q7
Zeven, Ger. 109/G2
Zevenaar, Neth. 108/D5
Zevenbergen, Neth. 108/B5
Zevgolation, Gre. 105/H4
Zevio, It. 117/E2
Zeya (res.), Rus. 125/M4
Zeya (riv.), Rus. 123/N4
Zeya-Bureya (plain), Rus. 123/N4
Zeytindağ, Turk. 148/A2
Zêzere (riv.), Port. 102/A3
Zghartā, Leb. 149/D2
Zgierz, Pol. 99/K3
Zgorzelec, Pol. 99/H3
Zhambyl (obl.), Kaz. 145/F4
Zhambyl, Kaz. 145/F4
Zhanaözen, Kaz. 121/K4
Zhangagazaly, Kaz. 145/D3
Zhangatas, Kaz. 145/E4
Zhanghei, Ger. 130/C2
Zhangjiakou, China 130/C2
Zhangping, China 137/C2
Zhangpu, China 137/C2
Zhangqiu, China 130/D3
Zhangshu, China 137/C2
Zhangwei (riv.), China 130/D3
Zhangye, China 128/H4
Zhangzhou, China 137/C3
Zhangzi (isl.), China 130/E3
Zhangzi, China 130/C3
Zhanhua, China 130/D3

Zhanjiang, China 141/K3
Zhao Xian, China 130/C3
Zhao'an, China 137/C3
Zhaojue, China 141/H2
Zhaoqing, China 141/K3
Zhaotong, China 141/H2
Zhaoyuan, China 130/E3
Zhaozhou, China 129/N2
Zhãyva (Ural) (riv.), Kaz.,Rus. 122/F5
Zhayyq (riv.), Kaz. 122/F5
Zhcheng, China 130/D3
Zhejiang (prov.), China 129/L6
Zhelaniya (cape), Rus. 122/G2
Zheleznodorozhnyy, Rus. 119/L3
Zheleznogorsk, Rus. 120/E1
Zheleznogorsk-Ilimskiy, Rus. 123/L4
Zhenfeng Bouyeizu Miaozu Zizhixian, China 141/J2
Zhengding, China 130/C3
Zhenglan, China 129/L3
Zhengning, China 130/B4
Zhengyang, China 130/C4
Zhengzhou, China 130/C4
Zhenhai, China 137/D2
Zhenjiang, China 130/D4
Zhenning Bouyeizu Miaozu Zizhixian, China 141/J2
Zhenping, China 130/C4
Zhentou (riv.), China 130/C4
Zhenwu (mtn.), China 130/B3
Zhenxiong, China 141/H2
Zhenyuan, China 137/A2
Zhenyuan, China 141/H3
Zhetiqara, Kaz. 121/M1
Zhezqazghan, Kaz. 145/E3
Zhezqazghan (obl.), Kaz. 145/E3
Zhicheng, China 137/B1
Zhigulevsk, Rus. 121/J1
Zhijiang, China 141/J2
Zhijin, China 141/J2
Zhiloy (isl.), Azer. 121/J4
Zhlobin, Bela. 120/D1
Zhmerynka, Ukr. 120/D2
Zhob, Pak. 147/J2
Zhob (riv.), Pak. 147/J2
Zhodino, Bela. 97/N4
Zhokhov (isl.), Rus. 123/R2
Zhongba, China 137/C3
Zhongshan, China 141/K3
Zhongxiang, China 130/C5
Zhongyang, China 130/B3
Zhoukou, China 130/C4
Zhoushan (isls.), China 137/D2
Zhouzhou, China 130/G7
Zhouzhuang, China 131/B3
Zhucheng, China 130/D4
Zhuhai, China 141/K3
Zhuji, China 137/D2
Zhujiang Kou (bay), China 129/T10
Zhukovka, Rus. 120/E1
Zhukovskiy, Rus. 119/X9
Zhumadian, China 130/C4
Zhuolu, China 130/G6
Zhuozi, China 130/C2
Zhushan, China 130/B4
Zhuxi, China 130/B4
Zhuzhou, China 141/K2
Zhuzhou, China 141/K2
Zhytomyr, Ukr. 99/K3
Zhytomyrs'ka Oblasti, Ukr. 99/K2
Zia (int'l arpt.), Bang. 143/H4
Zibo, China 130/D3
Ziębice, Pol. 99/J3
Zielona Góra, Pol. 99/H3
Zierenberg, Ger. 109/G6
Zierikzee, Neth. 108/A5
Zifta, Egypt 159/B4
Zigong, China 141/H2
Zigui, China 130/C4
Ziguinchor (int'l arpt.), Sen. 160/A3
Ziguinchor, Sen. 160/A3
Ziguinchor (pol. reg.), Sen. 160/A3
Zihuatanejo, Mex. 201/E5
Zijing (mtn.), China 130/B4
Zikhron Ya'aqov, Isr. 149/F6

Zile, Turk. 148/C1
Žilina, Slvk. 99/K4
Žilinský (pol. reg.), Slvk. 99/K4
Zillah, Libya 154/J2
Ziller (riv.), Aus. 101/J3
Zillisheim, Fr. 114/D2
Zimapán, Mex. 201/F4
Zimatlán de Alvarez, Mex. 202/B2
Zimba, Zam. 163/E4
Zimbabwe (ctry.) 163/E4
Zimla (well), Alg. 156/E4
Zimnicea, Rom. 107/G4
Zinapécuaro de Figueroa, Mex. 201/E5
Zinave, PN de, Moz. 163/F5
Zinder, Niger 161/H3
Zinder (dept.), Niger 161/H3
Ziniaré, Burk. 161/E3
Zinjin, China 137/C3
Zionland, Neth. 108/D3
Zion, Md, US 196/C4
Zion NP, Ut, US 186/D3
Zippori, Isr. 149/G6
Zirc, Hun. 106/C2
Žirje (isl.), Cro. 106/B4
Zirl, Aus. 115/H3
Ziro, India 141/F2
Zitácuaro, Mex. 201/E5
Žitava (riv.), Slvk. 99/K5
Zittau, Ger. 99/H3
Živinice, Bosn. 106/D3
Ziwa Magharibi (pol. reg.), Tanz. 162/A3
Zixi, China 137/C2
Zixing, China 141/K2
Ziya (riv.), China 130/D3
Ziyyon, Isr. 149/G8
Ziz, Oued (riv.), Mor. 156/D2
Zlatna, Rom. 107/F2
Zlatograd, Bul. 107/G5
Zlatorsko (lake), Serb. 106/D4
Zlatoust, Rus. 119/N5
Zlín, Czh. 99/J4
Zliv, Czh. 113/H4
Złocieniec, Pol. 99/J2
Zlot, Serb. 106/E3
Złotoryja, Pol. 99/H3
Złotów, Pol. 99/J2
Žlutice, Czh. 113/G2
Żmigród, Pol. 99/J3
Znam'yanka, Ukr. 120/E2
Znin, Pol. 99/J2
Znojmo, Czh. 99/J4
Zocca, It. 117/D4
Zoersel, Belg. 108/B6
Zoetermeer, Neth. 108/B4
Zoeterwoude, Neth. 108/B4
Zofingen, Swi. 114/D3
Zogang, China 141/G2
Zogno, It. 116/C1
Zográfos, Gre. 105/N9
Zohreh (riv.), Iran 146/F2
Zola, It. 117/E4
Zollikon, Swi. 115/E3
Zolotonosha, Ukr. 120/E2
Zomba, Malw. 163/G4
Zonguldak, Turk. 107/K5
Zonguldak (prov.), Turk. 107/K5
Zonhoven, Belg. 111/E2
Zonnebeke, Belg. 110/B2
Zonza, Fr. 104/A2
Zorge (riv.), Ger. 109/H5
Zorgo, Burk. 161/E3
Zorn, Fr. 98/D4
Zorneding, Ger. 113/E6
Zornheim, Ger. 112/B3
Zorritos, Peru 214/A1
Zossen, Ger. 98/Q7
Zottegem, Belg. 110/C2
Zou (prov.), Ben. 161/F5
Zou Xian, China 130/D4
Zouérat, Mrta. 156/B5
Zound-Wéogo (prov.), Burk. 161/E4
Zouping, China 130/D3
Zousfana, Oued (riv.), Alg. 157/E3
Zrenjanin, Serb. 106/E3
Zschopau (riv.), Ger. 113/F1
Zuata, Ven. 211/E2
Zubia, Sp. 102/D4
Zubūbā, Isr. 149/G6

Zucchero (peak), Swi. 115/E5
Zuckerhütl (peak), Aus. 115/H4
Zuehl, Tx, US 195/U21
Zug, Swi. 115/E3
Zugdidi, Geo. 121/G4
Zugersee (lake), Swi. 101/H3
Zughrār (well), Libya 157/H3
Zugspitze (peak), Ger. 115/G3
Zuid Holland (prov.), Neth. 108/A5
Zuid-Willemsvaart (canal), Belg.,Neth. 108/C6
Zuidbeveland (isl.), Neth. 108/A6
Zuidelijk Flevoland (polder), Neth. 108/C4
Zuidhorn, Neth. 108/D2
Zuidlaardermeer (lake), Neth. 108/D2
Zuidlaren, Neth. 108/D2
Zuidwolde, Neth. 108/D3
Zújar (riv.), Sp. 102/C3
Zújar, Sp. 102/D4
Zújar, Embalse del (res.), Sp. 102/C3
Zulia (riv.), Ven. 208/D2
Zulia (state), Ven. 210/C2
Zülpich, Ger. 111/F2
Zulte, Belg. 110/C2
Zululand (reg.), SAfr. 165/E2
Zumárraga, Sp. 102/D1
Zumba, Ecu. 214/B2
Zumbo, Moz. 163/F4
Zumpango de Ocampo, Mex. 201/K7
Zumpango del Río, Mex. 201/F5
Zundert, Neth. 108/B6
Zuni (riv.), Az,NM, US 186/E4
Zuni, NM, US 186/E4
Zuni (mts.), NM, US 190/A3
Zunyi, China 141/J2
Zuo Jiang (riv.), China 136/D1
Zuoquan, China 130/C3
Zuoyun, China 130/C3
Zuoz, Swi. 115/F4
Žur, Kos. 106/E4
Zurbāţiyah, Iraq 146/E2
Zürich (canton), Swi. 115/E2
Zürich (int'l arpt.), Swi. 115/E3
Zürich, Swi. 115/E3
Zürichsee (lake), Swi. 101/H3
Žuromin, Pol. 99/K2
Zurrieq, Malta 104/L7
Zurzach, Swi. 104/L7
Zusam (riv.), Ger. 101/J2
Zushi, Japan 135/D3
Zusmarshausen, Ger. 112/D6
Zutphen, Neth. 108/D4
Zuurberg NP, SAfr. 164/D4
Zuwārah, Libya 154/H1
Zuyevka, Rus. 119/L4
Zvishavane, Zim. 163/F5
Zvolen, Slvk. 99/K4
Zvorničko (lake), Bosn. 106/D3
Zvornik, Bosn. 106/D3
Zwartsluis, Neth. 108/C3
Zwedru, Libr. 160/C5
Zweibrücken, Ger. 111/G5
Zweisimmen, Swi. 114/D4
Zwesten, Ger. 109/G6
Zwevelgem, Belg. 110/C2
Zwickau, Ger. 101/K1
Zwickauer Mulde (riv.), Ger. 98/G3
Zwijndrecht, Belg. 111/D1
Zwischenahner Meer (lake), Ger. 109/F2
Zwischenwasser, Aus. 115/F3
Zwoleń, Pol. 99/L3
Żychlin, Pol. 99/K2
Żyrardów, Pol. 99/K2
Żywiec, Pol. 99/K4

Acknowledgements

Publisher Hammond World Atlas Corporation
Chairman Andreas Langenscheidt
President Marc Jennings
Vice President of Cartography Jennie Nichols
Director Database Resources Theophrastos E. Giouvanos

Cartography Walter H. Jones Jr., Sharon Lightner, Harry E. Morin, James Padykula, Thomas R. Rubino, Thomas J. Scheffer
Layout and Composition John A. DiGiorgio, Maribel Lopez
Cover Design Karen Prince

World Almanac Section
Content Development Consultant Richard W. Eiger
Editor Richard Hondula
Design and Page Layout Lee Goldstein

Photo Credits

Portraits on pages 10, 22, 36, 51, 55, 74 – APA Publication GMBH & Co. Verlag KG

Photos on pages 23, 27, 28, 33(L), 39, 40 – Vera Lorenz

Portraits on page 67 – Yang Zhao

Other photos, PhotoDisc™

Satellite images: NASA – Greece, Peloponnesus Peninsula – p.84

Pakistan, Indus River Delta – p.124; Egypt, Sinai Peninsula – p.150

Australia, Lake Eyre – p.166; United States, Grand Canyon – p.176

Argentina/Chile, Andes Mountains – p.204